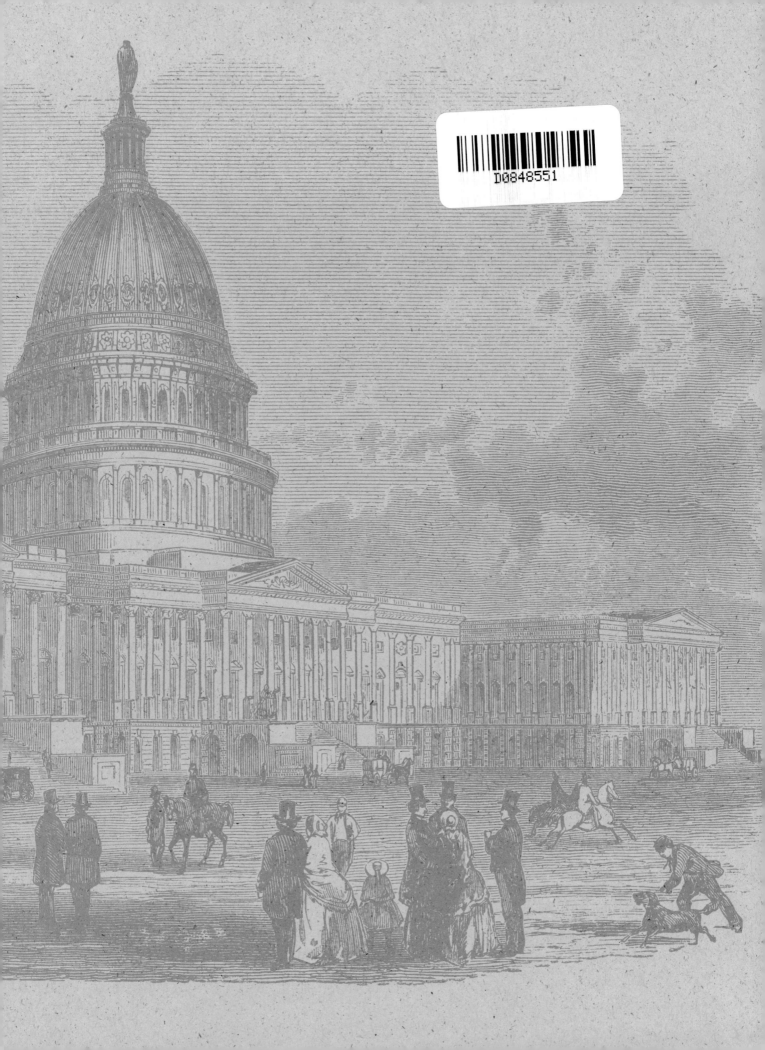

The Encyclopedia of the
United States Congress

Editorial Advisory Board

The
Encyclopedia
of the
United States Congress

Edited by

DONALD C. BACON
ROGER H. DAVIDSON
MORTON KELLER

Volume 2

SIMON & SCHUSTER

A Paramount Communications Company

New York   London   Toronto   Sydney   Tokyo   Singapore

Simon & Schuster
Academic Reference Division
15 Columbus Circle
New York, New York 10023

Printed in the United States of America

printing number
1 2 3 4 5 6 7 8 9 10

Library of Congress Cataloging-in-Publication Data
The encyclopedia of the United States Congress / edited by
Donald C. Bacon, Roger H. Davidson, Morton Keller.
p. cm.
ISBN 0-13-276361-3 (set : alk. paper)
ISBN 0-13-306663-0 (v.2 : alk. paper)
1. United States. Congress—Encyclopedias. I. Bacon,
Donald C. II. Davidson, Roger H. III. Keller, Morton.
JK1067.E63 1995
328.73′003—dc20 94-21203 CIP

Funding for this publication was received from
the Commission on the Bicentennial of the
United States Constitution. The University of Texas
at Austin and the Lyndon Baines Johnson Library recognize
with gratitude this and other assistance rendered by the
Commission in the development of this project.

Acknowledgments of sources, copyrights, and
permissions to use previously printed materials
are made throughout the work.

This paper meets the requirements of ANSI/NISO Z39.48-1992
(Permanence of Paper).

About the Editors

DONALD C. BACON is a Washington-based journalist specializing in Congress and the presidency. He has served as staff writer of the *Wall Street Journal* and assistant managing editor for congressional and political coverage of *U.S. News & World Report*. A former Congressional Fellow, he holds major prizes in journalism and has written and contributed to numerous books, including *Rayburn: A Biography* (1987) and *Congress and You* (1969).

ROGER H. DAVIDSON is Professor of Government and Politics at the University of Maryland, College Park. He has taught at several universities and served as a Capitol Hill staff member with the Bolling Committee, with the Stevenson Committee, and as Senior Specialist with the Congressional Research Service, Library of Congress. He is author or coauthor of numerous articles and books dealing with Congress and national policy-making, including the standard textbook, *Congress and Its Members* (4th edition, 1994).

MORTON KELLER is Spector Professor of History at Brandeis University. He has been a visiting professor at Yale, Harvard, and Oxford universities. Dr. Keller's books include *Regulating a New Society: Public Policy and Social Change in America, 1900–1933* (1994); *Regulating a New Economy: Public Policy and Economic Change in America, 1900–1933* (1990); *Parties, Congress, and Public Policy* (1985); and *Affairs of State: Public Life in Late Nineteenth Century America* (1977).

Abbreviations and Acronyms Used in This Work

AFL-CIO American Federation of Labor and Congress of Industrial Organizations
amend. amendment
app. appendix
Ala. Alabama
A.M. *ante meridiem*, before noon
Ariz. Arizona
Ark. Arkansas
Art. Article
b. born
c. *circa*, about, approximately
Calif. California
cf. *confer*, compare
chap. chapter (pl., chaps.)
CIA Central Intelligence Agency
Cir. Ct. Circuit Court
cl. clause
Cong. Congress
Colo. Colorado
Cong. Rec. Congressional Record
Conn. Connecticut
CRS Congressional Research Service
d. died
D Democrat, Democratic
D.C. District of Columbia
D.D.C. District Court (federal) of the District of Columbia
Del. Delaware
diss. dissertation
doc. document
DR Democratic-Republican
ed. editor (pl., eds); edition
e.g. *exempli gratia*, for example
enl. enlarged
esp. especially
et al. *et alii*, and others
etc. *et cetera*, and so forth

exp. expanded
F Federalist
f. and following (pl., ff.)
F. Federal Reporter
F.2d Federal Reporter, 2d series
FBI Federal Bureau of Investigation
Fed. Reg. Federal Register
Fla. Florida
F. Supp. Federal Supplement
Ga. Georgia
GAO General Accounting Office
GPO Government Printing Office
GS General Schedule (federal civil service grade level)
H. Con. Res. House Concurrent Resolution
H. Doc. House Document
H. Hrg. House Hearing
H.J. Res. House Joint Resolution
H.R. House of Representatives; when followed by a number, identifies a bill that originated in the House
H. Rept. House Report
H. Res. House Resolution
How. Howard (court reporter)
I Independent (party)
ibid. *ibidem*, in the same place (as the one immediately preceding)
i.e. *id est*, that is
Ill. Illinois
I.L.M. International Legal Materials
Ind. Indiana
J Jeffersonian
Jr. Junior
Kans. Kansas

Ky. Kentucky
La. Louisiana
M.A. Master of Arts
Mass. Massachusetts
Mich. Michigan
Minn. Minnesota
Miss. Mississippi
Mo. Missouri
Mont. Montana
n. note
N.C. North Carolina
n.d. no date
N.Dak. North Dakota
Nebr. Nebraska
Nev. Nevada
N.H. New Hampshire
N.J. New Jersey
N.Mex. New Mexico
no. number (pl., nos.)
n.p. no place
n.s. new series
N.Y. New York
Okla. Oklahoma
Oreg. Oregon
p. page (pl., pp.)
Pa. Pennsylvania
P.L. Public Law
Prog. Progressive
pt. part (pl., pts.)
Pub. Res. Public Resolution
R Republican
Rep. Representative
repr. reprint
rept. report
rev. revised
R.I. Rhode Island
S. Senate; when followed by a number, identifies a bill that originated in the Senate
S.C. South Carolina
S. Con. Res. Senate Concurrent Resolution
S. Ct. Supreme Court Reporter
S.Dak. South Dakota

S. Doc. Senate Document
sec. section (pl., secs.)
Sen. Senator
ser. series
sess. session
S. Hrg. Senate Hearing
S.J. Res. Senate Joint Resolution
S. Prt. Senate Print
S. Rept. Senate Report
S. Res. Senate Resolution
Stat. Statutes at Large
S. Treaty Doc. Senate Treaty Document
supp. supplement
Tenn. Tennessee
Tex. Texas
T.I.A.S. Treaties and Other International Acts Series
U.N. United Nations
U.S. United States, United States Reports
USA United States Army
USAF United States Air Force
U.S.C. United States Code
U.S.C.A. United States Code Annotated
USN United States Navy
U.S.S.R. Union of Soviet Socialist Republics
U.S.T. United States Treaties
v. versus
Va. Virginia
VA Veterans Administration
vol. volume (pl., vols.)
Vt. Vermont
W Whig
Wash. Washington
Wheat. Wheaton (court reporter)
Wis. Wisconsin
W.Va. West Virginia
Wyo. Wyoming

Years of Each Congress

This table provides a simple guide to the dates of each Congress, citing the year in which the following Congress begins as the year in which the previous Congress ends. For the exact opening and closing dates of each session of each Congress from the First Congress to the present, see the table accompanying the entry "Sessions of Congress."

1st	1789–1791	26th	1839–1841	51st	1889–1891	76th	1939–1941
2d	1791–1793	27th	1841–1843	52d	1891–1893	77th	1941–1943
3d	1793–1795	28th	1843–1845	53d	1893–1895	78th	1943–1945
4th	1795–1797	29th	1845–1847	54th	1895–1897	79th	1945–1947
5th	1797–1799	30th	1847–1849	55th	1897–1899	80th	1947–1949
6th	1799–1801	31st	1849–1851	56th	1899–1901	81st	1949–1951
7th	1801–1803	32d	1851–1853	57th	1901–1903	82d	1951–1953
8th	1803–1805	33d	1853–1855	58th	1903–1905	83d	1953–1955
9th	1805–1807	34th	1855–1857	59th	1905–1907	84th	1955–1957
10th	1807–1809	35th	1857–1859	60th	1907–1909	85th	1957–1959
11th	1809–1811	36th	1859–1861	61st	1909–1911	86th	1959–1961
12th	1811–1813	37th	1861–1863	62d	1911–1913	87th	1961–1963
13th	1813–1815	38th	1863–1865	63d	1913–1915	88th	1963–1965
14th	1815–1817	39th	1865–1867	64th	1915–1917	89th	1965–1967
15th	1817–1819	40th	1867–1869	65th	1917–1919	90th	1967–1969
16th	1819–1821	41st	1869–1871	66th	1919–1921	91st	1969–1971
17th	1821–1823	42d	1871–1873	67th	1921–1923	92d	1971–1973
18th	1823–1825	43d	1873–1875	68th	1923–1925	93d	1973–1975
19th	1825–1827	44th	1875–1877	69th	1925–1927	94th	1975–1977
20th	1827–1829	45th	1877–1879	70th	1927–1929	95th	1977–1979
21st	1829–1831	46th	1879–1881	71st	1929–1931	96th	1979–1981
22d	1831–1833	47th	1881–1883	72d	1931–1933	97th	1981–1983
23d	1833–1835	48th	1883–1885	73d	1933–1935	98th	1983–1985
24th	1835–1837	49th	1885–1887	74th	1935–1937	99th	1985–1987
25th	1837–1839	50th	1887–1889	75th	1937–1939	100th	1987–1989
						101st	1989–1991
						102d	1991–1993
						103d	1993–1995

CONNALLY, TOM T. (1877–1963), Democratic representative and senator from Texas, chairman of the Senate Foreign Relations Committee, and a strong internationalist. Born in central Texas, Connally inherited an interest in politics from his father, a successful farmer. After studying law, Connally entered politics, became a member of the Texas house of representatives, and then became county attorney. He was elected to the U.S. House of Representatives in 1916 after a contested Democratic primary in which all candidates were strong supporters of Woodrow Wilson. The campaign, like many campaigns in Texas's one-party system, was fought mainly over personalities of the candidates.

With the help of John Nance Garner, the powerful Texas representative, Connally was placed on the Foreign Affairs Committee, at the time an important committee given that Congress was being asked to declare war on Germany. Connally was a strong supporter of the war effort and of Wilson's proposed League of Nations. With Republican control of the government in the 1920s, Connally became a Democratic spokesman on foreign affairs. In 1928, he successfully ran for the Senate, defeating the Ku Klux Klan–backed incumbent, Earle B. Mayfield.

With the election of Franklin D. Roosevelt to the presidency, Connally became a supporter of the early New Deal. As a member of the Senate Finance Committee, he endorsed the reduction of the gold content of the dollar, a proposal ultimately backed by the Roosevelt administration. He also supported Roosevelt's farm programs, most of which were beneficial to Texas. He gained support within the Texas oil industry when he authored legislation that prohibited interstate shipments of oil that was produced in violation of state regulation. The so-called Hot Oil law increased the price of oil, put an end to chaos in the oil industry that resulted from overproduction after the discovery of the East Texas oil field, and eliminated the need for federal control of oil production.

Connally was known for his oratorical style and his unusual mode of dress. An admirer of William Jennings Bryan, he modeled his speech and appearance after Bryan. He cut his hair the way Bryan did, and usually wore a black suit with a frock coat, a stiff shirt, and a black string tie. Black silk ribbons held his watch and his glasses in place. Never at a loss for words, he was a master of sarcasm. His mastery of the language was considerable, and his words were often accompanied by dramatic facial expressions, gestures, and even pantomime. Con-

nally's speeches were favorites of the Senate galleries and brought out the Senate in force to watch the orator at work.

Although Connally is often considered a committed New Dealer, he did oppose Roosevelt's Court-packing plan, became increasingly unfriendly to labor during the 1940s, and frequently voted with the conservative coalition of Republicans and southern Democrats. He also supported states' rights against national power and was opposed to such civil rights laws as a federal antilynching statute.

His image as a liberal is largely due to his work on the Senate Foreign Relations Committee. He was either chairman of the committee or its ranking minority member from 1941 until his retirement in 1953. Connally was an internationalist, and his strong support for the United Nations, which he helped create, caused problems for him among conservative Texans. The Connally Resolution, which was a declaration of the war and peace aims of the United States, was introduced in 1943. It declared that the nation should achieve complete victory in the war but should then join in an international organization to preserve peace in the world and prevent aggression. Connally wanted to prevent a repetition of what he regarded as a tragic mistake after World War I, when U.S. participation in the League of Nations was blocked in the Senate. Connally attended the founding conference of the United Nations and teamed with Michigan senator

TOM T. CONNALLY.   LIBRARY OF CONGRESS

Arthur H. Vandenberg, the ranking Republican on the Senate Foreign Relations Committee, to rally support for American participation in the United Nations. When the Senate voted on the question of American participation, only two "nay" votes were cast. Connally's internationalist views, however, led him to be linked to the Truman administration, a link considered politically disastrous in 1952 Texas. Rather than run for a fifth term in the Senate, Connally chose to retire in 1953. He was succeeded by Texas's attorney general, Price Daniel, a pro-Eisenhower Democrat.

BIBLIOGRAPHY

Connally, Tom, as told to Alfred Steinberg. *My Name Is Tom Connally.* 1954.

Green, George Norris. *The Establishment in Texas Politics: The Primitive Years, 1938–1957.* 1979.

Miller, Otis, and Anita F. Alpern. "Tom Connally: One of the Senate Gallery's Favorites." In *Public Men In and Out of Office.* Edited by J. T. Salter. 1946.

Patenaude, Lionel V. *Texans, Politics, and the New Deal.* 1983.

ANTHONY CHAMPAGNE

CONNECTICUT. Since 1776 Connecticut has been the third-smallest state of the United States. Nevertheless, the Connecticut contingent at the Constitutional Convention of 1787, consisting of Roger Sherman, Oliver Ellsworth, and William Samuel Johnson, played a dynamic role there. Sherman, at sixty-six, a veteran of colonial and revolutionary politics, was the second-oldest member, after Benjamin Franklin, and, except for James Madison, spoke the most frequently. Eleven years earlier, at a meeting of the Second Continental Congress, Sherman had proposed the establishment of a bicameral legislature, with one house based on population and the other on equal representation for each state. The suggestion was ignored. Sherman revived the idea at the convention on 11 June as a way to resolve the acrimonious conflict between large and small states over representation. On 16 July the convention adopted the plan, thereafter called the Connecticut Compromise.

After the convention adjourned on 17 September, a strenuous campaign for the ratification of the Constitution began. In Connecticut, Ellsworth led the fight. On 9 January 1788, the delegates to the Connecticut ratifying convention finally voted 128 to 40 for unconditional approval, making Connecticut the fifth state to ratify.

Federal elections followed ratification. Initially, the Constitution allotted five House seats to Connecticut. As the censuses recorded population shifts, the number was altered. In 1793 Connecticut was assigned seven representatives; in 1823, six; in 1843, four; in 1901, five; and in 1931, six. All representatives were elected at large until 1837, when the state was divided into congressional districts. When Connecticut gained a representative in 1901, however, the new seat was filled by at-large elections until 1911. When it gained another seat in 1931, it was filled by at-large elections until 1964.

From 1788 to 1818, with one exception, Connecticut sent Federalists to Capitol Hill. Conservative candidates enjoyed a distinct advantage, largely because the state had retained its colonial charter, granted in 1662, which endowed the Congregational church with special privileges and placed restrictions on the franchise. Two Connecticut Federalists left their imprint in markedly different ways as the eighteenth century closed. Senator Ellsworth won national respect for drafting the Judiciary Act of 1789. In contrast, Rep. Roger Griswold was remembered for his unseemly behavior. A fierce quarrel between Griswold and Matthew Lyon, a Jeffersonian Republican representative from Vermont, over American policy toward France, led early in 1798 to a physical encounter. Lyon attacked Griswold with a hickory stick, Griswold responded with fire tongs, and a wrestling match ensued, all on the floor of the House.

In 1818 Connecticut adopted a state constitution that separated government and church and extended the suffrage to virtually all adult white males. Immediately, political patterns shifted. In 1819 five of the seven Connecticut representatives and one senator called themselves Democratic-Republicans.

Between the mid 1820s and the mid 1850s, a period of shifting alignments across the nation, Connecticut sent both Democrats and Whigs to Capitol Hill as well as a Free-Soiler in 1849 and two members of the Know-Nothing (American) party in 1855. The emergence of the Republican party, however, provided a focus. Beginning in 1859, voters favored Republicans over Democrats for House seats. In the choice of senators by the Connecticut General Assembly, the preference was clear; except for the years of economic depression from 1873 to 1881, only Republicans were selected for the Senate from 1856 to 1932.

Long tenures were common. Orville H. Platt, for example, took his senatorial seat in 1879; Joseph R.

CONNECTICUT POLITICS. This cartoon portrays the rivalry within Connecticut's governing Council of Twelve at the time of the ratification of the U.S. Constitution. The "Federals" represented trading interests and favored import taxes; the "Antifederals" represented agrarian interests and were more accepting of paper money. Connecticut appears here as a wagon laden with paper money and debt, sinking in mud, while the Federal members of the council pull to the left and the Antifederals pull right. Engraving attributed to Amos Doolittle, 1787.   LIBRARY OF CONGRESS

Hawley, his fellow Republican, took his two years later. Both remained senators until their deaths in 1905. Following the Spanish-American War, Platt, as chairman of the Committee on Relations with Cuba, introduced the amendment to the army appropriation bill of 1901 that established Cuba as a quasi-protectorate of the United States and that thereafter bore his name.

The Great Depression signaled the end of Republican dominance in Connecticut. In the 73d Congress (1933–1935) both senators and four of the six House members were Democrats. In the next Congress Democrats claimed all seats. With the outbreak of World War II, however, voters began to send a more heterogeneous group of lawmakers to Washington. In 1943 the first woman, Clare Boothe Luce, a Republican, was elected to the House; two years later, a second woman, Chase Going Woodhouse, a Democrat, won a seat. By 1991, when the 102d Congress convened, three representatives were women and three were men, the latter group including an African American. Three were Democrats; three, Republicans. The delegation included Protestants, Catholics, and Jews; the surnames indicated Yankee, Irish, and Italian forebears. The Connecticut congressional contingent, once the preserve of conservative white males, had become a study in diversity.

BIBLIOGRAPHY

Collier, Christopher, with Bonnie B. Collier. *The Literature of Connecticut History.* 1983.
Van Dusen, Albert E. *Connecticut.* 1961.

ESTELLE F. FEINSTEIN

CONSCRIPTION. Conscription or, as it is usually called in the United States, the draft has often been a contentious issue for Congress. It could hardly be otherwise in a nation whose political culture emphasizes individual liberty and limited government. The Constitution (Article I, section 8) granted Congress the "power to raise and support armies," but it neither mentioned nor prohibited conscription. For more than a century, the United States government relied upon volunteers to staff the army, navy, marines, and the ad hoc units—the U.S. Volunteers—that made up the bulk of the national wartime forces in the nineteenth century.

During the Civil War, the vast majority of soldiers in the Union army (92 percent) and the Confederate army (79 percent) were volunteers. The Confederate Congress adopted a national draft in 1862, initially to keep the veteran volunteers of 1861 in service. Its reach was soon expanded to compensate for the North's larger population base, but class-bound occupational exemptions caused much discontent. The U.S. Congress, pressed by the mili-

WORLD WAR I DRAFT. Published around the time of the passage of the Selective Draft Act of 1917, the cartoon refers to President Woodrow Wilson's request to Congress to pass conscription legislation. The president is shown rejecting the "U.S. Volunteer Mixture," asking for "the real stuff," that is, draftees, instead. Clifford K. Berryman, *Washington Evening Star,* c. 18 May 1917.

U.S. SENATE COLLECTION, CENTER FOR LEGISLATIVE ARCHIVES

tary and indirectly by the Lincoln administration, adopted national conscription in 1863. In response to pressure from middle-class voters and also from large manufacturers and railroad managers who wanted to exempt skilled workers, Sen. Henry Wilson (R-Mass.), the author of the bill, initially provided an escape provision for a commutation fee of three hundred dollars (the equivalent of a worker's annual wages) or the purchase of a substitute. "Peace Democrats" attacked the draft as class legislation, and its implementation led to massive antidraft riots in New York City and elsewhere. Congress eliminated the commutation provision in 1864, although those who could afford it could still hire substitutes directly.

In World War I, President Woodrow Wilson successfully pressed Congress to adopt the nation's first conscription for overseas service. The Selective Service Act of 1917 established a national conscription system based on four thousand civilian-led local draft boards and a national military Selective Service Headquarters. The draft law prohibited the use of substitutes, outlawed saloons or brothels near army camps, and authorized the deferment by local draft boards of individuals deemed indispen-

"FIGHT WITH THE MILITARY." Massive antidraft riot. Corner of Third Avenue and Forty-sixth Street, New York City, 13 July 1863.

HARPER'S PICTORIAL HISTORY OF THE GREAT REBELLION

sible to the economy. The Supreme Court upheld the law in 1918.

In World War II, following the German conquest of France in the spring of 1940, American interventionists persuaded President Franklin D. Roosevelt to support a compulsory military training bill. Despite considerable opposition, particularly from the midwestern isolationist wing of the Republican party, Congress adopted the Burke-Wadsworth Selective Service Training Act, the first national draft law to be adopted before the nation was at war. One year later, by a one-vote margin in the House, Congress voted to keep the draftees in the army beyond their one-year training period. After U.S. entry into the war in December 1941, nearly two-thirds of the sixteen million persons who served in the armed services were draftees.

The selective draft became a key part of national security policy during the Cold War. Congress rejected as too radical a system of universal military training and service (UMT&S) advocated by the Truman administration and the army. Instead, eighteen months after the expiration of the World War II conscription act, Congress adopted the Selective Service Act of 1948, which temporarily reestablished local draft boards and authorized conscription as needed to meet military force requirements.

The Korean War (1950–1953) played a decisive part in preventing a return to the traditional all-volunteer armed force. Despite its title, the Universal Military Training and Service Act of 1951 authorized a selective, not universal, draft; it did so for a four-year period. Quadrennially thereafter in non-election years, Congress regularly renewed the draft. As Sen. Richard B. Russell of Georgia, powerful Democratic chair of the Armed Services Committee, asserted in 1955, "The regular draft is a keystone of the arch of our national defense."

But conscription became one of the many casualties of the Vietnam War. Opposition mounted along with rising draft calls and the number of American casualties. Between 1965 and 1970, 170,000 young men became conscientious objectors, and perhaps as many as 570,000 evaded the draft illegally. In Congress the liberal wing of the Democratic party opposed the war, and it was joined by liberal Republicans from the north and the west.

Such controversy put increased pressure on Congress either to reform or to eliminate the draft. Many liberal Democrats supported draft reform, including an end to educational and occupational deferments and establishment of uniform standards and a national draft lottery for nineteen-year-olds. An initially small group in Congress advocated an all-volunteer armed force. In contrast, the House

Landmark Conscription Legislation

TITLE	YEAR ENACTED	REFERENCE NUMBER	DESCRIPTION
Enrollment Act	1863	12 Stat. 731	The first national draft law enacted by the U.S. Congress. It was amended in 1864; it expired in 1865. (Note: the Confederate Congress adopted national conscription with the Conscription Act of 16 April 1862.)
Selective Service Act of 18 May 1917	1917	40 Stat. 76	The act that established the modern draft and Selective Service System in World War I. Amended in 1918; expired in 1919.
Burke-Wadsworth Selective Service Training Act	1940	54 Stat. 885	The first peacetime national draft act in the United States. Provided for one year of military training for draftees. Extended by amendments until 31 March 1947.
Selective Service Act of 24 June 1948	1948	P.L. 80-759	The basic draft law in the United States. Amended and retitled the Universal Military Training and Service Act in 1951, readopted in 1955, 1959, 1963, and in 1967 retitled the Military Selective Service Act; readopted in 1971 (P.L. 92-129) with amendments. Presidential authority to induct persons into the armed forces expired on 1 July 1973. Compulsory registration resumed in 1980. Authorization for a standby draft as well as continued draft registration and classification by Selective Service Headquarters continues under the amended 1948 draft law.

Armed Services Committee's advisory board recommended maintaining the current Selective Service system. President Lyndon B. Johnson took a compromise position, but Congress rejected his moderate reform proposals and accepted the position of the conservatives in merely renewing the draft act without change in 1967.

After his election in 1968, Republican president Richard M. Nixon ended new occupational and dependency deferments, instituted an annual draft lottery for eighteen-year-olds (beginning in December 1969), removed Gen. Lewis B. Hershey from the directorship of the Selective Service System, and appointed a commission, headed by Thomas Gates, former secretary of Defense, which in 1970 recommended an All-Volunteer Armed Force (AVF) with a standby draft for emergency use.

But the lawmakers remained stymied by contending constituencies. Liberal internationalists challenged an AVF as too inflexible to meet emergencies, inequitable on class or racial grounds, and dangerous because it separated the army from society. Conservatives on Capitol Hill sought to avoid major alterations in the draft system, and they were temporarily successful.

Opposition to President Nixon's policy of gradual disengagement from the Vietnam War came to a head in Congress in 1971 over the issue of draft renewal. The administration appealed for a two-year extension of the draft. Congressional opponents sought to defeat renewal and to dismantle the Selective Service System. Only intensive appeals from the White House and the Pentagon persuaded a majority in Congress to extend the draft law. A coalition of conservative Republicans and southern Democrats enacted the Military Selective Service Act of 1971, commonly known as the Draft Extension Act, which extended presidential induction authority for two more years. It also authorized the president to eliminate student deferments and to create racially representative draft boards. In a move toward a peacetime AVF, Congress went far beyond the administration's request and provided a first-year pay increase for lower-rank service personnel totaling $2.4 billion. On 27 January 1973, the day a cease-fire was announced, the administration stopped conscripting young men—six months before presidential induction authority expired.

Compulsory draft registration was suspended in 1975 by President Gerald R. Ford, who also deactivated local draft boards. Following the Soviet invasion of Afghanistan, the draft was resumed in 1980 by President Jimmy Carter, who obtained a formal, if legally unnecessary, vote of support from Congress. Despite such symbolic actions and the continuance of Selective Service Headquarters and legislative authority for a standby draft, the United States has relied since 1973 upon an All-Volunteer Force.

[*See also* Armed Forces.]

BIBLIOGRAPHY

Chambers, John Whiteclay, II. *To Raise an Army: The Draft Comes to Modern America.* 1987.
Clifford, J. Garry, and Samuel R. Spencer, Jr. *The First Peacetime Draft.* 1986.
Flynn, George Q. *America and the Draft, 1940–1973.* 1993.
Geary, James W. *We Need Men: The Union Draft in the Civil War.* 1991.
O'Sullivan, John. *From Voluntarism to Conscription: Congress and Selective Service, 1940–1945.* 1982.
Segal, David R. *Recruiting for Uncle Sam: Citizenship and Military Manpower Policy.* 1989.

JOHN WHITECLAY CHAMBERS II

CONSENT. See Advice and Consent.

CONSERVATION. See Environment and Conservation.

CONSERVATISM. As applied to the U.S. Congress, the term *conservatism* lacks the meaning that it has for political systems in much of the world. There is no major conservative party in the United States capable of electing a majority of Congress and thereby gaining control of the policy process. Instead, conservatism has found strong individual proponents among leaders and factions of major political parties as well as, since the 1930s, by an informal cross-party coalition consisting of most Republicans and many southern Democrats.

Conservative Philosophy. One of the strongest conservative voices in congressional history was that of Sen. John C. Calhoun of South Carolina, who turned the Jeffersonian idea of states' rights into an argument against government activism on matters of economic regulation, slavery, and social welfare. Calhoun's concept of the "concurrent majority" of state governments, with power to interpose their will between Congress and the people of the United States, has often served to transform the debate over federalism into a controversy between supporters of federal action on behalf of citizens and supporters of state governments as bulwarks of the unequal status quo. Modern followers of the Calhoun philosophy, such as Sen. Jesse Helms of North Carolina, have applied the states' rights arguments to issues such as abortion, homosexuality, prayer in public schools, artistic freedom, and busing public school students to foster racial balance and equal educational opportunity.

These social policy arguments have mingled with another stream of conservative thought, one more closely connected to questions of the role of government in stimulating and regulating economic activity. Based on early Federalist doctrine, Whig (and, later, Republican) philosophy supported strong monetary and fiscal action to stimulate economic growth but opposed a major government role in establishing rules for the conduct of business. This blend of laissez-faire doctrine and government stimulation of the economy (with minimal business regulation) is generally endorsed by contemporary congressional conservatives, who believe that the interests of the nation are essentially identical to those of the private sector. They tend to oppose expanded power for labor unions, lower-income groups in society, and governmental agencies that oversee the government's role in the economy and provide benefits to consumers and workers as well as to business leaders. Although this is the political orientation of most congressional Republicans, many Democrats also agree with the basic tenets of free-enterprise capitalism.

Any attempt to explicate the role of conservatism in congressional policy-making is complicated by the diversity of issues that Congress must confront. However, certain policy perspectives, as reflected in roll-call voting patterns, are associated with congressional conservatism at the end of the twentieth century. The following discussion divides the assessment of conservatism in Congress along four major policy lines, based on the categories developed by Aage R. Clausen (1973). The policy achievements of congressional conservatives are measured by the rate of success that the conservative coalition of most Republicans and southern Democrats has had in roll-call votes against non-southern Democrats.

Four Major Policy Areas. On "big government" issues pertaining to public management of the economy, conservatives have opposed expansion of government economic controls, stimulation of the economy through budget deficits, more equitable distribution of taxation, and programs to make business more responsible for cleaning up or preventing pollution. They have favored limiting the rights and power of labor unions, maintaining the power of local political and economic elites against federal economic and social programs, congressional control over the District of Columbia, the lifting of federal control over business pricing policies, pursuit of a balanced federal budget, lower taxes, and tax advantages for businesses and entrepreneurs. This is the core cluster of issues over which conservatives and liberals struggle for control of the policy agenda.

On civil liberties issues, conservatives have had mixed success, with the House substantially more likely than the Senate to endorse their position. They have opposed the extension of government programs to foster school desegregation, particularly through resort to busing; opposed legislation supporting sexual equality; favored the expansion of police power over criminal suspects; supported the death penalty; opposed gun control; and opposed steps to facilitate voter registration.

Conservatives in Congress were generally isolationist on foreign policy issues prior to World War II, although many favored economic and strategic interventionism early in the twentieth century to support the overseas empire acquired following the Spanish-American War and to maintain advantages for U.S. corporations. The projection of American military strength and diplomacy during World War II and the Cold War led to a "sea change" among conservatives, who became strident supporters of an interventionist foreign policy. A leading example was Arthur H. Vandenberg, Republican senator from Michigan between 1928 and 1951. Originally an isolationist, Vandenberg afforded bipartisan support to the internationalist foreign policies of Roosevelt and Truman. Congressional conservatives have supported higher levels of defense spending, the adoption of new weapons systems, restrictive immigration policies, higher levels of foreign military aid, lower levels of foreign economic assistance, and U.S. participation in multinational defense institutions. Conservatives generally have opposed multilateral foreign aid programs, assistance to the United Nations and other nonmilitary international organizations, restrictions on military actions, and efforts to cut the defense budget.

On social welfare issues, congressional conservatives generally have opposed public housing; food stamps; the rights of labor unions to organize and pursue the interests of their members; federal efforts on behalf of more equal educational opportunities, urban needs, mass transit, and employee safety; and federal mandates of employment opportunities and increased compensation for labor (as with minimum wage legislation). Particularly in the Senate, conservatives have been relatively unsuccessful on this set of issues.

Other Issues. Congressional conservatism also has played a major role in areas of legislation that do not arise as frequently as government management of the economy, civil liberties, international involvement, or social welfare. On agricultural assistance issues, for example, conservatives have generally favored a laissez-faire approach that minimizes government intervention. Thus, they have opposed direct subsidy payments to farmers, federally mandated health standards for food growing and processing, and acreage restrictions.

On the internal governance and operation of Congress, conservatives generally have opposed expansion of legislative staff and have supported retaining most rules under which the legislature operates, particularly Rule XXII in the Senate, which governs filibusters. On issues of federalism and relations with the federal executive, conservative voting patterns have varied with the particular issues and with the party controlling the White House. For example, congressional conservatives have opposed federal involvement in redistricting state legislatures, favored limiting expansion of presidential staff under Democratic administrations, and attempted to limit the authority of the federal bureaucracy and of federal courts when those institutions were perceived as fostering a liberal agenda.

Measuring Conservatism. The measurement of conservatism in Congress is complicated and controversial. One common yardstick of the policies pursued by individual members and of the degree of conservative policy success in roll-call voting is Congressional Quarterly's index of conservative coalition support. The higher this score, the more conservative a member is said to be. When a majority of Republicans voting on a particular roll call are joined by a majority of voting southern Democrats (where the South includes the eleven states of the Confederacy, plus Kentucky and Oklahoma), and they are jointly opposed to a majority of voting northern (nonsouthern) Democrats, the "conservative coalition" is said to have formed. This particular voting pattern became less frequent during the 1980s than it had been in some sessions of Congress during the 1960s and 1970s when this cross-party coalition appeared consistently on more than one-fifth of all roll calls. These high rates of appearance were commonly interpreted as manifestations of ideologically based agreement linking like-minded members from both major parties. In 1992, the conservative coalition appeared on 48 (10.1 percent) of 473 House roll calls and won on 42, or 87.5 percent; it appeared on 38 (14.1 percent) of 270 Senate votes, winning 33, or 86.8 percent. In the same year, average conservative coalition support in the Senate was 65 percent among southern Democrats and 76 percent among Republicans, compared with just 26 percent among nonsouthern Democrats; in the House, mean levels of support were 62 percent for southern Democrats, 82 percent for Republicans, and 29 percent for nonsouthern Democrats. Mean conservative support was highest among southern Republicans (87 percent in each chamber) and lowest among Democrats from the East (21 percent in the Senate, 25 percent in the House).

Other measures of the philosophical leanings of members of Congress, as determined from their roll-call voting records, include indexes compiled by the Americans for Democratic Action, a liberal interest group, and the American Conservative Union, a conservative interest group. These scores consistently correlate strongly with Congressional Quarterly's conservative coalition support index. Many additional indexes of policy voting, usually on more narrowly defined issues, are reported by other interest groups and by other print media, notably the *National Journal*.

[*See also* Conservative Coalition; Southern Bloc.]

BIBLIOGRAPHY

Barone, Michael, and Grant Ujifusa. *The Almanac of American Politics, 1990.* 1991.
Clausen, Aage R. *How Congressmen Decide: A Policy Focus.* 1973.
Shelley, Mack C., II. *The Permanent Majority: The Conservative Coalition in the United States Congress.* 1983.

MACK C. SHELLEY II

CONSERVATIVE COALITION. The concept of a conservative coalition arose during the 1930s, when a combination of Republicans and southern Democrats acted informally to block legislation supporting the New Deal. This activity at first rarely occurred on formal roll-call votes. Rather, it initially was confined for the most part to decisions taken by standing committees, particularly the House Rules Committee, in opposition to Franklin D. Roosevelt's proposals and to actions favored principally by Democrats from nonsouthern states.

There is some roll-call evidence of occasional pre–New Deal appearances of commonly shared views by majorities of Republicans and southern Democrats against nonsouthern Democrats. It is generally agreed, however, that the controversies that arose in the wake of the Great Depression and World War II regarding the role of government in managing or stimulating the national economy were central to creating and sustaining a policy split dividing congressional Democrats into two distinctive groups. One was a southern wing, for the most part opposed to a major expansion of government's regulatory role in a capitalist economy; the other was a northern (really, a nonsouthern) wing, most of whom were more inclined than their southern copartisans to endorse stronger efforts by Washington to control the activities of the private economy and to carve out a larger role for government-owned or government-regulated enterprises.

With the passing of the economic crisis of the Depression, and as the economy expanded because of World War II, other issues served to continue, and in many respects deepen, the split within Democratic congressional ranks. But the issues pertaining to "big government" have continued far and away to be those on which Republicans have most frequently joined with southern Democrats against northern Democrats. Questions of social welfare, international involvement, and civil liberties have also been major catalysts for the appearance of the conservative coalition. With the important exception of social welfare votes, particularly in the Senate where liberal forces have been able to pass most of their legislative initiatives on roll-call votes, the conservative coalition has been a highly successful influence over national policy. On most other policy issues, when the cross-party conservative coalition has appeared, it has been successful most of the time.

The generally high party cohesion among Republicans and the comparatively weak cohesion among Democrats have fostered the continuation of the conservative coalition. The existence of a conservative coalition may be interpreted in at least three ways as a manifestation of the weakness of party structures in Congress. First, the very fact that a large regional segment of the Democratic party in Congress splits fairly regularly from its copartisans from other regions demonstrates the lack of centralized control by Democratic party leaders. Second, it makes sense to think of the conservative coalition as a cross-party substitute for a national conservative party (as exists, for example, in European parliamentary systems). Third, unlike what might be expected of a political system with strong political parties, the conservative coalition appears only episodically on selected issues. The sporadic nature of congressional policy coalitions, of which the conservative coalition is a particularly important and durable example, is best illustrated by considering the circumstances of southern Democrats, the swing bloc that decides whether the conservative coalition forms at all and, if it does, whether conservatives will be in the majority on a particular vote.

The cross-pressures brought to bear on southern Democrats, both to support their constituents' generally more conservative views and to provide at least episodic loyalty to their party's generally more liberal national leadership, mean that they are torn, both as a group and individually, on a wide array of issues. One practical consequence of this set of cross-pressures is that a substantial proportion of southern Democrats regularly defect from the predominant tendency of their regional colleagues to vote with Republicans when an appropriate issue arises. Some such defections also occur among Republicans, a few of whom consistently oppose the positions taken by majorities of both Republicans and southern Democrats, and among those northern Democrats who are more favorable to the stands commonly taken by congressional supporters of conservative policy preferences both in their own party and across the aisle. Based on 1992 roll-call votes, examples of defectors include, among southern Democrats, Georgia representative John Lewis and former Tennessee senator Albert A. Gore, Jr.; among Republicans, New York representative Bill Green and Vermont senator James M. Jeffords; and, among nonsouthern Democrats, former Wisconsin representative Les Aspin and Nebraska senator J. James Exon.

The 1980s produced a peculiar set of outcomes for the conservative coalition, which in one sense was overwhelmingly successful but in another became almost irrelevant. With strong support from the Ronald Reagan White House and helped greatly by Republican majorities in the Senate from 1981 to 1986, the conservative coalition was successful on virtually all votes on which it formed. This result is generally consistent with longer-term tendencies. The success rate of the conservative coalition is closely connected to the number of southern Democrats and Republicans elected. Nevertheless, the coalition's rate of appearance dropped markedly, to below 10 percent of recorded votes during the

1980s, as compared to more than a quarter of all roll-call votes in some sessions during the 1960s and 1970s. The dynamics of conservative coalition formation were altered during the Reagan years, perhaps as a consequence of the Reagan administration's ability to disconnect many Democratic members of Congress from their constituents' traditional policy liberalism and from their party's leadership, which often seemed unsure whether congressional Democrats could play the role of a loyal opposition to a generally popular president.

BIBLIOGRAPHY

Brady, David W., and Charles S. Bullock III. "Is There a Conservative Coalition in the House?" *Journal of Politics* 42 (1980): 549–559.

Patterson, James T. *Congressional Conservatism and the New Deal: The Growth of the Conservative Coalition in Congress, 1933–1939.* 1967.

Shelley, Mack C., II. *The Permanent Majority: The Conservative Coalition in the United States Congress.* 1983.

MACK C. SHELLEY II

CONSTITUENCY OUTREACH. Constituency outreach (or, to be more precise, attention to one's constituency) refers to the ways in which legislators serve and at the same time cultivate their constituencies, often with the objective of impressing voters back home and quelling their fears about the latitude that their legislators exercise away from the watchful eyes of constituents. Attention to one's constituents has always been a recognized activity of legislators, but it wasn't until Richard Fenno's classic *Home Style* (1978), a study of the behavior of members of Congress in their constituencies, that scholars began to appreciate the significance of constituency attention. For one thing, few realized the extent to which members were preoccupied with constituent matters; an even smaller number of scholars could boast of anything but a peripheral understanding of what legislators hoped to accomplish through their constituency activities. This is not to say that legislative scholars dismissed the constituency behavior of representatives and senators as unimportant; rather, the emphasis on the behavior of legislators while in Washington led researchers to focus on the study of congressional policy-making and institutions, to the exclusion of research on the activities of legislators that are directly related to constituents. What Fenno accomplished was to move critical questions about the constituency activities of representatives and senators to a more prominent position within legislative research. Fenno achieved this by introducing a rich conceptualization of the constituency behavior of legislators, the varieties of which he called "home styles," and suggesting how such activity was linked to their behavior while in Washington. There are three main expressions or categories of constituency outreach: casework, pork barreling, and constituent communication.

Casework. In casework, legislators help constituents deal with the federal bureaucracy. It would be a rare day in a congressional office that passed without letters, visits, or calls from constituents requesting the assistance of their legislator. The range of items on which constituents seek help is broad. Sometimes a government check is late in arriving, or some ambiguity in a federal regulation applicable to local businesses stimulates constituents to appeal to their representative or senator for help. In general, legislator-constituent contact occurs as incumbents seek to resolve or redress constituent grievances. When these problems involve the operations of the federal bureaucracy, the incumbent performs the role of legislative ombudsman. At other times, constituents contact their legislator to receive information or to express opinions.

Members actually spend little time themselves on casework problems; rather, their staffs bear the brunt of the daily casework. The legislator's personal involvement in casework normally is triggered only when staff are unsuccessful in resolving the problem or when the incumbent has a special interest in the case (e.g., a district dam or water project). Nevertheless, incumbents respond to constituent inquiries as if they were personally involved in resolving them. For instance, newsletters to constituents often point to the personal intercession of the senator or representative in resolving relatively minor constituent problems; responses to constituent inquiries carry the member's name in a smearable ink (to impress the truly skeptical), although probably few incumbents read or sign them. In this way, senators and representatives cultivate the image that they are personally involved in serving their constituents.

The key word here is "personally." Incumbents' personal involvement in such service is often exaggerated. Yet even if their personal involvement in casework is less than they would like their constituents to believe, members of Congress do allocate a large proportion of their staffs' time—only the legislator's own time is a more valuable resource—to constituent affairs. In addition to several staffers designated specifically as caseworkers, most legislative assistants, press aides, personal secretaries, and others without explicit constituent responsibilities also engage in casework from time to time.

The volume of casework processed in congressional offices is difficult to gauge, but one of the best estimates of the casework load is provided by John Johannes's survey of members and their staffs. Johannes asked about a number of issues regarding the processing of constituent requests; he then estimated that each week the average office in the Senate processed about 302 cases, and the average House office about 115 cases (Johannes, 1980, p. 519). Moreover, the casework load apparently was increasing, as 71 percent of the 193 staff surveyed by Johannes perceived an increase in the volume of casework reaching their offices, and more constituents were writing to their representatives and senators than in the past (Parker, 1986).

Members of Congress and their staffs cite different reasons for the growth in casework: the legislators point to growth in government, while their staffs attribute it to the efforts of legislators to stimulate casework. There is an indisputable logic to the members' argument: legislators have always engaged in casework, but the expansion of government programs resulting from Great Society legislation passed in the 1960s created more laws, regulations, bureaucracies, paperwork, and problems with government. Members found themselves besieged by constituents who were now more dependent than ever upon government action.

Despite the logic of the argument, incumbents must bear a significant proportion of the responsibility for the rise in casework, since senators and representatives clearly have exploited the resources of their offices to increase casework. Staffs and offices in the home district or state have expanded their operations, and mobile offices—vans equipped with office furniture—have become increasingly popular with legislators. Newsletters constantly remind constituents to bring their problems to their congressional representative; community forums and councils are encouraged to do the same. Johannes (1981) estimates that about half of members exploit at least two sources of contact with constituents to solicit casework.

Pork-Barreling. The processes through which members of Congress divert federal funds to their districts and states are known collectively as "pork-barreling." What better way to demonstrate con-

cern for the district or state than to bring home the bacon! And the opportunities to do so have never been greater. There is a variety of "pork" to be found in the federal budget: grants to local governments and universities, federal aid for specific constituent groups (e.g., subsidies for certain agricultural products), federal buildings and installations (e.g., military bases), and federal dollars in the form of contracts to local business for government work are just a few of the standard items available at the pork barrel.

Pork-barreling is one way in which legislators look after the interests of their constituents, ensuring that their districts and states receive their "fair share" of the federal pork barrel. Within their committees, in their interactions with agency officials, and on the floor of Congress, representatives and senators seek to further the interests of their constituents in a material fashion; federal projects, contracts, grants, installations, and federal office buildings bring money and jobs to the district or state—two benefits that most constituents appreciate. The value of a district or state project to constituents—rather than its efficiency, necessity, or worth to society—is the major consideration prompting legislators to raid the federal budget. Some may accuse members of expending too much effort procuring such benefits, but many members believe that such activity is what their constituents want and expect. And, indeed, constituents do expect their legislators to be on the watch for opportunities to further constituency interests. As a consequence, incumbents create and seize opportunities to benefit their constituencies. Their efforts often meet with remarkable success.

Another way in which legislators materially benefit their constituents is through their intercessions with federal agencies. For example, in the past members have used both legislative and extralegislative methods to assure that military bases or federal offices in their districts and states remain open. Notwithstanding the force of legislative imperatives, incumbents often need not resort to this drastic approach to assure that their constituents benefit from administrative decisions; phone calls, personal visits, political exchanges, and the exploitation of contacts within an agency may be equally successful. The main reason for the effectiveness of legislators in bureaucratic intercessions is that they are the ones who can provide what bureaucrats value most: higher budgets and program expansion. Agencies cannot even survive, much less thrive, without congressional support, since Congress controls the purse strings, authorizes new programs, and reauthorizes existing programs.

Constituent Communication. The two forms of constituent communication are personal contact with constituents and legislator (mass) mailings. How members of Congress allocate time between Washington and the district or state reveals a lot about their priorities, since time is the scarcest and most valuable resource at a legislator's command. If there is one perennial complaint among legislators, the lack of time is surely it. Incumbents jealously guard their own time, often erecting barriers of staff to protect them from claims on it; activities that squander a member's time are avoided—unless they involve constituents. Protecting their own time has become such a preoccupation of members that concerted efforts have been taken to reduce work loads. For instance, congressional leaders have frequently justified increases in legislative staff as a means of coping with demands made on the time of legislators. But while staff perform many constituency-related functions, their efforts only supplement those of their bosses. The personal time of the incumbent is often one resource without substitutes; for many constituents there is no adequate replacement for the personal attention of the member, and some things can only be done personally by the incumbent, like meeting with influential constituents or addressing large gatherings at home.

The personal time of the representative or senator is also a resource that is less divisible than the time of staff. Staff can be distributed between the Washington and home offices without disrupting either the lawmaking or constituency service responsibilities of congressional offices. Not so with the time of members. The allocation of time to constituent affairs poses a dilemma for most members of Congress, since the time spent in the constituency (or with constituents at any location) could also be spent in legislative activities that might enhance the realization of members' more personal goals. Thus there is a potential "zero-sum" relationship between the desire to attend to legislative business and the need to spend time on district and state matters. Most representatives and senators would rather devote their time to legislative business, and many see constituency matters as actually interfering with the performance of legislative responsibilities. Yet members willingly allocate large proportions of their personal time to constituent affairs.

John Saloma estimated that more than one-quarter (28 percent) of a representative's average work-week in Washington is devoted to constituency affairs and that a similar amount (25 percent) of the legislator's staff time is also spent on constituency matters (1969, pp. 184–185). More recent data suggest an even higher percentage of time may be devoted to constituency affairs, since a large proportion of a member's time in Washington and in the district or state is devoted to constituency matters. In Washington, about one-third of the average day of senators is spent dealing with constituent mail or talking with constituents and groups (U.S. Senate, 1976, p. 28), and representatives devote a similar proportion of time to district affairs while in their Washington offices (U.S. House of Representatives, 1977, pp. 18–19). In the district or state, almost all of a legislator's time is occupied with presentations to constituents, and incumbents spend considerable time there; in 1980, representatives spent about one of every three days in their districts, while senators spent one of every four days in their states (Parker, 1986).

In addition to personal contact, legislators express their attention to constituent problems and district or state interests through mass mailings sent to voters. Despite restrictions, a wide range of material qualifies for use of the congressional frank (free postage for mass mailings), such as newsletters, questionnaires, biographical material, federal laws and regulations, and nonpartisan election information (e.g., voter registration dates and places). These types of printed matter are exploited both to serve constituents and to promote the image that the incumbent is attentive to district or state interests. These two functions are almost impossible to separate.

Messages to Constituents: Content and Intent. The attentiveness that legislators shower upon their constituents conveys several messages that influence how members of Congress are perceived by voters. These messages are conveyed through the behavior and statements of legislators while in their constituencies and they can be both explicit and implicit. For example, a legislator may demonstrate concern for constituents by "bringing home" district projects, or by issuing statements designed to elicit voter trust; both actions convey the same message. In most instances, legislators rely upon both statements and actions, thereby serving to reinforce the messages they consider critical to their longevity in office. These messages present an image of a concerned representative, explain actions in Congress, and generally serve as self-promotion for the member. Legislators spend considerable time and effort in promulgating these messages, and their efforts seem to pay off, since voters tend to perceive legislators in terms of the images they project.

Presentations. Incumbents believe that support at home is won by the kind of individual self they portray, and they are not the least reluctant to manipulate their presentations of themselves. "So members of Congress go home," according to Fenno "to present themselves as a person and to win the accolade: 'he's a good man,' 'she's a good woman!'" (1975, p. 55). Fenno lists three personal characteristics that legislators emphasize: qualification, identification, and empathy. Every legislator creates the impression that he or she is qualified to hold office, that he or she can identify with the attitudes and beliefs of constituents, and that he or she can empathize with the problems of constituents. These personal characteristics are transmitted at each and every opportunity that a legislator has to communicate with constituents: newsletters, constituent mailings, meetings in the constituency, personal visits. The more personal and pervasive the contact, the greater the probability that the message will be retained. Incumbents make considerable use of these presentations to convey the image that they care about constituents, their problems, and their frustrations.

Explanations. Members of Congress also justify their Washington activities to constituents; Fenno (1978) refers to this as "explanations of Washington activities." Explanations are the mechanisms through which incumbents describe, interpret, and legitimize legislative pursuits, especially the two major preoccupations of senators and representatives: power and policy. The pursuit of power, for example, can be justified by claiming that influence is used to further district or state interests within Congress.

Even though they probably have little to fear from electoral reprisals for one or two unpopular votes, incumbent legislators make a point of explaining their votes and policy positions to their constituents when they are called upon to do so. Since most constituents are unaware of the specific votes and perceive their representative as voting in line with constituent sentiment (Parker, 1989), explaining roll-call votes generally creates few problems for incumbents. A string of "wrong" votes could pose problems, but most members avoid creating such patterns in their votes by developing a good sense of the policy stands that are likely to produce adverse constituent reaction. In fact, since

there is always some uncertainty as to what votes a member may be called upon to explain, legislators tend to "stockpile" more explanations than they actually need.

It is impossible for constituents to keep tabs on their legislators, especially when they are in Washington; hence, voters are largely uninformed about the behavior of their representatives and senators. But while the actions of incumbents may be invisible to their constituents, the incumbents themselves are not. Constituents normally find their legislators willing and prepared to explain their Washington activities, and their frequent appearances within their constituencies provide ample opportunities to question them about these activities. The fact that members frequently make themselves available to voters reinforces constituent trust, thereby assuring incumbents some measure of latitude in their Washington activities.

Self-promotion. John Saloma (1969) analyzed printed matter sent to constituents by representatives and senators (newsletters, news releases, form letters, and policy statements) during the first session of the 89th Congress. Saloma found that more than one-half of the representatives (55 percent) and senators (63 percent) used their written communications to enhance their own personal image and to advance their private interests (reelection). Three activities associated with such self-promotion have been identified: advertising, credit claiming, and position taking (Mayhew, 1974). Advertising activities are designed to disseminate a legislator's name widely among constituents and to associate it with a positive image. Credit-claiming activities involve the efforts of incumbents to create the belief that constituency benefits are solely attributable to their unique efforts. The notion of constituency benefits generally conjures images of the legislative pork barrel, but, in fact, a large proportion of the benefits that members funnel to their constituents do not even involve legislative action; rather, casework forms the bulk of the particularized benefits distributed to voters. Finally, position taking characterizes the efforts of incumbents to take policy stands that are pleasing to their constituents. There is no better way for a legislator to endear himself to his constituents than by publicly voicing policy positions that are strongly supported in the district or state.

These home activities are not entirely self-serving, since they meet legitimate representational responsibilities. Constituents expect to be kept informed about issues that are relevant to their concerns, and incumbents oblige them by providing such information while also taking the opportunity to further their own interests through these communications. Diana Yiannakis's study (1982) of the newsletters and press releases produced by a sample of members during the first six months of both the 94th and 95th Congresses demonstrates exactly how adept incumbents are at fulfilling these dual objectives. Yiannakis found that 42 percent of the paragraphs in these newsletters and press releases were devoted to explaining the incumbents' stands on national issues, and less than 10 percent were devoted to national or local information of a more general sort—an amount of space smaller than that allocated to claiming credit for particularized district benefits (11.6 percent).

Constituent perceptions. Since representatives and senators work exceedingly hard to promote the image that they care about their districts and states, it should not be too surprising to find that constituents see them in exactly these terms. Table 1 presents data describing the content of what voters liked or disliked about their representatives and senators in 1988 and 1990. It is clear from this table that constituency outreach was mentioned frequently by voters in evaluating their representative but considerably less often in voter evaluations of senators. This was the major difference in constituent perceptions of representatives and senators. This should not be construed, however, to suggest that the constituency service provided by senators cannot rival the level or quality of district service; few constituents had anything negative to say about the constituency behavior of senators. We should not ignore the fact that while constituency attention was mentioned less frequently in evaluations of senators than representatives, it remained a central ingredient in the images of both. The other important conclusion that can be derived from this table is that constituents rarely saw their legislators in terms of political issues. This is even more surprising because of the degree to which senators talk about public policies. No matter how much senators talk about political issues, however, voters were no more likely to mention issues in their evaluations of senators than they did in evaluating their representative. In both cases, the images carried only a wisp of issue content.

Why are the popular images of senators less colored by constituency outreach? The differing responsibilities and representational arrangements of representatives and senators, such as length of term, may make constituency attention less central to voter perceptions of senators. Or, perhaps, senators have more to "lose" by spending time with constituents than do representatives, in the sense that

TABLE 1. *Voter Perceptions of House and Senate Incumbents, 1988 and 1990*[1]

CONTENT OF LIKES/DISLIKES	1988 REPRESENTATIVES LIKES		DISLIKES		1990 REPRESENTATIVES LIKES		DISLIKES		1988 SENATORS LIKES		DISLIKES		1990 SENATORS LIKES		DISLIKES	
	No.	%	No.	%	No.	%	No.	%	No.	%	No.	%	No.	%	No.	%
LEADERSHIP	10	1	9	5	25	2	8	2	42	3	21	4	79	2	47	4
EXPERIENCE	78	11	7	4	176	14	10	3	226	14	19	3	623	19	20	2
CONSTITUENCY ATTENTION	192	28	19	11	343	27	43	11	260	17	50	9	585	18	128	12
TRUST	71	10	20	12	126	10	76	19	242	15	71	12	420	13	155	14
PERSONAL CHARACTERISTICS	68	10	11	6	144	11	25	6	174	11	26	5	280	9	51	5
PARTY	25	4	26	15	67	5	57	14	46	3	91	16	145	4	168	15
IDEOLOGY	64	9	24	14	70	6	41	10	171	11	99	17	233	7	149	13
DOMESTIC ISSUES	66	10	19	11	164	13	63	16	181	12	97	17	449	14	199	16
FOREIGN POLICY ISSUES	10	1	5	3	11	1	12	3	33	2	24	4	67	2	46	4
GROUP SUPPORT	59	9	14	8	92	7	19	5	103	7	34	6	175	5	57	5
MISCELLANEOUS	49	7	17	10	54	4	42	11	87	6	43	7	183	6	92	8

[1]Voters were asked: Was there anything in particular you liked or disliked about the incumbent candidate? Poll group sizes varied. The candidates were running in elections involving both House and Senate incumbents.
SOURCE: National Election Studies, 1988–1990 (University of Michigan)

they possess and exercise greater power than the average representative; the lawmaking activities that must be given up are more valuable to senators than to representatives. Since constituency outreach requires more of a sacrifice on the part of senators, they might be expected to devote less time to it. In any event, senators do spend less time with constituents than do representatives, and it shows in their images among voters.

One reason why constituency service may be important to constituents is that they do not perceive representatives and senators, in general, as devoting a great deal of time to district or state affairs. It seems clear, therefore, that legislators can create a sacred place for themselves in the minds of their constituents by being attentive to constituency matters. It is a good way to distinguish oneself from others in Congress who are perceived to spend more of their time on legislative business than on constituency affairs. This may explain why over one-third of the reasons given by respondents in a national survey (U.S. House, 1977, p. 820) for believing their representative to be better than most other incumbents made mention of some aspect of his or her service to the district (communicates with constituents, cares about constituents, tries to solve constituent problems, obtains federal funds for the district). It is easy to understand why attentive legislators are so popular with their constituents: they are spending time on activities that are important to constituents but are perceived as generally getting too little attention.

Impact of Outreach. One of the basic motivations of legislators is the desire to be reelected; no other goal (e.g., attaining a position of congressional leadership) can be entertained without first assuring reelection. Given the amount of time that legislators devote to constituency outreach activity, we might expect such actions to yield clearly identifiable reelection benefits. Indeed, many of the outreach activities that legislators engage in are designed to help them get reelected; the empirical evidence, however, remains inconclusive. Regardless of the electoral effects of constituency attention, there is less uncertainty about the effects of outreach efforts in promoting the efficiency and effectiveness of congressional oversight of federal programs: constituent contact provides legislators with valuable feedback about the operation of bureaucratic agencies and the programs they implement.

Electoral effects. Many of the services that members provide to constituents, such as mass mailings, fulfill representational obligations. A newsletter is one means through which constituents can learn about the activities of their representative or senator and about the impact of national policies on the district or state. On the other hand, fulfilling such a representational obligation may simultaneously satisfy electoral needs; the same newsletter that keeps constituents informed about government can be packaged to convey images that have electoral appeal. For instance, claiming credit for a federal project or advertising one's record of constituency service can be easily integrated with less political information. Government-subsidized travel to the state or district helps incumbents maintain contact with their constituents, but meetings with constituents also provide legislators with a ubiquitous channel for disseminating the types of messages that elicit voter support. The similarity of the member's messages between and during congressional campaigns testifies to the dual objectives that these incumbent resources serve—it is precisely the intertwining of electoral and representational purposes in their use that makes it difficult to regulate usage effectively without impairing representational responsibilities. The constituent contact that results from the utilization of most of these resources provides opportunities for incumbents to engage in electioneering. Incumbents use these contacts to enhance their visibility among constituents, to project electorally rewarding home-style images, and to mobilize supporters for an approaching election.

Senators face more obstacles than representatives in exploiting their contacts with their constituents for electoral advantage. One obstacle is that senators exercise less control over the dissemination of information about themselves than do representatives; for example, the higher levels of "free" (e.g., media supplied) information in Senate elections make challengers far more visible to voters than in House elections. This is not to say that senators gain less from the exploitation of office resources; rather, the nature of the office—the greater prestige, power, competitiveness, and campaign costs—makes senators more vulnerable to forces beyond their control.

Newsletters, trips to the state or district, and the use of other office resources do more than increase constituent contact and, therefore, voter support. These resources also discourage competitive challenges by influencing perceptions of vulnerability. If an incumbent can convince potential opponents, and those who would financially support their candidacies, that he or she is unbeatable, few formidable challenges will be made by the opposition party. It is difficult to recruit a candidate to run against a popular incumbent; often the activity degenerates into recruiting "losers" rather than highly qualified candidates. Thus, by maintaining extensive contact with voters, incumbents are able to weaken the opposition they face in primaries or at the next election.

The empirical link between constituency attention and electoral safety has stirred considerable research and controversy. Some constituency activities appear to influence elections, while others seem to have little or no effect; in still other instances, constituency activities and their impact on electoral safety remain an issue for debate. For example, the effects of mass mailings on electoral margins seem weak, if at all apparent. John Ferejohn (1977) found no evidence that an increase in mass mailings increased the visibility of incumbents, thereby giving them an electoral edge; an ingenious quasi-experimental study of the distribution of baby books to new parents by one representative found an immediate, but not a lasting, effect on the incumbent's electoral support (Cover and Brumberg, 1982). There is also no evidence that pork-barreling increases electoral safety; Paul Feldman and James Jondrow (1984) report that bringing government employment and money to the district appears to have no pronounced effect in increasing an incumbent's vote support.

Personal visits to the district and state, however, appear to increase electoral safety; representatives and senators who secured their previous reelection with a small margin of victory in states electorally dominated by the opposition party increased their election margins as they increased the time they spent in their constituencies (Parker, 1986). The results are less definitive with respect to casework. Morris Fiorina (1977) contends that legislators seize upon bureaucratic errors of omission and commission to curry favor with voters; resolving constituent grievances in a manner favorable to one's constituents impresses voters and solidifies electoral support within the district or state. Diana Yiannakis's study (1982) supports Fiorina's hypothesis; she found that levels of voter satisfaction with an incumbent's service to constituents was related to voter choice, especially among partisans of the challenger's party. John Johannes and John McAdams (1981), in contrast, contend that casework fails to affect an incumbent's reelection because constituents fully expect their legislators to render such service. Perhaps the issue is not whether constituency outreach affects electoral support, but what facets of such attention are most effective in doing so.

Oversight. Representatives and senators devote time and resources (staff) to addressing constituent problems, and they are quite effective in these efforts. Legislators intervene between constituents and bureaucrats in a whole range of matters—disagreements over a regulation, delays in federal grants (e.g., welfare), absence of administrative action, and others. In some instances, the incumbent may actually serve as a lobbyist for special interests within the constituency vis-à-vis his or her committees and the federal bureaucracy. These "errand boy" activities, as they are unflatteringly called, are viewed by members and constituents as basic elements of the job.

One result of the emphasis on pursuing constituent complaints is that oversight of the executive branch is provided on a continuous and timely basis. Casework sometimes even leads directly to formal oversight hearings or to the introduction of remedial legislation. Constituent reaction to agency programs and regulations may be the quickest way to alert agency officials and committee leaders to problems involved in the administration of a policy or program. It provides the type of scrutiny that neither Congress nor its administration watchdog, the General Accounting Office, can supply. Since legislative goals are stated so vaguely in legislation, it is difficult to determine whether any violation has occurred unless some citizen or group registers a complaint; the large number of constituents affected by a program ensures that any violation that seriously harms an organized group will be identified. Such a system of decentralized "alarms" may serve as an efficient check on the great authority that Congress has delegated to executive agencies:

Although Congress may, to some extent, have allowed the bureaucracy to make law, it may also have devised a reasonably effective and non-costly way to articulate and promulgate its own legislative goals—a way that depends on the fire-alarm oversight system. It is convenient for Congress to adopt broad legislative mandates and give substantial rule-making authority to the bureaucracy. The problem with doing so, of course, is that the bureaucracy might not pursue Congress's goals. But citizens and interest groups can be counted on to sound an alarm in most cases in which the bureaucracy has arguably violated Congress's goal. Then Congress can intervene to rectify the violation. (McCubbins and Schwartz, 1984, pp. 174–175).

Constituency outreach involves the ways in which incumbent legislators serve and at the same time cultivate their constituencies with the aim of improving their standing among constituents and reducing voter fears about the latitude their representatives and senators exercise in Washington. There are three categories of constituency attention: casework (helping constituents dealing with the federal bureaucracy); pork-barreling (bringing federal funds to the district or state); and constituent communication (personal and impersonal contacts with constituents). These "services" to constituents are designed to convey images that win voter approval, justify Washington behavior such as legislative votes, and promote one's standing within the constituency by advertising on-the-job accomplishments, claiming credit for constituency benefits (e.g., federal contracts), and taking policy positions that voters strongly favor. These activities and the messages they contain leave an indelible mark on voter evaluations and perceptions of their legislators—and the imprint is likely to create positive images of incumbent legislators. Constituency attention can be linked to the electoral safety of incumbents, though the relationship appears to vary by constituency activity (e.g., personal visits, mass mailings, casework, pork-barreling) and the effectiveness of legislative oversight of the federal bureaucracy.

[See also Broadcasting of Congressional Proceedings; C-SPAN; Circular Letters; Congress, article on Public Perceptions of Congress; Constituency Service; Correspondence to Congress; Franking; Petitions and Memorials; Pork Barrel; Press; Private Bills; Visitors to Capitol Hill; Voting in Congress, article on Ratings by Interest Groups.]

BIBLIOGRAPHY

Cain, Bruce, John Ferejohn, and Morris Fiorina. The Personal Vote. 1987.

Cover, Albert, and Bruce Brumberg. "Baby Books and Ballots: The Impact of Congressional Mail on Constituent Opinion." American Political Science Review 76 (June 1982): 347–359.

Dodd, Lawrence C. "Congress and the Quest for Power." In Studies of Congress. Edited by Glenn R. Parker. 1985. Pp. 489–520.

Feldman, Paul, and James Jondrow. "Congressional Elections and Local Federal Spending." American Journal of Political Science 28 (May 1984): 147–163.

Fenno, Richard F. Home Style. 1978.

Ferejohn, John. "On the Decline of Competition in Congressional Elections." American Political Science Review 71 (March 1977): 166–176.

Fiorina, Morris P. Congress: Keystone of the Washington Establishment. 1977.

Johannes, John R. "Casework in the House." In The House at Work. Edited by Joseph Cooper and G. Calvin MacKenzie. 1981. Pp. 78–96.

Johannes, John R., and John C. McAdams. "The Congressional Incumbency Effect: Is It Casework, Policy Compatibility, or Something Else?" American Journal of Political Science 25 (August 1981): 512–542.

Kingdon, John. Congressmen's Voting Decisions. 1973.

Mayhew, David R. Congress: The Electoral Connection. 1974.

McCubbins, Matthew, and Thomas Schwartz. "Congressional Oversight Overlooked: Police Patrols Versus Fire Alarms." American Journal of Political Science 28 (February 1984): 165–179.

Parker, Glenn R. Characteristics of Congress. 1989.

Parker, Glenn R. Homeward Bound. 1986.

Saloma, John S., III. Congress and the New Politics. 1969.

U.S. House of Representatives. Final Report of the Commission on Administrative Review. 95th Cong., 1st sess., 1977. H. Doc. 95-276.

U.S. Senate. Commission on the Operation of the Senate. Toward A More Modern Senate. 94th Cong., 2d sess., 1976. S. Doc. 94-278.

Yiannakis, Diana E. "House Members' Communication Styles: Newsletters and Press Releases." Journal of Politics 44 (November 1982): 1049–1071.

GLENN R. PARKER

CONSTITUENCY SERVICE. From the first meeting of the First Congress, senators and representatives have been attending to the needs, requests, and demands of their constituents for help in dealing with governmental problems. Over time, such constituency service has become a regular feature of the congressional landscape. Demands have grown; the process for handling constituent requests has become institutionalized; and controversies have arisen over the utility and consequences of the practice.

The Nature of Constituency Service. The range of constituency service is immense. Legislators routinely secure White House tour tickets for visitors, mail out pamphlets and government documents on a host of topics, answer constituents' questions about government policies or regulations, expedite the purchase of flags that have flown over the Capitol, help job seekers, and select young men and women for the armed service academies. More importantly, they engage in individual casework and federal projects assistance.

Individual ("low-level") casework involves intervening on behalf of citizens or, occasionally, resident aliens who feel aggrieved by or need assistance in dealing with federal (and sometimes state or local) agencies. Usually such people come to Congress after having failed to get what they want from the appropriate executive source, although a noticeable proportion go directly to Congress before exhausting administrative remedies. They may want to know what is holding up their applications or claims, for example, or be demanding explanations for denials, asking for help in expediting requests, or complaining about poor treatment at the hands of bureaucrats. Although no federal agency or program is immune to citizens' dissatisfaction, the most common cases involve social security, health insurance, and pension claims; military and veterans' affairs; job-related matters; immigration and visa issues; housing; and taxes. At times the petitioner is a group of constituents seeking, perhaps, a transfer of federal property or aid for a community project.

Federal projects assistance, sometimes called high-level casework, involves helping states and localities to win grants from federal departments and agencies. Because most federal funding for state and local governments is determined by statutory formulas, the amount of discretionary funding controlled by the executive branch is limited; thus congressional intervention becomes important to state and local governments that want to tap the federal "pork barrel." These projects rarely constitute more than 7 or 8 percent of the requests coming into congressional offices, but because of their importance and complexity, they may take up to a quarter or more of the time a legislative office devotes to constituency service.

Although throughout the nineteenth century senators and representatives complained of the excessive burden that petitioning citizens laid upon them, the volume of casework increased greatly after the New Deal establishment of new agencies and programs in the 1930s and then again after the explosion of Great Society programs in the 1960s. Both the New Deal and Great Society dramatically increased government benefits and regulations. National public-opinion surveys begun in 1978 have revealed that about 15 percent of Americans claim that they or their families have contacted their senators or representatives and that about two-fifths to one-half that number did so to request help. The others wrote or called to express opinions or seek information.

Precise numbers of case requests coming to Con-gress are hard to pin down, because until the onset of the computer age accurate records were seldom kept and because cases pour into both Washington and home-state or district congressional offices. The most accurate counts available come from surveys taken in 1977–1978 and 1982 by John R. Johannes and John C. McAdams. In the 95th Congress, the mean number of new requests received by 136 House offices was 108 per week (with a median of 100), about 90 percent of which were individual cases; in 53 Senate offices studied, the average was 302, but the median was only 175. By the 97th Congress, 204 House offices reported an average of 103 cases (again, 90 percent of which were "low-level" casework items), but the median fell to 70. The 28 Senate offices surveyed averaged 175 cases.

Explanations of who asks for casework help and why fall into two categories. One focuses on the demand side, picturing the legislator as an agent of the state or district, with the demand for casework services primarily determined by objective constituency needs, expectations, and abilities. The other, "supply-side," view sees senators and representatives as active entrepreneurs, urging their constituents to seek their services. Both explanations have some validity. Research (mostly on the House) indicates that senior representatives from constituencies with generally lower levels of education (and, presumably, higher need) are more likely to receive large numbers of casework requests. Members representing districts with concentrations of very highly educated citizens and large numbers of government employees—in other words, constituents, who are very capable of making demands—also attract heavy case loads. Finally, constituencies in regions of the country that share what Daniel Elazar terms a "traditionalistic" political culture (paternalistic, antibureaucratic, focusing on "friends and neighbors" politics) tend to make greater demands; conversely, those in "moralistic" (issue-oriented, "clean government") regions are distinctly less likely to do so.

The supply-side explanation also stands up to analysis. One of the clearest predictors of heavy caseloads is member seniority. Constituents also seem more inclined to seek help from representatives with whom they have come into contact. Thus, for example, in late 1981 and 1982, members who made the most trips back home were more likely to have heavy caseloads than those making fewer trips to their districts, all other factors being equal.

Contact need not always be in person, of course, and legislators have accordingly devised all sorts of tactics to advertise their services: newsletters; general or targeted mailings; personal appearances that include reminders of their willingness to help constituents; mobile offices; special seminars with local government officials or major constituency groups; staff members generously sprinkled in local offices; radio, television, and newspaper advertisements; and even matchbook covers and billboards—all are part of the casework "hustling" enterprise. By 1982, only 3 percent of the offices surveyed claimed to do nothing to solicit cases and projects; more than half the representatives employed four or more distinct devices (Johannes and McAdams, 1987). Younger representatives developed and deployed many of these aggressive tactics in the 1970s, but no matter when or by whom they were introduced, they have become standard fare in the House and, to a lesser degree, in the Senate. There is little doubt that they are at least somewhat effective.

A legislator's reputation for successful casework service is likely to bring in additional cases. Word-of-mouth advertising is considered by congressional staff assistants to be one of the best techniques for generating more case requests. (Scholarly research has only begun to test this claim.)

Decades of increased constituency service have created a strong set of casework expectations on the part of constituents and legislators alike, and local governments positively bank on cooperation from, and often leadership by, their Washington representatives in the search for federal dollars. Surveys conducted biennially by the University of Michigan's Center for Political Studies as well as those commissioned in 1977 by the House Commission on Administrative Review (the Obey commission) have revealed the extent to which the public believes that constituency service is important. For example, 37 percent of respondents in the Obey commission's poll responded to an open-ended question about what things were most important for representatives to do by pointing to district service; 70 percent agreed that it was "very important" for Congress to provide people with a direct link to the federal government. Ninety percent thought it very or fairly important for their representatives to help people in their districts who have problems with the government, and 94 percent said the same about getting a fair share of money for the district. A quarter to a third of respondents to the Center for Political Studies poll have told interviewers that

if they have a problem with the government, they expect their representatives to be very helpful in resolving it; only about one in ten anticipate little or no help. Members of Congress understand what all this means: when the Obey commission asked members what sorts of duties they thought they were expected to perform, four-fifths mentioned the constituent service role.

Members themselves see casework and projects as important, though not so important as legislative and policy-related duties. Their reasons include the obvious implications constituency service has for reelection and the attendant freedom to pursue policies that might otherwise find little support in their districts, but their reasoning goes further than this. Members of Congress are probably as compassionate as other Americans, and, as politicians, they are naturally sensitive to others; they genuinely care about their constituents and want to help them when they can. There are simply too many electorally safe or retiring senators and representatives who work diligently on constituency service without any electoral incentive to believe otherwise. Moreover, some members believe that casework carries other payoffs: inspiring ideas for legislation, for example, or strengthening congressional oversight of the executive branch. Some members harbor a deep-seated disdain for bureaucrats; several believe that casework prevents public alienation and cynicism or has symbolic importance; and a few see casework as a link to the "real world" outside Washington. Finally, almost all perceive casework as part of a legislator's job. Studies of legislatures around the world show that such views are almost universal. In short, motives for and the importance of constituency service are complex; no single reason can adequately explain why case and projects work has become "big business" in Washington.

The Casework System. Casework and federal projects assistance have become institutionalized in a routine and substantially bureaucratized system of exchanges. Constituents, in effect, are perceived to barter votes for congressional help with their problems, and executive agencies scurry to provide timely responses and, if possible, favorable decisions for congressional offices in return for legislative support for their programs.

All but a tiny portion of constituency service work is performed by the personal staffs of senators and representatives. Between the mid 1950s and 1980, these staffs roughly tripled in size, and staff positions became more specialized. Among

RAISING AND LOWERING FLAGS. Constituents often request a flag that has flown at the U.S. Capitol.

OFFICE OF THE ARCHITECT OF THE CAPITOL

about 23 percent in 1972 to more than 41 percent in 1990, while the increase in Senate staff in home-state offices went from 12 to 35 percent. Doing casework and projects work back home is a mixed blessing, since staff members must often contact executive agencies in Washington; conversely, Capitol Hill staffs frequently need to deal with local or regionally based executive officials. Over time, a variety of elaborate schemes for coordination have developed.

Casework staffs tend to be young, well educated, and female. Because constituency service is emotionally fatiguing and often perceived as the first step on the staff career ladder, there is considerable turnover. By and large, however, these women and men are dedicated to their work and share a great variety of casework-related motivations and attitudes, as do their employers.

The executive-branch casework bureaucracy is equally well developed. Almost all departments and agencies have congressional relations offices, whose primary functions include handling requests and inquiries from congressional staffs. Most of these offices are located in Washington; but congressional caseworkers frequently bypass them, going directly to agencies' regional and local offices around the country. Both sides perceive advantages in bringing cases to a successful resolution and maintaining good working relationships with their counterparts. However, rivalry and resentment do appear, especially when House and Senate staffs push harder for a particular resolution than agency people deem warranted or when a congressional staffer treats an agency official improperly.

In short, the casework process has become routinized at both ends, with clear expectations, standard operating procedures, and behavioral norms in place. So long as congressional staff are polite and sincere, and provided they don't push agencies to violate laws or administrative rules, executive officials will take care of their Capitol Hill counterparts by expediting the process of review. The interbranch politics of constituency service has its ups and downs, but most participants realize that they must get along with each other.

Issues in Constituency Service. Four overriding and often controversial issues surround constituency service: Does it work? Is it fair? Does it help or hinder the primary congressional duty of policy making? Does it pay off in votes and thus contribute to keeping legislators in office?

Effectiveness. Congressional interventions on behalf of constituents usually (but far from always)

those specializations is constituency service. Today a senator from a large state commonly has twenty or more aides doing little more than handling cases and projects, while a representative may assign half of his or her entire staff to such chores.

Led by the newest cohorts of legislators, especially those from urban areas and electorally marginal districts, members in the 1970s placed increasing portions of their staffs in offices located in their states and districts precisely to handle casework and, to a lesser extent, projects work. According to *Vital Statistics on Congress, 1991–1992,* the proportion of House staff in district offices jumped from

are effective in moving their questions, requests, and complaints through the executive bureaucracy more quickly than would otherwise happen and in getting the agencies involved to take a more thorough look at the cases, often at higher bureaucratic levels. The rule in agency offices is to settle cases as soon as possible. Occasionally, however, a congressional inquiry can actually delay the processing of a request, since the time devoted to giving special attention to the matter and replying to Congress might exceed the normal processing period.

Congressional staff estimates place the proportion of cases in which the original executive decision is modified in the range of 30 to 50 percent. In almost all cases, such changes are simply the result of taking a second and closer look at a constituent's problem and seeing that an error had been made, that new information is available to alter the original decision, or that there is in fact enough leeway in the relevant law or regulation to be more accommodating than was originally believed. Many of these cases probably would have been decided in the same fashion without congressional intervention if the constituent had made the appeal directly to the agency involved. Considering that perhaps as many as one-fifth of all cases are utterly lacking in merit (and are usually instantly recognized as such by both congressional and executive participants), the overall success rate is rather high.

Not all casework staffs and not all congressional offices are equally successful. Clearly, some staff members are more experienced and skillful at getting along with their executive counterparts. Personal intervention by senators and representatives is relatively rare, occurring when cases are particularly delicate or important or, more often, when the staff faces strong resistance from executive officials. Sometimes such personal intervention by the member makes a difference; at other times it does not. Much depends on the case, the executive official handling it, and the legislator's skills and influence.

Fairness, equity, and ethics. On the whole, relatively few outright violations of the equity principle seem to occur. Legislators and their staffs seldom ask agency personnel to break a law or a regulation (though they do ask that regulations be stretched), and only rarely do executive actors comply with such requests. The primary reason is that professional casework teams in both Congress and the executive branch are sensitive to the fairness issue and share a sense of casework ethics; legislators and their staffs also fear that public revelations of improper pressure will backfire and prove politically embarrassing.

Such was the case in the Charles H. Keating, Jr., affair of the 1980s. Keating, chairman of Lincoln Savings and Loan Association, had made substantial campaign contributions and other political donations to five senators, as well as loans and gifts to their family members and staff assistants. These senators were discovered to have held meetings with Federal Home Loan Bank Board regulators on behalf of Lincoln Savings. In November 1991, after two years of investigations and hearings, the Senate Select Ethics Committee publicly and formally reprimanded Sen. Alan Cranston (D-Calif.) for his involvement in the scandal. Cranston and the four other senators involved defended their actions as merely helping a constituent in need.

Such spectacular cases are relatively rare. Still, several questions deserve attention. At a superficial level, casework can be unfair because congressional or executive staffs might act arbitrarily, because a constituent might get away with a lie, or because only citizens who ask for help are likely to get it. Even among those who are being helped, not all receive the same quality of attention. Many of those involved in casework operations report that a legislator's friends, relatives, major contributors, and other VIPs occasionally receive special treatment, although most contend that they seek to treat all similar cases—certainly all routine cases—alike, regardless of the petitioner. Partisanship plays no significant role. Agency officials also admit to providing faster and more careful service to important senators and representatives (such as those on key committees), but even here there is some disagreement.

The real question is whether congressional intervention affects the substance, rather than the speed or care, of an agency's response. The best available evidence suggests that the answer is yes, but only rarely, and that this applies more to federal projects than to individual citizens' requests. In short, to the extent that there is unfairness or inequity in casework, it is not systematic in ways that might be expected. Rather, lack of perfect equity can be attributed as much to personalities and the peculiar nature of a given case as to partisanship and politics.

The Keating scandal is not unique. Anytime a senator or representative intervenes in the administrative process on behalf of a constituent, there arises the possibility of some impropriety, whether bribery (usually in the form of campaign financing), illegal gratuities, conflicts of interest, or even extortion or conspiracy to defraud. The courts have had to handle a number of such cases, and the House and Senate ethics committees have issued rules, ethics codes, and principles bearing on the problem. In all instances, however, the burden of judgment rests on the office of the member who is assisting constituents. In the vast majority of cases, no problems emerge, but constituency service sometimes crosses into a gray area of congressional ethics.

Policy-making implications. One common view of constituency service is that it is a necessary evil, a burden to be endured so that senators and representatives can remain in office to attend to the important work of legislation and oversight. Arguments in support of this thesis focus on the time spent by legislators on constituency service, the dedication of staff resources to casework, and the disruption to the administrative process that occurs when agencies must review cases already decided and respond to congressional staffs. Although there is truth to all these charges, they are exaggerated.

The fact is that senators and representatives spend relatively little time on cases and projects per se; they do, of course, spend endless hours with their constituencies explaining their positions, building political support, raising funds, and campaigning. Studies by the House Commission on Administrative Review (1977), Robert Klonoff (1979), and John R. Johannes (1984) have shown that the vast majority of members spend less, often far less, than 10 percent of their time pursuing case and project results for constituents. Their involvement typically comes when they meet constituents back in the state or district and pick up numerous requests for help or when they contact agencies directly because their staffs have come up against resistance. Legislators from highly educated districts, where voters are more concerned with policy issues, and those in leadership positions are less involved than others.

An estimated 40 percent or more of the average member's staff time and resources is dedicated to constituency service, and home-based staff devote virtually all their time to serving constituent needs. These facts raise three questions: (1) Is such resource allocation excessive or wasteful? (2) Does constituency work detract from legislative or oversight work staff might otherwise do? (3) Would these staff positions exist at all were it not for the enormous growth in casework? Obviously, if the staff positions existed and if constituency service volume were low, there would be more time for policy matters. These, of course, are hypothetical questions that cannot be answered empirically. What is known is that staffing is generally perceived as adequate, even though some legislators could clearly use more help.

Casework and projects work play a significant and costly role in departments and agencies. Thus it may be surprising that agency personnel take a benign or, frequently, positive view of the process, sharing the view that citizens often deserve a second chance. As for disruption to administrative procedures and efficiency, the results of a survey of executive personnel (Johannes, 1984) are surprising: for every official agreeing that casework disrupted his or her agency or detracted from more important things, nearly three disagreed. Four-fifths of legislators and their staffs disagreed as well. In terms of their own jobs, only one-fifth of the agency officials surveyed viewed handling cases as an interference or a problem. Their primary complaint concerned the time involved; other complaints involved cost, potential loss of respect for executive agencies, and damage to morale.

Dealing with constituent grievances and inquiries contributes positively to congressional oversight of the bureaucracy, to the legislative function, and to internal executive branch oversight. Hearing from constituents provides much of the raw data for oversight. Casework allows ad hoc correction of bureaucratic error, impropriety, and laxity, and can lead a senator or representative to consider changes in laws because of particularly flagrant or persistent problems that casework staffs have discovered. Cases provide opportunities for legislators to raise issues at hearings, and they are cited in speeches on the floors of the House and Senate. Johannes's 1984 survey revealed that about one-third of representatives regularly reviewed cases with their staffs, whereas only about one-fifth said they never did so.

But casework proves less effective and useful than it might be in terms of systematic use of its data for formal committee-based oversight. There are several reasons for this. One has to do with the volume and type of cases received. Frequently the weekly deluge of cases does not allow caseworkers sufficient time to do anything more than passively process constituent requests and complaints; most cases, moreover, are routine and do not raise issues relevant to oversight or legislation.

A second problem concerns how staffs are structured. Although congressional offices are now more able to rely on computers to keep track of cases, the separation of casework staff from policy staff in most offices means that caseworkers have little incentive to think in terms of overall policy or oversight when handling particular problems or requests. Records are kept, but systematic searches—especially searches across a number of House or Senate offices—are rare. Rather, staff members take an anecdotal approach and rely on their memories to identify recurring problems, unusually troublesome executive agencies, or apparent flaws in laws or agency regulations. Most congressional casework staff members, at least in Washington, claim that they generalize from specific cases to broader issues, but their frequent inability to attract the attention of the legislative staff or administrative assistants constrains the efficacy of their efforts. Obviously, the problem is compounded when casework is done in district or state offices. Conversely, when staffers handle both casework and legislation on a particular topic, the prospects increase for using casework for policy making.

Finally, to make the linkage between citizen problems and oversight or legislation requires active involvement at the subcommittee and committee level, where yet another cadre of legislators and staffers, with their own interests and priorities, holds sway. Only when a committee member or aide is intrigued by the information provided via casework experience and is in a position to employ it actively can casework contribute systematically to oversight or the legislative process.

Casework's greatest impact on policy may occur not through congressional procedures but through internal executive-agency responses to congressional interventions. In a survey of 212 executive officials, two-thirds indicated that congressional inquiries helped to highlight problems, and one-third indicated that some sort of systematic attempts were made to utilize them to examine agency policies and operations (Johannes, 1984, p. 171). Granted, the frequency of such use is minimal in most agencies, and often the problems being addressed are already known to agency officials, but even a low level of attention can be useful to police an agency's operations, reevaluate procedures, reconsider rules and regulations, or observe particular bureaucrats' behavior. All things considered, therefore, constituency service often contributes positively, if only rarely in a profound fashion, to Congress's legislative function and to both congressional and internal administrative oversight.

Electoral impact. One of the most important phenomena in American politics is the extremely high frequency with which representatives and, to a lesser extent, senators are able to return to Congress after each election. House reelection rates in the 95-to-98-percent range have been common since the 1960s or before. Documenting this phenomenon is easy; explaining it has proved a greater challenge. In addition to partisan and economic factors, presidential popularity, and particular national and local policy issues, a major explanatory factor is the "personal vote." In a 1987 book that takes its title from this term, Bruce Cain, John Ferejohn, and Morris Fiorina articulated better than anyone else the commonly accepted argument that legislator visibility and constituency service produce enough votes to win close elections or to turn marginal congressional seats into electorally safe ones. That legislators and staffs believe this is beyond dispute, as is the proposition that electorally threatened members are the most aggressive in courting their constituencies and advertising their casework, federal projects, and pork-barrel expertise. Scholars, however, are in disagreement; nearly all concede the logic of the argument, but many dispute the evidence.

Although it has many variants, the argument essentially runs as follows. Citizens seeking help from their representatives and senators are given excellent treatment, even if their requests cannot be granted. They are highly satisfied with what senators and representatives do for them. Constituents observe how diligently their representatives attend to the district (by means of frequent visits and staff allocations), remember what the legislators have done for them, their friends, or the constituency generally, and then come to believe firmly that, should they have difficulties in the future, they can depend on their senators and representatives for help. Voters' satisfaction with and favorable evaluations of legislator constituency service positively affect how they view their representatives' policy positions and actions and contribute to an overall positive job rating. All these factors together—partisanship, name recognition, expectation of helpfulness, favorable job rating, high levels of district service—make voters inclined to cast their ballots for incumbents. Furthermore, the reputation for excellent constituency service will deter challengers and weaken their chances of attracting financial and electoral support.

In the words of Morris Fiorina, "Pork barrelling and casework . . . are basically pure profit" (1977,

p. 45). Fiorina goes a step further, suggesting that Congress's inability or unwillingness to legislate clearly and carefully allows and perhaps causes bureaucratic imprecision and error, which triggers the citizen requests that lead to support for incumbents.

The primary means used to prove the case are sophisticated "multivariate" analyses of national election survey data, bolstered by some district-level information on legislator resource allocation and casework effort. If one accepts as valid the questions and the coding of the national election surveys conducted by the University of Michigan's Center for Political Studies, and if one agrees with the models and methodologies employed, the Fiorina thesis stands up to analysis.

Some scholars, however, dispute the validity of the data as well as the methodology employed to support the hypothesis. In one dissenting view John C. McAdams and John R. Johannes (1988) have argued that if the long chain of linkages (that casework for oneself or a friend brings satisfaction, which causes an expectation of helpfulness, which in turn produces a favorable evaluation that leads to a vote for the incumbent) holds, then one should be able to demonstrate a direct causal effect between casework and the vote. But such a link has yet to be demonstrated.

Critics argue that survey responses are often invalid or represent generalized affect toward incumbents rather than careful assessments of them. Analysts always run the risk of confusing correlation with causality, and the surveys on which analyses are based do not determine which came first: exposure to legislators' constituency service, voters' contacts with incumbents, expectations of helpfulness, or positive attitudes toward the incumbents. Faced with such uncertainties, scholars have attempted to use aggregate data—actual casework loads, dollars of federal spending, district election results, legislative resource allocation, and so on—rather than relying on individual survey data to tackle the problem. Again, results are mixed; the casework effect cannot be clearly demonstrated or even carefully measured.

Future Possibilities. Without doubt, constituency service will remain a major occupation of senators, representatives, and their staffs, and it probably will grow somewhat in complexity, if not in volume. For several reasons—because it is so time consuming, because ethical considerations occasionally loom large, and because of the possibility of systematically using casework for oversight purposes—some legislators have advocated centralizing the function and even turning the function over to a specialized congressional staff, a sort of congressional ombudsman. Arguments in favor of establishing such a central casework operation include greater ease of access for constituents, higher quality service from better-trained professional assistants, reduction of workload, elimination of many ethical problems, and enhanced use of casework for legislative and oversight purposes. Objections include the loss of the personal touch, loss of possible electoral benefits, and higher costs. To date, none of the bills introduced to establish such an institution have been successful, most likely because senators and representatives perceive a need to remain in the business of helping their constituents "fight city hall."

[See also Constituency Outreach.]

BIBLIOGRAPHY

Cain, Bruce E., John A. Ferejohn, and Morris P. Fiorina. *The Personal Vote: Constituency Service and Electoral Independence.* 1987.

Fiorina, Morris P. *Congress: The Keystone of the Washington Establishment.* 1977.

Johannes, John R. *To Serve the People: Congress and Constituency Service.* 1984.

Johannes, John R., and John C. McAdams. "The Congressional Incumbency Effect: Is it Casework, Policy Compatibility, or Something Else?" *American Journal of Political Science* 25 (1981): 512–542.

Johannes, John R., and John C. McAdams. "Entrepreneurs or Agents: Congressmen and the Distribution of Casework in the House: 1977–1978." *Western Political Quarterly* 40 (1987): 535–553.

Klonoff, Robert. "The Congressman as Mediator between Citizens and Government Agencies: Problems and Prospects." *Harvard Journal on Legislation* 16 (1979): 701–734.

McAdams, John C., and John R. Johannes. "Congressmen, Perquisites, and Elections." *Journal of Politics* 50 (1988): 412–439.

U.S. House of Representatives. Commission on Administrative Review. *Final Report.* 2 vols. 95th Cong., 1st sess., 1977.

JOHN R. JOHANNES

CONSTITUTION. [*This entry includes two articles,* Congress in the Constitution, *a discussion of the powers and limitations of Congress as set forth in the Constitution, and* Congressional Interpretation of the Constitution, *a discussion of the ways in which congressional actions have shaped the evolution of the Constitution. For further discussion of the* *debate over congressional powers and the relationship between Congress and the other branches of the U.S. government, see* Congress, *article on* Powers of Congress; Executive Branch; Legislative Branch; Judiciary and Congress; Oversight; President and Congress. *See also* Articles of Confederation; Bill of Rights; Constitutional Convention of 1787; *and articles on particular Amendments to the Constitution. For further discussion of particular Supreme Court cases concerning congressional powers, see* Buckley v. Valeo; Gravel v. United States; Immigration and Naturalization Service v. Chadha; McCullock v. Maryland; McGrain v. Daugherty; Marbury v. Madison; Morrison v. Olson; Myers v. United States; United States v. Curtiss-Wright Export Corporation; Youngstown Sheet and Tube Company v. Sawyer; Wesberry v. Sanders.]

Congress in the Constitution

The existence of a Congress in America predates the Constitution. The first Continental Congress was formed in 1774 as an assembly of delegates from the American colonies. By 1775 the Continental Congress had assumed governmental responsibilities, and in 1776 it declared the United States of America independent from Great Britain.

In 1777 Congress proposed the Articles of Confederation, which the states approved over the next four years. The Articles provided for governance of the new confederacy by "[t]he United States in Congress assembled." During and following the Revolutionary War, defects in the Articles became apparent. Congress lacked power to levy taxes or to regulate commerce among the states or with foreign countries, and laws, which required the approval of nine of the thirteen states represented in Congress, and amendments to the Articles, which required the unanimous approval of state legislatures, were difficult to adopt. Also, the Articles established no executive independent of Congress.

In 1787 Congress agreed to organize a convention to consider and report proposed revisions to the Articles of Confederation. Meeting throughout the summer of 1787 in Philadelphia, the convention reported to Congress a draft of a new Constitution instead of limited revisions to the Articles. Congress submitted the new Constitution for state approval. Following ratification by eleven states, Congress passed a resolution in September 1788 initiating the new government under the Constitution.

The Constitution established three separate branches of government: Congress, the executive, and the judiciary. The most important provisions for Congress are concentrated in Article I, which establishes Congress, makes rules for its election and governance, and assigns it legislative powers. Because the Constitution establishes a system of mutually checking (as well as separated) powers among the branches, succeeding articles of the Constitution govern congressional interaction with the executive and judicial branches. Provisions throughout the Constitution and its amendments limit Congress's powers.

Election and Governance of the Congress. The Constitution establishes rules for the election and governance of the Congress. It addresses the structure, membership, and election of Congress; its officers, meeting, and operations; and the compensation and privileges of its members.

Structure, membership, and election. Article I, section 1 creates "a Congress of the United States, which shall consist of a Senate and House of Representatives." In *Federalist* 51, James Madison explained that "the weight of the legislative authority" made it necessary "to divide the legislature into different branches; and to render them, by different modes of election and different principles of action, as little connected with each other as the nature of their common functions and their common dependence on the society will admit."

Initially, members of the House of Representatives were popularly elected (Art. I, sec. 2, cl. 1), while senators were chosen by the state legislatures (Art. I, sec. 3, cl. 1). By 1913, dissatisfaction with legislatures' selection of senators and support for popular enfranchisement led to ratification of the Seventeenth Amendment, which provided that senators, too, would be popularly elected.

The original idea that members of the House were direct representatives of the people was manifested by the requirement, preserved in the Fourteenth Amendment, that "Representatives shall be apportioned among the several States according to their respective numbers," except that each state was entitled to at least one representative (Amend. XIV, sec. 2, superseding Art. I, sec. 2, cl. 3). The Supreme Court ruled in *Wesberry v. Sanders* (1964) that each state's congressional districts must include as equal a number of inhabitants as is practical.

In contrast, the Senate consists of two members from every state (Amend. XVII, superseding Art. I, sec. 3, cl. 1). The determination that the House would be apportioned by population, while the Senate would represent the states equally, regardless of size, is known as the Great Compromise of

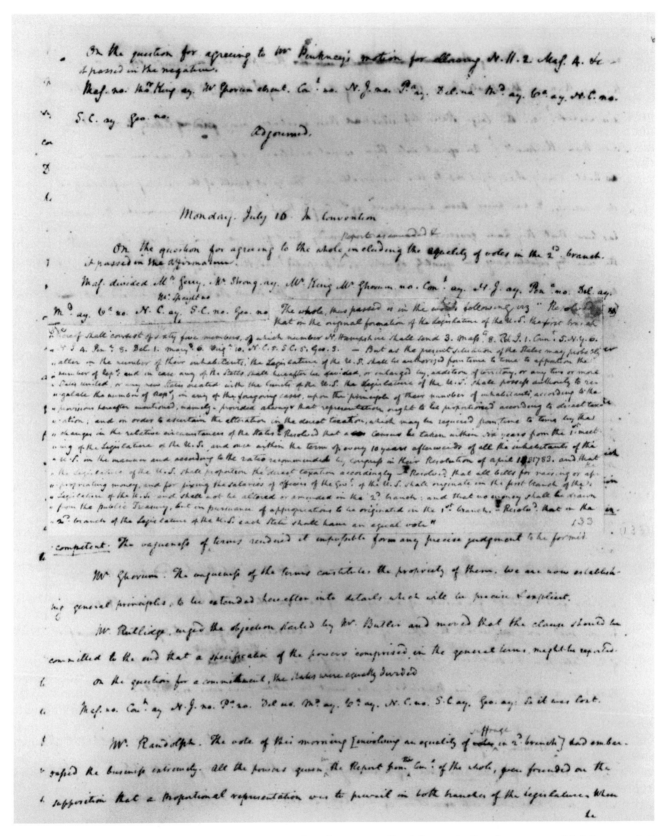

DEBATE ON THE CONSTITUTION. A page of James Madison's notes on the debates. A slip of paper on which he recorded the details of the "Great Compromise" is pasted on the sheet and begins with the words "The whole" and ends with "an equal vote." 16 July 1787.

the Constitutional Convention and was key to the Constitution's ratification. Equal state representation was so basic to the plan that no constitutional amendment may deprive a state of equal representation in the Senate without its consent (Art. V).

Because the more representative body of Congress "should have an immediate dependence on, and an intimate sympathy with, the people" (*Federalist* 52), representatives are chosen every two years (Art. I, sec. 2). Senators are elected for six-year terms (Amend. XVII, superseding Art. I, sec. 3, cl. 1), after initially having been divided as evenly as possible into three groups so that one-third of them are selected every two years (Art. I, sec. 3, cl. 2). Congressional terms begin and end at noon on 3 January (Amend. XX, sec. 1).

The Constitution established the House initially at sixty-five members, allocated among the states by population. It required an "actual Enumeration," or population census, within three years and every ten years thereafter, to reapportion seats. The Constitution did not permanently fix the House's size, except to stipulate that there not be more than one representative per thirty thousand people (Art. I, sec. 2, cl. 3).

For the House of Representatives, special elections, called by the state governors, are the sole method of choosing members to fill unexpired terms (Art. I, sec. 2, cl. 4). No temporary representatives are appointed pending a special election.

The Constitution also authorizes governors to call elections for filling vacancies in the Senate. However, unlike House vacancies—and even though the election of senators by state legislatures was replaced by direct popular election under the Seventeenth Amendment—the Constitution permits state legislatures to empower governors to fill vacancies temporarily until special elections are held (Amend. XVII, superseding Art. I, sec. 3, cl. 2). The states may act quickly, therefore, to assure equality of state representation in the Senate.

The Constitution specifies only a few uniform qualifications for service in each house. A member of Congress must, at the time of election, be an inhabitant of the state from which he or she is elected (Art. I, sec. 2, cl. 2; Art. I, sec. 3, cl. 3). Representatives and senators must also meet age and length of citizenship requirements before taking office. A representative must be at least twenty-five years of age and a citizen for at least seven years (Art. I, sec. 2, cl. 2); a senator must be a minimum of thirty years old and a citizen for at least nine years (Art. I, sec. 3, cl. 3). Madison justified these distinctions

"by the nature of the senatorial trust, which . . . requir[es the] greater extent of information and stability of character" that comes with age, and which, because of the Senate's foreign affairs role, warrants greater distance "from the prepossessions and habits incident to foreign birth and education" (*Federalist* 62). Members also must take an "Oath or Affirmation, to support this Constitution" (Art. VI, sec. 3).

The Framers' rejection of other qualifications expressed their democratic conviction that "under these reasonable limitations, the door of this part of the federal government is open to merit of every description, whether native or adoptive, whether young or old, and without regard to poverty or wealth, or to any particular profession or religious faith" (*Federalist* 52). The Supreme Court ruled in *Powell v. McCormack* (1969) that Congress may not add to the qualifications in the Constitution.

In addition, the Constitution establishes disqualifications for federal legislators. The incompatibility clause prohibits members from simultaneously holding judicial or executive office: "no Person holding any Office under the United States, shall be a Member of either House during his Continuance in Office" (Art. I, sec. 6, cl. 2). There are also two disqualifications applying to government officials generally. Thus, "no person shall be a Senator or Representative in Congress, . . . who, having previously taken an oath, as a . . . [federal or state official], to support the Constitution of the United States, shall have engaged in insurrection or rebellion against the same, or given aid or comfort to the enemies thereof," unless both houses vote by two-thirds majorities to waive this provision (Amend. XIV, sec. 3). Further, officers who have been convicted on impeachment charges may be disqualified from ever holding "any Office of honor, Trust, or Profit under the United States" (Art. I, sec. 3, cl. 7).

The Framers believed that qualifications for service in Congress were "more susceptible of uniformity" than qualifications for voting for Congress (*Federalist* 52). Therefore, the Constitution states only that "the Electors in each State shall have the Qualifications requisite for Electors of the most numerous Branch of the State Legislature" (Art. I, sec. 2, cl. 1). In accordance with Madison's belief that "the right of suffrage is very justly regarded as a fundamental article of republican government" (*Federalist* 52), constitutional amendments bar Congress or the states from denying voting rights on grounds of race (Amend. XV), sex (Amend. XIX), nonpayment of poll or other taxes (Amend. XXIV), or age, for people eighteen or older (Amend. XXVI).

Although the Constitution gives Congress no power to enlarge qualifications for congressional office, Congress has reserved plenary power over the congressional election process and final authority over election results. The Constitution provides that state legislatures may prescribe the "Time, Places and Manner" of holding congressional elections (Art. I, sec. 4, cl. 1). However, fearful that granting exclusive power over national elections to the states "would leave the existence of the Union entirely at their mercy" (*Federalist* 59), the Framers authorized Congress to "make or alter such Regulations, except as to the Places of chusing Senators" (Art. I, sec. 4, cl. 1).

After elections, the elections or qualifications clause provides that "each House shall be the Judge of the Elections, Returns, and Qualifications of its own Members" (Art. I, sec. 5, cl. 1). The Supreme Court held in *Roudebush v. Hartke* (1972) that Congress's power to determine winners of its elections is final.

Power to discipline members of Congress is similarly reserved to each house, which may "punish its Members for disorderly Behaviour, and, with the Concurrence of two thirds, expel a Member" (Art. I, sec. 5, cl. 2). Members are not subject to recall, nor, as the Senate established in 1799 in the case of Sen. William Blount, to impeachment. Blount was the first member of Congress to be expelled. Subsequently, during the Civil War, fourteen senators and three representatives were expelled for rebellion, and one representative was expelled in 1980 for criminal misconduct.

Officers, meeting, and operation. The Constitution grants each house of Congress broad power to "determine the Rules of its Proceedings" (Art. I, sec. 5, cl. 2). The Supreme Court has stated that Congress "may not by its rules ignore constitutional restraints or violate fundamental rights," but "within these limitations all matters of method are open to the determination of the house" (*United States v. Ballin* [1892]). The Constitution prescribes a few specific requirements as to Congress's officers, meetings, and business.

Regarding Congress's leadership, the Constitution creates one House and two Senate officers and grants both houses authority to appoint other officers. "The House of Representatives shall chuse their Speaker and other Officers" (Art. I, sec. 2, cl. 5), but the Constitution also specifies that the vice president is to be president of the Senate (Art. I, sec. 3, cl. 4). The vice president is without a vote except in case of a tie. The Constitution authorizes the Senate to choose other officers, including a president pro tempore, to serve when the vice president is either absent or serving as president of the United States" (Art. I, sec. 3, cl. 5). Both houses have appointed other officers, and each party's members have selected leaders in each house.

The Constitution sets specifications for Congress's meeting, establishment of a quorum, and adjournment. The Constitution requires Congress to "assemble at least once in every Year" (Art. I, sec. 4, cl. 2; Amend. XX, sec. 2). Originally, the Constitution directed annual assembly "on the first Monday in December, unless they shall by Law appoint a different Day" (Art. I, sec. 4, cl. 2). In 1933, the Constitution was amended, in conjunction with moving presidential inaugurations to 20 January, so that 3 January became the date for the annual convening of Congress, unless Congress should legislate a different day (Amend. XX, sec. 2).

The only other time that Congress is required to assemble is when the president uses the power "on extraordinary Occasions, [to] convene both Houses, or either of them" (Art. II, sec. 3). This power has been used only rarely. The Constitution also directs the president "from time to time [to] give to the Congress Information of the State of the Union, and recommend to their Consideration such Measures as he shall judge necessary and expedient" (Art. II, sec. 3). Although the first two presidents addressed Congress on the state of the Union in person, subsequent chief executives communicated in writing, until President Woodrow Wilson returned to the original practice in 1913. President Harry S. Truman initiated the current formal State of the Union address in 1947.

Regarding Congress's day-to-day meetings, a majority of each house "shall constitute a Quorum to do Business" (Art. I, sec. 5, cl. 1). The congressional majority may not, by absenting itself, prevent either house from functioning, as "a smaller Number may adjourn from day to day, and may be authorized to compel the Attendance of absent Members, in such Manner, and under such Penalties as each House may provide" (Art. I, sec. 5, cl. 1).

Longer adjournments are regulated by the restriction that "neither House, during the Session of Congress, shall, without the Consent of the other, adjourn for more than three days, nor to any other Place than that in which the two Houses shall be sitting" (Art. I, sec. 5, cl. 4). Although the power has never been used, the president may, when the houses cannot agree on the time of adjournment, "adjourn them to such Time as he shall think proper" (Art. II, sec. 3).

The Constitution imposes two other general requirements on Congress's operations. The publications or journal clause provides that "Each House shall keep a Journal of its Proceedings, and from time to time publish the same, excepting such Parts as may in their Judgment require Secrecy; and the Yeas and Nays of the Members of either House on any question shall, at the Desire of one fifth of those Present, be entered on the Journal" (Art. I, sec. 5, cl. 3). Also, when Congress votes on overriding a presidential veto, the Constitution requires that "the Votes of both Houses shall be determined by yeas and Nays, and the Names of the Persons voting for and against the Bill shall be entered on the Journal of each House respectively" (Art. I, sec. 7, cl. 2).

Each House acts by majority vote, except where the Constitution specifies a two-thirds vote. The two-thirds provision applies to both houses for overrides of presidential vetoes (Art. I, sec. 7, cl. 2–3), proposals of constitutional amendments (Art. V), and declarations of presidential disability (Amend. XXV, sec. 4); to either house's expulsion of members (Art. I, sec. 3, cl. 6); and to the Senate's impeachment conviction (Art. I, sec. 5, cl. 2) and consent to ratification of treaties (Art. II, sec. 2, cl. 2).

Compensation and privileges. The Constitution guarantees that senators and representatives will be paid, but leaves the amount to be determined by legislation, with the compensation to be disbursed from the U.S. Treasury (Art. I, sec. 6, cl. 1). In 1992, the states ratified an amendment, which the First Congress had proposed with the Bill of Rights in 1789, regulating the timing of congressional pay legislation. It states that no legislation changing the compensation of senators and representatives shall take effect until after the next election of representatives (Amend. XXVII).

The Constitution provides members of Congress with two legal privileges. The arrest clause states that "Senators and Representatives . . . shall in all Cases, except Treason, Felony and Breach of the Peace, be privileged from Arrest during their Attendance at the Session of their respective Houses, and in going to and returning from the same (Art. I, sec. 6, cl. 1). The arrest clause is of limited contemporary significance because arrests in civil suits, its intended target, are no longer common. The arrest clause offers no protection against arrest on criminal charges.

Of more lasting importance is the speech or debate clause, which provides that "for any Speech or Debate in either House, [senators and representatives] shall not be questioned in any other Place" (Art. I, sec. 6, cl. 1). To ensure legislative independence from the judiciary and executive, the clause protects members and their staffs from civil or criminal liability or compulsory testimony for their actions within the legislative sphere, including speeches, debates, voting on the floor or in committee, committee reports, and resolutions. The Supreme Court reads the speech or debate clause broadly and has held that, where applicable, its protection is absolute (*United States v. Johnson* [1966]; *Gravel v. United States* [1972]; *Eastland v. United States Servicemen's Fund* [1974]). The Court has also ruled, however, that the clause does not protect nonlegislative activities, including press relations, constituent service, and lobbying executive agencies (*Hutchinson v. Proxmire* [1979]).

Congress's Legislative Powers. Article I, section 1, vests "all legislative Powers herein granted . . . in a Congress of the United States." Although the federal legislative power is defined and limited by the Constitution, it consists of a formidable complex of powers enumerated in Article I and elsewhere and implied from the enumerated powers. The supremacy clause makes the "Constitution, and the Laws of the United States which shall be made in Pursuance thereof; and all Treaties made . . . the supreme Law of the Land" (Art. VI, cl. 2). Beyond stipulating the reach of Congress's legislative authority, the Constitution also specifies the procedures for making laws.

Enumerated powers. Congress's primary legislative authority is detailed in Article I, section 8, which empowers Congress, most significantly,

"To lay and collect Taxes . . . , to pay the Debts and provide for the common Defence and general Welfare of the United States" (cl. 1)

"To borrow Money" (cl. 2)

"To regulate Commerce with foreign Nations, and among the several States, and with the Indian tribes" (cl. 3)

"To establish an uniform Rule of Naturalization, and uniform Laws on . . . Bankruptcies" (cl. 4)

"To coin Money" (cl. 5)

"To establish Post Offices and post Roads" (cl. 7)

To grant patents and copyrights (cl. 8)

"To declare War" (cl. 11)

"To raise and support Armies" and a Navy (cl. 12–13)

"To exercise exclusive Legislation in all Cases whatsoever" over the District of Columbia (cl. 17).

The final clause of the section, known as the necessary and proper clause, authorizes Congress "To make all Laws which shall be necessary and proper for carrying into Execution the foregoing Powers, and all other Powers vested by this Constitution in the Government of the United States, or in any Department or Officer thereof" (Art. I, sec. 8, cl. 18). The relationship between Congress's specifically enumerated powers and the necessary and proper clause was the first great issue raised about Congress's legislative authority. Defending the clause from attack, Alexander Hamilton stated that "the constitutional operation of the intended government would be precisely the same" without the clause, as it was "only declaratory of a truth which would have resulted by necessary and unavoidable implication from the very act of constituting a federal government, and vesting it with certain specified powers" (Federalist 33). Madison affirmed that "without the substance of this power, the whole Constitution would be a dead letter" (Federalist 44).

In 1819, the Supreme Court upheld an expansive reading of the necessary and proper clause in McCulloch v. Maryland. Rejecting a challenge to Congress's chartering of a national bank based on the argument that Article I, section 8, did not specifically grant power to do so, the Court held that the necessary and proper clause gives Congress broad authority to implement the enumerated powers: "Let the end be legitimate, let it be within the scope of the constitution, and all means which are appropriate, which are plainly adapted to that end, which are not prohibited, but consist with the letter and spirit of the constitution, are constitutional."

Throughout U.S. history, the significance of Congress's individual enumerated powers has fluctuated with the nation's particular needs. Two powers—to tax and spend for the general welfare and to regulate interstate and foreign commerce—have figured critically in all stages of the nation's domestic development. Not coincidentally, the powers to tax and to regulate commerce were the two principal subjects of legislative authority that had been lacking under the Articles of Confederation.

Hamilton believed taxation was the most significant power given to Congress (Federalist 33) and stated that "As revenue is the essential engine by which the means of answering the national exigencies must be procured, . . . the federal government

must of necessity be invested with an unqualified power of taxation in the ordinary modes" (Federalist 31).

Although Madison viewed the taxing power as limited by the purposes enumerated in Article I, section 8 (Federalist 41), the Supreme Court in United States v. Butler (1936) ultimately adopted Hamilton's broader understanding that the taxing and spending clause "confers a power separate and distinct from those later enumerated, is not restricted in meaning by the grant of them, and Congress consequently has a substantive power to tax and to appropriate, limited only by the requirement that it shall be exercised to provide for the general welfare of the United States." The potency of Congress's "power of the purse" is reinforced by the express confirmation of Article I, section 9, clause 7 that the executive has no independent spending power: "No Money shall be drawn from the Treasury, but in Consequence of Appropriations made by Law."

The other enumerated power that proved central to national development is the authority to regulate interstate commerce (Art. I, sec. 8, cl. 3). The eventual dominance of Supreme Court decisions broadly interpreting interstate commerce sustained congressional regulation of a vast array of activities with a "substantial economic effect on interstate commerce" (Wickard v. Filburn [1942]; National Labor Relations Board v. Jones & Laughlin Steel Corporation [1937]; Gibbons v. Ogden [1824]).

The Constitution also assigns Congress critical responsibilities over national security, but by designating the president as "Commander in Chief of the Army and Navy" (Art. II, sec. 2, cl. 1), it divides war powers between Congress and the president. Congress is given power to declare war and to raise, support, and regulate military forces (Art. I, sec. 8, cl. 11–14). Congress has formally declared five wars: the War of 1812, the Mexican War, the Spanish-American War, and the two world wars. Congress has also periodically authorized use of armed force against hostile foreign powers without declaring war.

The Supreme Court has stated in United States v. Curtiss-Wright Export Corporation (1936) that war powers stand on a different footing from the federal government's enumerated domestic powers, because "the investment of the federal government with the powers of external sovereignty did not depend upon the affirmative grants of the Constitution. The powers to declare and wage war . . . if they had never been mentioned in the Constitution, would have vested in the federal government as necessary concomitants of nationality."

Clauses other than Article I, section 8 grant Congress legislative power. Article IV, section 3, clauses 1 and 2, for example, empower Congress to admit states into the Union and to make "all needful Rules and Regulations respecting the Territory or other Property belonging to the United States." The territory clause, the Supreme Court has declared in *Simms v. Simms* (1899), gives Congress "entire dominion and sovereignty, national and local, Federal and state, and . . . full legislative power over all subjects upon which the legislature of a State might legislate within the State."

Several constitutional amendments have expanded Congress's lawmaking authority by empowering Congress to enforce rights guaranteed by the amendments through "appropriate legislation." Thus, Congress has legislative power to enforce freedom from slavery (Amend. XIII), due process of law and equal protection of the laws (Amend. XIV), and voting rights (Amend. XV, XIX, XXIV, XXVI). Coupled with the commerce power, these grants give Congress broad authority over civil rights in employment, housing, public accommodations, education, and voting.

Implied powers and lawmaking procedures. In addition to the legislative powers expressly granted in the Constitution, Congress possesses implied powers essential to the exercise of the express powers, such as the power to investigate, which includes power to compel testimony. The investigatory power inheres in the power to make laws, as a "legislative body cannot legislate wisely or effectively in the absence of information respecting the conditions which the legislation is intended to affect or change" (*McGrain v. Daugherty* [1927]).

Along with vesting substantive legislative power in Congress, Article I prescribes procedures for lawmaking. Either house may initiate legislation, except for the origination clause's proviso: "All Bills for raising Revenue shall originate in the House of Representatives; but the Senate may propose or concur with Amendments as on other Bills" (Art. I, sec. 7, cl. 1). The House's prerogative to initiate revenue legislation derives from the Framers' conception of that chamber as being closer to the people. By custom, general spending and borrowing bills also originate in the House.

Article I, section 7, clause 2 provides that laws must be passed by both houses of Congress and presented to the president for signature or, if vetoed, repassed by two-thirds of each house. The president must return the bill to the originating house within ten days (excluding Sundays) or it becomes law without signature, unless under the pocket veto clause, "Congress by their Adjournment prevent its Return, in which Case it shall not be a Law" (Art. I, sec. 7, cl. 2).

The president's veto, or "qualified negative," accomplishes two purposes: it "serves as a shield to the Executive" and "furnishes an additional security against the enaction of improper laws" (*Federalist* 73). The Supreme Court has stated that this process of bicameral action and presentation reflects "the Framers' decision that the legislative power of the Federal Government be exercised in accord with a single, finely wrought and exhaustively considered, procedure" (*Immigration and Naturalization Service v. Chadha* [1983]).

Congress has broad power to delegate legislative power to the executive and judicial branches so long as it prescribes in legislation the terms of the delegation. The Supreme Court last invalidated acts of Congress on undue delegation grounds early in the New Deal (*Panama Refining Company v. Ryan* [1935]; *A.L.A. Schechter Poultry Corporation v. United States* [1935]). The Court has upheld every challenged delegation of power since then, including laws granting the president very broad regulatory discretion.

The Constitution does not grant the president inherent lawmaking power. In *Youngstown Sheet and Tube Company v. Sawyer* (1952), the Supreme Court stated, "The Founders of this Nation entrusted the lawmaking power to the Congress alone in both good and bad times." Justice Robert Jackson, in a concurring opinion, stated that presidential power is strongest when supported by congressional authorization and weakest when "incompatible with the expressed or implied will of Congress."

Congress's Relationship with the Other Branches. The Constitution vests Congress not only with legislative power but also with several controls over, and shared responsibilities with, the other government branches, including a role in selecting, retaining, and compensating officers of the other branches; a role in treaty making; and various duties regarding the judicial branch.

In *Federalist* 48, Madison reconciled this system of mutually checking powers with the principle of a strict separation of powers by explaining that "unless these departments be so far connected and blended as to give to each a constitutional control over the others, the degree of separation which the maxim requires, as essential to a free government, can never in practice be duly maintained."

Appointment and removal. The question of who should appoint judges and high executive officials occupied much attention at the Constitutional Convention. Some delegates thought presidential appointment would ensure "responsibility"; others thought the power too important for one individual. The Framers ultimately divided the power, providing that the president "shall nominate, and by and with the Advice and Consent of the Senate, shall appoint" judges and principal executive officers, including "Ambassadors, other public Ministers and Consuls" (Art. II, sec. 2, cl. 2). The appointments clause achieves both responsibility, because only one person selects officers, and security, because the Senate can block the president's choice. As Hamilton explained in *Federalist* 76, Senate confirmation is "an excellent check upon a spirit of favoritism in the President, and would tend greatly to prevent the appointment of unfit characters." Furthermore, before any officer may be appointed, Congress must establish the office by law.

For lesser officers, Congress may forgo Senate confirmation and vest appointment "in the President alone, in the Courts of Law, or in the Heads of Departments" (Art. II, sec. 2, cl. 2). The Supreme Court has ruled that, in selecting among these appointing authorities, Congress has significant discretion, needing to avoid only "incongruous" interbranch appointments (*Morrison v. Olson* [1988]). The Court has also held that because Congress is not itself a listed appointing authority, Congress may not appoint nonlegislative officers (*Buckley v. Valeo* [1976]).

Article II, section 2, clause 3 authorizes the president to make temporary appointments to fill vacant offices when the Senate is adjourned. Such "recess appointments" last only through the next congressional session.

Other than through impeachment, the Constitution is silent on removal of officers. When the First Congress established the original cabinet positions (Foreign Affairs, War, and the Treasury) in 1789, it decided that only the president, not the Senate, could remove executive officers. Citing this decision, the Supreme Court has held that the Senate may not participate in the president's decision to dismiss cabinet officers (*Myers v. United States* [1926]) but that Congress may limit the president's discretion to remove other officers (*Humphrey's Executor v. United States* [1935]; *Morrison v. Olson* [1988]).

Impeachment. Impeachment is the only constitutional mechanism through which Congress can remove federal judges, who serve "during good Behaviour" (Art. III, sec. 1), and top executive officers. Because officers are impeachable only for serious misconduct, "high Crimes and Misdemeanors," impeachment is infrequent. Although the Framers drew upon English parliamentary practice in drafting impeachment provisions, they departed from English experience by limiting impeachment to offenses by government officers and barring the use of impeachment for criminal punishment.

Article II, section 4 provides that "the President, Vice President and all civil Officers of the United States, shall be removed from Office on Impeachment for, and Conviction of, Treason, Bribery, or other high Crimes and Misdemeanors." Hamilton explained in *Federalist* 65 that impeachment is "a method of NATIONAL INQUEST" into the conduct of public officials for "the abuse or violation of some public trust." He described impeachment "as a bridle in the hands of the legislative body upon the executive servants of the government."

To prevent misuse, impeachment is divided between the two houses. The House of Representatives alone may initiate charges, or impeach, by majority vote (Art. I, sec. 2, cl. 5). Only the Senate may try impeachments—that is, determine guilt after receiving evidence on the charges (Art. I, sec. 3, cl. 6). On conviction, which requires concurrence of two-thirds of those senators present, the guilty official automatically loses his or her office (Art. I, sec. 3, cl. 7). The Senate also may disqualify convicted officers from holding future office but may not impose any further sanction. The Supreme Court has determined that the Senate's impeachment trial procedures are not subject to judicial review (*Nixon v. United States* [1993]).

In all, the House has impeached fifteen officers, seven of whom (all judges) were convicted. In addition to eleven lower-court judges, the House has impeached President Andrew Johnson, Supreme Court Justice Samuel Chase, Secretary of War William W. Belknap, and Senator Blount, although the Senate ruled that senators cannot be impeached but only expelled by the Senate. President Richard M. Nixon resigned while the House was preparing to impeach him.

Tenure and compensation. The Constitution regulates the compensation of officers to preserve the balance among the branches. As Hamilton stated in *Federalist* 79, "a power over a man's subsistence amounts to a power over his will." To safeguard judicial independence, the Constitution stipulates that the compensation of judges is not to be reduced while they are in office (Art. III, sec. 1). The Constitution likewise guarantees the president "a Compensation, which shall neither be encreased nor diminished during the Period for which he shall have been elected" (Art. II, sec. 1, cl. 7).

To "guard . . . against the danger of executive influence upon the legislative body" (*Federalist* 76) through inducements, the ineligibility and incompatibility clauses provide that

> No Senator or Representative shall, during the Time for which he was elected, be appointed to any civil Office under the Authority of the United States, which shall have been created, or the Emoluments whereof shall have been encreased during such time; and no Person holding any Office under the United States, shall be a Member of either House during his Continuance in Office. (Art. I, sec. 6, cl. 2)

Foreign affairs. The Constitution divides responsibility for foreign affairs between the Senate and the president through several provisions aside from those conferring the legislative and war powers on the House and Senate jointly. The power to make treaties is distributed much like the appointing power. The president is assigned the initial role, subject to Senate approval by a two-thirds majority (Art. II, sec. 2, cl. 2). Hamilton explained that the power to make "agreements between sovereign and sovereign . . . seems to form a distinct department, and to belong, properly, neither to the legislative nor to the executive" (*Federalist* 75). The Framers authorized the president to negotiate treaties so that he could act with "secrecy and despatch" (*Federalist* 64); they required Senate approval to ensure caution, steadiness, and conformity with law (*Federalist* 75).

The Framers also split the responsibility for appointing those officers who communicate between the United States and foreign governments. The power to appoint the nation's representatives abroad is divided under the appointments clause, with the president nominating and the Senate approving them (Art. II, sec. 2, cl. 2).

The Constitution gives to the president alone the duty to "receive Ambassadors and other public Ministers" from foreign countries (Art. II, sec. 3). Along with Madison, Hamilton initially viewed this function as unimportant (*Federalist* 69). However, Hamilton subsequently relied on this duty as a source of presidential authority in foreign affairs, and the provision has come to be cited as a consti-

tutional basis for presidential power over recognizing foreign governments and the president's role as the nation's sole organ in communicating with them.

Presidential election and succession. Congress has an important, but rarely triggered, role in the selection of the president. If no presidential candidate is supported by a majority of the electoral college, the House of Representatives selects the president from the three top candidates (Amend. XII, superseding Art. II, sec. 1, cl. 2). Each state delegation has one vote, and a majority is necessary to select a president. Similarly, if the electors do not cast a majority for a vice-presidential candidate, the Senate chooses one of the top two candidates as vice president. This procedure elected the president in 1800 and 1824 and the vice president in 1836.

The Constitution initially addressed the prospect of a vacancy in the presidency only by authorizing Congress to legislate the order of succession after the vice president (Art. II, sec. 1, cl. 6). Under this authority, Congress has mandated succession by the Speaker of the House, then the president pro tempore of the Senate, and then through the cabinet. The Twenty-fifth Amendment additionally provides that, if the vice presidency is vacant, the president nominates a vice president subject to approval by a majority vote of both houses. This provision was used in 1973, when Gerald Ford was selected to fill the vacancy caused by Vice President Spiro T. Agnew's resignation, and in 1974, when Nelson A. Rockefeller replaced Ford as vice president after Ford became president on Richard M. Nixon's resignation.

The Twenty-fifth Amendment also establishes procedures in the event of presidential disability. If the vice president and a majority of the cabinet determine "that the President is unable to discharge the powers and duties of his office, the Vice President shall immediately assume the powers and duties of the office as Acting President." The president resumes his or her powers on declaring in writing that he or she is not disabled, unless the vice president and a majority of the cabinet disagree, in which case Congress makes the final decision. The president resumes his or her duties unless two-thirds of both houses determine that he or she is unable to function.

Courts and constitutional amendments. In addition to confirmation and impeachment, the Constitution grants Congress three powers affecting the courts. First, Congress has the duty to establish all courts inferior to the Supreme Court, which is the only court established in the Constitution (Art. III, sec. 1). Second, Congress has authority to regulate the Supreme Court's exercise of appellate jurisdiction over cases filed in the inferior courts (Art. III, sec. 2, cl. 2). The Supreme Court held in *Marbury v. Madison* (1803) that Congress may not add to the original jurisdiction that the Constitution assigns to the Supreme Court. By invalidating a law expanding its original jurisdiction, the Court established in that case the principle of judicial review regarding the constitutionality of acts of Congress.

Third, Article V grants Congress a role in overruling constitutional decisions of the Supreme Court or otherwise altering the Constitution by empowering Congress to propose amendments to the Constitution. In addition to a never-used mechanism for calling a constitutional convention, the Constitution provides that, by two-thirds vote of both houses, Congress may propose amendments, which become effective if ratified by three-fourths of the states. The Constitution has been amended twenty-seven times this way, including the ten amendments in the Bill of Rights.

Limitations on Congressional Power. Congress's broad legislative powers are limited by several specific restrictions. Because of states' dissatisfaction with the paucity of limitations in the original text, the Bill of Rights was added to the Constitution to ensure additional limits on federal power.

Original constitutional limitations. Two important original limitations on congressional power were temporary. First, the Constitutional Convention compromised its bitter disagreement over the slave trade by providing that "the Migration or Importation of such Persons as any of the States now existing shall think proper to admit, shall not be prohibited by the Congress prior to the Year one thousand eight hundred and eight" (Art. I, sec. 9, cl. 1). In 1807 Congress passed a law banning the slave trade as of 1 January 1808, and slavery was abolished by the Thirteenth Amendment in 1865.

Another key original limitation on congressional power survived until this century. Article I, section 9, clause 4 provided that "no Capitation, or other direct, Tax shall be laid, unless in Proportion to the Census or Enumeration herein before directed to be taken." Following the Supreme Court's decision that this provision barred income taxes (*Pollock v. Farmers' Loan and Trust Company* [1895]), the Sixteenth Amendment was adopted in 1913 to permit direct levying of income taxes, irrespective of apportionment or population.

The Constitution also imposes restrictions on legislative authority that remain in force. Article I guarantees open and nondiscriminatory trade by the states with each other and with foreign countries by providing that "no Tax or Duty shall be laid on Articles exported from any State" and "no Preference shall be given by any Regulation of Commerce or Revenue to the Ports of one State over those of another" (Art. I, sec. 9, cl. 5–6).

Even prior to the Bill of Rights, the Constitution limited legislative action in order to safeguard individual liberty. Article I guarantees that "the Privilege of the Writ of Habeas Corpus shall not be suspended, unless when in Cases of Rebellion or Invasion the public Safety may require it" (Art. I, sec. 9, cl. 2). Habeas corpus has been suspended four times in American history, most notably during the Civil War.

Article I also bars bills of attainder and ex post facto laws (Art. I, sec. 9, cl. 3). The Supreme Court ruled in *United States v. Lovett* (1946) that laws which "apply either to named individuals or to easily ascertainable members of a group in such a way as to inflict punishment on them without a judicial trial are bills of attainder prohibited by the Constitution." The Court has defined an ex post facto law as a criminal law "that makes an action done before the passing of the law, and which was innocent when done, criminal; and punishes such action," or "aggravates a crime, or makes it greater than it was, when committed," or "inflicts a greater punishment, than the law annexed to the crime, when committed" (*Calder v. Bull* [1798]). Article III guarantees that "the trial of all Crimes, except in Cases of Impeachment, shall be by Jury" (Art. III, sec. 2, cl. 3). Article III also limits legislative power over the crime of treason by defining the offense, prescribing the evidence required for conviction, and limiting punishment (Art. III, sec. 3, cl. 1–2). Finally, the Constitution provides that "no religious Test shall ever be required as a Qualification to any Office or public Trust under the United States" (Art. VI, cl. 3).

The Bill of Rights and subsequent amendment. The omission of a formal bill of individual rights was one of the most controversial aspects of the proposed Constitution. Notwithstanding Hamilton's insistence that the restrictions enumerated in the text sufficed and that a more general bill of rights was "not only unnecessary in the proposed Constitution, but would even be dangerous" (*Federalist* 84), the lack of a bill of rights generated potent criticism. Several state conventions coupled ratification with proposed amendments guaranteeing individual rights or conditioned ratification on the addition of a bill of rights.

Following an election campaign dominated by controversy over amending the Constitution, the First Congress proposed the Bill of Rights in 1789. As ratified, it comprises ten amendments limiting federal power. Only the First Amendment specifically restricts Congress. It declares that "Congress shall make no law respecting an establishment of religion, or prohibiting the free exercise thereof; or abridging the freedom of speech, or of the press; or the right of the people peaceably to assemble, and to petition the Government for a redress of grievances."

The balance of the Bill of Rights likewise guarantees individual rights against governmental intrusion. Worded as general limitations on government power, the amendments restrict legislative actions, as well as those of the other branches. These amendments guarantee procedural rights for persons accused in criminal cases (Amend. VI); the right to jury trial in civil cases (Amend. VII); rights against unreasonable searches and seizures (Amend. IV); rights against double jeopardy, compelled self-incrimination, deprivation of life, liberty, or property without due process of law or the taking of private property without just compensation (Amend. V); and rights against excessive bail and cruel and unusual punishment (Amend. VIII).

Further extension of individual rights by constitutional amendment after the Civil War also limited legislative power by guaranteeing "the equal protection of the laws" (Amend. XIV, sec. 1), which is applied to the federal government through the due process clause of the Fifth Amendment.

[*See also* Advice and Consent; Checks and Balances; Concurrent Powers; Delegation of Powers; Emergency Powers; Enacting Clause; Enumerated Powers; General Welfare Clause; Implied Powers; Separation of Powers; Speech or Debate Clause; War Powers.]

BIBLIOGRAPHY

Elliot, Jonathan, ed. *The Debates in the Several State Conventions on the Adoption of the Federal Constitution.* 1974.

Farrand, Max, ed. *The Records of the Federal Convention of 1787.* 1974.

Fisher, Louis. *Constitutional Conflicts between Congress and the President.* 3d ed. 1991.

Henkin, Louis. *Foreign Affairs and the Constitution.* 1975.

Kurland, Philip B., and Ralph Lerner, eds. *The Founders' Constitution.* 1987.

Story, Joseph. *Commentaries on the Constitution of the United States.* Edited by Ronald D. Rotunda and John E. Nowak. 1987.

U.S. House of Representatives. *Constitution, Jefferson's Manual, and Rules of the House of Representatives, 103d Congress.* 102d Cong., 2d sess., 1993. H. Doc. 102-405.

U.S. House of Representatives. *Documents Illustrative of the Formation of the Union of the American States,* edited by Charles C. Tansill. 69th Cong., 1st sess., 1927. H. Doc. 398.

U.S. Senate. *The Constitution of the United States of America,* edited by Johnny H. Killian. 99th Cong., 1st sess., 1987. S. Doc. 16. Supplemented by *1990 Supplement.* 101st Cong., 2d sess., 1990. S. Doc. 36.

Wood, Gordon S. *The Creation of the American Republic, 1776–1787.* 1969.

Wright, Benjamin F., ed. *The Federalist.* 1961.

MICHAEL DAVIDSON, MORGAN J. FRANKEL,
and CLAIRE M. SYLVIA

Congressional Interpretation of the Constitution

Throughout its history, Congress has played an integral part in interpreting the meaning of the Constitution. Amendments to the Constitution represent one opportunity for congressional influence, but the principal way in which Congress defines constitutional values is through the regular statutory process. Congress is constantly engaged in balancing constitutional interests when it legislates on commerce, criminal law, federalism, the separation of powers, and other matters that require legislative attention. It is thus superficial to believe that the Supreme Court exercises some kind of monopoly on constitutional interpretation. In the U.S. system, all three branches are intimately involved in protecting and defending the Constitution.

Early Precedents. When members of the First Congress assembled, they had a clean slate for interpretation of the Constitution. The Supreme Court was not yet functioning, and it would be many years before the Court explored the constitutional issues that members of Congress had to grapple with in 1789. To the best of their ability, members studied the constitutional text and the intent of the Framers without judicial rulings to guide them. During the Republic's first decade, the scope of confronting Congress that required interpretation of the Constitution was impressive: they included judicial review, the president's power to remove executive officials, federalism, the Bank of the United States, treaties and foreign relations, war-making powers, interstate commerce, slavery, and the power of Congress to investigate executive activities. The reader of the *Annals of Congress* for 1789 finds a constitutional debate by members of Congress that was intense, informed, and diligent.

Independent legislative judgments of the Constitution were needed for two reasons. One was practical: members of Congress had constitutional questions thrown at them that they had to field as best they could. The second reason was constitutional in nature. Members of Congress, under Article VI, clause 3, are constitutionally required to take an oath "to support the Constitution." As later elaborated by statute (5 U.S.C. 3331), members "solemnly swear [to] support and defend the Constitution of the United States against all enemies, foreign and domestic; [to] bear true faith and allegiance to the same; [to] take this obligation freely, without any mental reservation or purpose of evasion; and [to] well and faithfully discharge the duties [of their office]."

Members have a duty to debate constitutional questions when a bill is under consideration or when the president threatens to operate outside constitutional boundaries. Although many members happen to be lawyers, that is irrelevant to this duty, for they all swear or affirm to defend the Constitution "without any mental reservation or purpose of evasion." Because Article I, section 9 mandates that "No Bill of Attainder or ex post facto Law shall be passed," they need to address those issues before a bill passes, not after. The First Amendment commands that Congress "shall make no law" respecting an establishment of religion, prohibiting the free exercise of religion, or abridging the freedom of speech or of the press. Congress is not at liberty to legislate on those subjects blindly, hoping that the president or the judiciary will catch any infringement of the Constitution. As Sen. Slade Gorton (R-Wash.) told his colleagues during debate in 1984: "You swore an oath, as I did, when you became Members of this body to uphold the Constitution of the United States. You cannot hide behind the fact that the Supreme Court of the United States has final authority on constitutional questions. . . . It is your duty to make a judgment as to whether or not this amendment is constitutional."

When Congress in 1789 created the first executive departments—Foreign Affairs, War, and Treasury—it had to decide whether the president had the implied power to remove the heads of those departments. The debates on this issue take up several hundred pages of the *Annals of Congress* and con-

stitute an exceptionally penetrating examination of the doctrine of implied powers. Although some members argued that the Senate should participate with the president in the removal of executive officials, others believed that these officials could be removed only through the constitutional process of impeachment. A third camp argued that since Congress creates an office, it may attach to that office any condition it deems appropriate for tenure and removal. A fourth school insisted that the power of removal belonged exclusively to the president as a function of his executive power.

Should Congress have submitted this constitutional question to the courts for resolution? James Madison, who led the implied powers debate, refused to defer to the judiciary. He strongly rejected the advice of those who said that "it would be officious in this branch of the Legislature to expound the Constitution, so far as it relates to the division of power between the President and the Senate." To Madison it was "incontrovertibly of as much importance to this branch of the Government as to any other, that the Constitution should be preserved entire. It is our duty, so far as it depends upon us, to take care that the powers of the Government be preserved entire to every department of Government." He continued:

> But the great objection drawn from the source to which the last arguments would lead us is, that the Legislature itself has no right to expound the Constitution; that wherever its meaning is doubtful, you must leave it to take its course, until the Judiciary is called upon to declare its meaning. I acknowledge, in the ordinary course of Government, that the exposition of the laws and Constitution devolves upon the Judiciary. But I beg to know, upon what principles it can be contended, that any one department draws from the Constitution greater powers than another, in marking out the limits of the powers of the several departments? The Constitution is the charter of the people to the Government; it specifies certain great powers as absolutely granted, and marks out the departments to exercise them. If the Constitutional boundary of either be brought into question, I do not see that any one of these independent departments has more right than another to declare their sentiments on that point.

After extensive debate, Congress agreed that the president had the power to remove the heads of the executive departments. The statutes creating those departments provided that the subordinate officers would have charge and custody of all records whenever the secretary "shall be removed from of-

U.S. CONSTITUTION. First page.

fice by the President of the United States." At the same time, it recognized some constitutional limitations on the president's removal power. When Congress debated the formation of the Treasury Department, Madison noted that the tenure of the comptroller required independence from presidential control because the properties of that office were not "purely of an Executive nature." It seemed to Madison that the comptroller exercised duties partly of "a Judiciary quality" and thus needed protection from presidential removals. That insight by Madison would later apply to other agency officials who exercised adjudicative duties. In particular, it applied to the comptroller general of the United States, created in 1921 as the successor to the comptroller.

In 1792, Congress had to decide by itself whether it possessed the constitutional power to investigate the executive branch. Just as the Constitution has no mention of the president's power of removal, so is it silent on the power of Congress to investigate the executive branch. When the House of Representatives learned that the troops of Maj. Gen. Arthur St. Clair had suffered heavy losses during an Indian attack, it first considered a resolution to request the president to institute an inquiry. The resolution was defeated by a vote of 35 to 21. The House then passed a resolution to empower a committee to inquire into the causes of the military failure and "to call for such persons, papers, and records, as may be necessary to assist their inquiries." According to the account of Thomas Jefferson, who at that time was secretary of State, President George Washington convened the cabinet to consider the extent to which the House could call for papers. The cabinet debated the issue and agreed,

> first, that the House was an inquest, and therefore might institute inquiries. Second, that it might call for papers generally. Third, that the Executive ought to communicate such papers as the public good would permit, and ought to refuse those, the disclosure of which would injure the public: consequently were to exercise a discretion. Fourth, that neither the committee nor House had a right to call on the Head of a Department, who and whose papers were under the President alone; but that the committee should instruct their chairman to move the House to address the President.

The cabinet concluded that there was not a paper "which might not be properly produced." The committee examined papers furnished by the executive branch, including papers and accounts furnished by the Treasury and the War departments, and listened to explanations from the heads of those departments and from other witnesses. St. Clair supplied the committee with written remarks on the expedition. The cabinet's advice that the House could call on the heads of departments only through the president was a formality that has long since been abandoned.

Although Congress exercised its investigative power on numerous occasions after 1792, it was not until *McGrain v. Daugherty* (1927) that the Supreme Court acknowledged the constitutional power of Congress to investigate activities in the executive branch. The Court had no alternative. It could not at that time, or even earlier, deny that such power existed. It could merely give its blessing to a power already recognized as legitimate by Congress and the president.

Congress again established precedents for its attention to constitutional issues in 1796, when President Washington notified the House of Representatives that Jay's Treaty had been ratified. Rep. Edward Livingston of New York offered a resolution requesting the president to transmit to the House a copy of the instructions that had been given to the American minister who had negotiated the treaty, together with correspondence and other related documents. The resolution was later modified to permit the president to withhold any papers that existing negotiations might render improper to disclose. In support of the resolution, Livingston argued that the House possessed "a discretionary power of carrying the Treaty into effect, or refusing it their sanction." In other words, agreement to a treaty by the president and the Senate did not compel the House to furnish funds or enact legislation to implement it. Rep. Albert Gallatin of Pennsylvania argued that this was particularly true when the Constitution gave certain powers, such as the authority to regulate foreign commerce or to establish tariffs, to both houses of Congress.

After weeks of debate, the Livingston resolution passed by a vote of 62 to 37. At that point Washington denied the request for papers and documents, citing the need for caution and discretion in foreign negotiations and maintaining the exclusive role of the Senate in the treaty-making process. (This controversy is wrongly characterized as an example of the president exercising "executive privilege" in withholding documents from Congress. Washington did not withhold papers from the Senate but only from the House.) The House adopted a resolution, sponsored by Rep. Thomas Blount of North Carolina, conceding the

House's exclusion from the treaty-making process. But the resolution noted

> that when a Treaty stipulates regulations of any of the subjects submitted by the Constitution to the power of Congress, it must depend, for its execution, as to such stipulations, on a law or laws to be passed by Congress. And it is the Constitutional right and duty of the House of Representatives, in all such cases, to deliberate on the expediency or inexpediency of carrying such Treaty into effect, and to determine and act thereon, as, in their judgment, may be most conducive to the public good.

Over the years, the House has blocked certain treaties that required appropriations, two examples being the Gadsden purchase treaty with Mexico in 1853 and the 1867 treaty with Russia that effected the U.S. purchase of Alaska. It is now commonplace for treaties expressly to recognize that their effectiveness depends on legislative consent by both houses.

Constitutional Amendments. Whenever two-thirds of both houses of Congress deem it necessary, they may propose amendments to the Constitution. On four occasions Congress has used the amendment process to reverse Supreme Court decisions. The Eleventh Amendment was passed in response to *Chisholm v. Georgia* (1793), in which the Court decided that a state could be sued in federal court by a plaintiff from another state. To protect states from a flood of costly citizen suits, Congress quickly passed a constitutional amendment declaring that "the Judicial power of the United States shall not be construed to extend to any suit in law or equity, commenced or prosecuted against one of the United States by Citizens of another State, or by Citizens or Subjects of any foreign States."

The Civil War amendments—the Thirteenth, Fourteenth, and Fifteenth—nullifed the Court's Dred Scott decision of 1857, which held that Congress could not prohibit slavery in the territories and that blacks as a class were not citizens protected under the Constitution. The Thirteenth Amendment abolished slavery; the Fourteenth Amendment provided that all persons born or naturalized in the United States "are citizens of the United States and of the State wherein they reside"; and the Fifteenth Amendment gave black men the right to vote. Before these amendments were ratified (in 1865, 1868, and 1870), Congress had already passed legislation in 1862 prohibiting slavery in the territories.

The Sixteenth Amendment overruled *Pollock v. Farmers' Loan and Trust Company* (1895), which struck down a federal income tax. In 1909, the Senate debated whether to reenact an income tax and let the Supreme Court reconsider the issue. Other senators cautioned that a confrontation with the Court might lead either to the Court yielding, and thereby losing the confidence of the people, or reaffirming its ruling and creating a breach between the judiciary and the legislature. To avert either outcome, Congress chose to pass a constitutional amendment in 1909, which was ratified in 1913. The Sixteenth Amendment gives Congress the power "to lay and collect taxes on incomes, from whatever source derived, without apportionment among the several States, and without regard to any census or enumeration."

The Twenty-sixth Amendment, ratified in 1971, overturned *Oregon v. Mitchell* (1970), a Supreme Court decision that voided a congressional effort to lower the minimum voting age in state elections to eighteen. The Court held that Congress could fix the voting age for national elections but not for state contests. Within a matter of months the states had ratified the amendment, which reads, "The right of citizens of the United States, who are eighteen years of age or older, to vote shall not be denied or abridged by the United States or any State on account of age."

On a number of other occasions Congress has challenged Court decisions first by passing new legislation and, when that has failed, by attempting to amend the Constitution. A child labor law enacted in 1916, relying on the commerce power of Congress, was declared unconstitutional by the Court in *Hammer v. Dagenhart* (1918). Congress refused to accept that verdict. In 1919 it enacted another child labor statute, this time based on its power to tax. Congress was criticized for trying to evade the Supreme Court by doing indirectly what could not be done directly. Sen. Henry Cabot Lodge (R-Mass.) countered that child labor was such a "great evil" that Congress could legitimately act by whatever means were at its disposal. Nevertheless, the Court struck down the second statute in *Bailey v. Drexel Furniture Company* (1922).

Undaunted, Congress passed a constitutional amendment in 1924 to give it the power to regulate child labor. By 1937, only twenty-eight of the necessary thirty-six states had ratified the amendment. By that time, however, the composition of the Supreme Court had begun to change, and Congress included a child labor provision in the Fair Labor Standards Act of 1938. The issue was taken to the Supreme Court, which in *United States v. Darby*

(1941) unanimously upheld the child labor provision.

In general, over the course of the twentieth century Congress increasingly came to question narrow judicial constructions adopted during the century's early decades, and in such contests Congress is likely to prevail. As the Court later admitted in *Prudential Insurance Company v. Benjamin* (1946), "The history of judicial limitation of congressional power over commerce, when exercised affirmatively, has been more largely one of retreat than of ultimate victory." After retiring from the Court in 1945, Justice Owen Roberts explained why the Court chose to back off in the face of congressional efforts to regulate the economy: "Looking back, it is difficult to see how the Court could have resisted the popular urge for uniform standards throughout the country—for what in effect was a unified economy."

Statutory Action. Interpretation of constitutional text, constitutional amendments, and judicial rulings on constitutional questions are of undeniable importance, but the principal road to constitutional change is statutory action. Congress constantly addresses constitutional issues when it legislates, and the president considers constitutional issues when deciding to sign or veto a bill. A major function of the Supreme Court is statutory construction, and through that function it interacts with other branches of government in a process that refines the meaning of the Constitution.

When judicial decisions are restricted to the meaning of a congressional statute, Congress may overturn the ruling simply by passing a new statute that clarifies legislative intent. This process is called statutory reversal. The private sector often uses Congress as an "appellate court" to reverse judicial interpretations of a statute. Corporations, trade unions, environmental groups, and other organizations come to Congress every year, urging it to pass legislation that will nullify judicial decisions. Although in a technical sense these are statutory and not constitutional interpretations, that distinction is largely meaningless. Many congressional statutes, such as those covering civil rights, pronounce constitutional values of great moment.

For example, a statute concerning the rights of women, enacted shortly after the Civil War, illustrates how the regular legislative process can redefine constitutional rights. In *Bradwell v. State* (1873), the Supreme Court denied that women had a constitutional right under the privileges and immunities clause of the Fourteenth Amendment to practice law. Concurring in that judgment, Justice Joseph P. Bradley reflected traditional judicial doctrines by arguing that the "paramount destiny and mission of women are to fulfil the noble and benign offices of wife and mother. This is the law of the Creator." Elsewhere in his concurrence Bradley gave other reasons, including "the divine ordinance," for excluding women from engaging in professional work. Other judicial opinions by the Supreme Court and state courts were based on similar arguments.

Although women won the right to practice law in some states, a rule adopted by the U.S. Supreme Court prohibited women from arguing there. In 1878, the House of Representatives began debate on a bill to authorize women to practice before the Court. The bill passed the House easily, 169 to 87, but was held up when the Senate Judiciary Committee reported the bill adversely, preferring to leave the question to the discretion of the Court. A year later, the Senate passed the bill by the vote of 39 to 20. It provided that any woman who was a member of the bar of the highest court of any state or territory or of the Supreme Court of the District of Columbia for at least three years, and was a person of good moral character, should be admitted to practice before the U.S. Supreme Court.

Sen. Aaron A. Sargent (R-Calif.) delivered a powerful statement that broke free from judicial stereotypes and drew on principles established by the Declaration of Independence. Calling attention to the progress of women in the medical and legal professions, he said that men had no right to circumscribe the ambitions of women in any way: "The enjoyment of liberty, the pursuit of happiness in her own way, is as much the birthright of woman as of man. In this land man has ceased to dominate over his fellow—let him cease to dominate over his sister; for he has no higher right to do the latter than the former."

During this period, Congress was ahead of the judiciary in many areas of constitutional rights. Congress passed legislation in 1875 to guarantee blacks equal access to public accommodations. The preamble of the statute also reflected the philosophy of the Declaration of Independence, beginning with the phrase, "Whereas, it is essential to just government we recognize the equality of all men before the law." The debate over the bill reveals an eloquent commitment on the part of Congress to provide for basic constitutional rights that would not have been protected by many of the states or by the courts. Much of the 1875 statute was declared unconstitutional by the Supreme Court in the *Civil Rights Cases* (1883).

The constitutional rights of African Americans remained in a constitutional backwater for decades, until the Supreme Court in the 1930s and 1940s began to invalidate many state laws that segregated blacks from whites, especially in universities and law schools. These decisions culminated in *Brown v. Board of Education* (1954), which represented a giant step forward in the establishment of civil rights for blacks. In important ways, it aroused the public conscience and articulated fundamental constitutional values. By itself, however, the decision did little to integrate public schools. As late as 1964, the Court complained in its decisions that there had been too much deliberation and not enough speed in enforcing *Brown*.

What finally turned the tide was a series of congressional enactments, including the Civil Rights Act of 1964, the Voting Rights Act of 1965, and the Fair Housing Act of 1968. The struggle against racial discrimination required a bipartisan consensus within Congress and the strong leadership of President Lyndon B. Johnson. In upholding these statutes, the Court recognized that much of constitutional law depends on fact-finding, which is a particular strength of Congress. The Court adopted a broad interpretation of the power of Congress "to enforce, by appropriate legislation," the provisions of the Fourteenth Amendment.

For example, section 4(e) of the Voting Rights Act of 1965 prohibited New York's literacy requirement as a precondition for voting. Congress provided that no person who had completed the sixth grade in Puerto Rico could be denied the right to vote in any election because of an inability to read or write in English. Upholding that law in *Katzenbach v. Morgan* (1966), the Court noted that fact-finding was a legislative, not a judicial, responsibility.

> It was for Congress, as the branch that made this judgment, to assess and weigh the various conflicting considerations—the risk of pervasiveness of the discrimination in governmental services, the effectiveness of eliminating the state restriction on the right to vote as a means of dealing with the evil, the adequacy or availability of alternative remedies, and the nature and significance of the state interests that would be affected by the nullification of the English literacy requirement as applied to residents who have successfully completed the sixth grade in a Puerto Rican school. It is not for us to review the congressional resolution of these factors. It is enough that we be able to perceive a basis upon which the Congress might resolve the conflict as it did.

The Civil Rights Act of 1964 included a title that gave African Americans equal access to public accommodations, reopening an issue that had lain dormant since the *Civil Rights Cases* of 1883. That decision, in fact, had never been overturned and raised the danger of a confrontation between the Court and Congress. The framers of the Civil Rights Act of 1964 saw a way to defuse the issue, and in so doing to give the Court a graceful retreat. They offered two constitutional arguments in support of equal access: the Fourteenth Amendment (at issue in the *Civil Rights Cases*) and the commerce clause. In *Heart of Atlanta Motel v. United States* (1964), the Court held that Congress had "ample power" under the commerce clause to enact the equal access provision. On this fundamental issue of giving blacks equal access to public accommodations, the guardians of minority rights and constitutional liberties were Congress and the president, not the courts. Once again, as for nearly a century, congressional persistence and ingenuity triumphed over judicial obstacles. Interestingly, majoritarian branches driven by majoritarian pressures took the lead in defending the constitutional rights of minorities, who are supposed to look to the courts for protection.

The power of Congress under the commerce clause was also at issue in a legislative-judicial conflict over federal minimum-wage legislation in the 1970s. In *National League of Cities v. Usery* (1976), the Supreme Court struck down a congressional statute that extended federal wage and hour provisions to almost all state employees. Although Congress had justified the legislation under the commerce clause, the Court held in a vote of 5 to 4 that the statute threatened the independent existence of the states. The fifth vote was supplied by Justice Harry Blackmun, who admitted, however, that he was "not untroubled by certain possible implications of the Court's opinion." If he decided in later years to swing to the other side, the Court's ruling could be easily overturned.

Justice Blackmun had the opportunity to do precisely that in a case involving local mass transit systems, which the Department of Labor considered a "nontraditional" state function and therefore within the reach of federal legislation. The San Antonio Metropolitan Transit Authority (SAMTA) challenged the department's interpretation, while several SAMTA employees brought suit against SAMTA for overtime pay under the Fair Labor Standards Act. During oral argument, the Justice Department conceded that mass transit was not a traditional function and was therefore subject to the commerce power of Congress.

In *Garcia v. San Antonio Metropolitan Transit Authority* (1985), Justice Blackmun abandoned the majority of 1976 and voted to overturn the *National League* decision, which he now regarded as having proved itself too impractical and abstract to apply in the lower courts. He also emphasized that the essential safeguard for federalism was not the judiciary but rather the political dynamics that operate within Congress: "[T]he principal and basic limit on the federal commerce power is that inherent in all congressional action—the built-in restraints that our system provides through state participation in federal governmental action. The political process ensures that laws that unduly burden the States will not be promulgated."

In the 1980s and 1990s, several cases have illustrated the constant interaction between Congress and the courts in defining and recognizing constitutional rights. In *Grove City College v. Bell* (1984), the Supreme Court interpreted the meaning of Title IX of the Education Amendments of 1972, which prohibits sex discrimination in any education program or activity that receives federal funds. The specific issue before the Court was whether the statute required federal funds to be terminated only for specific programs—or for the entire educational institution—in which discrimination was found to exist. The Court decided that the narrower interpretation should apply. Within four months, the House of Representatives, voting 375 to 32, passed legislation to overturn the decision. Action on the Senate side was delayed for several years because of disputes over the extent to which the issue involved abortion and the separation of church and state. In 1988, however, Congress passed legislation to reverse the *Grove City* decision. President Ronald Reagan vetoed the bill, but both houses overrode him, reasserting Congress's commerce power and its application to sex discrimination.

Another face-off between Congress and the Supreme Court, this time involving religious freedom, occurred in 1986 when the Court, in *Goldman v. Weinberger*, upheld a U.S. Air Force regulation that prohibited an officer from wearing a yarmulke indoors while on duty. The officer, an Orthodox Jew and an ordained rabbi, had worn a yarmulke for years without incident, until he appeared at a military trial and testified against the U.S. Air Force. When the case appeared before the Supreme Court, the Court ruled by a vote of 5 to 4 that the air force regulation was justified because

the military services required discipline, unity, and order. In a dissenting opinion, Justice William J. Brennan rebuked the Court for abdicating "its role as primary expositor of the Constitution and protector of individual liberties [and lending its support to] credulous deference to unsupported assertions of military necessity." Later in his dissent he acknowledged that other institutions of government, including Congress, are available to protect individual liberties.

Congress mobilized its forces to overturn the Court's decision. Each year Congress passes an authorization bill for the Defense Department. Just one year after the *Goldman* decision Congress attached an amendment to this bill to require the air force to change its regulation. Congress now permitted military personnel to wear conservative, unobtrusive religious apparel indoors, provided that the apparel does not interfere with their military duties. Thus basic rights unavailable from the courts were successfully secured by congressional action.

In another dialogue between Congress and the Court, Congress passed the Civil Rights Act of 1991, overturning or modifying nine Supreme Court decisions. The ruling that provoked legislative action was *Wards Cove Packing Company v. Atonio* (1989), which shifted the burden to employees to prove that racial disparities resulted from employment practices and were not justified by business needs. Earlier judicial doctrines, dating back to 1971, appeared to require an employee to demonstrate only disparate results, not intent.

To overturn this decision and several others that gave a narrow interpretation of constitutional civil rights, Congress passed legislation in 1990. President George Bush vetoed the bill, claiming that it would require employers to institute quotas for racial minorities to avoid expensive and time-consuming litigation. In 1991, Congress again pushed for the legislation, this time with what appeared to be sufficient votes for both houses to override a Bush veto. With only minor changes in the bill's language, and with the knowledge that his override-free record was in jeopardy, Bush signed the bill. Congressional initiatives once again were effective in securing the rights of members of racial minorities and of women.

The sometimes tenuous relationship between judicial decisions and congressional practices is borne out by the history of the legislative veto. In the prominent case of *Immigration and Naturalization Service v. Chadha* (1983), the Supreme Court held that legislative vetoes are an invalid form of congressional control over the executive branch. Not only did the Court strike down one-house vetoes (for violating the principle of bicameralism), it also ruled legislative vetoes unconstitutional because they are not presented to the president for his signature or veto. The broad principles announced by the Court nullified all existing legislative vetoes, which covered such diverse areas as executive reorganization, rule making, impoundment, foreign trade, and national emergencies. In his dissent, Justice Byron White claimed that the Court in "one fell swoop" struck down provisions in more laws enacted by Congress than the Court had cumulatively invalidated in its entire history.

Nevertheless, from the moment of the *Chadha* decision on 23 June 1983 to the end of the 103d Congress in 1995, Congress continued to rely on the legislative veto to control agency actions. Over that period of time, Congress created more than two hundred *new* legislative vetoes, and Presidents Reagan and Bush signed them into law. Instead of acting through the full legislative process required by *Chadha* (action by both houses and the presentment of a bill to the president), these new statutes enable Congress to rely on controls short of passing a public law. The usual method is to require committee or subcommittee approval of agency proposals. This practice continued under President Bill Clinton.

This record may appear to be one of congressional contempt for a judicial decision, but the institutional dynamics are more complex than that. A better explanation is that the Court reached too far and failed to understand the practical needs that led Congress and the executive branch to adopt the legislative veto in the first place. Those needs existed before the *Chadha* decision and persist after it.

Following the Court's ruling, Congress amended a number of statutes by deleting legislative vetoes and replacing them with joint resolutions (which must pass both houses and be presented to the president). The statutes that were changed to comply with *Chadha* include the District of Columbia Home Rule Act as well as laws dealing with executive reorganization, national emergencies, export administration, and federal pay. But Congress also added language to statutes requiring the executive branch to obtain the approval of specified committees. Congress no longer attempted to use one-house or two-house resolutions to control agency actions. The effect of *Chadha* was thus to drive leg-

islative vetoes underground, operating at the committee and subcommittee level.

Executive agencies accepted this committee oversight because they understood the risks of challenging Congress on the constitutionality of legislative vetoes. Pushed on this question, Congress was willing to repeal the committee vetoes and, at the same time, repeal discretionary authority it had granted to the agencies over the years. Instead of agency officials having to obtain the approval of designated committees for these discretionary actions, they would have to approach Congress and seek what the Court in *Chadha* demanded: action by both houses on a bill that is presented to the president. The committee veto represents a much less taxing procedure.

This accommodation between congressional committees and executive agencies is unlikely to be challenged in the courts. It is difficult to imagine who would have the standing necessary to bring suit. Plaintiffs would have an uphill battle in convincing the judiciary that the committee veto constituted an injury to them. Judges, sensing that lawsuits of this sort would be more on the order of academic or abstract exercises, would refuse to hear them. Courts now have a more sophisticated understanding of the complexities and varieties of executive-legislative relations and the practical limits of judicial directives.

Constitutional Dialogues. It is simplistic to believe that the judiciary is peculiarly equipped to protect individual and minority rights. That thesis was advanced in 1937, at the time of President Franklin D. Roosevelt's effort to pack the Supreme Court with six additional justices. Opponents condemned his plan as a threat to the independence of the judiciary, which was widely described as the guardian of individual rights. Roosevelt's proposal was soundly rejected, but Henry W. Edgerton, who later became a federal appellate judge, wrote an article at that time that examined the proposition that judicial supremacy is necessary to restrain Congress from infringing on personal liberty. Edgerton studied the Court's record and found little evidence to show that the judiciary was especially sensitive to individual and minority rights. With few exceptions, from 1789 to the time of Edgerton's study, the Supreme Court consistently favored governmental power over individual rights, lent support to harmful business practices, deprived African Americans of protection, upheld business interests over labor interests, and defended private wealth against taxation. For most of that period, individual rights were more likely to be protected by Congress and the president.

The interests of constitutional law and the political process are best served when members of Congress form independent judgments about constitutional issues. Most of these issues are comprehensible to members, whether or not they have legal training. Constitutional issues often turn not so much on technical legal points but on a balancing of competing political and social interests. Collisions occur between congressional regulation and federalism, states' rights and civil rights, government regulation and individual privacy, a free press and the right to a fair trial, congressional investigation and executive privilege, and other questions of constitutional priorities. Congress has adequate resources to analyze those issues. Although members should form their judgments with an awareness of what courts have decided, there is no need to follow those rulings in mechanical fashion. Legislators should not behave like district judges. That congressional interpretations or understandings of the Constitution differ from those of the Supreme Court is hardly reason for concluding that Congress ignores the Constitution—a charge that imputes bad faith.

Even after courts hand down a decision, there are opportunities for Congress to test the soundness of the decision by passing new legislation and supporting further litigation. The Supreme Court often makes room for congressional involvement by deciding an issue on statutory, not constitutional, grounds. This strategy invites Congress to reenter the arena and modify judicial decrees.

No single institution, including the judiciary, has the final word on constitutional questions. All citizens have a responsibility to review what judges decide. It is not true, as Justice Robert H. Jackson once remarked, that justices of the Supreme Court "are not final because we are infallible, but we are infallible only because we are final." The Court is neither final nor infallible. Judicial decisions rest undisturbed only to the extent that Congress, the president, and the general public find the rulings convincing, reasonable, and acceptable.

The courts therefore find themselves engaged in what Alexander Bickel once called a "continuing colloquy" with political institutions and with society at large, a process in which constitutional principle is "evolved conversationally, not perfected unilaterally." This process of give and take and mutual respect permits judges—who are appointed, not elected—to function and survive in a democratic society. The rough-and-tumble character of political debate lacks some of the amenities and dignity of the judicial process, but legislative products are not for that reason inferior to court rulings. The historical record provides convincing evidence that the collective wisdom of Congress, working in concert with the president and the executive branch, is often superior to judicial decisions.

Each decision by a court is subject to scrutiny and rejection by private citizens and public officials. What is final at one stage of judicial proceedings may be reopened by Congress at a later date, leading to revisions, fresh interpretation, and reversals of Supreme Court decisions. Members of Congress have both the authority and the capacity to participate constructively in constitutional interpretation. Their duty to support and defend the Constitution is not erased or nullified by doubts about personal or institutional competence. Much of constitutional law depends on fact-finding and the balancing of competing values, areas in which Congress justifiably can claim substantial expertise.

[See also Civil Rights Act of 1964; Fair Labor Standards Act; Immigration and Naturalization Service v. Chadha; McGrain v. Daugherty; Scott v. Sandford; Voting Rights Act of 1965.]

BIBLIOGRAPHY

Agresto, John. *The Supreme Court and Constitutional Democracy.* 1984.

Andrews, William G., ed. *Coordinate Magistrates: Constitutional Law by Congress and the President.* 1969.

Brest, Paul. "The Conscientious Legislator's Guide to Constitutional Interpretation." *Stanford Law Review* 27 (1975): 585–601.

Cox, Archibald. "The Role of Congress in Constitutional Determinations." *University of Cincinnati Law Review* 40 (1971): 199–261.

Fisher, Louis. *American Constitutional Law.* 2d ed. 1995.

Fisher, Louis. "Constitutional Interpretation by Members of Congress." *North Carolina Law Review* 63 (1985): 707–747.

Fisher, Louis. "The Curious Belief in Judicial Supremacy." *Suffolk University Law Review* 25 (1991): 85–116.

Mikva, Abner J. "How Well Does Congress Support and Defend the Constitution?" *North Carolina Law Review* 61 (1983): 587–611.

Morgan, Donald G. *Congress and the Constitution.* 1966.

Murphy, Walter F. "Who Shall Interpret: The Quest for the Ultimate Constitutional Interpreter." *Review of Politics* 48 (1986): 401–423.

Pritchett, C. Herman. *Congress versus the Supreme Court.* 1961.

Schmidhauser, John R., and Larry L. Berg. *The Supreme Court and Congress.* 1972.

Stumpf, Harry P. "Congressional Response to Supreme Court Rulings: The Interaction of Law and Politics." *Journal of Public Law* 14 (1965): 377–395.

LOUIS FISHER

CONSTITUTIONAL CONVENTION OF 1787.

A central irony of the founding era was that the American political elite, subscribers to the Radical Whig tradition that traced its ancestry back to John Locke, the Glorious Revolution of 1689, and the influential "Cato" articles published by John Trenchard and Thomas Gordon in London in the 1720s and widely reproduced in eighteenth-century America, were fundamentally committed to the principle of legislative supremacy. Thomas Jefferson, Benjamin Franklin, John Adams, Robert Livingston, and Roger Sherman, the drafters of the Declaration of Independence, went to great lengths in that document to absolve Parliament of infringing American liberties, in the process transforming King George III into a sort of Henry VIII. As the Founders were hardly barefoot backwoodsmen, it is fair to assume that their attempt to preserve the legitimacy of the Lockean model of representative government was purposeful.

This is reinforced by the fact that in every state constitution enacted after independence, save that of Massachusetts, the power of the chief executive was virtually eliminated. Only in New York and the New England states was the governor popularly elected; elsewhere, the legislature chose the governor. Similarly, everywhere but in Massachusetts, judges were treated in Lockean fashion as an arm of the executive, chosen and easily removable by the legislature. John Adams's design for the Massachusetts Constitution of 1780 prefigured the federal model, namely, with tenure dependent on "good behavior," but even he hedged the governor's power of judicial appointment, requiring "advice and consent" by a council composed of legislators and permitting removal by the governor and a legislative majority. Thus, "separation of powers" was given rhetorical respect.

Why and how, then, did the delegates come to shape the legislative power in a way that reflected a 180-degree turn from James Madison's original proposal (the Virginia Plan), creating a governmental structure with some quite distinctive features, including a strong executive and an independent judiciary? One of the remarkable characteristics of the delegates was the breadth of their political, administrative, and judicial background. The Framers had, collectively, well over a thousand years of experience in the work of governance at every level: they had been mayors, justices of the peace, provincial (or, later, state) legislators, state governors or presidents, and colonial agents in London.

The gathering convened in May 1787. Once George Washington had been chosen to preside and a set of rules—including one establishing the complete secrecy of the proceedings—had been adopted, the Framers turned to the Virginia Plan as a basis for discussion. What was remarkable about this decision was the absence of dissent. Madison's draft established nothing less than a republican version of the British Parliament: an omnicompetent national legislature with a lower house popularly elected "by the people of the several states" and an upper house chosen by the members of the lower house from nominees put forward by the state legislatures, with the executive and judiciary to be selected by both houses. As further protection against executive usurpations, a New York–style "council of revision" was included; to this body would be referred legislation vetoed by the executive, for eventual resubmission to the legislature.

Substantively, the plan demolished the power of the states. It gave the national legislature the power to

> legislate in all cases to which the separate states are incompetent, or in which the harmony of the United States may be interrupted [by state laws], to negative all laws passed by the several States contravening in the opinion of the national Legislature the articles of Union; and to call forth the force of the Union against any member . . . failing to fulfill its duty.

This "amendment" to the Articles of Confederation totally shifted the locus of power from the states to the center.

The delegates (about forty were usually present) initially seemed much taken with Madison's plan. At a certain point in June, however, the reality principle took hold; a number of delegates gradually realized that, while Madison's plan manifestly worked to the advantage of Virginia, it in effect invited them to commit political suicide. The composite "amendment" required approval by the states. Led by William Paterson of New Jersey, a solid phalanx emerged, not in opposition to a stronger national government but rather behind an effort to craft such reforms as would be acceptable to their constituents. The key issue became the equal representation of the states in one of the legislative chambers. Maneuvering on this issue continued until the Connecticut Compromise (or Great Compromise), which provided for equal representation in the Senate, was narrowly adopted on 17 July.

Article I of the Constitution, which designed legislative power, was changed from the plenary grant of authority in the Virginia Plan to a list of specific and strong delegated powers. The explicit emasculation of the states was modified in Article VI, which simply asserted the supremacy of national laws (and treaties) over state jurisdiction. There is no positive proof that the Framers assumed that the federal judiciary could enforce the supremacy clause, but it is a reasonable conclusion. Moreover, it became the obligation of the president to "take care that the laws be faithfully executed." Unfortunately, there was little substantive discussion of the powers of the president vis-à-vis Congress. The bulk of the discussion was structural: How was the president to be chosen and for what term? Would he be reeligible?

Article II gave the president a veto (modeled on the Massachusetts Constitution) with the understanding he would employ it only to defend the Constitution. As Secretary of State Jefferson re-

minded President Washington in 1791, "It is chiefly for cases where [the Congress is] clearly misled by error, ambition, or interest, that the constitution has placed a check in the negative of the President." Before Andrew Jackson, presidents sent only eight bills back to Congress, all on constitutional rather than policy grounds. The Senate also acted as a council on senior appointments and a massive check on treaty-making.

Since everybody knew that Washington would be the first president but disagreed about the selection mechanism, the bizarre Electoral College was improvised. No one anticipated that within a decade the nationalist elite would split to form a two-party system. Hence, George Mason was not being foolish when he casually stated that, after Washington, the presidential selection would go to the House nineteen times in twenty, with each state having one vote. (Thus would be maintained the equality of states irrespective of size or population, the rule in the Convention itself.)

While the Framers clearly saw the Congress as the matrix of the new government, another check on ephemeral passion, the Supreme Court, was included. There is strong evidence, although the matter was not discussed explicitly, of a consensus that the judiciary could block congressional action on constitutional grounds. Alexander Hamilton stated this explicitly in *Federalist* 78, but one has to be careful with that source. More compelling is the 1795 letter from Attorney General William Bradford imploring Hamilton to succeed John Jay as chief justice because the Court had "the power of paralyzing the measures of the government by declaring a law unconstitutional." In *Hylton v. United States* (1795), the Court placidly exercised this jurisdiction, however, sustaining the challenged statute.

The Congress that emerged from the Constitutional Convention's deliberations was clearly the dominant branch of the new government. The early American quest for absolute legislative supremacy had, however, been tempered by experience. Thus, any serious legislative action had to run a constitutional gauntlet of the states (which picked the Senate), the president, and, finally, the Supreme Court. To the founding elite, an imperial president, Congress, or Court was inconceivable.

[*See also* Anti-Federalists; Articles of Confederation; Constitution; Federalist Papers; Legislative Branch.]

DRAFTING THE CONSTITUTION. In Benjamin Franklin's garden. Members of the Constitutional Convention, *left to right*, Alexander Hamilton, James Wilson, James Madison, and Benjamin Franklin. Charcoal drawing by Allyn Cox.   LIBRARY OF CONGRESS

BIBLIOGRAPHY

Farrand, Max. *The Framing of the Constitution of the United States.* 1913.

Hutson, James H. *Supplement of the Records of the Federal Convention.* 1987.

Roche, John P. *Shadow and Substance.* 1964. Chap. 2, "The Founding Fathers: A Reform Caucus in Action."

Roche, John P. *Sentenced to Life.* 1973. Chap. 3, "The Strange Case of the Revolutionary 'Establishment.'"

JOHN P. ROCHE

CONTEMPT OF CONGRESS.

Contempt of Congress is an act of disrespect or disobedience to an official congressional body. Holding a party in contempt of Congress was once deemed an inherent and summary power, but since 1857 the offense has been defined by statute (11 Stat. 155), now in 2 U.S. Code (1958). Typical acts punished as contempt of Congress are refusing to testify or to submit documents ordered by a committee, or misbehavior before a legislative body.

Historically, the congressional contempt power derives from the judicial contempt of court power. The reason is that American law is rooted in English common law, under which Parliament originally was deemed to be exercising quasi-judicial functions as well as legislative powers. The king could do no wrong under English common law, and courts and Parliament were administrators of the king's will. Nowadays, the House of Lords exercises these quasi-judicial powers, while Commons carries out the purely legislative role.

The rationale for a contempt power is necessity as well as custom. The reasoning is that without such a power a legislative body could not function; there would be no way to deter disrespect or to encourage cooperation. So essential has it seemed that it has been deemed an inherent power of any legislature by scholars, historians, and judges.

The American colonies adopted many common-law procedures, and contempt of the legislature was one. State assemblies early exercised the contempt power to compel testimony and to protect their dignity. The federal Constitution is silent on the subject of congressional contempt; according to some commentators, it was deemed axiomatic that the power was inherent and thus did not need to be explicitly listed.

In any event, Congress always believed it had a contempt power, whatever its source and legal basis. As early as 1795 a House committee summarily imprisoned a nonmember for contempt. During the next fifty years the House and Senate did so regularly. The power of Congress to summarily punish contempt was first adjudicated and upheld in 1821 in *Anderson v. Dunn* (19 U.S. [6 Wheat] 204), though the power was later questioned in a landmark case, *Kilbourn v. Thompson* (103 U.S. 168 [1880]).

To clarify the confusion caused by reliance on dated English common law and conflicting American cases concerning the summary contempt power, Congress passed a law in 1857 authorizing punishment for contempt of Congress, but only after indictment and trial. Presently, when a congressional committee decides it has been offended by contempt, the Speaker of the House or the president of the Senate must certify this contempt to the attorney general, who then proceeds to prosecute the case as he would any other criminal offense.

In the mid-twentieth century the congressional contempt statute has been used frequently, often in contentious cases. Congressional committees have actively investigated crime, subversion, and security cases, for example, and they have resorted to contempt proceedings as a means of retribution. So the nature of the use of the congressional contempt power has evolved, as have its source and its procedural implementation. In the ninety-two years between 1857 and 1949, 113 witnesses were cited for contempt of Congress, while from 1950 to 1952, 117 witnesses were cited.

Has Congress been more active, or have witnesses become more obstinate? Between 1789 and 1925 Congress authorized 285 investigations, while between 1950 and 1952 it authorized 225. It is interesting to consider how the courts have disposed of congressional contempt cases. In the District of Columbia, where most contempt of Congress cases arise, between 1950 and 1959 there were 83 indictments for contempt of Congress, while grand juries refused to indict in 17 proposed cases. Of those indicted, 30 defendants were convicted and 47 were acquitted. Of the 30 convictions, 15 were reversed on appeal.

In the late twentieth century, resort to the congressional contempt power has decreased. The wrong itself has come to be regarded as an ordinary criminal offense to be treated no differently from other offenses.

[*See also* Investigations; Kilbourn v. Thompson; Witnesses, Rights of.]

BIBLIOGRAPHY

Aiyar, Krishna Jagavisa. *The Law of Contempt of Court, Parliament and Public Servants.* 1949.

Beck, Carl. *Contempt of Congress: A Study of the Prosecutions Initiated by the Committee on Un-American Activities, 1945–1947.* 1959.

Galloway, George Barnes. *Congress and Parliament: Their Organization and Operation in the U.S. and the U.K.* 1955.

Goldfarb, Ronald L. *The Contempt of Power.* 1971.

RONALD GOLDFARB

CONTESTED ELECTIONS. [*This entry discusses contested congressional elections. For discussion of Congress's role in resolving disputes concerning the election of the president, see* Electoral College; Electoral Commission of 1877; Electoral Count Act; Presidential Elections.] Borrowing from the British parliamentary model, Article I, section 5 of the U.S. Constitution provides that "Each House shall be the Judge of the Elections, Returns and Qualifications of its own Members." In addition, Article I, section 4 provides, "The Times, Places and Manner of holding Elections for Senators and Representatives shall be prescribed in each State by the Legislature thereof; but the Congress may at any time by Law make or alter such Regulations." Taken together, these sections invest Congress with near-complete authority to establish the procedures and render final decisions relating to the election of its members.

In exercising its authority to judge election returns, each house of Congress is essentially free from judicial review. The Supreme Court has declined jurisdiction over congressional election contests, finding that the authority to resolve contests is constitutionally committed to each of the respective houses and therefore is not justiciable.

Although Congress could assume complete responsibility for resolving election contests by enacting a comprehensive election code and thereby preempting state law, it has so far declined to do so. Instead, both houses have recognized and indeed relied on state contest (challenge) and recount procedures to clarify and resolve issues relating to election contests of their members.

In the absence of federal preempting legislation, the authority of states to enact contest and recount procedures governing federal elections seems well grounded in law. In the case of *Roudebush v. Hartke* (1972), the Supreme Court upheld Indiana's right to conduct a recount of a U.S. Senate election notwithstanding the power of the Senate to render the ultimate judgment as to which claimant was entitled to the seat. This case is in keeping with a long line of cases (*Ex Parte Siebold* [1880], *Minor v. Happersett* [1875], and *Smiley v. Holm* [1932]) in which the Court has found states to have broad authority to devise laws and set procedures governing federal elections provided that Congress has not legislated to the contrary.

It should be noted that, notwithstanding these cases and Congress's clear acquiescence in state exercise of jurisdiction, a number of states have chosen not to assert jurisdiction. Three states claim no jurisdiction and lack any procedures for resolving election disputes in federal elections. Another four do not provide for recounts in federal elections but do have contest procedures. Five states take the opposite position, allowing recounts but not contests.

Regardless of whether a state provides procedures for challenging the results of a congressional election, final authority to resolve a dispute clearly rests with the house of Congress to which the challenge pertains. The rules and precedents of each house establish the methods under which a challenge is considered. In the House of Representatives a contest may be initiated by any of four methods: (1) a contest filed by a losing candidate pursuant to the Federal Contested Election Act of 1969 (FCEA), (2) a protest or memorial filed by an elector of the district involved, (3) a protest or memorial filed by any other person, or (4) a privileged motion of any member.

Although the House of Representatives has considered contests brought by each of these methods, in practice the vast majority of contests are filed pursuant to the FCEA. Only under extraordinary circumstances would a contest brought by any other method stand any chance of success. Election contests in the House of Representatives are referred to the Committee on House Administration for investigation. The findings and recommendations of the committee are reported to the full House for final decision.

As the House of Representatives has come to rely on state fact-finding and issue resolution, the burden on a contestant to sustain a challenge has increased. Before the committee institutes a full investigation, a contestant must demonstrate, without the advantage of the panel's discovery procedures, that sufficient evidence exists to reverse the presumption of regularity in the election and establish the likelihood that the contestant will prevail on the merits.

An example of a privileged motion by a member is the contest titled McIntyre v. McCloskey (1985), in which the House refused to seat the state certified winner from Indiana's 8th Congressional District (Richard McIntyre) in a close election pending

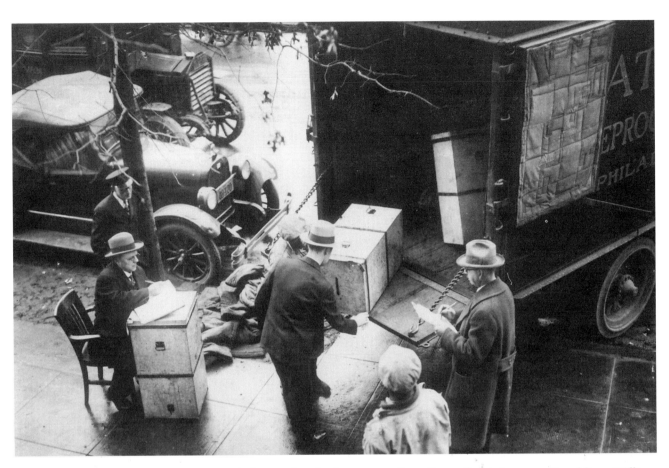

BALLOT BOXES. From the 1926 contested election for the Senate seat from Pennsylvania between Republican William S. Vare and ex–secretary of Labor, Democrat William B. Wilson. Newspapers had reported illegal activities by Vare's supporters during the 1926 primary. When Congress convened, Vare was not sworn in with the other senators-elect, pending a decision by a committee appointed by the Senate to investigate the Pennsylvania elections. On 22 February 1929, the committee reported that Vare was not entitled to a seat because of excessive campaign expenditures. Although the Senate Committee on Privileges and Elections decided that Vare had received a plurality of the legal votes, the Senate voted to give neither Vare nor Wilson the Senate seat. The governor of Pennsylvania then appointed Republican Joseph R. Grundy to the vacancy. LIBRARY OF CONGRESS

an investigation by the Committee on House Administration of alleged irregularities. General Accounting Office detailers, supervised by a professional recount director, counted ballots on site in the state, following which the House adopted a resolution seating Frank McCloskey as the winner by four votes.

The Senate's approach to election contests varies greatly from that of the House. There is no federal legislation governing Senate contests, nor has the Senate formally adopted general rules or procedures governing the conduct of contests. While two or three House contests can be anticipated per Congress, Senate contests are rare. The Senate considers each contest to present a unique case for adjudication.

Examining the decisions of the Senate, certain principles and procedures can be gleaned. The Senate has considered contests brought by private citizens, private and public associations, state governmental entities, and losing candidates. No particular form is required for a petition challenging an election result, nor are there any prescribed filing deadlines. It is generally expected that a petition will set forth sufficient grounds, supported by specific allegations, to justify an investigation. The petition is generally referred to the Committee on Rules and Administration, which adopts procedures for consideration of the petition. The committee then conducts such investigation as it deems necessary and reports its findings and recommendations to the full Senate for decision.

In 1974, after an unsuccessful seven-month Senate effort to determine the winning candidate in the hotly disputed race between Rep. Louis C. Wyman and John A. Durkin, which was caused by tie votes in the Senate Committee on Rules and Administration and a filibuster on the Senate floor, the Senate finally adopted a resolution that simply declared the seat vacant, thereby resulting in a new election.

Although the two houses take different approaches to the resolution of election contests, they share the same objective. Each attempts to discharge its constitutional responsibility in a manner that recognizes the evolution and general reliability of state election procedures while at the same time protecting its constitutional prerogative to be the final judge of the elections, returns, and qualifications of its members.

BIBLIOGRAPHY

U.S. House of Representatives. *Deschler's Precedents of the United States House of Representatives,* by Lewis Deschler. 94th Cong., 2d sess., 1977. H. Doc. 94-661. Vol. 2, chap. 9.

U.S. House of Representatives. Committee on House Administration. *Report Relating to Election of a Representative from the Eighth Congressional District of Indiana.* 99th Cong., 1st sess., 1985. H. Rept. 99-58.

U.S. Senate. *Senate Election, Expulsion, and Censure Cases, 1793–1972.* 92d Cong., 1st sess., 1972. S. Doc. 92-7.

CHARLES T. HOWELL

CONTINENTAL CONGRESS. *See* History of Congress, *articles on* The Origins of Congress *and* The Road to Nationhood.

CONTINGENT FUND. The term *contingent fund* refers to an account in appropriations legislation that funds expenses for which specific and separate appropriations have not been made. The term *contingent expenses* was first used in a legislative appropriations statute in the Act Making Appropriations for Support of Government of 11 February 1791. At that time, the account included almost all funding for the House and Senate. Over the years, however, statutory language regarding the account became quite specific, designating certain expenditures in detail while prohibiting others.

Today, there is no contingent fund, per se, in either the House or Senate. The Senate has an account titled Contingent Expenses of the Senate. Appropriations for this account defray the cost of various administrative and salary expenditures of the Senate and its officers, members, and committees. These appropriations are made for specific dollar amounts and for specific purposes. Within the account are nine components for which specific appropriations are made each year: Senate Policy Committees, Inquiries and Investigations (by committees), Caucus on International Narcotics Control, Secretary of the Senate, Sergeant at Arms and Doorkeeper of the Senate, Senator's Official Personnel and Office Expense Account, Office of Fair Employment Practices, Stationery Revolving Fund, and Miscellaneous Items. Any transfer of funds in excess of 10 percent of any entity must be approved by the Senate Committee on Appropriations.

Appropriations language of the House does not contain a similar account. In recent years, House language has included an account titled Contingent Expenses of the House. As in the Senate account, appropriations within the account were made for specific dollar amounts and for specific purposes. Some appropriations could be transferred to meet unanticipated fiscal responsibilities. Transfers could be accomplished only upon approval of both the ranking majority and minority members of the House Subcommittee on Legislative Branch Appropriations.

BIBLIOGRAPHY

U.S. House of Representatives. Committee on Appropriations. *Legislative Branch Appropriations Bill, 1992: Report to Accompany* H.R. 2506, 102d Cong., 1st sess., 1991. H. Rept. 102-82.

U.S. House of Representatives. Committee on Appropriations. Subcommittee on Legislative Branch Appropriations. *Legislative Branch Appropriations for 1992, Hearings.* Part 2. 102d Cong., 1st sess., 1991.

U.S. House of Representatives. Commission on Administrative Review. *Administrative Reorganization and Legislative Management: A Report Pursuant to Section 5 of House Resolution 1968, 94th Congress.* Vol. 1: *Administrative Units.* 95th Cong., 1st sess., 1977. H. Doc. 95-232.

U.S. Senate. Committee on Appropriations. *Legislative Branch Appropriations, 1993. Report to Accompany* H.R. 5427. 102d Cong., 2d sess. 1992. S. Rept. 102-481.

PAUL E. DWYER

CONTINUING RESOLUTION. Congress normally funds federal agencies for a fiscal year by annual enactment of thirteen general appropriation bills. If Congress fails to complete action on one or more of these bills before the start of a fiscal year, it enacts a joint resolution specifying that appropriations continue at some specified rate.

First enacted in 1876, continuing resolutions were intended to provide the funding necessary for the orderly continuation of government between the expiration of one fiscal year's appropriations and the delayed enactment of new appropriations. These measures are usually of a specific, limited duration and restrict funding to a specified rate of operations—usually the previous year's rate, the rate set by either the House or Senate version of the pertinent regular appropriation act for the upcoming fiscal year, or possibly the lowest of these alternatives. Congress is criticized, both inside and outside of its ranks, for also using continuing resolutions as a means of enacting one or more regular annual appropriations measures by specifying new levels and new objects of expenditure and extending their availability for the entire fiscal year.

The House treats continuing resolutions as a class apart from general appropriations and thus allows different procedural rules to govern their consideration. (For example, the prohibitions in Rule XXI against unauthorized appropriations and legislation in general appropriation bills do not apply.) Although the rules of the Senate do not make this distinction, their greater flexibility in general reduces the need for such.

BIBLIOGRAPHY

Keith, Robert A. *An Overview of the Use of Continuing Appropriations.* Congressional Research Service, Library of Congress. CRS Rept. 1980.
U.S. Congress. General Accounting Office. *Principles of Federal Appropriations Law.* GAO Doc. OGC-92-13. 2d ed. 1992. Vol. 2, chap. 8, "Continuing Resolutions."
U.S. House of Representatives. *Deschler's Precedents of the United States House of Representatives,* by Lewis Deschler. 94th Cong., 2d sess., 1977. H. Doc. 94-661. Vol. 7, chap. 25.

JAMES V. SATURNO

COOLIDGE, CALVIN

COOLIDGE, CALVIN (1872–1933), thirtieth president of the United States and an advocate of economy in government. Brought up in the tiny community of Plymouth Notch, Vermont, John Calvin Coolidge graduated from Amherst College, read law in the office of a Northampton, Massachusetts, lawyer, and was admitted to the bar in 1897. The following year he was elected to Northamp-

ton's city council and began his political ascent: city solicitor, clerk of the county courts, state representative, mayor, state senator, lieutenant governor, and governor. A Republican, he was elected in 1920 to the vice presidency, and on 2 August 1923 he succeeded Warren G. Harding as president, winning a landslide election in his own right in 1924.

In many ways Coolidge's was a notable presidency. The president managed a considerable reduction in the national debt, maintained the probity of the executive office through a long national airing of the Harding scandals, conducted foreign policy with aplomb by sponsoring the Kellogg-Briand pact for renouncing and outlawing war, and presided over a short-lived "Coolidge boom" in the national economy.

Coolidge's most notable failures were with Congress. The president was not an outgoing man; he did not possess any of the arts of private persuasion. Moreover, he believed that after he expounded what Congress ought to do, it was Congress's business to do it. He desired development of hydroelectric power at Muscle Shoals on the Tennessee River through private rather than public initiative. But Sen. George W. Norris (R-Neb.) espied a "steal" of public resources and delayed the project until the time of the New Deal. Coolidge also tangled with Congress over bonus legislation for World War I veterans, and Congress in 1924 passed a bill over his veto by large majorities. Nor could he easily contain Congress's enthusiasm for a succession of farm bills that would have propped up domestic farm prices by buying excess production and dumping it abroad. Coolidge was of farm origin— his father was a farmer and rural storekeeper. He had managed to escape the farm and wondered why other farmers did not also want to do so. Citing a variety of constitutional and fiscal objections, he easily vetoed the McNary-Haugen dumping legislation.

His most awkward dealings with Congress came over the Teapot Dome and other Harding administration scandals; Congress wanted to judge them, while the president determined to clean what he considered his own house. The Senate sought control through an investigation headed by Thomas J. Walsh of Montana, a Democrat. Coolidge countered with a special counsel—a former Democratic senator from Ohio, Atlee Pomerene, and a distinguished Republican lawyer, Owen J. Roberts. Fortunately, both Walsh and the president moved slowly, and everything became so stretched out that a dire confrontation was avoided.

CALVIN COOLIDGE. As president, addressing members of Congress in the House chamber, mid 1920s.

Last, the Senate in 1925 refused to confirm Charles B. Warren as attorney general. The senators were irritated with Vice President Charles G. Dawes, who during his inaugural address had castigated them for wasting time through their rule of unlimited debate. When Dawes was out of the chair, taking a nap in his suite in the Willard Hotel, they produced a tie vote on Warren's nomination; while Dawes was racing for Capitol Hill in a taxicab the nomination was lost when Sen. Lee S. Overman (D-N.C.) changed his vote.

Coolidge left the presidency in 1929, during the Indian summer of national prosperity. He died of a heart attack in January 1933.

BIBLIOGRAPHY

Fuess, Claude M. *Calvin Coolidge: The Man from Vermont.* 1940.

McCoy, Donald R. *Calvin Coolidge: The Quiet President.* 1962.

ROBERT H. FERRELL

COPYRIGHT, TRADEMARKS, AND PATENTS.

Copyright, trademark, and patent laws represent Congress's efforts to construct a legal framework to deal with ideas. Unlike other property, intellectual property (patents, copyrights, trade-

Landmark Legislation on Copyrights, Trademarks, and Patents

COPYRIGHTS			
TITLE	YEAR ENACTED	REFERENCE NUMBER	DESCRIPTION
Copyright Act of 1790	1790	1 Stat. 14	First federal copyright act.
Copyright Act of 1831	1831	4 Stat. 436	Consolidated copyright law; extended original term from 14 to 28 years, but left renewal term at 14 years.
Copyright Act of 1870	1870	16 Stat. 198	Consolidated copyright law including deposit requirements and coverage of dramatic works and photographs; added paintings, drawings, chromolithographs, statuaries, models, and fine art designs; and transferred copyright responsibilities to the Librarian of Congress.
Copyright Act of 1909	1909	35 Stat. pt. 1, 1075	Major copyright revision that governed U.S. copyright until Copyright Act of 1976; extended renewal term to 28 years; made publication, not recordation, the effective date of the copyright term; provided guidance as to ownership of renewal interest and distinguished new work from underlying work; and codified "First Sale Doctrine."
Record Piracy Act of 1971	1971	P.L. 92-140	Provided federal protection for sound recordings.
Copyright Revision Act of 1976	1976	P.L. 94-553	The current U.S. copyright statute as of 1994, it preempted state common law copyright; changed the term of copyright to life of the author plus 50 years, with other provisions where there is no measuring life; provided a nontransferable right in the author and specified heirs to terminate any transfers of rights under the copyright after 35 years; codified the judicial "fair use" doctrine; provided certain library, nonprofit educational, and other limitations on copyright; created compulsory licenses applicable to jukeboxes and cable television systems with a Copyright Royalty Tribunal to oversee them; and provided a mechanism for review of the need to address computer software concerns.
Semiconductor Chip Protection Act of 1984	1984	P.L. 98-620	Provided protection similar to copyright for mask works embodied in semiconductor chips.
Judicial Improvements Act of 1990	1990	P.L. 101-650	Expanded "moral" rights in works of visual art and in architectural works, and prohibited unlicensed leasing of computer software except by nonprofit libraries or educational institutions.

TRADEMARKS			
TITLE	YEAR ENACTED	REFERENCE NUMBER	DESCRIPTION
Trademark Act of 1870 and Trademark Act of 1876	1870, 1876	16 Stat. 210, 19 Stat. 141	First federal trademark acts; held unconstitutional in the *Trademark Cases (United States v. Steffens,* 100 U.S. 82 [1879]).
Trademark Act of 1881	1881	21 Stat. 502	Provided for registration of marks used in foreign commerce or in trade with Indian tribes.
Trademark Act of 1905	1905	33 Stat. 724	Provided 20-year renewable registration for nondescriptive trademarks used in interstate commerce.
Trademark Act of 1920	1920	41 Stat. 533	Added 20-year nonrenewable term for descriptive terms used in interstate commerce.
Trademark Act of 1946 (Lanham Act)	1946	P.L. 79-489	The U.S. trademark statute of the late twentieth century; although restricted to marks used in interstate commerce, its scope is broader than any since the 1870 and 1876 acts. It provided certain presumptions and procedural advantages for marks registered under it.

Landmark Legislation on Copyright, Trademarks, and Patents (Continued)

TRADEMARKS *(Continued)*			
TITLE	YEAR ENACTED	REFERENCE NUMBER	DESCRIPTION
Trademark Counterfeiting Act of 1984	1984	P.L. 98-473	Provided enhanced penalties and *ex parte* seizure procedures for counterfeits of registered marks.
Trademark Law Revision Act of 1988	1988	P.L. 100-667	Permitted registration prior to use of the mark, abolished "token use" registrability, reduced original term to 10 years, and created federal "dilution" cause of action.

PATENTS			
TITLE	YEAR ENACTED	REFERENCE NUMBER	DESCRIPTION
Patent Act of 1790	1790	1 Stat. 109	First federal patent act.
Patent Act of 1836	1836	5 Stat. 117	Established the Patent Office and modern administration system for patent examination.
Patent Act of 1870	1870	16 Stat. 198	Consolidated earlier changes made in the patent law and empowered the patent commissioner to promulgate rules and regulations.
Patent Act of 1952	1952	P.L. 82-593	The current U.S. patent law as of 1994, it codified all amendments since 1870, incorporated or overturned judicial constructions, created presumption of patent validity, expanded coverage to new uses, and delineated patent misuse and contributory infringement standard.
Amendments to Patent Act of 1952	1982	P.L. 97-164 P.L. 97-247 P.L. 97-256	Created the Court of Appeals for the Federal Circuit to resolve differences that had existed among the circuits, and made certain substantive changes.

marks, trade secrets, unfair competition) is by its nature subject to exclusive control only if kept secret. Disclosure results in dispersion: an idea disclosed to another is thereafter possessed by both. This simple difference has profound implications. Inventors and authors are discouraged from devoting resources and talents to the creation of new devices or books that others are free to take and exploit. The legislature, therefore, has created an exclusive patent right for inventors and copyright for authors, and lends federal support to trademark rights that protect the reputation of a product or service.

Congress strikes a balance between rewarding the idea by monopoly and encouraging its further exploitation by making it free. Patents only protect inventions that are novel, not obvious, and useful. The exclusive right does not extend to abstract ideas, scientific principles, and things that exist in nature or are already known or obvious. Others are free to develop new inventions from those ideas. Similarly, copyright extends only to the form of the author's expression, not to the ideas that are expressed.

Colonial legislatures awarded patents through private acts until the adoption of the Constitution, which granted Congress the power "to promote the Progress of Science and useful Arts, by securing for Limited Times to Authors and Inventors the exclusive Right to their respective Writings and Discoveries." The First Congress passed the Patent Act of 1790 and the Copyright Act of 1790. A patent was granted only after an examination to determine utility and "importance." Copyright was a simple registration system.

In 1870 and 1876 trademarks—words or symbols that indicate a single source of marked goods—were brought under federal law on the basis of the patent and copyright power. But the U.S. Supreme Court in the *Trademark Cases* (1879) held the application of those powers to trademarks to be unconstitutional on the ground that these were neither writings nor discoveries. Not until 1905 did Congress again provide a federal scheme for domestic trademarks, this time under the commerce power.

The dramatic modern evolution of commerce and technology has prompted congressional adaptation of intellectual property law. Copyright now covers not only printed materials but movies, sound recordings, television (broadcast and cable), computer software, and semiconductor chips. This has required new concepts of expression, publication, copying, and authorship. A 1978 congressional act preempted the copyright field from action by the states. In 1989, the legislature brought U.S. copyright law into conformity with the international Berne Convention. This compliance with Berne renewed attention to the so-called moral rights of the author to control a work after having sold it or to profit from resales by others. Also of concern is the scope of the fair use of a copyrighted work by others without permission.

The patent statute has undergone occasional revisions to avoid overly restrictive judicial standards. Congress abolished the court-created requirement that an invention result from a "flash of genius," made inventions presumptively valid, expanded process patents to cover new uses of old inventions, delineated patent misuse from contributory infringement, created a reexamination procedure, provided for extension of the term of drug patents affected by Federal Drug Administration delays, and made importation of goods produced abroad by domestically patented processes an infringement. Late-twentieth-century issues are whether or not to replace the U.S. practice (which awards the patent to the first to invent) with the standard of the first to file an application, used virtually everywhere else, and whether or not to impose restrictions on the patenting of new life forms.

The trademark law has undergone major changes. In 1993 state law continued to define the existence of a mark, and state registration was still permitted. But federal registration creates a presumption of validity and offers the registrant federal remedies. There are special provisions designed to address the problem of trademark counterfeiting. In order to protect the substantial investment required before a mark can be used, federal registration has been made available prior to actual use of the mark. Federal intellectual property law is Congress's response to the accelerating development and internationalization of high technology. These rapid changes will require closer congressional attention to the area and frequent legislative responses.

BIBLIOGRAPHY

Klitzke, Ramon A. "History of Patents—U.S." In *The Encyclopedia of Patent Practice and Invention Management.* 1964.

Latman, Alan. "Introduction." In *The Copyright Law.* 5th ed. 1979.

McCarthy, J. Thomas. "The Historical Basis of Trademarks and Legislative History." In *Trademarks and Unfair Competition.* 3d ed. 1992.

HAROLD F. SEE

CORRESPONDENCE TO CONGRESS.

Mail is the most important communications link between members of Congress and their constituents. Since the early 1970s the volume of correspondence to members has increased sharply, rising, for example, more than tenfold by 1990 to over 200 million pieces a year to members of the House of Representatives. The increase reflects the growing use of mail by interest groups engaged in grassroots lobbying and the advances in technology employed in organized mail campaigns. By far the largest share of mail to members deals with legislative issues. Other mail includes requests for assistance and invitations.

Members answer almost all their mail. About half the time of members' staffs is devoted to handling incoming and outgoing mail. High priority is given to reading and answering mail in most congressional offices. Form mail that can be answered with a form response is normally handled by a computer operator. Staff assistants prepare responses for other mail dealing with legislative issues. Computerized lists enable members to send more mail under the congressional frank to targeted groups of constituents. Requests for assistance are handled by case workers who are often located in the members' state or district offices.

Members encourage and highly value mail from their constituents. Although most members read or see only a small part of their mail, they are well informed as to its contents. The mail informs them about constituent interests and desires and thereby helps them to serve more effectively in their representative role. The mail also helps members to get reelected. Answering the mail offers members an opportunity to build political support by being responsive to constituent interests and concerns. Mail is also useful to members in reaching decisions on some issues before Congress.

The influence of the mail on particular voting decisions varies greatly and is affected by factors such as origin, form, issue, and volume of the correspondence. Influence also varies with the members' voting history, the intensity of their views on the issues, and their own expertise. Mail that is most likely to influence a member's decisions (1) comes from constituents, particularly those who are important to the member's reelection; (2) is individually composed by the sender and reflects informed and strongly held views; and (3) deals with an issue that affects the sender in a direct or personal way. The influence of mail is likely to be diminished if the member has a voting history or holds strong personal convictions on the issues or is an expert on the subject.

Influence does not necessarily increase with volume. A smaller volume of mail reflecting the informed views of senders who are not part of an organized campaign is given much more weight than a high volume of form mail inspired by an interest group. In some instances mass mailings promoted by interest groups can have a strong influence on decisions in Congress. Such mail campaigns can be effective if they deal with a salient issue that stirs the emotions or affects the pocketbook of senders and if, in addition to form mail, there is other mail on the subject that was clearly originated by individual senders.

Mass mailings forced Congress to repeal a law requiring withholding of taxes on interest and dividend income. The National Rifle Association has made very effective use of mail to oppose gun control legislation. Organized campaigns are much more likely than spontaneous letter writing to be the source of mail on major issues before Congress, particularly economic issues. In the 98th Congress, for example, for issues that inspired the most mail, organized campaigns generated twice as much correspondence as individual letter writers.

BIBLIOGRAPHY

Frantzich, Stephen E. *Computers in Congress: The Politics of Information.* 1982.
Hansen, Orval. *Congressional Operations: The Role of Mail in Decision-Making in Congress.* 1987.

ORVAL HANSEN

THOMAS CORWIN.   LIBRARY OF CONGRESS

CORWIN, THOMAS (1794–1865), senator and representative from Ohio, governor of Ohio, secretary of the Treasury, and minister to Mexico. Born in Kentucky and raised in Lebanon, Ohio, Corwin had a political career that reflected the growth of urban interests and antislavery sentiment in Ohio. When Corwin entered politics in the early 1820s, Cincinnati and surrounding counties were still feeling the effects of the severe deflation following the panic of 1819. Because this region opposed paper currency, Corwin, like most of the creators of the new Whig party, championed a strong protective tariff and a powerful central bank. Corwin also shared the Whig interest in proposing public works projects: in his case, canals and waterways, which were vital to Ohio's commerce.

Corwin was a typical Whig also in his belief that government should protect moral purity. Antislavery sentiment had originated largely with the Whigs' New England constituency. Aware of strong abolitionist currents in the nonslaveholding states, Corwin successfully convinced Whig leaders of the importance of garnering antislavery support. This was a tactical position designed to appeal to the principles of liberty while attacking President James K. Polk and fostering Whig party unity.

Corwin's responsiveness to major economic and social issues enabled him to attain high office. After serving as U.S. representative from 1831 to 1840, Corwin became governor of Ohio in 1840. Although he lost the 1842 gubernatorial race by 1,842 votes, he won election as U.S. senator and served from 1845 to 1850. Thereafter, Corwin was secretary of the Treasury under Millard Fillmore from 1850 to 1853.

Corwin attracted great attention as an opponent of the Mexican War. He condemned the war on moral grounds, characterizing the conflict as organized thievery. Like many Ohioans, Corwin linked expansionism with the spread of slavery. He demanded that U.S. troops be withdrawn from Mexico and refused to vote for appropriations to support the war.

Corwin was hostile to President Polk. Polk's veto of a harbor and rivers improvement bill and his tariff reductions incensed Corwin and other Whigs. As a critic of the Polk administration and a leading member of the Whig party, Corwin was considered a potential presidential candidate in 1848.

But his political importance diminished after 1848. Despite his opposition to slavery, Corwin supported the temporizing Zachary Taylor for the Whig leadership. Because he believed that party unity was paramount, Corwin repeatedly declined opportunities to advance personal interests. He attacked the emerging Free-Soil party and maintained that Taylor would never veto the Wilmot Proviso.

At the same time, Corwin continued to consider the Democrats dangerous prosoutherners. He even declared his willingness to vote for John C. Fremont in 1856. That year Corwin was elected to Congress as a Republican, and he supported Abraham Lincoln's rise to power. In 1860, Corwin chaired a select committee of the House convened to consider the country's peril. He finished his career by serving as minister to Mexico from 1861 to 1864. Corwin's career reflected the increasingly fierce sectional conflicts that gradually led to civil war.

BIBLIOGRAPHY

Knepper, George. *Ohio and Its People.* 1989.
Maizlish, Stephen E. *The Triumph of Sectionalism: The Transformation of Ohio Politics, 1844–1856.* 1983.
Morrow, Josiah. *Life and Speeches of Thomas Corwin.* 1896.

DOUGLAS W. RICHMOND

COURT-PACKING FIGHT. President Franklin D. Roosevelt's attempt to enlarge the Supreme Court, and thereby secure a liberal Court majority, triggered a bitter constitutional confrontation, known as the Court-packing fight of 1937. In a string of decisions, starting in 1935 with its invalidation of the National Industrial Recovery Act (1933), a closely divided Court had blocked significant portions of the New Deal's attempt to cope with the nation's then-raging industrial, agricultural, and social problems.

The Court scheme, secretly drafted by Roosevelt and Attorney General Homer S. Cummings, was part of a package of ideas labeled the judiciary reform act, ostensibly intended to improve efficiency in the federal judiciary system. Congestion in the court system was blamed largely on judges who had grown old and infirm and yet refused to retire. The measure would have allowed the president to appoint one additional Supreme Court justice, up to a maximum of six, for every justice who had served for ten years and remained on the bench after age seventy-and-a-half. With six of the nine justices already past age seventy, Roosevelt could have appointed as many additional justices, all of them presumably sympathetic to New Deal philosophy.

From 5 February 1937, when Roosevelt unveiled his proposal to stunned congressional leaders, until 22 July 1937, when the Senate buried his idea once and for all, the Court-expansion issue divided Congress as have few others. It opened wounds in the Democratic party that festered for half a century and encouraged the movement of conservatives into a bipartisan alliance that would harass liberal programs for decades.

Congress, whose power to determine the Court's size was well established, was not averse to a Court shakeup. Roosevelt's fatal error was to exclude congressional leaders from his early consideration of the expansion idea. Many members of

COURT-PACKING PROPOSAL. President Franklin D. Roosevelt, depicted as the quarterback, wanted six new Supreme Court Justices for each of the six on the bench who were over seventy years old, shown here as the players in the background. Clifford K. Berryman, 6 February 1937.   LIBRARY OF CONGRESS

Congress agreed that the Court needed new blood and almost certainly would have endorsed a less drastic solution. Even New Deal skeptics such as Chairman Hatton W. Sumners of the House Judiciary Committee supported measures to entice senior justices into retirement with generous pensions. But FDR's plan was a frontal attack on the independence of the judiciary, and thus an assault on the Constitution itself. "Boys, here's where I cash in my chips," Sumners informed colleagues after his White House briefing on the proposal. Sumners vowed to oppose the bill, forcing proponents to seek passage first in the Senate and hope that the House would follow. Other key lawmakers, such as Senate majority leader Joseph T. Robinson, who favored a constitutional limit on Court tenure, were also dismayed, although Robinson, ever loyal to the presidency, agreed to lead the Senate fight. Capitalizing on Robinson's popularity among his colleagues, the White House signaled that Robinson himself would be the president's choice for the first available Court seat.

Robinson believed that a majority of the Senate would support a scaled-down bill, but Roosevelt would not compromise. He held firm even when the Court gestured its capitulation to the New Deal in the spring by affirming the Wagner-Connery National Labor Relations Act and the Social Security Act. When conservative justice Willis Van Devanter chose to announce his retirement, assuring that Roosevelt would have his liberal majority, on the very day the Senate Judiciary Committee released a scathing condemnation of the bill, the fight became superfluous and unwinnable.

In June 1937, the president yielded. Still hoping for a face-saving partial victory, he advised the Senate majority leader to take the best deal he could get. When Senate debate opened on 6 July 1937, Robinson believed he had sufficient votes to pass his modified bill, which raised to seventy-five the age for appointing an additional justice and limited such expansion to one seat a year. But any remaining hope for the measure faded when its chief Senate advocate was struck by a fatal heart attack at the height of the debate. No longer bound by their pledges to Robinson, the senators rushed to recommit the bill to the Judiciary Committee and thus to oblivion.

BIBLIOGRAPHY

Alsop, Joseph, and Turner Catledge. *The 168 Days.* 1938.
Bacon, Donald C. "Joseph T. Robinson: The Good Soldier." In *Senate Leaders of the Twentieth Century.* Edited by Richard A. Baker and Roger H. Davidson. 1991.
Leuchtenburg, William E. "Franklin D. Roosevelt's Supreme Court 'Packing' Plan." In *Essays on the New Deal.* Edited by Harold M. Hollingsworth and William F. Holmes. 1969.
Pusey, Merlo J. "F.D.R. v. the Supreme Court." In *Times of Trial: Great Crises in the American Past.* Edited by Allen Nevins. 1958.

DONALD C. BACON

COVODE COMMITTEE. Established in 1860 by the Republican-controlled House of the 36th Congress, the Select Committee to Investigate Alleged Corruptions in Government, popularly known as the Covode committee, was meant less to uncover facts than to confirm widely believed suspicions that the administration of James Buchanan had abused the funds and offices at its command for political ends. The committee's report, issued in June 1860, was rightly denounced as partisan.

REP. JOHN COVODE (R-PA.).   LIBRARY OF CONGRESS

Chairman "Honest John" Covode, a hard-nosed Pennsylvania Republican, had proposed the investigation to repay the president for his charge of corrupt practices by Covode's political friends; no one dreamed that a Democratic Senate would convict anyone the House impeached. Yet the committee found more than enough evidence to make a solid case for the last two administrations' abuse of printing contracts and diversion of government funds to prop up faltering party presses, naturalization frauds in the 1856 Pennsylvania election, and the importation of outsiders to vote in Philadelphia two years later. Touching on Buchanan's maneuvers to pass the rigged Lecompton constitution that virtually imposed slavery on Kansas, witnesses described a systematic campaign in which offices, cash, contracts, and threats were used to suborn House members.

Covode could not tie the president directly to impeachable offenses, but the House did pass a resolution of censure. In the 1860 presidential campaign, Covode became one of the Republicans' biggest draws, and his committee report was a best-seller. On the more substantive side, the Covode report helped push Congress to reform the practice of public printing. Instead of contracting with private firms at exorbitant rates, Congress sent much of the work out to the Government Printing Office. Prices were set for binding, and outside printing contracts were restricted to the lowest bidder.

BIBLIOGRAPHY

Nichols, Roy F. *The Disruption of American Democracy.* 1948.
Summers, Mark. *The Plundering Generation.* 1988.
U.S. House of Representatives. *The Covode Investigation.* 36th Cong., 1st sess., 1860. H. Rept. 648.

MARK WAHLGREN SUMMERS

SAMUEL S. (SUNSET) COX.   LIBRARY OF CONGRESS

COX, SAMUEL S. (SUNSET) (1824–1889), Democratic representative from Ohio and New York, advocate of peaceful adjustment of nineteenth-century sectional interests. After a brief career in journalism as editor and chief owner of the Columbus (Ohio) *Statesman* (which published the glowing description of a sunset that won him his nickname), Cox entered politics. He served in the House from 1857 to 1865 and as a pro-Union Democrat supported measures designed to ease sectional conflict. He voted consistently for money and men to sustain the Union cause but at the same time backed efforts to restore peace. As a member of the Committee on Foreign Affairs, he aided in settling the *Trent* affair and helped to bring about the Hampton Roads Conference.

Defeated for reelection in 1864, Cox moved to New York, where he practiced law. He returned to Congress in 1869 and served almost continuously until his death. He was Speaker pro tempore in 1876. In the postwar era Cox labored for amnesty for those who had led the South against the Union. He advocated reform of the tariff and the civil service. As chairman of various House committees, he was primarily responsible for legislation establishing the Life Saving Service, broadening the scope of the census enumeration of 1890, and securing increased pay and vacation privileges for letter carriers. Cox was the author of several books, including *Union-Disunion-Reunion: Three Decades of Federal Legislation* (1885), *Why We Laugh* (1876), and *Eight Years in Congress* (1865).

BIBLIOGRAPHY

Lindsey, David. *"Sunset" Cox: Irrepressible Democrat.* 1959.

MONROE LEE BILLINGTON

COXEY'S ARMY. The first national protest action against unemployment was popularly known as Coxey's Army after its leader, Jacob Sechler Coxey, a wealthy quarry owner from Massillon, Ohio. Coxey proposed to march a large contingent of the nation's jobless to Capitol Hill in the spring of 1894 to demand that Congress fund public-works jobs during a time of severe economic depression. The often bizarre protest, officially labeled the "Commonweal of Christ," attracted unprecedented press coverage across the United States, which inspired numerous imitators. Many of them, mostly on the West Coast, raised "armies" of their own to rendezvous with Coxey on Capitol Hill.

Coxey led from two to three hundred marchers on a four-hundred-mile, month-long odyssey across the eastern United States. Hundreds more joined them on 1 May 1894, when they marched down Pennsylvania Avenue to present Congress with their "petition in boots." Coxey planned to give a brief speech summarizing their grievances, but police arrested him before he could address the several thousand onlookers gathered at the Capitol's east entrance. Officers charged him with violating laws that prohibited walking on the grass or displaying banners on the grounds, although Coxey's only "banner" was the small American flag affixed to his lapel. Nonetheless, a judge sentenced Coxey and his lieutenant, Carl Browne, to twenty days in jail.

Coxey's idea of putting the nation's unemployed to work building roads had been introduced in Congress in 1892 but had attracted little support. Browne, a self-described professional agitator from California, in early 1894 originated the idea of a march on Washington to publicize Coxey's proposal and to show Congress the need to approve it.

On 1 May 1944, the fiftieth anniversary of the great march and in the ninetieth year of his long life, Coxey again mounted the Capitol steps and, with the permission of House Speaker Sam Rayburn and Vice President Henry A. Wallace, completed his original speech.

BIBLIOGRAPHY

McMurry, Donald L. *Coxey's Army: A Study of the Industrial Army Movement of 1894.* 1929. Repr. 1968.
Schwantes, Carlos A. *Coxey's Army: An American Odyssey.* 1985.

CARLOS A. SCHWANTES

CRÉDIT MOBILIER. The Crédit Mobilier was a Pennsylvania-chartered construction company created to build the Union Pacific Railroad on the proceeds of bonds otherwise unsellable. In effect, the railroad directors hired themselves as contractors at exorbitant prices. Profits for shareholders were immense.

The fact that the government underwrote the project could have led to an embarrassing investigation. Late in 1867, therefore, a leading participant, Republican representative Oakes Ames of Massachusetts, decided to win friends on Capitol Hill by selling them shares on terms so generous that they verged on bribery. Beneficiaries included Representatives Henry L. Dawes of Massachusetts, John A. Bingham and James A. Garfield of Ohio, William D. "Pig Iron" Kelley of Pennsylvania, and Speaker Schuyler Colfax; together they constituted the Republican House leadership. At the same time, in an apparent shakedown, House Democratic floor-leader and Union Pacific government director James Brooks got a large block of shares. Most participants returned their stock within months of making the original arrangement and forswore the rich return possible over the long run; Garfield's profit, for example, amounted to $329.

Not until a late 1872 exposé in the New York *Sun* did the transactions become public. A House investigation led by Luke P. Poland (R-Vt.) cleared everyone but Brooks and Ames. For all the public allegations of whitewash, this may have been as far as justice could safely go; except for Ames's own letters, which proved no one's motive but his own, the evidence narrowed down to his word against his colleagues', and everyone dissembled or misremembered. The House censured Brooks and Ames (who died soon after, unrepentant); Garfield, Dawes, and Kelley would serve long, useful careers in spite of their involvement in the scandal.

BIBLIOGRAPHY

Ames, Charles E. *Pioneering the Union Pacific: A Reappraisal of the Builders of the Railroad.* 1969.
Crawford, J. B. *The Crédit Mobilier of America.* 1880.
Noonan, John. *Bribes.* 1986.

MARK WAHLGREN SUMMERS

CRIME AND JUSTICE. Issues of crime and justice attracted relatively little attention in the first Congresses. The new Constitution reinforced the tradition of law enforcement as preeminently a state and local problem. The first ten amendments (the Bill of Rights) placed still further restrictions on Congress, and the early courts ruled that there would be no common law crimes against the central government. Given the vast size of the new nation, an extensive federal criminal justice system would have strained the financial resources of the central government and violated the people's commitment to low taxes, localism, and individual freedom. A rural, decentralized people, just emerging from a revolution against abusive foreign authority, understandably opted to keep police powers as far from the federal government as possible.

Under the Constitution, however, Congress did have certain responsibilities in the criminal justice field. The new government had to define and fix penalties in cases involving counterfeiting, piracy, felonies on the high seas, and treason. The central government had exclusive jurisdiction over criminal justice in federal forts, magazines, and arsenals as well as in the District of Columbia and federal territories. And the Constitution's necessary-and-proper clause certainly suggested that Congress might act to fix criminal penalties for those interfering with certain delegated or implied powers the new government possessed, such as the operation of a postal system and post roads, the collection of federal taxes, and the protection of the currency and federally chartered banks.

The Nineteenth Century. Although Congress began to act in these areas with passage of the first Criminal Code in 1789, in only three areas might its actions reasonably have touched the ordinary citizen during the nineteenth century. First, for the federal territories in the West, Congress created the post of U.S. marshal. Serving the federal courts in civil matters and enforcing the criminal law, marshals acted in cases involving mail theft, murder, and crimes against railroad property. Second, during the Civil War, Congress created the Secret Service within the Treasury Department to protect the newly issued paper currency from counterfeiters. (Previously, the U.S. Mint had produced only coin.) During the late nineteenth century, the Secret Service gradually came to provide investigative and policing functions for other executive departments that requested its services, and in 1901, after the assassination of President William McKinley, Congress assigned it the duty of protecting the president. Legislators, however, remained fearful of both the costs and possible abuses of any federal police force. In 1908, after several powerful politicians charged President Theodore Roosevelt with using the Secret Service to embarrass his political enemies, Congress restricted the Secret Service to its anticounterfeiting and presidential protection duties.

The third area, the federal government's obliga-tion to protect the postal system, was the one most likely to bring it into contact with the ordinary citizen. In 1789, Congress declared it a criminal offense to interfere with the mails, and in 1836 it created a small force of special postal investigators to deal with mail robbery, lottery fraud, and other abuses. Because most Post Office officials were patronage appointees with congressional ties, the new corps of postal inspectors learned to be extremely circumspect in its work.

Responding to public pressures after the Civil War, however, Congress began to move beyond its obligations to protect the mails. Increasingly, it used its postal authority to assist in the emerging purity crusades of the time. In 1868, it banned from the mails any materials promoting lotteries. More important still, Congress in 1873 passed the so-called Comstock law, which drastically expanded the definition of obscenity and banned "obscene" literature and objects from the mails. Led by moral purist Anthony Comstock, who served as a New York postal inspector without pay, government officials seized obscene letters, pornography, abortion literature, and birth-control information and contraceptive devices. Since, with a few notable exceptions, local juries refused to convict those accused of violating the Comstock law, the precise success of the statute is difficult to gauge.

Industrialization and technological change were rapidly transforming the nation by the end of the century. Unprecedented economic growth produced powerful monopolies, massive immigration, labor-management strife, urban congestion, and political and consumer insurgency. Drawing on its constitutional powers over interstate commerce, Congress established machinery to regulate the railroads in 1887 and three years later struck out at monopolies in the Sherman Antitrust Act.

The Early Twentieth Century. Not surprisingly, Congress also began to use its interstate commerce powers in the criminal field. Going beyond its previous ban of lottery materials in the mails, legislators in 1895 prohibited the transportation of lottery tickets in interstate commerce. When the Supreme Court upheld this bold use of the commerce powers in *Champion v. Ames* (1903), Congress rapidly invoked the same authority to forbid the movement across state lines of obscene literature, contraceptives, impure or misbranded food and drugs, and uninspected meats. Responding to growing fears of prostitution rings, the legislators in 1910 passed the Mann Act, forbidding the transportation of women across state lines for immoral purposes. Three years later, the legislators overrode President

William H. Taft's veto of the Webb-Kenyon Act, which prohibited the use of interstate commerce for the movement of liquor into dry states.

An emboldened Congress also sought to employ its taxing powers against dangerous products and criminal activities. It taxed poisonous phosphorous matches out of the marketplace. Following considerable agitation by medical professionals and drug companies, Congress in 1914 enacted the landmark Harrison Act, which required the registration of professionals dealing in narcotic drugs, payment by them of special registration taxes, and their maintenance of detailed records of prescriptions and sales. Enforcement of this legislation by an agency in the Treasury Department increasingly criminalized drug trafficking and the use of narcotics, a development that, in turn, prompted still further federal legislation.

Enforcement of federal criminal law in the early twentieth century remained a problem for Congress, concerned as it was by both costs and possible abuse of power. Still conscious of Theodore Roosevelt's expansive use of the Secret Service, lawmakers in 1908 rejected his proposed creation of a Bureau of Investigation within the Department of Justice. When the defiant chief executive then created the bureau by executive order, Congress waited until Roosevelt was safely out of office before entrusting the new agency with additional responsibilities. In 1910, it gave the bureau the obligation of enforcing the Mann Act. During World War I and the subsequent red scare, the bureau also assumed important responsibilities in the internal security area. Overgrown and riddled with political infighting, the agency was reorganized in the 1920s as the Federal Bureau of Investigation (FBI) by Director J. Edgar Hoover, a staunch advocate of police professionalism.

Prohibition, the FBI, and the New Deal. Fortunately for the FBI, Congress did not assign it responsibility for enforcing the prohibition laws. The Eighteenth Amendment, which in 1920 made prohibition the law of the land, was to be enforced concurrently by U.S. Treasury agents and state and local officials. In the Volstead Act of 1919, the amendment's enabling legislation, Congress did not provide a sufficient number of reliable federal agents, nor did it pay them adequately for their services. As public contempt for prohibition mounted in the late 1920s, local officials increasingly abdicated their enforcement responsibilities. By the time the amendment was repealed in 1933, more than a quarter of federal prohibition agents had

been dismissed on a variety of charges, and the status of law enforcement generally had descended to an all-time low.

Spared the grief of prohibition, the FBI would in the 1930s become the chosen instrument for a dramatic "war on crime" by Congress and the White House. During the Great Depression, a series of highly publicized kidnappings and midwestern bank robberies transformed such felons as John Dillinger, Bonnie Parker and Clyde Barrow, and Charles Arthur "Pretty Boy" Floyd into minor folk heroes. Their frequent use of motor vehicles to flee across state boundaries precipitated a congressional crackdown. Drawing on a 1919 law forbidding the transportation of stolen motor vehicles across state lines, Congress again projected its powers over interstate commerce into the criminal justice field. After the heartrending kidnapping and slaying of aviator Charles Lindbergh's infant son, lawmakers in 1932 enacted a statute making the movement of kidnapped persons across state lines a federal felony. Congress placed enforcement in the ready hands of Hoover's FBI.

An even more ambitious spate of legislation followed during the New Deal's "war on crime." Attorney General Homer S. Cummings and Rep. Hatton W. Sumners (D-Tex.), chairman of the House Judiciary Committee, pushed some ten pieces of anticrime legislation through Congress. Most were based on Congress's interstate commerce, taxing, and postal powers, and a disproportionate share of enforcement responsibilities fell to the FBI. Lawmakers armed FBI agents and authorized them to move more aggressively against kidnappers, bank robbers, and those fleeing prosecution or transporting stolen property across state lines. Congress provided for the registration of machine guns, sawed-off shotguns, and rifles; attempted to upgrade federal criminal justice procedures; and granted prior approval for certain state law enforcement compacts. While the "war on crime" involved only a few new areas of federal activity, the highly publicized FBI campaigns against kidnappers and bank robbers gave the appearance of great vigor and success.

The Late Twentieth Century. In the last half of the twentieth century, a series of developments prompted a quantum increase in federal involvement in crime and justice issues. These included the growing concern over organized crime and racketeering, the intense public anxiety over drug abuse and personal safety, and the emerging civil liberties and civil rights movements. Caught among the conflicting pressures activated by these issues, Congress sought to negotiate acceptable public policies.

Organized crime. While the forerunners of modern racketeering had existed in pre–World War I America, Congress had considered such activities a problem for the states and localities. If the experience with prohibition brought notoriety and organizational skills to the underworld, it did not at first fundamentally alter the federal government's ideas about organized crime. The celebrated Chicago gangster Al Capone ultimately fell victim to federal tax officials, not to any concerted campaign against racketeering. Hoover's FBI seemed to prefer the statistical successes it could achieve in the pursuit of bank robbers and car thieves and sought to

avoid the temptations and corruption that might accompany a campaign against organized vice. Federal antiracketeering statutes enacted in 1934 and 1946 proved of little long-term significance. The FBI director, as well as prominent members of Congress, warned that any extensive campaign against organized crime would necessitate a costly and dangerous national police force and might prompt states and localities to abdicate their responsibilities in that area.

Three highly publicized Senate investigations helped alter these perspectives. In 1950 and 1951, Sen. Estes Kefauver (D-Tenn.) chaired a special committee (Senate Special Committee to Investigate Organized Crime in Interstate Commerce) that explored the problem of organized crime in inter-

KEFAUVER CRIME COMMITTEE. *Left to right,* Senators Charles W. Tobey (R-N.H.), Lester C. Hunt (D-Wyo.), committee chairman Estes Kefauver (D-Tenn.), Alexander Wiley (R-Wis.), and Herbert R. O'Conor (D-Md.) gathered for the first meeting of the committee, officially named the Senate Special Committee to Investigate Organized Crime in Interstate Commerce, 11 May 1950.   OFFICE OF THE HISTORIAN OF THE U.S. SENATE

state commerce. The Kefauver committee concluded that illegal gambling had a powerful and corrupting influence on local law enforcement and that the underworld was largely controlled by a sinister conspiracy called the Mafia. Between 1957 and 1960, Sen. John L. McClellan (D-Ark.) held hearings for a select committee looking into labor-management racketeering (Senate Select Committee on Improper Activities in the Labor or Management Field). McClellan's group established the existence of close ties between underworld figures and leaders of major unions, especially the Teamsters. Finally, in 1963, McClellan's Permanent Subcommittee on Investigations heard Joseph Valachi, an underling in a New York crime "family," provide sensational details about "Cosa Nostra," an extensive secret criminal organization run by an all-powerful "Commission."

While a few commentators and academics dismissed the Mafia–Cosa Nostra publicity as exaggeration, Congress and the public at large seemed to accept it. In the early 1960s, Attorney General Robert F. Kennedy, who had been chief counsel for the McClellan labor racketeering hearings, won congressional enactment of four anticrime statutes that were directed for the most part at gambling activities and based on Congress's interstate commerce powers. Also, Kennedy tried on his own to mobilize executive department agencies into a concerted attack on racketeering.

Street crime. By the mid 1960s concern over racketeering began to share equal billing with street violence. Most statistics pointed to a bewildering increase in the incidence of crime, a development that some linked to protests against the Vietnam War and a growing permissiveness in American society. With crime and street violence becoming a political issue, President Lyndon B. Johnson took two actions in 1965. First, he appointed the blue-ribbon Commission on Law Enforcement and Administration of Justice to conduct the first comprehensive review of American criminal justice in more than three decades. Second, he won congressional approval of the Law Enforcement Assistance Act, designed to provide federal funds to state and local governments for modernizing their law enforcement and corrections agencies. Johnson thought of his "war on crime" as part of his Great Society program. Crime was as multifaceted as its causes, he reasoned, but street violence could generally be traced to conditions of poverty in the nation's big cities.

In 1967, the president's crime commission reported its findings and recommendations, and Johnson used them as a basis for his proposed Omnibus Safe Streets and Crime Control Act. Conservative lawmakers, however, reworked Johnson's bill so thoroughly before passing it in 1968 that some liberals actually recommended a veto to the disappointed president. Contrary to Johnson's wishes, funds channeled through the Law Enforcement Assistance Administration (LEAA) would go to the states rather than directly to local communities; three Supreme Court decisions protecting suspects in federal criminal cases were reversed; the Johnson proposals on gun control were weakened; and Senator McClellan succeeded in getting expanded authority for police wiretapping and bugging without court warrants. Whatever the merits of the Safe Streets Act of 1968, the movement of LEAA moneys to state and local governments, as well as the act's wiretapping and criminal justice features, brought Congress, through its oversight functions, much closer than ever before to the day-to-day problems of law enforcement.

Passage of the 1968 legislation did not keep crime and justice from becoming a major political issue. Indeed, Republican presidential candidate Richard M. Nixon made "law and order" a central part of

JOSEPH VALACHI. Cosa Nostra member, testifying before the Senate Permanent Subcommittee on Investigations, 27 September 1963.   LIBRARY OF CONGRESS

Landmark Legislation on Crime and Justice

TITLE	YEAR ENACTED	REFERENCE NUMBER	DESCRIPTION
Act of 2 March 1895	1895	28 Stat. 963	Invoked congressional powers over interstate commerce in the criminal justice field, prohibiting the transportation of lottery materials across state lines.
White Slave-Trade Act (Mann Act)	1910	36 Stat. 825	Again drawing on Congress's interstate commerce powers, prohibited the transportation of women across state lines for purposes of prostitution.
Harrison Narcotics Act	1914	38 Stat. 785	First major use by Congress of its taxing power in the criminal justice field.
National Prohibition Act (Volstead Act)	1919	41 Stat. 305	Implemented the Eighteenth Amendment and concurrent federal and state jurisdiction over enforcement of prohibition.
Lindbergh Law	1932	47 Stat. 326	Drawing on Congress's interstate commerce powers, prohibited the movement of kidnapped persons across state lines. Typical of 1930s "war on crime" legislation.
Omnibus Crime Control and Safe Streets Act	1968	P.L. 90-351; 82 Stat. 197	Brought significant amounts of federal moneys to states and local governments for improvements in law enforcement.
Organized Crime Control Act	1970	P.L. 91-452; 84 Stat. 922	Title IX, the Racketeer Influenced and Corrupt Organizations (RICO) statute, set the stage for a concerted campaign against organized crime but also engulfed the criminal justice system in a host of complicated civil suits.

his campaign that year. His administration then sponsored model legislation for the District of Columbia that included highly controversial provisions dealing with pretrial detention and "no-knock" entry by police into the residences of criminal suspects. The Nixon administration also enthusiastically embraced a 1969 bill aimed at racketeering that was sponsored by McClellan and Sen. Samuel J. Ervin, Jr. (D-N.C.). This legislation, the Organized Crime Control Act, would be one of four approved by Congress and signed by the president in 1970.

The RICO statute and antidrug campaign. The complicated Organized Crime Control Act ultimately produced far-ranging and unexpected results. Because its sponsors were among the most conservative in the Congress and because it strengthened the police and prosecutors in their collection and use of evidence, civil libertarians feared that its real targets would be antiwar protestors rather than mobsters. For almost a decade, federal officials had little success in using the act against organized crime. By the early 1980s, however, prosecutors had begun to perfect their use of the act's "racketeer influenced and corrupt organization" (RICO)

title, which provided drastic criminal and civil penalties for those using racketeering money or methods in legitimate business. The RICO statute then became the basis for a series of dramatically successful prosecutions of organized crime "families" and of attempts to clean up corrupt labor unions.

Some in Congress found other uses of RICO troubling. Employing the act's civil as well as criminal provisions, prosecutors launched cases against stock brokers and others accused of white-collar offenses. Hoping to win treble damages and possibly label rivals as "racketeers," private businesses began to file RICO suits against competitors. Victims of sexual harassment initiated suits against their employers under RICO, as did abortion clinics against right-to-life demonstrators. Clearly sensing the abuses possible under the vaguely drafted RICO, Congress began a process of reevaluating the statute.

The growing problem of drug abuse proved even more controversial than RICO. Encouraged by the Nixon administration, Congress in 1970 passed the Comprehensive Drug Abuse Prevention and Control Act, which tightened penalties and set up procedures for the classification of psychoactive substances. This legislation proved ineffective, and the mounting drug problem became part of the bitter cultural wars of the 1980s. Congress seemingly returned to the issue each election year. In 1988, lawmakers passed the Anti–Drug Abuse Act, which created a cabinet-level "drug czar" to coordinate federal programs, increased penalties for users as well as drug dealers, and provided $2.8 billion in additional funds to combat illegal drugs. The Bush administration used this legislation as the basis for its controversial campaign to reduce the demand for illicit drugs and end the widespread smuggling of illegal substances into the country.

Civil liberties issues. Calls for harsher penalities to combat racketeering, drug abuse, and street violence did not alone account for the enlarged role of Congress in law enforcement and justice. Almost as important were demands for federal protection of civil liberties and civil rights. Certain provisions of legislation such as the Safe Streets Act and RICO seemed to impinge on traditional individual freedoms, and Congress seemed constantly to be seeking adjustments. By the late 1960s, the Supreme Court under Chief Justice Earl Warren had largely completed the process of "incorporating" the federal Bill of Rights into the Fourteenth Amendment's due process clause. As a consequence, much of the criminal justice dispensed in state and local courts was reviewable by the federal judiciary. The work load of the federal courts consequently swelled, raising for Congress the issues of increasing costs and the need for legislative fine tuning. Legislators, for example, debated both the costs and benefits of the "nationalized" corrections policy seemingly mandated by the judiciary. In the budget battles of the early 1980s, LEAA was phased out and federal funding for law enforcement became more problematic.

The involvement of lawmakers in the debates over RICO, drug abuse, and civil liberties reflected the much more extensive responsibilities Congress had assumed over crime and justice issues. By the 1990s, legislators also found themselves grappling with criminal activities spawned by the computer age. Notable among these problems were computer invasion and copyright infringement. Aware of the mushrooming problems, Congress in 1966 appointed a commission to make recommendations for a massive recodification of the federal criminal code. The commission reported back in the early 1970s with an omnibus proposal. The recodification scheme soon attracted the ire of civil libertarians, state and local law enforcement officials, and other interest groups, each maintaining that the proposed modifications posed grave dangers to existing traditions and liberties. Gridlocked over comprehensive recodification, Congress could only debate complicated criminal justice problems on a piecemeal basis.

[*For discussion of related public policy issues, see* Civil Liberties; Commerce Power; Communism and Anticommunism; Gun Control; Internal Security; Investigations; Judiciary and Congress; Military Justice, Uniform Code of; Narcotics and Other Dangerous Drugs; Presidential Assassinations and Protection; Prohibition; Regulation and Deregulation. *See also* Kefauver Crime Committee; Racketeer Influenced and Corrupt Organizations Act; White Slave-Trade Act.]

BIBLIOGRAPHY

Block, Alan A. "The Organized Crime Control Act, 1970: Historical Issues and Public Policy." *The Public Historian* 2 (1980): 39–59.

Goldberg-Ambrose, Carole E. "Criminal Law Code: Reform Must Be Piecemeal." *The Center Magazine* 41 (1981): 56–64.

Grisham, James Harvey. "Crime Control: A Study in American Federalism." Ph.D. diss., University of Texas at Austin, 1953.

Johnson, David R. *American Law Enforcement: A History.* 1981.

Moore, William Howard. *The Kefauver Committee and the Politics of Crime, 1950–1952.* 1974.

Sanders, Alain L. "Showdown at Gucci Gulch." *Time,* 21 August 1989.

WILLIAM HOWARD MOORE

CRISP, CHARLES F. (1845–1896), Democratic representative from Georgia, Speaker of the House (1891–1895). The child of English parents who settled in Georgia, Charles Frederick Crisp enlisted in the Confederate army in 1861 and eventually became a lieutenant in the 10th Virginia Infantry. He fought for three years, spent a year as a prisoner of war, and in June 1865 returned home to prepare for a career in law.

Crisp was admitted to the Georgia bar in 1866 and beginning in 1872 served as a state solicitor general and then as a superior court judge. In September 1882, Crisp resigned from the bench to run as a Democrat for the U.S. House of Representatives. He easily won election to the 48th Congress and held his congressional seat until his death in 1896.

CHARLES F. CRISP. Painting by Robert Hinckley.

LIBRARY OF CONGRESS

During his seven terms in Congress, Crisp participated in many of the most significant legislative battles of the time. His knowledge of parliamentary rules, his skill in disputation, and his commanding physical presence marked him as a leading Democrat. He played a major role in the passage of the Interstate Commerce Act of 1887. During the 51st Congress, Crisp waged a skillful battle against the force bill to protect blacks voting in federal elections, a measure much despised in the South. He worked for a low tariff and for an income tax and strongly supported the Sherman Silver Purchase Act of 1890.

In 1891, the popular and hardworking Crisp was selected Speaker of the House. He used the powers that he inherited from "Czar" Thomas B. Reed and added substantially to them, primarily by bringing the Committee on Rules into the Speaker's domain. This Committee on Rules, under Democratic direction, virtually dictated the legislative business of the House. His leadership during the 52d and 53d Congresses (1891–1895) proved stormy, for he frequently clashed with the Cleveland administration, particularly on the currency question. Though a conservative southern Democrat who opposed most Populist and Farmers' Alliance proposals, Crisp

nevertheless championed free silver, which strongly appealed to his agrarian constituency.

In 1896 Crisp announced his candidacy for the Senate seat of the retiring John B. Gordon. During his campaign, he engaged in a famous series of debates with Hoke Smith. Crisp easily won the primary that fall because free-silver inflationists dominated Georgia, and he assuredly would have been confirmed by the legislature as Georgia's senator had his health not failed. On 23 October 1896, one week before the general assembly met, he died in Atlanta.

BIBLIOGRAPHY

Knight, Lucian Lamar. *Reminiscences of Famous Georgians.* 1908.

Martin, S. Walter. "Charles F. Crisp: Speaker of the House." *Georgia Review* 8 (1954): 167–177.

RALPH LOWELL ECKERT

CRITTENDEN, JOHN J. (1787–1863), representative and senator from Kentucky, prominent border-state leader. Born in Kentucky, Crittenden

JOHN J. CRITTENDEN.

HARPER'S PICTORIAL HISTORY OF THE GREAT REBELLION

A CURE FOR REPUBLICAN LOCK-JAW

CRITTENDEN COMPROMISE. Cartoon presenting the compromise as the means of overcoming the inflexibility of Republicans on the slavery issue. In the lithograph, a sick man in a dressing gown, holding a paper inscribed "Republican Platform No Compromise," resists swallowing an enormous pill labeled "Crittenden Compromise," which a man shoves down his throat with a "Petition of 63,000." Although it enjoyed considerable public and congressional support, the compromise measure failed to pass. Benjamin H. Day, Jr., 1861.   LIBRARY OF CONGRESS

graduated from Virginia's William and Mary College, was admitted to the Kentucky bar, and soon entered the state legislature. In 1817 he was chosen to fill an unexpired term in the U.S. Senate. Retiring in 1819, he became a highly successful defense attorney, held several state and federal offices, and in 1835 was again elected to the Senate as a Whig.

In Congress he supported a protective tariff and a national bank and opposed Andrew Jackson's and Martin Van Buren's financial policies. He was reelected to the Senate in 1840 but resigned to become attorney general in William Henry Harrison's

cabinet. Leaving this post after John Tyler, Harrison's successor, scuttled the Whigs' legislative program, Crittenden was once again elected to the Senate in 1842. He opposed the annexation of Texas, advocated a peaceful settlement of the Oregon controversy, and criticized James K. Polk for the Mexican War. Like other Whigs, Crittenden voted for men and supplies to conduct the war, but he urged peace negotiations to end the conflict quickly.

In 1848 he was elected governor of Kentucky. He served as attorney general under Millard Fillmore, and in 1854 returned to the Senate, where he was a leading spokesman for border-state moderates. In 1854, he denounced the reopening of the slavery controversy by the Kansas-Nebraska Act, and called subsequently for restoration of the Missouri Compromise; in 1858 he voted against the proslavery Lecompton constitution, which he considered a fraud, and consistently worked to end the slavery controversy. Following the collapse of the Whigs, he joined the American party and in 1860 supported the Constitutional Union movement.

Crittenden offered the most important compromise proposal in Congress during the secession crisis of 1860 and 1861. His plan, which was a complicated set of laws, resolutions, and constitutional amendments, attracted the greatest support of any compromise package presented in Congress. Its most important aspects were a provision applying the Missouri Compromise line of 36° 30′ to all the territories and an unamendable amendment forever protecting slavery in states where it already existed. Despite his strenuous efforts, Congress rejected his plan as well as his novel idea to hold a national plebiscite on it.

He stood by the Union when the Civil War began in 1861 and, despite his earlier-announced intention to retire, bowed to popular pressure to run for the U.S. House of Representatives and was triumphantly elected. In the special session that summer he introduced a resolution declaring that the war was being fought solely to save the Union and not to end slavery, and it passed overwhelmingly. When he reintroduced it six months later, however, it was defeated.

Crittenden's Unionism never faltered, but he was increasingly at odds with the Lincoln administration and the prevailing sentiment in Congress. He opposed the creation of West Virginia, the confiscation acts against slavery, the Emancipation Proclamation, and the recruitment of black troops. He was also critical of the Union army's interference with slavery and civil liberties in Kentucky. A sectional moderate and devoted supporter of the Union, he found himself swept aside by the surging emotions unleashed by the war. He died in 1863 while preparing to run for reelection.

BIBLIOGRAPHY

Coleman, Ann M. B. *The Life of John J. Crittenden.* 2 vols. 1871.
Kirwan, Albert D. *John J. Crittenden: The Struggle for the Union.* 1962.

WILLIAM E. GIENAPP

CROCKETT, DAVID (1786–1836), representative from Tennessee, legendary frontiersman and humorist. Separating Davy Crockett the myth from Crockett the man can be difficult. His views, his appearance, and even the circumstances of his death have all been the subjects of debate. What is known is that he was independent, impulsive, and an exceptional humorist and public speaker.

Crockett was an Indian fighter in the Tennessee militia in 1813 and 1814. By 1816 he was involved in politics, first running for offices in the militia, then for justice of the peace, town commissioner, and state legislator. Between 1823 and 1827 he became a conspicuous opponent of Andrew Jackson, even though his social and political style were what is usually described as Jacksonian.

Crockett entered Congress in 1827. He dutifully supported land reform that favored West Tennessee settlers; hostile to a professional military, he opposed funding the West Point academy. But he continued to oppose his fellow Tennesseean Jackson, even fighting the new president's bill to remove Indians to the west. Defeated in 1831 partly because of his opposition to Jackson, Crockett was again elected to Congress in 1833.

DAVID CROCKETT.   *PERLEY'S REMINISCENCES*, VOL. 1

His opposition to Jackson and his flamboyant, story-telling campaign style attracted attention from eastern Whigs, and Crockett was discussed as a possible presidential candidate. But he was defeated for Congress in 1835.

After that, Crockett moved to Texas, where he quickly became a public figure. Joining the Alamo defenders, he survived the battle but was executed on orders of the victorious Mexican general Antonio López de Santa Anna.

BIBLIOGRAPHY

Hauck, Richard Boyd. *Crockett: A Bio-Bibliography.* 1982.
Shackford, James A. *David Crockett: The Man and the Legend.* 1956.

ANTHONY CHAMPAGNE

C-SPAN. *See page 239.*

CUISINE OF CONGRESS. Congress's fascination with food is as old as the Republic. In his classic work, *The Senate of the United States* (1938), George H. Haynes found the assessment of a Boston observer particularly interesting: "The vagaries in opinion and in voting of some of our statesmen could be better explained by complications of digestion than by the psychology of today, and if the records of their convivial meetings were at hand, the effect might be traced in the measures for which the good livers were responsible."

From Congress's earliest sessions, representatives and senators considered the dinner table a wel-

DOWNING'S RESTAURANT. Described as "one of the best restaurants in the Union," Downing's occupied two rooms on the ground floor of the House of Representatives. Wood engraving in J. B. Ellis, *The Sights and Secrets of the National Capital*, 1869.

LIBRARY OF CONGRESS

SENATE DINING ROOM. *Left to right,* Senators John A. Danaher (R-Conn.), Harold H. Burton (R-Ohio), and C. Wayland Brooks (R-Ill.), January 1941. LIBRARY OF CONGRESS.

come setting for discussing affairs of state. Sen. William Maclay's *Diary* for 1790 recorded the origin of the Pennsylvania Mess at which his state's congressional delegation dined together once a week. These Monday afternoon gatherings, which began with wine and oysters, often lasted far into the evening. Sometimes members of the cabinet were invited to join the assembled legislators.

Congress had barely arrived at the unfinished Capitol building in Washington before its members' eating habits were being called into question. During the 1805 impeachment trial of Supreme Court Justice Samuel Chase, Vice President Aaron Burr admonished senators for eating apples and cake while sitting in judgment in the Senate chamber.

When the central section of the Capitol was completed, areas were set aside for serving food and drink. In *Notations of the Americans* (1828), James Fenimore Cooper wrote of a visit to the building in

1826, when, entering through a subbasement door, he passed "among a multitude of eating rooms." In a letter to his family, a young Marine officer from Ohio described these chambers as "Refectories or Eating houses for the members" and continued: "Towards the close of the session the houses sit from 10 A.M. till 2 A.M. of the following day sometime, and then it is that they make use particularly of these houses—they call for Mutton Soup, or turtle soup, or Oyster Soup, or beef stake or Coffee or tea or rum, just as they choose, and get whatever they call for." Not only did the refectories serve the members of Congress and the Supreme Court, but the public was also welcome.

Of all the Capitol dining spots in the mid-nineteenth century, none was more popular with the members than the Hole-in-the-Wall. A tiny, circular room ten feet in diameter, it was adjacent to the Senate post office. Because the public was not allowed within its confines, the Hole-in-the-Wall provided a haven for uninhibited discussion. Senate doorkeeper and assistant sergeant at arms Isaac Basset described the setting in an unpublished memoir:

> It was no uncommon thing to see congregated there [Henry] Clay, [Daniel] Webster [John C.] Calhoun, [Thomas Hart] Benton, [Lewis] Cass, [William Ballard?] Preston, [Samuel S.] Phelps, [Stephen A.] Douglas, [William?] Wright, [John] Slidell, [James M.] Mason and others. What momentous questions have been discussed and what results have come to this country from plans laid in that small room . . . . [T]he lunch consisted principally of ham and bread and other simple eatables, but the supply of liquors was quite liberal.

From the beginning, liquor was available in the Capitol. Fruit vendors sold it in the public corridors; dining rooms and food bars on every floor plied their patrons with alcohol; and senior members were known to stash a good supply in committee rooms. Periodically, both houses would place restrictions on the sale of "intoxicating liquors," but such prohibitions were usually ignored. Offending beverages were simply served in porcelain cups and referred to as "cold tea." Often, such drinks appeared in this form in the chambers of the House and Senate.

For nearly two centuries, the proceedings of Congress have been filled with statements by its members singing the praises of regional dishes. Daniel Webster championed fish chowder before the Senate, Speaker Joseph G. Cannon made certain that bean soup would always be available in the dining rooms of the House of Representatives, and Huey P. Long's filibusters resounded with tributes to pot-likker and corn pone. In recent times, favorite recipes have been published in booklet form and handed out on the campaign trail. Detailed instructions for curing a ham, distributed for years by Virginia senator Harry Flood Byrd, Sr., began with the admonition, "Kill your hogs when the wind is from the northwest."

Chili con carne wars have occasionally erupted in Congress, causing debates to rage for weeks on the merits of a particular region's version of this often highly seasoned dish. These debates have led to chili cook-offs at which members prepare their special recipes and the Washington press corps acts as judge and jury. Members have also promoted various foods from their home states by offering free samples to colleagues.

The bills of fare of the Senate and House dining rooms have always featured some members' favorite dishes. Often southern dishes, these preferences are served year after year before losing their distinction and being stricken from the menu. From collard greens to black-eyed peas, vegetables cooked with a southern flair have long been a tradition in the House. But of all the favorites, no dish has enjoyed the enduring popularity of bean soup. Its origin has been the subject of disagreement between the Senate and the House for decades, each side claiming to have served the soup first. The House credits Speaker Cannon as having insisted in 1904 that bean soup remain forever on the dining room's menu, while the Senate claims that Sen. Knute Nelson of Minnesota made the dish a permanent part of the Capitol's fare in 1903.

[*See also* Alcoholic Beverages in Congress.]

BIBLIOGRAPHY

Carpenter, Frank G. *Carp's Washington.* 1960.
Haynes, George H. *The Senate of the United States: Its History and Practice.* 1938.
Hazelton, George C., Jr. *The National Capitol: Its Architecture, Art and History.* 1902.

JAMES ROE KETCHUM

CULLOM, SHELBY M. (1829–1914), Republican representative and senator from Illinois, sponsor of the Interstate Commerce Act of 1887. Shelby Moore Cullom was elected to the U.S. House of Representatives as a Republican in 1864 and served three terms. Failing to win renomination in 1870, he briefly engaged in banking, returned to the state legislature, and won the governorship in 1876. Reelected governor in 1880, he left the state to accept a seat in the U.S. Senate, a post he would occupy for thirty years.

Cullom's major legislative achievement was the enactment of the Interstate Commerce Act of 1887. He chaired the Committee on Interstate Commerce for many years, surrendering his chairmanship in 1901 to assume the chair of the Committee on Foreign Relations, a post he held until 1913.

Senator Cullom was a minor presidential hopeful in 1888, 1892, and 1896. His moderation and balance on the major questions debated during his career, including reconstruction and the tariff, led many to refer to him as a "man on the fence."

Cullom saw the interests of his state and region as primarily agricultural; much of his political success resulted from his ability to rationalize the position of the Midwest in the Republican fold. Ultimately, his basically conservative nature clashed with the Progressive movement, which he detested, and he suffered defeat in 1912.

BIBLIOGRAPHY

Cullom, Shelby M. *Fifty Years of Public Service.* 1911.
Neilson, James Warren. *Shelby M. Cullom: Prairie State Republican.* 1962.

JAMES WARREN NEILSON

CUMMINS, ALBERT B. (1850–1926), governor of Iowa and U.S. senator, a leader of the insurgent (or reform) wing of the Republican party during the Progressive era. A lawyer ambitious for public office, Albert Baird Cummins unsuccessfully sought a U.S. Senate seat in 1894 and 1900. In 1901 he won the Republican gubernatorial nomination and during his successful race became identified with the "Iowa Idea" of tariff revision to reduce the

ALBERT B. CUMMINS.   LIBRARY OF CONGRESS

duties on trust-made articles. He was reelected in 1903 and 1906. During his governorship he pushed through legislation for stricter railroad and insurance company regulation, pure food and child labor laws, prison reform, and the direct primary for party nominations.

In June 1908, Cummins was defeated in the preferential primary for the Republican nomination to the U.S. Senate by the incumbent, his longtime factional rival William B. Allison, who died that August. A special session of the state legislature amended the primary law to require a second primary in the case of the death, resignation, or removal of a regular primary nominee. After Cummins won that contest, the legislature formally elected him to complete the rest of Allison's term and to serve the full term to follow.

Cummins joined senatorial insurgents in 1909. These were mostly fellow middle-westerners in revolt against the Payne-Aldrich tariff bill. He supported Theodore Roosevelt's bid for the Republican presidential nomination in 1912. After Roosevelt bolted to head the Progressive party, Cummins announced he would vote for Roosevelt but refused to join the new party.

Cummins was reelected to the Senate in 1914, but his support for further reform—like that of most Republican progressives—waned during the presidency of Woodrow Wilson. When the Republicans regained control of the upper chamber as a result of 1918 elections, he became chairman of the Senate Committee on Interstate Commerce and thereby one of the chief architects of the Transportation (or Esch-Cummins) Act of 1920, which terminated wartime federal government control of the railroads. Like Wilson, Cummins stood firm against calls for government ownership of the railroads. His efforts to incorporate into the final legislation proposals for prohibiting railroad strikes and for consolidation of existing railway lines were unsuccessful. Nonetheless, Cummins was regarded as being largely responsible for the generous financial terms governing the railroads' return to private hands.

By a narrow margin Cummins defeated Smith W. Brookhart for the Republican Senate nomination in 1920 and went on to win reelection. He served as president pro tempore of the Senate from 1919 to 1925, but growing farmer discontent over low prices and Cummins's increasingly conservative stance resulted in his defeat by Brookhart in the 1926 primary. He died of a heart attack on 30 July 1926.

BIBLIOGRAPHY

Harrington, Elbert W. "A Survey of the Political Ideas of Albert Baird Cummins." *Iowa Journal of History and Politics* 39 (1941): 339–386.

Sage, Leland L. *A History of Iowa.* 1974.

Sayre, Ralph M. "Albert Baird Cummins and the Progressive Movement in Iowa." Ph.D. diss., Columbia University, 1958.

JOHN BRAEMAN

CURRENCY AND FINANCE. Colonial money consisted primarily of Spanish coins and some British gold coins, which the colonies supplemented after 1690 with their own paper money. The colonial legislatures issued their own bills of credit to meet government expenditures, and by 1775 almost every colony had engaged in note issue of some sort. Colonial governments maintained the value of the notes by receiving them for taxes. Conversely, during the War of Independence, the Continental Congress issued its own paper money— "Continentals"—but failed to tax vigorously enough to keep the notes from depreciating. In 1781, the superintendent of finance, Robert Morris, issued his own notes, popularly known as "Morris notes," secured by his reputation, which kept George Washington's troops supplied. Morris and others recognized the need for a privately owned bank to provide a sound currency. Beginning in 1782, a number of private banks, led by the Bank of North America, supplied circulating paper to the colonies.

After independence the new federal government, at the initiation of Secretary of the Treasury Alexander Hamilton, determined that it had to assume all of the debts incurred during the Revolutionary War, including those of the states. In his *Report on Public Credit* (1790), Hamilton argued that by assuming the states' debts the federal government would reduce the fiscal cost of borrowing and improve the government's creditworthiness. He also envisioned creating a market for government bonds, which would be given a stable and credible value when the government assumed the states' debts. Hamilton recognized the dangers of deficit spending by Congress, however; to control that urge, he planned for a sinking fund to retire the debt, and he stipulated that new debt would have to be subordinated to the old. To raise revenue, he proposed a series of import tariffs, as well as an excise tax on whiskey (an extraneous measure designed to bring farmers under the control of the government). Hamilton's concern that Congress would spend beyond its means appeared again in his second report on public credit in 1795, in which he recommended that no new debt be incurred without simultaneous provisions for its retirement.

One key proposal, made by Hamilton at the end of 1790, was the *Report on a National Bank,* in which he advocated a national bank to act as the agent of the Treasury in the marketplace. Several members of Congress objected, stating that nowhere in the Constitution did the government have the express authority to charter a bank. But Hamilton and his supporters argued from the "necessary and proper" clause that the government had "implied powers." Congress finally chartered the Bank of the United States (BUS) in 1791 with a twenty-year charter and a capital of $10 million, of which four-fifths would be private.

Another major element in Hamilton's plans was the establishment of an American currency system. In the *Report on the Establishment of a Mint,* Hamilton followed Thomas Jefferson's proposals for a decimal currency, placed at par with the Spanish milled dollar, the most widely used specie at the time. Hamilton also proposed a bimetallic standard to provide a more flexible means to increase the money supply. He set a 15:1 silver-to-gold ratio, which undervalued gold and attracted little of the precious metal to the government's vaults.

Albert Gallatin, who followed Hamilton as Treasury secretary, found the sinking fund—which he disliked—still in place. However, the public debt had grown to more than $82 million, and he designed a schedule to pay it. He also fought to preserve the whiskey tax, although he had previously denounced it. By 1806, thanks largely to his efforts, the Treasury had a $4 million surplus. He had, however, a problem Hamilton had not faced, namely a quasi-war with England that had resulted in the Embargo Act of 1807, which severely damaged the U.S. economy. When war broke out in 1812, the nation faced a $20 million deficit, only partially covered by private lenders. Making matters worse, Congress the previous year had refused to recharter the BUS, a potential source of funds.

The financial dislocations caused by the war persuaded Congress to charter a second Bank of the United States in 1816 with a capital stock of $35 million and an immediate bonus to the government of $1.5 million as a reward for approving the charter. While the new bank contributed to the circulating medium of the country, the vast majority of the currency still came from private notes issued through state-chartered commercial banks. Banks thus backed their note issues with reserves of specie, typically between 10 and 20 percent. Other organizations also received note issue privileges, including railroads and some cities. Occasionally, companies, such as steamship lines, issued small change notes (paper money that was valued at under a dollar).

As the economy grew, the role of the BUS in financial affairs also increased. The BUS had survived the panic of 1819, and some historians suggest that it effected a credit contraction that exacerbated the panic. In 1823, Philadelphian Nicholas Biddle took over the presidency of the BUS and directed its activities admirably until 1832, when he attempted to get the bank rechartered four years ahead of schedule, hoping that in an election year President Andrew Jackson would not dare veto the recharter bill. But Biddle miscalculated, and Jackson vetoed the bill, touching off the famous "Bank War." Jackson had the deposits of the federal government removed from the bank after the recharter veto was sustained, and the second BUS was a mere shell for the last two years of its life.

Meanwhile, the Jacksonian Democrats, whose own views on the proper monetary system ranged from "hard money" (coin only) to a national bank of their own, started to retool the nation's currency. In the Coinage Act of 1834, Congress reduced the gold content of the dollar, thereby hoping to bring more gold into the nation. During the previous few years, in fact, a large inflow of specie had occurred, upon which the commercial banks expanded their note issues. Some Democrats saw that as inflation and wanted the banks' issues controlled, especially when the paper money was used to buy western lands. In response, Jackson in 1836 issued his "specie circular," which required that federal lands be paid for in gold or silver. Jackson further confused the financial picture by redistributing the $35 million surplus in the budget to the states; but the states that contributed to the surplus did not necessarily get back what they put in. Jackson's actions—killing the BUS, redistributing the surplus, putting the government's deposits in favored banks, and issuing the specie circular—all contributed to financial chaos. They did not, however, cause the inflation prior to 1837 nor the panic of 1837. Those developments can be attributed rather to international specie flows drying up and the British government raising interest rates, chilling investment in the United States. Whatever the cause as people

at the time perceived it, the panic resulted in the money stock falling by one-third and prices dropping by 42 percent.

The panic convinced many legislators that the banks had been at fault. Many states responded by prohibiting all banks. Other states took a different tack: since part of the problem was that the charters seemed to run counter to egalitarian access to the market, why not open banking to anyone who had the money and eliminate legislative charters? Indeed, the result was "free banking," the forerunner of general incorporation laws. Anyone who could put up the required capital in bonds deposited with the state could open a bank. Michigan passed the first free banking law in 1837.

Meanwhile, without a national bank to hold the U.S. government's deposits, a new institution was needed. In 1840 Congress established the Independent Treasury system (sometimes called the Sub-Treasury), which held the receipts of the federal government in vaults around the country; it could disburse money, but not issue notes. All collections and disbursements were in gold, silver, or drafts on other subtreasuries. In reality, it acted more as a storage house than a bank, and while it survived

SALMON P. CHASE (R-OHIO). Secretary of the Treasury under President Abraham Lincoln.

HARPER'S PICTORIAL HISTORY OF THE GREAT REBELLION

until 1921, the difficult business of raising revenue for large government projects shifted back to the private market, especially into the hands of securities specialists such as Jay Cooke.

With the onset of the Civil War, Treasury secretary Salmon P. Chase, confronted with the unprecedented financial demands of modern warfare, turned to the securities markets and to Cooke, who sold $400 million worth of bonds in less than two years. The government, under Chase's guidance, eventually borrowed more than $500 million, and negotiated three other specie loans of $50 million. Chase also pursued other avenues of fundraising. He suggested that Congress issue paper money that would not be immediately convertible into gold, and Congress responded on 25 February 1862 with the Legal Tender Act, issuing $100 million worth of interest-free notes called "greenbacks," United States notes that carried a red seal.

Eventually the amount of greenbacks issued came to $450 million. In 1863, Congress passed the National Bank Act, which gave the federal government the authority to charter national banks that would hold government securities as collateral for their notes and hold an amount of bonds equal to one-third of their capital. National bank notes, while uniform in appearance, bore the name of the national bank that issued them—a lucrative form of advertisement.

Congress also established a $300 million ceiling on the total number of notes that the national banks could issue, which it raised on several occasions. Nevertheless, congressional acts could not keep up with seasonal fluctuations in the economy or regional demands for money. As a result, complaints arose about the need for a more elastic currency. The government had frozen the quantity of greenbacks in 1868, knowing that it had to reduce the total number if it intended to pay specie for the notes in the future. In 1875, Congress passed the Resumption Act, which traded off increases in the quantity of national bank notes for reductions in the quantity of greenbacks until it could convert greenbacks into gold at pre-Civil War parity in 1879. During the Civil War, the Confederacy, too, issued its own bonds and currency, but these became worthless after the South's defeat.

If the deflation prior to 1879 was a deliberate course chosen by the government to return to specie redemption, the deflation after that year was the result of international forces. Congress, of course, was happy to reduce the nation's debt (total outlays came to $3.2 billion on the Union side alone), and surpluses in the 1880s successfully eliminated the debt. But one side effect involved the reduction in a circulating medium and a general shortage of currency in areas of the country, particularly the West. "In-kind," or barter, still constituted a regular means of transacting business in some areas. Western groups turned first to greenbacks, then to silver for relief. But greenbacks, even when conversion to gold returned in 1879, and even when supplemented with "gold certificates"—notes issued from 1882 to 1900 with a brown seal and convertible into gold—did not adequately expand the money supply. New silver discoveries were promising, but Congress had just demonetized silver in 1873 (the "Crime of '73") when insufficient silver had flowed into the country to maintain coinage. Suddenly, large new discoveries made a return to bimetallism attractive, and, responding to western agitation, on 28 February 1878 Congress passed the Bland-Allison Act, requiring the Trea-

REP. RICHARD P. BLAND (D-MO.). Veteran free silverite and sponsor of the Bland-Allison Act of 1878, which passed over President Rutherford B. Hayes's veto.

NEW YORK STATE HISTORICAL ASSOCIATION, COOPERSTOWN

SEN. FRANCIS M. COCKRELL (D-MO.). Making an impassioned speech advocating free coinage of silver at a special session of Congress in 1893. As silver supplies became more abundant following the Civil War, western miners advocated free coinage of silver to increase the federal government's purchases of the metal. Farmers, who were usually burdened with high mortgage debt, supported free coinage as an inflationary measure that would shrink the long-term value of their debt.

NEW YORK STATE HISTORICAL ASSOCIATION, COOPERSTOWN

sury to purchase $2–4 million of silver a month at market prices and to issue legal tender silver dollars as well as notes called "silver certificates."

For decades the ratio of silver to gold had stayed at 16:1, devaluing silver slightly from its Hamiltonian ratio. By the 1870s, silver actually came out of the mines at a ratio closer to 17:1. Any law that required monetization at a different ratio would trigger silver inflows and a gold drain. Bland-Allison, by requiring purchase of a dollar value at market prices, did not result in any change in the relationship of the two metals. Hence it did not generate the inflation that silver advocates and Western groups hoped. As the price of silver continued to fall, however, new pressures on Congress appeared. In 1890, Congress passed the Sherman Silver Purchase Act, which required the Treasury to buy 4.5 million ounces at market price and to issue legal tender currency redeemable in gold or silver. People rushed to exchange their silver for paper and their paper for gold, especially international speculators. The subsequent gold drain caused the panic of 1893, as U.S. gold reserves fell perilously low. President Grover Cleveland called Congress into special session to repeal the Sherman Act, and in 1900 Congress placed the country on the gold standard with the Gold Standard Act. Under that law (also called the Currency Act of 1900), the U.S. dollar was defined as 23.22 grains of pure gold and was established as the unit of value.

By then, national bank notes constituted most of the circulating currency in the nation. Between 1897 and 1914, the money stock of the nation grew at a pace of 7.5 percent annually. Still, the problem of inelasticity in the currency remained, leading to calls for banking reform. Following the panic of 1907, Congress passed the Aldrich-Vreeland Emergency Currency Act authorizing the secretary of the Treasury to issue emergency currency in time of panic. It also created the National Monetary Commission, which in turn came up with a plan for a new national banking system. It took final form in the Federal Reserve Act of 1913, which created twelve Federal Reserve District Banks that could expand the monetary base by lending to the member banks of the Federal Reserve System at a uniform interest rate (the rediscount rate). In 1914 it also created Federal Reserve notes, a new form of paper money to supplant the national bank notes. Since all national banks had to join the Federal Reserve System, they no longer issued national bank notes; instead, they circulated the Federal Reserve notes as currency.

During World War I, the government again turned to the banks to purchase bonds. The nation emerged from war with a large deficit—$24 billion in 1921—which supply-side tax cuts designed by Secretary of the Treasury Andrew W. Mellon reduced to $16 billion during Calvin Coolidge's administration. Although farmers were suffering financially, the nation entered a decade of prosperity, in some measure due to the tax cuts in the Revenue Act of 1926, which actually produced more revenue from the groups receiving the cuts.

A decade of bank failures had already eroded the nation's financial system in rural areas, and after 1930 new waves of bank failures started to contract the money supply. Between 1930 and 1933 it declined by one-third. President Herbert Hoover tried to lend troubled institutions money from an independent source, the Reconstruction Finance Corporation (RFC), funded by $1.5 billion in bond sales and $500 million from the U.S. Treasury. The RFC provided loans, but under less than optimal terms, and it published the names of loan recipients. In the case of banks, that simply caused further runs, for depositors took news that a bank held an RFC loan as a sure sign that the bank was in trouble. Before long, the RFC loans, many thought, depended on political contacts rather than need. Meanwhile, the Federal Reserve Bank proved helpless in stopping the continued bank failures.

By 1933, incoming president Franklin D. Roosevelt faced a total national financial collapse. On 6 March he declared a national bank holiday, and Congress rushed through sweeping banking and securities legislation, including the Emergency Banking Relief Act and the Glass-Steagall Act (Banking Act of 1933), which provided deposit insurance and which separated banking and securities activities. In 1935, the Federal Deposit Insurance Corporation (FDIC), which Glass-Steagall had created as an emergency measure, became permanent, with a few of its provisions modified. Roosevelt used the Emergency Banking Act to recall all gold coin, bullion, and gold certificates on 5 April 1933 (although collectors could retain gold coins and individuals could hold coin or certificates under $100). With this legislation, together with Roosevelt's proclamation prohibiting the export of gold on 20 April 1933, the country abandoned the gold standard. With the subsequent Gold Reserve Act of 1934, gold would no longer be coined for domestic use, and the Federal Reserve banks transferred all gold to the U.S. Treasury in exchange for dollars. All existing gold coins were made into gold bars. The offi-

COTTON CAMPAIGN BANDANNA. For the 1896 race of Democratic presidential candidate William Jennings Bryan and his running mate, Arthur Sewell, who ran on a free-silver plank advocating the coining of silver and gold at a ratio of 16 to 1. Bimetallism was a central issue in the election, which William McKinley won, maintaining his "hard money," gold standard stance.

COLLECTION OF DAVID J. AND JANICE L. FRENT

cial price of gold also increased to $35.00 an ounce, with the content of the dollar reduced to 13.71 grains. Another act in 1934, the Silver Purchase Act, required that the Treasury purchase silver in the United States and abroad until the stock of silver equaled one-third the value of the monetary gold stock. Additional silver certificates were issued as a part of the circulating money supply as silver bullion was acquired, but had little net effect on the money stock.

Effectively, then, the composition of U.S. money stock was set for the next thirty years, consisting of still-circulating silver certificates (whose issues were stopped in 1963), U.S. notes, and Federal Reserve notes. Virtually all of the old national bank notes had cleared out of the system. Silver coins remained in circulation, but private ownership of gold coins generally remained restricted to collectors for many years.

The United States returned to the gold standard after World War II in accordance with the Bretton Woods Agreement of July 1944. The Bretton Woods proposals created two international organizations, the International Monetary Fund (IMF), designed to help nations solve short-term international debt problems, and the International Bank for Reconstruction and Development, usually called the World Bank. For the U.S. financial system, another important component of Bretton Woods involved the open, multilateral trading system, the General Agreement on Tariffs and Trade (GATT). The combined effect of the Bretton Woods provisions was to create a built-in demand for U.S. dollars, which became the world's currency, acting both as a reserve for foreign banks and as an exchange currency.

Throughout the 1950s and early 1960s the system worked well for two reasons: the United States remained the world's dominant economy (meaning everyone had to use U.S. money for trade), and the nation maintained balanced budgets. After the Great Society and Vietnam War expenditures, however, the U.S. budget fell out of balance, and foreign nations could no longer exchange dollars at par for gold. In 1968, Congress passed the Act to Eliminate the Gold Reserve against Federal Reserve Notes, and three years later, President Richard M. Nixon essentially terminated the Bretton Woods system by ending the convertibility of the dollar into gold for purposes of foreign exchange.

Meanwhile, rising federal expenditures authorized by Congress contributed to the inflationary spiral of the 1970s. Federal Reserve Board chairman Arthur Burns, a Nixon appointee, proved unable to restrain monetary growth by targeting interest rates. Inflation continued to plague the economy until Paul Volcker took over as Federal Reserve Board chairman in 1979 and announced a new policy focused on money supply that by 1982 had squeezed much of the inflation out of the system.

After his election in 1980, President Ronald Reagan, with a large new Republican bloc and a group of southern Democrats supporting him, pushed through a series of tax cuts. Inflation continued to fall or remain low, while government revenues, after the 1982 recession, rose. But expenditures continued to grow more rapidly, and the deficit grew. President George Bush, elected in 1988 on a campaign promise of "no new taxes" reversed himself and signed yet another tax increase sent to him by Congress as a "deficit reduction measure." But despite tax increases in 1986 (under President Ronald Reagan) and in 1990, deficits have only grown worse.

By 1992, Congress and the executive branch had proved unable to reduce federal expenditures, and

only tight policies by the Federal Reserve Bank kept inflation in check. Internationally, the dollar had sunk to new lows against foreign currencies; at home, huge inflows of foreign capital supported the deficits. In 1992, the House voted down a proposal for an amendment that would mandate a balanced budget. From the perspective of more than two hundred years, Hamilton's plan to have government debt funded before it could be assumed, which had provided the basis for a stable currency and financial system, clearly had been abandoned. Only the faith of the American public and those abroad in the inherent strength of the U.S. economy has staved off massive economic dislocation, suggesting that faith often becomes fact.

[See also Banking; Taxation.]

BIBLIOGRAPHY

Cargill, Thomas F., and Gillian Garcia. *Financial Reform in the 1980s.* 1985.
Degen, Robert A. *The American Monetary System.* 1987.
Krooss, Herman E., ed. *Documentary History of Banking and Currency in the United States.* 4 vols. 1969.
Schweikart, Larry, ed. *The Encyclopedia of American Business History and Biography: Banking and Finance to 1913.* 1990.
Schweikart, Larry, ed. *The Encyclopedia of American Business History and Biography: Banking and Finance, 1913–1989.* 1990.
Studenski, Paul, and Herman E. Krooss. *Financial History of the United States: Fiscal, Monetary, Banking, and Tariff, Including Financial Administration and State and Local Finance.* 2d ed. 1963.

LARRY SCHWEIKART

CURTIS, CHARLES (1860–1936), Republican representative and senator from Kansas and vice president of the United States (1929–1933) under Herbert Hoover. Born in Topeka to a quarter-blood Kansa (Kaw) Indian mother and a white father, Curtis as a child spent a short time on his tribe's reservation in Kansas. He then returned to Topeka, where he became an attorney and entered local and state politics before his election to the U.S. House of Representatives in 1892.

In Congress, Curtis served on committees dealing with expenditures and public lands and was chairman of the Committee on Indian Affairs. A strong advocate of the government's allotment program for Indians, he sponsored the Curtis Act of 1898, which abolished tribal courts, led to the dissolution of the Five Civilized Tribes, and established the grounds for Oklahoma statehood. Working behind the scenes, a hallmark of his political style, Curtis also championed the gold standard, high protective tariffs, and the partitioning of the future state of Oklahoma to major oil and gas interests.

In 1907 Curtis was designated to fill the unexpired term of Kansas senator Joseph R. Burton, and in 1914 he was returned to the Senate by popular vote. In recognition of his stand-pat Republican regularity he was selected to head the Rules Committee and then became party whip under Henry Cabot Lodge. An intractible supporter of diplomatic isolation, conservative farm policy, veterans' benefits, prohibition, and the economic interests of his home state, Curtis nevertheless was one of the first national leaders to advocate woman suffrage, and he was no less supportive of fair labor practices for children.

Following the death of Lodge one week after the election of Calvin Coolidge to the presidency in 1924, Curtis became the Senate's majority leader. He then served for a term as Hoover's vice president, presiding over the chamber of which he had been a member for two decades.

BIBLIOGRAPHY

Ewy, Marvin. "Charles Curtis of Kansas: Vice President of the United States, 1929–1933." *Emporia State Research Studies* 10 (December 1961): 1–58.

Unrau, William E. *Mixed-Bloods and Tribal Dissolution: Charles Curtis and the Quest for Indian Identity.* 1989.

WILLIAM E. UNRAU

CUSTOMS AND MORES OF CONGRESS. *See* Congress, *article on* Customs and Mores of Congress.

D

DAVIS, HENRY WINTER (1817–1865), representative from Maryland and Radical Republican leader during the Civil War. As a youth, Davis was warned by his father, a prominent Episcopalian minister, to "beware of the follies of Jacksonism," and he never forgot the admonition. In the early 1850s, when the Whig party collapsed, Davis joined the antiforeign, anti-Catholic Know-Nothing party to continue the battle against the Democrats. Elected to the 34th Congress in 1855 to represent Maryland's 4th Congressional District (which encompassed the central and western parts of Baltimore), Davis was one of only two southerners who refused to vote for the Democratic candidate in the speakership controversy of 1855–1856. Despite charges of sectional disloyalty, the Baltimore representative—handsome, cultivated, and a gifted orator—was able to win reelection to the 35th and 36th Congresses.

As sectional hostilities increased, however, Davis's popularity among constituents declined. Strongly pro-southern, Baltimore voters took issue with their representative, who in early 1860 cast the deciding ballot for William Pennington, the Republican candidate for the speakership. Davis's support of unconditional Unionism during the secession crisis of 1860–1861 served further to alienate many of his constituents, who ultimately denied his bid for a fourth term in Congress.

By the fall of 1863, as Confederate armies suffered defeat, the political situation in Baltimore had changed in favor of the Unionists. Davis, who at the time was leading Maryland's emancipationist movement, easily regained his congressional seat. Second only to Thaddeus Stevens as the most pow-

HENRY WINTER DAVIS. LIBRARY OF CONGRESS

erful Radical Republican in the House, Davis was responsible for drafting the Wade-Davis Reconstruction bill of 1864. Though pocket-vetoed by President Abraham Lincoln, the bill served as a blueprint for postwar Reconstruction legislation. On 30 December 1865, after having contracted pneumonia, Davis died at the age of forty-eight.

BIBLIOGRAPHY

Henig, Gerald S. "Henry Winter Davis and the Speakership Controversy of 1859–1860." *Maryland Historical Magazine* 68 (1973): 1–19.
Henig, Gerald S. *Henry Winter Davis: Antebellum and Civil War Congressman from Maryland.* 1973.

GERALD S. HENIG

DAVIS, JEFFERSON (1808–1889), Democratic representative and senator from Mississippi, secretary of War, only president of the Confederate States of America. Davis was born in Kentucky on 3 June 1808. At an early age he moved with his family to southwestern Mississippi. At the urging and with the help of his brother Joseph, twenty-four years older and like a second father to his younger sibling, Jefferson entered West Point in 1824. After graduating in 1828, he served seven years on the western frontier. His West Point education and army service were critically important to his later public career. They also imbued him with a powerful belief in an American nation.

Davis resigned from the army in 1835 to marry and become a planter on land made available by Joseph. Although his wife died only three months after the wedding, he remained at Davis Bend, on the Mississippi River just south of Vicksburg, where he became a slaveholding cotton planter. Thereafter, he ardently embraced the particular interests of the slave South. Following eight years of almost total seclusion, except for close association with Joseph, he emerged with strong political ambitions.

Although most planters in his part of Mississippi were Whigs, Davis was a staunch Democrat, probably because of his brother's influence and early family connections with Andrew Jackson, who would always be a hero for Davis. He upheld Democratic doctrine on critical financial issues, opposing a national bank and favoring a tariff for revenue only. His public life began in 1843 with an unsuccessful try for the state legislature. But in 1844 the state Democratic party chose him as one of its presidential electors, and he canvassed Mis-

JEFFERSON DAVIS. Pre–Civil War portrait by Mathew Brady, c. 1860.   NATIONAL ARCHIVES

sissippi for the victorious ticket headed by James K. Polk.

In 1845 he won election to the U.S. House of Representatives for the 29th Congress. Again he had to canvass the state, for at the time Mississippi had a general ticket system that required all candidates for Congress to run at large. Thus, from the beginning of his political life, Davis was intimately involved with voters, showing himself most willing to mingle with the adult white male electorate.

As a representative, Davis stood foursquare behind the policies of the Polk administration. He supported lowering the tariff and re-creating the Independent Treasury, which divorced the government from banks. A vigorous expansionist, he believed in America's manifest destiny to become a continental nation. Following Polk's lead, he was willing to compromise with Great Britain on Oregon but refused to bend in the quarrel with Mexico over the status of Texas, especially concerning its southern boundary.

The Mexican War, which resulted from the clash

between American ambitions and Mexican determination, had a momentous impact on Davis's political future. Elected colonel of a Mississippi volunteer regiment, he resigned from Congress in 1846 to go to war. In Mexico he became a legitimate war hero, which provided him with enormous political capital. On his return to Mississippi in 1847, the governor appointed him to fill an unexpired term in the U.S. Senate.

He took his seat in December 1847, and the next month the legislature elected him to a full term. At the outset, he became involved in two areas that occupied much of his Senate time: military affairs and the fateful question of slavery in the territories. A member of the Military Affairs Committee, he always advocated modernization and professionalism in the army. His concerns ranged from the well-being of West Point, which he always defended, to military organization. His chief concern, however, was to protect what he saw as the constitutional right of white southerners to take their black slaves into the vast territory newly won from Mexico. He became a major opponent of the Compromise of 1850, which in his mind failed to guarantee that right.

The passage of the compromise led to the transformation of political parties in some southern states, including Mississippi, that affected Davis. In 1851 he resigned from the Senate to run as his party's candidate for governor, but he lost narrowly. The defeat left him without political office until 1853, when President Franklin Pierce appointed him secretary of War, a post he held throughout Pierce's term. While in the cabinet, he remained powerful in Mississippi politics, and in January 1856 the legislature chose him for a Senate seat that would open in 1857.

On 4 March 1857, he moved from the cabinet back to the Senate. Now a leader among southern Democrats and chairman of the Military Affairs Committee as well as a confidant of President James Buchanan, Davis became a powerful force in the Senate. During his second tour as senator, the same two topics absorbed most of his energy; as before, he advocated professionalism in and the enhancement of the army.

Slavery, southern rights, and the territories were the paramount issues of the late 1850s. Davis was a stalwart backer of the controversial Lecompton constitution, which would have made Kansas a slave state. When the bitter sectional dispute over Kansas's status broke apart the Democratic party in 1858, he demanded the proscription of anti-Lecompton Democrats, a policy Buchanan's administration implemented. To impose a doctrinal test on the party, Davis in 1859 had the Senate Democratic caucus adopt resolutions requiring the federal government to protect slavery in the territories.

Even though Davis championed southern rights, he was not a secessionist, not even after Abraham Lincoln's election as president in 1860. During the fateful second session of the 36th Congress, Davis served on the select Committee of Thirteen, which failed in its attempt to find a compromise between southern and Republican demands. Reluctantly, he went along when Mississippi seceded. On 21 January 1861, he made his farewell speech to the Senate and returned home.

Davis's unique combination of political and military experience guaranteed him a prominent place in the new Confederate States of America. That role turned out to be the presidency, which he held until the Confederacy's collapse in 1865. Following the Confederate defeat, he lived for almost another quarter century, but he never again held public office. He never requested a pardon and was never given one during his lifetime, although Congress posthumously restored his citizenship in 1979.

BIBLIOGRAPHY

Crist, Lynda L., et al., eds. *The Papers of Jefferson Davis.* 7 vols. to date. 1971–.

Davis, Jefferson. *Rise and Fall of the Confederate Government.* 2 vols. 1881.

Davis, William C. *Jefferson Davis: The Man and His Hour: A Biography.* 1991.

WILLIAM J. COOPER, JR.

DAVIS ET AL. V. BANDEMER ET AL.

(478 U.S. 109 [1986]). Implementation of "one person, one vote" has resulted in congressional districting that is almost mathematically exact in equal populations, but "fair and effective representation" can be denied groups through partisan manipulation of district lines. This case was brought by Indiana Democrats who alleged that Republicans had drawn a mixture of single-member and multimember districts so that while Democrats received a majority of statewide votes they obtained a minority of the legislature. The Court held that an allegation of partisan gerrymandering states a claim under the equal protection clause that may be adjudicated by the courts. But the Supreme Court majority that had ruled on justiciability split on the rules for proving a denial of equal protec-

tion, leading to a negligible impact in the real world of politics. The prevailing justices found that equal protection is denied only when an electoral system is arranged so as to "consistently degrade" a group of voters' influence on the political process as a whole. The failure of a party to win seats in proportion to its total vote is not sufficient, because there is no right to proportional representation. The result of one election also is insufficient, because it is the operation of the system over time that counts. A showing of "continued frustration of the will of the majority of the voters" or of a denial of fair influence to the minority is necessary. Two justices would have allowed gerrymandering to be shown by looking at objective actions, such as drawing sprawling, irregular shapes, disregarding political subdivision lines, and other such factors.

No impermissible partisan gerrymandering was since found, but in *Shaw v. Reno* (1993), the Court held that some race-conscious districtings favoring minorities could deny equal protection. White voters in North Carolina challenged a plan enacted by the legislature to meet the Voting Rights Act mandate (as interpreted by the Department of Justice) that when districts *could* be drawn in which minorities were a majority they *must* be so drawn. One of the districts was shaped very irregularly in order to achieve a majority of African Americans. A decision of 5 to 4 held that, when districts were so strangely shaped as to leave no doubt that the only purpose was to include voters only on the basis of color, an equal protection violation was proved, unless a compelling reason justified the plan. Apparently, more compact districts drawn on a racial basis are not constitutionally suspect. The case was remanded for trial, and it has upset the electoral situation in a number of states. Under one reading, the case could invalidate the Voting Rights Act, but even more moderate readings could set back electoral successes of African Americans, Hispanics, and others.

BIBLIOGRAPHY

Alfange, Dean, Jr. "Gerrymandering and the Constitution: Into the Thorns of the Thicket at Last." *1986 Supreme Court Review* (1986): 175.

Schuck, Peter H. "The Thickest Thicket: Partisan Gerrymandering and Judicial Regulation of Politics." *Columbia Law Review* 87 (1987): 1325.

Symposium. "The Future of Voting Rights after *Shaw v. Reno.*" *Michigan Law Review* 92 (1993): 482.

JOHNNY H. KILLIAN

DAWES SEVERALTY ACT (1887; 24 Stat. 388–391). Also known as the General Allotment Act, the Dawes Severalty Act was sponsored in the Senate by Henry L. Dawes (R-Mass.) and passed on 8 February 1887. It represented a consensus view of American Indian policy. While discussions of allotment divided legislators along regional and party lines earlier in the decade, the Dawes bill passed without serious opposition. In effect for half a century (it was effectively repealed by the Indian Reorganization Act of 1934), the act disrupted life in every Indian community in the United States. Its destructive effects are still felt by Native Americans.

The Dawes Severalty Act authorized the president to order a survey of individual Indian reservations and the distribution of homesteads to tribal members. Each head of household would receive 160 acres of land, with single adults and unmarried children receiving 80 and 40 acres, respectively. The Indian Office would negotiate with tribes for the sale to non-Indians of all lands remaining un-

SEN. HENRY L. DAWES (R-MASS.).

claimed within their reservations once the allotment process was complete. Indians receiving allotments would be exempt from local property taxes for twenty-five years and prohibited from selling their lands for the same period. All allotted Indians were declared citizens of the United States.

Allotment appealed to self-styled "friends of the Indian," but it undermined both the social coherence and the economic health of tribal communities. Allotment also was favored by commercial interests eager to reduce Indian landholdings, and in fact, the law led to the transfer of ninety million acres of land from Indian to non-Indian ownership.

BIBLIOGRAPHY:

McDonnell, Janet A. *The Dispossession of the American Indian, 1887–1934.* 1991.
Prucha, Francis Paul. *American Indian Policy in Crisis: Christian Reformers and the Indian, 1865–1900.* 1976.

FREDERICK E. HOXIE

DAYTON, JONATHAN (1760–1824), New Jersey Revolutionary War patriot, soldier, delegate to the Federal Convention, and United States representative and senator. At the age of twenty-seven, Dayton was a New Jersey delegate to (and the youngest member of) the Constitutional Convention of 1787, promoting the interests of small states and endeavoring to prevent southern states from counting slaves when determining representation. He was elected to the First Federal Congress, but preferred the state assembly, where he became Speaker of the House. As a member of the Second Congress, he advocated an expanded army and defended Secretary of the Treasury Hamilton's economic policies from Republican critics.

Dayton's popularity won him the House speakership in the Fourth and Fifth Congresses. An enigmatic Federalist, he disapproved of Jay's Treaty, yet forcefully argued that Congress could not refuse appropriations to carry it out. In 1796 Dayton backed Aaron Burr for the presidency, thereby incurring Hamilton's ire. And as Speaker he tempered the demand for war with France during the XYZ crisis. A Federalist newspaper castigated him as "a shallow, superficial fellow . . . unfit to play the cunning part he has undertaken." He served one term (1799–1805) as a senator from New Jersey. He opposed the Republican-sponsored repeal of the Judiciary Act of 1801 and supported Justice Samuel Chase in his impeachment trial.

Dayton joined the Burr-Wilkinson conspiracy of 1804 and 1805, hoping to increase the value of his Ohio lands and was indicted in 1807 for treason, but escaped conviction on Burr's acquittal.

BIBLIOGRAPHY

Lomask, Milton. *Aaron Burr: The Conspiracy and Years of Exile, 1805–1836.* Vol. 2. 1982.
McCormick, Richard P. *Experiment in Independence: New Jersey in the Critical Period.* 1950.

WINFRED E. A. BERNHARD

DEBATE, REPORTERS OF. Congress's official reporters of debate provide more than verbatim transcripts of House and Senate proceedings. Unlike court reporters, they are expected to edit, amplify, and, when clarity or their own best judgment demands, revise spoken words of the participants. The debate reporter, observed *Shorthand Writer* magazine in 1917, must assure that the "imperfect utterances" of the lawmakers "shall not appear on the printed page, where their nakedness is open to the world."

Congress first established its own staff of official reporters in 1873. Before then, reporting was left to outsiders, mostly private entrepreneurs and journalists, and members of Congress were often disappointed in the results. House members as early as 1789 had complained about inaccurate, biased, or otherwise distorted reporting of that body's actions.

Debate reporters of Congress's early years faced daunting obstacles. Stenography was new and clumsy. Noise and poor acoustics made hearing difficult, and reporters had to contend with peculiar regional accents. The result: many major debates were lost to history because the reporter could not hear or, in some cases, identify the speakers. Thomas Lloyd, who reported the debates of the First Congress, occasionally had to resort to vague descriptions such as "the bald-headed man" or "the man in the blue coat and wig" to identify debate participants.

The history of reporting the debates and proceedings of Congress was divided by scholar Elizabeth Gregory McPherson into two distinct periods: 1789 to 1848, when private entrepreneurs provided the stenographic reports of both houses, and 1848 to the present, when Congress financed the publication of the debates and proceedings and accuracy improved with the development of phonetic stenography.

In the early 1800s, Joseph Gales and William Seaton were the leading specialists in reporting

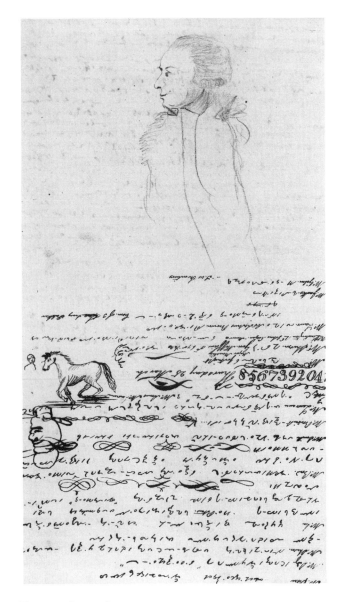

THOMAS LLOYD'S NOTES ON DEBATES FROM THE FIRST CONGRESS. Although Lloyd's published debate records serve as the principal source of information about the framing of the Bill of Rights, his doodles indicate that he was not a particularly reliable reporter.

LIBRARY OF CONGRESS

House and Senate debates. In various ventures, starting with the *National Intelligencer* in 1807, these brothers-in-law weathered several political upheavals to retain their positions as Congress's semiofficial reporters. Gales, seated next to the presiding officer, covered the Senate, and Seaton, similarly perched beside the Speaker, covered the House. Their reports appeared at first in the columns of their newspaper. In 1824 they launched the *Register of Debates,* devoted exclusively to the proceedings of Congress, and in 1833, they compiled and published the *Annals of Congress,* covering debates from 1789 to 1824. With the arrival in 1833 of the *Congressional Globe,* an organ of the ascendant Jacksonian Democrats, Gales and Seaton lost their lucrative business as Congress's official printer and were forced to fold the *Register of Debates.*

The Senate's decision in 1848 to employ the *National Intelligencer* and the *Union* to report and publish its proceedings brought Congress its first corps of skilled stenographers, under the supervision of Henry W. Parkhurst. Two years later, the House followed by awarding a contract to *Congressional Globe* editors John C. Rives and Francis P. Blair to report its debates.

Even these quasi-official publications, many members complained, mangled their speeches and mistreated opponents of the ruling party, problems that were finally resolved in 1873 when the legislators created the *Congressional Record* and hired a staff of official reporters answerable solely to Congress.

[*See also* Congressional Record.]

BIBLIOGRAPHY

McPherson, Elizabeth Gregory. "The History of Reporting Debates and Proceedings of Congress." Ph.D. diss., University of North Carolina, 1940.

Ritchie, Donald A. *Press Gallery: Congress and the Washington Correspondents.* 1991.

U.S. Senate. Senate Historical Office. *Official Reporters of Debate of the United States Senate.* 1990.

DONALD C. BACON

DEBATE AND ORATORY. When Alexis de Tocqueville visited Washington, D.C., in 1831, he criticized what he called the "petty side" of oratory in the U.S. Congress. "The debates of that great assembly," he wrote, "are frequently vague and perplexed and . . . seem to drag their slow length along rather than to advance towards a distinct object. Some such state of things will, I believe, always arise in the public assemblies of democracies." At the same time, Tocqueville noted that there was also an "imposing" side to congressional discourse. He praised the Senate as a body of "eloquent advocates, distinguished generals, wise magistrates, and statesmen of note, whose language would at times do honor to the most remarkable parliamentary debates in Europe." So impressed was Tocqueville with the best speakers he heard in Congress that he exclaimed, "I can conceive of nothing more admirable or more powerful than a great orator debating great questions of state in a democratic assembly."

Tocqueville was neither the first nor the last commentator to express ambivalence about the level of congressional speech making. In the two centuries since its founding in 1789, Congress has provided the stage for some of the most celebrated oratory in American history. It has also furnished a setting for numbing displays of triviality, bombast, false pathos, and coarse straining after effect. The tenor of its discourse has ranged from the elegant periods of Rufus Choate to the homespun homilies of David Crockett, the patrician eloquence of Lucius Q. C. Lamar to the mean-spirited mendacity of Joseph R. McCarthy, the philosophic lucubrations of J. William Fulbright to the vapid commonplaces of Warren G. Harding, the brawling pugnacity of Henry S. Foote to the stately dignity of Margaret Chase Smith. In its oratory, as in other respects, Congress has reflected the virtues, talents, and shortcomings of the American people in general.

The Early House. Throughout its history, Congress has functioned as a forum for debate on major issues of national policy. At first this role was fulfilled primarily by the House of Representatives. Preoccupied with the dignity and decorum of its proceedings, the Senate met behind closed doors until 1795 and would not move to center stage for another three decades. In keeping with the importance accorded the colonial assemblies before independence, the popularly elected House initially drew the lion's share of public attention, had longer sessions, and was far more active in debate. So prominent was the House in the early republic that Henry Clay resigned his seat in the Senate to stand for election to the House in 1811. Already a renowned orator despite his youth, Clay preferred what he called "the turbulence . . . of a numerous body to the solemn stillness of the Senate Chamber."

During the first thirty years of its existence, the House boasted a galaxy of accomplished speakers that included, in addition to Clay, James Madison, Albert Gallatin, William B. Giles, Robert G. Harper, John Randolph, Josiah Quincy, and John C. Calhoun. None, however, exceeded Fisher Ames, the mercurial arch-Federalist from Massachusetts, whose speech in defense of Jay's Treaty remains the acknowledged masterpiece of House oratory. Delivered on 28 April 1796 before packed galleries that included members of the Senate and the Supreme Court, both of which had adjourned for the occasion, Ames's dramatic address secured the passage of appropriations for the treaty, was deemed by British visitor Joseph Priestley "the most bewitching piece of parliamentary oratory" he had ever heard, and provided a touchstone of political discourse for generations of U.S. statesmen.

For the most part, however, the métier of speech making in the House was less the formal set speech than the ability to hold one's own in the rough-and-tumble of extemporaneous debate. It was this ability that made John Quincy Adams perhaps the most formidable rhetorical antagonist ever to sit in Congress. Standing at the center of the growing sectional controversy in the House from 1831 to 1848, he captured the imagination of the public with his spirited battles against the gag rule, the annexation of Texas, and the Mexican War. Using every rhetorical weapon available to him, he was feared in debate as much for the ferocity of his invective as for the power of his reasoning. Asking no quarter and giving none, he flayed his opponents without mercy, provoking in response a barrage of verbal abuse. Twice southern representatives moved formal resolutions of censure against him, and twice he repelled them with brilliant defenses. In 1842, after defeating the second attempt at censure, he gleefully noted in his diary that he had left Thomas F. Marshall, the chief speaker against him, "sprawling in his own compost." By the time Adams died in 1848, he had become revered as "Old Man Eloquent."

The Senate's Golden Age of Oratory. Long before Adams's death, changes in American politics and in Congress itself had swung the oratorical balance away from the House and toward the Senate, a development that produced the most concentrated outpouring of political eloquence in the nation's history. Beginning with the Compromise of 1820 and continuing until the Civil War, the Senate chamber served as what John J. Crittenden called a "grand theatre"—a stage upon which the great issues of the day were debated and upon which the most eminent figures of American politics played their roles. The leading actors in these debates—Clay, Calhoun, Daniel Webster, Robert Y. Hayne, William H. Seward, Charles Sumner, Stephen A. Douglas, Lewis Cass, Thomas Hart Benton, Robert Toombs—saw their speeches not just as instruments of political action but as artistic creations in the tradition of the great orations of antiquity.

SEN. HENRY CLAY (W-KY.). Addressing the Senate in 1850. Engraving by Robert Whitechurch after a drawing by Peter Rothermel, 1855.

Newspapers and magazines regularly reprinted the public addresses of lesser Senate speakers as well as the productions of titans such as Webster and Sumner. And once reprinted, the speeches touched off heated discussion in the press not just about their subject matter, but also about their rhetorical techniques and aesthetic qualities. It was the golden age of American oratory. Ralph Waldo Emerson captured its spirit when he exclaimed that "the highest bribes of society are at the feet of the successful orator. . . . All other fames must hush before his. He is the true potentate."

The quintessential Senate debate of the golden age—and arguably the greatest oratorical contest in the history of Congress—took place between Webster and Hayne over the course of nine days in late January 1830. The ostensible issue was the disposition of western lands, but the true subject became the nature of the Union and the meaning of the Constitution. In his legendary second reply to Hayne, immortalized in the massive painting by George Healy that hangs in Boston's Faneuil Hall, Webster destroyed Hayne's quest to create an entente between the South and the West, excoriated the doctrine of nullification, and established in the public mind the idea that the Union was founded on the collective sovereignty of the American people rather than as a confederation among sovereign states.

As with other major Senate debates of the time, the clash between Webster and Hayne was relished as much for its personal drama as for its political doctrines. To Hayne's partisans, his speech of 21 and 25 January seemed unanswerable, but Webster was confident that he would "grind" the South Carolinian "as fine as a pinch of snuff." On the day of Webster's reply, the Senate chamber was overflowing with spectators who began arriving early in the morning. Women occupied so many seats on the floor that most senators were obliged to stand, while, in the words of one observer, "the halls and stairways were packed with men who clung to one another, like bees in a swarm." And Webster did not disappoint. His voice was hypnotic, his bearing regal, his countenance captivating. "Eye, brow, each feature, every line of the face," Charles W. March recalled in his *Reminiscences of Congress* (1850), "seemed touched, as with a celestial fire." By the time Webster finished his peroration, with its moving eulogy to the Union, men and women in the gallery were weeping openly. It was an oratorical triumph worthy of the ages. Massachusetts representative Edward Everett deemed it the equal of Demosthenes' "On the Crown."

Twenty years later, Webster was again a participant in one of the great set pieces in the chronicles of American oratory—this time in conjunction with Clay and Calhoun during the Senate debates over the Compromise of 1850. Seeking to avert the destruction of the Union in the aftermath of the Mexican War, Clay had come out of retirement to reclaim his seat in the Senate. On 29 January 1850 he introduced eight compromise resolutions, which he supported on 5 and 6 February in the most acclaimed oration of his long and distinguished career. On 4 March Calhoun countered with a prolonged attack on the North for usurping the rights and power of the South. The country, he insisted, could be saved only by adopting measures that would allow the southern states to remain in the Union "consistently with their honor and safety." On the brink of death and too weak to deliver the speech himself, Calhoun had it read to the Senate by James M. Mason of Virginia. Three days later, Webster presented his celebrated "Seventh of March" oration, a masterful plea for compromise that condemned both the moral absolutism of the abolitionists and the extremism of southern secessionists. Coming at the end of their careers and in the most serious crisis facing the Union before the Civil War, the orations of the great triad quickly took on legendary status and remain classic exemplars of the art of deliberative oratory.

Other notable Senate orations during the golden age included Calhoun's closely reasoned speech of 15 and 16 February 1833, attacking the tariff and defending his doctrine of nullification as a constitutional remedy to tyranny of the federal government; Webster's dexterous response to Calhoun of 16 February 1833, excoriating nullification as theoretically bankrupt and historically contrary to the principles of the Constitution; Benton's highly praised address of 12 January 1837, calling for expunction of the resolution of censure against President Andrew Jackson; Thomas Corwin's eloquent philippic of 11 February 1847, denouncing the war with Mexico as an unjust crusade of conquest; Seward's famous presentation of 11 March 1850, arguing that slavery in the western territories was regulated by "a higher law than the Constitution"; Douglas's climactic speech of 30 January 1854, concluding debate on the ill-fated Kansas-Nebraska bill; Sumner's recklessly vitriolic "The Crime against Kansas" of 19–20 May 1856, a million copies of which were distributed in pamphlet form; and Jefferson Davis's dignified farewell to the Senate on 21 January 1861, before leaving Washington to attend the convention launching the Confederacy.

Not all congressional oratory during the golden age was golden. For every highly polished rhetorical jewel there were dozens of sophistic baubles. John Quincy Adams, who earlier in his career had been the first Boylston Professor of Rhetoric and Oratory at Harvard, often deplored the pedestrian blather and ostentatious nonsense he heard daily in the House. In a futile effort to emulate the eloquence of Congress's best speakers, the worst produced volumes of what the *North American Review* lambasted in 1841 as "wretched babble." When presented by the likes of Adams, Clay, or Webster, a speech of three to four hours in length was a source of edification and entertainment; in the hands of a lesser orator, it was too often an exercise in pretentious verbiage, pointless storytelling, jumbled imagery, pompous grandiloquence, and gratuitous classical allusions. Webster himself despaired that "the vernacular tongue of the country" had become "greatly vitiated, depraved, and corrupted by the style of our Congressional debates." "If it were possible for those debates to vitiate the principles of the people as much as they have depraved their tastes," he lamented, "I should cry out, 'God save the Republic!'"

As with other observers of congressional oratory, Webster also had ample opportunity to remark the personal invective that frequently attended debate in the House and Senate. To help ensure free and open debate in Congress, the Founders had stipulated in the Constitution that senators and representatives "shall not be questioned in any other

Place . . . for any Speech or Debate in either House." Historically, the only formal restraints on the content of congressional speeches have come from rules of decorum prohibiting "unparliamentary language," rules that were considerably looser and less strictly enforced before the Civil War than today. As early as 1790, Massachusetts representative Fisher Ames complained about the "low, indecent, and profane" idiom of speech making in the House, and during the turbulent debates over slavery, aspersions on the motives, character, patriotism, and values of other members abounded in both chambers. Not only were speeches on the floor often punctuated with epithets such as "liar," "coward," and "scoundrel," but at times hecklers in the gallery became so disruptive that the sergeant at arms had to be summoned to clear the chamber of spectators.

Nor were violations of decorum solely verbal. Fistfights were commonplace in the House during much of the nineteenth century, and more than a few debates were punctuated with freestyle brawling. In one instance, John B. Dawson of Louisiana cocked his pistol and might well have killed Joshua R. Giddings of Ohio had he not been restrained by colleagues. During another debate, more than thirty representatives brandished guns on the floor of the House. Though less raucous than its counterpart, the Senate was hardly immune from violence. The brutal caning of Charles Sumner by Preston S. Brooks in 1856 in retaliation for his "Crime against Kansas" oration is the most notorious physical assault in Senate annals, but it is far from the only one. As late as 1902 two southern senators came to blows during debate, prompting a revision of the rules to stipulate that "No Senator in debate shall directly or indirectly, by any form of words, impute to another Senator or to other Senators any conduct or motive unworthy or unbecoming a Senator" and that "No Senator in debate shall refer offensively to any State of the Union."

The Decline of Debate and Oratory. Although decorum is much improved in the late twentieth century, the same cannot be said for the state of congressional oratory. One reason debate stirred such passions during the golden age is that it played a significant role in the proceedings of Congress. Senators and representatives fought over words because they believed that words mattered. "Politics," as Webster stated, was the "master topic of the age" and oratory was the preeminent mode of political expression. In the decades after Appomattox, however, the nation's attention turned to

business, the fervor of the sectional controversy cooled in the quest for profits, and monumental orations such as those of the golden age no longer echoed in the halls of Congress. So precipitously did congressional oratory decline during the last decades of the nineteenth century that writer Edward Everett Hale declared it to be a lost art.

Although Hale's judgment turned out to be premature with respect to the Senate, it was acutely true of the House of Representatives. By 1840 the increase in U.S. population and the admission of new states to the Union had swelled the membership of the House to over 240, and the next year the House adopted a rule limiting each representative to one hour of speaking time on a given subject. In 1847 it imposed a rule limiting debate on amendments to five minutes per speaker, and in 1860 it allowed debate on amendments to be closed off altogether by vote of a majority of the members in attendance. These rules are still in effect, and they constitute one of the major differences in procedure between the House and the Senate, where unlimited debate remains the norm in most cases. As Woodrow Wilson stated in his classic study of congressional government, "The House once debated. Now it does not debate. It has not the time. There would be too many debaters, and there are too many subjects to debate. It is a business body and it must get its business done."

In the late twentieth century, the House seldom devotes more than two afternoons of debate to even the most important legislation, while on minor questions the entire body may have a total of one hour of debate to divide among all 435 members. There are dozens of speeches by representatives in any issue of the *Congressional Record*, but only a fraction of them are actually delivered on the floor of the House. Most are inserted under the House's indulgent "revise and extend" rule, which allows any member five legislative days after a measure has been voted upon not only to amend whatever remarks he or she may have made during debate, but also to compose entire "speeches" solely for the purpose of appearing in the *Record* and of being reprinted thereafter for readers back home. The business of the House is dominated by its committees, and with few exceptions oratory has little discernible impact in the process of proposing, drafting, and voting upon legislation.

Because of its smaller size and minimal restrictions on debate, the modern Senate has provided a more congenial arena for oratory than has the House. During the twentieth century, a number of talented speakers have made their voices heard in the Senate, including Albert J. Beveridge, George F. Hoar, Henry Cabot Lodge, Robert M. La Follette, William E. Borah, Everett M. Dirksen, Huey P. Long, Hubert H. Humphrey, Frank Church, Eugene J. McCarthy, and Robert C. Byrd. In few instances, though, has Senate debate galvanized the nation as it did during the golden age. While Americans often pay great attention to what the Senate does on issues of national policy, they seldom give much heed to what senators say in their speeches about those issues.

Contrary to conventional wisdom, this has not resulted simply from a general decline in speech making. Although orations in the grand style of the nineteenth century have long been the reliquiae of a departed age, the twentieth century has produced its share of historically significant public addresses. The fact that relatively few have been uttered on the Senate floor is less a reflection of the oratorical ability of individual senators than of the changing balance between the executive and legislative branches of government. Ever since Theodore Roosevelt transformed the White House into a "bully pulpit," the rhetorical presence and power of the presidency have grown steadily, with a commensurate decline in the rhetorical presence and power of Congress. In times of national crisis, the nation looks to the president, rather than to Congress, for rhetorical direction. It is no accident that the most anthologized speeches of the twentieth century include a large number of presidential addresses but almost none presented by senators or representatives during the course of debate in Congress.

[See also Eulogies; Humor and Satire, article In Congress; Language.]

BIBLIOGRAPHY

Baskerville, Barnet. *The People's Voice: The Orator in American Society.* 1979.

Byrd, Robert C. *The Senate, 1789–1989: Addresses on the History of the United States Senate.* 2 vols. 1988–1991.

Duffy, Bernard K., and Halford R. Ryan, eds. *American Orators before 1900: Critical Studies and Sources.* 1987.

Duffy, Bernard K., and Halford R. Ryan, eds. *American Orators of the Twentieth Century: Critical Studies and Sources.* 1987.

MacNeil, Neil. *Forge of Democracy: The House of Representatives.* 1963.

Oliver, Robert T. *History of Public Speaking in America.* 1965.

STEPHEN E. LUCAS

DEBT LIMIT. The restriction, by statute, of the amount of federal debt that may be issued and outstanding at any given time is referred to as the federal debt limit. Under current law the ceiling applies to almost all (over 99.3 percent) of the federal debt. The modern limit traces its origins to the Second Liberty Bond Act of 1917. Since passage of that act, the nature of debt limitation has evolved into today's comprehensive limit on federal debt.

The debt limit covers almost all Treasury debt, known as *public debt*, whether held by the public or in government accounts. The limit also covers the small amount of debt issued by agencies for which the government specifically guarantees the principle and interest. (A number of federal agencies can issue debt to the public, debt that is subject not to the general limit but to its own specific statutory limit.) The debt subject to the general limit includes an accounting adjustment for Treasury securities sold at a discount. The adjustment is considered necessary to avoid misrepresenting the amount of debt issued compared to the amount of cash received from the borrowing.

Most of the public debt not subject to limit was issued in fiscal year 1986 by the Federal Financing Bank (FFB), a part of the Treasury. The FFB can issue up to, and in 1993 had outstanding, $15 billion in public debt that is not subject to limit.

History of the Debt Limit. Before a general debt limit was adopted in 1917, Congress needed to approve each issuance of federal debt, including a determination of its term and interest rate. With the approach of World War I, Congress found it increasingly difficult to stay ahead of the expanding borrowing needs of the government. The newly enacted debt ceiling provided the government with a more efficient method of borrowing to help finance the costs of the war. As the borrowing grew, the original limits were periodically increased and widened to other classes of federal securities.

During and after World War I, the debt limit was found to be a convenient means for Congress to provide the Treasury with authority to issue debt. In 1941, Congress consolidated the previously separate limits on different types of federal debt—bills, notes, and bonds—into a single limit that nearly covered the total amount of federal debt. This is essentially the form of today's debt limit.

In the 1950s, Congress began to use temporary limits, with expiration dates, that were then combined with the permanent limit to produce the total debt limit. The original hope for this modification was that in the future the debt could be reduced to the level of the permanent limit, a hope that almost always went unfulfilled. The separate temporary and permanent debt limits were merged in 1983 and have, with some limited and short-term exceptions, remained combined ever since. In mid 1992 the permanent limit stood at $4.145 trillion, having risen rapidly from less than $1 billion at the end of fiscal year 1981. The increase resulted mostly from consistently large federal budget deficits and the growing debt holdings in federal government accounts.

Changing the Limit. Throughout most of its existence the debt limit has been changed by the introduction of legislation specifically written for that purpose. As the debt limit was approached or a temporary limit was about to expire, the Treasury would often request that Congress increase or extend the debt limit. The requested increase generally would be large enough to accommodate the borrowing needs of the government for some period into the future.

Debt limit bills provided Congress with one of its few opportunities to debate overall fiscal and budgetary policies before the advent of the formal congressional budget process in 1974. The debates sometimes delayed adoption of the legislation until a permanent limit had been reached or a temporary limit had expired. In addition, the necessity of adopting the legislation has made it a target for unrelated amendments. Raising the limit is necessary since a failure to raise the limit could severely limit the government's ability to pay for its existing obligations. Raising or extending the limit has been fairly common, occurring approximately fifty times between 1970 and 1993.

A change in the internal House rules (Rule XLIX) adopted in 1979 produced a new method of generating legislation to raise the debt limit. Under the House rule, upon adoption of the concurrent resolution on the budget by both houses of Congress, a new joint resolution containing the debt limit increase is created, deemed passed by the House, and sent to the Senate. The debt limit increase in this joint resolution is based on the increase or increases in the public debt subject to limit for the upcoming fiscal year or years contained in the congressionally adopted concurrent resolution on the budget.

The Senate, which has not changed its rules, treats the debt-limit-changing resolution like any other resolution sent from the House. It can accept, reject, or modify the straightforward increase in the debt limit. Acceptance sends the resolution to the president; rejecting or modifying the resolution sends it back to the House or to a conference committee for further consideration. One such Senate modification occurred in 1985, with the amendment that eventually became the Balanced Budget and Emergency Deficit Control Act of 1985, more commonly known as the Gramm-Rudman-Hollings Act (P.L. 99-177). Eventually, if Congress wants the government to fulfill its fiscal obligations, a debt-limit bill, with or without modifications, will emerge from Congress and be sent to the president.

The changed House rule has not eliminated the need for specific legislation to raise the limit, as had once been hoped. The Senate's continued authority to modify the House-adopted joint resolution on increasing the debt limit and the use of debt-limit legislation as a vehicle for other legislation have resulted in the continued need and desire for separate debt-limit bills. And if the limit needs to be raised at any time other than during the budget resolution deliberations, separate legislation is still necessary.

The debt limit also can be and has been changed by attaching it to or including it in some other piece of legislation as an amendment. Although this procedure is not common, it is used; the Omnibus Budget Reconciliation Act of 1990 (P.L. 101-508), for example, contained a title raising the debt limit.

[*See also* Budget Process.]

BIBLIOGRAPHY

Shuman, Howard E. *Politics and the Budget: The Struggle between the President and the Congress.* 2d ed. 1988.

PHILIP D. WINTERS

DECLARATIONS OF WAR. *See* Constitution, *article on* Congress in the Constitution; Foreign Policy; War Powers.

DEFENSE. Before there was a United States—before there was an American Constitution—before there was a U.S. army or navy, there was the Continental Congress, predecessor to today's national legislature. Then and later the representatives' first duty was to provide for the common defense. That task posed the most basic question about the role of force in a democracy: how to ensure the preservation of security from threats abroad and of liberty from the concentration of power at home.

The spirit that informed the Constitution and the statutes flowing from it reflected the special sensitivity of military policy. Quartering of British soldiers in private homes, impressment of Americans for British sea duty, and the use of force to repress legitimate grievances by loyal subjects had bred deep suspicion of executive power among the American colonists. Those royal abuses spawned an American tradition of close congressional involvement in defense affairs. In the new republic the instruments of defense were tightly controlled, ultimately by the Congress.

The Constitution grounds that policy in the enumerated powers of Congress (Art. I, sec. 8); of sixteen subsections, seven bear directly and others indirectly on the control of military forces. Not only was the legislature to have general authority to provide for defense, but it was to "raise and support Armies" under appropriations limited to two years, to establish a navy, to provide for organizing the militia, and to make regulations for the discipline and use of all forces. Capping those authorities was the power to declare war, a provision that would be the center of much later dispute. Paired with these extensive specifications of congressional power over defense was the singular designation of the president as "commander in chief."

While the quality and depth of congressional involvement in national security matters has varied widely, the penetration of American legislators into this sphere is unparalleled among the parliaments of the world. The history of that involvement falls broadly into two divisions, before and after World War II. For most of the nation's existence peacetime military forces were small in scale and limited in function. Only in times of war did military and defense issues require congressional debate and action, yet those episodes provoked frequent frictions between the executive and legislative branches.

Presidents and generals have rarely had an easy time with Congress. Even during wartime, when deference to those conducting the country's defense is at its peak, Congress has often intruded into the details of military plans and operations. The legislature has at times pressed for more vigorous prosecution of war and at other times urged restraint in the use of force. House and Senate chambers have rung to voices of war hawks and war skeptics, of imperialists and isolationists, of ideologues demanding victory at any cost and protesters urging peace at any price. Congressional attitudes have been too mixed and too complex to characterize as consistently either more pacific or more militant than the executive branch.

Influenced by both the history of king-made wars and the tradition of state militia organization under the Articles of Confederation, the First Congress was not inclined to create a permanent army and navy of any substantial size even though George Washington favored a professional force. It did establish the Department of War as one of the first three government agencies, providing a skeletal structure for lightly manned armed forces. At the same time, Congress was immediately attentive to operational failures. When President Washington reported that Gen. Arthur St. Clair, governor of the Northwest Territories, had led the entire regular army of less than two thousand men into an Indian ambush near Fort Wayne, Indiana, on 4 November 1791, the House of Representatives ordered an inquiry into the disaster. From that investigation evolved a basic legislative pattern of examining military performance and civilian-military relations, typified in modern times by the massive hearings on the surprise attack at Pearl Harbor in 1941 and the congressional review of President Truman's dismissal of Gen. Douglas MacArthur during the Korean War.

Contrasting with Congress's wariness of standing military forces was the recurrent tendency of many in Congress to demand military initiatives at crucial moments in the nation's history. Thus, the "War Hawks" of 1812, led by the young House Speaker, Henry Clay of Kentucky, proposed ejecting the British from Canada and seizing the entire continent. That early expansionist impulse echoed later in the surges of congressional support for action against Mexico in 1848 and Spain in 1898, aroused on both occasions by "manifest destiny" ambitions for territorial expansion as well as by political and humanitarian considerations.

In the Mexican episode one of the most eloquent voices calling for Congress to restrain the executive's use of force was that of Rep. Abraham Lincoln, whose reticence about presidential power would later yield to the exigencies of civil war. From 1861 to 1865 Lincoln's dramatic assertion of executive prerogative in time of war came against the backdrop not only of the Union's gravest crisis, but also of unprecedented congressional interference in military affairs, notably through the joint Committee on the Conduct of the War. Despite congressional dissatisfaction with executive management of military operations, the Civil War forced legislative acquiescence in abandoning voluntary recruitment in favor of conscription. The initial draft law of 1863, intended mainly to spur voluntary enlistments, allowed potential conscripts to buy their way out of service by finding substitutes, an unsavory practice that Congress would eliminate in the Selective Service Act of 1917 and later measures.

The intensifying violence of modern war tempered the nationalist sentiments that animated congressional debates during the nineteenth century and revived members' respect for the warnings of George Washington and Thomas Jefferson against entanglement in the conflicts of others. Before and after World War I isolationism was the familiar theme of public opinion and congressional attitudes. In 1934, hearings of the Senate Special Committee to Investigate the Munitions Industry chaired by Sen. Gerald P. Nye (R-N.D.) placed the blame on bankers and munitions makers for America's entry into World War I; those hearings in turn led Congress to pass neutrality laws that undermined whatever potential there was for the United States to help deter the aggressions that triggered World War II. During 1940 and 1941 Congress was the focus and the forum for the struggle between isolationists in the America First Committee and interventionists in the Committee to Defend America by Aiding the Allies.

Intense debate centered on the Selective Training

FIRSTHAND VIEW. Members of Congress examine the fuselage of a bomber under construction in the Glen L. Martin airplane plant, Baltimore, Md., 1942.

LIBRARY OF CONGRESS

and Service Act of 16 September 1940, the nation's first peacetime draft. By the narrowest of margins in the House and with the addition of eighteen amendments in the Senate, Congress approved a system that would register 17,000,000 men in fifteen months and actually induct more than 900,000 before war came. The high-water mark of U.S. isolationism came with its failure to deny Franklin D. Roosevelt a third presidential term in 1940 and to defeat the Lend-Lease Act of 1941.

For most of the nation's history a clear pattern persisted: Congress would support only minimal military forces in peacetime and would insist on prompt demobilization of the larger armed services after the end of major conflicts. For example, after World War II, the call to "bring the boys home" produced abrupt drawdowns in personnel and equipment. The advent of the Cold War, however, broke the pattern. Following protracted hearings and sharp argument, Congress enacted the Selective Service Act of 1948, adding obligations for service in the reserves after active duty. Periodically renewed, the law served as the basic structure for military recruitment through the Korean and Vietnam conflicts, until the "volunteer army" concept won favor during the presidency of Richard Nixon.

The post–World War II years saw Congress's intermittent concern with defense policy give way to nearly constant attention. The experience of total war against the Axis and perpetual conflict with communism called into question the legislature's capacity to address urgent threats in time to protect the nation. In an age of long-range bombers and strategic missiles, America's ocean barricades were no longer sufficient for safety. Many legislators were haunted by the memory of Congress's uncertain performance in the months before Pearl Harbor. The creation of nuclear weapons and other radical changes in technology reinforced the view that only the president was capable of coping with the high-tempo crises likely to dominate world politics.

Although sobered by self-doubt and alarmed by the nuclear perils, Congress was not a passive player in the reshaping of America's defense posture. Four persistent issues drew the legislature into this realm: (1) the architecture of the defense establishment; (2) defense procurement, basing, and manpower policy; (3) the diplomacy of national security; and (4) decisions to use military force.

The Architecture of Defense. The modern Congress of the last half-century recognized that ad hoc responses would not be adequate for future emer-

gencies, that new dangers required a systematic approach to military preparedness. As defense budgets shrank drastically and forces demobilized in 1945 and 1946, decisions were made to reconfigure the defense establishment. Foremost among these decisions were those that concerned management of nuclear programs. Congress moved control of such efforts out of the military and into the Atomic Energy Commission (AEC), closely monitored by a Congressional Joint Committee on Atomic Energy (JCAE). The partnership of AEC and JCAE, which expressed the legislature's historic commitment to civilian control of the military, for many years would be a central channel for congressional influence over vital strategic programs.

A similar perspective shaped the National Security Act (1947). In creating the new Department of the Air Force and realigning the other services under a civilian secretary of Defense, Congress struck a careful balance among the executive agencies and between the two branches of government. The legislation also created a Joint Chiefs of Staff (JCS), comprising a chairman and the heads of the U.S. Army, Navy, and Air Force, to advise the president and the secretary of Defense. (The Marine Corps commandant would gain a vote in the JCS in 1952.) The National Security Act Amendments of 1949 strengthened the legislature's access to senior military advice by providing statutory authority for any member of the JCS to offer Congress "on his own initiative . . . any recommendation relating to the Department of Defense that he may deem proper." At the same time, there were strict safeguards against any tendency toward the type of general staff that many felt had contributed to Germany's historic aggressions. Indeed, congressional resistance to service unification was part of a longstanding inclination to exploit interservice rivalry as a tool of legislative control. Later reforms would weaken that device as Congress authorized greater reliance on unified commands, on centralized Department of Defense management of the services, and (in the Goldwater-Nichols Defense Reorganization Act of 1986) an enlarged role for the JCS chairman.

At crucial junctures Congress also initiated institutional and program changes that affected the larger framework of national defense. Responding to the 1957 Soviet launch of *Sputnik I* Congress promoted an invigorated national space program. It did so, however, by moving control of major space operations from the military to a civilian agency, the National Aeronautics and Space Admin-

SEN. RICHARD B. RUSSELL (D-GA.). *At right,* chairman of the Senate Armed Services Committee (1951–1953, 1955–1969), addressing Department of Defense officials and ranking officers of the armed forces during a meeting in the Armed Services Committee room.   OFFICE OF THE HISTORIAN OF THE U.S. SENATE

istration, while at the same time consolidating military research and development under a director of Defense Research and Engineering. Congress also pressed for more intensive training of qualified scientists and engineers by passing the National Defense Education Act of 1958 (P.L. 85–864), which would support tens of thousands of graduate students. It was also from Congress that innovations arose to ensure consideration of nonmilitary factors in national security. The Arms Control and Disarmament Act of 1961 had numerous sponsors, including particularly Sen. Hubert H. Humphrey (D-Minn.), a pioneer in the field as a leader in the Foreign Relations Committee.

Some organizational issues proved especially troubling for Congress. Following creation of the Central Intelligence Agency (CIA) in 1947, an extensive community of intelligence collectors and analysts emerged, but legislative oversight was attenu-

ated, at best. To a degree a self-denying ordinance kept Congress, afflicted by fear that it would be incapable of keeping secrets, in the dark. In the mid 1970s abuses of intelligence resources—some related to the Watergate scandal, others ranging from inappropriate drug experimentation on unknowing subjects to assassination plots—led Congress to tighten controls by establishing separate House and Senate committees, that built responsible and effective relations with the CIA. Difficulties with intelligence oversight recurred, however, during the Reagan administration (1981–1988) when CIA director William Casey, without advising Congress, carried out such exploits as mining Nicaraguan harbors to aid the Contra rebels against a Marxist regime.

A more straightforward problem for legislative-executive relations evolved from the role assumed by the National Security Council (NSC) staff and its

Landmark Defense Legislation

TITLE	YEAR ENACTED	REFERENCE NUMBER	DESCRIPTION
War Department Act	1789	1 Stat. 49, Chap. 7	Established a Department of War.
Militia Act	1792	1 Stat. 264, Chap. 28	Established a national militia.
Navy Armaments Act	1794	1 Stat. 350, Chap. 12	Established a U. S. Navy.
Militia Act	1795	1 Stat. 424, Chap. 36	Authorized the president to call out the militia to suppress insurrection or repel invasion.
Marine Corps Act	1798	1 Stat. 594, Chap. 72	Established a distinct Marine Corps.
Militia Act	1861	12 Stat. 281, Chap. 25	Authorized the president to use military force to suppress the rebellion.
Selective Service Act	1863	12 Stat. 731, Chap. 75	Subjected all white males aged 25–35 to the draft; allowed draftees to hire substitutes.
Militia Act	1903	32 Stat. 775, Chap. 196	Gave the War Department more control over the National Guard in peacetime.
Selective Service Act	1917	40 Stat. 76, Chap. 15	Established the second wartime draft.
War Risk Insurance Act	1917	40 Stat. 398, Chap. 105	Replaced a chaotic military pension system with uniform death-and-disability benefits for service personnel and their dependents.
Neutrality Act	1935	49 Stat. 1081, Chap. 837	Prohibited export of arms and other implements of war to belligerent countries and barred U.S. citizens from traveling on ships of belligerent countries.
Neutrality Act Amendments	1939	54 Stat. 4, Chap. 2	Eased restrictions imposed by the 1935 Act.
Selective Training and Service Act	1940	54 Stat. 885, Chap. 720	Established the first peacetime draft.
Lend-Lease Act	1941	55 Stat. 31, Chap. 11	Authorized the manufacture and transfer of weapons and other defense articles to "any country whose defense the President deems vital to the defense of the United States."
Servicemen's Readjustment Act (GI Bill of Rights)	1944	58 Stat. 284, Chap. 268	Defined a program of benefits World War II veterans.
Atomic Energy Act of 1946 (McMahon Act)	1946	P.L. 79-585	Vested control of atomic energy in a civilian commission.
National Security Act	1947	P.L. 80-253	Created basic national security structure.
Defense Production Act	1950	P.L. 81-774	Defined emergency powers over economy.
Defense Reorganization Act of 1958	1958	P.L. 85-599	Established Defense Research Directorate and other reforms for space age.
Arms Control and Disarmament Agency	1961	P.L. 87-297	Created Arms Control and Disarmament Agency.
War Powers Resolution	1973	P.L. 93-148	Reasserted power of Congress over use of U.S. forces.
Defense Reorganization Act of 1986 (Goldwater-Nichols)	1986	P.L. 99-433	Strengthened role of Joint Chiefs of Staff chairman and promoted interservice cooperation.

director, the assistant to the president for national security. Beginning in the Nixon administration (1969–1974) with disputes about the Vietnam War and an embryonic détente with the Soviet Union, some members of Congress raised questions about the dominance of National Security Adviser Henry A. Kissinger and suggested that the appointee for the office of NSC director be subject to Senate confirmation. While resisting statutory congressional oversight of his office, Kissinger devised informal

Figure 1
Defense Outlays as a Percent of U.S. GNP, 1950–1990

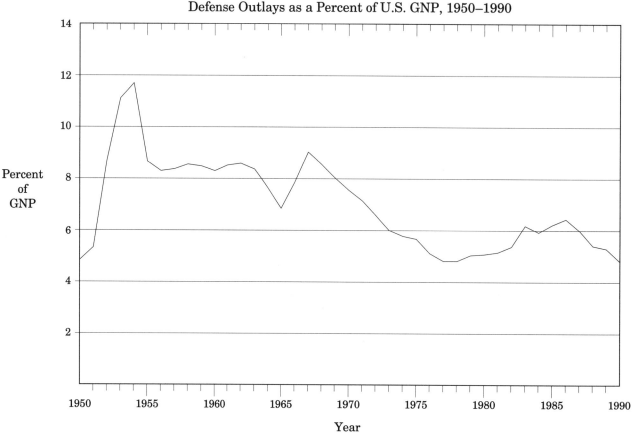

SOURCE: Department of Defense, *Report of the Secretary of Defense to the President and the Congress*, January 1990, p. 11; Kruzel, Joseph, ed., *1990–1991 American Defense Annual*, 1991.

arrangements to meet with congressional committees, a practice followed by a number of his successors. Still, the extra-constitutional activities of Oliver North and other NSC officials during the Iran-contra episode of the 1980s showed the hazards of lodging national security operations in a White House staff shielded from legislative scrutiny.

Procurement, Basing, and Manpower. The president can command only those forces that Congress puts at the executive's disposal. Historically, much debate centered on the size and shape of naval forces because it was the navy that could most readily engage the nation in foreign wars. In recent decades Congress has participated actively in choosing the principal weapons systems for all services, viewing procurement decisions as crucial to its influence on national strategy.

So important to the navy was the support of leading legislators that major ships bear their names—

for example, Carl Vinson (D-Ga.), longtime chairman of the House Armed Services Committee, and Henry M. (Scoop) Jackson (D-Wash.), a vigorous pro-defense senator. Congress favored the power-projection capabilities advocated by admirals seeking aircraft carriers, and it sped development of ballistic missile–launching submarines by underwriting larger budgets than the Eisenhower administration (1953–1961) preferred for that purpose. By contrast, when the navy sought a fleet of so-called fast deployment logistics ships (FDLS) in the late 1960s, Senate Armed Services chairman Richard B. Russell (D-Ga.) reacted memorably, saying, "If you have the capability to go anywhere and do anything, you'll always be going somewhere and doing something."

Conventional weapons programs consumed most appropriations, but strategic nuclear systems triggered the most intense legislative struggles. Those struggles illustrate both the alliances of bureaucratic factions of members of Congress and the development of independent legislative capacity to evaluate weapon programs. The results were sometimes surprising. For example, when President Lyndon B. Johnson reluctantly acceded in 1967 to pressure from some legislators to deploy an antiballistic missile (ABM) system, he did not foresee how divisive the plan would become. A combination of skepticism about the plan's strategic wisdom and opposition from constituents who feared that the deployment might draw attacks that it could not defeat resulted in mounting congressional resistance. Perennial arguments over ABM funding contributed to the conclusion of a 1972 treaty limiting Soviet and American deployments. That outcome virtually eliminated the army, the original manager of the U.S. ABM system, from a role in strategic nuclear activities.

Congressional action on procurement and basing decisions blends high politics and low politics, considerations of national interest and narrow calculations of constituency interest. Because of their direct connection to the nation's security, defense programs may be less susceptible to pork-barrel politics than other programs, but this is not always the case. This theme was captured in a colleague's rebuke of Rep. L. Mendel Rivers's (D-S.C.) perennial campaign for defense expenditures in his locality: "Mendel, you put anything more in that district and it'll sink." With enormous budgets and hundreds of installations providing jobs and voters, the defense establishment regularly attracted close interest of legislators. More than once Congress distorted defense investment by extending production of unneeded systems and resisting the closure of surplus bases. In the late 1980s Congress took steps to constrain its own behavior by establishing an independent commission to facilitate base closings and by supporting dramatic cuts in defense spending.

The Diplomacy of National Security. Despite Congress's pluralistic structure, it has shown remarkable consistency in strengthening diplomatic instruments of security policy. It was instrumental in the incorporation of arms control as an integral part of U.S. defense planning and operations. At the outset of the space age, Congress pressed to keep outer space free of weapons, while opening it to other military operations (e.g., reconnaissance and communications). Nuclear proliferation has been a permanent concern, prompting Congress to place strict limits on nuclear cooperation with other nations and to impose sanctions against

those who violate the 1968 Non-Proliferation Treaty (NPT). The 1972 Antiballistic Missile (ABM) Systems Treaty won overwhelming approval in the Senate, where only two senators objected.

Congressional behavior regarding arms diplomacy displays the tendency to hedge against bad outcomes that is a hallmark of defense policy generally. Thus, Congress has usually endorsed the goal of negotiated restraint in arms, but it has set high standards for verification of agreements. As arms diplomacy has increased in importance, legislators have insinuated themselves into direct contact with negotiators, sometimes serving as channels for significant information exchange between governments.

In a number of cases Congress has also set goals and criteria for negotiations. In 1963 a resolution sponsored by Senator Humphrey and Sen. Thomas J. Dodd (D-Conn.) paved the way for a nuclear test ban by inviting an agreement limited to those areas where confidence in verification was high (i.e., the atmosphere, under water, and outer space). Seven years later the Senate was far more ambitious than the administration in its approach to the Strategic Arms Limitation Talks (SALT) with the Soviet Union; by a vote of 72 to 6 in April 1970 it urged the president to seek mutual suspension of further deployments of strategic offensive and defensive weapons systems, specifically pressing for a halt to testing missiles with multiple warheads (MIRV), which would later undermine stability. An amendment to the resolution ratifying the ABM treaty made clear that no further strategic agreement would win approval unless it met several requirements set by Senator Jackson and others.

One of the most notable congressional interventions in arms diplomacy occurred when Reagan administration officials attempted to reinterpret the ABM treaty. When President Reagan's Strategic Defense Initiative of 1983 rekindled interest in the possibility of ballistic missile defense, officials in the Defense and State departments identified potential loopholes in the ABM treaty's negotiating record that they contended entitled the United States to go far beyond the limits of the accord as originally explained to the Senate. At the same time, the administration denied senators the opportunity to review the negotiating record for themselves. That position was directly counter to the precedent set by George Washington in 1796 when he conveyed to the Senate the full instructions and negotiating record for Jay's Treaty, the first treaty concluded under the Constitution. Sen. Sam Nunn

(D-Ga.), chairman of the Senate Armed Services Committee, waged a decisive campaign to obtain access to relevant negotiating materials and to confirm that commitments made to the Senate in support of treaty ratification were binding upon the executive. The exercise reaffirmed Senate prerogatives in making and interpreting treaties.

Throughout its engagement in arms control, Congress has acted as a balance, restraining presidents who overemphasized diplomacy at the expense of sound defense policy and energizing those who disdained negotiations. From Jimmy Carter (1977–1981) legislative leaders extracted greater investment in defense in conjunction with the abortive SALT II agreement of 1979; from Ronald Reagan, they coaxed a more forthcoming negotiating stance in exchange for partial support of his strategic missile program.

Decisions to Use Force. Nothing has so confounded classical doctrines of constitutional authority over defense as the declining relevance of formal declarations of war. Most uses of military force in U.S. history have fallen short of declared war, with its implications for international and domestic legal regimes. Only in modern times, however, have those uses tended toward prolonged, large-scale military operations that would have presumed a congressional declaration. While the Founders intended that presidents have the power to respond to attacks on the United States, its citizens, or its forces, the idea that the president could initiate or sustain such operations without legislative approval is constitutionally suspect.

A number of dubious precedents have raised difficulties between the branches. Franklin D. Roosevelt directed an undeclared naval war against German submarines in the Atlantic for much of 1940 and 1941. The concept of protracted but limited war without formal declaration developed in the Korean conflict (1950–1953) and in Vietnam (1963–1973). Congressional discomfort both with the frustration of limited war and with the erosion of legislative control over war making grew steadily into the 1970s. Although Congress repeatedly authorized and appropriated funds for U.S. operations in those conflicts, and Congress's passage of the 1964 Gulf of Tonkin Resolution would be described by executive officials as tantamount to a declaration of war, there was a growing conviction that general resolutions of political support to bolster a president's hand in crisis and repeated appropriations to support troops already committed to battle did not satisfy constitutional scruples.

Over strenuous objections by some members and a presidential veto, Congress sought to regain its slipping power by enacting the War Powers Resolution of 1973. Far from settling the issue, the law became part of the ongoing struggle to clarify the most perplexing dilemmas of national security. Presidents from Gerald R. Ford on have criticized the law as an unconstitutional encroachment on the presidency, although they filed reports meeting the statute's requirements on most occasions when U.S. forces were exposed to the risk of hostilities. Lost in the controversy was the original intention of the resolution's principal author, Sen. Jacob K. Javits (R-N.Y.), who sought not to enervate the presidency but to ensure that Congress could not evade responsibility for judging the wisdom of committing forces to combat. Dissatisfaction with the act's effects moved a number of legislators, especially in the Senate, to propose simplifying the provision and modifying its fixed timetable for removal of U.S. forces from combat unless Congress acted to affirm their engagement.

Quarrels over war powers arose repeatedly during the administrations of Ronald Reagan and George Bush (1989–1993). Congress supported presidential requests for U.S. ships to perform escort duty in the Persian Gulf during the Iran-Iraq War, but interventions in Grenada and Lebanon evoked less sympathetic congressional reactions. Before the tragedy that cost almost three hundred lives in the 1983 terrorist attack on the U.S. Marine barracks in Beirut, Senator Nunn was warning prophetically that the forces deployed were "too few to fight, too many to die." More encouraging was the legislative-executive performance in sharing responsibility for the U.S. commitment to help repel Iraqi aggression against Kuwait (1990–1991). The House and Senate debates on President Bush's request for authority constituted statecraft of a high order, as did the work of the president and Secretary of State James Baker in mobilizing an international coalition against Iraq. If the interbranch collaboration in that instance did not guarantee future consensus, it did offer a model to be emulated.

Conclusion. Legislative-executive relations in defense policy have often revolved around the double-track machinery of congressional authorization and appropriations. Dominant figures in these processes have been the chairmen of the House and Senate Armed Services committees, which share responsibility for authorizing and overseeing defense programs and budgets, and the chairmen of the two houses' Defense Appropriations subcommittees, which are responsible for funding the military establishment. Since World War II these four chairmen have shared a generally pro-defense outlook, working closely with Defense Department officials and with each other. While in the House the roles are always separated, in the Senate they have sometimes merged, as in the 1960s through the 1980s, when first Richard Russell and then John C. Stennis (D-Miss.) led both the Armed Services Committee and the Defense Appropriations Subcommittee. The creation of independent budget committees in 1974 opened a third window on military activities and increased pressure to relate defense expenditures to general economic policy. The result was occasional, not unhelpful, tension between the czars of defense policy in the traditional standing committees and those they considered interlopers from the budget committees.

As the twentieth century wound toward its end, Congress moved far beyond the relative passivity it once exhibited toward defense policy. The large measure of deference paid to presidential leadership during and after World War II has been replaced by a skepticism that blends respect for executive responsibilities with keener congressional oversight of national security institutions and activities.

Experienced and highly knowledgeable legislators have emerged in both the Senate and House, whose Armed Services chairman Les Aspin (D-Wis.) became secretary of Defense in 1993, following the path of two previous colleagues, Melvin R. Laird (R-Wis.) in 1969 and Richard B. Cheney (R-Wyo.) in 1987. Aspin's Senate counterpart, Sam Nunn, has attained magisterial sway over defense policy exceeding even that of his two Georgia predecessors as postwar chairmen, Senator Russell and Representative Vinson. What remains uncertain is whether a more assertive Congress will produce more effective national defense or more frequent deadlock between the branches. The outcome hinges not only on an enlightened Congress, confident of its own capacities, but on a responsive executive branch, dedicated to forging consensus with its legislative partner.

[See also Armed Forces; Armed Services Committee, House; Armed Services Committee, Senate; Conscription; Intelligence Policy; War Powers. For further discussion of the armed services, see Air Force; Army; Marine Corps; Navy. See also Central Intelligence Agency; Defense Production Act of 1950; Iran-Contra Committees; National Security Act; Nuclear Weapons; Nye Committee; and entries on particular wars in which the United States has fought.]

BIBLIOGRAPHY

Blechman, Barry. *The Politics of National Security: Congress and U.S. Defense Policy*. 1990.

Fisher, Louis. *President and Congress: Power and Policy*. 1972.

Frye, Alton. *A Responsible Congress: The Politics of National Security*. 1975.

Galloway, George B. *History of the United States House of Representatives*. 1961.

Huntington, Samuel P. *The Common Defense: Strategic Programs in National Politics*. 1961.

Koh, Harold. *The National Security Constitution: Sharing Power after the Iran-Contra Affair*. 1990.

Mann, Thomas, ed. *A Question of Balance: The President, the Congress and Foreign Policy*. 1990.

Nolan, Janne. *Guardians of the Arsenal: The Politics of Nuclear Strategy*. 1989.

Reveley, W. Taylor, III. *War Powers of the President and Congress: Who Holds the Arrows and the Olive Branch?* 1981.

Russett, Bruce M. *What Price Vigilance? The Burdens of National Defense*. 1970.

Schlesinger, Arthur M., Jr. *The Imperial Presidency*. 1973.

Sofaer, Abraham. *War, Foreign Affairs, and Constitutional Power: The Origins*. 1976.

ALTON FRYE

DEFENSE PRODUCTION ACT OF 1950

(64 Stat. 798–822). Innocently named but fiercely debated at birth, the Defense Production Act (DPA) remained the focus of intense controversy for years after its enactment. At its core, the legislation posed fundamental questions of executive authority, not only over defense policy but also over the entire U.S. economy.

By the spring of 1950, with factories operating near capacity, the Truman administration's plans for major rearmament to meet the Soviet buildup threatened serious production bottlenecks and inflationary pressures. With the outbreak of war in Korea in June, the president pressed for expanded powers to control credit and provide financing for defense programs; he also raised the prospect of price controls and rationing, a grim echo of World War II. Sen. Robert A. Taft (R-Ohio) and others saw such a sweeping grant of power as menacing economic freedom in the United States, but a confused and shifting debate produced an act signed by Truman on 8 September 1950.

Among other powers, the DPA (P.L. 81-774) authorized the president to impose wage and price controls, selectively as well as generally; to limit consumer credit; to set priorities for allocating scarce materials; and to use up to $2 billion for loans to ensure defense production. These authorities were to terminate on 30 June 1951. To monitor the act, Congress established the Joint Committee on Defense Production, whose longevity would reflect the fact that the DPA was to prove more than temporary. To implement the legislation, Truman established the Office of Defense Mobilization to energize production and the Economic Stabilization Agency to restrain inflation.

The DPA became an interbranch battleground over the ensuing decades. Truman's use of the DPA set the pattern; even with lingering military stalemate in Korea, public reaction to his application of economic controls prompted Congress to add weakening amendments to the 1951 extension of the act. The ultimate attempt to maximize the act's scope came when Truman used it, instead of the Taft-Hartley Act, to prevent a steel strike by taking over the industry until the Supreme Court, in *Youngstown Sheet and Tube Co. v. Sawyer* (1952), ruled that he had exceeded his authority.

From the Eisenhower administration on, periodic renewals of the DPA triggered arguments over a wide array of economic policies: the possible exemption from antitrust restrictions of defense firms collaborating on key projects, installment credit regulation; the stockpiling of critical materials; and the use of government procurement to induce strategic industries to disperse their factories. By the 1990s, debate over extending the DPA was marked by anxiety in the Defense Department and Congress regarding the U.S. defense mobilization base (i.e., the industrial infrastructure required to expand military production rapidly in wartime). A serious concern was the increased amount of foreign-produced components incorporated in the nation's most modern weapons systems. Legislators pressed the administration of George Bush for preferential treatment of domestic producers of specified items; they also proposed that government regulators deny foreign investors the right to acquire U.S. defense firms, a question raised in acute form by French attempts to acquire a major American missile manufacturer at the very time that U.S. intelligence was reporting extensive industrial espionage by France. More positively, the 1992 extension of the act carried significant provisions to modernize the act's thrust by promoting development of dual-use technologies that would benefit civilian as well as military sectors. In Congress, the DPA remained a focus of mixed emotions in the 1990s: apprehension about excessive grants to the executive of power over the economy persisted alongside a desire for protection of U.S. defense capacity.

[*See also* Youngstown Sheet and Tube Co. v. Sawyer.]

BIBLIOGRAPHY

Truman, Harry S. *Memoirs by Harry S. Truman: Years of Trial and Hope.* 1956.
Congressional Quarterly Inc. *Congress and the Nation, 1945–1964.* 1965.

ALTON FRYE

DEFERRAL. The temporary delay of spending provided by law is known as a *deferral*. It is one of two types of impoundment (an executive action to withhold spending) defined in the Impoundment Control Act of 1974. The other type, *rescission* (an action to cancel spending permanently), is discussed under its own entry.

The Impoundment Control Act of 1974 establishes procedures for congressional consideration of impoundments and sets forth the conditions under which the president may rescind or defer spending. It was enacted after the unprecedented impoundments in the late 1960s and early 1970s by President Richard M. Nixon.

With respect to deferrals, the act requires the president to submit a special message to Congress specifying the amounts to be deferred and identifying the reasons for the proposed deferrals. Deferrals are permissible under the act only for contingencies, to promote efficiency, or as provided by law—in other words, only for these three routine administrative reasons, not for making policy changes. Deferred funds may be withheld from obligation only until the end of the fiscal year. If Congress wishes to disapprove a proposed deferral, it must enact legislation to do so.

The Impoundment Control Act originally permitted either house of Congress to reject proposed deferrals by simple resolution. The Supreme Court, in *Immigration and Naturalization Service v. Chadha* (1983), however, declared the legislative veto unconstitutional, thereby invalidating the use of simple resolutions for disapproving deferrals and creating the possibility that the president could propose deferrals for policy reasons without the congressional controls originally contemplated. In 1987, Congress amended the act to limit proposed deferrals to the three specific criteria listed above.

[*See also* Congressional Budget and Impoundment Control Act of 1974; Rescission.]

BIBLIOGRAPHY

Middlekauff, William Bradford. "Twisting the President's Arm: The Impoundment Control Act as a Tool for Enforcing the Principle of Appropriation Expenditure." *Yale Law Journal* 100 (1990): 209–228.

Thurber, James A., and Samantha L. Durst. "Delay, Deadlock, and Deficits: Evaluating Proposals for Congressional Budget Reform." In *Federal Budget and Financial Management Reform*. Edited by Thomas D. Lynch. 1991.

EDWARD DAVIS

DEFICIENCY BILLS.

Up through the late 1950s, Congress used deficiency bills, to provide additional appropriations to federal departments or agencies that had obligated their regular appropriations too rapidly during a given fiscal year. Under the Antideficiency Act of 1906 (31 U.S.C. 1512–1519), as amended in 1950, appropriations may not be obligated "at a rate that would indicate a necessity for a deficiency or supplemental appropriation" unless required by certain subsequent laws or specified emergencies. Deficiency bills were distinguished from supplemental appropriations bills, which generally provided additional funds for new or unanticipated needs.

After World War II, congressional action on separate deficiency bills became more and more infrequent and eventually ended altogether. In modern practice, supplemental appropriations measures are generally used for all additional funding needs that may arise during the current fiscal year. Occasionally, regular or continuing appropriations measures also may be used to provide supplemental appropriations.

BIBLIOGRAPHY

Fisher, Louis. "Supplemental Appropriations: History, Controls, Recent Record." Congressional Research Service, Library of Congress. CRS Rept. 79-101. 1979.

U.S. Congressional Budget Office. *Supplemental Appropriations in the 1980s*. February 1990.

EDWARD DAVIS

DELAWARE.

One of the thirteen original states, Delaware established itself as the first state when, on 7 December 1787, its state convention unanimously ratified the Constitution. The least populous state in 1787, Delaware sent a delegation of five men to the Constitutional Convention in Philadelphia dedicated both to protect small-state interests and to construct a more powerful national government. At the insistence of delegate George Read, who was the most influential figure in Delaware politics, Delaware bound its delegates to a pledge not to surrender the one-vote-per-state principle of the government established by the Articles of Confederation. At the Convention, John Dickinson—Delaware's most famous delegate, with revolutionary experience dating from the Stamp Act Congress in 1765—warned James Madison that Delaware would prefer an alliance with a foreign power to surrendering its interests to a union dominated by Virginia and other large states. More constructively, Dickinson also suggested that a plan to base representation in one house of the national legislature on population while preserving the equality of states in the other would be a suitable compromise. The Delaware delegation opposed Madison's Virginia Plan, supported the alternative New Jersey Plan, and endorsed the Great Compromise that established how representation in the House and Senate would be determined.

The political history of Delaware has been marked by alternating eras of single-party dominance. From 1789 to the early 1820s, the Federalist party controlled Delaware politics, a longevity unmatched by the Federalists in any other state. After the reshuffling of parties occasioned by the John Quincy Adams–Andrew Jackson rivalry of the 1820s, the Whig party emerged triumphant in Delaware and controlled state politics in the 1830s and 1840s. With the founding of the Republican party and a more concerted opposition to slavery on the national scene in the 1850s, however, Delaware turned solidly Democratic and remained so until the end of the nineteenth century. Delaware rejected the Reconstruction amendments, for example, and bitterly opposed congressional Reconstruction of the South. From the start of the twentieth century through the mid 1930s, an alliance of the Republican party and Delaware industrialists, including the Du Pont family, dominated Delaware politics. Only the Great Depression and the political skills of Franklin D. Roosevelt ended Republican control. Since then, Democrats and Republicans have waged a more balanced struggle for political control of Delaware, with party success often following national political trends.

With the exception of the period from 1813 to 1823, when Delaware sent two representatives to the House of Representatives, the state has been represented by a single member in the House. Notable among Delaware's members of Congress is

James A. Bayard, Sr., a Federalist senator and the single Federalist member of the U.S. delegation to negotiate the Treaty of Ghent, which ended the War of 1812. He was the first of five Bayards to represent Delaware in Congress. In addition, Louis McLane, a former Federalist who joined the Jacksonian Democrats, set an unequaled Delaware record of being elected to the House for six consecutive Congresses. McLane also served in Jackson's cabinet until he opposed the president's plan to destroy the Second Bank of the United States.

BIBLIOGRAPHY

Munroe, John A. *History of Delaware.* 1979.
Rossiter, Clinton. *1787: The Grand Convention.* 1966.

RICHARD HUNT

DELEGATES, NONVOTING. Nonvoting delegates to Congress were authorized by the Continental Congress in the Ordinance of 1784. The ordinance provided for the political organization of territories outside of the original thirteen states and authorized these territories, once a territorial government had been established, to "keep a member in Congress, with a right of debating, but not of voting." The 1784 measure was restated in the Northwest Ordinance of 1787, which recognized the status of territorial legislatures in the Northwest Territory to "elect a delegate to Congress, who shall have a seat in Congress, with a right of debating but not of voting." In 1789, one of the earliest acts of the First Congress under the Constitution was to reenact the provisions of the Northwest Ordinance. The position of territorial delegate has been recognized continuously since then.

Initially, organized territories were clearly on the road to ultimate admission to statehood, but with the United States' acquisition of noncontiguous overseas territories (Hawaii, Puerto Rico, and the Philippines) in the 1890s, and other territories (e.g., the U.S. Virgin Islands and Guam) at later dates, territories came to be distinguished as either "incorporated" or "unincorporated"; the former were clearly likely to become states and the latter had a less clearly determined status. Congress created the post of resident commissioner for these indeterminate-status territories; the Philippines (until 1946) and Puerto Rico were granted representation status through commissioners whose formal duties were identical to those of delegates with the exception that commissioners were chosen for four-year terms while delegates served two-year terms.

House historical records are unclear, but it appears that delegates were permitted to vote in the House committees to which they were assigned at least until the 1840s. Thereafter, the practice evidently ended (a proposal was offered in 1884 to allow delegates committee-voting rights, but it was not acted on). At the time of that proposal, delegates and resident commissioners were assigned only to committees concerned with territorial affairs and not panels with broader jurisdictions. Delegates never accrued seniority on the committees and were not counted in determining the party ratios on panels.

During consideration of the Legislative Reorganization Act of 1970, the House agreed by voice vote to an amendment by Resident Commissioner Jorge Cordova of Puerto Rico to elect the commissioner (then, the only House delegate) to standing committees in the same manner as other members and "to possess in such committees the same powers and privileges as the other Members." Through this language, delegates were permitted to accrue seniority, to chair committees and subcommittees, to serve on conference committees, and to vote in committee.

Later that year, the House authorized the post of delegate from the District of Columbia. In 1972 delegates from Guam and the Virgin Islands were authorized in law, and a delegate from American Samoa was authorized in 1980. The resident commissioner from Puerto Rico is still elected for a four-year term, while the other delegates are chosen for two-year terms. Each receives the same salary, staffing allowance, and other benefits as members of the House. Since 1980, proposals have been offered to authorize nonvoting delegates to represent American Indians and Americans residing abroad, but these proposals, have not been acted upon.

In 1993, the House changed its rules to allow delegates to vote on issues (primarily amendments to bills) considered in the Committee of the Whole. Complex procedures were adopted to ensure that delegate votes would not affect the ultimate outcome of Committee of the Whole votes. House Republicans charged that the new rules were unconstitutional, but the U.S. District Court and the U.S. Court of Appeals for the Washington, D.C. circuit denied the lawsuit.

[*See also* Shadow Senators.]

BIBLIOGRAPHY

Berkhofer, Robert F. "Jefferson, the Ordinance of 1784, and the Origins of the American Territorial System." *William and Mary Quarterly* 29 (April 1972): 231–262.

Harlow, Ralph V. *History of Legislative Methods before 1824.* 1917.

U.S. House of Representatives. *Cannon's Precedents of the House of Representatives of the United States,* by Clarence Cannon. 74th Cong., 1st sess., 1935. Vol. 6, ch. 73.

U.S. House of Representatives. *Constitution, Jefferson's Manual, and Rules of the House of Representatives, 103d Congress.* Compiled by William Holmes Brown. 102d Cong., 2d sess., 1992. H. Doc. 102-405.

U.S. House of Representatives. *Hinds' Precedents of the House of Representatives of the United States,* by Asher C. Hinds. 59th Cong., 2d. sess., 1907. Vol 2, chap. 43.

PAUL S. RUNDQUIST

DELEGATION OF POWERS. Following the political philosophy of John Locke, as exemplified by the U.S. constitutional system of separate powers, it is thought that a power originally given cannot be delegated away. This nondelegation doctrine would appear to limit Congress's authority to transfer power to another branch of government. In reality, however, Congress has been forced to delegate to accomplish the breadth of its policy-making tasks, so that "the exertion of legislative power does not become a futility."

Historically, the Supreme Court has given a variety of interpretations to the delegation doctrine. The Court first approved congressional delegation to the executive in *The Brig Aurora v. United States* (1813). Then, in 1935, the Court invalidated legislative delegation in two domestic cases involving the National Industrial Recovery Act (NIRA): *Panama Refining Co. v. Ryan* and *Schechter Poultry Corp. v. United States.* Delegating to the president the right to take statutory action under NIRA to alter prices, production, and competition, the Court ruled that the transfer of power was too broad a delegation of independent authority. It would leave the executive branch virtually "unfettered" in its authority to regulate trade and industry.

Only one year after the *Panama* and *Schechter* cases, the Court sustained a congressional delegation of authority to the executive branch in the area of foreign affairs. In *United States v. Curtiss-Wright Corp.* (1936), Congress had given the president permission to ban the sale of arms to two South American countries involved in armed conflict. More than half a century later, during the 1987 Iran-contra hearings, several individuals testified that actions taken under the Reagan administration in the area of foreign affairs could be traced to the delegation of power articulated and upheld in *Curtiss-Wright.* The Iran-contra committee (the House Select Committee to Investigate Covert Arms Transactions with Iran), however, rejected such a "blanket endorsement of plenary presidential power" in the area of a delegated foreign policy. Although the *Curtiss-Wright* decision was not used to justify action in the Iran-contra controversy, the decision did represent the Court's firm commitment to validating legislative delegation in the majority of its future cases.

Congress has continued to use its power to delegate to administrative agencies the authority to implement certain public policies. For example, in *Skinner v. Mid-American Pipelines* (1989), Congress delegated to the Department of Transportation the right to establish fees for pipeline users, and in *Mistretta v. United States* (1989), the Supreme Court upheld legislative delegation to the U.S. Sentencing Commission of the responsibility to formulate guidelines for federal judges in establishing sentences for federal offenses. Although delegation of legislative authority remains a significant part of the U.S. constitutional system, compelling questions remain. For example, what are the limits of delegated authority? How does Congress monitor the power it delegates and, finally, how are administrative agencies held accountable for the authority they are delegated? These will remain important concerns for the Supreme Court as it continues to interpret the delegation doctrine.

[*See also* United States v. Curtiss-Wright Corp.]

BIBLIOGRAPHY

Corwin, Edward, and Jack Peltason. *Understanding the Constitution.* 1991.

Rossum, Ralph, and Alan Tarr. *American Constitutional Law.* 1991.

JANIS JUDSON

DEMOCRATIC PARTY. The Democratic party emerged in the latter years of the eighteenth century in opposition to the dominant Federalist party. Some adherents were followers of Thomas Jefferson and his limited-government theories. Others took the side of France against England in the wars in Europe. Still others joined the party in opposition to Alexander Hamilton's economic program. Regionally, its strength was greatest in the frontier areas of the South and West and among farmers.

In Congress, the first open expression of Democratic partisanship was a meeting of followers of Jefferson who caucused on 2 April 1796 to formulate a strategy to defeat the appropriations bill attached to Jay's Treaty with Britain. Jefferson's followers in Congress were called, variously, Republicans, Democratic-Republicans, or Jeffersonians. It is difficult to detect patterns of party voting in the first three Congresses, but by the Fourth Congress (1795–1797) a majority of Republicans were voting en bloc against a majority of Federalists.

The Democratic Party in the Jacksonian Era.
In the period between 1804 and 1824, Democratic-Republican strength in the House ranged from a high of 87 percent of all seats in 1824 to a low, during the War of 1812, of 58 percent. In the Senate, party strength never dipped below 65 percent of the total membership and was as high as 91 percent.

The party in this early period was less a reflection of consistent ideological or policy agreement among members than it was a loose alignment of factions headed by such political notables as Henry Clay of Kentucky, John Quincy Adams of Massachusetts, and Andrew Jackson of Tennessee. By 1824, the common interests uniting these groups had come apart as each of the principals vied for the presidency. While Adams won the 1824 presidential election, the use of the party caucus in Congress to nominate the party's presidential candidates was abandoned, and alternative nominating devices came into use. The chief antagonist of the caucus system of nomination was Andrew Jackson, who won the presidency in 1828.

Jackson's liaison to his supporters in Congress was former senator Martin Van Buren, a powerful political leader from New York. Jackson had serious political differences with John C. Calhoun, his first vice president, and the Senate, where Calhoun presided, was less friendly territory to Jackson than the House, where, until the election of 1836, Jacksonians predominated. In institutional terms, Jackson's two terms marked a turning away from legislative dominance. Party strategy was set by a "kitchen cabinet" of Jackson advisers, only some of whom were members of Congress.

A combination of the economic crisis in 1837 and agitation over slavery came to divide the Democratic-Republican forces in Congress. The political opposition, the National Republicans (later the Whigs), increased their strength in both houses and frustrated the legislative initiatives of Jackson's successor, Martin Van Buren.

The Jackson–Van Buren period was one of greatly broadened political participation through the vehicle of the mass party. The prerogatives of the presidency were asserted against the claims of Congress for supremacy, but Jackson continued the Jeffersonian tradition of small government.

A Divided Party in the Era of Sectionalism.
Southern sectionalism was strongest within the Democratic party, and a split between Jackson and Calhoun caused the latter to resign from the vice presidency in 1833. Although the proximate cause of the split was Calhoun's opposition to higher tariffs, slavery was to be the issue that would plague the party in the next two decades. Given the party's strong geographical base in the South, maintaining a national majority resulted in Democratic presidential candidates who were, typically, "northern men with southern principles."

The year 1840 marked the first time that the name *Democratic party* was formally used, but in that year the Democrats lost both the presidency and both houses of Congress.

After the death of victorious Whig presidential candidate William Henry Harrison, his successor, John Tyler, encountered political problems, and the Democrats regained control in the 1842 election. But the abiding question of slavery and the prosecution of the Mexican War by Democrat James K. Polk, who was elected in 1844, gave the House back to the Whigs in 1846. Overall in this period, the Democrats were dominant in Congress, controlling both houses in five of seven Congresses between 1840 and 1854.

The preeminent Democratic figure throughout the 1830s and 1840s in Congress was unquestionably John C. Calhoun. Until his death in 1850, he symbolized the powerful southern wing of the party in the Senate. Because the balance of forces between North and South was more nearly equal in the Senate and because the increasing size of the House made it necessary to limit debate, the great sectional debates took place in the Senate.

The congressional Democrat who was the major figure of the 1850s was Stephen A. Douglas of Illinois. His Kansas-Nebraska bill set the agenda for Congress at mid-decade, but his efforts to advance the bill, which Douglas saw as a compromise to avert civil war, were stoutly resisted in the North. Democrats remained comfortably in control in the Senate in the late 1850s, outnumbering Whigs and others in the 34th Congress (1855–1857) by almost 3 to 1. In the House, the forces were more evenly balanced, with Republicans and Whigs outnumbering Democrats in the 34th Congress 108 to 83 and maintaining a bare majority in the two succeeding Congresses that preceded the Civil War.

The election of 1856 changed the composition of the Democratic membership of the House and Senate in an ominous way. Before the Kansas-Nebraska Act was passed, the Democrats in both houses were

CINCINNATI DEMOCRATIC CONVENTION. Voting for presidential candidates on the seventeenth and final ballot. Wood engraving, *Frank Leslie's Illustrated Newspaper,* June 1856.   LIBRARY OF CONGRESS

regionally balanced. Now southern Democrats predominated: 75 to 53 in the House and 25 to 12 in the Senate. This intrapartisan realignment stripped Douglas of much of his power base.

In December 1858, the Democratic caucus in the Senate, which had responsibility for the party's committee assignments, stripped Douglas of his chairmanship of the Committee on Territories. This was the first time on record that a senator had ever been ousted from a chairmanship.

The Civil War and Republican Dominance. The coming of the Civil War and the resignation of Southern members hit the Democrats hardest because of their strong base in the seceding states. But even some Northern Democrats came under a cloud of suspicion for harboring pro-Southern sympathies. The most dramatic evidence of the effects of the secession on congressional Democrats was the number of seats they lost. In the 37th Congress (1861–1863) Senate Republicans outnumbered Democrats 31 to 10. So small was their number that they suspended caucus meetings. There were 101 House Democrats in the 36th Congress, only 42 in the 37th.

If the Democrats dominated the pre–Civil War House and Senate, the postwar period was one of Republican supremacy. It would be 1875 before the Democrats would again be the majority party in the House and 1879 before they would outnumber Republicans in the Senate. By 1877, Reconstruction had set the stage for a measure of party competition in Congress that had been lacking so long as the Democrats' southern wing was not represented. The resumption of their seats by southern Democrats coincided roughly with a financial panic that swept the country in 1875. This, combined with scandals in the administration of Ulysses S. Grant, led to a Democratic takeover of the House in the election of 1874. But the financial problems of the mid-1870s also had the effect of introducing a major new policy dimension to party competition, with newly invigorated Democrats championing a

DEMOCRATIC RALLY. Union Square, New York City. Engraving, after Thomas Nast, *Frank Leslie's Illustrated Newspaper*, September 1856.

variety of inflationist policies and Republicans, in general, adhering to hard money and tight credit. Tariffs, monetary policies, and race relations in the South were the dominant issues of the period after the Civil War, with congressional Democrats generally in favor of low tariffs and inflationary monetary policies, and opposed to the Republican "force bills" designed to prevent intimidation of blacks in the South.

Among the leading congressional Democrats of the post–Civil War era were Ohio senator George H. Pendleton, who introduced an important measure to pay off the national debt in greenback currency. He was also author of the Pendleton Act, which created the federal civil service. House Speaker Samuel J. Randall of Pennsylvania (1876–1881) made important institutional changes, such as a major revision of House rules, the establishment of a five-member Rules Committee chaired by the Speaker, and the use of committee assignments to advance legislation that he favored. John G. Carlisle of Ken-

tucky became Speaker in 1883 and served until 1889. He was the first Speaker to use his power of recognition to dispose of motions with which he disagreed, but even that assertion of power failed to give him the ability to work the majority's will in the face of delaying tactics by the Republicans.

Throughout the 1890s, partisan control in the House shifted back and forth between Democrats and Republicans, with Thomas B. Reed wielding the gavel for the Republicans and Charles F. Crisp of Georgia for the Democrats. Crisp expanded still further the powers of the Rules Committee as an instrument of the Speaker.

While the Senate lends itself less to strong leaders, one figure did emerge in the last decade of the nineteenth century: Arthur Pue Gorman of Maryland. Chosen to head the party caucus in 1889, Gorman not only was a major figure in the Senate but had been an influential backer of Grover Cleveland in his first presidential campaign. Democratic influence in the Senate was limited in the period between 1885 and 1900. Democrats controlled the Senate only for the two-year period of the 53d Congress (1893–1895). This was not a period of glory for either party in the Senate. The term *pork barrel* arose, as Democratic and Republican senators agreeably endorsed one another's river and harbors bills. But it was an era that also saw the creation of the Interstate Commerce Commission, in response to abuses by the railroads, as well as the landmark Sherman Antitrust Act. Splits within the Democratic party over such things as monetary policy reduced the effectiveness of its members in both the House and Senate.

The Democrats from Progressivism to the New Deal. A split in the Republican party at the end of the first decade of the twentieth century gave Democrats their first opportunity in forty years to challenge Republican dominance in Congress. In the House, Democrats led by James Beauchamp (Champ) Clark of Missouri joined with progressive Republicans to limit the power of Speaker Joseph G. Cannon. The first election after the "revolt against Cannonism" in 1910 saw control of the chamber pass to the Democrats for the first time since 1895. Having stripped the speakership of much of its power, House Democrats used the caucus to organize. While Champ Clark was chosen Speaker, real power resided in the hands of Oscar W. Underwood of Alabama, the majority leader.

In the Senate, a leadership vacuum that had prevailed since the death of Gorman in 1906 was filled by John Worth Kern of Indiana, who was elected caucus chairman in 1913. Kern in the Senate and Clark and Underwood in the House worked closely with Woodrow Wilson after his 1912 election to the presidency, and Congress saw an unprecedented degree of coordination between a Democratic president and Democratic leaders on Capitol Hill. Landmark legislation enacted during this period was the resolution that initiated the income tax amendment, the creation of the Federal Reserve System, and the Seventeenth Amendment, which provided for direct election of senators. These reforms were an outgrowth of the progressive movement, which had influenced the party since William Jennings Bryan's nomination in 1896.

The split within the Democratic ranks over the course of foreign policy after World War I, the loss of both houses to the Republicans in the 1918 elections, and the loss of the White House in 1920 ushered in a decade of Republican dominance in Congress. It was not until the 1930 elections, in the midst of the Great Depression, that the party was able to organize the House by a narrow margin, and it was 1933 before the Democrats were again the majority in the Senate.

The New Deal and Fair Deal Democrats. In the 1930s, economic issues were paramount and served to unite the party. President Franklin D. Roosevelt's leaders in Congress were Sen. Joseph T. Robinson of Arkansas and Senate Finance Committee chairman Pat Harrison of Mississippi. Roosevelt's 1932 running mate was House Speaker John Nance Garner of Texas, who played an important role in coordinating New Deal activity with his successor in the speakership, Henry T. Rainey of Illinois, and floor leader Joseph W. Byrns of Tennessee. Another important presidential ally was Rules Committee chairman Edward W. Pou of North Carolina, whose use of the closed rule limiting debate and floor amendments facilitated the passage of New Deal legislation.

Roosevelt's successful first term culminated in his victory over Gov. Alfred M. Landon in 1936, but his second term was clouded by his effort to expand the size of the Supreme Court to dilute the strength of conservative justices who had invalidated some New Deal legislation. The so-called Court-packing scheme of 1937 prompted the arrival of a conservative coalition of Republicans and southern Democrats who united to foil Roosevelt's plan. The coalition has endured as one of the more or less permanent ideological alignments in Congress. Relations between the White House and Congress suffered further by Roosevelt's decision to "purge" conservatives by campaigning actively for their defeat in the 1938 congressional elections. His three main targets were all reelected.

Roosevelt's foreign policy in the late 1930s involved working around a series of neutrality acts passed by Congress, and his effort to extend the temporary draft in 1940 required the energetic efforts of the new House Speaker, Sam Rayburn of Texas, who became one of the president's most reliable allies. Alben W. Barkley of Kentucky was Roosevelt's loyal ally in the Senate until 1944, when the president vetoed a wartime appropriations bill against Barkley's advice. The majority leader resigned his post in protest but was reelected overwhelmingly at the same time that Roosevelt's veto was overridden.

Roosevelt died in April 1945, never having repaired his breach with congressional Democrats. His successor, former Missouri senator Harry S. Truman, was frustrated by southern conservatives in his efforts to pass a fair-employment-practices bill as part of his Fair Deal, an extension of the New Deal. International-minded Democrats provided the support for Truman's Greek-Turkish aid bill, the Marshall Plan to rebuild Western Europe after World War II, and the North Atlantic Treaty, and thus established the party as committed to active U.S. involvement in world affairs.

Democrats lost control of the 80th Congress in the 1946 elections, but Truman's upset victory over Thomas E. Dewey in 1948 swept the Democrats back into the majority in both houses. However, the victory of Republican Dwight D. Eisenhower in the 1952 presidential election provided long enough coattails for the Republicans to recapture both houses.

Toward a New Frontier and a Great Society. The advent of the Eisenhower years set the stage for a unique period in Senate history. In the eight years between 1951 and 1959, Democratic and Republican strength differed by only one or two seats. It was in this environment that Lyndon B. Johnson of Texas became the Democrats' floor leader, a position in which he exerted an unprecedented degree of control. Johnson's slender majorities in the 84th and 85th Congresses (1955–1959) brought him into close cooperation with the Eisenhower White House to pass seemingly incremental but symbolically important legislation such as the 1957 Civil Rights Act.

Johnson's dominant position was undermined by the very success that Senate Democratic candidates encountered in the 1958 elections. An increase of fifteen seats, mostly northern and western liberals, filled the Senate with members more anxious for combat than cooperation with the Republican president.

The election also increased the Democratic majority in the House, but the control by conservatives of key House committees threatened the program of President John F. Kennedy, elected in 1960. Liberal House Democrats in that year established the Democratic Study Group (DSG) to develop strategy to use against the conservative Rules Committee chairman, Howard W. Smith of Virginia. Cooperating with Speaker Rayburn, the DSG defeated Smith's forces narrowly to "liberalize" the committee and open the way for Kennedy's New Frontier legislation. Kennedy did somewhat better with his legislative program in the Senate than in the House, where southern conservative Democrats held about one hundred seats, or slightly less than 40 percent of the total of Democratic seats in the chamber. By the beginning of the next decade that

percentage had fallen to about 30 percent. Southern Democrats in the Senate declined from about a third of the membership in 1960 to only about a quarter in the 1980s, but it was more than the regional composition of the two chambers that changed during the 1960s and 1970s.

After the assassination of President Kennedy and the victory of his successor, Lyndon B. Johnson, in 1964, a huge Democratic House class of 295 members entered with the 89th Congress and, with the leadership of the DSG, served as a major force for institutional reform. While Democratic numbers in the House diminished somewhat after 1964, another peak in Democratic strength in the House after the election of 1974—the so-called Watergate class—gave new impetus to reform.

Democrats and Congressional Reform. Reform in the early 1970s included the creation of a twenty-four-member Steering and Policy Committee, under control of the Speaker, to make Democratic committee assignments. That power was formerly vested in the Ways and Means Committee. With support from the Democratic class of 1974, DSG chairman Philip Burton of California led a revolt against senior committee chairmen. During this period, the Speaker was given the power to select members of the Rules Committee, and the power of the caucus to approve nominations of committee chairs and other assignments was established. These reforms had the effect of restoring some of the powers of the speakership that had been taken away in the revolt against Cannonism in 1910, but they also strengthened the membership through the enhancement of the caucus. While the role of the caucus had waxed and waned over the years, it assumed an important role in the 1981–1983 period, with the attempt to delineate party policy in the aftermath of the party's loss of the White House and Senate in the 1980 elections.

The Democratic imprint on the Senate was less dramatic. The modification of Rule XXII in 1975, which facilitated cloture, and Senate Resolution 60 of the same year, which expanded committee staff for senators, were products of Democratic majorities but are less distinctively partisan reforms. The bipartisan nature of the Senate and the narrower margins by which the party has typically controlled the body since 1954 (except for the years 1981–1987) made for a different pattern of reform. Some modest diffusion of leadership responsibilities was implemented by Majority Leader George J. Mitchell, who was chosen in 1989.

America's oldest political party used its time out

of presidential power in the 1980s to debate whether the traditional egalitarianism of the party had become too hostile to economic growth and whether the party had become too rigidly antibusiness. Recapturing the White House in 1992 on a traditional Democratic promise to create jobs, the Democrats, under President Bill Clinton, altered some of their stimulative fiscal policies to accommodate deficit reduction and incentives to investment. What differentiates Democrats most starkly from Republicans in the 1990s are issues of social policy. Democrats are consistently more supportive of the extension of civil rights and privacy rights than Republicans and inclined to press more strongly for environmental controls and consumer protection.

[*See also* Democratic Study Group. *For discussion of Thomas Jefferson's followers in Congress, see* Jeffersonian Republicans.]

BIBLIOGRAPHY

Goldman, Ralph M. *Search for Consensus: The Story of the Democratic Party.* 1979.

Ladd, Everett Carll, Jr., and Charles D. Hadley. *Transformations of the American Party System.* 1978.

Nichols, Roy F. *The Invention of the American Political Parties.* 1967.

Parmet, Herbert S. *The Democrats.* 1976.

Rutland, Robert A. *The Democrats.* 1979.

Silbey, Joel H. *The Partisan Imperative.* 1985.

ROSS K. BAKER

DEMOCRATIC-REPUBLICANS. *See* Jeffersonian Republicans.

DEMOCRATIC STUDY GROUP. The Democratic Study Group (DSG) is a legislative service organization (LSO) in the House of Representatives. Founded in 1959 as a liberal counterpoint to the influence of senior conservatives and southern Democrats, it now consists of nearly all Democratic members of the House. The oldest and best known LSO in Congress, it has the largest budget and staff. While only Democrats may join formally, any House member can subscribe to the DSG's numerous legislative reports, policy analyses, and research services.

The DSG is led by a chairman, who is limited to a single two-year term of service, elected by the entire membership at the beginning of each Congress. An executive committee, also elected biennially,

meets several times each month to discuss political and legislative issues and to receive guest speakers. The full membership normally convenes only to elect officers at the beginning of a Congress. The DSG is managed on a day-to-day basis by an executive director hired by the chairman and executive committee.

The DSG's principal activity is to disseminate detailed written materials to members of the House about upcoming legislation and policy issues, which it does on a daily basis when the chamber is in session. It has become so closely identified with this function that Democratic members normally look first to the DSG, rather than to the party leadership or House committees, as the primary source for analysis of legislation. Its publications are widely respected for their accuracy, thoroughness, political relevance, and timeliness.

The DSG evolved during the 1950s, when many progressive Democrats saw their policy goals frustrated by a conservative coalition that dominated the institution through the seniority system, often with the support of Democratic party leaders, committee chairmen, and other senior members. A group of liberals, led initially by Rep. Eugene J. McCarthy (Minn.), met from 1956 to 1959 to discuss strategies for change and to organize a continuing entity that would serve their policy goals, "whip" members on key votes, and promote major institutional reforms. The first chairman of the new organization was Rep. Lee Metcalf (Mont.). Two later chairmen of the DSG went on to hold major leadership roles in the House—Thomas S. Foley (Wash.), who became Speaker in 1989, and Phillip Burton (Calif.), Democratic Caucus chairman (1974–1976) and unsuccessful candidate for majority leader. Other prominent leaders in the organization during its early years and through the House's most active reform period of the 1970s were John A. Blatnik (Minn.), Frank Thompson, Jr. (N.J.), James G. O'Hara (Mich.), Donald M. Fraser (Minn.), Abner Mikva (Ill.), David Obey (Wis.), and the DSG's influential executive director from 1968 to 1988, Richard P. Conlon.

The DSG instigated and coordinated many of the reforms that democratized the House, weakened the seniority system, restrained the independence of committee chairs, and strengthened the political and procedural powers of the House leadership.

Major reforms in which the DSG played a significant role were: expanding the size of the Rules Committee to prevent its blockage of President Kennedy's legislative program (1961); requiring regular monthly meetings of the Democratic Caucus (1969); requiring recorded votes in the Committee of the Whole (1971); limiting the ability of senior members to hold multiple subcommittee chairmanships (1971); giving subcommittees a "Bill of Rights" that delineated their powers and permitted subcommittee chairs to hire at least one staffer (1971, 1973); requiring automatic secret ballot election of committee chairs by the Democratic Caucus (1973); opening House committee meetings to the public (1973); creating a Steering and Policy Committee chaired by the Speaker to make recommendations on policy (1973) and assign members to committees (1974); and letting the Speaker nominate all Rules Committee Democrats (1974).

Following the reformist zeal of the 1970s, the DSG's original insurgent role in the House evolved into one of close cooperation with the party leadership and increased focus on legislative policy studies. With the return of institutional reform as a major issue in 1992 and during the 103d Congress, the DSG advocated more rapid organization of the House and its committees and more effective scheduling of business on the House floor, and served as the prime mover in the creation of the Speaker's Working Group on Policy Development, which was intended to become the House's agenda-setting mechanism and to promote the Clinton administration's legislative program.

BIBLIOGRAPHY

Democratic Study Group. *Reform in the House of Representatives.* 1 December 1992. Internal report prepared for the organization of the 103d Congress.

U.S. Congress. *Congressional Record.* 100th Cong., 2d sess., 31 March 1988. See Mike Lowry, "Tribute to Richard P. Conlon on Twentieth Anniversary at DSG," pp. E936–E938.

MATT PINKUS

DEMOGRAPHICS OF CONGRESS. *See* Members, *article on* Demographic Profile.

DEPOSITORY INSTITUTIONS DEREGULATION AND MONETARY CONTROL ACT OF 1980 (94 Stat. 132–193). Aimed at deregulating financial institutions, the Depository Institutions Deregulation and Monetary Control Act (DIDMCA) of 1980 in many ways extended federal control over the financial sector. In the 1970s, scores of businesses started to encroach on financial activities that traditionally had been the domain of banks—stock brokers offered money market funds on which clients could write checks, department stores such as Sears expanded their credit card programs, and savings and loans institutions and credit unions broadened their activities to offer special accounts that resembled checking accounts but paid higher rates. At the same time as banks faced increased competition from nonbank businesses, their own profit margins started to shrink due to the rising interest rates of the late 1970s. Banks lobbied for the privilege of offering similar accounts and pressed for reductions in Federal Reserve capital requirements. Federal Reserve officials supported the concept of lowering the requirements on banks if the banks would acquiesce in giving the Federal Reserve greater power to regulate banking and money in other areas. Paul Volcker, chairman of the Federal Reserve, and two former chairmen, Arther Burns and G. William Miller, also supported a bill that would trade private financial deregulation for increased federal control over the monetary system. The result was DIDMCA, which passed with virtually no dissenting votes. Thus Congress leveled the playing field between savings and loans and banks. DIDMCA also phased out Federal Reserve Bank ceilings on interest rates paid on time deposits, allowing the rate to fluctuate with the market.

Some provisions of the law, such as restricting the conditions under which foreign institutions could take over U.S. banks, reflected the economic and political climate of the day. Title I, however, expanded the Federal Reserve Board's regulatory powers by extending its control over the reserve requirements of all banks, including nonmembers. Any institution that issued checks or was eligible for deposit insurance fell under the Federal Reserve's newly expanded scope.

Finally, DIDMCA allowed "eligible collateral" for Federal Reserve Notes to include foreign obligations, meaning that the United States could intervene in foreign securities markets, even to the extent of monetizing the debt of a bankrupt country.

BIBLIOGRAPHY

McNeill, Charles R. "The Depository Institutions Deregulation and Monetary Control Act of 1980." *Federal Reserve Bulletin* 66 (June 1980): 444–453.

Timberlake, Richard H., Jr. "Legislative Construction of the Monetary Control Act of 1980." *American Economic Review* 75 (May 1985): 97–102.

LARRY SCHWEIKART

DE PRIEST, OSCAR

DE PRIEST, OSCAR (1871–1951), Republican from Illinois, first African American representative ever elected from a northern state. Oscar De Priest was born in Florence, Alabama, to former slaves. He grew up in Salina, Kansas, where he attended an integrated grade school. In 1889, De Priest moved to Chicago, where he became the first black alderman. Active in pursuing civil rights and employment opportunities for blacks, De Priest was noted for his skills as a propagandist and an organizer, and he generally kept a high profile.

In 1929, De Priest became the first black representative elected to Congress in thirty years. Thus, in a sense, he represented all eleven million African Americans in the United States and had to respond to constituency claims from all over the nation. He became a national celebrity. To the ire of southern whites, First Lady Lou Hoover invited Mrs. Jesse De Priest, along with other congressional wives, to a White House tea. Mrs. De Priest's presence triggered state resolutions condemning the social mixing of blacks and whites.

De Priest tried unsuccessfully to desegregate the House restaurant. Most of his efforts, however, were directed toward legislation protecting his national black constituency. In 1931, he introduced a bill proposing monthly pensions to ex-slaves over the age of seventy-five, and in 1933 he added an antidiscrimination clause to a $300 million bill for unemployment relief and reforestation. In 1934, he tried unsuccessfully to pass a bill holding local officials responsible for the lynching of prisoners held in their care.

Other than lobbying for improved civil rights legislation, De Priest was not particularly active in Congress. He served on the committees on Enrolled Bills, Indian Affairs, and Invalid Pensions. Reelected in 1932, De Priest was defeated by Arthur W. Mitchell, a black Democrat, in 1934.

BIBLIOGRAPHY

Christopher, Maurine. *Black Americans in Congress.* 1976.
Ragsdale, Bruce, and Joel D. Treese. *Black Americans in Congress, 1870–1989.* 1990.
Gosnell, Harold F. *Negro Politicians: The Rise of Negro Politics in Chicago.* 1935.

CAROL M. SWAIN

DEREGULATION. *See* Regulation and Deregulation.

DESCHLER, LEWIS

DESCHLER, LEWIS (1905–1976), parliamentarian of the House of Representatives from 1928 until 1974. Born in Chillocothe, Ohio, in 1905, he attended Miami University and came to Washington in 1925 to continue his higher education at George Washington University. He was appointed by Nicholas Longworth, the Republican representative from Ohio who was then serving as Speaker of the House, to the position of timekeeper, a job that placed him at the rostrum of the House and provided the unique opportunity to observe and learn House procedure. A student of the House rules, he learned quickly, advanced to the position of assistant parliamentarian in 1927, and succeeded Lehr Fess as parliamentarian in 1928. He continued to serve in that position for the next forty-four years, during the speakerships of Henry T. Rainey, Joseph W. Byrns, William B. Bankhead, Sam Rayburn, Joseph W. Martin, Jr., John W. McCormack, and Carl B. Albert. He stepped down as parliamentarian in July 1974, but continued as a special parliamentary consultant to the Speaker and began a compilation of the precedents of the House. His compilation efforts were suspended on his death in 1976, but the project was renewed by his successor as parliamentarian, William Holmes Brown, and by others in that office.

Deschler's expertise in shepherding legislation through the House was widely recognized, and as a confidant and adviser of Speaker Rayburn his

OSCAR DE PRIEST.   LIBRARY OF CONGRESS

knowledge of the precedents was instrumental in various legislative victories, such as the quick passage of the early New Deal legislative package in the famous one hundred days of activity at the beginning of the Franklin D. Roosevelt era, and the admission of Alaska and Hawaii into the Union. An acknowledged expert on parliamentary procedure, he authored *Deschler's Rules of Order*, published shortly before his death.

BIBLIOGRAPHY

U.S. House of Representatives. *Deschler's Precedents of the United States House of Representatives*, by Lewis Deschler. 94th Cong., 2d sess., 1977. H. Doc. 94-661.

WILLIAM HOLMES BROWN

DILATORY MOTIONS.

Dilatory motions are proposed by representatives and senators solely or primarily to delay legislative action, not to achieve a constructive policy or procedural effect.

Clause 10 of House Rule XVI directs that "[n]o dilatory motion shall be entertained by the Speaker." The House first adopted this rule in 1890 to codify the principle that members should not be able to make motions that are intended only to prevent the House from working its will. This principle is especially important in the House because the general theory underlying its procedures is that a majority of its members should be able to control their legislative agenda and the amount of time they devote to debating each matter they consider.

The Senate has no comparable rule. Since the late 1970s, however, the Senate has established several precedents that permit the presiding officer to rule amendments, motions, and other actions out of order as being dilatory after cloture has been invoked on a matter. The rationale for these precedents is that dilatory actions are incompatible with the purpose of cloture, which is to enable the Senate to vote on a matter by limiting further consideration of it while still giving senators ample opportunities to debate seriously and to amend it.

There are no fixed criteria for determining when a proposed action is dilatory. The decision necessarily involves a subjective judgment. The Speaker and the Senate's presiding officer rule actions to be dilatory only under what they consider to be extreme and obvious circumstances.

[*See also* Cloture.]

BIBLIOGRAPHY

U.S. House of Representatives. *Deschler's Precedents of the United States House of Representatives*, by Lewis Deschler. 94th Cong., 2d sess., 1977. H. Doc. 94-661. Vol. 7, pp. 77–84.

STANLEY BACH

DIRKSEN, EVERETT M.

(1896–1969), Republican representative and senator from Illinois, Senate minority leader (1959–1969). Forsaking early endeavors in small business and the theater, Everett McKinley Dirksen won a seat in the U.S. House of Representatives in 1932, first defeating a Republican incumbent in the primary and then overcoming the Democratic landslide that elected Franklin D. Roosevelt president in the general election. Representing the Republican heartland around Peoria, Illinois, he served eighteen years in the House and built a solid record as a constructive minority member. He served on the Appropriations Committee from 1937 to 1949, and in September 1941, he renounced his traditional isolationism in foreign affairs. During the 80th Congress (1947–1949), he served as chairman of the District of Columbia Committee and the Appropriations Subcommittee on Agriculture. In one magazine's 1946 rankings, he was listed as overall the second most able member in the House. With his eyesight failing, however, he retired from the House in 1949, only to have his health improve to the extent that he could run for the U.S. Senate in 1950 against the sitting majority leader, Scott W. Lucas. Dirksen triumphed and entered the Senate in 1951, where he was to begin a distinguished eighteen-year career.

Dirksen's first few years in the Senate, however, bore only the faintest glimmers of distinction. He quickly became identified with the conservative "old guard" within the body and, perhaps more significantly, he distanced himself from his internationalist positions of the 1940s. Ambitious for national office, he squelched his chances in the 1952 Republican convention with a public attack on former presidential candidate Thomas E. Dewey. Still, Dirksen maintained good relations with President Dwight D. Eisenhower, who nurtured continuing ties with him despite the senator's conservative rhetoric. By 1955 Dirksen had begun his movement back to moderate conservatism and toward leadership positions within the Senate.

Republican senators chose Dirksen as their whip in 1957 and elected him minority leader two years later. Although some moderates opposed his elevation to this position, within two years virtually all factions backed him as an effective leader. Dirksen essentially refashioned the role of the Senate minority leader. He forged very strong working rela-

EVERETT M. DIRKSEN. In April 1965.
LIBRARY OF CONGRESS

tionships with Democratic Senate majority leaders Lyndon B. Johnson and, especially, Mike Mansfield. Dirksen served as the public leader of the Republicans during much of the 1960s, and worked closely with Presidents John F. Kennedy and Lyndon Johnson. Holding weekly news conferences, Dirksen, nicknamed the "Wizard of Ooze," would rhapsodize on the policies and politics of the day and by doing so kept Republican views in the news in an era of Democratic dominance. Faced with the difficult task of affecting policy while leading a legislative faction that never exceeded thirty-eight senators between 1958 and 1968, Dirksen led by cajoling his peers, not by attempting to coerce them.

With his ever-present cigarette, substantial stature, carefully tousled white mane, and almost lyrical orations, Dirksen found a ready audience in the press corps. The minority leader would dole out bits of new information, which he often gleaned from his ongoing communications with Democratic presidents and legislative leaders. Indeed, Dirksen's influence began with his press relations and his close personal relationships with Lyndon Johnson and Senate majority leader Mike Mansfield. Republican Senate colleague James Pearson (R-Kans.) observed that "He and Mansfield were enormously close . . . close personal friends. With Johnson it was different. They were close, but it was more an honor among thieves. They understood—they knew what was going on in each other's mind."

Minority Leader Dirksen managed to have a policy impact by carefully husbanding his resources of close ties to Democratic presidents and majority leaders while employing the threat of extended debate (filibuster) to bring the Senate to a halt. With his lifelong penchant for drama, Dirksen became a key actor in various major legislative battles of the 1960s, including the 1963 Limited Nuclear Test Ban Treaty and, especially, the Civil Rights Act of 1964 and the Voting Rights Act of 1965, in which he rallied substantial Republican support that provided the margin of victory for the legislation. At the same time, Dirksen could not effectively press for the enactment of his own ideas, such as an amendment to the Constitution permitting prayer in public schools. There were distinct limits to the power of the minority, no matter how skillfully it was led.

In the late 1960s, leadership became somewhat more problematic for Dirksen. New Republican senators, such as his Illinois colleague Charles H. Percy, were less open to his cajoling style. Moreover, with the election of Richard M. Nixon as president in 1968, Dirksen was no longer the most visible Republican in Washington; ironically, his relations with Nixon were much less cordial than with either Kennedy or Johnson. Never mindful of his health, Dirksen became less vigorous in his seventies. He died in September 1969.

Although only minority leader, Dirksen nevertheless succeeded in having a great impact on the policies of the 1960s; indeed, he may well have been, in those heady times, "the most powerful member of the Senate," as one colleague described him.

BIBLIOGRAPHY

Loomis, Burdett A. "Everett McKinley Dirksen: The Consummate Minority Leader." In *First among Equals.* Edited by Roger Davidson and Richard Baker. 1991.
MacNeil, Neil. *Dirksen.* 1970.
Schapsmeier, Edward L., and Frederick H. Shapsmeier. *Dirksen of Illinois.* 1985.

BURDETT A. LOOMIS

DISABILITY LEGISLATION. Before 1920, Congress dealt with the matter of disability at a distance, such as by granting land for an asylum. The 1920 vocational rehabilitation program provided federal grants for states to counsel people on how to overcome disability and find work.

On 6 July 1943, President Franklin D. Roosevelt signed a new civilian rehabilitation law that permitted the states to fund "corrective surgery." Rep. Graham A. Barden (D-N.C.) and Sen. Robert M. La Follette, Jr. (R-Wis.) worked within the education committees to gain support for the law. The program eventually obtained bipartisan backing. Liberals, such as Sen. Paul H. Douglas (D-Ill.), wanted to expand social services. Conservatives, such as Rep. Daniel A. Reed (R-N.Y.), hoped to put disabled persons to work and reduce welfare loads.

In the 1950s and 1960s, the rehabilitation program benefited from the same forces that aided medical research. Sen. Lister Hill (D-Ala.) and Rep. John E. Fogarty (D-R.I.) used their influence on the appropriations subcommittees and on the authorizing committees to channel money to vocational rehabilitation. The process began with passage of a new rehabilitation law, signed by President Dwight D. Eisenhower on 3 August 1954, that provided training grants for rehabilitation counselors. The expansion of vocational rehabilitation reached a climax in 1968, when Congress increased the federal share of rehabilitation grants to 80 percent.

By 1970, the program was attracting criticism for not attempting to rehabilitate people with severe disabilities and for not respecting its clients' civil rights. In 1973, negotiations between Senators Alan Cranston (D-Calif.) and Jennings Randolph (D-W.Va.) and the White House produced new legislation that highlighted the rehabilitation of the severely disabled. After President Richard M. Nixon vetoed two earlier versions, Congress dropped a demand that this legislation also initiate federal grants for independent living centers (i.e., peer-run residential and vocational assistance centers). In 1978 a new law, signed by President Jimmy Carter with the understanding that its more costly provisions would not be put into effect immediately, provided federal funding for independent living centers. Dramatic oversight hearings by the House Committee on Education and Labor, held in Berkeley, California, a major center of the independent living movement, paved the way for the 1978 law.

In 1973, Congress set disability policy off in new directions by including Section 504 in the rehabilitation law. A staffer who worked for Sen. Jacob K. Javits (R-N.Y.) wanted to apply the protections of Title VI of the Civil Rights Act of 1964 to disabled people. Without further discussion, Congress legislated that someone could not be excluded from the benefits of a federal program "solely by reason of his handicap." After a protracted fight to get the president to sign regulations for this provision, which lasted until 1977, pressure arose to extend civil rights protection beyond public-sector activities to reach private employment and public accommodations. First, Sen. Lowell P. Weicker, Jr. (R-Conn.), and later, Sen. Tom Harkin (D-Iowa), highlighted the issue in the Senate Committee on Labor and Public Welfare. Harkin chaired a Subcommittee on Disability Policy that helped to prepare legislation in the summer of 1989. Sen. Edward M. Kennedy (D-Mass.) and Rep. Tony Coehlo (D-Calif.) also lent their strong support to the Americans with Disabilities Act, which President George Bush signed into law on 26 July 1990.

Even though laws attempting to guarantee civil rights to disabled people have attracted attention in recent years, the nation's primary response to disability remains the awarding of disability pensions through the social security program. This program originated during a Senate debate on 17 July 1956. After the House Committee on Ways and Means, chaired by Jere Cooper (D-Tenn.), had voted to include disability benefits in omnibus social security legislation, the Senate Finance Committee, influenced by Harry Flood Byrd, Sr. (D-Va.), voted to remove disability insurance from the bill. A fight on the Senate floor to restore disability benefits ensued. Sen. Lyndon B. Johnson (D-Tex.) kept wavering Democrats in line, and union representatives marshaled votes from reluctant Republicans (including Wisconsin senator Alexander Wiley). The bill, passed by a two-vote margin, initiated disability benefits for social security contributors, fifty or older, who could prove that they were unable to engage in "substantial gainful employment." Between 1958 and 1972, Congress liberalized the law, adding dependents' benefits (1958), removing the age limitation (1960), liberalizing the definition of disability (1965), and providing disability insurance beneficiaries with health insurance coverage (1972). The House Ways and Means Committee, under the direction of Wilbur D. Mills (D-Ark.), took the lead in permitting each of these expansions.

By the end of the 1970s, disability insurance encountered controversy. Rep. James A. Burke (D-Mass.) headed a newly formed Subcommittee on Social Security. Refined between 1976 and 1978, Burke's bill attempted to reduce the maximum amount a family could receive from disability insurance. When Rep. J. J. (Jake) Pickle (D-Tex.) took over as subcommittee chairman in 1979, he contin-

Landmark Disability Legislation

TITLE	YEAR ENACTED	REFERENCE NUMBER	DESCRIPTION
Smith-Fess Act	1920	P.L. 66-236	Starts rehabilitation program.
Barden–La Follette Act	1943	P.L. 78-113	Expands rehabilitation program.
Vocational Rehabilitation Amendments of 1954	1954	P.L. 83-565	Establishes grants for rehabilitation research and training.
Social Security Amendments of 1956	1956	P.L. 84-880	Begins disability insurance program.
Rehabilitation Act of 1973	1973	P.L. 93-112	Guarantees civil rights of disabled persons.
Rehabilitation, Comprehensive Services, and Developmental Disabilities Amendments	1978	P.L. 95-602	Starts independent living program.
Social Security Disability Amendments of 1980	1980	P.L. 96-265	Attempts cutback on the growth of the disability rolls.
Social Security Disability Benefits Reform Act of 1984	1984	P.L. 98-460	Protects beneficiaries from being removed from the disability rolls.
Americans with Disabilities Act	1990	P.L. 101-336	Extends civil rights protection to private sector activities.

ued Burke's efforts and, with the full committee's acquiescence, brought a disability insurance bill to the House floor on 6 September 1979. Despite opposition from the Rules Committee, this measure cleared both houses, and President Carter signed it on 9 June 1980. The law reduced the chance that someone could make more from disability insurance than from working, and it made it less likely that younger workers could receive higher disability benefits than older, retired workers.

Soon a bitter controversy erupted over an obscure provision of the 1980 law that required "nonpermanently disabled individuals" to be reexamined every three years. The Reagan administration implemented this section with an intensity that had not been foreseen by Congress. By fall 1984, the administration had reviewed the cases of 1.2 million people and informed 490,000 of them that they would lose their benefits.

Congressional indignation led to hearings by oversight committees such as the Senate Governmental Affairs Committee. Between 1981 and 1984, Congress held twenty-seven hearings on removing people from the rolls. In September 1984, a conference committee, led by Representative Pickle and Sen. Bob Dole (R-Mo.), agreed to a measure that put the burden of proof on the government to demonstrate that a person's medical condition had improved before the person could be removed from the disability rolls.

The 1984 law made it harder to remove someone from the disability insurance rolls; the 1990 Americans with Disabilities Act made it easier for people

with disabilities to work. Congress faced the difficult task of reconciling rehabilitation and civil rights policies, on the one hand, with policies granting disabled persons a retirement pension, on the other. This reconciliation lay at the cutting edge of disability policy in the 1990s.

[*See also* Occupational Safety and Health Act of 1970; Social Security Act; Social Welfare and Poverty.]

BIBLIOGRAPHY
Berkowitz, Edward D. *Disabled Policy: America's Programs for the Handicapped—A Twentieth-Century Fund Report.* 1987.
Scotch, Richard. *From Goodwill to Civil Rights.* 1984.
Stone, Deborah. *The Disabled State.* 1984.

EDWARD D. BERKOWITZ

DISCHARGE RULES. Especially in the House, congressional committees play a gatekeeping role, because introduced measures are normally referred to committee and cannot receive floor consideration unless reported. Discharge circumvents this obstacle by taking an unreported measure from the committee charged with it.

The Senate has no explicit discharge rule, but permits a discharge motion. Senators seldom move discharge on a measure, because they can more readily place an identical measure directly on the calendar or offer its text as a nongermane amendment. Discharge occasionally occurs on nominations, where those alternatives are unavailable because only the president can initiate nominations.

The House discharge rule originated from the 1910 revolt against Speaker Joseph G. Cannon's total control of floor action. Though amended several times before 1931, this rule remained vulnerable to dilatory tactics, so that the leadership was able to prevent any measure passing the House by discharge, notably in a session-long blockage of railway labor arbitration (1924–1925). Since 1931, a more effective rule framed by Charles R. Crisp (D-Ga.; former House parliamentarian) has been in effect.

House Rule XXVII, clause 3 today permits a discharge petition to be filed at the clerk's desk on any measure (except a private bill) that a committee has held for thirty legislative days. If half the House membership (218) then signs this petition, the motion is "entered" on a special discharge calendar. On any second or fourth Monday falling at least seven legislative days later, any signer may move discharge. After twenty minutes debate, a majority vote may adopt the motion. The measure then goes to the appropriate calendar unless a nondebatable motion to consider is then offered and agreed to. If this happens, the measure comes up under the general rules of the House (i.e., money bills in Committee of the Whole; others under the one-hour rule). If the discharge motion is rejected, no further discharge action on the same subject can be taken during that session of Congress.

The rule also permits a second method of discharge, designed as the principal one, in which the petition is filed not on the measure itself, but on a special rule for considering it. If supporters of an unreported measure introduce such a rule, and the Rules Committee does not report it within seven legislative days, the supporters may file a petition to discharge that committee. If discharge succeeds and the rule is adopted, the underlying measure comes to the floor under the terms of the special rule rather than the general rules. (Until 1991, a special rule coming up by discharge was neither debatable nor amendable.)

The Rules Committee under conservative coalition control (ca. 1937–1960) often declined to report special rules for considering reported measures, especially New Deal and racial equality legislation. The House often attempted to discharge the committee from special rules on these reported measures. Discharge attempts for special rules on unreported measures were largely forgotten until the 1960s. The Rules Committee then began to su-

persede such attempts by reporting alternative special rules that set the Committee's own terms for considering the measure. By the 1990s, some discharge proponents succeeded in forestalling this response and securing adoption of their own special rules.

Only by discharge can the House consider a measure without cooperation from either the committee of jurisdiction, the Speaker, or the Rules Committee. Yet success by this procedure is difficult. The signature requirement exceeds the majority normally needed for passage. Proponents must hold their majority through several complicated stages. Committee and floor leaders generally oppose discharge as infringing their prerogatives and disruptive, and have several opportunities to recover control of the floor.

Consequently, of 447 petitions filed from 1935 to 1992, only thirty-three were entered, and only two measures became law through use of the rule. Yet discharge may be more successful as a threat. Over the same years, discharge was attempted on twenty-six measures that then came up through other procedures. Of these, twenty-two passed the House and fifteen received final approval.

From 1931 through 1934, only one-third of the House had to sign a discharge petition. Petitions were filed on forty-three measures and entered on eleven (including the veterans' bonus and repeal of prohibition), but only two passed the House. The change to a higher requirement reflected leadership desires to keep from the floor measures that could not pass. Since 1970, discharge has been attempted disproportionately on proposed constitutional amendments (e.g., school busing, school prayer, balanced budget), which require greater support to pass than to discharge.

Discharge petition signatures used to be considered confidential until the full required number signed, with the intent of protecting members from pressure to sign. Nevertheless, signatures to at least five petitions were revealed without authorization, notably on the 1960 civil rights bill. In the 1980s the argument gained strength that abolishing confidentiality would foster accountability, and in 1993, discharge was attempted on a resolution for this purpose. After signatures to this petition were disclosed, the required number were obtained, and the House adopted the rules change.

BIBLIOGRAPHY

U.S. House of Representatives. *Cannon's Precedents of the House of Representatives of the United States*, by

Clarence Cannon. 74th Cong., 1st sess., 1935. Vol. 7, secs. 1007–1023.

U.S. House of Representatives. Committee on Rules. Subcommittee on Rules of the House. *Discharge Petition Disclosure.* 103d Cong., 1st sess., 1993. Hearing.

U.S. House of Representatives. *Deschler's Precedents of the United States House of Representatives.* 94th Cong., 2d sess., 1977. H. Doc. 94-661. Vol. 5, chap. 18.

RICHARD S. BETH

DISCIPLINE OF MEMBERS.

The Constitution expressly authorizes each house of Congress to discipline its own members. Article I, section 5, clause 2 states that "Each House may determine the Rules of its Proceedings, punish its Members for disorderly behavior, and, with the Concurrence of two thirds, expel a Member." Even without express constitutional authority to do so, however, the disciplining of members of a legislative body has been recognized as an inherent authority of the institution to protect its own integrity and proceedings.

Discipline of a member by the House or the Senate may take several forms. The most common are expulsion and censure. A censure is a formal procedure in which the full House or the full Senate, by majority vote on a resolution, expresses disapproval of the conduct of a member of that body. An expulsion is a removal of a member from the House or the Senate by a two-thirds vote of that particular body.

In addition, Congress may discipline its members in other ways, including fines, loss of seniority, reprimand, and suspension or loss of certain privileges. It has been suggested in the past that congressional punishment might even extend to imprisonment by the sergeant at arms.

Congress may generally discipline its own members for violations of statutory law, including crimes; for violations of internal congressional rules; or for any conduct that either house of Congress believes reflects discredit upon the institution. Both houses have thus disciplined their own members for conduct that has not necessarily violated any specific rule or law but that was found to demonstrate contempt for the institution or to discredit the House or Senate. When the most severe sanction of expulsion has been employed, however, the conduct has historically involved either disloyalty to the United States or the conviction of a crime, such as bribery, involving the abuse of one's official position.

While resolutions for censure or expulsion in the House or Senate once were routinely referred either to ad hoc special committees or to standing committees with jurisdictions in other areas, such as the Judiciary or Rules committees, in the 1960s standing committees were created in both the House and Senate to deal exclusively with internal ethics and matters of official conduct. The House Committee on Standards of Official Conduct, formed in 1967, and the Senate Select Committee on Ethics, originally formed in 1964 as the Select Committee on Standards and Conduct, have promulgated detailed procedures to ensure fairness and to protect due process rights in investigations of and proceedings regarding members charged with ethical improprieties

A resolution introduced for disciplining a member will generally be referred to the respective ethics committee in the House or the Senate. Both committees may also initiate investigations and ethics proceedings on their own accord or investigate a matter raised by a formal complaint filed with the committee by a member of Congress or an outside party. Unlike most other congressional committees, the ethics panels are made up of an equal number of Democrats and Republicans to ensure some degree of bipartisanship and consensus. If discipline of a member is deemed warranted by a majority of the committee after proceedings have been held, the committee brings a resolution, along with a report, to the full House or Senate for consideration. The House or Senate may accept the committee's recommendation for discipline, reject it, or substitute the body's own chosen form of discipline, which may be more or less severe than that recommended by the committee.

Expulsion. Expulsion is the form of discipline in which the Senate or the House, after a member has taken the oath of office, removes that senator or representative from membership by a two-thirds vote of the respective body. An expulsion is considered a disciplinary matter and a matter of protecting the integrity of the institution and its proceedings. An exclusion, on the other hand, is the denial of a member-elect's seat by a simple majority vote prior to his or her seating because of the member-elect's failure to meet the constitutional qualifications for office; exclusion is not intended as a disciplinary procedure.

Other than the two-thirds requirement, there is no apparent limitation, either in the text of the Constitution or in the deliberations of the Framers, on the authority to expel a member of Congress.

The Supreme Court has found an expansive authority and discretion within each house of Congress regarding the grounds and procedures for expulsion, noting that either house may expel a member for conduct which, in the judgment of the body, "is inconsistent with the trust and duty of a member" even if such conduct was "not a statutable offense nor was it committed in his official character, nor was it committed during the session of Congress, nor at the seat of government" (*In re Chapman* [1897]; see also *United States v. Brewster* [1972]). Although the authority to expel seems very broad, Congress has shown self-restraint in employing this form of discipline; generally, it has deferred to the will of the electorate.

Fifteen senators have been expelled, fourteen early in the Civil War for disloyalty to the Union. Ten of them were expelled in a single resolution of 11 July 1861 for having engaged in a "conspiracy for the destruction of the Union and Government, or with full knowledge of such conspiracy hav[ing] failed to advise the Government of its progress or aid in its suppression"; four others were expelled separately in 1861 and 1862 for disloyalty to the Union. The fifteenth was Sen. William Blount of Tennessee, expelled in 1797 for attempting to incite Indians against U.S. government officials as part of a scheme to seize Spanish Florida and Louisiana with British and Indian help.

The House of Representatives has expelled four members, three in 1861 for disloyalty to the Union. The fourth was Michael O. Myers of Pennsylvania, expelled on 2 October 1980. Myers had been convicted of bribery for receiving a payment in return for promising to use his official influence on immigration bills in the so-called Abscam sting operation run by the FBI.

In addition to these expulsions, both House and Senate committees investigating matters of conduct have from time to time recommended the expulsion of other members. In those cases, however, the members resigned from Congress before an expulsion vote could be taken by the full House or Senate.

The authority and power of each house of Congress to expel appears to be at the virtually unbridled discretion of those bodies. However, policy considerations, as opposed to questions of power, have generally restrained the House and Senate in their authority when the conduct complained of occurred before the individual became a member of that chamber or when it occurred in a prior Congress and the electorate, knowing of the conduct, still reelected the member. Such restraint has not necessarily been exercised in censure cases.

Censure. The term *censure*, unlike the term *expel*, does not appear in the Constitution. The concept derives, however, from the same clause in the Constitution that stipulates expulsion—Article I, section 5, clause 2. That article authorizes each house of Congress to "punish its Members for disorderly Behaviour."

In the Senate, a censure has traditionally meant the punishment imposed by the Senate on a member when it adopts, by majority vote, a resolution condemning or disapproving his or her behavior. "Censure" is used to describe the formal action of the Senate in adopting a resolution expressing the Senate's "censure," "condemnation," "denouncement," or general disapproval of a member's conduct, even when the word is not expressly included in the language of the resolution. No forfeiture of rights or privileges automatically follows a censure by the Senate.

In the House of Representatives, a censure is similarly a vote of disapproval by the majority of members present and voting, generally with the additional requirement that the member stand at the well of the House chamber to receive a verbal rebuke and the reading of the censure resolution by the Speaker of the House.

The authority of either house of Congress to discipline its own members by censure has come to be recognized and accepted in congressional practice as extending to cases of misconduct, even outside Congress, that the Senate or House finds to be reprehensible and to reflect discredit on the institution. As the Senate report on the 1954 censure of Sen. Joseph R. McCarthy (R-Wis.) stated: "It seems clear that if a Senator should be guilty of reprehensible conduct unconnected with his official duties and position, but which conduct brings the Senate into disrepute, the Senate has the power to censure."

The House of Representatives has similarly taken a broad view of its authority to discipline its members by way of expulsion or censure. In the 63d Congress, the House Judiciary Committee described the power of the House to punish for disorderly behavior as a power that is "full and plenary and may be enforced by summary proceedings. It is discretionary in character, . . . restricted by no limitation except in case of expulsion the requirement of the concurrence of a two-thirds vote." In the 1967 report on Rep. Adam Clayton Powell, Jr. (D-N.Y.), the House Select Committee described cen-

Disciplinary Actions Taken by the Full House or Senate against a Member

HOUSE OF REPRESENTATIVES[1]

CENSURE

Date	Member of Congress	Conduct
11 July 1832	William Stanbery (Ohio)	Insulting the Speaker of the House.
22 March 1842	Joshua R. Giddings (Ohio)	Introducing resolution relating to delicate international negotiations, deemed "incendiary."
15 July 1856	Laurence M. Keitt (S.C.)	Assisting in assault on a member.
9 April 1864	Benjamin G. Harris (Md.)	Treasonous conduct in opposing subjugation of the South.
14 April 1864	Alexander Long (Ohio)	Supporting recognition of the Confederacy.
14 May 1866	John W. Chanler (N.Y.)	Insulting the House by introduction of resolution containing unparliamentary language.
24 July 1866	Lovell H. Rousseau (Ky.)	Assaulting another member.
26 January 1867	John W. Hunter (N.Y.)	Unparliamentary language.
15 January 1868	Fernando Wood (N.Y.)	Unparliamentary language.
14 February 1869	Edward D. Holbrook (Idaho)	Unparliamentary language.
24 February 1870	B. Frank Whittemore (S.C.)	Selling military academy appointments.
1 March 1870	John T. Deweese (N.C.)	Selling military academy appointments.
16 March 1870	Roderick R. Butler (Tenn.)	Selling military academy appointments.
27 February 1873	Oakes Ames (Mass.)	Bribery in Crédit Mobilier case.
27 February 1873	James Brooks (N.Y.)	Bribery in Crédit Mobilier case.
4 February 1875	John Y. Brown (Ky.)	Unparliamentary language.
17 May 1890	William D. Bynum (Ind.)	Unparliamentary language.
27 October 1921	Thomas L. Blanton (Tex.)	Unparliamentary language.
31 July 1979	Charles C. Diggs, Jr. (Mich.)	Salary kickbacks from staff.
6 June 1980	Charles H. Wilson (Calif.)	Receipt of improper gifts; maintaining persons on official payroll who were not performing duties commensurate with pay; improper personal use of campaign funds.
20 July 1983	Gerry E. Studds (Mass.)	Sexual misconduct with House pages.
20 July 1983	Daniel B. Crane (Ill.)	Sexual misconduct with House pages.

REPRIMAND

Date	Member of Congress	Conduct
29 July 1976	Robert L. F. Sikes (Fla.)	Use of office for personal gain; failure to disclose interest in legislation.
13 October 1978	Charles H. Wilson (Calif.)	False statement before Standards of Official Conduct Committee investigating Korean influence matter.
13 October 1978	John J. McFall (Calif.)	Failure to report campaign contributions from Korean lobbyist.
13 October 1978	Edward R. Roybal (Calif.)	Failure to report campaign contributions; false sworn statement before Standards of Official Conduct Committee investigating Korean influence matter.
31 July 1984	George Hansen (Idaho)	False statements on financial disclosure form; conviction under 18 U.S.C. sec. 1001 for such false statements.
18 December 1987	Austin J. Murphy (Pa.)	Ghost voting (allowing another person to cast his vote on the floor when he was absent); maintaining on payroll persons not performing official duties commensurate with pay.

[1] Not a censure, reprimand, or expulsion, on 1 March 1967 the House refused to seat Adam Clayton Powell, Jr. (D-N.Y.), in connection with charges of income tax evasion, misuse of committee funds, and a high absentee record. Powell challenged the exclusion and in June 1969 the Supreme Court ruled in his favor. Powell was reelected and seated in the 91st Congress, but was stripped of his seniority and fined $25,000.

Disciplinary Actions Taken by the Full House or Senate against a Member (Continued)

HOUSE OF REPRESENTATIVES (*Continued*)

REPRIMAND (*Continued*)

Date	Member of Congress	Conduct
26 July 1990	Barney Frank (Mass.)	Use of political influence to fix parking tickets and influence probation officers.

EXPULSION

Date	Member of Congress	Conduct
13 July 1861	John B. Clark, Jr. (Mo.)	Disloyalty to the Union—taking up arms against the United States.
2 December 1861	John W. Reid (Mo.)	Disloyalty to the Union—taking up arms against the United States.
3 December 1861	Henry C. Burnett (Ky.)	Disloyalty to the Union—open rebellion against the government.
2 October 1980	Michael O. Myers (Pa.)	Bribery conviction for accepting money in return for promise to use influence in immigration matters during FBI's Abscam sting investigation.

SENATE[2]

CENSURE

Date	Member of Congress	Conduct
2 January 1811	Timothy Pickering (Mass.)	Violation of rules on secrecy.
10 May 1844	Benjamin Tappan (Ohio)	Release of confidential information.
28 February 1902	John L. McLaurin (S.C.)	Fighting with another member in the Senate.
28 February 1902	Benjamin R. Tillman (S.C.)	Fighting with another member in the Senate.
4 November 1929	Hiram Bingham (Conn.)	Placing on the Senate committee payroll, with access to confidential information, a paid lobbyist having a direct interest in legislation before the committee.
2 December 1954	Joseph R. McCarthy (Wis.)	Noncooperation with and abuse of Senate committees.
23 June 1967	Thomas J. Dodd (Conn.)	Use of political and campaign funds received at testimonials and fundraisers for personal purposes.
11 October 1979	Herman E. Talmadge (Ga.)	Financial irregularities in official reimbursements, financial disclosures, and personal use of political funds.
25 July 1990	David F. Durenberger (Minn.)	Use of "book promotion" arrangement to evade statutory limit on honoraria fees for outside speaking; improper receipt of official Senate reimbursement for stays in his own apartment.

[2]In November 1991 Alan Cranston (D-Calif.) was reprimanded by the Ethics Committee before the full Senate, which did not vote as a body, for links between fundraising and official activities, in connection with the "Keating Five" Scandal, resulting in "an impermissible pattern of conduct."

sure to be "appropriate in cases of a breach of the privileges of the House [including those] affecting the rights of the House collectively, its safety, dignity, and the integrity of its proceedings; and the other, affecting the rights, reputation, and conduct of Members, individually, in their representative capacity." The Select Committee also noted, "This discretionary power to punish for disorderly behavior is vested by the Constitution in the House of Representatives and its exercise is appropriate where a Member has been guilty of misconduct relating to his official duties, noncooperation with committees of this House, or nonofficial acts of a kind likely to bring this House into disrepute."

In the Senate, nine members have been censured by way of resolutions using the terms *censure, con-*

Disciplinary Actions Taken by the Full House or Senate against a Member (Continued)

SENATE *(Continued)*

EXPULSION

Date	Member of Congress	Conduct
8 July 1797	William Blount (Tenn.)	Was found to have written a letter to a U.S. government interpreter seeking his aid in a plan to seize Spanish Florida and Louisiana with British and Indian help.
11 July 1861	James M. Mason and Robert M. T. Hunter (Va.); Thomas L. Clingman and Thomas Bragg (N.C.); James Chestnut, Jr. (S.C.); Alfred O. P. Nicholson (Tenn.); William K. Sebastian[3] and Charles B. Mitchel (Ark.); John Hemphill and Louis T. Wigfall (Tex.)	Disloyalty to the Union—"Said Senators are engaged in said conspiracy for the destruction of the Union and Government, or with full knowledge of such conspiracy have failed to advise the Government of its progress or aid in its suppression."
4 December 1861	John C. Breckinridge (Ky.)	Disloyalty to the Union—the senator "has joined the enemies of his country, and is now in arms against the Government he had sworn to support."
5 February 1862	Jesse D. Bright (Ind.)	Disloyalty to the Union by writing a letter in 1861 recommending an arms manufacturer to Jefferson Davis, president of the Confederacy.
10 January 1862	Waldo Porter Johnson (Mo.)	Disloyalty to the Union.
10 January 1862	Trusten Polk (Mo.)	Disloyalty to the Union

[3]The resolution of expulsion as it pertained to William K. Sebastian was "revoked and annulled" by the Senate on 3 March 1877; note S. Rept. 513, 44th Cong., 1st sess.

demn, or *denounce,* or in resolutions using no specific term at all, for various forms of misconduct. These have included fighting in the Senate; breaches of Senate confidentiality; allowing a lobbyist with interests in particular legislation to be on the staff of a committee considering such legislation, with access to the secret meetings and considerations of the committee; noncooperation with and abuse of investigating committees of the Senate; using political funds for personal purposes; financial irregularities regarding gifts, accounts, and contributions; circumventing the limits on speaking fees that a senator may earn; and taking official Senate expense reimbursements for living in an apartment that the senator owned.

In the House of Representatives, there have been twenty-two censures of members of or delegates to the House, including two censures of former members who, in 1870, resigned just prior to the House's consideration of expulsion motions against them. Most of the House censures occurred in the nineteenth century and involved the use of unparliamentary and insulting language on the floor of the House or acts of violence and assault on fellow members. However, corruption in office and the use of one's official position to obtain gifts, bribes, payments, or salary kickbacks have also been grounds for censure in the House.

Reprimand. The term *reprimand* currently means different things in the House and Senate. In the House of Representatives prior to the 1970s, the terms *reprimand* and *censure* were often considered synonymous and were used together or interchangeably in a resolution, as were the terms *censure* and *condemn.* In 1921, for example, a resolution adopted by the House instructed the Speaker to summon Rep. Thomas L. Blanton (D-Tex.) to the well of the House "and deliver to him its reprimand and censure."

Since then, however, there has come to be a distinction of usage in the House, so that a reprimand involves a lesser level of disapproval than a censure. The term *reprimand* was expressly used by the House to indicate a less severe rebuke for the first time in 1976. Rep. Robert L. F. Sikes (D-Fla.) was reprimanded for his failure to disclose certain personal interests in official matters and for using his office to further personal financial interests. Since 1976 a total of seven House members have been reprimanded by the full House for a variety of misconduct, including misrepresentations to investigating committees, failure to report gifts or contributions, misuse of political influence, and ghost voting (allowing one member to cast a vote on the floor for an absent member).

Procedurally, in the House a censure resolution will generally instruct the member to go to the well of the House, as noted above. In the case of a reprimand, however, this dramatic element is omitted.

There is no precedent for the full Senate to vote a resolution reprimanding a member for misconduct, although that term was considered and rejected by the full Senate in the censure of a senator in 1967. In 1991 the Senate Select Committee on Ethics issued a reprimand on its own accord to Sen. Alan Cranston (D-Calif.) for his part in the so-called Keating Five scandal, involving an improper intervention by a senator's office into an administrative investigation. Such an action by the committee, because it is not voted by the full Senate, is clearly different from, and considered a lesser form of rebuke or disapproval than, a resolution of censure formally adopted by the full Senate.

[*See also* Ethics and Corruption in Congress; Ethics Committee, Senate Select; Standards of Official Conduct Committee, House.]

BIBLIOGRAPHY

Bowman, Dorian, and Judith Farris-Bowman. "Article I, Section 5: Congress' Power to Expel—An Exercise in Self-Restraint." *Syracuse Law Review* 29 (1978): 1071, 1089–1090.

U.S. House of Representatives. Committee on Standards of Official Conduct. *Historical Summary of Conduct Cases in the House of Representatives.* 102d Cong., 2d sess., 1992.

U.S. House of Representatives. Joint Committee on Congressional Operations. *House of Representatives Exclusion, Censure, and Expulsion Cases from 1789 to 1973.* 93d Cong., 1st sess., 1973. Committee Print.

U.S. Senate. Committee on Rules and Administration. *Senate Election, Expulsion, and Censure Cases from 1793 to 1972.* 92d Cong., 1st sess., 1972. S. Doc. 92-7.

JACK H. MASKELL

DISCLOSURE. *See* Financial Disclosure.

DISCRIMINATION. *See* Civil Rights.

DISTRICTING. *See* Apportionment and Districting.

DISTRICT OF COLUMBIA. The seat of government of the United States, the District of Columbia is a unique jurisdiction with a controversial history that dates back to the Revolutionary War. From the time of the meeting of the First Continental Congress in 1774 until 1800, when the U.S. Congress moved to the District of Columbia, Congress met, and the related functions of government were performed, in eight different cities—Baltimore; York, Pennsylvania; Lancaster, Pennsylvania; Princeton, New Jersey; Trenton, New Jersey; Annapolis, Maryland; New York City; and Philadelphia. While the Continental Congress was in session in Philadelphia in 1783, veterans of the Revolutionary War who had not been paid for their services marched on that body in protest. Congress viewed this action as a threat and an insult and appealed in vain to Pennsylvania officials to disperse the soldiers. As a consequence of its failure to obtain protection, Congress was forced to move to other towns to conduct its business. Having been put to flight by a group of mutinous soldiers, members of Congress were determined to establish a seat of government where they could conduct their business without fear of intimidation. The Framers of the Constitution did not want the national capital to be dependent on any state for service or protection. As a result, the Constitutional Convention of 1787 adopted Article I, section 8, clause 17, which states: "The Congress shall have power . . . to exercise exclusive legislation in all cases whatsoever over such district (not exceeding 10 miles square) as may by the cession of particular States, and the acceptance of Congress, become the seat of government of the United States."

Intense rivalry between northern and southern states over where the capital would be located was finally ended in 1790 in a compromise engineered by Alexander Hamilton and Thomas Jefferson. The capital was to be located on the Potomac River on land ceded by Maryland and Virginia. In 1790, this land was accepted by Congress, which authorized President George Washington to select the exact site of the federal district and to appoint a board of commissioners to take over the planning and building of the new capital city. The three commissioners were empowered to acquire lands and provide buildings for the accommodation of the national government but were not given general governmental authority.

The laws of Maryland and Virginia remained in effect until Congress assumed jurisdiction over the ceded territory, and residents of the federal district

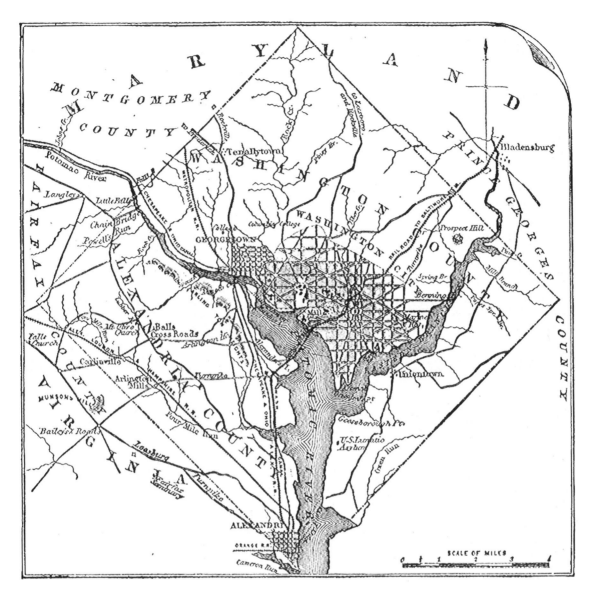

MAP OF THE ORIGINAL DISTRICT OF COLUMBIA.   *PERLEY'S REMINISCENCES*, VOL. 1

voted in their respective states until December 1800. By an act of 27 February 1801, Congress assumed jurisdiction over the federal district and rescinded the jurisdiction of Maryland and Virginia over the area. The City and County of Washington were created from the Maryland portion and Alexandria County was created from the Virginia portion. The cities of Georgetown and Alexandria maintained their own political structures. Neither the Constitution nor Congress addressed the issue of providing for voting representation in Congress for the District's residents.

The board of commissioners was abolished in 1802, and its power was conferred on a superinten-dent appointed by the president. In the same year Congress enacted the charter for the City of Washington, which gave the city its first government, consisting of a mayor appointed by the president and an elected city council. The first municipal election was held in 1802. Only free white males who had lived in the city for one year and owned property could vote.

The charter was materially altered in 1812 to provide for an eight-member board of aldermen, elected biennially, and a twelve-member board of common council, elected annually. The mayor was elected annually by a majority vote of both boards. An entirely new charter, providing for biennial elections of both the mayor and the aldermen, was enacted in 1820. This charter remained in force until 1871.

The residents of the Virginia portion of the federal district were dissatisfied with their economic and political status, and in 1846 they successfully sought retrocession to Virginia, thus reducing the federal district to its present size of sixty-nine square miles. In 1870 a movement to establish a single centralized government for the federal district was started. Many residents believed that the separate governments of Georgetown, Washington City, and Washington County could not handle the social and physical problems facing the District. In their view, Congress had not lived up to its obligation to support the city financially. Frederick Douglass, however, recognized in these arguments an effort to reduce the influence of the City's black population, the vote having been extended to black males after the Civil War. In 1871 the separate governments of the cities of Washington and Georgetown and the County of Washington were abolished, and a territorial government was established under a new name, the District of Columbia. The local government was managed by a presidentially appointed governor and an elected legislative assembly, and the District was granted a nonvoting delegate to the U.S. House of Representatives.

Tremendous physical improvements were made during the period of the territorial government, but their great cost produced substantial indebtedness. District taxpayers rebelled at the resulting higher property assessments and taxes and petitioned Congress to investigate alleged malfeasance. As a result Congress in 1874 abolished the local government and the office of nonvoting delegate. The president appointed an interim three-member commission to govern the District, with final approval of the District's budget being reserved to the Congress (as it is to this day). In 1878 Congress made the commission form of government permanent, and it lasted until 1967.

This one-hundred-year drought of self-government can be attributed in part to the fact that the District's population became increasingly African American; by the 1970s, more than two-thirds of the District's residents were black. Whites had moved to the Maryland and Virginia suburbs, where they enjoyed self-government and full voting rights. With southern Democrats in control of the congressional committees that governed the federal district, there was little concern for, and substantial opposition to, establishing self-government or extending voting rights to District residents. In 1961, however, the Twenty-third Amendment to the Constitution gave District citizens the right to vote in the presidential election, with three electors participating in the Electoral College. In 1978 Congress passed the District of Columbia Elected Board of Education Act, giving the District's citizens direct control over the development and conduct of their public education system by providing for the nonpartisan election of an eleven-member board of education.

As the issue of local government reorganization gained prominence in the years following World War II, so did the issue of an elected government for the District. The local government had become an administrative quagmire, with government powers and authority divided among independent entities. The result was an administration that was tangled, complex, and uncontrolled.

Frustrated by congressional failure to pass home rule legislation for the District, President Lyndon B. Johnson in 1967 used his reorganization authority to revamp the city government. Under Johnson's reorganization plan, the three-commissioner structure was abolished and replaced by a single commissioner (who was afterward called mayor) and a nine-member bipartisan council, all appointed by the president with the advice and consent of the Senate. The Congress did not disapprove the proposed plan during its sixty-day review period, and Reorganization Plan Number 3 became effective on 11 August 1967.

Efforts to provide the District with representation in Congress continued to gain momentum, and in 1970 President Richard M. Nixon signed authorizing legislation for a nonvoting delegate to Congress from the District of Columbia. In 1971 Walter E. Fauntroy became the first nonvoting delegate under this legislation, serving until 1991, when he was succeeded by Eleanor Holmes Norton.

The years of struggle for home rule by District of Columbia citizens and supporters in Congress finally came to fruition in 1973, when Congress enacted the Home Rule Charter, providing considerable self-government for the District. The charter provides for an elected mayor, a governing council of thirteen members, and advisory neighborhood councils. Congress retained important powers over the District's government, including line-item approval of its budget and the power to overturn (within thirty legislative days), amend, or repeal acts passed by the council.

To compensate for the loss of tax revenues that results from the federal presence in the city, the District receives an annual federal payment that, before 1991, averaged about 15 percent of the District budget; in 1991 the amount was increased to about 24 percent of the budget. The remainder of the District's resources come from local revenues.

In 1978 Congress proposed a constitutional amendment to give the District full voting representation in both the House and the Senate, but only sixteen of the required thirty-eight states ratified the amendment before the 1985 deadline. As it became clear that this amendment would not win approval, the movement for statehood for the District, which could be attained through simple majorities in both houses, gained support. A constitutional convention was held in 1982, and District voters approved a draft statehood constitution. In 1983 the District petitioned Congress to admit it to the Union as the state of New Columbia.

In 1980 District voters approved a statehood proposal that included a provision for the election, prior to statehood, of two "shadow" senators and one shadow representative, but not until 1990 was legislation approved to schedule the election of these officials. Among the first three persons elected to these positions was former presidential candidate Jesse Jackson, who vowed to bring statehood to the District. Statehood as well as alternative proposals to secure congressional representation for residents of the District were the subject matter of bills introduced in the 101st and 102d (1989–1993) Congresses. Hearings on the statehood bill were concluded in the House in April 1992 and a vote by the full body was expected during the year. As the year wound down, however, supporters of statehood decided not to put the issue before the House because of what was termed "an artificially low vote potential" related to election year politics. The 1992 election results renewed hope for passage: endorsement of statehood in the Democratic Party Platform and by newly elected President Bill Clinton encouraged optimism that the issue would move forward during the 103d Congress. By mid 1993 both the Senate and the House had announced plans to hold hearings on the issue during the year.

The bill to admit the state of New Columbia into the Union was brought to the House floor for full debate and a vote in November 1993. Although the statehood bill was defeated by a vote of 277 to 153, sponsors and supporters of the measure portrayed the vote as a victory. The affirmative votes exceeded expectations, and it was the first time in history that either the House or Senate had debated statehood for the District. The Senate took no action on the bill during 1993.

Although Mayor Marion Barry, who held office from 1979 to 1991, had strong local support, congressional mistrust of his administration harmed Congress's relations with the District during the 1980s. The election of Mayor Sharon Pratt Dixon in 1990 brought new congressional confidence in the District's ability to manage its own affairs.

[See also Capitol Hill; Twenty-third Amendment.]

BIBLIOGRAPHY

Schmeckebier, Laurence F. The District of Columbia: Its Government and Administration. 1928.
Smith, Sam. Captive Capital. 1974.
U.S. House of Representatives. Committee on the District of Columbia. Governance of the Nation's Capital: A Summary History of the Forms and Powers of Local Government for the District of Columbia, 1790 to 1973. 101st Cong., 2d sess., 1990. Committee Print.

CHARLES W. HARRIS

DISTRICT OF COLUMBIA COMMITTEE, HOUSE. Congressional oversight of the District of Columbia is concentrated in four bodies. The House Committee on the District of Columbia and the Senate Governmental Affairs Subcommittee on General Services, Federalism, and the District of Columbia have jurisdiction over legislative authorizations for the District; the House and Senate Appropriations committees, both with subcommittees on the District of Columbia, have jurisdiction over expenditures.

The House Committee for the District of Columbia was established as a standing committee in 1808, eight years earlier than its Senate counterpart. It was the first standing committee created by Congress to assist in exercising its exclusive authority over the seat of federal government. The establishing resolution, offered by Rep. Philip B. Key of Maryland (subsequently its first chairman), stated: "It shall be the duty of this committee to take into consideration all petitions and memorials relating to the affairs of the District of Columbia, and report from time to time, by bill or otherwise." The objective was to simplify the process of legislating for the District, whose citizens were not represented on the floor of the House.

In 1880 the House revised its rules so that subjects "relating to the District of Columbia other than appropriations therefor" were referred to the committee, meaning that the committee was given general and usually exclusive jurisdiction over bills relating to District affairs. Starting with eighteen members, the size of the committee has ranged from a high of twenty-six in the early 1970s to a low of eleven members (seven majority and four minority). The District's nonvoting delegate to the committee is not included in the ratio.

Over the years, the number of subcommittees has ranged between three and six. In the 102d Congress (1991–1993) there were three subcommittees: Fiscal Affairs and Health, Government Operations and Metropolitan Affairs, and Judiciary and Education.

Before the reorganization of the District government in 1967, the House and Senate District committees were in fact the local legislative bodies for the District of Columbia. Despite the broad jurisdiction of the House committee, however, many subjects relating to the District are handled by or shared with other standing committees. For example, public reservations and parks within the District are largely under the jurisdiction of the Committee on Interior and Insular Affairs. Because of the geographical nature of its jurisdiction, the District Committee has had few conflicts with other committees, although problems have arisen with, for example, the Committee on Education and Labor (regarding D.C. hospitals), the Judiciary Committee (regarding federal chartering of organizations), and the Public Works Committee (regarding transportation, federal lands and buildings, and Robert Fitzgerald Kennedy Stadium).

In the pre–home rule era, the District Committee was dominated by southern conservatives from rural areas who had little understanding of or sympathy for the problems of the city. The most notable—and controversial—of the leaders was Rep. John L. McMillan (D-S.C.), who chaired the committee from 1948 to 1972. During his twenty-four years as chairman, Representative McMillan was viewed as the holder of ultimate authority over almost every aspect of District life, from parking-space assignments to public employee payrolls, and home-rule legislation was bottled up for years.

McMillan's authority over city affairs began to erode in 1965, when the House, spurred by lobbying from the administration of Lyndon B. Johnson, took a home-rule bill out of the hands of his committee. The bill was eventually defeated, but the rare vote to wrest it from the District Committee was a watershed in District politics. McMillan is credited with successfully sponsoring or supporting a substantial amount of legislation geared to the city's development and covering such areas as antipollution authority, education (e.g., establishing

Washington Technical Institute and Federal City College), health and hospitals (e.g., Washington Hospital Center and Cafritz Hospital), reorganization of the courts, public safety, and welfare. In 1967, McMillan himself introduced the bill that gave the District an elected eleven-member board of education. During the same year, however, he stood in the well of the House of Representatives in an effort to persuade his colleagues to vote against Reorganization Plan Number 3, submitted to Congress by President Johnson, which replaced the District's three-member board of commissioners with an appointed mayor and council and was widely viewed as a step toward full home rule.

A staunch conservative and segregationist, McMillan displayed little sympathy for the will and views of the District's African American population. In addition to accusing him of racism, leaders in the black community contended that he ignored their needs in such critical areas as housing, welfare, and law enforcement. McMillan was defeated in his bid for reelection in 1972. The District Committee was then chaired by Charles C. Diggs, Jr. (D-Mich., 1973–1979) and Ronald V. Dellums (D-Calif., 1979–1993), both African Americans. Since 1979, a majority of the Democratic members have been black (four of seven members in 1992).

After the passage of the Home Rule Act of 1973 the committee still sponsored legislation connected with the federal interest, but its main activities were in the area of oversight and review of legislative action by the District city council. The change to a stable, African American–dominated committee resulted in large part from the committee's downsizing and from a strengthened norm of self-selection for committee membership in the House. The committee is still a low priority for most of its members except the chairman, the District's delegate, and the ranking minority member. Because most of its members (of both parties) are not very active, the committee's Democratic leadership can usually count on a stable pro-District majority. And because the committee's counterpart in the Senate is relatively passive, only three resolutions disapproving District legislation have been passed during the home-rule era.

This pro-District role has not been without costs to the committee, however. Viewed by other representatives as "captured" by the interests it oversees, the committee has found it difficult to win floor approval for its own agenda. As the referral body for disapproval resolutions, the committee has the arduous task of trying to determine legitimate federal interests. This has largely resulted in a negative agenda, one designed to block federal initiatives that challenge local autonomy.

[*See also* District of Columbia.]

BIBLIOGRAPHY

Harris, Charles W. "Federal and Local Interests in the Nation's Capital." *Public Budgeting and Finance* 9 (1989): 66–82.

Weaver, R. Kent, and Charles W. Harris. "Who's in Charge Here: Congress and the Nation's Capital." *The Brookings Review* 7 (1989): 39–45.

CHARLES W. HARRIS

DISTRICTS. A congressional district is a legally defined and delimited geographic area in which all qualified voters have the right to select a representative to the U.S. House of Representatives. From the First Congress to the present, the vast majority of representatives elected to the House have been selected by single-member, geographically defined districts. Over congressional history, however, several other methods have also been used to select representatives.

The first in a series of laws requiring the district method of election appeared in the Apportionment Act of 1842, which stated that for the extent of the law (ten years) members of the House were to be "elected by districts composed of contiguous territory equal in number to the representatives to which said state may be entitled" (5 Stat. 491). Although alternative methods of election were used before and after this statute, the act began the legal precedent that codified the single-member, geographically defined congressional district as part of the American political system. The most recent law (as of 1992) mandating House elections by district was passed on 14 December 1967 (81 Stat. 581). This statute, as well as court rulings in the 1960s against malapportionment, mandates that all states having two or more representatives must divide into districts of somewhat equal population after each decennial reapportionment. After the apportionment of the 1990 census, six states were assigned one representative apiece and the remaining 429 members of the House were elected from states that were subdivided into districts.

Origin of Political Representation by Geographic Area. The origin of political representation by geographic area can be traced back through Western civilization, the British heritage of the American political system, and the American colo-

nial experience. Ancient tribal councils, royal tribunals, Greek and Roman assemblies, and councils of the Middle Ages are in a sense the precursors of modern democratic legislatures. The medieval assemblies of Europe represented class and corporate interests and were, of course, dominated by an absolute ruler. During the Middle Ages, membership in these assemblies also gradually began to be drawn from towns or other settled areas—the genesis of the idea of representation by place rather than by rank, status, or class.

In medieval England, representation on the king's assembly was generally divided between nobility, clergy, and townsmen. Parliamentary representation by geographic area evolved with the gradual emergence of constitutional government. Eventually, a bicameral parliament emerged, with the House of Lords representing class interests and the House of Commons representing the various towns, boroughs, and counties from which its members were selected. The American tradition of colonial legislative assemblies whose members were elected by geographic area undoubtedly derives from this British heritage. The House of Burgesses, the first American colonial legislature, convened in Jamestown, Virginia in 1619. As Virginia expanded the burgesses were selected by and represented the various plantations and towns of the European-settled portion of Virginia. As other North American colonies were established by England, they also instituted assemblies that followed the British and Virginian traditions of representation by geographical area.

During the latter colonial period, the assemblies were often arenas for debate over economic and political freedom, and their existence became a point of contention between leading citizens and the royal appointed governor. After the Revolution, the Constitutional Convention of 1787 grappled with the meaning of democracy and how the concerns of the people should be represented through elected assemblies. The Connecticut Compromise established a bicameral national legislature composed of the Senate and the House of Representatives. The Senate consisted of two members from each state regardless of population, elected by the state legislature. The House consisted of state delegations apportioned according to population. The Constitution, however, does not state that House members are to be elected by districts. Despite this omission, there is evidence in the Constitution, in the proceedings of the Constitutional Convention, and in political writings of the day to support the assertion that the Framers intended the House to be elected by districts, as was the custom in the colonial assemblies.

Alternatives to Single-Member Districts. Because the Framers determined that the number of representatives from each state should be roughly proportional to a state's population relative to the total population of the nation, they probably intended that each state be divided into districts whose boundaries would be drawn according to the same proportional idea. The first five federal apportionment laws (1792–1832), however, simply provided the apportionment ratio and the resultant specific number of representatives for each state. After reapportionment the task of devising the electoral procedures for electing House members was up to the respective states. This created a situation in which individual states could, and did, elect representatives to the House of Representatives in different ways. Although single-member, geographically defined district representation was dominant, the lack of legal precedent and guidance from the Constitution spawned three other electoral and representative formats: statewide election of the entire delegation (general tickets, multimember geographically defined districts (plural districts), and a combination format, in which some members of a state delegation were elected by single-member, geographically defined districts and some members by statewide election (at-large representation).

General ticket representation. In spite of custom and the probable intentions of the Framers, a number of states in the 1790s and the early nineteenth century did not divide into congressional districts. These states elected their entire House delegations through statewide elections—that is, all the eligible voters of the state voted for all the seats in Congress from that state. This type of election is called a general ticket election to differentiate it from the at-large election, discussed below. One political effect of general ticket representation is that geographic areas of a state that are not in political agreement with the majority have their political power diluted. If a state is divided into congressional districts, such areas can elect representatives of political persuasions different from those of the statewide majority. General ticket elections hit their peak in the Third Congress (1793–1795), when nearly a third of House members (33 out of 105) were elected by this method. In the first fifty years of Congress an average of 10 to 20 percent of the House was elected by general ticket. General ticket elections were first discouraged by the district provisions of the 1842 apportionment law, but they

were in use through the 91st Congress (1969–1971), until the 1967 law mandating districts.

Plural district representation. Plural, or multimember, district representation occurs when one geographically defined district elects more than one person. Over the first fifty years of congressional history there were plural districts that elected two, three, or even four members to the House. This type of election ended after the Apportionment Act of 1842. In the plural district method one populous county or group of counties usually comprised one district. In most cases this was an attempt to keep the county unit as the entity of legal description while recognizing urban areas that deserved greater representation. Plural districts were extensively used in New York, Pennsylvania, and Maryland, states with areas of high population density and other vast areas of virtual wilderness. For example, in the 14th Congress (1815–1817) New York elected 12 out of 27, Pennsylvania 14 out of 23, and Maryland 2 out of 9 representatives by way of plural districts. Although plural district elections kept the county unit intact, abuses similar to the potential abuses of general ticket elections were possible. Several representatives could in effect be elected by a city, diluting the power of other areas, which might elect a representative of a different political persuasion under a single-member-district scheme.

At-large representation. The term *at-large election* refers to cases in which the majority of a state congressional delegation is elected from single-member, geographically defined districts but one, two, three, or four additional representatives are elected statewide. Representatives elected statewide are labeled *at-large representatives* when the majority of a state delegation is elected by districts. It is important to differentiate this method from the general ticket, in which the entire delegation is elected statewide.

The first at-large representative was elected from Mississippi to the 33d Congress (1853–1855); the last three were elected from Maryland, Ohio, and Texas to the 89th Congress (1965–1967). At-large representation was most often used after a decennial reapportionment by states that were given a greater number of House seats. At-large representation usually occurred when the state legislature either (1) could not convene in time to perform redistricting, (2) could not agree on a new redistricting plan, (3) used this representative method in its new redistricting plan, or (4) decided not to redistrict. Again, partisan advantage could be attained by the majority party by the election of several representatives statewide. In many cases, the majority-party congressional delegation did not want to redistrict because its members were satisfied and did not want to tamper with existing, "safe" districts. The 63d Congress (1913–1915), elected immediately after the 1910 census apportionment, had the greatest number of at-large representatives, with twelve states electing twenty-one members at-large.

Federal Provisions concerning Congressional Districts. To achieve the Framers' intentions—electoral equity within states and a systematic form of representation—Congress passed a series of provisions, usually included in apportionment laws, mandating single-member districts as the method by which members of the House should be elected. Over time, the establishment of single-member districts eliminated the general ticket, plural district, and at-large methods of election. In addition, Congress has historically given directives to the states with respect to the actual drawing of district boundaries. For example, the precedent-setting Apportionment Act of 1842 not only mandated single-member districts but also directed that, for the time the law was in force, congressional districts must be "contiguous" (5 Stat. 491). This temporarily slowed the practice of creating districts with geographically separate portions. The 1872 apportionment law was the first to direct that each district contain "as nearly as practicable an equal number of inhabitants" (17 Stat. 192). And the 1901 apportionment law, besides specifying that districts should be contiguous, also prescribed that each district be a "compact territory" (31 Stat. 733). This stipulation targeted the practice of gerrymandering, that is, the drawing of congressional districts with odd or peculiar shapes, so as to favor the party or group in power, with results that seem to defy geography. Again, these provisions were in effect for the ten-year period of the particular law. Because the general Apportionment Act of 1929 (46 Stat. 21) and later apportionment laws did not carry provisions concerning compactness, contiguity, or equal population, numerous examples of malapportioned, gerrymandered, and even split districts occurred in the latter portion of the twentieth century.

The federal courts have also played a role in the drawing of congressional districts. In the 1960s the Supreme Court ruled that malapportionment, the drawing of districts of significantly unequal population, is unconstitutional. In the 1970s the Court ruled that gerrymandering to deprive or dilute minority representation is unconstitutional. In the 1980s the Court ruled in *Davis et al. v. Bandemer et al.* that even partisan gerrymanders were subject to judicial review and possible alteration.

Congressional Redistricting Process. The original purpose of holding a census every ten years was to reallocate House seats to the states and, ideally, to allow the states to redraw congressional districts according to population changes. This has not always been the result. The longest interval without a new redistricting law was in New Hampshire, where the congressional district law of 19 February 1881 remained in effect until 3 July 1969. The Supreme Court rulings in malapportionment cases of the 1960s now ensure that after each decennial census states must pass redistricting laws to alter boundaries to reflect population changes even when a state's number of representatives remains the same.

Although some redistricting guidance has historically been given by Congress, the state legislatures finally define and draw district boundaries. The congressional redistricting process is usually accomplished by a law passed by both chambers of a state legislature and signed by the governor. Of course, if the same political party controls both chambers and the governorship it completely controls the redistricting process.

Historically, state legislatures have used given political entities to construct congressional districts. The county (in New England, the town) has been the basic building block of congressional districts and congressional redistricting statutes. In densely populated urban areas the counterpart to the county, the ward, was used extensively, especially in the 150 years after the First Congress. Many times these common political units were divided by gerrymanders to achieve majority-party objectives. As metropolitan areas became larger and more complex, streets became common boundaries dividing the expanding cities into congressional districts. The stringent Supreme Court equal-population rulings of the 1960s necessitated using numerous other fine divisions (census tracts, precinct boundaries, etc.) to draw district boundaries, resulting in increasingly complicated and lengthy districting laws. Many states have codes regulating congressional redistricting, including directives for compactness and contiguity and using current boundaries of counties, cities, and other political units where possible.

Districts and Political Representation. States can be subdivided into congressional districts in many ways. Even when boundaries are drawn in a nonpartisan way, different schemes for creating compact districts will yield different political results, though the district populations remain equal. Even when performed most fairly, the district method of representation carries an inherent electoral bias. Under a bad, gerrymandered districting, the results can be significantly skewed in favor of the party in power.

Virtually all Western-style democratic national legislatures elect representatives by district. In most parliamentary systems, however, the elected members view themselves as representatives of the party and agents in the promotion of its platform and ideology. Within these parliaments, voting virtually always follows party lines. In the parliamentary model, election by district only occasionally affects representative behavior. Additionally, numerous parliamentary election laws have integrated proportional representation schemes with voting districts to produce a more representative electoral result and lessen the need for gerrymandering since seats are distributed to political parties based upon the percentage of the total vote. In the United States the representative philosophy of the House is quite different. Representatives partly view their role as that of agents of their districts and see themselves as charged with the promotion of local concerns. The freedom of roll-call voting in the U.S. Congress is unsurpassed in the world. In the U.S. model, concern for district affairs has a great effect on the behavior and actions of representatives. The election of House members by district is therefore fundamental to understanding the functioning of Congress and representative democracy in the United States.

[*See also* Apportionment and Redistricting; Davis et al. v. Bandemer et al.; Gerrymandering.]

BIBLIOGRAPHY

Grofman, Bernard, ed. *Political Gerrymandering and the Courts.* 1990.
Hacker, Andrew. *Congressional Districting.* 1963.
Luce, Robert. *Legislative Principles.* 1930.
Martis, Kenneth C. *The Historical Atlas of United States Congressional Districts, 1789–1983.* 1982.
Morrill, Richard L. *Political Redistricting and Geographic Theory.* 1981.
Pitkin, Hanna F. *The Concept of Representation.* 1967.

KENNETH C. MARTIS

DIVIDED GOVERNMENT.

The condition that exists when the majority party in either or both houses of Congress differs from the party of the president is called *divided government.* The constitutional structure of the U.S. government, which separates the legislative and executive branches, sets differing terms of office for representatives, senators, and the president, and ensures that they will be chosen from different constituency bases, makes divided government possible. In parliamentary systems, where the executive is selected by the legislature, divided government cannot occur, although coalition governments are possible. In countries with more unified election systems than in the United States, divided government is less likely to occur.

Until the late 1960s divided government was an infrequent and short-lived phenomenon in American politics. It occurred primarily when neither political party was dominant and control of the presidency and Congress shifted a great deal (1876–1896), or when a major-party realignment was in progress and there was a lag in the ascendent party's winning control of all the institutions (1930–1932), or when, in what are known as deviating elections, particularly popular presidential candidates of the minority party won office without their party maintaining a majority in Congress throughout their terms. Under none of these conditions was divided government an enduring circumstance.

However, between 1969 and 1992 divided government became the rule, not the exception. Republican presidents held office for twenty of those twenty-four years, with only Jimmy Carter's single term interrupting the string of Republican succession from Richard M. Nixon through George Bush. Yet the Democrats held their majority in the House of Representatives throughout the period and in the Senate for eighteen of those years. Republican presidential candidates won three of the six elections (1972, 1980, 1984) by landslides in both the popular vote and the electoral college but never held more than 192 of the 435 seats in the House of Representatives. When Bush handily won office in 1988, the Democrats actually made small gains in their House and Senate majorities.

Why was there such a long period of divided government? Researchers have offered several explanations. Some have focused on voting behavior. After the late 1960s voters became less strongly attached to political parties. More and more voters claimed to be independents or identified only weakly with a political party. Fewer voters relied on partisanship in making their choices in elections. Weakened attachment to parties resulted in increases in split-ticket voting. It also allowed congressional incumbents to insulate themselves from the short-term partisan effects of presidential elections.

Still, this analysis does not explain why the effect led to Republican presidential success and Democratic congressional success. A few scholars have tried to make the case that some voters consciously voted for divided government, arguing that these voters wanted a Democratic Congress and a Republican presidency so that the excesses of the party controlling one branch would be offset by the party controlling the other.

Some think that the Democrats' success in House elections has been due to the advantages of incumbency. This analysis points out that incumbents have been winning reelection at higher rates and by larger margins and argues that because Democrats comprise a majority in the House, their incumbency advantage has allowed them to remain in the majority. This contention, however, fails to recognize the fact that Democrats continue to win about the same percentage of contests for open House seats as they do contests for incumbents' seats.

The success of Democrats in open-seat House contests coupled with their failure in presidential elections has focused attention on candidate recruitment and selection as an explanation for divided government. Because Democrats hold an overwhelming majority of state legislative seats—the "farm teams" on which many future congressional candidates gain experience of running for and serving in office—they have a larger pool of congressional candidates than do the Republicans. By comparison, Republicans may have better control of the process of recruiting presidential candidates. Democrats may be less likely than Republicans to select their strongest candidate for president, and the arduous process of winning the Democratic nomination may leave the candidate weakened for the general election.

Finally, Democratic success in House elections and Republican success in presidential races may in part reflect differences in these contests' apportionment bases. House seats are apportioned on the basis of population, not registered voters. Although House districts have about the same populations, they have substantially different numbers of voters. For a variety of reasons Democrats have tended to do better in districts with lower numbers of voters, while Republicans have tended to win districts with high numbers of voters. Thus the Democratic party has done better in the House, which is population based, while the Republican party has excelled in presidential and senatorial elections, which, in apportionment terms, are more voter-based.

The impact of divided government is the subject of considerable debate. Critics contend that it leads to governmental stalemate, because each party has the ability to block the policy initiatives of the other. Congress is unwilling to pass what the president requests, and the president vetoes or threatens to veto what Congress approves. Major policy problems may remain unresolved. This leads to a situation in which Congress and the president have little incentive to act responsibly because each knows it can blame policy failures on the other. Voters find it difficult to hold elected officials accountable because it is unclear whom to credit for policy successes and whom to blame for failures.

Others view divided government less harshly. They note that unified party control, as during the Carter years, provides no guarantee against stalemate between Congress and the executive. During the period of divided government from 1970 to 1972, many major policy changes were enacted, including the economic proposals of the Reagan administration, the 1986 Tax Reform Act, and welfare reform. Vetoes or threats of veto usually resulted in policy compromises, not paralysis.

In fact, the policy consequences of divided government have changed with the context of American politics. During much of the twentieth century, divided government did not create insurmountable problems. Because American political parties were not highly cohesive, congressional decisions were often structured by coalitions that cut across parties. Thus, Republican presidents like Eisenhower, Nixon, and Ford faced with Democratic majorities in Congress were able to pass many of their legislative programs by winning the support of conservative southern Democrats in Congress. When a sufficient number of these southerners joined with the Republican minority to form what became known as the conservative coalition, Republican presidents often were able to produce majorities in the House and the Senate.

With the passage of the Voting Rights Act in 1965, the context for congressional politics started to change. To appeal to a growing number of black voters in the South who were enfranchised through enforcement of the Voting Rights Act, Democratic candidates were forced to take less conservative policy stances. (Conservative voters in the South increasingly supported Republican candidates.) And southern Democrats elected to Congress gradually came to resemble nonsouthern Democrats in their roll-call vote decisions. The passage of the Reagan economic program in 1981 may well have been the last major policy victory for the conservative coalition.

The dwindling of the conservative southern Dem-

Congress and the President, 1798–1993[1]

CONGRESS	SENATE			HOUSE			PRESIDENT
	MAJ	MIN	OTHER	MAJ	MIN	OTHER	
1st 1789–1791	**17 Ad**	9 Op		**38 Ad**	26 Op		**Washington, F**
2d 1791–1793	**16 F**	13 DR		**37 F**	33 DR		**Washington, F**
3d 1793–1795	**17 F**	13 DR		57 DR	48 F		Washington, F
4th 1795–1797	**19 F**	13 DR		**54 F**	52 DR		**Washington, F**
5th 1797–1799	**20 F**	12 DR		**58 F**	48 DR		**J. Adams, F**
6th 1799–1801	**19 F**	13 DR		**64 F**	42 DR		**J. Adams, F**
7th 1801–1803	**18 DR**	13 F		**69 DR**	36 F		**Jefferson, DR**
8th 1803–1805	**25 DR**	9 F		**102 DR**	39 F		**Jefferson, DR**
9th 1805–1807	**27 DR**	7 F		**116 DR**	25 F		**Jefferson, DR**
10th 1807–1809	**28 DR**	6 F		**118 DR**	24 F		**Jefferson, DR**
11th 1809–1811	**28 DR**	6 F		**94 DR**	48 F		**Madison, DR**
12th 1811–1813	**30 DR**	6 F		**108 DR**	36 F		**Madison, DR**
13th 1813–1815	**27 DR**	9 F		**112 DR**	68 F		**Madison, DR**
14th 1815–1817	**25 DR**	11 F		**117 DR**	65 F		**Madison, DR**
15th 1817–1819	**34 DR**	10 F		**141 DR**	42 F		**Monroe, DR**
16th 1819–1821	**35 DR**	7 F		**156 DR**	27 F		**Monroe, DR**
17th 1821–1823	**44 DR**	4 F		**158 DR**	25 F		**Monroe, DR**
18th 1823–1825	**44 DR**	4 F		**187 DR**	26 F		**Monroe, DR**
19th 1825–1827	**26 Ad**	20 J		**105 Ad**	97 J		**J. Q. Adams, C**
20th 1827–1829	28 J	20 Ad		119 J	94 Ad		J. Q. Adams, C
21st 1829–1831	**26 D**	22 NR		**139 D**	74 NR		**Jackson, D**
22d 1831–1833	**25 D**	21 NR	2	**141 D**	58 NR	14	**Jackson, D**
23d 1833–1835	20 D	20 NR	8	147 D	53 AM	60	Jackson, D
24th 1835–1837	**27 D**	25 W		**145 D**	98 W		**Jackson, D**
25th 1837–1839	**30 D**	18 W	4	**108 D**	107 W	24	**Van Buren, D**
26th 1839–1841	**28 D**	22 W		**124 D**	118 W		**Van Buren, D**
27th 1841–1843	**28 W**	22 D	2	**133 W**	102 D	6	**W. Harrison, W** **Tyler, W**
28th 1843–1845	**28 W**	25 D	1	142 D	79 W	1	Tyler, W
29th 1845–1847	**31 D**	25 W		**143 D**	77 W	6	**Polk, D**
30th 1847–1849	**36 D**	21 W	1	115 W	108 D	4	Polk, D
31st 1849–1851	35 D	25 W	2	112 D	109 W	9	Taylor, W Fillmore, W
32d 1851–1853	35 D	24 W	3	140 D	88 W	5	Fillmore, W
33d 1853–1855	**38 D**	22 W	2	**159 D**	71 W	4	**Pierce, D**
34th 1855–1857	**40 D**	15 W	5	108 R	83 D	43	Pierce, D
35th 1857–1859	**36 D**	20 R	8	**118 D**	92 R	26	**Buchanan, D**
36th 1859–1861	**36 D**	26 R	4	114 R	92 D	31	Buchanan, D
37th 1861–1863	**31 R**	10 D	8	**105 R**	43 D	30	**Lincoln, R**
38th 1863–1865	**36 R**	9 D	5	**102 R**	75 D	9	**Lincoln, R**

[1]Division in each house of Congress between the majority party, the principal minority party, and other members (independents and members of minority parties) at the beginning of each Congress. When the majority party is the party of the president, it is printed in boldface. When the majority party in both houses is the party of the president, the president's name and the number of the Congress are also printed in boldface.

Congress and the President, 1798–1993 (Continued)

CONGRESS	SENATE			HOUSE			PRESIDENT
	MAJ	MIN	OTHER	MAJ	MIN	OTHER	
39th 1865–1867	42 R	10 D		149 R	42 D		Lincoln, R A. Johnson, R
40th 1867–1869	42 R	11 D		143 R	49 D		A. Johnson, R
41st 1869–1871	56 R	11 D		149 R	63 D		Grant, R
42d 1871–1873	52 R	17 D	5	134 R	104 D	5	Grant, R
43d 1873–1875	49 D	19 D	5	194 R	92 D	14	Grant, R
44th 1875–1877	45 R	29 D	2	169 D	109 R	14	Grant, R
45th 1877–1879	39 R	36 D	1	153 D	140 R		Hayes, R
46th 1879–1881	42 D	33 R	1	149 D	130 R	14	Hayes, R
47th 1881–1883	37 R	37 D	1	147 R	135 D	11	Garfield, R Arthur, R
48th 1883–1885	38 R	36 D	2	197 D	118 R	10	Arthur, R
49th 1885–1887	43 R	34 D		183 D	140 R	2	Cleveland, D
50th 1887–1889	39 R	37 D		169 D	152 R	4	Cleveland, D
51st 1889–1891	39 R	37 D		166 R	159 D		B. Harrison, R
52d 1891–1893	47 R	39 D	2	235 D	88 R	9	B. Harrison, R
53d 1893–1895	44 D	38 R	3	218 D	127 R	11	Cleveland, D
54th 1895–1897	43 R	39 D	6	244 R	105 D	7	Cleveland, D
55th 1897–1899	47 R	34 D	7	204 R	113 D	40	McKinley, R
56th 1899–1901	53 R	26 D	8	185 R	163 D	9	McKinley, R
57th 1901–1903	55 R	31 D	4	197 R	151 D	9	McKinley, R T. Roosevelt, R
58th 1903–1905	57 R	33 D		208 R	178 D		T. Roosevelt, R
59th 1905–1907	57 R	33 D		250 R	136 D		T. Roosevelt, R
60th 1907–1909	61 R	31 D		222 R	164 D		T. Roosevelt, R
61st 1909–1911	61 R	32 D		219 R	172 D		Taft, R
62d 1911–1913	51 R	41 D		228 D	161 R	1	Taft, R
63d 1913–1915	51 D	44 R	1	291 D	127 R	17	Wilson, D
64th 1915–1917	56 D	40 R		230 D	196 R	9	Wilson, D
65th 1917–1919	53 D	42 R		216 D	210 R	6	Wilson, D
66th 1919–1921	49 R	47 D		240 R	190 D	3	Wilson, D
67th 1921–1923	59 R	37 D		301 R	131 D	1	Harding, R
68th 1923–1925	51 R	43 R	2	225 R	205 D	5	Coolidge, R
69th 1925–1927	56 R	39 D	1	247 R	183 D	4	Coolidge, R
70th 1927–1929	49 R	46 D	1	237 R	195 D	3	Coolidge, R
71st 1929–1931	56 R	39 D	1	267 R	167 D	1	Hoover, R
72d 1931–1933	48 R	47 D	1	220 D	214 R	1	Hoover, R
73d 1933–1935	60 D	35 R	1	310 D	117 R	5	F. Roosevelt, D
74th 1935–1937	69 D	25 R	2	319 D	103 R	10	F. Roosevelt, D
75th 1937–1939	76 D	16 R	4	331 D	89 R	13	F. Roosevelt, D

Abbreviations: Ad, supporters of the president's administration; AM, Anti-Masonic; C, coalition president; D, Democratic; DR, Democratic-Republican (sometimes known as Jeffersonian Republican); F, Federalist; J, Jacksonian; Maj, majority party; Min, principal minority party; NR, National Republication; Op, opposition; R, Republican; U, Unionist; W, Whig

Congress and the President, 1798–1993 (Continued)

CONGRESS	SENATE			HOUSE			PRESIDENT
	MAJ	MIN	OTHER	MAJ	MIN	OTHER	
76th 1939–1941	**69 D**	23 R	4	**261 D**	164 R	4	**F. Roosevelt, D**
77th 1941–1943	**66 D**	28 R	2	**268 D**	162 R	5	**F. Roosevelt, D**
78th 1943–1945	**58 D**	37 R	1	**218 D**	208 R	4	**F. Roosevelt, D**
79th 1945–1947	**56 D**	38 R	1	**242 D**	190 R	2	**F. Roosevelt, D** **Truman, D**
80th 1947–1949	51 R	45 D		245 R	188 D	1	Truman, D
81st 1949–1951	**54 D**	42 R		**263 D**	171 R	1	**Truman, D**
82d 1951–1953	**49 D**	47 R		**234 D**	199 R	1	**Truman, D**
83d 1953–1955	**48 R**	47 D	1	**221 R**	211 D	1	**Eisenhower, R**
84th 1955–1957	48 D	47 R	1	232 D	203 R		Eisenhower, R
85th 1957–1959	49 D	47 R		233 D	200 R		Eisenhower, R
86th 1959–1961	64 D	34 R		283 D	153 R		Eisenhower, R
87th 1961–1963	**65 D**	35 R		**263 D**	174 R		**Kennedy, D**
88th 1963–1965	**67 D**	33 R		**258 D**	177 R		**Kennedy, D** **L. Johnson, D**
89th 1965–1967	**68 D**	32 R		**295 D**	140 R		**L. Johnson, D**
90th 1967–1969	**64 D**	36 R		**247 D**	187 R		**L. Johnson, D**
91st 1969–1971	57 D	43 R		243 D	192 R		Nixon, R
92d 1971–1973	54 D	44 R	2	254 D	180 R		Nixon, R
93d 1973–1975	56 D	42 R	2	239 D	192 R	1	Nixon, R Ford, R
94th 1975–1977	60 D	37 R	2	291 D	144 R		Ford, R
95th 1977–1979	**61 D**	38 R	1	**292 D**	143 R		**Carter, D**
96th 1979–1981	**58 D**	41 R	1	**276 D**	157 R		**Carter, D**
97th 1981–1983	**53 R**	46 D	1	243 D	192 R		Reagan, R
98th 1983–1985	**54 R**	46 D		269 D	165 R		Reagan, R
99th 1985–1987	**53 R**	47 D		252 D	182 R		Reagan, R
100th 1987–1989	55 D	45 R		258 D	177 R		Reagan, R
101st 1989–1991	55 D	45 R		260 D	175 R		Bush, R
102d 1991–1993	57 D	43 R		266 D	166 R	1	Bush, R
103d 1993–1995	**57 D**	43 R		**258 D**	176 R	1	**Clinton, D**

SOURCE: Adapted from the *Encyclopedia of the American Presidency,* edited by Leonard W. Levy and Louis Fisher (Simon & Schuster, 1994).

ocratic membership in Congress and, in turn, the decline in the conservative coalition as a meaningful force in decision making gave divided government greater significance. With more cohesive political parties in Congress—especially the Democrats—the coalition strategy of Republican presidents was no longer successful. It became increasingly difficult for Republican presidents Reagan and Bush to win legislative victories when confronted with a more united Democratic party. In fact, it is only in this context that the debate about the policy consequences of divided government has occurred.

Since divided government ended in 1992 with the victory of Democratic presidential candidate Bill Clinton, it may be possible to better evaluate the claims of its critics. If the critics are correct, then unified party control of Congress and the presidency, especially with relatively cohesive parties, should bring an end to gridlock and stalemate on critical policy areas like the budget, economic policy, and health care. Under such conditions, voters' ties to political parties may strengthen as voters may more easily hold parties accountable for policy successes and failures. This, in turn, will undermine one of the major causes of divided government.

BIBLIOGRAPHY

Jacobson, Gary C. *The Electoral Origins of Divided Government.* 1990.

Rohde, David W. *Parties and Leaders in the Postreform House.* 1991.

BRUCE I. OPPENHEIMER

BIBLIOGRAPHY

Hechler, Kenneth W. *Insurgency: Personalities and Politics of the Taft Era.* 1940.

Ross, Thomas R. *Jonathan Prentiss Dolliver: A Study in Political Integrity and Independence.* 1958.

Sage, Leland L. *A History of Iowa.* 1974.

JOHN BRAEMAN

DOLLIVER, JONATHAN P. (1858–1910), representative and senator from Iowa and long-time Republican party regular who later joined the insurgent revolt against old-guard Republicans. His abilities as a spellbinding stump speaker brought Jonathan Prentiss Dolliver, a lawyer, to the attention of Iowa Republican leaders. In 1888 he won election to the United States House of Representatives from Iowa's 10th District and went on to win five reelections. His major legislative interests were protective tariffs and higher pensions for veterans.

Within Iowa politics, Dolliver was a loyal cog in the Republican political machine headed by Sen. William B. Allison, who saw to it that Dolliver was chosen to succeed John H. Gear, Iowa's other senator, who died in 1900. Dolliver was elected to a full term in 1907. Increasingly aware of Iowa voters' discontent over railroad abuses and high tariff rates, Dolliver gradually cut loose from the standpatters, who wished to maintain the status quo. He backed the proposed national child labor law and supported the Meat Inspection, Pure Food and Drug, and Employers' Liability acts of 1906. Most important, he was Theodore Roosevelt's leading Senate supporter in the 1906 fight over the Hepburn bill authorizing the Interstate Commerce Commission to fix railroad rates.

Allison's death in August 1908 broke Dolliver's last emotional link to the party's old guard. When Nelson W. Aldrich of Rhode Island blocked Dolliver's bid for a seat on the Senate Finance Committee, Dolliver joined the insurgent revolt against party regulars over the Payne-Aldrich tariff bill. He was on the insurgent side in the controversy between Gifford Pinchot and Richard A. Ballinger over conservation policy, in the conflict over new railroad rate legislation resulting in the adoption of the Mann-Elkins Act of 1910, and in the fight over the postal savings bank measure. When the insurgents battled with the standpatters for control of Iowa's 1910 Republican state convention, Dolliver tirelessly stumped the state despite his precarious health. He died on 15 October 1910 from heart disease.

DOME. *See* Capitol, *article on* Dome and Great Rotunda.

DOORKEEPER OF THE HOUSE. The doorkeeper is an elected officer of the House of Representatives. The office has its origins in the First Congress on 2 April 1789, when the House passed a resolution "That a door-keeper and an assistant door-keeper be appointed for service of this House." Two days later the House voted in favor of Gifford Dalley as the first doorkeeper and Thomas Claxton as his assistant. Claxton was elected doorkeeper in 1795 and held the post until 1821, the longest tenure in the office. In 1994 the doorkeeper was James T. Molloy of Buffalo, New York, the thirtieth person to hold the office since 1789; he was

Doorkeepers of the House

CONGRESS	YEAR OF ELECTION	DOORKEEPER
1st	1789	Gifford Dalley
2d	1791	Gifford Dalley
3d	1793	Gifford Dalley
4th	1795	Thomas Claxton
5th	1797	Thomas Claxton
6th	1799	Thomas Claxton
7th	1801	Thomas Claxton
8th	1803	Thomas Claxton
9th	1805	Thomas Claxton
10th	1807	Thomas Claxton
11th	1809	Thomas Claxton
12th	1811	Thomas Claxton
13th	1813	Thomas Claxton
14th	1815	Thomas Claxton
15th	1817	Thomas Claxton
16th	1819	Thomas Claxton
17th	1821	Benjamin Burch
18th	1823	Benjamin Burch
19th	1825	Benjamin Burch
20th	1827	Benjamin Burch
21st	1829	Benjamin Burch

Doorkeepers of the House (Continued)

Congress	Year of Election	Doorkeeper	Congress	Year of Election	Doorkeeper
22d	1831	Overton Carr	63d	1913	Joseph J. Sinnott
23d	1833	Overton Carr	64th	1915	Joseph J. Sinnott
24th	1835	Overton Carr	65th	1917	Joseph J. Sinnott
25th	1837	Overton Carr	66th	1919	Bert W. Kennedy
26th	1839	Joseph Follansbee	67th	1921	Bert W. Kennedy
27th	1841	Joseph Follansbee	68th	1923	Bert W. Kennedy
28th	1843	Jesse E. Dow	69th	1925	Bert W. Kennedy
29th	1845	C. S. Whitney	70th	1927	Bert W. Kennedy
30th	1847	Robert B. Hackney	71st	1929	Bert W. Kennedy
31st	1849	Robert B. Hackney	72d	1931	Bert W. Kennedy
32d	1851	Z. W. McKnew	73d	1933	Joseph J. Sinnott
33d	1853	Z. W. McKnew	74th	1935	Joseph J. Sinnott
34th	1855	Nathan Darling	75th	1937	Joseph J. Sinnott
35th	1857	Robert B. Hackney	76th	1939	Joseph J. Sinnott
36th	1859	George Marston	77th	1941	Joseph J. Sinnott
37th	1861	Ira Goodnow	78th	1943	Joseph J. Sinnott
38th	1863	Ira Goodnow	79th	1945	Ralph R. Roberts
39th	1865	Ira Goodnow	80th	1947	M. M. Meletio
40th	1867	Charles E. Lippincott	81st	1949	William M. Miller
	1868	Otis S. Buxton	82d	1951	William M. Miller
41st	1869	Otis S. Buxton	83d	1953	Tom Kennamer
42d	1871	Otis S. Buxton	84th	1955	William M. Miller
43d	1873	Otis S. Buxton	85th	1957	William M. Miller
44th	1875	Lafayette H. Fitzhugh	86th	1959	William M. Miller
45th	1877	John W. Polk	87th	1961	William M. Miller
46th	1879	Charles W. Field	88th	1963	William M. Miller
47th	1881	W. P. Brownlow	89th	1965	William M. Miller
48th	1883	James G. Wintersmith	90th	1967	William M. Miller
49th	1885	James G. Wintersmith	91st	1969	William M. Miller
50th	1887	A. B. Hurt	92d	1971	William M. Miller
51st	1889	Charles W. Adams	93d	1973	William M. Miller[1]
52d	1891	Charles W. Adams			James T. Molloy[2]
53d	1893	A. B. Hurt	94th	1975	James T. Molloy
54th	1895	W. J. Glenn	95th	1977	James T. Molloy
55th	1897	W. J. Glenn	96th	1979	James T. Molloy
56th	1899	W. J. Glenn	97th	1981	James T. Molloy
57th	1901	W. J. Glenn	98th	1983	James T. Molloy
58th	1903	F. B. Lyon	99th	1985	James T. Molloy
59th	1905	F. B. Lyon	100th	1987	James T. Molloy
60th	1907	F. B. Lyon	101st	1989	James T. Molloy
61st	1909	F. B. Lyon	102d	1991	James T. Molloy
62d	1911	Joseph J. Sinnott	103d	1993	James T. Molloy

[1]Resigned 31 December 1974
[2]Acted as doorkeeper in the interim

elected for the first time in 1975. Perhaps the most colorful of the recent doorkeepers was William M. (Fishbait) Miller of Pascagoula, Mississippi, who served as doorkeeper from 1949 to 1953 and again from 1955 until his defeat for reelection in the House Democratic Caucus in 1974. The doorkeeper is elected by the entire House after nominations from the majority and minority parties.

Since the advent of radio and television, public recognition of the doorkeeper comes from his ceremonial role of announcing the president of the United States and other visiting dignitaries to the House chamber. The doorkeeper's duties have always included the enforcement of rules concerning the privileges of the House chamber. The doorkeeper oversees the pages, the doormen, publication and distribution services (which includes the mailing of House members' newsletters), the document room, cloakrooms, and the office of photography. The doorkeeper also administers the galleries and work areas set aside for daily newspapers and wire services, radio and television, and periodicals, which function under authorization of the Speaker.

BIBLIOGRAPHY

De Pauw, Linda Grant, et al., eds. *Documentary History of the First Federal Congress 1789–1791.* Vol. 3: *House of Representatives Journal.* 1977.

Miller, William M. *Fishbait: The Memoirs of the Congressional Doorkeeper.* 1977.

U.S. House of Representatives. *Constitution, Jefferson's Manual, and Rules of the House of Representatives, 103d Congress.* Compiled by William Holmes Brown. 102d Cong., 2d sess., 1992. H. Doc. 102-405.

RAYMOND W. SMOCK

DOUGHTON, ROBERT L. (1863–1954),

Democratic representative from North Carolina, chairman of the House Committee on Ways and Means, 1933–1947 and 1949–1953. A farmer and small-town banker before entering the House in 1911, Doughton served first on the Banking and Currency Committee and later chaired the Committee on Expenditures in the Department of Agriculture. He moved to the Ways and Means Committee in 1925 and, climbing in seniority rapidly on a rash of vacancies, became chairman seven years later. Critics argued that he was unprepared to direct the prestigious committee, but they were soon silenced by the panel's outpouring of innovative legislation early in the New Deal period. His talent for com-

promise was especially evident in the passage of the Social Security Act of 1935, which he sponsored and shepherded through a committee deeply divided over the bill's old-age and other provisions.

Nicknamed Muley, a reference to his stubbornness, Doughton was a rough-hewn man of simple attributes. He supported much of the New Deal but rebuffed President Franklin D. Roosevelt's efforts to dictate tax policy. "The Committee on Ways and Means is not going to delegate to any department, agency, person, or persons its duties and its responsibilities," he said. Doughton resisted Roosevelt's plans to tax the rich heavily and impose a national sales tax. After helping enact several tax increases to finance World War II, he balked when FDR sought still another increase in 1943. He supported, and Congress passed, a bill that left existing tax rates intact. Both houses subsequently overrode a presidential veto of the measure. Doughton retired in 1953, having served as Ways and Means chairman for eighteen years, longer than any predecessor.

BIBLIOGRAPHY

Kennon, Donald R., and Rebecca M. Rogers. *The Committee on Ways and Means: A Bicentennial History, 1789–1989.* 1989.

Rankin, Robert S. "Robert Lee Doughton: Hard Work and No Vacation." In *Public Men In and Out of Office.* Edited by J. T. Salter. 1946.

DONALD C. BACON

DOUGLAS, HELEN GAHAGAN (1900–

1980), representative from California (1945–1950), Democratic liberal defeated by Richard M. Nixon in the 1950 race for the U.S. Senate. Born into a wealthy Brooklyn family, educated in private schools, including two years at Barnard College, Douglas performed on Broadway and in operatic starring roles in the 1920s. She and actor Melvyn Douglas married in 1931, moved to Los Angeles, and had two children. Her husband's political activity and her own visibility in urging aid to migrant farm workers resulted in an invitation to the White House in 1939. The resulting friendship with the Roosevelts drew her into Democratic party politics, particularly the Women's Division. She won her first congressional campaign in 1944 running on a New Deal platform.

In Congress, Douglas, a speaker in high demand, viewed herself as a generalist who was concerned about a broad range of issues, from postwar inflation, housing, and civil rights to equal status for women and cancer research funds. Organized labor provided her with substantial campaign funding. A member of the Committee on Foreign Affairs, Douglas cosponsored the Atomic Energy Act of 1946, worked particularly diligently on legislation to implement the Marshall Plan, and generally followed the Truman line. Her opposition to Greek-Turkish aid, however, cost her reappointment to the U.N. delegation in 1947. Douglas's actions in Washington were well received in her district, particularly by her large black constituency, which resulted in increasing victory margins. Douglas deserves recognition in large measure because she challenged the political system as an "outsider," motivated people to political action, and served as a voice for the liberal conscience. Despite political success, marital and parenting challenges complicated her life. Characteristic restlessness led Douglas to run for the Senate, but it is likely that she would have lost the race, even without Nixon's infamous "red-smear" tactics, because of the political climate and her gender. After the campaign, she and her family returned to New York, where she continued to be an important voice for liberal causes and a model for women moving into electoral politics, particularly in the 1970s.

BIBLIOGRAPHY

Douglas, Helen Gahagan. *A Full Life*. 1982.

Helen Douglas Project. Vols. 1–4. Regional Oral History Office, The Bancroft Library, University of California, Berkeley.

Scobie, Ingrid Winther. *Center Stage: Helen Gahagan Douglas, A Life*. 1992.

INGRID WINTHER SCOBIE

PAUL H. DOUGLAS. In August 1965.

LIBRARY OF CONGRESS

DOUGLAS, PAUL H. (1892–1976), senator from Illinois (1949–1967) and a leader in the Senate of the liberal and progressive wing of the Democratic party. Paul Howard Douglas was a pathfinder and social reformer, Chicago alderman, a pre–World War II interventionist, president of the American Economic Association, and the author of eighteen books. A Quaker, he joined the Marine Corps in 1942 at age fifty and was wounded in combat.

Douglas served on the Banking, Labor, and Finance committees and as chairman of the Joint Economic Committee. He authored the 1955 Minimum Wage Act, the Union-Management Pension and Welfare Fund Disclosure Act, the Truth in Lending Act, the Area Redevelopment Act, and numerous housing and banking bills. He was an expert on unemployment, housing, welfare, Social Security, reciprocal trade, taxes, Medicare, and Medicaid.

Over the opposition of the Senate's powerful southern Democratic–conservative Republican coalition, he led the struggle for civil rights and the reform of the Senate filibuster rule; opposed water, tax, and commodity subsidies; and fought waste in military procurement. (He coined the phrase "a liberal need not be a wastrel.") He authored a famous Senate report *Ethics in Government* after the Reconstruction Finance Corporation scandals in the early 1950s. He successfully fought President Harry S. Truman's attempt to do away with the Marine Corps. Douglas was both the watchdog and conscience of the Senate. "When the chips are down," he said, "a Senator should vote his profound individual convictions . . . regardless of who is with him or against him."

Douglas's battles for civil rights and the Indiana Dunes National Seashore were vindicated by congressional passage of the Civil Rights Act of 1964 and the Voting Rights Act of 1965 and, the following year, a bill to make the Indiana dunes a national lakeshore. "When I was a young man," he said, "I wanted to save the world. In my middle years I wanted to save the country. Now I just want to save the Dunes."

BIBLIOGRAPHY

Douglas, Paul H. *Economy in the National Government.* 1952.
Douglas, Paul H. *In the Fullness of Time: The Memoirs of Paul H. Douglas.* 1972.

HOWARD E. SHUMAN

DOUGLAS, STEPHEN A. (1813–1861), representative and senator from Illinois, Democratic party leader, and presidential candidate. Stephen Arnold Douglas was born in Brandon, Vermont, the son of a physician who died while Douglas was an infant. He moved to upstate New York in 1830, where he continued his education in the local academy and began his study of the law. In 1833 he left home, determined to settle in the "western country," where the requirements for the bar would be less formal. He settled in Jacksonville, Illinois, and a few months later was licensed to practice law in the state.

Douglas's interest in politics was first aroused when he was captivated by the image of Andrew Jackson during the 1828 campaign. The tenets of Jacksonian democracy became his creed. His vigorous defense of Jackson's anti–Bank of the United States policy won the support of the Kentucky and Tennessee farmers who had settled in the vicinity of Jacksonville. Standing only five feet four inches in height, exuding energy and intensity of feeling, Douglas soon became known as the Little Giant.

Douglas applied new techniques of party organization to Democratic politics in Illinois. A committee structure was developed, nominating conventions were introduced, and tight party discipline was imposed. More than any other, Douglas was instrumental in bringing the second-party system to the state. Brash, hard-driving, and ambitious, he had an instinct for leadership that appealed to the citizenry. The Democratic party became the vehicle for his ambition, and he was soon recognized as its head.

In 1838, barely twenty-five years old, Douglas was narrowly defeated in his first race for Congress by

STEPHEN A. DOUGLAS.   LIBRARY OF CONGRESS

his Whig opponent, John T. Stuart, Abraham Lincoln's law partner, losing by a margin of only thirty-six votes in a total vote of over thirty-six thousand. Following the state's redistricting in 1843, he again ran for Congress, as the Democratic candidate in the new 5th Congressional District, ten counties lying principally between the Illinois and Mississippi rivers. In a successful campaign that stressed national issues, Douglas denounced a national bank as dangerous to popular liberty and condemned the protective tariff as favoring the rich at the expense of the poor, arguments that the largely rural electorate found appealing. For the next eighteen years, Douglas's name would be linked with all the great movements of national political life. He was reelected to a second term in 1844 and to a third in 1846, each time by an increasing majority.

Douglas joined the first session of the 28th Congress in December 1843. His first major speech, appropriately, was a zealous defense of Andrew Jackson and in support of a bill to refund the fine imposed on Jackson during the campaign against the British at New Orleans. The bill passed, and Douglas established his credentials as a leader of the Democratic party in Congress. He held an unshakable faith in popular rule, or what he would later call popular sovereignty, and strongly believed that the people spoke through the majority. He was dedicated to the idea that a strong, viable, and disciplined party organization provided the most effective channel for the expression of the popular will. Douglas was devoted to the Constitution, although he could not always be termed a strict constructionist, and he insisted that the rights of the states be consistently and scrupulously protected. The Union, to Douglas as to Jackson, was sacred and perpetual, a confederation of sovereign states rather than a consolidated empire. But Douglas was not doctrinaire. Compromise, a willingness to adapt principles to circumstances, and the ability to yield a little in order to gain support for larger measures were for him marks of the wise politician.

The nation's future, Douglas believed, lay in the expansion and development of what he often called the Great West. His first move as a congressman was to unfold a legislative program that included territorial expansion, the construction of a transcontinental railroad, the encouragement of western settlement through a free land or homestead policy, and the organization of territorial governments. He placed himself almost immediately in the forefront of the movement to annex Texas, and he was a leader in demanding the acquisition of all of Oregon. He enthusiastically supported the Mexican War, which he viewed as advancing the cause of freedom and democracy. The extension of the United States' boundaries to the Pacific, he believed, was but the fulfillment of the nation's destiny. Advances in technology such as railroads and the telegraph, the flexibility of the federal system of government, and, especially, America's role as the model republic—all these factors defied limits to national growth. In recognition of his aggressive stand in support of western expansion and development, Douglas was chosen to serve as chairman of the House Committee on Territories.

In December 1846, shortly after his reelection to a third term in the House and after months of careful preparation and lobbying, Douglas fulfilled a long-held ambition by being elected to the U.S. Senate by the Illinois legislature. Reelected twice, in 1853 and 1859—the latter following a strenuous campaign against Abraham Lincoln—Douglas reached the peak of his reputation and notoriety as a national leader in the Senate. He took his Senate seat at a time when the conflict between the North and the South over the status of slavery in the territories was heating to the boiling point. The end of the Mexican War and the introduction of the Wilmot Proviso, which would have banned slavery in all the lands acquired from Mexico, initiated a constitutional debate that polarized the nation and moved it by degrees to the brink of civil conflict. The Senate played a significant role in the debate, and in the Senate Douglas stood at the vortex of controversy.

In the Senate as in the House, Douglas was elected to the chairmanship of the Committee on Territories, a key position in the debate. The committee was new, its scope still uncertain. Douglas insisted on a broad and comprehensive definition of its authority. He argued that all territorial business, whether it involved military, judicial, postal, or other affairs, fell within the purview of his committee. He insisted that the admission of new states came under the jurisdiction of his committee as well. Douglas's position often involved him in bitter clashes with other committee chairmen, but it brought him recognition as one of the most powerful members of the Senate. Until his removal from the chairmanship by a southern-dominated Democratic caucus following his reelection campaign in 1858, Douglas wrote, modified, and sponsored legislation creating seven territories.

During the debates over slavery in the territories, Douglas refined and developed his doctrine of popular sovereignty as a middle ground between the northern antislavery position and the southern proslavery stand. The people of a territory, he contended, must be allowed to decide the question for themselves, without the intervention of the national government. In keeping with his faith in popular rule, he found this solution fair and just to both sides. He was convinced, however, that by allowing the people of the territories to make their own democratic decision, freedom, not slavery, would be extended, for he believed that slavery would prove uneconomical in the western regions. The doctrine was first implemented in the Compromise of 1850, a sectional accord in which Douglas played a significant part, when California was admitted as a free state in accordance with the wishes of its inhabitants, and the territories of Utah and New Mexico were organized on the basis of popular sovereignty.

In 1854, Douglas followed up with the introduction of the Kansas-Nebraska Act, arguably the decade's most explosive piece of legislation—and one that would be inseparably linked with his name. Although the two territories lay north of the Missouri Compromise line, Douglas declared that the act's true intent was neither to introduce nor to exclude slavery but to leave the people free to form and regulate their "domestic institutions" in their own way. To guarantee its passage, Douglas bowed to pressure from southern senators and added an explicit repeal of the Missouri Compromise. The move was greeted by a storm of denunciation from northern antislavery elements. Douglas was singled out for vilification and charged with being insensitive to the moral issue of slavery, with betraying freedom in the territories in the interest of his own presidential ambitions, and with being a member of a "slave power" conspiracy bent on spreading slavery throughout the free states as well as the territories. The furor resulted in a realignment of political parties, as the Whig party gave way to the new sectional Republican party and the Kansas Territory was plunged into disorder and chaos.

Douglas became the focus of controversy in Congress as he defended popular sovereignty against his attackers. Crowds packed the Senate galleries to witness the Little Giant in action. His mind had the rapidity of lightning, it was said, and his words were like red-hot nails hurled at his opponents. In 1856, he wrote and submitted a territorial committee report on Kansas in which he blamed the interference of northern and southern extremists for the disorder and violence and reaffirmed his doctrine of popular sovereignty as the only practical means for restoring order. Undaunted by the Supreme Court's decision in *Scott v. Sandford* a year later, which he insisted did not properly involve popular sovereignty, Douglas opposed the admission of Kansas as a slave state under the dubious Lecompton constitution, enacted by a fraudulently elected territorial convention. Defying President James Buchanan and the southern Democratic leadership, he denounced the measure as a travesty of popular sovereignty, for, he said, it clearly did not express the will of the people of Kansas. He further sharpened his position during the Lincoln-Douglas debates of 1858, when he argued that the people of a territory could still exclude slavery in spite of the Dred Scott decision simply by enacting legislation unfriendly toward the institution and by depriving slavery of legal protection, a view that became known as the Freeport doctrine. Southern leaders were so angered by Douglas's statement that they removed him from the Committee on Territories and sought to strip him of his Senate power.

Douglas was nominated for the presidency in 1860, but the action split the Democratic party. Convinced that the election of Republican Abraham Lincoln would destroy the Union, Douglas appealed to southerners to forsake their leadership and turn back the tide of disunion. His effort was to no avail. Lincoln was elected, and the secession of southern states became a reality. Douglas spent the last months of his life in a desperate search for a Senate compromise that would preserve the Union and avoid civil war. Popular sovereignty remained his solution to the crisis. Lincoln's refusal to countenance compromise and his inauguration, followed by the bombardment and surrender of Fort Sumter, South Carolina, dashed Douglas's hopes that the nation might yet be reunited. Broken in body and spirit, Douglas died in Chicago on 3 June 1861, at the age of forty-eight.

BIBLIOGRAPHY

Johannsen, Robert W. *The Frontier, the Union, and Stephen A. Douglas.* 1989.

Johannsen, Robert W. *The Letters of Stephen A. Douglas.* 1961.

Johannsen, Robert W. *Stephen A. Douglas.* 1973.

Wells, Damon. *Stephen Douglas: The Last Years, 1857–1861.* 1971.

ROBERT W. JOHANNSEN

DRAFTING. The terms *legislative drafting* and *bill drafting* are often used to describe the act of sitting down and committing legislative language to paper. More accurately, however, they describe the entire multifaceted process of converting raw ideas into legislative language that will effectively carry them out. Actually writing the words is merely the last stage in this process, although it is obviously a critical stage, and one that differs in a number of important respects from other literary activities.

Legislative language requires an unusually high degree of accuracy and precision; it cannot tolerate the minor ambiguities that are common in everyday speech and in most other kinds of writing. Because a bill is meant to become law it must be written with careful attention to how it and existing laws will interrelate. It must be cast in a form and style that is highly specialized yet varies from setting to setting, and its passage often depends on a maze of procedural and parliamentary questions that can only be guessed at in advance.

A legislative proposal starts on its way because someone—the sponsor—believes there is a problem that should be addressed by legislation and calls upon a drafter for assistance. Whoever originates this legislative idea is the sponsor during the preliminary drafting, but a legislator must take over this sponsoring function once the product is ready for introduction.

The drafter's job is to help put into legislative form what the sponsor envisions. In many cases, however, the sponsor's ideas are imperfectly formed; he or she often provides no more than a set of general objectives that must be refined before a practical means for achieving them can be devised or may have no appreciation of the collateral problems that the proposal might raise.

The sponsor's initial generalities must be converted into specifics: problems, gaps, inconsistencies, or ambiguities in the proposal must be identified and dealt with; substantive, legal, administrative, and technical questions that may arise along the way must be anticipated; and an arrangement of the bill's various elements that will effectively communicate its message to the intended audience must be found. The drafter's efforts in these areas often constitute the best way—sometimes the only way—of identifying those aspects of the sponsor's policy that need modification or further refinement.

The final product must be cast in language that is clear, consistent, legally effective, technically sound, administrable, enforceable, and constitutional; be correct in terms of form and style; be as readable as possible; and not create unintended any side effects.

Producing a bill that is objectively correct in terms of form and style is complicated by the fact that four different drafting styles (with occasional variants) are currently used in federal legislation: (1) the older or "traditional" style, which has the fewest arbitrary requirements and is the least demanding in a technical sense; (2) "Code" style, which is used in the positive-law titles of the United States Code; (3) revenue style, which is used in all tax laws, has many formal requirements, and is the most demanding; and (4) a modified version of revenue style that incorporates most of the features of that style while avoiding its extremes. Any bill could be written in any of these styles, although in most cases the drafter will feel constrained to conform with the style of existing law in the field or to accommodate the stylistic preferences of the committees that will consider the bill. Revenue style is increasingly becoming the style of choice in federal legislation when no such constraints are present.

Language that can be easily comprehended by readers is always desirable, but bills that are inescapably complex or deal with highly technical subjects cannot be couched in the language of everyday speech and frequently cannot be made "readable" at all. In any event, most important federal legislation today is addressed to an audience of administrators or specialists rather than to ordinary people, even if ordinary people are the ones who will ultimately benefit or suffer under it.

Legislative drafting is a highly pragmatic operation, not an academic exercise. The drafter's overriding objective with any bill is to develop a full understanding of the underlying problem and the sponsor's policy for solving it and then to give expression to that policy clearly and accurately. All other drafting rules and principles, though they are normally quite consistent with and supportive of that objective, are secondary; stylistic deviations and lack of readability become virtues (or at least are forgivable) when they are unavoidable consequences of the effort to achieve it.

[See also Bills; Lawmaking; Legislative Counsel; Public Law; Resolutions.]

BIBLIOGRAPHY

Dickerson, Reed. *The Fundamentals of Legal Drafting.* 1965.

Filson, Lawrence E. *The Legislative Drafter's Desk Reference.* 1992.

Hirsch, Donald. *Drafting Federal Law.* Published for the Department of Health and Human Services, 1980. Revised for the use of the Office of the Legislative Counsel, U.S. House of Representatives, 1989.

LAWRENCE E. FILSON

DRED SCOTT DECISION. *See* Scott v. Sandford.

DRUGS. *See* Narcotics and Other Dangerous Drugs.

DYNASTIES, POLITICAL. *See* Political Dynasties.

E

EASTLAND, JAMES O. (1904–1986), Democratic senator from Mississippi, president pro tempore of the Senate, Judiciary Committee chairman, and implacable foe of civil rights legislation. Chairman of the Senate Judiciary Committee (1956–1978) during the height of the civil rights movement, James Oliver Eastland made his committee the burying ground for civil rights legislation. Of the scores of civil rights bills assigned to Judiciary, few emerged until 1965, when the Senate leadership began to attach directives to bills requiring the committee to report them by certain fixed deadlines. Eastland was fond of telling white audiences in Mississippi that he once had special pockets sewn into his trousers so he could carry such bills around with him and take care of them.

Eastland first went to the Senate in 1941 when his father's boyhood friend, Governor Paul B. Johnson, Sr., appointed Eastland to the seat left vacant upon the death of Pat Harrison. He served but three months, declining to enter the special election, won by Rep. Wall Doxey, to fill the remainder of Harrison's term. The following year, however, Eastland successfully challenged Doxey's bid for re-election to a full term of his own. Reclaiming his seat in January 1943, Eastland retained it for thirty-six years.

At age fifty-one he became the youngest chairman of the Judiciary Committee to that point in the history of the Senate and held that post longer than anyone in the twentieth century. He also served as chairman of the Subcommittee on Internal Security, having helped to secure passage of the McCarran Internal Security Act of 1950 over President Harry S. Truman's veto. As chairman of the Sub-

JAMES O. EASTLAND.
OFFICE OF THE HISTORIAN OF THE U.S. SENATE

committee on Soil Conservation and Forestry, Eastland guarded the interests of southern agriculture, especially in the Mississippi Delta, where he owned a 5,800-acre plantation that reaped thousands of dollars in annual farm subsidies. In 1972 he became president pro tempore, twice coming within a heartbeat of the presidency when both Spiro T. Agnew's resignation in 1973 and Gerald R. Ford's succession to the presidency after Richard M. Nixon resigned in 1974 briefly left the nation without a vice president.

Reticent to the point of shyness in public, Eastland was a master of cloakroom politics. His parlia-

667

mentary skills, his seniority, and his surprising capacity to pacify his committee members earned him the grudging respect, although certainly not the affection, of most of his colleagues. In an era of intense racial tension, he was the cigar-chomping caricature of segregationist intransigence, and he reveled in the image.

BIBLIOGRAPHY

Chandler, David Leon. *The Natural Superiority of Southern Politicians: A Revisionist History.* 1977.
Johnston, Earle. *Mississippi's Defiant Years, 1953–1973: An Interpretive Documentary with Personal Experiences.* 1990.

CHESTER M. MORGAN

ECONOMIC COMMITTEE, JOINT. The Joint Economic Committee (JEC) is a permanent committee of Congress that includes members of the House and Senate. The JEC has no power to report legislation. Rather, its purpose is to gather and analyze information concerning the state of the U.S. economy and to convey to Congress policy recommendations intended to address economic problems facing the nation. The committee also scrutinizes the views and actions of economic policymakers in the executive branch, such as the Federal Reserve Board. In carrying out these tasks the JEC holds public hearings, undertakes studies of the economy, and issues reports. Similar to its counterpart in the executive branch, the Council of Economic Advisers (CEA), the JEC is the only committee in Congress that takes a broad, encompassing view of U.S. economic policy and performance.

The JEC was established under the Employment Act of 1946. One of the purposes of that legislation was to strengthen the federal government's capacity to monitor economic performance and undertake needed intervention. Coming after the Great Depression of the 1930s, the Employment Act formally acknowledged the federal government's responsibility for avoiding a repeat of that cataclysm and for maintaining prosperity. Along with the CEA, the JEC has helped to systematize economic policymaking and has brought professional economists into the highest levels of the federal government.

Membership on the JEC is drawn from both chambers and both parties. When a senator serves as chairman, the vice chairman usually is a House member, and vice versa. (Occupants of these posts are drawn from the majority party of the respective chamber.) The chairmanship traditionally rotates from one chamber to the other at the beginning of each Congress. For the 103d Congress (1993–1995), the JEC included ten members each from the House and Senate—twelve Democrats and eight Republicans. The JEC has had ten to twelve subcommittees in the past, although currently it has none. The JEC's jurisdiction covers such topics as monetary and fiscal policies, trade, productivity, economic growth, investment, jobs, and prices. Professional staff positions on the committee are almost exclusively filled by economists.

As with other joint committees of Congress, the JEC has received scant attention by scholars, no doubt because of its lack of authority to report legislation. Nevertheless, the committee is frequently at the center of economic policy debates in Washington. The JEC has become an important forum for generating policy advice and monitoring U.S. economic performance. Its hearings are frequently covered by the news media, particularly during appearances by top executive branch officials. The committee holds annual hearings to examine the *Economic Report of the President*, regularly calls the chairman of the Federal Reserve Board, and receives testimony on labor-market conditions from the commissioner of labor statistics on the first Friday of each month, when monthly employment data are released.

When one party controls the executive branch and another controls Congress, it is not unusual for the majority to use the JEC as a forum for scrutinizing and criticizing the president's economic policy. However, like Congress as a whole, the committee is much less effective in building a consensus around an alternative economic policy.

[See also Employment Act of 1946.]

BIBLIOGRAPHY

Schick, Allen. *Making Economic Policy in Congress.* 1983.
Sundquist, James L. *The Decline and Resurgence of Congress.* 1981.

GARY MUCCIARONI

ECONOMIC OPPORTUNITY ACT OF 1964 (78 Stat. 508–534). The Economic Opportunity Act of 1964 is better known as the "poverty program," or "war on poverty," launched during the administration of President Lyndon B. Johnson. The act created an Office of Economic Opportunity (OEO) to administer several programs intended to lift millions of Americans above the poverty level. Its centerpiece was the Community Action Program, which created and funded in each local community an agency that would mobilize the poor and launch a comprehensive program to "focus" federal, state, and local resources and social services on the poverty problem. It also created the Job Corps, a residential training program for disadvantaged school dropouts, the Neighborhood Youth Corps, which provided part-time work experience for disadvantaged youths still in school, an adult education program, a program to enable talented disadvantaged students to go on to college (Upward Bound), preschool education (Head Start), legal services, and Volunteers in Service to America (VISTA), which was billed as a domestic Peace Corps. Reform-minded intellectuals played a key role in getting the issue on the agenda and supplying policy options, such as the community action concept, while other programs (e.g., the Job Corps) had been introduced earlier in Congress.

Despite Johnson's lofty declaration of an "unconditional war" on poverty, the first year's appropriation of barely $1 billion fell far below the estimated $15 billion believed necessary. Funding remained low throughout the decade. An ambitious long-term budget for the poverty programs was proposed by the OEO in 1966. But the escalating war in Vietnam, plus Johnson's refusal to raise taxes in an election year, killed the idea.

The Community Action Program became highly controversial when militant advocates for the poor and the poor themselves used the community action agencies to challenge the power of local political establishments. Congress took strong action against the program in response. After persistent efforts to abolish the OEO, the Republicans succeeded during the Nixon administration. Some parts of the original act remained in the early 1990s and are generally regarded as successes, particularly the Job Corps and Head Start.

BIBLIOGRAPHY

Levitan, Sar A. *The Great Society's Poor Law: A New Approach to Poverty.* 1969.

Moynihan, Daniel P. *Maximum Feasible Misunderstanding: Community Action in the War on Poverty.* 1969.

GARY MUCCIARONI

ECONOMIC POLICY. [*This entry discusses congressional economic policy in two separate articles, one on nineteenth- and the other on twentieth-century policies. For discussion of related issues, see* Banking; Currency and Finance; Internal Improve-

ments; Public Lands; Regulation and Deregulation; Tariffs and Trade; Taxation; Transportation.]

Nineteenth Century

The federal system adopted in 1789 dispersed power to all levels of government, thereby enabling towns, cities, counties, states, and many other public and private institutions to join Congress in promoting economic enterprise. Sometimes the different levels of government competed or clashed, but more often their efforts complemented and reinforced each other (as in the local, state, and national aid to western railroads). While many historians think that the impact of Congress on economic development was greater in the first half of the nineteenth century than in the second, and greater still in the twentieth century, Congress in fact has been preoccupied with economic growth throughout the history of the nation. However, its tactics and policies did change as cities grew, the arable public land disappeared, transportation improved, local gave way to national markets, and gigantic manufacturing corporations supplanted relatively small businesses. Congress intervened in the economy in a wide variety of ways, but its major areas of concern were banking and currency, the tariff, transportation, and the public domain.

Rampant inflation during and after the Revolutionary War persuaded Congress to protect the nation's credit and the stability of its currency. The first Bank of the United States (BUS), chartered in 1791, was a quasi-public institution that maintained large reserves of specie and followed prudent lending policies. It became the repository of most federal revenue from customs duties, excise taxes, and public land sales. However, rapid population growth, territorial expansion, and the first phase of industrialization prompted a dramatic increase in the number of state banks chartered in the two decades before the War of 1812. During the war, many of these new banks in the South and West suspended payments in specie, and the Bank of the United States was compelled to accept heavily discounted notes in payment of customs duties and taxes. For this reason, Congress chartered a second Bank of the United States in 1816 and gave it greater control over state banks—which increased from 5 in 1791 to 28 in 1800 to 338 in 1818. By threatening to demand payment in specie, the new national bank served as a powerful check on the loan and currency policies of state banks—at the price of keeping the money supply small and promoting mild deflation during most of the four decades before the Civil War. After President Andrew Jackson refused to recharter the Bank of the United States in 1836, federal involvement in banking waned until the Civil War, but this was due in large part to increasing state banking regulation through the process of incorporation.

The financial needs of the Civil War deeply influenced currency and banking and inevitably led to tighter federal control. In 1863 Congress invited state banks to accept federal charters, on condition that they purchase government bonds in the amount of one third of their capital stock, and many did. By the end of 1866 the national bank network embraced 1,600 units, which held about 75 percent of the nation's total deposits.

In 1865, Congress imposed a 10 percent tax on state bank notes in an attempt to create a national currency by driving the state bank notes—which constituted the bulk of the circulating paper issued before the Civil War—out of circulation. It also decided to finance the war by issuing greenbacks and notes rather than by levying heavy taxes on personal income or business. Only about 25 percent of the

cost of fighting the war was raised through taxes, and the personal income tax adopted during the war—a modest 3 to 5 percent levy that was phased out by 1872—contributed no more than 10 percent. Despite these policies, state banks increased rapidly in the 1880s and 1890s, especially in the South, and there was no national banking system until Congress enacted the Federal Reserve Act in 1913.

Banking policy took a back seat to currency management after the Civil War, as Congress was caught up in an extended debate between those (including most bankers and industrialists) who wanted to maintain the money supply at the same level or shrink it to keep prices up and those (including most farmers) who wanted to expand the money supply and lower prices. The inflationists favored issuing more greenbacks to pay off the nation's postwar bonded debt, but the contractionists won out, and gradually the bills were retired. Thereafter, much of the debate was over whether gold or silver should be the basic circulating medium. Congress in 1873 dictated that silver should be coined at a ratio of 16 to 1 relative to gold. But in that year silver dollars were worth $1.02 in gold, so silver money virtually disappeared. The supply of silver, increased during the 1870s, however. Various European countries adopted the gold standard in that decade, and Nevada's Comstock Lode reached its peak productivity in those years. Silver fell to 96 cents in 1876, and the old ratio of 16 to 1 became inflationary. Whether the money supply should be determined by the supply of gold or silver, the size of the population, or the price of basic commodities was debated until the century ended, but no clear monetary policy emerged (though the "gold bugs" generally dominated in Congress).

Another ongoing congressional debate that spanned much of the nineteenth century had to do with the tariff. The first tax on imported goods—taxes on exported goods were specifically prohibited by the Constitution—was adopted soon after Washington's first inauguration. But for the new nation's first two decades tariffs were a source of revenue, not a device to protect fledgling industries. However, after the War of 1812 many lawmakers feared that Europe would flood the United States with cheap goods. In 1816 they enacted the first protective tariff, which levied duties of 7.5 to 30 percent, with special protection for cottons, woolens, iron, and other manufactured goods.

At the end of the 1820s, customs duties took on new meaning as part of Henry Clay's "American System," which envisioned the protective tariff as a

PEWTER MEDAL. Bearing slogan "Equal and full protection to American industry," espousing a protective tariff favored by northern industrialists and Whig candidates in the 1836 elections.

COLLECTION OF DAVID J. AND JANICE L. FRENT

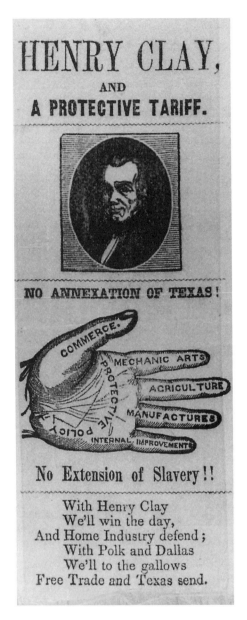

HENRY CLAY,
AND
A PROTECTIVE TARIFF.

NO ANNEXATION OF TEXAS!

COMMERCE.
MECHANIC ARTS
PROTECTIVE POLICY
AGRICULTURE
MANUFACTURES
INTERNAL IMPROVEMENTS

No Extension of Slavery!!

With Henry Clay
We'll win the day,
And Home Industry defend;
With Polk and Dallas
We'll to the gallows
Free Trade and Texas send.

SILK CAMPAIGN RIBBON. Reflecting the main positions of the economic platform for Henry Clay's (W-Ky.) 1844 presidential campaign.

COLLECTION OF DAVID J. AND JANICE L. FRENT

tool for building home markets for agricultural and domestic products and for unifying the nation by providing money for education, transportation, and other internal improvements. But political opposition from the South—and from many shippers, banks, and businesses involved in foreign trade—undermined this early attempt at economic planning.

From 1832 to the Civil War, southern opposition to high protective tariffs restrained the protection-

ists. The Tariff of 1857 reduced the maximum rate to 24 percent and the average duty to the lowest level since 1815. Nevertheless, the tariff remained the major source of federal revenue, bringing in five to ten times more than all other sources combined. After secession, protectionists dominated Congress until the close of the century, despite a treasury surplus and charges that high tariffs increased the cost of living and contributed to the squeeze on workers during the depressions of the 1870s and 1890s. During the Civil War, average rates more than doubled, and duties remained high for the rest of the century, whether Democrats or Republicans held power. Industrial development, the rise of large corporations, and the prevalent belief that a high tariff guaranteed the American wage scale added to the strength of protectionist sentiment in Congress. The 1897 Dingley tariff, the highest in American history, set average rates at 52 percent. The tariff was largely a bipartisan issue because it was the product of the tug-and-pull of a multitude of local industries and interests, not an incipient form of centralized economic planning. And while Congress successfully protected from competition many industries—such as steel and wool in the last decades of the century—they might have grown as fast, or perhaps even faster, without high tariffs.

The power of localism in nineteenth-century America also left its mark on transportation policies. Thomas Jefferson asked Congress in 1806 to apply surplus federal revenue to the construction of roads and canals, to river improvements, and to education. Secretary of the Treasury Albert Gallatin subsequently produced a comprehensive plan for a national transportation system, and every president before Andrew Jackson favored federally financed internal improvements. But the National, or Cumberland, Road from Cumberland, Maryland, to Wheeling, Virginia (now West Virginia), built along the Ohio River after the War of 1812, was the only substantial accomplishment. Constitutional objections and sectional jealousies blocked congressional adoption of a comprehensive transportation plan.

In an effort to reduce divisive trade barriers and to promote nationalism, the Constitution had designated the Mississippi and Saint Lawrence rivers and their navigable tributaries as common highways, open to all. Congress extended this principle to all the nation's navigable streams in 1803. After the War of 1812 the promotion of trade and national security went hand in hand to advance the idea of keeping interior waterways open. During the 1820s the Army Corps of Engineers assumed most of the work of river improvement, including dredging, clearing snags, building levees, and lining stream banks. The first river-and-harbor bill was passed in 1824, and expenditures increased until 1837, when shrinking federal revenue and state and sectional conflicts temporarily put an end to the work of the corps. By 1837 about ninety projects had been undertaken on the Mississippi, Ohio, Red, Arkansas, Missouri, Cumberland, Hudson, Cape Fear, and Savannah rivers at a cost of about $9 million.

After the Civil War, dissatisfaction with the railroad, a new nationalism, and the ballooning treasury surplus led to annual rather than intermittent rivers and harbors appropriations. But rewarding constituents and building up home districts took precedence in Congress; lawmakers never asked the corps to prepare comprehensive plans for water transportation, nor did they require it to gather and compile commercial statistics. Until 1884, when Congress finally gave the corps the power to veto infeasible surveys ordered by members of Congress, the mere investigation of a project almost invariably led to its construction. As a result, corps projects were often wasteful, inefficient, and poorly coordinated. They were designed as much to distribute the treasury surplus as to promote commerce, and internal improvements became a crude form of what in the twentieth century would be called "revenue sharing."

As early as the 1820s, Congress began to provide land grants to a handful of states to encourage the construction of turnpikes and canals and the improvement of rivers. But it was not until 1850, when Congress promised land to the Illinois Central, that the public domain was used to subsidize a railroad. By 1871, when land grants were terminated, seventy railroads had been given nearly 156 million acres, although they registered only 131 million. This was 10 percent of the entire public domain, and because the railroads ran along streams and through valleys, much of that land was the best in the West.

The federal government also provided many other forms of aid, including surveys of the best transcontinental routes, free timber for ties and fuel, and low duties on iron used for rails. Most railroads were eager to sell their land as rapidly as possible so that they could increase the carrying trade and raise revenue to expand operations; consequently, the land from the federal government

sold for an average price of only $3.38 an acre. Some lines would have been built without the grants, but the West was settled much more rapidly as a result of congressional policy. Moreover, the benefits—creating a new sense of union and developing national markets, stimulating the fledgling steel industry, and standardizing rail gauges—cannot be overemphasized.

Still, Congress never produced a coherent program to develop a national transportation system or even to populate the West. Most members supported subsidies to transportation, but they did not favor increasing the power of executive agencies in Washington. The Union Pacific Railroad is a case in point. The federal government's "policy" when it incorporated that railroad in 1862 was, in the words of historian Wallace Farnham, "a blend of neglect and unresolution." The Plains Indians had not been "subdued" when construction began, and there was little or no federal presence in Wyoming Territory. Although the government was represented on the company's board of directors, Congress made no effort to supervise construction, set tolls, regulate the issuance or sale of company stock, or administer the corporation's daily operations.

The Union Pacific and Central Pacific were the first private corporations chartered by the federal government (aside from the Bank of the United States). Congress subsequently incorporated the Northern Pacific (1864), the Atlantic & Pacific (1866), and the Texas & Pacific (1871). Federal incorporation might have inaugurated a new era of rate regulation, but the government remained quick to subsidize and slow to rule. "To say that the government created the robber barons," Farnham concluded, "is to utter at least part of the truth." In short, the Union Pacific did not corrupt government, government corrupted the Union Pacific, which was forced to create its own commercial law in part because Congress would not. In many ways business served as a surrogate for an unwilling federal government, especially in the West, where state and local government was generally too poor and too weak to undertake public works.

The same commitment to economic growth and the same lack of vision were evident in land policy. The public domain served many purposes, and Congress had a hard time sorting them out. At one time or another public land policy was intended to provide homes for the homeless, to increase the loyalty of frontier inhabitants to the central government, to expand domestic markets for manufactured goods, to keep agricultural and industrial wages high in the East (by draining off surplus workers), and (by promoting the small family farm) to resist the spread of slavery. Initially, the public lands were seen as a source of revenue to pay the nation's debts. In 1796 Congress provided for land sales in minimum parcels of 640 acres at a minimum auction price of $2 per acre. Because the only land offices were located on the East Coast, it was anticipated that the land would be purchased by nonresident speculators who would, in turn, retail it to actual settlers. But Congress came under heavy pressure from squatters, who often moved to the frontier well ahead of government surveyors and defied all attempts by the U.S. Army to drive them away, and from Massachusetts and Virginia, which were selling their surplus land at a much lower price. Because land sales were slow in the 1790s, Congress in 1800 lowered the minimum amount of land to 320 acres. In 1820 acreage was cut to 80 acres and the price was reduced to $1.25 an acre. The 1800 and 1820 laws allowed buyers to purchase their land on credit, but by the 1830s and 1840s pressure for free land had mounted. Southerners opposed this policy, lest it disrupt the balance between slave and free states. The Homestead Act did not pass until 1862.

Critics of nineteenth-century land policy have complained that American land laws played into the hands of speculators because the laws were filled with loopholes that allowed cattle, land, timber, railroad, and other companies to monopolize the public domain, and because they were rooted in the increasingly anachronistic idea that land was the primary expense in setting up a farm. Both these criticisms miss the point that U.S. land policy was designed not just to dispose of land as rapidly as possible and keep prices low but also to eliminate the bureaucratic cost of a more active federal role in land management (as in leasing the grazing lands or operating federally managed timber farms or coal mines). Instead of having a federal agency classify the timber, grazing, mineral, and farming land within the public domain, Congress in effect paid speculators to do so.

This disposal policy had many woeful effects. It encouraged farmers to exhaust the soil and move rather than conserve what they had. Because almost all land sold for the minimum price, only the best was taken and the rest was left for later waves of settlers. And because many farmers speculated in land as a sideline and held tracts for longer than needed to raise crops, early settlements were scattered rather than compact, which dramatically in-

CAMPAIGN POSTER. For the 1884 presidential campaign of James G. Blaine (R-Maine), stating solutions to regional economic problems: "Public Lands for Actual Settlers," "Increased Commercial Intercourse with Friendly Neighboring States," and "No Tribute to England for American Fish."

COLLECTION OF DAVID J. AND JANICE L. FRENT

creased the cost of roads, schools, jails, and social services. Speculation also contributed to higher taxes because unimproved land was generally taxed at much lower rates than improved land. Finally, the public domain was one of the chief sources of corruption in nineteenth-century politics; in the South and West that corruption suggested that neither wisdom nor justice could ever prevail in Washington. Congress encouraged the settlement of the West, but it did so at a very high price.

Congress participated in economic development in other ways as well. The absence of direct federal taxes contributed to the growth of American industry and encouraged investment. At the end of the century federal taxes absorbed only 3 percent of the national income, and other taxes took a scant 6 percent—about $20 per capita per year for *all* taxes. In 1885 most federal revenue (more than 60 percent) still came from customs duties and most of the remainder from levies on alcohol and tobacco. Federal taxes were regressive because they targeted consumer goods rather than income or profits. Congress also stimulated investment by allowing almost open immigration in the nineteenth century, thus assuring manufacturers that the steady supply of unskilled workers from southern and eastern

Europe would not be interrupted. Finally, it refused to exercise the national power of incorporation granted by the Constitution, except for national banks and a few railroads. By not exercising the power it had, Congress allowed private corporations to shop for charters in states that offered them the best terms and the highest profits.

Congress and the nation paid dearly for making economic growth the paramount goal. Natural resources were squandered and wasted; community values were repeatedly subordinated to the cult of individualism and self-advancement; slavery and the dispossession of the American Indian were encouraged; and powerful economic groups won disproportionate power in Washington. But congressional economic policy in the nineteenth century reflected powerful social realities. The United States was a huge nation with a multitude of ethnic groups and religions. Born fearful of centralized power, Americans lacked an established church, aristocracy, military caste, and intelligentsia. They could not rely on many of the traditional leadership elites available to European nations, and the absence of foreign enemies allowed the government to remain small and taxes low. The United States became a nation with the energy and will to tap its vast economic potential, but Congress—like the people it represented—seldom stopped to ponder where the nation was headed. Many nineteenth-century Americans recognized that the pursuit of wealth had become a religion in the United States, an end in itself. That quest became the central dynamic of nineteenth-century America.

[*See also* Bank of the United States; Railroads; Silver Issue.]

BIBLIOGRAPHY

Brownlee, W. Elliott. *Dynamics of Ascent: A History of the American Economy.* 1974.
Bruchey, Stuart. *Enterprise: The Dynamic History of a Free People.* 1990.
Farnham, Wallace D. "'The Weakened Spring of Government': A Study in Nineteenth-Century American History." *American Historical Review* 68 (1963): 662–680.
Gates, Paul W. *History of Public Land Law Development.* 1979.
Hacker, Louis M. *The Course of American Economic Growth and Development.* 1970.
Hughes, Jonathan R. T. *The Governmental Habit Redux: Economic Controls from Colonial Times to the Present.* 1991.

DONALD J. PISANI

Twentieth Century

Throughout the twentieth century, Congress has paid very close attention to economic policy-making. Congressional authority to tax and spend has been the legislature's chief means of subsidizing, stimulating, and directing economic development.

During the nineteenth century, the national legislature protected domestic industry through tariffs, promoted railroad construction, encouraged agricultural exports, and acquired and developed millions of acres of land. By 1887, however, Congress could not ignore the problems and power of large corporations. Directed at railroads, the Act to Regulate Commerce (1887) created the Interstate Commerce Commission (ICC), outlawed pooling, and prohibited various forms of price discrimination. It was followed by the Sherman Antitrust Act (1890) to "protect trade and commerce against unlawful restraints and monopolies." These initiatives were intended to protect competition and restrict monopoly power.

The Roosevelt and Taft Administrations. Large corporations were a "natural development," declared the new president, Theodore Roosevelt, in 1901. But, he continued, the coming of big business required "practical efforts" to address the "real and grave evils" this development posed to U.S. polity. Roosevelt called for the creation of a Department of Commerce with its own Bureau of Corporations to collect information on interstate industry, and in 1902 Congress complied. The Elkins (1903) and Hepburn (1906) acts strengthened the ICC's rate-regulating authority. And the 1906 Meat Inspection Act and Pure Food and Drugs Act authorized federal inspection of the meat, food, and drug industries.

The pace of progressive economic legislation slowed during William Howard Taft's presidency (1909–1913). In 1910, the president and Congress hammered out new railroad regulation. The Mann-Elkins Act empowered the ICC to initiate rate-making proceedings, with its decisions subject to review by a special Commerce Court. A year later, a special subcommittee of the House Banking Committee, chaired by Arsène P. Pujo (D-La.) and charged with investigating the "money trust," conducted hearings on the interrelations among the nation's largest financial interests.

Woodrow Wilson's Presidency. Democrat Woodrow Wilson won the presidency in 1912, having campaigned for an end to the special privileges enjoyed by monopolies and a restoration of unfettered competition. The Democrats also gained control of both houses of Congress. Wilson called the 63d Congress (1913–1915) into special session to make good on the Democratic promise of tariff revision. The resulting Underwood Tariff (1913) lowered average rates to approximately 29 percent and added numerous consumer goods to the duty-free list. To make up for the resulting revenue loss, Congress levied a moderately progressive income tax, which the recently ratified Sixteenth Amendment had legalized.

Acting on the findings of the Pujo Committee, the president urged Congress to reform the country's banking system. The Federal Reserve Act of 1913 established a centralized banking network composed of twelve regional districts and a supervisory Board of Governors. Charged with controlling credit and currency, the Federal Reserve System was the first national banking network since the Second Bank of the United States (1816–1833).

In early 1914, Congress took up the antitrust issue. Henry D. Clayton (D-Ala.), chairman of the House Judiciary Committee, introduced four bills prohibiting interlocking directorates, certain price-cutting measures, and other practices inhibiting competition. The Clayton Antitrust Act became law in October. Companion legislation passed the month before had provided for the establishment of an interstate trade commission. Known as the Federal Trade Commission (FTC), it was authorized to issue cease and desist orders in the instance of "unfair methods of competition." The FTC also took over the investigative function of the Bureau of Corporations.

In mid 1916, President Wilson signed the Federal Farm Loan Act to supply long-term credit to farmers at low interest rates. He also sanctioned congressional legislation establishing an eight-hour day for railroad workers and the Keating-Owen Child Labor Act, which barred products made with child labor from interstate trade.

United States entry into World War I in April 1917 forced Congress into the all-consuming business of military and industrial mobilization. At the administration's behest, the legislature established the War Industries Board to allocate resources, set targets, and fix prices in the production of war materials; the War Finance Corporation to provide credit to military industries; and the National War Labor Board to arbitrate labor disputes. Congress also authorized the federal government to take control of domestic railroad operations. This expansion in the scale and scope of government economic authority set new precedents for the concentration of federal power.

The war effort cost unprecedented sums of money. Most expenditures were financed by borrowing, and the federal debt climbed from $1 billion in 1916 to over $25 billion three years later. To meet the interest charges on the debt and to help finance war expenses, Congress was forced to raise taxes significantly, especially income taxes. The revenue acts of 1917 and 1918 placed most of the war's fiscal burden on wealthy individuals and corporations. But almost all Americans paid more taxes.

The 1920s. The postwar U.S. economy proved remarkably efficient at converting production and resource allocation to peacetime challenges. The real gross national product increased 45 percent between 1920 and 1929, and during much of the 1920s the nation enjoyed general prosperity.

As the country entered the age of mass consumption, political support for progressivism and strict governmental supervision of big business waned. Both Congress and the executive generally gave large enterprises relatively free rein in the economic sphere. During the 1920s, Congress rarely discussed new antitrust legislation. In industries such as chemicals, autos, and utilities, businesses consolidated without significant government interference.

Agriculture, however, did not thrive. Although farm prices had soared during World War I, they fell precipitously with peace and remained depressed for much of the 1920s. Through a variety of new laws, the farm bloc in Congress tried to address declining commodity prices. In 1921, the Grain Futures Act and the Packers and Stockyards Act established government controls on grain exchanges and stockyards, and the Capper-Volstead Act exempted agricultural cooperatives from antitrust prosecution. Designed to maintain the domestic prices of wheat, corn, meat, and other farm products, the Fordney-McCumber Act of 1922 raised U.S. tariff rates to an average level of 33 percent. Following extensive debate and political infighting, the Agricultural Marketing Act became law in 1929. This legislation created the Federal Farm Board and gave it control of a $500 million fund from which the agency could buy, sell, or store farm products to prevent a market glut. But the act made no provision for controlling production. With the government as a guaranteed buyer, farmers simply expanded output. None of these measures significantly relieved agrarian economic distress.

The Great Depression and the Franklin D. Roosevelt Era. The stock market crash of 24 October 1929 and the massive economic downturn that followed shattered Americans' confidence in the economy's viability. But the federal government lacked the political and practical capital needed to confront an economic crisis of such magnitude. Economists could offer policymakers little advice beyond general (and ineffective) opposition to the Hawley-Smoot Tariff of 1930, which raised ad valorem rates to 40 percent on manufactured and some farm products.

In 1930 the Democrats won control of the House for the first time since 1919 and reduced the Republican majority in the upper house to one. Facing a deepening domestic and international economic crisis, the Hoover administration proposed, and the 72d Congress (1931–1933) passed, a number of emergency relief measures. These included the establishment of the Reconstruction Finance Corporation (RFC) to offer loans to troubled banks, railroads, and insurance companies; the Glass-Steagall Bank Credit Act to enable the United States to remain on the gold standard; and the Federal Home Loan Bank Act to assist savings and loan institutions in providing mortgage and housing construction funds. But Congress and the outgoing president proved incapable of remedial policy-making.

Franklin D. Roosevelt's inauguration in March 1933 ushered in a new era of government activism. Calling Congress into special session on 9 March, he proposed the Emergency Banking Relief Act, which prohibited the hoarding of gold, provided for the orderly reopening of banks, and gave the chief executive broad power over the Federal Reserve. In less than eight hours, both the House and Senate passed the bill. Most banks were able to reopen immediately, restoring depositors' confidence and avoiding a large-scale financial panic.

In the first hundred days of his administration, Roosevelt sent a virtual torrent of legislation to Capitol Hill. It moved swiftly through Congress, with eleven major initiatives receiving less than forty hours of total debate in the two houses. Most measures were directed toward relief and recovery for specific groups. They included the establishment of the Civilian Conservation Corps, which provided reforestation and conservation work for 250,000 jobless Americans; the Federal Emergency Relief Act for distributing $500 million to states and localities; and the Agricultural Adjustment Act (AAA), which aimed to lift farm prices to parity with industrial prices by inducing farmers to reduce production.

Less than a week after passage of the AAA, Congress enacted the Tennessee Valley Authority Act, designed to build dams and power plants, provide electricity, and develop the economy of the Tennessee River basin. Soon after, both houses passed the Banking Act of 1933 creating a Federal Bank Deposit Insurance Corporation to guarantee deposits up to $5000 and the Emergency Railroad Transportation Act to aid in the financial reorganization of the railroads. At the same time, Congress also approved the innovative National Industrial Recovery Act. Business leaders were pleased that the act created a National Recovery Administration with responsibility for developing industry-specific codes of fair competition to raise prices and limit production, free from antitrust prosecution. Labor leaders welcomed the provision (section 7A) guaranteeing workers the right to organize unions and bargain collectively. Public spending proponents applauded the establishment of the Public Works Administration (PWA) with appropriations of over $3 billion to put unemployed Americans to work building roads, bridges, and other public projects.

Roosevelt continued to bombard Congress with economic initiatives, some targeted at recovery and others at longer-term economic reform. The Securities and Exchange Commission was created in 1934 to regulate the capital markets. The Works Progress Administration, established in 1935, put millions of jobless Americans to work on public projects. The National Labor Relations Board was created in 1935 to supervise specific labor-management regulations, including provisions banning managerial interference with union labor organizing efforts. In August 1935, as a result of congressional and administration efforts, both houses passed the Social Security Act, which set up a system of old-age and survivors' insurance as well as a federal and state program of unemployment compensation. This legislation marked the federal government's assumption of responsibility for the material well-being of elderly and indigent citizens—an important first step toward a more comprehensive welfare state.

In sum, New Deal measures greatly expanded the federal government's role in the economy. The myriad of agencies and public projects increased administrative expertise, improved public planning techniques, and enlarged the precedents for governmental intervention in the economy. Amounting to the most significant reform movement in U.S. history, these measures reflected executive initiative and bipartisan congressional commitment to alleviate unprecedented economic distress.

The coming to World War II vindicated the Keynesian prescription of countercyclical fiscal measures to restore full employment. The economic recovery that had eluded the nation for so long arrived quickly as economic preparation for war stepped up. Over the course of the war, the federal government spent over $320 billion (some $3 trillion in 1990 dollars). More than half of wartime government expenditures was paid for through deficit financing. But personal and corporate taxes also rose substantially. In real terms, federal revenues grew more than fivefold between 1939 and 1945.

The Postwar Years. In the closing years of the war, policymakers, business representatives, labor leaders, and others feared a return of the Great Depression. How would the nation absorb the 12 million Americans in the armed forces? How could the country's resources be efficiently converted to peacetime conditions? The Servicemen's Readjustment Act of 1944, better known as the GI Bill, and the Employment Act of 1946 responded to these concerns. The GI Bill provided veterans a college education, vocational training, and medical care. Introduced by Sen. James E. Murray (D-Mont.), the Employment Act committed the government to a Keynesian fiscal program for maintaining full employment. The legislation assigned responsibility for economic policy-making to the president (with congressional advice), established the Council of Economic Advisers, and created what was to become the congressional Joint Economic Committee to analyze the president's economic report.

Despite earlier fears, the postwar economy prospered. During the Truman and Eisenhower administrations (1945–1961), real output and gross private investment each grew at an average rate of over 3 percent per year. Annual unemployment averaged less than 4.5 percent, and real average weekly wages increased by 33 percent. The index of industrial production climbed 68 percent.

It was an economic tour de force. In its midst, congressional conservatives tried to reverse New Deal reforms, while both houses struggled to regain political authority from the executive. In 1947, over President Harry S. Truman's veto, a Republican-dominated Congress passed the Taft-Hartley Act, which prohibited the closed shop, union political contributions, and secondary boycotts. Truman administration efforts to create a permanent Fair Employment Practices Committee, authorize federal assistance to education, and repeal Taft-Hartley all

failed on Capitol Hill. In 1949, Congress approved the administration's Housing Act, which financed construction of more than 800,000 housing units for lower-income Americans and provided mortgage assistance to middle income groups.

During Dwight D. Eisenhower's presidency, House and Senate conservatives continued their attempts to dismantle New Deal legislation. In 1953 and 1954, the Reconstruction Finance Corporation was liquidated, and Congress enacted legislation that granted title to offshore oil to the states (Texas and Louisiana). However, most such attempts proved unsuccessful. For example, an administration-sponsored attempt to reduce the scope of TVA activity failed. So too did conservative efforts to prevent extensions of Social Security, unemployment compensation, and agricultural benefits. Instead, the most important congressional economic initiative of the 1950s was the Federal Highway Act of 1956, which authorized federal financing of an extensive interstate highway system. The system greatly facilitated a geographical redistribution of the nation's people, as the railroads had done in the nineteenth century. New urban centers and suburbs in the South and Southwest boomed, while older cities deteriorated.

The Kennedy and Johnson Years. President John F. Kennedy's New Frontier (1961–1963) encompassed a variety of ambitious economic proposals: elimination of structural unemployment and regional poverty, federal assistance to education, a comprehensive system of medical care for the elderly, and fiscal incentives for economic expansion. However, most of these were defeated by a Congress under the sway of a conservative Republican–southern Democrat coalition. Preferring tax reduction to government spending as a Keynesian stimulus to growth, Kennedy in 1962 proposed and Congress approved an investment tax credit for business. But until 1964, the legislature refused to adopt the president's recommended cuts in individual income taxes.

Lyndon B. Johnson pursued economic policies similar to those of Kennedy, but the Texan enjoyed more success in persuading Congress to enact his economic program. Johnson used his significant legislative experience and the outpouring of national grief over Kennedy's assassination to push a $12 billion tax-reduction bill and other economic initiatives through the House and Senate. To wage war on the poverty afflicting one in five Americans, Congress created the Office of Economic Opportunity in 1964. During the same period, the legislature authorized $375 million for urban mass transit, expansion of the National Defense Education Act, and a food stamp program.

The 1964 elections increased the Democratic majorities in both houses of Congress, assuring the Johnson administration of significant leverage. The president wasted little time in exploiting the working progressive majority on Capitol Hill. Over the next three years, the House and Senate approved federal health insurance for the aged (Medicare) and indigent (Medicaid); a broader, higher minimum wage; a manpower training program; federal aid to education; block grants to urban areas; rent subsidies for the poor; truth-in-packaging regulations; and the creation of two new cabinet departments, Housing and Urban Development and Transportation. From 1964 to 1970, federal expenditures for health, welfare services, education, and income maintenance grew more than 200 percent in real terms.

The ambitious economic and social programs enacted during the 1960s changed the composition of federal spending. In the years immediately after World War II, total government outlays constituted approximately 25 percent of the gross national product (GNP). Defense expenditures comprised 15 percent of the national product, with nondefense outlays at 10 percent. The "welfare shift" of the 1960s helped push total government expenditures to almost one-third of GNP, with nondefense spending accounting for almost 25 percent of national output.

As Johnson and his staff became entangled in the Vietnam War, the administration's legislative victories declined. With federal expenditures enlarged by the war and growing at an average annual rate of over 12 percent, inflation accelerated. In 1968, Johnson sought and Congress passed a temporary 10 percent tax surcharge to finance the war. Although the measure produced a government surplus in 1969, it did not slow the rate of inflation.

The 1970s. Richard M. Nixon inherited a high and rapidly rising price level. Controlling inflation became Nixon's central economic objective. Through tight monetary policy, and eventually a wage-price freeze, the administration tried unsuccessfully to slow the rate of inflation. Congress played little direct role in the administration's antiinflationary efforts, but the legislature was active in other areas of economic policy-making. In 1970, Congress passed the Occupational Safety and Health Act to monitor and enforce workplace health and safety standards. Two years later, Congress increased Social Security benefits by 20 percent and added cost-of-living ad-

justments to the program. The State and Local Fiscal Assistance Act of 1972 authorized $50 billion in federal funds to states and municipalities. In 1973, the House and Senate enacted the Comprehensive Employment and Training Act, which provided training and public service jobs for unemployed Americans. The liberal tide that had helped shape congressional action on economic and social initiatives during the Kennedy and Johnson administrations ran strong through the Nixon presidency.

Stagflation (inflation coupled with low growth and high unemployment) continued in the mid 1970s. In response, Congress in 1974 established the Congressional Budget Office and charged it with coordinating the size and timing of federal spending programs. To encourage energy conservation and the development of alternative energy sources in the wake of the OPEC oil embargo of 1973, Congress in 1975 passed the Energy Policy and Conservation Act and in 1977 created the Department of Energy. Two years later, Congress deregulated domestic crude oil prices and implemented a windfall profits tax.

Despite legislative attempts to reduce U.S. dependence on foreign petroleum, energy shocks continued to buffet the national economy, driving the general price level higher. As president, Jimmy Carter tried to use tight monetary policy to fight inflation, and in 1979 and 1980 the country endured a painful recession, with 7.8 percent unemployment. But in 1980, the consumer price index rose by more than 13 percent.

Inflation was not the only ailment afflicting the United States. During the 1970s, annual productivity growth slipped below 1 percent from nearly 3 percent per year in the first two postwar decades. In 1978, Congress passed the Full Employment and Balanced Growth Act, amending the full employment legislation of 1946. The new legislation reaffirmed the federal government's responsibility "to use all practicable programs and policies to promote full employment," and it committed the president to reducing unemployment to 4 percent within six years.

The Reagan Administration. The economy continued to stagnate. Capitalizing on the situation, Ronald Reagan won the presidential election against Carter in 1980. In addition, the Republicans also gained control of the Senate for the first time since 1955. Declaring that the country was "in the worst mess since the Great Depression," Reagan quickly sent his administration's economic plan to Capitol Hill. "Reaganomics" encompassed a combi-

REAGANOMICS. Two-sided cloth doll satirizing the supply-side economic policies of the Reagan administration.

COLLECTION OF DAVID J. AND JANICE L. FRENT

nation of targeted spending reductions, significant tax cuts, and a large-scale defense buildup. In 1981, Congress passed the Economic Recovery Tax Act, which cut taxes through a three-year, 25 percent reduction in marginal rates; expanded depreciation allowances; and permitted larger investment credits. Reagan's legislative victories owed much to administrative and special interest lobbying support, the defection of conservative House Democrats, and the president's enormous popular appeal.

The net fiscal effect of the Reagan initiatives was expansionary. But in 1982, the economy slid into a recession, a product of the Federal Reserve's restrictive monetary policy. GNP fell and unemployment rose, but inflation dropped precipitously from over 10 percent in 1981 to less than 4 percent in 1983. By 1984, the economy was in the midst of a strong recovery, which persisted for three more years. Although Americans welcomed the return of stable prices and economic expansion, many began to worry about the unprecedented growth in peacetime deficits that accompanied the president's economic policies. The gap between government revenues and outlays climbed from $74 billion in 1980 to $212 billion in 1985, an increase of over 180 percent.

With rising deficits came mounting debt service

costs. In 1985, interest charges on the national debt amounted to 13 percent of the federal budget. Reagan refused to consider tax increases or cuts in defense spending, which grew from $143 billion in 1980 to $259 billion in 1985. Instead, the president blamed the Congress for excessive social spending. In 1985, recognizing its own inability to curtail spending on entitlement programs or defense, the House and Senate approved the Gramm-Rudman Balanced Budget Act. This law imposed a five-year schedule of targeted deficit reductions that Congress proved consistently unable to meet.

By the end of the 1980s, defense spending constituted 25 percent of the federal budget. Income security programs, including Social Security and Medicare, comprised 44 percent of all federal expenditures. Interest on the government debt accounted for 13 percent, and discretionary civil spending, such as community development and education programs, made up the remaining 18 percent. With Congress and the executive branch unwilling to countenance reductions in the first two categories and with interest charges fixed, only discretionary spending remained open for political debate. Under the budgetary regime of the late 1980s, fiscal policy had been greatly weakened as a weapon of short or longer-term economic stabilization.

The 1990s. As the 1990s opened, President George Bush and Congress could offer few policy solutions to the economic challenges confronting the United States. Declining savings rates, structural unemployment, and a large, stubborn trade deficit coupled with continued massive government shortfalls, the deterioration of the U.S. infrastructure, including the nation's public schools, and rising income inequality all demanded political attention. As President Bill Clinton and his administration took office in 1993, numerous signs pointed to a return to the government activism of the 1930s and 1960s. But the gigantic federal debt made it difficult for Congress to enact new programs. Passed in August of 1993, the Omnibus Budget Reconciliation Act aimed to reduce the annual federal deficit from 4 percent of GDP in 1993 to 2.2 percent in 1998. But over the late 1990s, deficits are expected to grow again, from 3.3 percent of GDP in 2004 to 10 percent by 2020.

Throughout the first ninety years of the twentieth century, Congress has been critically involved in the functioning of the national economy. From the Progressive era, through the Great Depression and the New Deal, across the postwar period and through

Landmark Legislation

Title	Year Enacted	Reference Number	Description
Interstate Commerce Act	1887	P.L. 49-104	Directed at railroads; outlawed rebates, pooling, and specific forms of price discrimination, and established the Interstate Commerce Commission.
Sherman Antitrust Act	1890	P.L. 51-647	Declared "every contract, combination in the form of trust or otherwise, or conspiracy, in restraint of trade or commerce among the several States, or with foreign nations" to be illegal.
Pure Food and Drugs Act	1906	P.L. 59-3915	Authorized government inspection of food, meat, and drug industries.
Federal Reserve Bank Act	1913	P.L. 63-6	Established a centralized banking network, composed of twelve regional districts and a supervisory Board of Governors, responsible for controlling credit and currency.
Federal Trade Commission Act	1914	P.L. 63-311	Designed to prevent "unfair methods of competition in commerce"; established the Federal Trade Commission with the power to investigate individual and corporate actions.
Clayton Antitrust Act	1914	P.L. 63-323	Declared price discrimination and interlocking directorates to be illegal under certain circumstances.
Hawley-Smoot Tariff	1930	P.L. 71-497	Raised ad valorem rates to 40 percent on manufactured and some farm products.
Reconstruction Finance Corporation Act	1932	P.L. 72-8	Established the RFC to offer loans to distressed banks, railroads, and insurance companies.
Agricultural Adjustment Act	1933	P.L. 72-25	Aimed to lift agricultural prices to parity with industrial prices by controlling farm production, including granting subsidies to farmers who withdrew land from cultivation and plowed under crops in surplus.
Tennessee Valley Authority Act of 1933	1933	P.L. 73-32	Developed the economy of the Tennessee River basin through constructing dams and power plants, providing electricity, rebuilding forests, and replenishing topsoil.
Banking Act of 1933	1933	P.L. 73-66	Created the Federal Bank Deposit Insurance Corporation to guarantee deposits up to $5000.
National Industrial Recovery Act	1933	P.L. 73-90	Created the National Recovery Administration with responsibility for developing industry-specific codes of fair competition to raise prices and limit production; established the Public Works Administration to put unemployed Americans to work on public projects; and guaranteed workers the right to organize and collectively bargain.

the 1960s, 1970s, and 1980s, legislative activism toward the economy had ebbed and flowed, shaped by political imperatives and precedents, executive initiative, macroeconomic change, and the ideological heritage of the United States. Over the next decades, beginning with the 1990s, the economic future of the United States will depend in no small measure on how these factors play themselves out on Capitol Hill.

[*For general discussion of related issues, see* Appropriations; Budget Process. *See also* Budget Committee, House; Budget Committee, Senate; Congressional Budget Office; Great Society; New Deal; Office of Management and Budget. *For discussion of particular legislation, see* Agricultural Adjustment Acts; Balanced Budget and Emergency Deficit Control Act; Banking Act of 1933; Budget Reconciliation Act; Clayton Antitrust Act; Congressional Budget and Impoundment Control Act of 1974; Economic Opportunity Act; Emergency Banking Relief Act; Federal Reserve Bank Act; Federal Securities Act; Federal Trade Commission Act; GI Bill of Rights; Hawley-Smoot Tariff Act; Interstate Commerce Act; National Defense Educa-

Landmark Legislation (Continued)

TITLE	YEAR ENACTED	REFERENCE NUMBER	DESCRIPTION
Securities Exchange	1934	P.L. 73-404	Created the Securities and Exchange Commission to regulate the U.S. capital markets.
Emergency Relief Appropriation Act	1935	P.L. 74-48	Established the Works Progress Administration to put millions of unemployed Americans back to work.
Wagner Act	1935	P.L. 74-372	Created the National Labor Relations Board to supervise labor-management relations.
Social Security Act	1935	P.L. 74-531	Established a system of old-age survivors' insurance and a federal-state program of unemployment compensation.
Employment Act of 1946	1946	P.L. 79-33	Committed the federal government to a Keynesian fiscal program to maintain full employment; established the Council of Economic Advisers; and created what was to become the Joint Economic Committee.
Taft-Hartley Act	1947	P.L. 80-120	Prohibited the closed shop, union political contributions, and secondary boycotts.
Economic Opportunity Act	1964	P.L. 88-452	Initiated a broad-ranging war on poverty that included Head Start, Upward Bound, VISTA, and other programs.
Medicare Act	1965	P.L. 89-97	Provided federal health insurance for the aged and poor.
Congressional Budget and Impoundment Control Act of 1974	1974	P.L. 93-344	Established the Congressional Budget Office, charged with coordinating the size and timing of federal spending programs.
Energy Policy and Conservation Act	1975	P.L. 94-163	Encouraged energy conservation and development of alternative sources (Department of Energy established in 1977).
Economic Recovery Tax Act of 1981	1981	P.L. 97-34	Reduced individual tax rates and expanded depreciation allowances and investment tax credits.
Gramm-Rudman-Hollings Act	1985	P.L. 99-177	Imposed a five-year schedule of targeted reductions in the federal deficit.
Omnibus Budget Reconciliation Act of 1993	1993	P.L. 103-66	A broad-based attempt to reduce the federal deficit through raising revenues and cutting government spending. The legislation aimed to lower the U.S. deficit by $473 billion between 1994 and 1998.

tion Act of 1958; National Industrial Recovery Act; Pure Food and Drugs Act; Sherman Antitrust Act; Sixteenth Amendment; Social Security Act; Taft-Hartley Labor-Management Relations Act; Wagner-Connery National Labor Relations Act.]

BIBLIOGRAPHY

Hamby, Alonzo L. *The Imperial Years: The United States since 1939.* 1976.

Keller, Morton. *Parties, Congress, and Public Policy.* 1985.

Leuchtenberg, William E. *The New Deal: A Documentary History.* 1968.

Link, Arthur Stanley. *Woodrow Wilson and the Progressive Era.* 1954.

Matusow, Allen J. *The Unraveling of America: A History of Liberalism in the 1960s.* 1984.

Mowry, George Edwin. *The Era of Theodore Roosevelt and the Birth of Modern America.* 1962.

NANCY F. KOEHN

EDMUNDS, GEORGE F. (1828–1919), senator from Vermont and a leader of the Republican party's "Half-Breed" faction. Appointed to the Senate in April 1866, Edmunds was reelected in 1868 and then for three subsequent terms. His habitually close scrutiny of all government money grants earned him the appellation "watchdog of the Senate." Possessing a keen legal mind, Edmunds was generally acknowledged to be the Senate's leading parliamentarian and most able constitutional lawyer. He served on the Judiciary Committee from 1871 to 1891 and was chairman from December 1872 until his resignation in 1891, except for two years of Democratic control (1879–1881). He also served on the Pensions (1869–1873) and Foreign Relations (1881–1883) committees. Edmunds's acid tongue and contrary disposition did not prevent his election as president pro tempore of the Senate and thus acting vice president from 1883 to 1885.

Throughout his Senate tenure Edmunds maintained a hostile attitude toward the South. His constant waving of the "bloody shirt" and opposition to southern Democrat–supported assaults on black and white Republicans in the region gained him a reputation as one of the South's principal adversaries. Edmunds supported high tariffs, the gold standard, and civil service reform. As a member of the 1877 Electoral Commission, he helped to draft the legislation that decided the disputed Hayes-Tilden presidential election. The only Senate bills carrying his name—the 1882 Edmunds Anti-Polygamy Act and the 1887 Edmunds-Tucker Act—were instrumental in eventually ending polygamy in America and destroying Mormon political hegemony in Utah. Edmunds also wrote much of the 1890 Sherman Antitrust Act. Ill health forced him to submit his resignation in 1891.

BIBLIOGRAPHY

Adler, Selig. "The Senatorial Career of George Franklin Edmunds, 1866–1891." Ph.D. diss., University of Illinois, 1934.

Welch, Richard E., Jr. "George Edmunds of Vermont: Republican Half-Breed." *Vermont History* 36 (Spring 1968): 64–73.

Robert S. Salisbury

EDUCATION.

The Constitution contains no specific license for the federal government to establish or regulate educational institutions, and some cite education as an example of the Tenth Amendment's principle that powers not explicitly given to the federal government are reserved to the states. Indeed, federal initiatives in education have been carefully scrutinized and frequently opposed because of the strong tradition of local and state control. Community school boards control personnel, finance, and other matters, while states regulate teacher training and certification, length of the school year, and many aspects of the curriculum.

However, even in the early national period, many leaders deemed education critical for republican government and national unity. Since the founding of the military academies in the early nineteenth century (the U.S. Military Academy at West Point in 1802 and the U.S. Naval Academy at Annapolis in 1845), Congress has been willing to invest in certain categories of research and advanced education deemed to be in the national interest. That willingness expanded greatly with the land-grant college movement after the Civil War. The scope of federal activity has increased a great deal in the twentieth century, particularly since World War II. In the absence of explicit constitutional endorsement of a federal role in education, some advocates cited the Constitution's general welfare clause of Article I, and the Supreme Court eventually endorsed this view in *Hamilton v. Regents* (1934) and *Wickard v. Filburn* (1942). Then, with the Supreme Court's increased sanction for civil rights stemming from the Fourteenth Amendment's equal protection clause, especially in *Brown v. Board of Education* (1954), Congress took an increasing interest in equal educational opportunity. After World War II, in the face of the Cold War and international economic competition, the federal government invested heavily in research and education in the name of national defense and economic productivity.

Early Federal Policy. Although the Founders characteristically viewed education as beneficial to public order, no early federal action was taken in this regard except for the founding of West Point, which was justified by Congress's national defense responsibility. Between 1790 and 1795 George Washington urged Congress to create a national university in the nation's capital to promote science and literature. Congress declined to act on the proposal; opponents thought it was an inappropriate role for the federal government. Thomas Jefferson, who favored government involvement in schooling at the state level, believed that Congress did not have the authority to establish a national university without a constitutional amendment. Schooling was very much a local prerogative, and even the states took little or no initiative in providing education in the early national period. Proposals for mandatory, statewide systems of education fell on deaf ears. In the 1780s Jefferson in Virginia and Benjamin Rush in Pennsylvania urged their state legislatures to erect common school systems, but to no avail.

Although Congress balked at any involvement in education in the established states, the western territories were another matter. Promoters of western settlement, who were often investors in the land companies as well as legislators at the state or national level, were eager that the new territories attract settlers, develop concentrated settlements, and become states with sound, republican governments. Toward those ends, they guaranteed that common schools would be provided in every town. In 1785, the Continental Congress passed the Northwest Ordinance, which directed that one of the thirty-six sections in each town be rented out and the income from it devoted to common schooling. A companion law in 1787 stated the rationale: "religion, morality and knowledge, being necessary for good government and the happiness of mankind, schools and the means of education shall forever be encouraged." But the system was not direct or local; the moneys were collected and put in territorial or state funds to accrue income for schools. The lands were not highly profitable because unimproved land was available in abundance. Furthermore, the territorial governments were starved for capital; abuses emerged, often because the school moneys were invested in other improvement schemes that collapsed. Therefore, the land grants resulted in little actual aid for local schooling in the early nineteenth century. In the second half of the century, Congress improved the system, eliminating fraud and allowing for the sale rather than the rental of the land; thus, a substantial amount of aid resulted from the land grants to the territories farther west.

Meanwhile, Congress in 1826 refused to extend such land-grant support of schools to the already established states. In the same year, a proposal to create a federal fund for education failed, as did a plan to create a standing committee on education in the House of Representatives in 1829. Although Congress resisted proposals to get involved with the schooling of the population in general, the federal government did begin allocating funds and making policies regarding the education of Native Americans during this period.

Nineteenth-Century Initiatives. Only in the 1850s did a proposal for federal aid to education in the states gain majority support, again using land grants. Rep. Justin S. Morrill from Vermont introduced a bill in 1857 to provide land grants to each state to support college-level training in agriculture and the "mechanical arts." The bill was not only an attempt to foster scientific agriculture and industrial education, but also a means of ingratiating the Republican party to farmers. Despite some southern and western opposition, it passed both houses, but President James Buchanan vetoed it as an extravagant, unconstitutional infringement upon states' rights. However, in 1862, with Abraham Lincoln in the White House and no southern Democrats left in the Congress, Morrill introduced the bill again, adding military education to the targeted programs. Again it passed, and this time it was signed into law.

The Morrill Land-Grant College Act (12 Stat. 503–505) provided 30,000 acres of federal land, or scrip equal to that acreage, for each senator and representative from a state, the proceeds to be invested to support the technical education specified in the legislation. The definitions were vague, and regulation was minimal, so several different types of institutions benefited. Some states (such as Michigan and Iowa) established new colleges for the stated purposes, many of which came to be known as the "A & M" (agricultural and mechanical) colleges. Other states (such as Wisconsin and North Carolina) gave the proceeds to their existing state universities to develop programs, and in other states private universities, such as the Sheffield Scientific School at Yale and the Massachusetts Institute of Technology, developed programs that fit the legislation. The Hatch Act, approved in 1887, provided for agricultural experiment stations to be operated in connection with the agricultural schools established through the Morrill Act. A second Morrill Act of 1890 (26 Stat. 417) provided outright annual grants for technical education in the land-grant colleges.

After the Morrill Act of 1862, Congress took no major steps during the nineteenth century to support education. However, two pieces of education legislation, one temporary and the other begrudging, deserve mention. When Congress created the Freedman's Bureau as a war measure in 1865, the agency had no explicit educational mission. (It was to provide food, medical assistance, and resettlement help.) But Congress, overriding a presidential veto in 1866, continued the agency and added $500,000 for education. Subsequently the agency collaborated with freed blacks and with workers from northern missionary societies to support 2,677 black schools by 1870, when the bureau was abolished.

During this same period, education enthusiasts lobbied strenuously for the creation of a department of education at the federal level. Congress revived various plans for a federal department of education pressed earlier by educational reformer Henry Barnard, the National Teachers Association, and others. Opponents feared encroachment on state and local authority, but proponents convinced a majority in Congress that the agency would be modest, devoted largely to gathering statistics and promoting awareness of education's importance. The Department of Education Act (14 Stat. 434) passed in 1867 and was signed by a skeptical President Andrew Johnson in March 1867. The next year, however, an ambivalent Congress demoted the organization to an office within the Interior Department (15 Stat. 92, 106). It was known as the Bureau of Education from 1870 to 1939, when it moved to the new Federal Security Agency, later the Department of Health, Education and Welfare. There it resided until its reelevation to department status in 1980. Prior to World War II, its activities were confined to gathering statistics and issuing reports.

Despite widespread hostility to expanded federal initiatives in education, a small coalition in Congress supported general aid to local schools in the late nineteenth century. Support came from Republicans interested in reconstruction in the South; labor groups supporting increased educational opportunity; and some professional educators, led by John Eaton, the second commissioner of education, who succeeded Henry Barnard in 1870. In that year, George F. Hoar (R-Mass.) introduced a bill in the House to establish a national education system, under which the federal government could declare a state's common school system inadequate, appoint a superintendent of schools and inspectors, designate textbooks, establish schools, and tax the inhabitants of the state. A striking proposal for the assertion of federal power, the Hoar bill was opposed by Democrats, the Catholic Church, and some organizations of public school educators. The bill never came to a vote, and less far-reaching versions of federal aid to local common schools also failed in the remainder of the nineteenth century. Four times in the 1880s Sen. Henry W. Blair of New Hampshire introduced legislation for general aid to education in the states, but it never passed both houses.

General aid to schools was not popular with the public or Congress, and federal regulation of mandatory programs was even less so. Increasing federal involvement went along a different path, following the precedent of the Morrill Act; federal money was used to encourage voluntary participation in programs targeted at specific categories of educational activity. Thus began the distinction between categorical aid, which Congress has long preferred, and general aid, which Congress has long resisted.

Twentieth-Century Aid to Vocational Education. When Congress again became active in the field of education in the second decade of the twentieth century, the Morrill Act stood as a precedent in two ways. First, it was categorical aid on a voluntary basis. Second, it was aimed at practical, vocational education. By 1900 American industrialists were both worried about international competition and convinced of the value of vocational education for teenagers. The National Association of Manufacturers (NAM), organized in 1895, began to lobby for federal legislation in support of vocational education in high schools. Organized labor, initially resistant, became convinced that such legislation would not undermine its interests. With the American Federation of Labor as well as the NAM in favor, the stage was set for the first federal initiative applying to local elementary and secondary education in all the states. In 1907 the National Society for the Promotion of Industrial Education (NSPIE) was founded with the endorsement of President Theodore Roosevelt, and it soon became a highly effective lobby group for vocational education legislation.

Although early bills for federal support of vocational education in agriculture, industrial arts, and home economics failed, momentum was building to overcome traditional objections. In 1914 Congress passed the Smith-Lever Act establishing extension work in agriculture and home economics emanating from the land-grant colleges; this, however, was not aid to public schools. In the same year, though, Congress empaneled a National Commission on Aid to Vocational Education that included congressional supporters of federal aid and leading members of the NSPIE. It held hearings and promptly proposed federal legislation that was enacted with only minor revisions in 1917. The skilled lobbying of this growing coalition, the promotion of vocational education as a war preparedness measure, and President Woodrow Wilson's endorsement of the legislation ensured passage of the Smith-Hughes Act (the Federal Vocational Education Act, 39 Stat. 929–936). It provided $1.6 million in the first year to support the salaries of vocational education teachers in agriculture, industrial arts, and home economics. School districts were required at least to match the federal sums. Annual appropriations rose to $7.2 million in 1926. At that time, the federal dollars were about 25 percent of the funds being devoted to vocational education at the local level; however, these federal funds were only 0.3 percent of all funds expended on public education.

The money had a stimulating effect, popularizing the idea that high schools should prepare youth for practical work roles. Subsequent legislation in the 1950s (George-Reed Act, 1929, 45 Stat. 1151; George-Ellzey Act, 1934, 48 Stat. 79; George-Deen Act, 1936, 49 Stat. 775; George-Barden Act, 1946, 60 Stat. 775; and Education Amendments of 1956,

P.L. 911) provided enhanced funding, included commercial and business education, and authorized expenditures for guidance and teacher training, but did not substantially change the purpose or procedures for federal aid to vocational education. Periodic reports stated that federal aid had not significantly increased the percentage of students receiving vocational education and, worse, that not very many graduates got jobs in the vocational fields they had studied. Still, the NSPIE (renamed the National Vocational Education Association in 1920) and the American Vocational Association (formed in 1926) remained effective lobby groups. Vocational education developed strong constituencies among educators, labor leaders, and members of Congress.

In the 1960s recurrent criticisms led to more substantial changes but not to a retreat from vocational education. A continual stream of legislation allowed states to shift funds among the old regulated categories; use funds for research on vocational education; establish and maintain vocational-technical schools at the postsecondary level; and support programs for work study, school-to-work transition, workplace literacy, and job retraining. As the definition of vocational education broadened from the initial emphasis on specific job skills to more general abilities, and as the target audience broadened to include those already in the work force and the unemployed, the distinction between vocational education and adult basic education became blurred.

New Deal and World War II Legislation. Although vocational education was the recipient of substantial and continuing federal aid from the 1920s to the 1950s, Congress did not extend the strategy to other areas. In the 1930s and 1940s proposals for general aid to public elementary and secondary schools were introduced but got nowhere for some of the same reasons that they failed in the 1870s and 1880s: fears about the erosion of local control; the opposition of the Catholic Church; and Congress's disinclination to give money with no categorical strings attached. Some New Deal legislation affected education: the Civilian Conservation Corps and the National Youth Administration had educational programs (albeit more or less incidental to those organizations' purposes), the Works Progress Administration constructed some schools, and the Federal Emergency Relief Administration supported some educational activities. But long-term federal assistance to local schools was not part of the New Deal agenda.

World War II added three more pieces of federal education aid to Congress's repertoire. The mobilization of matériel and the training of personnel in 1939 and 1940 caused rapid population increases in areas of the United States with military installations and consequent strain on housing and social institutions in those areas. The Lanham Act of 1940 (P.L. 76-849) provided assistance for housing. After a report from the War Department on severe school overcrowding in these areas, Congress passed an amendment to the Lanham Act in 1941 (P.L. 77-137) that provided assistance for the construction, maintenance, and operation of schools while assuring local authorities that the federal government would never "exercise any supervision or control over any school" thus assisted. Such assurances, plus the emergency atmosphere of the war, allayed most people's anxieties about federal control, and subsequent amendments passed with little opposition. With the end of World War II, new school construction was halted; Congress expected the Lanham Act to be phased out. Local officials, however, urgently argued that the schools in federally affected areas were swollen with students and that state and local governments could never make up the lost federal aid. After much debate and study, Congress decided in the late 1940s to continue federal aid in lieu of the local property taxes not paid on federally owned property. The anchors of postwar legislation in this area were passed in 1950: Public Law 815 for school construction and Public Law 874 for the operation of schools. These established the pattern for later "impacted areas" bills.

Two other pieces of World War II educational legislation outlasted the war. As a reward for serving the country, Congress in 1944 passed the GI Bill (the Servicemen's Readjustment Act, P.L. 78-346). There had been some federal vocational rehabilitation programs for disabled veterans after World War I, but the GI Bill was unprecedented. Besides provisions for home mortgages and unemployment benefits, its most famous feature, Title II, provided tuition costs for the further education of veterans, who could use the grants to return to high school, attend college, or receive other types of specialized training. Much to college officials' surprise, over a million veterans had enrolled in college under this program by the fall of 1946. Higher education was expanding anyway, with or without the GI Bill, so its independent impact is difficult to estimate; but about 12 percent of all men who received their college degrees between 1940 and 1955 said they would not have been able to finish without the GI Bill, and vast numbers of students pursued further training other than college. The original GI Bill covered service up to 1947. In 1952 Congress passed a similar bill, the Veterans Readjustment Assistance Act (P.L. 82-550), covering service from 1950 to 1955, including the Korean War, and in 1966 a post-Korea bill (P.L. 89-358) covered service beyond 1955. Participation rates by veterans in some kind of training after they left the armed services were, according to a 1973 report to Congress, about 48 percent for the World War II era, 42 percent for Korea, and 41 percent for Vietnam. Because of the gender composition of the military (1 to 2 percent women in all three eras), the benefits were realized largely by men.

If the war enhanced academic opportunity at home, it also expanded America's intellectual horizons abroad. Higher education, with increasing assistance from Congress, became more international, for many reasons: the continuation of studies begun during the war, the pressure after the war for continuing leadership and international involvement by the United States, the continuing competition among nations, and the expansion and specialization of higher education. Language study became more diverse, research universities began interdisciplinary area studies programs, and exchanges of students and faculty increased. One early sign of Congress's interest in fostering such study was the Fulbright Act for student and faculty exchanges (P.L. 584), passed in 1946. Begun modestly enough with funds from foreign currency debts, the program stood the test of time and was expanded in the Fulbright-Hays Act of 1961, the basic governing law of federally funded foreign academic exchanges.

World War II, then, expanded federal involvement in education, but only in a few specific categories: returning veterans' tuition, scholarly exchange programs, and supplementing local funds in areas where federal activities impacted local schools. Even when these were added to ongoing aid to vocational education and some special activities like Native American education, the agenda still was modest. As of 1958 the total share of federal money in expenditures on local elementary and secondary education was about 4 percent. In the next twenty years, that percentage would rise to about 10 percent largely in response, first, to Cold War technological concerns and then, second, to concerns about both poverty and equality of opportunity.

Cold War Motivation. The question of America's global status raised its head urgently in 1957,

spurring Congress to expand the vocational education precedent into other categories of school learning. During the 1940s and 1950s, educators had continued their long, unsuccessful fight to get general federal aid for local schooling. Meanwhile, in the early 1950s, academic critics developed a critique of American public schooling, blaming weak-minded progressive education for a lack of academic emphasis and results. They made little impact until 1957, when the Soviet Union launched the *Sputnik* satellite. Then, diverse impulses—public anxiety about the Cold War, academic critics' desire to improve traditional, discipline-based learning in the public schools, and public school advocates' yearning for federal assistance—combined, somewhat uncomfortably, to support the National Defense Education Act (NDEA) of 1958 (P.L. 85-864).

The perception of a Cold War crisis overcame congressional critics' reluctance to extend federal aid further. President Dwight D. Eisenhower told Secretary of Health, Education and Welfare Marion B. Folsom that "anything you could hook on the defense situation would get by," and in a subcommittee meeting Sen. Lyndon B. Johnson said, "We meet today in the atmosphere of another Pearl Harbor." These justifications also stymied some educators' efforts to broaden the bill to cover nontechnical areas such as English and history. For secondary education, the NDEA provided assistance to school districts to improve science, math, and language instruction; to enhance guidance and testing activities; and to expand the use of technology in the classroom. At the college level, it provided loans and fellowships for work in teacher preparation, international areas studies, and languages. With the assistance of the National Science Foundation and various curriculum development consortia, new curricula in mathematics and science were developed. In the aftermath of *Sputnik* and the NDEA, more high school students took foreign languages and more graduate students studied cultures and languages of developing nations. NDEA also established a new level of congressional involvement and activism with regard to precollegiate public schooling.

Expanded Assistance for Elementary and Secondary Education. Seven years later, Congress passed a major education bill with very different premises and purposes. The Elementary and Secondary Education Act (ESEA) of 1965 (P.L. 89-10) was not purely a product of the 1960s. Its roots went back to the civil rights movement, including the long struggle of the National Association for the

Advancement of Colored People for schools that were equal and, eventually, that were integrated, culminating in the Supreme Court's decision in *Brown v. Board of Education* (1954). In the 1960s such civil rights concerns combined with issues of poverty to shift the emphasis from the NDEA's focus on developing talent in science and technology to an agenda concerned with equality of opportunity and the development of basic skills in all children. Support for this agenda came from the continuing civil rights struggles in the South; a public shocked by increasingly violent reactions against that movement, dramatically publicized on television; increasing awareness of inequality and despair among the poor of northern cities; and the skillful politics of Lyndon B. Johnson, who made education a central part of his agenda when he succeeded John F. Kennedy as president in 1963. The Civil Rights Act of 1964 (78 Stat. 241-268) had an important bearing on education through its Title VI, which stipulated the policy of cutting off funds to any federally assisted program that discriminated on the basis of race. This provision gained greater potential weight when, the following year, the ESEA offered expanded aid to local school systems. The Department of Education actually withheld funds very infrequently, and the threat of such denial aroused great backlash and political conflict; nonetheless, Title VI was frequently cited in later court cases as the charter for nondiscrimination in federally funded education programs.

The ESEA provided aid for compensatory education in basic skills for children in schools with a large proportion of low-income families (Title I). It also provided aid to libraries, support services, pilot projects, educational research, and state education agencies. But Title I was the largest category, and it has been reauthorized and funded regularly since 1965 (in education bills since 1981 it has been called "Chapter I").

Although the Vietnam War distracted attention and resources from President Johnson's Great Soci-

POSTCARD. President Dwight D. Eisenhower, *center*, in his White House office, following a conference on school integration and other civil rights matters, 23 June 1958, with, *left to right*, Lester B. Granger, executive secretary of the National Urban League; Martin Luther King, Jr., president of the Southern Christian Leadership Conference; E. Frederick Morrow, administrative officer, White House; A. Philip Randolph, vice president of the AFL-CIO; and Roy Wilkins, executive secretary of the NAACP.
COLLECTION OF DAVID J. AND JANICE L. FRENT

ety programs, the 1970s saw a continuation and expansion of the emphasis on group rights. Various omnibus education bills included items focusing on new groups that, in the judgment of Congress, had suffered discrimination or needed special help. In response to congressional investigations revealing the high dropout rates and low educational achievement of Spanish-speaking American students, Congress added a voluntary aid title (Title VII) to the ESEA in 1968 (P.L. 90-247) popularly called the Bilingual Education Act, which gave assistance to local districts to provide bilingual education, which was defined loosely. But the late 1960s saw disruptions, including school boycotts in Los Angeles, San Antonio, Chicago, and Denver, that dramatized the demands of Latino students; the development of the bilingual lobby; and a growing number of court cases, culminating in the Supreme Court decision in *Lau v. Nichols* (1974) requiring all school systems to accommodate the problems of students with limited English proficiency. In the Education Amendments of 1974 (P.L. 93-380) Congress defined bilingual education further and urged schools to develop a multicultural curriculum. Subsequent controversies about bilingual education led Congress to mandate studies to determine which methods worked best for transition to English and whether some programs in practice encouraged continued use of non-English languages rather than a transition to English. In 1988 a reauthorization of Title VII for five years allowed 25 percent of the funds to be used on other techniques, such as English as a Second Language or the so-called "immersion" approaches, rather than transitional bilingual education in the students' languages.

In the meantime, sex discrimination received attention in Title IX of the Education Amendments of 1972 (P.L. 92-318). In language modeled on Title VI of the Civil Rights Act, Title IX forbade discrimination based on sex in any federally funded education program. Many exceptions were specified, including the admissions policies of religious schools, military schools, and many sorts of colleges, as well as organizations like the Boy Scouts and Girl Scouts. The most highly publicized applications of Title IX have been those requiring sex equity in athletic programs, though Title IX over the years has also involved matters of employment, pay, and other concerns in educational institutions.

Turning to another disadvantaged group, Congress passed the Rehabilitation Act of 1973 (P.L. 93-112), the "Civil Rights Act for the Handicapped," which called for greater physical access and opportunity for handicapped people. Following upon that mandate, Congress enacted in 1975 the Education for all Handicapped Children Act (P.L. 94-142). Congress had long provided small amounts of funding for the education of handicapped children, and from 1965 to 1975 the financial commitment grew in response to effective political involvement by parent groups. The 1975 legislation reinforced parental involvement in handicapped education and escalated the financial commitment and the shift toward the mainstreaming of handicapped children in elementary and secondary education. Public Law 94-142 required schools to provide all handicapped children with transportation and appropriate instruction in the "least restrictive" setting that was feasible, and it called upon the schools to collaborate with parents in developing an Individualized Education Program (IEP) for each handicapped child. Levels of funding and policy interpretation continue to be controversial, but Congress has regularly reauthorized and funded handicapped education legislation since 1975, and the mainstreaming feature of the legislation has had considerable impact on teacher training and on elementary and secondary classrooms.

Because enforcement lies with the executive branch, the vigor of these antidiscrimination programs has depended not only upon congressional continuation and refinement, but also upon the actions of the executive agencies involved. However, in many areas, such as sex equity and handicapped equity, congressional action has led to state and local action, so that the equity concepts are now woven into a larger institutional fabric and do not depend upon federal action alone.

Aid to Higher Education. In the flurry of collaboration between Congress and the executive branch under President Johnson, when the federal role in education was greatly escalated, Congress applied the central theme of equal opportunity to higher education legislation; this resulted in the Higher Education Act of 1965 (P.L. 89-329), a companion piece to the Elementary and Secondary Education Act of 1965. Johnson called these two acts the "keystones of the great fabulous 89th Congress." In subsequent years the frequently amended and expanding student aid provisions of the Higher Education Act became the largest single expenditure in the federal education budget. Precedents for higher education student aid had focused on particular groups or programs, particularly veterans and the study of science. Congress had also assisted in the

Landmark Education Legislation

Title	Year Enacted	Reference Number	Description
Northwest Ordinances	1785, 1787	—	Reserved the rental income from one section of land for education in each town of the Northwest Territory.
Morrill Land-Grant College Act	1862	12 Stat. 503–505	Provided grant of federal lands to states to establish and operate college programs in agricultural and scientific education.
Smith-Hughes Vocational Education Act	1917	39 Stat. 929–936	Provided federal grants to vocational education in local elementary and secondary schools.
Amended Lanham Act	1941	P.L. 77-137	Impact aid: provided federal grants to areas with schoolchildren living on nontaxable federal property.
Servicemen's Readjustment Act (GI Bill)	1944	P.L. 78-346	Provided federal grants to individual veterans for further education.
Fulbright Act	1946	P.L. 79-584	Arranged college student and faculty exchanges abroad.
National Defense Education Act	1958	P.L. 85-864	Provided federal grants to local elementary and secondary schools for improved education in math, science, and foreign languages, and to universities for improved programs and graduate fellowships in these areas.
Vocational Education Act of 1963	1963	P.L. 88-210	Increased the level of federal funding for vocational education; broadened the definition of vocational education, making more programs eligible for funding.
Elementary and Secondary Education Act	1965	P.L. 89-10	Provided aid to local elementary and secondary schools for compensatory education for children in low-income districts; also for improved libraries, pilot projects, and educational research.
Higher Education Act	1965	P.L. 89-329	Created a general system of federal loans and scholarships for undergraduates.
Education Amendments	1972	P.L. 92-318	Title I expanded college scholarships and loans. Title IX forbade discrimination based on sex.
Education Consolidation and Improvement Act	1981	P.L. 97-35	Allowed more discretion to local districts through block grants.
Goals 2000: Educate America Act	1994	P.L. 103-227	Title II created a board to certify voluntary national content, performance, and opportunity-to-learn standards and related assessment systems. Title III provided funds for states to develop such standards at the state level.

expansion of physical facilities with such efforts as the Higher Education Facilities Act of 1963. But the 1965 act brought these sorts of assistance together in an omnibus bill; increased the level of support; and provided, for the first time, outright scholarships for undergraduates from low-income families. (Such a provision, advocated by President Eisenhower, had failed when proposed as part of the National Defense Education Act of 1958.) The 1965 act provided aid for college libraries, aid to "developing" (for example, traditionally black) institutions, and student aid in the form of both loans and scholarships. Of the funds authorized, 68 percent was for institutional support and only 32 percent for student aid. (By 1986, these figures had become 10 percent for institutions and 90 percent for student aid.) When these new ventures in facilities construction and student financial aid were added to the expanding federal support of research and training, the result was a 400-percent increase in federal expenditures on higher education between 1956 and 1966.

In the late 1960s and early 1970s, several influential reports cited the remaining obstacles to equal opportunity in higher education. As a result, Congress passed the Higher Education Act of 1972 (Title I of the 1972 Education Amendments, P.L. 92-318), a comprehensive, highly detailed bill that greatly expanded scholarships through a program called Basic Educational Opportunity Grants, also known as Pell Grants after Sen. Claiborne Pell (D-R.I.), chairman of the Senate Education Subcommittee and author of the new program. The acts of 1965 and 1972 established the basic structure of federal aid to higher education for subsequent legislation. During the late 1970s, Congress and the Carter administration worried that the costs of the Guaranteed Student Loan provisions had mushroomed and that the program was being utilized more by middle-income families than low-income families. In the 1980s and early 1990s, Congress acquiesced in some cuts requested by the Reagan and Bush administrations, which were beset by budget deficits and recession and less committed than their predecessors to a high level of federal assistance to education. Nonetheless, despite mixed enthusiasm about the effectiveness and equity of federal financial assistance, the programs laid out in 1972, especially the Pell Grants, have become a fixture in federal legislation on higher education.

Reversal and Limitation. By the late 1970s, both Democrats and Republicans were considering the limits of federal intervention in education. Interest in deregulation, in local variation, and in capping federal expenditures was evident across party lines. Thus, when Ronald Reagan became president, he was able to reverse the expansion of federal assistance and control in his first education bill, which established the patterns of his later bills. The Education Consolidation and Improvement Act (ECIA) of 1981 (P.L. 97-35) continued Title I for the basic skills education of children from poor neighborhoods (now called Chapter I); it blocked together about forty smaller federal programs, distributed the money on the basis of school-age population throughout the country, and allowed local districts latitude to spend the money on any of the included programs. Thus, the federal aid was spread out more widely, especially since every district got aid,

whether it applied or not. Furthermore, some of the blocked programs, notably the Emergency School Assistance Act, which provided money to districts attempting to racially integrate their schools, had focused on urban problems. Therefore, the ECIA represented a shift from aid to cities toward aid to rural and suburban communities. Because substantial lobbies existed for bilingual education, handicapped education, and some other categorical programs, and because Congress resisted administration efforts to block those areas, separate bills continued programs in those areas.

Still, the ECIA came at a time of recession as well as a shift in administration philosophy; thus, the states had not only more discretion but less federal aid. The federal share of local elementary and secondary budgets fell from its peak of 9 percent in 1980 to 7.5 percent in the first year of the Reagan administration, and by the end of the second Reagan administration in 1988, it was 6.3 percent. Thus, the Reagan and Bush administrations effected a substantial retreat from federal activism in education but were restrained from a more dramatic reversal by a Democratic congressional majority along with education-minded Republican allies.

Issues of the 1990s. In the 1990s some reform impetus returned to the federal government. The 1980s, however, left a legacy: many of the education reform proposals flowed from concerns shared across party lines by the governors and their chief state school officers in the 1980s, as well as by various nongovernmental groups at the national level. As the Clinton administration set out to foster the movement toward national goals, curriculum content standards and assessment procedures, members of Congress and of the Education Department often stressed that compliance of the states was voluntary, that much variation across school districts and states was expected, and that the reform movement was more "national" than "federal." Their efforts to combine the goals of equity and productivity can be seen in the major education bills of the 103d Congress. In the Goals 2000 Act, Congress endorsed the development of voluntary content standards and achievement goals, with Democrats in the Congress insisting that students not be penalized by high-stakes tests until some way was devised to also measure whether they had had an opportunity to learn the content. In the School-to-Work Act, Congress encouraged states to develop tighter links between their school systems and their workplaces, through the development of apprenticeships and the incorporation of occupationally relevant content in the academic curriculum of the high schools. In the reauthorization of the Elementary and Secondary Education Act (ESEA), the administration asked Congress to redirect compensatory education funds (Title I) toward the poorer districts; at the same time, the administration's bill required assessment and accountability of the districts receiving such funds. In addition, Title II of the proposed ESEA reduced the amount of discretionary block grants to local districts and increased funding for the professional development of teachers. Thus, by the mid 1990s, the federal government was more actively engaged in educational reform than during the administrations of Ronald Reagan and George Bush, but federal initiatives included a more collaborative relationship to the states and to national groups outside the government than had been the case in the Kennedy-Johnson years.

Conclusion. Education is a function left largely to local and state government; the federal share of local elementary and secondary public school budgets has never exceeded 10 percent. Aid to higher education is targeted to individuals or individual institutions that apply for the assistance; it is not highly regulatory, except on some issues of discrimination and research safety. The general inclination of Congress has been to leave the funding and control of education to states and localities. When this inclination has been overcome, it has usually been on issues of equal opportunity or of international military and economic competition. Although the two goals are often seen as contrasting, even competing, they are sometimes invoked simultaneously. For example, in the discussion surrounding the 1965 Higher Education Act, it was argued that the nation could not afford to lose the talent represented by academically able students who could not afford to go to college.

The durability of the federal government's limited but important role in education seems evident from its continuation, largely intact, through three Republican administrations (1980–1992) unsympathetic to a large federal role in this area. This continuity was maintained partly because of the continuing control of Congress by the Democratic party, but on issues of education, they have always been assisted by Republican allies. Given this positive commitment, balanced by the constraints of budget deficits and other strong domestic priorities, one should probably not expect a radically different federal role in education in the future.

[*For discussion of related congressional committees, see* Education and Labor Committee, House; Labor and Human Resources Committee, Senate. *See also* Elementary and Secondary Education Act of 1965; Fulbright Scholars Act; GI Bill of Rights; Higher Education Act of 1965; Library of Congress; Morrill Land-Grant College Act; National Defense Education Act of 1958; Science and Technology; Service Academies; Smithsonian Institution; Vocational Education Act of 1963.]

BIBLIOGRAPHY

Clowse, Barbara Barksdale. *Brainpower for the Cold War: The Sputnik Crisis and the National Defense Education Act of 1958.* 1981.

Gladieux, Lawrence E., and Thomas R. Wolanin. *Congress and the Colleges: The National Politics of Higher Education.* 1976.

Graham, Hugh Davis. *The Uncertain Triumph: Federal Education Policy in the Kennedy and Johnson Years.* 1984.

Jeffrey, Julie Roy. *Education for Children of the Poor: A Study of the Origins and Implementation of the Elementary and Secondary Education Act of 1965.* 1978.

Olson, Keith W. *The GI Bill, the Veterans, and the Colleges.* 1974.

Rainsford, George N. *Congress and Higher Education in the Nineteenth Century.* 1972.

Salamone, Rosemary C. *Equal Education under Law: Legal Rights and Federal Policy.* 1986.

Spring, Joel. *The Sorting Machine Revisited: National Educational Policy since 1945.* 1989.

Warren, Donald R. *To Enforce Education: A History of the Founding Years of the United States Office of Education.* 1974.

CARL KAESTLE

EDUCATION AND LABOR COMMITTEE, HOUSE. The Committee on Education and Labor owes its origins to the Legislative Reorganization Act of 1946 (60 Stat. 812), which combined the Committee on Education, established in 1967, with the Committee on Labor, created in 1883. Education and Labor's jurisdiction includes measures concerning education and labor generally, school lunch programs, vocational rehabilitation, miners' welfare, the U.S. Employees' Compensation Commission, and Gallaudet University, the Washington, D.C., school for the deaf. In intercommittee contests, Education and Labor won jurisdiction over juvenile delinquency, runaway youth, certain human services programs, Native Americans' education, additional school food programs, and retirement income. It shares jurisdiction over employment discrimination aspects of civil rights laws.

Beyond reviewing all legislation under (and tax policies affecting) its jurisdiction, Education and Labor also oversees activities of the Education and Labor departments. Special oversight rules direct it to review, study, and coordinate all domestic education laws, programs, and government activities as well as student assistance programs under the jurisdiction of other committees.

Committee jurisdiction expanded as new issues surfaced, coming to include antipoverty programs, national education standards and assessment, drug and alcohol abuse prevention and education, refugee education, computer-related education, AIDS education, elderly care, child care, missing children education and prevention programs, family leave, workers' compensation, victims' survivors' compensation, and training programs for the disadvantaged.

Membership and Leadership. From the 1950s through the 1980s, Education and Labor earned the reputation of being a middle-ranking committee in attractiveness to members seeking assignments. It has tended to attract liberal Democrats and relatively conservative Republicans with safe seats. Scores tabulated by interest groups (including Americans for Democratic Action, Americans for Constitutional Action, and the AFL-CIO) since the 1950s have consistently shown that Education and Labor Democrats tend to be more liberal than their party colleagues in the House. Since the mid 1960s, committee Republicans on average have scored slightly more liberal than all House Republicans, although they still rate as conservative.

Drawn heavily from mid-Atlantic and eastern north-central states, members often represent large urban areas where organized labor is strong. Representation from western, north-central, and southern states has increased in recent years.

The committee's reputation for being partisan, ideological, and contentious stems from the controversial issues that so often come before it. Committee debates over these issues reflect basic party divisions. Committee Democrats, among the most liberal in the House, have traditionally favored labor unions and big government in the form of federal intervention to create jobs and fund public education. Committee Republicans have been conservative—although usually slightly less so than their House colleagues—preferring state control of education and private-sector solutions to unemployment. Although the minority tends to be more

cohesive than the majority, members have generally voted with party colleagues both in committee and on the floor.

Since the late 1950s, Education and Labor has been fractious, raucous, and sometimes rebellious—the committee that subscribes least to Sam Rayburn's philosophy of "to get along, go along." Because of the unorthodox behavior of Chairmen Graham A. Barden (D-N.C.; 1950–1953, 1955–1960) and Adam Clayton Powell, Jr. (D-N.Y.; 1961–1966), it has operated under strict rules longer than have most committees. The committee has been described as pluralistic and party-led and has been categorized as policy-oriented, with members motivated primarily by policy interests. Members have, in fact, often had the making of good public policy as their goal, but the committee has been characterized by a permeable decision-making process, little emphasis on expertise, and limited success on the House floor.

Operations. Conservative southerner Barden chaired the committee during most of the 1950s, exercising nearly absolute power over its internal structure and workings. He used it to stem the flow of progressive or liberal legislation. With few exceptions, the full committee conducted most business, allowing the chairman to retain control. In 1957, committee Democrats revolted, forcing the adoption of rules, something few committee then had. Rules required regular meeting dates and the establishment of standing subcommittees with specified jurisdictions. When, despite this, the chairman still prevailed, members adopted more stringent rules the next term.

When he took over in 1961, Powell became one of the few committee chairmen to be constrained by rules, and so his position was relatively weak compared to that of other committee chairmen. The chairmanship change afforded members an opportunity to adopt additional rules that further curtailed the chairman's discretion, including a requirement that ranking minority members chair subcommittees. Having considerable autonomy, Powell's subcommittee chairmen conducted most committee business, holding more than 99 percent of the committee's hearings. With power thus decentralized, more members participated in decision making. Nevertheless, subcommittee decisions were often overruled or amended in full committee. If members could not get amendments approved in subcommittee, they would resubmit them during full committee markup or floor debate. Powell generally facilitated members' efforts. The number of measures considered, bills reported, and laws enacted under his chairmanship was unprecedented for the committee.

By 1967, when Carl D. Perkins (D-Ky.) took over, majority members controlled the creation, number, and jurisdictions of subcommittees. They changed subcommittee names, added units, or reorganized over the next few sessions as issues or politics demanded. Members held two or three subcommittee assignments per term. The permeable structure allowed any member to participate (but not vote) in subcommittee deliberations even if the member was not on that subcommittee. Under Perkins, subcommittees held 97 percent of the hearings. Nonetheless, subcommittees did not receive deference from the full committee. Despite rules limitations, Perkins's political skills afforded him considerable power in the committee and in the House. Subsequent chairmen, such as Augustus F. Hawkins (D-Calif.) and William D. Ford (D-Mich.), also had to rely on their own resources rather than on the inherent powers of their post.

Education and Labor often interacts with labor unions and the education establishment. Among the organizations that have been particularly active in trying to influence labor policies are the AFL-CIO, the United Mine Workers, the National Association of Manufacturers, the U.S. Chamber of Commerce, the International Ladies' Garment Workers Union, the International Brotherhood of Electrical Workers, and the International Brotherhood of Teamsters. Organizations that have been particularly important in education matters include the National Education Association, the American Federation of Teachers, the National School Boards Association, the American Council on Education, and the National Parent-Teacher Association. Other groups that have regularly lobbied Education and Labor members include organizations representing the interests of higher education, libraries, vocational education, school nutrition, and public employees. Representatives of minorities, children, women, the elderly, persons with disabilities, the poor and homeless, state and local governments, and various religious groups have also lobbied members of the committee.

The departments of Education and of Labor are the committee's primary executive-branch contacts. It also interacts with the departments of Agriculture and of Health and Human Services.

The committee interacts with several executive-branch agencies. For example, it works with the Department of Education on student loans and bilingual education. It deals with the Labor Department on wage and hour laws, pension programs, employment discrimination, mine safety, and occupational safety and health. The committee cooperates with the Department of Justice on juvenile justice programs, with the Interior Department on Native American education, and with Agriculture on the school lunch program and the women, infants, and children (WIC) nutrition program. The Department of Health and Human Services administers the Older Americans Act and the Americans with Disabilities Act, parts of which fall under the committee's jurisdiction; Education and Labor also deals with HHS concerning the Head Start program and community services block grants.

Performance. Notable laws emerging from Education and Labor include the Fair Labor Standards Act of 1938 (P.L. 75-718, from the Committee on Labor), which established the minimum wage; the Taft-Hartley Act, or the Labor-Management Relations Act of 1947 (P.L. 80-101); the National Defense Education Act of 1958 (P.L. 85-864); the Landrum-Griffin Act, or the Labor-Management Reporting and Disclosure Act of 1959 (P.L. 86-257); the Vocational Education Act of 1963 (P.L. 88-210); the Economic Opportunity Act of 1964 (P.L. 88-452), which created the Great Society's antipoverty program; the Elementary and Secondary Education Act of 1965 (P.L. 89-19); the Occupational Safety and Health Act of 1970 (OSHA; P.L. 91-596); the Comprehensive Employment and Training Act of 1973 (CETA; P.L. 93-203); the Job Training Partnership Act of 1982 (P.L. 97-300); and the Americans with Disabilities Act of 1990 (P.L. 101-336).

Despite producing landmark legislation in the 1960s, the committee became less productive and attractive to members than it otherwise might have been because of internal conflicts and a decline in jurisdictional salience resulting from external events. Members' perceived lack of expertise, particularly on education, also contributed to frequent House challenges to committee decisions. Because most House members had received their schooling from the nation's public educational system, committee members had difficulty claiming exclusive skill in designing education policy. Consequently, the House deferred to the committee's judgment less often than to the opinions of committees considering more arcane issues. Thus, it has been less successful than some committees in moving its bills through the House.

In the 1950s, controversies over aid to racially segregated schools and religious schools and the intractability of the chairman combined to limit the committee's accomplishments. The 1960s gave rise to the committee's most important legislative accomplishments, which were furthered by the fact that the goals of the progressive chairman (Powell) coincided with the domestic policy agenda of Presidents John F. Kennedy and Lyndon B. Johnson—much of which fell under the purview of Education and Labor. But the legal difficulties faced by Chairman Powell affected the committee's credibility, and the escalation of the Vietnam War deflected attention and funds away from matters under its jurisdiction. Moreover, by the late 1960s and early 1970s many major issues had been settled. The resulting slide of its jurisdiction from the top of the legislative agenda reduced the committee's importance. In the late 1980s and early 1990s, issues such as child care and a renewed emphasis on education and employment reversed the slide, again moving the committee toward the forefront of domestic policy-making.

[See also Labor and Human Resources Committee, Senate.]

BIBLIOGRAPHY

Fenno, Richard F. *Congressmen in Committees.* 1973.

Hall, Richard F. "Participation and Purpose in Committee Decision Making." *American Political Science Review* 81 (1987): 105–121.

Parker, Glen R., and Suzanne L. Parker. *Factions in House Committees.* 1985.

Reeves, André E. *Congressional Committee Chairmen: Three Who Made an Evolution.* 1993.

Smith, Steven S., and Christopher J. Deering. *Committees in Congress.* 2d ed. 1990.

Unekis, Joseph K., and Leroy N. Rieselbach. *Congressional Committee Politics: Continuity and Change.* 1984.

ANDRÉE E. REEVES

EIGHTEENTH AMENDMENT (1919; 40 Stat. 1050). The Eighteenth Amendment to the Constitution, adopted in 1919 and commonly referred to as national prohibition, became the only constitutional amendment ever repealed. It rendered illegal "the manufacture, sale, or transportation of intoxicating liquors within, the importation thereof into, or the exportation thereof from the United States and all territory subject to the jurisdiction thereof for beverage purposes." A century-long, broadly based temperance crusade had gradually concluded that only a national ban on alcoholic beverages could solve the social, economic, political, and moral problems they caused. Only a constitu-

tional amendment, difficult to achieve but thereafter equally hard to repeal, would insure against the backsliding that had often occurred after the passage of prohibition laws within the states. Therefore, in 1913 a coalition of church groups, feminists, social and political reformers, and businessmen began pressing Congress for a national prohibition amendment.

Congress had previously treated alcohol prohibition as a state and local matter. Before adoption of an income tax in 1913, Congress used liquor taxes as a major source of federal revenue. That year, however, the first federal liquor restriction, the Webb-Kenyon Act, outlawed interstate shipment of alcohol into states that barred its internal manufacture and sale. By December 1914 a majority of representatives indicated their approval of constitutional prohibition. The Anti-Saloon League, an effective single-issue pressure group, and others then campaigned successfully for the election in 1916 of enough additional sympathetic congressmen to assemble the two-thirds majority required to pass an amendment resolution.

The Senate approved a prohibition amendment by a bipartisan vote of 65 to 20 on 1 August 1917. The House, after revising the Senate resolution to specifically grant federal and state governments concurrent power to enforce prohibition, endorsed it by a 282 to 128 margin on 17 December 1917. Senators reluctant to vote for the amendment but under pressure to do so attached a requirement that ratification be completed within seven years, calculating that this innovation would thwart final approval. However, the necessary three fourths of the state legislatures ratified the amendment by 16 January 1919, a span of only thirteen months, and every state but Illinois, Indiana, and Rhode Island did so by 1922. An Ohio referendum of November 1919 seeking to overturn the general assembly's act of ratification was invalidated by the Supreme Court in *Hawke v. Smith* (1920), but it fostered an impression that Congress and state legislatures had imposed a measure lacking in popular support.

Opponents of prohibition bore responsibility for another distinctive feature of the amendment: a one-year delay in its taking effect to cushion the blow to the liquor industry. Nevertheless, prohibition devastated the previously legal manufacturing, distribution, and retail liquor business, at the time the seventh largest industry in the country. In two centuries of constitutional development, only the Thirteenth Amendment, ending slavery, had a greater impact on property rights.

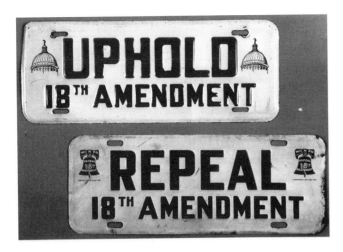

PUBLIC OPINION. Views on both sides of the debate over the continuance of prohibition were expressed on a variety of novelty items, such as license plate attachments.
COLLECTION OF DAVID J. AND JANICE L. FRENT

Enforced by Congress through the Volstead Act (1919), the Eighteenth Amendment proved controversial in practice. While most Americans observed the liquor ban, a significant minority, concentrated in cities, visibly did not. Growing disenchantment with national prohibition led to its repeal by the Twenty-first Amendment in December 1933.

[*See also* National Prohibition Act; Prohibition; Twenty-first Amendment.]

BIBLIOGRAPHY

Blocker, Jack S., Jr. *American Temperance Movements: Cycles of Reform.* 1989.
Timberlake, James H. *Prohibition and the Progressive Movement, 1900–1920.* 1963.

DAVID E. KYVIG

EISENHOWER, DWIGHT D. (1890–1969),

general of the U.S. Army in World War II and Supreme Allied Commander in Europe, president of Columbia University, thirty-fourth president of the United States (1953–1961). One of the most popular presidents in U.S. history, Eisenhower took office on 20 January 1953, when a majority of Americans had grown tired of the tumult of the Roosevelt and Truman administrations. Through his two terms Eisenhower conducted himself with restraint, mostly keeping his policies noncontroversial. When duty demanded he took dramatic steps, as when he dispatched federal troops to Little Rock, Arkansas, in 1957 to enforce a Supreme

Court order to desegregate public schools there. Otherwise he declined to exercise strong leadership in the growing civil rights struggle largely because of his apprehension over the effect of desegregation on the South; on the other hand, he objected to the South's contrivance to keep African Americans from voting.

In 1956 he proposed that Congress establish a Civil Rights Commission to investigate the violations. This led to the Civil Rights Act of 1957, which empowered the attorney general to seek an injunction when an individual was deprived of the right to vote. Conviction was punishable by six months in jail or a one-thousand-dollar fine, or both. As Democratic majority leader in the Senate, Lyndon B. Johnson commanded the successful fight for the bill. Afterward he wrote, "We obtained only half a loaf in that fight, but it was an essential half-loaf, the first civil rights legislation in eighty-two years."

Eisenhower was not a reformist president. He did not bombard Congress with legislation anywhere near the scale of the New Deal and Fair Deal years. Nevertheless Eisenhower did push legislation to build the Interstate Highway System, to develop the Saint Lawrence Seaway (with Canada), to bring an additional ten million persons under Social Security, and to provite a tax cut of $7.4 billion in 1954.

There were other satisfactions as well. When the McClellan Committee (the Permanent Subcommittee on Investigations) in the Senate aroused public indignation with disclosures of corruption and malpractice in labor unions, a flood of recommendations swept over Capitol Hill, including a message from Eisenhower in 1958 containing a variety of proposals for correcting the abuses. The upshot was the passage of the Labor-Management Reporting and Disclosure Act of 1959, better known as the Landrum-Griffin bill. The comprehensive measure included some changes favored by Eisenhower, including safeguards against misuse of union funds by union officials.

Eisenhower's relations with Congress were often troubled, however, and in ways that could not have been anticipated. In the years before the war he had frequently testified before congressional committees as a spokesman for the War Department and was well liked on Capitol Hill. Later, Congress fairly gushed over him as the victor in Normandy and was filled with respect for him when he was elected president. Nevertheless, nothing in his eight years in office brought him such unhappiness— even wrath—as his experiences with Congress.

The ultimate irony is that it was Republicans, above all Sen. Joseph R. McCarthy and the notorious Army-McCarthy hearings of 1954, who caused him the most pain. Eisenhower usually got on very well with Democrats, particularly with Sam Rayburn and Lyndon Johnson, two powerful figures from Texas, his native state (though he grew up in Abilene, Kansas).

In the 1952 election, Eisenhower defeated Gov. Adlai E. Stevenson of Illinois so overwhelmingly that the tide swept the Democrats out of control of Congress for only the second time since the Hoover administration. Rayburn became the House minority leader and Johnson the Senate minority leader. In the 1954 off-year elections, however, the Democrats regained control, and for the last six years of the Eisenhower presidency Rayburn was the Speaker of the House and Johnson the Senate majority leader. These two offices must be reckoned with by any president, and for Eisenhower the relationships with the men who held them were gratifying. He often entertained them at the White House to talk over legislative strategy. On at least one foreign-policy question, namely, whether the United States should intervene militarily to help the French against the Communists at Dien Bien Phu in northern Vietnam in 1954, Eisenhower privately conferred with the Democratic leaders, and his course was influenced by them. They opposed air power intervention without Allied participation. When Eisenhower appealed to British prime minister Winston Churchill to join a united action, Churchill declined, and the United States did not intervene in Vietnam with armed forces during the Eisenhower administration. The president did, however, send a military advisory and assistance group to undertake covert action against the Communist National Liberation Front and sent money and military equipment to the government of South Vietnam. Hence Eisenhower kept the United States out of war in Vietnam, but continued the American involvement.

While the Republicans were in congressional control in 1952 and 1953, the Speaker of the House was Joseph W. Martin, Jr., a gentlemanly party wheel from North Attleboro, Massachusetts. Martin

DWIGHT D. EISENHOWER. In keeping with his belief that personal acquaintance would ease the tensions of partisanship, the president talks jovially with House Speaker Sam Rayburn and other members of Congress.

OFFICE OF THE HISTORIAN OF THE U.S. SENATE

admired Eisenhower personally and cooperated with him on legislation, but his views on world affairs were so different from Eisenhower's that there was little rapport between them. Eisenhower had an internationalist outlook, whereas Martin, a former Republican national chairman, had long had isolationist leanings.

The unquestioned Republican leader of the Senate in 1953 was Robert A. Taft of Ohio, Eisenhower's unsuccessful rival for the presidential nomination at the 1952 Republican national convention. Eisenhower's strong internationalist viewpoint, as against Taft's history of isolationism, was a vital factor in his nomination. From the start of the Eisenhower administration, however, Taft strove to help the president. The only blowup between them occurred over the budget. When, at a meeting at the White House on 30 April 1953, Taft learned that the first Eisenhower budget would not be balanced, he accused the president of "taking us down the same road Truman traveled." He asserted, "It's a repudiation of everything we promised in the campaign." Shocked as he was over Taft's outburst, Eisenhower was genuinely upset when he learned soon afterward that Taft was dying of cancer. Taft was succeeded as Senate Republican leader by William F. Knowland of California, with whom Eisenhower had little in common.

Eisenhower's troubles with conservative Republicans began almost immediately after his inauguration, when Sen. John W. Bricker of Ohio introduced an amendment to the Constitution that Eisenhower believed would restrict a president's authority to conduct foreign policy. Bricker and his conservative supporters wanted to amend the Constitution to prohibit presidents from entering into international agreements like the one Franklin D. Roosevelt signed at Yalta late in World War II. (Conservatives blamed the Yalta agreement for Soviet control of Eastern Europe.) The Constitution makes treaties the "supreme law of the land." The Bricker amendment carried a "which" clause, declaring that "a treaty shall become effective as internal law. . . only through legislation which would be valid in the absence of a treaty." Utter confusion reigned over its meaning. Eisenhower said that the Constitution was being demolished "bit by bit by Bricker." He endured months of exasperation before a substitute amendment, which he also opposed, fell one vote short of the two-thirds Senate vote required to send a constitutional amendment to the states for ratification.

Eisenhower's second term was slowed, if imperceptibly, by illnesses. Near the end of his first term,

on 24 September 1955, he suffered a serious heart attack while vacationing in Denver. On 7 June 1956, he was stricken with ileitis and underwent abdominal surgery. And on 25 November 1957, he collapsed in the Oval Office with a mild stroke, which slightly affected his speech for a time. The three illnesses, however, caused no material change in his presidency.

Of all the speeches he delivered in eight years, the most remembered was his Farewell Address. He warned the country against the influence springing from the "conjunction of an immense military establishment and a large arms industry," advising that "in the councils of government, we must guard against the acquisition of unwarranted influence, whether sought or unsought, by the military-industrial complex."

BIBLIOGRAPHY

Ambrose, Stephen E. *Eisenhower*. Vol. 2: *The Presidency*. 1984.
Donovan, Robert J. *Eisenhower: The Inside Story*. 1956.
Griffith, Robert. *The Politics of Fear: Joseph R. McCarthy and the Senate*. 2d ed. 1987.

ROBERT J. DONOVAN

ELECTIONS, CONGRESSIONAL. [*This entry includes six articles on the election of members of Congress:*

    Theory and Law
    Becoming a Candidate
    Nomination to Candidacy
    Congressional Campaigns
    Voting
    Election Results

For discussion of congressional policies concerning the election of president, see Presidential Elections.]

Theory and Law

Any electoral system represents decisions made about voters' eligibility (whether suffrage will be exclusive or inclusive), the size of the geographic areas that will be represented (whether representatives will be elected from small districts or larger regions such as states or provinces or the nation as a whole), and the number of representatives that will be chosen from a given electoral area. Different electoral systems weigh votes differently, allow voters to name their preferences in different ways, and use different rules for determining who wins and who loses an election. These differing choices have consequences for a given system's fairness and equitability, affecting how voters vote and determining whom representatives represent.

Like all election systems, the American congressional election system is grounded in law and precedent.

Voting Eligibility. In congressional elections in the United States, suffrage is regulated by both federal and state law. The U.S. Constitution allows the states to determine their eligible electorates, but with a few caveats: a state must apply the same suffrage rules in U.S. congressional elections as it applies in elections to the most numerous house of its state legislature, and a state cannot pass suffrage laws that are discriminatory or that in any other way violate the U.S. Constitution. (State suffrage laws applied only to U.S. House elections until 1913, when the Seventeenth Amendment to the U.S. Constitution provided for direct election of U.S. senators as well.) The Constitution also provides that elections be held every two years for all members of the House of Representatives and every two years for one-third of the members of the U.S. Senate.

Early state suffrage laws were exclusive rather than inclusive. Suffrage was restricted along lines of race, sex, and class. Blacks, women, and men without certain landed or personal property could not vote. Suffrage was soon extended to white male taxpayers, and by 1860 most states had achieved universal white male suffrage. The Fifteenth Amendment (1870) to the Constitution allowed black men to vote. Several states allowed women to vote in the period from 1890 to 1919, but it took the passage of the Nineteenth Amendment in 1920 to give women throughout the country the right to vote—which thereby established universal suffrage. Throughout the nineteenth century, then, voting for U.S. representatives was based on restricted suffrage, and the elected representatives reflected this fact: all were white males of the upper or middle class. As states expanded their suffrage, nonwhite, female, and lower-class interests were expressed in congressional voting, and candidates reflecting their areas' demographic characteristics had a better chance of being elected to congressional office.

Number of Representatives. Determining a state's eligible voters is one component of an electoral system; determining the number of representatives to be elected is another. The Constitution (Article I, section 2) stipulates that the number of U.S. representatives from any state is to be based on that state's population relative to other states' populations and that the figure is to be revised every ten years according to the results of the federal census. Each decade, the U.S. Congress passes apportionment laws detailing the apportionment formula used and giving the total number of representatives in the House of Representatives and the number of representatives each state receives. The Constitution (Article I, section 3) also stipulates that each state shall have the same number of senators: that is, two.

Area of Representation. The Constitution is silent on whether representatives should be elected by districts or statewide or whether, if election is by district, how many should be elected from each district. The Constitution specifies only that representatives (and senators) must be inhabitants of their states. Today, Americans take for granted that representatives are elected in single-member districts, but this has not always been the case. Because of the ambiguity in the U.S. Constitution, during the early part of the nation's history states used four different methods: electing one member per district (single-member district), electing several members per district (plural or multimember district), electing some members from single-member districts and some statewide (mixed single-member district and at-large system), and electing all members statewide (completely at-large system). In 1842, a congressional apportionment law called for the election of representatives by the single-member district system, bringing an end to plural-member districts. At-large systems were discouraged, but some states continued to use mixed at-large systems until 1967 and completely at-large systems until 1970. A congressional act in 1967 declared these two types of at-large systems invalid. This act allowed only two exceptions: New Mexico and Hawaii could retain their completely at-large systems. However, New Mexico passed a law in 1968 adopting the single-member district system and, in 1970, Hawaii followed suit. The year 1970 marked the universal acceptance of the popular single-member district system of representation in the United States.

How Are Votes Cast? How one's vote is counted is also determined by state law. Throughout American history, states have weighted votes equally in congressional and other elections. No one's vote is counted more than once nor is any person allowed to vote more than once. Of course, vote fraud did occur and was particularly prevalent throughout the nineteenth century in large urban areas that did not have secret ballots or personal registration systems to prevent people from voting more than once. The passage by most states of personal registration laws in the period from 1890 to 1920 and the passage of secret ballot acts in the period from 1888 to 1896 eliminated much of the corrupt voting.

Americans' preference for unweighted voting also means that state laws prohibit voters from transferring their votes to other candidates for the same office on the ballot. Nor can voters rank their candidate preferences for an office on the ballot. In a congressional race, a voter can vote for only one candidate in his or her district. In essence, Americans have single-preference, unweighted voting: each voter selects only one candidate per office, and that vote is counted only once in the vote tabulation.

Among the various rules governing congressional elections, Americans are most used to the plurality (winner-take-all) voting rule for determining winners and losers. All states adopted this rule on entry into the Union. Basically, plurality voting means that the candidate who receives the most votes wins the contest; if candidate A receives one more vote than candidates B, C, D, etc., candidate A wins the congressional seat. This rule is easy to apply in a single-member district system. When, as sometimes happened in the earlier part of the nation's history, a state had a plural-member district or at-large election system, the rule extended to the number of congressional seats at stake: if, for example, four seats were in contention, then the four candidates with the highest vote totals would be declared winners. Most scholars believe that the plurality voting rule in single-member districts sustains and reinforces a two-party system in congressional elections. These and other election laws make it very difficult for third parties to compete for congressional seats.

Comparative Voting Systems. The electoral systems of the United States and other democracies have much in common. There is a shared belief in universal suffrage, the secret ballot, and some form of voter registration. Most democratic nations have followed the same historical progression in extending suffrage from upper-class males to middle- and then lower-class males and finally to women. Some other democracies (e.g., England, Canada, India, New Zealand) even have plurality voting rules and single-member districts similar to those in the United States. But in many parliamentary democracies, voting rules are very different from those in U.S. congressional elections. Some democracies, particularly in continental Europe, use party lists for voting, multimember or plural districts, and proportional representation. A few of these countries also permit votes to be transferred and have runoff elections. A few of these countries once permitted plural voting as well. This practice allowed certain individuals in a country to vote more than once on election day; for example, from 1918 to 1948, England allowed university graduates and occupants of most business premises to vote both in the election districts of their places of residence and their places of graduation or business.

Proportional representation is the central feature of many European voting systems. Parties are represented in legislatures in proportion to the numbers of voters supporting them. In an ideal system, a party's share of seats in parliament would exactly correspond to the proportion of the vote it receives. While in a few countries (e.g., the Netherlands) the entire nation is a single constituency, most countries use proportional representation at the district level, leading to results that only approximate the ideal. Proportional representation only works at the district level if each district sends multiple members to the legislature; otherwise, not all votes would be represented.

An example will illustrate how proportional representation works. If a given district has ten seats in its country's parliament, party A receives four of these seats if it wins 40 percent of the district's vote; Party B receives three seats if it wins 30 percent of the district's vote; and so on. In proportional representation systems, the focus is on voting for a political party; choice of a particular candidate is considered less important and, in some countries, is not even permitted. Parties prepare party lists at election time to facilitate voting along party lines. In closed-list countries, the voter can vote only for the party of his or her choice. In open-list countries, the voter must first vote for a party but then can exercise the option to vote for particular candidates printed on the party list. Under either system, the order in which the candidates are placed on the list by the party organization determines which party members get elected unless candidate-preference voting is large enough to counteract the party organization's ranking of candidates. The only way all candidates of a given party can be elected in a district is if the party receives close to 100 percent of the district's vote.

Norway, in its 1814 constitution, was the first to use proportional representation with multimember districts. Today the majority of the world's democracies use proportional representation. These countries define the quotas of votes needed to obtain parliamentary seats by various mathematical formulas; still other mathematical formulas are used to set rules regarding how seats are allocated among parties when the breakdown of votes for the various parties is not exactly proportional to the number of seats in a district.

Some countries have also legislated variants to the basic proportional representation voting system. A prime example is Ireland, which allows voters to rank in order of preference candidates so that when one candidate is successfully elected in the district, his or her surplus votes go to the second-ranked choice of voters, and so on. (The last-place candidate also has his or her votes transferred to the second-ranked preference in the same way.) This concept of transferring or rank-ordering votes stands in direct contrast to the American system and to most proportional representation systems, which allow only a single preference vote (i.e., one vote for a legislative candidate or party in a given district). The transferable (or alternative) vote is also used in elections for the lower house of the Australian parliament, but in a voting system more reminiscent of congressional voting in the United States: single-member districts with a majority (not plurality) voting rule. In this case, only the second preferences of the last-place candidate's votes are transferred until one candidate has a majority vote. France, with a single-member district system similar to Australia's, has at times in its history used a second ballot runoff election for parliament if no candidate has received a majority vote in the district in the first election. Some of these voting schemes seem to weaken the party voting that is a basic feature of the proportional representation voting system.

Comparative Effects of Voting Systems. The differences between the American system of congressional elections and these other voting systems have implications not only for legislative representation but for candidate campaign strategies and voter psychology as well. The American single-member district is a narrow territorial base that has a political life of its own. This may lead congressional candidates to stress local issues, pork-barrel projects, and service to the district to the detriment of national issues and national party policy. It may also lead congressional candidates to stress individual personality more than their European counterparts do. On the other hand, party-list ballots and proportional representation in multi-member districts can lead to a too-great focus on

party, with a correspondingly lopsided emphasis on national party platforms and national issues. Such differences are a matter of degree rather than absolute, but the kind of electoral system that is used does influence voter psychology and affects how campaign strategies are developed.

Historically, nations that were more culturally and ethnically homogeneous tended to adopt plurality-based voting systems for legislative elections. Countries that were more socially heterogeneous seemed to adopt proportional representation systems so that the many, diverse opinions in their societies might be represented. These diverse opinions often crystalized into intense and formidable political cleavages; the histories of many European countries, for example, show major ethnic, religious, cultural, and social conflicts.

Whether a nation adopts a plurality or a proportional representation voting system also influences the system of political parties that develops, which in turn reflects the social homogeneity or heterogeneity of that society. Plurality voting is usually associated with two-party systems in more homogeneous societies, proportional representation voting with multiparty systems in more heterogeneous societies. Two parties seem able to represent most opinions in a homogeneous society, for the large mass of political opinion in such societies (e.g., the United States) is often moderate or centrist in character. Plurality voting reinforces the two-party system by mandating that only one candidate can be a winner in a political race. Translated into the context of U.S. congressional elections, this means that only two parties will field candidates that can meaningfully compete for a congressional seat in a single-member district. Both candidates will often take moderate views on many issues, reflecting majority opinion in their district. By contrast, in a socially heterogeneous society more extreme views on the left and right of the ideological spectrum need to be taken into account. Proportional representation encourages many parties to compete for political office since they will receive seats in parliament roughly proportional to the votes cast for them in each district. No votes are wasted and no votes (beyond a minimum vote threshold required by law) go unrepresented because there is never only one winner in a legislative race in any district. Given this incentive to sustain multiparty competition for parliamentary seats, political parties are encouraged to run party slates, which cumulatively reflect the diversity of opinion in society.

Advocates of plurality voting in congressional

elections argue that it leads to clear-cut results and that government is made more stable because one party often controls Congress. They also argue that plurality voting reflects the moderate ideological stance of most Americans. (Others argue instead that it reflects the natural duality of opinion on issues in American politics.) Advocates further stress that plurality, district-based voting allows for stronger representation of vital local interests, issues, and constituencies. Supporters of proportional representation in parliamentary elections contend, however, that their system of voting permits many different points of view to be represented. They also assert that the political focus in such systems is on national issues, national party policy, and party responsibility in government. They do concede that clear-cut results are often difficult to obtain, since coalition governments are the likely electoral outcome. Most important, advocates of proportional representation emphasize that their system allows virtually every voter to be represented, unlike the American plurality system, in which all votes for the losing congressional candidate are wasted and, hence, all those voters go unrepresented. Supporters of proportional representation also believe that the American election system leads to an overrepresentation of parochial concerns to the detriment of the national interest.

Each system of elections reflects and serves the culture and society that uses it. Europeans and others with proportional representation systems want to represent diversity of opinion and minority interests in their parliaments. Given their cultural history, proportional representation was the way to achieve these goals. Americans in their early history formulated election laws to ensure local or geographic representation in congressional elections. They balanced this with the establishment of a presidential system representing the national interest. Plurality, single-member-district voting rules also ensured the maintenance of a two-party system in what was then a reasonably homogeneous society. It may be that the sharply dualistic nature of political opinion in early American history was the original motivation for plurality voting, but the more moderate views of most Americans today still make this same system of voting suitable for congressional elections. Also, the modern American tendency toward candidate-oriented voting fits well with locally based plurality voting in congressional elections. Plurality voting does not produce correspondences between voting and party-seat allocation as accurately as does proportional representa-

tion, but the benefits of the plurality system seem to outweigh the disadvantages for the American experience.

[See also Apportionment and Redistricting; Districts; Gerrymandering; Voting and Suffrage.]

BIBLIOGRAPHY

Bogdanor, Vernon, and David Butler. *Democracy and Elections: Electoral Systems and their Political Consequences.* 1983.

Katz, Richard S. *A Theory of Parties and Electoral Systems.* 1980.

Lijphart, Arend, and Bernard Grofman, eds. *Choosing an Electoral System: Issues and Alternatives.* 1984.

Mackie, Thomas T., and Richard Rose. *The International Almanac of Electoral History.* 3d ed. 1991.

Martis, Kenneth C. *The Historical Atlas of United States Congressional Districts, 1789–1983.* 1982.

Rae, Douglas W. *The Political Consequences of Electoral Laws.* Rev. ed. 1971.

Rusk, Jerrold G. "The American Electoral Universe: Speculation and Evidence." *American Political Science Review* 68 (September 1974): 1028–1049.

Rokkan, Stein. *Citizens, Elections, Parties.* 1970.

Taagepera, Rein, and Matthew Shugart. *Seats and Votes: The Effects and Determinants of Electoral Systems.* 1989.

JERROLD G. RUSK

Becoming a Candidate

Who runs for Congress, and why? Of people who are similarly situated in society, why do some enter politics while others do not? Approximately 150 million Americans could run for Congress every two years, but only about one thousand run in a typical year, and only a fraction of those conduct serious campaigns. (The average number of challengers for House races in the years 1972 to 1988 was 1,017; this figure excludes incumbents as well as the approximately one hundred people who run for Senate seats in a given election year.) This winnowing of the politically active from the inactive, and of the potential candidate from the political observer, is known to scholars as the process of recruitment, or "candidate emergence." Two approaches have been used to examine the process: one proceeds at the individual level, the other at the institutional level.

Individual-Level Theories. Individual-level approaches include the following: an approach that focuses on psychological dispositions and personality traits as the basis for explaining political motivation and behavior; the traditional sociological approach that points to the importance of occupation, social status, and social mobility; and the rationalist approach that views potential candidates as rational actors who assess the costs and benefits of running for office.

Psychological approach. Proponents of the psychological approach argue that people with certain personality types are most likely to enter politics. The pioneer of this approach, Harold Lasswell, believed that because politics involves the quest for and exercise of power, the successful political personality must be power-centered (Lasswell, 1948). The pursuit of power was seen as a basis for overcoming low self-esteem, either by changing the traits of the self or altering the environment in which the person lives. To support this theory of political motivation, Lasswell examined individual life histories to discover the traumatic experiences that create the power-centered personality. Early childhood experiences and indoctrination by parents were generally viewed in the psychological literature as central in forming the political personality.

Though the theory is appealing, practical and theoretical problems limit the applicability of the approach. First, it is difficult to get high-level politicians to take the personality tests (such as the thematic apperception tests) required to assess the theories. In fact, no member of Congress has ever subjected himself or herself to such tests, although research at the state and local levels shows that politicians do not have a distinctive concern for power or affiliation. Second, the interpretation of behavior and the methods for determining important personality traits are not agreed upon. Even Lasswell backed away from his early focus on power-centered personalities, recognizing that such people were not likely to be effective in politics, and proposed a natural selection process that weeds out the intensely power-oriented person because his or her personality precludes the flexible give-and-take that is required in politics.

Sociological approach. Do elected officials differ from the people they represent? Are certain groups or classes of people advantaged in the pursuit of a seat in Congress? Not surprisingly, the upper and upper-middle classes are heavily overrepresented in the top levels of elected public office. At the federal level, almost no politicians have working-class or blue-collar backgrounds. Nearly half of all members of Congress are lawyers, and the next largest percentage comes from business and banking. Also, members of Congress are mostly male and white. In the 103d Congress (1993–1995), there were only

6 women in the Senate and 48 in the House (11 percent of the latter chamber's membership). There was only one African American in the Senate and 38 in the House (8.7 percent; if one includes Eleanor Holmes Norton, the District of Columbia's nonvoting delegate, there were 39). That members of Congress are not cut from the same cloth as the broader public is well established, but the link between background variables and behavior has been more difficult to determine. In fact, there is virtually no link between background variables and behavior in office, once other factors, such as constituency, are controlled. For most issues there are not even correlations between background and behavior, so trying to establish actual causation has not been an issue in the research. Indeed, the weakness of any such links has led most scholars to reject the sociological approach.

The most important aspect of occupational data is whether or not the congressional aspirant is a current officeholder. This is a key variable in the rational approach outlined below, but it is not emphasized in the social-background research, which tends to focus on occupations at the time of entry into politics. The sociological approach makes sense for studies of lower-level offices, most of whose occupants enter politics from other careers. But most new members of Congress are being "promoted" rather than recruited—that is, they enter Congress from some lower office. Thus, to understand why most candidates run for Congress, the rational calculations of career politicians must be examined.

Rational approach. The rational approach to studying recruitment to Congress looks at the costs and benefits associated with the decision to run for higher office. While those who work from this perspective recognize that psychological and background differences may be important, they do not see them as central. The costs and benefits approach is relatively new, though it had become dominant by the early 1980s, coincident with a change in the nature of congressional elections. In the 1960s, scholars noted the advent of candidate-centered campaigns and the declining role of political parties. By the 1980s, the notion that contemporary congressional elections were dominated by candidates rather than parties had become conventional wisdom. Once political campaigns were viewed in these terms, it made analytical sense to focus on the rational calculations of the individual political entrepreneur. If, indeed, the candidate bore the "risks, rewards, and pains" of campaigns, then the specification and measurement of those factors should be made from an individual-level perspective.

Research looking at individual-level influences on the strategic calculations of politicians was extended and formalized by David Rohde in 1979 with his article on risk bearing and progressive ambition (that is, the desire to move from a lower to a higher office). Rohde moved toward predicting who would run for Congress by focusing on the decision to run for higher office rather than on the initial decision to enter politics. The first formal statement of an ambitious politician's decision calculus reads: $Uo = PB - R$ where

   Uo = utility of the target office O
   P = probability of winning election to office O
   B = value of office O
   R = risk of running

This equation has two important implications. First, it states that ambitious politicians will always aspire to higher office if expected net benefits are positive (i.e., $PB > R$). In making strategic calculations, a potential candidate for Congress who already holds a lower office will consider the probability of winning a House (or Senate) race and the chances of winning reelection to his or her current office, times the benefits of the respective offices, minus the costs associated with running. The benefits of holding office include the power and prestige of the office and the excitement of being in the public limelight.

The costs of running are both financial and personal. Fund-raising is the most demeaning and difficult task to be performed in running for Congress. The cost of mounting a strong challenge to an incumbent or running for an open seat in the House started at about $500,000 in 1992. Fund-raising can easily consume a majority of the candidate's time. The personal costs are also high. The lack of privacy and the pressures on families that come with being a member of Congress deter many potential candidates from running. Furthermore, politicians must consider the opportunity costs associated with a campaign for Congress—that is, the value of the political office or other job they would have to give up to serve in Congress.

The second implication of this simple calculation is also important; the greater the risk of running, the greater the probability of winning must be before a politician would decide to run for Congress. This observation illuminates an important distinction between amateur and experienced candidates. Candidates who already hold political office have many advantages over inexperienced candidates in seeking higher office, but they also have more to lose if they are not elected. Thus, experienced politicians attempt to time their campaigns for higher office with periods when there is a higher probability of winning, while amateurs may not be as sensitive to electoral goals. Therefore, experienced candidates are less likely to challenge a sitting incumbent and are more likely to attempt to gain higher office when the seat is open (by a ratio of more than two to one from 1972 to 1990). They are also sensitive to national economic conditions and various district-level variables. Amateurs, on the other hand, are more likely to be motivated by nonelectoral concerns such as a sense of duty to the party and policy goals, though many "ambitious amateurs" are also motivated by electoral goals (Canon, 1990).

Two historical patterns in the political backgrounds of House candidates are worthy of brief mention. First, consistent with the rational calculus outlined above, experienced Democratic challengers were far more likely to run in 1974 and 1982 (because of Watergate and the recession, respectively) than in other elections over the period 1972 to 1988, while experienced Republican challengers were more likely to run in 1972. For example, 30.5 percent of Democratic challengers in 1982 had previous elective experience, compared to an average of only 17.3 percent during the entire period 1972 to 1988. Second, there was a general trend toward fewer challengers with previous elective experience through the 1980s (dropping from 22.3 percent of all challengers to incumbents in 1982, to 13.4 percent in 1984, to 11.5 percent in 1986, to 8.5 percent in 1988). Not surprisingly, about 98 percent of all incumbents who ran for reelection in 1986 and 1988 were reelected. These trends, however, are generally cyclical. In 1992 about 14 percent of all challengers had some previous elective experience—a figure nearly identical to the average of all challengers during the years 1972 to 1988.

Institutional Theories. The institutional approach to studying political recruitment examines the context of the decision to run for Congress rather than individual motivations or backgrounds. It points to the importance of political-career structures, the rules of the game, and political parties.

Career structure. One central aspect of this context is the nature of the political-career structure—the tiering of local, state, and national offices with thousands of opportunities at the bottom of the pyramid and only a handful at the top. In general, this career structure charts out the path of least resistance because it indicates to aspiring politicians which lower office is most likely to serve as a stepping-stone to a higher office. (For example, in many states, a majority of U.S. House members previously served in the state legislature.) There is, however, great variation in the nature of these paths. In some districts, politicians must serve long apprenticeship in lower-level offices or in the party organization. In others, the career structure is more open to amateurs who attempt to make Congress their initial public office.

The theoretical contribution of this perspective was its focus on the importance of political ambition and political careers. Joseph Schlesinger (1966) built a theory of ambition on the notion that political opportunities were structured by ambitious people looking to further their political careers. When a series of challengers uses a state legislative seat as a stepping-stone to the House, it becomes more firmly entrenched as the preferred route or, as he calls it, the "manifest office." The use of manifest offices for the House and Senate has undergone significant changes since 1960. More House members have been elected from state legislatures (slightly more than half in the years 1980–1992, compared with 30 percent in the 1930s and 1940s), while fewer senators have used the common stepping-stone of holding a governorship before running for the Senate (13.7 percent between 1960 and 1987, compared with 23.2 percent between 1913 and 1959).

Candidates with previous political experience, especially in the manifest office, have many advantages in running for Congress: an existing voter base, which enhances name recognition; a campaign organization and fund-raising network in place from previous races; and greater attention from the media, which are more likely to treat their candidacies seriously. Survey research indicates that voters value political experience in candidates for public office. Of some thirty desirable qualities for political candidates ranked in various polls, ranging from youth and good health to courage and intelligence, political experience was the only one consistently mentioned as the most important characteristic. Given this public attitude, previous political experience is typically viewed as a necessary requirement for serving in Congress.

Aggregate-level results provide some evidence for the link between experience and votes. On the average, experienced challengers received 7 percent more of the two-party vote than inexperienced candidates from 1972 to 1978 (Jacobson and Kernell, 1983, p. 31). Some of the experienced candidates' relative success may be explained by their tendency to challenge vulnerable incumbents (that is, experienced challengers may not receive more votes in elections because they are better candidates than amateurs but because they run against incumbents who are not very popular). Even after controlling for other variables that would reduce the incumbent's vote, however, the relationship between previous experience and votes remains very strong. It has been shown that a highly experienced challenger receives 10 percent more of the vote than a complete amateur, even after controlling for the candidates' relative ability to raise campaign money.

A majority of those who make it to Congress have climbed their way up the political ladder, but a sizable number of amateurs do not follow the typical path. These amateurs are at a disadvantage for several reasons: the absence of prior campaign experience, low name recognition (celebrities are the exception), and a general preference among voters for candidates with prior experience. But these obstacles are not insurmountable. The successful campaigns of Senators Herb Kohl (D-Wis.) and Frank R. Lautenberg (D-N.J.) and former representative Ed Zschau (R-Calif.), among many others, indicate that large expenditures on consultants, staff, and advertising can permit amateurs to overcome initial deficits. The careers of some celebrities, such as astronaut John Glenn (D-Ohio), basketball players Bill Bradley (D-N.J.) and Tom McMillen (D-Md.), football player Jack Kemp (R-N.Y.), and actor Fred Grandy (R-Iowa), demonstrate that name recognition from careers outside politics can be parlayed into a House or Senate seat. Overall, about one-fourth of the members of the U.S. Congress do not have prior elective experience.

A 1990 study found that more amateurs are elected during periods of generally increased political opportunity, such as the 1930s were for the Democrats or 1980 was for the Republicans (Canon, 1990, chap. 3). In such elections, amateurs take advantage of a desire for political change and exploit the relative openness of the career structure in the United States. Compared to nations with stronger party systems, the United States requires little in the way of party or office apprenticeship, even for the highest offices. Furthermore, all voters do not necessarily prefer experience. The suspicions many Americans hold about career politicians and the long-standing tradition of "running against Washington" can be exploited by amateurs who can credibly claim that they are not part of the power structure.

Rules governing elections. The rules of the game set the boundaries and guide the ambitions of politicians, amateurs, and experienced politicians alike. Two types of rules are central: those that define office availability and term restrictions (if any) and those that define electoral conditions. Provisions that establish the number of elective offices define the number of opportunities to run for office at various levels of government. These rules shape political careers by ensuring that the outlets for initial political ambitions are usually at the local level, where opportunities are the most numerous. Term restrictions also direct ambition. An office with a one- or two-term limit does not arouse the same ambition as an office in which one could make a career. Thus, congressional office is a more likely outlet for those wishing to establish a long-term career (though this would obviously change if term limits were imposed).

While office availability and term restrictions must be accepted as givens by ambitious politicians, one factor that helps define the nature of political opportunities is subject to manipulation: the drawing of district lines. Gerrymandering, the practice of tinkering with district lines for partisan advantage, can create substantial distortions in the geographic distribution of votes. The courts throw out the most blatant cases, but in many states the decennial practice of redistricting can affect the strategic calculations of candidates for office.

The second set of rules of the game defines the electoral conditions. Runoff primaries in the South have often discriminated against blacks, while third parties have never taken hold in the United States, largely because of single-member districts and winner-take-all elections. Both the transition from the party ballot to the secret ballot and the implementation of the direct primary had significant impact on the party's control over general elections and nominations. The Seventeenth Amendment, which provided for the direct election of U.S. senators, took their selection away from the party elite and gave it to the public. Both of these changes opened up the political process to a broader range of candidates. On the other hand, closed primaries, in which only members of a given party can vote, still serve as a tool, albeit a limited one, for maintaining some party control over who runs for office.

Political parties. Political parties influence who runs for Congress by structuring competition through the two-party system and by nominating political candidates, minimally through supplying them with a party label and more substantially through participating in their recruitment and selection. The two-party system's profound impact on the field of candidates has several dimensions. Most basically, having a two-party system means that third parties do not compete realistically for public office; few candidates have an actual chance of winning without the Democratic or Republican label. Each party's competitive standing in a given congressional district further defines potential candidates' ambitions and careers. Republicans considering a career in politics face a different set of opportunities on the south side of Chicago than in the suburbs of Dallas. The competitive positions of the parties at the national level also affect the types of candidates who are elected in a given year. Thus 1932, 1964, and 1974 were years in which many Democratic candidates were swept into office; in 1980, some Republicans who formerly would not have had much of a chance found themselves in Washington.

Parties also influence the career structure through nominations for political office. It is obviously in the party's interest to field the strongest possible candidate for the general election. Ideally, this is done by grooming candidates as they work their way up through party ranks. Parties also like to control politicians' ambitions and so act to stop or inhibit challengers to the strongest candidate in a primary race. Preprimary endorsements can provide an effective means of choking off outside candidacies. In 1986, for example, 99 percent of those endorsed by the Minnesota Democratic-Farmer-Labor party (the Democratic party in Minnesota) won in open seat and incumbent primary races (373 of 377). The closed primary—in which voters must be registered members of a party to vote in that party's primary—is another minimally effective but widely used step for exerting some party control. Parties have recently attempted to play a larger role in candidate recruitment through aggressive recruitment and candidate training schools. An expanding resource base enhances the party's role in recruitment. In the 1989–1990 election cycle, the various Democratic party committees raised $86.7 million, while the Republicans raised $207.2 million, compared with only $16.1 million and $44.1 million for the two parties, respectively, in the 1975–1976 cycle.

While parties clearly have some impact on the types of candidates who emerge in congressional elections, their role can be overstated. Studies of recruitment consistently reveal that the party does not play a central role in a candidate's decision to run for office. Candidates usually seek the blessing of the party organization, but, with a few exceptions, nominations are not rewards handed out to the party faithful.

The various perspectives discussed here offer insights into how people become candidates for Congress. The psychological and sociological approaches best explain initial recruitment (why someone chooses politics as a career). For example, early studies of the social backgrounds of political leaders demonstrated that the opportunity to enter politics is strongly skewed toward highly educated, upper-middle-class professionals. On the other hand, social backgrounds do not help predict which lower-level politicians will seek higher office. Thus, social background analysis provides little analytical leverage in explaining patterns of advancement to the U.S. Congress. The rational and institutional approaches have the opposite strengths and weaknesses: they do an excellent job of explaining the logic behind promotion to higher office, but they provide little assistance in helping explain which of the eligible millions will enter politics. A comprehensive understanding of who becomes a candidate for Congress must combine the several approaches.

[See also Members, articles on Demographic Profile and Qualifications.]

BIBLIOGRAPHY

Canon, David T. *Actors, Athletes, and Astronauts: Political Amateurs in the United States Congress.* 1990.

Jacobson, Gary C., and Samuel Kernell. *Strategy and Choice in Congressional Elections.* 1983.

Lasswell, Harold D. *Power and Personality.* 1948.

Matthews, Donald R. "Legislative Recruitment and Legislative Careers." *Legislative Studies Quarterly* 9 (1984): 547–585.

Matthews, Donald R. *U.S. Senators and Their World.* 1960.

Rohde, David W. "Risk Bearing and Progressive Ambition: The Case of Members of the United States House of Representatives." *American Journal of Political Science* 23 (1979): 1–26.

Schlesinger, Joseph A. *Ambition and Politics: Political Careers in the United States.* 1966.

DAVID T. CANON

Nomination to Candidacy

When machines dominated American politics, one of the most important aspects of their control was the ability to control political nominations. As Boss Tweed of Tammany Hall is reported to have claimed, "I don't care who does the electing, just so I do the nominating." Machines no longer dominate congressional and senatorial nominations as they once did, but what has replaced them?

This question can be answered in a number of ways. The fifty states have fifty different sets of laws that govern nominations. Normally, the procedures governing congressional and senatorial nominations parallel those for other partisan offices within the state. In the vast majority of the states, nomination is by direct primary election, but primaries vary according to who may run, who may vote, the role played by formal party organizations, and what is necessary to win. In the remaining states, party organization plays a more determinative role in deciding nominations.

When are nominations contested? When are they hotly contested? What difference do nomination contests make for the general election prospects of winners? No incumbent U.S. senator and only seven incumbent U.S. representatives lost primary elections between 1982 and 1990. In 1992 primaries played a more significant role, in part because of redistricting, in part because of the House bank scandal, and in part because of an anti-incumbent mood in the electorate. Whether this election represents an aberration or the breaking of a long pattern remains in doubt. Given the success of incumbents in other years, seeking reelection, it might be asked: do those who oppose them necessarily represent the challengers who would provide the most competition? If not, why are the best challengers not nominated? An understanding of the legal mechanisms of party nomination for the House and Senate and of the political ramifications of the nominating process will point toward answers to all these questions.

The Legal Environment. States with strong party organizations and intense two-party competition were among the last to adopt the direct primary as a means of nominating candidates for office. But by 1955, when Connecticut adopted a challenge primary as a means for contesting the party organization's convention- or caucus-nominated candidate through a primary, all states had instituted some form of primary for statewide offices and thus for congressional nominations. In several southern states, however, parties are given the option of nominating either by primaries or by convention. In Virginia, for instance, each party has used the convention system on occasion.

Within the framework of the primary nominating system, there are differences among legal environments in the states. State primary systems are distinguished from one another by the formal role played by political parties, by the definition of the electorate, and by provisions regarding how the winner is determined.

Eight states (Colorado, Connecticut, Delaware, New Mexico, New York, North Dakota, Rhode Island, and Utah) permit political parties formally to endorse candidates before primary elections. In each case, the endorsee has certain advantages in the primary itself—for example, automatic placement on the ballot or a preferred ballot position. A number of other states have informal endorsement procedures, but these do not have the impact of those specified by law. Endorsed candidates in those states with legal provisions for expression of party preference are rarely challenged for nominations, and when challenged they are rarely defeated, except for the seemingly aberrant cases of the Democrats in New York and the Republicans in Utah.

The most frequently noted legal distinction among primary systems is how the electorate is defined. The question is whether a citizen must be enrolled in a political party to vote in that party's primary. Twelve states (California, Connecticut, Kentucky, Maine, Maryland, Nebraska, Nevada, New Hampshire, New Jersey, New Mexico, New York, Oklahoma) hold closed primaries, that is, primaries in which a citizen must enroll in a party some time well in advance of the primary election to be eligible to vote in that primary. Typically, public records of partisan involvement are available to candidates and others, and citizens wishing to change their affiliation must do so long before the primary election. Fifteen additional states (Arizona, Colorado, Delaware, Florida, Iowa, Kansas, Massachusetts, North Carolina, Ohio, Oregon, Pennsylvania, Rhode Island, South Dakota, West Virginia, Wyoming) have closed primaries in which the rules are more flexible: either the record of affiliations is not published, or switches are permitted right up to primary day. In some of these states, independents can enroll in either party on primary day, but partisans cannot switch from one party to the other.

Twenty states (Alabama*, Arkansas*, Georgia*, Hawaii, Idaho, Illinois*, Indiana*, Michigan, Minnesota, Mississippi*, Missouri*, Montana, North Dakota, South Carolina*, Tennessee*, Texas*, Utah, Vermont, Virginia*, and Wisconsin) have open primaries, that is, primary elections in which any reg-

istered voter can vote in either party's primary. Among these states there is some variation. In eleven of them (those marked with an asterisk in the list above), mostly in the South, the choice of party must be made publicly though no permanent record is kept. In the remaining states, the choice is made in the secrecy of the voting booth.

Alaska and Washington employ a variation of the open primary called the blanket primary, a system in which citizens can vote in the Republican primary for some offices and the Democratic primary for other offices on the same ballot (but not in both primaries for the same office). Finally, Louisiana has a unique nonpartisan primary in which candidates for both parties appear on the same ballot. A runoff is held between the top two finishers, regardless of party affiliation, unless one candidate achieves a majority of the votes cast on primary day, in which case that candidate is declared the winner without opposition at the general election.

State nominating systems also vary according to the percentage of votes needed to win a primary. Normally, primaries are won by the candidate with a plurality of the votes, that is, more votes than any other candidate. However, in a number of states (mostly southern and border states, for example, Georgia and North Carolina) in order to win a primary a candidate must win a majority of the votes; if no candidate wins a majority, a runoff is held between the top two finishers. This procedure has engendered a good deal of criticism from activists who claim it disadvantages African American candidates in the South, but it has been defended by others who refute that claim.

The Political Environment. The most important element in the political environment for the nominating process is the presence or absence of an incumbent. Incumbent representatives and senators are rarely defeated. More to the point, they are rarely challenged in primaries. In the congressional elections from 1982 through 1990, 69.5 percent of the incumbents running for reelection to the House of Representatives were nominated without any opposition. In the majority of the other cases, opposition has been only token. Incumbent senators are challenged more frequently; 43.3 percent were challenged during the 1982 through 1990 elections, and many more of those challenges than House challenges were significant.

The differences between the positions of House and Senate incumbents are significant. First, Senate seats are seen as more prestigious than are House seats. In addition, these seats come up only once every six years rather than every other year. But just as important, representatives are perceived to be nearly invulnerable; they build up positive name recognition and, barring personal moral or ethical problems, are rarely harshly criticized in the press. Senators, on the other hand, because they represent larger constituencies (except in the case of those senators from states with only one representative), build up less of a personal relationship with their constituents; also, they are viewed more as national figures and so as more legitimate targets for criticism on policy stands. Challengers—and particularly serious challengers—are more likely to appear when the prize is more valued and when the chances for success seem higher.

The following theme is a constant no matter how one looks at the politics of House nominations: incumbents are less likely to be challenged in their own party if the party has legal endorsing powers. That is, if the party is strong and backs the incumbent, challengers are even less likely to emerge than otherwise. If one turns to the party of the challenger, the norm is for the nomination to go by default to a self-starter, an ambitious politician who thinks he or she has the key to beating the incumbent. Few find that key. The role of a political party organization is frequently to find a challenger; in fact, over the past five elections, an average of more than fifty seats per election have had no major party opposition to the incumbent; the nomination, viewed as of little value, went begging.

In cases where incumbents are viewed as vulnerable—perhaps because of scandal or advancing age or a close race in the preceding general election—contested primaries in the other party are more common. Of the few challengers who beat incumbent representatives, most do so after having won a contested primary. In contested primaries, the definition of the electorate becomes important. Obviously, political strategists have an easier time in states with closed primaries, because they know who is eligible and likely to vote in the primary. On the other hand, in open primary states, strategists can appeal to those in the other party who favor their candidates.

Other challengers have beaten incumbents without having to contest for the party nomination. In some cases, strong party organizations, often armed with legal endorsement procedures, have dissuaded those who would oppose the anointed challenger. In other cases, an incumbent's vulnerability was not apparent when nomination contests were planned. A challenger with a free ride through the nominating process has the advantage of a unit-ed party, though some argue that such challengers are disadvantaged because contested primaries enhance name recognition.

Most Senate challengers do face primary elections, because a Senate seat is viewed as having more value than a House seat and as more likely to turn over. Prospective candidates are more difficult to dissuade, because their turn will not come up again very soon. Thus, not only are more senators challenged in primaries than is true of representatives, but more Senate challengers have to win primary contests to garner nominations than is true of House challengers. Again, some of these are divisive primaries that harm general election chances; others are less divisive and serve to enhance the challenger's name recognition throughout the state.

Finally, the same pattern appears in a more exaggerated form in open seats. When House or Senate incumbents retire, ambitious politicians see an all-too-infrequent opportunity to win a seat in Congress. For open seats, the norm is contested primaries in both parties. The exceptions to this rule prove the point. Nominations go uncontested—and on rare occasion even begging—only when they are viewed as not having much worth, for instance in the minority party in a strong one-party area.

The congressional nominating process is highly significant because a responsive legislature depends on competitive elections, and competitive elections depend on high-quality nominees. At least since the 1970s, few congressional elections have been very competitive. One reason is that few nominees have been capable of running serious races, and the reason is that high-quality challengers have decided to forego congressional races.

The nominating process all but guarantees this result. For the most part, except in those few states with strong party organizations and formal endorsement procedures, congressional and senatorial nominees are self-starters, ambitious politicians who want to move into the national legislature or to "promote" themselves from the House to the Senate. And ambitious politicians only run when they think they stand a good chance for victory. Thus, incumbent representatives are rarely challenged, incumbent senators are rarely defeated for nomination, and challengers frequently are nominated by default. Only when elections are viewed as potentially winnable, as when incumbents appear vulnerable or seats are vacated, do the strongest candidates put themselves forth and compete for congressional nominations.

[*See also* Political Parties.]

BIBLIOGRAPHY

Jacobson, Gary C. *The Politics of Congressional Elections.* 3d ed. 1992.

Jewell, Malcolm E., and David M. Olson. *Political Parties and Elections in American States.* 3d ed. 1988.

Key, V. O., Jr. *American State Parties: An Introduction.* 1956.

Maisel, L. Sandy, Linda L. Fowler, Ruth S. Jones, and Walter J. Stone. "The Naming of Candidates: Recruitment or Emergence?" In *The Parties Respond: Changes in the American Party System.* Edited by L. Sandy Maisel, 1990. Pp. 137–159.

L. SANDY MAISEL

Congressional Campaigns

Modern congressional campaigns can be characterized as "candidate-centered." Party organizations no longer play a major role in the nomination and election of candidates; candidates are typically self-starters who were not recruited by political parties. These candidates raise the bulk of their campaign funds from their own direct contacts with contributors, are responsible for the conduct and content of their own campaigns, and generate their own publicity and advertising. In presenting themselves to the voters, they may choose to emphasize or to deemphasize their party affiliation, depending on what kind of strategy they believe will enable them to win the election.

Party Loyalties. Although party organizations are no longer as involved in congressional campaigns as they used to be, most voters still identify with one of the two major parties, and party identification is the single best predictor of how a citizen will vote. For these reasons, candidates representing the majority party in a district generally choose to emphasize their party affiliation, while those representing the minority party usually deemphasize it. In some states and congressional districts, one party has such a strong advantage in party affiliation among voters that candidates of the minority party have little or no chance of winning elections. Still, in most states and districts, there are enough voters without a party identification, or willing to vote contrary to their party identification, to elect a candidate from either party.

Voters who reject the simple cue of voting based on party may consider a variety of factors in their ballot decisions. Although national issues and candidates' ideologies can be important, they clearly do not dominate some other dimensions of voter choice, such as candidates' personal qualities. Certainly, it is difficult for candidates to communicate complex messages about issues in the brief time or space available in advertisements. Furthermore, commentators and journalists tend to focus their attention on the personal attributes of the candidates or on the closeness of the race, factors that, they argue, are of more interest to citizens. For these reasons, much of the information that citizens receive about candidates has little issue content.

CAMPAIGN BADGE. For Matthew S. Quay's race for a U.S. Senate seat from Pennsylvania in 1893. Lavish badges and ribbons were often employed in campaigns around the end of the nineteenth century.

LIBRARY OF CONGRESS

Incumbents and Challengers. Incumbents themselves are nonetheless responsible for much of the content of campaigns. Over his or her term of office, an incumbent seeks to build constituent support in various ways. The incumbent serves constituents by voting for popular legislation, by sponsoring and promoting legislation that meets the particular needs and interests of constituents, and by acting as an intermediary between constituents and the federal government.

Service to their constituents has become a much more prominent part of a representative's job. Starting with Lyndon B. Johnson's Great Society, the federal government vastly expanded the level of services it provided to state and local governments and to individuals. This expanded federal role gave representatives a greater opportunity to intervene with the government on behalf of constituents. Constituents came to expect that a representative would not just vote to represent their opinions in Congress but would actually help them in their dealings with the federal government, in ways ranging from aiding them in getting disability benefits, for example, to securing a tax exemption for a small business.

Morris Fiorina (1977) argues that House members have taken such advantage of these opportunities for constituency service that their reelection prospects have been noticeably enhanced. In the 1980s, an average of 92.2 percent of all House races involved an incumbent seeking reelection, and 94.8 percent of these incumbents were successful.

The high reelection rates of House incumbents are not a result simply of their constituency work in Congress but also of their success in advertising their accomplishments. The franking privilege allows representatives to send postage-free mailings to constituents. This is a tremendously valuable resource enabling incumbents to inform constituents of their activities. In addition, representatives seek as much newspaper and television coverage of their work as possible. Thus, by the time an election campaign begins, an incumbent generally has a substantial name-recognition advantage over any challenger, and the campaign itself seldom redresses this imbalance. Surveys have established that, by election day, voters are much more likely to recognize or to recall the names of incumbents than of their challengers.

Although senators and House members have similar opportunities to serve their constituents and to publicize their service, senators do not achieve the same security of reelection. During the 1980s, an average of 87.5 percent of all Senate races involved an incumbent seeking reelection, and of those incumbents, 82.5 percent were successful.

There are several explanations for the greater advantage of House incumbency. One focuses on the different expectations citizens have of senators as compared to House members. Surveys indicate that citizens, especially in the larger states, believe national issues are a more important part of the job of a senator than of a House member. Senators themselves give greater emphasis to national issues in their public activities and reelection campaigns than do House members. Such emphasis is a response to constituent expectations and also contributes to the formation of their future expectations.

Senators' reelection prospects are more closely tied than are House members' prospects to swings of national opinion on the major issues of the day, and senators are more likely to be held accountable for failures of national public policy. In contrast, House members are more likely to be evaluated in terms of local service. Unlike major national policy issues, local service is generally not controversial. Helping a Democratic constituent who has a problem with the government does not preclude helping a Republican who also has a problem. Both constituents will be grateful, but one may decide to cross party lines and vote for the helpful House member at election time. Similarly, local public works projects are generally popular among constituents regardless of party affiliation.

A second, related explanation for the more favorable reelection prospects of House members focuses on differences in the constituencies of House members and of Senators. The populations of House members' districts are about equal, and with the exception of a few states with small populations, House members represent fewer constituents than do senators. In fact, the average senator represents about nine times as many constituents as the average House member. Thus, it is much easier for individual House members to meet and serve individual constituents and to build support on that basis. This further reinforces the differences in expectations that constituents have of a House member compared to a senator and illustrates how House members can more easily build support based on constituency service than can senators.

House and Senate constituencies also differ in terms of partisan competition. House districts are more likely than states to be dominated by one party. When a large majority of citizens identifies with one party, it is much less likely that other factors will be strong enough to override this partisan imbalance and affect the outcome of an election. Thus, many House districts often reelect the candidate representing the majority party again and again, contributing to the higher reelection rate of House members as compared to senators.

Finally, the quality of challengers in House and Senate races differs sharply. Only high-quality challengers are at all likely to defeat incumbents. A challenger must be considered competitive from the start in order to get the media attention and campaign contributions necessary to mount a strong challenge. One characteristic common to good challengers is prior elective office. A successful run for election in the district, albeit for another office, helps give the challenger the visibility, experience, and fund-raising contacts necessary to wage an effective campaign.

Few such high-quality challengers choose to run against incumbents in House races. By contrast, Senate races more often involve a challenger of high caliber. Because the Senate term is six years long, as opposed to two for the House, a Senate challenger has much more time to raise funds and wage an effective campaign than does a House challenger. House seats and statewide elective offices are logical stepping-stones, providing a ready pool of potentially interested candidates with the visibility and other resources needed to run for the Senate.

The relative lack of high-quality challengers in House races compared to Senate races is more a consequence than a cause of the apparent safety of House incumbents. Challengers, whatever their qualifications, must choose to enter a race. The greater a potential challenger's belief that he or she can win, the more likely he or she is to enter the race. Incumbents, of course, use the resources at their disposal to convince prospective challengers of the futility of a challenge. House incumbents generally succeed at this more often than do Senate incumbents.

For all these reasons, House members have a greater advantage in retaining office than do senators. Recent studies have estimated the incumbency advantage to be worth about 8.5 percent of the vote in House elections (Jacobson, 1990) and between 3 and 4 percent of the vote in Senate elections (Erikson, 1991).

Levels of Competitiveness. Despite the difficulties and long odds of a successful challenge, most races for the House and Senate are contested.

Strong challengers are more likely to enter the race when they perceive the incumbent to be vulnerable. Such vulnerability is often a product of the incumbent's real or supposed personal failings and may reflect scandal, such as the 1991 House banking scandal, or an inattention to the wishes of the district. A close election result in the most recent prior election may suggest that an incumbent is vulnerable, even if there are no other obvious signs of trouble.

Factors beyond the incumbent's control can also increase vulnerability. Changes in House district partisanship or geographic composition may make a district more competitive. The outcome of a House or Senate election may also be influenced by voters' approval or disapproval of the president's program or by their views on other national issues, most often the state of the economy. Quality challengers are more likely to enter races when they judge that national or local constituency factors favor their party.

While there clearly are difficulties in mounting a challenge to a House or Senate incumbent, many challengers nevertheless enter these races. Those that choose to run against incumbents seek to negate the advantages of incumbency during the course of the election campaign. Their disadvantages in this regard, however, are tremendous, because so little is generally known about them and what is known about the incumbent tends to be quite favorable, since it is based largely on the incumbent's own publicity efforts.

The Money Factor. Challengers also begin their campaigns with severe disadvantages in organization and fund-raising ability. Fund-raising is essential; the cost of a congressional campaign almost quadrupled between 1976 and 1990. In 1976, the average cost of a House campaign was $73,316; in 1990, it was $284,257. The Senate has seen a similar increase in the cost of campaigning. In 1976, the average cost of a Senate campaign was $595,449; in 1990, it was $2,574,868. These averages include noncompetitive as well as competitive races; competitive races cost even more.

Funds are raised from several sources, but primarily from individual contributors and political action committees. Parties play a very small financial role in both House and Senate races; in 1990, they provided only 4 percent of the total funds for House races and 7 percent of the total funds in Senate races (Ornstein, Mann, and Malbin, 1992).

Money is especially crucial for challengers because of their lack of name recognition, for which they must compensate through television, radio, and newspaper advertisements and campaign flyers and pamphlets. While an incumbent is guaranteed a certain amount of publicity by virtue of his or her office, the challenger has to buy that same publicity.

The importance of money in congressional campaigns is well documented. Gary Jacobson (1990) has demonstrated the importance of campaign contributions in reinforcing the disparities between incumbents and challengers. Incumbents can raise much more money than challengers because of their established contacts with constituents and interest groups. Furthermore, they are, as the numbers show, good bets to win reelection, and there is more to be gained from giving to a winner than to a loser. Challengers are likely to be able to raise enough money to mount a strong campaign only if they can convince others that they have a good chance of winning, and this is a difficult task at the start of a campaign.

Interestingly, though, if a challenger manages to raise sufficient funds, every dollar he or she spends is worth more votes than the dollar spent by an incumbent (Jacobson, 1990). Given the electorate's relative unfamiliarity with the challenger, spending by the challenger has a greater effect than spending by the incumbent in increasing voters' familiarity.

Money is crucial to waging a campaign not only for the advertising it buys, but also because it is needed to build an organization that will coordinate additional campaign activities, such as fundraising, polling, and turning out the vote. In the past, a representative could rely on the local party organization to carry out many of these tasks; the party informed the majority of voters about its candidates through publicity and personal contact with the voters. David Olson (1978) has documented how, more recently, representatives have developed their own personal organizations independent of local parties. Furthermore, as an incumbent's seniority increases, he or she becomes better known in the district and has less need for party assistance.

Contacting Constituents. Part of the ability of representatives to develop their own organizations must be attributed directly to television. Starting with the 1952 presidential race, television permanently changed the face of American political campaigns. With television, voters could see candidates for themselves and listen to their messages instead of relying on the parties to deliver those messages.

Generally, television and other direct means of communicating with the voter, such as newspaper

LIGHTHEARTED TELEVISED CAMPAIGN ADVERTISEMENT. With an Elvis Presley impersonator, for Democrat Russell D. Feingold's successful 1992 campaign for a U.S. Senate seat from Wisconsin.

R. MICHAEL JENKINS, CONGRESSIONAL QUARTERLY INC.

or radio, are most effective if the media market closely fits the constituency of the candidate. One study has shown that voters are more familiar with House candidates when the House constituency closely matches a natural community boundary (Niemi, Powell, and Bicknell, 1986). Voters are less likely to be confused about which district they live in because in such communities everyone lives in the same House district. Furthermore, since all media coverage is devoted to a single House district news attention is directed toward only one district and purchased advertising time is cost-effective.

In contrast, a large city may contain many House districts. In such cities, voters are likely to be confused about which district they live in and who their representative is. The news media seldom devote much attention to candidates in any one district, because only a small portion of their audience is interested in any single district, and purchased advertising is relatively expensive because it generally must be aimed at a city-wide audience larger than the district. Television is the most expensive of advertising media, and for this reason its use is not practical in some House districts. Challengers are at a particular disadvantage in such fragmented communities; although incumbents are somewhat less well known in fragmented than in single-district communities, challengers are *much* less well known in fragmented communities. Thus, incumbents have a bigger net familiarity advantage in fragmented communities.

LYNDON B. JOHNSON. Campaigning by helicopter for a U.S. Senate seat from Texas, 1948.

LIBRARY OF CONGRESS

Surveys of constituents are another form of direct contact between candidate and constituent. Beginning in the 1970s, the use of these surveys became common, especially in Senate campaigns. This was only one aspect of the increasing professionalism of campaigns. In the past, campaign staff consisted mostly of volunteers from the district who made phone calls and personally contacted voters. Today, most members of campaign staffs are still volunteers, but candidates, especially Senate candidates, often hire professionals for advice on campaign strategy, media, and polling (Herrnson, 1988).

Parties have begun to reassert themselves in this area of professional campaign services. Both the Republican and Democratic parties have Senate and House campaign committees. While they help raise funds for candidates, the bulk of their contribution lies in providing polling and advertising advice and, in some cases, the recruitment of candidates. While these national party organizations do not constitute the primary campaign organizations for candidates, they have become more and more involved, especially in House races (Herrnson, 1988).

Open seat races, that is, races in which the incumbent does not seek reelection, are typically more competitive than races with incumbents running for reelection. Nonetheless, studies have shown that in House elections, the outcome in open seat races is strongly influenced by the partisan composition of the district and the popularity of the former incumbent. Thus, although candidates whose party has not held the seat have a much better chance of winning, on average, in open seat races, the incumbent's party typically retains the seat. In 203 open seat races in the 1980s only 49 were won by the opposing party. In the Senate, the outcome of the race seems to depend more on the quality of the two candidates. Of the 25 open seats in the 1980s, 12 changed party hands, a much higher proportion than for the House.

Open seat races by definition result in the election of new members. The disproportionately large number of open seats in 1992 resulted from three factors: redistricting reduced the electoral security of some members; the House banking scandal threatened the electoral prospects of House incumbents, especially the forty-six incumbents with one hundred or more overdrafts; and, finally, 1992 was the last year in which an incumbent could retire and retain for personal use moneys collected for political campaigns. Although twenty House and Senate incumbents were defeated in primaries in 1992, the large number of freshmen members in the 103d Congress was primarily a result of retirements, not electoral defeats of incumbents. Contrary to popular belief, H. Ross Perot's presidential campaign—and all the anti-incumbent fervor that accompanied it—was of little importance in the general election, where the typical party and incumbency factors worked much as usual.

The consequences of "candidate-centered" campaigns are clear. Incumbents in both House and Senate races have a distinct advantage because of the resources that incumbency provides. Over time, they can build support by virtue of their service to their constituents, an opportunity challengers do not have. District service translates into campaign contributions and publicity that in turn build further support. These advantages frequently deter strong challengers from entering a race, and those who do run seldom win. House members, by virtue of their smaller constituencies and the more particular expectations that voters have of them, are better able to use these resources to establish electoral safety than are senators. In the absence of any major change in the electoral system, these patterns are likely to persist.

[See also Campaign Committees; Campaign Financing.]

BIBLIOGRAPHY

Erikson, Robert S. "Incumbency and U.S. Senators." Paper presented at Stanford Conference on Senate Elections. 1991.

Fiorina, Morris. *Congress: Keystone of the Washington Establishment.* 1977.

Herrnson, Paul. *Party Campaigning in the 1980's.* 1988.

Jacobson, Gary. *Electoral Origins of Divided Government.* 1990.

Niemi, Richard G., Linda W. Powell, and Patricia L. Bicknell. "The Effects of Congruity between Community and District on Salience of U.S. House Candidates." *Legislative Studies Quarterly* 11 (1986): 187–201.

Olson, David. "U.S. Congressmen and Their Diverse Congressional District Parties." *Legislative Studies Quarterly* 3 (1978): 239–264.

Ornstein, Norman J., Thomas E. Mann, and Michael J. Malbin. *Vital Statistics on Congress, 1991–1992.* 1992.

LYNDA W. POWELL and WENDY SCHILLER

Voting

"Few die and none retire" was the adage applied to incumbent members of the House of Representatives in the 1950s. Only in the Democratic landslide of 1958 did fewer than 90 percent—89.9 percent—of incumbents fail to win reelection during that decade. Senators were not quite so fortunate; only in 1956 were more than three-quarters of incumbent senators successful in winning new terms. Reelection rates to the House fell slightly during the turbulent 1960s but crept back over the 90 percent mark in the 1970s. By the mid-to-late 1980s, it seemed that only a scandal could unseat an incumbent representative. Not only were reelection rates high, but the margins of victory had become ever larger. Senators continued to have a more difficult time achieving reelection, but by the 1980s incumbents had become more secure than they had been in decades (see table 1).

The incumbency advantage in the House is a twentieth-century phenomenon. For most of the nineteenth century representatives were not career politicians. Henry Clay served as Speaker of the House in his first term. Reelection rates began to rise in the mid-nineteenth century as more members became career politicians, peaking in 1920 before falling again. Prior to the 1960s, reelection rates tracked the fortunes of the president's party. Since then, incumbents have increasingly won new terms regardless of national tides.

Twentieth-century House elections have become less competitive over time, while contests for the Senate have become slightly more competitive. The post–World War II House incumbency reelection rates have increased more steadily over time than those for the Senate. Not only have fewer Senate incumbents won reelection than their House coun-

TABLE 1. *House and Senate Reelection Rates, 1946–1990*[1]

YEAR	HOUSE	SENATE
1946	82.4	56.7
1948	79.3	60.0
1950	90.5	68.8
1952	91.0	64.5
1954	93.1	75.0
1956	94.6	86.2
1958	89.9	64.3
1960	92.6	96.6
1962	91.5	82.9
1964	86.6	84.8
1966	88.1	87.5
1968	96.8	71.4
1970	94.5	77.4
1972	93.6	74.1
1974	87.7	85.2
1976	95.8	64.0
1978	93.7	60.0
1980	90.7	55.2
1982	90.1	93.3
1984	95.4	89.6
1986	98.0	75.0
1988	98.3	85.2
1990	96.0	96.9
1992	88.3	82.1
Mean	91.6	76.5
Standard deviation	4.6	12.5

[1]Percent winning of members who sought reelection.
SOURCE: Norman J. Ornstein, Thomas E. Mann, and Michael J. Malbin, comps., *Vital Statistics on Congress, 1991–1992.* Mean and standard deviation figures calculated by the author.

terparts (76 percent compared to 92 percent in the postwar era), but Senate elections have demonstrated considerably more volatility. The standard deviation for Senate incumbency victories is almost three times as large as that for the House (12.9 compared to 4.7). The fortunes of Senate incumbents can change quickly, even as House incumbents remain relatively insulated from national trends. Incumbent senators' success rates plummeted in 1958, only to rise to near record levels two years later. Barely more than half of incumbent senators won reelection in 1980, yet more than 90 percent won just two years later. Some of the variation in Senate reelection rates is attributable to the peculiar cycle in which just one-third of senators face the electorate every two years, but the wide swings over time suggest that other, more systematic factors are also at work.

House and Senate elections are fundamentally different from each other. The aggregate correlation between House and Senate incumbent reelection rates in the twenty-three postwar elections is just .31. House contests are marked by weak challengers who have had little prior experience and have difficulty raising enough money to compete with well-funded incumbents. Senators face much stronger challengers, often House members or governors, with widespread name recognition and the ability to raise substantial amounts of money. Representatives come from more homogenous constituencies, which limits the role of issues in elections. Senators' more heterogenous constituencies highlight the controversial policy stands that legislators are expected to take in the "world's greatest deliberative body." Most House districts are more compact than states, so representatives can establish personal relationships with their constituents. Senators are forced to rely mostly on the media to reach voters; they cannot establish the same trusting relationship with constituents that comes from one-on-one contact.

The decline of parties made voters more likely to support incumbents. Presidents could no longer carry large majorities of their partisans into Congress, but they were also less likely to lose many seats in the midterm "referenda" on the president's popularity. Weaker partisanship made House incumbents more secure, but not senators.

Students of congressional elections agree that senators have greater difficulty winning reelection than members of the House. Yet that is one of the few assertions about congressional elections that is unchallenged. There are few disputes over what drives Senate elections, but largely because they have not been studied in great detail. The sources of the incumbency advantage for the House remain controversial. Indeed, it is not even clear whether House incumbents became safer in the 1970s and early 1980s. From 1946 to 1964, 61 percent of House incumbents won more than 60 percent of the vote in their reelection bids; from 1966 to 1984, 73 percent achieved this measure of security. Yet Gary Jacobson (1991) demonstrates that incumbents elected with supposedly secure margins of between 60 and 65 percent of the vote in the 1970s were just as likely to lose the next time around as members who garnered from 55 to 60 percent of the vote in the 1950s. Not until 1986 and 1988 did increased vote margins bring greater short-term se-

curity. Ten percent fewer incumbents won by more than 60 percent in 1990 than in 1986 and 1988, presaging the high retirement and defeat rates of 1992.

Ironically, the members who supposedly were most secure—those with the longest tenure—were more likely to lose than they had been in the era when seniority equaled power in the House. Freshman members, in contrast, became more secure than they had once been. The "sophomore surge," the boost in votes from an initial victory to the first reelection campaign, tripled from the 1960s to the 1970s and has remained high. Currently there is both more uniformity and greater volatility in House contests. The seniority of members is not so strongly related to their prospects of victory.

Voters are becoming more fickle in House races as well as in Senate contests. Members with "safe" margins can no longer rest assured of victory. Voters now shift their loyalties in less predictable ways than before. What has saved many incumbents from defeat in light of these trends is a decrease in the "swing ratio," a measure of how many seats change for every percentage of aggregate vote change. In races involving incumbents, the House swing ratio was cut in half from the period between 1946 and 1964 to the period between 1966 and 1986. Higher vote margins protected incumbents from being swept out of office when national tides went against their party. Even large swings in the national two-party vote would not spell defeat for the increasing share of members who had won by comfortable margins. Senators, who usually won by smaller margins than their House counterparts, were less insulated from national trends, as the elections of 1958, 1980, and 1986 indicate.

The elections of 1984 through 1988 signaled a sharp increase in the electoral security of House members. While only fifteen incumbents were defeated in the 1990 general elections—still two and a half times as many as in 1986 or 1988—sitting members' vote shares declined to just under two-thirds of the vote, the lowest average since 1974. The average vote shares dropped for members of both parties, although more precipitously for Republicans than for Democrats. Thus, 1990 set the stage for the sea change of 1992, which began setting a record for retirements as sixty-five House members decided not to seek new terms. Historically, representatives have had long-established auras of invincibility, especially in comparison to their Senate counterparts. What kept them so secure for so long and why did their advantages atrophy so quickly?

House Incumbency Advantages. A range of interrelated factors has made House incumbents more secure since the 1960s. They include (1) the waning of party identification; (2) the correspondent deemphasizing of issues in House elections; (3) legislators' development of "home styles" designed to enhance reelection prospects; (4) increasing perquisites of office that help members develop nonpartisan home styles; (5) spending patterns that strongly favor incumbents over challengers; and (6) weaker challengers with less political experience and feeble party support. Overall, incumbents now run largely on their own merits and demerits. Weaker parties rob challengers of auxiliary campaign organizations. They eviscerate the ties between presidential popularity and party-line voting, thus insulating incumbents from trends that would harm their party nationally. Legislators are now free to develop their own style, deemphasizing issues and highlighting the delivery of services and personal style. The more popular members are, the more money they can raise—and the less money challengers can amass. Faced with very popular incumbents who can raise a lot of money, the strongest challengers are likely to opt out and leave weaker candidates as the sole contestants in House races.

Party identification. Party identification has become less central to American politics since the 1970s. Americans no longer identify as strongly with parties as they did in the 1950s and 1960s. The percentage of those without party identification doubled—from approximately 10 percent to about 20 percent—in House and Senate elections from the 1950s to the 1980s. From the 1940s through 1952, about 20 percent of congressional districts split their partisan tickets between the presidency and the House; by the 1970s and 1980s, approximately one-third of the districts regularly did so, with that portion rising to 44 percent in the presidential landslides of 1972 and 1984. Even when national trends strongly favored one party, incumbents won approximately 90 percent of their contests.

Issues and home style. As partisanship became less important in House races, sitting legislators increasingly relied on their own resources to win new terms. Representatives sought to develop home styles that downplayed controversial issues and highlighted the bonds of trust between legislators and their constituents. Members told voters that they were primarily concerned with looking out for local interests. Some studies (e.g., Johannes, 1984) show that policy agreement between legislators and constituents does affect incumbents' reelection success.

The development of a successful home style usually, though not always, depends on a representative's ability to sidestep controversial issues. If members want to appeal to a sufficient number of voters to take 70 percent of the vote, then they must avoid contention. Jacobson (1992) shows why incumbents should avoid issues and focus on the personal contact that is essential to establishing trust between voters and members. In 1988, 19 percent of respondents to the American National Election Study said that they liked the incumbents' ideology and policy positions, while 35 percent disliked their members' stands on issues. Given this two-to-one balance against issues, incumbents try to shift attention away from ideology. If a district is homogenous, so the range of ideological positions is not wide, members may be able to benefit from highlighting issues. The more diverse the district—or if the incumbent represents the disadvantaged party—the more the incumbent will steer the campaign away from issues.

Development of a successful home style requires being known and liked. Throughout the 1980s an average of 92 percent of constituents recognized their incumbent's name, compared to 54 percent name-recognition for challengers. Half of the respondents who recognized the incumbent's name liked something about the member; only 12 percent disliked anything. By contrast, only 21 percent of those who recognized the challenger's name liked something about the candidate, while 14 percent disliked something (Jacobson, 1992).

Incumbents have a presence that challengers lack. More than twice as many voters report some contact with the incumbent compared to the challenger in House races. Almost all voters (91 percent) report some contact with the incumbent. About two-thirds received mail from their legislator, compared to just 15 percent from the challenger. On the specific dimensions of contact—personal, attending a meeting, talking to staff, read about in newspaper, saw on television, heard on radio, or indirect contact through family or friends—incumbents' advantages ranged from 2 to 1 to 10 to 1. The better known and liked incumbents are, the more votes they get, especially from people who identify with the opposition party. Contact develops both name recognition and likability; more critically, it develops positive evaluations of the incumbent's job performance and reputation for helpfulness (Jacobson, 1992).

Perquisites. Incumbents grant themselves a wide array of perquisites, estimated to be worth up to $1.5 million over a two-year term, to increase their name recognition and likability. Members have unlimited mailing ("franking") privileges to their districts and very generous office expenditures that permit them to travel back to their districts as often as they wish, to make unlimited long-distance phone calls (and to receive them on toll-free numbers), to send newsletters to their constituents, and to maintain office staffs considerably larger than those of any other legislature in the world. Both the House and Senate have television studios in which members can produce programs and relay them via satellite to stations in their districts without charge.

Members of Congress have always paid attention to their constituents. The new era of powerful incumbents has been marked by a sharp increase in perquisites. There was a tenfold increase in the volume of congressional mailings from the 1950s to the 1970s and a further doubling over the next decade. The initial big spurt occurred in the 1970s, as incumbent vote shares shot up. The number of House employees jumped from 1,440 in 1947 to 7,569 in 1989. More critically, an ever-increasing number of legislators—in the Senate as well as the House—shifted office staff to their constituencies. By 1990, 42 percent of House staff (and 35 percent of Senate staff) were constituency-based. Most of the district staff handles mail, constituents' requests, and casework designed to resolve peoples' problems with the government.

Perquisites enhance name recognition. They also buy likability at relatively little cost. Casework and publicity are noncontroversial. They appeal to voters across partisan and ideological lines, whereas stances on issues are more divisive. Do perquisites attract votes? The evidence is mixed. Johannes (1984) finds that the volume of casework done by a congressional office has little impact on the member's vote margin and that voters are moved more by a legislator's policy positions than by specific benefits. Few constituents, after all, ask members for help in casework. Yet even if casework does not directly produce votes, it does lead to a reputation for helpfulness, which generates support for incumbents.

Legislative Spending. Incumbents also use legislative spending to build coalitions. The increasing incumbency advantage has been traced in part to the growing expenditures on pork-barrel projects that often provide more political than economic benefit. Legislators like such projects—a new dam, a post office—because they are visible. The electoral impact of the pork barrel is unclear, however. The amount of money spent on such programs does not seem to affect the share of the votes incumbents receive. Rather, a member's reputation for helping the district seems more important than actual dollars spent, and reputations do not seem to have suffered in the mid 1980s, when funds for such projects were severely limited. Morris P. Fiorina (1991) argues that it is not pork-barrel spending on specific projects that matters. Much more important, he claims, is the overall increase, beginning in the 1960s and 1970s, in government expenditures on a wide range of social programs. This spending changed people's expectations of government. Members of Congress can claim credit for these entitlement programs and offer constituents real assistance in getting benefits—thus securing votes from a grateful electorate.

Campaign funding and spending. The greatly expanded role of the federal government has led to the proliferation of new interest groups seeking to influence policy. These organizations not only lobby; they increasingly have formed political action committees (PACs) to influence the outcome of congressional elections. PACs burgeoned after the enactment of the Federal Election Campaign Act of 1974, which sought to curb the accountability-free cash campaign contributions that had figured so importantly in the Watergate scandal. The number of political action committees rose from 608 in 1974 to more than 4,000 by 1990. PAC contributions to House candidates rose from $30 million in 1974 to $147.9 million in 1988 (both in 1988 dollars). PAC contributions rose from 17 percent of all House receipts in 1974 to 43 percent in 1988. The largest source of campaign funds was still individuals, but their share nevertheless declined from 60 percent to 49 percent during the same period. Most PAC contributions go to incumbents. Even business-oriented PACs usually pursue a pragmatic strategy of rewarding those who hold power and so give more money to Democratic than to Republican incumbents.

Congressional campaigns have become very expensive. The average House incumbent spent $79,000 in 1976 but almost $400,000 in 1990. Challengers were reasonably competitive in 1976, spending $51,000; but by 1990 they had fallen to just $109,000. Challengers need money to buy name recognition. Their name recognition increases with spending, although the rate of increase tapers off as spending goes up and stops increasing altogether after a plateau of about $500,000 is reached. Increased expenditures bring votes, so the amount a challenger spends is one of the most important, if not the most important, determinant of whether the incumbent or the challenger wins in a House election.

There was a long-standing debate about the effect of incumbent expenditures. For all the money that sitting members raised, there appeared to be little payoff. The more incumbents spend, the *worse* they do—a most anomalous result. Members who spend the most face the strongest challenges; they must react in turn. Incumbents garner large war chests to scare off high-quality challengers. There is now agreement that incumbent spending does lead to at least some increment in vote shares for the sitting member. Sitting members who spend virtually nothing already start with virtually universal name recognition—greater than even the highest spending challenger can hope to achieve. Therefore, the impact of incumbent spending is bound to be less than it is for challengers.

As the gap between challenger and incumbent spending increases, incumbents' advantages grow. Most challengers from 1972 to 1990 spent under $100,000 (1990 dollars); this level of spending gave them just a 1 percent chance of unseating an incumbent. Even the best-funded challengers—the 14 percent who spend more than $300,000 (1990 dollars)—stood only a one-in-four chance of besting the incumbent.

Challenger quality.   Most challengers are amateurs, with no background in politics. High-quality challengers, who have previously held elective office, are experienced in running campaigns and begin with greater name recognition. Jacobson (1991) finds that from 1946 to 1988, 17.3 percent of experienced challengers defeated incumbents, compared to a mere 4.3 percent of amateurs. A high-quality challenger can, on average, expect to win an additional 3 percent of the vote against an incumbent. Beyond that, high-quality challengers are also able to raise more money, so that their competitive advantage over amateur challengers is magnified. Yet the quality of challengers—especially Republicans—declined markedly in the late 1980s and in 1990. The share of incumbents who ran unopposed rose sharply.

Senators' Lower Incumbency Advantage. Senators have fared less well than representatives in winning reelection because they do not have some of the latter's incumbency advantages. The decline of partisanship benefits incumbents in both chambers, but senators do not gain as much from it as House members, because they are not as sheltered by nonpartisan, constituency-oriented activities. Issues play a greater role in Senate elections than in House contests. Voters expect senators to take more prominent roles than representatives in debates on national policy. Also, the six-year term encourages senators to take greater risks on policy issues.

Senators have different home styles than representatives. Their constituencies are usually larger and more diverse. They cannot—or will not—engage in the personal contact that House members do. Senators are less likely than are House members to meet constituents personally. They go home less often. They pay less attention to constituents in the middle years of their terms and have less direct contact with them during election campaigns. When they campaign, they are more likely to do so through the media. Here they are at a disadvantage, because they cannot control what television or newspapers report about them. Senators also find it more difficult to claim credit for legislative accomplishments than do representatives.

Most critically, senators face stronger and better-financed challengers than do representatives. About two-thirds of Senate challengers in the 1970s and 1980s have held prior elective office—often serving in the House or as governor—while still others have achieved celebrity status as, for example, astronauts or athletes. While Senate incumbents are slightly more likely than their House counterparts to be recognized by constituents (97 compared to 92 percent), Senate challengers are substantially more likely to be known than are House challengers (78 percent compared to 54 percent). While Senate challengers are about as well liked as their House counterparts, more voters know who they are. Incumbent senators are not as well liked as representatives, perhaps because they do not perform the wide array of constituent service functions that House members do. Senators are more likely to face primary challenges—and to lose them—than are House members.

Senate elections are far more expensive to mount than House campaigns. Incumbent expenditures rose from $623,000 in 1976 to $3.55 million in 1990. Challengers spent $452,000 in 1976 and $1.7 million in 1990. The spending gap between incumbents and challengers has widened, reflecting the somewhat greater security senators had in the early

1990s as compared to the 1970s and early 1980s. Yet the gap is far narrower than in House races. Strong challengers need not match incumbent spending. They need only spend enough to gain widespread name recognition. Challenger spending, according to Alan I. Abramowitz (1988), is the most important factor in Senate elections, followed by the closeness of a primary challenge, the ideology and partisanship of the state, and the voters' judgment of which party can best handle national problems.

Yet all Senate constituencies are not alike. As Mark C. Westlye (1991) shows, only 48 percent of the Senate elections between 1968 and 1984 fit the category of hard-fought races. The remainder are very much like House contests, with little competition and moderate amounts of money spent. There are two distinct types of Senate incumbents: the vulnerable (mostly in large, heterogenous, competitive states) and the relatively safe (mostly in small, homogenous, one-party states).

National Party Trends. Even though partisanship has waned, party identification still exerts a strong pull on individual voting behavior in congressional elections. Most voters still cast ballots consistent with party identification. When a president and his party become unpopular—most often on account of a weak economy—do voters take out their frustrations on his congressional party? There is substantial historical evidence for such "retrospective" voting. In five midterm elections from 1874 to 1938, the president's party lost seventy or more seats. Since 1950, no House election has cost either party even fifty seats. Yet Senate elections remain volatile and more subject to national trends than contemporary House contests.

There is stronger evidence for retrospective voting in aggregate studies of vote and seat shifts than in voters' motivations as expressed through survey research. Voters now punish presidents for their mistakes when they come up for reelection and are less likely to take out their frustrations on the president's partisans in the House. On the other hand, they are also less likely to reward the chief executive with sizable majorities in presidential election years. Coattails are substantially less important than they were before partisan ties atrophied. Dwight D. Eisenhower's 55 percent victory in 1952 brought him a Republican Congress; George Bush's slightly smaller victory in 1988 saw the Democrats pad their majority by three House seats.

Even though more modest, there are still partisan shifts in the House and Senate that track presidential popularity and the national economy, as in the elections of 1974, 1980, 1982, and 1986. Because many analyses had failed to find any direct link between evaluations of the president and the economy and voters' choices for Congress, Jacobson and Kernell (1983) suggested that it was candidates, not voters, who behaved strategically. Better quality candidates run during their party's "good years." Donors are more likely to contribute to the campaigns of these high-quality challengers. Even though voters do not behave strategically, candidates and donors do, thus creating the impression that voters respond to the political and economic environment.

While House elections are more insulated from national trends than they were in the nineteenth century and the first half of the twentieth, at least some voters do respond to presidential popularity and the state of the economy. In the 1974 referendum on Watergate and a weak economy, voters who backed Republican candidates in 1972 cast their ballots retrospectively, while those who had voted for the Democrats two years earlier logically continued to back their own party (Uslaner and Conway, 1985). Senate elections suggest the weakness of the "strategic politicians" thesis. In several postwar elections (1946, 1958, 1980, 1986), Senate turnover has appeared far more responsive to national trends than House results. Yet there is far less variation in challenger quality for the Senate than for the House. There is still the potential for retrospective voting, even if party ties no longer bring about the massive seat changes that marked earlier elections.

What Happened to the Incumbency Advantage? The first crack in the House incumbency advantage came in 1990, when incumbents' vote shares dropped precipitously in both chambers. Yet few House incumbents lost, and Senate turnover set a postwar low (one incumbent defeated, three retired). We know that weak challengers who were poorly funded saved many House incumbents (Jacobson, 1992). (Senate incumbents, especially Democrats, did face strong challengers—including some of the Republicans' best and brightest House members.)

Incumbents in both chambers possessed all the advantages of previous campaigns, yet their vote shares fell. Something was happening. Congress and the president were stymied over the federal budget deficit in 1990; the confrontation proved embarrassing to both, and confidence in the government fell. The level of the public's confidence in government has, however, borne an inconsistent relationship to electoral outcomes for Congress. Discontent in 1974 and 1980 produced massive partisan shifts, first toward the Democrats and then toward the Republicans. Yet similarly high levels of distrust had no measurable effect in 1976 or 1978.

In 1990 and again in 1992, confidence in leaders plummeted after having recovered to some degree. For most of the 1980s, confidence in government had been higher than during the 1970s. In 1990 it fell sharply, right before the election. It rose in 1991 with the Persian Gulf War but then slid rapidly throughout 1992. These dips resembled the 1974 decline, but with a difference. The Watergate-inspired fall let voters take out their frustration on one party. The 1990 and 1992 declines were directed at both parties. In 1990, Republican House incumbents lost more races than did Democratic incumbents. The House bank scandal and the independent presidential candidacy of H. Ross Perot in 1992 encouraged stronger challengers in both parties. With Democrats holding substantial majorities, they had more to lose.

Democratic incumbents lost twice as many seats (16 compared to 8) as Republicans in 1992. Nevertheless, the net partisan swing was small. The electorate took out its frustrations on both parties. The success rate of House incumbents running for reelection fell to 88.3 percent, the lowest level since 1974. Senate victory rates are more volatile, so 1992 did not stand out. For both chambers, incumbents' share of the vote plummeted—to the lowest level for the House since 1974 and for the Senate since 1980. Rising distrust of government, the anti-incumbent theme that resonated from Ross Perot's campaign, and a sharp rise in the quality of challengers (especially for the House) all contributed to the weakening of the incumbency advantage. Even incumbents tried to campaign as outsiders. Legislators worried whether the electoral security of the 1980s would give way to increased volatility in the 1990s and in the twenty-first century, which might look more like the nineteenth century than the twentieth.

BIBLIOGRAPHY

Abramowitz, Alan I. "Explaining Senate Election Outcomes." *American Political Science Review* 82 (1988): 385–404.

Canon, David T. *Actors, Athletes, and Astronauts.* 1990.

Fenno, Richard F., Jr. *Home Style.* 1978.

Fenno, Richard F., Jr. *The United States Senate: A Bicameral Perspective.* 1982.

Fiorina, Morris P. *Congress: Keystone of the Washington Establishment.* 2d ed. 1991.

Green, Donald Philip, and Jonathan S. Krasno. "Salvation for the Spendthrift Incumbent." *American Journal of Political Science* 32 (1988): 884–907.

Gross, Donald, and David Breaux. "Historical Trends in U.S. Senate Elections, 1912–1988." *American Politics Quarterly* 19 (1991): 284–309.

Jacobson, Gary C. *The Electoral Origins of Divided Government.* 1991.

Jacobson, Gary C. *The Politics of Congressional Elections.* 3d ed. 1992.

Jacobson, Gary C., and Samuel Kernell. *Strategy and Choice in Congressional Elections.* 2d ed. 1983.

Johannes, John R. *To Serve the People: Congress and Constituency Service.* 1984.

Uslaner, Eric M., and M. Margaret Conway. "The Responsible Congressional Electorate." *American Political Science Review* 79 (1985): 788–803.

Westlye, Mark C. *Senate Elections and Campaign Intensity.* 1991.

ERIC M. USLANER

Election Results

The Framers intended the U.S. Congress to represent the people. The House of Representatives was to be especially responsive because all its members were subject to election every two years and because House seats were to be apportioned to the states based on population. The Senate was more removed from popular sentiment because of its members' six-year terms and because its members were chosen by state legislatures rather than ordinary voters. The Seventeenth Amendment made senators subject to direct popular election, but the six-year term remains in place. Together the two chambers were intended to provide complementary strengths: the House would be subject to the immediate pressures of popular sentiment; the Senate would be free to exert a brake on the whims of public opinion. This balance would ensure both responsiveness and deliberation in the making of national policy.

Two Concepts of Representation. Implicit in the American political experience are two concepts of representation: the Madisonian concept and the party concept (Stone, 1990). The Madisonian concept is most clearly spelled out in James Madison's defense of the Constitution in *Federalist Papers* 10 and 51. In *Federalist* 10, Madison argued that a complex society was made up of many factions or interests, each agitating for governmental policy favorable to its interests. Through representation,

Figure 1
Democratic Presidential Votes and House Seats, 1868–1992

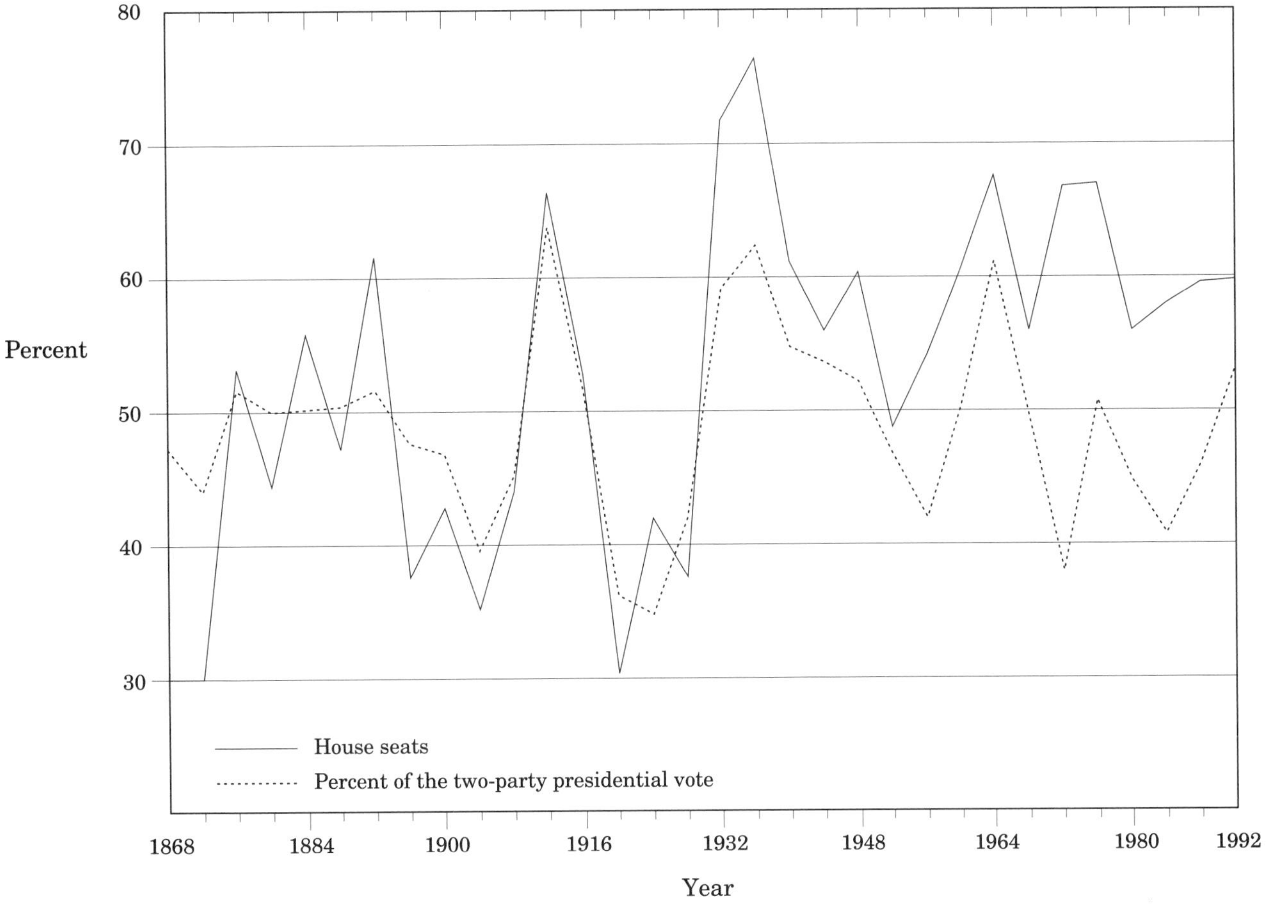

SOURCE: *Guide to U.S. Elections*, 3d ed., Washington, D.C.: Congressional Quarterly Press, 1994.

Madison sought to bring as many interests into government as possible in order to prevent a majority from single-handedly controlling the government.

In *Federalist* 51, Madison extended this argument to ensure the so-called separation of powers. Each institution of government was to represent different interests by being based on different rules of apportionment, by having different constituencies, and the like. The resulting conflict among institutions would prevent any single institution or interest from dominating governmental affairs.

The partisan concept of representation stands in direct contrast to the Madisonian view. Despite Madison's explicit attempts to limit parties, national political parties developed early in the nation's history (Chambers and Burnham, 1967). Parties seek to control institutions of political power by electing their candidates to public office. Once in power, the parties become responsible for keeping their campaign promises and for successfully managing governmental affairs. If the governing party succeeds, the voters reward it with another term of office; if it fails, voters punish it by voting in the opposition party. Since the Civil War, the Democratic and Republican parties have dominated American politics.

One problem for proponents of party representation is that under the separation of powers it is possible for one party to control one or both houses of Congress while the other controls the presidency. Such "divided government" exacerbates the natural rivalry between the legislative and executive branches, making it difficult for voters to determine which party is responsible for setting policy. Thus, the Madisonian system tends to favor diversity in government and to limit party responsibility; party government tends to foster responsibility but gives power to a majority.

The modern Congress is often criticized as unrepresentative and unresponsive to the popular will. Critics often point to high reelection rates among incumbents, and some call for reform such as limitations on congressional terms. In evaluating congressional representation, it is important to keep in mind the two competing concepts of representation that help define a fundamental tension in the American experience with representative government. Data on the partisan division of support and rates of turnover in Congress are presented below in order to examine the relationship between election results and representation; some of the links between these results and the Madisonian and partisan concepts of representation are discussed. In this way, the nature of congressional representation and how it might be improved or damaged by reform proposals (such as term limitations) can be better understood.

Partisan Control of Congress and Presidency. The partisan division of seats in the House of Representatives and Senate between 1868 and 1992 is compared with the two-party division of the vote for president in figures 1 and 2. The fact that the partisan division of seats and presidential votes tend to move together through time demonstrates

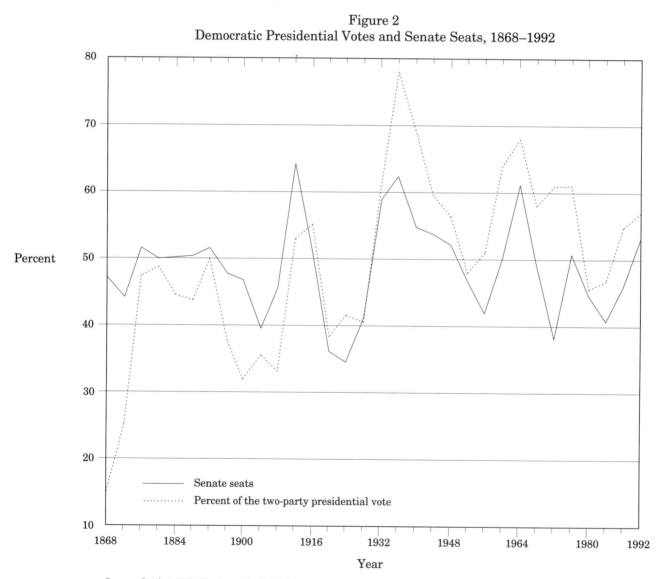

Figure 2
Democratic Presidential Votes and Senate Seats, 1868–1992

SOURCE: *Guide to U.S. Elections*, 3d ed., Washington, D.C.: Congressional Quarterly Press, 1994.

Figure 3
Districts Splitting Their Votes for President and Congress by Party, 1900–1992

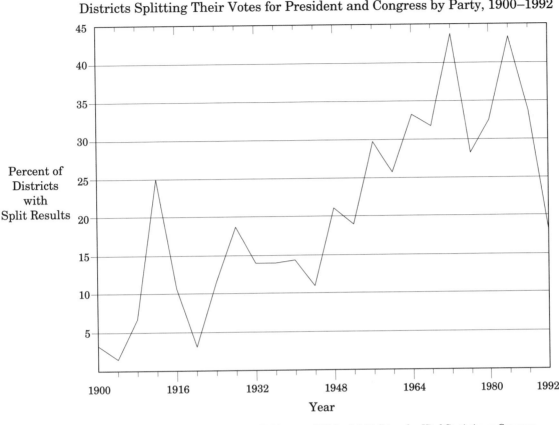

SOURCE: Norman J. Ornstein, Thomas E. Mann, and Michael J. Malbin, eds., *Vital Statistics on Congress, 1993–1994*, Washington, D.C.: Congressional Quarterly Press, 1994.

the importance of party in American national elections. Political scientists speak of eras of party alignments characterized by fairly stable divisions of the two-party vote and by enduring coalitions of interests supporting each party (Burnham, 1970). The major shifts in partisanship among American voters are reflected in both figures. Madison championed separated institutions in conflict with one another, but common bonds of partisanship tend to bridge these institutional differences.

For much of U.S. history party alignments have been strong enough to ensure that the party winning a majority in the Congress has also won the presidency. Divided government resulted from a presidential election only twice between 1868 and 1956 (in 1876 and 1888). However, beginning in the 1930s, a noticeable gap between presidential votes and the party division in Congress developed, especially in the House. Between 1876 (after Reconstruction) and 1928, the average gap between the partisan division in the House and the two-party vote for president

was less than 3 percent. Between 1932 and 1992, the gap increased to about 11 percent.

In the post–World War II period, divided government became quite common. The dominant pattern was one of a Republican president facing Democratic majorities in Congress. For the first two years of Dwight D. Eisenhower's term, the Republicans held the presidency and Congress. During the Kennedy and Johnson administrations, the four years of Jimmy Carter's presidency, and again following the election of Bill Clinton in 1992, Congress and the presidency were both held by the Democratic party. During the first six years of Ronald Reagan's presidency, the Republicans also held the Senate, but the Democrats controlled the House. For the last six years of Eisenhower's presidency, for all of the Nixon-Ford years, and for the Reagan-Bush era, divided government was the norm.

Divided government occurs because a significant proportion of voters vote for a president of one party and for a representative or senator of the

Figure 4
Turnover in the House

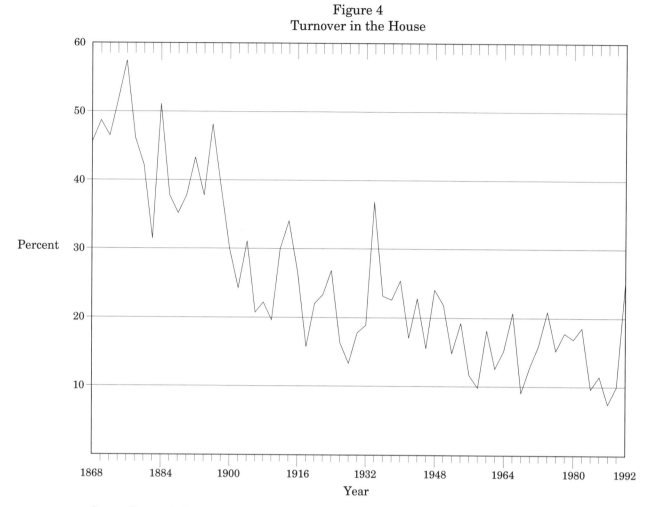

SOURCE: Norman J. Ornstein, Thomas E. Mann, and Michael J. Malbin, eds., *Vital Statistics on Congress, 1993–1994,* Washington, D.C.: Congressional Quarterly Press, 1994.

other party. This split-ticket voting is contrary to party representation because voters are sending mixed signals. Since the partisan concept of representation turns on giving one party governing responsibility for a limited period of time, voters cannot signal a clear preference for one party's program by splitting their vote.

Figure 3 shows a clear increase in the proportion of districts splitting their vote by party. The presidential election of 1956 was the first in the twentieth century in which a president of one party and a Congress of the other were elected. Not surprisingly, the average percentage of districts with split results before 1956 is substantially lower (13 percent) than the average since 1956 (34 percent).

Divided government is contrary to the partisan concept of representation because it denies one party control over the major policy-making institutions of the national government. Because the parties have different underlying philosophies and policy agendas, conflict between Congress and president goes up, and government has more difficulty acting (Kelly, 1994). At the same time, voters have greater difficulty assessing responsibility. In campaigns, presidents tend to blame Congress for policy failures while the majority in Congress blames the chief executive.

If divided government is contrary to the partisan concept of representation, it is perfectly consistent with the Madisonian concept. Madison distrusted a government capable of quick action; he certainly worried about a government in the hands of a single faction, even if that faction were a majority. Moreover, because congressional districts and states have unique interests, the fact that voters sometimes choose candidates of one party for Congress at the same time that they vote for the opposition party's candidate for president is also consistent with the Madisonian view. It simply means that the individuals involved are judged by voters to be the best representatives of their particular interests.

To understand better why voters have increasingly split their tickets, patterns of turnover in Congress must be examined. Trends are clearer in the House of Representatives, the legislative institution intended to be closer to the people. Declining rates of turnover in the House have led some to question the quality of representation it offers.

Patterns of Turnover in Congress. Turnover rates in the House of Representatives from 1868 through 1992 appear in figure 4. There are substantial fluctuations in the series, but the percentage of members exiting the House of Representatives in any given election has been declining over the past

century. For example, the average rate of turnover before 1900 was around 40 percent; after 1946 it dropped to less than 20 percent. The meaning of declining turnover for representation is unclear. High rates of turnover are not a guarantee of good representation, nor is low turnover a sure sign that legislatures are unrepresentative. After all, if members of Congress were perfectly attentive to constituency interests, the House would meet an important standard of representation, voters would be satisfied with their representative's service, and reelection rates would be very high.

Table 1 breaks down the sources of turnover for both House and Senate since 1946. Turnover in the House of Representatives due to electoral defeat—whether in a primary or a general election—has been in steady decline since World War II. In the years between 1946 and 1966, 11 percent of House members who sought reelection were defeated. Between 1968 and 1992, the rate of electoral defeat in

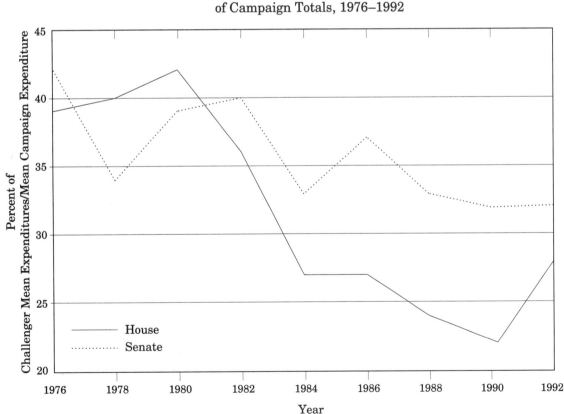

Figure 5
Senate and House Challengers' Spending as Proportions
of Campaign Totals, 1976–1992

SOURCE: Norman J. Ornstein, Thomas E. Mann, and Michael J. Malbin, eds., *Vital Statistics on Congress, 1993–1994*, Washington, D.C.: Congressional Quarterly Press, 1994.

TABLE 1. *Sources of Turnover in Congress, 1946–1990*

YEAR	HOUSE		SENATE	
	ELECTORAL DEFEAT	RETIREMENT	ELECTORAL DEFEAT	RETIREMENT
1946	18%	7%	43%	9%
1948	21	7	40	8
1950	10	7	31	4
1952	9	10	35	4
1954	7	6	25	6
1956	5	5	14	6
1958	8	6	36	6
1960	7	6	3	5
1962	8	5	17	4
1964	13	8	15	2
1966	12	5	13	3
1968	3	5	29	6
1970	5	7	23	4
1972	6	9	26	6
1974	12	10	15	7
1976	4	11	36	8
1978	6	11	40	10
1980	9	8	45	5
1982	10	9	7	3
1984	5	5	10	4
1986	2	9	25	6
1988	2	5	15	6
1990	4	6	3	3
1992	12	15	18	7

SOURCE: Norman J. Ornstein, Thomas E. Mann, and Michael J. Malbin, eds. *Vital Statistics on Congress, 1993–1994.* Washington, D.C., 1994.

the House dropped to only 6 percent. No such trend is evident in the Senate. The average level of defeat in the first half of the period was 25 percent; in the second half, it was 23 percent.

Changes in House and Senate turnover cannot be attributed to retirement trends. The average retirement rate in the House before 1966 was 6 percent; after 1966, it was 8 percent. The situation was similar in the Senate, where retirements ran at 5 percent before 1966 and at 6 percent after. Although a fair proportion of turnover in an average year is due to retirements, the trend showing a marked decrease in the electoral vulnerability of House members is not due to retirement decisions. Why have incumbent members of the House become increasingly immune to electoral defeat?

Explaining Electoral Safety in the House.
Since 1946, 92 percent of House incumbents seeking reelection have won, whereas the success rate among Senators is a much lower 76 percent. High

reelection rates are related to divided government: if the Democratic majority in Congress is relatively secure because party members gain reelection at very high rates, the partisan swings manifested in alternating party control of the presidency are unlikely to be matched in Congress. This is contrary to party representation because the government fails to respond in full measure to party swings. On the other hand, it may reflect a movement toward the Madisonian concept of representation in that government is not subject to a party majority and representatives are tied to diverse constituency interests.

David Mayhew (1974) argues that increased safety results from incumbents' ability to pursue name recognition in their districts by taking advantage of free mailing privileges (franking) and other perquisites of office. In addition, representatives use their positions of power in Congress to engage in casework and the provision of particularized benefits designed to curry favor with constituents. Because only incumbents have these resources, they enjoy an increasing electoral advantage over challengers (Jacobson, 1987). Voters are more likely to hear positive things about the incumbent in their district than about the challenger simply because they are more likely to hear from the incumbent than from the challenger (Mann and Wolfinger, 1980).

Incumbents also have the advantage of having more money than their challengers. Figure 5 shows the percentage of campaign money in the average district spent by challengers in House and Senate campaigns since 1976. If challengers ran on an equal financial footing with incumbents, the proportion of all funds spent by challengers would be 50 percent. The advantage House incumbents have over their challengers is evident in their relative expenditures. Figure 5 also shows that while Senate incumbents also enjoy an advantage in spending, the incumbency benefit in the House is greater. Moreover, during this period, House challengers slipped badly.

The incumbent advantage in spending is a major factor in accounting for the increased electoral safety of incumbents in the House of Representatives (Jacobson and Kernell, 1983). Because incumbents can raise more money than challengers, high-quality challengers choose not to run. Of course, if experienced, visible, and highly qualified candidates decide not to enter a race against incumbents, contributors react by not giving as much money to challengers, which reduces their ability to unseat incumbents even further. The spiral of challenger disadvantage (and incumbency advantage) continues, contributing to the declining rate of incumbent defeat.

With increased incumbent safety, House elections since the mid 1960s have increasingly become candidate-centered rather than party-centered (Alford and Brady, 1989). This means that voters increasingly consider the personal characteristics of the candidates rather than evaluating party records (Cain, Ferejohn, and Fiorina, 1987). House elections are therefore insulated from national political trends, including voters' evaluations of presidential performance.

Senate incumbents are not as safe as House incumbents, but Senate elections also turn powerfully on candidate qualities (Abramowitz, 1980). Senate contests are more visible than House elections, and Senate constituencies are larger and more diverse. As a result, it is difficult for senators to contact all their constituents or to respond to personal requests for assistance. Senate seats are also more desirable than House seats, so Senate races are more likely to attract highly qualified and visible challengers. Thus, in Senate elections, both incumbent and challenger are likely to be well known. The consequence is a more competitive situation than in House elections, although the competition is preeminently between individual candidates rather than spokespersons for partisan policy agendas.

Implications for Representation in Congress. The American experience of congressional representation is a hybrid of the Madisonian and party concepts. The years since World War II have brought more frequent periods of divided government and increased incumbent safety, especially in the House of Representatives. Divided government reinforces the separation of powers, a principle comfortably within the Madisonian tradition. Incumbent safety may also be consistent with the Madisonian ideal to the degree that it results from House members being especially attentive to constituency interests. Though some evidence of this exists, there is also evidence that incumbent safety results from incumbents' use of perquisites and from various factors that discourage well-qualified challengers from running. These developments are not consistent with either concept of representation, and they rightly generate pressures for reform.

The idea behind imposing limits on the terms of representatives and senators is to ensure that incumbents do not develop a "lock" on their office and become insulated from constituency interests. Term limits, however, could have other consequences that might weaken representative government. For example, they would be likely to reduce the overall level of experience and expertise in the legislative branch. This in turn could shift power to other, less democratic, centers of influence, especially the permanent bureaucracy.

An alternative solution might emphasize the importance of making congressional elections more competitive rather than arbitrarily limiting the time in office of otherwise acceptable candidates. Elections could be made more competitive by giving challengers resources that are roughly equivalent to those enjoyed by incumbents so that they can attain comparable levels of visibility.

Members of Congress, even incumbents who have successfully won reelection many times, worry a great deal about what their constituents want (Fiorina, 1974). Understandably enough, incumbents enjoy being in Congress and they want to remain there, often for their entire careers. This ambition to stay in office is what gives voters control over incumbents' behavior. That control is by no means perfect, and the incumbency effect is a genuine source of concern, but representatives and senators do not routinely ignore their constituents' interests. They are adept at balancing competing demands from their districts and states as they pursue their legislative careers.

Perhaps the question of greater importance is how Americans are likely to balance the tension between the Madisonian and partisan concepts of representation. The presidential election of 1992 ended a twelve-year period of divided government. Many saw the election as turning on voters' frustration with "gridlock" in Washington and their dissatisfaction with the tendency for politicians of both parties to deny responsibility for chronic national problems such as the deficit. One expression of this discontent was the substantial portion of the 1992 vote attracted by H. Ross Perot, a presidential candidate with no partisan affiliation. Voters turned Republican president George Bush out of office in favor of Democrat Bill Clinton, while at the same time electing substantial Democratic majorities in Congress, but, rather than view this result as a strong endorsement for the Democratic party, most observers acknowledged that the victory put the Democrats on probation. If they could succeed in making headway against a host of difficult policy issues, the electorate would be likely to vote for continued united government under their leadership. If they could not succeed, they ran the risk of incurring the wrath of the voters and suffering defeat.

Whatever one makes of the return to united government in 1992, Congress and the president must operate within the constraints of a system designed to foster the Madisonian ideal. This means that party discipline is always difficult to establish and enforce. Members of Congress must face the voters in their states and districts and justify their actions to win support for another term. This is the essence of representative government, but in American politics it is done largely without organized party assistance. The diversity that Madison saw in American society continually generates debate, conflict, delay, and compromise, and Americans must always grapple with the question of whether these are desirable features of government and public life.

[See also Members, articles on Demographic Profile, Congressional Careers, and Tenure and Turnover.]

BIBLIOGRAPHY

Abramowitz, Alan. "A Comparison of Voting for U.S. Senators and Representatives in 1978." *American Political Science Review* 74 (1980): 633–640.

Alford, John, and David Brady. "Personal and Partisan Advantage in U.S. Congressional Elections, 1846–1986." In *Congress Reconsidered*, edited by Lawrence C. Dodd and Bruce I. Oppenheimer. 4th ed. 1989.

Burnham, Walter Dean. *Critical Elections: The Mainsprings of American Politics.* 1970.

Cain, Bruce, John Ferejohn, and Morris Fiorina. *The Personal Vote: Constituency Service and Electoral Independence.* 1987.

Chambers, William N., and Walter Dean Burnham, eds. *The American Party System: Stages of Political Development.* 1967.

Fiorina, Morris. *Representatives, Roll Calls, and Constituencies.* 1974.

Jacobson, Gary. "Enough Is Too Much: Money and Competition in House Elections, 1972–1984." In *Elections in America*, edited by Kay L. Scholzman. 1987.

Jacobson, Gary, and Samuel Kernell. *Strategy and Choice in Congressional Elections.* 2d ed. 1983.

Kelly, Sean. "Punctuated Change and the Era of Divided Government." In *New Perspectives on American Politics.* Edited by Lawrence C. Dodd and Calvin Jillson. 1994.

Mann, Thomas, and Raymond Wolfinger. "Candidates and Parties in Congressional Elections." *American Political Science Review* 74 (1980): 617–632.

Mayhew, David. *Congress: The Electoral Connection.* 1974.

Stone, Walter. *Republic at Risk: Self-Interest in American Politics.* 1990.

SEAN Q KELLY and WALTER J. STONE

ELECTIONS, PRESIDENTIAL. See Presidential Elections.

ELECTORAL COLLEGE. The Framers of the Constitution invented the Electoral College as a compromise between those who favored a direct popular election of the president and those who advocated letting Congress select the president. Both the Virginia Plan and the New Jersey Plan, the foundation documents of the Constitution, called for the election of the executive by the legislature, as was the practice in all but three of the states. Fearing that legislative selection would make the executive subservient to the legislature, a group of delegates led by two Pennsylvanians—James Wilson and Governeur Morris—proposed instead that the executive be elected by the people. To give Congress that power, they argued, would tend to violate the principle of separation of powers, which the Framers regarded as sacrosanct.

The delegates to the Constitutional Convention virtually ignored the proposal for popular election. The idea aroused their fears of direct democracy. Furthermore, by requiring voters to pass judgment on candidates from distant states of whom they knew little or nothing, popular election seemed impractical.

Wilson countered with a proposal, adopted in modified form, for an electoral college that would choose the executive with combined popular and legislative participation. As stipulated by Article II, section 1 of the Constitution, the president would be selected by a majority vote of electors, who would be chosen by the states using whatever methods they individually adopted. The number of electoral votes each state would receive would be equal to its total representation in Congress (i.e., two for the two senators plus one vote for each representative). If no presidential candidate received votes from a majority of electors, the House of Representatives would elect the president from among the five candidates receiving the highest number of electoral votes. To prevent a cabal from forming in the Electoral College, electors would never meet as a national body; instead, they would vote in their own state capitols and then send the results to the Senate for counting. Finally, to ensure that the electors would not simply support a variety of home-state favorites, each was required to vote for two candidates for president from two different states, with the runner-up in the presidential election filling the office of vice president.

Not foreseeing the development of a two-party system, most delegates believed that after George Washington (the obvious choice for the first president) left office, majorities would seldom form in the Electoral College and the House would choose most presidents. The Framers' concerns about congressional participation in presidential elections were confirmed in the elections of 1800 and 1824, in which the House decided the result. The unhappy circumstances of these contests led to the view, even on the part of those favoring legislative supremacy, that the existing auxiliary plan for selection by the House was a great evil—in the words of Thomas Jefferson, "the most dangerous blot in our Constitution."

The Electoral College no longer operates as it was first designed. The original plan was for electors to select the president in a nonpartisan fashion by elevating individuals of outstanding reputation;

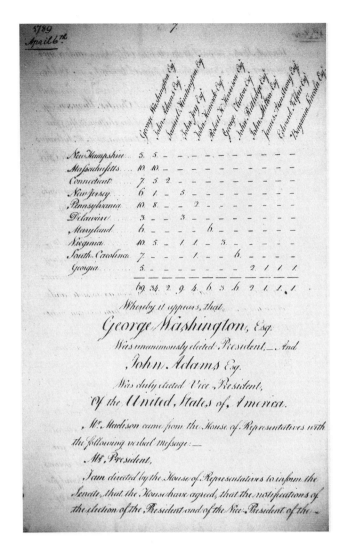

FIRST PRESIDENTIAL ELECTION. Page seven of the Senate Journal showing the electoral vote, 6 April 1789.

NATIONAL ARCHIVES

the vice president was selected not as a candidate on a ticket with a presidential candidate but as the runner-up in the electoral vote for the president. As political parties emerged at the end of the eighteenth century, however, electors lost the independent status envisioned by the Framers. Instead, they became instruments of party will. Party organization, taking form first in congressional caucuses (1800–1824) and later in nominating conventions (from 1832 on) transformed electors into instructed agents who pledged to cast their ballots for the party's presidential and vice-presidential candidates. In 1804, the Twelfth Amendment was adopted; it implicitly acknowledged the existence of political parties and provided for separate balloting by the electors for president and vice president.

VOTE COUNTING. Depiction of the House chamber on 2 March 1877, packed full for the opening of electoral ballots by President Pro Tempore of the Senate Thomas W. Ferry for the contested election between Rutherford B. Hayes and Samuel J. Tilden.

OFFICE OF THE HISTORIAN OF THE U.S. SENATE

The emergence of a two-party system helped remedy a deficiency in the Framers' method of presidential selection—the possibility that no candidate would receive a majority of electoral votes, thus exposing the nation to the problems caused by the House of Representatives electing the president. By the 1830s, party conventions controlled the only gates to consideration for the presidency, thus tending to concentrate popular support behind two major candidates. Correlatively, each major party held large-scale popular allegiance, virtually ensuring that presidential elections would be decided by electors without having to go to the House.

Although no presidential election was thrown into the House after 1824, the Electoral College and the specter of congressional participation in choosing the executive continued to provoke controversy. The election of Republican Rutherford B. Hayes in 1876 was decided only after Congress had formed a fifteen-member commission to resolve a conflict over disputed electoral votes in four states. The choice of Hayes over the popular Democratic governor of New York, Samuel Tilden, came under serious question because it resulted from a deal between House Democrats and Republicans that appeared to thwart the will of the people. So that the events of 1876 would not be repeated, Congress in 1887 enacted legislation that delegated to each state the final authority to determine the legality of its choice of electors and required a concurrent majority of both houses of Congress to reject any electoral vote.

By the end of the twentieth century, the emergence of candidate-centered campaigns, dominated by direct primaries and mass media, and the decline of partisan loyalties among the electorate had reopened the question of whether one presidential candidate could always win the support of a national majority. Once again, the fear of congressional participation in the choice of the executive haunted the political landscape. Whether this fear was justified was a matter of debate. Nevertheless, it was a fear borne of fundamental constitutional traditions and conflicts.

[*See also* Twelfth Amendment.]

BIBLIOGRAPHY

Ceaser, James. *Presidential Selection: Theory and Development.* 1979.

Sindler, Allan P. "Presidential Selection and Succession in Special Situations." In *Presidential Selection.* Edited by Alexander Heard and Michael Nelson. 1987.

Slonim, Shlomo. "Designing the Electoral College." In *Inventing the American Presidency.* Edited by Thomas E. Cronin. 1989.

SIDNEY M. MILKIS

ELECTORAL COMMISSION OF 1877.

The disputed presidential election of 1876 between Republican Rutherford B. Hayes and Democrat Samuel J. Tilden created an unprecedented crisis in the American political system. Tilden, the popular-vote winner, had 184 undisputed electoral votes, only one vote shy of the 185 needed to elect, and Hayes had 165, but both parties claimed 20 contested votes. One vote, that of a disputed elector

JOINT SESSION OF CONGRESS COUNTING THE ELECTORAL VOTE. Rep. David Dudley Field (D-N.Y.) objects to Florida's vote. Wood engraving from a sketch by Theodore R. Davis. Originally published in *Harper's Weekly,* 17 February 1877.

OFFICE OF THE ARCHITECT OF THE CAPITOL

from Oregon, would be readily resolved in Hayes's favor. But 19 came from Florida, Louisiana, and South Carolina, the last remaining reconstructed states with Republican regimes. There, Democrats' intimidation of voters had produced electoral returns for Tilden, and Republican-controlled election boards had done the same for Hayes.

When Congress reconvened in December following the election, it immediately faced a stalemate between the Republican-controlled Senate and the Democrat-controlled House over who should determine which electoral returns from the three southern states should be counted. The Twelfth Amendment provided only that "the President of the Senate shall, in the presence of the Senate and House of Representatives, open all the certificates and the votes shall then be counted." Lacking clear guidelines, Republicans thought the president of the Senate should count the disputed electoral

votes—obviously in behalf of Hayes. Democrats, however, argued that only the two houses acting concurrently could determine which votes to count.

In a highly charged political atmosphere, the Senate and House created select committees to consider compromise solutions. Meeting jointly in January 1877, they recommended creating an electoral commission of five representatives (three Democrats and two Republicans), five senators (two Democrats and three Republicans), and five members of the Supreme Court. The last group was allegedly nonpartisan, but the committee chose two justices who were known Republicans and two who were Democrats, who together were then to select the fifth justice—whom everyone understood would be David Davis of Illinois, an independent. After hearing legal arguments from each side, the fifteen-member commission was to decide whether or not to go behind the returns to investigate the circumstances of each disputed election. Only the concurrence of both houses could reverse the tribunal's final decision.

Congress approved the Electoral Commission bill on 26 January with much heavier Democratic (181 to 19) than Republican (57 to 84) support, primarily because Democrats were confident that Davis would favor at least some of Tilden's claims. At this point, however, the Illinois legislature elected Davis to the U.S. Senate, and he promptly declined to serve on the commission. The fifteenth seat then went to Justice Joseph P. Bradley, an independent-leaning Republican.

Congress began the count on 1 February, and when Florida was reached, it referred the dispute to the commission. By a partisan vote of 8 to 7, that body decided not to go behind the returns and to accept those signed by Florida's Republican governor for Hayes. The Democratic House rejected the commission's finding, but the Republican Senate approved, so Hayes received Florida's votes. The same 8 to 7 commission vote and Senate approval gave Hayes Louisiana on 16 February and South Carolina on 28 February. Although House Democrats threatened a filibuster to delay the count beyond 4 March, when the new president was to be sworn in, northern Democrats feared the consequences of an interregnum, and southern Democrats busily extracted pledges from Hayes's backers that he would agree to "home rule" for the South by discontinuing support for the lingering Republican administrations in Louisiana and South Carolina. Democrats thus allowed the completion of the count on the eve of Hayes's inauguration.

[*See also* Electoral College; Electoral Count Act.]

BIBLIOGRAPHY

Benedict, Michael Les. "Southern Democrats in the Crisis of 1876–1877: A Reconsideration of *Reunion and Reaction.*" *Journal of Southern History* 46 (1980): 489–524.

Polakoff, Keith Ian. *The Politics of Inertia: The Election of 1876 and the End of Reconstruction.* 1973.

Woodward, C. Vann. *Reunion and Reaction: The Compromise of 1877 and the End of Reconstruction.* 1951.

TERRY L. SEIP

ELECTORAL COUNT ACT (1887; 24 Stat. 373–375). The disputed Hayes-Tilden presidential contest of 1876, resolved only by the hastily created and controversial Electoral Commission of 1877, prompted the act of 3 February 1887 to "regulate the counting of the votes for President and Vice-President." The Twelfth Amendment did not specify who was to count or decide which electoral returns were legitimate when there were dual or contested returns, as in 1876. With the necessary and proper clause as their constitutional justification, in 1887 the two chambers finally agreed to embody in statutory form various traditional congressional practices for counting the vote. The resulting legislation placed the burden for settling electoral disputes on the states and established procedures for certifying and forwarding certifications of electors to Washington. At a joint session of Congress (which now occurs on 6 January), the presiding officer of the Senate opens the electoral certificates from each state in alphabetical order and hands them to two tellers from each house. The tellers read each certificate, call for objections (which must be in writing and signed by at least one senator and one representative), and list the undisputed votes for each candidate for president and vice president. When all returns have been so handled, the Senate and the House meet separately, follow guidelines for resolving the contested returns, and then reconvene in joint session to complete the count. A rejection of electoral votes requires separate action by both houses, but generally Congress must accept all "regularly given" and "lawfully certified" returns. With the exception of changes in timing necessitated by the Twentieth Amendment, the procedures established in 1887 still stand.

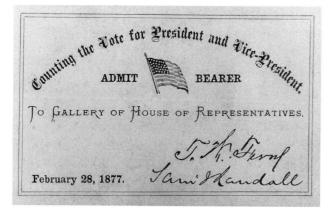

ADMISSION TICKET. For entrance to the House chamber for the counting of the electoral vote. Although the joint session of Congress counted the vote on 2 March 1877, tickets bearing several dates had been printed in advance.   COLLECTION OF DAVID J. AND JANICE L. FRENT

[*See also* Electoral College; Electoral Commission of 1877.]

BIBLIOGRAPHY

Burgess, John W. "The Law of the Electoral Count." *Political Science Quarterly* 3 (1888): 633–653.
Dougherty, J. Hampden. *The Electoral System of the United States.* 1906.

TERRY L. SEIP

ELEMENTARY AND SECONDARY EDUCATION ACT OF 1965

(79 Stat. 27–58). The Elementary and Secondary Education Act (ESEA) was a centerpiece of President Lyndon B. Johnson's Great Society legislation, a response to the escalating racial and urban problems of the 1960s. Important precedents for the ESEA were the National Defense Education Act of 1958; various employee training measures of the Kennedy administration; and the Civil Rights Act of 1964, which authorized the federal government to withhold federal funds from discriminatory programs. Civil rights activism and the crisis of the cities, as well as the political skills of Johnson and his allies in the strongly Democratic Congress, helped overcome opposition to federal aid. Commissioner of Education Francis Keppel and key congressional leaders worked out delicate compromises on aid to religious schools and gained Catholic support. The House passed the bill in March 1965 by 263 to 153. The Senate passed it by an even wider majority, 73 to 18, and President Johnson signed the bill on 11 April at a one-room schoolhouse in Texas.

Most of the funds authorized for ESEA were assigned to Title I, which provided compensatory instruction in basic skills for schoolchildren in high poverty areas. Title II provided library books and textbooks to elementary and secondary schools; substantial aid to parochial schools under this title helped win support for ESEA. Title III provided grants for educational innovations at the local level. Title IV created federal research and training facilities in education, and Title V aimed to strengthen state education departments.

ESEA has had immense impact on local education in an organizational sense; Title I programs have become a familiar feature of elementary schools, and school districts have come to rely upon these funds. It is difficult to assess whether the instruction resulting from Title I has been effective. There is a mountainous history of evaluation efforts that indicate mixed results, but successful constituencies have developed to sustain continual reenactment of Title I (now called Chapter I). ESEA expressed Congress's belief that compensatory education can be used to fight poverty and to create equal opportunity.

[*See also* Civil Rights Act of 1964; Higher Education Act of 1965; National Defense Education Act of 1958.]

BIBLIOGRAPHY

Eidenberg, Eugene, and Roy D. Morey. *An Act of Congress: The Legislative Process and the Making of Educational Policy.* 1969.
Jeffrey, Julie Roy. *Education and the Children of the Poor: A Study of the Origins and Implementation of the Elementary and Secondary Education Act of 1965.* 1978.

CARL F. KAESTLE

ELEVENTH AMENDMENT. It was both inevitable and appropriate that the first amendment to the Constitution proposed by Congress after the Bill of Rights concerned the major structural issue of the new Republic: the relationship between the states and the federal government. The United States had assumed the remaining Revolutionary War debts of the states, but it remained unclear whether the states could be required to meet their obligations to private citizens. The matter came to a head in February 1793 when the Supreme Court in *Chisholm v. Georgia,* its first constitutional case, rejected Georgia's contention that it could not be sued by a British creditor.

The Court's decision met with much indignation in Georgia, Massachusetts, and other states and led to calls for a constitutional amendment that would negate the ruling. The Second Congress, however, nearing the end of its lame-duck session, did not act, and before the Third Congress convened in late 1793, war resumed between Britain and France, which served to heighten popular anti-English sentiment in the United States. The dominant Federalists had to respond, and did so with the Eleventh Amendment. The proposed amendment was approved by the Senate on 14 January 1794 by a vote of 23 to 2 and by the House on 4 March by a vote of 81 to 9. As sent to the states for ratification, it read, "The Judicial power of the United States shall not be construed to extend to any suit in law or equity, commenced or prosecuted against one of the United States by citizens of another State, or by Citizens or Subjects of any Foreign State."

This effectively defused anti-*Chisholm* sentiment.

Not until January 1798 was the amendment ratified by enough states to make it part of the Constitution. The Supreme Court then quickly dropped its jurisdiction in such cases.

BIBLIOGRAPHY

Gibbons, John J. "The Eleventh Amendment and State Sovereign Immunity: A Reinterpretation." *Columbia Law Review* 83 (1983): 1889–2005.
Jacobs, Clyde E. *The Eleventh Amendment and Sovereign Immunity.* 1972.

MORTON KELLER

EMBARGO. The embargo of 1807–1809 was the most ambitious and controversial of the trade restrictions adopted by the United States during the Napoleonic Wars to force Great Britain and France to show greater respect for neutral rights. Enacted by Congress on 22 December 1807 at the request of the administration of Thomas Jefferson, the embargo was essentially a nonexportation law that prohibited American ships and goods from leaving port.

At first the law had numerous loopholes. Many ships were able to slip out of port before official news of the embargo arrived, and once at sea, they did not return. Merchants could legally dispatch ships to pick up American property abroad, and about six hundred vessels sailed on this pretext. Some ships left port illegally, while others—nominally plying the coasting trade—were "blown off course" to ports in the West Indies or Canada. There was also a good deal of smuggling across the Canadian frontier.

To enforce the embargo, Secretary of the Treasury Albert Gallatin told President Jefferson that government officials would need "arbitrary powers" that were "equally dangerous & odious." The president was undeterred. "Congress," he replied, "must legalise all *means* which may be necessary to obtain it's [*sic*] *end.*" In response to administration requests, Congress adopted four supplemental laws. The most sweeping was the enforcement act of 1809, which gave government officials such extraordinary powers that the Fourth Amendment guarantee against unreasonable searches and seizures was seriously eroded.

The enforcement campaign was largely successful, but the cost to the young republic was enormous. Economically, the embargo drove the nation into a deep depression. Farmers could not ship their produce to foreign markets, and merchants could not send their ships to sea. Exports, which had peaked at $108 million in 1807, plummeted (officially at least) to $22 million in 1808. Government revenue, heavily dependent on trade, fell from $17 million in 1808 to $7.7 million in 1809. Only the nation's small manufacturing establishment benefited from the embargo.

Politically, the embargo generated talk of nullification and secession in New England and rejuvenated the Federalist party, which only a year or two before had seemed headed for extinction. Constitutionally, the embargo raised serious questions about the limits of government power. So determined was Jefferson to enforce the measure that he used the army and navy without proper authority, endorsed the death penalty for smugglers, and even defied a federal judge who challenged his power.

Despite all this, the embargo won no concessions from England or France. Napoléon Bonaparte used the measure as a pretext for seizing American vessels, claiming that they must be British ships in disguise. England was deprived of some of her customary imports but found new markets for her exports in South America and welcomed the withdrawal of a commercial rival.

On 1 March 1809, after fifteen months of national suffering, Congress repealed the embargo as of 15 March. Although sometimes hailed as an innovative alternative to war, the embargo was an ill-starred measure that did far more harm to the United States than to its intended targets.

[*See also* War Hawks; War of 1812.]

BIBLIOGRAPHY

Jennings, Walter W. *The American Embargo, 1807–1809.* 1921.
Spivak, Burton. *Jefferson's English Crisis: Commerce, Embargo, and the Republican Revolution.* 1979.

DONALD R. HICKEY

EMERGENCY BANKING RELIEF ACT (1933; 48 Stat. 1–7). When George Wingfield's chain of banks in Nevada failed in 1932, it triggered the collapse of the banking system in that state. Nevada declared a business moratorium (in reality, a "bank holiday") to stop the runs and to allow the banks to reorganize, banks had been failing throughout the 1920s, but with the coming of the Great Depression, the character of the bank failures seemed to change. By March 1933, depositor withdrawals had changed a drain into a full-fledged money panic. Accordingly, President Franklin D. Roosevelt's first official act on 4 March 1933 was to close all of the nation's banks. On 9 March 1933 Congress quickly and with almost no debate passed the Emergency Banking Relief Act, which provided for the banks to reopen under private ownership after they met basic criteria in a bank examination and received a license. Another provision authorized the Reconstruction Finance Corporation (RFC) to invest in preferred stock and capital notes of banks. On the surface, that appeared beneficial to banks, but the bankers soon learned that the RFC expected to appoint directors to the banks' boards. Occasionally, the fact that the RFC invested in a bank proved sufficient to destabilize a bank by suggesting that it was in trouble. Finally, the act gave the president the authority to take the United States off the gold standard.

The bank holiday and the subsequent Emergency Banking Relief Act, as well as the Banking Act of 1933 (Glass-Steagall Act), which created federal deposit insurance, met with success in good part because of the little-appreciated clause allowing the president to abandon the gold standard. Once gold stopped flowing out of the country, depositors again felt safe in putting their money in banks, because they could redeem their dollars in gold.

[*See also* Banking Act of 1933.]

BIBLIOGRAPHY

Degen, Robert A. *The American Monetary System: A Concise Survey of Its Evolution since 1896.* 1987.
Klebaner, Benjamin J. *American Commercial Banking: A History.* 1990.

LARRY SCHWEIKART

EMERGENCY POWERS. Federal law makes available to the president a variety of powers for use in crises or emergency conditions threatening the nation. This authority is not limited to military or war situations. Some of these powers, deriving from the Constitution or statutory law, are continuously available to the president, with little or no qualification. Others—statutory delegations from Congress—exist on a standby basis and remain dormant until the president formally declares a national emergency. Using the powers delegated by such statutes, the president may seize property and commodities, organize and control the means of production, assign military forces abroad, institute martial law, seize and control all transportation and communication, regulate the operation of private enterprise, and restrict travel.

There are, however, limits and restraints on the president in his exercise of emergency powers. With the exception of the habeas corpus clause, the Constitution makes no allowance for the suspension of any of its provisions during a national emergency. Disputes over the constitutionality or legality of the exercise of emergency powers are subject to judicial review. Indeed, the courts and Congress can restrain the president regarding emergency powers, as can public opinion. Certainly Congress may modify, rescind, or render dormant its delegations of emergency authority.

Until World War I, U.S. presidents utilized emergency powers at their own discretion. However, during and after the war, chief executives had available to them a growing body of standby emergency law, which became operative upon the proclamation of a national emergency. Sometimes these proclamations confined the matter of crisis to a specific policy sphere, such as during the banking crisis of 1933; at other times, such as in the general proclamation of 1950, they placed no limitation on the pronouncement.

These activations of standby emergency authority remained acceptable until the era of the Vietnam War. In 1976, Congress curtailed this practice with the passage of the National Emergencies Act (90 Stat. 1255). This act grew out of the recommendations of the Senate Special Committee on National Emergencies and Delegated Emergency Powers, a temporary study panel. According to the statute's procedures, the president, when declaring a national emergency, must specify the standby authorities he is activating. Congress may negate this action through a resolution disapproving the emergency declaration or the activation of a particular statutory power. The act was amended in 1985 (99 Stat. 448) to require the use of a joint resolution in this regard, which must be approved through the constitutionally provided legislative process. Originally, a so-called legislative veto could be effected via a concurrent resolution approved by both houses of Congress.

Any national emergency declared by the president that is not previously terminated by Congress expires automatically on the anniversary of the declaration, unless the president, within the ninety-day period prior to each anniversary date, gives notice to Congress and in the *Federal Register* that the emergency is to continue in effect. In practice, Congress did not find it necessary to rescind the national emergencies subsequently declared by Presidents Jimmy Carter, Ronald Reagan, and George Bush.

BIBLIOGRAPHY

U.S. Senate. Committee on Government Operations and Special Committee on National Emergencies and Delegated Emergency Powers. *The National Emergencies Act (Public Law 94-412)—Source Book: Legislative History, Texts, and Other Documents.* 94th Cong., 2d sess., 1976. Committee Print.

U.S. Senate. Special Committee on National Emergencies and Delegated Emergency Powers. *A Brief History of Emergency Powers in the United States.* 93d Cong., 2d sess., 1974. Committee Print.

HAROLD C. RELYEA

EMPLOYMENT ACT OF 1946 (60 Stat. 23–26).

The Employment Act of 1946 is rooted in two events: the Great Depression of the 1930s and the Keynesian revolution in economics. The experience of the 1930s created fears that after World War II the United States might return to economic stagnation. Keynesian economics provided a persuasive intellectual justification for the government to manage the macroeconomy.

A full-employment bill was introduced in Congress in 1945 by Sen. James E. Murray, a liberal Democrat from Montana. Murray's bill declared that every American had a "right to employment" and provided mechanisms to achieve this goal. If the anticipated level of private investment was insufficient to absorb the entire labor force, the federal government would provide such additional investment and spending needed to reach full employment.

The full-employment bill was considered in a highly charged ideological atmosphere. It met its demise in the House of Representatives, where Republicans and southern Democrats rewrote the bill and eliminated the right to employment and the mechanisms to achieve full employment. This less ambitious legislation, the Employment Act of 1946, nevertheless gave formal recognition to the federal government's responsibility for maintaining economic prosperity. Embodying the spirit, if not the letter, of the original bill, the act served as a reminder of liberal aspirations to establish guaranteed full employment. The act also instituted several innovations: the annual submission of the *Economic Report of the President,* the Council of Economic Advisers, and the Joint Economic Committee of Congress. These all helped systematize economic policy-making and brought professional economists into the highest levels of the federal government.

BIBLIOGRAPHY

Bailey, Stephen K. *Congress Makes a Law: The Story behind the Employment Act of 1946.* 1951.

GARY MUCCIARONI

ENACTING CLAUSE.

Every bill begins with an enacting clause, and every resolution with a resolving clause, as a formal declaration that the substantive language that follows has been duly adopted in accordance with the constitutionally mandated procedures. The exact form of these clauses was first prescribed by statute in 1871 and is at present set forth in Title 1 of the United States Code.

The enacting clause reads as follows:

> Be it enacted by the Senate and House of Representatives of the United States of America in Congress assembled, . . .

The resolving clause in a joint resolution uses the single word *Resolved* in place of *Be it enacted* with *two thirds of each House concurring therein* inserted before the final comma if the resolution is one proposing a constitutional amendment. In either case, the Senate is always mentioned first, regardless of where the measure originates.

In a concurrent resolution the clause reads *Resolved by the House of Representatives (the Senate concurring)* (with the names of the two houses reversed if it originates in the Senate). In a simple resolution it consists of the single word *Resolved.*

In the early days of the Republic, it was thought necessary to give every subdivision of a bill its own separate enacting clause, and the sections were not numbered. This practice gradually disappeared, and today Title 1 of the Code provides that "no enacting or resolving clause shall be used in any section of an Act or resolution of Congress except the first."

[*See also* Bills; Resolutions.]

BIBLIOGRAPHY

Filson, Lawrence E. *The Legislative Drafter's Desk Reference.* 1992.

U.S. House of Representatives. Law Revision Counsel. *How Our Laws Are Made.* Published periodically.

LAWRENCE E. FILSON

ENDANGERED SPECIES ACT OF 1973 (87 Stat. 884–903).

The Endangered Species Act (P.L. 93-205) passed without controversy in 1973. Previous legislation had directed the secretary of the Interior to draw up a list of endangered fish and wildlife and had prohibited importation or interstate shipment of these endangered species. The 1973 law authorized the secretary to protect plants as well as animals, extended protection to "threatened" species, and, most important, prohibited federal agencies from taking actions that would modify or destroy a habitat critical to the survival of an endangered species. By 1976 the department had listed more than six hundred species as "endangered."

The act became controversial when environmental groups discovered its potential for blocking major federal projects. In 1978 the Supreme Court ruled that the Tennessee Valley Authority could not open the floodgates of the nearly complete $130 million Tellico Dam because it threatened the survival of a tiny fish, the snail darter. This was one of several projects blocked by the federal courts under the act.

Shortly after the Supreme Court handed down its decision in *TVA v. Hill* (1978), Congress enacted legislation creating an Endangered Species Committee, which included the secretaries of the Interior, Army, and Agriculture and the administrators of the Environmental Protection Agency and the National Oceanic and Atmospheric Administration. Quickly dubbed the "God Squad," this body was authorized to grant exemptions to the Endangered Species Act in carefully circumscribed circumstances. The committee's first official act was to deny an exemption to the Tellico Dam. That led Congress to pass further legislation specifically exempting the project.

The Endangered Species Act is a good example of the type of across-the-board environmental protection mandate Congress imposed on federal agencies in the 1970s. As was frequently the case, environmentalists resorted to the federal courts to enforce the legislative mandate, and Congress desperately sought mechanisms for arbitrating disputes between those advocating environmental protection and those pushing economic growth.

BIBLIOGRAPHY

Congressional Quarterly Inc. *Congress and the Nation.* Vol. 4 (1977), pp. 289–291; vol. 5 (1981), pp. 563–565, 573–574.

R. Shep Melnick

ENERGY AND COMMERCE COMMITTEE, HOUSE.

The Committee on Energy and Commerce is one of the three or four most important of the twenty-two standing committees in the House of Representatives. Formally established in 1795 as the Committee on Commerce and Manufactures, it was the third standing committee created by the House. In 1821, it was renamed the Commerce Committee. In 1891 it became the Committee on Interstate and Foreign Commerce, and in 1980 it assumed its current name, the Committee on Energy and Commerce. In short, the core of the committee's jurisdiction has always included matters related to commerce, but the other policy issues under its purview have changed considerably over its two-hundred-year history.

The Committee's Changing Jurisdiction. The formal jurisdiction of each standing committee is laid out in the Standing Rules of the House, which are typically adopted at the beginning of each new congress. However, as David C. King has argued (in *Border Wars: Congress and the Politics of Jurisdictional Change,* forthcoming), such a formal, institutionalized view of committee jurisdictions is incomplete and frequently misleading. King distinguishes between two components of committee jurisdiction, which he refers to as their "statutory" and "common law" components.

Statutory jurisdiction is what is laid out in the official House rules, the "letter of the jurisdictional law," which is rewritten at relatively rare moments of major congressional reform. However, King demonstrates that these episodic reorganizations are largely ratifications of the more incremental "common law" changes in committee jurisdictions that accumulate, Congress by Congress, as a result of new issues emerging on the national agenda and the evolving interests of committees and their chairs. To understand the past, present, and future of a committee's jurisdiction, then, it is important to look beyond the official jurisdictional grants laid out in the House rules.

The first major jurisdictional reform after the 1946 Legislative Reorganization Act occurred in October 1974, when the House Select Committee on Committees passed a set of amendments to the chamber's jurisdictional arrangements. These reforms largely allowed the Interstate and Foreign Commerce Committee to continue considering the issues that had been on its legislative agenda in the recent past. For instance, the committee was given official jurisdiction over most health care and consumer affairs issues, areas into which it had been slowly moving for two decades. At the same time, it largely relinquished several areas that it had been neglecting, such as surface transportation (except railroads), civil aviation, weather, energy (other than interstate regulation of oil and natural gas), and environmental research and development.

In the aftermath of the OPEC oil embargo of 1974 and the ensuing salience of energy policy and closely related environmental issues, the Interstate and Foreign Commerce Committee aggressively reasserted its claim to these two policy domains. In 1975, the committee created a new Subcommittee on Energy and Power. By the late 1970s, common law jurisdiction over energy issues was thus spread across several committees, the most active of which, however, was Interstate and Foreign Commerce. In 1980, the House Select Committee on Committees proposed a formal reorganization designed to create a new Committee on Energy, which would consolidate all energy issues variously handled by the Commerce, Interior, and Public Works committees. John D. Dingell (D-Mich.), then chairman of the Commerce Subcommittee on Energy and Power, led the fight against the Select Committee's proposal, offering an alternative that essentially designated the Interstate and Foreign Commerce Committee as the panel with principal jurisdiction over national energy policy. The latter alternative won, and to make this apparent to everyone, the committee was renamed the Committee on Energy and Commerce.

After 1980, the committee's jurisdiction continued to change, moving slowly into a number of important areas. For instance, the committee began successfully to address new issues of foreign trade policy, banking reforms, product liability law, magnetically levitated trains, and university administration of federal grants, few of which fit easily into the committee's statutory jurisdiction and most of which fit quite easily under the statutory jurisdictions of other committees. In any case, the committee's jurisdiction in the 1990s spanned the domains of health, including public health services, health research and training, health insurance, and major aspects of federal Medicare and Medicaid policy; the environment, including hazardous waste control and cleanup, clean air and clean water policy, and ozone depletion; energy, including federal programs relating to natural gas, oil and other fossil fuels, nuclear power, energy conservation and affordability, and utilities regulation; consumer protection and product liability; railroads and inland waterways; travel and tourism; telecommunications; private insurance regulation; and public securities exchange policy. In sum, the evolving jurisdiction of Energy and Commerce includes important policies and programs that affect virtually every citizen in the country (and many beyond) virtually every day.

Committee Leadership. Leadership on Energy and Commerce has been relatively stable since the mid 1960s. From 1966 until his retirement in 1980, the chairman was Harley O. Staggers, a moderate-to-liberal Democrat from West Virginia. According to David Price (*Who Makes the Laws*, 1972), Staggers was principally interested in the opportunities that chairing the committee gave him to secure federal benefits for his district, particularly projects and grants awarded by the Department of Transportation. On larger policy matters, Staggers was cautious and averse to conflict, even to the point of blocking or delaying many of his fellow Democrats' initiatives. Most other accounts describe Staggers as a weak leader who rarely exploited his formal position to expeditiously push matters on the committee's agenda to expeditious legislative fruition. Reacting to Staggers's weak leadership, John E. Moss (D-Calif.), Dingell, and several other Democrats pressed for greater devolution of agenda control and legislative authority to Energy and Commerce subcommittees, which they succeeded in achieving in 1975.

Staggers retired in 1980, and Dingell assumed the chair of the now more decentralized committee in the following year. Despite the decentralization that Dingell had helped to bring about, his leadership of the committee proved very strong in a number of respects. In particular, Dingell used his procedural prerogatives as chair to achieve his policy goals over the objections of the subcommittees of his own jurisdiction and sometimes against the preferences of a committee majority. In addition, Dingell was active in negotiating with the House leadership over the assignment of new members to the committee in an attempt to populate it with members sympathetic to his own positions on major issues likely to come before the panel.

Dingell was largely responsible for the incremental but significant expansion of the committee's common law jurisdiction into areas previously untouched by the panel. His main vehicle was the Energy and Commerce Oversight and Investigations Subcommittee, which he elected to chair in every Congress after becoming chairman of the full committee. Dingell used the subcommittee to pursue waste and fraud in Pentagon procurement, banking deregulation, federal grants to universities, and a host of other issues. Such investigations did not always produce legislation from the committee, though that occurred frequently enough. But even when not proposing legislation, Dingell expanded the committee's power as an agenda setter for other committees, agency officials, interest group activists, and even the White House.

Under Dingell, as under Staggers, leadership on the committee was not limited to the full committee chair. Subcommittee chairs and other policy entrepreneurs sometimes pursued ambitious agendas of their own. Especially noteworthy were the group of new Democrats who joined the committee after the post-Watergate elections of 1974. One of the most prominent members of that cohort was Henry A. Waxman (D-Calif.), who won the chairmanship of the Subcommittee on Health and the Environment in 1979 over two more senior committee members and who subsequently became an aggressive legislative entrepreneur. For instance, Waxman used his subcommittee to push further into various health issues previously controlled by Ways and Means, health education issues previously controlled by Education and Labor, and environmental matters officially under the jurisdictions of Interior and Public Works. Some of Waxman's efforts, in fact, provoked major fights with Dingell, particularly Waxman's initiatives regarding clean air policy. For over a decade, Waxman, a representative of the smog-ridden Los Angeles area, locked horns on these issues with Dingell, who represented a Detroit-area automobile manufacturing district.

Given that top committee Democrats were not always in agreement, and given further that the White House was controlled by Republicans for all but four years in the 1970s and 1980s, Republican leaders on the committee sometimes played significant roles in shaping the direction of the panel's initiatives during this era. Indeed, Dingell was not above forming alliances with minority leaders when disagreeing with the majority of his Democratic colleagues. Such bipartisan cooperation on a wide variety of issues was common between Dingell and Norman F. Lent (R-N.Y.), the committee's ranking minority member from 1988 to 1992.

Committee Composition. For decades, congressional scholars have characterized most committees in the House as relatively homogeneous and biased, compared to their parent chamber, on policy questions within their jurisdictions. The underlying logic is that the assignment of members to committees is roughly self-selective, so that agriculture panels, say, are highly biased in favor agricultural programs and urban affairs panels are biased in favor of federal housing subsidies, mass transit funds, and other programs that provide aid to cities. This logic does not hold up in the case of the Energy and Commerce Committee for two reasons, both of which are related to the breadth and salience of the committee's jurisdiction. First, given that the committee addresses issues that interest so many states, districts, and organized interests, it is a highly coveted assignment. Self-selection to the committee is thus limited by the competition of interested members for available committee seats. Second, the diversity of issues within Energy and Commerce's jurisdiction guarantees that members will seek assignment to it with different interests in mind.

Thus, the committee has members from virtually every region of the country, and committee fights often break out along regional lines. In legislative debates over energy pricing, for example, representatives of energy-producing states of the middle South are at odds with representatives from the energy-consuming states of the North and Northeast. The committee tends to be ideologically diverse as well, with various wings of each party well represented. Finally, the committee tends to be mixed regarding the motivations that attract and retain its members. Various committee activities affect district constituencies in direct ways, including the high-profile issues of clean air and water policy, oil and gas deregulation, hazardous waste cleanup, and even Amtrak reauthorizations. But at the same time, many other issues evoke members' deeply felt personal policy interests or ideological commitments, including many of the larger environmental and health care issues, various forms of in-kind benefits to the poor and unemployed, and gender equity in insurance. Given the diverse range of opportunities for legislative action regarding members' various interests, turnover rates on the committee are among the lowest in the House.

Committee Decision Making. By the beginning of the 103d Congress (1993–1995), Energy and Commerce had six subcommittees: Dingell's Oversight and Investigations Subcommittee plus five others with jurisdiction over specific substantive areas. Despite Chairman Dingell's unusually strong role, the subcommittees remain the arenas where most of the important legislative work is done, including holding hearings and developing expertise relevant to setting policy, drafting legislation and negotiating compromises among diverse members and groups, and deciding which matters to take up and which to ignore, thereby influencing the legislative agenda of the full committee. Almost all legislative hearings are held in subcommittee; only rarely is a bill marked up (considered and amended) in full committee without first having been marked up in the subcommittee of jurisdiction. As Richard L. Hall and C. Lawrence Evans (1990) have shown, once bills move to full committee markup, they typically reflect most of what the originating subcommittees want, but bills are not automatically ratified. Given the regional, parochial, and ideological interests of the committee membership, significant legislative battles frequently play out on the full committee stage so that subcommittees seldom get everything they want.

The typical subcommittee size ranges from one-fourth to one-half of the forty or more members of the full committee. But even these relatively small figures overstate the number of members who participate in decision making on a typical bill. More often than not, a few players drive the action. When a bill moves from subcommittee to full committee, participation is similarly selective. For instance, Hall (1994) found that less than a third of the Energy and Commerce members were active during either full or subcommittee consideration of a typical bill. Whether a nominal member becomes a player in a particular legislative game before his or her panel depends on such things as the member's district and personal policy interests, the opportunity costs of involvement in the issue relative to some other issue, and the time and political resources the member has to invest relative to potential committee competitors.

Given the key deliberative roles played by the few who are able and willing to participate, too much can be (and often is) made of committee voting and voting alignments. Most decisions in Energy and Commerce are made by voice vote or unanimous consent, reflecting the fact that the central bargains have already been struck by the principal players' pre-markup. When decisions do come to a roll-call vote, many committee members are not on hand to vote, choosing instead to give their proxy to a colleague (a practice allowed in most congressional committees but prohibited on the floors of both chambers). Still, this is not to say that committee voting does not matter; it does, in both visible and not-so-visible ways. Frequently, bargains are struck behind the scenes by Energy and Commerce actors who anticipate what the larger panel membership will allow. Especially on major and controversial decisions, majority-rule roll-call votes determine the committee policy. As in other committees, the usual pattern in such votes is for the committee to split along party lines, but as suggested above, voting patterns on some issues reflect regional and other constituency-based cleavages as well.

Another important feature of committee decision making concerns the committee's relationship with external groups and actors. Given the scope of Energy and Commerce's jurisdiction, many public and private groups lobby and otherwise communicate with committee members and their staffs. Indeed, the importance of the committee's decisions to commercial interests gives members a substantial campaign fund-raising advantage with private political action committees (PACs). Such funds and the lobbying that accompanies them enable private interests to mobilize their supporters on matters about which those interests care most.

Staff play an important role in committee decision making. For over a decade, Energy and Commerce has been known for having one of the largest, most experienced, and most expert staffs of any committee in the House. Many ideas for new initiatives or legislative amendments bubble up from staff investigations. The expansive nature of the committee's jurisdiction and the ambitious nature of its legislative agenda are probably both consequence and cause of the committee's large and talented staff.

The Committee and the Parent House. Although it enjoys one of the broadest and most salient jurisdictions of any committee, Energy and Commerce is not without constraints in the House. At the early stages of drafting and negotiation, committee and subcommittee members may dominate the action, but even then they must anticipate what the reactions of their interested colleagues might be at subsequent stages of the legislative process. In many other cases, bills referred to Energy and Commerce are also referred to other committees with overlapping jurisdiction, often producing an intercommittee struggle. Because so many Energy and Commerce bills are of general interest, only infrequently do they pass the floor without scrutiny by party leaders or members of other committees. Usually, Energy and Commerce bills come to the House floor under "open rules," which allow amendments from the floor by (perhaps disaffected) committee members and nonmembers.

Still, the scope and salience of the House Energy and Commerce Committee make it one of the most important and coveted in the House. Its influence over the chamber's legislative agenda is more substantial than that of most committees, and in terms of both legislation generated and investigations held, it has been one of the two or three most productive committees since the early 1970s.

[See also Commerce, Science, and Transportation Committee, Senate; Energy and Natural Resources Committee, Senate.]

BIBLIOGRAPHY

Hall, Richard L. *Participation in Congress.* 1995.

Hall, Richard L., and C. Lawrence Evans. "The Power of Subcommittees." *Journal of Politics* 52 (1990): 335–355.

King, David C. *Border Wars: Congress and the Politics of Jurisdictional Change.* Forthcoming.

Price, David E. *The Commerce Committees.* 1975.

U.S. House of Representatives. Committee on Interstate and Foreign Commerce. *180 Years of Service: A Brief History of the Committee on Interstate and Foreign Commerce, U.S. House of Representatives.* 94th Cong., 1st sess., 1976. Committee print.

RICHARD L. HALL

ENERGY AND NATURAL RESOURCES.

U.S. energy and natural resources policy reflects, as few others do so clearly, the core values in American society. For most of American history, energy policy was predicated on the credos of unlimited opportunity, the burgeoning frontier, and ever-expanding supplies (Katz, 1984). This changed in the 1970s, when two energy crises shattered the belief that resources, especially energy supplies, were unlimited and destroyed the certainty that the future would be better than the past.

Before the 1970s, few people spoke of energy policy. Instead, they referred to the distinct areas of oil, gas, coal, electricity, and nuclear power. Fuels rarely competed, and, because the supplies of each were sufficient, they were rarely seen as alternatives to one another. Many fuel policies focused on curtailing oversupply. Nor did the fuels compete on the basis of their relative impact on the environment. The central issues in the myriad fuel policies were ideological battles between private and public power, consumers and producers, and industries and labor. The government aided the industries through legislation designed to protect them from wide swings in market prices. This situation ended in the 1970s when energy crises and growing environmental awareness pitted fuels against each other and changed the mix of interests on energy policy.

So abundant were resources that there were no energy policies until the twentieth century, a reflection of the restricted role of the federal government on a wide range of policies. States imposed a few regulations but largely left the industries untouched. Most companies did business in wide areas, leaving the states with little effective control. Monopolies developed in many areas, especially in oil. The Rockefeller cartel of Standard Oil amassed control of more than 80 percent of the United States' crude oil supplies, refining capacity, and kerosene. The Commerce Department in 1906, backed by a Supreme Court decision in 1911 *(Standard Oil Company v. the United States),* ruled that the monopoly violated the Sherman Antitrust Act of 1890. Standard Oil was broken up. The era of federal intervention in energy markets had begun.

Policies on oil, gas, coal, electricity, and nuclear power reflected a few fundamental cleavages for most of the twentieth century. The dominant conflict was between producers and consumers. The fights between public and private power and between labor and management were similar. From the New Deal through the late 1960s, few issues elicited such consistent and pervasive left-right tensions as did energy.

Coming at the same time as the rise of environmental consciousness, the price shocks of the 1973 to 1974 and 1979 Arab oil embargoes pitted fuels against each other for the first time. Shortages of oil and natural gas led to the search for alternatives. Oil and gas producers battled one another and with advocates of coal and nuclear power. Ecological concerns led to a new emphasis on conservation and a push for renewable fuels such as solar energy. Synthetic fuels, previously an issue of interest only to the few prophets of doom in energy markets, became politically salient. The energy shocks and the rise of environmentalism also disrupted traditional coalitions. The producer-consumer animosity gave way to fights among different types of producers and alternative classes of consumers. The new politics of energy were more a war of each against all than a straight fight between ideologies.

Oil Policy. The federal government's policy toward oil quickly became solicitous of industry. President William Howard Taft set aside some publicly held lands in 1912 for naval oil reserves. In 1918, Congress amended the Revenue Act of 1916 to allow mineral companies, including oil firms, to deplete asset values on their taxes. The Mineral Leasing Act of 1920 permitted the secretary of the Interior to lease federally owned mineral rights, granting three-eights of the revenues to the states. The naval reserves (one of which was located at Teapot Dome, Wyoming) were transferred to the Interior Department in 1922 by Interior Secretary Albert B. Fall. In return for bribes in what became known as the Teapot Dome scandal, Fall leased the fields to private firms without competitive bidding. The affair led to public revulsion against government-industry collusion on oil. No federal initiatives on oil were proffered until soaring production in the 1930s led to a drop of more than 75 percent in crude oil prices. Under President Franklin D. Roosevelt's National Industrial Recovery Act in 1933, the American Petroleum Institute was permitted to establish regional coordinating committees that limited oil production. Surpluses continued, and the Supreme Court later ruled the entire National Recovery Administration unconstitutional. In 1935, Congress enacted the Connally Hot Oil Act, which established a system of prorationing of oil supplies and prohibited the interstate transmission of surplus oil. Congress also enacted the Interstate Compact to Conserve Oil and Gas Act of 1935, which allowed states to coordinate their own prorationing legislation.

The major oil producers were the leading supporters of the Connally Hot Oil Act and the Interstate Compact. Independent producers, who generally bear much greater risks than major producers, have more consistently opposed government intervention in oil markets. The independents argued that the majors controlled so much of the oil market that they effectively reestablished a cartel. Independents have often formed an unusual coalition against the majors with consumers, who have sought more government intervention in the marketplace.

After World War II, splits developed among the major producers over a new threat: imported oil. Domestic producers worried that cheap imported oil threatened the economic security of the domestic industry. The majors split over controlling supply, with the sides reflecting whether the firms were purely domestic or had foreign investments. The majors preferred voluntary import quotas to government intervention. The voluntary system collapsed in 1957 when President Dwight D. Eisenhower established a mandatory quota system, claiming national security interests were at stake. The federal system broke down in the 1960s as the Oil Import Appeals Board granted many exemptions from the mandatory system.

Another conflict reappeared with a more distinctly ideological overtone: who controlled offshore oil reserves? The Mineral Leasing Act of 1920 left the question, known as the tidelands issue, unresolved. States—and conservative Republicans and southern Democrats—maintained that offshore reserves belonged to them, while liberal Democrats backed federal control of these resources. The Supreme Court ruled (in *United States v. California*, 33 U.S. 19) in 1947 that the federal government owned the mineral rights under the sea for twenty-seven miles off the California coast. The court reached similar decisions in claims by Louisiana and Texas in 1950 (*United States v. Texas*, 339 U.S. 707, and *United States v. Louisiana*, 339 U.S. 699). These decisions provoked an ideological conflict between conservatives backing states' rights and liberals favoring expanding the powers of the federal government. A Republican president and Congress enacted the Submerged Lands of Act of 1953, which granted title to offshore resources to the states according to their historic boundaries. The Outer Continental Shelf Lands Act of 1953 gave control of reserves outside these boundaries to the Department of the Interior. More than 85 percent of offshore reserves remained under federal control, provoking Louisiana in 1954 and Alabama two years later to extend their borders.

Increasing energy use and real prices that continued to drop inevitably produced a supply-demand imbalance. Energy consumption grew at 3.5 percent per year for fifteen years after 1950 and at 4.5 percent a year from 1965 to 1973, as prices declined in real dollars (Kash and Rycroft, 1984). Some observers predicted a supply crisis in the late 1960s, but few people took their concerns seriously. Even before the first embargo, the predictions proved true. President Richard M. Nixon included oil in his general price controls in 1971. When the cold winter of 1972–1973 led to heating oil shortages in the Northeast, oil price controls were reestablished in the Emergency Petroleum Allocation Act of 1973. The legislation also created the Federal Energy Agency, granting it authority to ration petroleum products among regions and users. The Energy Emergency Act of 1973 gave the president the power to reduce speed limits, restrict outdoor fuel use, require lower indoor temperatures, require industries and utilities to shift fuel types depending on availability, and to force refineries to adjust their fuel mixes.

The next several years brought a flurry of legislation on oil and energy, but little was done to overcome the nation's dependence on expensive imported oil that was subject to disruption without notice. The Energy Policy and Conservation Act of 1975 reimposed price controls for four years and pushed back the price of domestic oil. It also established a Strategic Petroleum Reserve, under which the United States was to stockpile as much as 1 billion barrels of oil for use in the event of future embargoes.

The legislation also mandated that utilities switch to coal from oil and natural gas, established mandatory fuel economy standards, and gave the president authority to impose conservation initiatives. In the Tax Reform Act of 1969, Congress had reduced the 27.5 percent depletion allowance for oil to 22 percent. The Tax Reduction Act of 1975 abolished the depletion allowance.

Congress also took initiatives to expand domestic production but had to face the growing power of environmentalists. The Trans-Alaska Pipeline Authorization Act of 1973 authorized the construction of a 789-mile pipeline carrying oil to the lower forty-eight states, overriding sections of the National Environmental Policy Act of 1969 that required environmental impact assessments. The Federal Land Policy and Management Act of 1976 required the government to balance energy development and wilderness in the management of federal lands. The Alaska Lands Act of 1980 set aside 104 million acres of federal lands on which energy development would be either restricted or prohibited. The Outer Continental Shelf Lands Act Amendments of 1978 established a federal fund to clean up offshore oil pollution and mandated environmental impact studies for offshore drilling.

President Jimmy Carter proposed a national energy strategy in 1977. It quickly passed the House as a single bill but was largely emasculated in the Senate. The two chambers finally agreed on a package of five bills in 1978. The package included the National Energy Conservation Policy Act, the Energy Tax Act, the Natural Gas Policy Act, the Power-plant and Industrial Fuel Use Act, and the Public Utilities Regulatory Policy Act. The impact on oil was indirect, accomplished through conservation measures. The National Energy Conservation Policy Act established grants to low-income families for insulation, loans to install solar collectors, and conservation programs. The Energy Tax Act provided tax credits for solar energy and imposed an extra duty on gas-guzzling automobiles. The Emergency Energy Conservation Act of 1979 permitted the president to impose oil rationing if a shortage of 20 percent of demand existed for thirty days and if neither house objected. In 1980, Congress sought to recover some of the profits that had increasingly accrued to oil companies because prices had begun to rise. The Crude Oil Windfall Profits Tax Act of 1980 was the biggest single tax ever levied on a U.S. industry.

Under President Ronald Reagan there were few energy initiatives. The Democratic House opposed the market-oriented approach of the Republican president and Senate (controlled by Republicans from 1981 through 1987). The Emergency Petroleum Allocation Act and its price controls on oil expired in 1981, and Reagan decontrolled oil prices on taking office. Reagan and Congress jousted over federal land-management practices, mostly producing stalemate. There were few initiatives on oil under President George Bush. When Bush and the Democratic Congress agreed on the Energy Policy Act of 1992 they could not find much accord on oil policy. The legislation provided for the development of fleets of alternative-fuel and electric vehicles, mandated faster filling of the Strategic Petroleum Reserve, streamlined procedures for setting rates for interstate oil pipelines, and eased some terms for oil and gas leasing.

Although oil producers divided on many issues, the conflicts that reached Congress were largely ideological even after the first energy crisis. Roll-call votes on oil regulation issues reflected left-right divisions more than anything else. Self-interest mattered, although not as much as ideology. Producing-state legislators were more likely than other conservatives to favor deregulation, while consuming-state members were more likely than other liberals to back stronger controls on the industry (Kalt, 1981). In the late 1970s, oil politics became more complicated. Oil producers were more united than gas producers but had to compete with gas producers and other fuel firms for market share. Oil did have one captive market—the automobile—but post-1973 energy policy was dedicated to reducing the country's dependence on foreign oil. Conflicts became so intense that the post-1973 energy agenda largely took oil issues off the table.

Natural Gas. The cleanest fuel, natural gas, has had some of the dirtiest politics. For many years, its politics were intertwined with those of oil. It has historically been produced as a by-product of oil, yet its economics are distinct. Gas production is not as concentrated in a few producers as oil is, nor are the production, transportation, and distribution integrated.

The Supreme Court, in *Munn v. Illinois* (1877), ruled that states could regulate natural gas production and marketing. Congress established the Federal Power Commission in 1920 to regulate interstate gas pipelines. The growth of federal initiatives during the New Deal set the stage for regulating natural gas. The Public Utility Holding Company Act of 1935 blocked concentration in the industry by barring distribution companies from transporting gas across state lines. The law also prohibited companies from establishing multiple layers of control, each of which could pass on higher costs to consumers.

The producer-consumer animosity continued throughout the New Deal. The Natural Gas Act of 1938, the landmark regulatory legislation on energy, gave the Federal Power Commission the authority to set wholesale rates for gas marketed across more than one state. Gas became the only mineral so regulated. Ideological battles over this issue continued for almost five decades. Congress repeatedly tried to restrict the power of the Federal Power Commission from 1947 on, provoking vetoes from an unsympathetic President Harry S. Truman in 1950 and a sympathetic Eisenhower in 1956 after Sen. Francis H. Case (R-S.D.) stated on the Senate floor that an oil lobbyist had tried to bribe him.

The conflicts on natural gas were largely ideological, pitting consumers and their northern Democratic allies in Congress against producers and their southern Democratic and Republican supporters. The ideological battles mirrored constituency interests (M. Elizabeth Sanders, *The Regulation of Natural Gas*, 1981). The severe winter of 1976 led to shortages, forcing the antagonists to agree to the Emergency Natural Gas Act of 1977, which gave the president authority to declare an emergency if severe shortages occurred and permitted the purchase of gas from the intrastate market for the first time.

The Natural Gas Policy Act of 1978, part of President Carter's energy package, set the opposing forces on gas politics in disarray, creating a variety of group pressures. The law extended federal control over the intrastate market, provided for the gradual deregulation of prices, and established twenty-seven categories of gas subject to different rates and regulations. Producers split according to the type of gas they produced, most distributors sided with residential consumers, and industrial and commercial users were divided, as were pipeline companies. The conflicts on gas policy became so complex that Congress could take no action at all during the Reagan administration, despite strong pressures in 1982–1983 as prices skyrocketed and supplies perversely increased (Uslaner, 1989).

Gas politics were more convoluted than oil issues because gas had been subject to federal controls since 1938. Separate markets—and distinct politics—had developed in the interstate and intrastate arenas. When the federal government intervened in the intrastate markets in 1978, the traditional conflicts were upset. There was no hope for any progress on gas policy until the 1978 price controls expired and the demand for new regulations subsided. With low prices in 1992, the Energy Policy Act loosened restrictions on importing Canadian gas. A more controversial proposal, to prohibit states from imposing production restrictions, failed.

Coal and Synthetic Fuels. When the energy shocks of the 1970s shook the oil and gas policy domains as shortages replaced surpluses, coal should have been the primary beneficiary. The United States has been called the Saudi Arabia of coal. In the 1980s, world coal supplies were estimated to be 350 times those of oil, and much of those reserves were located in the United States. Yet coal remains the stepchild of the energy industry, with few federal initiatives and much controversy.

More than any other fuel, coal has been subject to boom-and-bust cycles. It is distinctive among energy sources in its long-standing labor-management disputes. In contrast to clean natural gas, dirty coal has no environmental constituency and many enemies among the ecologically minded. These conflicts hurt further development of coal and hampered investments in synthetic fuels, including liquefied coal and less conventional sources such as oil shale, methane from coal seams, and biomass. Synthetic fuels were subject to environmental and safety issues similar to those that affect coal.

As with natural gas, the first federal initiatives on coal came during the New Deal. The Bituminous Coal Act of 1935 sought to stabilize prices and wages simultaneously. As with many of Roosevelt's early initiatives, the Supreme Court found the act unconstitutional. The Bituminous Coal Act of 1937 eliminated the wage provisions, focusing instead on setting a floor price for coal. When the law lapsed in 1943, Congress refused to renew it. It enacted no additional legislation on coal until 1969, when labor-management conflict forged the Coal Mine and Safety Act of 1969. The law established mandatory health and safety standards for all coal mines, established restrictions on dust and noise, and directed companies to provide benefits to disabled miners.

The coal industry was particularly hard hit by the rise of environmentalism. The National Environmental Policy Act of 1969, the Clean Air Act amendments of 1970, the Federal Water Pollution Control Act of 1972, and the Surface Mining Control and Reclamation Act of 1977 imposed restrictions on coal, making it less competitive than other fuels. Coal producers had to bear extra costs for cleaning up the environment, removing pollution from coal as it burns, and correcting the environmental devastation produced by strip mining. Environmental concerns made low-sulfur western coal more competitive with high-sulfur eastern coal; the West's share of the coal market increased from 15 percent in 1973 to 36 percent in 1983. Producers were racked by regional divisions as well as conflicts with labor and environmentalists.

Some attempts were made to boost the use of coal. The Energy Supply and Environmental Coordination Act of 1974 provided for utility conversion from oil and gas to coal, but the act had many loopholes. As part of Carter's energy package, the Powerplant and Industrial Fuel Use Act of 1978 restricted industrial users and utilities from using oil and gas when they could convert to coal. The industry faced additional pressure under the Coal Leasing Amendments Act of 1974, which required competitive bidding for leasing coal reserves on federal lands. Mining companies could not persuade Congress to grant rights of way for slurry pipelines to provide cheaper transportation for coal than railroads.

The Reagan administration was kinder to coal, expediting leases of federal land until Congress imposed a two-year moratorium in 1983. Coal policy, so long stymied, finally came into its own in the Energy Policy Act of 1992, which provided something for everybody in the coal community. The industry and environmentalists received a $278 million grant for fiscal 1993 and a virtual blank check for the next four years toward the development of clean coal technology. Small operators received subsidies, retired workers health benefits, environmentalists a temporary ban on opening wilderness and park lands to further leasing, and industry relief from conflicting legal claims over the ownership of coal-based methane gas as well as a promise that the government would seek to export more coal.

Synthetic fuels, some of which are coal based, have long been the "answer" to long-term supply problems for those who have seen energy supplies as limited and likely to run out. Until the 1970s, as the embargo constricted supplies and the environmental movement stressed the limits to growth, few advocated this position. Nevertheless, there were a few attempts to develop "synfuels." The Oil Placer Act of 1872, arguably the first federal initiative on energy, permitted private companies to file claims on oil shale lands. President Woodrow Wilson reversed this policy for naval reserves during World War I, and the Mineral Leasing Act of 1920 banned further claims.

Synthetic fuels were brought to the fore during World War II when much of the nation's energy capacity was devoted to the military effort. The Synthetic Liquid Fuels Act of 1944 provided $30 million for synfuels development. The Truman administration proposed a $10-billion program that foundered when industry objected to a government role in synfuels development. There were small pilot programs under the Truman and Johnson administrations. Carter had grand visions for synthetic fuels: the Energy Security Act of 1980 provided $20 billion for the immediate development of synfuels and as much as $68 billion more for the future. The legislation also proposed to expedite environmental review of synthetic fuels, but environmentalists defeated this provision. Almost immediately after enactment, the program became controversial. Congressional Republicans blocked Carter's initial nominees for directors of the Synthetic Fuels Corporation. The projects and the board became mired in controversy and cost overruns. Congress cut funding for the corporation in half in 1984; it terminated the program the next year.

Coal had been one of the most ideological of all energy issues. The 1970s changed all that. Many traditional liberal opponents of Big Oil saw coal as the solution to the country's energy needs when coal prices became more competitive in the 1970s. Ecological consciousness dampened the enthusiasm for coal just as its economics made it an attractive alternative. Synthetic fuels had never been controversial, because they ranked so low on the nation's energy agenda and the public knew little about them. The 1980s brought synfuels to the fore, along with controversies over public versus private power and energy development versus the environment. Without a long-standing constituency to fight for synthetic fuels, they quickly fell out of favor and off the agenda.

Electricity and Nuclear Power. Struggles over electricity and nuclear power reflected the ideological debate over public versus private power. Additionally, utility regulation involved issues of state versus federal responsibility, while nuclear power since the 1960s has been plagued by questions of safety.

Most regulation of utilities occurs in the states. The first such federal law, the Federal Water Power

Landmark Energy Legislation

TITLE	YEAR ENACTED	REFERENCE NUMBER	DESCRIPTION
Mineral Leasing Act	1920	41 Stat. 437	Permitted the secretary of the Interior to lease federally owned mineral rights, granting three-eighths of the revenues to the states.
Federal Water Power Act	1920	41 Stat. 1063	Mandated that public utilities be given preference over private firms in the construction of hydroelectric plants.
Tennessee Valley Authority Act	1933	48 Stat. 58	Provided for the development of hydroelectric power through the construction of dams in a large part of the underdeveloped South.
Connally Hot Oil Act	1935	49 Stat. 30	Established a system of prorationing of oil supplies and prohibited the interstate transmission of surplus oil.
Bituminous Coal Act	1937	50 Stat. 72	Set a floor price for coal.
Natural Gas Act	1938	52 Stat. 821	Gave the Federal Power Commission the authority to set wholesale rates for gas marketed across more than one state. Gas became the only mineral so regulated.
Synthetic Liquid Fuels Act	1944	58 Stat. 189	Provided $30 million for synfuels development.
Flood Control Act	1944	58 Stat. 887	Established the primacy of public power over private initiatives by dictating that power generated at reservoirs be delivered to the Interior Department, which would determine whether to sell it to public or private utilities.
Atomic Energy Act of 1946	1946	60 Stat. 755	Gave the government a monopoly over nuclear power.
Submerged Lands Act	1953	67 Stat. 29	Granted title to offshore resources to the states, according to their historic boundaries.
Outer Continental Shelf Lands Act	1953	67 Stat. 462	Gave control of oil reserves outside the states' historic boundaries to the Department of the Interior.
Atomic Energy Act of 1954	1954	68 Stat. 919	Barred the Atomic Energy Commission from the commercial production of nuclear energy, permitting it to issue licenses to private firms that could produce and market power.
Price-Anderson Act	1957	P.L. 85-256	Limited the liability of industry to $560 million for any single nuclear accident; guaranteed compensation to accident victims. Congress extended the act in 1974.
Trans-Alaska Pipeline Authorization Act	1973	P.L. 93-153	Authorized the construction of a 789-mile pipeline carrying oil to the lower forty-eight states, overriding sections of the National Environmental Policy Act of 1969 that required environmental impact assessments.
Emergency Petroleum Allocation Act	1973	P.L. 93-159	Reestablished price controls on oil and created the Federal Energy Agency, with the power to ration all petroleum products among regions and users.
Energy Policy and Conservation Act	1975	P.L. 94-163	Reimposed oil price controls for four years and pushed back the price of domestic oil. It also established the Strategic Petroleum Reserve, under which the U. S. was to stockpile up to a billion barrels of oil for use in the event of future embargoes. It also mandated that utilities switch to coal from oil and natural gas, established mandatory fuel economy standards, and gave the president authority to impose conservation initiatives.

Landmark Energy Legislation (Continued)

Title	Year Enacted	Reference Number	Description
Tax Reduction Act	1975	P.L. 94-12	Abolished the depletion allowance for oil and gas.
Department of Energy Organization Act	1977	P.L. 95-91	Melded some of the energy agencies in the Department of Interior with the Federal Energy Administration, the Federal Power Commission, and the Energy Research and Development Administration (ERDA) into a single cabinet department. The Federal Power Commission was replaced by the Federal Energy Regulatory Commission, which remained virtually autonomous.
Energy Tax Act	1978	P.L. 95-618	Provided tax credits for solar energy and imposed an extra duty on gas-guzzling automobiles.
Powerplant and Industrial Fuel Use Act	1978	P.L. 95-620	Restricted industrial users and utilities from using oil and gas when they could convert to coal.
Natural Gas Policy Act	1978	P.L. 95-621	Extended federal control over the intrastate gas market, provided for the gradual deregulation of prices, and established 27 categories of gas subject to different rates and regulations.
Energy Conservation Policy Act	1978	92 Stat. 3206	Mandated conservation standards for major appliances. Utilities were required to give consumers information about energy conservation devices and could give small loans to consumers to enhance efficiency. The legislation provided for grants to schools and hospitals to install energy-saving equipment and subsidies to low-income families for conservation.
Energy Security Act	1980	P.L. 96-294	Provided $20 billion for the immediate development of synfuels and as much as $68 billion more for the future, as well as lesser amounts for renewable fuels and conservation.
Crude Oil Windfall Profits Tax Act	1980	P.L. 96-471	The biggest single tax ever levied on a U.S. industry, imposing an excess-profits tax on oil designed to capture $227 billion.
Nuclear Waste Policy Act	1982	P.L. 97-425	Required the president to select a single site as the permanent repository for wastes by 1987. The law required that the criteria be scientific and without political interference, and expedited nuclear plant licensing.
Energy Policy Act of 1992	1992	P.L. 102-486	Mandated development of federal, state, and local fleets of vehicles running on alternative fuels. It also loosened restrictions on importing Canadian gas. The legislation provided funding for the development of clean coal technology, as well as subsidies for operators of small mines, health benefits for retired workers, and a temporary ban on opening wilderness and park lands to further leasing. The law permitted utilities to operate wholesale plants outside their service areas and wholesalers to request that utilities function as common carriers. The act streamlined licensing requirements for nuclear power plants.

Act of 1920, mandated that public utilities be given preference over private firms in the construction of hydroelectric plants. The New Deal sought to use the power of the federal government to bring electric power to people who could not obtain it. The Tennessee Valley Authority Act of 1933 provided for the development of hydroelectric power through the construction of dams in much of the underdeveloped South. The same year saw the establishment of the Bonneville Power Administration in the more prosperous Northwest. The Emergency Relief Act of 1935 codified Roosevelt's executive order establishing the Rural Electrification Administration, which provided loans to cooperatives that would bring power to rural areas.

The Flood Control Act of 1944 further established the primacy of public power over private initiatives. It dictated that power generated at reservoirs be delivered to the Interior Department, which would determine whether to sell it to public or private utilities. The public-private debate continued through the Eisenhower administration, which sought to further the development of private utilities. Congress forced the administration to cancel a plan to sell power from the Tennessee Valley Authority to the private Dixon-Yates firm in 1954 and again established the primacy of public power in 1957 when it dictated that at least half the power generated by the Niagara Falls dam be granted to public utilities. Private utilities did not score a major victory until 1967, when southern Democrats and Republicans joined forces to deny funds for the Dickey-Lincoln School public electricity-generating project in Maine.

The energy shocks of the 1970s led Congress to regulate fuel use by utilities. The Energy Supply and Environmental Coordination Act of 1974 attempted to dictate that utilities switch from scarce oil and natural gas to abundant coal, but the law was full of exemptions. The Powerplant and Industrial Fuel Use Act of 1978 contained stricter switching requirements, which remained in force until its 1987 repeal. Congress made a feeble attempt to set utility rates in the Public Utility Regulatory Policy Act of 1978, another part of the Carter energy program. Then, under Ronald Reagan and George Bush, utility policy took a major shift toward the market and away from public power. Congress reversed the preference for public utilities, first established in 1920, in the Hydroelectric Re-Licensing Act of 1986. The Energy Policy Act of 1992 exempted some wholesale power suppliers from the 1935 Public Utility Holding Company Act to allow utili-

ties to operate wholesale plants outside their service areas. It also permitted wholesale generators to request that the Federal Energy Regulatory Commission order utilities to transmit their power as common carriers when doing so would not disrupt existing systems. The great ideological conflicts that had dominated electricity politics even before the New Deal gave way to bipartisan coalitions for both the 1986 and 1992 bills.

Nuclear power began—after World War II—as a relatively noncontroversial alternative energy source. It was to become the most contentious energy issue of all. Nuclear power supporters saw the new fuel, an offshoot of nuclear weapons technology, as a source of cheap reliable power. The strongest backers of nuclear power at the outset were liberals, who favored both the cheap electricity it would produce and the government control of utilities that would be dictated by the sensitive technology. The Atomic Energy Act of 1946 gave the government a monopoly over nuclear power. The Atomic Energy Act of 1954, enacted by a Republican president and Congress, shifted the balance, banning the Atomic Energy Commission from the commercial production of nuclear energy and permitting it to issue licenses to private firms that could produce and market power.

As early as 1957 there were concerns about nuclear accidents. The Price-Anderson Act of 1957 limited the liability of industry to $560 million for any single nuclear accident and guaranteed compensation to accident victims. Congress extended the act in 1974. In 1964, Congress required that nuclear power be competitive with other fuels. Power companies purchasing nuclear electricity from the Atomic Energy Commission would pay market prices for other fuels, not subsidized rates.

Environmental criticism of nuclear energy stepped up after a 1966 accident at the Enrico Fermi nuclear power plant in Detroit, although no radiation was released. The National Environmental Policy Act of 1969 directed all federal agencies to prepare and weigh the environmental effects of their functions; environmentalists relied on the law in their attempts, often successful, to block the construction of nuclear plants. Nuclear power had become the most controversial of all fuels. The accident at the Three-Mile Island plant in Pennsylvania in 1979 energized opponents more than anything before that time.

The decade-long fight over funding for the Clinch River Breeder Reactor in Tennessee, whose initial costs of $700 million in 1973 had escalated to $1.5

billion by the time Congress terminated the program in 1983, is an example of only one type of controversy involving nuclear power. Another is the handling of nuclear wastes. The Nuclear Waste Policy Act of 1982 required the president to select a single site as the permanent repository for wastes by 1987. The law required that the criteria be scientific, without political interference, and sought to expedite nuclear plant licensing. Congress circumvented its own criteria in 1987 when it required two sites, one in the East and the other in the West. Site selection was not so easy; not until the Waste Isolation Pilot Project Act of 1992 was Carlsbad, New Mexico, selected as a test location. Despite the rancor over much nuclear policy, the Energy Policy Act of 1992 significantly advanced the role of nuclear power in the energy mix. It took steps to privatize the Energy Department's energy enrichment program, streamlined licensing requirements for nuclear power plants, and provided $213 million in fiscal 1993 for research and development of advanced reactor technologies. Only $60 million was ultimately appropriated in 1993.

Electricity and nuclear power were initially marked by the ideological fight over public versus private power. Electric power is a secondary resource; electricity must be generated from some other source. When fuels began competing with each other in the 1970s, the utility industry divided along the lines of the primary fuels each plant employed. Public versus private power remained a key concern, but the politics of utilities otherwise fractured. The public versus private issue faded on nuclear power; environmental and safety concerns dominated everything else. Nuclear politics kept its ideological veneer, but votes in Congress, as revealed in the unending search for a waste repository, reflected the "not-in-my-backyard" syndrome more than deep-seated beliefs.

Conservation and Alternative Fuels. The oil embargo and resulting energy shock transformed energy policy in another way. It changed the meaning of a word. *Conservation* had meant preserving supplies through managed production. It was largely synonymous with *prorationing*, protection of supplies for producers. Beginning in the 1970s, conservation acquired a consumerist twist: preservation of energy supplies by using less. Beginning in 1973, Congress pursued energy conservation with a zeal matched only by the painlessness of the largely exhortatory programs enacted. When people were asked to change their behavior, they were induced to do so by tax credits. Appliance and automobile manufacturers had the responsibility for developing more efficient products, and they were generally given considerable time to make the changes—most of which would hardly be noticed by the average voter except, ideally, through lower energy bills.

The initial efforts included lowering the speed limit to 55 miles per hour to save gasoline (Emergency Highway Energy Conservation Act of 1973) and the establishment of year-round daylight savings time to save electricity (Emergency Daylight Savings Time Energy Conservation Act of 1973). The Automobile Fuel Economy Act of 1975 authorized the Transportation Department to raise the average fuel-economy standards for automobiles to 21 miles per gallon by 1980 and to 28 miles per gallon by 1985. The Energy Conservation and Production Act of 1976 established efficiency standards for new commercial and residential buildings. Two 1975 laws—the Solar Heating and Cooling Demonstration Act and the National Energy Extension Service Act—merely set up centers to disseminate information on solar energy and conservation.

Two elements of Carter's 1978 energy package included significant conservation provisions. The Energy Conservation Policy Act of 1978 mandated conservation standards for major appliances. Utilities were required to give consumers information about energy conservation devices and could give small loans to consumers to enhance efficiency. The legislation provided for grants to schools and hospitals to install energy-saving equipment and subsidies to low-income families for conservation. The Energy Tax Act of 1978 provided a wide range of tax credits for energy-saving devices. Federal research and development on conservation grew from $105 million in 1974 to $568 million in 1980, then were cut by 80 percent in the Reagan years.

Congressional support for alternative fuels was never great. The Carter package of 1978 provided tax credits, mostly for solar energy and conservation. To make synthetic fuels more palatable to environmentalists, the Energy Security Act of 1980 contained subsidies for renewable fuels such as solar, biomass from urban wastes, wind and hydroelectric power, and geothermal energy. Yet the funds were small compared to spending on conservation and even that was less than one-fortieth of what Congress and the president provided for synthetic fuels (Uslaner, 1989).

Congress provided all sorts of funding for minor demonstration projects such as the electric car, but few had any effect on energy usage. Conservation,

REP. RICHARD L. OTTINGER (D-N.Y.). With an electric car at the Capitol, January 1967.   LIBRARY OF CONGRESS

renewables, and coal support were hit particularly hard by the Reagan budget cuts and never recovered. Even the major provision in the Energy Policy Act of 1992, which mandated the development of alternative-fuel fleets for state and federal governments and local school districts, provided little money for the transition. Methanol, ethanol, and other alcohol-based fuels have long received federal subsidies in agriculture bills. They are congressional favorites, because they provide guaranteed markets to farmers in uncertain times.

Institutions of Energy Policy. Until the 1970s, energy management in the legislative and executive branches reflected the varying politics of individual fuels. There was no central energy agency in either branch. In 1974, Congress established the Federal Energy Administration to handle shortages and the Energy Research and Development Administration (ERDA) to coordinate long-range planning. ERDA, authorized in the Energy Reorganization Act of 1974, took on most of the functions of the Atomic Energy Commission but also focused—for the first time—on renewable fuels. Three years later, Congress enacted the Department of Energy Organization Act, melding some of the energy agencies in the Department of Interior with the Federal Energy Administration, the Federal Power Commission, and ERDA into a single cabinet department. The Federal Power Commission was replaced by the Federal Energy Regulatory Commission, which remained virtually autonomous. Environmental groups insisted that the Interior Department maintain control of federal lands, so they were excluded from the new department. The Department of Energy was a patchwork of existing agencies with little coherence or sense of mission (Vietor, 1984). The Reagan administration tried to abolish it in 1982, but Congress objected.

Congressional institutions were as fragmented as executive organizations. Each fuel was considered separately until the 1970s. While oil, gas, coal, and electricity all fell under the jurisdictions of the House and Senate Commerce committees, public lands came under the western-dominated Public Works and Interior panels. The House Interstate and Foreign Commerce Committee, chaired for many years by Harley O. Staggers (D-Ky.), was dominated by coal interests. Oil and gas producers were well represented in both chambers by Speaker Sam Rayburn (D-Tex.), Senate majority leader Lyndon B. Johnson (D-Tex.), and Senators Robert S. Kerr (D-Okla.) and Russell B. Long (D-La.). As a key member—and later chairman—of the Senate Finance Committee, Long effectively blocked repeal of the oil depletion allowance for many years. The dominance of the Democratic party, and thus the congressional committee system, by southern conservatives made producers dominant over consumers from the late 1930s until the 1970s. During the New Deal, consumers and labor had often triumphed over producers. With the rise of the conservative coalition of southern Democrats and Republicans in the late 1930s, the balance shifted.

In the 1970s, several trends came together to disrupt producer dominance. The energy crises led many people to believe that producers had conspired with oil-exporting countries to raise prices greatly. Affiliation with producers became a liability for many politicians. The rise of environmentalism added a previously unknown dimension to energy politics. The nationalization of party politics narrowed the differences between northern and southern Democrats, leaving many producer states without strong proponents of the energy industry in the majority party.

The retirement or death of many key producer officials in the 1960s and 1970s undermined the industry's dominant position, as did changes in the congressional committee system at around the same time that the first energy crisis hit the country. Committee reforms in the House in the 1970s took much power from committees and moved it either to subcommittees or to the floor. Powerful committee chairmen could no longer protect the industries effectively as Staggers had been renowned for doing for coal.

Both the House and Senate permitted bills to be sent to more than one committee beginning in the 1970s. Because energy affects virtually everything, the number of claimants was huge. Five House committees claimed primary jurisdiction over energy: Interstate and Foreign Commerce, Interior, Public Works, Science and Technology, and Foreign Affairs. In the 95th Congress (1977–1979), eighty-three committees and subcommittees, including every member who served in the House, held hearings on energy-related bills. Only the Budget Committee and four minor panels did not handle energy issues; almost 14 percent of all multiply referred bills concerned energy. The House attempted to restructure its energy jurisdictions in a single committee that would have virtual control over fuels policy, but the House decisively rejected the reorganization. It did create an "energy committee" by renaming Interstate and Foreign Commerce as Energy and Commerce. Committee jurisdictions were left largely intact (for an account, see Uslaner, 1989).

Other jurisdictional changes did little to centralize decision-making. After World War II, Congress established a Joint Committee on Atomic Energy to handle nuclear power issues, mostly in secret for national security reasons. By the mid 1970s, nuclear power had become highly controversial, and the joint committee was viewed as too much a protector of industry. In 1977, the House and Senate abolished it and split its functions among five other panels. The Senate gained the Energy and Natural Resources Committee in 1976 as part of a broader committee reorganization; the new panel was largely a renamed Interior Committee without significantly enhanced jurisdiction.

The House increasingly used Speaker's task forces to coordinate decision making on energy. Such a panel, consisting of members of many committees chosen for their loyalty to the party program, was effective in getting Carter's energy package through the House of Representatives in 1977. A task force was also used in the 1992 legislation. These organizational alternatives point to the weakness of the contemporary committee system and the diverse range of interests on energy. Carter's 1977 legislation was drastically watered down in the Senate once opponents had time to mobilize; the 1992 bill was a patchwork of small steps. Not even a task force could take action on the more controversial issues such as oil production and regulation.

Because energy affects everyone and everything, policy-making will continue to be marked by a wide range of interests and the potential for deep conflict. When prices are high, tempers flare. When costs subside, there is greater potential for action but less interest.

[*See also* Energy and Commerce Committee, House; Energy and Natural Resources Committee, Senate; Nuclear Power.]

BIBLIOGRAPHY

Davis, David Howard. *Energy Politics.* 3d ed. 1982.

Chubb, John E. *Interest Groups and the Bureaucracy.* 1983.

Engler, Robert. *The Politics of Oil.* 1961.

Goodwin, Craufurd, ed. *Energy Policy in Perspective.* 1981.

Jones, Charles O. "Congress and the Making of Energy Policy." In *New Dimensions to Energy Policy.* Edited by Robert Lawrence. 1979.

Kalt, Joseph P. *The Economics and Politics of Oil Price Regulation.* 1981.

Kash, Don E., and Robert W. Rycroft. *U.S. Energy Policy: Crisis and Complacency.* 1984.

Katz, James Everett. *Congress and National Energy Policy.* 1984.

Tugwell, Franklin. *The Energy Crisis and the American Political Economy.* 1988.

Uslaner, Eric M. *Shale Barrel Politics.* 1989.

Vietor, Richard A. *Energy Policy in America since 1945.* 1984.

ERIC M. USLANER

ENERGY AND NATURAL RESOURCES COMMITTEE, SENATE.

The Committee on Energy and Natural Resources is responsible for processing legislation and conducting oversight on issues pertaining to national energy policy and the development of nonmineral energy resources such as nuclear, solar, and hydroelectric power.

The committee is also responsible for policies governing the nation's natural resources. Energy-producing resources such as oil, gas, and coal fall under the purview of the committee. Energy and Natural Resources also handles policies directing the use of America's public lands, including forests, parks, wilderness areas, historical sites, and wild and scenic rivers. Energy and Natural Resources was one of seventeen standing committees in the U.S. Senate in the 103d Congress (1993–1995).

History and Development. The Senate organized its first group of standing committees in 1816. Among the eleven committees was a Committee on Public Lands. Since 1816, the name of the committee has been changed several times and its jurisdiction has been repeatedly expanded. The basic responsibility of the Committee on Energy and Natural Resources remains the same as the duty of the original Public Lands Committee, however: to handle issues governing America's vast wealth in natural resources.

The evolution of the Energy and Natural Resources Committee corresponds closely to the territorial growth of the United States. The Public Lands Committee was formed after the Louisiana Purchase of 1803 had doubled the size and greatly enhanced the economic resources of the nation. The committee oversaw the nation's public lands during the massive changes of the nineteenth century. Issues facing the committee included settlement of the West and the 1862 Homestead Act; whether territories should be admitted to the Union as slave states; and establishment of the nation's first national park in 1872, the first national forest in 1891, and the first national wildlife refuge in 1902.

The Public Lands Committee's work also expanded as federal and state governments began creating agencies to administer public lands. The Department of the Interior was established in 1849, and in 1916 the National Park Service was created as a part of the Interior Department. By 1910, most states had also created their own wildlife and fisheries departments.

The Senate continued to expand the responsibilities of its public land panel during the twentieth century. In a 1921 reorganization, the committee was given jurisdiction over geological surveys and was renamed the Committee on Public Lands and Surveys.

The Legislative Reorganization Act of 1946 again changed the committee's name and expanded its jurisdiction. The Senate consolidated public lands, surveys, Indian affairs, offshore territories, irrigation and reclamation, and mining under a new Committee on Interior and Insular Affairs. In its traditional role of overseeing the public lands, the Interior and Insular Affairs Committee developed legislation that led to statehood for Alaska and Hawaii in the 1950s.

During the late 1960s and the 1970s, public debate on environmental policy issues and then on energy policy issues began. The Interior and Insular Affairs Committee became increasingly active in these new areas of legislative policy-making. It fashioned and reported the National Environmental Policy Act of 1969, ground-breaking legislation that required the study of federal actions that might affect the environment. When energy issues became a top priority following the OPEC oil embargo of 1973, legislation was developed by the Interior Committee.

A 1977 Senate reorganization again renamed and restructured the committee. The name was changed from Interior and Insular Affairs to Energy and Natural Resources, a change that underscored the committee's role in energy policy-making. The 1977 re-organization solidified the committee's jurisdiction over energy issues. Jurisdiction over issues concerning Native Americans was moved from the committee to a newly organized Select Committee on Indian Affairs.

The Committee on Energy and Natural Resources considers a wide variety of legislative initiatives. For example, in 1991 it held hearings on the Bush administration's national energy strategy; the Department of Energy's civilian nuclear waste program; designation of a section of Hawaii's shoreline as a national park; and the impact on future timber supplies of planned sales of timber logged in national forests.

The variety of issues considered by Energy and Natural Resources reflects the committee's broad jurisdiction. Senate Rule XXV provides the Energy and Natural Resources Committee with jurisdiction over the following areas: (1) coal production, distribution, and utilization; (2) energy policy; (3) energy regulation and conservation; (4) energy-related aspects of deep-water ports; (5) energy research and development; (6) extraction of minerals from oceans and outer continental shelf lands; (7) hydro-electric power, irrigation, and reclamation; (8) mining education and research; (9) mining, mineral lands, mining claims, and mineral conservation; (10) national parks, recreation areas, wilderness areas, wild and scenic rivers, historical sites, and military parks and battlefields as well as preservation of prehistoric ruins and objects of interest on the public domain; (11) naval petroleum reserves in Alaska; (12) nonmilitary development of nuclear energy; (13) oil and gas production and distribution; (14) public lands and forests, including farming and grazing thereon and mineral extraction therefrom; (15) solar energy systems; and (16) territorial possessions of the United States, including trusteeships. The committee is also responsible for oversight on matters relating to energy and resources development.

Membership and Chairmen. Energy and Natural Resources can be characterized as primarily a nonpartisan, constituency-oriented committee. Senators generally seek appointment to Energy and Natural Resources so they can provide constituent services at home that, in turn, enhance their chances for reelection. The committee allows members to bring projects into their states and to depict themselves as leaders on high-profile energy and environmental issues.

Traditionally, committee members have dispro-portionately come from the western states; in the 103d Congress, 45 percent of committee members came from the West. Western states have large areas of public land within their borders, often more than 50 percent of a western state's total area. The public lands include wilderness areas, national forests, and national parks. These lands are utilized by a number of interests: cattleraisers graze their cattle, loggers cut timber, mining interests extract coal and minerals, and drillers extract oil and gas from public lands. Groups and the public at large use the public lands for hiking, camping, and other recreational sports. Issues such as public land use, access by commercial interests, and fees charged for usage provide western senators numerous opportunities for constituent services.

Most of the senators from nonwestern states who serve on the committee also do so for reasons related to constituent interests. Some of these senators are from coal- or oil- and gas-producing states, for example. Others are from energy poor states that have interests at stake when energy legislation is drafted.

The Energy and Natural Resources Committee has had a series of illustrious chairmen. Henry M. Jackson (D-Wash.) was chairman of Interior and then Energy and Natural Resources from the 88th through the 96th Congress (1963–1981). Senator Jackson was responsible for the consolidation of energy matters under the jurisdiction of his committee in 1977, during a time when intense public debate about energy policy was taking place. Senator Jackson, long interested in both national defense and public lands issues, was among the first to link energy independence to national security.

After the Republican party gained control of the Senate in the 1980 elections, James A. McClure (R-Idaho) served as chairman from the 97th through the 99th Congress (1981–1987). Senator McClure used the chairmanship to advance the Reagan administration's policies of deregulation and construction of nuclear power plants.

J. Bennett Johnston (D-La.) became chairman of Energy and Natural Resources when the Democratic party regained control of the Senate in 1987 and has continued in that position as of 1994. Senator Johnston took a lead in developing programs to invigorate the energy industries of the United States, particularly nuclear power and oil and gas, through exploration along the nation's coastlines.

Senators Jackson, McClure, and Johnston were all leaders within their respective political parties, positions that bolstered the power of the chairman to move the committee's legislation favorably through the legislative process. Senator Jackson was chairman of the Democratic National Committee in 1960 and a candidate for president in 1972 and 1976. Senator McClure was chairman of the Republican Conference from 1981 to 1984. Senator Johnston served as chairman of the Democratic Senatorial Campaign Committee in 1975 and 1976.

The Committee on Energy and Natural Resources has one of the heaviest work loads of all Senate committees. The committee is sent more legislative measures than are most Senate panels. In the 1980s, Energy and Natural Resources ranked third (after Judiciary and Finance) in the number of legislative measures referred for processing. In the 97th Congress, for example, 341 legislative proposals were referred to Energy and Natural Resources. This represented 7.8 percent of all measures referred to Senate committees during the 1981–1982 period.

[*See also* Homestead Act; National Parks and Forests; Natural Resources Committee, House; Public Lands; Territories and Possessions.]

BIBLIOGRAPHY

Kriz, Margaret E. "The Power Broker." *National Journal* 24 (1992): 494–499.

Magida, Arthur J. "The House and Senate Interior and Insular Affairs Committees." In *The Ralph Nader Congress Project: The Environment Committees.* 1975.

U.S. Senate. Committee on Energy and Natural Resources. *History of the Committee on Energy and Natural Resources.* 100th Cong., 2d sess., 1989. S. Doc. 100-46.

MARY ETTA BOESL

ENFORCEMENT. The U.S. constitutional system permits change through the amendment process, but such change does not come easily. After Congress or the states have proposed an amendment, it must be ratified by three-fourths of the state legislatures or by a national convention composed of representatives from three-fourths of the states. Since the Civil War amendments, Congress has been given the dubious task of ensuring the enforcement of the substance of these respective amendments. For example, although section 1 of the Thirteenth Amendment abolished slavery, section 2 was written to ensure that the actual burdens of slavery would be permanently eliminated— "Congress shall have the power to enforce this article by appropriate legislation." And while the

Fourteenth Amendment's section 1 promised equal protection under the laws, section 5—"Congress shall have the power to enforce, by appropriate legislation, the provisions of this article"—was necessary to guarantee those very protections. In the case of the Fourteenth Amendment, however, Congress's enforcement power was often weakened by the Supreme Court's narrow interpretation of the enforcement clause. For example, Congress passed the Civil Rights Act of 1875, which intended to secure for all people the "full and equal enjoyment" of public accommodations, such as inns or theaters. Yet the Supreme Court found that act unconstitutional. The law, the Court argued, attempted to control, for example, the private discriminatory action of innkeepers, and that limit was not intended to be within the scope of the Fourteenth Amendment. Only state action that discriminated was limitable under the amendment.

Congress's enforcement power under the Thirteenth Amendment actually received a more generous reading by the Court, but not until the 1968 decision of *Jones v. Alfred H. Mayer Co.* At issue in *Jones* was a modern legislative act (42 U.S.C. 1982) based on the older Civil Rights Act of 1866, an act that attempted to ensure that all citizens enjoy the right to sell, lease, or purchase real and personal property. This time the Court interpreted Congress's enforcement power in a way that would permit the antidiscrimination act. The law could be used to reach private as well as state and public conduct, a result the Court had refused to consider in its reading of the Civil Rights Act of 1875. By broadly interpreting 42 U.S.C. 1982 to protect the right of all people to purchase property, the Court had expanded the very meaning of the enforcement clause under the Thirteenth Amendment. Eliminating the badges of slavery in 1865 meant obliterating any obstacles to the acquisition of property in 1968.

Congress's enforcement power of the Fifteenth Amendment has also had a slow and protracted history. Before the Voting Rights Act of 1965, which was extended in 1970, 1975, and 1982, Congress rarely used its power to enforce voting rights. But with the 1965 legislation firmly in place, Congress has used a variety of procedures such as bilingual elections and changes in state residence requirements to guarantee the right to vote and to prevent the "dilution" of minority voting power. Critics of the Voting Rights Act argue that it has encouraged federal intervention in state and local voting matters. Yet even the Supreme Court has upheld an expansive view of Congress's authority, under the enforcement clause, to implement and secure voting rights. It remains to be seen how well Congress achieves its commitment to equality as it aggressively utilizes its enforcement powers to guarantee the protections of all the Civil War amendments.

BIBLIOGRAPHY

Peltason, Jack W. *Understanding the Constitution.* 1994.
Rossum, Ralph, and Alan Tarr. *American Constitutional Law.* 1991.

JANIS JUDSON

ENFORCEMENT ACTS. *See* Force Acts.

ENTITLEMENT. A provision of law that requires the federal government to make payments to individuals or governments who meet particular eligibility requirements is called an entitlement. Entitlements constitute binding obligations on the part of the federal government; an eligible individual or government may seek legal recourse if the obligation is not met. Among the better-known entitlement programs are Social Security, Medicare, unemployment compensation, and Aid to Families with Dependent Children (AFDC).

Entitlement laws do not specify or limit the amounts to be spent on these programs. Instead, these laws detail eligibility criteria and outline the formulas for determining individual payment amounts. The total amount of money spent on any particular entitlement program depends on the number of eligible recipients and the size of the benefit each is entitled to receive. Because entitlements are structured this way, Congress must appropriate sufficient funds to cover payments to all individuals who qualify.

Entitlements are funded through either permanent or annual appropriations acts. Social Security receives its funds through a permanent appropriation; the necessary monies become available without any annual action by Congress. In other cases, the money for entitlements is included in one of the annual appropriations bills. But since they must approve enough money to cover all payments, congressional appropriators have no direct control over this spending.

In the context of the budget process, entitlement programs fall under the broad category of mandatory, or direct, spending. Broadly defined, mandatory spending is spending that is not directly controlled by the annual appropriations process. Entitlement programs make up the bulk of mandatory spending. In fact, entitlements by 1993 accounted for approximately half of all federal spending. Entitlement spending outlays for fiscal 1993 exceeded $750 billion.

While there are many different entitlement programs, a fairly small number account for most of the spending in this category. For fiscal 1993, the twenty-one largest entitlement programs accounted for 97 percent of entitlement and other mandatory spending. Most of these large entitlements (those with outlays of at least $1 billion) are social welfare programs. Besides those already discussed, they include the food stamp program, Civil Service Retirement system, child nutrition programs, social services block grants to states, and the Guaranteed Student Loan program. All told, there were 357 entitlement and other mandatory spending accounts in 1993.

Eligibility for entitlement benefits is determined on the basis of two criteria. Some, such as medicare or unemployment compensation, are work-related entitlements, with eligibility and benefits determined by past work experience. Others, such as medicaid, food stamps, and AFDC, are means tested; eligibility is determined, in part, by a recipient's low income. The vast majority of entitlement programs are work-related benefits.

[*See also* Backdoor Spending; Medicare; Social Security Act.]

BIBLIOGRAPHY

Cahill, Kenneth. *Entitlements and Other Mandatory Spending.* Congressional Research Service, Library of Congress. CRS Rept. 92-376 EPW. 1992.
Schick, Allen. *Reconciliation and the Congressional Budget Process.* 1981.

KATHLEEN DOLAN

ENUMERATED POWERS. The enumerated powers of Congress, found chiefly in Article I, section 8 of the Constitution, consist of seventeen specific grants of authority. A number of constitutional amendments, beginning with the Civil War amendments, grant Congress further enumerated prerogatives.

Among the initial enumerated grants are the economic powers of taxation and spending, the permission to pay debts, the borrowing of money, the management of commerce, and the regulation of currency. Other expressly stated powers include the authority to build post offices and roads, create inferior courts, declare war, and raise and support armies and navies. These powers were of considerable importance in 1791, as the Continental Congress had failed to resolve the financial crisis created by the Revolutionary War and its aftermath. Furthermore, the expanded economic ability of Congress was expected to solve the problem of an unpaid war debt, stem the flow of inflated currency, and facilitate the movement of interstate commerce.

The power to tax and spend is particularly vital because it allows Congress to provide for, as the Constitution states, "the general welfare" of the United States. In 1791 this broadly stated power gave Congress the flexibility it needed to raise revenues to meet the demands of a growing nation. Today, taxing and spending in the name of the general welfare result in the allocation of federal dollars for housing, aid to the poor, education, health care, and other public policy areas. Occasional conflicts with states over how a particular expenditure of funds intrudes upon the reserved powers of the states is usually resolved in favor of Congress. For example, in *South Dakota v. Dole* (1987), South Dakota challenged Congress's restraint of federal highway funds to states that allowed those under the age of twenty-one to purchase alcohol. The Court decided in favor of the congressional spending plan and reaffirmed the concept of welfare as that which is "shaped" by the vision of Congress alone.

Congress's enumerated power to regulate commerce with foreign nations and among the states permits the legislature to act in a wide range of areas. For example, in *Gibbons v. Odgen* (1824) the Supreme Court interpreted commerce as more than the mere buying and selling of goods, and expanded the definition to include a new realm of commercial exchanges, such as navigation and licensing. In *National Labor Relations Board v. Jones & Laughlin Steel Corporation* (1937), the Supreme Court read Congress's commerce power to incorporate labor relations and the conditions of employment. The commerce clause has even been used to vindicate civil rights claims (*Heart of Atlanta Motel v. United States* [1964]) and to control the spread of crime (*Perez v. United States* [1971]). In these instances, the enumerated commerce power did not limit the legislature from devising a set of implied powers to achieve its objectives, nor did it confine Congress to the precise and narrow language of the Constitution.

The final section of Article I guarantees Congress its latitude in decision making. The necessary and proper clause of section 18 allows Congress to use a variety of means to expedite its enumerated powers. For example, Congress's authority to raise and support armies and navies implies that personnel may be drafted to secure that objective. The elastic clause, as it is also known, enhances all of the enumerated powers and provides a more accurate picture of the full scope of congressional influence. From the early days of the ratification debates to contemporary times, controversy has raged over the extent of the necessary and proper clause's flexibility. Yet, Thomas Jefferson's belief in a narrow construction of the necessary and proper clause could not withstand John Marshall's challenge that the phrase be used more comprehensively to accommodate legislative policy-making. And while the debate was settled in *McCulloch v. Maryland* (17 U.S. [4 Wheat.] 316 [1819]), the legacy of enumerated and implied powers still demands, as the Framers intended, a government mindful as well of its constitutional limits.

[*See also* Implied Powers; McCulloch v. Maryland.]

BIBLIOGRAPHY

Murphy, Walter, James Fleming, and William Harris. *American Constitutional Interpretation.* 1986.
Peltason, Jack W. *Understanding the Constitution.* 1994.

JANIS JUDSON

ENVIRONMENT AND CONSERVATION.

The Constitution grants Congress vast authority over the nation's public domain—the 729 million acres of land owned by the federal government and held in trust for the people. Article IV, section 3 invests Congress with the "Power to dispose and make all needful Rules and Regulations respecting the Territory and other Property belonging to the United States." This authority supersedes any conflicting state laws that might otherwise apply to the public domain. Additionally, Congress may exercise any of its constitutionally enumerated powers, such as collecting taxes and regulating commerce, on the public lands as elsewhere.

Congressional policies affecting natural resources and the environment have changed immensely over the nation's history. Public lands and resources were initially treated as a transient public asset to be transferred rapidly to state and private interests for economic exploitation and development. Only gradually, with a great deal of political difficulty and economic cost to the nation, did Congress recognize a compelling public interest in preserving, protecting, and cultivating the bountiful natural and economic riches of the public domain. The congressional commitment to stewardship of public resources as a public trust, a legacy of the conservation movement, has been transformed by modern environmentalism into a broader, more difficult, and more costly congressional effort to control environmental degradation and promote ecological vitality throughout the nation, on the public domain and elsewhere.

Many interests and influences have shaped the congressional response to the nation's need for resource and environmental conservation since the mid-nineteenth century. In addition to the many competing state, regional, and economic interests represented in Congress itself, other important factors include the scientific, professional, and academic organizations concerned with resource and environmental issues; public opinion and changes in public values; the many organizations representing major resource consumers; increasing technological innovation and scientific information affecting conservation; the mounting importance of domestic resources for foreign trade and national security; widespread media attention to conservation issues; and changes in the U.S. economy.

The Great Giveaway: Public Land Policies, 1789–1872. The earliest public land policies were intended to raise revenue and to reward soldiers for Revolutionary War service. Within a few decades, however, Congress began to view public land sales primarily as a powerful inducement to westward expansion. During the nation's first century, Congress added vast tracts of resource-rich lands to the public domain and then ceded, gave away, or sold at bargain prices many millions of acres from this natural bounty to promote western expansion and economic growth. In 1802, the public domain (mostly lands ceded to the federal government by the original thirteen states) consisted of 236.8 million acres between the Atlantic seaboard and the Mississippi River. Beginning with the Louisiana Purchase in 1803, Congress added to the public domain an additional 1.6 billion acres, a territory larger than Western Europe, Great Britain, and Mexico combined, and eventually ceded much of it back to the new states.

Western interests, riding a wave of nationalistic fervor for continental expansion, dominated congressional land policies in the years preceding the Civil War. While farmers, settlers, and squatters benefited from the cheap-land policies in the years immediately preceding and following the Civil War, the railroads and their allied economic interests were the biggest beneficiaries. Congress directly granted the railroads 93 million acres of western public lands and ceded an additional 37.7 million acres to the new western states, which, in turn, quickly transferred most of it to the railroads. Altogether, the land transferred to the railroads constituted an area larger than France, England, Scotland, and Wales. Land speculators, who often managed to obtain public lands that Congress had intended for farmers and settlers, also benefited from this ready availability of cheap land and from inadequate state and federal supervision of land settlement and sales.

These land policies did hasten westward expansion. But congressional oversight of public land management, negligent or indifferent at best, also permitted profligate waste, corruption, and disregard of land laws. The federal government's General Land Office and its state counterparts, responsible for supervising the settlement and transfer of the public domain according to law, were notorious for the ease with which their oversight could be subverted for the benefit of land speculators and others out to turn a quick profit without regard for protecting or cultivating natural resources on the public lands. The era from 1800 to 1870 was characterized by great forest devastation caused by "strip-and-run" lumbering, mostly on forested public domain. As much as twenty-five million acres of forests were lost annually to uncontrolled fires. Western farmers and stockmen often degraded grasslands by overgrazing and excessive plowing. This unstabilized soil would eventually create heavy stream sedimentation, massive topsoil erosion, and dust storms—the last culminating in the catastrophic dust bowls of the years 1920 to 1940.

By the end of the Grant administration (1869–1877), mismanagement of the public lands had become a national scandal. A movement for radical reform of public land policies gathered political strength in the next two decades. During Benjamin Harrison's presidency (1889–1893) Congress enacted the first major laws inspired by the new land-reform philosophy, which would eventually inspire the nationally influential conservation movement.

Conservation Begins. The conservation movement's unifying principles sharply departed from the earlier public land policies. Conservationists believed that government should act as a steward of the public domain, managing it wisely as a public trust whose benefits should serve the public interest. This meant that government should preserve, protect, and enhance for public enjoyment public lands of unique historical or scenic value such as the Yosemite Valley or the Alaskan wilderness; should "conserve for use" the rich economic resources within the public domain, such as timber, minerals, and water, so that economic benefits flowed to the public rather than to private interests; and should practice rational planning to assure efficient development of public land resources through expert, professional management that would produce the maximum economic return compatible with "wise use."

These goals also created political struggles within the conservation movement itself. "Conservation for use" contradicted the goal of resource preservation, setting "preservationists" at odds with proponents of "wise" resource consumption from the public lands. Resource users, recreationists, and scientists disagreed over which kind of land use was "most efficient." Competing conservation values were manifested in congressional disagreements over allocation of forest lands for timber production, recreation, or national parks and in conflicts between western grazing interests and eastern proponents of watershed protection over forest land priorities. The bitter congressional controversy between 1900 and 1920 over the Forest Service's attempt to control the national parks was, in good part, a battle between preservationists and "wise use" resource proponents within the conservation movement. In later years, Congress encouraged further governmental battles over competing conservation goals by enacting legislation, such as the National Forests Multiple Use–Sustained Yield Act of 1960, that mandates "multiple use" of the nation's national forests and leaves the responsible federal agencies to resolve the intense battles over which uses should prevail in forest reserves.

The conservationist movement's congressional impact was first apparent in the Forestry Reserves Act of 1891, a turning point in the history of American land politics. The act, promoted by Secretary of the Interior John W. Noble, his chief forester, Bernard E. Fernow, and a coalition of eastern and midwestern legislators, repealed earlier laws giving farmers, squatters, and speculators easy access to federal timberlands. But its most important provision authorized the president to "set apart and reserve . . . public lands, wholly or in part covered with timber or undergrowth . . . as public reserva-

tions." The law, overcoming decades of opposition to timber reservations by many western legislators, exemplified congressional awareness that the frontier's closing marked the end of cheap resources and testified to legislative concern about continual scandals involving fraudulent acquisition of federal timberlands. The law also demonstrated the growing policy influence of forest and agricultural scientists who recognized the economic importance of protecting western watersheds. Using the act's authority, the president could reserve timberlands for public development, national parks, or water supply protection. The law virtually closed the public domain to settlers and speculators. During the law's first year, President Harrison created six forest reservations, including the Yellowstone Park Forest Reserve, together exceeding three million acres, and during his last year in office he created nine more reservations totaling more than ten million acres.

The First Conservation Era. The first major era of congressional conservation policy emerged under the aggressive leadership of President Theodore Roosevelt (1901–1909), an ardent and influential spokesman for the conservation movement, who acted in collaboration with a bipartisan congressional coalition of Progressive Republicans and Democrats.

The nation's emerging conservation consciousness was, in large part, a response to rapidly expanding research by natural scientists and to major transformations in the country's economy and land use. New federal surveys revealed that western irrigation water could support sustained agricultural production only if scientifically conserved and managed. Many eastern and midwestern conservationists and congressmen feared that private capital would quickly gain control of western water rights and exploit them at the expense of small farmers and ranchers. The frontier's closing also stimulated public support for the principles of scientific management and economic efficiency increasingly promoted by resource managers. Muckraking newspapers had aroused public indignation over fraud and profligate waste involving the public lands. Among the influential leaders of the bipartisan congressional coalition promoting resource conservation were Senators Francis G. Newlands (R-Nev.), Jeter C. Pritchard (R-N.C.), Joseph R. Burton (R-Kan.), and William Warner (R-Mo.), and Representatives John F. Lacey (R-Iowa), Thomas C. McRae (D-Ark.), John W. Weeks (R-Mass.), Walter P. Brownlow (R-Tenn.), James M. Moody (R-N.C.), and Theodore E. Burton (R-Ohio).

A major enactment of the period was the Rivers and Harbors Act of 1899 (Refuse Act), an indication of congressional commitment to the development and improvement of inland waterways for transportation, flood control, and navigation. Congressional support for inland waterways had been slowly growing since the Civil War. Members of Congress from inland areas, particularly the Mississippi valley, expected improved waterways to stimulate economic development. The act drew additional support from businesses angered by the rise in railroad rates at the beginning of the Spanish-American War.

Among the Refuse Act's most enduring conservation impacts was the provision authorizing the U.S. Army Corps of Engineers to control by permit any construction, or obstruction, of any navigable U.S. waterway or its tributary. In the early 1970s the Refuse Act provided the authority for the first major federal permit system to control industrial pollution of navigable waters until the act was superseded by the Federal Water Pollution Control Act Amendments of 1972.

The Newlands Reclamation Act of 1902 (Newlands Act) ended a dispute among the federal government, the states, and private interests over who should develop the rivers of the seventeen western states by vesting development authority with the secretary of the Interior. Other provisions restricted corporate access to irrigated public lands to encourage their cultivation by family farmers. The Newlands Act also created the U.S. Reclamation Service (later the Bureau of Reclamation) and established a fund, underwritten by land sales and mineral royalties, to finance irrigation projects to be chosen at the discretion of the secretary of the Interior. Eastern and midwestern farming spokesmen, led by the delegations from Ohio and Indiana, bitterly opposed the legislation, which they feared would stimulate western agricultural competition. Led by Representatives James M. Robinson (D-Ind.), William P. Hepburn (R-Iowa), and John S. Snook (D-Ohio), and with encouragement from House Speaker Joseph G. Cannon (R-Ill.), opponents asserted that western irrigation projects would not repay their federal investments and charged that the act subsidized western farmers at the expense of eastern agriculture. The successful legislative coalition supporting the act was led by western proponents of the bill, especially Rep. Francis Newlands and Senators Clarence D. Clark (R-Wyo.) and Henry C. Hansbrough (R-N.D.). They were supported by a politically powerful legislative

alignment of representatives for major eastern industries, commerce, and labor organizations.

Among the most enduring achievements of the first conservation era was the creation of the national forests and the development of professional governmental forestry under Gifford Pinchot, the first chief of the Forest Service in the Department of Agriculture. Creation of the forest reserves provoked intense regional, economic, and ideological controversies within Congress. Big timber companies such as the Weyerhaeuser Corporation, having exhausted their eastern forest resources, fought any restriction on western timber in the public domain and also fought the smaller timber interests, which expected the reserves to enhance their own competitive position. Many western legislators, led by Sen. William E. Borah (R-Idaho) and Rep. Frank W. Mondell (R-Wyo.), feared that western forest reserves would inhibit regional economic development. Among conservationists bitter arguments arose between advocates of scientifically managed timber harvesting and "preservationists" determined to keep forested wilderness untouched by economic development. The successful congressional coalition supporting the reserves included eastern (especially Appalachian) and southern legislators led by Senators Jeter Pritchard and Joseph Burton and Representatives Walter Brownlow and James Moody, who hoped that the legislation would also subsidize the reforestation of local timberlands degraded by "cut-and-burn" timbering. They were joined by western irrigation interests expecting watershed protection and by ranchers hoping for new grazing land on the reserves. Many Republican legislators saw patronage opportunities in the management of forest reserves. And a powerful coalition of horticulturalists, botanists, gardeners, and landscape architects, led by the American Forestry Association, added additional support.

The foundations for the national forests had been laid by Congress with the passage of the Forest Service Organic Act of 1897, granting authority to the secretary of the Interior, whose jurisdiction then embraced forests on the public domain, to regulate almost all important forest uses, to limit timber sales, and to control mineral exploration in the forests. In 1905, Congress, at President Roosevelt's initiative, authorized the transfer of most federal forest lands to Pinchot's Forest Service; soon thereafter these timberlands were designated the national forests. Chief Forester Pinchot, a superb administrator, skillful public leader and passionate conservationist, became Roosevelt's principal advis-

Landmark Conservation and Environmental Legislation

Title	Year Enacted	Reference Number	Description
Forestry Reserves Act	1891	26 Stat. 1103	Authorized the president to create forest reserves and to reserve timberlands as national parks and as protection of water supply.
Rivers and Harbors Act (Refuse Act)	1899	30 Stat. 331	Authorized the U.S. Army Corps of Engineers to investigate, regulate, and prohibit the dumping of wastes into navigable U.S. waterways.
Lacey Act	1900	31 Stat. 187	Prohibited the importation and interstate shipment of any wild bird or mammal taken or posessed in violation of the laws of any state or foreign country.
Newlands Reclamation Act	1902	P.L. 57-161	Authorized federal government to develop western waterways, created U.S. Reclamation Service, and provided for a revolving fund to finance dams and irrigation projects.
American Antiquities Act	1906	P.L. 59-209	Authorized the federal government to preserve historic and prehistoric ruins, monuments, and other valuable historic artifacts on public domain.
Establishment of the Office of National Parks, Buildings, and Reservations Act (National Park Service Act)	1916	P.L 64-235	Created the Office of National Parks, Buildings, and Reservations, which was renamed the National Park Service in 1934.
Civilian Conservation Corps Act	1933	P.L. 73-5	Authorized creation of the Civilian Conservation Corps, defined its mission, and established authority for its planning.
Tennessee Valley Authority Act	1933	P.L. 73-17	Authorized creation of the Tennessee Valley Authority as a public corporation with broad powers for resource development.
Grazing Act (Taylor Act)	1934	P.L. 73-482	Authorized the Department of the Interior to regulate grazing on public lands, issue permits and collect fees for grazing, and restrict access to public grazing lands.
Soil Conservation Act	1935	P.L. 74-46	Established soil conservation as a federal responsibility, created the Soil Conservation Service, and authorized its programs.
Rural Electrification Act	1936	P.L. 74-605	Created the Rural Electrification Administration and authorized it to market electric power and make loans to underwrite purchase of its services.
Flood Control Act	1936	P.L. 74-738	Authorized the U.S. Army Corps of Engineers to acquire rights-of-way reservoir land for flood control purposes.
Water Pollution Control Act	1948	P.L. 80-845	Authorized federal enforcement of state water pollution laws at state request; provides loans for waste treatment plants.
Clean Air Act of 1963	1963	P.L. 88-206	Authorized federal enforcement of state air pollution laws at state request.
Water Quality Act	1965	P.L. 89-234	Created first federal-state water quality standard setting process; established the Federal Water Pollution Control Administration to provide federal grants for waste treatment research and facilities.
Motor Vehicle Air Pollution Control Act	1965	P.L. 89-272	Authorized the secretary of Health, Education, and Welfare to establish regulations to control auto air pollution.

Landmark Conservation and Environmental Legislation (Continued)

TITLE	YEAR ENACTED	REFERENCE NUMBER	DESCRIPTION
Air Quality Control Act of 1967	1967	P.L. 90-148	Established federal-state process for creating air pollution control regions; created new enforcement procedure for state air pollution regulations; authorized federal grants and research on air pollution.
National Environmental Policy Act	1969	P.L. 91-190	Required environmental impact statements for federal actions affecting the environment; created President's Council on Environmental Quality; declared national policy to preserve and protect the environment.
Clean Air Act Amendments of 1970	1970	P.L. 91-604	Required EPA to set national air quality standards and auto emissions limits; required states to develop implementation plans; established enforcement process.
Federal Water Pollution Control Act Amendments of 1972	1972	P.L. 92-500	Set national water quality goals and state responsibility for their implementation; created pollution discharge permit system and greatly increased federal grants for waste treatment plant construction.
Coastal Zone Management Act	1972	P.L. 92-583	Created federal guidelines for state coastal management plans and authorized grants to encourage state coastal planning.
Endangered Species Act	1973	P.L. 93-205	Enlarged federal authority to protect both threatened and endangered species.
Safe Drinking Water Act of 1974	1974	P.L. 93-523	Authorized federal government to set national drinking water standards and regulate state groundwater protection programs.
Toxic Substances Control Act	1976	P.L. 94-369	Required premarket testing of chemicals; permitted EPA to ban or regulate the manufacture, sale, or use of chemicals creating an "unreasonable risk of injury to health or the environment."
Resource Conservation and Recovery Act	1976	P.L. 94-580	Required EPA to create regulations for hazardous waste treatment, storage, transportation, and disposal.
Surface Mining Control and Reclamation Act	1977	P.L. 95-87	Established national regulatory controls for surface mining and vested enforcement authority in Department of the Interior.
Clean Air Act Amendments of 1977	1977	P.L. 95-95	Amended and extended Clean Air Act; created new deadlines for compliance with auto and stationary source emissions standards; created new compliance requirements for state implementation plans.
Clean Water Act of 1977	1977	P.L. 95-217	Extended deadlines for industrial and urban compliance with water quality standards; set national standards for industrial pretreatment of wastes and increased federal grants for waste treatment facilities.
Comprehensive Environmental Response, Compensation, and Liability Act ("Superfund")	1980	P.L. 96-510	Authorized federal government to create national inventory of abandoned hazardous waste sites; authorized federal government to clean up sites and establish regulations for cleanup; created $1.6 billion fund for cleanup and established liabilities.
Resource Conservation and Recovery Act Amendments of 1984	1984	P.L. 98-616	Revised and strengthened federal hazardous waste management controls; set new standards and limits for land disposal of waste.
Safe Drinking Water Act of 1986	1986	P.L. 99-339	Reauthorized Safe Drinking Water Act of 1974; accelerated schedule for setting federal standards for 83 toxic pollutants.

Landmark Conservation and Environmental Legislation (Continued)

TITLE	YEAR ENACTED	REFERENCE NUMBER	DESCRIPTION
Superfund Amendments and Reauthorization Act of 1986	1986	P.L. 99-499	Created $8.5 billion fund to clean up most dangerous abandoned hazardous waste sites; established new standards and schedules for cleanups; required industries to inform local communities about nature and amount of hazardous chemicals used or emitted.
Clean Air Act Amendments	1990	P.L. 101-549	Set new deadlines for urban areas failing to meet national air quality standards; established new, stricter auto emissions standards; created deadlines for identifying and reducing industrial toxic air emissions; created new limits on air pollutants causing acid precipitation and atmospheric ozone depletion; authorized the creation of a market for "emissions trading" between industrial air pollution sources.

er on natural resources. Under Pinchot's leadership, the Forest Service soon developed a reputation for professional competence, dedication, and effectiveness in managing the new national forests. Their creation and professional management were strongly supported by most western legislators of both parties and by Progressive Republicans, who were assisted by newly formed conservationist organizations throughout the country. Over the course of his administration, Roosevelt expanded the national forests from 42 million to 172 million acres and created 138 new national forests in twenty-one states.

In 1900, Congress passed the Lacey Act (Fish and Wildlife Coordination Act), a testimonial to the dedication of conservationist representative John Lacey of Iowa and his major collaborators, Senate Judiciary Committee chairman George F. Hoar (R-Mass.) and Sen. Henry M. Teller (R.-Colo.). The act was the first federal legislation prohibiting the importation or interstate shipment of wild birds or mammals that had been taken in violation of the laws of any state or foreign country. It gave the federal government authority to control interstate commerce in illegally secured game. It was also the first federal legislation that acknowledged the importance of protecting animal species and the public interest in limiting their destruction.

The Lacey Act was Congress's response to rising public indignation over the growing endangerment of game birds and mammals and the wholesale slaughter of nongame birds whose feathers were coveted for millinery decoration. The legislation, though vigorously opposed by the nation's game dealers and milliners, was strongly supported by most sportsmen, scientific naturalists, and conser-

vationists, aided by the popular press. The act created an important precedent by establishing congressional authority to use the Constitution's commerce clause for wildlife protection.

A few years later, Congress passed the American Antiquities Act of 1906, authorizing the president to designate as national monuments "historic landmarks, historic and prehistoric structures, and other objects of historic of scientific interest" situated on federal lands. Other provisions of the act limited private access to historic or archaeological sites on federal lands by requiring entry permits.

The American Antiquities Act provided the basis for the designation in succeeding years of more than seventy-nine national monuments and for the first time gave the president the continuing discretionary authority to identify cultural properties of great national significance. It was also a powerful impetus for the development of the national park system. The act eventually enabled Theodore Roosevelt to designate eighteen national monuments, of which four—Grand Canyon, Olympic, Lassen, and Petrified Forest—were ultimately to become national parks.

The national park system developed gradually, without an initial comprehensive plan or a management strategy for individual parks. Congress had designated the headwaters of the Yellowstone River as the first national park in 1872. Competition quickly intensified between state and regional delegations for additional parks or for money to maintain existing ones, since Congress spent grudgingly for park management. Competition for park appropriations also involved aggressive lobbying by the private park concessionaires who provided most park services. Early attempts to create a centralized federal park administration in the executive branch were rejected, however, because of the expense and because many members of Congress wanted to use federal park jobs for patronage.

By 1916, eleven national parks had been created, more were planned, and a centralized park administration seemed imperative. That year, proponents led by Sen. Reed Smoot (R-Utah) and Representatives Frederick C. Stevens (R-Minn.) and William Kent (I-Calif.) proposed legislation creating a national park service in the Department of the Interior, which was responsible for supervising the existing parks. Major opposition came from western congressmen who feared the loss of grazing rights in the parks; from other legislators who hoped to get parks for their own constituencies; from the Forest Service and its legislative allies, who wanted park administration vested in the Forest Service; and from conservationists who opposed the "lock-up" of natural resources in the parks. Proponents of improved park management won the battle, and the Establishment of the Office of National Parks, Buildings, and Reservations Act of 1916 became the first important step in the federal planning of park development. Besides creating the Office of National Parks, Buildings, and Reservations— which became the National Park Service in 1934— the act explicitly designated recreation as the primary park use by directing that the parks were to be managed "to conserve the scenery and the natural and historic objects and wildlife therein and to provide for the enjoyment of the same in such manner and by such means as will leave them unimpaired for the enjoyment of future generations." Not until the New Deal, however, were the parks planned and administered as part of a coordinated national system.

The Struggle to Protect Conservation Policies. The first conservation era ended with Republican William Howard Taft's election to succeed Roosevelt in 1909. A struggle then transpired between congressional partisans of Roosevelt's conservation programs and opponents determined to revise or repeal many of them. Congressional support for conservation had always been fitful and unpredictable. Disagreements between Roosevelt and Congress were grounded in differing institutional and political viewpoints that continually reappeared in federal policy-making concerning natural resources. Congress, reluctant to surrender to the executive branch its collective authority to designate public land uses and the conditions for resource development, fought the transfer of the forest reserves to the Forest Service and delayed for decades the creation of centralized national park planning.

Congress also showed scant enthusiasm for Roosevelt's comprehensive resource-planning ideas. In 1907, legislative waterways committees, protecting their own authority, had thwarted Roosevelt's plans for a coordinated, multipurpose federal waterways program by rejecting his proposed Inland Waterways Commission. A year later, congressional opposition had ended Roosevelt's National Conservation Commission, which was promoting comprehensive federal resource planning and management. Joining this opposition were many private interests, especially resource developers such as timber, mining, and cattle companies, who believed that a shift of public land authority to executive agencies would weaken their access to public resources. And Congress lacked Roosevelt's confidence in professional public resource managers employed by executive agencies such as the Forest Service, preferring instead to retain for itself the authority to determine matters such as the amount of timber allowed to be cut on the public domain.

A crucial test of strength between congressional conservationists and their critics grew from a nasty public dispute involving Gifford Pinchot and Richard A. Ballinger, Taft's secretary of the Interior. The conflict culminated in 1910 with a nationally publicized joint congressional committee investigation of the Forest Service and the Department of the Interior. Secretary Ballinger started the controversy shortly after assuming office in 1909, when he initiated a number of department actions intended to release to private ownership valuable public land and reservoir sites previously reserved for public projects. To conservationists, these actions appeared to prove that Taft and his resource administrators intended to undo much of Roosevelt's conservation program. Soon thereafter, Ballinger also ended the cooperative management of federal forests previously established between his department and the Department of Agriculture. He also made clear his general opposition to extensive federal powers over resource development. These actions and others were interpreted by Pinchot and other conservationists as proof that Taft intended to destroy many of their most important achievements. Pinchot assumed the leadership in aggressively attacking Ballinger's policies and, in turn, incurred Taft's displeasure. When in late 1909 Pinchot charged that Ballinger had illegally attempted to turn over Alaskan public land leases to coal interests, President Taft fired the chief forester for insubordination.

In early 1910, a joint congressional committee publicly investigated the charges in the Pinchot-Ballinger dispute, giving both men an opportunity to present their cases. The hearings failed to confirm Pinchot's charges of malfeasance and administrative incompetence against Ballinger. But conservationists nonetheless viewed the hearings as a vindication of their accusations and a victory for the conservation movement. They contended that the hearings had embarrassed the Taft administration by revealing its anticonservation sentiments and had thus rallied national opposition to its resource policies. They had succeeded in elevating conservation to a great moral crusade and had rallied conservationist forces in Congress and throughout the country to defend Roosevelt's policies against the Taft administration and future congressional or executive attacks. The Taft administration soon after abandoned the several additional anticonservation initiatives it had contemplated, and for several decades congressional critics of conservationist policies remained relatively silent.

Conservation Renewed: The New Deal Era. Congress, following the national mood, did not again give conservation sustained attention until the Great Depression and Franklin D. Roosevelt's presidency. During the Wilson administration, Congress and the White House were preoccupied with World War I and its aftermath. In the 1920s, the Republican majority in Congress had little interest in ambitious social programs and, with the exception of the intense conflict leading to federal protection of dam sites along Muscle Shoals in the Tennessee River, made few significant resource decisions. But the absence of strong, continuing federal government regulation of the public domain during these years permitted severe degradation of many federal grazing lands and forests and encouraged negligence in the administration of the national parks. The Teapot Dome scandal of 1922, which revealed that Secretary of the Interior Albert B. Fall had illicitly leased vast federal oil reserves to private petroleum companies, exemplified the governmental negligence about critical public resource conservation that persisted throughout the 1920s.

By the time Franklin Roosevelt entered the White House in 1933, the nation's economy and politics had been profoundly altered by the Great Depression and the environmental disasters that followed like retribution for a century's worth of land abuse. Powerful continental winds swept up unstable farm soil across the Midwest and Great Plains and hurled it into massive dust clouds that obliterated the sun and produced the great dust bowls of the 1930s. Massive soil erosion on public and private lands caused severe stream sedimentation, flooding, and other natural disasters, all of which further intensified an already crippling economic depression by robbing thousands of farm families of land and livelihood.

Like his cousin Theodore, Franklin Roosevelt was a zealous conservationist. He believed that the restoration and wise economic development of public and private lands was inherently valuable—as well as being an immediately effective, politically attractive strategy for national economic recovery. During Roosevelt's first two terms, large Democratic majorities and moderate Republicans in both houses of Congress generally supported the president's conservation initiatives. The result was a continuing stream of federal conservation legislation whose sweep, economic impact, and administrative requirements overshadowed the achievements of Theodore Roosevelt's era. The New Deal marked the greatest period of conservation policymaking in American history, an era of unprecedented expansion of federal government responsibility for land conservation and resource development and management. But these programs, which generally left a legacy of economic and social improvement, never produced the coordinated national resource planning that Franklin Roosevelt sought. Some programs, such as the Tennessee Valley Authority (TVA), demonstrated competent, efficient governmental resource planning on a massive scale. But congressional opposition and bureaucratic rivalries thwarted a national water development plan, and other resource agencies seldom sought or welcomed coordinated planning.

From TVA to REA: An Outpouring of New Programs. Franklin Roosevelt's first conservation initiative, the most successful and spectacular of the New Deal resource programs, was the Tennessee Valley Authority Act, which Congress passed in 1933. The act created the Tennessee Valley Authority, a public corporation eventually responsible for the comprehensive economic development of the entire Tennessee River valley through power generation, flood control, soil conservation, rural electrification, and related activities. TVA had its origins in the latter years of World War I as a federal facility consisting of a hydroelectric dam and two nitrate-manufacturing facilities intended largely for military purposes. The eleven-year evolution of this facility into the revolutionary, multipurpose regional development agency that would become TVA resulted, in large measure, from the visionary efforts of Sen. George W. Norris (D-Neb.), chairman of the Senate Committee on Agriculture and Forestry during the critical early years of TVA's development.

In its first decade, TVA created seven hundred miles of navigable streams, planted 200 million trees, and erected or planned a multitude of new dams for hydroelectric power and flood control. TVA instituted "source to mouth" river management on an unprecedented scale and demonstrated the federal government's capacity for highly professional, effective, and efficient planning. While TVA's accomplishments during World War II and thereafter constitute perhaps the greatest memorial to cooperative congressional–White House conservation management in the New Deal period, TVA's political independence could annoy legislators in whose constituencies it operated. Sen. Kenneth D. McKellar (D-Tenn.) fought a bitter if unsuccessful battle against the TVA's Douglas Dam near Knoxville because it would eliminate large vegetable crop production. Some local congressmen, including McKellar, also found TVA's resistance to political patronage irritating.

Other major conservation laws and programs quickly appeared. Early in 1933, Congress approved Roosevelt's proposal for a Civilian Conservation Corps (CCC) to employ thousands of young, unemployed American men in a national program of land reclamation, reforestation, flood control, and related activities. Before World War II, the CCC had employed almost three million men, who, among other achievements, had planted more than two billion trees in reforestation and land stabilization projects. Congress also passed the Soil Conservation Act in 1935, creating the Soil Conservation Service to assist farmers and industry in developing and using effective soil stabilization procedures. The Grazing Act of 1934 (Taylor Act) authorized the federal government for the first time to regulate grazing on the public domain and to collect fees from cattle owners who grazed their herds there.

Second only to TVA in its regional impact, the Rural Electrification Administration (REA) was established by Congress in 1936. At the president's initiative, with important legislative leadership by Representatives Sam Rayburn (D-Tex.) and John E. Rankin (D-Miss.) and Sen. George Norris, the REA was intended to provide abundant, cheap power to the great majority of the nation's thirty million rural residents then living without electricity. Rural

electric service proved to be extremely popular in Congress, particularly among members from the rural Southeast and Midwest. Private power companies, after initially opposing the REA, soon attempted to compete with REA in creating rural electric cooperatives, thereby persuading Congress to increase REA's scope and funding in its first crucial decade. The REA encouraged the development of a large network of rural electric cooperatives, which became the chief recipients of REA loans and the major means of electrifying America's farms. REA's major role in improving the quality of rural life was a significant contribution to preserving the American family farm in the Depression era. Congress further enlarged the federal government's role in farm conservation by passage of the Flood Control Act of 1936, which established the federal government's responsibility for flood control and watershed development and expanded federal authority to obtain rights-of-way and reservoir land for flood control projects.

By the time World War II ended most of the New Deal's conservation programs, the federal government had assumed a vast, continuing authority for conservation of the public domain that constituted a revolution in federal public land management. Congress and the executive-branch resource agencies had become the permanent trustees, managers, and planners of the public domain.

The Beginnings of Environmentalism. After World War II, Congress cautiously began to establish a federal role in national pollution management in response to growing air and water pollution problems. Between 1950 and 1970, Congress for the first time invested the federal government with limited authority to combat water and air pollution. The first federal pollution legislation after World War II, the Water Pollution Control Act of 1948 and its 1956 amendments, like later enactments in the 1960s, defined pollution control as a state and local governmental responsibility. The federal government's role was confined to modest financial support for pollution control research and facilities.

The Clean Air Act of 1963 authorized the federal government to initiate, at state request, abatement proceedings against violators of state air quality standards. The Motor Vehicle Air Pollution Control Act of 1965 authorized federal regulations for new-automobile emissions, and the Air Quality Control Act of 1967 required the federal and state governments to cooperate in setting emissions standards for most nonautomotive pollution sources. The

Water Pollution Control Act Amendments of 1956 authorized the federal government, with state approval, to initiate enforcement proceedings against violators of state pollution laws; the Water Quality Act of 1965 authorized the federal government to initiate cooperative federal-state standard setting for water quality. The last two bills provided modest grants and technical assistance to the states for water quality improvement.

Enforcement provisions in these laws were typically cumbersome and ineffective. This legislation nonetheless created the statutory framework for later, far more rigorous regulation through amendment. During the 1960s, many congressional members and committees gained expertise and influence in pollution control policy. From this group originated many initiatives that eventually became landmark environmental legislation in the 1970s. Among the most prominent of these legislators and legislative committees were Edmund S. Muskie (D-Maine) and his Senate Subcommittee on Air and Water Pollution; the Senate Interior and Insular Affairs Committee, chaired by Henry M. Jackson (D-Wash.); the House Health and Science Subcommittee; the Public Works committees of both chambers; and Representatives Paul G. Rogers (D-Fla.), John A. Blatnik (D-Minn.), and Emilio Q. Daddario (D-Conn.).

Congress Enters the Environmental Era. By the early 1970s, environmental pollution had become a major national problem. Most states were reluctant to regulate air or water pollution aggressively, and Washington lacked the authority to do so. But environmentalism had developed into a major social movement, and environmental protection became a compelling public, presidential, and congressional concern. Congress, impatient with state inaction, decisively shifted authority for pollution regulation to the federal government. Between 1970 and 1990, Congress passed twenty-seven major environmental laws that radically redefined the federal role in national pollution control, brought almost all major forms of environmental degradation within federal regulatory authority, and established a vast, complex new federal regulatory process to enforce these laws. This remarkable outpouring of new policies, the legislative signature of the nation's environmental era, profoundly affected the U.S. economy as well as the environment. It was the product of a broadly bipartisan, durable legislative coalition in both chambers. Unlike earlier conservation policies, the achievements were largely the result of congressional initiative, persistence, and talent.

Environmentalism has affected congressional policies, structure, and politics in many important ways. Beginning with the 1970 amendments to the Clean Air Act, the federal government has assumed the primary authority for creating and enforcing national air and water pollution standards and for scientific and technical research to support these activities. The states were made responsible for implementing and enforcing the new standards in collaboration with the federal government. Congress vested the primary responsibility for implementing these laws in the Environmental Protection Agency (EPA), created by a 1970 executive order by President Richard M. Nixon. The EPA and its ten regional offices, in turn, were expected to write regulations and provide assistance to the state environmental agencies in carrying out their regulatory duties.

The enormous economic, political, and environmental impact of these new programs has compelled Congress to commit a large and increasing amount of its time and resources to legislative oversight of environmental programs and the bureaucracies implementing them. At least twenty-eight agencies, involving eight cabinet departments and four independent commissions, share responsibility for environmental programs. Environmentalism also encouraged the proliferation of congressional committees and subcommittees between 1970 and 1990, as more legislators sought to participate in environmental policy-making. By 1993, eleven Senate standing committees, thirteen House standing committees, and perhaps one hundred of their collective subcommittees claimed some environmentally related jurisdiction. And members of Congress have had to respond to legislative pressures from an increasingly active environmental lobby. The five most important national lobbying organizations, all created after 1967, grew in collective membership between 1972 and 1990 from about 52,000 to 368,000 members and in 1990 had budgets collectively exceeding $33 million. Environmentalists today are among the most influential and visible of Washington's pressure groups.

The relationship between Congress and the EPA has been especially intense and adversarial. This conflict has often been exacerbated, as in the 1980s, by partisan disputes between congressional Democrats and Republican presidents about their respective authority to direct EPA's programs and to define its mission. Until the late 1970s, Congress had often left significant discretion to EPA in implementing environmental programs. But legislators became increasingly dissatisfied with EPA's slowness and difficulties in program implementation and distrustful of EPA's competence or commitment in its work. Congressional supervision of EPA became extremely rigorous and unrelenting: perhaps no federal regulatory agency has been more closely scrutinized. Congress now annually requires of EPA between 100 and 150 written reports and initiates more than five thousand individual inquiries to the agency. In recent sessions, EPA officials have been asked to appear before congressional committees between 92 and 214 times. During a single session of the 101st Congress (1989–1991), congressional committees received testimony from EPA 142 times. Congress now routinely writes numerous deadlines into new legislation to limit EPA's discretion in implementing the law. More than eight hundred deadlines had been mandated by 1990. The Superfund Amendments and Reauthorization Act of 1986, for instance, alone contains more than seventy-five major program deadlines for EPA.

Institutional tensions between Congress and the White House erupted into a conflict especially damaging to EPA during Ronald Reagan's first presidential term. Numerous congressional committees accused the White House and EPA administrator Anne Burford of using their administrative powers to subvert the agency's regulatory programs in violation of congressional mandates. The struggle, badly disrupting EPA's programs, ended in 1983 with Burford's resignation and White House concessions. But the larger issue of White House influence within EPA would continue to trouble Congress. Many legislators believed that several White House practices diminished EPA's responsiveness to Congress by creating for the White House an inappropriate backdoor influence in EPA's regulatory process. Among these were the requirement that the Office of Management and Budget (OMB) review all newly proposed EPA regulations to ensure that they were compatible with the White House agenda, the requirement that EPA prepare for OMB review a cost-benefit analysis for all newly proposed regulations, and the appointment of committees within the White House to review the economic impact of existing regulations.

Environmentalism also transformed federal conservation policies by creating new ecological values and standards that Congress and federal agencies now must consider in managing the public domain. One of the most comprehensive changes in conservation policies was created by the National Environmental Policy Act of 1969, which requires federal agencies to prepare for every proposed program

significantly affecting the environment a detailed environmental impact statement (EIS) in which its ecological impact must be carefully documented and evaluated. These impact statements, required of all federal resource agencies, relate to most important resource decisions. The Forest Service, for instance, must prepare for congressional and public review an EIS when setting quotas for timber cutting on any national forest. So must the Department of Transportation when proposing a new segment of interstate highway. The EIS process has created growing public awareness of the ecological implications in federal resource decisions and greater congressional attention to the environmental issues involved in bureaucratic activities over which it has oversight.

Two Decades of New Environmental Law. Among the major pieces of legislation passed between 1970 and 1990, the National Environmental Policy Act of 1969 also created the President's

ALTERNATIVE FUEL SOURCES. Sen. Larry Pressler (R-S.Dak.) demonstrates an alcohol-fuel distillery in front of the Capitol.

Council on Environmental Quality. Amendments to two earlier laws fundamentally altered the federal government's approach to air and water pollution regulation by creating the "command and control" regulatory structure that currently prevails. The Clean Air Act amendments of 1970, 1977, and 1990 required the federal government to set national air quality standards to be enforced by the states, set emissions limits for automobile pollutants, established a regulatory program for industrial toxic air emissions, and required additional controls on air emissions related to acid precipitation. The 1977 and 1990 amendments also marked a major departure from more traditional approaches to regulation by allowing "emissions trading" between regulated facilities. This new approach, considered by many economists to be more economically efficient than older methods, permitted firms to receive credits for reducing their pollution emissions below the required levels and to use the credits to offset excessive emissions elsewhere in their own facilities or to sell the credits to other firms that might need them. The Federal Water Pollution Control Act Amendments of 1972 set national water quality standards, required a state-enforced permit system to control pollution discharges into navigable waters, and authorized federal grants to the states to build waste treatment facilities.

Other laws extended federal regulation to new environmental domains. The Safe Drinking Water Act of 1974 authorized the federal government to set national drinking water safety standards and to regulate state underground pollution control programs. The Toxic Substances Control Act of 1976 similarly empowered federal authorities to ban or regulate dangerous chemicals in commerce and industry and to require testing of new chemicals. The Resource Conservation and Recovery Act of 1976 required the federal government to create regulations for the treatment, storage, transportation, and disposal of hazardous wastes. The Surface Mining Control and Reclamation Act of 1977 established national regulatory standards and enforcement procedures for the control of surface ("strip") mining. The Comprehensive Environmental Response, Compensation and Liability Act of 1980, or "Superfund," authorized the federal government to identify abandoned hazardous waste sites and to clean up the most dangerous of them.

During the 1980s, major amendments, often amounting to significant new legislative programs, were added to most of these laws. Environmental policies generally were supported in the 1970s by a broad bipartisan congressional coalition collaborating with the White House. But during President Reagan's first term, White House opposition to many existing environmental programs enforced by the EPA caused bitter conflict between environmentally minded congressional Democrats and Reagan Republicans, who were joined by conservative Democrats. The policy gridlock during this period resulted in no significant new laws until Democrats regained control of both congressional chambers in 1984. Thereafter, comprehensive amendments to the existing laws were frequently enacted. Among the most significant were the Superfund Amendments and Reauthorization Act of 1986, which increased funding for abandoned waste site cleanups and required industry to provide local communities with information on hazardous chemicals used or emitted. The Safe Drinking Water Act of 1986 reauthorized the Safe Drinking Water Act of 1976 and mandated accelerated schedules for EPA to set standards for eighty-three water pollutants.

New Challenges. George Bush's election to the presidency in 1988 was followed by few environmental initiatives from Congress or the White House. A bipartisan congressional coalition did successfully work with the president to create the Clean Air Act Amendments of 1990. This legislation for the first time required industrial controls to reduce emissions contributing to acid precipitation and created a new system of "emissions trading" to reduce the cost of industrial pollution regulation. But the White House grew increasingly averse to new environmental regulations during the serious economic recession beginning in 1990, and Congress preferred to concentrate on other issues. Nonetheless, Congress has confronted several significant environmental issues in the early 1990s.

One major challenge is to increase American involvement in global environmental management. In particular, the United States needs to make a firm commitment with other nations to reduce significantly the global emission of air pollutants associated with acid precipitation and climate warming (the greenhouse effect), to preserve global biodiversity, and to combat global deforestation. Scientific research increasingly demonstrates that global and domestic environmental degradation are intimately related. Congress can significantly increase U.S. support for research on global environmental problems, can encourage greater attention to global issues from the White House and EPA, and can create legislative initiatives for greater consultation on global issues with other nations. But legislators will inevitably be highly divided over the policies to achieve these goals. Economic interests likely to bear heavy regulatory costs for these policies, such as electric utilities and steel and automobile manufacturing, assert that scientific evidence about climate warming is too inconclusive to justify new regulations and that further study is necessary, a viewpoint shared by most congressional Republicans but opposed by environmentalists and the majority of congressional Democrats. Also, regional conflicts over the seriousness of acid precipitation and the need to remedy it exist between northeastern legislators, where the problem seems most dire, and Ohio River valley legislators, whose economies may have to assume heavy costs for controlling this pollution.

A second challenge is to create effective economic strategies for controlling air and water pollutants as an alternative to the present cumbersome and often unsuccessful approaches. The "command and control" regulatory structure embodied in the amendments to the Clean Air Act and to the Federal Water Pollution Control Act needs to be supplemented with newer approaches that use economic incentives to obtain compliance more effectively. These newer approaches should in particular be directed toward creating more economic incentives for materials recycling and for pollution prevention rather than pollution cleanup. Many environmentalists and congressional Democrats are ideologically opposed to such a marketplace approach to regulation, however. Compulsory recycling is generally opposed by primary metal refiners, the manufacturers and users of disposable containers and their materials, and numerous western legislators representing areas in which metal refining is a major industry.

Another major challenge will be the creation of a federal program to compel state and local land-use controls for nonpoint water pollution. Congress will confront few environmental tasks more difficult, yet essential, than finding a means to achieve local land-use controls, without which a major source of surface water and groundwater contamination will remain unregulated. Congress has in the past been reluctant to assert vigorous federal authority in local land-use planning because it directly threatens state and local government controls of land use. Agriculture interests, a major source of nonpoint pollution, have joined farm-state members in opposing such regulation. They are often joined by urban interests and the housing industry, where significant nonpoint pollution also

originates. But unless the federal government assumes significant authority for land-use planning or creates a regulatory structure compelling state and local governments to control nonpoint pollution, the nation's waters will become gravely degraded within a few decades.

It is also desirable that Congress provide the EPA with far greater administrative resources. At present, EPA is extremely deficient in staff and budget, and its resources are far from commensurate with its responsibilities. Congress should allow EPA more freedom in implementing mandated programs and provide the agency with a legislative charter explicitly defining what EPA's program priorities should be. Current congressional oversight of EPA's activities and the congressional tradition of writing environmental laws that permit little administrative flexibility have stifled EPA's regulatory procedures. Efforts to increase EPA's regulatory effectiveness, like other proposals for increased federal economic regulation, will also provoke strong partisan conflicts within Congress. Finally, Congress can facilitate federal environmental planning by greatly reducing the number of committees with environmental jurisdiction in each chamber. While Congress has produced a remarkable record of environmental legislation and has often assumed the leadership in national environmental policy-making, some of its greatest challenges and possibly its most important achievements lie ahead.

[*For discussion of related public policy issues, see* Agriculture; Energy and Natural Resources; National Parks and Forests; Public Lands. *See also* Energy and Natural Resources Committee, Senate; Environment and Public Works Committee, Senate; Natural Resources Committee, House; Public Works and Transportation Committee, House. *For discussion of related legislation, see* Clean Air Act; Comprehensive Environmental Response, Compensation, and Liability Act of 1980; Endangered Species Act of 1973; National Environmental Policy Act of 1969.]

BIBLIOGRAPHY

Congressional Quarterly. *The Battle for Natural Resources.* 1983.

Cooley, Richard A., and Geoffrey Wandesforde-Smith. *Congress and the Environment.* 1969.

Culhane, Paul J. *Public Land Politics: Interest Group Influence on the Forest Service and the Bureau of Land Management.* 1981.

Dunlap, Riley E., and Angela G. Mertig, eds. *American Environmentalism: The U.S. Environmental Movement, 1970–1990.* 1992.

Hays, Samuel P. *Beauty, Health and Permanence: Environmental Politics in the United States, 1955–1985.* 1987.

Hays, Samuel P. *Conservation and the Gospel of Efficiency.* 1959.

Harris, Richard A., and Sidney M. Milkis. *The Politics of Regulatory Change.* 1989.

Foss, Philip O. *Politics and Grass.* 1960.

Rosenbaum, Walter A. *Environmental Politics and Policy.* 1991.

Smith, Frank E. *The Politics of Conservation.* 1966.

Udall, Steward L. *The Quiet Crisis.* 1963.

Vig, Norman J., and Michael E. Kraft, eds. *Environmental Politics in the 1990s.* 1990.

Wilkinson, Charles E., and H. Michael Anderson. *Land and Resource Planning in the National Forests.* 1987.

WALTER A. ROSENBAUM

ENVIRONMENT AND PUBLIC WORKS COMMITTEE, SENATE.

As its name indicates, two quite different sets of issues fall within the jurisdiction of the Senate Environment and Public Works Committee. Until the late 1960s the committee's central concern was public works: highways, bridges, dams, rivers and harbor projects, public buildings, and regional development efforts such as the Tennessee Valley Authority. During the 1970s environmental issues absorbed more and more of the committee's attention. Many senators joined the committee to deal with high-profile environmental matters. The committee's jurisdiction now includes air, noise, and water pollution; regulation of nonmilitary nuclear power; hazardous waste and toxic substances control; drinking water safety; ocean dumping and environmental aspects of the outer continental shelf; endangered species protection; solid waste disposal and recycling; and environmental research. While the House has distributed jurisdiction for environmental issues to several committees, the Senate has placed most environmental matters within this one committee. In 1977 the word *environment* was added to the committee's name to signify the importance of the new set of issues.

When the committee dealt primarily with public works projects, it was viewed as a pork barrel committee suitable for senators eager to deliver tangible benefits to their constituents. This side of the committee was personified by Jennings Randolph (D-W.Va.), who chaired the committee from 1966 to 1980, and Quentin N. Burdick (D-N.D.), who served as chairman from 1986 to 1992. First elected to Congress in 1932, Randolph never abandoned his New Deal commitment to using public works to bolster the economy in his poverty-ridden state. His greatest interest was in road building.

Neither Randolph nor Burdick devoted much attention to environmental issues. They gave subcommittee chairmen great latitude, so long as they did not trample on local concerns—such as high-sulfur West Virginia coal. Most important work, including markup sessions, occurred in subcommittee. The full committee usually limited its role to exercising quality control in the final stages of the bill-writing process.

The principal architect of the committee's transformation in the 1970s was Edmund S. Muskie (D-Me.). Ironically, Muskie never sought the committee assignment. Majority leader Lyndon B. Johnson placed Muskie on the Public Works Committee in 1958 to punish him for an early display of independence. Muskie was instrumental in the formation of a new subcommittee on air and water pollution, which he chaired for many years. The Muskie subcommittee—as it became known—played a central role in writing the Clean Air Act, the Clean Water Act, Superfund legislation, and other important environmental statutes of the 1970s.

The change in the committee's business is reflected in the composition of its subcommittees. As late as 1972 four of its six subcommittees dealt with public works and economic development. In 1992 five of its six subcommittees focused on environmental protection.

One of the committee's most important characteristics is bipartisanship. The Republicans on the committee share the Democrats' commitment to both public works and environmental protection. When Republicans took control of the committee in 1981, the new chairman, Robert T. Stafford of Vermont, frequently clashed with the Reagan administration on environmental issues. He had worked closely with Muskie for many years and was even more devoted to the cause than were many Democrats. His successor as ranking Republican, John H. Chafee of Rhode Island, resembled Stafford in that regard. Republicans appointed to the committee in recent years, however, have been considerably more conservative and probusiness than Stafford and Chafee. If this trend continues, committee deliberations could become more partisan and ideologically charged.

Despite the importance of public works projects for the West, only five of the committee's seventeen members come from that region. Moreover, easterners chair all but one of the subcommittees. For many years the committee has had an unusually high proportion of New Englanders, many of whom were attracted by the panel's jurisdiction over environmental matters.

The committee's bipartisanship allowed its subcommittees to develop aggressive staffs. Muskie's subcommittee not only wrote key parts of environmental laws but carefully monitored the activities of the Environmental Protection Agency. The tradition lived on after Muskie left the committee in 1979 to become secretary of State. Subcommittee staff members developed close ties with environmental groups, which viewed Environment and Public Works as the "conscience of the Senate." Industry lobbyists, in contrast, have at times dismissed the committee as a "wholly owned subsidiary of the environmental community" (Bryner, 1993, p. 99).

The history of two important bills sheds light on the operation of the committee. During the 1980s it took the lead in pushing for stronger air pollution control, particularly measures to reduce acid rain. The committee repeatedly reported out legislation that pleased environmentalists but lacked sufficient support to pass the Senate. Several times party leaders refused to schedule its clear air bills for floor debate. The Clean Air Act of 1990 passed only after Senate majority leader George E. Mitchell (himself a former chairman of the pollution control subcommittee) ignored the committee's bill and negotiated a separate deal with the White House.

These events weakened the committee's reputation within the Senate. When Burdick, the last of the old guard, died in 1992, Max Baucus (D-Mont.) became chairman of the full committee. Baucus had previously chaired the subcommittee that wrote the clean air bill rejected by party leaders. In his new role Baucus has had to search for compromises that will appease both the committee's environmentally conscious majority and its increasingly vocal critics on the floor.

A year later Congress passed a bill that made major changes in federal spending on transportation. The subcommittee on Water Resources, Transportation, and Infrastructure, chaired by Sen. Daniel Patrick Moynihan (D-N.Y.), played a major role in writing the Surface Transportation Reauthorization Act of 1991. The law reversed the committee's longstanding commitment to road building. It gave states much more flexibility to use federal funds for mass transit; it also emphasized regional planning and efforts to reduce automobile pollution in urban areas. The act demonstrated that environmental protection had replaced public works construction as the committee's dominant concern.

[See also Public Works and Transportation, Committee, House.]

BIBLIOGRAPHY

Asbell, Bernard. *The Senate Nobody Knows.* 1978.
Bryner, Gary. *Blue Skies, Green Politics: The Clean Air Act of 1990.* 1993.
Cohen, Richard. *Washington at Work: Back Rooms and Clean Air.* 1992.
Congressional Quarterly Inc. "Highways, Mass Transit Funded." In *Congressional Quarterly Almanac.* 1991. Pp. 137–151.

R. SHEP MELNICK

EQUAL RIGHTS AMENDMENT. Although the Equal Rights Amendment (ERA) is most closely identified with the women's movement of the 1970s, the first version was introduced on 10 December 1923 by Rep. Daniel R. Anthony, Jr., a Republican from Kansas and the nephew of suffragist Susan B. Anthony. Three days later another Kansan, Sen. Charles Curtis, the Republican whip, introduced a parallel bill in the Senate. The amendment, drafted by Alice Paul of the National Woman's party (NWP), read: "Men and women shall have equal rights throughout the United States and every place subject to its jurisdiction."

The first ERA quickly became the focal point of disagreement between women activists over the issue of special labor laws for women. Attempts to compromise came to nothing, and the rift obstructed further action in Congress until World War II produced a brief spate of interest in recognition of women's work in the war effort. ERA proponents managed to persuade committees in both the House and the Senate to hold hearings and report the bills. In May 1943 the Senate Judiciary Committee approved an ERA by a vote of 12 to 4, changing the wording to bring it in line with the Nineteenth Amendment. The new version, also supplied by Alice Paul, read: "Equality of rights under the law shall not be denied or abridged by the United States, or by any State, on account of sex." The first floor vote took place in the Senate in 1946, its proponents winning 38 to 35, a majority but not the two-thirds majority needed to send the amendment to the states for ratification.

Opponents found a successful strategy to thwart the ERA. Named for its introducer, Sen. Carl Hayden (D-Ariz.), the "Hayden rider" stated that the

Ratification of the Equal Rights Amendment

STATES RATIFYING

1972

Hawaii, Delaware, Nebraska, New Hampshire, Idaho, Iowa, Kansas, Texas, Maryland, Tennessee, Alaska, Rhode Island, New Jersey, Wisconsin, West Virginia, Colorado, New York, Michigan, Kentucky, Massachusetts, Pennsylvania, California

1973

Wyoming, South Dakota, Minnesota, Oregon, New Mexico, Vermont, Connecticut, Washington

1974

Maine, Montana, Ohio

1975

North Dakota

1977

Nebraska

STATES RESCINDING

1973

Indiana

1974

Tennessee

1977

Idaho

1978

Kentucky (rescission bill vetoed by the acting governor)

STATES NOT RATIFYING

Alabama, Arizona, Arkansas, Florida, Georgia, Illinois, Louisiana, Mississippi, Missouri, Nevada, North Carolina, Oklahoma, South Carolina, Utah, Virginia

---

first provision "shall not be construed to impair any rights, benefits, or exemptions . . . conferred by law upon members of the female sex." In 1950, to the dismay of ERA proponents, the Senate voted for both equality for women and special treatment, adopting the rider on the floor by a vote of 51 to 31 and the ERA by a vote of 63 to 19. In 1953 the Senate again adopted both. In the 86th Congress (1959–1961), Senate sponsors withdrew the resolution after the rider was again adopted on the floor. The opposition of House Judiciary Committee chair Emanuel Celler (D-N.Y.), who wanted to preserve labor laws for women, kept the amendment from reaching the floor of that chamber.

Two factors invigorated the ERA by the 1970s: a ban against discrimination in employment passed in 1964 led to the elimination of labor laws for women only, thus removing one source of opposition to the ERA; and a reborn women's rights movement now united around the goal of constitutional equality for women through constitutional amendment. Congress responded quickly. In June 1970 Martha W. Griffiths (D-Mich.) gathered the signatures needed to bring the ERA to the floor despite the opposition of committee chair Emanuel Celler. After only a brief debate, on 10 August the House approved the amendment by a vote of 350 to 15. Supporters then confronted a brief setback: on 13 October the Senate, by a vote of 36 to 33, added a provision exempting women from the draft; ERA proponents asked that the bill be killed for the session.

Meanwhile, women's organizations inundated Congress members with mail and telephone calls;

letters arrived in the tens of thousands. In March 1971 the House Judiciary Committee added a new version of the old rider, but in October the House bowed to the wishes of feminists and rejected the proviso 104 to 254, adopting the original ERA by a vote of 354 to 23. On 29 February 1972 the Senate Judiciary Committee voted 15 to 1 to report the original amendment. ERA opponent Samuel J. Ervin, Jr. (D.-N.C.) introduced nine amendments on the Senate floor, but all were defeated; none received more than 18 votes. On 22 March 1972 the Senate passed the ERA by a vote of 84 to 8, sending it to the states with a seven-year deadline for ratification.

Twenty-two states ratified by the end of the year and eight states more in early 1973, all either unanimously or by wide margins. But as before, success generated powerful opposition. The Supreme Court's *Roe v. Wade* decision in January 1973 legalizing abortion facilitated the mobilization of a conservative anti-ERA coalition. Arguments that the ERA and abortion were linked, and that the amendment would legalize homosexual marriage, eliminate support laws, abolish single-sex public rest rooms, and require the military to use women in combat succeeded in stalling the amendment's progress. Three states ratified in 1974, only one in 1975, and one in 1977. Between 1973 and 1977 three states voted to rescind their ratifications, a gesture whose legal effect remained ambiguous.

Supporters now feared that the amendment would not win the additional three states needed before its ratification deadline in March 1979. Rep. Elizabeth Holtzman (D-N.Y.) and Sen. Birch Bayh (D-Ind.) initiated a successful effort to extend the ratification deadline, finally winning an additional thirty-nine months in the fall of 1978. But the additional time brought no further successes, and on 30 June 1982 the deadline arrived without ratification by a three-fourths majority of the states, as required by the Constitution.

Although the amendment continued to be prominent on the agenda of feminist organizations, after 1982 feminist activity focused on changing the membership of the state legislatures to improve chances for a future ratification attempt.

[*See also* Women's Issues and Rights.]

BIBLIOGRAPHY

Berry, Mary Frances. *Why ERA Failed: Politics, Women's Rights, and the Amending Process of the Constitution.* 1986.
Boles, Janet K. *The Politics of the Equal Rights Amendment: Conflict and the Decision Process.* 1979.
Harrison, Cynthia. *On Account of Sex: The Politics of Women's Issues, 1945 to 1968.* 1988.
Hoff-Wilson, Joan, ed. *Rights of Passage: The Past and Future of the ERA.* 1986.

Cynthia Harrison

ERVIN, SAMUEL J., JR. (1896–1985), Democratic senator from North Carolina (1954–1974); leading opponent of civil rights legislation in the 1950s, 1960s, and 1970s; champion of civil liberties; chair of the Senate Watergate Committee. When a Republican senator challenged Sam Ervin's aggressive questioning of a witness during the Senate's televised investigation into the Watergate affair, nicknamed the "Ervin hearings," the North Carolinian drawled, "Well, I'm just an old country lawyer and I don't know the finer ways to do it. I just have to do it my way." During his twenty years in the Senate, Ervin often relied on mountain stories, biblical quotations, and old-fashioned southern manners to disarm political opponents and sway public opinion. But Ervin's simple country-lawyer charm masked his sophisticated political acumen as well as his complex background.

After graduating from the University of North Carolina at Chapel Hill in 1917, Ervin served with distinction in World War I, earned a degree from Harvard Law School in 1924, and practiced law in North Carolina for thirty-one years. He served as a defense attorney, a district judge, a superior court

SAMUEL J. ERVIN, JR. At his desk, with some of the letters he received protesting government snooping, February 1971.   LIBRARY OF CONGRESS

judge, and an associate justice on the North Carolina Supreme Court. Ervin, who was born in 1896, the year of the *Plessy v. Ferguson* decision, was appointed to the Senate just a month after the *Brown v. Board of Education* ruling in 1954. His steadfast opposition to civil rights legislation, which he attacked as "unwise and unconstitutional," earned him a reputation among his friends as one of the Senate's foremost constitutional experts and a reputation among his critics as a rational segregationist who used the Constitution as a cloak for political obstruction. Ervin insisted, however, that he only opposed civil rights measures in order to "preserve the Constitution," and he explained, "It is not the 'civil rights' of some, but the civil liberty of all on which I take my stand."

In the 1960s, Ervin expanded his political agenda not only by fighting against civil rights but by fighting for civil liberties. As chairman of the Senate's Subcommittee on Constitutional Rights, he championed the political rights of Native Americans, the legal rights of the mentally ill, and the privacy rights of employees of the federal government. He sponsored the Indian Bill of Rights and the Bail Reform Act, and he surprised his southern colleagues by supporting the Supreme Court's ban on prayer in the public schools. However, on most issues Ervin remained a loyal southern conservative in his political positions, including his support of the Vietnam War and his opposition to welfare programs, consumer protection, labor unions, civil rights, and the Equal Rights Amendment. In the early 1970s, Ervin's concern for civil liberties led him into a series of constitutional clashes with President Richard M. Nixon that culminated in his appointment as the chair of the Senate's Watergate investigation.

In the summer of 1973, Ervin became a national folk hero during the televised Watergate hearings. The senator's concern for constitutional government and his genuine moral outrage served as a dramatic foil to the unrepentant intransigence of the Nixon officials who testified before him. It was during these hearings that Nixon's popular support began to wither under the mounting revelations of what Attorney General John Mitchell called "the White House Horrors."

At the time of his death in 1985, Ervin's reputation as a foe of civil rights, a protector of civil liberties, and a defender of the Constitution ironically prompted politicians from both the left and right to praise him as "the last of the Founding Fathers."

BIBLIOGRAPHY

Clancy, Paul R. *Just a Country Lawyer: A Biography of Senator Sam Ervin.* 1974.
Ervin, Sam J., Jr. *Preserving The Constitution: The Autobiography of Senator Sam Ervin.* 1984.

KARL E. CAMPBELL

ESPIONAGE ACT (1917; 40 Stat. 217–231).

America's April 1917 entry into World War I brought with it the first congressional legislation aimed at espionage and treason since the Alien and Sedition Acts of 1798: the Espionage Act of 1917 and the group of amendments to it that were passed as the Sedition Act of 1918.

Bills aimed at both espionage and criticism of American policy were introduced by two southern Democrats, Rep. Edwin Y. Webb of North Carolina and Sen. Charles A. Culberson of Texas. They provided for press censorship, restrictions on the use of the mails for "treasonable" matter, and penalties for interference with the military effort. The censorship portion set off a storm of congressional controversy. House Speaker James Beauchamp (Champ) Clark declared that censorship of the press was "in flat contradiction of the Constitution" and progressive Hiram W. Johnson and conservative Henry Cabot Lodge condemned it. Congress dropped the provision, but the rest of the bill sped through, and President Woodrow Wilson signed it on 5 June 1917.

Postmaster General Albert S. Burleson and Attorney General Thomas W. Gregory vied with one another in clamping down on what they considered to be treasonable utterances. And within a year the president asked Congress for amendments to strengthen the Espionage Act by extending its reach to "profane, scurrilous, or abusive language about the form of government . . . the Constitution . . . or the flag of the United States, or the uniform of the Army and Navy." The result—the Sedition Act—became law on 16 May 1918.

Under these statutes some pro-German newspapers and speakers and, far more often, socialist and other radical antiwar voices were suppressed and punished. In its 1919 *Schenck v. United States* and *Abrams v. United States* decisions, the Supreme Court upheld the constitutionality of this legislation. Congress allowed the law to expire in 1921.

BIBLIOGRAPHY

Kennedy, David M. *Over Here: The First World War and American Society.* 1980.

Murphy, Paul L. *World War I and the Origin of Civil Liberties in the United States.* 1979.

Scheiber, Harry N. *The Wilson Administration and Civil Liberties, 1917–1921.* 1960.

MORTON KELLER

ETHICS AND CORRUPTION IN CONGRESS.

In American society, distrust of politics and politicians is a deeply ingrained cultural feature. Many people assume that members of Congress cannot be trusted and that "political ethics" is a contradiction in terms.

That assumption has constituted a staple of humorists at least since Mark Twain wrote that there is no criminal class in America—except Congress. Although popular cynicism about political ethics has not stopped people from running for Congress or from getting elected and reelected, it has added to the natural tension within the political system over how congressional standards and ethics are set and enforced.

According to the U.S. Constitution, Article I, section 5, Congress has the unique power of governing itself and its members: "Each House may determine the Rules of its Proceedings, punish its Members for disorderly Behavior, and with the concurrence of two thirds, expel a Member." This constitutional power serves as the basis for the congressional system of ethics. It means, obviously, that Congress has the responsibility to police itself, even though members of Congress are still subject to the dictates of criminal law and, except for official responsibilities and speech and debate, to civil proceedings as well. At the same time, lawmakers are judged individually every two or six years by the voters.

The self-regulatory aspect of Congress has fueled public suspicion; it has also produced within Congress substantial tension and frustration—a frustration compounded by the reality that standards of official conduct regularly change as overall standards and ethics evolve. Because of the contradictory nature of representative government, establishing sound ethical guidelines that balance the public interest against the private concerns of representatives has proved complex. Members of Congress must live with this inherent tension, and the ethics codes and standards intended to guide congressional behavior often simply add to their frustration.

Nonetheless, ethical standards and a system of oversight and discipline are necessary if Congress is to maintain its institutional legitimacy. To be sure, ethical standards are constantly changing as society changes; what would clearly be considered corruption today was perfectly acceptable in an earlier era. For example, in 1833, Sen. Daniel Webster argued vigorously in the Senate for the protection of Nicholas Biddle's Bank of the United States against attack from President Andrew Jackson. Subsequently, he wrote to Biddle, "If it is wished that my relation to the Bank should be continued, it may be well to send me the usual retainers." Webster ultimately received $32,000 for his efforts on behalf of the bank.

Whatever the definition of graft and corruption, however, they have always existed in government to some extent. The onset of organized interest group lobbying in the 1830s has often been credited with bringing more extensive corruption, more bribery, and monumental conflicts of interest. Industrialization in the 1850s expanded lobbying and group involvement, thereby augmenting congressional corruption. Popular gambling houses of the time, such as Edward Pendleton's Palace of Fortune, worked closely with lobbyists. If a legislator fell into debt with a house, the manager could steer his vote on a piece of legislation by threatening exposure or demanding payment. Lobbyists reciprocated managers' efforts through patronage as well as special gifts. One wealthy industrialist arrived at Pendleton's offering a team of horses. If such events occurred frequently, they could still generate public outrage whenever they were uncovered and reported.

Lobbying, and attendant corruption, grew steadily until the Grant administration of the early 1870s, an era particularly marked by political debauchery. The most famous scandal during this period was one involving Crédit Mobilier, a joint stock company controlled by Union Pacific Railroad. Rep. Oakes Ames (R-Mass.), also a director of Crédit Mobilier and Union Pacific, bribed his fellow congressmen with stock to guarantee federal subsidies to the railroad. The exposure of the scheme in 1872 revealed a list of eighteen current or former legislators in both parties who allegedly received stock. Although Congress officially censured only two representatives, Ames and Democratic leader James Brooks of New York, the event fomented strong public distrust in the institution.

Soon after the Crédit Mobilier incident, Congress made a bad situation worse when it voted itself a pay raise, increasing legislators' remuneration from $5,000 to $7,000 per year. The public might have grudgingly accepted the raise in itself, but it became outraged when Congress voted to apply it retroactively, granting members back pay for that Congress even though the measure was passed on the last day of the session and more than half of those who benefited were lame ducks.

In other scandals of the era, Secretary of War William W. Belknap was impeached for selling Indian trading posts to the highest bidders, and a number of candidates or their supporters were accused of bribing voters for support or intimidating them from going to the polls at all. There were also sex scandals, including one involving Senators Roscoe Conkling (R-N.Y.) and William Sprague (R-R.I.) and Sprague's wife, that caught public attention and intensified the sense of corruption inside government.

Periodically throughout American history, scandals or allegations of scandal have erupted to reinforce public outrage over Washington's illicit politics; examples include the Whiskey Ring of 1875, the Teapot Dome scandal of 1922–1923, the Internal Revenue Service scandal of 1950–1951, Watergate and "Koreagate" in the 1970s, and Abscam and the savings and loan scandals in the 1980s. There followed the House bank and post office scandals, accusations of misconduct against Speaker James C. Wright, Jr. (D-Tex.), and scandals involving members under fire for allegations ranging from sexual misconduct to personal use of government funds. In several cases, ethics or lobbying reforms ensued. These scandals contributed to the delegitimation of Congress and its self-policing mechanisms and helped shape the system that exists today.

Understanding the present system involves reviewing the historical precedents, evaluating the structural and legal approaches adopted through the years, and outlining the current set of ethical codes and standards. Furthermore, because reform has often evolved in response to some scandal or case of ethical wrongdoing, a few examples can furnish valuable insight into the conduct of members of Congress and the rationale behind the system they have devised.

Expulsion and Censure. In its original form Article I, section 5 did not include the phrase "with the concurrence of two thirds." This was added at the suggestion of James Madison during debate at the Constitutional Convention of 1787. Madison asserted that the right of expulsion was "too important to be exercised by a bare majority of a quorum, and in emergencies might be dangerously abused."

Belying Madison's concerns, Congress has exercised its disciplinary powers sparingly through the years. Lawmakers have been reluctant to punish their own, and when possible they have adopted less stringent and often symbolic forms of punishment. By 1993, only fifteen senators and four representatives had been expelled in the history of Congress. Expulsion is the most severe form of punishment and has traditionally been reserved for cases involving criminal abuse of the office or disloyalty. All but two cases of expulsion occurred during the tumultuous years of the Civil War, when some Southern members were charged with supporting a rebellion. At one point ten Senators were expelled in a single day, 11 July 1861, though one expulsion was later annulled. Of the two remaining cases, one involved a charge of conspiracy in 1797, and the other, expelling Rep. Michael O. Myers (D-Pa.), involved personal corruption and bribery in the Abscam scandal of the late 1970s and early 1980s.

Unsuccessful attempts at expelling members of Congress have arisen from charges such as assault on a fellow member, killing another member in a duel, sedition, corruption, and even Mormonism. In the case of the duel, the surviving member was not even subjected to censure, a less severe form of punishment than expulsion. In 1838, Rep. Jonathan Cilley, a Democrat from Maine, was fatally wounded by Rep. William J. Graves, a Whig from Kentucky. While a majority of the investigating committee recommended that Graves be expelled, their report was never taken up by the full House. Apparently dueling among members was not infrequent and had commonly gone unremarked.

The more lenient punishment, censure, requires only a majority vote, as opposed to the two-thirds required for a vote of expulsion. The House and Senate differ somewhat in their approaches to censure. In the Senate, members may speak before the chamber in their own behalf, whereas in the House, members come before the Speaker and are formally denounced without any opportunity to defend themselves. Some of the offenses that have warranted censure in the House include insulting the Speaker or another representative, assaulting a senator, treasonable and offensive utterances, corruption, and financial misconduct.

Over time, the House has censured a total of twenty-two members; the Senate has censured (or "denounced" or "condemned") nine. The first formal House censure was in 1832, issued to Rep. William Stanbery, an Ohio anti-Jacksonian, for what was considered unacceptable and offensive

SENATE SELECT COMMITTEE ON INVESTIGATION OF CHARGES AGAINST BURTON K. WHEELER. *Left to right at the table,* Senators William E. Borah (R-Idaho), chairman, Claude A. Swanson (D-Va.), Thaddeus H. Caraway (D-Ark.), Charles L. McNary (R-Oreg.), and Thomas Sterling (R-S.Dak.), 1924.   LIBRARY OF CONGRESS

language. He had said, "The eyes of the Speaker [Andrew Stevenson] are too frequently turned from the chair you occupy toward the White House."

Senators have been censured for breach of confidence, assault, bringing the Senate into disrepute, obstruction of the legislative process, and financial misconduct. One of the more notorious cases of censure in the Senate involved Sen. Joseph R. McCarthy (R-Wis.). In 1954, McCarthy was disciplined by his Senate colleagues for failing to cooperate with the Subcommittee on Privileges and Elections in their investigation of his behavior, for obstructing the constitutional process by harassing the members of that committee, and for generally bringing the Senate into disrepute. Although McCarthy went on record as having been censured, the actual term used by the Senate was *condemned.*

Another important case was that of Sen. Thomas J. Dodd (D-Conn.) in 1967. Dodd was censured for

using campaign funds to cover personal expenses and for fraudulently billing travel costs to the government. His was the first case taken on by the newly established Select Committee on Standards and Conduct.

In the late 1980s, both the House and the Senate witnessed cases of censure and denouncement that involved financial wrongdoing. This trend primarily reflected the increasing importance of money in the campaign process and Congress's inability to devise an adequate system of codes and standards to guide members in handling their congressional finances. Many members accused of financial wrongdoing have pleaded their own uncertainty over the boundaries of propriety in serving constituents.

In addition to expulsion and censure Congress has through the years come up with lesser forms of punishment, such as reprimand, condemnation, and loss of chairmanship or seniority. These penalties are largely symbolic and are designed to quell public anxiety without ruining a member's political career.

Evolution of Ethical Standards. The institutionalization of ethical standards and practices in Congress has been an evolutionary process. In early Congresses, the rules were loose and often inconsistently applied. The establishment of House and Senate ethics committees in the 1960s represented a major step toward uniformity. These committees were formed in the wake of a series of scandals in the early 1960s, highlighted by revelations about Robert G. "Bobby" Baker. As secretary to the Democratic majority in the Senate, Baker was accused of influence peddling and bribery; his actions tarnished the entire Senate leadership.

The Senate Ethics Committee, established in 1964, was originally called the Select Committee on Standards and Conduct. It was given the task of drawing up a code of conduct and was authorized to receive complaints and recommend disciplinary action. Members hoped that the bipartisan composition of the committee would shield it against the charges of prejudice and partisanship that had marred ethics investigations in the past. As already mentioned, the committee's first official action involved an inquiry into the activities of Senator Dodd.

The Powell case. In the House, the Committee on Standards of Official Conduct gained permanent status and was given investigative and enforcement powers in 1968. The committee was formed largely in reaction to the case of Rep. Adam Clayton Powell, Jr. (D-N.Y.). Within the scope of congressional ethics, the Powell case remains significant because it resulted in a precedent-setting Supreme Court ruling that limited Congress's power to exclude recalcitrant members.

Powell, who was first elected to Congress in 1944 and served as chairman of the Education and Labor Committee from 1961 to 1967, was widely considered the most powerful African American of his time. He got into trouble with the Internal Revenue Service and was indicted on a charge of tax evasion. He was also involved in two civil suits, one in which he was sued for libel by a constituent and the other involving the fraudulent transfer of property.

Many members, upset by Powell's behavior and blatant disregard for the law, sought to take action against him. First, the House Democratic Caucus removed him as chairman of the Education and Labor Committee (the last time a committee chairman had been deposed was in 1925). This occurred in January 1967, after Powell's Harlem constituents had elected him to a twelfth term in Congress.

In March 1967, against the recommendation of a select committee established to investigate Powell's "qualifications," the full House adopted a resolution to exclude him from the 90th Congress—the first such exclusion since 1919. Because Powell had not yet been seated, a simple majority of the House was able to vote to exclude him; had he been seated, only a vote for expulsion—requiring a two-thirds majority—could have removed him from office. The final resolution to exclude Powell was adopted by a vote of 307 to 116.

Powell filed suit against the House, and the proceedings eventually reached the Supreme Court. With his case pending before the Court, Powell entered his name in the special election held to fill his own vacant seat. He won the election but never applied to the House to be seated. Powell ran again in 1968 and again was victorious. In January 1969, he was sworn in as a member of the 91st Congress, after a two-year exile (during which his district went unrepresented). Later that year, the Court ruled that because Powell met the constitutional requirements for membership, the House had wrongly excluded him. Powell's case made clear that the House needed to develop some form of internal discipline—a code of conduct and a means of enforcing it.

The original codes of conduct established by the House and Senate ethics committees were general in nature and vague in content. Congress intended them largely to restore public confidence, eroded by certain ethical scandals of the mid 1970s.

The Hays scandal. One impropriety with significant consequences involved Rep. Wayne L. Hays, a Democrat from Ohio, and his employee-mistress, Elizabeth Ray. Although Hays resigned from the House before being officially disciplined, his case marked an important turning point in the level of scrutiny given to the personal lives of members of Congress. The scandal was uncovered by a pair of *Washington Post* reporters. Because of the ground swell of attention and publicity generated by the story, similar charges of sexual scandals involving other members of Congress and top government officials readily surfaced. Ben Bradlee, the *Post*'s executive editor, likened the Hays affair to Watergate: it brought public and especially press attention to congressional abuses and excesses, just as Watergate had for the executive branch.

This and subsequent scandals seemed to affect the behavior of many members of Congress profoundly. More caution was evident in their handling of financial and personnel issues, and many were more discreet in their personal affairs.

Strengthening the codes. Pressure built both within and outside Congress to toughen the ethics codes. In 1976 the House formed a fifteen-member bipartisan group—the Commission on Administrative Review, commonly known as the Obey Commission—to draft a new code of ethics that would address a whole host of issues, including congressional perquisites, acceptance of outside gifts and favors, financial disclosure, and limits on campaign financing. To no one's surprise, opinions among House members conflicted. Ultimately the commission came up with a series of proposals that would substantially change procedures and regulations regarding members' financial accountability. The proposals included a ban on office accounts; a limitation on outside earned income, including fees or honoraria; limitations on acceptance of gifts, use of the frank (or free postage), and reimbursed travel; and a more rigorous system of financial disclosure.

The commission's proposals survived the scrutiny of three separate House committees and were adopted in March 1977, nearly intact. The most controversial issue was the proposed limit on earned income. Because the limitation did not apply to unearned income derived from financial investments such as stocks and bonds, opponents argued that it would unduly burden less wealthy members. In the end Speaker Thomas P. (Tip) O'Neill, Jr. (D-Mass.), reminded his colleagues that the credibility of the institution was at stake and urged that all members would have to make sacrifices toward restoring public confidence in Congress.

In 1977 the Senate set about devising its own official code of ethics by establishing the Special Committee on Official Conduct. The committee came up with a plan that, in general terms, greatly resembled that of the House. One difference was that the Senate code extended many of its provisions to cover key staff members. In addition, the Senate code forbade all lobbying activities of former Senators and Senate employees for a specified period after leaving the Senate, prohibited certain kinds of employment discrimination by senators in hiring their staffs, and required that the Senate ethics committee publicly justify all decisions regarding allegations against members or staff.

The final vote of 86 to 9 in support of the code's passage in no way reflected the depth of conflict that characterized the debate. Many senators voted to institute the code mainly because they feared the political ramifications of voting against it. Arguments against limitations on earned income echoed those in the House. In the end, the new Senate code was a clear improvement over the previous one, which had been largely symbolic, offering little guidance, few means of enforcement, and many gaps and inconsistencies.

Adoption of these new ethics codes in both the House and Senate was closely tied to a congressional pay raise that took effect in February 1977. Members knew that in order to make a pay raise more palatable to the public, they would have to clean up their act, so to speak. In fact the commission that recommended the pay raise in 1976 issued a strong statement warning that a new code of ethics represented "the indispensable prelude to a popular acceptance of a general increase in executive, legislative and judicial salaries."

Ethics in Government Act (1978). With each house having passed its own new code of conduct, Congress moved to draft a comprehensive code of ethics that could be enacted into law. The Ethics in Government Act was signed into law in October 1978. It mandated detailed financial disclosure by federal officials and placed new restrictions on the license of former federal officials (not including members of Congress and their staffs) to lobby their former agencies. In addition, the bill encompassed most of the major elements of the House and Senate ethics codes. It did not refer only to Congress, though, as it was in part a response to the Watergate scandal of the mid 1970s, which had cast a dark shadow over the executive branch. In fact, one important provision of the bill set up an Office of Government Ethics to oversee financial disclosures and possible conflicts of interest within the executive branch.

Another important provision of the 1978 law authorized special prosecutors to investigate and prosecute high-ranking executive-branch officials, separate and apart from the activities of the attorney general's office. Supporters of the provision aimed to eliminate the conflict inherent in a system in which the attorney general might be responsible for investigating the president who appointed him or her. The position of special prosecutor—or independent counsel, as it was renamed in 1983—was devised to operate outside the reach of executive-branch coercion. The 1978 law was also intended to restore public confidence in the political system, particularly in the wake of the Watergate scandal.

In the early 1990s a great debate was raging over whether the law had served its purpose or had become a blunt weapon for Congress and ambitious, unchecked prosecutors to use against executive-branch officials for political purposes. Although prosecutorial independence had generally been maintained, the power wielded by independent counsels had been politicized and in some cases abused. Critics of the office further claimed that it reflected a double standard: if the executive branch cannot be trusted to police its own, neither can Congress, so the independent counsel law should have applied to the legislature as well.

That argument suffers from two problems. First, the Framers specifically charged Congress with policing itself, believing that voters would prove the ultimate judges of elected officials. Appointed officials are treated by a different standard. Second, Congress is in fact policed by others, including executive-branch prosecutors—as occurred in the Abscam case, discussed below. In addition, the attorney general can choose to appoint a special counsel to investigate wrongdoing by members of Congress. Attorney General William Barr exercised this prerogative to investigate overdrafts by representatives from the House bank in 1992, when he appointed retired federal judge Malcolm Wilkey to take over the investigation from the U.S. attorney in Washington.

Even though some criticism might have been overstated or misguided, the independent counsel law still had problems. Some analysts believe that the law contributed in the long run to the culture of scandal pervading Washington in the late twentieth century. They argue further that Congress wielded an inordinate amount of power over the executive branch and that this power threatened the traditional integrity of the system of checks and balances.

The Iran-contra scandal and subsequent legal proceedings have been cited by some as evidence of the current system's inadequacy. Independent counsel Lawrence Walsh came for many to symbolize a process in which tens of millions of taxpayer dollars were spent on political prosecutions that some considered abusive and ultimately obstructive of the normal functioning of the criminal justice system. Furthermore, critics of the system express doubt that Justice Earl Warren's support of Congress's investigative powers for the "furtherance of a legislative purpose" was intended to generate what they perceive as political harassment, character assassination, and partisan bickering.

The creation of the independent counsel can be linked in large part to the Watergate scandal of 1972–1974. Watergate really ushered in the modern era of ethics reform, not only because it brought into question the standard of ethical behavior proper for public officials, but also because of the instrumental role the media played in uncovering the scandal. In the past, reporters had hesitated to publicize allegations concerning ethics abuses by elected officials; the Watergate affair paved the way for more active and aggressive involvement. In essence the press adopted a much more assertive role as watchdog over the government establishment, heightening public awareness of and interest in the ethical behavior of government officials.

Developments during the 1980s. The development of congressional codes of conduct and the passage of the Ethics in Government Act were indeed important steps toward developing a system of responsible and ethical government. As a series of ethical scandals during the 1980s demonstrated, however, inherent weaknesses remained in the system. Evidently members of Congress either failed to comprehend the regulations and standards laid out in their own codes of conduct or assumed that fellow members would show leniency in enforcing those codes, especially because ethical indiscretions by individual members often reflect poorly on the institution as a whole. In addition, with campaign costs escalating in the 1980s, members were under increasing pressure to solicit new donors and maintain large campaign funds. Simultaneously, the public was becoming increasingly cynical about Congress as an institution.

During the 1980s little was accomplished in the way of ethics reform. At the same time there were many scandals and investigations involving members of Congress, perhaps indicating the need for reform and clarification of the standards established in the late 1970s. That only a small percentage of these investigations resulted in any real disciplinary action caused many to question the effectiveness of the system. During the 1980s, in the view of many, there was not much a member of Congress could do short of criminal indictment to incur expulsion or even censure. As a result, Congress was criticized for failing to punish its members adequately for ethical infractions.

Abscam. The new decade was ushered in by what may have been the biggest scandal in congressional history. The incident, commonly known as Abscam, involved six representatives and one senator and resulted in the expulsion of one House member and the resignation of three. The three other lawmakers escaped congressional discipline when they were defeated at the polls before their investigations could be completed.

The scandal arose out of an undercover operation in which FBI agents disguised as businessmen and Arab sheiks enticed several members of Congress into accepting bribes in return for certain legislative and political favors. Five of the seven members implicated were actually videotaped accepting cash or stocks, and those videotapes were seen widely by TV viewers throughout the country. In the end, seven members of Congress were convicted of criminal wrongdoing.

The speed and severity of Congress's action in dealing with the Abscam scandal contrasted with its usual disposition of ethical scandals. Perhaps actual criminal wrongdoing provided an unmistakable motivation. Congress has had more difficulty in dealing with infractions that fall within the written law but outside the boundaries of what is popularly accepted as proper behavior for public officials.

Sex scandals. In 1982 the media played a prominent role in bringing to light allegations concerning a sex and drug ring that involved members of Congress and teenage congressional pages. Assertions of misconduct were aired on TV and printed in the papers before any official inquiry had been made. The ethics committee found the claims to be without merit, and it was later revealed that several of the allegations made by former pages had been exaggerations or outright lies. This incident raised important questions about press coverage of ethical scandals. Many members of Congress felt that the media had no business reporting unsubstantiated accusations, which could significantly damage the reputations of members of Congress and the body as a whole.

In 1983 it became apparent that not all the allegations of sexual misconduct had been unfounded. Two members of the House, Daniel B. Crane (R-Ill.) and Gerry E. Studds (D-Mass.), were censured for sexual misconduct with congressional pages, marking the first time any member had been censured for a sexual offense. Although the ethics committee had recommended a reprimand, the House chose the more severe form of discipline.

Attempts at ethics reform. During the late 1980s a good deal of concern was brewing over government ethics. First came the Iran-contra scandal, which implicated members of the executive branch and also cast a spotlight on Congress, where a select committee was given the task of investigating the incident and making recommendations. In addition, questions were being raised, both within Congress and repeatedly by the press, about illegal office accounts, free travel provided by lobbyists and interest groups, and large sums of money paid to members for speeches made to interest groups.

Finally, two major attempts at ethics reform in Congress emerged from other highly publicized investigations into wrongdoing by prominent members of Congress. One reform attempt was successful and one was not. During an investigation into the Speaker of the House Jim Wright, when a general feeling of unease prevailed among members about the rules governing financial disclosure, Congress attempted to broaden the reach of the 1978 Ethics in Government Act. That act restricted lobbying by certain executive-branch employees after they left the government; the 1988 bill would have extended those restrictions to members of Congress and high-ranking staff members. Many felt that such legislation was necessary to counter the public perception of a revolving door between government and the world of lobbyists and interest groups. In the end the bill was pocket vetoed by President Ronald Reagan; many members breathed a sigh of relief, having voted for the bill less because they supported its provisions than because they were afraid to go on record as being against ethics reform.

The other major attempt at ethics reform came in 1989. The House passed and the president signed into law a combination ethics and pay-raise package. This law came on the heels of the resignation of Speaker Wright, who had been under investigation for questionable financial dealings. Never before had a Speaker resigned in midterm; in fact, no previous Speaker had ever been formally charged with violating House ethics rules. Wright's troubles and eventual resignation seemed to act as catalysts for reform. Wright himself, in his resignation speech, called for an overhaul of the entire ethics process and the outright abolition of honoraria.

A task force had been created in January 1988 to review ethics standards and make recommendations for reform. In the following months, not only had the Speaker resigned, but the majority whip had also resigned, one member had been convicted in a state court of sexual misconduct, another had admitted to involvement with a male prostitute, and still another had been tried for bribery. In the Senate, the public focus on the so-called Keating Five—senators who had helped savings and loan magnate Charles Keating by intervening with regulatory offices—had further put congressional ethics under scrutiny and attack. The new Speaker of the House, Thomas S. Foley (D-Wash.), made ethics legislation one of his top priorities and, on assuming the role of Speaker, directed the task force to report on its findings within ninety days.

Passage of HR 3660, the ethics-pay package, in November 1989 resulted in significant changes in the congressional codes of ethics. The bill effectively overhauled the 1978 Ethics in Government Act. It included a pay raise for members of the House, federal judges, and top executive-branch officials. At the same time it prohibited House members, staff, and some other federal officials from keeping any honoraria, effective January 1991; in lieu of paying honoraria, organizations could make charitable contributions of up to $2,000. The amount of honoraria senators would be allowed to keep was lowered from 40 percent of their salary to 27 percent.

The bill also imposed further restrictions on members' earned income and tightened existing restrictions on gifts and travel. In addition, more detail was required in financial disclosure statements, and the ban on lobbying activities after leaving office was extended to members of Congress and their staffs.

In the end, many praised Congress's efforts in coming up with this latest ethics reform package. Even Common Cause, a citizens' group usually quite critical of Congress, hailed the bill, saying that it "could well spell the beginning of the end of the anything-goes ethics era that dominated Washington during the 1980s."

The 1989 bill by no means resolved the troublesome issues involved in congressional ethics, but many argue that a real change in congressional behavior followed the 1989 reforms. In fact, after the bill was passed many members gave up accepting honoraria altogether, although the new law banning honoraria was not scheduled to take effect until 1991 and even then would apply only to House members.

Lobbying. One important aspect of congressional politics that further complicates the ethical equation is lobbying, which has a powerful—many would say corrupting—effect on the legislative process. Lobbyists representing a whole host of special interests exert significant influence over both individual legislators and the content of legislation.

While the propriety of lobbying activities has often been questioned, the lobbying system has proven difficult to regulate. Because the right to "lobby" falls under the rubric of the rights of free speech and petition, it is very hard to draw the line between influence peddling and these constitutional freedoms.

The only comprehensive law to affect lobbying was passed in 1946. The Federal Regulation of Lobbying Act required lobbyists to register, indicate their legislative interests, and report on how much money they spend in pursuing those interests. This legislation was intended to expose the pressures brought to bear on public policy. Because the law is vaguely worded and has been narrowly interpreted by the Supreme Court, however, its effectiveness has often been questioned and there have been numerous attempts to reform it.

Later efforts aimed at regulating the lobbying industry focused on the need to create a uniform code for lobby registration. Reformers maintain that such a code would encourage more compliance and allow for a more effective means of enforcement. In addition, there have been calls to tighten the requirements for financial disclosure. Both initiatives have been met with opposition from lobbyists themselves.

Lobbyists gain access and influence through many channels, including financial ones. While corporations and labor unions are barred from making direct campaign contributions, they can collect, aggregate, and distribute contributions through political action committees (PACs). Campaign contributions to members of Congress serve the dual purpose of keeping "friendly" members in power and ensuring access to lawmakers when they consider important pieces of legislation. While this strategy has worked well for the lobbyists, it has exacerbated the ethical problems and dilemmas faced by members of Congress. Often members have difficulty in putting a safe distance between the money they receive from special interests and the actions they take on behalf of those interests.

The issues and controversies surrounding lobbying are closely tied to the debate over campaign finance. As long as money continues to play so important a part in campaigns and elections, it will remain a powerful tool for the organized groups that come to Washington to pursue specific legislative interests and broad policy goals.

Despite the recurring preoccupation with congressional ethics and ethics reform, public and press unhappiness with Congress and its standards has, if anything, increased. Ironically, this disillusionment has been fed by the reforms themselves—

notably, by the many ensuing disclosures concerning unsavory congressional activity and campaign contributions. As more reports of PAC contributions, congressional travel, and gifts received are made public, more media stories appear on the subjects and more public outrage is expressed—regardless of the extent of corruption, contributions, or trips, which may actually have declined. As a matter of fact, in the early 1990s, many veteran observers of Washington and Congress believed that, in part because of ethics reform, the level of personal corruption had declined sharply since the period from 1940 to 1970.

The "Keating Five" Case. In the late 1980s, the continuing problems and confusion that plague the congressional ethics system were epitomized by the highly publicized example of the so-called Keating Five. This case illustrated how the world of political fund-raising had become a veritable minefield for many politicians. The five senators involved collectively accepted some $1.5 million in political contributions from a savings and loan executive named Charles H. Keating, Jr. In return Keating asked the senators to intervene on his behalf with the federal regulators who were investigating the failing Lincoln Savings and Loan Bank of California. Eventually the government was forced to seize the bank, and the subsequent bailout cost taxpayers an estimated $2 billion.

The central question faced by the committee investigating this case concerned the extent to which members of Congress can properly intercede with federal agencies for campaign contributors while actively soliciting and accepting donations from these same contributors.

In the end, two senators, John McCain (R-Ariz.) and John Glenn (D-Ohio), were found guilty only of exercising poor judgment. Two other senators, Donald W. Riegle, Jr. (D-Mich.), and Dennis DeConcini (D-Ariz.), were held in slightly stronger reproach by the Senate Ethics Committee. The committee concluded that the senators had indeed acted improperly and that their actions could not be condoned. Ultimately, however, it determined that no formal punishment could be warranted for any of the four under existing ethics codes.

The fifth senator, Alan Cranston (D-Calif.), was found to have violated the Senate's general rule against improper behavior. Following a formal investigation, Cranston was reprimanded by the ethics panel. This punishment represented a new form of discipline, with the committee's reprimand falling somewhere between a committee rebuke and a full censure. The committee's findings and ultimate determination were presented to the full chamber as a fait accompli; the full Senate did not vote on the matter.

In the end, speaking before his Senate colleagues, Cranston maintained that although his behavior might have appeared improper to some, at no time had he violated the established norms of behavior in the Senate. He suggested that virtually all senators were at risk because they all had at one time or another engaged in similar behavior. Cranston's comments angered many of his colleagues, illustrating the lack of consensus within the Senate regarding standards of behavior. Without clear guidelines, disciplinary measures must remain difficult to impose and enforce.

The details of the Keating case are less important than its broader implications for congressional ethics. One of the most critical questions raised by this case involved the proper boundaries of constituent service: How far should senators go in helping their constituents? Over time many senators have complained of unclear standards in this area. The Ethics Committee had the important task of clarifying these standards. While the committee members conceded that the relevant written guidelines were less than adequate, it stopped short of redrawing those guidelines, leaving that duty for yet another task force.

The Keating Five investigation also brought out the need for campaign finance reform. Clearly, a system in which special interests contribute money and expect favors in return will inevitably generate conflicts of interest. The ethics panel stated that senators can indeed intervene on behalf of contributors when such action will promote the public interest, but that campaign contributions should not be a factor. This left most senators just as bewildered about operating within the standards of proper behavior as they had been prior to the Keating case. One area of confusion arose from the absence of PAC money in the Keating case; the contributions Keating gave to the senators took the form of personal money or so-called soft money—contributions not to individual senators but to state parties for get-out-the-vote or voter registration efforts.

Even before the Keating deliberations had been concluded, both the Senate and the House began work on new guidelines for campaign finance. Similar efforts were under way in 1990, but a comprehensive bill was never passed. Regulating campaign finance is a tricky business, in part because certain constitutional protections—free speech and freedom of association—guarantee individuals the right to raise money for and contribute to politicians.

Many members of Congress believe that avoiding such scandals in the future will necessitate instituting a system of public finance, although significant partisan differences exist on this subject. While Democrats favor spending limits and public financing, Republicans oppose both. Furthermore, the House and Senate differ in their approaches to reform. For example, in the 1992 Senate version of campaign finance reform, PAC contributions had been banned, while most House incumbents who relied heavily on PAC contributions strongly opposed any such stricture.

While some had hoped that the Keating Five scandal would provide just the spark needed to bring about some compromise on campaign finance reform, it was not clear in 1993 whether the lessons learned would translate into any real change in the system. The Ethics Committee clearly passed the buck on establishing a more stringent set of standards. The House and Senate subsequently came up with their own respective proposals for reform. In addition a certain degree of public pressure must be brought to bear on legislators if substantive reform is to be achieved. If the past is any indication, an atmosphere of increased public scrutiny, usually present in the wake of some highly publicized scandal, is often conducive to the reevaluation and rewriting of old standards.

Unresolved Issues. The congressional ethics system operating in the late twentieth century retains many gaps and inconsistencies. Some have suggested that the problem lies more with the system of enforcement than with the ethics codes themselves, pointing out that members must be willing to punish their colleagues in order to deter future transgressions. Certainly standards need to be made clear, but beyond that, many believe that members must have some incentive—if only a negative incentive—to adhere to even the broadest guidelines for proper behavior.

While House and Senate ethics committees composed of sitting lawmakers from their respective chambers have generally been conscientious at evaluating charges of ethical violations by their colleagues, the simple fact that sitting members are charged with evaluating their colleagues carries a built-in suspicion of unfairness—either that members will more harshly punish their colleagues for political advantage or will try to soft-pedal allegations to protect their friends.

Given the constitutional requirement that Congress police itself, many members of the 1993 Joint Committee on the Organization of Congress made the following suggestion: that Congress create ethics committees consisting of former members of Congress—people with sensitivity to the requirements of a legislative, inherently political, body but without the inherent conflicts of judging their current peers. Any findings from their investigations, or requirements for action, could then be referred to the appropriate committee or chamber for action by the full House or Senate as the Constitution mandates.

Furthermore, while critical examination of the congressional ethics system is indisputably worthwhile, any heightened awareness of and focus on the personal and professional lives of members of Congress creates a certain danger—namely, that such a focus could dissuade people from entering public life.

It seems we have reached the point now where the press and the public have come to believe that every detail of a government official's life ought to

CIGAR BOX. From the 1924 presidential campaign, making use of the cigar brand Crooks to refer to the scandal involving the improper leasing of the Teapot Dome and Elk Hills oil reserves during the Harding administration. Following an investigation launched by the Senate Committee on Public Lands, Warren G. Harding's secretary of the Interior Albert B. Fall, a former senator, was fined and served a prison term for his involvement in the affair. Although Teapot Dome was actually an administration scandal and the Senate conducted a rather successful inquiry, Teapot Dome damaged the reputation of the Senate because Fall had served for many years in that house.

COLLECTION OF DAVID J. AND JANICE L. FRENT

be available for public consumption and considered relevant to his or her job. Certainly any behavior that impinges on an official's job or ability to carry out his or her duties is relevant and should be treated with a certain degree of scrutiny.

Most people would agree that elected officials are bound to some degree by the public trust, and perhaps the standards to which they are held ought to be higher than those of the average citizen. There is an increased risk, however, that if the most qualified individuals feel their talents and abilities will be taken into consideration only after they have passed some sort of ethical litmus test, they will likely take those talents and abilities elsewhere. It seems obvious that without the best minds at work in government, we have little hope of solving the many public policy crises we face, crises which by far surpass this issue of ethics reform in terms of their urgency and gravity.

[See also Abscam; Campaign Financing; Crédit Mobilier; Discipline of Members; Ethics Committee, Senate Select; Financial Disclosure; Honoraria; House Bank; Interest Groups; Lobbying; Members, article on Qualifications; Organization of Congress Committee, Joint; Political Action Committees; Savings and Loan Crisis; Standards of Official Conduct Committee, House; Teapot Dome.]

BIBLIOGRAPHY

Association of the Bar of the City of New York. Special Committee on Congressional Ethics. *Congress and the Public Trust.* 1970.

Beard, Edmund, and Stephen Horn. *Congressional Ethics: The View from the House.* 1975.

Berg, Larry, et al. *Corruption in the American Political System.* 1976.

Clark, Marion, and Rudy Maxa. *Public Trust, Private Lust.* 1977.

Congressional Quarterly. *Congressional Ethics.* 1980.

Congressional Quarterly. *Guide to Congress.* 3d ed. 1982.

Douglas, Paul H. *Ethics in Government.* 1952.

Garment, Suzanne. *Scandal—The Culture of Mistrust in American Politics.* 1991.

Getz, Robert. *Congressional Ethics—The Conflict of Interest Issue.* 1966.

Jennings, Bruce, and Daniel Callahan. *Representation and Responsibility: Exploring Legislative Ethics.* 1985.

Simmons, Charlene Wear. "Thoughts on Legislative Ethics Reform and Representation." *PS: Political Science & Politics* 24 (June 1991): 193–200.

Thompson, Margaret Susan. *The "Spider Web": Congress and Lobbying in the Age of Grant.* 1985.

Weeks, Kent M. *Adam Clayton Powell and the Supreme Court.* 1971.

NORMAN J. ORNSTEIN

ETHICS COMMITTEE, HOUSE. *See* Standards of Official Conduct Committee, House.

ETHICS COMMITTEE, SENATE SELECT. The U.S. Senate first established an ethics committee on 24 July 1964. Known as the Select Committee on Standards and Conduct, its name was changed to the Select Committee on Ethics in February 1977 following Senate-wide committee reorganization. The six-member, bipartisan committee has been vested by the Senate to oversee the elements of its self-discipline authority embedded in Article I, section 5 of the Constitution.

Often referred to as the Senate Ethics Committee, it is authorized to (1) recommend rules or regulations necessary to ensure appropriate Senate standards of conduct; (2) receive complaints and investigate allegations of improper conduct and violations of law or of the Senate Code of Official Conduct by members, officers, or employees of the Senate in the performance of their official duties; (3) investigate unauthorized disclosures of intelligence information; (4) implement the Senate public financial disclosure requirements of the Ethics in Government Act; and (5) review, upon request, any decision of the Senate Office of Fair Employment Practices established in 1991 to protect Senate employees from discrimination.

The committee may investigate any allegations brought by members, officers, or employees of the Senate; those brought against them by any other citizen or group; or it may initiate an inquiry on its own. It has formal procedures for the filing of complaints and is careful not to publicize allegations that do not merit full review. After several stages in an investigative process, the committee may recommend to the Senate any appropriate sanction, including expulsion of a senator.

Since 1964, the Senate Ethics Committee has acknowledged working on allegations involving some twenty-one senators as well as three investigations in which the number involved was not made public. As a result, one senator resigned before certain expulsion for a bribery conviction; one senator was censured and two were denounced (a form of censure) by the Senate for financial misconduct; one senator was rebuked by the committee for the improper acceptance of gifts; and one senator involved in the "Keating Five" case was reprimanded by the committee. The other four senators in the latter case were criticized in written statements from the committee for showing poor judgment

SENATE ETHICS COMMITTEE HEARING. *At right*, Sen. Thomas J. Dodd (D-Conn.) listens to his former personal secretary Marjorie Carpenter testifying before the Senate Ethics Committee, which is investigating charges of misconduct brought against him. At center is Dodd's attorney, James Waters. Dodd, angered at a suggestion that he might have received a $10,000 payoff from lobbyist Julius Klein, asked the Justice Department to bring perjury action against Carpenter, June 1966.   OFFICE OF THE HISTORIAN OF THE U.S. SENATE

and giving the appearance of acting improperly. In some cases, no disciplinary action was recommended by the committee or taken by the Senate.

Most of the work of the first ethics committee, the Select Committee on Standards and Conduct, was not publicized. It undertook several investigations, but only one member of the Senate was disciplined. Both committees have often been criticized for lack of action, partly because of their desire to protect the "due process" rights of those investigated.

Moreover, the Senate and the House of Representatives have traditionally exercised their powers of self-discipline with caution. The Senate historian Richard Baker notes in *The History of Congressional Ethics* (1985), "For nearly two centuries, a simple and informal code of behavior existed with prevailing norms of decency the chief determinants of

proper conduct. Congress has chosen to deal with only the most obvious acts of wrongdoing." Until the 1960s, when the Senate and House first established ethics committees and codes of conduct, any allegations investigated were conducted by special or select committees created for the purpose or were considered by the Senate without prior committee action.

Attention to congressional ethics began gradually in the 1940s when legislation calling for annual public financial disclosure reports by senators was first introduced by Sen. Wayne L. Morse (D-Oreg.). During the 1950s and early 1960s, when several unsuccessful attempts were made to create joint or select congressional committees to monitor and impose codes of official conduct, there was continued concern over the official conduct of members and employees of the Senate. This concern gathered momentum after Robert G. (Bobby) Baker, secretary to the Democratic majority, resigned from his job in October 1963 amid speculation that he had misused his official position for personal financial gain.

For the next year and a half the Senate Rules and Administration Committee held hearings to investigate the business interests and activities of Senate officials and employees to ascertain what, if any, conflicts of interest or other improprieties existed and whether any additional laws or regulations were needed. The Senate recognized that serious allegations had been made against a former employee and that it had no specific rules or regulations governing the duties and scope of activities of members, officers, and employees.

During the next year, the Rules Committee made several recommendations for ethical guidelines based on Baker's outside activities, which it found to be in conflict with his official duties. Subsequently, additions to the Senate rules—calling for public financial disclosure reports and more controls on staff involvement in Senate campaign funds—were introduced to implement the committee's Baker investigation recommendations.

On 24 July 1964, during debate on the proposed ethics rules and a resolution to give the Rules Committee authority to investigate future alleged violations of Senate rules, the Senate adopted a substitute proposal by Sen. John Sherman Cooper (R-Ky.) to establish a permanent Senate Select Committee on Standards and Conduct. This committee, similar to the one he had advocated during several stages of the Baker investigation, was authorized to investigate allegations of improper conduct, to recommend disciplinary action, and to suggest new Senate rules defining and ensuring proper standards of conduct. With the creation of this committee, an internal disciplinary body was established in Congress for the first time on a continuing basis.

The members of the new committee, appointed a year later, included John C. Stennis (D-Miss.) as chairman and Wallace F. Bennett (R-Utah) as vice chairman, positions they held for ten years. The committee's work on a code of conduct for the Senate was diverted for the next year by its first case, that of Sen. Thomas J. Dodd (D-Conn.), who was censured by the Senate in June 1967 for the conversion of campaign funds to personal use.

Because of the interruption by another investigation, it was not until March 1968 that the committee reported and the Senate adopted its first standards of conduct. This so-called Code of Conduct covered outside employment by officers and employees, the raising and reporting of campaign funds, political fund activity by Senate employees, and limited public financial disclosure requirements for members, officers, and designated employees of the Senate and senatorial candidates.

On 1 April 1977, the Senate Code of Conduct, often criticized as insufficient, was revised and amended, and the procedures and duties of the Ethics Committee were further developed. One impetus was the Watergate scandal; others were a congressional pay raise, several studies recommending limitations on outside earned income and more explicit standards of senatorial conduct, and a number of polls and studies that indicated a decline in the public's confidence in all three branches of government, Congress in particular. Included in the revised code were the first public financial disclosure requirements for members, officers, and employees of the Senate, as well as the first limit on gifts, outside earnings, the franking privilege, unofficial office accounts, lame-duck foreign travel, and discrimination in staff employment.

Unlike its House counterpart, the Senate Ethics Committee has undergone no major revitalization since established. However, the roles, makeup, and practices of both congressional ethics committees have increasingly been scrutinized in recent years. In 1993, the Joint Committee on the Organization of Congress and a bipartisan Senate ethics study commission studied and held hearings on several options to improve Senate ethics procedures, often criticized because of the difficulty inherent in the current system of senators judging their colleagues, the drawn out investigative process, the absence of a fixed set of disciplinary sanctions, the lack of public accountability, and the demands on the time of senators serving on the Select Committee on Ethics.

In its final report, the joint committee deferred to the Senate ethics study commission, which made several recommendations to the Senate leadership in March 1994. These included streamlining the Ethics Committee's formal investigative procedures, establishing a set of standard disciplinary sanctions, terminating so-called plea bargaining with senators under investigation by the Ethics Committee, and better educating senators and staff about ethics. The commission rejected a statute of limitation on charges that could be investigated by the Ethics Committee, and discussed, but did not recommend, bifurcation (dividing the investigative and adjudicatory steps) of the disciplinary process and the use of outsiders such as judges or former senators.

[*See also* Financial Disclosures; Rules and Administration Committee, Senate; Standards of Official Conduct Committee, House.]

BIBLIOGRAPHY

Calmes, Jacqueline. "The Ethics Committees: Shield or Sword?" *Congressional Quarterly Weekly Report,* 4 April 1987, pp. 591–597.

Dewar, Helen. "Senate Ethics Panel at a Crossroads." *Washington Post,* 3 January 1993, pp. A1, A16.

Gettinger, Stephen. "Senate Ethics Revisions Aim to Ease Process." *Congressional Quarterly Weekly Report,* 5 March 1994, pp. 522–523.

Sasser, James. "Learning from the Past: The Senate Code of Conduct in Historical Perspective." *Cumberland Law Review* 8 (Fall 1977): 357–384.

MILDRED LEHMANN AMER

EULOGIES. On 26 December 1799, Rep. Henry Lee of Virginia, speaking at the funeral ceremonies for George Washington in the nation's capital, eulogized the former president, who had died twelve days earlier, as "first in war, first in peace and first in the hearts of his countrymen." Although the great bulk of speaking in the House and Senate is necessarily deliberative in nature, there is also a substantial tradition of congressional oratory eulogizing deceased colleagues, presidents, and other figures of note. As illustrated by Lee's famous anaphora, this tradition has produced some memorable discourse.

Perhaps the most memorable was delivered on 28 April 1874 by Lucius Q. C. Lamar. A representative from Mississippi, Lamar had been a slaveholder and a colonel in the Confederate army. Yet he believed that the South, if it were to move forward, had to develop a spirit of genuine conciliation with the North. When the abolitionist senator Charles Sumner died in the spring of 1874, Lamar joined his eulogists, praising his "instinctive love of freedom" and self-sacrificing patriotism. Stressing the "common heritage of American valor" that united the sections of the nation, Lamar concluded by appealing, "My countrymen! know one another, and you will love one another." The speech enraptured its listeners, many of whom were moved to tears; won lavish praise when it was reprinted in newspapers throughout the land; and remains one of the great public addresses in U.S. history.

Although not on the same order as Lamar's oration, other congressional eulogies of note include Thomas Hart Benton's 1848 tribute to John Quincy Adams, Henry Clay's commemoration of John C. Calhoun after the latter's death in 1850, James G. Blaine's address of 27 February 1882 on the assassination of President James A. Garfield, and Mike Mansfield's speech honoring the slain John F. Kennedy in November 1963.

BIBLIOGRAPHY

Baskerville, Barnet. *The People's Voice: The Orator in American Society.* 1979.

Oliver, Robert T. *History of Public Speaking in America.* 1965.

STEPHEN E. LUCAS

EXECUTIVE AGREEMENT. The term *executive agreement* is used in the United States for an international agreement that is not submitted to the Senate for its advice and consent. Since the beginning of World War II, the number of executive agreements entered into by the United States has escalated rapidly. Of the approximately thirteen thousand international agreements concluded between 1946 and 1992, more than twelve thousand fell into this category.

Most executive agreements might better be called congressional-executive agreements. In many cases legislation authorizes the president to conclude specified agreements. For example, a 1792 act authorized the postmaster general to make arrangements with foreign countries for reciprocal delivery of mail. In other cases the president submits agreements after their conclusion for the explicit approval of Congress, as in the case of the constitution of the World Health Organization. Still other agreements are signed pursuant to treaties earlier approved by the Senate, such as hundreds of military agreements implementing the North Atlantic Treaty.

Congress has been concerned particularly with what have been called sole executive agreements—international agreements concluded by a president solely on his own authority, without any congressional authorization or approval. Examples include the destroyers-for-bases agreement with Great Britain of 1940 and the Yalta agreement of 1945. To supervise the use of executive agreements, in 1972 Congress passed the Case Act (P.L. 92-403). This act requires the secretary of State to transmit all executive agreements to Congress within sixty days, including oral agreements reduced to writing and secret agreements on a classified basis.

[*See also* Advice and Consent; Treaties.]

BIBLIOGRAPHY

Johnson, Loch K. *The Making of International Agreements: Congress Confronts the Executive.* 1984.

McClure, Wallace M. *International Executive Agreements: Democratic Procedure under the Constitution of the United States.* 1941.

U.S. Senate. Committee on the Judiciary. Subcommittee on Separation of Powers. *Congressional Oversight of Executive Agreements: 1975.* Hearings, 13 May–25 July 1975.

ELLEN C. COLLIER

EXECUTIVE BRANCH. Cooperation and conflict characterize the relationship between the executive branch and Congress, the parameters of which are established by the Constitution. The relationship is further delineated by statutory law that defines the organization of the executive branch and may establish formal rules and procedures of operation and interaction; occasionally by court decision; by congressional resolutions affecting the organization, rules, and procedures of the legislative branch; by executive orders of the president; and by informal norms, procedures, and expectations that over time have become accepted by both branches.

The separation-of-powers system requires cooperation but also offers opportunity for conflict. In Article I on Congress and Article II on the executive, the Constitution outlines the powers of each branch; responsibility for national policy-making is shared. Because action by both branches is needed to achieve most policies, presidents and congresses have struggled to prevail virtually since the beginning of the Republic.

The president nominates ambassadors, judges, and high-level executive branch officials and other "officers of the United States," but the Senate must approve the nominations. The president negotiates treaties, but the Senate must approve treaties. Congress approves legislation; the president may veto it; if each house of Congress subsequently approves a measure by a two-thirds majority, the bill becomes law without the president's signature (in practice vetoes are rarely overridden).

In other areas, the distinctions are less clear. Although the president is commander in chief of the armed forces, Congress has the responsibility to "raise and support" armies and "provide and maintain a navy." Congress declares war. How are these shared—and, to some degree, overlapping and conflicting—war powers used in an era of increased presidential foreign-policy responsibilities and air transport of troops? Section 3 of Article II charges the president to "take Care that the Laws be faithfully executed." In practice, what does this mean for the role of the president vis-à-vis Congress? The advise-and-consent power on nominations, the appropriations power, the stipulation that "no Money shall be drawn from the Treasury, but in Consequence of Appropriations made by Law," and the general legislative power under Article I, section 1 and section 8 (the latter gives Congress the power "to make all Laws which shall be necessary and proper for carrying into Execution the foregoing Powers, and all other Powers vested by this Constitution in the Government of the United States, or in any Department or Officer thereof") establish a system of overlapping responsibilities.

Because the authority for policy-making is shared, the views of one branch affect policy proposals of the other; for example, congressional views affect executive-branch negotiations on and the provisions of treaties. Or there may be a stalemate, as occurred in the 1980s; there are numerous opportunities, both in Congress and in the executive branch, to kill proposed policies. In the contemporary era, the president and the executive branch are deeply involved in developing legislation and in legislative strategy and coalition building on the Hill.

The lines between establishing and implementing policy are not clear: the executive branch and Congress are involved in both. Congress has both specific and general rights under the Constitution that give it the authority directly to affect the executive branch and to conduct oversight inquiries on executive-branch operations, programs, and policies. In addition, complex issues that cut across traditional committee and agency jurisdictions, as well as party and ideological lines, blur the separation between the branches.

Statutory law further defines the parameters of the relationship. Legislation establishes executive departments and agencies and executive-branch procedures. The Budget Act of 1921, for example, established a unified executive branch budget and the Bureau of the Budget in the Treasury Department (now the Office of Management and Budget [OMB] in the Executive Office of the President). The Budget Act of 1974 directed changes in execu-

EXECUTIVE BRANCH

EXECUTIVE DEPARTMENTS

Department of Agriculture

Department of Congress

Department of Defense
Joint Chiefs of Staff

Department of Education

Department of Energy

Department of Health and Human Services
Social Security Administration

Department of Housing and Urban Development

Department of the Interior

Department of Justice
Attorney General
Solicitor General
Office of Legal Counsel
Federal Bureau of Investigation
Office of the Pardon Attorney

Department of Labor

Department of State

Department of Transportation
Saint Lawrence Seaway Development Corporation

Department of the Treasury
United States Secret Service

Department of Veterans' Affairs

INDEPENDENT COMMISSIONS

Commodity Futures Trading Commission (CFTC)

Consumer Product Safety Commission (CPSC)

Federal Communications Commission (FCC)

Federal Election Commission (FEC)

Federal Energy Regulatory Commission (FERC)

Federal Maritime Commission (FMC)

Federal Mine Safety and Health Review Commission

Federal Reserve System, Board of Governors of the Federal Trade Commission (FTC)

Interstate Commerce Commission (ICC)

National Labor Relations Board (NLRB)

Nuclear Regulatory Commission (NRC)

Occupational Safety and Health Review Commission

Postal Rate Commission

Securities and Exchange Commission (SEC)

U.S. International Trade Commission (ITC)

GOVERNMENT CORPORATIONS

African Development Foundation

Export-Import Bank of the United States

Farm Credit Administration

Federal Deposit Insurance Corporation (FDIC)

Federal Housing Finance Board

Inter-American Foundation

Legal Services Corporation

National Railroad Passenger Corporation (Amtrak)

Pennsylvania Avenue Development Corporation

Pension Benefit Guaranty Corporation

Resolution Trust Corporation

Tennessee Valley Authority (TVA)

OTHER AGENCIES AND BOARDS

Administrative Conference of the U.S.

Central Intelligence Agency (CIA)

Commission on the Bicentennial of the U.S. Constitution

Commission on Civil Rights

Defense Nuclear Facilities Safety Board

Environmental Protection Agency (EPA)

Equal Employment Opportunity Commission (EEOC)

Federal Emergency Management Agency (FEMA)

Federal Labor Relations Authority

Federal Mediation and Conciliation Service

Federal Retirement Thrift Investment Board

General Services Administration

Merit Systems Protection Board (MSPB)

National Aeronautics and Space Administration (NASA)

National Archives and Records Administration

National Capitol Planning Commission

National Credit Union Administration

National Foundation on the Arts and the Humanities

National Mediation Board

National Science Foundation

National Transportation Safety Board

Office of Government Ethics

Office of Personnel Management

Oversight Board for the Resolution Trust Corporation

Peace Corps

Railroad Retirement Board

Selective Service System

U.S. Arms Control and Disarmament Agency (ACDA)

U.S. Information Agency (USIA)

U.S. International Development Cooperation Agency

Agency for International Development (AID)

U.S. Office of Special Counsel

U.S. Postal Service

tive impoundment procedures. Other statutes establish reporting requirements, used by Congress to monitor executive actions (sending troops abroad), to obtain information (the annual Economic Report of the President), or to focus executive attention on specific matters or continuing issues (human rights). Statutes also direct or prohibit executive actions: the Boland (and similar) amendments during the 1980s prohibited U.S. support of the Nicaraguan Contras.

The relationship between the branches is also affected by unilateral actions of Congress regarding its own organization and procedures. In the 103d Congress (1993–1995), the executive branch worked with 252 committees and subcommittees established by Congress. In early 1993, President Bill Clinton's economic stimulus package was defeated because the Democratic majority could not muster the needed 60 votes under Senate Rule XXII to stop a Republican filibuster.

Similarly, executive orders of presidents, and departmental authority to write regulations implementing legislation, affect both branches. An executive order may reorganize an executive department or agency. Or a procedural executive order, such as that which established a central review by OMB of proposed executive-branch regulations, changed long-established congressional committee–executive agency relationships on specific regulatory matters and shifted decision making to a different arena. If Congress opposes the effect of proposed action, the order can be overturned by legislation—as Congress threatened to do at the start of the 103d Congress in 1993 if there were an executive order on gays in the military.

Court decisions also affect the relationship between the two branches. Late-twentieth-century court decisions held that executive privilege did not extend to all the taped conversations in the Oval Office during the Nixon presidency (*United States v. Nixon*, 1974), limited the president's impoundment actions (for example, *Train v. New York*, 1975), nullified the legislative veto (*U.S. Immigration and Naturalization Service v. Chadha*, 1983), and held unconstitutional the sequester provisions of the 1985 Gramm-Rudman-Hollings Act (*Bowsher v. Synar*, 1986).

The president is chief executive and head of the executive branch—or the "executive establishment," as Ronald Moe termed it in a report prepared for the Senate Governmental Affairs Committee (*The Federal Executive Establishment: Evolution and Trends*, 1980). The First Congress (1789–1791) established the cabinet departments of State, Treasury, and War to handle the major governmental functions. Three additional departments were established during the nineteenth century, and eight have been established since. Typically, cabinet departments have been formed by elevating an independent agency to cabinet status (e.g., Veterans' Affairs in 1989) or dividing an existing department (e.g., Health, Education, and Welfare, which in 1979 became the departments of Health and Human Services and of Education). Independent executive agencies have been established with increasing increasing frequency (the National Aeronautics and Space Administration [NASA] and the Environmental Protection Agency [EPA], for example). And new government units have been established within an existing unit, as the Council of Economic Advisors was in the Executive Office of the President in 1946.

The contemporary executive is characterized by organizational complexity and dispersion. In January 1993, at the start of the Clinton presidency, the executive establishment included fourteen cabinet departments (State, Treasury, Defense, Justice, Interior, Agriculture, Commerce, Labor, Transportation, Housing and Urban Development, Health and Human Services, Energy, Education, and Veterans' Affairs); the Executive Office of the President, which includes White House staff, the Office of Management and Budget, and other agencies such as the Council of Economic Advisors; and numerous independent agencies such as the Federal Trade Commission, the Securities and Exchange Commission, and NASA. The independent executive agencies vary in organization, in autonomy, and in accountability to the president. The tension between centralized integrative management and decentralization and unit autonomy, so evident in congressional organization, also characterizes the executive branch.

About three million civilians and about two million armed services personnel worked in the executive bureaucracy in 1991. Twelve percent of the civilians worked in Washington, D.C.; others were deployed throughout the country and abroad. Departments vary in size: Defense employs the most civilians, 969,059 in 1991, and Education the fewest, 4,603 (figures are from *Budget of the United States, Fiscal Year 1993*). Political appointees (department secretaries, under secretaries, deputy and assistant secretaries, and agency administrators and commissioners), who are nominated by the president and confirmed by the Senate, lead the ex-

VIEW OF WASHINGTON, D.C. From the Treasury, looking toward the Capitol. Engraving by W. Wellstood, Jr., c. 1840.

ecutive establishment. In *A Government of Strangers* (1977), Hugh Heclo reports an increasing number of political executives and compares the Interior Department of 1924—which had a secretary, three assistant secretaries, and ten bureau heads—with the political executives of 1976: a secretary, an under secretary, seven assistant secretaries, and twenty-six bureau heads.

Structural, procedural, and perceptual differences affect the interaction of the two branches and national policy. The executive branch, although complex, is organized hierarchically. The president heads the executive branch; cabinet officials, nominated by the president, head departments. Those at the top—political executives and ultimately the president—are responsible for decisions. Political executives and the bureaucracy work for the president. Lines of authority and command are clear.

In contrast, Congress is a collegial institution, with a flat organizational structure. Congressional leaders do not control who becomes a member of the institution, and members of Congress are accountable to constituents outside the institution, not to congressional leaders within it. Congress is decentralized structurally; the major work is accomplished through the committee system. And committee jurisdictions do not necessarily match the jurisdictions of executive-branch agencies. Congressional leaders seek to coordinate the work of the institution primarily through persuasion; although leaders have the responsibility to achieve legislation, leaders do not make the final decision on its content. Congressional procedures, particularly in the Senate, permit and even encourage participation by members in deliberation and decision making. And in contrast to the executive branch, as decisions move through the legislative process from subcommittee to committee to the floor, the number of decision makers becomes larger. The legislative process is characterized by norms of participation, an open and lengthy decision process with numerous points of access by outside individuals and groups, including the executive, and the real possibility of major change at each point in the process. The decentralized structure and decision processes mean that political executives must testify on legislation or report on policy frequently—too frequently, they say—before congressional subcommittees and committees.

In contrast to the executive branch, in 1993 Congress and the four legislative support agencies (the Congressional Budget Office, the Congressional Research Service, the General Accounting Office, and the Office of Technology Assessment) employed 22,434. Congress is dependent on the executive for information and analysis of executive-branch operations and programs and for assistance in developing legislation. And although congressional staff increased in the 1970s because Congress wanted independent information and analysis on policy issues, congressional staff members are generalists, in contrast to the much larger and more specialized executive bureaucracy.

Shaped by terms of office and average tenures, time frames differ for the two branches. A president's horizon is constrained by the four-year, or at most eight-year, term. As Carl Brauer notes (in *The In-and-Outers*, edited by G. Calvin Mackenzie), the average tenure of political executives is 2.2 years. Members of Congress, and particularly committee chairs, have longer tenures: 11.5 years in the 102d Congress (1991–1993). They can outlast both political executives and presidents. Bureaucrats too, with average tenure of slightly more than 13 years, can outlast presidents and at least some members of Congress. It therefore may not be as compelling for Congress as it is for a president to approve proposed policy quickly.

Perceptions and perspectives also differ. Congress, particularly since the Vietnam War and the events of Watergate, when members felt that institutional prerogatives had been badly threatened, has been watchful and at times wary of executive-branch actions. Policy actions that a majority in Congress consider legitimate—such as legislative provisions during the 1980s that forbade assistance to the Contras in Nicaragua—are considered by the executive interference in policy implementation. Committee reports directing a departmental action may be viewed as micromanagement. However, the congressional view is different. The War Powers Resolution of 1973, for example, which requires that presidents report to Congress when troops are sent into a conflict situation, was passed after Congress felt left out of decision making during the Vietnam War. Similarly, the impoundment provisions of the Budget and Impoundment Control Act of 1974 were considered a response to President Richard M. Nixon's efforts to rescind congressional policy directives by not spending funds that had been appropriated.

In the contemporary era, a president sets the national agenda, is a legislative leader who develops policy, proposes legislation and works with Congress to get his programs passed, and as head of the executive implements policy. At every stage there is interaction with Congress. Presidents are assisted by legislative liaison staff in the White House and executive agencies. Presidents, and their delegates, are important in the negotiations and compromises that lead to a policy acceptable to both branches.

There are both formal and informal processes for coordination between the two branches. A president uses the annual State of the Union address to set the national agenda and to establish the framework for cooperation; he identifies issues and concerns, lays out the broad outlines of needed policy, recites joint accomplishments of the two branches, thanks members of Congress for their assistance in the past, and asks for help in the coming year. Other reports, such as the president's annual economic report, assess specific policy areas. Presidential nominations and appointments and the signing or vetoing of legislation are also used. Through mandated reports to Congress on specific programs or issue areas, and through formal appearances before congressional committees to testify on behalf of departments and agencies, political executives lay out the positions and concerns of the executive branch and shape the context of policy-making.

But the executive establishment also has informal tools that presidents and others use to shape the executive-congressional relationship and policy outcomes. Speeches, press conferences, and statements by presidents and political executives are important. Presidents may appeal to the American public on issues; President Ronald Reagan (1981–1989) made masterful use of the presidential speech from the White House to seek public support for policy issues, urging that the public write Congress. The president can use the cabinet, the press, the bureaucracy, the White House staff, and agencies in the Executive Office of the President to help achieve presidential and executive branch goals. Political executives and high-level bureaucrats work with committees to draft legislation and build voting coalitions and during conference committee consideration. Other informal processes include the lines of regular communication between the branches established by staff members at all levels, the social exchange of the Washington community, and in recent years the growing group of professionals that works first for one branch and then for the other. After the change of administration in 1993, Clinton appointed three members of

Congress to his cabinet, and numerous staff members from Capitol Hill went to senior positions in the departments and agencies.

For Congress, passing legislation, exercising oversight, confirming presidential nominations, and using other formal tools of congressional power are significant in shaping the relationship with the executive. The press, public opinion, the bureaucracy, lateral lines of communication and relationships built up over a number of years, and the movement of personnel—both to the executive from Congress and to Congress from the executive—present opportunities as well as constraints, as they do for the president.

The relationship between the executive and Congress is a changing one within the broad parameters established by the Constitution. At any particular time it is affected by organizational structure, the issues on the government agenda, control of the White House and of Congress, and the leadership of the two branches. Both formal and informal factors determine the interaction between the two branches and ultimately, of course, national policy.

[*See also* Bureaucracy; Cabinet and Congress; Oversight. *For broad discussion of congressional relations with the executive branch, see* President and Congress.]

BIBLIOGRAPHY

Aberbach, Joel D. *Keeping a Watchful Eye: The Politics of Congressional Oversight.* 1990.
Fisher, Louis. *The Politics of Shared Power: Congress and the Executive.* 1992.
Jones, Charles O. *The Trusteeship Presidency: Jimmy Carter and the United States Congress.* 1988.
Mayhew, David. *Divided We Govern.* 1992.
Peterson, Mark A. *Legislating Together: The White House and Capitol Hill from Eisenhower to Reagan.* 1990.

SUSAN WEBB HAMMOND

EXECUTIVE COMMUNICATIONS.

Both the House and Senate receive a continuous flow of information from the executive branch that includes myriad messages and communications from the president and various department and bureau heads. Among these communications are reports and statements in response to provisions of law, congressional resolutions and requests for comment on pending legislation, nominations, and notice of executive action and drafts of legislative proposals.

The House makes a distinction between presidential messages, which are laid before the House and entered in the *Journal* and the *Congressional Record*, and other executive communications. These other communications are usually referred to the appropriate standing committee(s) under the direction of the Speaker without any action by the House; occasionally, however, they too may be laid before the House, as in the case of letters from the president or other executive officials advocating certain legislative action or responding to a resolution of inquiry.

After the *Journal* is read at the beginning of a legislative day, or when the Senate is engaged in morning business by unanimous consent, the presiding officer is to lay before the Senate messages from the president and reports and communications from the heads of departments. In addition, Rule VII provides that it shall be in order at any time to lay before the Senate any bill or other matter sent to the Senate by the president. All communications submitted to the Senate are received at the Desk and, unless otherwise disposed of, are referred to the appropriate standing committee. A 1908 Senate resolution prohibits the receipt of executive communications, except when authorized by law, made in response to a resolution, or transmitted by the president.

BIBLIOGRAPHY

U.S. House of Representatives. *Constitution, Jefferson's Manual, and Rules of the House of Representatives, 102d Congress.* Compiled by William Holmes Brown. 101st Cong., 2d sess., 1991. H. Doc. 101-256. Rule XVI.
U.S. Senate. *Senate Procedure, Precedents, and Practices,* by Floyd M. Riddick. 97th Cong., 1st sess. S. Doc. 97-2.

JAMES V. SATURNO

EXECUTIVE PRIVILEGE.

In requesting information necessary for carrying out its investigative and oversight functions, Congress sometimes runs up against claims of executive privilege. Executive, or governmental, privilege is a multifaceted concept, including privilege against disclosing various types of information in certain contexts. Disputes regarding congressional access to information from the executive branch are often infused with separation-of-powers considerations. Beyond congressional-executive conflict over the scope and applicability of executive privilege, executive privilege is sometimes invoked to shield documents from private parties engaged in civil litigation against the government. The Freedom of Information Act and other disclosure laws contain provisions designed to protect from disclosure the deliberations of government officials during the period before a policy decision is reached; such provisions are based on traditional ideas of executive privilege.

Not until the mid 1970s did the courts begin to explore the contours of executive privilege and congressional access to information. For the previous two hundred years, disputes between the president and Congress over access to documents were invariably settled in the political arena. Judicial involvement was hardly contemplated as presidents from George Washington to Lyndon B. Johnson periodically struggled with congressional demands for information. Most demands were complied with; others fell subject to political give-and-take and were resolved in a variety of ways, depending on the relative political strength of the parties. Practically, this remains the case today, despite judicial involvement, which began in the 1970s. Recent presidents have issued guidelines on responding to congressional requests, and both parties usually ultimately enter into negotiations over access to sensitive information.

The Watergate years spawned the first court cases on executive privilege and ushered in a contentious period in congressional-executive relations. In *United States v. Nixon* (1974), the Supreme Court ruled in a case involving the Watergate special prosecutor's access to tape recordings of conversations between President Richard M. Nixon and his advisers. The Court found that "to the extent [executive privilege] relates to the effective discharge of a President's powers, it is constitutionally based" and that "the protection of the confidentiality of presidential communications has . . . constitutional underpinnings." Also constitutionally based, however, were the rights of criminal defendants and courts to have access to relevant evidence in criminal cases. The Court held that the generalized assertion of confidentiality in the president's privilege claim must give way to the focused and critical need for the information in a criminal trial. It noted that the outcome might be different if national security information was being sought. It also reserved the question of the balance between privilege and congressional demands for information.

In some other disputes over executive privilege, lower federal courts have declined to enter the fray. In *United States v. AT&T* (551 F.2d 384 [1976] and 567 F.2d 121 [1977]), the federal circuit court acted as a mediator, guiding the parties to a negotiated settlement in a case involving committee access to wiretap information. In *United States v. House of Representatives* (556 F.Supp. 150 [1983]), a case involving congressional access to investigatory material compiled by the Environmental Protection Agency, the federal district court declined the invitation of the executive to adjudicate the case. In both cases, the courts recognized competing constitutionally based claims: Congress's power to investigate and oversee the executive and to compile information relevant to the legislative process and the president's interests in confidentiality in fulfilling his executive responsibilities. It may be that because of what one court described as "nerve-center constitutional questions," the courts will continue to demur and leave the resolution of executive privilege claims to the political arena.

[*See also* Freedom of Information Act; Watergate.]

BIBLIOGRAPHY

Hamilton, James, and John C. Grabow. "A Legislative Proposal for Resolving Executive Privilege Disputes Precipitated by Congressional Subpoenas." *Harvard Journal of Legislation* 21 (1984): 145–172.

Hoffman, Daniel N. *Governmental Secrecy and the Founding Fathers.* 1981.

Shane, Peter M. "Negotiability for Knowledge: Administrative Responses to Congressional Demands for Information." *Administrative Law Review* 44 (1992): 197–244.

RICHARD EHLKE

EXECUTIVE REORGANIZATION. A process intended or undertaken to increase the economy or efficiency of executive branch agencies, executive reorganization increased after the late nineteenth century as government expanded. Constitutionally, Congress has the predominant authority over the organization of executive agencies. After the Civil War, Congress sought economy through reorganization, establishing select committees to undertake the process. In 1869 the Joint Select Committee on Retrenchment was created. In 1887 the Senate Select Committee on Methods of Business of the Executive Departments was established, and in 1893 Congress created the Joint Commission to Inquire into the Status of the Laws Organizing the Executive Departments, popularly called the Dockery-Cockrell Commission.

Before 1900 Congress monopolized reorganization for two reasons. First, it was widely thought that the executive should be subordinate to Congress. Second, Congress could protect its interest in the patronage within the federal agencies by controlling any changes in them. Thus, there was no role made for the president in these congressional initiatives.

In 1905 President Theodore Roosevelt challenged Congress's monopoly of executive reorganization by appointing the Keep Commission (Committee on Department Methods) to improve executive organization. It was named after its chairman Charles Keep, assistant secretary of the Treasury. In 1911 President William Howard Taft created the President's Commission on Economy and Efficiency, composed of prominent experts on administration. The commission made the first official recommendation for an executive budget.

The 1920 Joint Committee on Reorganization reflected the changing roles of Congress and the presidency in reorganization. The committee was created by Congress after the presidential election, but, after his inauguration, President Warren G. Harding demanded the authority to name the committee's chair. Congress assented, and Harding named Walter F. Brown, who was his assistant for administration. In fact, the joint committee's 1924 report to Congress was written in the executive branch. Most notably, the report recommended delegating executive reorganization authority to the president. The Economy Act of 1932 implemented that recommendation.

The Economy Act began a line of reorganization acts that joined the delegation of reorganization authority to the president with a new instrument, the legislative veto. Presidential orders for executive reorganization were to be submitted to Congress and could be rejected within a specified time limit.

From the 1930s into the 1980s presidents dominated executive reorganization, using ad hoc reorganization planning groups, the increased capacity of the Bureau of the Budget (later the Office of Management and Budget), and the reorganization authority. The most prominent of these presidential vehicles for executive reorganization were President Franklin D. Roosevelt's 1936 Committee on Administrative Management (Brownlow Committee), President Dwight D. Eisenhower's 1953 Advisory Committee on Government Organization, President Lyndon B. Johnson's 1966 Task Force on Governmental Organization, President Richard M. Nixon's 1969 Advisory Council on Government Organization (Ash Council), and President Jimmy Carter's 1977 President's Reorganization Project.

Congress created two reorganization initiatives during this period of presidential dominance, the first and second Commissions on the Organization of the Executive Branch, both chaired by Herbert Hoover and known as the Hoover Commissions. The first was created in 1947 by the Republican 80th Congress (1947–1949), and the second in 1953 by the Republican 83d Congress (1953–1955). In each case Congress's aim was executive reorganization that would reverse the executive branch's post-1930s expansion.

In 1983 the Supreme Court ruled in *Immigration and Naturalization Service v. Chadha* that the legislative veto was unconstitutional, thereby destroying the basis for congressional delegation of reorganization authority to the president. Since 1983 the president has been able to propose reorganization, but those proposals must be enacted into law by Congress.

[*See also* Bureaucracy; Immigration and Naturalization Service v. Chadha.]

BIBLIOGRAPHY

Arnold, Peri E. *Making the Managerial Presidency: Comprehensive Reorganization Planning, 1905–1980.* 1986.

U.S. House of Representatives. Committee on Rules. *Studies on the Legislative Veto.* 96th Cong., 2d sess., 1980. See especially Louis Fisher and Ronald Moe, "Delegating with Ambivalence: The Legislative Veto and Executive Reorganization," pp. 164–247.

White, Leonard D. *The Republican Era: 1896–1901.* 1958.

PERI E. ARNOLD

EXPANSION. *See* Territorial Expansion.

EXPEDITED CONSIDERATION. Expedited consideration stems from procedures established to ensure that a measure moves from introduction to conclusive floor action within a short or definite time frame. Expedited procedures are usually included in statutes as rule-making provisions, enacted pursuant to the constitutional authority of each chamber to "determine the rules of its proceedings."

Historically, expedited procedures have often been enacted as part of legislative veto provisions. Expedited procedures have also been enacted for consideration of recurring legislation, such as concurrent resolutions on the budget and reconciliation bills in the Congressional Budget Act of 1974, and for special purpose measures such as consideration of the North American Free Trade Agreement in 1993 or the recommendations of the Commission on Base Realignment and Closure established in the Base Closure and Realignment Act of 1988.

Typically, expedited procedures provide a time limit for a committee to report the specified legislation and a means of discharging the committee if it fails to report. This discharge mechanism can be either automatic or a privileged motion with little or no debate allowed. There is also generally a method for the measure to reach the floor for prompt consideration, such as making it privileged. These provisions are more important in the House, where control of the agenda rests with the chamber and committee leadership, than in the Senate.

Often these procedures prohibit amendments, even committee amendments, to the measure and impose a time limit on its consideration. These characteristics are more important in the Senate, due to its greater vulnerability to dilatory tactics.

BIBLIOGRAPHY

Nickels, Ilona. *Fast-Track and the North American Free Trade Agreement.* Congressional Research Service, Library of Congress. CRS Rept. 93-116. 1993.

U.S. House of Representatives. *Constitution, Jefferson's Manual, and Rules of the House of Representatives, 103d Congress.* Compiled by William Holmes Brown. 102d Cong., 2d sess., 1992. H. Doc. 102-405.

U.S. House of Representatives. Committee on Rules. *Legislative Veto after Chadha.* 98th Cong., 2d sess., 1984. See Stanley Bach, "Statement on Expedited Procedures."

JAMES V. SATURNO

EXPLORATION. It is unlikely that members of the first Congress under the Constitution viewed exploration as one of their primary issues. Making the new government operational while dealing with problems of taxation, foreign affairs, Indians, and the public domain absorbed all their time, and yet prudent legislation on these matters demanded knowledge of the northern, southern, and especially the western frontiers. Article I, section 8 of the Constitution gave Congress the right to regulate commerce with the Indian tribes; Article IV, section 3 gave the federal government rights over the territories. Exploration as a federal activity was easily justified by these and other sections of the Constitution.

In the years from 1789 to 1803 Congress was well aware of the vast, unknown land mass leading to the "South Sea" (the Pacific Ocean). Its members knew of Capt. Robert Gray's discovery of the Columbia River (1792) and of Alexander Mackenzie's trek across Canada to the Pacific (1793). Some probably knew that in December 1789 the War Department had proposed that Lt. John Armstrong ascend the Missouri in an attempt to reach the Pacific but had been dissuaded from doing so after he reached St. Louis. Nevertheless congressional action involving exploration had to await the Louisiana Purchase and President Thomas Jefferson's interests in the West.

Jefferson initially planned to request funds for a western exploration in his annual message to Congress, but Secretary of the Treasury Albert Gallatin urged him instead to submit his proposal in a confidential communication. Gallatin may have feared that constitutional questions would be raised because the explorers would be leaving American territory. Jefferson used commerce with the Indians as constitutional justification for the endeavor. On 28 February 1803 Congress accepted Jefferson's request for $2,500. (More than three times that sum was spent for supplies and equipment, and the total bill exceeded $49,000.) Meriwether Lewis and William Clark were chosen to lead the expedition. Because of opposition from the Federalists, Jefferson remained tight-lipped about the expedition until it was under way.

The president, aware that the citizenry was excited about Lewis and Clark's expedition and about continued overland exploration, requested funding for other exploration projects. Congress appropriated $3,000 (rather than the $12,000 requested) for William Dunbar and George Hunter to explore the Red River to its source; although because of Spanish opposition the two men explored the Ouachita River instead. In 1805 Jefferson wrung $5,000 from Congress for another Red River expedition under the leadership of Thomas Freeman; it also failed in the face of Spanish hostility.

Worsening international relations and the War of 1812 halted this first wave of Congress-subsidized exploration. For a quarter of a century thereafter, private parties—fur trappers and traders or European sportsmen—were more likely than government officials to explore, but a few government expeditions were sent out to locate and construct frontier army posts. An exception was Maj. Stephen H. Long's expedition to the Rocky Mountains. In 1819 the major, having bungled an expedition bound for the Mandan villages at the great bend of the Missouri in present North Dakota—and facing an embarrassing congressional investigation—was hastily sent west to find the source of the Red River. Although he failed to find it he did succeed in fostering the concept of the Great Plains as "the Great American Desert."

President John Quincy Adams suggested to Congress in 1825 that the United States, as one of the world's great nations, should make contributions to exploration and increased knowledge. The House of Representatives concurred by passing a resolution in 1828—without an appropriation—suggesting that the president send out a small vessel for exploratory purposes.

This was a portent of increasing interest, which culminated in the 1830s in allotments of up to $300,000 to the Navy Department for exploration. After considerable bickering, in August 1838 the United States Exploring Expedition, led by Lt. Charles Wilkes, left Hampton Roads, Virginia. This voyage of nearly four years' duration made extraordinary contributions to geographical knowledge. It discovered that Antarctica is of continental size, charted the Fiji Islands, and mapped the Columbia River region. Yet upon its return in 1842 the results of the expedition were virtually ignored. Administrations had changed and other concerns commanded the attention of the nation and Congress; even today the Wilkes Expedition is but slightly known.

In the same year Wilkes returned, Missouri senator Thomas Hart Benton's son-in-law John C. Fremont began his explorations. In four expeditions between 1842 and 1849 (the first three financed by the government, the fourth by private subscription) Fremont explored the route to Oregon, Great Salt Lake, the California Trail, the Great Basin, and the southern Rockies. By now the expanding American West had become a political concern, and Senator Benton was one of several members of Congress to advocate expansion. They promoted expansion by influencing the policies of the Corps of Topographical Engineers, the army branch that was directly involved in western exploration. They wanted Oregon, Texas, the Southwest, and California for the United States, and harbors on the Pacific to expedite U.S. trade with the Orient. Inevitably, exploration entered into their plans.

With the end of the Mexican War, the acquisition of Oregon, and the discovery of gold in California, the demand arose for a transcontinental railroad. Sectional rivalries, reflected in congressional politics, played a large part in debate and discussion about the railroad. The common belief was that the country could afford only one transcontinental line, and thus its location was of considerable importance. Although the Topographical Engineers had reconnoitered, and favored, a southern route, it was clear that members of Congress from the central and northern sections of the United States would never agree to it. The result was authorization by Congress for a series of Pacific Railroad Surveys conducted primarily by officers of the Topographical Corps. Although sectional difficulties blocked the choice of a particular route or a Pacific railroad act until the Civil War, the results of the surveys were impressive. They revealed that several feasible routes, not just one, existed. Scientific studies carried out during the surveys were published by the government in impressive quarto volumes. Thus, congressional action to solve a political problem had resulted in advances in scientific and geographic knowledge.

After the Civil War, mapping of the West and knowledge of its geology and flora and fauna expanded rapidly. Two congressionally sponsored geographical and geological surveys and two under army auspices were undertaken from 1867 to 1878. The former were the U.S. Geological and Geographical Survey of the Territories and the U.S. Geographical and Geological Survey of the Rocky Mountain Region; the latter were the U.S. Geological Exploration of the Fortieth Parallel and the U.S. Geographical Survey West of the One Hundredth Meridian. These surveys are commonly known by the names of their leaders: the Hayden, Powell, King, and Wheeler surveys.

Congress was aware of the wastefulness brought on by the duplication of tasks by these expeditions even as funds were appropriated annually for their continuation. In 1874 and again in 1878 congressional hearings discussed the problem. The latter were aided by congressional mandate that the National Academy of Sciences make recommendations, and the academy's guidance was reflected in the legislation that materialized on 3 March 1879. The surveys were consolidated into one civilian U.S. Geological Survey (USGS) under the Interior Department. The survey has received nearly consistent congressional support and today is involved in research in the Arctic, Antarctica, and the islands of the Pacific; in mapping the moon; in astrogeology research; and in satellite surveys.

Congress was early aware of the need for explorations in Alaska and allowed funding for the purpose to come from appropriations to the army and navy. Rear Admiral Robert E. Peary's Arctic explorations, which culminated in his discovery of the North Pole on 6 April 1909, were financed by private groups, but he understood the value of good public relations and was careful to keep Congress informed of his exploits. In 1909 a congressional subcommittee recommended that Peary be officially recognized as discoverer of the North Pole, and that he be retired from the navy with the rank of rear admiral. Congress concurred. Rear Admiral Richard E. Byrd, also a navy officer, received considerable financial aid from Congress in the post–World War I era for his explorations in Antarctica, and Congress continues to support American research there.

The launching of *Sputnik* by the Soviet Union in 1957 aroused Congress to increase federal activities in space research and exploration. Congress had created the National Advisory Committee for Aeronautics (NACA) in 1915, and by 1958 it had some eight thousand employees. Legislation renamed NACA the National Aeronautics and Space Administration (NASA) and specified new responsibilities and authority. With congressional support, NASA conducted the Apollo missions to the moon and manages the space shuttle. In response to public attitudes, Congress has cooled NASA's more ambitious plans for a space station and planetary exploration, but the space program, and NASA, continue to secure large appropriations.

Several patterns are evident in Congress's relation to exploration. First, Congress often follows the leadership of the chief executive, as in the case of Jefferson's Lewis and Clark expedition. Second, Congress follows the public: if the public is interested, then so is Congress; if public interest lags, so does Congress lag in its support. Finally, Congress can be aroused when larger political issues are involved, as during the Pacific Railroad surveys and the creation of NASA.

[*See also* Aerospace; Territorial Expansion.]

BIBLIOGRAPHY

Dupree, A. Hunter. *Science in the Federal Government.* 1957.
Goetzmann, William H. *New Lands, New Men.* 1986.
Jackson, Donald. *Thomas Jefferson and the Stony Mountains.* 1981.
Manning, Thomas G. *Government in Science: The U.S. Geological Survey, 1867–1894.* 1967.

RICHARD A. BARTLETT

EX POST FACTO LAWS. Laws that alter the definition of a crime to punish an activity that was not a violation when committed, that increase the punishment for a crime after its commission, and

that limit defenses that were available when the crime was committed are all ex post facto laws prohibited by the Constitution. Article I, section 9, clause 3 imposes the prohibition on Congress; Article I, section 10, clause 1 imposes it on the states. The Supreme Court determined in 1798 in *Calder v. Bull* that the prohibition applies only to penal or criminal laws, and this limitation has been maintained ever since. There is no corresponding restriction on enactment of retroactive civil laws, nor is there a prohibition on federal laws impairing the obligation of contracts; such laws are tested instead under due process principles.

Substance, not form, governs analysis of whether a law imposes punishment that is criminal in nature. A law that limited federal court practice to attorneys who would swear that they had not aided the Confederate cause during the Civil War was held to violate the clause (*Ex parte Garland*, 1867), but laws providing for deportation of aliens were held not to impose punishment in the criminal sense (*Harisiades v. Shaughnessy*, 1952). Other issues have arisen over whether a law's retroactive effects bring it within one of the forbidden categories. Not all retroactive procedural and evidentiary changes that disadvantage a defendant are prohibited, the Court reiterated in *Collins v. Youngblood* (1990); only those (e.g., the elimination of a defense) that significantly reduce the proof necessary to convict are barred.

BIBLIOGRAPHY

Crosskey, William. "The True Meaning of the Constitutional Prohibition of Ex-Post-Facto Laws." *University of Chicago Law Review* 14 (1947): 539–566.
Singer, Norman J. *Statutes and Statutory Construction.* 1986.

GEORGE A. COSTELLO

EXPUNGEMENT. Adopted from the practices of the British House of Commons and Colonial legislatures, *expungement* is the legislative process by which specific words are struck from the record of proceedings of either the Senate or the House of Representatives. Expungement is tied to traditions of congressional decorum and helps to promote order during debate. Rules governing debate in both the House and the Senate require members to observe proper protocol. For example, members may be critical of legislation but may not engage in personal attacks.

Disorderly, derogatory, and unparliamentary language of any form may be expunged. Most typically, language expunged consists of words spoken on the floor. But words inserted into the *Congressional Record* from letters, telegrams, or charts may also be expunged. A motion to expunge may be made by the individual who entered the words, by the target of the offending remarks, or by a third party not directly involved.

When a senator or representative wishes to have material struck from the record, that member objects to the words and makes a motion that they be expunged. The motion may be accepted by unanimous consent, or a vote on the motion may be held. If the motion carries, the words are crossed out of the record by the clerk.

Words may be expunged immediately after they are spoken or well after the fact. For example, language uttered in 1834 that censured President Andrew Jackson was not expunged until 1837.

[*See also* Congress, *article on* Congressional Publications; Congressional Record.]

BIBLIOGRAPHY

Luce, Robert. *Legislative Procedure.* 1922. Pp. 527–534.
U.S. House of Representatives. *Deschler's Precedents of the United States House of Representatives,* by Lewis Deschler. 94th Cong., 2d sess., 1977. H. Doc. 94-661. Vol. 1, chap. 29.

MARY ETTA BOESL

EXTENSIONS OF REMARKS. The section of each day's *Congressional Record* that follows the proceedings of the House and Senate is known as the Extensions of Remarks. It is primarily used by members of the House to include the text of bills and additional legislative statements not delivered on the House floor as well as matters not germane to the proceedings, such as speeches delivered outside Congress, letters from and tributes to constituents, and published articles. A member must get permission from the House to have an item published in the Extensions of Remarks.

Although the laws and rules for publication of the *Record* provide direction for the use of this section by the Senate as well, it is only on rare occasions that remarks by senators are included here. Their so-called extraneous remarks are found in the Senate portion of the *Record* under the heading Additional Statements.

Until 1968 (90th Cong., 2d sess.), what is now known as the Extensions of Remarks section was called the Appendix. The Appendix formed part of both the daily and permanent editions of the *Record.* Beginning in 1941 (77th Cong., 1st sess.), each page number was preceded by the designation "A." Beginning in 1954 (83d Cong., 2d sess.), the Appendix pages were omitted from the permanent editions of the *Record* and could only be found in the daily editions. However, material from the Appendix considered germane to legislation was inserted in the permanent *Record* at the point where the legislation was under discussion.

Since 1968 the Extensions of Remarks have replaced the Appendix and been published in both the daily and permanent editions. At the same time the *Record* began publishing on the last page of each daily edition an alphabetical listing of members whose Extensions of Remarks appear in that issue. All of these actions were at the direction of the Joint Committee on Printing.

[*See also* Congressional Record.]

BIBLIOGRAPHY

U.S. Congress. Joint Committee on Printing. "Laws and Rules for Publication of the *Congressional Record.*" (Appears periodically in editions of the *Congressional Record* following the Extensions of Remarks.)
U.S. House of Representatives. *Deschler's Precedents of the United States House of Representatives,* by Lewis Deschler. 94th Cong., 2d sess., 1977. H. Doc. 94-661. Vol. 1, pp. 407–430.

MILDRED LEHMANN AMER

F

FAIR LABOR STANDARDS ACT (1938; 52 Stat. 1060–1069). Until Congress passed the Fair Labor Standards Act (FLSA) in 1938, federally legislated protection of labor extended only to railroad and maritime workers and federal employees. In 1918 and 1922 the Supreme Court had held federal child-labor laws invalid. States had begun to legislate safety and health standards and to regulate child labor and working hours in the last quarter of the nineteenth century, but, even here, judicial interpretation and employer opposition sharply limited what could be done.

Federal wage and hour standards first appeared in the 1930s with the industry codes promulgated by the National Recovery Administration (NRA). But the Supreme Court declared the NRA's industry codes unconstitutional in 1935. The Walsh-Healey Act (1936), setting the minimum labor standards in federal contracts, was only a partial substitute.

Drafted under the general direction of Secretary of Labor Frances Perkins, FLSA set a national minimum wage ($.25 per hour rising to $.40 over seven years). Maximum hours were not set as such, but FLSA required that work in excess of a forty-four-hour standard week (dropping to forty hours over two years) be paid at time and a half. But protected workers had clearly to be engaged in interstate commerce if the regulations were to survive court inspection. Consequently, FLSA excluded many workers: retail and service employees, local transportation personnel, employees in fishing and agriculture, and seasonal workers. The Congress of Industrial Organizations backed the legislation strongly, but the American Federation of Labor's support was much less emphatic. Employers were divided, with southern and rural interests seeking to preserve competitive regional differences.

The drive to enact FLSA came from within the administration of Franklin D. Roosevelt, notably from Secretary Perkins and the president himself. Cooperating closely with key congressional advocates—Sen. Hugo L. Black (D-Ala.) and Rep. William P. Connery, Jr. (D-Mass.)—Roosevelt and Perkins saw the bill pass the Senate in July 1937 by a vote of 56 to 28. But it was held up in the House by the AFL, which feared that mandated minimum wages would weaken collective bargaining, and by southern representatives opposed to wage increases in their region's industries. Overwhelming southern popular support for the bill became clear during the early stages of the 1938 election campaign, however, and in May 1938 the House passed a modified version of the Senate bill by a vote of 314 to 97. The final bill was written in conference and signed into law in June.

FSLA was the first successful attempt to implement wage and hour standards on a comprehensive national scale and remains the basis of federal labor standards to this day. Despite the act, many of the poorest workers—women, African Americans, migratory workers—remained severely disadvantaged, but some 300,000 people saw immediate gains from higher wages, and 1.3 million benefited from shorter hours.

BIBLIOGRAPHY

Boris, Eileen. "The Regulation of Homework and the Devolution of the Postwar Labor Standards Regime: Beyond Dichotomy." In *Labor Law in America: Historical and Critical Essays.* Edited by Christopher L. Tomlins and Andrew J. King. 1992.

Brandeis, Elizabeth. "Organized Labor and Protective Labor Legislation." In *Labor and the New Deal.* Edited by Milton Derber and Edwin Young. 1957.

Hart, Vivien. "Minimum-Wage Policy and Constitutional Inequality: The Paradox of the Fair Labor Standards Act of 1938." *Journal of Policy History* 1 (1989): 319–343.

CHRISTOPHER L. TOMLINS

FAMILIES OF MEMBERS. *See* Members, *article on* Spouses and Families.

FAMILY POLICIES. Family policy as a concern of the federal government is a phenomenon of the last quarter of the twentieth century. It became an item on the federal agenda with the beginning of the Carter administration in 1977. According to Gilbert Steiner in *The Futility of Family Policy* (1981), throughout most of the twentieth century, "the dominant ethic [had] discouraged civil intervention in family affairs." Although some still argue for that perspective, most national legislators in the 1990s favor proposals that assist both traditional and nontraditional families.

Early Legislation. In earlier years, there had been occasional federal attempts to assist individuals within the context of the family, but they had not been framed as attempts to strengthen or protect the family or to deal with the problems of dysfunctional families. In 1912, for example, Congress established the Children's Bureau in the Labor Department to conduct research on "all matters pertaining to the welfare of children and child life among all classes." After World War I, dozens of bills were introduced allocating economic and symbolic rewards to the veterans of that conflict and their surviving spouses, often extending benefits to wives of veterans whose disabilities and deaths were not service-connected. Other proposals provided assistance to widows of foreign service officers, to Gold Star Mothers, and to veterans' widows who, after remarrying, became single again.

In 1921 Congress enacted the Sheppard-Towner Maternity and Infancy Protection Act, the first major grant-in-aid program established by the federal government for state welfare programs. The law provided for instruction in the hygiene of maternity and infancy through public-health nurses, visiting nurses, consultation centers, child-care conferences, and literature distribution. It authorized $1.25 million distributed over a five-year period. States were eligible for the funds if they devised a plan for transmitting health information that received Children's Bureau approval. The legislation was allowed to lapse in 1929 but was reborn in the 1935 Social Security Act, Title V of which provided grants to the states for maternal and child health. Three programs were included under this title: maternal and child health services, crippled children's services, and child welfare services. Title IV initiated federal government financial aid to dependent children.

With the New Deal, national legislation such as the Social Security Act began to focus on support for poor families. William Henry Chafe, in *The American Woman* (1972), stated that government "ceased to be extraneous to the concerns of the family but instead provided school lunches, aid to dependent children, and relief checks which helped the family to survive." Aid to Dependent Children (ADC) was aimed principally at widows and their offspring. The Great Society legislation of the 1960s broadened the federal commitment to social welfare policies that assisted families.

Expanding the Family Policy Agenda. Over time, Congress has extended its attention beyond poor families to concern itself with dysfunctional families, issues of women's equality, and families pressured by changing cultural values. It can be argued that only one member of the House of Representatives in the 1970s—George Miller (D-Calif.)—considered family policy as his major priority. Sen. Walter F. Mondale (D-Minn.) also made children and family a major part of his focus in the 1970s. Under the Carter administration, "scholars and politicians recast a plethora of old social policy questions—child development, social services, public welfare—as issues of family policy" (Steiner, 1981).

In the 1980s Congress played a more direct and prominent role regarding family policy. In 1982, the House established a Select Committee on Children, Youth and Families. Advocates for the committee's establishment argued that with jurisdiction over programs affecting children and families scattered throughout the committee structure of Congress, no forum existed in which to carry out comprehensive review and oversight regarding issues concerning the nation's children. The panel's official charge included "problems of children, youth and families, including income maintenance, health, nutrition, education, welfare, employment and recreation." Initially, the select committee's focus was on children only, but it was expanded to include families after the lobbying efforts of family groups. The select committee could conduct studies and report findings to the House, but it could not report legislation. In a cost-cutting move, Congress abolished this select committee, along with others, in 1993.

In 1983 two caucuses were formed in the Senate to focus attention on the needs of children and families—the Senate Caucus on the Family and the Senate Children's Caucus. The Caucus on the Family studied such topics as the growing rate of family disintegration, teenage alcohol and drug abuse, adolescent pregnancy, teenage suicide, and juvenile delinquency. The Children's Caucus focus included the status of foster children, the cause and prevention of accidents among children, and juveniles in jail.

Another caucus instrumental in keeping family policy issues prominent in Congress in the 1980s was the Congressional Caucus on Women's Issues (CCWI). The CCWI has promoted a number of bills affecting women as family members, including measures on parental and disability leave, spousal retirement and social security pension equity, divorce reform, and dependent care.

In 1981 the CCWI introduced the Economic Equity Act, a compendium of bills, some affecting women as individuals and others in their roles as wives and mothers. The 97th Congress (1983–1985) passed several bills under the Economic Equity Act umbrella affecting women in the family context. Pension laws were changed to give spouses a right to the pensions of workers who died before retirement age but who had worked at least ten years and reached the age of forty-five. The Child Support Enforcement Amendments of 1984 required states to withhold money from the paychecks and state income tax refunds of parents delinquent in child support payments. The Civil Service Spouse Retirement Equity Act of 1984 protected the rights of former spouses of federal employees to survivor pension benefits and federal employee health plan coverage.

In 1985, after Ronald Reagan's landslide reelection victory, the CCWI devised a new strategy to make "women's issues" more palatable in the conservative era. Measures that might previously have been described as women's legislation were now labeled *pro-family*, a politically popular term normally associated with the political and religious right. Legislation for parental leave was the first proposal

to which this approach was applied. The next was child care legislation.

Some conservatives have opposed federal aid to dysfunctional families, arguing that such assistance is not a proper function of the federal government and is contrary to the rights of families to decide what is best for their children. However, others have promoted federal projects to protect the family, at least the traditional two-parent family with the mother at home and the father the economic provider.

Republicans were perceived to be the champions of family values and made "the family" their issue in the 1980s; but by 1988, congressional Democrats began to see the usefulness of making theirs the family-oriented party. The House Democratic leadership even devoted the party's annual conference that year to the theme "Our Family, Our Future." The core items in the late 1980s Democratic family agenda included elementary and secondary education reauthorization, welfare reform, job-protected family leave, mandatory worker health insurance, and expanded child care.

Child care topped the domestic agenda for both parties at the start of the 101st Congress (1989–1991); for the first time, Congress passed and the president signed into law a major child-care bill. The measure allowed $18.3 billion in tax credits to help low- and moderate-income families deal with the costs of child care and $4.25 billion for new grant programs to help states improve the quality and availability of such care. Those who owed no taxes received a refund from the government for child care expenses under this program. Previously, direct federal child care services had helped only poor families.

Congress also passed a law granting family and medical leave in 1990, an idea that was first introduced in 1985 by Rep. Patricia Schroeder (D-Colo.) The House, however, upheld President George Bush's veto of the measure; he again vetoed such legislation in 1992. In February 1993, as one of his earliest acts, President Bill Clinton signed into law the Family and Medical Leave Act. The legislation requires businesses employing fifty people or more to grant unpaid leave of up to twelve weeks per year to workers for the birth or adoption of a child or the illness of a close family member.

Although advocates of children's programs said political momentum had been building for several years, it accelerated after a September 1987 opinion survey, prepared for KIDSPAC (a political action committee promoting the welfare of children)

Landmark Legislation on Families

TITLE	YEAR ENACTED	REFERENCE NUMBER	DESCRIPTION
Sheppard-Towner Maternity and Infancy Protection Act	1921	P.L. 67-95	Provided matching federal grants-in-aid to states for the purpose of promoting child and maternal health services; provided for instruction through public health nurses, visiting nurses, consultation centers, child care conferences, and literature distribution.
Social Security Act	1935	P.L. 74-271	Provided payments to children deprived of parental support because of death, continued absence from the home, or incapacity of a parent.
Child Nutrition Act	1966	P.L. 89-642	Expanded the federal government school food aid program; authorized a pilot breakfast program and a nonfood assistance program (food preparation and storage equipment) for schools in poor areas.
Family Planning Services and Population Research (Title X of the Public Health Services Act)	1970	P.L. 91-572	Authorized $382 million for fiscal years 1971–1973 to coordinate and expand family planning services and population research activities of the federal government.
Child Nutrition Act Amendments	1972	P.L. 92-433	Established the Special Supplemental Food Program for Women, Infants, and Children (WIC)
Child Abuse Prevention and Treatment Act	1974	P.L. 93-247	Provided federal aid for the prevention and treatment of child abuse and neglect.
Health Services and Centers Act	1978	P.L. 95-626	Authorized health and social service programs for pregnant teenagers.
Title IV-E of the Social Security Act	1980	P.L. 96-272	Aimed to remove welfare children from foster care for placement either with their birth families or in permanent adoptive homes.
Adolescent Family Life Act	1981	P.L. 97-35	Provided pregnant teenagers with prenatal care and counseling; funded prevention services aimed at discouraging sexual activity among teenagers.

by Democratic pollster Peter D. Hart, showed public support for federal programs for children. Pressure by outside groups, usually organized from local communities, has served as a catalyst for congressional action on family policy, as in the case of domestic violence legislation in the late 1970s. Congress has also often been motivated to develop a policy on a particular family problem by the publication of national statistics showing the magnitude of the problem.

Controversies in the development of federal family policy have involved debates about money as much as about values. Arguments have developed over whether one's commitment to family is proportional to the amount of money one is willing to spend on federal programs to aid poor families, dysfunctional families, and families with children in general. Conservatives argue that their opposition to more federal spending to create family programs does not mean they are less committed to strengthening families, as liberals charge.

Federal programs for dealing with family problems other than poverty (which has often generated entitlement legislation) have usually begun with

Landmark Legislation on Families (Continued)

TITLE	YEAR ENACTED	REFERENCE NUMBER	DESCRIPTION
Child Support Enforcement Amendments	1984	P.L. 98-378	Required the withholding of money from the paychecks of parents delinquent in court-ordered child support payments.
Retirement Equity Act	1984	P.L. 98-397	Expanded pension coverage for employees who left and subsequently returned to a job; ensured the pension rights of homemakers whose working spouses died before reaching retirement age; lowered the age at which young workers could start building up pension credits.
Child Abuse Amendments	1984	P.L. 98-457	Established a program of matching grants for states that set up special funds for the prevention of child abuse.
Family Support Act	1988	P.L. 100-485	Required states to provide education, training, and work programs for welfare mothers; extended child care and medical benefits to families in which parents left the welfare rolls for jobs.
Budget-Reconciliation Bill, Title V: Child Care	1990	P.L. 101-508	Provided funding for child-care assistance.
Family and Medical Leave Act	1993	P.L. 103-3	Required businesses employing fifty people or more to grant unpaid leave of up to twelve weeks per year to workers for the birth or adoption of a child or the illness of a close family member.
Title IV-12, Social Security Act of the Budget Reconciliation Act	1993	P.L. 103-66	Informally referred to as "family preservation," this act provided funds for states to help troubled families stay together. It guaranteed each state a fixed amount of money for family preservation efforts, such as intense temporary counseling at home.

narrow-focused demonstration projects or matching grants to the states for community projects with a specific dollar amount allocated. Research has often been a component of the legislation. The programs have usually been authorized for a two- or four-year period. Renewals have involved increased appropriations and expansion of the program (e.g., to include child abuse) although just maintaining funding has required a constant struggle.

Many family policy items have been on Congress's agenda since the 1970s, causing considerable friction and debate. For example, Congress first passed a comprehensive child care bill in 1971, but it was vetoed by President Richard M. Nixon on grounds that it might undermine the family by encouraging women to work outside the home. His

veto was sustained. For nearly twenty years, Congress struggled with the issue before enacting the 1990 child care bill.

Poverty Programs. Having created the welfare state and expanded its services, Congress had to control what it had wrought. Thus, welfare reform became a major agenda item in the 1970s and remained so for nearly twenty years before Congress and the president enacted major changes in the welfare system with the Family Support Act of 1988.

As noted above, Aid to Dependent Children (ADC) provided funds only for dependent children; not until 1950 did Congress add a caretaker grant to provide for the mother's essential expenses and change the program's name to Aid to Families with

Dependent Children (AFDC). ADC was administered at the state and local levels, with grants from the federal government to supplement its financing. In 1961, Congress amended the AFDC title of the Social Security Act to allow states to provide benefits to two-parent families where both parents were unemployed. Only twenty-six states have elected to use this option.

The welfare rolls grew significantly during the 1960s. Congress, at the urging of President Lyndon B. Johnson during the Great Society years of 1964 to 1968, responded with an expansion of poverty programs. The Food Stamp Program was established in 1964. Medicare and Medicaid legislation passed in 1965. In 1966 Congress enacted the Child Nutrition Act, which targeted more money to poor communities, and, as part of the Economic Opportunity Amendments, initiated the Head Start program, which was designed to prepare preschool children from deprived families to enter kindergarten or first grade.

In 1972, Congress initiated a two-year pilot program to provide supplemental food assistance to pregnant and lactating women and infants up to age four in the form of a $20 million amendment to the 1966 Child Nutrition Act. The Women, Infants, and Children program (WIC) has become one of the most popular social programs on Capitol Hill, but unlike most other welfare programs, it is not an entitlement program. It requires an annual appropriation from Congress, which is then spread only as far as the money allows. This means that not all eligible women and children receive benefits. Along with the successful Head Start education program, full funding of WIC has been championed in recent Congresses. But although its supporters have shown that it saves money in the long run, increased spending for such a social program runs afoul of budget constraint considerations that have dominated Congresses since 1980.

In 1970 President Nixon proposed the Family Assistance Plan, which would have guaranteed a federal payment of $1,600 a year to a family of four with no income and assistance to the "working poor." Under the Social Security Act, the states determined who would receive assistance and how much they would receive. Under Nixon's proposal, the amount of federal assistance would no longer be tied to the level of state appropriations. It passed the House easily but was rejected by the Senate Finance Committee. Liberals felt that the benefits were too small and the work requirements too stringent, while for conservatives, the bill was too expensive.

For eighteen years afterward, Congress grappled with the question of welfare reform, mainly in terms of controlling costs. In 1988 Congress passed the Family Support Act with the intent to promote economic self-reliance for low-income families, particularly those headed by single mothers. The bill required states to establish education, training, and work programs designed to move welfare recipients to full-time jobs (through the Job Opportunities and Basic Skills Training [JOBS] program). It would guarantee welfare mothers the child care, transportation, and other support they might need to participate in the program. And it stiffened child-support enforcement to ensure that noncustodial parents provide financial assistance to their families.

The welfare reform agenda in Congress has included changes in the foster care system. In 1980 Congress passed legislation (Title IV-E of the Social Security Act) aimed at removing children from foster care for placement with either their birth families or permanent adoptive homes. It limited federal support for foster care by limiting matching payments to states and established a program of federal adoption assistance to encourage the adoption of children with special problems that made unsubsidized adoption unlikely.

Dysfunctional Families. Federal concern with dysfunctional families has centered on child abuse, domestic violence, and teenage sexuality and pregnancy. In this domain of family policy, philosophical conflict over the proper role of government, particularly the federal government, has been especially sharp. Congress has also struggled with the question of whether these programs should be restricted to low-income families or be unrelated to income. The passage of the Child Abuse Prevention and Treatment Act in 1973 initiated the federal government's involvement in fighting child abuse, mainly through demonstration programs and research. In 1978 the act was extended for four years and expanded to initiate a modest attack on the problem of sexual abuse of children. Opponents argued that these programs were not a federal responsibility. Rep. Earl F. Landgrebe (R-Ind.) stated that provisions allowing states to remove children from their parents were reminiscent of the practices of totalitarian states such as Nazi Germany and the Soviet Union. However, the law was repeatedly reauthorized. The 1989 version included funds to provide "respite" care for families of severely ill or disabled children as well as for referral or support services for families of children who were disabled or at risk of being abused.

In the 1970s, proponents of federal legislation concerning domestic violence were not as fortunate as the proponents of child abuse legislation. In 1979, Congress debated the first such proposal, the Domestic Violence Prevention and Services Act. It would have funded direct service programs to the states for community-based, nonprofit groups to provide shelter and other services to victims of domestic violence. Opponents sent a "Dear Colleague" letter to all senators, stating "This legislation represents one giant step by the federal social service bureaucracy into family matters which are properly, more effectively and democratically represented by the states and local communities." The bill was defeated.

However, legislation was enacted in 1984 authorizing $63 million over three years for programs to prevent family violence and aid state efforts to provide shelter to victims of domestic abuse. The authorization was part of the Child Abuse Amendments of 1984, the central portion of which was legislation designed to ensure that severely handicapped infants received appropriate medical care. Although the authorization for federal family violence assistance was opposed by the Reagan administration, it met little opposition in Congress.

Teenage pregnancy and sexual activity in general constitute a third major family problem that Congress has tackled. Congress initiated action in this area in 1978, when it authorized $210 million for fiscal year 1979–1981 for health and social service programs for pregnant teenagers. In 1981 Congress enacted an adolescent family life program that provided funds for initiatives to discourage teenage sexual activity. It also continued the 1978 initiative for pregnant teenagers and appropriated money for "scientific research on the causes and consequences of premarital adolescent sexual relations and pregnancy." The legislation prohibited any reference to abortion during counseling sessions funded under the program. The law was nicknamed "the chastity bill."

Abortion. The abortion issue has hampered the passage of some bills dealing with family concerns, especially the authorization of funds for family planning services. Major federal involvement in family planning began in 1970 with passage of Title X of the Public Health Services Act, which among other things established an Office of Population Affairs in the Department of Heath, Education and Welfare. Of the funds authorized, $91.7 million was budgeted for services to 2.2 million of the estimated 5 million low-income women who needed and wanted birth control information but did not have

access to family planning services. The rest was to go to research and international population activities. The law mandated that none of the funds appropriated could be used in programs where abortion was a method of family planning. Its renewal expired in 1985 because Congress failed to settle abortion disputes. Disagreements over abortion also led to the lapse of the Adolescent Family Life Act in 1990.

Near the end of the twentieth century, congressional interest in family policy was expected to grow. "Pro-family" legislative initiatives were high on the agenda of many members of the 103d Congress. It was anticipated that in addition to new proposals, great attention would also be given to the consolidation and coordination of existing programs.

[*See also* Abortion; Aging Committee, House Select; Aging Committee, Senate Special; Children, Youth, and Families Committee, House Select; Labor and Human Resources Committee, Senate; Social Welfare and Poverty.]

BIBLIOGRAPHY

Langley, Patricia A. "The Coming of Age of Family Policy." *Families in Society: The Journal of Contemporary Human Services* 72 (1991): 116–120.

Nelson, Barbara. *Making an Issue of Child Abuse.* 1984.

Nutting, Brian. "Two Caucuses on Children, Families Formed." *Congressional Quarterly Weekly Report* (18 June 1983): 1236.

Rovner, Julie. "Congress Clears Overhaul of Welfare System." *Congressional Quarterly Weekly Report* (1 October 1988): 2699–2701.

Rovner, Julie. "Democrats Lining Up Behind 'Family' Banner." *Congressional Quarterly Weekly Report* (30 January 1988): 183–188.

Steiner, Gilbert. *The Futility of Family Policy.* 1981.

BARBARA C. BURRELL

FAREWELL ADDRESS, WASHINGTON'S. *See* Washington's Farewell Address.

FARM BLOC. Jolted by a severe post–World War I economic slump, the American Farm Federation Bureau facilitated the organization of a short-lived, formal congressional farm bloc in the early 1920s. On 9 May 1921, at a bipartisan meeting of midwestern and southern senators in Farm Bureau offices in Washington, D.C., an equal number of Republicans and Democrats founded the bloc, agreeing to seek farm-relief legislation by acting in unison without regard to party. The size of the bloc

FARMERS' PROTEST MARCH. On the Capitol steps, 1978.

doubled to twenty-four when six senators of each party subsequently joined.

Republican-led, first by William S. Kenyon of Iowa and then by Arthur Capper of Kansas, the bloc included many influential senators, such as George W. Norris (R-Nebr.), Charles L. McNary (R-Oreg.), Claude A. Swanson (D-Va.), and Morris Sheppard (D-Tex.). A less-structured corollary bloc of approximately one hundred members in the House of Representatives was headed by Republican Lester J. Dickinson of Iowa.

With ample nonbloc support, this wobbly coalition took credit for voluminous legislation in the 67th Congress (1921–1923), including the regulation of meat packers, stockyards, and trading in grain futures; increasing the capital of federal land banks; extending immunity from antitrust prosecution to agricultural cooperatives; and raising tariff rates on foreign agricultural products.

Sectional clashes shattered the bloc in the next Congress. However, the Farm Bureau strenuously promoted cooperation between the Midwest and the South during the 1920s in an effort to restore the bloc to optimum strength. Congressional passage of the McNary-Haugen bill in 1927 and 1928 signified partial reconciliation, but genuine unity occurred only when Franklin D. Roosevelt entered the White House.

The bloc flourished in the New Deal atmosphere of congeniality toward agriculture and coalition politics. Recognition of farm interests in major legislation—such as the Agricultural Adjustment Acts of 1933 and 1938 and the Tobacco and Cotton Control Acts of 1934—demonstrated the bloc's political power. Reciprocity between the various farm groups maintained the bloc's equilibrium, and its members wielded vast influence by virtue of committee assignments, seniority, and ties to farm lobbies and the government's agricultural bureaucracy. Particularly noted for skillfully securing largess for bloc constituents were Senators John H. Bankhead II (D-Ala.), J. W. Elmer Thomas (D-Okla.), and Clyde M. Reed (R-Kans.), as well as Representatives Clarence Cannon (D-Mo.) and Everett M. Dirksen (R-Ill.). The bloc secured strong price supports during World War II and after, and its influence continued nearly undiminished in the 1950s.

Although the term *farm bloc* has almost vanished from the political vocabulary in recent decades, legislators employing bloc tactics still exert enormous clout on behalf of farmers. They have less strength than before, however, as urban and labor interests have become less supportive, environmental and consumer groups more active in shaping agricultural policy, and the number of farmers steadily fewer. Fundamental farm problems persist, however, often reflecting not so much declining political power as the difficulty of finding solutions to economic and technological dislocations in agriculture.

An integral feature of twentieth-century politics, the farm bloc has adeptly represented a shrinking farm population. One of the best examples of American interest-group politics, the bloc illustrates the process by which a group exerts an influence on public policy disproportionate to its size.

[*See also* McNary-Haugen Farm Relief Bill.]

BIBLIOGRAPHY

McCune, Wesley. *The Farm Bloc*. 1943.
Shideler, James H. *Farm Crisis, 1919–1923*. 1957.

PATRICK G. O'BRIEN

FEDERAL AID ROAD ACT. *See* Rural Post Roads Act.

FEDERAL ANTI–PRICE DISCRIMINATION ACT (1936; 49 Stat. 1526–1528). During the 1920s many socioeconomic changes combined to transform the retail grocery and drug business. According to a Federal Trade Commission (FTC) report released in 1934, large chain stores such as Kroger and Piggly Wiggly had been competing unfairly with more modest retailers. Because of the enormous quantity of goods that chains bought as compared with the purchases of individual shopkeepers, the supermarkets were able to demand and to receive preferential prices, thereby undercutting the financial viability of their smaller competitors. Besides quantity discounts, such companies exacted advertising allowances, which served as rebates, since few stores actually publicized individual products. Chains also used price leaders (selling merchandise at cost) and loss leaders (selling goods below cost) to weaken their competition, offsetting their losses by charging higher prices in other markets or by raising prices once their rivals had been eliminated.

When the FTC report appeared, the problem seemed to have been solved through National Recovery Administration (NRA) codes outlawing most of these questionable practices. But this relief was short-lived, for on 27 May 1935, the Supreme Court, in *Schechter Poultry Corp. v. United States*, unanimously declared the NRA unconstitutional. Members of Congress quickly launched an offensive to outlaw price discrimination. H. B. Teegarden, general counsel for the Wholesale Grocers' Association, already had an amendment to the Clayton Antitrust Act (1914) ready for use when the NRA ceased to exist. On 11 June 1935, he convinced Rep. Wright Patman (D-Tex.) to sponsor the measure (H.R. 8442). Two weeks later, Senate Majority Leader Joseph T. Robinson (D-Ark.) introduced an identical bill in the Senate (S. 3154). The bills proposed to ban price discrimination on similar goods if that practice helped to create a monopoly or substantially lessened competition. They even allowed the FTC to bring prima facie cases, forcing manufacturers to prove their innocence. Retailers were also liable, since the act outlawed receiving a discriminatory price.

The measure did not sail through Congress rapidly or easily. Before it could be considered, President Franklin D. Roosevelt temporarily derailed it by first pushing through his Second Hundred Days programs. Then the bill bogged down in hearings in the House before finally passing late in May 1936. In the Senate, business interests tried to sidetrack it by supporting the less rigorous Borah-Van Nuys proposal. The Institute of Distribution, a lobby for chain stores, began a publicity campaign, charging that the proposal would hurt farmers, consumers, and laborers. Without any White House aid, Robinson forced the bill through the Senate and into a conference committee, where he, Patman, and Teegarden formulated the final draft. Roosevelt then signed the Federal Anti–Price Discrimination (Robinson-Patman) Act into law on 19 June 1936.

Seen as a way to protect modest businesses from being destroyed by the chain stores, the Robinson-Patman Act failed to stop the demise of small, independent grocers and druggists. The consumer appeal of supermarkets and national chains proved too great. Several court decisions also weakened the law by allowing some discriminatory pricing. Yet the Robinson-Patman Act does permit the FTC to intervene in cases of unfair price fixing, and it gives small businesses access to the courts when their owners can point to predatory pricing practices.

[See also National Industrial Recovery Act.]

BIBLIOGRAPHY

Patman, Wright. *Complete Guide to the Robinson-Patman Act.* 1963.
U.S. Federal Trade Commission. *Final Report on the Chain Store Investigation.* 74th Cong., 1st sess., 1934. S. Doc. 4.
Weller, Cecil E., Jr. "Joseph Taylor Robinson and the Robinson-Patman Act," *Arkansas Historical Quarterly* 47 (Spring 1988): 29–36.

CECIL E. WELLER, JR.

FEDERAL COMMUNICATIONS ACT. *See* Communications Act of 1934.

FEDERAL CORRUPT PRACTICES ACT OF 1925 (43 Stat. 1070–1074).

The Federal Corrupt Practices Act of 1925 repealed and replaced provisions of earlier federal statutes enacted by Congress in 1910 and 1911 that regulated federal elections. These early campaign financing regulations required the reporting and filing of financial statements that itemized campaign contributions and expenses of candidates for both primary and general elections to congressional offices. A Supreme Court decision in 1921 ruled that Congress did not have the authority to regulate primary election campaigns. Subsequently, Congress passed the 1925 act, which included many provisions of the earlier acts but applied coverage only to general elections.

Major provisions of the 1925 Corrupt Practices Act required political committees and candidates to file financial statements of political contributions and expenditures, limited the amount of expenditures that could be made by congressional candidates, and prohibited political contributions by corporations.

Although the 1925 act gave the appearance of effectively controlling federal election contributions and spending, loopholes in the law made it largely ineffective. The reporting requirements and limitations on expenditures by candidates applied only to congressional, not to presidential, candidates, and covered only general or special elections. Primary elections were left unregulated, as was spending for nominating conventions. Required reports were neither sufficiently detailed nor accessible to provide for public monitoring. In later years, the expenditure limitations on congressional candidates, which had not been adjusted since 1925, became unrealistically low, and the expenditure limitations on political committees were easily evaded by the use of multiple committees.

In 1971, Congress sought to address the law's inadequacies with a new comprehensive campaign reform act, the Federal Election Campaign Act of 1971, which, among its other provisions, repealed the 1925 act.

BIBLIOGRAPHY

Yadlosky, Elizabeth, and Jack Maskell. "Reform of Federal Campaign Finance Procedures." *Forensic Quarterly* 48 (November 1974): 452–455.

RICHARD C. SACHS

FEDERAL ELECTION COMMISSION.

The Federal Election Commission (F.E.C.) is responsible for administering and enforcing the Federal Election Campaign Act (F.E.C.A.). The F.E.C., created in 1974 when the Federal Election Campaign Act was amended, has six voting commissioners (three Republicans and three Democrats) as well as two nonvoting members, the clerk of the House of Representatives and the secretary of the Senate. The 1974 amendments to the F.E.C.A. required two of the six commissioners to be appointed by the president, two to be appointed by the Speaker of the House, and two to be appointed by the president pro tempore of the Senate. In 1976 the Supreme Court ruled in *Buckley v. Valeo* (424 U.S. 1 [1976]) that the original composition of the Federal Election Commission violated the separation of powers clause because, although the F.E.C. was an agency within the executive branch, four of its six commissioners were appointed by Congress. As a result of the Supreme Court's ruling the commission was reconstituted, and all six commissioners are appointed by the president and subject to confirmation by the Senate.

The Federal Election Commission has three main responsibilities: to enforce the Federal Election Campaign Act, to administer the public funding of presidential campaigns, and to collect and disclose campaign finance reports filed by candidates, political action committees (PACs), and the political party campaign committees. Candidates for federal office are required to regularly report campaign receipts and expenditures to the Federal Election Commission. Political parties and PACs are also required to report to the F.E.C. expenditures on behalf of federal candidates. Information on campaign receipts and expenditures is public information and is made available by the commission.

While the Federal Election Commission receives high praise for its disclosure of candidate, political action committee, and party financial reports, it is routinely criticized for its enforcement activities. The commission is criticized for its inability to act in a bipartisan or nonpartisan fashion, the slowness of its enforcement procedures, and the lack of severity of its fines. However, the major criticisms levied against the F.E.C. are a result of the structures and procedures established by Congress. For example, while most independent agencies have an uneven number of commissioners, the F.E.C. has three Democratic and three Republican commissioners, thus making the agency a partisan, rather than a bipartisan or nonpartisan agency. On controversial partisan questions the commission often splits its votes 3 to 3, thus ensuring inaction. Similarly, the slowness of the enforcement procedures is largely a result of the statutory provisions under which the F.E.C. operates.

The F.E.C. is also criticized for the slowness of its audit procedures of presidential election campaigns. By law, all presidential candidates who receive public funds for their campaigns must be audited by the Federal Election Commission. The F.E.C. audits often drag on for years after the election, requiring the campaign to have someone, usually the campaign treasurer, available to answer F.E.C. inquiries. However, while members of Congress criticize the commission's slowness and inaction, they also have been unwilling to expand the F.E.C.'s powers and responsibilities.

BIBLIOGRAPHY

Jackson, Brooks. *Broken Promise: Why the Federal Election Commission Failed.* 1990.
Magleby, David B., and Candice J. Nelson. *The Money Chase: Congressional Campaign Finance Reform.* 1990.

CANDICE J. NELSON

FEDERAL HOLIDAYS.

Since 1870 more than eleven hundred different proposals have been offered to establish federal holidays. Only eleven have been approved: New Year's Day (1870), Independence Day (1870), Christmas Day (1870), Washington's Birthday (1879), Memorial Day (1887), Labor Day (1894), Veterans Day (1938), Thanksgiving Day (1941), Inauguration Day (1957), Columbus Day (1968), and the Birthday of Martin Luther King, Jr., (1983). Although these patriotic celebrations are frequently referred to as national holidays, they are legally applicable only to federal employees. All federal employees receive ten holidays. The eleventh, Inauguration Day, is a holiday only for federal employees in the Washington, D.C., metropolitan area. Although federal holidays are not binding on the country as a whole, most are observed by state and local governments as well as by private industry.

The first holiday law in 1870 was apparently prompted by a memorial drafted by bankers and businessmen in the nation's capital. It was applicable only to the 5,500 federal workers in the District of Columbia. In 1879 Congress added Washington's Birthday to the holidays observed by federal workers in the District of Columbia. Congress chose not to extend the holiday to federal employees in other parts of the country until 1885.

Congress's decision to approve Decoration Day (also known as Memorial Day) in 1887 largely resulted from the lobbying efforts of federal employees who had served in the Civil War. This legislation was preceded by twenty years of varied observances throughout the country. When Congress approved the Labor Day holiday on 28 June 1894, it joined twenty-one states that had already set a day honoring the labor movement.

In 1938 the twentieth anniversary of the signing of the armistice ending World War I prompted a second holiday to honor America's war dead. Before Congress approved the Armistice Day holiday, the occasion had been marked by ad hoc civic and religious commemorations for two decades. In 1954 the name of Armistice Day was changed to Veterans Day to commemorate the efforts of American servicemen and servicewomen in World War II and Korea as well.

Thanksgiving Day gained approval as a federal holiday in 1941, following eighty years of annual presidential Thanksgiving proclamations. Inauguration Day became a federal holiday in the metropolitan area of the District of Columbia in 1957 for practical reasons and also to allow federal employees an opportunity to observe the historic events associated with presidential inaugurations.

A grassroots lobbying effort led by business and public interest groups provided the impetus for the

Federal Holidays

Holiday	Date Established	Date Celebrated
New Year's Day	28 June 1870	1 January
Birthday of Martin Luther King, Jr.	2 November 1983	Third Monday in January
Inauguration Day	11 January 1957	20 January of each fourth year after 1965
Washington's Birthday[1]	31 January 1879	Third Monday in February[2]
Memorial Day	23 February 1887	Last Monday in May[3]
Independence Day	28 June 1870	4 July
Labor Day	28 June 1894	First Monday in September
Columbus Day	28 June 1968	First Monday in October
Veterans Day[4]	13 May 1938	11 November[5]
Thanksgiving Day	26 December 1941	Fourth Thursday in November
Christmas Day	28 June 1870	25 December

[1]Although popularly known as Presidents' Day and Washington–Lincoln Day, this holiday remains officially Washington's Birthday.
[2]Originally celebrated on 22 February.
[3]Originally celebrated on 30 May.
[4]Originally called Armistice Day.
[5]Originally celebrated on 11 November. The date of the celebration was changed to the fourth Monday in October in 1968 and then was changed back to 11 November in 1975.

Monday Holiday Law of 1968, which changed the observance of Washington's Birthday, Memorial Day, and Veterans Day to Mondays and created an additional federal holiday—Columbus Day. Supporters argued that the three-day weekend measure would reduce employee absenteeism, eliminate costly production interruptions caused by midweek holidays, afford increased opportunities for family activities, stimulate tourism, and enhance sales in a broad range of businesses. Opponents contended that long-weekend holidays would adversely affect the spiritual life of the nation and lead to a substantial increase in traffic deaths. Seven years later, Congress determined that changing Veterans Day to a Monday had resulted in confusion as well as resentment over tampering with traditional holidays and returned celebration of the holiday to 11 November.

On 3 November 1983, President Ronald Reagan signed legislation designating the third Monday of January as a paid holiday for federal employees to honor Rev. Martin Luther King, Jr. The King Birthday Law climaxed a fifteen-year, occasionally acrimonious struggle in Congress. Civil rights groups supported the holiday as a tribute to the martyred civil rights leader. Others derided King's worthiness for such recognition and declared the public-sector and private-sector cost of an additional holiday unacceptably high. Ultimately, Congress decided that the symbolic value of honoring Dr. King outweighed the holiday's impact on the economy and voted to approve the holiday.

[*See also* Commemorative Legislation.]

BIBLIOGRAPHY

Hatch, Jane M. *The American Book of Days*. 1978.
Myers, Robert J. *Celebrations: The Complete Book of American Holidays*. 1972.

STEPHEN W. STATHIS

FEDERAL HOUSING ACTS. Federal housing laws of the 1930s were designed for two main purposes: to provide reliable sources of mortgage funds for housing, which had largely dried up during the Great Depression, and to stimulate construction activity and thereby provide employment. Other objectives were to promote home ownership, clear slums, and help low-income families get decent housing that was within their means.

The first major legislation of the period was the Federal Home Loan Bank Act (P.L. 72-304), enacted in 1932, the last year of the Hoover administration. This law laid the groundwork for a federally regulated system of savings and loan associations specializing in financing home mortgages. With the addition of deposit insurance by the National Housing Act (P.L. 73-479), passed in 1934, the savings and loans evolved into the leading source of long-term credit for housing until the 1980s.

An early New Deal measure was the Home Owners' Loan Act of 1933 (P.L. 73-43), which created the Home Owners' Loan Corporation (HOLC). This agency made direct loans to owners who were unable to get loans elsewhere and were facing loss of their properties. The HOLC made more than one million loans by mid 1936, of which 138,000 were foreclosed by the end of May 1939, and is credited with helping to stabilize real estate values.

The Federal Housing Administration (FHA) was also established by the National Housing Act. This agency was authorized to insure mortgage lenders against loss on residential loans that met government standards. From 1934 through 1993, FHA insured more than 21 million home mortgages and mortgages on multifamily buildings containing about 4 million dwelling units.

Still another provision of the 1934 act permitted creation of national mortgage associations to purchase and sell first mortgages in a secondary market, using the proceeds of notes and debentures issued in capital markets. The reluctance of private groups to go into this business led to the establishment, in 1938, of a government agency, the Federal National Mortgage Association, or Fannie Mae, to function as a secondary market facility.

Fannie Mae evolved into a major secondary market supplier of long-term housing credit in the postwar period. It was transformed into a government-chartered, stockholder-owned enterprise in 1968; some of its responsibilities in support of assisted housing and government-insured housing were assigned to a new government agency named the Government National Mortgage Association, or Ginnie Mae. Another entity patterned on Fannie Mae, the Federal Home Loan Mortgage Corporation, or Freddie Mae, was created within the Home Loan Bank System in 1970 and has since grown rapidly. The 1934 law thus laid the foundation for a nationwide system of residential mortgage finance still operational in the 1990s.

Low-rent public housing was another creation of 1930s legislation. A coalition of labor groups, social workers, architects, and others who were concerned about the grim housing conditions of millions of low-wage earners and other low-income families urged the government to provide such housing. For low-income families, the financial reforms brought by the FHA and the FHLB system were not enough; they needed deep rent or income subsidies. Real estate groups called for rent certificates for use in ex-

isting housing. After a long legislative struggle, Congress passed the United States Housing Act of 1937 (P.L. 75-412), which authorized federal payments to cover the capital cost of low-rent housing projects built and owned by local housing authorities. The need to stimulate construction activity and the desire to clear slums were persuasive arguments in the choice of this approach.

By 1942, public housing authorities were functioning in more than 500 localities, but the program had achieved only modest results—fewer than 200,000 units approved when the war effort required a reallocation of building resources. In 1993, there were about 1.4 million public housing units in the nation, providing shelter for 3 million persons.

Amendments to the 1937 act have created other programs to assist low-income housing, notably the Section 8 rental assistance program, under which about 2.5 million households were getting rent certificates or vouchers in 1993. Additionally, more than half a million low-income households were living in private developments with rents lowered under mortgage interest subsidy programs of the Department of Housing and Urban Development. About 400,000 low-income households in rural communities received rental housing subsidies through programs of the Farmers Home Administration.

Some of the issues confronting the framers of early housing laws have been debated ever since. Is there a need for financial institutions that specialize in residential loans? What risk does the government take in insuring private savings deposits or mortgage loans, and how can it protect itself against undue risk? (The savings and loan debacle of the 1980s showed how costly government guarantee programs can be.) What types of housing assistance and related services are most likely to enable low-income families to gain dignity and become self-reliant? Should families receiving assistance represent a cross section of the lower income community or should they be limited to the most deprived and deeply disadvantaged in terms of income, household type, and potential for upward mobility? How much discretion should be vested in local authorities, and what role should tenants themselves play in initiating, constructing, and managing housing? Should the federal government overlook or attempt to alter local patterns and practices of racial discrimination in providing housing aid?

Policy issues have often been intertwined with difficult technical questions: How should the degree of risk in setting insurance premiums for government insurance programs like FHA be determined? What is substandard or inadequate housing? What percentage of income can a low- or moderate-income family afford to spend on shelter? Should locations and amenities of assisted housing meet standards of market-level developments or properties? Such questions remain part of the ongoing housing debate.

BIBLIOGRAPHY

Colean, Miles, *American Housing.* 1944.

Fish, Gertrude Sipperly, ed. *The Story of Housing.* 1979.

U.S. House of Representatives. Committee on Banking, Finance, and Urban Affairs. Subcommittee on Housing and Community Development. *A Chronology of Housing Legislation and Selected Executive Actions, 1892–1992.* 103d Cong., 1st sess., 1993. Committee Print 103-2.

MORTON J. SCHUSSHEIM

FEDERALISM. The Framers faced a fundamental dilemma as they gathered in Philadelphia during the summer of 1787. The existing confederation, which provided states a large degree of independence from the national government, had proved unsatisfactory. The national economy was in a depression, the continental dollar was unstable, the navy was unable to adequately protect international shipping, and the army was unable to maintain domestic order. Given these deficiencies, the Framers decided to change the entire governmental structure, including existing intergovernmental relationships. However, they could not adopt a unitary system of governance in which all governmental power is vested in the central government and is delegated, at the central government's discretion, to constituent governments. The states had just won their independence from a nation governed by unitary principles, and they were not willing to give up their political autonomy. Therefore, the Framers invented a new intergovernmental system that was subsequently called American federalism.

The Constitution is the binding legal document that defines American federalism. However, it does not precisely delineate what the relationship between the federal government and states ought to be. As James Madison wrote in *The Federalist*, the Constitution is "neither wholly federal nor wholly national." For example, several constitutional provisions suggest that the relationship between the federal government and states should be a unitary one, with the federal government playing the pre-dominant role in domestic policy. Article VI states that the federal government's laws "shall be the Supreme Law of the Land." Article I, section 8 empowers Congress to provide for the common defense and general welfare of the United States. Moreover, Article 1, section 8 empowers Congress to take any action deemed "necessary and proper" to carry out its assigned duties.

However, other constitutional provisions suggest that the relationship between the federal government and states should be a confederal one, with states playing the predominant role in domestic policy. For example, Article I, section 8 specifically lists seventeen "enumerated" congressional powers, including the power to lay and collect taxes, coin money, establish post offices, fix a standard of weights and measures, and declare war. This has suggested to many that the Framers intended congressional powers to be limited to these seventeen specific activities. Otherwise, why would they have gone to the trouble of listing them? Moreover, the Tenth Amendment explicitly guarantees that all powers not granted to the federal government are reserved to the states or to the people.

These constitutional ambiguities have led to a number of theories concerning what the relationship between the federal government and states ought to be. For example, the most important political disputes during the 1800s, including the Civil War, arose primarily from disagreements between those who believed in the states' rights, or compact, theory of American federalism and those who believed in the nationalist theory of American federalism.

Advocates of the states' rights interpretation of the Constitution, including Thomas Jefferson, Andrew Jackson, and John C. Calhoun, argued that states created the federal government when they ratified the Constitution. Since states were jealous of their domestic prerogatives, they would not have ratified the Constitution had they thought the federal government would deprive them of their predominant role in domestic policy. The states' insistence on the adoption of the Bill of Rights as a condition for ratifying the Constitution is further proof, they argued, that states were worried about federal encroachment on their powers. As a result, states' rights advocates argued (1) that constitutional provisions such as the Tenth Amendment, which suggest a passive federal government, overrule constitutional provisions that suggest an activist federal government; (2) that certain constitutional phrases, such as granting Congress authority to "promote the general welfare," should be read as useful literary devices rather than as indications that the Framers intended Congress to exercise broad powers in domestic policy; and (3) that the Constitution should be read narrowly, limiting congressional powers to the seventeen specific powers listed in Article 1, section 8.

Calhoun articulated the extreme view of the states' rights argument in 1828. He argued that because the federal government received its authority to govern from the states, the states retained the right to declare any federal law null and void within its boundaries.

Advocates of the nationalist interpretation of the Constitution, including John Marshall, Henry Clay, and Abraham Lincoln, disagreed. They argued that the Constitution was ratified not by state legislatures but by state conventions specially elected by the people for that purpose. They also pointed out that the first three words of the Constitution are "We the People," not "We the States." Therefore, they believed, the Constitution is not an interstate compact but a compact among the American people. And thus, in their view, constitutional provisions suggesting an activist federal government, such as the "necessary and proper" clause, are just as meaningful and forceful as those suggesting a more passive federal government. Moreover, from this perspective, constitutional phrases like that granting Congress authority to "promote the general welfare" are not just literary devices but phrases placed in the Constitution to give future generations flexibility in defining the nature of American federalism. They argued that the Framers wisely allowed each generation to determine whether the federal government was to be activist or passive, depending on what was necessary and proper for its time.

The Framers recognized that the Constitution created a somewhat ambiguous American federalism. Concern over the extent of federal powers, particularly regarding slavery, was hotly debated at the Philadelphia Convention. The famous Connecticut Compromise is generally credited with ending debate and saving the Constitutional Convention.

The Framers' Expectations for Congress. The Connecticut Compromise established Congress as the primary arbitrator of American federalism. The interests of smaller-population states, which generally advocated states' rights, were protected by giving each state equal representation in the Senate. The interests of more populous states, which generally advocated a more activist federal government,

were protected by basing representation in the House of Representatives on population. Since a bill cannot become law without approval of both legislative bodies, advocates of both states' rights and nationalist interpretations of the Constitution were convinced that their interests would be represented equally in Congress. Moreover, in Article I, section 10, the Constitution prohibited states from entering into any agreement or compact with another state without Congress's consent. Thus, the controversy over the relationship between the federal government and states (often referred to as vertical federalism) and among states (often referred to as horizontal federalism) was deferred to future congressional battles.

The differing roles of the House and Senate in determining the nature of American federalism also affected the Framers' decision concerning how senators were selected. Unlike members of the House, senators were not elected directly by the people. Instead, reflecting their role as representatives of states' interests, senators were selected by state legislatures. The Framers were convinced that this provision would further ensure that the Senate protected states' rights, because any senators opposing their state legislatures' views on important issues would not be reelected by those legislatures once the senators' terms of office had expired. Moreover, states were expected to follow the practice of subjecting senators to recall if they failed to vote on important issues as instructed by their state legislatures.

Although Congress's role in approving laws has provided it with an important role in determining the nature of American federalism throughout American history, it did not fulfill the Framers' expectations as the primary arbitrator of American federalism until the late 1960s. Instead, the U.S. Supreme Court served as the primary arbitrator of American federalism from 1803 to 1937, the presidency served as the primary arbitrator from 1937 to 1968, and the presidency and Congress have shared the role of primary arbitrator since 1968.

The Supreme Court's Role As Arbitrator. The Framers did not anticipate John Marshall's ruling in *Marbury v. Madison* (1803), in which the Supreme Court asserted its power of judicial review. Nor did they anticipate Marshall's subsequent ruling in *McCulloch v. Maryland* (1819), which supported the nationalist view of the Constitution by broadly interpreting Congress's authority under the necessary and proper clause and establishing the supremacy clause as predominant over the Tenth

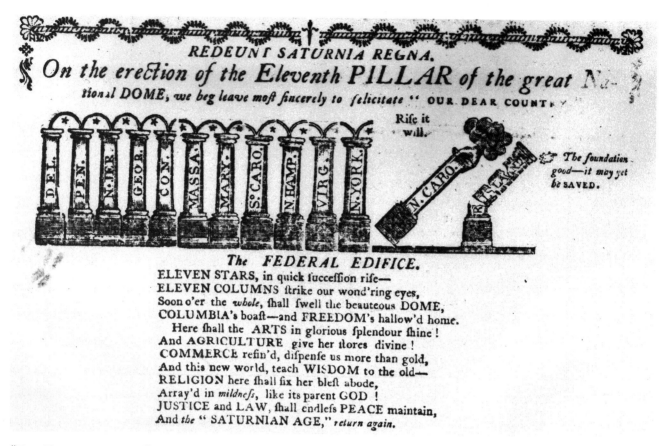

REDEUNT SATURNIA REGNA.

On the erection of the Eleventh PILLAR of the great Na-tional DOME, we beg leave most sincerely to felicitate "OUR DEAR COUNTRY."

Rise it will.

The foundation good—it may yet be SAVED.

The FEDERAL EDIFICE.

ELEVEN STARS, in quick succession rise—
ELEVEN COLUMNS strike our wond'ring eyes,
Soon o'er the *whole*, shall swell the beauteous DOME,
COLUMBIA's boast—and FREEDOM's hallow'd home.
Here shall the ARTS in glorious splendour shine!
And AGRICULTURE give her stores divine!
COMMERCE refin'd, dispense us more than gold,
And this new world, teach WISDOM to the old—
RELIGION here shall fix her blest abode,
Array'd in *mildness*, like its parent GOD!
JUSTICE and LAW, shall endless PEACE maintain,
And *the* " SATURNIAN AGE," *return again.*

"THE FEDERAL EDIFICE." A cartoon that appeared in Benjamin Russell's *Massachusetts Centinel* in celebration of the ratification of the Constitution by the eleventh state, New York. Woodcut, 1788.   LIBRARY OF CONGRESS

Amendment. Marshall's ruling in *Gibbons v. Ogden* (1824) widened Congress's authority over interstate commerce to include most aspects of intrastate commerce. Although Congress benefited from Marshall's rulings because they broadened its authority to act in domestic policy, the rulings also clearly established the Supreme Court as the primary arbitrator of the broad contours of American federalism.

Although the Supreme Court thus usurped Congress's anticipated role as primary arbitrator during the 1800s, Congress still played an important role in shaping the nature of American federalism within the framework established by the courts. For example, in an effort to promote economic development, Congress approved legislation giving states over 3 million acres of federal land to help pay for wagon roads, 4.5 million acres for canal construction, 2.25 million acres for improving river navigation, and 64 million acres for flood control. Congress also approved legislation giving states more than 2.6 million acres of federal land to help pay

for universities and 1.3 million acres for primary and secondary schools. Congress also approved, from time to time, legislation establishing joint-stock companies with states to undertake internal improvement projects and providing states the services of the U.S. Army Corps of Engineers to assist state government officials in surveying and planning their states' respective internal improvement projects.

The President's Role as Arbitrator. The relationship between the federal government and states began to change in a fundamental way during the Great Depression, as did the courts' role in shaping American federalism. Facing a national economic crisis, President Franklin D. Roosevelt secured passage of the National Industrial Recovery Act of 1933, the centerpiece of his First New Deal. It created a massive public works program to combat unemployment and the National Recovery Administration to negotiate and enforce "code agreements" with the nation's major industries. These agreements regulated nearly all business activities, including wages, hours of employment, and production levels. However, the Supreme Court ruled in the case of *Schechter Poultry Corporation v. United States* (1935) that this centralized system of code agreements was an unconstitutional infringement on the right of states to regulate intrastate commerce. On behalf of the Court, Chief Justice Charles Evans Hughes wrote that "where the effect of intrastate transactions upon interstate commerce is merely indirect, such transactions remain within the domain of state power."

Fearing that the Supreme Court's narrow reading of the interstate commerce clause would gut the centerpieces of his Second New Deal—the National Labor Relations Act of 1935 (which guaranteed labor's right to collective bargaining in the private sector) and the Social Security Act of 1935—President Roosevelt proposed the court bill of 1937. It would have allowed the president to add up to six new justices to the Supreme Court, one for each justice who had served on the court for at least ten years and who was at least seventy years and six months old. Roosevelt's obvious attempt to "pack" the court with justices who would interpret the Constitution broadly divided the nation. However, although the bill did not pass, it had the desired effect. Using a broad interpretation of Congress's interstate commerce powers, the Court declared in *National Labor Relations Board v. Laughlin Steel Corporation* (1937) that the National Labor Relations Act of 1935 was not an unconstitutional infringement on states' rights. Moreover, it ruled in *Stewart Machine Company v. Davis* (1937) and *Helvering, Welch, and Edison Electric Illuminating Company v. Davis* (1937) that the Social Security Act of 1935 did not infringe on states' rights because, in the Court's words: "when money is spent to promote the general welfare, the concept of welfare or the opposite is shaped by Congress, not by the states."

With the Supreme Court out of its way, Roosevelt's Second New Deal could proceed. It represented a major turning point for American federalism. The Social Security Act of 1935, for example, established the precedent for the expansion of federal government involvement in domestic welfare policy. It created the old-age retirement system, unemployment compensation, and federal intergovernmental grants for the blind, for crippled children, for maternal and child care, and for dependent children.

Moreover, not only had the substance of American federalism changed, with the federal government becoming much more active; the courts' acceptance of Roosevelt's Second New Deal legislation also marked the ascendancy of the president as the primary arbitrator of American federalism. Although the courts continued to play an important role in fine-tuning the contours of American federalism, particularly concerning civil rights, civil liberties, abortion, and political processes, the broad contours of American federalism were now determined primarily by the legislative process, as the Framers had originally intended. However, the nature of that process was now dramatically different from what the Framers had envisioned.

The president's role in the contemporary legislative process is much greater than the Framers anticipated. Presidents provide legislative policy leadership through the preparation of the executive budget and the presentation of major policy initiatives. They are intimately involved in legislative deliberations. Instead of reserving the presidential veto for extraordinary circumstances, such as when they believe a bill to be unconstitutional, presidents now routinely veto legislation on policy grounds. They also routinely use the threat of vetoing legislation as a bargaining chip with legislators.

Moreover, Congress has changed as well. The constitutional ties that once bound senators to the role of protecting state governmental interests have been severed. Since the adoption of the Seventeenth Amendment in 1913, senators have been elected directly by the people, and they have not been subject to recall or censure for failing to obey instructions from state legislatures since the Civil War. Although senators are still interested in fostering their states' interests, they recognize that their reelection prospects are no longer necessarily enhanced by responding to the demands of state and local government officials. Instead, they realize, they must respond to their states' residents' demands, which often conflict with the wishes of state and local government officials. Thus, the Framers' expectation that the House and Senate would routinely take fundamentally opposite positions on issues pertaining to federalism was not realized.

From 1940 to 1964, both the House and the Senate for the most part resisted efforts to involve the federal government in areas traditionally viewed as state responsibilities. During those years, the House was dominated by rural interests that had little to gain from bold new federal initiatives to address urban needs. Moreover, congressional structures and procedures reinforced Congress's tendency to resist federal intrusion on states' rights. For example, the seniority system that was used to distribute committee chairmanships, the highly autonomous committee system (primarily chaired by southern conservative Democrats who advocated states' rights), and the Senate's filibuster and cloture rules were major obstacles to legislation that expanded the federal government's responsibilities in domestic governance. Moreover, the "conservative coalition" of conservative southern Democrats and Republicans, which often formed a majority in Congress and especially in the House of Representatives, frustrated efforts to expand significantly the federal government's role in domestic policy. Combined, these factors protected the states' primacy in most areas of domestic policy.

Congress Rivals the President as Arbitrator. The Democratic party's landslide election victory in 1964 altered Congress's role in American federalism. Reflecting their belief in Keynesian economic thought, the new members of Congress advocated an activist federal government. They were convinced that economic growth could best be assured if the federal government regulated the economy, redistributed income from the wealthy to the poor, and spent money during recessions. It was believed that these actions would stimulate demand for goods and services and even out the downturns in the business cycle.

The major consequence of this approach was the deployment of federal intergovernmental grants. Their use avoided the constitutional issues that would have been raised by the direct federal provision of services. The constitutionality of intergovernmental grants had been settled in 1923 when the Supreme Court ruled, in *Massachusetts v. Mellon* and *Frothingham v. Mellon*, that states and individuals did not have legal standing to bring suit against the spending of federal intergovernmental funds. Individuals could not sue because since they could not prove that it was their specific tax dollars that were being spent, they could not prove harm. States could not sue because federal intergovernmental grants are voluntary; thus, states could not prove harm. As a result, intergovernmental grants were convenient, constitutionally tested vehicles through which newly elected Democrats could satisfy their twin desires to stimulate the economy and, at the same time, address social problems.

Instead of protecting states' rights as they had done during the 1940–1964 era, members of both the House and Senate eagerly accepted presidential initiatives to expand the federal government's responsibilities in domestic policy. Also, to an extent never seen before, individual lawmakers assumed the role of policy innovators, pressing for the enactment and expansion of new and existing federal programs.

At the same time that Congress asserted its role as a policy innovator, it began to dismantle congressional structures and procedures that had reinforced Congress's tendency to resist federal intrusion on states' rights. Among other changes, the seniority system was challenged, reformed, and reduced in importance, the powers of committee chairmen were challenged and weakened, the number of subcommittees was increased and the powers of subcommittee chairmen were strengthened, legislative staffs were increased, and the filibuster was challenged and weakened by making it easier to invoke cloture. These changes enhanced the ability of rank-and-file members of Congress to have an impact on the congressional decision-making process. Thus, the decentralization of power within the House and Senate fostered a political environment conducive to a more activist and intrusive role for the federal government in American federalism.

Although Congress's shift toward greater acceptance of a more activist federal government resulted mostly from the emergence of Democratic majorities in the House and Senate, that shift was also due to fundamental changes in the nature of congressional elections. First, the Supreme Court's ruling in *Wesberry v. Sanders* (1964) requiring that congressional districts in the House be based on the one person, one vote principle reduced the number of rural, conservative districts in the House. Although representatives from these rural districts advocated federal subsidies for agriculture, they opposed legislation to expand the federal government's role in most other areas of domestic policy. The representatives who replaced them advocated a more active federal government, particularly in dealing with urban problems, civil rights, health, education, and welfare.

Second, and perhaps most important, the decline of political party influence in American politics increased the political anxiety of many members of Congress. They were no longer able to count on loyal party voters to elect them; nor, given the increasing cost of campaigns, could they count on their party organizations to provide sufficient campaign funds. Therefore, they sought to pave their own road to reelection and power: (1) by mobilizing issue-oriented volunteers to staff their campaigns; (2) by responding to the demands of organized interest groups in order to obtain financing for their campaigns; and (3) by cultivating media attention to obtain name recognition and a reputation as a responsible political actor capable of being trusted with governmental power. All three of these goals were enhanced by becoming an independent policy entrepreneur in the Congress. Initiating new federal programs and securing more funding for existing federal programs appealed to issue-oriented volunteers, strengthened alliances with organized interest groups, and provided demonstrable evidence to reporters that the member was worthy of their attention.

The Shift from Cooperative to Coercive Federalism. The shift from a state-centered domestic policy to a federal-centered one escalated with the enactment of President Lyndon B. Johnson's Great Society legislation during the mid 1960s. The enactment of the Civil Rights Act of 1964, Medicaid in 1965, and the Water Quality Act of 1965, among others, moved the federal government into many areas of domestic policy that had previously been considered primarily state responsibilities, including environmental protection, education, transportation, health, and welfare. Moreover, the relationship between the federal government and states began to shift from one primarily marked by cooperation and mutual respect to one mostly characterized by coercion and mutual suspicion. Instead of enacting policies, like land grants, designed to assist state and local government officials in achieving their own goals through their own means, the federal government increasingly used (1) the carrot of federal grants-in-aid assistance to encourage state and local government officials to undertake certain activities that they might otherwise not have undertaken; (2) the stick of intergovernmental grants-in-aid regulations to ensure that federal intergovernmental grants-in-aid funds were spent "wisely"; and (3) the stick of intergovernmental mandates, such as meeting national clean water standards, to force state and local government officials to undertake certain activities that they might otherwise not have taken.

The trend toward a more centralized political system has continued, despite two major presidential initiatives to reverse the trend (President Richard M. Nixon's New Federalism proposals in 1969 and President Ronald Reagan's New Federalism proposals in 1981 and 1982). The centralization of governmental power is evidenced in a number of ways, including the rising number and cost of federal inter-

governmental grants-in-aid programs (see figures 1 and 2). In 1960, there were 132 such programs, costing approximately $7 billion. In 1981, the number of grants reached a then-record high of 539 and cost a then-record high of $95 billion. Bolstered by a Republican majority in the Senate from 1981 to 1986, President Reagan convinced Congress to reduce the number of federal grants during his first term in office. The number fell to 405 in 1984. Since then, however, it has continued to increase, particularly after the Democratic party regained control of the Senate in 1987, reaching a new all-time high of 557 in 1993. The cost of these grants has also increased, reaching $199 billion in 1993.

In addition, despite academic studies indicating that administrative regulations attached to federal grants-in-aid programs are too numerous; that they are often too expensive, inflexible, inefficient, inconsistent, intrusive, and ineffective; and that they create a policy system that lacks accountability, their numbers have also continued to increase. Moreover, the number and intrusiveness of federal mandates has also increased (see figure 3). The federal government adopted fourteen laws containing mandates with significant intergovernmental effects during the 1960s, twenty-two additional laws with significant mandates during the 1970s, and twenty-seven more during the 1980s. In 1993, federal mandates imposed more than $3.6 billion in additional costs to state and local governments. Among the most costly are mandates requiring state and local government officials to pay for meeting national clean water and clean air standards, providing the handicapped access to educational and transportation services, and removing asbestos from local schools.

Advocates of a more active federal presence in domestic policy relied primarily on Keynesian economic thought to justify their actions. They also cited one or more of the following reasons to justify establishing and continuing federally financed, intergovernmental grants-in-aid programs, regulations, and mandates:

1. Since the federal government's fiscal resources are superior to those of the states and localities, it must take the initiative to ensure that fundamental national goals, such as protecting civil rights and providing the poor with a minimum standard of living, are achieved.
2. Since the federal government funds intergovernmental programs, it has the right to determine which governmental services deserve assistance

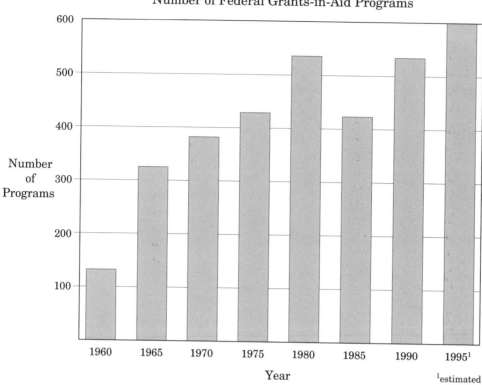

Figure 1
Number of Federal Grants-in-Aid Programs

SOURCE: U.S. Advisory Commission on Intergovernmental Relations, *Characteristics of Federal Grant-in-Aid Programs to State and Local Governments Funded FY 1993*, 1994; *Categorical Grants: Their Role and Design*, 1978.

and to ensure that the funds are spent "wisely."

3. States and localities are unable to levy sufficient taxes to provide acceptable levels of governmental services because they compete with other states and localities for business investment and taxpaying residents.

4. States and localities often fail adequately to fund or engage in programs, such as air and water pollution controls, that have either costs or benefits that spill over onto other states and localities.

5. Intergovernmental grants encourage states to experiment with various policy alternatives so as to create new approaches to solving the nation's domestic problems.

6. State and local government officials often overlook the needs of the poor when allocating public resources because the poor generally do not vote and are often not formally represented by organized interest groups.

Critics of the federal government's growing influ-

ence in domestic policy countered these arguments, arguing that

1. The federal government's fiscal resources are not superior to those of the states, especially given the size of the federal government's deficit.

2. Recent reforms have improved the capacity of state and local government officials to govern both efficiently and effectively.

3. States and localities would levy sufficient taxes to provide "acceptable" levels of public services if the federal government reduced its taxes.

4. The best means to protect the poor and disadvantaged is to provide them with jobs through a strong national economy. Turning back many intergovernmental programs to states and localities and using the saved revenue to reduce federal taxes will, in turn, stimulate economic growth.

They also argued that

1. Active state and local governments promote a

sense of self-reliance that is the cornerstone of political freedom.

2. State and local government officials are closer to the people and are better able than federal officials to adapt public programs to state and local needs and conditions.

3. More active state and local governments allow more people to become involved in the policy process.

4. State and local governments encourage experimentation and innovation in solving U.S. domestic problems.

5. Active state and local governments reduce the political turmoil that often results from single policies that govern the entire nation.

Contemporary American Federalism. States and localities continue to play an important role in domestic policy. In 1993, they spent more than $1 billion, 14 percent of the gross national product.

Moreover, they continue to play a major role in many areas of domestic policy, especially primary and secondary education, law enforcement, corrections, fire protection, sanitation, parks and recreation, and transportation. They also continue their traditional role as policy innovators and experimenters, providing policymakers at all levels of government an opportunity to learn from the different approaches used to combat the many problems that confront them. Since the mid 1980s, states and localities have been particularly active in experimenting with new approaches to solving problems in the areas of primary and secondary education, health care, welfare, energy planning and conservation, criminal justice, international economic development policy, capital formation, and economic development strategies.

Although many states have improved their capacity to govern well by reforming their institutional structures and their revenue-generating capabilities,

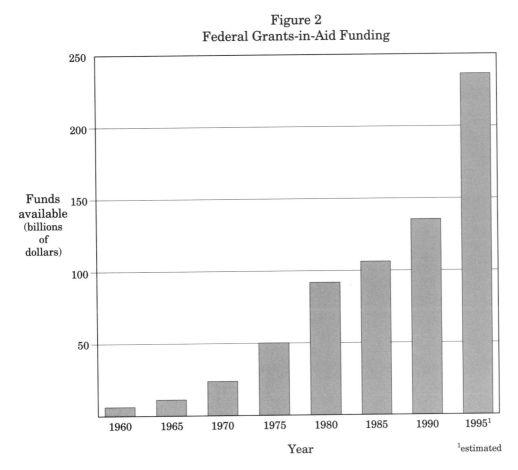

Figure 2
Federal Grants-in-Aid Funding

Funds available (billions of dollars)

¹estimated

SOURCE: U.S. Advisory Commission on Intergovernmental Relations, *Significant Features of Fiscal Federalism*, vol. 2, 1993.

Figure 3
Number of Federal Mandates

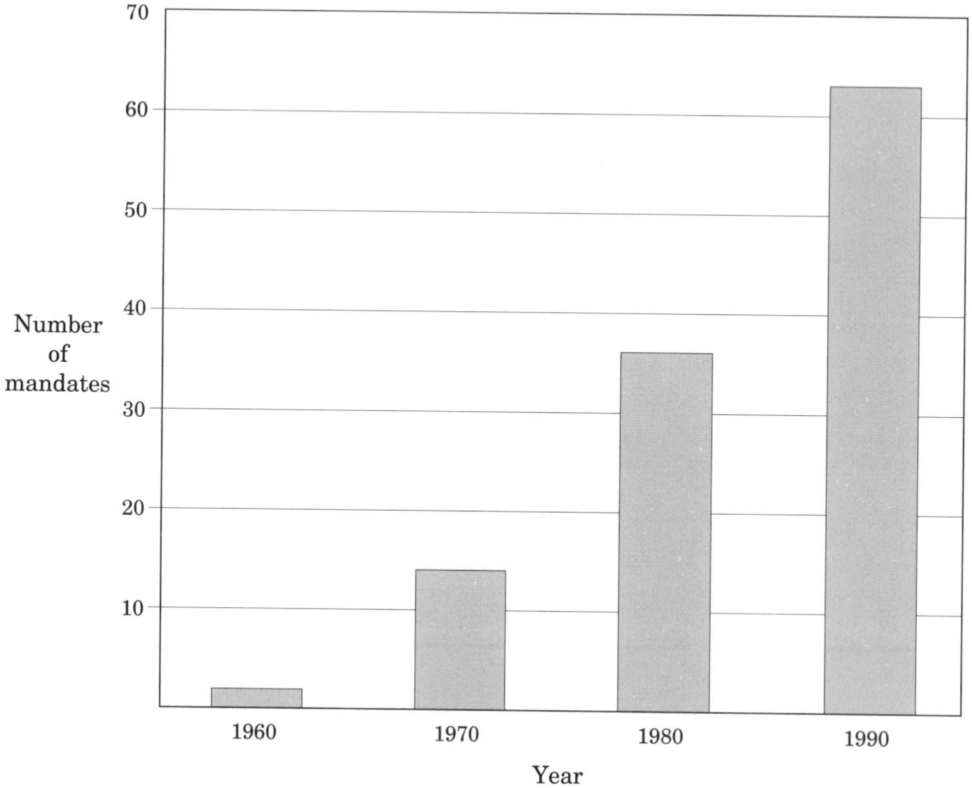

Number
of
mandates

Year

SOURCE: Timothy J. Conlan and David R. Beam, "Federal Mandates: The Record of Reform and Future Prospects, *Intergovernmental Perspective* (Fall 1992): 7–11, 15.

most scholars agree that the federal government has superseded the states as the preeminent force in American domestic policy. As of 1993, government spent more than $1.5 trillion annually, 24 percent of the gross national product. The federal government's fiscal and monetary policies, coupled with its regulatory powers, shape the national economy, and its 557 grants-in-aid programs, thousands of intergovernmental regulations, and scores of intergovernmental mandates strongly influence how state and local governments operate and which goods and services they provide its residents. For example, the federal government is credited or blamed, depending on one's political values, for stimulating state and local expenditures in the areas of income maintenance (primarily through the cost matching requirements in the Aid to Families with Dependent Children program), health care (primarily through the cost matching requirements in the Medicaid program), highways and mass transit (primarily through the cost matching re-

quirements in the Aid to Highways program), and environmental protection (primarily through intergovernmental mandates regarding the attainment of specific air and water pollution standards and the low-interest loan program for wastewater treatment facilities construction).

The federal government also supplements state and local efforts in many areas of domestic policy, including the construction of schools and the provision of remedial education services (primarily through the Compensatory Education for the Disadvantaged program), the feeding of the poor (primarily through the school lunch and Food Stamps programs), the provision of social services such as day care and drug and alcohol abuse counseling (primarily through the Social Services Block Grant), and job training (primarily through the Job Training Partnership program). Nationally, the Medicaid program alone accounted for more than 12 percent of all state government expenditures in 1993.

Congress's Role in Shaping Contemporary American Federalism. Congress has played a very important role in shaping the nature of contemporary American federalism. It first asserted its role as an equal partner with the presidency in 1969 when it rejected most of President Nixon's New Federalism proposals. Congress's role in accepting, rejecting, or revising presidential federalism initiatives, such as President Reagan's swap proposal in 1982 (whereby the federal government would have taken full responsibility for Medicaid in exchange for states taking full responsibility for Aid to Families with Dependent Children and Food Stamps), continues to generate extensive media coverage and public interest. However, Congress's role as an arbitrator of contemporary American federalism extends beyond its reaction to presidential initiatives. For example, its preference for narrowly defined categorical grants with numerous administrative requirements and for federal mandates has played an equally important role in moving the federal government to the preeminent position in American federalism.

Congress's preference for categorical grants over block grants and general revenue sharing arises from several sources. First, categorical grants provide legislators an opportunity to claim political credit for providing tangible benefits to their constituencies. Block grants and general revenue sharing also provide an opportunity for credit claiming, but members of Congress must share credit because state and local government officials decide how to allocate the funds.

Second, since categorical grants, unlike block grants and general revenue sharing, are used for only one programmatic purpose, they can be defined narrowly to emphasize program goals with broad congressional support. Thus, categorical grants are perceived as being easier to maneuver through the legislative process than block grants and general revenue sharing.

Third, unlike block grants and general revenue sharing, most categorical grants require potential recipients to apply to the federal bureaucracy for funding. This provides members of Congress with an opportunity, through their executive oversight functions, to exercise greater control over the use of categorical grant funds than over either block grant or general revenue sharing funds.

Thus, when asked to devise intergovernmental programs to address America's problems, Congress has shown a preference for categorical grants. Of the 557 intergovernmental grant-in-aid programs in 1993, 543 were categorical grants, collectively accounting for 89 percent of all federal intergovernmental grants-in-aid funding.

Electoral politics also plays a role in explaining why Congress prefers categorical grants. In most instances, organized interest groups vigorously defend categorical grants against grant consolidation efforts. They perceive consolidation as a threat to "their" program and established operating procedures that, in many instances, they helped to devise. Thus, the so-called iron triangles (subcommittee chairs, bureau chiefs, and clientele interest groups) and issue networks usually encourage Congress to resist initiatives to replace categorical grants with either block grants or general revenue sharing. They also encourage Congress to reject initiatives, such as President George Bush's 1991 turn back and regulatory relief proposals, that would decentralize programmatic authority.

Another reason Congress prefers categorical grants is that many members believe that a great number of state and local government officials are either unwilling (due to prejudice) or unable (due to pressures to appease middle- and upper-income voters or to attract business investment) to target resources to the poor and disadvantaged.

For these reasons, most of the federal grants adopted since the 1960s have had numerous administrative regulations attached to ensure that the federal government's money is spent "wisely." For example, the federal government requires states that participate in Medicaid to provide the poor with thirteen specific medical services, including inpatient hospital services, outpatient hospital services, physician services, and laboratory and X-ray services. The federal government also encourages states to provide the poor with thirty-five other health care services, including dental care, optometrist services, and prescription drugs, by making them eligible for Medicaid matching grants. At the same time, it discourages states from offering other health care services to the poor by making them ineligible for Medicaid reimbursement.

In the transportation area, the federal government has used the threat of withdrawing its highway assistance to "encourage" states to adopt uniform standards concerning the content of driver education courses, the training and certification of driver education instructors, testing procedures for obtaining a driver's license, record-keeping systems for accidents and vehicle registration, highway design and maintenance, traffic control, vehicle codes and inspections, and surveillance of traffic for detection of potential high-accident areas. It also uses the threat of the withdrawal of highway assistance to "encourage" states to remove advertising billboards within 660 feet of interstate highways, to limit highway speeds to either fifty-five miles per hour in urban areas or sixty-five miles per hour in rural areas, to adopt a twenty-one-year-old minimum drinking age, and to adopt a mandatory motorcycle helmet and automotive seat-belt law.

State and local government officials object to federal intergovernmental regulations on the grounds that they create a lot of paperwork, which increases the cost of providing government services; often prevents them from taking advantage of circumstances that are unique to their state or locality; and distorts their spending decisions, because the grants usually require a nonfederal match, typically one-third to one-half of program costs. These complaints have led state and local officials routinely to ask their lobbying organizations in Washington, D.C.—principally the National Governors' Association, National Conference of State Legislatures, National League of Cities, U.S. Conference of Mayors, and National Association of Counties—to fight for regulatory reform. Although these efforts have led to many changes, most of the officials still consider the administrative requirements attached to intergovernmental grants to be burdensome, expensive, and unnecessary infringements on their authority. However, because of political opposition to state and local government tax increases and the public's seemingly unquenchable desire for public goods and services, very few states and localities have ever refused federal assistance.

State and local officials also object to the relatively recent proliferation of federal intergovernmental mandates. However, in an era of fiscal austerity and mounting federal deficits, many members of Congress see federal intergovernmental mandates as a viable means of achieving their policy goals without increasing the federal deficit because mandates place the burden of financing those policies on the states and localities.

Congress's Future Role in American Federalism. Congress's role in determining the nature of American federalism is not static. Like a living organism, Congress has evolved over time, both reacting to and influencing changes in the broader political environment. The constitutional ties that once bound the Senate to states' rights and the House to the nationalist interpretation of the Constitution have been severed, and the nature of contemporary congressional elections encourages

members of both houses to make decisions consistent with the nationalist interpretation. Moreover, reflecting changes in their electoral environment, Congress has reformed its rules and procedures, which makes it easier for members to arrive at decisions consistent with the nationalist interpretation.

Although changes in Congress's broader political environment suggest that it is likely to continue to proceed with the centralization of governmental authority, there are several factors that may reverse this trend. The two most important are the growing impact of the federal deficit on economic growth and the globalization of the national economy.

The deficit and American consumers' appetite for imported goods has many members of Congress worried that Keynesian solutions to the nation's economic troubles (which are another reason given to justify federal intergovernmental expenditures) may no longer be appropriate. Keynesian economic policies stimulate demand for goods and services, but if that demand is for foreign-made products, the stimulus benefits the nation that made the product, not the United States. Moreover, Keynesian economic thought relied on government surpluses during periods of economic growth to compensate for deficits incurred during recessions. However, the federal government has not had a surplus since 1969, and its cumulative debt is expected to exceed $3.6 trillion in 1994. Many economists have argued that government borrowing to finance the deficit hinders economic growth because it encourages interest rates to rise. Moreover, interest on the federal deficit (currently amounting to over $220 billion annually) inhibits the federal government's ability to spend money on other programs.

The impact of the federal deficit on Congress's decisions concerning federalism has already been evidenced by its increasing use of federal mandates to achieve its policy goals. Also, although the magnitude of the deficit has not stopped the number and cost of federal intergovernmental grants-in-aid from increasing in recent years, the deficit is likely to restrain future growth in both the number and cost of federal intergovernmental programs.

Another important change in Congress's broader political environment that may influence its decisions concerning federalism is the enactment of recent reforms in many states that have enhanced their capacity to govern both efficiently and effectively. This may encourage members of Congress to rethink their traditional opposition to block grants and their insistence on imposing strict regulatory controls over the use of categorical grant funding.

These countervailing forces in Congress's broader political environment make it difficult to predict the outcome of future congressional decisions that bear on the issue of federalism. The most likely scenario is that Congress will continue to enact policies that centralize governmental power. However, the means to achieve that end may change. Although Congress will continue to rely on categorical grants and intergovernmental regulations to ensure that state and local government officials make "good" public policy decisions, its dependence on federal mandates to achieve policy objectives is likely to increase.

While predicting future congressional actions pertaining to federalism is difficult, one thing is clear. Congress no longer plays second fiddle to either the Supreme Court or the president in determining the nature of American federalism.

[See also Anti-Federalists; Bill of Rights; Constitution; Constitutional Convention of 1787; Federalist Papers; Federalists; General Welfare Clause; Grant-in-Aid; History of Congress, articles on The Origins of Congress and The Road to Nationhood; Internal Improvements; Interstate Compacts; Judicial Review; Judiciary and Congress; President and Congress, overview article; Revenue Sharing; States' Rights.]

BIBLIOGRAPHY

Beam, David R. "Washington's Regulation of States and Localities: Origins and Issues." Intergovernmental Perspective 7 (1981): 8–18.

Colella, Cynthia Cates. "The Breakdown of Constitutional Constraints: Interpretative Variations from the First Constitutional Revolution to the Fourth." In The Condition of Contemporary Federalism: Conflicting Theories and Collapsing Constraints. Edited by David B. Walker. 1981. Pp. 27–110.

Conlan, Timothy J. "Congress and the Contemporary Intergovernmental System." In American Intergovernmental Relations Today: Perspectives and Controversies. Edited by Robert Jay Dilger. 1986. Pp. 89–108.

Conlan, Timothy J., and David R. Beam. "Federal Mandates: The Record of Reform and Future Prospects." Intergovernmental Perspective 18 (1992): 7–11, 15.

Dilger, Robert Jay. National Intergovernmental Programs. 1989.

Fiorina, Morris P. Congress: Keystone of the Washington Establishment. 1989.

Riker, William H. The Development of American Federalism. 1987.

ROBERT JAY DILGER

FEDERALIST PAPERS. *The Federalist* is the most authoritative, comprehensive, and profound contemporary interpretation of the political intention of the Framers. Strictly speaking, the treatment of Congress comprises fifteen of the *Federalist* papers, numbers 52 to 61 on the House of Representatives and 62 to 66 on the Senate. But it would be more accurate to say that discussion of the legislative power pervades the work.

The authors, and the Founders in general, believed that a legislature chosen by and responsible to the people was the dominant department of government. For all their policy differences, Alexander Hamilton and James Madison (*The Federalist's* chief authors, under the nom de plume "Publius") agreed on the generous grant of powers to Congress in Article 1, section 8 and elsewhere in the Constitution. They strengthened the case for a strong Congress by endorsing the Constitution's "necessary and proper" clause on the commonsense ground that the grant of a general legislative power implies the grant of the means necessary to achieve that end, so long as those means are not contrary to the letter and spirit of the Constitution.

The Federalist's readiness to grant broadly defined powers to the Congress was balanced by an awareness of the danger that passion and interests, unchecked, could lead to abuses of power. The primary control over an imperious national legislature, its authors believed, was republican government itself: the sovereignty of the people. This would be manifested most directly by the election to Congress, of those who met age, residency, and citizenship requirements, by a broad constituency at frequent intervals. A qualified executive veto and judicial review of legislation were additional checks on congressional power, as was the division of the legislature into the House and the Senate.

Publius passed lightly over the Senate's most conspicuous features, the equal representation of the states and the selection of senators by state legislatures, defending them as necessary concessions to public opinion and the demands of the smaller states. The Senate's small size, its six-year terms, and the importance of its agenda, *The Federalist* suggested, would transform its members into statesmen. The Senate would also offer a necessary counter to the executive and judicial branches. In any event the House, intimately bound to the people, would more than hold its own. And rotating one-third of the Senate's seats every two years gave ample opportunity to the popularly elected state legislatures to check senatorial power.

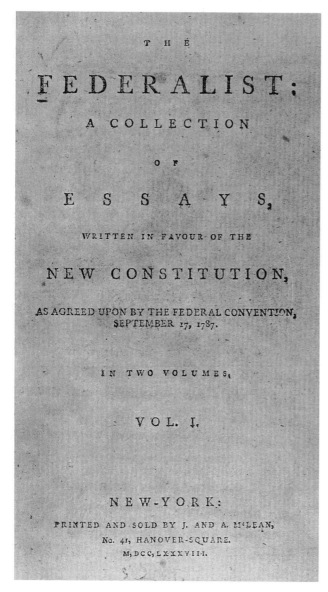

THE FEDERALIST. Volume 1, 1788. Cover page.
RARE BOOKS AND MANUSCRIPT DIVISION, THE NEW YORK
PUBLIC LIBRARY, ASTOR, LENOX, AND TILDEN FOUNDATIONS

By leaving in the hands of the state legislatures a large mass of residual powers touching on the life, liberty, and property of citizens, the Constitution, argued *The Federalist's* authors, in effect limited Congress to those powers necessary to manage the common concerns of the Union. More important, the federal principle greatly extended the practicable orbit of government, thus creating a more numerous and diverse constituency for Congress. Large electoral districts were likely to have a higher proportion of representatives able to perform the difficult work of government, and to lessen the risk of elections carried by corruption and intrigue.

As Madison argued in *Federalist* 10 (the most famous of the *Federalist* papers), the sheer number and variety of interests in a large republic offered the best security against the threats of instability and tyranny posed by an unjust majority or an oppressive minority. Confidence in self-government by the American people within the bounds of a republican Constitution, a shared heritage, and common belief in the Union led the authors of *The Federalist* to argue that Congress would govern both energetically and prudently.

BIBLIOGRAPHY

Epstein, David F. *The Political Theory of The Federalist.* 1984.

Hamilton, Alexander, James Madison, and John Jay. *The Federalist Papers.* Edited by Clinton Rossiter. 1961.

Kurland, Philip, and Ralph Lerner, eds. *The Founders' Constitution.* Vols. 1–3. 1986.

MARVIN MEYERS

FEDERALISTS. The Federalist party (or, more appropriately, proto-party, since it lacked most of the characteristics of a modern political party) developed in Congress in the early years of George Washington's presidency in support of his administration. Although Federalists might be found in all the states, their strength was concentrated mainly in the North, especially in New England.

As the federal government was installed in New York under the newly ratified Constitution in 1789, it was the Founders' fervent hope that factionalism and parties might be avoided. The Founders believed that citizens in a republic should be represented by a virtuous elite who would legislate not for partial or selfish interests, but for the general good of all of society. Within a relatively short time, however, members of Congress began to divide over domestic and foreign policy issues into two loose partisan groupings—Federalists and Jeffersonian Republicans. The Federalists adopted the name of those who had supported ratification of the Constitution and, by doing so, implied that those who opposed them were Anti-Federalists who, refusing to accept their defeat over ratification, continued their opposition to the Constitution even after it had been adopted.

The first major division in Congress came in early 1790 when Alexander Hamilton, Washington's secretary of the Treasury, issued his first Report on

Public Credit, calling for the payment of the national debt at par value to current holders of debt and for the assumption of the states' debts by the federal government. Both issues were controversial, but it was the assumption of state debts that threatened to destroy the new union. States that still were carrying large debts incurred during the Revolution, such as Massachusetts and South Carolina, were enthusiastic in their support of assumption, while states that had retired much of their debt, such as Maryland, Virginia, North Carolina, and Georgia, were strenuous in their criticism, fearing that by assuming the state debts, the federal government would gain considerable power at the expense of the states. After being defeated once in the House of Representatives, assumption was later passed 34 to 27, with the northern states supporting it 24 to 9, while southerners were mainly against it, with 18 opposed and 10 in favor.

Later the same year Hamilton submitted an even more controversial plan, proposing that the Bank of the United States be created. This national bank, owned largely by private investors, would be the federal government's fiscal agent, thus having enormous financial power; this would create, Hamilton believed, a bond of self-interest between the wealthy citizens of the Republic and the government. The division in Congress, for the most part, followed the same lines as the earlier conflict over funding and assumption, with the northerners largely in favor and the southerners opposed. Ultimately the bank was established after Hamilton satisfied Washington's concerns that the Constitution did not grant the federal government the power to create a bank. The acrimonious debate and partisan division over Hamilton's financial program was the first step in creating an alignment between those who supported the policies of Washington and Hamilton—the Federalists—and those who opposed them—the Jeffersonian Republicans.

But divisive as Hamilton's program was, it was the pressure of foreign policy that further polarized the two proto-parties. The growing radicalism of the French Revolution in the early 1790s and the outbreak of war between revolutionary France and imperial Britain convinced the Federalists that the Republicans were not merely domestic colleagues who honestly differed with them over policy. Indeed, neither side accepted the idea of a loyal opposition. The Federalists believed that they were, rather than a political party, the government itself; any opposition to them therefore challenged the government and the Constitution. And by the late 1790s, many Federalists came to view their opponents as nothing less than seditious agents of France.

The congressional battle over Jay's Treaty in 1795 and 1796 not only was an important factor in the defining of Federalists and Republicans, but also was crucial in stimulating proto-party caucuses in the House of Representatives and in promoting popular meetings in order to influence congressional action. In 1794, in an effort to settle a number of long-standing and potentially war-producing differences between England and the United States, President Washington had sent Supreme Court Chief Justice John Jay to London in an effort to settle the controversy. The resulting treaty was immensely divisive. The Federalists supported it, claiming that despite Great Britain's refusal to compromise certain key issues, it was a better alternative than war. After the Senate approved the treaty and the president signed it, Washington called upon the House of Representatives to appropriate funds for the implementation of the treaty. After a prolonged and acrimonious debate and despite intense Republican opposition, the Federalists and the Washington administration prevailed.

The height of Federalist power in Congress came in the Fifth and Sixth Congresses (1797–1801), during which Federalists enjoyed a 64 to 53 and 67 to 47 advantage, respectively, over their Republican opponents. In 1798, France's insulting refusal to meet with a delegation sent by Federalist president John Adams to settle serious differences between the two countries intensified distrust of the Republicans, whom Federalists believed sympathetic to France. Congressional Federalists, led by South Carolina's Robert G. Harper, attempted to destroy their domestic opposition. The resulting Alien and Sedition Acts restricted the activities of aliens, many of whom were sympathetic to the Republicans, and drastically restricted freedom to criticize the government.

The unpopular John Adams's unsuccessful campaign for a second term as president bitterly split the Federalists in 1800. Despite some resurgence of Federalist strength during Thomas Jefferson's presidency and during the War of 1812 and despite their continued vitality in New England and Delaware, the Federalists never regained their national prominence or power. Federalist spokesmen like Rufus King of New York continued to serve in Congress. King was the last Federalist presidential candidate in 1816; as a U.S. senator in 1820, he opposed the expansion of slavery under the Missouri

LIVERPOOL PITCHER. Commemorating Thomas Jefferson's presidential inauguration. The jug (1801) bears a quotation from his inaugural address: "We are all Republicans . . . all Federalists," an attempt at reconciliation with his political opponents.

COLLECTION OF DAVID J. AND JANICE L. FRENT

Compromise. By the 1820s, however, Federalists had virtually disappeared from the American political landscape as they aligned themselves behind the two emerging and opposing wings of the Republican party.

[*See also* Alien and Sedition Acts; Anti-Federalists; Jay's Treaty; Jeffersonian Republicans.]

BIBLIOGRAPHY

Bell, Rudolph M. *Party and Faction in American Politics: The House of Representatives, 1789–1801.* 1973.
Sharp, James Roger. *American Politics in the Early Republic: The New Nation in Crisis.* 1993.

JAMES ROGER SHARP

FEDERAL REGISTER. The official gazette of the federal government, the *Federal Register* was mandated by the Federal Register Act of 1935 (49 Stat. 500) in response to the increasing number of agency regulations, rules, and related administrative actions and the fugitive status of these instruments. The expansion of the government during World War I and again during the New Deal resulted in the presidential and agency issuance of a growing quantity of administrative law. However, there was no central repository or accountability for keeping track of this material. By the early days of the New Deal, federal administrative law was in such disarray that, on one occasion, government attorneys arguing a case (*United States v. Smith* [1934]) before the Supreme Court were embarrassed to find their lawsuit was based on a nonexistent regulation. A short time later, government attorneys discovered they were pursuing litigation that was based on a revoked executive order (*Panama Refining Co. v. Ryan* [1935]).

An influential call for reform was made by Erwin N. Griswold in the *Harvard Law Review*. Congress responded with the Federal Register Act, which became law in July 1935. Produced in magazine format, the *Federal Register* contains a variety of presidential directives, agency notices, and administrative law. Published each workday by the Office of the Federal Register, National Archives and Records Administration, the *Register* may be found in university law libraries, major public libraries, and many federal depository libraries and agency reading rooms. It is available in electronic form from government and commercial sources.

BIBLIOGRAPHY

Griswold, Erwin N. "Government in Ignorance of the Law—A Plea for Better Publication of Executive Legislation." *Harvard Law Review* 48 (1934): 198–214.
Newman, Frank C. "Government and Ignorance—A Progress Report on Publication of Federal Regulations." *Harvard Law Review* 63 (1950): 929–956.
Springer, Randy S. "Gatekeeping and the *Federal Register:* An Analysis of the Publication Requirement of Section 552(a)(1)(D) of the Administrative Procedure Act." *Administrative Law Review* 41 (1989): 533–548.

HAROLD C. RELYEA

FEDERAL RESERVE BANK ACT (1913; 38 Stat. 251–275). Banking and currency reform stood side by side with antitrust as a leading economic issue of the Progressive era. Easier access to credit and money had been a mainstay of southern and western agrarian protest for decades. And by the early 1900s, bankers and businessmen felt the need for a more rationalized banking and currency system.

The first substantial plan emerged from a National Monetary Commission chaired by Sen. Nelson W. Aldrich of Rhode Island, a prominent "old guard" Republican. It called for a central bank substantially under the control of the nation's major private banks. Democrats of the South and the West strongly opposed the Aldrich approach, and in 1913 newly elected president Woodrow Wilson found it necessary to opt for an alternative plan. William Jennings Bryan and his followers wanted tighter government control; Treasury secretary William Gibbs McAdoo surprised no one by wanting the bank subject to greater Treasury control.

Sen. Carter Glass of Virginia played a leading role in fashioning the result, a system of twelve regional reserve banks, privately controlled but supervised by a Federal Reserve Board that received government deposits and issued Federal Reserve notes as currency. This (and an agricultural credit amendment) minimally satisfied Bryan and the agrarian wing and was accepted by most of the business community.

The act became law on 23 December 1913. The Federal Reserve System was far from being a central bank on the European model and was frequently subject to private banking influence (as in the runup to the Great Depression). But the Federal Reserve System has continued, essentially unchanged into the 1990s.

BIBLIOGRAPHY

Livingston, James L. *Origins of the Federal Reserve System: Money, Class, and Corporate Capitalism, 1890–1913.* 1986.

White, Eugene N. *The Regulation and Reform of the American Banking System, 1900–1929.* 1983.

MORTON KELLER

FEDERAL SECURITIES ACT. *See* Securities Acts.

FEDERAL TRADE COMMISSION ACT

(1914; 38 Stat. 717–724). A Federal Trade Commission—or, to use a common term of the time, an Interstate Trade Commission—modeled after the Interstate Commerce Commission was a major part of Woodrow Wilson's antitrust program of 1913 and 1914. The federal courts' interpretation of the Sherman Antitrust Act had come under growing assault. Louis D. Brandeis and other critics warned that the Supreme Court's "rule of reason," which distinguished between acceptable and unacceptable corporate consolidations, did not adequately check the growth and power of big business. At the same time, influential voices of the business community, among them the U.S. Chamber of Commerce, wanted an administrative agency that would bring greater predictability and stability to business regulation (and, they thought, be more responsive to their interests).

Brandeis and New York lawyer George D. Rublee drafted a trade commission bill that was introduced in Congress by New Hampshire representative Raymond B. Stevens. It designated those unfair trade practices to be outlawed and provided for the creation of a Federal Trade Commission (FTC) with the power to issue cease and desist orders against those business activities that in its view fostered the illegal suppression of competition. This was, said one observer, to be an "expert machinery" to prevent "unfair methods of competition in commerce."

House Commerce Committee chairman William C. Adamson of Georgia and others opposed what they regarded as a new regulatory agency empowered to make law that was properly within the province of Congress. But Wilson strongly backed an instrument that he thought would foster better business-government relations and strengthen antitrust regulation. He told Congress: "The business men of the country desire . . . the advice, the definite guidance and information which can be supplied by an administrative body." Later, he buoyantly declared that the FTC "has transformed the government of the United States from being an antagonist of business into being a friend of business." With both political parties, almost all trade associations, Brandeis, and the Chamber of Commerce supporting it, the Federal Trade Commission Act breezed through Congress with almost no opposition and became law in September 1914.

But this supposed milestone in the rise of administrative regulation fulfilled neither the expectations of its supporters nor the fears of its few opponents. In practice, the FTC (often hobbled by incompetent or overly probusiness commissioners) limited itself almost entirely to fraudulent or deceptive trade practices—most notably, false and misleading advertising. Beyond this, adverse court decisions entirely eviscerated the FTC. A study in the mid 1920s found it "not uncommon for the Commission to be under fire in the Senate for exercising its powers too gingerly and in the House for daring to use them at all." The steady growth of the consumer economy has given the FTC a continuing role (however attenuated) in the complex business of federal regulation of American business.

[*See also* Clayton Antitrust Act; Sherman Antitrust Act.]

BIBLIOGRAPHY

Henderson, Gerard C. *The Federal Trade Commission: A Study in Administrative Law and Procedure.* 1924.
Link, Arthur. *Wilson: The New Freedom.* 1956. Pp. 425–442.

MORTON KELLER

FELLOWSHIP PROGRAMS. *See* Intern and Fellowship Programs.

FERRARO, GERALDINE A. (1935–), representative from New York and the first woman to be nominated by a major party as a candidate for vice president. Ferraro served as representative from New York's 9th Congressional District in the 96th, 97th, and 98th Congresses (1979–1985). While in the House, she tackled several issues of particular interest to women, including pay equity, the Equal Rights Amendment, and programs to reduce the disproportionate number of women and children living in poverty in the United States. Representative Ferraro's committee assignments included the committees on Post Office and Civil Service, Budget, Public Works and Transportation, and Aging. During her three terms in the House, Ferraro rose to a position of influence within the House Democratic leadership. She served as secretary of the Democratic caucus and was appointed to the prestigious Democratic Steering and Policy Committee, which is responsible for all Democratic House committee assignments.

Considered a protégé of Speaker Thomas P. (Tip) O'Neill, Jr. (D-Mass.), Ferraro successfully used her House leadership position as a launching pad for her bid as the Democratic candidate for vice president in 1984. Geraldine Ferraro's nomination for the vice presidency created an emotional outpouring at the Democratic convention and among women across America. Many Republicans as well as Democrats applauded what Rep. Barbara B. Kennelly (D-Conn.) called the "breaking down [of] another barrier to full equality and justice."

Ferraro, the daughter of working-class immigrant parents, had risen through the ranks to achieve the "American dream." While teaching school in New York City, Ferraro had attended law school at night.

Mondale/Ferraro: for the Family of America

CAMPAIGN POSTER. Geraldine A. Ferraro, *right*, with Walter F. Mondale (D-Minn.), during the 1984 Democratic presidential campaign.

COLLECTION OF DAVID J. AND JANICE L. FRENT

She served as an assistant district attorney, then as a member of the House, and finally as the vice presidential running mate of Walter F. Mondale in their unsuccessful race against incumbent President Ronald Reagan and Vice President George Bush. Characteristically, equality was the theme of her vice presidential nomination acceptance speech. She quoted Dr. Martin Luther King, Jr., and then added, "America is the land where dreams can come true for all of us."

BIBLIOGRAPHY

Breslin, Rosemary. *Gerry: A Woman Making History.* 1984.
Ferraro, Geraldine. *Ferraro: My Story.* 1985.

MARY ETTA BOESL

FESSENDEN, WILLIAM PITT (1806–1869), Whig representative and Republican senator from Maine, chairman of the Joint Committee on Reconstruction. After graduation from Bowdoin

College, William Pitt Fessenden studied law and was admitted to the bar in 1827. He was a Whig representative in the 27th Congress (1841–1843) and a senator from 1854 until his death in 1869, except for a hiatus of eight months in 1864–1865 while he served as secretary of the Treasury.

While a senator, Fessenden distinguished himself by his work on the the Finance Committee, of which he became chairman in 1861; by his opposition to the Kansas-Nebraska bill; by his chairmanship of the Joint Committee on Reconstruction in 1866; and by his opposition to the impeachment of Andrew Johnson. Fessenden was one of the great Senate debaters of his era. He worked tirelessly with Salmon P. Chase in formulating the appropriation and loan bills to finance the Civil War, as well as the national banking acts, and in pushing the legislation through Congress.

Although critical of Lincoln's plan of reconstruction in December 1863, Fessenden refused to vote for the Wade-Davis bill in July 1864 and supported Lincoln's pocket veto. As chairman of the Joint Committee on Reconstruction, he tried to prevent a clash between President Andrew Johnson and Congress, but the stubborn and suspicious Johnson would not be propitiated. Fessenden was the pri-

mary author of the joint committee's report, for which he was praised by contemporaries and continues to receive praise from historians. Friendship between Fessenden and Charles Sumner in the 1850s turned to bitter animosity during the war, and Fessenden probably accepted the chairmanship of the joint committee to prevent Sumner from getting it.

Although he distrusted and disliked President Johnson, Fessenden opposed impeachment from its first suggestion in 1866 and was one of the seven Senate Republican recusants who voted to acquit the president. He was persuasive and courageous in arguing both the impropriety and the illegality of the impeachment. This often acerbic and morose man was one of the ablest members of the founding generation of congressional Republicans.

BIBLIOGRAPHY

Fessenden, Francis. *Life and Public Services of William Pitt Fessenden.* 2 vols. 1907.

Jellison, Charles A. *Fessenden of Maine: Civil War Senator.* 1962.

PATRICK W. RIDDLEBERGER

WILLIAM PITT FESSENDEN.

FIFTEENTH AMENDMENT (1870; 15 Stat. 346). In the years following the Civil War, the political difficulties of establishing peace in the reconstituted Union proved as formidable as the military difficulties leading to the Northern victory had been. To legalize the end of slavery, Republican state legislatures in 1865 ratified the Thirteenth Amendment to the federal Constitution. To achieve political control of the South, Republicans of the 39th Congress in 1867 began congressional Reconstruction by imposing black suffrage on ten previously rebel states. In 1868 the Fourteenth Amendment was ratified, nationalizing civil (but not voting) rights. Thus, while blacks could vote in the South under Reconstruction, all the border and lower northern states still prohibited black suffrage.

During the lame-duck session of the 40th Congress, in early 1869, the Republican congressional leadership decided to enfranchise adult black males outside the South as a possible counterweight against a resurgent Democratic party. Some Republicans also wished to advance the cause of equal rights and impartial justice. The idealistic motive reinforced the pragmatic one. As a black clergyman from Pittsburgh observed, the "Republican Party had done the negro good but they were doing themselves good at the same time."

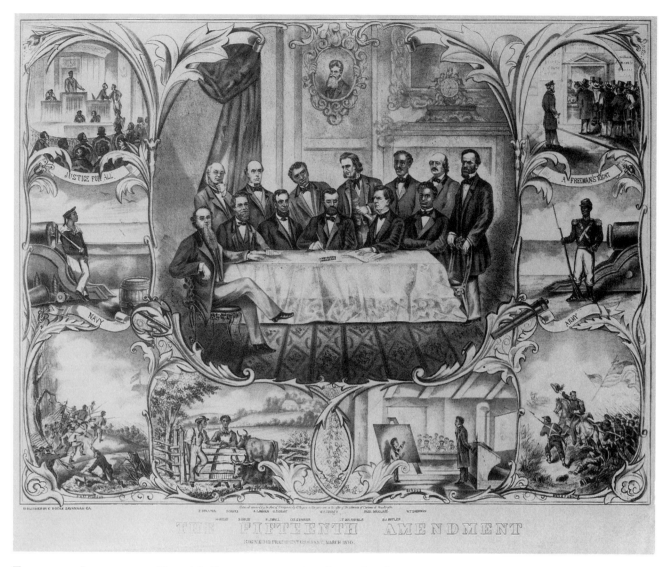

FIFTEENTH AMENDMENT. Pictorial allegory representing the civil rights promised to African Americans. *At center,* the political figures that pushed for civil rights for black Americans, including President Ulysses S. Grant signing the amendment, with slain president Abraham Lincoln beside him. LIBRARY OF CONGRESS

Although the principal objective remained the enfranchisement of blacks in northern and border states, Republicans had an important secondary objective in mind. They intended to protect black voting in the South by federal election enforcement. To safeguard both objectives, they settled on a constitutional amendment affirming black suffrage instead of a federal statute, which would have been potentially more vulnerable to repeal. While agreeing on these goals, Republican members of Congress had divergent outlooks and regional priorities, and they differed over how to achieve their common goals. Striking a compromise, they framed an amendment asserting that neither the

states nor the federal government could limit citizens' voting rights "on account of race, color, or previous condition of servitude." This did not protect blacks' access to public office, nor did it prohibit literacy, property, or nativity tests for suffrage. Members feared such far-reaching reform might be politically dangerous and imperil chances for ratification. The amendment represented more the pragmatic instincts of moderate Republicans and practical Radicals than the idealistic views of doctrinaire Radical Republicans.

The struggle for ratification in 1869 and 1870 followed party lines. Most Republicans supported the amendment, and most Democrats opposed it. The fight for ratification was fiercest in the lower North, where political forces were evenly divided and journalists and politicians regarded the potential black voter as holding the balance of power. Despite Republican control of most state legislatures, ratification remained uncertain. National party pressure as well as presidential and congressional intervention proved decisive. As one Ohio Republican advised Republican governor Rutherford B. Hayes, "By hook or by crook you must get the 15th amendment through or we are gone up." Declared ratified on 30 March 1870, the amendment enabled blacks to vote in seventeen northern and border states. Their votes counted significantly in close contests, helping Republicans in Connecticut, New Jersey, Pennsylvania, and elsewhere.

Although Republicans regarded the Fifteenth Amendment as the supreme achievement of Reconstruction, it eventually became a dead letter in the fifteen former slave states. As national retreat from Reconstruction gained momentum during the late nineteenth and early twentieth centuries, most border state and southern blacks lost the franchise. With repression in the South, indifference in the North, inaction in Washington, and conservatism in the nation, the Fifteenth Amendment was rarely enforced. Federal courts often interpreted the Fifteenth Amendment narrowly, thus limiting enforcement. The Republican-led 51st Congress (1891–1893) failed to enact a new enforcement measure. In 1894 the Democrat-led 53d Congress repealed existing legislation and so virtually ended federal enforcement. In the face of federal paralysis, Democrats in their one-party states used force, fraud, law, and discriminatory practice to prevent blacks from registering and voting.

With the rise of the civil rights movement during and after World War II, a series of pivotal decisions by the U.S. Supreme Court poured new meaning into the Fifteenth Amendment. Under prodding from civil rights leaders, notably Martin Luther King, Jr., and from President Lyndon B. Johnson, the liberal, Democrat-led 89th Congress approved the landmark Voting Rights Act in 1965. Other major civil rights acts were approved during the 1960s. This legislation spurred enfranchisement and revolutionized the politics of the South. Millions of African Americans became registered voters and in turn elected thousands of black public officials, including members of Congress from southern and border states. White southerners in Congress rapidly accommodated to this new political force and moderated their positions. Once again

fruitful, the Fifteenth Amendment had come full circle.

BIBLIOGRAPHY

Gillette, William. *Retreat from Reconstruction, 1869–1879.* 1979.
Gillette, William. *The Right to Vote: Politics and the Passage of the Fifteenth Amendment.* 1969.

WILLIAM GILLETTE

FILIBUSTER. A word of Dutch and Spanish origin meaning *freebooter, filibuster* was first used in a legislative context in the mid-nineteenth century in reference to delaying tactics employed to prevent a vote on a legislative matter that would pass if a vote were allowed. Such obstructive tactics predate the application of the term, however. There is evidence of their employment, for example, in American colonial legislatures; and in the First Congress, what became known as a filibuster was used in the House of Representatives against a bill to establish the nation's permanent capital.

Currently, the term is primarily applied to tactics used in the U.S. Senate. Originally, however, it was also applicable to practices that were a common feature of House activity. As the House grew in size, it adopted rules changes that restricted the opportunities for filibuster. These included the use of a previous-question motion whereby a House majority could end debate, limitations on the time members are allowed to speak during general debate and on amendments, and enforcement of a rule of germaneness requiring that members speak to the subject under consideration. Although obstructive and delaying tactics still exist in the House, the vehicles are far more limited and less effective than in the Senate.

The Senate's smaller size allowed it the luxury of a tradition of unlimited debate and thus an environment favorable to filibusters. Until 1917, Senate debate could only be ended by unanimous consent. If a single senator objected to a request to end debate and vote on a measure, that request was denied and debate continued.

From the 1840s until the 1880s filibusters in the Senate were common but rarely successful. Underlying the filibuster strategy was an assumption that the filibuster not only prevented a vote on the item of legislation under consideration but also delayed the disposal of other matters on the Senate floor. Thus, senators concerned to move these other matters forward might be willing to make concessions to those filibustering in order to break the logjam. A filibuster's success depended on the presence of one of two conditions: either a sizable minority of the Senate had to be so intensely opposed to the bill under consideration that it could sustain debate indefinitely or the filibuster had to occur near the end of a session, when a handful of senators or even a single senator could threaten the completion of other legislative business.

In the late nineteenth century, with party divisions in the Senate more equal in number, the frequency, intensity, and success of filibusters increased. Debate was extended not only through filibusters but also through use of a range of parliamentary delaying tactics, such as frequent votes and quorum calls. Efforts to change Senate rules to allow for cloture, a formal means whereby the Senate could vote to end debate, failed.

Although several modest changes in Senate rules in the early years of the twentieth century placed curbs on obstructionism, it was not until 1917 that the Senate adopted its first cloture rule. During the lame-duck session of the 64th Congress (1915–1917), eleven senators successfully filibustered a bill to arm merchant ships favored by the administration of Woodrow Wilson. Wilson then called the Senate into special session and demanded that it change its rules, which it did with Rule XXII. As adopted, Rule XXII provided that sixteen senators could submit a cloture petition requesting a vote on ending debate on a matter before the Senate. Two days after the filing a vote would be taken, and if two-thirds or more of the senators present and voting supported the cloture motion, further debate would then be limited to one hour for each senator.

If cloture votes are used as an indicator of the frequency of filibusters, Rule XXII appears to have had the desired impact. From 1917 to 1960 only twenty-three cloture votes occurred. Clearly, there were more than twenty-three filibusters during this time, but the threat of cloture had somewhat changed the nature of the tactic itself. In some cases senators engaged in individual filibusters intended to dramatize an issue rather than to defeat a bill. In 1957, for example, after other southerners had decided against trying to block a modest civil rights bill, Strom Thurmond, then a Democratic senator from South Carolina, held the floor for a record twenty-four hours and eighteen minutes. In other instances, no cloture vote took place, either because a compromise was reached or because the Senate surrendered to the filibuster.

With the adoption of a cloture rule, then, the fili-

SEN. HUGH SCOTT (R-PA.). Resting on a makeshift bed during the filibuster against the Civil Rights Act of 1964.
OFFICE OF THE HISTORIAN OF THE U.S. SENATE

buster became a less effective weapon and its use declined. On occasion, the filibuster could still be a valued tactic, as at the end of a session, or when a sizable number of members were vehement in their opposition to a bill (as southern Democrats were to most civil rights legislation from 1937 through the 1960s) and thus there were likely insufficient votes to invoke cloture.

The adoption of Rule XXII also signaled a change in Senate norms regarding the use of the filibuster. It became accepted practice that the filibuster would be reserved for only the most major issues. It was understood that to employ the filibuster for relatively trivial matters would result in new efforts to put restrictions on debate. In addition, as civil rights votes began to dominate filibusters and cloture efforts, civil rights advocates became reluctant to engage the tactic. The pro–civil rights senators realized that were they to engage in filibusters themselves, they would be deprived of a major ground for criticizing civil rights opponents in the Senate.

In the late 1960s and 1970s filibuster use rose again, dramatically, and new means had to be developed to manage Senate business. The primary reason for the filibuster's increased use was that it had again become an effective tactic. Senate workload had grown significantly and Senate sessions started to run year-round; time pressure became severe. Under these conditions, a filibuster—or even the threat of one—took on important implications. The floor time needed to indulge those wanting to filibuster and still assure completion of other business had simply disappeared. Moreover, the threat of a filibuster from an individual senator was often enough to bring concessions. In addition, the filibuster was now used by others besides southern Democrats and against initiatives other than civil rights bills.

In an effort to manage floor business in this changed environment, Senate leaders developed new methods of dealing with the filibuster. A traditional method had been to keep the Senate in session day and night. This not only wears down the filibusterers but also gives other senators, who are inconvenienced by around-the-clock sessions, a strong incentive to vote for cloture. This tactic was used successfully to pass the 1964 Civil Rights Bill. Understandably, Senate leaders are reluctant to resort to this strategy frequently.

Two now more commonly used methods, the "track system" and "holds," came into use in the early 1970s under Majority Leader Mike Mansfield (D-Mont.). Under the track system an agreement is reached with those filibustering that part of each day will be devoted to the legislation being filibustered and part of the day to other legislation. This allows the Senate to complete other business while the filibuster proceeds. It does help the leadership manage the Senate's work, but it also takes pressure off those engaging in the filibuster.

The hold is a more informal way for party leaders to respond to a filibuster threat. A senator or a group of senators may place a hold on a piece of Senate business by making a request of the leadership. This means that no action will be taken until the hold is released. It allows senators to work out disagreements over legislation before tying up the Senate floor with a filibuster. In 1983, Senate leaders of both parties agreed to restrict the use of holds and refused to guarantee them for indefinite periods.

These tactics for coping with the filibuster did not reduce its frequency. From 1961 to 1970, there were sixteen cloture votes; from 1971 until 1975, when Rule XXII was changed, there were twenty-four cloture votes. With use of the filibuster getting out of hand, the Senate was forced to make cloture easier. In 1975, Rule XXII was amended to require that three-fifths of the total membership of the Senate—instead of two-thirds of those present and voting—be required to end debate.

Two major effects have ensued from this change. First, efforts to invoke cloture have been more successful. Prior to the change, cloture was successfully voted 22 percent of the time, but from 1975 through 1987 cloture was voted 41 percent of the time. Second, senators resurrected another form of filibuster, the post-cloture filibuster. By appending hundreds of amendments to a bill, demanding that the amendments be read, requesting roll-call votes, and through other tactics, a filibuster could be extended long after cloture. Sen. James B. Allen (D-Ala.) was the first to uncover the post-cloture filibuster strategy, and others soon followed his lead. In response, the Senate has twice restricted Senate debate after cloture. In 1979, the rules were amended to limit all Senate activity following cloture to one hundred hours, and in 1986, as part of the effort to allow for the televising of Senate floor proceedings, post-cloture activity was reduced to thirty hours.

Although the changes in the cloture rule may have slowed the growth of filibusters and filibuster threats, they had not led to an overall decline in their use. In the 100th Congress (1987–1989), forty-three cloture votes were taken. Despite efforts to control its excesses and its lower rate of success, the filibuster remains a tactic with which any senator can derail the schedule of business.

[See also Cloture; Extension of Remarks; Germaneness; Previous Question; Unanimous Consent Agreements.]

BIBLIOGRAPHY

Oppenheimer, Bruce I. "Changing Time Constraints on Congress: Historical Perspectives on the Use of Cloture." In *Congress Reconsidered*, 3d ed. Edited by Lawrence C. Dodd and Bruce I. Oppenheimer. 1985. Pp. 393–413.

Smith, Steven S. *Call to Order*. 1989.

BRUCE I. OPPENHEIMER

FILLMORE, MILLARD (1800–1874), Whig representative from New York, vice president, thirteenth president of the United States (1850–1853). Born into a desperately poor family in Cayuga County, New York, Fillmore educated himself and became a successful Buffalo lawyer. In the House of Representatives from 1833 to 1835 and 1837 to 1843, he chaired the powerful Ways and Means

MILLARD FILLMORE.   *PERLEY'S REMINISCENCES*, VOL. 1

Committee. As New York State comptroller from 1847 to 1848, he framed a new banking code and designed a sound state currency system. Fillmore, as the vice presidential nominee, was an asset to the Whig ticket in 1848 because his opposition to the expansion of slavery offset the fact that presidential candidate Zachary Taylor was a slaveowner.

In 1850, Henry Clay (W-Ky.) offered compromise measures to settle the bitter sectional quarrel over the expansion of slavery: He would admit California as a free state; allow New Mexico to decide for itself on slavery; compromise on the Texas land claim, giving the state two-thirds of present-day New Mexico (half of what the Texans wanted); give the South a federal fugitive slave law; and abolish the slave trade in the District of Columbia. Southerners persuaded Clay to accept a combination of the measures into a single omnibus bill, which could not pass and which inspired numerous amendment efforts and fierce debates by extremists on both sides. Taylor opposed the omnibus because he wanted to avoid congressional debate by admitting California and New Mexico immediately as states and because he supported New Mexico against the claims of Texas. Vice President Fill-

more, presiding over the Senate, agreed with Taylor, but in case of a tie, he was ready to vote for the omnibus if he should find an amended version acceptable.

On 9 July 1850, Taylor died, and Fillmore became president. The omnibus bill failed on 31 July, but with Fillmore's strong support its parts were soon passed as separate bills in what came to be known as the Compromise of 1850. The Texas settlement, which left New Mexico intact, came after Fillmore warned that he would defend New Mexico with force. The Fugitive Slave Act, though a necessary part of the compromise, violated Fillmore's conscience. Fillmore enforced it nominally to enable Unionists to defeat secessionists in southern elections of 1851 and 1852. He also sent additional troops to the Carolinas and strengthened the forts in Charleston, South Carolina.

After the 1850 compromise Fillmore was extremely popular, but he did not want another term as president and supported the candidacy of his secretary of State, Daniel Webster. But when the antislavery senator William H. Seward (W-N.Y.), who was bitterly hated in the South, mustered Whig delegates for Gen. Winfield Scott, Fillmore recognized the danger to the Whig party and became a candidate. He was too late. Though he led the convention for several ballots, Webster's small number of delegates finally switched to Scott. Southern Whigs voted en masse for the Democratic candidate, Franklin Pierce, thereby destroying the national Whig party.

Within two years Fillmore had joined the nativist Know-Nothing (American) party, which many Whigs saw as an alternative to the radically antislavery Free-Soilers and the southern-dominated Democrats. In 1856, the Know-Nothings nominated Fillmore for president. He ignored the party's nativist platform and spoke out strongly for an end to sectional conflict; he received 28.6 percent of the vote, carrying only Maryland. Ultimately returning to Buffalo, he supported the Union effort in the Civil War with time and money. He died on 8 March 1874.

BIBLIOGRAPHY

Hamilton, Holman. *Prologue to Conflict: The Crisis and Compromise of 1850.* 1964.

Rayback, Robert. *Millard Fillmore: Biography of a President.* 1959.

Smith, Elbert B. *The Presidencies of Zachary Taylor and Millard Fillmore.* 1988.

ELBERT B. SMITH

FILMS. *See* Movies on Congress.

FINANCE COMMITTEE, SENATE.

The Finance Committee is reputed to be the most powerful and prestigious committee in the U.S. Senate. It is certainly one of the oldest and most active Senate committees, with responsibility for federal tax and foreign trade legislation, public borrowing and debt, and approximately half of all federal spending (including social security). With twenty members, it is also one of the largest Senate committees. In the 103d Congress (1993–1995), its members included eleven Democrats and nine Republicans, and it was chaired by Sen. Daniel Patrick Moynihan (D-N.Y.). Since its founding, prominent committee members have included three future presidents, eight vice presidents, numerous cabinet officers, and such Senate notables as Henry Clay, Daniel Webster, John C. Calhoun, Robert M. La Follette, Robert A. Taft, Russell B. Long, and Bob Dole.

Committee History and Evolving Jurisdiction.

The Senate Finance Committee was established in 1816 to succeed the Select Committee on Finance and a Uniform National Currency. Reflecting the original Senate practice of creating temporary, ad hoc committees for specific legislation, the select committee was organized in 1815 to report on tariff legislation and a bill reauthorizing the Bank of the United States. The following year, the Senate established a series of permanent, or standing, committees to deal more effectively with subjects of recurring legislative interest. Among these were committees on Foreign Relations, Military Affairs, Public Lands, the Judiciary—and Finance.

Since its creation, the Finance Committee has been the most important Senate committee in economic and fiscal affairs, although its specific jurisdiction has varied considerably, at one time or another encompassing all or most revenue, tariff, trade, appropriations, veterans, banking, and currency legislation. Tariff and trade legislation was especially important during the nineteenth century, when customs duties and tariffs provided the major source of federal government revenues and conflicts over tariff rates sharply divided the nation along regional and party lines. Low tariffs and free-trade policies were generally favored by rural and agricultural interests in the South and West—typically represented by the Democratic party—while high protective tariffs were favored by northern industrial interests, which were represented first by

the Federalists and later by the Whig and Republican parties.

Originally, efforts were made to divide jurisdiction over tariff bills between the Senate Committee on Finance and the Committee on Commerce and Manufactures. Bills on tariffs and duties intended strictly to raise federal revenues were referred to the Committee on Finance, while legislation establishing higher, protective tariffs was referred to the Commerce Committee. This distinction proved difficult to maintain, both politically and conceptually, and after 1834 virtually all tariff legislation was referred to the Committee on Finance.

Consolidation of the Finance Committee's jurisdiction over tariff legislation placed it at the center of economic policy and partisan controversies for the next century. Reflecting changing partisan control of the Congress and evolving economic conditions in the country, major tariff increases were enacted in 1828, 1861, 1890, and 1930, while tariff reductions were enacted in 1833, 1913, and 1934.

Initially, the Senate Finance Committee was also given responsibility for most military and general governmental appropriations bills. By the 1830s, it had expanded its jurisdiction to include naval and Indian affairs appropriations as well. This concentration of authority became especially burdensome and controversial during the Civil War, however, and the House moved to create a separate Appropriations Committee in 1865. The Senate followed suit in 1867, dividing responsibility over revenue and spending bills between the committees on Finance and Appropriations.

The Senate Finance Committee's jurisdiction was divided further in 1913, when the new Committee on Banking and Currency was established. Prior to this, the issuance of paper currency—so-called greenbacks—and the expanded coinage and circulation of money redeemable in silver rather than gold generated important economic and political disputes in which the Finance Committee played a major role. For example, the Sherman Silver Purchase Act of 1890, named after committee chairman John Sherman (R-Ohio), enlarged the money supply through expanded government purchases of silver. Its repeal in 1894 contributed to the bitter battle between gold and silver Democrats in 1896 and the subsequent regional realignment of political parties.

Finance Committee responsibilities were also expanded in 1913 with the ratification of the Sixteenth Amendment. This amendment reestablished congressional authority to impose an income tax on individual citizens, complementing the corporate income tax enacted in 1909. Over the next forty years, the income tax became the predominant source of revenue for a greatly expanded federal government, and the complex system of exemptions, exclusions, and deductions from income became an important feature of tax politics.

Another important expansion of committee responsibilities occurred in 1935, when legislation to establish the Social Security system was enacted. Because of the system's reliance on payroll taxes, this and all subsequent social, unemployment, and medical insurance legislation was referred to the Committee on Finance.

In 1994, the Committee on Finance had jurisdiction, by Senate Rule XXV, over legislation in eleven key areas: taxation, Social Security, Medicare, Medicaid, Supplemental Security Income, cash welfare assistance for poor families, social services, unemployment compensation, maternal and child health grants, tariff and trade legislation, and public debt. Although this broad jurisdiction creates many opportunities for conflict and overlap with other Senate committees, the Finance Committee has developed a reputation for vigorously defending its domain, and during the 1980s it consistently ranked among those committees with the smallest percentage of bills receiving multiple referrals (see Roger Davidson, "Multiple Referral of Legislation in the U.S. Senate," *Legislative Studies Quarterly* 14 (1989): 385, 388). The committee also made recommendations concerning the confirmation of presidential nominations for the secretaries of Treasury and Health and Human Services, the U.S. trade representative, the commissioners of the Social Security Administration and the Internal Revenue Service, and a number of other subcabinet positions.

Committee Culture and Decision Making. Historically, the Finance Committee's decision-making culture and its patterns of policy-making have been shaped by three principal factors: the scope of the committee's jurisdiction, the constitutional requirement that revenue bills originate in the House of Representatives, and the Senate's relatively open rules governing floor debate and amendment.

The scope and economic significance of the Finance Committee's jurisdiction have made it one of the Senate's most important and desirable committee assignments. Donald Matthews's analysis of committee recruitment patterns during the 1950s (in *U.S. Senators and Their World*, 1960) indicates that the Finance Committee ranked third in attractiveness among committee assignments in the Senate. Between 1947 and 1957, for example, thirteen senators transferred to the Finance Committee from other Senate committees, but only three transferred away from Finance in favor of assignments on the Foreign Relations and Appropriations committees. Subsequent research on Senate committee assignments by Steven Smith and Christopher Deering indicates that Finance remained one of only three Senate committees whose power and prestige were listed as a reason for selecting the assignment in the 1970s and 1980s (*Committees in Congress*, 1990). Smith and Deering also demonstrate that the committee ranks relatively high in media visibility and overall levels of legislative activity. Although the Finance Committee traditionally had a rather conservative ideological complexion, as Senate leaders sought to restrict committee membership to more conservative senior members, this pattern weakened after the 1970s.

Even more important in shaping the committee's role in legislative matters has been the constitutional requirement in Article I, section 7 that "all bills for raising revenue shall originate in the House of Representatives." This stricture has generally required that the House act first on tax and trade legislation, allowing it to define the basic contours of such laws. Acting second, the Senate has tended to adopt an "appeals court" role: groups and individuals who are dissatisfied with legislation passed by the House focus their energies on obtaining favorable changes and amendments in the Senate (John F. Manley, *The Politics of Finance*, 1970).

These distinctive roles have been reinforced by the rules of procedure in the two chambers. House rules have traditionally restricted or prohibited floor amendments to revenue bills, while Senate rules and traditions have permitted much more open floor debate and broader legislative participation. Consequently, in considering appeals by disgruntled parties, the Senate has generally found it difficult to restrict consideration of amendments that members, either on or off the Finance Committee, have been determined to offer.

Neither of these factors has kept the Finance Committee from exerting an important influence over the content of fiscal legislation, but they have combined to shape the patterns of committee deliberations and coalition building over time. In particular, committee chairmen have traditionally sought consensus or unanimity within the committee in order to bolster support for its legislation on the Senate floor. Chairmen have also tended to struc-

SENATE FINANCE COMMITTEE MEETING.

OFFICE OF THE HISTORIAN OF THE U.S. SENATE

ture bills within committee in anticipation of expected floor amendments. Such considerations encourage coalition building through logrolling and the accumulation of provisions attractive to diverse and often narrow economic interests.

Scholars and critics sometimes claim that Senate Finance Committee bills resemble "Christmas trees," on which relatively clean and simple legislation from the House is loaded down with popular amendments and costly ornaments. For example, John Witte's detailed study of the origins of twentieth-century tax legislation found that, of provisions originating in the Senate, expanded "loopholes" and other revenue-losing provisions outnumbered revenue increases by a ratio of more than 4 to 1 (*The Politics and Development of the Federal Income Tax*, 1985). In contrast, revenue gainers and losers were roughly equal among those provisions originating in the executive branch or the House.

Similar patterns in earlier tariff legislation showed that the Senate aggressively used its constitutional authority to "propose or concur with amendments" to House-passed revenue bills, typically adding hundreds and even thousands of amendments to major tariff bills. In one extreme

example, an 1872 tariff reduction bill was only four lines long when it passed the House, but it was modified in the Senate with twenty pages of amendments, revising various tariff duties and abolishing the Civil War–era income tax.

As these examples indicate, the constitutional prescription that the House originate revenue bills has not prevented the Senate generally and the Finance Committee in particular from playing an important role in shaping tax and trade policy. In fact, as Witte has shown, the Senate's activism in sponsoring new tax legislation increased appreciably during the 1970s and reached a pinnacle during the early 1980s. Major revenue bills enacted in the 1980s, including the historic Tax Reform Act of 1986, bore a heavy Senate imprint.

The most striking example occurred in 1982, when the Finance Committee, led by chairman Sen. Bob Dole (R-Kans.), took the initiative in developing one of the largest tax hikes in history (see Catherine Rudder, "Fiscal Responsibility, Fairness, and the Revenue Committees," in *Congress Reconsidered*, edited by Lawrence C. Dodd and Bruce I. Oppenheimer, 1989). When the House proved unable to act first on this politically sensitive matter, the Senate proceeded on its own, circumventing the constitutional limitation by attaching its provisions to a minor fiscal bill already passed by the House.

Historically, Dole and other Finance Committee chairmen have been further aided by the committee's tradition of centralized resources. The committee did not establish a system of permanent subcommittees until the 93d Congress (1973–1974), and staff resources remain firmly under the control of the full committee. This is particularly important for tax legislation, in which effective legislative action is often contingent on authoritative cost estimates prepared by the staff of the Joint Committee on Taxation.

[*See also* Appropriations Committee, Senate; Banking, Finance, and Urban Affairs Committee, House; Banking, Housing, and Urban Affairs Committee, Senate; Taxation Committee, Joint.]

BIBLIOGRAPHY

Conlan, Timothy J., Margaret T. Wrightson, and David R. Beam. *Taxing Choices: The Politics of Tax Reform.* 1990.
Price, David E. *Who Makes the Laws? Creativity and Power in Senate Committees.* 1972.
Schick, Allen. *Congress and Money: Budgeting, Spending, and Taxing.* 1980.
U.S. Senate. *History of the Committee on Finance.* 97th Cong., 1st sess., 1981. S. Doc. 97-5.

TIMOTHY J. CONLAN

FINANCIAL DISCLOSURE. Members of Congress and certain congressional staff are required to file annual financial disclosure reports. These reports publicly detail information about the member's or employee's personal financial affairs and also provide certain information about the personal finances of the member's or employee's spouse and dependent children.

The financial disclosure requirements for members of Congress and other high-ranking officials in the U.S. government were originally enacted into law in the Ethics in Government Act of 1978. The amended and current requirements for financial disclosure by federal officials may now be found codified in the United States Code, in the appendix to Title 5 (5 U.S.C.A. app. 6, sec. 101 et seq.).

Requirements. Financial disclosure reports must be filed by 15 May of each year by all members of Congress and by those congressional staffers who are compensated at a rate of pay equal to 120 percent of the base salary for a GS-15 (General Schedule, grade 15) government employee. If no one on a member's staff receives that high a salary, then the member must designate at least one principal assistant to file a disclosure report.

Members and employees of the House of Representatives file with the clerk of the House, while senators and those Senate staff members covered by the regulation file with the secretary of the Senate. Copies of the reports are forwarded for review to the respective ethics committees in each house of Congress: the House Committee on Standards of Official Conduct and the Senate Select Committee on Ethics.

Within thirty days of filing, the reports are available to the public for inspection and copying. Those requesting disclosure information must identify themselves and must state that they are aware of the prohibitions against the use of the reports for commercial, credit, or fund-raising purposes. Reports are kept for public inspection for six years.

The required contents of the disclosure statements include the reporting of the sources and types of outside earned and unearned income received by the filer in amounts in excess of $200; gifts received in excess of $100; gifts of travel, food, or lodging accepted, or reimbursements for such expenses, along with an itinerary of such travel when aggregating $250 or more; interests in income-producing assets and investments of more than $1,000 (including bank accounts in excess of $5,000); liabilities owed exceeding $10,000; the description and date of transactions in real property or stocks, bonds, or other financial instruments that exceed $1,000 in value; positions held in businesses and organizations, including whether any compensation exceeding $5,000 has been received from any one source during the preceding two years; and any agreements or arrangements for future employment, leaves of absence, or continuing compensation from any source other than the federal government. Information must also be provided about the income, gifts, reimbursements, assets, liabilities, and financial transactions of the member's or employee's spouse and dependent children. When dollar amounts are disclosed in the financial reports, the exact amount of income, assets, debts, or transactions need not be listed, but rather a range of value is reported for each asset or item.

Although the identity of the specific holdings in a trust must also generally be disclosed by members and employees, if one has a qualified blind trust approved by the House or Senate ethics committee, then only the income from such a trust need be disclosed, and not the identity of the assets in it. Blind trusts shield officials from knowing what assets they own, thereby protecting them from potential undue influences from those financial interests.

History of Disclosure Requirements. After World War II, legislative recommendations were regularly drafted and introduced in Congress by supporters of financial disclosure. Not until the 1970s, however, was uniform, public financial disclosure for Congress formally mandated in congressional rules or law.

In 1946, revelations were made of profiteering in the commodities market by certain members of Congress who had received valuable inside information while serving on the House and Senate committees on Agriculture. Sen. Wayne L. Morse (R-Ore.), a persistent and early supporter of public financial disclosure requirements, began in that year and in each successive Congress to introduce bills requiring public financial disclosure by members and other high-level officials (see, for example, S. Res. 306, 79th Cong., 2d sess., 1946). In addition to calls for financial disclosure laws by President Harry S. Truman during this time, Sen. Paul H. Douglas (D-Ill.) chaired a special subcommittee of the Senate Labor Committee that looked into issues of ethics in government service. (Senator Morse also served on the subcommittee.) The Douglas subcommittee included financial disclosure as part of its ethics recommendations in its respected report on ethics in government in 1951. That special subcommittee of the Senate Labor and Public Welfare Committee, however, did not formally introduce legislation requiring disclosure, and its other principal recommendations were not adopted.

Although financial disclosure was not recommended as part of the major conflict-of-interest law revisions examined in the late 1950s and enacted in 1962 (P.L. 87-849), the call for financial disclosure in Congress again gained impetus in the 1960s with the revelation of financial wrongdoing by the powerful Senate staff aide Robert G. (Bobby) Baker. The Senate Rules Committee, which investigated the Baker case, recommended the creation of a Senate committee on standards of conduct (S. Res. 338, 88th Cong., 2d sess., 1964) and the adoption of limited, confidential financial disclosure for members (S. Res. 337, 88th Cong., 2d sess., 1964). The recommendation to establish the Senate Select Committee on Standards and Conduct (now the Senate Select Committee on Ethics), strengthened by a floor amendment by Sen. John Sherman Coop-

er (R-Ky.), was eventually approved. Detailed public financial disclosure requirements sponsored by Sen. Clifford P. Case (R-N.J.) were, however, defeated in Senate debate in 1964, as were other attempts to adopt even the limited disclosure requirements recommended by the Rules Committee.

The House of Representatives in 1967 followed the Senate lead and authorized its own standing ethics committee, the House Committee on Standards of Official Conduct. Led in large part by further allegations of wrongdoing by members of Congress, specifically Sen. Thomas J. Dodd (D-Conn.), and Rep. Adam Clayton Powell, Jr. (D-N.Y.), both the Senate and the House ethics committees for the first time recommended an official written "code of conduct." This code was formally adopted as rules by the House (H. Res. 1099, 90th Cong., 2d sess.) and by the Senate (S. Res. 266, 90th Cong., 2d sess.) in 1968. These rules included provisions for "limited" financial disclosure by members. The disclosure required by the Senate was a confidential filing with the General Accounting Office that would be opened by the select committee only if allegations of wrongdoing were made against the member. The disclosure required by the House was a very limited public disclosure of particular holdings and ownerships in entities that did business with the government.

The Watergate scandal of the 1970s led to substantial review and revision of ethical standards and laws in the federal government generally, including rules changes in the House and Senate. In 1977, both the House and the Senate adopted much more detailed, public financial disclosure requirements in their respective rules (S. Res. 110, 95th Cong., 1st sess.; H. Res. 287, 95th Cong., 1st sess.). The next year, when the comprehensive Ethics in Government Act of 1978 (P.L. 95-521) was passed, annual public financial disclosure for top officials in all three branches of the federal government was enacted into law for the first time in Titles I, II, and III of that act. In 1989, the Ethics Reform Act (P.L. 101-191; see also P.L. 101-280), amended and recodified the disclosure provisions to combine the separate financial disclosure requirements for officials in the three branches of government into one title of the Ethics in Government Act.

Purpose of Disclosure Requirements. Disclosure requirements are now an important part of conflict-of-interest regulation, deterrence, and supervision in all three branches of government. In the legislative branch, disclosure is one of the principal conflict-of-interest regulators, since other forms of conflict-of-interest regulation, specifically divestiture of assets and disqualification from voting, were considered largely unworkable for members of Congress.

Members of Congress, unlike most regulators in the executive branch, must vote on and perform official duties with respect to issues that affect virtually the entire spectrum of economic and business matters. Divestiture of all conflicting assets, therefore, was seen as impractical because members could not reasonably be required to divest themselves of all their assets on taking congressional office. Disqualifying a member from acting on a matter in which he or she might have a personal interest would also raise serious difficulties because of members' function and role in a representative democracy. If members had to disqualify themselves on particular matters, this would in effect disenfranchise their entire constituencies on those matters and might even deprive their constituents of representation on matters that are of particular interest to them.

Financial disclosure was thus seen as a more practical method of dealing with members' potential conflicts of interest. Supporters of financial disclosure initially argued that the openness of full disclosure of a member's financial affairs could, in itself, help restore public confidence in elected officials and could help to dispel some of the suspicion and cynicism about the workings of government so pervasive in the post-Watergate era. Furthermore, since members of Congress must regularly submit themselves to the collective will of the voters in regular elections, it was believed that full disclosure of their finances would provide the information and data on which the electorate could reasonably and knowledgeably evaluate the conflict-of-interest issue. A member's decision in obtaining or retaining an asset could then be judged by his or her constituents, and the will of the people could thus be exercised.

The public availability of financial information reported under financial disclosure requirements was intended to deter members from obtaining or holding interests that created obvious or serious conflicts of interest with the members' official duties. Finally, financial disclosure was seen as a mechanism for providing the information to enforce and oversee more substantive conflict-of-interest prohibitions.

Opposition and Constitutional Challenges. Opponents of financial disclosure see it as an onerous, irrelevant, and burdensome requirement. Many of the items to be disclosed in a full disclosure, such as a member's bank accounts or certificates of deposit, are believed irrelevant to any substantial conflict-of-interest issues. Since the disclosure requirements for members or employees of Congress and members' or employees' spouses and children can seem burdensome and intrusive, some view such comprehensive disclosure requirements as a possible obstacle to recruiting qualified personnel in Congress and in the government generally.

Some also believe that the public disclosure of members' financial holdings and assets constitutes an invitation to demagogic attacks. According to critics of disclosure, disclosure alone fails to do the job of conflict-of-interest regulation because the disclosure of assets does not prohibit, regulate, or provide any guidance or rules about proper or improper conduct but only provides information.

The most persistent objection to financial disclosure is that it relegates officials to the status of "second-class" citizens and unduly interferes with their rights of privacy in matters of personal and family finances. During the consideration of the statutory requirements of the Ethics in Government Act, issues regarding how mandatory financial disclosure might violate a constitutional right to privacy were examined, particularly through reference to the experience of those states that had been very active in passing comprehensive ethics regulations, including financial disclosure provisions. State provisions were, however, generally upheld against constitutional challenges by the courts reviewing them. The federal disclosure provisions of the Ethics in Government Act of 1978 were themselves eventually upheld against a constitutional challenge in *Duplantier v. United States* (606 F.2d 654 [1979]), which the Supreme Court refused to review. The federal circuit court found that although privacy is an important personal interest, disclosure requirements for public officials do not impermissibly intrude into "the sphere of family life constitutionally protected by the right of privacy." The court concluded that there exist important governmental interests advanced by public financial disclosure that outweigh incidental intrusions into public officials' financial privacy.

Penalties. The financial disclosure law provides for a civil penalty and fine to be enforced by the attorney general for violations. Although the disclosure provisions do not state express criminal penalties for failure to file or for false filings, a person knowingly filing a false financial disclosure report may still be subject to possible criminal penalties under general provisions of federal criminal law, at 18 U.S.C., sec. 1001, for false or fraudulent statements to the U.S. government. The application of the general criminal penalties for violations of the disclosure law was sustained in *United States v. Hansen* (772 F.2d 940 [1985]) for George V. Hansen (R-Idaho), who while a member of Congress was found to have filed intentionally false statements in his disclosure report.

BIBLIOGRAPHY

Association of the Bar of the City of New York. Special Committee on Congressional Ethics. *Congress and the Public Trust.* 1970.

Getz, Robert S. *Congressional Ethics: The Conflicts of Interest Issue.* 1966.

U.S. House of Representatives. Commission on Administrative Review. *Financial Ethics.* 95th Cong., 1st sess., 1977. H. Doc. 95–73.

U.S. House of Representatives. Select Committee on Ethics. *Legislative Branch Disclosure Act of 1977.* 95th Cong., 1st sess., 1977. H. Rept. 95–574.

U.S. Senate. Special Committee on Official Conduct. *Senate Code of Conduct.* 95th Cong., 1st sess., 1977. S. Rept. 95-49.

U.S. Senate. Committee on Governmental Affairs. *Public Officials Integrity Act of 1977.* 95th Cong., 1st sess., 1977. S. Rept. 95–170.

JACK H. MASKELL

FIRST CONGRESS. Meeting in New York's Federal Hall for its 1789 and 1790 sessions and in Philadelphia's Congress Hall for its 1790–1791 session, the First Congress made decisions and enacted legislation that fleshed out the structure of the new United States of America, further defined federalism, set precedents and established a republican tone for the new government, defused opposition to the Constitution, and held the Union together when a breakup was threatened.

Congress focused on establishing a federal revenue during its first session. Although House debate sometimes revealed both sectional and economic divisions, the members accomplished the most pressing part of their agenda by establishing duties on imports and the tonnage of ships as well as a system for duty collection.

Congress also addressed three issues left unresolved by the Constitutional Convention: establishing executive departments, shaping the federal judiciary, and crafting a bill of rights. Rep. James Madison (Va.), informal House floor leader during the first session, introduced a resolution to estab-

lish departments of Treasury, War, and Foreign Affairs. The question of who had the power to remove the secretaries of these departments touched off a debate on constitutional interpretation. The conclusion, that implicitly this power rests with the president, expanded the powers of the presidency and defined executive lines of authority.

Under the leadership of Oliver Ellsworth (Conn.), the Senate defined the structure, jurisdiction, and procedures of the federal judiciary. The Senate met behind closed doors, but Pennsylvania senator William Maclay's diary reveals that debate on the Judiciary Act of 1789 focused on the meaning of the Constitution and the nature of federalism. The bill established a system of lower federal courts but avoided complete usurpation of the state courts' original jurisdiction.

In June 1789, Madison proposed constitutional amendments to protect individuals' and states' rights from federal interference. His amendments were seen as an unwelcome diversion by most Federal-

FEDERAL HALL, NEW YORK. Seat of the First Congress during the first and second sessions. Designed by architect Pierre-Charles L'Enfant. Engraving by A. Doolittle, 1790, after a drawing by Peter Lacour.

LIBRARY OF CONGRESS

FEDERAL HALL, NEW YORK. Chamber of the House of Representatives, 1789. Drawing.

ists and as not going far enough to curb federal government powers by the small group of Anti-Federalists in Congress. But Madison persisted, convincing the House that the amendments would settle public unease and bring North Carolina and Rhode Island into the Union. Connecticut representative Roger Sherman's insistence that the amendments be placed at the end of the Constitution rather than integrated into it created an identifiable Bill of Rights. The Senate significantly edited the seventeen amendments passed by the House, and twelve were sent to the states.

In 1790 Congress confronted the difficult problems of funding debts incurred by the former Congress and the states during the Revolutionary War and of choosing the site for the capital city. At the request of Congress, Secretary of the Treasury Alexander Hamilton submitted his plan for funding the foreign and domestic debt of the United States and for assuming the state debts. Assumption proved a volatile sectional issue, with members from debtor states faced off against representatives from states that had either paid or substantially reduced their debts. Despite the House defeat of assumption in April, its supporters continued to attempt to force House reconsideration.

The Senate took up a bill to establish the temporary and permanent seats of the federal government, and by 2 June confronted both this issue and the Funding Act, passed by the House without provision for assumption. Both houses were nearly equally divided; Congress had reached its first impasse. Prominent men in both the North and South began to question the Union's viability, raising the possibility of civil war. Eventually a meeting among Hamilton, Madison, and Secretary of State Thomas Jefferson produced an agreement. Madison would supply the southern votes needed for assumption if Hamilton would convince the New Englanders not to interfere with a southern offer to Pennsylvania that would place the capital at Philadelphia for ten years, after which the government would move permanently to a site on the Potomac River. This "compromise of 1790" was the first of three great compromises (the others being the Missouri Compromise and the Compromise of 1850) designed to maintain the sectionally divided Union. The final acts of the compromise occurred during the third session, when the same individuals who had agreed to change their votes also supported the other two vital components of Hamilton's plan: an excise on distilled spirits and a national bank.

The First Congress also adopted legislation regulating the military establishment, the territories, and Indian trade; establishing a census, rules of naturalization, and copyright and patent procedures; and admitting Kentucky and Vermont into the Union. More than 180 bills and resolutions were introduced, including annual budgets. The Senate addressed the executive business laid before it: nominations, treaties, boundary disputes, and a hostage situation, among other issues. The Congress also dealt with more than six hundred petitions. Second-session memorials from Quaker groups and the Pennsylvania Abolition Society caused a divisive House debate on slavery and the slave trade, without resolution of the issues.

A friend of Vice President John Adams summed up the accomplishments of the First Congress: "In no nation, by no Legislature, was ever so much done in so short a period for the establishment of Government, Order, public Credit & general tranquility."

BIBLIOGRAPHY

Bickford, Charlene Bangs, and Kenneth R. Bowling. *Birth of the Nation: The First Federal Congress, 1789–1791.* 1989.

Bowling, Kenneth R. *Politics in the First Congress, 1789–1791.* 1990.

DePauw, Linda Grant, Charlene Bangs Bickford, Kenneth R. Bowling, and Helen Veit, eds. *The Documentary History of the First Federal Congress, 1789–1791.* 1972–.

CHARLENE BANGS BICKFORD

FISCAL YEAR. The term *fiscal year* (FY) refers to any yearly accounting period, without regard to its relationship to the calendar year. The federal government's fiscal year begins on 1 October and ends on 30 September. Before FY 1977, the federal fiscal year ran from 1 July to 30 June. This was changed to the present October to September year by the Congressional Budget and Impoundment Control Act of 1974 [P.L. 93-344] to give Congress more time to prepare the budget and to better ensure that the necessary legislation could be passed before the fiscal year began.

A fiscal year is designated by the calendar year in which it ends; for example, FY 1994 began on 1 October 1993 and ended on 30 September 1994.

Related budget terms include *budget year*, which refers to the fiscal year for which a budget is being considered, that is, the fiscal year following the current year. *Current year* refers to the fiscal year in progress, and *prior year* indicates the fiscal year immediately preceding the current year.

The beginning of the fiscal year, 1 October, marks the date by which that fiscal year's budget must be completed. Work on the budget for a particular fiscal year begins approximately one year before its start, with federal agencies preparing their budget requests. The president submits his budget in the February before the start of a new fiscal year, and Congress acts on it throughout the spring and summer. If a new fiscal year begins without a budget in place, one of two things can occur: the federal government shuts down operations until a budget is finalized, or, more likely, Congress passes legislation, known as a continuing resolution, to provide the necessary funds to allow the government to operate in the absence of a final budget.

[*See also* Congressional Budget and Impoundment Control Act of 1974.]

BIBLIOGRAPHY

LeLoup, Lance. *Budgetary Politics.* 3d ed. 1986.

Schick, Allen, Robert Keith, and Edward Davis. *Manual on the Federal Budget Process.* Congressional Research Service, Library of Congress. CRS Rept. 91-902 GOV. 1991.

U.S. Congress. General Accounting Office. *A Glossary of Terms Used in the Federal Budget Process.* 1981.

KATHLEEN DOLAN

FISH, HAMILTON (1888–1991), representative from New York, leading isolationist, and foe of President Franklin D. Roosevelt, whose home district he represented. Fish became a third-generation member of Congress in a special election in 1919 and, in time, the ranking Republican on the House Rules and Foreign Affairs committees. During the 1920s, he devoted himself to patriotic and veterans' causes—he was an early advocate of the bill to make "The Star-Spangled Banner" the national anthem—but also supported the antilynching bill, equality for women, and a Jewish homeland in Palestine. In 1930 he proposed and then chaired the short-lived Special Committee to Investigate Communist Propaganda.

Fish emerged as a militant isolationist in the 1930s, promoting strict neutrality legislation and taking his anti-involvement message to the public. He became notorious for speaking at a German Day rally at swastika-bedecked Madison Square Garden in 1938, but he also endorsed the peace resolutions of the American Socialist party. In the spring of 1939 he formed the National Committee to Keep America Out of War, with headquarters in his Washington, D.C., office, and that summer he met with German foreign minister Joachim von Ribbentrop, offered to mediate the Danzig dispute, and proposed a thirty-day moratorium on war preparations at the Interparliamentary Union meeting in Oslo.

His biting attacks on Roosevelt's "war policies" continued until Pearl Harbor, and he voted against the draft, lend-lease, and neutrality revision. During the 1940 presidential campaign, Roosevelt often used the cadenced refrain "Martin [Joseph W., Jr., R-Mass.], Barton [Bruce, D-N.Y.], and Fish" to castigate his isolationist opponents.

After the attack on Pearl Harbor, Fish closed ranks behind the president, but he had become an embarrassment even to his own party and was defeated for reelection in 1944.

BIBLIOGRAPHY

Current, Richard N. "Hamilton Fish: 'Crusading Isolationist.'" In *Public Men In and Out of Office.* Edited by J. T. Salter. 1941.
Hanks, Richard K. "Hamilton Fish and American Isolationism, 1929–1944." Ph.D. diss., University of California at Riverside, 1971.

MANFRED JONAS

FIVE-MINUTE RULE. The five-minute rule in clause 5(a) of the House of Representatives Rule XXIII governs the reading of bills for amendment when the House resolves into the Committee of the Whole. The provision of five minutes in which to explain an amendment was adopted by the House in 1847. The provision of five minutes to speak in opposition was adopted in 1850. Five-minute debate also occurs in the House as in Committee of the Whole on any motion to recommit a bill or joint resolution with instructions pursuant to clause 4 of Rule XVI and in committee proceedings.

Through pro forma amendments, five-minute debate theoretically may continue until each member has spoken. The right to explain or oppose an amendment has precedence over motions to amend it. Recognition typically alternates between members of the majority and minority parties, but priority is accorded to members of a reporting committee. Debate must be confined to the pending subject. Time may not be yielded or reserved. Debate on the pending text and its amendments may be limited by nondebatable motion after one speech, however brief. This motion is amendable but may not allocate time.

A preferential motion to rise and report a recommendation to strike the enacting clause is debated under the five-minute rule: the proponent may not reserve time, and an opponent is not recognized until the proponent has spoken. Five-minute debate on an appeal in Committee of the Whole continues at the discretion of the chairman.

BIBLIOGRAPHY

U.S. House of Representatives. *Constitution, Jefferson's Manual, and Rules of the House of Representatives, 103d Congress.* Compiled by William Holmes Brown. 102d Cong., 2d sess., 1992. H. Doc. 102–405.

JOHN V. SULLIVAN

FLAG OF THE UNITED STATES. On 14 June 1777 the Continental Congress passed a resolution establishing the flag of the United States: "*Resolved,* That the flag of the thirteen United States be thirteen stripes, alternate red and white: that the union be thirteen stars, white in a blue field, representing a new constellation." The resolution was not referred to committee or discussed, but subsequent records indicate that the flag was designed by Francis Hopkinson, a delegate from New Jersey and signer of the Declaration of Independence. After the admission of Vermont and Kentucky the Third Congress in 1794 voted to add two stars and two stripes to the flag effective 1 May 1795, despite opposition from some who said that the flag should have a permanent design.

The current flag design of thirteen stripes and one star for each state was established by law in 1818 after the admission of Tennessee, Ohio, Louisiana, Indiana, and Mississippi. The act describes a flag of thirteen stripes and twenty stars and requires the addition of a star to the flag's union on the admission of each new state. The new star is added to the flag on the Fourth of July following the admission of the new state. Although codified in 1874 as part of the Revised Statutes (specifying thirty-seven stars) and in 1947 as part

THE FIRST FLIGHT OF OLD GLORY. Painting by E. Percy Moran.   LIBRARY OF CONGRESS

of the United States Code (specifying forty-eight stars), the basic design has not changed since 1818. Since 1912 the president has specified the exact design of the flag by executive order. The fifty-star flag is described by Executive Order 10,834 (21 August 1959), signed by President Dwight D. Eisenhower.

The 77th Congress codified the rules and customs concerning use of the flag in 1942. The Flag Code was derived from the uniform code of flag etiquette drafted in 1923 and 1924 by various patriotic and civic organizations based on army and navy customs. The Flag Code not only sets forth specific rules for display of the flag but also describes proper conduct during the playing of the national anthem and recitation of the pledge of allegiance. The 94th Congress made significant amendments to the Flag Code in 1976. In a separate 1939 law the 76th Congress prohibited foreign vessels from using the flag.

The Flag Code provides that the flag be flown, usually from sunrise to sunset, on the following specific days: New Year's Day (1 January), Inauguration Day (20 January), Lincoln's Birthday (12 February), Washington's Birthday (third Monday in February), Easter Sunday (variable), Mother's Day (second Sunday in May), Armed Forces Day (third Saturday in May), Memorial Day (half-staff until noon, last Monday in May), Flag Day (14 June), Independence Day (4 July), Labor Day (first Monday in September), Constitution Day (17 September), Columbus Day (second Monday in October), Navy Day (27 October), Veterans Day (11 November), Thanksgiving Day (fourth Thursday in November), Christmas Day (25 December), the birthdays of states (dates of admission), and on state holidays. In addition to the dates specified in the Flag Code, Congress has directed that the flag be flown on government buildings and homes on National Maritime Day (22 May) and Gold Star Mother's Day (last Sunday in September) and on government buildings on Thomas Jefferson's Birthday (13 April), Loyalty Day and Law Day, U.S.A. (1 May), Father's Day (third Sunday in June), National Aviation Day (19 August), and Citizenship Day (17 September). Although the Flag Code allows an illuminated flag to be flown at night, Congress also has specifically permitted twenty-four-hour flying of the flag at Flag House Square, Baltimore, Maryland; on the town green at Lexington, Massachusetts; over the USS *Utah* at Pearl Harbor; on the grounds of the National Memorial Arch at Valley Forge State Park, Pennsylvania; and at all national cemeteries. The president by proclamation has specifically permitted twenty-four-hour flying of the flag at the Fort McHenry National Monument and Historic Shrine, the U.S. Marine Corps Memorial, the White House, the Washington Monument, and U.S. customs ports of entry that are continually open.

Flag Day (14 June) was recognized in a 1916 proclamation by President Woodrow Wilson for what may have been the first official celebration of the holiday. Since 1941, presidents have recognized Flag Day as an annual national holiday, and the 81st Congress in 1949 recognized the celebration. The 89th Congress in 1966 also declared the week in which June 14 occurs as National Flag Week and directed all citizens to display the flag.

The 78th Congress in 1943 required the military to provide burial flags for deceased veterans who served in periods of war or national emergency, and in 1988 the 100th Congress extended this privilege to deceased individuals who served in the United States merchant marine. In 1954 the 83d Congress also directed that burial flags be presented to the next of kin or a close friend of a deceased member of the armed forces.

The first act concerning flag desecration was passed in 1905 to curtail commercial use of the flag. The act prohibits the federal trademark office from registering any design containing the flag or coat of arms or other insignia of the United States. In 1917 the 64th Congress passed a broad act applicable only to the District of Columbia that makes it a misdemeanor to place marks or advertisements on the flag or to use the flag on merchandise. During World War I the 65th Congress passed an espionage act, in effect until 1921, that made it a crime to speak, write, or publish disloyal, profane, scurrilous, or abusive language about the flag when the United States was at war.

The protests over U.S. military action in Vietnam spurred the 90th Congress in 1968 to pass a national antidesecration act. Although courts had previously held state antidesecration laws to be constitutional, a Texas law similar to the 1968 federal statute was declared unconstitutional under the First Amendment by a Texas state appellate court in 1988. The case, *Texas v. Johnson*, involved the burning of a U.S. flag at the 1984 Republican National Convention in Dallas, but it provoked little controversy until the Supreme Court affirmed the Texas court in 1989. The Supreme Court in a 5 to 4 decision declared that the act of burning the flag is symbolic speech protected by the First Amendment. The Senate expressed "profound disappointment" over the Supreme Court's action. The House of Representatives expressed "profound concern," and several House members denounced the Court itself. President George Bush and some members of Congress proposed a constitutional amendment to protect the flag; the 101st Congress eventually passed the Flag Protection Act of 1989, amending the 1968 antidesecration law in an attempt to circumvent the free speech concerns raised by the Supreme Court in the *Johnson* case. This effort was rebuffed when the Supreme Court in 1990 declared the new federal law unconstitutional as violating the First Amendment in the combined cases of *United States v. Eichman* and *United States v. Haggerty*. President Bush and some members of Congress renewed their effort to amend the Constitution, but this failed in 1990 when the 101st Congress was unable to secure a two-thirds majority in favor of the amendment in either the Senate or House of Representatives.

BIBLIOGRAPHY

Furlong, William R., and Byron McCandless. *So Proudly We Hail: The History of the United States Flag.* 1981.

Goldstein, Robert J. "The Great 1989–1990 Flag Flap: An Historical, Political, and Legal Analysis." *University of Miami Law Review* 45 (September 1990): 19–106.

CHARLES A. SPAIN, JR.

FLOOR LEADER. [*This entry includes two separate discussions of floor leadership, the first on the House and the second on the Senate.*]

In the House

Party floor leaders are mentioned in neither the Constitution nor the rules of the House of Representatives. Technically they are unofficial officers of the House, yet the institution could not function efficiently without them. There are two floor leaders, one for the majority and one for the minority. The majority floor leader, often called simply the majority leader, performs numerous duties, but principally the majority leader works with the Speaker to manage the flow and substance of floor debate. The minority floor leader, serves as field marshal for the opposing party and guardian of the minority's right to share in the legislative process. Both leaders have the prestige of heirs apparent to the speakership, depending on which party controls the House when the vacancy occurs.

Originally the House had no formal leader other than the Speaker, whose role was restricted to that of an impartial moderator. Legislative and political leadership came from outside the institution, mainly the White House or, when run by Alexander Hamilton, the Treasury Department. President Thomas Jefferson (1801–1809) was first to grasp the full potential of party politics in Congress. Jefferson organized his House supporters and designated one of his trusted lieutenants to lead them. The main responsibility of these early floor leaders was, as historian George B. Galloway noted, "to see that members 'voted right.'" Their obedience to the executive was clear, and at least one, Rep. William B. Giles, was actually called the premier, or prime minister.

Subsequent presidents could not dominate Congress as had Jefferson. By 1811, a new generation of lawmakers, exemplified by two young representatives, Henry Clay of Kentucky and John C. Calhoun of South Carolina, were giving the legislative branch its own strong and independent voice. Elected Speaker his first day as a House member, Clay was determined to enhance the Speaker's influence in House and party affairs and to develop a

Floor Leaders of the House of Representatives

CONGRESS	MAJORITY	MINORITY
56th (1899–1901)	Sereno E. Payne, R-N.Y.	James D. Richardson, D-Tenn.
57th (1901–1903)	Sereno E. Payne, R-N.Y.	James D. Richardson, D-Tenn.
58th (1903–1905)	Sereno E. Payne, R-N.Y.	John Sharp Williams, D-Miss.
59th (1905–1907)	Sereno E. Payne, R-N.Y.	John Sharp Williams, D-Miss.
60th (1907–1908)	Sereno E. Payne, R-N.Y.	John Sharp Williams, D-Miss.
(1908–1909)	Sereno E. Payne, R-N.Y.	James Beauchamp (Champ) Clark, D-Mo.
61st (1909–1911)	Sereno E. Payne, R-N.Y.	James Beauchamp (Champ) Clark, D-Mo.
62d (1911–1913)	Oscar W. Underwood, D-Ala.	James R. Mann, R-Ill.
63d (1913–1915)	Oscar W. Underwood, D-Ala.	James R. Mann, R-Ill.
64th (1915–1917)	Claude Kitchin, D-N.C.	James R. Mann, R-Ill.
65th (1917–1919)	Claude Kitchin, D-N.C.	James R. Mann, R-Ill.
66th (1919–1921)	Frank W. Mondell, R-Wyo.	James Beauchamp (Champ) Clark, D-Mo.
67th (1921–1923)	Frank W. Mondell, R-Wyo.	Claude Kitchin, D-N.C.
68th (1923–1925)	Nicholas Longworth, R-Ohio	Finis J. Garrett, D-Tenn.
69th (1925–1927)	John Q. Tilson, R-Conn.	Finis J. Garrett, D-Tenn.
70th (1927–1929)	John Q. Tilson, R-Conn.	Finis J. Garrett, D-Tenn.
71st (1929–1931)	John Q. Tilson, R-Conn.	John Nance Garner, D-Tx.
72d (1931–1933)	Henry T. Rainey, D-Ill.	Bertrand H. Snell, R-N.Y.
73d (1933–1935)	Joseph W. Byrns, D-Tenn.	Bertrand H. Snell, R-N.Y.
74th (1935–1937)	William B. Bankhead, D-Ala.	Bertrand H. Snell, R-N.Y.
75th (1937–1939)	Sam Rayburn, D-Tex.	Bertrand H. Snell, R-N.Y.
76th (1939–1940)	Sam Rayburn, D-Tex.	Joseph W. Martin, Jr., R-Mass.
(1940–1941)	John W. McCormack, D-Mass.	Joseph W. Martin, Jr., R-Mass.
77th (1941–1943)	John W. McCormack, D-Mass.	Joseph W. Martin, Jr., R-Mass.
78th (1943–1945)	John W. McCormack, D-Mass.	Joseph W. Martin, Jr., R-Mass.
79th (1945–1947)	John W. McCormack, D-Mass.	Joseph W. Martin, Jr., R-Mass.
80th (1947–1949)	Charles A. Halleck, R-Ind.	Sam Rayburn, D-Tex.
81st (1949–1951)	John W. McCormack, D-Mass.	Joseph W. Martin, Jr., R-Mass.
82d (1951–1953)	John W. McCormack, D-Mass.	Joseph W. Martin, Jr., R-Mass.
83d (1953–1955)	Charles A. Halleck, R-Ind.	Sam Rayburn, D-Tex.
84th (1955–1957)	John W. McCormack, D-Mass.	Joseph, W. Martin, Jr., R-Mass.
85th (1957–1959)	John W. McCormack, D-Mass.	Joseph W. Martin, Jr., R-Mass.
86th (1959–1961)	John W. McCormack, D-Mass.	Charles A. Halleck, R-Ind.
87th (1961–1962)	John W. McCormack, D-Mass.	Charles A. Halleck, R-Ind.
(1962–1963)	Carl B. Albert, D-Okla.	Charles A. Halleck, R-Ind.
88th (1963–1965)	Carl B. Albert, D-Okla.	Charles A. Halleck, R-Ind.
89th (1965–1967)	Carl B. Albert, D-Okla.	Gerald R. Ford, R-Mich.
90th (1967–1969)	Carl B. Albert, D-Okla.	Gerald R. Ford, R-Mich.
91st (1969–1971)	Carl B. Albert, D-Okla.	Gerald R. Ford, R-Mich.
92d (1971–1973)	Hale Boggs, D-La.	Gerald R. Ford, R-Mich.
93d (1973)	Thomas P. (Tip) O'Neill, Jr., D-Mass.	Gerald R. Ford, R-Mich.
93d (1974–1975)	Thomas P. (Tip) O'Neill, Jr., D-Mass.	John J. Rhodes, R-Ariz.
94th (1975–1977)	Thomas P. (Tip) O'Neill, Jr., D-Mass.	John J. Rhodes, R-Ariz.
95th (1977–1979)	James C. Wright, Jr., D-Tex.	John J. Rhodes, R-Ariz.
96th (1979–1981)	James C. Wright, Jr., D-Tex.	John J. Rhodes, R-Ariz.
97th (1981–1983)	James C. Wright, Jr., D-Tex.	Robert H. (Bob) Michel, R-Ill.

Floor Leaders of the House of Representatives (Continued)

CONGRESS	MAJORITY	MINORITY
98th (1983–1985)	James C. Wright, Jr., D-Tex.	Robert H. (Bob) Michel, R-Ill.
99th (1985–1987)	James C. Wright, Jr., D-Tex.	Robert H. (Bob) Michel, R-Ill.
100th (1987–1989)	Thomas S. Foley, D-Wash.	Robert H. (Bob) Michel, R-Ill.
101st (1989–1991)	Richard A. Gephardt, D-Mo.	Robert H. (Bob) Michel, R-Ill.
102d (1991–1993)	Richard A. Gephardt, D-Mo.	Robert H. (Bob) Michel, R-Ill.
103d (1993–1995)	Richard A. Gephardt, D-Mo.	Robert H. (Bob) Michel, R-Ill.

more formal and efficient leadership structure. Previously, the Speaker had less real power than the presidentially designated floor leader. That changed under Clay. When the House created its first standing committees in 1816, Clay picked the committee members and the chairmen. He also assumed the political leadership of his party in the House and insisted on selecting his own floor leader, leaving no doubt about the Speaker's supremacy.

Thereafter, until the responsibility was taken over by the party caucuses in 1910, floor leaders were personally chosen by the Speaker. Sometimes the Speaker selected a trusted associate or, to promote party harmony, a close rival for the speakership. Normally the job went to the chairman of either the Ways and Means Committee or the Appropriations Committee, primarily because those panels handled most of the important legislation and attracted the ablest and most respected members. House records do not always make it clear who served as floor leader, especially for the minority, in some periods prior to the late 1800s.

In 1910, the House rebelled against the accumulated power of the Speaker and, among other reforms, bolstered the floor leader's prestige and independence by making the position an elective party office. The first majority floor leader elected by the Democratic Caucus, Oscar W. Underwood of Alabama, had more power, in fact, than Speaker James Beauchamp (Champ) Clark of Missouri, whom he ostensibly served. Underwood chaired the party caucus and through it controlled the Rules Committee. He also continued to chair the Ways and Means Committee, whose Democratic members, serving as their party's Committee on Committees, assigned Democrats to all other committees. "Clark was given the shadow, Underwood the substance of power," wrote Galloway. No floor leader before or since has matched Underwood's supremacy within his party and the House generally.

Underwood moved to the Senate in 1915, and his successors gradually surrendered much of the power that he had acquired for the office. The cau-

cus proved awkward and divisive as a decision-making body and fell into disuse; the Rules Committee began to resist outside influence, and the task of managing the House's increasingly heavy work load, stimulated by the war and its aftermath, left floor leaders little time for other obligations, such as chairing a major committee. Deprived of independent power bases, the floor leaders soon resumed their traditional place as the Speaker's loyal subordinates.

By the early 1920s, both parties had relieved their floor leaders of all committee assignments—described by Neil MacNeil as "a revolutionary change"—reflecting the House's judgment that the government would continue to expand and that management of the House's legislative business had become a full-time job. "The elevation of the party floor leader to an independent rank, second only to the Speaker himself, had a profound influence on the attitude of the House toward the man chosen for the post," MacNeil wrote in *Forge of Democracy* (1963). Since 1919, he observed, "the House has elected not a single Speaker who had not been the party leader."

Floor leader chosen since 1910 have tended to share certain characteristics. All have been men, most in their mid fifties, who had served in the House, on average, about eighteen years. They were viewed as Speakers-in-training. With few exceptions, they enjoyed good health and seemed likely to remain in the House for many more years. Each had a reputation for party and personal loyalty, forcefulness, knowledge of House rules, agility and persuasiveness in debate, and fondness for partisan repartee.

The duties of the floor leader, especially the majority floor leader, have multiplied in number and complexity over the years. As described by House parliamentarian Lewis Deschler,

a party's floor leader, in conjunction with other party leaders, plays an influential role in the formulation of party policy and programs. He is instrumental in guiding legislation favored by his party through the House, or in resisting those programs of the other party that are considered undesirable by his own party. He is instrumental in devising and implementing his party's strategy on the floor with respect to promoting or opposing legislation. He is kept constantly informed as to the status of legislative business and as to the sentiment of his party respecting particular legislation under consideration. (1977)

The majority leader serves in more than a partisan capacity, as he or she is chiefly responsible for scheduling legislation for debate and arranging the order of business. Using intricate knowledge of the House rules—an essential job requirement—the majority leader collaborates with the Speaker to expedite noncontroversial House business and assure timely and orderly handling of controversial matters. Positioned at the majority table to the right of the center aisle, as viewed from the Speaker's rostrum, the majority floor leader has the right of first recognition whenever he seeks the Speaker's attention. The Speaker usually looks to the majority leader for time-saving unanimous-consent motions, by which the House conducts much of its routine business, and substantive resolutions affecting the operation of the House or the government as a whole. The leader's duties range from housekeeping chores, such as announcing the coming week's schedule, to serving as Speaker pro tempore in the Speaker's absence.

Both leaders make certain appointments, such as their party's representatives on ceremonial committees and official objectors for the private and consent calendars. The Democratic leader, with the Speaker's concurrence, named his party's whip prior to 1987; after that the position became an elective office of the Democratic caucus. Also, in an exception to the custom of exempting floor leaders from committee service, the majority leader represents the House leadership on the Budget Committee.

BIBLIOGRAPHY

Galloway, George B. *History of the House of Representatives.* 1962.

Hasbrouck, Paul DeWitt. *Party Government in the House of Representatives.* 1927.

Peabody, Robert L. *Leadership in Congress: Stability, Succession, and Change.* 1976.

Ripley, Randall B. *Party Leaders in the House of Representatives.* 1967.

U.S. House of Representatives. *Deschler's Precedents of the United States House of Representatives,* by Lewis Deschler. 94th Cong., 2d sess., 1977. H. Doc. 94-661. Vol.1.

DONALD C. BACON

In the Senate

For most of the twentieth century, specially designated party floor leaders have directed Senate proceedings. This development would have surprised the Framers of the U.S. Constitution. Those architects of Congress gave little thought to Senate floor leadership because they viewed the Senate as a collegial congregation of senior statesmen whose principal function was to review the legislative handiwork of the House of Representatives. Failing to anticipate the rise of political parties as instruments for organizing the Senate's business, they evidently assumed that leadership, when needed, would be the province of energetic sponsors and opponents of specific legislation.

From 1789 until the early twentieth century, committee chairmen and various personally influential members provided the primary source of Senate floor leadership. As late as 1885 Professor Woodrow Wilson could observe that "No one is *the* Senator. No one may speak for his party as well as for himself; no one exercises the special trust of acknowledged leadership." By the early twentieth century, however, increasingly assertive Democratic and Republican party caucuses began regularly to elect floor leaders.

The Democrats acted first, under the prodding of President Woodrow Wilson, who owed his 1912 election to a split in Republican ranks. Recognizing that he had a precarious majority and a limited time to enact an ambitious legislative program, Wilson sought a Senate floor leader to advance his priorities and enforce party unity in voting. The Senate Democratic caucus accommodated the president by electing as its chairman and floor leader John Worth Kern (1913–1917, Ind.), a progressive senator only two years into his first term. Following his predecessors' custom, however, Wilson relied also on his party's committee chairmen and selected Senate political allies. By the mid 1920s, both parties routinely designated floor leaders, with the leader serving as majority or minority leader, depending on which party was in control. In recognition of the floor leader's emerging "first among equals" status, the Democratic leader in 1927 began the custom of occupying a front-row, center-aisle desk; the Republican leader took a corresponding position starting in 1937.

A succession of strong Democratic leaders began during that era with Joseph T. Robinson (1923–1937, Ark.) and continued through the term of Alben W. Barkley (1937–1949, Ky.). Barkley helped shape the position during a time of major institu-

Senate Majority and Minority Leaders

CONGRESS	PARTY RATIOS			MAJORITY LEADER	MINORITY LEADER	PRESIDENT
66th/3d sess. 1920–1921	R49	D47	—	[Henry Cabot Lodge[1] (R-Mass.)]	Oscar W. Underwood[2] (D-Ala.)	Wilson
67th 1921–1923	R59	D37	—	[Henry Cabot Lodge]	Oscar W. Underwood	Harding
68th 1923–1925	R53	D42	I1	[Henry Cabot Lodge/ Charles Curtis (R-Kans.)]	Oscar W. Underwood	Harding/ Coolidge
69th 1925–1927	R54	D41	I1	Charles Curtis	Joseph T. Robinson (D-Ark.)	Coolidge
70th 1927–1929	R48	D46	I1	Charles Curtis James E. Watson (R-Ind.)	Joseph T. Robinson	Coolidge
71st 1929–1931	R56	D39	I1	James E. Watson	Joseph T. Robinson	Hoover
72d 1931–1933	R48	D47	I1	James E. Watson	Joseph T. Robinson	Hoover
73d 1933–1935	D59	R36	I1	Joseph T. Robinson	Charles L. McNary (R-Oreg.)	F. D. Roosevelt
74th 1935–1937	D69	R25	I2	Joseph T. Robinson	Charles L. McNary	F. D. Roosevelt
75th 1937–1939	D76	R16	I4	Joseph T. Robinson/ Alben W. Barkley (D-Ky.)	Charles L. McNary	F. D. Roosevelt
76th 1939–1941	D69	R23	I4	Alben W. Barkley	Charles L. McNary[3]	F. D. Roosevelt
77th 1941–1943	D66	R28	I2	Alben W. Barkley	Charles L. McNary	F. D. Roosevelt
78th 1943–1945	D57	R38	I1	Alben W. Barkley	Wallace H. White, Jr. (R-Maine) (acting)	F. D. Roosevelt
79th 1945–1947	D57	R38	I1	Alben W. Barkley	Wallace H. White, Jr.	F. D. Roosevelt Truman
80th 1947–1949	R51	D45	—	Wallace H. White, Jr.	Alben W. Barkley (D-Ky.)	Truman
81st 1949–1951	D54	R42	—	Scott W. Lucas (D-Ill.)	Kenneth S. Wherry (R-Nebr.)	Truman
82d 1951–1953	D49	R47	—	Ernest W. McFarland	Kenneth S. Wherry/ H. Styles Bridges (R-N.H.)	Truman
83d 1953–1955	R48	D47	I1	Robert A. Taft (R-Ohio) William F. Knowland (R-Calif.)	Lyndon B. Johnson (D-Tex.)	Eisenhower

[1]Lodge's title was party conference chairman; he did not hold the official title of Republican floor leader. On 5 March 1925 Charles Curtis became the first Republican to be designated floor leader.
[2]Underwood was elected as the first Democratic floor leader in 1920.
[3]In 1940, at the request of Senator McNary, Sen. Warren R. Austin (Vt.) served as acting leader. In succeeding years, although McNary was still officially listed as minority leader until his death on 25 February 1944, Wallace H. White, Jr., served as acting leader.

tional change within the Senate. His two successors, Scott W. Lucas (1949–1951, Ill.) and Ernest W. McFarland (1951–1953, Ariz.) proved less successful and suffered embarrassing reelection defeats at home while preoccupied with leadership responsibilities in Washington. In 1953 the Democrats selected Lyndon B. Johnson (Tex.), who had served in the body only four years, confirming that seniority—essential for committee chairmen—is not a prerequisite for floor leadership. A protégé of powerful committee chairmen, Johnson proved to be the most forceful among all who had held the office to

Senate Majority and Minority Leaders (Continued)

CONGRESS	PARTY RATIOS			MAJORITY LEADER	MINORITY LEADER	PRESIDENT
84th 1955–1957	D47	R47	I2	Lyndon B. Johnson	William F. Knowland	Eisenhower
85th 1957–1959	D49	R47	—	Lyndon B. Johnson	William F. Knowland	Eisenhower
86th 1959–1961	D65	R35	—	Lyndon B. Johnson	Everett M. Dirksen (R-Ill.)	Eisenhower
87th 1961–1963	D64	R36	—	Mike Mansfield (D-Mont.)	Everett M. Dirksen	Kennedy
88th 1963–1965	D66	R34	—	Mike Mansfield	Everett M. Dirksen	Kennedy/ L. B. Johnson
89th 1965–1967	D68	R32	—	Mike Mansfield	Everett M. Dirksen	L. B. Johnson
90th 1967–1969	D64	R36	—	Mike Mansfield	Everett M. Dirksen	L. B. Johnson
91st 1969–1971	D57	R43	—	Mike Mansfield	Everett M. Dirksen/ Hugh Scott (R-Pa.)	Nixon
92d 1971–1973	D54	R44	I2	Mike Mansfield	Hugh Scott	Nixon
93d 1973–1975	D56	R42	I2	Mike Mansfield	Hugh Scott	Nixon/Ford
94th 1975–1977	D60	R38	I2	Mike Mansfield	Hugh Scott	Ford
95th 1977–1979	D61	R38	I1	Robert C. Byrd (D-W.Va.)	Howard H. Baker, Jr. (R-Tenn.)	Carter
96th 1979–1981	D58	R41	I1	Robert C. Byrd	Howard H. Baker, Jr.	Carter
97th 1981–1983	R53	D46	I1	Howard H. Baker, Jr. (R-Tenn.)	Robert C. Byrd	Reagan
98th 1983–1985	R54	D46	—	Howard H. Baker, Jr.	Robert C. Byrd	Reagan
99th 1985–1987	R53	D47	—	Bob Dole (R-Kans.)	Robert C. Byrd	Reagan
100th 1987–1989	D55	R45	—	Robert C. Byrd	Bob Dole	Reagan
101st 1989–1991	D55	R45	—	George J. Mitchell (D-Maine)	Bob Dole	Bush
102d[4] 1991–1993	D57	R43	—	George J. Mitchell	Bob Dole	Bush
103d 1993–	D57	R43	—	George J. Mitchell	Bob Dole	Clinton

[4]Party ratio after 9 May 1991.

SOURCE: U.S. Congress and Senate information are adapted from *Majority and Minority Leaders of the Senate* by Floyd M. Riddick, S. Doc. 100-29, 100th Cong., 2d sess., 1988; party ratios are from Kenneth C. Martis, *The Historical Atlas of Political Parties in the United ed States Congress, 1789–1989,* 1989.

that time. When he left for the vice presidency in 1961, Democrats spurned his arm-twisting style for the conciliatory manner of Mike Mansfield (1961–1977, Mont.). Mansfield provided a greater degree of autonomy for his party colleagues during his record-setting tenure in that post. Successors Robert C. Byrd (1977–1989, W.Va.) and George J. Mitchell (1989–, Maine) sought to balance the firmness of Johnson with the reasonableness of Mansfield.

After the start of the New Deal era, Republicans controlled the Senate for only one Congress each in the 1940s and 1950s, and three in the 1980s. This limited period of majority leadership, combined with the party's tradition of dividing its leadership posts, has reduced the opportunity for the emergence of a line of influential leaders. Among the most significant to serve in recent years have been Everett M. Dirksen (1959–1969, Ill.), Howard H. Baker, Jr. (1977–1985, Tenn.), and Bob Dole (1985–, Kans.).

Floor leaders are elected to a two-year term by a majority vote of their respective party conferences. When there are more than two candidates, the senator receiving the lowest number of votes on the first ballot drops out of the race. Successive ballots are taken until one candidate secures a majority. Party leaders seeking reelection customarily try to obtain commitments from a majority of party members before the formal vote. When they succeed, potential challengers often step aside, allowing the leader the appearance of unanimous support from party colleagues.

The majority leader, in consultation with the minority leader, committee chairmen, and other members, serves as the Senate's chief legislative agenda setter. To expedite business, the leader relies heavily on unanimous consent agreements to limit time, amendments, and motions on measures during their floor consideration. Inasmuch as an objection by a single member can disrupt such agreements, they are devised in frequently complex behind-the-scenes negotiations. Because they manage unanimous consent agreements and because they have the right to be recognized by the presiding officer before other senators who wish to speak, the leaders exercise significant, but not always conclusive, discipline over the chamber's proceedings.

Floor leaders seek, often with great frustration, to accommodate the scheduling desires of their party colleagues, most notably in the timing of roll-call votes. Yet, with varying degrees of success, leaders also enforce discipline. Seldom does a session pass without a leader threatening to cancel scheduled recesses or keep the Senate in session late into the evening to accomplish previously agreed upon legislative goals. Through their influence over committee assignments, legislative scheduling, and Senate administrative operations, leaders can render valuable assistance to cooperative party members and convey annoyance with recalcitrant colleagues.

In an environment where one objection can block proceedings, party floor leaders place a high priority on maintaining open communications with one another, scrupulously honoring pledges and avoiding surprises. A floor leader whose party controls both the Senate and the White House experiences conflicting institutional loyalties as leader of the Senate and chief legislator for the president. From issue to issue, the leader may be obligated to advocate the interests of party colleagues, the full Senate, or the president.

Everett Dirksen, leader of Senate Republicans from 1959 to 1969, captured the modern floor leader's sense of challenge and frustration when he observed, "There are 100 diverse personalities in the U.S. Senate. O Great God, what an amazing and dissonant 100 personalities they are! What an amazing thing it is to harmonize them. What a job it is." A generation later, Democratic leader Robert Byrd echoed identical themes: "The leaders are often the prisoners of their own troops and should ever expect the unexpected to happen and foil their best-laid plans."

Senate floor leaders have acquired significant statutory responsibilities in recent years. They serve on the Senate Joint Leadership Group with the president pro tempore and the chairmen and ranking members of several administrative committees. They make key appointments to offices, boards, and commissions through recommendations to the president pro tempore. Democratic floor leaders traditionally chair their party conference and the committees that set party policy and designate committee members; Republican floor leaders, in contrast, do not preside over these additional panels. In recognition of their added responsibilities, floor leaders, with the president pro tempore, are compensated at a higher rate than other members, receive additional allowances for staff and office expenses, and are provided leadership office suites that are adjacent to the Senate floor.

BIBLIOGRAPHY

Baker, Richard A., and Roger H. Davidson, eds. *First among Equals: Outstanding Senate Party Leaders of the Twentieth Century.* 1991.

Byrd, Robert C. *The Senate, 1789–1989: Addresses on the History of the United States Senate.* Vol. 2. 1991.

RICHARD A. BAKER

FLORIDA. The Adams-Onís Treaty, concluded on 22 February 1819, ceded Florida to the United States and included assurances of U.S. citizenship for the territory's inhabitants. Moving quickly to fulfill that promise, Congress incorporated Florida into the United States on 3 March 1821, nine days after Spain formally relinquished it. Within a year Congress had created a government for the territory that, with some border adjustments, would later become the twenty-seventh state.

Despite that initially smooth beginning, Florida faced numerous obstacles on the road to statehood. Its sparse population was a problem. Another hurdle was a dispute between Florida's three distinct sections: West Floridians wanted to be annexed to Alabama and Georgia, middle Floridians favored immediate statehood, and East Floridians were skeptical of both objectives. Finally, there was the issue of slavery. As a slave territory, whose admission would upset the delicate balance between slave and nonslave states in Congress, Florida's best hope for statehood depended on a compromise in which Florida would enter the Union jointly with a free state. But the only free territory ready for statehood was Iowa, whose residents had twice rejected plans to petition Congress.

In 1838 Florida voters approved a "state" constitution and a statehood petition. Opponents said Florida had too few people and too weak an economy to be self-sufficient as a state; proponents countered that the Adams-Onís Treaty guaranteed its statehood regardless of such factors. The issue languished until 1841, when Florida's prospects took a positive turn with the election of David Levy Yulee, a fervently pro-statehood Democrat, as the new territorial delegate to Congress. Yulee, sometimes known as David Levy, worked tirelessly to sell Floridians on the advantages of statehood. He also proved an effective advocate for Florida in Congress, later becoming the state's first senator and the first Jew to serve in the Senate.

In 1844 Iowans reversed course by approving their own draft constitution and petition for statehood. Yulee stepped up his lobbying efforts, and within three months the House Committee on Territories had reported a bill for the joint admission of both territories. The measure quickly cleared the House, 145 to 46, the Senate adding its approval on 24 February 1845. President John Tyler signed the act of admission for Florida and Iowa on 3 March 1845. The ceremony proved premature for Iowa, whose residents balked at boundary changes required by the statute. Its admission delayed until the dispute was resolved, Iowa joined the Union as the twenty-ninth state in December 1846.

Florida sided with the Confederacy in the Civil War and seceded from the Union on 11 January 1861. Absent from Congress for seven years, it was readmitted on 25 June 1868. Its first postwar delegation, elected under Reconstruction rules, was all Republican. It continued to elect Republicans, as well as Democrats, until 1886, when Democrats regained all the seats. From then until the 1950s, when newly arriving retirees from other states began to influence its politics, Florida remained a one-party state. The election of William C. Cramer in 1954 marked the turning point for Republican fortunes in the state. In 1993 and 1994, Florida had a Republican and a Democrat in the Senate, and thirteen Republicans and ten Democrats in the House.

From one representative and two senators prior to the Civil War, Florida's congressional delegation has expanded steadily. The growth, fueled by a population boom, has been most dramatic in the last half of the twentieth century. From 1913 to 1953 Florida gained one House member every decade. Since the 1950 census, which added two representatives for a total of eight, its House membership has risen rapidly—to twelve in 1963, fifteen in 1973, nineteen in 1983, and twenty-three in 1993.

Prominent Floridians in Congress have included Duncan U. Fletcher, a senator (1909–1936) and chairman of the committee on Commerce and Banking and the Committee on Currency; Claude Pepper, who as a senator (1936–1951) eloquently defended the New Deal and as a representative (1963–1989) advocated programs for the elderly and chaired the Committee on Rules; Dante B. Fascell, a representative (1955–1993) and chairman of the Committee on Foreign Affairs; James A. Haley, a representative (1953–1977) and chairman of the Committee on Interior and Insular Affairs; and Sam M. Gibbons, a representative (1963–) and chairman of the Committee on Ways and Means. Florida's first black member of Congress was Josiah T. Walls, elected to the House in 1870. Ruth Bryan Owen, elected to the House in 1928, was the state's first woman member. In 1994, Florida's delegation included five women and three African Americans.

[*See also* West Florida.]

BIBLIOGRAPHY

Dinnerstein, Leonard, and Mary Dale Palsson. *Jews in the South*. 1973. Pp. 52–67.

González-Montaner, Teresita, and Luis R. Dávila-Colón. "Florida: The 27th State." In *Breakthrough from Colonialism: An Interdisciplinary Study of Statehood*. Edited by Luis R. Dávila-Colón et al. Vol. 1. 1984. Pp. 313–334.

U.S. Congress. *Congressional Record*. 99th Cong., 1st sess., 22 April 1985. Pp. S4443–S4444.

DONALD C. BACON

FOOTE, HENRY S.

FOOTE, HENRY S. (1804–1880), senator from Mississippi, combative Unionist, and author. Henry Stuart Foote was elected to the Senate as a Democrat in 1847 and became chairman of the Foreign Relations Committee two years later. He quit the Senate in 1852 to run for governor as a Unionist and defeated Jefferson Davis. As secessionism flourished Foote moved to California and later to Tennessee, where he was elected to the Confederate Congress. In that body he was denounced for opposing President of the Confederacy Jefferson Davis's war policies and supporting President Abraham Lincoln's 1863–1864 peace terms.

Though slight of stature, Foote was violent and fearless in defense of his views. His clashes with other members of Congress were legend. He brawled in the aisles with Sen. Simon Cameron of Pennsylvania and threatened to hang Sen. John P. Hale of New Hampshire if Hale ever came to Mississippi. He fought in four duels, including two with Rep. Sergeant S. Prentiss of Mississippi, and was wounded three times.

In 1850 Foote provoked one of the Senate's most famous confrontations. Angry at Sen. Thomas Hart Benton for stubbornly opposing Kentucky senator Henry Clay's compromise on slavery, he chided Benton for weeks until, finally, on 17 April,

he pushed the ill-tempered Missourian too far. Benton turned on his tormentor and began stalking him menacingly across the chamber. Foote responded by drawing a pistol from his pocket and pointing it at Benton. According to one popular account, Benton immediately ripped open his vest and defiantly shouted, "Let the assassin fire!" Foote, in his *Casket of Reminiscences* (1874), said he had acted in the belief that Benton was armed and, upon seeing that he was not, had quickly handed his own weapon to a senator who had rushed to intervene. He belittled Benton's dramatic gesture, claiming that it occurred well after the pistol was put away. The Senate investigated the incident but took no action.

BIBLIOGRAPHY

Foote, Henry Stuart. *Bench and Bar of the South and Southwest.* 1876.
Foote, Henry Stuart. *Texas and the Texans.* 1841.
Foote, Henry Stuart. *The War of the Rebellion.* 1866.
Gonzales, John E. "The Public Career of Henry Stuart Foote (1804–1880)." Ph.D. diss., University of North Carolina, 1958.

DONALD C. BACON

FORCE ACTS. During the nineteenth century, Congress occasionally authorized the use of federal force against resistance or rebellion at the state or local level. The most notable cases of such legislation, often dubbed force acts by their opponents, came during the nullification crisis of the early 1830s and the Reconstruction period after the Civil War.

When South Carolina nullified the tariffs of 1828 and 1832, President Andrew Jackson denounced the action and in January 1833 asked Congress for authority to use military force to coerce South Carolina into paying the tariff. The Senate Judiciary Committee responded with a bill providing for alternative ways of collecting tariff revenue and authorizing the use of military force should South Carolina refuse to back down. Officially known as the Revenue Collection bill, the measure was greeted with reservations in both houses, not only among nullifiers and those distrusting Jackson, but also among those seeking compromise, such as Henry Clay of Kentucky. Working with John C. Calhoun, the South Carolina architect of nullification, Clay authored a compromise tariff bill in February, and it was only in conjunction with this measure that the Force Bill passed both houses by 1 March 1833. Satisfied with the compromise tariff, South

HENRY S. FOOTE.   NATIONAL ARCHIVES

Carolina repealed its ordinance of nullification but defiantly nullified the Force Bill—an action Congress and Jackson quietly overlooked—and the crisis was resolved.

A second major instance of force legislation occurred during Reconstruction, when congressional Republicans, responding to appeals from southern Republicans for protection from Democratic intimidation and terrorist organizations, passed three overlapping acts to enforce the Fourteenth and Fifteenth Amendments. The first Enforcement Act (31 May 1870) provided penalties for state officials and others using fraud, intimidation, and violence to limit voting rights and authorized federal authorities to initiate proceedings against violators. Aimed more at Democratic election fraud in northern urban areas, the second Enforcement Act (28 February 1871) created federal supervisors to oversee voter registration and congressional elections. The final measure (20 April 1871), often referred to as the Ku Klux Klan Act, targeted private (even individual) conspiracies and terrorist groups operating in disguise, established the denial of civil and political rights as federal felonies, and empowered the president to suspend the writ of habeas corpus and to use military force to suppress "insurrection, domestic violence, unlawful combinations, or conspiracies" in areas where a state was unable or unwilling to do so.

While this legislation temporarily helped curb terrorist activity, federal officials, wary of their expansion of federal jurisdiction into areas traditionally reserved for state authority, applied the habeas corpus and military force features in only one instance, in South Carolina. Southern resistance continued, and northern enthusiasm for enforcement quickly waned as the North retreated from Reconstruction. Additional enforcement legislation failed to pass in 1875 and again in 1890, when a Republican-controlled Congress, upset over election fraud and intimidation, tried to pass another federal elections bill (the Lodge force bill) providing for court-appointed federal election supervisors to oversee registration and election procedures.

Meanwhile, in a series of decisions, the Supreme Court imposed strict interpretations on the Fourteenth and Fifteenth Amendments and overturned some provisions of all three Enforcement acts. In 1894, a Democrat-controlled Congress repealed most remaining sections, but some fragments survived to be applied by a more forceful government during the civil rights revolution of the 1960s and afterward.

[See also Nullification.]

BIBLIOGRAPHY

Ellis, Richard E. *The Union at Risk: Jacksonian Democracy, States' Rights, and the Nullification Crisis.* 1987.

Freehling, William W. *Prelude to Civil War: The Nullification Controversy in South Carolina, 1816–1836.* 1966.

Gillette, William. *Retreat from Reconstruction, 1869–1879.* 1979.

Welch, Richard E., Jr. "The Federal Elections Bill of 1890: Postscripts and Prelude." *Journal of American History* 52 (1965): 511–526.

TERRY L. SEIP

FORD, GERALD R., JR. (1913–), Republican representative from Michigan, House minority leader, appointed vice president (1973), succeeded Richard M. Nixon to become thirty-eighth president of the United States (1974–1977). Gerald Rudolph Ford, Jr., was born Leslie Lynch King, Jr., in Omaha, Nebraska. His parents' marriage soon failed, and mother and infant returned to her family. They moved to Grand Rapids, Michigan, where she remarried and the child took his stepfather's name.

A solid student who excelled at sports, Ford graduated from the University of Michigan in 1935 and Yale Law School in 1941. A Grand Rapids anti-bossism movement and Wendell Willkie's 1940 presidential campaign first engaged his political interest. He saw combat in World War II as a naval officer and returned home a proponent of U.S. activism in world affairs.

In 1948, Ford defeated isolationist incumbent Bartel J. Jonkman in the Republican primary in Michigan's 5th Congressional District. He then won the general election, a feat he repeated twelve times by comfortable margins. Ford seldom challenged the conservative sensibilities of his electorate, and he cemented his ties in the district with exceptional attention to constituent services.

Ford's committee assignments reflected his policy interests. He soon joined the Appropriations subcommittees on Foreign Operations and Defense, where his budget expertise became widely acknowledged. His low-key but effective committee work earned him a reputation as a "congressman's congressman," in the words of a 1961 American Political Science Association award. In 1963 and 1964, Ford served on the Warren Commission, investigating the assassination of President John F. Kennedy. However, no major legislation would ever bear his name.

Ford thrived in House Republican affairs as well. In 1949, he befriended Rep. Richard M.

PRESIDENT GERALD R. FORD. Ford's first appearance as president before a joint session of Congress, 12 August 1974. He is being greeted by House Speaker Carl B. Albert (D-Okla.), who is shaking hands with the president, and President Pro Tempore of the Senate James O. Eastland (D-Miss.), standing to Albert's left.

OFFICE OF THE HISTORIAN OF THE U.S. SENATE

Nixon, and they joined others to form the Chowder and Marching Society, a discussion and social group. In 1952, Ford and seventeen colleagues sent a much-publicized letter to General Dwight D. Eisenhower, urging him to seek the Republican presidential nomination. A succession of leadership challenges, organized by "Young Turk" colleagues, eventually made Ford the House minority leader in 1965, replacing Charles A. Halleck of Indiana. Differences in leadership style, not policy, prompted these challenges, and the former Turks later cited as Ford's virtues his fair dealing, inclusive style, and energy in key but unglamorous tasks.

During the debates over President Lyndon B. Johnson's Great Society, Ford encouraged Republicans to forge policy alternatives rather than align with southern Democrats. He criticized Johnson's conduct of the Vietnam War as "pulling our best punches." During the Nixon administration, a loyal Ford chafed at the administration's disdain for Congress and saw his goal of becoming House Speaker recede. He considered retirement, but the Watergate scandal changed everything.

Vice President Spiro T. Agnew resigned in 1973 after pleading no contest to bribery and related tax charges. A besieged Nixon, facing growing accusations himself, nominated the easily confirmable Ford under the Twenty-fifth Amendment. The national press was initially disappointed, with a typical editorial calling him a "routine partisan of narrow views." After his Senate confirmation hearings, a more sympathetic press portrait stressed Ford's hardworking decency and integrity.

Vice President Ford struggled to avoid Watergate entanglement while remaining loyal to Nixon, and he became president 9 August 1974 upon Nixon's resignation. Unhappy about Watergate, Ford's pardon of Nixon, and the economy, voters that November gave the Democrats an overwhelming majority in Congress, the largest in the House since 1936.

President Ford's relationship with Congress was complex. On one hand, Ford and congressional leaders had close personal ties, and several presidential staff members had worked or served in Congress. Counterposed, however, were deep party differences over policies, unsettling internal reforms in Congress, and Congress's determination to strengthen its own powers while checking the growth and abuse of executive-branch powers. Emblematic of the situation was the aftermath of Ford's decision to pardon Nixon in an attempt to refocus the national agenda, freeing the former president from a threat of prosecution. There was real congressional outrage, accompanied by the conciliatory tone of Ford's subsequent, nearly unprecedented personal appearance before a House Judiciary subcommittee.

In foreign affairs, Congress strove to use its appropriations and other powers to alter Ford's policies, notably in refusing further military aid to South Vietnam. Ford accepted Congress's role, and he complied, albeit unhappily, with the War Powers Resolution's consultation provisions on several occasions.

In domestic affairs, Ford's fiscal conservatism and budget expertise propelled him into frequent conflict with Congress over spending levels. Because 1974 legislation had ended a president's power to impound unwanted funds, Ford launched a veto strategy to limit spending. He successfully relied on "floating coalitions" to sustain his vetoes. When Ford was done, he had achieved a record-breaking pace of sixty-six public bill vetoes in thirty months.

Nonetheless, these tactical victories masked a strategic defeat. Ford failed to galvanize the public for a debate on the budget and spending priorities, and, for many voters, he failed generally to articulate a vision for future policy. Ford barely survived former California governor Ronald Reagan's challenge for the presidential nomination in 1976. Then, he closed a twenty-nine-point polling gap only to lose the presidency to Jimmy Carter by the puniest of margins. Ford's valedictory speech before Congress tapped a large reservoir of goodwill for restoring integrity and public trust to the presidency.

BIBLIOGRAPHY

Cannon, James M. *Time and Chance: Gerald R. Ford's Appointment with History.* 1994.
Ford, Gerald R. *A Time to Heal: The Autobiography of Gerald Ford.* 1979.
Reichley, A. James. *Conservatives in an Age of Change: The Nixon and Ford Administrations.* 1981.

DAVID A. HORROCKS

FOREIGN AFFAIRS COMMITTEE, HOUSE.

The House Committee on Foreign Affairs has a long and rich tradition in U.S. history and within the congressional committee systems. Its lineage dates to the Committee of Correspondence, established in 1775 by the Continental Congress to represent the emerging nation abroad. After independence, that committee eventually emerged as the Committee for Foreign Affairs, although several select and temporary committees were used to address foreign policy in the early Congresses. In 1822, when the House committee structure was changed, the Committee on Foreign Affairs was made a standing committee. It has retained that name and designation to the present, except when it was temporarily renamed the Committee on International Relations between 1975 and 1979.

Despite its longevity, the House Committee on Foreign Affairs has usually been viewed as a weak and ineffective committee, largely overshadowed by its Senate counterpart, the Committee on Foreign Relations. Unlike the Senate committee, which has authority over treaties and the appointments of foreign policy officials, Foreign Affairs has had a more limited foreign policy agenda, mainly confined to foreign aid and State Department authorization bills. As the committee's activity expanded after World War II, its policy impact was judged by Holbert Carroll (1966) and Richard F. Fenno (1973) as limited and mainly responsive to presidential wishes.

In the aftermath of the Vietnam War and the House internal reforms of the 1970s, however, the committee's influence has grown modestly. The change in its subcommittees' responsibilities, the composition of its membership, and a more effective leadership have been the important factors contributing to the committee's expanded foreign policy role. Several incipient institutional factors (e.g., the trend toward centralization of foreign policy-making within the House leadership and the activism of other committees with foreign policy interests), however, militate against Foreign Affairs playing a dominant foreign policy role in the House or the Congress as a whole.

Structure and Operation of Subcommittees. Since its subcommittee system was established in 1945, Foreign Affairs has usually had five (sometimes four) regional subcommittees (e.g., Europe and the Middle East, Asia and Pacific Affairs, Western Hemisphere Affairs, and Africa) and four functional subcommittees (e.g., Arms Control, International Operations, International Security and Science, International Economic Policy and Trade, and Human Rights and International Organizations). Prior to the 1970s, however, these subcommittees were not central to committee operations. They had no delegated legislative responsibilities, possessed no separate staff, and were under the control of the committee chairman.

Since the House reforms, the powers of the subcommittees and their chairmen have been considerably enlarged. First, the subcommittees are now assigned jurisdictional and legislative responsibilities; all legislation within their domain must be referred to them by the committee chairman within two weeks after he or she receives it. Second, in conjunction with the full committee chairman, the subcommittee chairmen now set legislative hearing dates, take up issues within their jurisdiction at their discretion, and meet to coordinate legislative activities. Finally, subcommittee chairmen have now been allowed to appoint separate staffs. Previously, the only staff assistance came from the full committee. In fact, the combined size of all subcommittee staffs is now roughly equal to the size of the full committee staff.

Membership. Since the end of World War II, the membership of Foreign Affairs has been mainly drawn from the Midwest and the East. From the 91st Congress (1969–1971) through the 100th Congress (1987–1989), for instance, about 70 percent of the members came from those two regions, a figure 10 to 15 percent higher than the proportion of all

House representatives from those areas. Likewise, the percentage of representatives from other regions changed only modestly during this period. The West's committee representation has increased to the point that its overall percentage exceeds its proportion of the entire House, but the South's committee representation remains below its overall representational size.

While the aggregate composition of the committee has remained relatively stable, the internal makeup of the committee has not. Because this committee assignment is viewed as unlikely to assist (and may actually hurt) a member's reelection chances, the committee has had difficulty in attracting and retaining members. Since the mid 1970s, transfers from Foreign Affairs and committee vacancies have been frequent. From the beginning of the 93d Congress (1973–1975) through the 102d Congress (1991–1993), for example, twenty-two members gave up their seats on Foreign Affairs to transfer to other committees. By contrast, only five transfers occurred from the 84th (1955–1957) to the 92d Congress (1971–1973). Some members left to join more prestigious House committees (e.g., Appropriations, Ways and Means, Rules), but others transferred to committees with seemingly more constituency importance (e.g., Armed Services, Energy and Commerce). Coupled with the usual reasons for committee vacancies (i.e., electoral defeat, retirement, death), Foreign Affairs has had an average of nine vacancies at the beginning of each new Congress since 1973. These vacancies have sometimes been difficult to fill and on two or three occasions had to be filled with temporary assignments.

Second, the political character of Foreign Affairs membership has also changed. Although the committee remains generally more liberal than the House as a whole, the ideological gulf between the parties widened in the 1980s and 1990s. By the 100th Congress (1987–1989), for instance, both very liberal and very conservative members of the House were serving on the committee. These ideological differences translated into differences on foreign policy issues and into greater policy activism by individual members and subcommittees. Bipartisan committee decision making suffered as a result. One indicator of this changed decision making was the decline in committee member support for the president's foreign policy agenda—which Foreign Affairs members typically had always supported, at least until the Nixon administration. The greater ideological division and erosion in committee support on foreign policy matters

was no doubt attributable to the presence of an ideological president, Ronald Reagan, in the White House during most of the 1980s, but part of the change must also be attributed to the more assertive and independent members serving on Foreign Affairs during this period.

Despite a committee that has become more ideologically and politically divided, several factors have aided the committee in completing its legislative business. First, some of the political divisiveness has been channeled into the subcommittee system, and thus not all political battles have to be fought at the full committee level. Second, Foreign Affairs has retained a core set of moderates and liberals who have sought policy compromises to make the committee function effectively. Third, and perhaps most critical, the committee leadership—at both the full committee and subcommittee levels—has been more effective than in the past.

Leadership. From the late 1950s through 1993, Foreign Affairs had only four chairmen. The first two committee chairmen during that period were Thomas E. Morgan (D-Pa.) and Clement J. Zablocki (D-Wis.), who had difficulty managing the committee and yielded power to the subcommittees. Dante B. Fascell (D-Fla.), who assumed the chairmanship in 1983 and served through 1992, was better able to strike a balance between the full committee and the subcommittees. The full committee functioned more effectively as a result.

Four factors helped Fascell. First, he was able to exercise more direct control than either Morgan or Zablocki. He set out to achieve greater organizational coordination between the committee and its subcommittees and largely succeeded (although Christopher Madison [1991] raised some doubts about this). Second, Fascell had a good command of the issues facing the committee. Even when he lacked immediate knowledge, he was a quick study. Third, he had the ability to know when a bill stood a chance of passage, both within the committee and within the House. Finally, Fascell (and the committee) had several very able subcommittee chairs during his tenure (e.g., Lee H. Hamilton, Stephen J. Solarz, Michael D. Barnes, and Howard Wolpe). Since most policy initiatives start within the subcommittees, effective subcommittee chairs are thus always crucial to making the process operate. During Fascell's tenure about 90 percent of the subcommittees' recommendations were usually approved by the full committee.

The fourth chairman of the committee, Lee H. Hamilton (D-Ind.), assumed that position in January 1993. In the short term, his approach to the position appears to have been to continue Fascell's style of coordinating actions between the subcommittees and the full committee. In the long term, Hamilton will probably exercise more centralized control of Foreign Affairs than his immediate predecessor because that approach more closely comports with his personal style and with his desire to achieve results.

Jurisdiction and Oversight. Although the House reforms of the 1970s provided new jurisdictional responsibilities for Foreign Affairs, the principal legislative activities of the committee have remained the foreign assistance and the foreign relations (State Department) authorization bills. While the State Department bill has been routinely passed by Foreign Affairs and the House, passage of the foreign aid bill has proved more difficult, especially in the 1980s and early 1990s.

The authorization bills have increasingly served, however, as vehicles for the committee and the House to put their stamp on a broad range of foreign policy concerns through the use of amendments and "earmarks," specific legislative language requiring or prohibiting executive action. In the 1970s and 1980s, for example, the House used the foreign aid bill to require the president to allow Congress to review all arms sales abroad and to place human rights conditions on countries receiving U.S. assistance. At times the foreign aid bill has also been routinely earmarked to provide funds (and even specific amounts) to some countries (e.g., Egypt, Israel) and to forbid or restrict funds to others (e.g., Guatemala, El Salvador). In 1990, a State Department authorization bill was used by Congress to challenge presidential prerogatives in executing foreign policy, prompting President George Bush to claim the right to interpret the bill's controversial provisions unilaterally.

Although these two authorizations are the focal points for committee activity, Foreign Affairs has worked on an increasing number of other measures. From the 93d Congress (1973–1975) to 1992, an average of about twenty-seven measures annually were reviewed by Foreign Affairs and eventually became law—a significant increase from the immediate post–World War II era. Some of these measures have had enormous impact on American foreign policy, including the war powers legislation of the 1970s and antiapartheid legislation of the 1980s.

The extent of committee oversight has also grown. One important aggregate indicator of the increased activities of Foreign Affairs subcommittees is the number of hearings they have held. Hearings conducted by both full committee and subcommittees roughly doubled in number in the 1970s and 1980s. In the 91st Congress (1969–1971), there were 91 full committee hearings and 267 subcommittee hearings. In the 98th Congress (1983–1985), the totals were 210 and 398, respectively.

Both the regional and the functional subcommittees regularly review developments in their areas of responsibility and routinely invite administration representatives (e.g., an assistant secretary of State) to explain current policy. The regional subcommittees' approach to such reviews is, to borrow the language of Mathew D. McCubbins and Thomas Schwartz (1984), a "police patrol" oversight model, in which oversight is exercised on a continuous basis. Functional subcommittee reviews, in contrast, reflect a combination of the "police patrol" model and "fire alarm" model, in which oversight is exercised more sporadically and in response to a specific important issue of the moment.

Institutional Challenges. While internal committee dynamics have produced both problems and opportunities for Foreign Affairs, at least three institutional changes within the House have limited the committee's efforts to achieve preeminence in foreign policy matters.

First, other committees that deal with foreign and national security matters have begun to play a larger role in the congressional process. Most notably, the Armed Services Committee assumed a much larger role in congressional decision making in the 1980s and 1990s, especially with defense buildup during the Reagan years and the outbreak of the Persian Gulf War and defense cuts during the Bush years. The Permanent Select Committee on Intelligence, created during the mid 1970s, also became more actively involved in foreign policy issues, especially on questions related to Central America and the Iran-contra affair.

Second, the Appropriations Committee, and especially its Subcommittee on Foreign Operations, has become more pivotal in the foreign policy process. When Congress has been unsuccessful in getting foreign aid authorizations passed—a common phenomenon in the 1980s—the Appropriations Committee has successfully sought waivers or congressional consent to appropriate funds. The practical effect of this action has been to reduce the influence of the authorizing committee and to increase the power and influence of the appropriating committee.

Third, congressional policy-making has become increasingly centralized within the House leadership, and the role of Foreign Affairs has declined as a result. Congressional responses on key foreign policy issues are increasingly formulated through the direct personal involvement of the leadership (e.g., Speaker James C. Wright, Jr.'s 1987 peace initiative for Central America and the congressional resolutions on the Persian Gulf War), through the use of task forces outside the committee structure (as in, e.g., the development policies toward Nicaragua and El Salvador in the 1980s), or through the appointment of select committees by the leadership (as in the investigation of the Iran-contra affair). While Foreign Affairs (or at least some members of the committee) was not entirely bypassed by these approaches, the committee was not at the center of policy-making.

BIBLIOGRAPHY

Carroll, Holbert. *The House of Representatives and Foreign Policy.* Rev. ed. 1966.

Fenno, Richard F. *Congressmen in Committees.* 1973.

Kaiser, Fred M. "Oversight of Foreign Policy: The U.S. Committee on International Relations." *Legislative Studies Quarterly* 2 (1977): 255–279.

Madison, Christopher. "Paper Tiger." *National Journal* 23 (1991): 1434–1437.

McCormick, James M. "The Changing Role of the House Foreign Affairs Committee." *Congress and the Presidency* 12 (1985): 1–20.

McCormick, James M. "Decision Making in the Foreign Affairs and Foreign Relations Committees." In *Congress Resurgent: Foreign and Defense Policy on Capitol Hill.* Edited by Randall B. Ripley and James M. Lindsay. 1993.

McCubbins, Mathew D., and Thomas Schwartz. "Congressional Oversight Overlooked: Police Patrols versus Fire Alarms." *American Journal of Political Science* 28 (1984): 165–179.

U.S. House of Representatives. Select Committee on Committees. *Monographs on the Committees of the House of Representatives.* 93d Cong., 2d sess., 1974. See especially Roger H. Davidson, "Committee on Foreign Affairs," pp. 47–58.

Westphal, Albert C. F. *The House Committee on Foreign Affairs.* 1942.

JAMES M. MCCORMICK

FOREIGN AID. Foreign assistance as a formal, ongoing function of governmental policy is a post–World War II phenomenon. Assistance activities in the nineteenth and early twentieth centuries were merely isolated incidents of governments providing relief to foreign victims of natural disasters and of European powers expending resources on their colonies.

Early assistance by the U.S. government occurred as a result of military intervention in Latin America and security concerns during World War II. The U.S. military administration of Cuba (1899–1902) stamped out tropical diseases, notably yellow fever, through scientific research, quarantine regulations, and construction of sanitary works. During the U.S. occupation of Haiti (1915–1934) the United States not only reorganized and rationalized the collection of customs duties (as it did in various Latin American countries) but also built one thousand miles of roads and 210 bridges and supported technical education, agricultural experiments, importation of new breeds of livestock, and development of sisal cultivation. Under the Stabilization Fund, established by the Department of the Treasury in 1934 from "profits" from the revaluation of the gold dollar, the U.S. government entered into agreements with Brazil (1937), Argentina (1940), and Mexico (1941) to assist currency stabilization. During World War II (commencing with the outbreak of war in Europe, which preceded U.S. entry by two years) the United States extended to numerous countries a total of $48 billion in grants and $1 billion in credits. The bulk of this assistance was in the form of war matériel and equipment through the Lend-Lease Program ($46.7 billion), with smaller amounts provided for refugee relief and other assistance.

There is no agreed-upon definition or concept of *foreign assistance.* The term includes such activities as providing loans and grants to foreign governments, providing guarantees for exports and direct foreign investment, furnishing technical assistance and commodities, extending relief from disasters, and financing exchange programs.

Structure of U.S. Assistance

The U.S. foreign assistance program is generally considered to date from 1947, with initiation of the Marshall Plan for the reconstruction of Europe. Designed to assist Europe after the vast economic and human dislocation of World War II, the Marshall Plan was the initiative of President Harry S. Truman and Secretary of State George Marshall and garnered little public support or congressional enthusiasm. Like most subsequent U.S. foreign assistance programs, the rationale of the Marshall Plan was a combination of (1) "altruism" to alleviate human suffering and rekindle economic activity; (2) "realpolitik" to make the world safe from communism; and (3) "economic self-interest" to make Europe a profitable commercial partner and to finance the export of U.S. goods and services. The

MARSHALL PLAN. On 1 December 1947, by an 83 to 6 vote, the Senate passed an interim bill (S. 1774) that provided $597 million for emergency winter aid to Austria, China, France, and Italy. Published a day after the vote in the Senate, this cartoon makes reference to the lopsided majority by which the bill was passed. Clifford K. Berryman, *Washington Evening Star*, 2 December 1947.

U.S. SENATE COLLECTION, CENTER FOR LEGISLATIVE ARCHIVES

Marshall Plan was a tremendous success, but unlike foreign assistance in the 1990s, it was not designed to introduce "development" to underdeveloped regions of the world. It involved providing short-term, massive amounts of U.S. capital and goods to a region of the world that had enjoyed well-developed human and physical resources that had been disoriented and destroyed by the war. This short-term assistance allowed Europe to begin to repair its infrastructure and to reemploy its population. Western Europe thereby was able to return to its earlier state of development. In contrast, most subsequent foreign assistance has been provided to countries that possess neither advanced physical nor human infrastructure. Development of these countries has been much more tedious than originally envisaged.

The forty-five-year history of U.S. foreign assistance can be segmented according to the priorities emphasized: technical assistance during the 1950s; capital projects during the 1960s; basic human needs during the 1970s; and institution building, the private sector, and democracy during the 1980s. Foreign assistance programs have grown in breadth and complexity over the years and include a panoply of activities and purposes. U.S. foreign assistance is provided both bilaterally and multilaterally.

The bilateral and multilateral assistance programs described below include only official U.S. government programs. The total amount appropriated for these programs was $14.6 billion in fiscal year 1993, most of which went to four categories—bilateral economic development assistance, economic support fund assistance, military assistance, and multilateral assistance. This amount does not include assistance provided from private U.S. sources to support overseas voluntary activities, which totaled some $3.5 billion in 1992.

Bilateral Assistance. Provided by a donor government to a recipient government or organization, bilateral assistance is programmed by the United States in many different forms and through multiple programs.

1. *Bilateral economic development assistance* is designed to promote long-term economic development and is administered principally through medium-term (five-to-seven-year) projects. The principal areas of activity are agriculture and rural development, health, family planning, child survival, education, promotion of the private sector, energy, environmental protection, and democracy and human rights. Special Assistance Initiatives is a category of assistance initiated in the late 1980s for countries or regions that required new and unique activity (e.g., the Philippines in the post-Marcos era and the emerging democracies of Eastern Europe and the former Soviet Union). The Development Fund for Africa (development assistance for the countries of Africa) has greater flexibility of implementation than does other development assistance.

2. *Economic Support Fund assistance* is provided to countries for political or security requirements and administered through three different mechanisms—as cash grants for budget and balance-of-payments support to governments (60 percent of the total), as development assistance projects (30 percent), and to finance U.S. commodity imports (10 percent).

3. *Military assistance* is provided through the Foreign Military Finance program, principally as grants but also as loans, to finance the purchase of U.S. military equipment; and through the International Military Education and Training program to finance training in U.S. military techniques and management.

4. *International organizations* provide voluntary contributions for the development activities of international organizations.

5. *Narcotics control* projects are designed specifically to discourage the planting of narcotics-producing crops, to encourage the planting of substitute crops, and to assist with enforcement of antinarcotics laws.

6. *Food assistance* programs provide donations of U.S. agricultural commodities for humanitarian purposes (for food-for-work programs, child nutrition, and emergency disaster relief) and sales of agricultural commodities through low-interest loans.

7. *Disaster assistance* includes emergency assistance (food, medicine and medical care, tents, blankets, etc.) to relieve human suffering from natural or man-made disasters and for disaster relief preparedness.

8. *American Schools and Hospitals Abroad* assistance includes grants to U.S.–associated overseas medical and educational institutions.

9. *Migration and refugee assistance* provides assistance for refugees.

10. *The Overseas Private Development Corporation* provides political risk insurance, loan guarantees, and small direct loans for joint ventures by U.S. corporations and local investors in order to promote economic development; Overseas Private Investment Corporation (OPIC) is self-financing through fees and earnings on reserves.

11. *Trade and Development Agency* partially funds feasibility studies and provides other support for U.S. firms to facilitate their involvement in the early stages of development of capital projects.

12. *Inter-American Foundation and the African Development Foundation* provide small grants for community development projects in Latin America and Africa, respectively.

13. *Debt forgiveness* is a process that forgives debt owed to U.S. government agencies.

Multilateral Assistance. Pooled by donor governments, multilateral assistance is channeled through various multilateral development institutions. The principal multilateral development banks are the International Bank for Reconstruction and Development (the World Bank) and its affiliates, the International Finance Corporation and the International Development Association; and the regional development banks for Europe (Eastern Europe and the former Soviet Union), Latin America, Africa, and Asia.

Shifting Aid Goals and Techniques

U.S. foreign assistance as a percentage of the U.S. gross national product (GNP) has declined steadily from 2 to 3 percent of GNP during the Marshall Plan to 1 percent of GNP during the late 1950s to approximately 0.2 percent in fiscal year 1993. The total amount of assistance increased during the early 1980s to peak at $18 billion in 1985.

The Development Assistance Committee (DAC) of the Organization for Economic Cooperation and Development (OECD) compiles foreign assistance statistics. It includes as Official Development Assistance (ODA) all aid that is development motivated, in contrast to that provided for purposes of security, military, or export promotion. U.S. ODA declined from 36 percent of assistance provided by DAC members from 1977 to 1987 to 22 percent in 1987. In the late 1980s and the early 1990s, Japan and the United States provided similar magnitudes of foreign assistance. However, with declining U.S. aid levels and rising Japanese levels, Japan has assumed the position as the world's number one provider of foreign assistance.

The relative importance of particular foreign assistance programs has shifted during the past four and a half decades. Food was the principal foreign assistance tool during the 1960s but subsequently declined in volume and importance. The Economic Support Fund (ESF) and its predecessors were substantial in the mid 1950s and the 1980s. Military assistance peaked in the early 1950s due to the Korean War and the strategic importance of Turkey and Greece to the North Atlantic Treaty Organization (NATO), in the early 1970s due to the Vietnam War, and in the mid 1980s due to instability in the Middle East and conflict in Central America.

Half of U.S. foreign assistance in the 1970s was provided in the form of loans, but by 1990, in response to the debt crisis among developing countries, U.S. assistance was provided almost entirely as grants.

U.S. assistance was concentrated in Europe in the late 1940s and early 1950s, in Asia from the mid 1950s to the mid 1970s, and in the Middle East since the mid 1970s. Beginning in the late 1970s as an outgrowth of the Camp David Accords, the majority of U.S. foreign assistance has been allocated to the Middle East; Israel and Egypt receive nearly half of U.S. bilateral assistance. Asia and Europe each received the next largest proportion of U.S. assistance, but that amount declined in the latter half of the 1980s. Assistance to Europe increased dramatically in the early 1990s with the implosion of communism in Eastern Europe and the Soviet Union. Assistance to Latin America was around $1 billion at the beginning of the 1980s, doubled during the middle years of the decade because of conflicts in Central America, but was declining by the beginning of the 1990s. Assistance to Africa increased slowly over the years, with a dramatic high of $2 billion in 1985 because of unusually high levels of assistance for famine relief. By the beginning of the 1990s, assistance to Africa had stabilized in the range of $800–900 million annually.

Principal Aid Statutes and Committee Jurisdictions. The core of U.S. foreign assistance is the bilateral foreign assistance program, the principal statutory base for which is the Foreign Assistance Act of 1961, as amended (P. L. 87-195). In addition, arms sales are authorized by the Arms Export Control Act (P. L. 90-629). Various other laws affect specific foreign assistance programs and policies. Jurisdiction for authorization of bilateral foreign assistance programs rests with the Committee on Foreign Affairs in the House and the Committee on Foreign Relations in the Senate. Appropriation of the funds for these programs is provided for in the annual Foreign Operations, Export Financing, and Related Programs appropriations bill, which falls within the jurisdiction of the Subcommittee on Foreign Operations, Export Finance, and Related Programs of the House Appropriations Committee and the Subcommittee on Foreign Operations of the Senate Appropriation Committee.

Multilateral assistance is provided through various multilateral financial institutions. U.S. participation in and policies toward these institutions are authorized in separate statutes for each institution. Jurisdiction for authorization of multilateral assistance programs rests in the House of Representatives with the Committee on Banking, Finance, and Urban Affairs and in the Senate jointly with the Committee on Foreign Relations and the Committee on Banking, Housing, and Urban Affairs. The appropriations jurisdiction rests with the Foreign Operations subcommittees.

Food assistance is authorized primarily by the Agricultural Trade Development and Assistance Act of 1954 (P.L. 83-480). Jurisdiction for food assistance is shared in the House of Representatives by the Committee on Agriculture and the Committee on Foreign Affairs, and in the Senate rests with the Committee on Agriculture, Nutrition, and Forestry. The responsibility for appropriations rests with the House and Senate Appropriations subcommittees on Agriculture, Rural Development, and Related Agencies.

These statutes have been amended by numerous subsequent laws, and provisions of law affecting foreign assistance also appear in other statutes. For example, in 1973 Congress amended the Foreign Assistance Act to refocus the U.S. foreign assistance program on basic human needs. In recent years foreign assistance authorizing legislation has been included in the annual Foreign Operations, Export Financing, and Related Programs Appropriations bill. The prohibition in the rules of the House and Senate against the inclusion of authorizing legislation (provisions defining policy and programs) in appropriations bills was repeatedly circumvented during the late 1980s and early 1990s because, despite enactment of several country- or region-specific authorization bills, a comprehensive foreign assistance authorization bill had not been enacted since 1985.

There are many reasons Congress has not enacted foreign assistance authorizing legislation in recent years. For several years the House passed legislation but the Senate did not; in 1991 the House failed to pass the conference report after both bodies had passed authorization bills and the Senate had approved the conference report. In addition, the executive branch developed a preference for having only an appropriations bill (which provides money, but theoretically not major policy directives and restrictions). The foreign aid coalition weakened as the program became more security and less development oriented. And the overarching rationale for foreign assistance—the Cold War anticommunist consensus—disappeared.

The Politics of Foreign Aid. The politics of foreign assistance defies ready explanation. Foreign assistance legislation normally entails a variety of objectives and purposes—humanitarian, foreign policy, national security, economic self-interest—and it generally is supported by a variety of interests—the executive branch, foreign governments, business interests, ethnic groups, and humanitarian, religious and other nongovernmental organizations (NGOs). Many of these entities support particular elements of foreign assistance and may oppose other aspects of the program. Thus, maintaining a coalition of these shifting and disparate interests is a complex task.

Among the most consistent and influential sources of support for foreign assistance legislation have been a variety of American Jewish organizations, especially the American-Israeli Political Action Committee (AIPAC), an umbrella organization in Washington that promotes assistance for Israel. The strength of that support is due to the high level of political activity of those groups: their strong commitment to Israel, their support for humanitarian and refugee assistance, and the high proportion of U.S. assistance that goes to Israel and Egypt in support of the Middle East peace process.

In the 1980s U.S. groups interested in Central America were particularly active in attempting to influence the content of legislation authorizing U.S. assistance to countries in Central America, and groups interested in Africa have become increasingly active in supporting assistance to Africa.

Another source of support for foreign assistance bills has been U.S. NGOs, including church groups, family planning and health organizations, cooperatives and credit unions, grass-roots development entities, universities, agricultural organizations, labor groups, and humanitarian organizations. These organizations are composed both of advocacy groups, which seek to influence public opinion, and development organizations, which implement programs in developing countries. Some of these groups became disenchanted with foreign assistance in the mid and late 1980s as the balance of foreign assistance shifted toward more politically motivated objectives and programs. With the end of the Cold War and a shift back to more development-based assistance, these groups have shifted their focus to advocate statutory reform of U.S. foreign assistance programs. The Support for Eastern European Democracy (SEED) Act, which Congress enacted in 1989 to provide assistance to Poland and Hungary and later amended to cover all countries in Eastern Europe and the Baltics, was passed with the active support of U.S. Eastern European ethnic groups and labor organizations. The Freedom for Russia and Emerging Eurasian Democracies and Open Markets (FREE-DOM) Support Act, enacted in 1992 to provide assistance to Russia and the other newly independent states, brought strong support from a range of U.S. NGOs, particularly business and farm groups, ethnic groups, and business schools.

The greatest overall influence on foreign assistance legislation comes from the executive branch. Foreign assistance bills are generally developed around the president's budget request for specific authorizations. The ability of the president to influence his party's members and to threaten to veto legislation can have a powerful influence on the substance of legislation. Some legislation is formally requested by the executive branch, while other measures originate in Congress. The SEED Act, for example, was submitted to Congress by the president, but was substantially revised and expanded by the committees of jurisdiction in close cooperation with the executive branch and interested NGOs.

Emerging Trends. The difficulty in enacting authorizing legislation, combined with a sense that the foreign assistance program was not necessarily keyed to U.S. foreign policy needs of the 1990s, led the Committee on Foreign Affairs in 1988 to undertake a year-long review of U.S. foreign assistance policies and programs. That study produced a complete rewrite of the Foreign Assistance Act, which passed the House in 1989 and again in 1991 but was not enacted into law. Other studies of U.S. foreign assistance also were undertaken during that period, primarily by academic institutions and by NGOs. Many analysts agreed that the foreign assistance program suffered from the following core problems:

Too many goals and objectives (thirty-three in the Foreign Assistance Act), which result in the absence of an overall, comprehensible mandate.

Too much micromanagement by Congress and by the Agency for International Development (AID) headquarters in Washington, which results in insufficient flexibility to effectively implement the program or to respond to the needs of intended recipients.

Inadequate strategic planning and management, which results in ad hoc decision making.

The public perception that U.S. government foreign assistance, unlike the assistance programs of other donors, benefits neither the needy nor U.S. business interests.

The challenge to development practitioners and policymakers is to identify emerging and future foreign assistance needs and to fashion a program that meets those needs and appeals to the American people. Proposals for change run the gamut from improving the management of the Agency for International Development according to the precepts of "reinventing government," to collapsing the agency into the Department of State, to creating a quasi-governmental foundation to operate the foreign assistance program.

BIBLIOGRAPHY

Michigan State University. Center for Advanced Study for International Development. *New Challenges, New Opportunities: U.S. Cooperation for International Growth and Development in the 1990's.* 1988.

Phoenix Group. International Trade and Development Education Foundation. *Reforms Needed in U.S. Assistance to Developing Countries.* 1989.

Sewell, John, and Peter Storm. *Challenges and Priorities in the 1990's: An Alternative U.S. International Affairs Budget, FY 1993.* 1992.

U.S. Congress. House Committee on Foreign Affairs and Senate Committee on Foreign Relations. *Legislation on Foreign Relations through 1993.* 103d Cong., 1st sess., 1994.

U.S. House of Representatives. Committee on Foreign Affairs. *Foreign Assistance Policy Studies: A Review of Major Reports and Recommendations.* 100th Cong., 2d sess., 1988.

U.S. House of Representatives. Committee on Foreign Affairs. *Report of the Task Force on Foreign Assistance.* 101st Cong., 1st sess., 1989.

GEORGE M. INGRAM

FOREIGN POLICY.

One of the most distinctive features of the American system of government is the role of the legislative branch in the foreign policy process. The Founders viewed Congress as the engine or motive force of American government. In view of their colonial experience, they were deeply suspicious of executive authority, yet the Framers were no less mindful of the turbulent and dangerous experience of the new republic under the Articles of Confederation, when Congress largely dominated the making and implementation of foreign affairs.

Accordingly, in the new scheme of government the Founders assigned several important powers in the foreign policy field to the chief executive, such as serving as the commander in chief of the armed forces and negotiating agreements with other nations. Nevertheless, under the Constitution the House and Senate still possessed impressive foreign policy prerogatives. As Edward S. Corwin expressed it, this division of authority created an "invitation to struggle" between the president and Congress for a preeminent position in foreign policy.

The dominant reality about the foreign policy process of the United States as it has evolved over two centuries is that the president has emerged as the ultimate decider. We frequently hear references to Franklin D. Roosevelt's or Ronald Reagan's foreign policy. Yet no external policy of the United States is named, say, for the 90th Congress or for influential leaders of the House and Senate.

The normal and overwhelming preoccupation of the House and Senate is domestic affairs, especially constituency concerns and business. Congressional participation in foreign policy, therefore, tends to be episodic and highly selective; it is often precipitated by some crisis abroad or by a widely publicized foreign policy failure. As a rule, Congress tends to have a brief attention span in foreign affairs and to lack an overall strategy.

Historically, the congressional role in foreign policy decision making has tended to be cyclical. Since the late eighteenth century, the pendulum of legislative involvement has swung in a very wide arc— between diplomatic activism and forceful assertions of congressional prerogatives, on the one hand, and the other pole of relative legislative passivity and acquiescence to presidential actions, on the other. Between these extreme positions, since World War II Congress has normally asserted its foreign policy powers on a limited basis and has somehow arrived at a modus vivendi with the White House in conducting foreign relations.

Treaties and Executive Appointments. The Constitution assigns to the Senate a unique role in the foreign policy process. Article II, section 2 provides that the president has the power "by and with the Advice and Consent of the Senate, to make Treaties, provided two thirds of the Senators present concur." Treaties are concluded as the result of a complex process of negotiation and ratification. After a treaty's terms have been agreed to and the document has been signed, the president submits the treaty to the Senate for its advice and consent.

At this stage, the Senate has three choices. It may approve the treaty by the required two-thirds majority. In the vast majority of cases, Senate deliberations have resulted in approval. Alternatively, the Senate may reject the treaty by failing to give it a two-thirds favorable majority. (This course includes the possibility that the Senate may fail to take any action at all on the treaty.) In this case, the president may simply abandon the treaty, may subsequently renegotiate the agreement to meet senatorial objections, or may resort to an executive agreement to accomplish the same purpose. Executive agreements are written or oral understandings between the president and other heads of state. Although legislators from time to time complain about executive agreements, since the New Deal Congress has increasingly recognized their legitimacy; in some instances, as in trade policy, Congress has expressly authorized the president to enter into them.

A third course—highlighted by the celebrated case of the Treaty of Versailles negotiated by President Woodrow Wilson after World War I—is for the Senate to attach amendments and reservations to the treaty, sometimes substantially altering its provisions. For example, Wilson refused to accept the treaty after the Senate had introduced a number of major and minor changes. Politically astute presidents will attempt to forestall adverse senatorial action on treaties by consulting key senators well in advance of, or during, negotiations and by including senators (and sometimes representatives) on the team that negotiates important treaties.

The other (and much less influential) power assigned to the Senate by the Constitution is the right to approve or confirm high-level presidential appointments. Relying on this prerogative, the Senate may conduct a detailed investigation of an appointee's background and qualification for the position, sometimes in the full glare of television cameras and the news media.

In practice, most presidential nominees receive routine senatorial confirmation. Occasionally, a presidential nominee is subjected to intense senatorial examination, and in rare cases the nominee fails to receive confirmation. Normally, however, legislators operate on the theory that a chief executive is entitled to have a team of advisers that has the president's confidence and shares his ideology or objectives. Resourceful chief executives may elude legislative control over their appointments by relying on presidential agents, such as the vice president, private citizens, and sometimes the First Lady, to undertake specific diplomatic missions.

General Legislative Authority in Foreign Affairs. The Senate and House jointly possess an impressive array of powers affecting the conduct of foreign affairs. Congress established, regulates, and provides the funds to operate the State Department and its vast network of U.S. embassies, consulates, and missions around the world. By the Rogers Act (1924) Congress created a professional Foreign Service for the United States, and it periodically reorganizes the diplomatic corps. Congress similarly established and provides the funds to support other executive departments—such as Commerce, Treasury, and Energy—with overseas programs and responsibilities. Other executive agencies—such as the United States Information Agency (USIA), the Agency for International Development (AID), and the Arms Control and Disarmament Agency (ACDA)—were created by acts of Congress and require annual appropriations. The Central Intelligence Agency (CIA), along with other agencies in what is called the intelligence community, were also created by Congress and depend on funds made available by the House and Senate.

In addition, Congress can and does regulate foreign travel by U.S. citizens and enacts laws dealing with immigration, the naturalization process, and the rights of aliens residing in the United States. Congress also makes laws regulating the nation's foreign trade, such as tariff legislation and the granting of trade concessions to other countries.

Three especially important prerogatives are shared by the House and Senate in the foreign policy realm: the war power, the "power of the purse," and several informal or extraconstitutional powers acquired by Congress throughout the course of U.S. history.

The war power. The Constitution (Art. I, sec. 8) confers on Congress a number of prerogatives related to the armed forces that are often referred to collectively as "the war power." Congress is empowered by the Constitution to provide for the common defense; to define and punish piracy and other crimes committed on the high seas, as well as offenses against international law; to declare war; to raise and support an army and to provide for and maintain a navy (and today, the air force); and to make rules governing the armed forces.

In Article II, sections 2 and 3, the Constitution designates the president as the commander in chief of the armed forces and directs the chief executive to "take Care that the Laws be faithfully executed." In taking the oath of office, the president pledges to "preserve, protect and defend the Constitution." The precise boundary between legislative and executive prerogatives in dealing with the armed forces has usually been determined more by experience than by the intentions of the Framers or the conflicting interpretations of legal experts.

Americans have always been profoundly suspicious of a standing army. One of the greatest threats to democratic government—the man on horseback, or military dictator—is usually associated with ground forces. Therefore, the Constitution (Art. I, sec. 8) distinguishes between congressional treatment of the land and naval forces of the United States. Appropriations to operate the army may be made available for no more than two years, while no such prohibition exists for the navy (or the air force).

Few clauses in the Constitution have been—and continue to be—as passionately debated as the right of Congress to declare war (Art. I, sec. 8). For more than two centuries widely differing interpretations have been given regarding what this constitutional provision really means and what its implications are for the congressional role in external policy.

Proponents of decisive legislative influence in foreign affairs have long contended that this prerogative means (or ought to mean) that Congress makes the decision to go to war, along with the collateral

CAMPAIGN POSTER. For the 1920 presidential election, suggesting that Democratic candidate James M. Cox was un-American in his support for the U.S. entrance into the League of Nations. Although Republican candidate Warren G. Harding courted voters from both sides of the League debate, as a senator from Ohio he had opposed the League of Nations and in 1919 voted against the Treaty of Versailles.

COLLECTION OF DAVID J. AND JANICE L. FRENT

decision to end military hostilities. An early draft of the Constitution empowered Congress to "make war." In the end the Founders conferred on Congress the right to "declare war," mainly to allow the president ample authority to repel invasions or respond to other imminent threats to national security. According to this constitutional interpretation, Congress also has the power to determine whether or when the nation's armed forces are deployed overseas.

Persuasive contrary arguments are made by proponents of presidential control over the military establishment. To begin with, declarations of war are associated with a particular period of history that came to an end in the twentieth century. Nazi Ger-

many's Blitzkrieg (or lightning war) on Poland in September 1939 marked the beginning of modern war in which nations routinely make surprise attacks on other nations. As Alexander Hamilton argued in supporting President Thomas Jefferson's reliance on military force to suppress the Barbary pirates, the notion that the United States cannot be at war without a formal "declaration" by Congress can lead to the possible and absurd conclusion that between two nations there may exist a state of war on one side and a state of peace on the other. War, Hamilton and other constitutional authorities have repeatedly emphasized, is a fact or condition, the existence of which does not depend upon verification by Congress.

SECRETARY OF STATE DEAN RUSK. Speaking before the Senate Foreign Relations Committee, February 1966.

LIBRARY OF CONGRESS

Precedents derived from U.S. history also strongly support this conception of the war power. The last declaration of war was in 1941, following Japan's surprise and devastating attack against Pearl Harbor. Overall, only five wars in U.S. history have been formally declared: the War of 1812, the Mexican War, the Spanish-American War, World War I, and World War II. By contrast, from the late eighteenth to the late twentieth century the United States engaged in upwards of two hundred wars and lesser conflicts in which the armed forces were used to achieve national goals abroad without a declaration of war by Congress.

Many of these aspects of the war power were brought into sharp relief when Congress debated and passed (over President Richard M. Nixon's veto) the War Powers Resolution of 1973. The basic purpose of the resolution was to avoid a repetition of the Vietnam War by imposing stringent limits on the powers of the chief executive to commit the armed forces abroad for an extended period without the explicit consent of Congress.

For a number of reasons, the War Powers Resolution failed to fulfill its proponents' hopes. Experience revealed that the resolution had a number of fundamental defects, and, beginning with Nixon, chief executives have viewed the resolution as unconstitutional and have refused to be bound by its terms. Several of the resolution's key provisions are vague and imprecise, leaving room for contradictory interpretations. Moreover, the resolution specifies no penalty for a president's violation of its provisions. Another weakness was that after 1973 legislators were reluctant to engage in heated and prolonged confrontations with the White House when the nation faced a serious external threat. But perhaps the War Powers Resolution's most fundamental problem is that its stipulations run counter to most Americans' feelings; when the nation confronts external threats to its security and diplomatic interests, people expect and demand forceful presidential leadership. This is especially true when, as during the period of the Persian Gulf War, public confidence in Congress consistently ranks below the level of approval for the president in the conduct of foreign affairs.

The ineffectiveness of the War Powers Resolution does not mean that Congress lacks important prerogatives in dealing with the armed forces. For example, legislators authorize and appropriate funds for the national defense budget (in excess of $280 billion in 1992). It is also within Congress's power to determine the size of the military establishment, its composition, and whether it relies on conscription or voluntary enlistment to meet its personnel needs. In addition, Congress authorizes and provides the funds for long-range research-and-development programs to modernize the armed forces. And committees of the House and Senate periodically investigate and report on a wide range of problems related to national defense—from the use of American arms-aid by foreign governments, to the conduct of the Vietnam and Persian Gulf wars and other instances of military intervention, to waste and mismanagement at the Pentagon.

The power of the purse. In *Federalist* 58 James Madison wrote that congressional control of the government's purse strings was "the most complete and effectual weapon" available to the legislative branch for determining public policy. The Constitution (Art. I, sec. 7) requires that all tax legislation originate in the House of Representatives and must ultimately be approved by majority vote in the House and Senate. The same article (sec. 9) provides that "No Money shall be drawn from the Treasury, but in Consequence of Appropriations made by Law."

The scope and importance of the power of the purse is highlighted by the American diplomatic record since World War II. During the war, the multibillion-dollar Lend-Lease program providing American assistance to the Allies had to be approved and funded by Congress. During this period Congress also secretly financed a crucial undertaking in national security and foreign policy: the Manhattan Project for the development of the atomic bomb.

Then, beginning in 1947, a series of major programs and undertakings set the course of postwar American foreign policy. These included the Greek-

CONGRESSIONAL CRITICS OF THE VIETNAM WAR. *Left to right,* Senators George McGovern (D-S.Dak.), Alan Cranston (D-Calif.), Mark O. Hatfield (R-Oreg.), Charles E. Goodell (R-N.Y.), and Harold E. Hughes (D-Iowa), c. 1970.

WASHINGTON STAR COLLECTION, WASHINGTON PUBLIC LIBRARY

Turkish Aid Program; the European Recovery Program (popularly called the Marshall Plan); the program of military aid to the North Atlantic Treaty Organization (NATO) and later other allies; and the Point Four Program of aid to developing nations.

In the years that followed, the White House requested, and Congress authorized and funded, a continuing program of U.S. economic aid to Israel. Similarly, Congress approved and made funds available for President John F. Kennedy's Alliance for Progress, a multibillion-dollar undertaking to promote long-range economic development in Latin America. For several years, the House and Senate (usually with little significant dissent) provided the money to support the Johnson administration's effort to defeat communism in Southeast Asia.

Again in the early 1990s, the massive military intervention carried out by President George Bush against Iraqi expansionism in the Persian Gulf—a war estimated to have cost the United States $1 billion for each day it was waged—would not have been possible without the legislative branch's provision of funds and other resources. After the war, several Persian Gulf allies requested economic assistance from Washington. During the same period Moscow sought large-scale financial assistance from the United States and other industrialized nations to preserve national cohesion and solve its critical domestic problems.

Congress's exercise of the power of the purse involves a complex two-stage process. In the first stage, any proposed expenditure must be authorized by majorities in the House and Senate. For external policy, this stage is the special province of the House Foreign Affairs and the Senate Foreign Relations committees, which scrutinize proposals and recommend spending projects to their respective chambers. (It must be emphasized, however, that jurisdictional lines among legislative committees have over time become increasingly shadowy and that nowadays nearly all other standing committees of the House and Senate claim some jurisdiction in foreign policy.) Authorizing legislation must ultimately be approved by majorities in the House and Senate.

Next comes the appropriations stage, the designated province of the influential House Appropriations Committee and its less prestigious counterpart, the Senate Appropriations Committee. In this phase, the key question is (or should be) whether, on the basis of projected revenue estimates, funds will be available to finance the long list of programs receiving congressional authorization. (Since World War II the total of authorized expenditures has nearly always exceeded anticipated federal revenues.) This means that Congress, led by the two Appropriations committees, must establish some scale of priorities among competing spending programs. In the end, the House and Senate must enact identical appropriations bills actually making funds available to pay for authorized projects and to operate agencies such as the State and Defense departments.

In exercising the power of the purse, Congress finds ample opportunity to leave its imprint on the nation's foreign policy. Congress may, for example, terminate all or any part of the highly varied programs that together constitute the nation's overall foreign relations by withholding funds for their continuation. In practice, this seldom happens. Since World War II, U.S. foreign policy has exhibited a high degree of continuity, which is contingent on the willingness of Congress to provide the funds required to continue these undertakings.

Another way Congress can and does use the power of the purse to influence U.S. diplomacy is by attaching conditions to the use of funds made available to the president. In the post–World War II period, such conditions have covered a wide range of issues, including restrictions against military intervention by the White House in Sub-Saharan Africa, prohibitions against the provision of U.S. military aid to anticommunist groups in Central America, and the denial of funds to governments violating human rights.

Yet in the final analysis, most legislators recognize that the chief executive must have considerable flexibility to conduct foreign affairs successfully. As a rule, therefore, congressionally imposed restrictions on the president's freedom of action contain escape clauses permitting the White House to waive the constraints if the president determines that doing so is required by some compelling national interest.

Informal and extraconstitutional powers. Congressional prerogatives in the foreign policy field extend beyond those specified in the Constitution and include powers and practices incident to lawmaking that have been acquired by the House and Senate since 1789. One major prerogative is the congressional power of investigation. During any legislative session, several investigations by committees of the House and Senate are under way, and a number of these will have significant implications for foreign affairs. Legislators might decide, for example, to inquire into the administration of the foreign aid program in one or more Latin

American nations, to examine the ability of the NATO partners to pay a higher proportion of the cost of the alliance's defense, or to look into Israel's need for greater U.S. economic assistance.

In such investigations, government officials, lobbyists for interest groups, and private citizens are called as witnesses before congressional committees. Committee staff members collect documents and other materials relevant to the inquiry. The committee normally issues a report (sometimes including a minority report as well) making recommendations related to the subject under investigation.

In the modern period such investigations have sometimes had a significant impact on the conduct of foreign relations. The inquiry headed by Sen. Harry S. Truman (D-Mo.) during World War II, for example, made a valuable contribution to resolving problems related to the war effort. During the Korean War a joint investigation by the Senate Foreign Relations and Armed Services committees into the dismissal of the highly popular Gen. Douglas MacArthur played a key role in averting what might have been a serious constitutional crisis. Certain other investigations in the same period, however (such as those focusing on why the United States "lost" China to communism and those seeking to uncover communist influence within the State Department), usually generated more publicity and partisan wrangling than enlightenment. In more recent years, the detailed congressional investigation of the Iran-contra affair sought to determine whether the Reagan White House had violated the law by providing military aid to anticommunist groups in Central America and, if so, which executive officials were responsible. Among their other results, such investigations often serve to focus public attention (usually preoccupied with domestic concerns) on important foreign policy issues.

Another informal power of Congress in the foreign policy field is the passage of simple resolutions by the House or the Senate (often called sense-of-the-House or sense-of-the-Senate resolutions). In any given legislative session the *Congressional Record* may contain literally hundreds of such resolutions. Unlike joint resolutions, these simple resolutions are merely expressions of opinion and have no binding force as law.

Although not legally enforceable, such resolutions are often taken seriously by the president and his foreign policy advisers because they are useful indicators of underlying public concern about important foreign policy questions. Moreover, as a general rule the White House wants to maintain cooperative relations with Congress and to give legislators the impression that their views have been heard and have been taken into account in policy formulation. Sometimes the State Department even assists in promoting the reelection of senators and representatives who have supported the president's foreign policy program. For example, the State Department may write speeches on foreign affairs for these legislators or may aid them in preparing resolutions or amendments to, say, the foreign aid bill. The legislators may then introduce these amendments on the floor of the House or Senate, thereby demonstrating to their constituents what zealous watchdogs of the public treasury they are.

Another of Congress's informal powers is travel abroad by members of the House, the Senate, their aides, and members of the increasingly large legislative staff. During any given year, hundreds of legislators and assistants travel to foreign countries or participate in international meetings and conferences. Sometimes denounced as foreign junkets at taxpayers' expense, overseas trips by legislators can usefully undergird the independent role Congress plays in foreign policy. Foreign trips provide legislators and their aides with firsthand information about conditions and problems abroad; in turn, this step does much to free the House and Senate from complete reliance on the executive branch for essential information. Overseas travel also gives lawmakers an opportunity to meet with foreign officials and political leaders and to acquire greater insight into the views and policies of other governments.

Other Legislative Contributions. In a democratic system, public policy must have the "consent of the governed"; it must be acceptable to and supported by the people and their elected representatives. The Vietnam War provided a graphic reminder of what can happen to the nation when this essential ingredient is lacking. The president and other high-level executive officials are aware that if their policies encounter fundamental questions or opposition on Capitol Hill, then serious doubts concerning those policies exist in the minds of American citizens.

A legislative contribution closely related to the conduct of foreign affairs is Congress's role as a conduit, providing citizens' organizations, interest groups, and individuals with direct access to the government. The Bill of Rights permits citizens "to petition the Government for a redress of grievances." Traditionally, Congress has been the channel through which such opinion is conveyed to policymakers, although citizens may also communicate their viewpoints to executive officials and agencies.

This phenomenon has a negative side. Many students of the legislative process in the United States believe that, if anything, Congress in the contemporary period listens too closely to political action committees (PACs) and other interest groups, whose conceptions of the national interest are often strongly colored by self-interest. A noteworthy example has been congressional receptivity to the views and demands of ethnic minorities who are keenly concerned about developments affecting the "old country." As a general rule, ethnic minorities have very strong opinions on a narrow range of foreign policy questions, and they tend to express their viewpoints frequently and with great intensity. A prominent example is the Irish American population, whose traditional anti-British position and vocal opposition to close association with Great Britain was a major factor in public rejection of the League of Nations after World War I. Later, during and after World War II, Polish Americans, Ukrainian Americans, and other minorities exerted considerable pressure on policymakers to protect the rights of people living in Russia and Eastern Europe. Another noteworthy example is the decisive influence of the American Jewish community in gaining Washington's support for the creation of the state of Israel and for large-scale U.S. military and economic support for Israel since 1948. (By contrast, Arab Americans have been considerably less successful in their lobbying activities, in part because, as in the Middle East itself, opinion among Arabs in the United States is often highly fragmented.) Similarly, African Americans in Congress and interest groups championing their causes have had a significant impact on legislative viewpoints and actions respecting South Africa and other African nations.

From time to time, Congress makes a valuable contribution by providing forceful evidence to foreign governments (whose officials are perennially mystified by the workings of the American democratic system) of the unity and constancy of the nation's foreign policy. Executive officials face the continuing challenge of convincing officials of other countries that the foreign policies of the United States are credible and have the people's enduring support. From Soviet leader Joseph Stalin during and after World War II to President Saddam Hussein of Iraq, a succession of foreign leaders in the modern period has seriously miscalculated on this score.

The willingness of Congress year after year to provide the funds, military power, and other resources needed for the United States to implement the containment strategy against expansive communism was an outstanding example of the ability of policymakers in Washington to collaborate on foreign policies and programs. Similarly, legislative support for the actions of the Bush White House in successfully opposing Iraqi expansionism in 1990 and 1991 left little doubt that the nation's goals had the overwhelming support of the American people and their leaders.

A related legislative contribution is Congress's role as what might be called a "policy amplifier." The 535 representatives and senators can together make Congress an "echo chamber," repeating and magnifying policy statements announced by the White House. When necessary, Congress can turn up the volume on America's diplomatic message, transmitting it loud and clear to governments and private groups overseas.

Two examples from postwar U.S. diplomatic experience illustrate the point. Beginning in the 1960s, Congress demanded that the NATO allies defray a larger share of the overall costs of Western defense. On more than one occasion, executive officials relied on the threat of an adverse reaction on Capitol Hill if the European allies failed to cooperate in achieving the goal. The same phenomenon has long been evident in United States–Japan relations. Legislators have complained vocally about allegedly unfair Japanese trade practices and about Tokyo's reluctance to pay a higher proportion of Asian defense costs—concerns widely shared by the American people.

Another contribution Congress makes to foreign policy was highlighted during the Persian Gulf War. On both sides of the political aisle, legislators repeatedly urged President Bush and his aides to state and publicly explain the administration's goals in the conflict. Initially, Washington's goals were limited to restoring independence to Kuwait and protecting the security of Saudi Arabia and the smaller nations of the Persian Gulf area. As the weeks passed, however, policymakers referred to other objectives of U.S. intervention, such as "teaching aggressors a lesson"; overthrowing Saddam Hussein's regime and establishing a new democratic order in Iraq; protecting the rights of the Kurds, the Shiites, and other political dissidents within the country; and creating (in President Bush's words) a "new world order." Although legislators from time to time attempted to compel the White House to clarify its goals in the conflict, it cannot be said that these efforts were conspicuously successful. Indeed, as a general phenomenon, throughout American diplomatic history the relationship between military force and political objectives has posed a recurrent problem for policymakers and citizens, and the problem has become especially acute in the era of limited war.

A different congressional contribution to foreign policy has been legislators' articulation of American ethical principles and the insistence that these be reflected in U.S. foreign policy. The American people have never been receptive to realpolitik principles of statecraft. To the contrary, since the end of the nineteenth century legislators have been at the forefront in supporting such idealistic undertakings as international efforts to limit steadily rising armaments and to outlaw war as an instrument of national policy. Even during World War II, when the Soviet Union and the United States were allies, legislators urged the Roosevelt administration to press the Stalin regime to end its harsh treatment of religious believers and political dissidents. After the war, on several occasions—from the issuance of the Truman Doctrine in 1947 to the Persian Gulf conflict of 1990 and 1991—legislators called on the White House to rely on the United Nations to achieve U.S. objectives abroad. Moreover, during the Persian Gulf conflict lawmakers repeatedly insisted that the Bush administration endeavor to solve the crisis by peaceful methods before using military force.

More than any other single example, perhaps, intensive legislative interest in and activity affecting international human rights issues illustrate the contribution of Congress to foreign policy decision making. Legislators became especially active on this front during the 1970s, when they often made U.S. economic and military aid or trade concessions conditional on the record of other governments in respecting human rights. A well-publicized example was congressional insistence that Moscow permit large-scale Jewish emigration and that it cease the oppression of political dissidents.

Finally, the House and Senate provide what might be called the congressional "yellow light" function. From time to time Congress prevails on the White House to reexamine its policies, to make certain that the nation is on the right diplomatic course, and in some cases it has compelled changes in established policies. For example, in the late 1940s the Truman administration considered recognition of the communist regime on the Chinese mainland, a move that encountered outspoken legislative opposition, reflecting in turn deepseated public resistance. (The Kennedy administration encountered much the same reaction to this proposed step in the early 1960s.) Mounting congressional opposition was a key factor compelling the Nixon administration to terminate the nation's involvement in the Vietnam War. During the 1980s, growing disaffection on Capitol Hill was a crucial factor in the Reagan administration's decision to withdraw U.S. forces from Lebanon. And in response to legislative demands, President Bush made several efforts to resolve the Persian Gulf conflict by diplomacy and to gain broad United Nations support for his position before resorting to military force against Iraq.

[See also Executive Agreement; Foreign Affairs Committee, House; Foreign Aid; Foreign Relations Committee, Senate; Tariffs and Trade; Treaties; War Powers; War Powers Resolution.]

BIBLIOGRAPHY

Barnhart, Michael, ed. Congress and United States Foreign Policy: Controlling the Use of Force in the Nuclear Age. 1987.

Blechman, Barry M. The Politics of National Security: Congress and U.S. Defense Policy. 1990.

Collier, Ellen. War Powers Resolution: Fifteen Years of Experience. 1988.

Crabb, Cecil V., Jr., and Pat Holt. Invitation to Struggle: Congress, the President, and Foreign Policy. 4th ed. 1992.

Forsythe, David P. Human Rights and U.S. Foreign Policy: Congress Reconsidered. 1988.

Johnson, Loch K. A Season of Inquiry: Congress and Intelligence. 1988.

Said, Abdul A., ed. Ethnicity and U.S. Foreign Policy. 1986.

Smist, Frank J., Jr. Congress Oversees the United States Intelligence Community, 1947–1989. 1990.

Tivnan, Edward. The Lobby: Jewish Political Power and American Foreign Policy. 1987.

Tonmasevski, Katarina. Development Aid and Human Rights. 1989.

Warburg, Gerald F. Conflict and Consensus: The Struggle between Congress and the President over Foreign Policymaking. 1989.

Williams, Phil. The Senate and U.S. Troops in Europe. 1985.

Wormuth, Francis D., and Edwin B. Firmage. To Chain the Dogs of War: The War Powers of Congress in History and Law. 1986.

CECIL V. CRABB, JR.

FOREIGN RELATIONS COMMITTEE, SENATE.

The Senate Foreign Relations Committee was created as a standing committee of the Senate in 1816. Originally it had five members; by the 1930s, it had twenty-three. In 1947, membership was cut back to thirteen. In the 103d Congress (1993–1995), it had nineteen—eleven Democrats and nine Republicans, reflecting the party division in the Senate as a whole.

More than 325 senators have served on the committee. Six of them have also been president, nine have been vice president, and nineteen have been secretary of State. The presidents were Andrew Jackson, James Buchanan, Andrew Johnson, Benjamin Harrison, Warren G. Harding, and John F. Kennedy. The vice presidents include John C. Calhoun, Alben W. Barkley, and Hubert H. Humphrey. The secretaries of State include Daniel Webster, William H. Seward, Hamilton Fish, John Sherman, Elihu Root, James F. Byrnes, and Edmund S. Muskie. Also, uncounted assistant secretaries and ambassadors served on the committee or its staff.

The committee's jurisdiction is specified in Senate Rule XXV 1 (j)(1). Its most important responsibilities are those relating to the Department of State, the Arms Control and Disarmament Agency, the United States Information Agency, and the United Nations. It has jurisdiction over foreign aid, international financial institutions, treaties, and nominations to high positions in the State Department and related agencies.

In the 103d Congress (1993–1995), the committee had seven subcommittees: European Affairs; International Economic Policy, Trade, Oceans, and Environment; East Asian and Pacific Affairs; Western Hemisphere and Peace Corps Affairs; Terrorism, Narcotics, and International Communications; African Affairs; and Near Eastern and South Asian Affairs. Subcommittees varied in size from five to eleven members.

In the 101st Congress (1989–1991), the committee and its subcommittees held 282 meetings. The committee reported 26 bills and joint resolutions, nine of which became law, and 31 other resolutions, of which 26 were agreed to by the Senate. In the same period, the committee and the Senate approved 24 treaties and 2,000 nominations out of 2,046 received, more than 1,700 of which were routine promotions in the Foreign Service. No nomination was rejected, but 11 were withdrawn by the president. When it does not wish to confirm a nomination, the committee's usual practice is simply not to act on it; the nomination then expires at the end of that session of Congress.

Many of the committee's hearings and reports are on nonlegislative subjects—for example, the threat of foreign terrorism or major issues of U.S. policy in East Asia. The committee thus provides a forum for public discussion and clarification of important issues. The committee's hearings on the Vietnam War in the 1960s, for example, became a focal point for opponents of the Johnson administration's policy.

By requiring the Senate's advice and consent to treaties and to the nomination of certain high officials, the Constitution gives the Senate a special role in foreign policy. The Foreign Relations Committee is the Senate's agent in playing this role as well as the broader constitutional role, which the Senate shares with the House, of declaring war and appropriating funds. (The committee has no jurisdiction over appropriations, but it does have the power to authorize appropriations and thereby to set ceilings on them.) Thus, the relationship between the committee, on the one hand, and the White House and the State Department, on the other, is of cardinal importance in the process of making foreign policy. Much of the history of the committee revolves around this relationship.

The Nineteenth Century. Few of the eminent senators who served on the Foreign Relations Committee in the nineteenth century held the position of chairman (Henry Clay and Charles Sumner were conspicuous exceptions), and many of the committee's prominent members (for example, Andrew Jackson and John C. Calhoun) were more interested in other matters.

Sumner (R-Mass., 1851–1874) is best remembered for his fervent campaign against slavery and his advocacy of a hard-line Reconstruction policy toward the South after the Civil War. But Sumner also played an important role as chairman of the Foreign Relations Committee (1861–1871), being the first of the committee's chairmen to attempt to use that position to influence foreign policy significantly.

In 1861, he intervened with President Abraham Lincoln to secure the release of two Confederate officials whom the U.S. Navy had taken from a British ship on the high seas. In a burst of patriotic fervor, Congress voted the U.S. naval commander a gold Medal of Honor, but the British delivered an ultimatum to Washington and sent troops to Canada in preparation for war. In urging Lincoln to release the men (whose seizure was contrary to international law), Sumner not only acted against a strong tide of congressional and public opinion, he also compromised his own strong anti-

Confederate feelings for the sake of upholding international law.

However, after the Civil War, Sumner opposed the Grant administration's policy to seek arbitration of claims against Great Britain arising from the war. He also demanded British withdrawal from Canada as part of any settlement. On an unrelated issue, Sumner led the opposition to a treaty (which the Senate rejected in 1870) annexing Santo Domingo (now the Dominican Republic).

With the support of President Ulysses S. Grant, Secretary of State Hamilton Fish, himself a former member of the committee (1855–1857), maneuvered to inspire a coup d'état against Sumner among Senate Republicans in 1871. Sumner was not only deposed as chairman but was also removed as a member of the committee. This represented a startling interference by the executive branch in the internal affairs of the Senate and an even more startling repudiation by the Senate of one of its own committee chairmen.

Spanish-American War to World War II. The committee began to establish itself as an enduring influence in the late 1890s as a result of two developments. One was the Spanish-American War of 1898. The war gave the committee favorable public exposure, thrust the United States more prominently onto the world stage, and increased the importance of foreign policy as a political issue. Prominent members of the committee, notably Chairman Cushman K. Davis (R-Minn.) and Henry Cabot Lodge (R-Mass.), took up the popular cry for war against Spain, which was declared on 25 April 1898. The war ended in August, and President William McKinley named three members of the committee to the five-man delegation to the peace negotiations.

The other development leading to increased committee influence was a trend toward greater continuity of membership. This, in turn, contributed to the establishment of recognized procedures and traditions. Whereas the giants of the nineteenth-century Senate who served on the committee did not pay it much attention, those of the twentieth-century Senate began to do so. Lodge served from 1895 until his death in 1924, the last five years as chairman. William E. Borah (R-Idaho) joined the committee in 1911 and served until his death in 1940. He was chairman from 1924 to 1933. Key Pittman (D-Nev.) came on in 1916 and stayed until 1940. He was chairman from 1933 to 1940. Hiram W. Johnson (R-Calif.) was on the committee from 1919 to 1945. These men and others with long-term service gave the committee an institutional memory.

Lodge, Borah, and Johnson led an isolationist bloc that in 1919 and 1920 defeated President Woodrow Wilson on the Treaty of Versailles and the League of Nations. They blocked ratification of the treaty, which incorporated the covenant of the League. After Lodge's death, Borah, Johnson, and their followers kept the United States out of the World Court despite the recommendations of Republican presidents in the 1920s. In the 1930s, even in a Democratic Congress and against the wishes of a Democratic president, they were able to pass three neutrality acts that provided, among other things, for an arms embargo against belligerent powers. It was not until September 1939, when World War II broke out in Europe, that President Franklin D. Roosevelt was finally able to persuade Congress to repeal the arms embargo.

Roosevelt was determined not to repeat Wilson's experience with the League of Nations, and early in World War II he involved the Foreign Relations Committee in postwar planning. In particular, he invited the committee chairman, Tom Connally (D-Tex.), and the ranking Republican, Arthur H. Vandenberg of Michigan, to the Dumbarton Oaks Conference that drew up preliminary plans for the United Nations in 1944. President Harry S. Truman made them delegates to the U.N. Conference itself in 1945. Partly as a consequence of this collaboration, the United Nations Charter was approved by the Senate 89 to 2. Connally and Vandenberg were members of the U.S. delegation to the first two sessions of the U.N. General Assembly.

After World War II. The Legislative Reorganization Act of 1946 brought about a transformation in the Senate and the Foreign Relations Committee, setting in motion enduring changes in procedures and modes of behavior. The act for the first time gave Senate committees their own professional staffs, selected on the basis of merit. Before 1947, committee reports were written by officials of the executive branch; after 1947, they were written by committee staffs. These staffs also greatly reinforced Senate independence by giving committees their own tools of research and inquiry.

In the Foreign Relations Committee, this change coincided with the assumption of the chairmanship by Vandenberg following the Republican victory in the 1946 election. Vandenberg selected the committee's chief of staff and gave him authority to hire the rest of the staff. Thus began a thirty-year committee tradition of nonpartisan career staffing.

Vandenberg did even more to influence committee traditions. He had decided that the Republican party must be led away from isolationism, and in

LEADING MEMBERS OF THE SENATE FOREIGN RELATIONS COMMITTEE. Looking over charges made by Patrick J. Hurley against the State Department, December 1945. *Left to right*, Senators Warren R. Austin (R-Vt.), Arthur H. Vandenberg (R-Mich.), and Tom T. Connally (D-Tex.), committee chairman.

OFFICE OF THE HISTORIAN OF THE U.S. SENATE

the effort to do so, he was energetically assisted by Lodge's grandson, Henry Cabot Lodge, Jr., himself now a Republican senator from Massachusetts and a member of the Foreign Relations Committee. Among other steps toward this end, Vandenberg (along with Connally, now the ranking Democratic member of the committee) established a tradition of nonpartisanship (a term he preferred to bipartisanship) in the committee's deliberations. Vandenberg prided himself on the number of unanimous 13 to 0 votes in the committee, but this unanimity came at a price: a committee that was not ideologically representative of the Senate. This meant that the committee faced constant battles to get its bills through the Senate without amendments being attached that would weaken the legislation.

The committee's nonpartisan approach continued, in the main, but its homogeneity did not. The price for its becoming more representative of the Senate was the loss of unanimity and an increase in contentiousness within the committee.

Studies and investigations. In the 1950s, the committee began to use its staff, usually working under the supervision of an ad hoc subcommittee, to make its own studies of foreign policy problems. The first of these was a study of proposals to revise the United Nations Charter (at a time when the charter was scarcely five years old). This was followed by a study of U.S. foreign information pro-

grams and by another of technical assistance programs. A larger study of foreign aid led to the creation of the Development Loan Fund. The recommendations of a study of Latin America anticipated some aspects of the Alliance for Progress. Many of these studies included segments that the committee contracted out to academic and other nongovernmental experts. The nondiplomatic lobbying of foreign governments in the United States was examined in depth in the 1960s. In the 1980s and the early 1990s, the committee investigated the international drug trade and the tangled affairs of the Bank of Commerce and Credit International (BCCI).

In the meantime, the committee staff, which grew slowly but steadily after 1947, traveled the world and reported back to the committee on the foreign aid program and other policy matters. Staff reporting on the Vietnam War and on American overseas military bases worldwide was especially important in laying the groundwork for public hearings. The committee's hearings on the Vietnam War in the 1960s had a good deal to do with increasing public opposition to the war. The committee's review of President Lyndon B. Johnson's intervention in the Dominican Republic in 1965 precipitated the break between the president and Chairman J. William Fulbright (D-Ark.), which was soon finalized by their differences over Vietnam.

In 1979, the committee abandoned the concept of a unified staff working for the committee as a whole, and the professional staff was split between the majority and the minority. This was first done mainly to satisfy the growing demand of senators for more staff, a Senate-wide phenomenon, but it also reflected the growing ideological diversity on the committee. During much of the 1980s and continuing into the 1990s, for example, committee members ranged from the very conservative Jesse Helms (R-N.C.) to liberals such as Paul S. Sarbanes (D-Md.), Christopher J. Dodd (D-Conn.), and John Kerry (D-Mass.).

Committee organization. The authority and jurisdiction of subcommittees became a contentious issue in the Foreign Relations Committee—and throughout Congress, for that matter—in the 1970s. Traditionally, Foreign Relations had operated without subcommittees, except occasionally on an ad hoc basis to deal with a technical subject, such as tax treaties, or to make a particular study, such as those discussed above. In 1950, the committee created a group of consultative subcommittees that corresponded generally to the organization of the

State Department. The purpose was to establish closer relations with the department. This produced indifferent results, since the subcommittees had no legislative jurisdiction. Their sole mission was to meet privately from time to time with assistant secretaries of State so as to become better informed and to transmit their views to the department informally. Some subcommittees did this; some did not.

In the 1950s, 1960s, and 1970s, a number of subcommittees were appointed to conduct long-range studies. Prominent among these were a subcommittee on disarmament in the 1950s, under the chairmanship of Hubert H. Humphrey (D-Minn.); a subcommittee on U.S. overseas commitments in the 1960s, under the chairmanship of Stuart Symington (D-Mo.); and a subcommittee on multinational corporations in the 1970s, headed by Frank Church (D-Idaho). These studies resulted in little significant legislation, but each had an impact on policy through hearings and reports.

During these same decades, tension was growing in the committee over the question of centralization versus decentralization. Those who favored centralization argued that foreign policy was a seamless web and that its problems were not susceptible to compartmentalization. Those who favored decentralization argued the reverse and added that the growing complexity of foreign policy demanded that problems be broken into smaller pieces.

More was involved, however. When Fulbright left the Senate at the end of 1974, he had been chairman of the Foreign Relations Committee for almost sixteen years, longer than anyone else. For most of that time, the ranking minority member had been either Bourke B. Hickenlooper (R-Iowa) or George D. Aiken (R-Vt.). These three men together served on the committee for a total of sixty-nine years. They agreed that the committee was not broken and so there was no reason to fix it. Other members were of a contrary view; they wanted a show of their own to run, with staff and budget. Prominent in this group were Humphrey and Church.

Fulbright and Aiken left the Senate at the same time; their departures were followed at the beginning of 1975 by the creation of a subcommittee on foreign aid, headed by Humphrey, with jurisdiction over the annual foreign aid legislation. Part of Humphrey's motivation in pushing for this subcommittee went beyond the organizational debate described above and to the substance of foreign aid. The full committee had been distinctly un-

friendly to foreign aid for at least ten years and, on occasion, had even tried to kill the program. Humphrey wanted to reform and revive it, and he saw a subcommittee as a better vehicle for accomplishing this. His effort was not completely successful, but it did reduce the level of controversy for a time.

The creation of the foreign aid subcommittee in 1975 was followed in 1977 by transformation of the subcommittee on multinational corporations. Converted into the subcommittee on economic policy, it now had a broader jurisdiction.

The subcommittee on foreign aid was abandoned after Humphrey died in 1978, and gradually the full committee reclaimed legislative jurisdiction. In the early 1990s, there was again a move to increase subcommittee autonomy, especially with respect to staffing. This was at least partly due to dissatisfaction among committee members with what they perceived to be gridlock in the full committee brought on by ideological divisiveness.

Legislative-executive relations. The committee's relations with the executive branch have varied over time and over different issues at the same time. The crucial determinant is whether the committee generally agrees with a given executive policy. If it agrees, its relations are cooperative; if it does not, its relations are adversarial. But there has been a long-term trend toward independence, with the corollary of declining executive influence on the committee.

Beginning in the Vandenberg-Connally era, senators were commonly included on delegations to international conferences, but by the 1960s, some senators (Hickenlooper, for one) were wondering whether this did not compromise the Senate's independence in considering any treaty that might result. Senators were notably reluctant to get involved in the long-running negotiations that led to the conclusion in 1977 of the Panama Canal treaties. (The primary reason was that senators smelled an unpopular political issue and did not want to become identified with it any sooner than necessary.) On the other hand, after the treaties were submitted to the Senate, Howard H. Baker (R-Tenn.), the chamber's minority leader and a member of the Foreign Relations Committee, went to Panama and in effect renegotiated important provisions of the treaties with Panamanian president Omar Torrijos.

Of necessity, the role of the Foreign Relations Committee is generally reactive: the executive makes a proposal, and then the committee considers it. But this is not always the case. A Senate resolution, originating with Vandenberg, set in motion the process that led to the North Atlantic Treaty. The Food-for-Peace program grew from a proposal (opposed by the Eisenhower administration) in a foreign-aid conference committee to earmark funds for surplus agricultural commodities. The educational exchange program grew from an amendment proposed to a surplus property bill by Fulbright when he was a junior senator.

After 1987, under the chairmanship of Claiborne Pell (D-R.I.), the committee was less active and generally less effective. Issues that would once have been addressed by the Foreign Relations Committee were taken up by the Armed Services Committee (the Persian Gulf War, reinterpretation of the treaty limiting antiballistic missiles) or by the Judiciary Committee (war powers, the antiballistic missile treaty).

At the same time, the committee has remained an independent force. Committee staff members travel widely and independently to places including Kurdish areas of Iraq in the aftermath of the Persian Gulf War and the remnants of Yugoslavia during the fighting among Serbs, Croats, and Muslims. So do committee members. Another sign of continued independence is the committee's readiness to assert its power over nominations.

BIBLIOGRAPHY

Austin, Anthony. *The President's War.* 1971.
Dennison, Eleanor E. *The Senate Foreign Relations Committee.* 1942.
Farnsworth, David N. *The Senate Committee on Foreign Relations.* 1961.
Gould, James W. "The Origins of the Senate Committee on Foreign Relations." *Western Political Quarterly* 12 (1959): 670–682.
U.S. Senate. Committee on Foreign Relations. *170th Anniversary, 1816–1986.* 99th Cong., 2d sess., 1986. S. Doc. 99-21.

PAT M. HOLT

FORESTS, NATIONAL. See National Parks and Forests.

FORMER MEMBERS OF CONGRESS.
The U.S. Association of Former Members of Congress (FMC) was incorporated by alumni of the House and Senate on 18 June 1970 "to promote the cause of good government at the national level by strengthening and improving the United States Congress as an institution." It received a federal charter in 1982.

Recipients, FMC Distinguished Service Award

1974	Gerald R. Ford
1975	John W. McCormack
1976	Lewis Deschler
1977	Samuel J. Ervin, Jr.
1978	Nelson A. Rockefeller
1979	George H. Mahon
1980	Clare Boothe Luce
1981	Edmund S. Muskie
1982	Hugh Scott
1983	Richard W. Bolling
1984	Jacob K. Javits
1985	J. William Fulbright
1986	Walter H. Judd
1987	Thomas P. (Tip) O'Neill, Jr.
1988	John J. Rhodes
1989	Edward P. Boland
1990	Edward J. Derwinski
1991	Corinne C. (Lindy) Boggs
1992	Richard B. Cheney
1993	Abner Mikva

Members meet each spring in the House of Representatives chamber to hear reports on activities and to present a Distinguished Service Award. Activities include hosting delegations from foreign legislatures, sponsoring scholarly studies, and arranging college campus visits by former senators and representatives.

In 1974 and 1975, FMC sponsored one hundred oral history interviews with former senators and representatives. Cassette recordings and transcripts, placed in the Manuscript Division of the Library of Congress, are available to scholars for research.

FMC's annual Distinguished Service Award recognizes exemplary political performance. The award, begun in 1974, is rotated between the Republicans and the Democrats.

[*See also* Members, *article on* Retirement.]

BIBLIOGRAPHY

U.S. Association of Former Members of Congress. *Report to the Congress.* 1983.
U.S. Congress. *Congressional Record.* 102d Cong., 2d sess., 2 April 1992. "Reception for Former Members of Congress," pp. H2262–H2269.

GEORGE MEADER

FORMOSA RESOLUTION (1955). On 24 January 1955, President Dwight D. Eisenhower sent a special message to Congress requesting au-

thority to take such military action as might be needed to repel any Communist Chinese aggression in the area of the Formosa (Taiwan) Straits and specifically to ensure the security of Formosa, where the Nationalist Chinese government had established itself after the Communist takeover of the mainland, and of the nearby Pescadores Islands. On the same day, the so-called Formosa Resolution was introduced in Congress. It passed the House 409 to 3 on 25 January and the Senate 85 to 3 on 28 January. In effect, Congress firmly backed the president in order to—in the president's words—"remove any doubt concerning our readiness to fight, if necessary, to preserve the vital stake of the free world in a free Formosa."

But neither the United States nor the People's Republic of China were anxious for war. In the next few weeks, the United States encouraged and assisted Nationalist Chinese forces in evacuating the hard-to-defend Tachen Islands for more defensible positions elsewhere. Beijing lowered its harsh anti-U.S. rhetoric and eased military pressure in anticipation of Premier Zhou Enlai's call at the Bandung nonaligned summit in April 1955 for Sino-American talks on Taiwan and other issues.

The Formosa Resolution's granting of congressional authority for possible presidential military action in the Taiwan Straits was periodically referred to in ensuing years, notably during the 1958 Taiwan Straits crisis prompted by heavy Communist Chinese bombardment of Nationalist garrisons on the offshore islands of Quemoy and Matsu. With the reevaluation of U.S. and Chinese policies in the early 1970s, the Formosa Resolution was seen as anachronistic and was repealed by the Senate in 1974.

BIBLIOGRAPHY

Barber, Hollis W., et al., eds. *The United States in World Affairs.* 1957. Pp. 88–99.

Barnett, A. Doak. *China and the Major Powers in East Asia.* 1977. Pp. 185–202.

Keesing's Contemporary Archives. Vol. 10. 1955–1956. Pp. 14,017–14,021, 14,117–14,119.

ROBERT G. SUTTER

FORNEY, JOHN W. (1817–1881), journalist, clerk of the House, secretary of the Senate, and political adventurer. As editor of the *Lancaster Journal,* Forney forged a political alliance with fellow Pennsylvanian James Buchanan that rewarded him with patronage during the administrations of James K. Polk and Franklin Pierce. Federal appointments enabled Forney to publish newspapers in Philadelphia and Washington. From 1851 to 1856 he served as clerk of the House of Representatives, presiding over that body during the battle to elect a Speaker in 1855 and 1856. With Buchanan's election as president, Forney expected a cabinet office or Senate seat. When political opponents blocked his advance, he felt betrayed by Buchanan. Returning to Philadelphia, Forney threw his newspaper's support to Sen. Stephen A. Douglas in his fight with Buchanan over Kansas. In 1860 Forney shifted his allegiance to the Republicans and was again elected clerk of the House.

Abraham Lincoln supported Forney's election as secretary of the Senate in 1861 and persuaded him to convert the Washington *Sunday Chronicle* to a daily paper, which the government distributed to the Army of the Potomac. Forney continued to write a widely read political column, signed "Occasional" (the best of these he later collected and published in his book, *Anecdotes of Public Men*). His rooms near the Capitol served as a regular meeting place for congressional insiders. Although he initially supported Lincoln's successor, Andrew Johnson, Forney broke with him over his veto of the Freedmen's Bureau bill. Forney left the office of secretary in 1868, sold the *Chronicle,* and accepted an appointment as collector of the Port of Philadelphia from President Ulysses S. Grant.

Forney epitomized the political journalism of the mid-nineteenth century, with its willing embrace of partisanship and its hunger for patronage. Showing considerable agility, Forney offered his pen and his paper to the service of whatever party or faction suited his purpose at the time. But while Forney harbored lofty ambitions, he squandered them in political brawls. Noted one of his editors, John Russell Young: "He never came up to his own."

BIBLIOGRAPHY

Carman, Harry J., and Reinhard H. Luthin. *Lincoln and the Patronage.* 1943.

Forney, John W. *Anecdotes of Public Men.* 2 vols. 1873–1881.

DONALD A. RITCHIE

FOURTEENTH AMENDMENT (1866; 14 Stat. 358–359). The origins of the Fourteenth Amendment lay in the growing disagreement between President Andrew Johnson and the Republican party over the treatment of the newly freed slaves and the terms of readmission to the Union of the former Confederate states in the years after the

Civil War. Johnson believed that the secessionist states should be allowed to determine the status of the freedmen and that, having complied with minimal conditions for readmission—ratifying the Thirteenth Amendment and framing a new state constitution—they should be readmitted. The Republican party, however, wanted to be certain that the freedmen's civil rights were protected and that the South was properly punished for its misdeeds. A potentially serious conflict was in the offing should neither side be willing to compromise its basic position.

Congress met in December 1865 and decided not to readmit senators and representatives from secessionist states. Instead it appointed the Joint Committee on Reconstruction, composed of six senators and nine representatives, to formulate a congressional reconstruction plan. The committee was controlled by moderates, who were led by its chairman, Sen. William Pitt Fessenden. There was hope that an accommodation with President Johnson could be worked out.

The first measure proposed was an extension of the Freedmen's Bureau, an agency created by Congress on 3 March 1865 to feed and care for southern refugees, white and black. The second measure granted civil rights to the freedmen and gave the federal courts authority to protect those rights. Most Republicans saw the Freedmen's Bureau bill as necessary to protect southern blacks and the civil rights bill as a way to make freedmen citizens with basic civil rights. These measures were passed and sent to the president for his signature. His veto of both measures and his subsequent denunciation of Congress provoked the confrontation that resulted in the Fourteenth Amendment. Though Congress overrode the veto of the Freedmen's Bureau and civil rights bills, few Republicans felt that civil rights for blacks were secure. The opposition of the president meant that something more permanent was needed.

The Joint Committee on Reconstruction worked over the winter and spring of 1866 to write a constitutional amendment that would guarantee the rights of freedmen, protect against the return of Confederates to political power, and repudiate the Confederate debt. Contrary to the view of earlier historians, the final amendment was a compromise between Radical Republicans and moderate elements of the Republican party. Despite strenuous efforts Radical Republicans were unable to win acceptance for their proposals. As Sen. John Sherman, a moderate Republican said of the amend-

REP. THADDEUS STEVENS (R-PA.). A leader of the Radical Republicans during the Civil War and Reconstruction.

HARPER'S PICTORIAL HISTORY OF THE GREAT REBELLION

ment's final form: "They talk about radicals; why, we defeated every radical proposition in it."

On 30 April 1866, the Joint Committee reported to Congress a five-part amendment to the Constitution. After six weeks of extensive debate, it was revised, passed by the necessary two-thirds majority in both houses, and sent to the states. The first clause made all persons born or naturalized in the United States citizens and prohibited states from abridging "the privileges or immunities of citizens," depriving "any person of life, liberty, or property without due process of law," or denying to any person "the equal protection of the law." The second clause provided for a reduction in a state's representation in direct proportion to the number of male citizens denied the suffrage. The third clause disqualified from federal or state office any person who had "engaged in insurrection or rebellion" against the United States. (This clause replaced a more severe recommendation that all who had participated in the rebellion be disenfranchised until 1870.) The fourth clause guaranteed "the validity of the public debt of the United States" and prohibited the payment of any part of the Confederate debt. The fifth and last clause gave Congress the power to enforce the provisions of the article "by appropriate legislation."

The most serious congressional debate was over the disqualification clause. Although many Republicans thought that the complete disenfranchisement of Confederates until 1870 was too harsh, some punishment was deemed necessary. A change was proposed prohibiting the holding of any office at the state or national level until a congressional pardon had been granted. The House of Representatives stood by the original clause (largely because of the efforts of Thaddeus Stevens of Pennsylvania), but the Senate substituted the milder provision, and it was passed.

Congress adjourned in July without resolving the question of what the southern states had to do to be readmitted. Tennessee quickly ratified the Fourteenth Amendment on 19 July 1866, and its congressmen were promptly readmitted, but it was not yet clear that ratification was a necessary condition for the readmission of the other former Confederate states. One year later, the passage of the Reconstruction Act of 1867 officially established it as a precondition. By that time the Republican party had been victorious in the election of 1866, and Congress was moving rapidly toward Reconstruction as advocated by Radical Republicans.

The meaning of the Fourteenth Amendment continues to be a matter of dispute. Much attention has been given to the question of "original intent"—what did the framers mean when they passed the amendment. It is difficult to be certain about the intentions of members of the Republican party since there were many close votes and numerous changes of wording on the floor of Congress. A number of scholars believe that, with the amendment's passage, states could no longer violate any of the rights included in the Bill of Rights; they are convinced that this was the express intention of the amendment's framers. Others argue the opposite: that the framers meant to protect the rights of the freedmen and not to interfere with state sovereignty over local affairs; they also worry that the original meaning of the amendment has been forgotten.

The most important part of the amendment is its first section, which includes the due process clause. A careful reading of the debates, especially the words of John A. Bingham, author of this section, and Jacob M. Howard, a moderate Republican leader in the Senate, shed light on the intentions of the Republican party. In his arguments Bingham stated, "Protection by national law from unconstitutional State enactments, is supplied by the first section of the amendment." Howard added that the section included "the personal rights guaranteed and secured by the first eight amendments of the Constitution." If these words are to be believed, the Republican party intended to enforce the Bill of Rights against any adverse action by individual states. Thus the due process clause was made binding on all states, making it a vitally important part of American legal tradition and a continuing vehicle for the protection of individual rights.

It seems unlikely, however, that there will be complete agreement in the foreseeable future over Congress's intention when it passed the Amendment. In the final analysis, the question of whether the courts should be bound by original intent remains more a political than a historical question.

[See also Reconstruction Committee, Joint.]

BIBLIOGRAPHY

Berger, Raoul. The Fourteenth Amendment and the Bill of Rights. 1989.

Curtis, Michael Kent. No State Shall Abridge: The Fourteenth Amendment and the Bill of Rights. 1986.

James, Joseph B. The Framing of the Fourteenth Amendment. 1965.

Nelson, William E. The Fourteenth Amendment: From Political Principle to Judicial Doctrine. 1988.

GLENN M. LINDEN

FRANKING. Franking is the marking of a piece of mail with an official signature or sign that indicates that the sender has the right to free mailing. Members of Congress have a franking privilege that permits them to send official mailings. Instead of a postage stamp or metered mail in the upper right-hand corner of the envelope, the member of Congress's signature on the envelope is called a frank and is recognized by the U.S. Postal Service.

Federal regulations (39 USC 3210 et seq.) provide that members of Congress may send through the mail without prepayment of postage the following materials:

Official correspondence including Mailgrams;
Public documents printed by order of Congress;
The Congressional Record and reprints of any part of its contents for official business, activities, or duties;
Seed and agriculture reports from the Department of Agriculture.

Congress has traditionally defined official correspondence to cover a wide range of matter including, but not limited to, comments on issues and legislation, newsletters, press releases, questionnaires, government reports and publications, congratulatory notes for a laudable achievement, responses to various inquiries, biographies and photographs of a member of Congress (if part of an official publication or in response to a request), and announcements.

A member may not send as franked mail personal correspondence, personal business correspondence, or political correspondence. The prohibition includes a personal letter to a friend or relative, an article or other text laudatory of any member of Congress on a personal level, rather than on an official level, a holiday greeting, a request of money or other campaign support, or a note of sympathy or congratulations, other than as a mention in otherwise frankable correspondence.

Others vested with the right to use the frank, though for fewer purposes than incumbent members of Congress, are the vice president and vice-president elect, House and Senate members-elect, resident commissioners and delegates in Congress, the Senate secretary and sergeant at arms, all elected House officers, House and Senate legislative counsels, and Senate legal counsel. Staff members working under a member or officer of Congress generally may use envelopes or labels bearing an imprint of that person's frank.

Franking privileges for members expire ninety days after they leave office, except that former Speakers of the House may use the frank as long as they deem necessary. The privileges for others expire immediately or, in some cases, no more than ninety days after leaving office.

While the word *frank* is derived from the Latin *francus* and means the right to send mail free, franking is not free. From 1972 to 1994, Congress appropriated and spent $1.5 billion on official mail. During the 1980s, Congress spent from a low of $43 million to a high of $113 million per year for postage. During fiscal year 1993, the House of Representatives received approximately 35.3 million pieces of mail and sent 159.2 million pieces, at a cost of $24.6 million for postage. That same year, the Senate received 42.4 million pieces of mail and sent 41.5 million pieces at a cost of $10.6 million. Of the total congressional mail costs, the House accounted for 79 percent, the Senate for 21 percent. Combined, Congress received 77.7 million pieces of mail and sent 200.6 million pieces, at a cost for postage of $35.2 million (see figure 1).

Historically, Congress has spent more for official mail costs in election years than in nonelection years. For example, Congress spent nearly $88 million in 1990 and $72 million in 1992, two election years, and only $43 million in 1991, a nonelection year. The decrease is primarily due to congressional reforms enacted in 1989 and 1990, which dramatically reduced franking costs.

The cost for franked mail is paid from the annual appropriation for the legislative branch in individual accounts entitled "official mail costs" for the House and Senate. Congress pays the cost of franked mail to the U.S. Postal Service as postal revenue.

The franking privilege helps to ensure that the public is kept well-informed of what their government and Congress are doing, and how Congress's leaders and elected representatives are carrying out their official duties.

History of the Franking Privilege. Franking dates back to 1660, when it was first instituted by the British House of Commons. In the United States, the franking privilege was accorded members of the Continental Congress before the adoption of the Constitution. In 1775, the First Continental Congress passed legislation that gave its legislators mailing privileges so as to better inform their constituents. It was one of the few direct means of communication between the members and their constituents.

The franking privilege began before the passage of the Post Office Act by the First Congress. According to the *Journal of the Continental Congress*, on Wednesday, 8 November 1775, it was "resolved, that all letters to and from the delegates of the United Colonies, during the session of Congress, pass, and be carried free of postage, the members having engaged upon honor not to frank or enclose any letters but their own."

On 13 October 1782 a general postal resolution was passed by the Continental Congress:

And be it further ordained by the authority aforesaid, that letters, packets, and dispatches to and from the members and secretary of Congress, while actually attending Congress, to and from the Commander in Chief of the armies of the United States, or commander of a separate army, to and from the heads of the departments or finance, or war, and of foreign affairs, of these United States, on public service shall pass and be carried free of postage. And be it ordained, that single letters, directed to any officers of the line, in actual service, shall be free of postage. (*Journal*, vol. 23, 1782, p. 678)

Figure 1
Official Mail Costs by Chamber, Fiscal Years 1972–1994

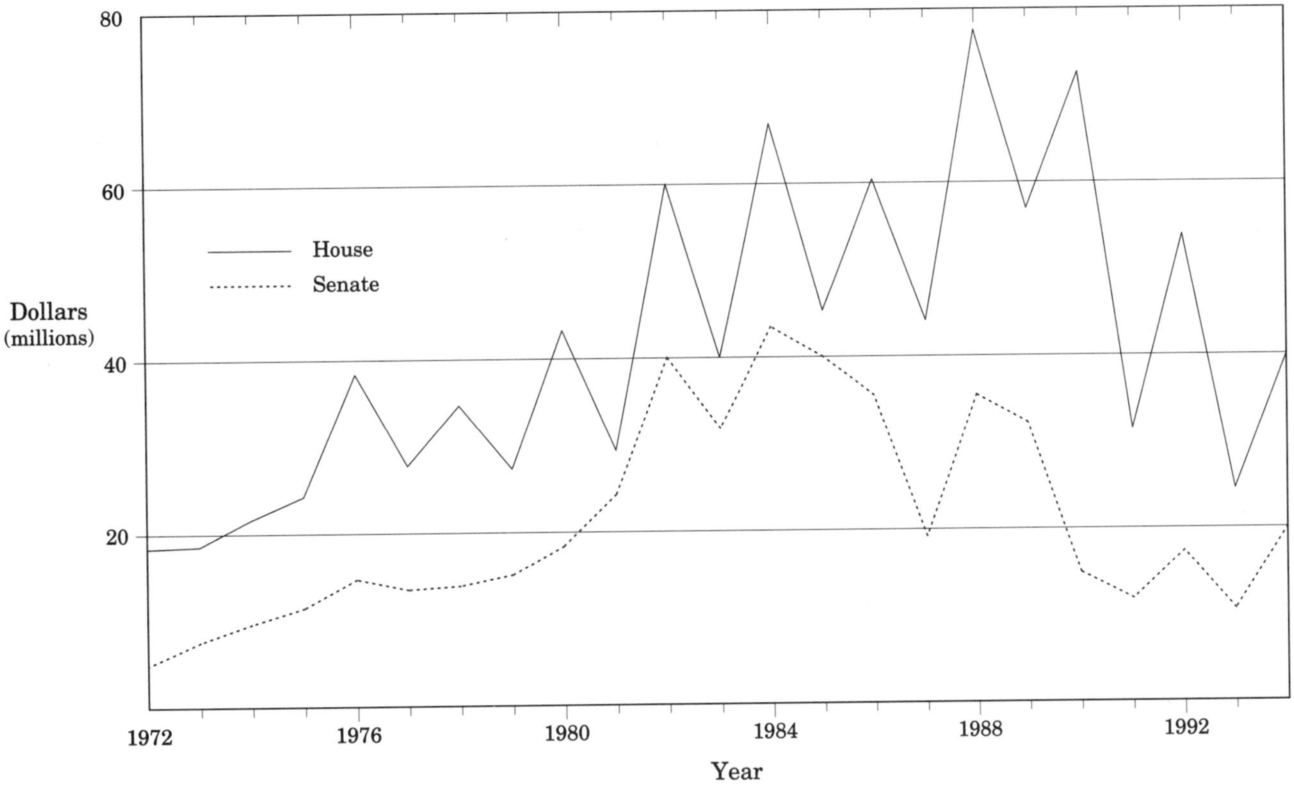

Note: Data for 1993 and 1994 estimated.

Source: John Samuels Pontius, *Official Mail Costs FY 1972 to FY 1994*, Congressional Research Service, Library of Congress, 1993.

During 1782 and 1783, the franking privilege was extended to army officers as well as to heads of departments.

In the Second Congress a committee was appointed to create a bill "to provide for the regulation of the Post Office and Post roads." Prior to passage of this bill by the House, two motions to strike the section of the bill that gave the members of Congress franking privileges were defeated. The legislation as finally passed contained the following provisions relative to the franking privilege:

That the following letters and packets, and no other, shall be received and conveyed by post, free of postage, under such restrictions as are hereinafter provided: that is to say, all letters and packets to or from the President or Vice President of the United States and all letters and packets, not exceeding two ounces in weight, or to or from any Member of the Senate or House of Representatives, the Secretary of the Senate or Clerk of the House of Representatives, during their actual attendance in any session

of the Congress and twenty days after such session. (1 Stat. 354)

Approximately this same law, with modifications, continued in force until the Act of 1845, which is the basis of the present law. According to Jack Maskell of the Congressional Research Service,

the franking privilege is granted to Members of Congress essentially to advance what is perceived as the public interest in facilitating official communications from elected officials to the citizens whom they represent. If Members were required to pay for postage from their own funds for official communications to their constituents, it is believed that few members could afford more than only selected correspondences and that therefore important exchanges of ideas, notices, reports, and assistance and services to constituents would be curtailed. (1981, p. 2)

The franking privilege has been controversial since the earliest days of the Continental Congress.

While few would quarrel with the intent behind the frank—to help members of Congress better communicate with their constituents—the privilege has, on occasion, been subject to abuse. As the frank has grown in size and cost to the government, so has the need to monitor these expenditures. Congress did terminate the frank throughout the government, for one year, in 1873. According to Doris Whitney of the Congressional Research Service,

> The Postmaster General was required to provide postage stamps or stamped envelopes of special design for each of the executive departments of the Government. The following year, Congress began to restore free franking. Since that time, the free use of the mail had been extended under three headings, namely Congressional franked mail, official penalty mail for certain departments of the Government in penalty envelopes, and personal free mail under signature for authorized persons. (1966, p. 4)

Prior to 1968, members of Congress generally turned to the Post Office Department for interpretive rulings and advisory opinions as to the frankability of materials under the "official business" test.

ABUSE OF FRANKING PRIVILEGES. Political cartoon lampooning inappropriate uses of franking by members of Congress. The cartoon portrays a congressman "who franks his clothes home to Wisconsin and has them cheaply laundered." *Harper's Weekly,* 1860.

OFFICE OF THE HISTORIAN OF THE U.S. SENATE

The Post Office ceased giving advisory opinions on the frank in December 1968, and until 1973, there were almost no restrictions on franking, when the first efforts at internal controls were undertaken.

Criticism of the Franking Privilege. In recent years, the cost of the franking privilege has been subject to scrutiny by the press and to public criticism. Opponents of the privilege claim that franking restrictions or an outright ban (either totally or only in election years) are required to eliminate the advantage franking gives to incumbents; alternatively, free mailing privileges could be accorded to qualified challengers. The present allowance is approximately $165,000 for House incumbents and about $190,000 for a senator depending on the number of addresses in a state. A 1993 Senate-passed campaign reform measure (S. 3) would have prohibited franked mass mail in any year the officeholder appeared on the ballot; this legislation is pending in the House.

Despite the use of the frank to keep constituents better informed, critics allege that the vast majority of franked mail is unsolicited. According to former Senate Rules Committee chairman Charles McC. Mathias, Jr., "mass mailings constituted 96% of the mail sent by Senators in 1982; of those, three-quarters were constituent newsletters. Only 4% were individual letters responding to inquiries or requests." (The rest, Mathias remarked, "we are casting out to the winds.")

Congress's volume of such mass mail increases noticeably during election years. While members are prohibited from sending mass mailings (five-hundred pieces of mail that are of substantially identical content) sixty days before a primary, runoff, or general election, they still manage to send a considerably higher volume of mail just before the election cutoff than during the rest of their term. The costs of the franking privilege have increased with the use of computer-generated mail and mass mailings (newsletters, town meetings notices, and other identical mail of five-hundred or more pieces), particularly in election years.

After reports of franking abuses in the 1972 elections, Common Cause challenged Congress's use of the frank, arguing in the law suit that the privilege allowed members to spend public funds for campaign purposes, giving them an unfair advantage over challengers. Undercutting the suit, Congress rushed in 1973 to amend the franking statute. The amendments prohibited mass mailings (defined as five hundred or more pieces with identical content)

United States Senate
COMMISSION ON ART
WASHINGTON, DC 20510–7102
OFFICIAL BUSINESS

Geo. J. Mitchell
U.S.S.

Mr. Michael Ross, Illustration Editor
Simon & Schuster Academic Reference Division
26th Floor
15 Columbus Circle
New York, NY 10023

A PIECE OF FRANKED MAIL. From the United States Senate Commission on Art, Sen. George J. Mitchell (D-Maine), chairman.
ACADEMIC REFERENCE DIVISION, SIMON & SCHUSTER

within four weeks of a primary or general election in which the member is a candidate for reelection. The House also established a Commission on Congressional Mailing Standards to resolve franking disputes, while the Senate empowered its Select Committee on Standards and Conduct to rule on frankable matter in that body.

In 1977 and 1981, Congress added more restrictions to franking. The preelection cutoff was extended from twenty-eight to sixty days. In 1977 the House banned the use of franked mass mailings printed and prepared with money from private or political funds; only money from appropriated funds can be used. Furthermore, the House took the cost-saving step of requiring that newsletters and other postal patron mailings be sent at the least costly postal rate.

In the Common Cause lawsuit, the Federal District Court found that the franking rules Congress adopted made a reasonable attempt to distinguish between official material that could be franked and political material that could not be sent under the frank. In 1983, the Supreme Court declined to reconsider lower court opinion in the lawsuit initiated by Common Cause. Yet the franking issue resumed in the late 1980s as the press, taxpayers groups, and members of Congress argued for greater franking reform.

Franking Reform. Recently, Congress passed a number of additional franking reforms. In 1989, the Senate and House agreed to include the Joint Item Account, "Official Mail Costs," within the Senate and House portions of the legislative branch appropriations bill, which gave each house greater control over its own franking budget.

To further reduce franking costs, the House in 1989 reduced the number of postal patron newsletter mailings from six to three. In 1989, the Senate, and in 1990, the House, established an official mail allowance from which each member pays the costs of his or her franked mail, thus limiting the amount that can be spent on official mail. The cost of franked mailings by each representative and the cost of mass mailings by each senator are publicly disclosed. Four times each year, the postmaster general issues a report, also publicly disclosed, that tabulates the estimated number of pieces and costs of franked mail for that quarter, with separate tabulations for the House and Senate.

A senator is permitted to mail the equivalent of approximately one piece of mail to each address annually. A House member's franking allowance allows three pieces to each nonbusiness address per year. The Senate in 1990 restricted senators from augmenting their franked mail funds with funds from any source, public or private. The Senate requires that mass mailings contain the public disclaimer: "Prepared, Published, and Mailed at Taxpayer Expense." In 1992, Congress prohibited House members from sending mass mailings outside their districts.

From 1991 to 1993, it was estimated that the House of Representatives saved over $100 million in franking costs as a direct result of franking reforms. The reduction has been attributed to the mail allotment system and to public disclosure. In the Senate, costs decreased from $43.6 million in fiscal year 1984 to $17.4 million in fiscal year 1992 (both election years), a dramatic reduction. Voter anger and an increase in congressional members' accountability were two major factors in the dramatic decrease in mail costs. This occurred during the time when first-class mail rates increased from 8 cents in 1972 to 29 cents in 1993.

Future Issues Surrounding Franking. Opponents of alleged franking abuse offer a number of suggestions intended to reduce franking costs still further. Some of the following ideas have been introduced as legislation by members of Congress; others come from citizen groups:

Abolish the franking privilege and establish a postage allowance.

Cut by half the official mail allowance.

Prohibit all mass mailings (five-hundred or more pieces of mail identical in content). This would eliminate newsletters, town hall meeting notices, and targeted mail. The frank would be banned unless mail is in direct response to a constituent's request for assistance. No unsolicited mail would be sent, except for press releases and correspondence with government agencies. This would dramatically reduce the use and cost of the frank, and put challengers on a more equal footing with incumbents regarding postage.

Publicly disclose all indirect costs of franking: costs of printing and acquiring mail lists; salary costs of all congressional employees who write the mass mailings; salary and costs of handling, folding, and processing the mail.

Reduce the current mail allowance in the House from three to one times the number of addresses in a member's district, an allowance similar to that in the Senate.

Prohibit House members from transferring money from other official payroll and office expense allowances to their official mail allowance. The Senate prohibits such transfers.

Prohibit postal patron mailings in an election year, which would reduce the burden challengers face against incumbents, as well as reduce franking costs.

Disclose quarterly in the *Congressional Record* individual House members' franked mailing costs.

Require a disclaimer on all House mass mailings similar to that required on all Senate mass mailings: "Prepared, Published, and Mailed at Taxpayer Expense."

Simply reduce official mail costs in the annual legislative branch appropriations bill (such amendments are typically introduced).

Defense of Franking Privilege. Against these proposals to reduce franking costs, it can be argued that further dollar or volume limits on the use of the frank may impair the ability of members of Congress to keep in touch with their constituents. Further franking limits may reduce the effectiveness of members who represent diverse constituencies—who frequently write not only from the member's district but also from across the nation.

Unlike the president, who can rely on mass media coverage to get his message to the public, members of Congress continue to rely heavily on franked mail to communicate with their constituencies. Further franking limits would put Congress at an institutional disadvantage when compared with the resources and facilities that the president and the executive branch are able to command.

[*See also* Constituency Outreach; Perquisites.]

BIBLIOGRAPHY

Congressional Quarterly Inc. *Congress A to Z.* 1988.
Congressional Quarterly Inc. *Congressional Quarterly's Guide to Congress.* 4th ed. Edited by Mary Cohn. 1991.
Maskell, Jack. *Summary of Guidelines for Congressional Franking.* Congressional Research Service, Library of Congress. CRS Rept. 81-271 A. 1981.
Pontius, John Samuels. *Official Mail Costs: Fiscal Year 1972 to Fiscal Year 1994.* Congressional Research Service, Library of Congress. 1993.
Whitney, Doris. *Origin and Development of the Franking Privilege in the United States.* Congressional Research Service, Library of Congress. 1966.
Yadlosky, Elizabeth, and Jack Maskell. *The Congressional Frank: Statutory Provision, Legislative History, Judicial Construction, and Some Proposals for Amending the Law.* Congressional Research Service, Library of Congress. CRS Rept. 80-132 D. 1980.

JOHN SAMUELS PONTIUS

FREEDOM OF INFORMATION ACT

(1966; 89 Stat. 250–251). Statutorily establishing the people's right to know about the activities and operations of government, the Freedom of Information Act provides any person—individual or corporate, regardless of nationality—with access to identifiable, unpublished, existing records of the federal departments and agencies. There is no requirement to demonstrate a need or indicate a reason for such a request. On the contrary, the government must defend its reasons for withholding, in whole or in part, responsive records.

Although the Freedom of Information (FOI) statute specifies nine categories of information that may be protected from disclosure, these exemptions do not require agencies to withhold records but merely permit access restriction. Allowance is made in the FOI law for the following exemptions:

1. Information properly classified for national defense or foreign policy purposes as secret under criteria established by an executive order
2. Information relating solely to agency internal personnel rules and practices
3. Data specifically excepted from disclosure by a statute that either requires that matters be withheld in a nondiscretionary manner or that establishes particular criteria for withholding or refers to particular types of matters to be withheld
4. Trade secrets and commercial or financial information obtained from a person and therefore privileged or confidential
5. Inter- or intra-agency memorandums or letters that would not be available by law except to an agency in litigation
6. Personnel, medical, and similar files the disclosure of which would constitute an unwarranted invasion of personal privacy
7. Certain kinds of investigatory records compiled for law enforcement purposes
8. Certain information relating to the regulation of financial institutions
9. Geological and geophysical information and data, including maps, concerning wells.

The FOI Act provides that disputes over the availability of agency records may be appealed to the head of an agency for resolution and ultimately settled in federal court.

When providing records in response to FOI Act requests, agencies may charge fees for certain activities (document search, duplication, and review) depending on the type of requester: commercial user, educational or noncommercial scientific institution whose purpose is scholarly or scientific research, news media representative, or the general public. Requested records may also be furnished by an agency without any charge or at a reduced cost, according to the law, "if disclosure of the information is in the public interest because it is likely to contribute significantly to public understanding of the operations or activities of the government, and is not primarily in the commercial interest of the requester." Both the Office of Management and Budget and the Department of Justice coordinate aspects of FOI Act policy and activities within the executive branch.

The product of eleven years of investigation and deliberation in the House of Representatives and half as many years of consideration in the Senate, the FOI Act became operative in July 1967, one year after its enactment. On three occasions—in 1974, 1976, and 1986—Congress has amended the statute to clarify its provisions or otherwise improve its functioning. As congressional source documents on and oversight evaluations of the FOI Act indicate, the statute was not generally supported as legislation or enthusiastically received as law by the departments and agencies. The 1974 amendments were adopted over a presidential veto. Diligent and continuous congressional monitoring of the administration and operation of the information access law has contributed significantly to its effective functioning. It is not, however, applicable to either house of Congress. This exclusion occurred because the withholding of information that the FOI Act was created to remedy was regarded as an executive branch problem. Congress, by contrast, published a large amount of literature concerning its activities. Furthermore, the committees developing the FOI Act focused on executive branch withholding of information and otherwise lacked jurisdiction over congressional operations. Finally, there were, and remain, constitutional restraints, such as the secret journal clause and the speech or debate clause, on applying the FOI Act to Congress.

The FOI Act has become a popular tool of inquiry and information gathering in various quarters of American society—the press, business, scholars, attorneys, consumers, and environmentalists, among others—as well as with some foreign interests. In the early 1990s, the annual volume of requests ran to about 500,000. The response to a request may amount to only a few sheets of paper or up to several linear feet of records or may provide information in an electronic format. Under the watchful eye of congressional overseers, agency information management professionals must efficiently and economically service FOI Act requests through timely supply, brokerage, or explanation.

A quarter century after its enactment, the FOI Act continued to sustain the sovereignty of the citizenry, providing a statutory declaration of the people's right to know about the activities and operations of government while offering procedures for realizing this claim. A model for similar laws adopted by foreign governments and by many of the states, the federal FOI Act remains one of the most generous expressions of information policy of its kind.

BIBLIOGRAPHY

Relyea, Harold C. "Access to Government Information: Rights and Restrictions." In *United States Government Information Policies: Views and Perspectives.* Edited by Charles R. McClure, Peter Hernon, and Harold C. Relyea. 1989. Pp. 141–160.
Relyea, Harold C. "Public Access through the Freedom of Information and Privacy Acts." In *Federal Information Policies in the 1980's: Conflicts and Issues.* Edited by Peter Hernon and Charles R. McClure. 1987. Pp. 52–82.
U.S. House of Representatives. Committee on Government Operations. *A Citizen's Guide on Using the Freedom of Information Act and the Privacy Act of 1974 to Request Government Records.* 102d Cong., 1st sess., 1991. H. Doc. 101-193.

HAROLD C. RELYEA

FREE TRADE. *See* Tariffs and Trade.

FRESHMEN. The status of freshmen members of Congress differs according to whether they are in the House or Senate and has varied dramatically over the course of American history.

In the House. In the nineteenth century, freshmen House members assumed such positions as Speaker of the House and other prominent posts. But as the House became institutionalized and the seniority system became more important, the status of the freshman declined significantly. By the mid-twentieth century, it was common to hear such admonitions as "Freshmen should be seen and not heard" and "To get along you go along." It was expected that freshmen members would serve a period of apprenticeship in which they sat back and learned the ropes. Freshmen were given the less de-

NEWLY ELECTED DEMOCRATIC REPRESENTATIVES. At a press conference, December 1992. *Left to right,* Pat Danner (Mo.), Elizabeth Furse (Oreg.), Karen Shepherd (Utah), Lynn Schenk (Calif.), and Marjorie Margolies-Mezvinsky (Pa.).

R. MICHAEL JENKINS, CONGRESSIONAL QUARTERLY INC.

sirable committee assignments and were discouraged from being too active and visible in the legislative process.

By the 1960s and 1970s, the tradition of apprenticeship had been substantially weakened. Although freshmen were still at a disadvantage vis-à-vis their more senior colleagues, they moved more rapidly than before into significant House roles. These changes occurred for a number of reasons. Certainly, the large influxes of new members chosen in the 1964, 1966, and 1974 elections were a factor. Also, societal pressures on Congress and its members made it more difficult for a newcomer to serve an apprenticeship and more difficult for senior members to keep them down. As the public's expectations for congressional action on a large number of domestic problems grew, freshmen members became more active, sometimes in response to the perceived inaction of senior members, many of whom were conservative, from the South, and hostile toward governmental problem-solving. Moreover, all House members, freshmen included, increasingly recognized that they controlled their own fate, and, as incumbents became more and more confident of reelection, the most meaningful sanctions they faced resided in their districts and their constituents—not in the party or Congress. The dramatic reforms adopted in 1975 resulted in the decentralization of power in the House, giving many more members a stake in the action, particularly through the enhancement of the subcommittee system. As freshmen with ambitions for higher office realized that positive media coverage and public recognition would facilitate their careers, they became much bolder in seeking the limelight. Since the 1970s, the seniority system has been further eroded and opportunities for freshmen have continued to open up.

Nevertheless, freshmen members still face some hurdles. They are put toward the back of the line for desired committee assignments and receive the smallest House offices. Most freshmen are at a natural disadvantage because of their unfamiliarity with House rules and procedures. Furthermore, since freshmen are less entrenched than their more senior colleagues, they will undoubtedly continue to devote the bulk of their efforts to ensuring their reelection.

According to *Congressional Quarterly*, in the post–World War II era up to 1992, the total turnover in the House has ranged from a high of 118 in 1948 to a low of 34 in 1988. The number of incumbents defeated in general elections has ranged from a high of 68 in 1948 to a low of 6 in 1986 and 1988. With the substantial turnover in 1992 due to the resignation or defeat of incumbent members, the opportunities for the freshmen of the 103d Congress to play an important role in the reform of the U.S. House were unusually great, although at the end of that Congress's first session it appeared that new members' impact would be less than originally thought. If the movement to limit members' terms continues to flourish, freshmen members of Congress may move even more quickly to become active and influential participants in the legislative process.

In the Senate. Writing about the Senate of the 1950s, Donald Matthews (1960) discussed the norm of apprenticeship as it applied to freshmen senators. Even then, Matthews quoted senior senators bemoaning the weakening of the apprenticeship norm. Since that time, apprenticeship has practically vanished from the Senate. Norman J. Ornstein and his coauthors (1993) argue that the apprenticeship norm died out because it had served the interests of only those conservative senators, in both parties, who had dominated the Senate in the 1950s. As this conservative domination weakened in the 1960s, 1970s, and 1980s, in large part because of the influx of new members who, generally, preferred a more activist Congress, the apprentice-

ship norm declined. Moreover, senators are now more likely to fashion their careers independently of their parties and are therefore less dependent on moving up the party ladder. Added to this is the fact that, increasingly, senators come to Congress from backgrounds in business, the military, or other non-political occupations—and such newcomers are simply unwilling to sit back and take a passive role.

[*See also* Members, *articles on* Congressional Careers *and* Tenure and Turnover.]

BIBLIOGRAPHY

Davidson, Roger H. *The Postreform Congress.* 1992.

Mann, Thomas E., and Norman J. Ornstein. *The New Congress.* 1981.

Matthews, Donald R. *U.S. Senators and Their World.* 1960

Ornstein, Norman J., Robert L. Peabody, and David W. Rohde. "The U.S. Senate in an Era of Change." In *Congress Reconsidered.* Edited by Lawrence C. Dodd and Bruce J. Oppenheimer. 5th ed. 1993.

HERB ASHER

FUGITIVE SLAVE ACT (1850; 9 Stat. 462–465). The most controversial part of the Compromise of 1850, the Fugitive Slave Act was designed to rectify southern complaints over the inadequacy of the 1793 statute that made the constitutional obligation to return runaway slaves to their owners a federal responsibility, a view upheld by the Supreme Court in *Prigg v. Pennsylvania* (1842).

In the supercharged sectional atmosphere of the pre–Civil War period, any law to return fugitives to slavery was bound to be controversial in the North. But the 1850 act contained several provisions, inserted at the behest of southern radicals, that were deliberately provocative. The law denied the accused fugitive a jury trial (to prevent sympathetic northern juries from ignoring the evidence and freeing the defendant), provided that cases would be heard before special commissioners rather than in regular federal courts, limited inquiry to the question of identity, and awarded the commissioner a fee of ten dollars if the alleged fugitive was returned to slavery but only five dollars if the person was freed (on the premise that additional forms had to be filled out in the first instance). Equally controversially, it empowered federal marshals to call on private citizens to assist in capturing runaway slaves and established stiff fines and jail sentences for individuals who aided fugitives or resisted the law. With a number of pro-compromise

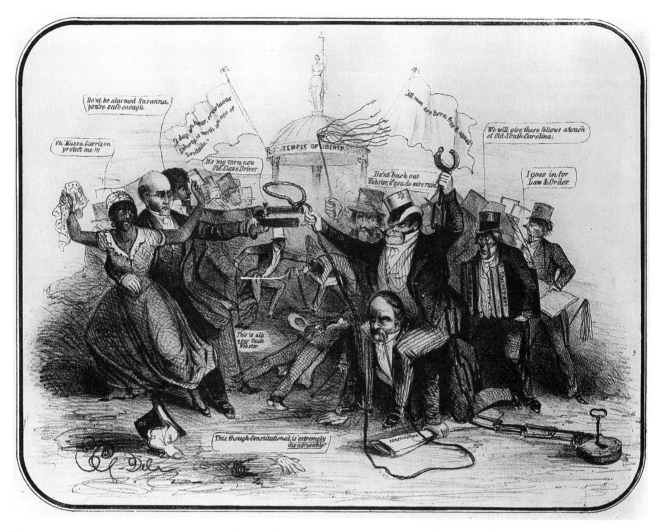

PROJECTED AFTERMATH OF THE LAW. Lithograph, c. 1850, bearing the caption, "Practical Illustration of the Fugitive Slave Law."

northerners dodging the vote, the bill passed Congress and became law in September 1850.

Precisely because antislavery people hated the law, southerners stipulated that its enforcement was a test of the North's fidelity to the Compromise of 1850. The controversy over the law was largely symbolic, for few fugitive slaves ever reached the free states, and hence southerners' economic loss was slight. In general, the law was enforced in the free states: approximately two hundred accused fugitives were seized under its provisions, and most of those were quietly returned to slavery. A handful of spectacular instances of resistance, however, greatly exacerbated sectional tensions and heightened southern anger. In several northern cities, antislavery mobs forcibly rescued blacks, acts that, while atypical, received widespread publicity. Moreover, federal efforts to convict prominent indi-

viduals in these rescue cases failed because of northerners' deep revulsion to the law.

Northern states initially refrained from interfering with the law, but, following approval of the Kansas-Nebraska Act in 1854, a number of states passed so-called personal liberty laws. These statutes, which generally prohibited state officials from cooperating with federal authorities in enforcing the Fugitive Slave Act and placed various legal roadblocks in the law's way, demonstrated the hardening of attitudes and the growing unwillingness of northerners, including many conservatives who initially supported the distasteful law, to sustain the Compromise of 1850. In 1855 the Wisconsin Supreme Court declared the Fugitive Slave Act unconstitutional, a ruling overturned by the U.S. Supreme Court in *Ableman v. Booth* (1859).

The controversy over the law was an important

factor in the unraveling of the compromise settlement of 1850. Southerners in Congress consistently rejected proposals to modify the law, and thus it remained a festering sore between the two sections. Intended to assuage southern anger, the Fugitive Slave Act accomplished little in this regard, instead revealing the growing moral chasm separating North and South in this decade.

BIBLIOGRAPHY

Campbell, Stanley W. *The Slave Catchers: Enforcement of the Fugitive Slave Law, 1850–1860.* 1970.

Hamilton, Holman. *Prologue to Conflict: The Crisis and Compromise of 1850.* 1964.

WILLIAM E. GIENAPP

FULBRIGHT, J. WILLIAM (1905–), Democratic representative and senator from Arkansas, chairman of Senate Foreign Relations Committee (1959–1974), outspoken internationalist whose criticism of U.S. foreign policy antagonized presidents from Harry S. Truman to Richard M. Nixon. Born in Sumner, Missouri, James William Fulbright moved with his parents to Fayetteville, Arkansas, a small university town in the foothills of the Ozark Mountains, when he was three. Following his father's death in 1923 and a brief stint managing his family's businesses, Fulbright graduated from the University of Arkansas and in 1925 received a Rhodes scholarship to attend Oxford University. After graduating from George Washington University Law School in 1934, he joined the antitrust division of the Justice Department, where he worked on the famous Schechter "sick chicken" case (*Schechter Poultry Corp. v. United States* [1935]), in which the Supreme Court struck down the National Industrial Recovery Act of 1933.

In 1936 he returned to Fayetteville to help with the family businesses and to teach part time at the University of Arkansas law school. In 1939 Arkansas governor Carl Bailey appointed Fulbright president of the university, making him one of the youngest college presidents in the country. Two years later he was fired by the new governor, Homer Adkins. He responded by running for the U.S. House of Representatives in the mostly rural 3d Congressional District.

During his single term as a representative (1942–1944), Fulbright made his mark as an outspoken internationalist. He lambasted latent isolationism and cosponsored the Fulbright-Connally resolution, which put Congress on record as favor-

J. WILLIAM FULBRIGHT. During Joint Economic Committee hearings, 31 January 1963.

LIBRARY OF CONGRESS

ing U.S. membership in a post–World War II collective security organization.

In 1944 Fulbright defeated his nemesis, Governor Adkins, in a run for a seat in the U.S. Senate, where he served continuously until his defeat by Dale Bumpers in 1974, after which Fulbright retired. Among his most significant legislative achievements were the Fulbright Scholars Act (1946), through which more than 200,000 Fulbright scholarships have been awarded; a measure creating a national cultural center (the Kennedy Center) in Washington, D.C.; reform of the Reconstruction Finance Corporation; and various measures stimulating the economies of the state of Arkansas and the South as a whole.

From 1952 until 1954, Fulbright waged open battle with Sen. Joseph R. McCarthy (R-Wis.) and his followers. He was the only senator to vote against renewed appropriations for McCarthy's investigative subcommittee, and he led the fight for that anticommunist demagogue's congressional censure in 1954. During the administration of John F. Kennedy, Fulbright incurred the wrath of the reactionary John Birch Society and others on the radical right by prompting Secretary of Defense Robert S. McNamara to ban political activity by anticommunist members of the military.

Throughout his early career, Fulbright's record on civil rights was segregationist. Although he worked to tone down the Southern Manifesto, a statement issued by southern Congress members condemning the 1954 *Brown v. Board of Education* decision, he nevertheless signed it. By 1965, however, Fulbright had come openly to support African Americans' right to vote and to enjoy equality under the law.

From first to last, Fulbright's major interest was foreign policy. He was initially appointed to the Senate Foreign Relations Committee in 1949. He became chairman in 1959, serving in that post for fifteen years—longer than any of his predecessors. He began his career as a "cold warrior" and a champion of executive prerogative, but by 1965 he had become convinced that the executive had been captured by hard-line anticommunists and that the Cold War and the conflict in Vietnam had spawned a military-industrial complex with a vested interest in continuing hostilities with the communist world.

In numerous speeches, interviews, and televised hearings, Fulbright championed the cause of détente and attacked such hallowed Cold War assumptions as the monolithic communist threat and the domino theory—the argument, by prowar activists, that maintenance of an independent South Vietnam was the key to preventing the fall of all Southeast Asia to communism. His criticism caused an open breach with his old friend and colleague President Lyndon B. Johnson, a breach that widened as Fulbright, his committee staff, and his allies in the press worked assiduously and successfully to destroy the popular consensus on Vietnam that Johnson had inherited.

Although he enjoyed a good working relationship with Henry Kissinger, President Nixon's national security adviser, and although he applauded Nixon's overtures to the Soviet Union and the People's Republic of China, Fulbright quickly came to believe that the Nixon administration was as committed as its predecessor to preserving American hegemony around the world and to winning a military victory in Vietnam. He uncovered the secret bombing of Cambodia, secret treaties with Thailand and Spain, and the clandestine war in Laos. His national commitments resolution of 1969 was later expanded and enacted as the War Powers Resolution of 1973. No modern political figure is more closely identified with restoring congressional prerogatives in the field of foreign policy or with reducing U.S. commitments overseas than this Arkansas intellectual, whose unbridled independence made him one of the most controversial and effective senators of his era.

BIBLIOGRAPHY

Berman, William C. *William Fulbright and the Vietnam War.* 1988.

Johnson, Haynes, and Bernard Gwertzman. *Fulbright: The Dissenter.* 1968.

RANDALL B. WOODS

FULBRIGHT SCHOLARS ACT (1946; 60 Stat. 754–755).

Sen. J. William Fulbright's experience as a Rhodes scholar coupled with his dismay over the inexperience and ignorance of U.S. leaders at the dawn of the Cold War prompted the Arkansas Democrat in 1946 to sponsor an amendment to the Surplus Property Act of 1944 that laid the foundation for the international exchange program that bears his name. At the close of World War II the United States owned millions of dollars worth of Lend-Lease matériel overseas. American manufacturers, fearing a glut of the domestic market, had compelled Congress to pass legislation forbidding its repatriation. Fulbright hit on the idea of using the proceeds from the sale of such matériel to finance study in the country in question by U.S. students and scholars. On 1 August 1946 President Harry S. Truman, with Fulbright standing beside him, signed the surplus property amendment (P.L. 584) into law.

The Fulbright Scholars Act, as it was called, provided that up to $20 million could be earmarked for educational exchanges with any one country. As the bill became law, the State Department announced that it had already completed a scholastic exchange agreement with Great Britain; soon similar agreements were being negotiated with more than twenty countries around the globe. Under the Fulbright Act, American students could receive grants to finance the cost of higher education or research in foreign countries. Academics from the United States were eligible for stipends that would fund research or lectureships at overseas universities. Foreign students were entitled to compete for money to pay for transportation to the United States for study at universities and colleges.

Over the years the Fulbright Act was expanded on several occasions. In 1948 the U.S. Information and Education Exchange Act (Smith-Mundt Act) made possible exchanges to countries that had not signed agreements. Congress began an annual appropriation to fund the program. In both 1953 and 1954, citing competition with the Communist bloc as justification, Congress doubled the number of countries eligible to enter into formal exchange agreements and substantially increased the money available. Finally, in 1961, the Fulbright-Hays Act brought together the various pieces of legislation affecting educational exchange. Very early in the exchange program, through the medium of binational commissions, host countries began contributing substantially to the exchange program. Between 1949 and 1991, 212,514 men and women participated in the Fulbright Exchange Program.

BIBLIOGRAPHY

Glazer, Nathan, ed. *The Fulbright Experience and Academic Exchanges*. The Annals of the American Academy of Political and Social Science, vol. 491. 1987.

Johnson, Walter, and Francis Colligan. *The Fulbright Program*. 1968.

RANDALL B. WOODS

G

GAG RULE. Since the late eighteenth century, in both the United States and Great Britain, the term *gag rule* has referred to formal restrictions on political speech. Then, as now, use of the word *gag* has implied a constraint that exceeded accepted rules of debate or violated established rights of free speech. Congressional critics of the Sedition Act of 1798 called the legislation a *gag law*. Within the first decade of the nineteenth century, American political writers used *gag rule* to refer to congressional limitations on floor debate.

The most notorious gag rule was that passed by the House of Representatives on 26 May 1836 in response to a petition campaign demanding the abolition of slavery and the slave trade in the District of Columbia. House Rule XXI ordered that all petitions dealing with slavery were to be laid on the table without printing or referral. The House renewed some form of the gag rule in each ensuing Congress until 3 December 1844, when John Quincy Adams's motion for repeal finally won approval. The Senate in March 1836 rejected John C. Calhoun's motion to refuse all antislavery petitions but approved James Buchanan's compromise motion that ostensibly affirmed the right of petition by allowing the Senate to receive antislavery petitions that would then be rejected without referral or consideration. Throughout the antebellum period, gag rule applied to any attempt to restrict debate on slavery.

In more recent years, gag rule has applied to unusual limits on the debate and amendment of legislation before the House of Representatives. One example is closed rules that allow only committee amendments.

BIBLIOGRAPHY

Peterson, Merrill D. *The Great Triumvirate: Webster, Clay, and Calhoun.* 1987.

BRUCE A. RAGSDALE

GALLERIES. Ringing the House and Senate chambers, galleries allow the public and media to view congressional floor proceedings. Although the Constitution did not mandate open sessions, the popularly elected House opened its gallery in Federal Hall in New York City to the public on 8 April 1789, two days after establishing its first quorum. Upstairs on the second floor the smaller Senate chamber contained no gallery. Even after moving to Congress Hall in Philadelphia, the Senate met in closed session until 9 December 1795, when construction of a gallery was completed, and even then opened only its legislative proceedings. Until 1929 the Senate routinely emptied the galleries during executive sessions dealing with treaties and nominations.

Doorkeepers under the supervision of the House and Senate sergeants at arms regulated traffic into the galleries and enforced the rules of each chamber. Nineteenth-century citizens and foreign visitors showed such interest in congressional debates that they packed the galleries to capacity. "Never were the amphitheaters of Rome more crowded by the highest ranks of both sexes than the Senate chamber," Margaret Bayard Smith wrote during the Webster-Hayne debate of 1830. "Every seat, every inch of ground, even the steps, were *completely* filled." Tickets to the public galleries were first is-

SILK CAMPAIGN RIBBON. For Democrat Martin Van Buren's 1840 presidential campaign. The ribbon disparagingly links the opposition Whig party to the defunct Federalist party, which had backed the Sedition Act of 1798, referred to as a gag law by its congressional critics. (*See previous page.*)

COLLECTION OF DAVID J. AND JANICE L. FRENT

sued in 1868 to meet the immense demand for admittance to the Senate's impeachment trial of President Andrew Johnson. Thereafter, visitors received gallery tickets from their senators and representatives.

In the 1850s, construction of new chambers provided greatly expanded gallery seating. Galleries to the left of the chair were assigned to women and their male escorts, while galleries to the right of the chair were open to men only. The central gallery above the chair was reserved for the press. Later, galleries were set aside for diplomats, staff, and members' families and guests. Although the galleries were never officially segregated by race, when segregation became common in Washington the doorkeepers tacitly steered African American visitors to separate seating.

Rules require that members of Congress neither address the galleries nor introduce special visitors in the galleries. During dramatic debates and votes, presiding officers often admonish the galleries against applause or other demonstrations and sometimes threaten to clear the galleries following outbursts. Gallery visitors may not read, write, or take photographs. These rules have arisen because of the long lines of visitors waiting for available seats in the galleries and the desire to prevent any disturbance to the floor proceedings. In 1916, when President Woodrow Wilson addressed a joint session of Congress, suffragists unfurled a banner over the gallery railing with the message: "Mr. President, What Will You Do for Woman Suffrage?" Since then, rules have restricted visitors from placing any items on the railings or from leaning over them.

After Puerto Rican nationalists fired shots from the House gallery and wounded several representatives in 1954, some members talked of installing glass partitions between the galleries and the chambers. Congress rejected these proposals, but in later years metal screening devices outside the gallery entrances helped augment security.

As a symbol of democratic government, the galleries remain open, day or night, whenever the Senate and House are in session. Only during rare executive sessions dealing with highly classified information is the public excluded from the congressional galleries.

[*See also* Press Galleries; Violence, *article on* Violence against Congress.]

BIBLIOGRAPHY

Byrd, Robert C. *The Senate, 1789–1989: Addresses on the History of the United States Senate.* Vol. 2. 1991.

Smith, Margaret Bayard. *The First Forty Years of Washington Society.* 1906.

DONALD A. RITCHIE

GAO. *See* General Accounting Office.

GARFIELD, JAMES A. (1831–1881), Republican representative from Ohio, twentieth president of the United States. The only American president to be elected directly from the House of Representatives to the White House, James Abram Garfield deserves to be at least as well remembered for his seventeen years' service in the Congress as for his two hundred days' tenure in the presidency. First elected to Congress in 1862 while still a general in the Union army, Garfield was naturally placed on the Military Affairs Committee. Along with Robert C. Schenck (R-Ohio) and Henry Winter Davis (Unconditional Unionist, Md.) he urged more vigorous prosecution of the Civil War and a program of radical reconstruction. His most notable legislative accomplishment was the creation of the Department of Education in 1867, but his real legislative passion was economic issues, where his moderate instincts and scholarly background led him to advocate hard money and lower tariffs.

His tariff policy was somewhat constrained by the conflicting interests of his constituents. Although the 19th Congressional District in the Western Reserve section of northeastern Ohio, which had been long represented by noted abolitionist Joshua R. Giddings, was united in its support of radical measures of reconstruction, it was sharply divided along economic lines, with iron furnaces at one end of the district, farms at the other, and sheep ranches in between.

Garfield's repeated reelections, usually by overwhelming margins, were testimony to his skill in reconciling these varied interests. At a time when few congressmen were able to win more than two terms, Garfield held his seat from 1863 to 1880, and was seriously challenged only in 1874, when his involvement in the Crédit Mobilier scandal and the "salary grab" rendered him vulnerable.

The seniority and experience accumulated during his long tenure carried Garfield to a position of leadership among congressional Republicans as he rose through the committee structure. In the post–Civil War years he was chairman of the Military Affairs Committee, presiding over the orderly reduction of the swollen military establishment. As

JAMES A. GARFIELD. As president.

chairman of the Committee on Banking and Currency in the 41st Congress (1869–1871), he led the investigation into the Black Friday stock-market collapse. He reached the peak of his influence as chairman of the House Appropriations Committee from 1871 to 1875, where he strove to establish congressional control over the previously haphazard budget-making process.

Had the Republican party retained control of Congress, Garfield would likely have become Speaker of the House, although his indecisive temperament might have proved a liability in that position. Instead, he served as Republican minority leader from 1875 to 1880, using his ready eloquence to harass the Democratic majority and his conciliatory personality to hold Republican factions together during the stormy administration of Rutherford B. Hayes.

It was this conciliatory quality that made Garfield acceptable as a dark-horse choice by the the Republican convention in 1880. Ironically, his brief presidential administration was marked by conflict, most notably with the powerful Republican senator from New York, Roscoe Conkling. Conkling and his junior colleague, Thomas C. Platt, objected to Garfield's nominee for collector of the Port of New York. They appealed to the principle of senatorial courtesy to defeat it, but after a struggle that consumed much of the first session of the 47th Congress, Garfield prevailed. Conkling and Platt resigned their seats, the tradition of senatorial courtesy was dealt a heavy blow, and the authority of the executive branch relative to the Senate was elevated from its post–Civil War low, thereby beginning that steady accretion of presidential power that characterizes the modern presidency.

Garfield himself would have little time to savor this triumph. On 2 July 1881 he was shot down by a demented religious fanatic, Charles J. Guiteau. He died on 19 September and was succeeded by Vice President Chester A. Arthur.

BIBLIOGRAPHY

Hinsdale, Burke A., ed. *The Works of James Abram Garfield.* 2 vols. 1882.
Peskin, Allan. *Garfield.* 1978.

ALLAN PESKIN

GARNER, JOHN NANCE (1868–1967), representative from Texas, Democratic floor leader (1929–1931), Speaker of the House (1931–1933), and vice president of the United States (1933–1941). Garner was known for his rough-hewn personality, legislative effectiveness, and his dramatic break with President Franklin D. Roosevelt. Labor leader John L. Lewis once referred to Garner as a "labor-baiting, poker-playing, whiskey-drinking, evil old man." There was enough truth in the characterization that decades later it was still commonly applied to Garner. Yet Garner was far more than that. He was a rugged representative of a rapidly disappearing frontier. Born in a log cabin in Red River County, Texas, only three years after the American Civil War, educated in country schools, unable to succeed at Vanderbilt Law School because of his poor educational background, Garner read law in the less academically challenging environment of a Red River County law office, became an attorney, and entered politics. Due to poor health, he sought a dry climate and moved to Uvalde, Texas, deep in the southwestern part of the state. There he became the representative of the scantly populated 15th Congressional District. Garner was elected to the House in 1902 and was continuously reelected until his resignation in 1933 to become vice president. Although from time to time Garner faced serious opposition, he never conducted a major reelection campaign and rarely even gave political speeches.

JOHN NANCE GARNER. On the steps of the Capitol.
LIBRARY OF CONGRESS

At the beginning of his congressional career, Garner was in the minority and assigned to minor committees. He quickly developed a network of personal ties in the House, however. Garner had a rough, homespun style, got along well with people, and enjoyed camaraderie, drinking, cards, and gambling. In his second term he was appointed to the Foreign Affairs Committee, an assignment that led to a close friendship with Rep. Nicholas Longworth (R-Ohio).

With the election of 1910, Democrats gained control of the House and Garner became party whip. In 1913, he passed up the chair of the House Foreign Affairs Committee to become a member of the Ways and Means Committee. He cultivated a reputation for being a watchdog of the federal purse, supported the creation of the Federal Reserve System, pushed for a graduated income tax, and supported a selective tariff to protect U.S. producers from cheap labor in other countries.

Speaker James Beauchamp (Champ) Clark's presidential ambitions had been thwarted by Woodrow Wilson, and the House majority leader, Claude Kitchin (D-N.C.), was opposed to U.S. entry in World War I. Wilson therefore could not work with the Democratic leadership, so Garner functioned as liaison between the White House and the House of Representatives. With the Republicans' return to power in both Congress and the White House in the 1920s, Garner devoted his energies to tariff and tax issues. He was especially critical of the fiscal policies pursued by the Harding and Coolidge administrations, which he viewed as benefiting the very rich.

In 1929, Garner became the minority leader while Longworth, his longtime friend, became the Republican Speaker. Much House business was transacted between the two men in an office in the Capitol nicknamed the Board (or Bureau) of Education. There, Longworth and Garner would meet after hours with their protégés to drink, swap political gossip, and make political deals.

The Republicans lost control of the House in 1931 after several of their members died in office and were replaced by Democrats. With his party back in power, Garner was elected Speaker on 7 December 1931. Although Garner had always opposed the sales tax, his most controversial act as Speaker was to support a balanced budget in 1932; he urged that new taxes be raised, even if those taxes were sales taxes. Garner clashed with President Herbert Hoover on measures to deal with the Depression, particularly over Garner's support for a major public works bill that Hoover denounced as a pork-barrel measure.

With the 1932 presidential election campaign, Garner became a candidate for the presidency. Backed by Texas as a favorite son and also by the Hearst newspapers, Garner refused to participate in a stop-Roosevelt movement. He accepted the Dem-

ocratic vice presidential nomination and in 1932 the Roosevelt-Garner ticket carried forty-two of the forty-eight states.

He was an active vice president, attending cabinet meetings and serving as a communications channel between the White House and Congress. Although Garner supported early New Deal programs, his views later diverged from those of the president. For example, while he embraced the recovery measures of Roosevelt's first administration, he was unhappy with and sometimes actively opposed the reform programs of the second administration, believing them to be spendthrift policies with a strong leftist tinge. Most significantly, Garner was against the president's serving a third term. By 1939, the conflicts between Garner and Roosevelt were irreparable. Garner mounted an ill-fated bid for the Democratic presidential nomination in 1940. His effort was doomed as it became increasingly clear that Roosevelt would seek a third term. With the Democratic convention's "draft" of Roosevelt for the nomination in 1940, Henry A. Wallace was chosen as Roosevelt's running mate.

Garner continued serving as vice president until the end of his term, then left Washington for retirement at his home in Uvalde, where he became a revered folk figure. He died on 7 November 1967, just two weeks before his ninety-ninth birthday.

BIBLIOGRAPHY

Fisher, O. C. *Cactus Jack*. 1982.
James, Marquis. *Mr. Garner of Texas*. 1939.
Timmons, Bascom N. *Garner of Texas: A Personal History*. 1948.

ANTHONY CHAMPAGNE

GENERAL ACCOUNTING OFFICE.

With 4,900 employees (as of 1993), the General Accounting Office (GAO) is the largest of the congressional support agencies. Created in 1921 by the Budget and Accounting Act, the GAO attempts to ferret out waste, fraud, and abuse in the management of federal programs. In addition, the GAO offers advice to Congress on a wide variety of policy-relevant topics.

The GAO differs from other congressional support agencies in several respects: it is much larger (twenty times larger than the Congressional Budget Office); it relies more heavily on regional offices (located in fourteen cities); it is more independent, thanks to a comptroller general who is appointed for a fifteen-year term; it is more controversial, because it routinely attacks federal agencies and federal programs; it is more visible, because its reports often generate considerable media publicity; and it has governmentwide duties, acting, in effect, as the audit agency of the federal government. Like other congressional support agencies, however, the GAO is guided by congressional moods and by specific congressional requests. The GAO is also subject to formal congressional oversight and to Congress's power of the purse.

Evolution of the GAO. Until the mid-1960s the GAO focused primarily on audits of federal agencies. To perform these tasks, the GAO hired accountants. Its work, though useful, received little attention in the mass media and was often taken for granted on Capitol Hill. This began to change in the mid-1960s, when Congress asked the GAO to evaluate new federal programs, especially antipoverty programs associated with Lyndon B. Johnson's Great Society. Although the GAO often focused on program implementation rather than program results, the latter received some attention.

The GAO's program-evaluation role became further institutionalized in 1970, when the Legislative Reorganization Act required the GAO to "review and analyze the results of Government programs and activities carried on under existing law, including the making of cost benefit studies." The Congressional Budget and Impoundment Control Act of 1974 expanded the GAO's program-evaluation role and required the GAO to set up a program review and evaluation office. This office eventually became the Program Evaluation and Methodology Division (PEMD), which hired social science academics to conduct increasingly sophisticated evaluations of federal programs.

At the same time, the GAO was placing less emphasis on traditional audits. The General Accounting Act of 1974 transferred some of the GAO's audit functions to the General Services Administration, thus relieving the GAO of these time-consuming responsibilities. Such steps transformed the GAO from a low-profile auditing agency into a highly visible source of policy advice.

The GAO's Agenda. Congressional interest in the GAO and its work heightened as a result of two developments. The first was the GAO's growing capacity for policy analysis and program evaluation. The second was Congress's growing interest in legislative oversight of the bureaucracy. The latter played to the GAO's strengths as a "counterbureaucracy"—that is, an agency required by law to monitor and report wrongdoing by other government agencies.

As a result of these changes, GAO reports proliferated. At the same time, congressional committees took a more active interest in the subject and content of GAO reports. When Elmer Staats took over as comptroller general in 1966, less than 10 percent of the GAO's reports were requested by members of Congress. In 1992, Comptroller General Charles Bowsher reported that 80 percent of the GAO's reports were requested by members of Congress, usually congressional committee or subcommittee chairmen. Although the importance of the distinction between requested and unrequested reports can be overdrawn, there has clearly been a trend toward more requested reports.

GAO reports encompass a wide range of topics, from defense procurement to transportation to environmental protection to welfare reform. In general, GAO reports reflect the current preoccupations of Congress. For example, in 1991 and 1992 the GAO issued numerous reports on health policy—a reflection of growing congressional interest in health care reform. Less visible issues receive less attention. By virtue of its size, however, the GAO can devote at least some attention to such obscure topics as Census Bureau methodology, Social Security Administration computers, and the spread of the Western spruce budworm.

Strategies and Tactics. The GAO serves Congress primarily by scrutinizing and criticizing federal administrative agencies. Most GAO reports are critical of federal agencies, and most include recommendations for administrative reform. Clearly, the GAO takes its role as a counterbureaucracy seriously.

Increasingly, the GAO has been willing to advise Congress directly, and GAO testimony on Capitol Hill has increased dramatically. In 1985, GAO officials testified on Capitol Hill a total of 117 times. In 1990, GAO officials testified a total of 306 times, more often than any other agency except for the Department of Defense.

Under Comptroller General Bowsher, the GAO has also made a concerted effort to offer policy recommendations. Bowsher also initiated an unusual series of transition reports, issued just after the 1988 presidential election. These reports, which aroused considerable interest and controversy, criticized the federal government's lack of progress in a number of policy areas and made explicit recommendations for reform.

Policy Impact. The GAO's impact on public policy has not been systematically evaluated. One recent study did find, however, that GAO reports are

ORGANIZATION OF THE GENERAL ACCOUNTING OFFICE

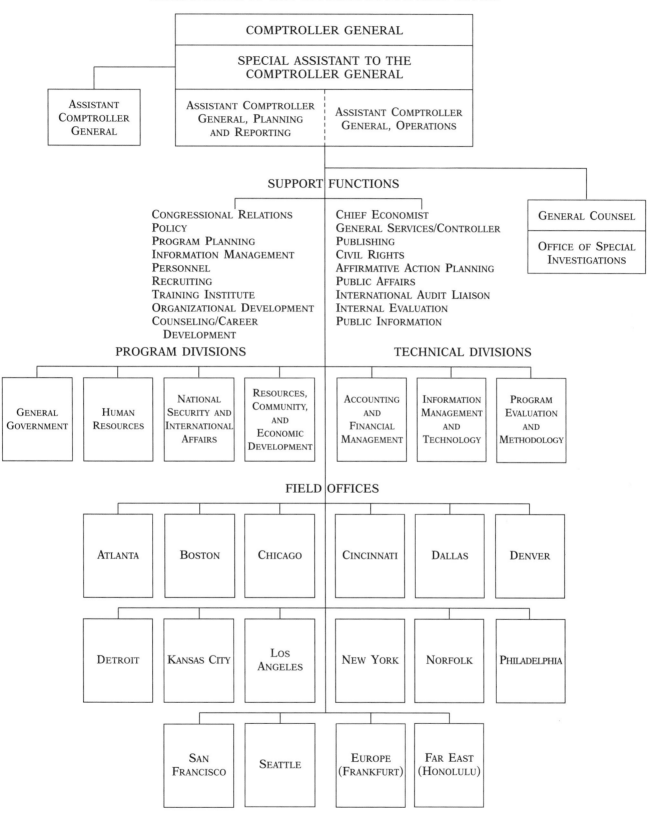

SOURCE: *U.S. Government Manual*

frequently cited by congressional staff members as examples of public policy reports with which they are personally familiar. Indeed, of eighty-three evaluation studies cited, 71 percent were GAO reports.

The impact of GAO reports on policy depends in part on the timeliness of their release. Recognizing this, the GAO attempts to issue reports without delay. Often, however, it is impossible to release a report as quickly as Congress would like. The clarity of GAO reports also seems to make a difference. With this in mind, the GAO has in recent years stressed readability and accessibility, achieved through crisply written summaries, the use of clearer typefaces, and improved graphics.

Beyond these factors, congressional committees are likely to differ in their receptiveness to GAO reports. Constituency committees, with well-established commitments to programs that benefit constituents, may be less receptive to GAO reports (which often criticize such programs) than are policy committees, whose members are less constrained by constituents. Thus the House Public Works and Transportation Committee might be less responsive to GAO reports than the House Energy and Commerce Committee. This generality has not, however, been fully investigated.

Role Conflicts. Like other congressional support agencies, the GAO sometimes experiences role conflicts. The GAO is called on to decide whether to pursue its own agenda or the agenda of congressional committee chairs, whether to criticize administrative agencies or Congress itself, and whether to be drawn into partisan debates or remain aloof. These conflicts are not easily resolved.

The most frequent conflict is between professionalism, on the one hand, and responsiveness, on the other. The GAO has hired large numbers of highly skilled auditors and analysts, whose professional norms structure their response to work assignments. At the same time, the GAO is extremely aware of its responsibilities to Congress. When members of Congress define the GAO's responsibilities in parochial or particularistic terms, problems may arise. For example, Sen. Christopher S. Bond (R-Mo.) became upset when, in 1992, the GAO conducted a study of the Missouri River basin and reached conclusions inimical to the interests of Bond's "downstream" constituents. Although Bond focused on methodological flaws in the GAO's research procedures, he appeared to be concerned above all with the GAO's conclusions and their implications for his state. Ironically, the GAO got embroiled in this controversy by acceding to a request for a report from two members of Congress who represented states "upstream" of Missouri.

Some of the most bitter disputes over the GAO's role arise during periods of divided government, when the legislative and executive branches are controlled by different political parties. By deferring to congressional committee chairs, the GAO inadvertently defers to members of one political party. If its reports are highly critical of the executive branch, the GAO may be accused of partisanship, even though it carried out its assignment in good faith. Thus, responsiveness may be mistaken for partisanship.

The General Accounting Office assists Congress in several different ways—through formal reports, prepared testimony, briefing sessions, and informal advice. Members of Congress, in turn, utilize GAO input in a variety of ways—to support positions they have already taken, to anticipate emerging problems, to fine-tune legislative proposals, and even to rethink fundamental assumptions. Although most GAO reports focus on administrative failures, some reports identify legislative mistakes and recommend legislative remedies. Moreover, the GAO's strong administrative oversight role seems fully consistent with renewed congressional interest in the oversight function. In this respect, as in many others, the GAO's activities seldom deviate very far from congressional expectations.

[*See also* Legislative Reorganization Acts; Oversight.]

BIBLIOGRAPHY

Boyer, John, and Laura Langbein. "Factors Influencing the Use of Health Evaluation Research in Congress." *Evaluation Review* 15, no. 5 (1991): 507–532.

Mosher, Frederick. *A Tale of Two Agencies: A Comparative Analysis of the GAO and the OMB.* 1984.

Weiss, Carol. "Congressional Committees as Users of Analysis." *Journal of Policy Analysis and Management* 8, no. 3 (1989): 411–431.

WILLIAM T. GORMLEY, JR.

GENERAL WELFARE CLAUSE. Among Congress's enumerated powers in Article I of the Constitution is the "Power to lay and collect Taxes, Duties, Imposts and Excises, to pay the Debts and provide for the common Defence and general Welfare of the United States." On its face, the "general Welfare" portion of the clause would seem to vest very broad powers in Congress. It is commonly accepted, however, that the power to provide for the general welfare is a qualification of the spending and taxing power. In other words, provision for the general welfare is the purpose for which taxes may be imposed and spending accomplished.

The *Federalist* reveals a difference of opinion as to the scope of the phrase "general Welfare" within this constraint. Alexander Hamilton argued for a broad interpretation. James Madison, on the other hand, contended that the clause was simply a reference to the other powers delegated to Congress elsewhere in Article I. In *United States v. Butler* (1936), the Supreme Court adopted Hamilton's view, holding that the power to tax and spend for the general welfare is not limited by the direct grants of power enumerated elsewhere in Article I. The general welfare clause combined with the necessary and proper clause thus creates broad authority to determine the best means to provide for the general welfare.

The Court defers to congressional judgments of what is necessary to promote the general welfare. Challenges based on the general welfare clause to two congressional actions—campaign finance reform legislation (*Buckley v. Valeo* [1974]) and a congressional requirement imposed on federal highway funds that states enact a minimum drinking age of twenty-one (*South Dakota v. Dole* [1987])—were unsuccessful. In both, the Court reiterated the broad power of Congress to promote the general welfare through its spending decisions. In the latter case, in fact, the Court noted that the level of deference that has been accorded to congressional judgment with respect to the general welfare raised questions about whether the general welfare clause presents a judicially enforceable limitation on congressional power. *South Dakota v. Dole* and numerous other cases also demonstrate Congress's formidable power to impose conditions and qualifications on the receipt of federal funds to provide for the general welfare and promote national goals.

[*See also* Buckley v. Valeo.]

BIBLIOGRAPHY

Tribe, Laurence. *American Constitutional Law.* 2d ed. 1988. P. 321.

U.S. Senate. *The Constitution of the United States of America, Analysis and Interpretation.* 99th Cong., 1st sess., 1988. S. Doc. 99-16.

RICHARD EHLKE

GENOCIDE CONVENTION.

The United Nations General Assembly adopted the Convention on the Prevention and Punishment of the Crime of Genocide on 9 December 1948. A response to Adolf Hitler's persecutions, the treaty binds its parties to prevent and punish persons committing genocide, defined as the intentional destruction of any national, ethnic, racial, or religious group by measures such as killing or harming its members. The treaty entered into force on 12 January 1951, after ratification or adherence by twenty nations. By 1992 more than one hundred countries had become parties.

The United States signed the convention on 11 December 1948, and on 16 June 1949 President Harry S. Truman submitted it to the Senate for advice and consent. Although senators agreed that genocide was abhorrent, the treaty remained pending in the Senate for almost thirty-seven years. The Senate Foreign Relations Committee favorably reported the treaty with three understandings and one declaration in 1970, 1971, 1973, 1976, and 1984. But strong Senate opposition arose on such issues as the scope of the treaty power, the balance of state and federal jurisdiction in criminal matters, and whether the treaty would require extradition of U.S. citizens to other countries where they might be charged with genocide.

On 18 July 1985, the committee reported the convention with two reservations, five understandings, and one declaration. The Senate gave its advice and consent with the eight conditions on 19 February 1986, by a vote of 83 to 11. The reservations required the consent of the United States to the submission of any dispute under the convention to the International Court of Justice and stated that nothing in the convention authorized U.S. action prohibited by the Constitution. Implementing legislation approved on 4 November 1988 (P.L. 100-606) established genocide as a crime in the federal criminal code. The treaty entered into force for the United States on 23 February 1989.

BIBLIOGRAPHY

U.S. Senate. Committee on Foreign Relations. *Report on the International Convention on the Prevention and Punishment of the Crime of Genocide.* 81st Cong., 1st sess., 1985. Exec. Rept. 99-2.

ELLEN C. COLLIER

GEORGE, JAMES Z.

(1826–1897), Democratic senator from Mississippi. George served as a member of the Mississippi secession convention and then in the Confederate army. In 1875 he led the Democratic party in wresting power from the Republican state government. Four years later, he became chief justice of the state supreme court.

After a bitterly contested election, George entered the Senate in 1881, joining fellow Mississippi Democrat Lucius Q. C. Lamar. Although sometimes associated with the conservative Democrats of the Cleveland administration, George usually opposed the eastern regional orientation and big business bias of the national party and often differed with the conservative Lamar wing of the Mississippi Democratic party. George favored federal antitrust legislation and regulation of railroads. He opposed protective tariffs as being unfair to farmers and laborers and obstructive to the South's prospects for attracting industry.

George's attempts to reverse what he considered economic distortion favoring the wealthier areas of the country included support for reforms in banking and bankruptcy laws and monetary inflation through coinage of silver; he believed these would make the financial system fairer to the economically weak and to his largely rural and agricultural region. For the same reason, he favored direct federal aid to education.

George participated in the Mississippi constitutional convention of 1890. He sponsored and later defended the constitutional provisions that dramatically curtailed voting by blacks and poor whites through literacy and tax requirements. Thus, he embodied the mix of relative economic liberalism and hostility to civil rights for blacks that so frequently characterized southern members of Congress until the late twentieth century. Twice reelected, George served as senator until his death on 14 August 1897.

BIBLIOGRAPHY

Peck, Lucy. "The Life and Times of James Z. George." Ph.D. diss., Mississippi State University, 1964.
Ringold, Mary Spencer. "Senator James Zachariah George of Mississippi: Bourbon or Liberal?" *Journal of Mississippi History* 12 (1954): 164–182.

JAMES B. MURPHY

GEORGE, WALTER F. (1879–1957), Democratic senator from Georgia, chairman of the committees on Finance and Foreign Relations, and patriarch of the Senate in his later years. Walter Franklin George rose from the status of tenant farmer's son to that of one of the most powerful members of the Senate. George earned a law de-

gree from Mercer University in 1901 and won his first political campaign in a race for district attorney in 1906. He later served as a superior court judge, a state appellate court judge, and a justice on the state's highest court. George won an election to fill an unexpired Senate term in 1922. He entered the Senate as an isolationist but became a strong supporter of increased American involvement in world affairs and led the fights for the Lend-Lease Act, the United Nations, the Marshall Plan, SEATO, foreign aid, and the creation of a bipartisan foreign policy after World War II.

George remained a fiscal conservative throughout his career and ably defended corporate interests. Although critics accused him of showing little concern for the disadvantaged, George did support vocational education, rural electrification, and social security. He became an authority on both finance and foreign affairs, serving as chairman of the Finance Committee for ten years (1941–1946 and 1949–1953) and the Foreign Relations Committee for six years (1939–1943 and 1955–1957). The seventy-eight-year-old George, facing a serious challenge from former governor Herman E. Talmadge, declined to seek reelection in 1956. President Dwight D. Eisenhower then appointed him ambassador to NATO, a position he held until his death in 1957. The *Atlanta Journal* lamented that the state had lost "one of the greatest of all Georgians." He represented his state in the Senate for thirty-four years.

BIBLIOGRAPHY

Cobb, James C. "Walter Franklin George." In *Famous Georgians*. Edited by Kenneth Coleman and Jackie Erney. 1976.
Mellichamp, Josephine. *Senators from Georgia*. 1976.
Robinson, James A. *Congress and Foreign Policy Making*. 1962. Pp. 54–55.
White, William H. "Senator George: Monumental, Determined." *New York Times Magazine*, 13 March 1955.

HAROLD P. HENDERSON

GEORGIA. Founded as an English colony by James Oglethorpe in 1733, Georgia was the fourth state to ratify the Constitution (31 December 1787) and join the Union. William Few and James Gunn were Georgia's first senators and Abraham Baldwin, James Jackson, and George Mathews the first representatives. In 1790 Georgia had only two seats in the House but was given four following the 1800 census. The state reached a high of twelve seats in 1910 but fell back to ten in 1930 and remained at

HOWELL COBB (D-GA.). Chairman of the convention of delegates from the seceded states, 1861–1862.

that level until 1990, when an eleventh seat was added.

Georgia's early congressional delegations were most interested in matters of trade and western expansion as evidenced by congressional involvement in solving the infamous Yazoo land fraud cases in 1795 and 1796 and the Georgia delegation's opposition to the Bank of the United States and the Hamiltonian economic program of 1791. Georgians supported the Indian Removal Act of 1830, which provoked serious controversy about the removal of the Cherokee Indians to western reservations, opposed protective tariffs in the 1830s and then supported them in the 1840s, and while supporting states rights, opposed the nullification doctrine espoused by neighboring South Carolina. Georgians

were split on the Wilmot Proviso but followed the leadership of Rep. Howell Cobb, Speaker of the House in the 31st Congress, who led the Unionist Democrats in Georgia in support of the Compromise of 1850.

Georgia joined other southern slave states in seceding from the Union on 18 January 1861. The state's congressional seats remained vacant until 25 July 1868 when six House members were temporarily seated. The state was formally readmitted to the Union 15 July 1870, and a full delegation was seated in January 1871. Important leaders in Congress in the pre–Civil War period included Sen. William H. Crawford and Speaker Howell Cobb. Notable Georgians in the post–Civil War period included Senators Robert Toombs and John B. Gordon and Representatives Alexander H. Stephens, populist Thomas E. Watson, Speaker Charles F. Crisp, and Georgia's first African American Congress member, Rep. Jefferson F. Long. In 1922, Rebecca L. Felton, a Georgian, became the first woman to serve in the Senate. Felton, at age eighty-seven, was also the oldest person to become a first-time senator, and served the shortest term—two days. Since the Civil War Georgia has been dominated by the Democratic party, which provided all of Georgia's elected officials to Congress until 1964, when Howard H. Callaway, a Republican, was elected to the House. Georgia's first Republican elected statewide since Reconstruction was Sen. Mack Mattingly, elected in 1980.

Georgians understood the value of seniority and continued to elect and reelect capable men to serve in Congress. In the House the best example is Rep. Carl Vinson, who served forty years (1914–1965), chaired the Naval Affairs and the Armed Services committees, and was the father of the two-ocean navy. In the Senate, Walter F. George (1922–1957) chaired the Foreign Affairs Committee, Richard B. Russell (1933–1971) chaired four committees including the Armed Services and Appropriations committees, Herman E. Talmadge (1957–1981) chaired the Agriculture Committee, and Sam Nunn (1973–), a great-nephew of Carl Vinson, chairs the Armed Services Committee. The longest serving Republican in 1993 was Rep. Newt Gingrich, first elected in 1979.

Georgians were leaders on both sides of the argument to end racial segregation in the 1960s. Sen. Richard B. Russell was the chief strategist of the southern states' rights Democrats in the Senate. Rep. Charles L. Weltner, elected as a civil rights moderate in 1963, refused to seek reelection in

1966 rather than swear loyalty to a segregationist Democrat. Two African American civil rights leaders, Andrew Young and John Lewis, later were elected to the House.

BIBLIOGRAPHY

Coleman, Kenneth, ed. *A History of Georgia.* 1977.

U.S. Senate. *Biographical Directory of the United States Congress.* 100th Cong., 2d sess., 1989. S. Doc. 100-34.

MELVIN STEELY

GERMANENESS.

The germaneness rule sets forth one of the fundamental procedures for deciding which bills will be considered, and how, on the floor of the House of Representatives. Whenever the House considers any proposed law, any House member may offer proposed changes, or amendments. However, the germaneness rule makes any nongermane amendment out of order, meaning, generally, that any amendment that is not fairly closely related to the subject of the bill is out of order. For example, when the House considers a bill for farm aid, the rule will allow representatives to offer amendments to raise or lower the levels of aid or adjust the workings of farm aid programs because these are germane, but it forbids representatives from offering amendments about environmental laws, for instance, or civil rights, because these are not germane to the legislation.

The House has followed the germaneness rule since 1822. In the House the rule enables the majority party to specify the legislative agenda. If the majority party in the House declines to let a proposal come to the floor as a proposed bill, a representative who disagrees cannot simply offer the proposal as an amendment to some other unrelated bill. By contrast, the Senate does not generally follow the germaneness rule, except in certain special situations such as cloture. Hence, generally, any senator can offer any amendment to any bill. This difference is one of several reasons that the House has a stricter and more majority-run process than does the Senate.

In 1982, for example, Congress enacted a provision requiring banks to withhold income taxes on the interest they pay. This provision produced a major public backlash; however, neither chamber's tax-writing committees would report a bill to repeal the provision, which produced needed revenue. The House germaneness requirement prevented any representatives from trying to repeal that provision by a floor amendment to unrelated bills. In contrast, the Senate's lack of a germaneness rule meant that senators could, and did, offer repeal measures in 1983 as amendments to various unrelated bills on the floor, such as farm bills, appropriations, and social security bills. Eventually, in this way, they enacted a repeal measure. Perhaps the most extreme example in congressional history of a nongermane amendment proposed a change in the Constitution to prevent reapportionment of state legislatures—this was offered on the Senate floor in 1964 as an amendment to a concurrent resolution on National Baseball Week.

[*See also* Amending.]

BIBLIOGRAPHY

Smith, Steven S. *Call to Order: Floor Politics in the House and Senate.* 1989.

Tiefer, Charles. *Congressional Practice and Procedure.* 1989.

CHARLES TIEFER

GERRYMANDERING.

The procedure of dividing a political unit into election districts with the objective of giving one group the greatest advantage in the largest number of districts is called *gerrymandering.* Gerrymandering most often results in oddly or peculiarly shaped districts, which may appear artificially elongated, protruded, fragmented, or perforated. A skillful gerrymander, however, may have the appearance of geographic symmetry but the real effect of culling out votes in one area or adding votes in another. Gerrymandering can be practiced on many different levels—in the creation of city council districts, county commissioner districts, state legislative districts, and U.S. congressional districts.

The most common form of this practice is the *partisan gerrymander,* in which one political party intentionally draws electoral districts to dilute or eliminate the electoral power of the opposition party. Also common is the *racial gerrymander,* in which the majority racial group draws electoral districts to dilute or eliminate the electoral power of minority voters, who are often geographically concentrated in certain areas. There have also been cases of gerrymandering against linguistic, religious, and ethnic groups and where urban-rural power conflicts exist.

Origin of the Term. The technique of drawing congressional district boundaries to favor a particular individual or party goes back to the First Congress and probably has roots in colonial assem-

THE GERRY-MANDER!

IN TWO CHAPTERS............WITH CUTS.

"Now I appeal to each bye-stander, If this is not a SALAMANDER. Dean Swift.

CHAP. I.....NATURAL HISTORY.

ALL that we can learn of the natural history of this remarkable animal, is contained in the following learned treatise, published in the newspapers of March, 1812, embellished by a drawing, which is pronounced by all competent judges, to be a most accurate likeness.

The horrid Monster of which this drawing is a correct representation, appeared in the County of Essex, during the last session of the Legislature. Various and manifold have been the speculations and conjectures, among learned naturalists respecting the *genus* and origin of this astonishing production. Some believe it to be the real *Basilisk*, a creature which had been supposed to exist only in the poet's imagination. Others pronounce it the *Serpens Monocephalus* of Pliny, or single-headed *Hydra*, a terrible animal of pagan extraction. Many are of opinion that it is the *Griffin* or *Hippogriff* of romance, which flourished in the dark ages, and has come hither to assist the knight of the rueful countenance in restoring that gloomy period of ignorance, fiction and imposition. Some think it the great Red Dragon, or Bunyan's *Apollyon* or the *Monstrum Horrendum* of Virgil, and all believe it a creature of infernal origin, both from its aspect, and from the circumstance of its birth.

But the learned Doctor Watergruel who is famous for peeping under the skirts of nature, has decided that it belongs to the *Salamander* tribe, and gives many plausible reasons for this opinion. He says though the Devil himself must undoubtedly have been concerned, either directly or indirectly in the procreation of this monster, yet many powerful causes must have concurred to give it existence, amongst which must be reckoned the present combustible and venomous state of affairs. There have been, (says the Doctor) many fiery ebullitions of party spirit, many explosions of democratic wrath and fulminations of gubernatorial vengeance within the year past, which would naturally produce an uncommon degree of inflammation and acrimony in the body politic. But as the Salamander cannot be generated except in the most potent degree of heat, he thinks these malignant causes, could not alone have produced such diabolical effects. He therefore ascribes the real birth and material existence of this monster, in all its horrors, to the alarm which his Excellency the Governor and his friends experienced last season, while they were under the influence of the Dog-star and the Comet—and while his Excellency was pregnant with his last speech, his libellous message, and a numerous litter of new judges and other animals, of which he has since been happily delivered. This fright and purturbation was occasioned by an incendiary letter threatening him with fire-brands, arrows and death; (if his proclamation is to be credited) which was sent to him by some mischievous wight, probably some rogue of his own party, to try the strength of his Excellency's mind. Now his Excellency being somewhat like a tinder-horn, and his party very liable to take fire, they must of course have been thrown into a most fearful panic, extremely dangerous to persons in their situation, and calculated to produce the most disastrous effects upon their unborn progeny.

From these premises the sagacious Doctor most solemnly avers there can be no doubt that this monster is a genuine Salamander, though by no means perfect in all its members; a circumstance however which goes far to prove its illegitimacy. But as this creature has been engendered and brought forth under the sublimest auspices, he proposes that a name should be given to it, expressive of its genus, at the same time conveying an elegant and very appropriate compliment to his Excellency the Governor, who is known to be the zealous patron and promoter of whatever is new, astonishing and erratic, especially of domestic growth and manufacture. For these reasons and other valuable considerations, the Doctor has decreed that this monster shall be denominated a

GERRY-MANDER!!

CHAP. II.......POLITICAL HISTORY.

...what has been said in the foregoing chapter, of this animal, the reader may be inclined ...ut it is altogether a fabulous being—a mere creature of poetic fancy, or of pagan my...t so, gentle reader. It is certain that it has had a positive existence—that it owed its ...lence of political faction—and that during the period of its existence, it had a very ...nce in the politics of this Commonwealth.

It is well known that the two political parties in Massachusetts have been for many years nearly equally divided, the balance however, generally inclining to the federal side. For six successive years previous to the birth of the GERRY-MANDER, the representation of the parties in the Senate, as chosen by the people, was divided in the following manner. The vacant districts were so equally divided, that no choice could be made by the people, and the vacancies were filled according to the political character of the other branch of the Legislature.

YEARS.		FEDERAL.	DEMOCRATIC.	VACANCIES.
1806,		19	20	1
1807,		19	21	0
1808,		20	18	2
1809,		22	18	0
1810,		20	19	1
1811,		19	21	0

In the year 1811, both the branches of the Legislature, and the Governor, were, with the exception of a single year, for the first time, democratic; but the experience of past years, taught the prevailing party, that the tenure of their power was extremely precarious, and that the smallness of their majority in the Senate was sometimes, from the superiority of talents on the other side, quite embarrassing.

The senatorial districts had been formed, according to the natural and most obvious construction of the constitution, without any division of counties. To effect the desired object of securing a decided majority in the Senate in all future years, the Legislature divided the State into new senatorial districts in such a manner as to procure the election of the greatest number of democratic Senators. They not only divided counties to effect their object in opposition to the powerful arguments of the federal members, who urged the unconstitutionality of such a measure, but they divided the counties of Essex and Worcester in a manner which showed that all considerations of convenience or propriety were disregarded, and that the only object was to form a democratic district from each of those federal counties. This will appear from the following plan of the two Essex Districts, in which the double dotted lines show the boundaries of the districts as they were formed by the districting law of 1811, commonly called the Gerry-Mander law.

In the plan given above of the Essex *outer* district, authorized by law to choose three Senators, while the federal towns enclosed within it formed another district to choose two, the reader will perceive all the features of the *Gerry-Mander*. It was the creature of the Legislature of 1811, and the design of its creation was to increase and secure the power of the democratic party in the Senate of the State.

The Gerry-Mander did not disappoint the expectations of its fond parents. The election of Senators in 1812 took place under the Gerry-Mander law, and the result was, that TWENTY NINE democratic, and only ELEVEN federal Senators were chosen. On the same day the federal candidate for Governor was chosen by a handsome majority; and what is more remarkable, such was the malignant influence of the animal of which we are giving the history, that it required fewer democratic votes to choose the twenty nine democratic Senators, than were actually given to the federal candidates, of whom only eleven were chosen.

The whole number of votes given for Senators was 101,930, of which 51,766 were given to the federal candidates, and 50,164 for the democratic candidates, making a federal majority of 1602 votes. Yet the democratic minority, with the help of the Gerry-Mander, outvoted the federal majority, almost three to one—that is, so as to constitute a Senate of 29 democratic and 11 federal members.

One fact remains to be recorded of this monster. Thus far his career had been prosperous, and all the fond hopes of his parents and friends were gratified in his complete success. But alas for the frailty of human expectations, especially when founded on schemes of fraud and injustice. The public were indignant at the gross usurpation upon their rights; they rose in their strength, burst the chains which had been imposed upon them, and overcame the monster, notwithstanding his great power. A new districting law was passed, by which he was deprived of all political authority, and it was reported that he was dead.* We have even seen an account of his funeral obsequies, but it is now, after a lapse of some years, when the apprehensions of the public have been quieted, confidently reported, that it was but an empty coffin that was followed to the tomb—that he still lives, and that it is the determination of his friends to restore him to his former power and dignity. It is to be hoped, for the reputation of the Commonwealth, that this attempt will not be successful.

FEDERALIST POLITICAL BROADSIDE, 1812. Including a satirical natural history of the gerrymander and a denunciation of the partisan manipulation of electoral districts in Essex County, Mass. LIBRARY OF CONGRESS

909

blies. The term *gerrymander* originated with the Massachusetts congressional redistricting law enacted after the 1810 census apportionment. This law was passed by the Democratic-Republican majority in the Massachusetts legislature specifically to dilute the power of the formerly majority Federalists. The statute was signed into law on 11 February 1812 by Democratic-Republican governor Elbridge Gerry. To reduce Federalist electoral power the law contained a number of districts that divided counties and had peculiar shapes. One particularly unusual configuration was the Essex (2d) district. This elongated district stretched north from Boston and then east along the New Hampshire border. Federalist politicians ridiculed the shape of the Essex district, saying it resembled an animal or monster. The "salamander"-shaped district was dubbed a *gerrymander* after Governor Gerry. The first appearance of *gerrymander* in print was probably in the Boston *Gazette* of 26 March 1812. The newspaper published a political cartoon by artist Elkanah Tisdale that showed a map of the Essex district embellished with the trappings of a prehistoric monster. The cartoon's caption was "Gerrymander," and Federalist newspapers throughout New England and the United States began using the term to describe the process of drawing legislative districts for partisan advantage.

The Process of Gerrymandering. The goal of the partisan congressional gerrymander is the enhancement of electoral power, leading to the election of representatives in numbers substantially greater than would otherwise result, given the gerrymandering party's share of the total statewide vote. This goal can be accomplished in either of two basic ways. The first gerrymandering method is "packing," that is, concentrating the voting strength of the opposition in as few electoral districts as possible. This puts a large surplus of votes in these districts, wasting opposition votes in the winner-take-all, one-member-to-a-district system of congressional representation (see table 1). The second gerrymandering method is "cracking," or splitting—that is, defusing or spreading out the opposi-

TABLE 1. *Districts, Election Methods, and Electoral Results: Statewide Election Results*[1]

METHOD AND TYPE	REAPPORTIONMENT, IF ANY	ELECTION RESULTS	
I GENERAL TICKET	—	4 Republicans	0 Democrats
II PROPORTIONAL REPRESENTATION	—	2 Republicans	2 Democrats[2]
III GERRYMANDERED DISTRICTS WITH DEMOCRATS SPLIT	District 1: 50,000 Republican 48,750 Democrat District 2: 50,000 Republican 48,750 Democrat District 3: 50,000 Republican 48,750 Democrat District 4: 50,000 Republican 48,750 Democrat	3 Republicans	1 Democrat
IV GERRYMANDERED DISTRICTS WITH REPUBLICANS PACKED	District 1: 80,000 Republican 18,750 Democrat District 2: 40,000 Republican 58,750 Democrat District 3: 40,000 Republican 58,750 Democrat District 4: 40,000 Republican 58,750 Democrat	1 Republican	3 Democrats
V POSSIBLE FAIR AND COMPETITIVE DISTRICTS, OR POSSIBLE BIPARTISAN GERRYMANDER	District 1: 52,000 Republican 46,750 Democrat District 2: 52,000 Republican 46,750 Democrat District 3: 48,000 Republican 50,750 Democrat District 4: 48,000 Republican 50,750 Democrat	2 Republicans	2 Democrats

[1]Concerning the election of four representatives. Statewide vote total: 200,000 Republican, 195,000 Democrat.
[2]Results depend upon the method and formula used.

tion vote by dividing the opposition areas and placing small portions in a number of different districts so as to deny the opposition a majority in any district. Packing and cracking are used together, depending on the geographic distribution of opposition voters.

Congressional redistricting laws are usually statutes passed by the state legislature and signed by the governor. A party's ability to gerrymander, then, first relies on its having control of both chambers of the state legislature and the governorship. If the opposition controls one of the three key actors, then it has the power to influence or stop the redistricting process. In such states, compromise redistricting laws are the norm. In many instances such compromise laws contain *bipartisan gerrymanders* that draw district boundaries to preserve the districts of incumbents of both parties or to gain or lose seats in proportion to the current partisan ratio of representatives (see table 1). These are *incumbent gerrymanders* of the *inclusionary* type. An *intraparty gerrymander* occurs when the party in power tampers with or eliminates the district of an unwanted incumbent because of a reduction in a state's number of House seats or because of intraparty fighting. These are also incumbent gerrymanders, but of the *exclusionary* type.

The art and science of gerrymandering relies on detailed knowledge of voter-registration statistics and historic voting patterns in precincts, wards, cities, and counties. The typical partisan congressional gerrymander manifests one or more of the following characteristics: (1) shaping districts in bizarre or unusual ways, (2) dividing well-known political entities (e.g., wards, cities, counties) between different districts, (3) splitting known communities of interest between different districts, (4) packing known communities of interest into a few districts, (5) placing the residences of opposition incumbents in new districts, and (6) dividing up the old districts of opposition incumbents and distributing the pieces among adjacent districts.

Historically, gerrymanders were hand-drawn maps painstakingly put together using voting statistics and arithmetic. Since the 1980s large census and voting databases and geographic information technologies have enabled computers to quickly calculate and draw a myriad of possible district configurations with different political-demographic characteristics.

Reforming the Congressional Redistricting Process.

The first national electoral provision addressing the practice of unusually configured congressional districts was the Apportionment Act of 1842 (5 Stat. 581), which mandated congressional districts of "contiguous" territory, thereby temporarily banning the physical splitting of a district into two or more geographically separated areas. The 1901 (31 Stat. 733) and 1911 (37 Stat. 13) apportionment laws specifically addressed gerrymandering by adding the word *compact* to the stipulation of contiguity. These prescriptions did not appear in the general census apportionment law of 1929 or in subsequent acts or amendments. Before and since the 1930s numerous gerrymandered and even split districts have appeared in congressional redistricting.

Historically, malapportionment and the gerrymander were practiced hand-in-hand to give the greatest possible advantage to the partisan political cartographer. Supreme Court rulings of the 1960s eliminated population malapportionment. The case against malapportionment has sound legal standing, and abuses can easily be identified and rectified. Gerrymandering, on the other hand, poses much tougher legal questions and involves courts in the partisan political process. However, the Court has ruled on certain gerrymander cases, and guidelines for measuring the practice have been developed.

Racial Gerrymandering.

Evidence of racial gerrymandering can be found in the post-Reconstruction South and in northern cities during the first half of the twentieth century. The disenfranchisement of African Americans in the South in the late nineteenth century lessened this practice, but after the voting rights acts of the 1960s, the practice of diluting minority votes surfaced again, mainly in the form of racial gerrymandering and at-large elections. Racial gerrymanders split highly concentrated urban and rural black populations between two or more election districts, making black voters the minority in each district. Similar cases of gerrymandering to dilute the power of Hispanic voters have also been demonstrated. In the 1970s court challenges were made to obvious, deliberate racial gerrymanders, mostly in the southern states. The courts ruled that conspicuous and premeditated gerrymandering against groups that had previously suffered discrimination was unconstitutional. The most famous case of racial gerrymandering on the statewide congressional-district level was that involving the Mississippi congressional redistrictings of 1966, 1972, and 1981, which split the concentration of African American voters in the Mississippi Delta region of the state. This and similar occurrences on the local and state levels prompted a 1982 amendment to the Voting Rights Act (96 Stat.

131) obligating election districts at all levels to be fashioned in such a way that racial or linguistic minorities would have the potential power to elect representatives. These so-called minority-majority districts in 1992 led to the election of more minority representatives to Congress. To accomplish the minority representation goal, however, some districts were drawn with erratic boundaries to connect minority concentrations, thereby packing minority groups into the same district. The exclusionary gerrymander of the past gave way to this type of inclusionary gerrymander.

Continuing Judicial Issues. Reformers of the redistricting process consider both partisan and racial gerrymandering inherently unfair, biased, and, because they weaken voter choice, inherently undemocratic. As mentioned, the courts have ruled racial gerrymandering unconstitutional. In 1984 the courts went one step further in an Indiana congressional redistricting case, *Bandemer v. Davis* (603 F. Supp. 1479), ruling that partisan gerrymandering was not only subject to judicial review but also unconstitutional. Although the Supreme Court ruled against the specifics in the Indiana case, the way was opened for judicial review of the intentional partisan gerrymander.

If the partisan gerrymander is justiciable (i.e., open to challenge in court), then defining criteria to prove the presence of the practice become important. Such proof is important in the case of either *intentional gerrymander* or *innocent gerrymander*. The most obvious test is the geographic compactness of the district. Geographers and mathematicians have developed formulas for measuring the spatial compactness of areas as well as models for dividing a given geographical space (for example, a state) into a certain number of districts in the most compact way. But a state may be divided into compact districts in a number of different ways, and even the most compact division may either intentionally or innocently pack or split votes.

Criteria other than shape are therefore also important in establishing a fair and unbiased redistricting. Three other geographic factors are (1) consideration of the boundaries of established political units, (2) recognition of geographic concentrations of communities of interest, and (3) correlation of new districts with previous district boundaries. These geographic considerations are quantifiable and can give objective, substantive evidence vital to the judicial review of redistricting.

A number of political criteria have also been considered in the analysis of gerrymandering, includ-

ing (1) political fairness (that is, that the ratio of elected members of both parties is roughly in proportion to the total partisan breakdown of a given region over several elections; see table 1), (2) electoral responsiveness (that is, that districts are competitive enough to react to electoral swings and the possible selection of new representatives), and (3) the intention of the lawmakers to establish a partisan advantage.

Some states have considered creating nonpartisan (or at least bipartisan) electoral commissions to draw congressional districts. Even under the best conditions, however, the district method of election carries an inherent electoral bias. Referring to table 1, a case can be made that Method III is actually a fair (and certainly a competitive) districting, even though skillfully gerrymandered for partisan advantage. Some observers say that this and like examples suggest that, without proof of intent, the gerrymander may be a political problem without judicial solution. Enough geographical and political standards do seem available, however, to establish initial criteria before the drawing of electoral districts and to judge their fairness after they have been drawn.

[*See also* Apportionment and Redistricting.]

BIBLIOGRAPHY

Davidson, Chandler, ed. *Minority Vote Dilution*. 1984.
Griffith, Elmer C. *The Rise and Development of the Gerrymander*. 1907.
Grofman, Bernard, ed. *Political Gerrymandering and the Courts*. 1990.
Morrill, Richard L. *Political Redistricting and Geographic Theory*. 1981.
Musgrove, Philip. *The General Theory of Gerrymandering*. 1977.
U.S. Senate. Committee on Government Affairs. *Congressional Anti-Gerrymandering Act of 1979, Hearings*. 91st Cong., 1st sess., 1979.

KENNETH C. MARTIS

GI BILL OF RIGHTS (1944; 58 Stat. 284–301). The Servicemen's Readjustment Act of 1944, better known as the GI Bill of Rights, entitled veterans of World War II to a wide range of benefits. The bill provided veterans with job training, hiring priority, and monthly allowances while they looked for work. For the almost nine million former soldiers who by 1956 had enrolled in educational or vocational programs, it furnished full tuition as well as a stipend for books and living expenses. Through the Veterans Administration (VA), it made available low-interest loans for buying homes, farms, and small businesses. Later legislation also granted comprehensive medical coverage to disabled veterans and mandated additional funds for the construction of VA hospitals.

The legislative history of the GI Bill began in the fall of 1943, when President Franklin D. Roosevelt asked Congress to pass several bills that would provide a generous package of benefits to veterans. The intent was to reward them for their services, cushion their reentry into the job market, stimulate the postwar economy, and prevent a return to the depression conditions of the 1930s. The administration was also confident that the proposal would gain praise from liberals eager to extend the New Deal, attract votes from grateful veterans in the upcoming presidential election, provide a wedge for the future extension of social provisions to society as a whole, and win quick passage from a conservative Congress that during the war had grown increasingly hostile to Roosevelt's domestic policies and enhanced executive power.

The administration's program stalled, however, until January 1944 when the American Legion presented an omnibus bill that consolidated the earlier proposals and centralized all benefits within the VA. Despite opposition from other veterans' organizations, the measure quickly gained approval from the Senate in March. But in the House, conservative John E. Rankin (D-Miss.), chairman of the Committee on World War Veterans' Legislation, objected to the unemployment benefits, which he viewed as overly generous, and to the educational provisions, which he saw as largely a device to lure unsuspecting veterans into college courses taught by communist sympathizers. Ultimately, his concerns led the House in May to adopt a relatively conservative measure, but the compromise bill drafted by the conference committee more closely resembled the Senate's version. In June 1944 the compromise bill won overwhelming support in both houses and was signed by Roosevelt, who described it as substantially similar to his original initiatives.

The GI Bill of 1944 (in conjunction with subsequent modifications) made a major contribution to America's postwar prosperity. It eased the demand for employment during demobilization and reconversion, boosted economic growth through government spending (by 1962 the VA had issued more than $50 billion in loans alone), made home ownership a realistic goal for most veterans, and transformed American higher education by enabling almost 500,000 former soldiers to go to college. The bill's success led to the extension of similar benefits to Korean War and Vietnam War veterans.

BIBLIOGRAPHY

Olson, Keith W. *The GI Bill, the Veterans, and the Colleges.* 1974.
Ross, Davis R. B. *Preparing for Ulysses: Politics and Veterans during World War II.* 1969.

MICHAEL W. FLAMM

GIDDINGS, JOSHUA R. (1795–1864), representative from northeastern Ohio and long-term leader in the political struggle against slavery. Joshua Reed Giddings was first elected to the U.S. House of Representatives in 1838 as a Whig. He represented perhaps the most completely "abolitionized" congressional district in the nation. Before the election he had been instrumental in organizing Ohio's Whig party, and he remained a fervent Whig until he joined the antislavery Free-Soil party in 1848.

Through the 1840s and 1850s, regardless of his party affiliation, Giddings led the fight in Congress to end the federal government's support of slavery and to prevent its expansion into the western territories. So unpopular were his activities with most other members of Congress that in 1842 he was censured by the House, after which he resigned in protest. Giddings's constituents immediately returned him to his seat with a nearly unanimous vote of confidence. He then served uninterrupted terms until he was passed over for renomination in 1858 because of ill health.

Giddings's long career as a legislator was closely intertwined with the political crises that led to the Civil War. Over the years, his close associates included abolitionist William Lloyd Garrison and antislavery political leaders John Quincy Adams, William H. Seward, Salmon P. Chase, and Abraham Lincoln. Working closely with these men, Giddings played an instrumental role in the formation of the Republican party between 1854 and 1860. Both in Congress and in the politics of his home state, Giddings was a consistently strong advocate of political rights and civil justice for African Americans.

BIBLIOGRAPHY

Giddings, Joshua R. *Speeches in Congress.* 1852.
Stewart, James Brewer. *Joshua R. Giddings and the Tactics of Radical Politics.* 1970.

JAMES BREWER STEWART

GILES, WILLIAM B.

GILES, WILLIAM B. (1762–1830), representative and senator from Virginia, governor of Virginia. A successful young Virginia lawyer, William Branch Giles was elected to the House of Representatives of the First Congress. He was a forceful and contentious spokesman for the emerging Democratic-Republican party and was closely associated with Jefferson. He vehemently opposed Hamilton's economic policies and introduced resolutions, drawn up by Jefferson, in February 1793 that accused Hamilton of maladministration of the Treasury. In a belligerent speech against Jay's Treaty, Giles stressed constitutional checks on the president's treaty-making power.

Disheartened by Republican failures during President John Adams's administration, Giles resigned from Congress in 1798. Jefferson's election two years later brought him back to the House, where he became the president's "prime minister" and adroitly carried out the Republican agenda.

As floor leader Giles attacked the Judiciary Act of 1801, calling instead for "the absolute repeal of the whole judiciary system." Illness forced his resignation from Congress in 1802, but he was appointed to the Senate in 1804. In the proceedings against Justice Samuel Chase, he endeavored to broaden the impeachment process to enable Congress to oust Chief Justice John Marshall. His loyalty to Jefferson led him to reject John Randolph's dissident "Quid" faction in 1806.

Giles supported the 1807 embargo—President Jefferson's experiment in prohibiting trade with Great Britain as retaliation against infringements of American neutrality. By 1810 Giles was demanding war against Great Britain. Ever hostile to Federalist institutions, he challenged the rechartering of the Bank of the United States in 1811.

With his influence waning, Giles left the Senate in 1815, continuing to attack Madison and Monroe for abandoning "true republicanism." As governor of Virginia (1827–1830) he espoused a narrow states' rights approach, always fearful of federal dominance.

BIBLIOGRAPHY

Anderson, Dice R. *William Branch Giles: A Study in the Politics of Virginia and the Nation from 1790 to 1830.* 1914.

Cunningham, Noble E., Jr. *The Jeffersonian Republicans in Power: Party Operations, 1801–1809.* 1963.

WINFRED E. A. BERNHARD

GLASS, CARTER

GLASS, CARTER (1858–1946), representative and senator from Virginia and author of some of the nation's most significant banking legislation. Glass was elected to the House of Representatives as a Democrat in 1902. He supported the key legislative reforms of the Progressive era, and his affinity for the individualistic reform philosophy of the New Freedom led to a close relationship with Woodrow Wilson. As chairman of the House Banking and Currency Committee after 1912, he was instrumental in writing and passing the Glass-Owen or Federal Reserve Act. Wilson named him secretary of the Treasury in 1918, and in 1920 Glass returned to Congress as a senator. After two decades as one of Virginia's antimachine Democrats he reconciled with the state organization in the early 1920s and became a close ally of its new leader, Harry Flood Byrd, Sr.

By the 1930s Glass was commonly regarded as the foremost congressional authority on banking, a reputation enhanced by his prescient warnings in the 1920s against speculation and predictions of collapse unless the Federal Reserve Board acted effectively to curb it. As chairman of the subcommittee of the Senate Banking and Currency Committee that considered all federal banking matters, he dominated banking and monetary legislation even while Republicans controlled the Senate. President Herbert Hoover considered his support essential to passage of the administration's 1932 credit expansion bill, and Glass agreed to sponsor it despite concerns that its liberalized lending provisions were unsound and superfluous. It became the first Glass-Steagall Act. Glass's own response to the Great Depression was to reform the banking system. The second Glass-Steagall Act (the Banking Act of 1933), separating commercial from investment banking, tightening the regulatory authority of the Federal Reserve, and creating deposit insurance, provided a half-century of banking stability.

Glass declined an invitation from Franklin D. Roosevelt to manage Treasury again. Instead, he claimed the chair of the Appropriations Committee while retaining de facto control of Banking and Currency by continuing to head its banking subcommittee. A devotee of the gold standard, a balanced budget, and individualism, he became an immediate critic of the New Deal, ultimately voting against more New Deal legislation than any other congressional Democrat. He and Roosevelt reconciled in the late 1930s over their common anti-isolationist views, and the administration used its influence to put Glass on the Foreign Relations Committee.

More fearless and individualistic than most politicians, Glass traveled an independent road within his party, the Senate, and the Byrd organization. He generally spoke what he thought and did what he wanted. Often he said the Senate had declined since the days of its nineteenth-century giants, becoming little more than a rubber stamp for the president. In 1939 a *Life* magazine poll of Washington press correspondents accorded him the highest integrity rating (defined as fidelity to principle and disregard for political expediency) of any member of Congress; writers called him "the Senate's only intellectually honest man" but added that he was "a nasty, bitter fighter, intensely prejudiced" and that "his vindictiveness tends to impair his influence." His efforts to protect the strength, independence, and high standards of the Federal Reserve never wavered; in 1938 Roosevelt dedicated a bronze bas-relief of Glass in the lobby of Washington's Federal Reserve Building, where it hangs opposite a similar memorial to Wilson. The inscription reads: "Defender of the Federal Reserve System."

BIBLIOGRAPHY

Koeniger, A. Cash. "Carter Glass and the National Recovery Administration." *South Atlantic Quarterly* 74 (1975): 349–364.

Koeniger, A. Cash. "The New Deal and the States: Roosevelt versus the Byrd Organization in Virginia." *Journal of American History* 68 (1982): 876–896.

Koeniger, A. Cash. "The Politics of Independence: Carter Glass and the Elections of 1936." *South Atlantic Quarterly* 80 (1981): 95–106.

Smith, Rixey, and Norman Beasley. *Carter Glass: A Biography.* 1939.

A. CASH KOENIGER

GLASS-STEAGALL ACT. *See* Banking Act of 1933.

GOLDWATER, BARRY (1909–), senator from Arizona, Republican party candidate for president in 1964, and a leading spokesman for American conservatism. Barry M. Goldwater was born in territorial Arizona, the grandson of a Jewish immigrant peddler. A prominent Phoenix businessman, Goldwater ran for the U.S. Senate in 1952. Taking advantage of incoming president Dwight D. Eisen-

BARRY GOLDWATER. Speaking at the National Press Club, Washington, D.C., 1963.   LIBRARY OF CONGRESS

hower's coattails, Goldwater defeated Senate Majority Leader Ernest W. McFarland. He quickly aligned with Senate conservatives, making federal spending, states' rights, and control of labor unions his main concerns. In the 1950s he served on the McClellan committee and was active in its investigation of labor union and management abuses. Goldwater's rise to influence accelerated with the death of Joseph R. McCarthy in 1957 and the defeat of Sen. William F. Knowland in the 1958 elections.

Goldwater soon emerged as the leading advocate of conservatism in the Senate and nation. He advocated a strong military establishment, with heavy reliance on air power, to counter the international communist threat, and he opposed the Limited Nuclear Test Ban Treaty on the grounds that it weakened American defenses against an expansionist Soviet Union. Determined to resist the growth of the federal bureaucracy and increased spending, he opposed New Frontier and, later, Great Society initiatives. Thus, he voted against both the Civil Rights Act of 1964 and Medicare as unconstitutional extensions of federal power. His books, *The Conscience of a Conservative* (1960) and *Why Not Victory?* (1963), prepared the ground for a presidential bid in 1964.

In the 1964 campaign, Goldwater appealed to Americans with a message of rugged individualism, fiscal conservatism, and anti-communism. Candid and quotable, he appeared to be a man who, unlike other politicians, voiced his convictions regardless of their consequences. His blunt, off-the-cuff remarks, however, embroiled him in controversies. In particular, Democrats exploited his words to scare voters with an image of a politically inept, irresponsible candidate eager to destroy Social Security and itchy to trigger nuclear war. Although Goldwater and many Republican candidates were buried in President Lyndon B. Johnson's landslide, the shift in party power from liberal, eastern Republicans to Sunbelt and western conservatives would prove long-lasting. In defeat, Goldwater became a martyr to the conservative cause. He would never again be a candidate in presidential politics, but his influence with the Republican party's conservative rank and file was unrivaled.

Arizona voters returned Goldwater to the Senate in 1968, 1974, and 1980. Peers described him as a man of courage and principle dedicated to the protection of individual freedom, a strong national defense, and conservative principles. As a respected elder statesman, he was chosen by Senate Republicans as one of their representatives to advise President Richard M. Nixon on the eve of his resignation in 1974. In the 1970s and 1980s Goldwater served on the Armed Services Committee and the Select Committee on Intelligence. While supporting President Ronald Reagan's military buildup, he was a sharp critic of Defense Department waste and inefficiency. Goldwater considered his greatest legislative achievement to be the Military Reorganization Act that restructured the military establishment. It became law in 1986 on the eve of his retirement from the Senate.

BIBLIOGRAPHY

Bell, Jack. *Mr. Conservative: Barry Goldwater.* 1962.
Goldwater, Barry. *With No Apologies.* 1979.
Goldwater, Barry, with Jack Casserly. *Goldwater.* 1988.
McDowell, Edwin. *Barry Goldwater: Portrait of an Arizonan.* 1964.

ROBERT A. GOLDBERG

GORE, THOMAS P. (1870–1949), Democratic senator from Oklahoma and author of the Gore Resolution of 1916. Totally blind as a result of two childhood accidents, Gore was elected to the Senate as a progressive Democrat when Oklahoma became a state in 1907. He became embroiled in the neutrality controversy in the early months of World War I. As a progressive-pacifist, he opposed President Woodrow Wilson's stand to uphold American neutrality. The Gore Resolution of 1916 was designed to express Congress's sense that U.S. citizens should not exercise their rights to travel on armed ships in time of war.

During World War I, Gore was chairman of the Agriculture Committee and concerned himself with food and agricultural legislation, displaying his independence and often disagreeing with the president's policies. Gore's pacifism manifested itself during the Senate's postwar battle over the League of Nations, when he took an isolationist stand, resulting in his not being reelected in 1920.

Gore served another term from 1931 to 1937. His continued independence and his evolution into a staunch economic conservative caused him to oppose most New Deal measures. A spokesman for Oklahoma's oil interests in the 1930s, Gore no longer represented Oklahoma farmers' interests as he criticized New Deal expenditures, government regulation, and social welfare programs.

BIBLIOGRAPHY

Billington, Monroe Lee. *Thomas P. Gore: The Blind Senator from Oklahoma.* 1967.

MONROE LEE BILLINGTON

GORMAN, ARTHUR PUE (1839–1906), Democratic senator from Maryland, Senate majority leader from 1893 to 1895, and the dominating figure of Maryland politics in the late nineteenth century. Born in Woodstock, Howard County, Maryland, Gorman attended local public schools until 1852. He then went to Washington, where he served as a congressional page and worked his way up from various subordinate offices to the postmastership of the Senate. Gorman subsequently held a wide succession of responsible political positions:

ARTHUR PUE GORMAN.   LIBRARY OF CONGRESS

collector of internal revenue for Maryland's 5th Congressional District; president of the Chesapeake and Ohio Canal Company; chairman of the Democratic State Central Committee; manager of the 1884 Democratic presidential campaign; and state legislator.

Elected four times by the state legislature, Gorman served as a U.S. senator from 1881 to 1899 and from 1903 until his death. An old guard leader of the Maryland Democracy, Gorman wielded power through force of character, parliamentary skill, and his awareness of the importance of the committee structure. A member of the powerful Appropriations Committee and the Committee on Rules, he assisted in the passage of the Interstate Commerce Act of 1887 and the Public Printing Act of 1894.

Gorman's stand in 1890 against the federal elections bill underscored his skills as a legislative leader. This Republican proposal sought supervision of federal elections and examination of voting irregularities, especially pertaining to black suffrage in the South. Gorman masterfully spearheaded a filibuster and forced a delay in the consideration of the measure while bargaining with "silver" Republicans on the currency issue, thus defeating the elections bill that had been approved by the House and endorsed by President Benjamin Harrison.

Gorman played a significant role in putting together the Wilson-Gorman Tariff Act of 1894. Occupying a middle ground between high protectionists and free traders, he devised a policy based on practical business principles. By adding hundreds of protective amendments, Gorman emasculated the Wilson bill passed by the House and favored by President Grover Cleveland. Gorman's verbal attacks on Cleveland further strained their relationship.

For most of Gorman's career, Republicans controlled the Senate and presidency. He served as minority leader from 1889 to 1893, 1895 to 1898, and again from 1903 to 1906. An anti-imperialist and an advocate of a sound money policy, Gorman led his party during a tumultuous period marked by political protest, economic discontent, and social tension. Remaining calm in the face of the free silver hysteria in 1896, he counseled moderation and patience.

Gorman championed party loyalty and regularity during his senatorial years, and he was often considered as a possible presidential nominee. He never bolted party lines when candidates he personally opposed won nominations. Gorman intertwined the fortunes of the Democratic party with his own, bringing conservative leadership to Senate Democrats while endeavoring through compromise to ease the transition from the politics of the pre–Civil War era to that of the Gilded Age.

BIBLIOGRAPHY

Lambert, John R. *Arthur Pue Gorman.* 1953.

LEONARD SCHLUP

GOVERNMENTAL AFFAIRS COMMITTEE, SENATE.

The Committee on Governmental Affairs is often regarded as the Senate's "good government committee." It is that and considerably more. In addition to the committee's historic mission to oversee government operations so as to ferret out inefficiency, waste, and official corruption and its characteristic concerns with organization and management issues, the latter-day committee (particularly since 1977) has had a substantial legislative jurisdiction as well. In the early 1990s the panel's jurisdiction consisted of budget and accounting measures (with exceptions as provided for in the Budget and Accounting Act of 1974); census,

PERMANENT INVESTIGATIONS SUBCOMMITTEE OF THE GOVERNMENTAL AFFAIRS COMMITTEE. *Left to right,* Sen. Samuel J. Ervin, Jr. (D-N.C.); Sen. John L. McClellan (D-Ark.), subcommittee chairman; Robert F. Kennedy, chief counsel; Carmine Bellino, staff investigator; Sen. Karl E. Mundt (R-S.D.); and Sen. Carl T. Curtis (R-Nebr.). Ruth Watt, chief clerk, stands behind McClellan.   OFFICE OF THE HISTORIAN OF THE U.S. SENATE

social, economic, and statistical data collection; congressional organization (excepting amendment of the rules of the Senate); the federal civil service, including the status and compensation of officers of the United States; governmental information; intergovernmental relations; municipal affairs of the District of Columbia; the U.S. Postal Service; the National Archives; and organization and management of U.S. nuclear export policy. The breadth of this jurisdiction affords the committee critical legislative and oversight controls over important agencies, including the General Accounting Office, the Office of Management and Budget, the Office of Personnel Management, and the General Services Administration.

The committee's broad and somewhat open-ended mandate has allowed members, particularly the chairmen and subcommittee chairs, to pursue virtually any subject that has attracted their interest. This range is further enhanced by the committee's authority to receive and examine reports of the comptroller general of the United States (the director of the General Accounting Office) and to study the efficiency, economy, effectiveness, and organization of all agencies and departments of the government, including Congress itself. For example, during the 101st Congress (1989–1991), the panel and its five subcommittees held a total of 138 hearings on a variety of legislative and oversight issues ranging from "Serious Management Problems at Our Domestic Agencies" to "Crisis in Science and Math Education," from "Chemical and Biological Warfare" to "Homeless Assistance," from "Department of Energy Radiation Health Effects Research Program and Working Conditions at DoE Sites" to "Drug Problems in Columbus, Ohio," and from "The Trade and Technology Promotion Act of 1989" to "Federal Advisory Committee Act Amendments," among many others. In addition, there have been advise and consent hearings for a number of presidential nominations.

Background. The committee's historical roots can be traced to the Committee on Retrenchment, established by the Senate in 1842 "to take into consideration the expenditures of the government in the several departments thereof, and to inquire whether . . . retrenchments can be made without injury to the public service." The Retrenchment Committee was abolished fifteen years later without being replaced until Congress in 1866 created the Joint Select Committee on Retrenchment, which it maintained for six years. In 1871, the Senate created its own Committee on Investigation and Retrenchment, then replaced it two years later with a Committee on Civil Service and Retrenchment, which remained in service until 1921. From the 1880s through the early decades of the twentieth century, the Senate experimented with a number of expenditure control committees and with what today would be called administrative and organizational oversight committees. The Committee on Expenditures of Public Money, for example, was created in 1884 and continued for five years, though it does not appear to have had a significant impact. It was replaced by the standing Committee on the Organization, Conduct, and Expenditures of the Executive Departments, which was continued in various relatively inactive organizational incarnations, including the Committee on Public Expenditures of 1909–1911.

It is to the Senate Resolution of 27 May 1920 creating the Committee on Expenditures in the Executive Departments that the contemporary Committee on Governmental Affairs traces its modern history. The Committee on Expenditures in the Executive Departments began its activities by receiving and rapidly reporting the bill that was to embrace one of the most important government organizational reforms of the twentieth century, the National Budget and Accounting Act of 1921. That legislation created both the Bureau of the Budget (now the Office of Management and Budget) and the General Accounting Office, and with them a centralized system for federal budgeting and auditing of accounts. For nearly a quarter century thereafter, however, the committee's legislative record was remarkably thin, and its expenditure controlling posture was weak and inattentive. All this changed dramatically with passage of the Legislative Reorganization Act of 1946, which for the first time officially recognized congressional responsi-

bility for administrative oversight and provided increased staffing to assist with this effort. The act reorganized the congressional committee structure, yet it retained the Committee on Expenditures in the Executive Departments, for the first time according it official jurisdiction over budget and accounting measures other than appropriations, mandating a new relationship between the committee and the comptroller general, and otherwise establishing the basics of the committee's contemporary authority.

With the changes established by the 1946 act, the Committee on Expenditures in the Executive Departments became a major Senate committee, and it moved relatively rapidly to capitalize on its new mandate. To conduct extensive probes into government economy and efficiency, the panel made extensive use of its Subcommittee on Senate Investigations, which could trace an independent lineage to the Senate Special Committee Investigating the National Defense Program led by Sen. Harry S. Truman (D-Mo.) during World War II. The Subcommittee on Reorganization, along with the full committee, was instrumental in handling directly or otherwise reviewing the dozens of legislative proposals stemming from the reports of the Commission on Organization of the Executive Branch of Government (the first Hoover Commission), which began to be released in 1949. As a follow-up to the Hoover Commission proposals, the committee was effectively involved in crafting the Executive Reorganization Act of 1949, which delegated executive reorganization powers to the president, subject to a legislative veto. The panel was, in addition, central to the development and passage of the Federal Property and Administrative Services Act of 1949 and the Budgeting and Accounting Procedures Act of 1950, which also followed up on Hoover Commission recommendations.

In 1952, near the outset of the second session of the 82d Congress, the name of the committee was changed to the Committee on Government Operations to reflect more accurately the nature of its broader mandate. At the same time, the Subcommittee on Senate Investigations was redesignated the Permanent Subcommittee on Investigations. In 1979, the full committee's name was changed yet again to the Committee on Governmental Affairs.

The Committee's Function. Much of the work of the full committee and its various subcommittees has proceeded in a relatively quiet, businesslike manner, beyond the glare of the klieg lights. As has been said, Governmental Affairs Committee hearings "don't attract many cameras." A singular exception must be made for the Permanent Subcommittee on Investigations (PSI). In the early 1950s, PSI provided the forum for Sen. Joseph R. McCarthy's (R-Wis.) famous investigations of domestic communism.

The Permanent Subcommittee on Investigations has continued to hold widely publicized if less controversial hearings on a wide variety of subjects. For example, Sen. John L. McClellan (D-Ark.), chairman of the full committee (1949–1952) and the PSI (1955–1972), conducted highly visible investigations of the Teamsters Union and its president, Jimmy Hoffa, and of white-collar crime and fraudulent use of government subsidies, as in the Billy Sol Estes affair, a multimillion-dollar swindle involving federally regulated cotton allotments. More recent PSI investigations have culminated in hearings on diverse topics, including organized crime, emerging criminal groups, offshore banks, "crack" cocaine, international drug-trafficking organizations, the entertainment industry and drugs, domestic money laundering, navy shipbuilding procurement, transfer of technology, child pornography and pedophile organizations, weight reduction products and plans, and abuses in the federal student aid program, among many others.

Legislatively, the committee and its subcommittees have remained highly productive in restructuring the organization and processes of government. During the particularly active chairmanship of Abraham A. Ribicoff (D-Conn.) (1975–1980), the committee was central to successful legislative efforts to secure major reforms, including the Civil Service Reform Act of 1978, which reorganized the Civil Service Commission as the Office of Personnel Management and the Merit Systems Protection Board and established the new Senior Executive Service; the Ethics in Government Act of 1978, which accomplished a major overhaul of prior law on misfeasance, malfeasance, and conflict of interest, requiring public financial disclosures of high-level public officials, restricting post-service activities, and authorizing the appointment of independent special prosecutors; the Inspector General Act of 1978, establishing an Office of Inspector General in twelve major departments and agencies; the Nuclear Non-Proliferation Act of 1978, for the first time establishing specific criteria to govern U.S. nuclear exports; and the Paperwork Reduction Act of 1980, which set up a procedural and institutional framework, centralized within the Office of Management and Budget, for reducing the burden of governmental paperwork requirements on the public. The committee also developed the legislation that created the Department of Energy and the Department of Education in 1977.

During the chairmanship of William V. Roth, Jr. (R-Del., 1981–1986), and John Glenn (D-Ohio, 1987–), the committee has remained at the forefront of legislative efforts to reform government structure and procedure. Major legislative accomplishments of the panel during this period include the Debt Collection Acts of 1981 and 1982; Prompt Payment Act of 1982; Ethics in Government Act Amendments of 1982; Single Financial Audit Act of 1983; Federal Debt Recovery Act of 1985; Federal Employees' Retirement System Act of 1986; the Nuclear Protections and Safety Act of 1988; the Department of Veterans Administration Act of 1988; and the Federal Financial Management Improvement Act of 1990.

In addition to the Permanent Subcommittee on Investigations, subcommittees of the Governmental Affairs Committee during the 103d Congress (1993–1995) were Oversight of Government Management; General Services, Federalism, and the District of Columbia; Federal Services, Post Office, and Civil Service; and Government Information and Regulation.

[See also Budget and Accounting Act; Civil Service Reform Act of 1978; General Accounting Office; Government Operations Committee, House; Investigations, Senate Permanent Subcommittee on; Legislative Reorganization Acts, article on Act of 1946; Office of Management and Budget.]

BIBLIOGRAPHY

Malbin, Michael J. Unelected Representatives: Congressional Staff and the Future of Representative Government. 1980. Chap. 4, "Shepherding a Bill through the Senate: The Sunset Bill."

McConachie, Lauros G. Congressional Committees: A Study of the Origins and Development of Our National and Local Legislative Methods. 1898.

U.S. Senate. Committee on Government Operations of the United States Senate: 50th Anniversary History, 1921–1971, by Arthur A. Sharpe. 92d Cong., 1st sess., 1971. S. Doc. 31.

U.S. Senate. Report: Activities of the Committee on Governmental Affairs. 97th Cong., 1st sess.–102d Cong., 1st sess., 1981–1991.

U.S. Senate. Committee on Governmental Affairs. Summary of Activities of the Committee on Governmental Affairs under the Chairmanship of Senator Abraham Ribicoff. 96th Cong., 2d sess., 1980. Committee Print.

Wilmerding, Lucius, Jr. The Spending Power: A History of the Efforts of Congress to Control Expenditures. 1943.

ROBERT S. GILMOUR

GOVERNMENT CORPORATIONS.

Since Congress created the Bank of the United States in 1791, the national government has used private-style organizations to pursue public purposes. The government has created a broad class of government corporations, separate legal entities that conduct quasi-commercial activities financed by the revenues they raise. They have been used to promote agriculture, run airports, support international trade, and develop consumer cooperatives, but most importantly they have been used to help expand the supply of credit for housing, agriculture, and education.

A befuddling array of organizations lies behind this concept, however. A *government corporation*, strictly speaking, is "a government entity created as a separate legal person by, or pursuant to, legislation," as a 1981 study by the National Academy of Public Administration defined it. Like private corporations, government corporations can sue and be sued. They are governed by administrators or boards appointed by the president or by the cabinet secretary who oversees their operations, and their finances are managed through the annual government appropriations process.

Some government corporations, such as the Government National Mortgage Association (Ginnie Mae) or the Export-Import Bank, are of a "pure" type, with the government itself owning the assets. Other corporations, such as the Communications Satellite Corporation (COMSAT), have been established by law but are entirely privately owned, with most—or all—board members chosen by their private stockholders. Some government enterprises are not incorporated, including the U.S. Postal Service and the authority that manages Washington, D.C.'s two airports. There are also government corporations, such as the Legal Services Corporation, that are not enterprises; that is, they do not finance their activities from revenues derived from commercial-type activities.

Many of the largest and most important "government corporations" (in the broad sense) are hybrids: government-sponsored enterprises with mixed public-private ownership, governed by board members chosen by the president as well as private stockholders. They include the Federal National Mortgage Association (Fannie Mae); the Federal Home Loan Mortgage Corporation (Freddie Mac); the Student Loan Marketing Association (Sallie Mae); the College Construction Loan Insurance Association (Connie Lee); the Federal Asset Disposition Association (FADA); and the Federal Agricultural Mortgage Association (Farmer Mac). By buying, bundling, and reselling loans of different kinds, these hybrid government-sponsored enterprises promote lending for purposes the government has determined are in the public interest.

Although the nation has experimented with such enterprises since its earliest days, their sustained use is more recent. The first purely governmental corporation was the Panama Railroad Company, created in 1904 to manage the construction of the Panama Canal. With World War I, Congress established new but temporary corporations to finance ship and housing construction. Not until the New Deal, with the establishment of the Federal Deposit Insurance Corporation, the Tennessee Valley Authority, and Fannie Mae, did widespread and permanent use of government corporations begin. The number has since increased rapidly, with twenty-six of the thirty-five government corporations counted in a 1981 census by the National Academy of Public Administration having been established after 1960.

Because the finances of government-sponsored enterprises are largely separate from the federal budget process, elected officials have found them a welcome alternative during deficit-reduction battles. Because the Treasury implicitly, but not always legally, stands behind their loan portfolios, investors have welcomed them as especially safe investments. That, in turn, has allowed government-sponsored enterprises to expand their portfolios at below-market rates. By the end of fiscal year 1990, these hybrids had supported the growth of federally assisted credit to more than $6 trillion, double the amount of just a decade before.

Despite the considerable problems of oversight that government corporations have created, Congress continues to turn to them for a variety of reasons. Members of Congress sometimes wish to promote an activity that they believe to be in the public interest and that they believe can be self-financing. A reliable source of nontax revenue could remove activities, such as the TVA, from annual budget battles. In some cases, members of Congress deemed activities like bank deposit insurance too important to be subjected to annual debate. More recently, in proposals like President Bill Clinton's plan for national service, government corporations have been attractive mechanisms to protect programs from frequent political tampering by removing the opportunities that come from budgetary review. Members of Congress have gradually moved from the first justification to the last as a strategy to insulate programs from close scrutiny and to promise more stable financing.

Congress rarely oversees government corporations carefully. Because the corporations largely escape annual budgetary review, members of Congress rarely have the opportunity or incentive to pay much attention to the corporations until scandals, such as the banking crisis of the late 1980s, arise. Because of the unusual financing structure of corporations, congressional leverage over government corporations is less direct than for other government programs. Limited expertise about government corporations in Congress, among both members and staff alike, further limits congressional oversight. This scant oversight has caused two problems. First, government corporations have developed in ad hoc fashion, with little consistency in form and little thought given to broader financial and governance questions they raise. Second, the growth of government corporations has created a huge contingent liability should the corporations fail.

These organizations have given the government substantial flexibility to deal with complex problems. They have made available a large supply of relatively cheap credit. That flexibility, however, has come at a cost: because they are government chartered, the federal government remains ultimately responsible for their operations, yet the government's leverage over them is weak. Most of all, the line dividing public from private purposes has become blurred.

BIBLIOGRAPHY

National Academy of Public Administration. *Report on Government Corporations.* 1981.
Seidman, Harold. "The Quasi World of the Federal Government." *Brookings Review* 6 (1988): 23–27.
Seidman, Harold, and Robert Gilmour. *Politics, Position, and Power: From the Positive to the Regulatory State.* 4th ed. 1986.
Stanton, Thomas H. *Government Sponsored Enterprises: Their Benefits and Costs as Instruments of Federal Policy.* 1988.

DONALD F. KETTL

GOVERNMENT IN THE SUNSHINE ACT

(90 Stat. 1241–1248). This act requires numerous federal agencies to open their meetings to the public when the meetings involve substantive discussion of official agency business. The act applies to collegial bodies composed of two or more members, a majority of whom are appointed by the president with the advice and consent of the Senate. The presumption is that all meetings should be open, although specific exemptions in the act permit meetings or portions of meetings to be closed when disclosure of information could be detrimental to the public interest.

Passed soon after Watergate, the act sought to restore public trust in the government and its institutions by allowing the public to observe how officials make their decisions. Reflecting the view that in a democratic society public officials should be accountable to the public, the act specifies that "the public is entitled to the fullest practicable information regarding the decision-making processes of the Federal Government."

The Sunshine Act has generated some debate over whether the extent of openness in government required by the act is compatible with collegial decision making. Those concerned about collegiality argue that the degree of openness has weakened collegial decision making. They want to allow agencies to close meetings when discussions are of a preliminary nature or deal with certain issues that are to be decided later in an open forum. Those concerned about openness, however, question whether collegial decision making has been affected significantly and fear that the changes proposed by those who want to amend the act would undermine its purpose.

[*See also* Executive Branch; Freedom of Information Act.]

BIBLIOGRAPHY

Berg, Richard K., and Stephen H. Klitzman. *An Interpretative Guide to the Government in the Sunshine Act.* 1978.

ROGELIO GARCIA

GOVERNMENT OPERATIONS COMMITTEE, HOUSE.

Primarily responsible for overseeing the expenditures of the executive branch, the House Committee on Government Operations oversees all aspects of economy and efficiency in government. The committee oversees executive branch practices such as procurement, organization of the executive branch, and revenue sharing, ensuring that executive agencies are spending taxpayers' money in ways that Congress intended when that money was appropriated. Government Operations is one of twenty-two standing committees in the U.S. House of Representatives in the 103d Congress (1993–1995).

History and Development. The House of Representatives has traditionally organized committee panels to oversee the expenditures of the executive agencies. This oversight responsibility was given to the Ways and Means Committee when that standing committee was organized in the Fourth Congress (1795–1797). Within a few years, however, the oversight of federal expenditures became too burdensome for Ways and Means to perform its duties adequately.

In 1814, Congress acted to relieve Ways and Means of the expenditures oversight function. During the 13th Congress (1813–1815) the House created the original standing Committee on Expenditures, which was to oversee the departments and the appropriation laws, watch for expenditure violations, and report to Congress concerning economy and accountability of public officers. This Committee on Expenditures continued to exist until December 1883.

During the 14th Congress, members decided to expand markedly Congress's capabilities to oversee executive-branch expenditures. Six additional standing committees were created in 1816 to examine agency accounts and expenditures. A committee was organized to oversee the expenditures of each of the five departments that existed at that time (State, Treasury, War, Navy, and Post Office). A sixth committee was established to oversee accounts and expenditures for public buildings.

Each of the new expenditure committees had specific oversight responsibilities: to examine the accounts and expenditures of the department for which it was responsible; ensure that expenditures were not inequitable or extravagant; and determine if the expenditures were justified by law, if claims were justified by vouchers, and if payments conformed to appropriations. Each committee was also to report to Congress on any savings that could be made and any abuses that were found.

When the 14th Congress created an expenditure committee for each existing department, it set a pattern that was to continue for nearly a century. As the executive branch established new federal agencies, the House established corresponding expenditures committees. The Committee on Expenditures in the Interior Department was established in 1860, the Committee on Expenditures in the Department of Justice in 1874, the Committee on Expenditures in the Department of Agriculture in 1889, and the Committee on Expenditures in the Department of Commerce and Labor in 1905.

The House of Representatives operated with eleven expenditures committees until 1927, when the 70th Congress abolished sixteen superfluous committees, including the eleven expenditures committees. In place of the expenditures committees, the House created the Committee on Expenditures in the Executive Departments, which had jurisdiction over expenditures in all the executive departments.

When the committee system was modernized by the Legislative Reorganization Act of 1946, the Committee on Expenditures in the Executive Departments was retained and its jurisdiction expanded. The committee was assigned legislative responsibility over budget and accounting measures other than appropriations and executive-branch reorganizations. The committee also was responsible for examining reports of the comptroller general; studying the economy and efficiency of government activities at all levels; evaluating the effects of government reorganization laws; and studying intergovernmental relationships between federal, state, and local governments as well as between the United States and international organizations.

In 1952, the House changed the panel's name to the Committee on Government Operations, and that name has been retained to the present. Jurisdiction over the National Archives and over general revenue sharing was added to its authority in 1975. Jurisdiction over measures providing for expenditures not included in the regular federal budget was added in 1985.

Characteristics. The House Government Operations Committee can be characterized as a congressional watchdog. It oversees expenditures throughout the executive branch and oversees many of the processes that affect costs, such as the organization of the executive branch and accounting measures.

The Government Operations Committee considers a wide and varied array of issues. For example, in 1991, the committee held hearings on the following subjects: the adequacy of laws and regulations governing the transportation of hazardous chemicals by railroad; worker safety in the petrochemical industry; costs of the Strategic Defense Initiative; race and sex discrimination in the operation of the Job Training Partnership Act; Federal Deposit Insurance reform; and funding by the National Endowment for the Arts for state and local art projects.

The diversity of issues considered by the committee reflects its broad jurisdiction. House rule prescribes that the committee have jurisdiction over the following: (1) budget and accounting measures, other than appropriations; (2) the overall economy and efficiency of government operations and activities, including federal procurement; (3) reorganizations in the executive branch of the government; (4) general revenue sharing and intergovernmental relations between the United States government and the states and municipalities; (5) the National Archives; (6) measures providing for off-budget treatment of federal agencies or programs; and (7) measures providing for the exemption of a federal agency or program from efforts to balance the budget and control the deficit.

Because of its broad jurisdiction it is impossible for the Government Operations Committee to address each and every government spending issue. Consequently, the committee chooses which issues it will address in a given Congress, an agenda that varies considerably from Congress to Congress, depending on the personal interests of the members of the committee and the public policy issues under national debate at the time.

This flexibility is reflected by changes in the committee's agenda in recent years. Jack Brooks (D-Tex.), Government Operations Committee chairman from the 94th through the 100th Congress (1975 to 1989), brought considerable notoriety to the committee as it uncovered one after another corrupt or excessive government procurement practice. John Conyers, Jr. (D-Mich.), who became chairman in 1989 and remained in that position in the 103d Congress (1993–1995), has nudged the committee into the social welfare arena. Under Chairman Conyers's guidance, the committee has investigated topics such as the effectiveness of federal moneys spent on substance abuse programs, and race and sex discrimination in procurement practices.

Occasionally, the work of the committee attracts national attention, particularly when procurement scandals are uncovered. Stories of outrageously overpriced supplies or of contracts awarded to friends of senior government officials create congressional and public uproars. But most of the work of the Government Operations Committee takes place outside the national spotlight, and most of the issues considered by the committee are of little interest to the general public.

Even though appointment to the Government Operations Committee is not a highly visible assignment, members serve on the committee so they can influence public policy. Steven Smith and Christopher Deering report (in *Committees in Congress*, 1990) that members who want to serve on a

policy committee often request appointment to the Government Operations Committee. Smith and Deering also report that service on the committee has become more desirable since the early 1970s, in part because of the importance of executive expenditures to the budget crisis, and in part because of the visibility the committee receives when it uncovers scandalous procurement practices.

Historically, committees responsible for executive expenditures were not as active and as prestigious as is the modern Government Operations Committee. Lauros McConachie (in *Congressional Committees*, 1898) depicted the several expenditure committees as do-nothing panels to which the Speaker appointed the representatives whom he believed to be the most incompetent. Similar observations were made during floor debate in 1927, when the House of Representatives decided to consolidate the eleven committees on expenditures into one Committee on Expenditures in the Executive Departments. Representatives favoring the 1927 consolidation contended that some of the committees had no work to do, did not meet regularly, and served only as another committee assignment possibility.

There are conflicting views about the effectiveness of the Government Operations Committee's oversight activities. Some House members believe it is advantageous to have a separate committee specializing in oversight investigation that can operate on a broad, government-wide basis. Others believe oversight should be conducted by the authorizing and appropriating panels that have jurisdiction over specific federal agencies and programs. While the Government Operations Committee has remained vigorous, Congress has also strengthened other oversight mechanisms. House rules were changed in the mid 1970s to require committees with twenty or more members to have an oversight subcommittee or to carry out oversight functions in their legislative subcommittees, and committees have been furnished additional funds and staff with which to conduct investigatory work.

The Government Operations Committee receives more communications from the executive branch than does any other House standing committee. In the 99th Congress the committee processed 764 executive communications, nearly 21 percent of all such communications referred to standing committees. Some of these communications may have been routine, others may have been in response to major congressional inquiries, but each required some work on the part of the committee. At a minimum, each communication had to be read and processed. Those that answered congressional questions about issues of major concern had to be analyzed, which may have prompted legislative or oversight hearings that consumed months of work by the committee.

[*See also* Government Affairs Committee, Senate.]

BIBLIOGRAPHY

Cohen, Richard E. "The King of Oversight." *Government Executive*, September 1988, 16–18.

Sugawara, Sandra. "Conyers Promises a More Stringent Vigil over Procurement." *Washington Post*, 27 August 1990, p. 5.

U.S. House of Representatives. *Interim Report of the Activities of the House Committee on Government Operations*. 102d Cong., 1st sess., 1992. H. Doc. 102-1086.

Oleszek, Walter J. *Congressional Procedures and the Policy Process*. 3d ed. 1989.

MARY ETTA BOESL

GOVERNMENT PRINTING OFFICE.

Statutorily established in 1860, the Government Printing Office (GPO) provides public printing for the entire federal government through its own facilities and the procurement of commercial services. An agency of the legislative branch, GPO is headed by the public printer, who is appointed by the president subject to the approval of the Senate.

During the initial meetings of Congress in 1789, many members recognized the practical need for printed documents to assist each chamber with the performance of its duties and responsibilities. If nothing more, printing would allow legislators to work with legible documents and would provide multiple copies of records. Members also appreciated the civic value served by the publication of government documents—informing the sovereign citizenry. Consequently, early Congresses quickly provided for the printing and distribution of both laws and treaties. Similar action was taken regarding the House and Senate journals in 1813. Publication of congressional floor proceedings was begun in 1824, and, later, in 1846, Congress provided for the routine printing of congressional reports, special documents (including executive branch material), and legislative proposals. All this work was performed by private printers under contract to Congress.

By the time of the Jefferson administration, if not earlier, public printing had become an instrument for patronage. Those receiving contracts were po-

COPIES OF THE FEDERAL BUDGET. Beginning of the press run at the Government Printing Office, 1980.

STEVE KARAFYLLAKIS, CONGRESSIONAL QUARTERLY INC.

litical friends (often newspaper publishers) who owned printing machinery. Both an administration press (faithful to the president) and a party press (loyal to congressional leaders) were developing in Washington, D.C. The ability of heads of executive branch agencies to procure printing was usually controlled by the president. To meet printing needs and to bestow patronage, the president might turn to House or Senate contract printers or to both. These congressional printers were selected on a partisan basis and according to their ability to publish a newspaper that would function as a party organ. Such printers produced a large volume of the printing required by each house, and they frequently received smaller amounts of executive-branch printing from the president. It was a profitable business for the printers and one that rapidly became corrupt.

A congressional investigation in 1840 revealed that printers utilized by Congress had made profits of almost $470,000 during the previous seven years. Similar revelations by other inquiries in 1846, 1852, and 1860 contributed to growing embarrassment and outcry over the deplorable ethics and the graft of the public printing industry.

The reform response was the establishment of GPO to produce all public printing, either using its own facilities or through the competitive procurement of commercial services. Additional aspects of government-wide printing and publication were set with the Printing Act of 1895, still the source of much of the basic policy found in the printing chapters of the U.S. Code. This statute also transferred to GPO a program begun in 1813 for distributing selected government publications to certain depository libraries throughout the country.

The Printing Act also relocated the superintendent of documents, previously an Interior Department official, to GPO, giving him responsibility for managing document sales and preparing periodic catalogs of federal publications. The sale stock available to the superintendent derived entirely from materials provided for this purpose by the departments and agencies or returned from depository libraries. In 1904, the superintendent was authorized to reprint any departmental publication, with the consent of the pertinent secretary, for public sale. Congress legislated comparable discretion to reproduce its documents in 1922.

When the Printing Act became law, GPO relied on electrically powered rotary presses with hand-set type. This technology was subsequently replaced by linotype composition, which eventually gave way to computer-assisted composition and printing. Paper copies of documents came to be supplemented by microform, computer tapes, and diskettes. Since the mid 1980s, electronic formats have been introduced in both fixed modes, such as CD-ROMs, and in on-line services.

When GPO was established, it came under the immediate scrutiny of an existing special oversight panel. The Joint Committee on Public Printing, mandated in 1846, continues to monitor GPO management and operations. Through the exercise of remedial powers, the joint committee sets government printing and binding regulations. Its ten members are drawn equally from the chairs and ranking members of the Committee on House Administration and the Senate Committee on Rules and Administration, which have legislative jurisdiction over GPO and matters pertaining to it, but the joint committee itself has no actual legislative authority. GPO must seek funding annually from the appropriations committees of both houses, and it is subject to audit by the General Accounting Office, another legislative branch agency.

[*See also* Congress, *article on* Congressional Publications.]

BIBLIOGRAPHY

Stathis, Stephen W. "The Evolution of Government Printing and Publishing in America." *Government Publications Review* 7A (1980): 377–390.

U.S. Government Printing Office. *100 GPO Years, 1861–1961.* 1961.

U.S. Government Printing Office. *GPO/2001: Vision for a New Millennium.* 1992.

HAROLD C. RELYEA

GRAMM-LATTA RESOLUTION (1981). The budget resolution for fiscal year 1982 (H.R. Con. Res. 115, 97th Cong., 1st sess.), adopted by the House in May 1981, is better known as the Gramm-Latta Resolution. It embodied the budgetary proposals of newly elected president Ronald Reagan. House action on the resolution was one of the first major tests of congressional support for Reagan's budget policies, which called for lower taxes, higher defense spending, and cuts in social programs.

In April 1981, the House Budget Committee reported a budget resolution that called for a shift in budget priorities along the lines recommended by the new president but did not endorse all of his proposals. The committee had rejected an alternative, developed by two of its members—Phil Gramm of Texas, then a conservative Democrat, and Delbert L. Latta of Ohio, the ranking Republican on the committee—that reflected the president's program and had his support. But the full House approved a special rule (a simple resolution reported by the House Rules Committee that establishes the conditions for House consideration of legislation) that made the Gramm-Latta alternative in order as a substitute amendment. The House approved the Gramm-Latta alternative 253 to 176 on 7 May 1981 and approved the resolution, as amended by the alternative, that same day.

The vote approving the Gramm-Latta substitute was one of the first indications of a new conservative coalition of House Republicans and conservative, mostly southern Democrats (the so-called boll weevil Democrats) that was to give President Reagan a working majority in the Democrat-controlled House for the remainder of the 97th Congress.

BIBLIOGRAPHY

"First Budget Resolution Follows Reagan Plan." In *Congressional Quarterly Almanac.* 1981. Pp. 247–253.
U.S. House of Representatives. Committee on the Budget. *A Review of the Reconciliation Process.* 1984. Committee Print 9.

EDWARD DAVIS

GRAMM-RUDMAN-HOLLINGS ACT. *See* Balanced Budget and Emergency Deficit Control Act.

GRANDFATHERING. The term *grandfather* has been defined to mean a specific legal exemption based on previously existing circumstances. The term originated with a provision (the "grandfather clause") in some southern state constitutions designed to enfranchise poor whites and disenfranchise blacks by waiving certain voting requirements for descendants of men voting before 1867. In recent times, it has been applied to some provisions in law that are included by reference and contain a specific exemption. Most frequently it has been used in connection with Congress, to describe certain exceptions and exemptions to limitations on committee assignments.

Members of Congress receive committee assignments according to a long-standing and interrelated series of party procedures and chamber rules, and the number of assignments per member is generally limited. Not all committees are equally attractive and sought after, however. Slots on the less appealing panels are often difficult to fill. To fill the requisite committee size allocation, party caucuses occasionally assign members to these less attractive committees in addition to, and notwithstanding, their regular assignments. Such an assignment is called a "grandfather." The term is further used to describe the continuation of the additional assignment, notwithstanding party rules. The member is thus seen as being grandfathered in to the additional slot. Members retain these grandfathers until other members seek the slot or they give them up voluntarily or lose them because of the adoption of stricter limitation rules. Grandfathered seats still

enable members to gain seniority on both the additional and legitimate committee assignments.

BIBLIOGRAPHY

U.S. House of Representatives. *Preamble and Rules of the House Democratic Caucus.* 103d Cong., 1st sess., 1993.

JUDY SCHNEIDER

GRANT, ULYSSES S. (1822–1885), army officer, general in chief of the U.S. Army, and eighteenth president of the United States. During the Civil War, Grant's dealings with Congress were limited to responding to inquiries made by the Committee on the Conduct of the War and the efforts of Rep. Elihu B. Washburne to promote Grant's career, most notably though the passage of a bill in February 1864 reestablishing the rank of lieutenant general with Grant in mind. During Reconstruction, Grant as general in chief of the U.S. Army worked closely with Congress. The army, in charge of administering federal policy in the defeated South, became embroiled in the struggle over reconstruction between President Andrew Johnson and the Republican-dominated Congress. Originally supportive of the president, Grant became disil-

INAUGURATION OF ULYSSES S. GRANT. In March 1869.
LIBRARY OF CONGRESS

lusioned with Johnson's excessive leniency toward former Confederates and indifference toward the fate of southern blacks, Unionists, and army personnel on occupation duty. He advised congressional Republicans in framing the Reconstruction Acts of 1867, which called upon the army to administer the reconstruction process; Congress protected Grant by attaching riders to appropriation bills directing Johnson to issue orders through Grant and forbidding the president from ordering Grant away from Washington. As relations between Johnson and Grant worsened, the general drew closer to congressional Republicans, and in 1868 he supported Johnson's impeachment.

Grant had been mentioned as a possible presidential candidate as early as 1864; by 1867, moderate Republicans and some Democrats were vying to nominate him in 1868. Republican setbacks in the off-year elections of 1867 ended whatever hopes Radical Republicans had of nominating one of their own for president; Grant thus emerged as the logical Republican nominee in 1868 because of his great popularity, an appeal enhanced by his image as a nonpolitician. In the fall election, proclaiming, "Let us have peace," he trounced his Democratic rival, Horatio Seymour.

Grant began his first term determined to resist further congressional encroachment on presidential powers. He chose his original cabinet slate without consulting congressional Republicans, and he forced Congress to modify the Tenure of Office Act to enhance his powers of appointment and removal. Within a year, however, he discovered that he had to forge a coalition of congressional supporters to enact policies, in particular a treaty to annex the Dominican Republic. Although Massachusetts senator Charles Sumner and his allies defeated annexation, Grant succeeded in forming a coterie of administration senators led by Roscoe Conkling of New York, Zachariah Chandler of Michigan, Simon Cameron of Pennsylvania, and Timothy O. Howe of Wisconsin; they ousted Sumner from his chairmanship of the Senate Foreign Relations Committee in 1871.

It is commonly believed that these senators dominated a hapless and confused Grant, who, surrendering to their dictation, thus eroded presidential power in executive-legislative relations. Recent scholarship offers a reevaluation of the Grant presidency, discovering that Grant demonstrated considerable political skill and chose to work with Congress to pass legislation and build political support. Most notable among these accomplishments was

ULYSSES S. GRANT. As president, in a portrait photograph by Mathew Brady. Shortly after his election, Grant came to realize the importance of forging a congressional coalition supportive of his policies. In his second term he came into conflict with Congress, especially the Democratic House.   LIBRARY OF CONGRESS

the passage of the series of Enforcement acts in 1870 and 1871 that authorized Grant to crush violence, intimidation, and fraud by Democrats in the South and in northern cities and the negotiation of a treaty with Great Britain to arbitrate damages arising out of British actions during the Civil War. Moreover, Grant's support of civil service reform impinged upon congressional efforts to dictate appointments as part of the patronage process. In fact, Grant's opponents, who included dissident Republicans (the so-called Liberal Republicans) as well as Democrats, characterized as "Caesarism" his supposedly high-handed exercise of executive power. But Grant easily won reelection in 1872 over newspaper editor Horace Greeley, the Liberal Republican–Democratic candidate.

Grant's second term proved troublesome. Revelations of corrupt behavior by congressmen in accepting stock in Crédit Mobilier, an investment scheme fronting as a construction company for the Union Pacific Railroad, overshadowed Grant's reelection triumph; Congress's decision to vote itself a retroactive pay raise served to worsen its image. An economic depression sparked by the panic of 1873, the growing unpopularity of Reconstruction, and the emergence of new issues led to the election of a Democratic majority in the House of Representatives in 1874. That year, Grant issued his most important veto, rejecting a bill that called for a modest inflation of the money supply; it was sustained, in part, because members of Congress remembered Senator Sumner's fate. Grant also called for the enactment of the line-item veto, the first president to do so, but Congress refused his request, much as it declined to add to the president's Reconstruction power and lost interest in civil service reform. Grant, frustrated by Congress's failure to resolve disputes in southern states, responded to criticism of his efforts to protect Republican regimes from violence in several strongly worded messages.

Once in power, House Democrats wasted no time in launching investigations of the administration. These hearings, along with a probe launched by Secretary of the Treasury Benjamin H. Bristow, revealed corrupt behavior by administration officials. Bristow's investigation of the Whiskey Ring, a revenue fraud conspiracy, implicated Grant's private secretary, Orville E. Babcock; a House committee investigation disclosed that the two wives of Secretary of War William W. Belknap had sold post traderships at frontier forts, and only Belknap's immediate resignation saved him from conviction in the ensuing impeachment trial. Additional investigations targeted other administration officials for malfeasance in office; Grant, denouncing the partisan motivation of such inquiries, often failed to assess the accuracy of their charges. His defensiveness over the charges and his inability to believe that his friends had betrayed him seriously damaged his reputation and dashed what hope remained for a third term.

Grant worked with Congress to provide an equitable solution to the disputed results of the 1876 presidential contest between Republican Rutherford B. Hayes and Democrat Samuel J. Tilden. He backed the formation of an electoral commission to determine the winner, then negotiated with southern envoys to end a House filibuster by promising not to support Republican regimes in Louisiana and South Carolina. Leaving the White House in March 1877, he returned from a world tour and made an unsuccessful bid for a third term in 1880. Several months before his death, as he struggled with throat cancer and financial distress while he composed his memoirs, Congress placed his name on the army retired list with his old rank of full general.

BIBLIOGRAPHY

Hesseltine, William B. *Ulysses S. Grant: Politician.* 1935.
McFeely, William S. *Grant: A Biography.* 1981.
Simpson, Brooks D. *Let Us Have Peace: Ulysses S. Grant and the Politics of War and Reconstruction, 1861–1868.* 1991.

BROOKS D. SIMPSON

GRANT-IN-AID. Grants-in-aid are a leading technique of intergovernmental relations in the U.S. federal system. Congress uses grants to state and local governments as instruments of national policy. They are typically given for a specified purpose, with conditions attached, and not just to redistribute public revenues.

Grants initially took the form of lands, although in one noteworthy measure in 1836 Congress distributed revenue that had been realized from land sales. Over the course of the nineteenth century, Congress made massive grants to state governments from the federal domain. By far the greatest amount, over eighty-one million acres, was for common schools. Far surpassing what was needed for school sites, this land was to be leased or sold, with the proceeds going to education. The statements of purpose accompanying grants were usually very general.

Grants-in-aid as a systematic technique of federal-state relations, applying to all states and employing a reasonably specific statement of purpose, are usually traced to the Morrill Land-Grant College Act (1862), which gave each state thirty thousand acres for each of its senators and representatives in Congress to endow colleges in the agricultural and mechanic arts. States that contained no public lands were given scrip.

Grants-in-aid financed out of appropriations followed, and they were well-established by the early twentieth century. Examples included the Hatch Act of 1887 (agricultural experiment stations); a second Morrill Act, in 1890 (annual appropriations for the land-grant colleges); the Weeks Act of 1911 (forest fire protection); the Smith-Lever Act of 1914 (agricultural and home economics extension work); the Federal Aid Highway Act of 1916; the Smith-Hughes Act of 1917 (vocational education); and the Sheppard-Towner Act of 1921 (maternal and infant hygiene).

Massachusetts challenged the constitutionality of the Sheppard-Towner Act, arguing that it lay beyond the scope of Congress's spending power. In *Massachusetts v. Mellon* (1923), the Supreme Court declined to rule on the merits, holding that a state is not entitled to a remedy in the courts against an allegedly unconstitutional appropriation of national funds.

Federal grants prior to the New Deal amounted to less than 10 percent of states' revenue from their own sources. With the Social Security Act (1935), which initiated grants for public assistance, the figure rose precipitously. With the Interstate Highway Act of 1956, which authorized a mammoth public works program, it jumped again. During the Johnson administration in the mid 1960s, Congress enacted scores of grant programs to combat poverty and inequality. Medicaid, providing medical care for the needy, and aid for elementary and secondary education, benefiting especially the poorest states and school districts having a high proportion of poor children, were passed in 1965. The election of Republican presidents did not slow the growth of grants. In particular, enactment of sewage treatment system grants in 1972 gave spending yet another big push. By 1978, federal grant programs numbered close to five hundred and totaled $79 billion, which approached a third of state and local governments' general revenues from their own sources and a fourth of federal domestic outlays. They had become pervasive.

Until the New Deal, federal grants went almost exclusively to state governments. With the enactment of aid for public housing in 1937 and urban redevelopment in 1949, grants to cities became routine. However, they remained a minor share of local revenues until the explosion of grant spending in the 1960s and 1970s, of which local governments were the principal beneficiaries.

Grants are allocated among recipient governments either by statutory formulas (formula grants) or at the discretion of federal administrators who pass judgment on applications (project grants). Most grants are distributed by formula, and much of the politics of grant-in-aid programs is linked to the construction of the formulas. While many formulas contain equalizing elements intended to compensate for interjurisdictional disparities in taxable wealth and socioeconomic composition, the normal tendency of grant politics is toward wide geographic dispersion of aid.

In the State and Local Fiscal Assistance Act of 1972, Congress enacted a program of grants-in-aid unrestricted by purpose. Called "general revenue sharing," this program was a radical departure, but after the federal government began to experience severe fiscal shortages at the end of the 1970s it was discontinued. Congress reverted to prescribing the purposes of grants. However, initiatives by Presidents Richard M. Nixon and Ronald Reagan led to the emergence of "broad-based" or "block" grants, which provided funds on relatively general and permissive terms. They were created by consolidating and simplifying clusters of related categorical grants, most importantly in regard to community development and employment and training.

Largely through such consolidations, the number of grant programs fell to 435 (422 "categorical" and 13 "block") by 1987. However, even as revenue sharing reached a peak and block grants took effect, categorical grants continued to predominate in terms of dollars.

The tendency over time, despite the introduction of block grants, has been for conditions to become more numerous, exacting, and varied. Included are sweeping prohibitions against discrimination on the basis of race, color, national origin, gender, age, and handicapped status, all products of the rights revolution of the 1960s and 1970s. Also, as grants exploded, Congress began threatening to withhold all or part of the biggest grants (e.g., for highways and medicaid) in order to influence actions of the states, sometimes in ways having no connection to the purpose of the grant. Thus, federal grants gradually have become more coercive, their conditions perceived by state and local governments as "mandates." This trend continued even as, after 1978, they began to decline as a share of federal domestic outlays and state and local expenditures.

It is not necessarily the case that conditioned grants-in-aid produce uniform policy. Interjurisdictional differences are reduced but not eliminated by this type of federal intervention. Gaps in federal laws and limits on the supervisory capacities of federal agencies leave room for the play of state and local politics and policy traditions.

The states' appeals to federal courts for relief from grant conditions have been futile. Courts have granted standing to challenge such conditions but invariably have found that they are not coercive because states are technically free to refuse the grants and that Congress has power to set the terms on which federal funds are disbursed. The precedent-setting case was *Oklahoma v. Civil Service Commission* (330 U.S. 127 [1947]). Additionally, after the late 1960s, federal judicial readings of the Constitution and federal statutes often specified the states' obligations in grant programs, especially in the field of welfare. Courts have admitted claims of private individuals against state governments under grant-in-aid statutes.

BIBLIOGRAPHY

Advisory Commission on Intergovernmental Relations. *Significant Features of Fiscal Federalism.* Published annually.
Advisory Commission on Intergovernmental Relations. *Regulatory Federalism: Policy, Process, Impact, and Reform.* 1984.
Clark, Jane Perry. *The Rise of a New Federalism.* 1938.

MARTHA DERTHICK

GRAVEL V. UNITED STATES (408 U.S. 606 [1972]). The Constitution provides that "for any Speech or Debate in either House, [senators and representatives] shall not be questioned in any other Place." This privilege was designed to protect members of Congress from intimidation in the form of prosecutions or other forms of questioning that directly impinge on the legislative process. The clause traces its roots to the English Bill of Rights and has been recognized as an important defense of legislative independence.

Gravel v. United States arose out of the 1971 disclosure of the Pentagon Papers, a secret history of the Vietnam War prepared by the Defense Depart-

ment. Sen. Mike Gravel (D-Alaska) read from the Pentagon Papers in a subcommittee meeting and placed them in the public record. A grand jury investigating possible criminal violations related to the Pentagon Papers' disclosure subpoenaed an aide to Senator Gravel and an employee of a publisher that had reportedly made arrangements with Gravel's office to publish the papers.

The Supreme Court held that the aide was protected insofar as his conduct would be protected legislative activity if performed by the member himself. Protected activity, the Court stated, embraces those matters that are an "integral part of the deliberative and communicative processes by which Members participate in committee and House proceedings with respect to the consideration and passage or rejection of proposed legislation or with respect to other matters which the Constitution places within the jurisdiction of either House." Thus, while the conduct of the hearing and its preparation were privileged, questioning about private publication of the papers was permissible. Subsequent cases have fleshed out the scope of protected legislative activity in the context of criminal prosecutions, libel suits, and employment discrimination claims by examining the extent to which the activities at issue were an integral part of the legislative process and therefore immune from criminal or civil process.

[*See also* Speech or Debate Clause.]

BIBLIOGRAPHY

Reinstein, Robert J., and Harvey A. Silvergate. "Legislative Privilege and the Separation of Powers." *Harvard Law Review* 86 (1973): 1113–1182.
U.S. Senate. *The Constitution of the United States of America: Analysis and Interpretation.* 99th Cong., 1st sess., 1987. S. Doc. 99-16.

RICHARD EHLKE

GREAT SOCIETY. *Great Society* is the term used by President Lyndon B. Johnson that signaled his intention to use the authority and resources of the federal government to improve the living conditions and opportunities for Americans, especially those deemed "disadvantaged." The Great Society served as a rubric for a wide range of domestic social welfare programs. Most Great Society programs were enacted in 1965, following Johnson's landslide election and that of large Democratic majorities to the 89th Congress. It was in Johnson's State of the Union speech of that year that he used the phrase in an exalted tone and presented specific legislative proposals.

By 1967 the Vietnam War had diminished Johnson's popularity, and the cost of the war had made Congress more reluctant to support large budgets for domestic social welfare programs. It was the 1970s, rather than the 1960s, that saw the growth of many Great Society programs and successor programs, such as the Comprehensive Employment and Training Act (CETA).

A key part of the Great Society was the Economic Opportunity Act of 1964, dubbed the "war on poverty." That act established the Office of Economic Opportunity to direct and coordinate a wide variety of education, employment, and training programs. The act created an Office of Economic Opportunity (OEO) to administer several programs intended to lift millions of Americans above the poverty level. Its centerpiece was the Community Action Program, which created and funded local community agencies that would mobilize the poor and launch a comprehensive program to "focus" federal, state, and local resources and services on the poverty problem. It also authorized a variety of training and work experience programs, such as the Job Corps and the Neighborhood Youth Corps, for disadvantaged youth.

The Medicare program expanded Social Security to provide health insurance for the elderly, and Medicaid, a grant-in-aid program to the states, funded health care for the poor. Great Society legislation also included civil rights laws for minorities (e.g., the Voting Rights Act of 1965), federal aid for education (the Higher Education Act of 1965), for public housing (the Housing and Urban Development Act of 1965), and a liberalization of benefits and eligibility for traditional welfare programs like Aid to Families with Dependent Children.

While particular programs like Medicare, the Job Corps, and Head Start are generally acknowledged as political and programmatic successes, the Great Society has been the subject of intense criticism and debate. Many have argued that politicians oversold these programs, creating unrealistic expectations of what they could achieve. Although certain groups, such as the elderly, have been lifted out of poverty in great numbers, the Great Society fell far short of perhaps its principal aim—to make economically self-sufficient and upwardly mobile groups in urban and rural areas that continue to suffer from persistent poverty.

Conservative critics of the Great Society have argued that these programs were ill-conceived be-

CAMPAIGN COMIC BOOK. Portraying Lyndon B. Johnson as a superhero who foresees the creation of the Great Society, 1964.   COLLECTION OF DAVID J. AND JANICE L. FRENT

cause they failed to strengthen families and communities and promote self-responsibility; instead, it is argued, the programs created dependency. Liberals counter that the programs suffered from poor implementation and inadequate funding and that more progress was not made because of changes in the U.S. economy.

[See also Civil Rights Act of 1964; Economic Opportunity Act of 1964; Elementary and Secondary Education Act of 1965; Higher Education Act of 1965; Medicare; National Foundation on the Arts and the Humanities Act of 1965; Urban Mass Transportation Act of 1964; Vocational Education Act of 1963; Voting Rights Act of 1965.]

BIBLIOGRAPHY

Levitan, Sar A. *The Great Society's Poor Law: A New Approach to Poverty.* 1969.

Levitan, Sar A., and Robert Taggart. *The Promise of Greatness*. 1976.

GARY MUCCIARONI

GREEN, EDITH S. (1910–1987), Democratic representative from Oregon (1954–1974) and innovative advocate for aid to higher education, equal rights, and social welfare. Initially a teacher, Edith Starrett Green became involved in politics through her work, and in 1952 was asked by members of the Oregon Democratic party to run for secretary of State; she did and suffered her only election loss. In 1954 she won election to the House of Representatives, a post she held until her voluntary retirement in 1974. Upon retirement, Edith Green returned home to Portland, where she worked as a professor of government and a member of the Oregon Board of Higher Education.

Edith Green is often called the "mother of higher education." Most notably, she authored and shepherded through Congress the Higher Education Act of 1965, which provided for federal student aid. For eighteen years, she served on the Committee on Education and Labor, where she became the second-ranking member. By 1973, in her final House term, Green was disenchanted with the liberal-leaning Education and Labor Committee, which she abandoned in favor of a junior slot on the Appropriations Subcommittee on Health, Education, and Welfare. Here she was directly involved in efforts to force the Republican administration to spend funds as appropriated by Congress, then controlled by the Democrats.

Representative Green was respected by friends and foes alike for her hard work, intelligence, and legislative acumen. Her toughness and independence led her to speak out on many of the controversial issues of her day and made it difficult to place Edith Green on the traditional liberal-conservative spectrum: for example, she was an early opponent of the Vietnam War; she joined with southern colleagues in opposing school busing; and she authored the Equal Pay for Equal Work Act.

BIBLIOGRAPHY

Dreifus, Claudia. "Women in Politics: An Interview with Edith Green." *Social Policy* 2 (1972): 16–22.
Green, Edith. "Fears and Fallacies: Equal Opportunities in the 1970s." University of Michigan, Ann Arbor, 1975.
Miller, Norman C. "Rep. Edith Green, a Bareknuckle Fighter." *Wall Street Journal*, 3 December 1969.

MARY ETTA BOESL

GRIFFITHS, MARTHA W. (1912–), Democratic representative from Michigan (1955–1974) and advocate for women's rights and social welfare. Trained as an attorney, Martha Wright Griffiths first entered public service in 1948, when she won a seat in the Michigan legislature. She resigned the state post to run for the U.S. Congress in 1952, a bid she narrowly lost. Martha Griffiths won the House seat when she ran again in 1954, even though the state Democratic party supported her opponent in the primary election. Twenty years later, in 1974, she voluntarily left Congress and returned to the Detroit area, where she planned to retire. In 1982 Griffiths came out of retirement to run successfully for lieutenant governor of Michigan, and she was reelected to the post in 1986.

While in Congress, Griffiths was known for her expertise in economics. She was the first woman to serve on the powerful Committee on Ways and Means. She was also a member of the Joint Committee on Budget Control and the Joint Economic Committee, where she chaired the Subcommittee on Fiscal Policy.

Martha Griffiths can be characterized as a hard-working legislator who frequently promoted bold

MARTHA W. GRIFFITHS.

initiatives. She had her share of successes, and her share of failures, in her legislative efforts. Many credit Griffiths with convincing southern representatives that prohibitions against sex discrimination should be added to the Civil Rights Act of 1964; she also pushed through amendments to the Social Security Act to benefit female workers. She was the major House sponsor of early national health insurance legislation and of the Equal Rights Amendment.

BIBLIOGRAPHY

George, Emily. *Martha W. Griffiths.* 1982.
Kool, Nancy. "Martha Griffiths: First among Firsts." *Monthly Detroit*, March 1984.

MARY ETTA BOESL

GROSS, HAROLD R. (1899–1987), Republican representative from Iowa, one of the "Great Objectors" of the House. Once described as "caretaker of the congressional conscience," Harold Royce Gross, a conservative with a booming voice, dedicated his twenty-six-year House career (1949–1975) to a single purpose: slowing the flow of federal dollars into programs that he deemed extravagant and wasteful. Gross served on no major committees, had no leadership role, and was shunned by many of his colleagues. Yet within the limits of his objectives—the exposure and demise of questionable legislation—he ranked among the most effective House members in history.

Noted for his careful scrutiny of all bills before the House, Gross religiously remained on the floor and took an active role in debate. His informed questioning of managers often exposed hidden costs and unintended consequences, revelations sufficient to keep certain bills from becoming law. "How much will this boondoggle cost?" was his favorite opening line. He was most effective at blocking bills brought before the House under expedited procedures that require unanimous consent, or near-unanimous consent, for passage. Throughout the 1950s and 1960s, his loud "I object" was for legislative activists the most dreaded utterance heard on Capitol Hill. He used various techniques, including frequent quorum calls, to protest the passage of bills that he could not block. *Reader's Digest* estimated in 1972 that he had requested more quorum calls than any other House member in history. For years he sponsored a bill to reduce federal spending, which by special arrangement with the House clerk was always numbered H.R. 144, the initials

and number creating a pun on his name.

Gross ranks among a half dozen representatives who, by sheer dedication to their self-appointed roles as Treasury watchdogs, have earned the House's informal title of "Great Objector." Others were Elisha Whittlesey, Elihu B. Washburne, William S. Holman, Constantine B. Kilgore, and Robert F. Rich.

BIBLIOGRAPHY

Leslie, Jacques. "H. R. Gross: Conscience of the House." *Reader's Digest*, August 1972, 92–96.
McNeil, Neil. *Forge of Democracy: The House of Representatives.* 1963. Pp. 132–133.

DONALD C. BACON

GROW, GALUSHA A. (1823–1907), representative from Pennsylvania, antislavery Republican, Speaker of the House (1861–1863), co-creator of the Homestead Act. Grow was a prominent member of the generation of northern Republicans that swept into Congress during the 1850s and gave the new party its distinctive initial character. Raised in Pennsylvania, he went to Amherst College, practiced law (including a partnership with David Wilmot, author of the Wilmot Proviso), was active in Pennsylvania Democratic politics, and in the 1850 election became the youngest new member of the 32d Congress. First as a Democrat and then as a Republican, he held his western Pennsylvania seat until 1863.

In the wake of Abraham Lincoln's victory in the 1860 election, and Republican domination of Congress after the southerners left, the thirty-seven-year old Grow was chosen in July 1861 to be the Speaker of the House, a tribute to his oratorical and leadership qualities and to his identification with Republican party principles. His long-championed Homestead Act finally was enacted in May 1862, a major item in the flood of legislation passed by this first Republican-dominated Congress.

However, Grow had to face a redrawn district and vengeful Democrats in the election of 1862, a time when the unpopularity of the war and his Radical Republicanism worked against him. He lost his seat, and over the course of a thirty-year effort to return—during which Grow was constantly blocked by the opposition of the Curtin-Cameron-Quay leadership of the Pennsylvania Republican machine—he managed to secure only one freak re-election in an 1883 by-election. Political issues, and the Republican party, had moved on past him.

GALUSHA A. GROW.
HARPER'S PICTORIAL HISTORY OF THE GREAT REBELLION

BIBLIOGRAPHY

Dubois, James T., and Gertrude S. Mathews. *Galusha A. Grow, Father of the Homestead Law.* 1917.
Ilesevich, Robert D. *Galusha A. Grow: The People's Candidate.* 1988.

MORTON KELLER

GRUNDY, FELIX (1777–1840), representative and senator from Tennessee, "War Hawk." Grundy grew up in frontier Virginia in the late eighteenth century and then moved to and came of political age on the new southwest frontier. He took an active part in the drafting of Kentucky's 1799 consti-

tution, served in the new state's legislature and on its supreme court, and then moved to Nashville, Tennessee. His eloquence and legal skills made him the area's leading criminal lawyer, and in 1811 he was elected to the House of Representatives as a Democratic-Republican.

Grundy came to Congress as one of the outspoken War Hawks, the name given to a group of young members of Congress imbued with the burgeoning popular nationalism of the new nation. They favored war with England (and if necessary with France as well) in defense of American rights at sea and in hopes of territorial gains in Canada and the Spanish Southwest.

After the War of 1812, Grundy allied himself with the rising political star of his fellow-Tennessean, the war hero Andrew Jackson. Nevertheless, he lost his seat to John Bell, who represented yet another generation in the fast-changing political culture of the region. Grundy replaced John H. Eaton as one of Tennessee's senators when Jackson made Eaton

FELIX GRUNDY. Engraving by T. B. Welch after a painting by W. B. Cooper. LIBRARY OF CONGRESS

his secretary of War. Although he was attracted by South Carolina's states' rights stand in the nullification controversy of 1832, Grundy's close ties to Jackson led him to steer a middle course. Grundy successfully resisted Jackson's efforts to restore his seat to Eaton while remaining a staunch Jacksonian, and he later served as Martin Van Buren's attorney general. Grundy was an evocative representative of the new, popular American nationalism that found its voice in the War of 1812 but could not easily adapt to the rising political pressures of sectionalism.

BIBLIOGRAPHY

Parks, Joseph. *Felix Grundy: Champion of Democracy.* 1940.

MORTON KELLER

GULF WAR. *See* Persian Gulf War.

GUN CONTROL. Firearms have played a prominent role in the nation's history. The Constitution recognizes "the right of the people to keep and bear arms"; it was only after notorious gun-related crimes in the twentieth century that Congress enacted major laws regulating firearms. The National Firearms Act, passed in 1934 after the attempted assassination of president-elect Franklin D. Roosevelt the previous year and a wave of organized-crime killings, imposed taxes on machine guns, sawed-off shotguns, and rifles and required that such firearms be registered with the Treasury Department. In 1938, Congress passed the Federal Firearms Act to require licenses for manufacturers, importers, and dealers, and to prohibit the selling of firearms to indicted suspects or convicted criminals. After the 1963 assassination of President John F. Kennedy, members of Congress introduced various gun control measures but none was enacted.

The assassinations in 1968 of civil rights leader Martin Luther King, Jr., and Sen. Robert F. Kennedy (D-N.Y.) provided the necessary momentum for the passage of two significant bills. On 6 June 1968, the day after Robert Kennedy was shot to death, President Lyndon B. Johnson called on Congress "to give America the gun control law it needs." Within two weeks, Congress had attached a provision to an omnibus crime bill that, in effect, banned mail-order sales of handguns by requiring them to be acquired from licensed dealers in the buyer's home state. Legislators then began work on the Gun Control Act of 1968, which extended the purchasing restrictions to all types of guns. Clauses involving regulation of dealers and collectors generated lengthy debates both in committee and on the floor. Eventually, Congress approved a bill that excluded Johnson's proposals for licensing gun owners and registering firearms.

Complaints by gun owners that the 1968 law was being enforced too strictly against those who did not intend to use guns criminally resulted in a new statute eighteen years later. The 1986 Firearms Owners Protection Act once again permitted interstate sales of long guns by dealers. The law included a ban sought by gun control advocates on the manufacture and sale of machine guns, and a separate measure restricted the sale of armor-piercing ammunition.

Attempts to challenge federal gun control laws as contrary to the Second Amendment have failed in the Supreme Court. Antigun organizations, citing the fact that the rate of violent crime associated with guns in the United States is among the world's highest, continue to press for more controls. Opponents, led by the National Rifle Association, argue that criminals can easily obtain one of the estimated 200 million guns in the nation and that more laws may infringe on the rights of those using firearms in sports. In 1993, Congress passed the so-called Brady Bill, named after White House press

Landmark Legislation on Gun Control

TITLE	YEAR ENACTED	REFERENCE NUMBER	DESCRIPTION
National Firearms Act	1934	48 Stat. 1236	Regulated machine guns, sawed-off shotguns, and rifles.
Gun Control Act	1968	82 Stat. 1213–1236	Barred interstate mail-order sales of firearms.
Firearms Owners Protection Act	1986	P.L. 99-308	Lifted interstate ban on sales of rifles and shotguns and banned machine guns.
Brady Handgun Violence Prevention Act (Brady Bill)	1993	P.L. 103-159	Imposed a five-day waiting period on handgun purchases.

BRADY BILL. *At front, left to right,* Rep. Charles E. Schumer (D-N.Y.), Sarah Brady, and Jim Brady at a press conference announcing the reintroduction of the Brady Bill to Congress.

R. MICHAEL JENKINS, CONGRESSIONAL QUARTERLY INC.

secretary James Brady, who was seriously wounded in the 1981 assassination attempt on President Ronald Reagan; the bill, which became effective in February 1994, imposed a five-day waiting period on prospective handgun purchases so that law-enforcement authorities could check the buyers' backgrounds. Opponents promptly went to court objecting to the required record checks. In 1994, Congress considered legislation that would ban certain military-style "assault weapons" that sometimes are used in urban crimes. New legislation was introduced that would require licenses and training for handgun purchasers. The intensity of arguments and political activity by opposing sides indicated that the gun control debate would continue through the 1990s and beyond.

BIBLIOGRAPHY

Kennett, Lee, and James LaVerne Anderson. *The Gun in America: The Origins of a National Dilemma.* 1976.

Kleck, Gary. *Point Blank: Guns and Violence in America.* 1991.

Wright, James D., Peter H. Rossi, and Kathleen Daly. *Under the Gun: Weapons, Crime and Violence in America.* 1983.

TED GEST

H

HALF-BREEDS. *See* History of Congress, *article on* The Age of the Machine.

HALLECK, CHARLES A. (1900–1986), a Republican representative from Indiana (1935–1969), self-styled "gut fighter" who served as House minority leader from 1959 to 1965. After service in the infantry in World War I, Halleck returned to his native state; he received an A.B. degree in 1922 and an LL.B. degree in 1924 from Indiana University. He started a law practice and was appointed prosecuting attorney for the 30th judicial circuit, where he served from 1924 to 1934. In 1935, he won a special election to fill the vacancy caused by the death of a Republican representative-elect. Halleck was reelected to the 75th Congress (1937–1939) and to fifteen successive Congresses.

Recognizing his loyalty to party, his basic midwestern, rural, conservative values, and his skills at party infighting, Republican leaders appointed him to the House Committee on Rules early in his career. His fund-raising skills and effective stump-speaking also brought him the chairmanship of the Republican National Campaign Committee in the early 1940s.

In 1946, Republicans rode the crest of an anti-Truman, anti-Democratic election surge to win outright control of the House for the first time since 1928. Joseph W. Martin, Jr., of Massachusetts, the Republican minority leader, was elevated to Speaker; Halleck leap-frogged over the minority whip, Leslie C. Arends of Illinois, to become the new Republican majority leader in the 80th Congress (1947–1949). But in 1948 Harry S. Truman upset New York governor Thomas E. Dewey, and the House and Senate reverted to Democratic control. (Halleck had for a time seemed assured of becoming Dewey's vice presidential candidate, but at the last minute, Dewey turned to California governor Earl Warren. Neither candidate on the ticket proved adept at turning back Truman's campaign criticisms of an "80th-do-nothing Congress," a task that Halleck would have relished.)

In late 1958, after years of frustration serving under Martin, Halleck finally secured the go-ahead from Republican president Dwight D. Eisenhower to challenge the senior ailing minority leader. Even with the support of "young turks" Melvin R. Laird of Wisconsin, Glenard P. Lipscomb of California, and others, Halleck was able to edge Martin only by one vote. Six years later, in January 1965, another band of young turks, this time led by Robert P. Griffin of Michigan, Charles E. Goodell of New York, and Donald Rumsfeld of Illinois, promoted Conference chairman Gerald R. Ford of Michigan over Halleck. Ford won by a vote of 73 to 67.

As floor leader, Halleck was especially effective in challenging Democratic party rhetoric or summarizing his own party's case in the closing moments of debate. But when he signed on to support the Kennedy-Johnson Civil Rights Act of 1964, he earned the ire of a number of his southern conservative colleagues.

After Halleck's loss to Ford in January 1965, several committee assignments were returned to him, but not the strategic Rules Committee post. Halleck from time to time unleashed his fiery debate style in the closing years of his congressional service. He died on 3 March 1986.

CHARLES A. HALLECK. *Left*, with Senate minority leader Everett M. Dirksen (R-Ill.) in Dirksen's office, 9 February 1961. LIBRARY OF CONGRESS

BIBLIOGRAPHY

Jones, Charles O. *The Minority Party in Congress.* 1970.

Peabody, Robert L. *Leadership in Congress: Stability, Succession and Change.* 1976.

Scheele, Henry. *Charles Halleck: A Political Biography.* 1966.

ROBERT L. PEABODY

HARDING, WARREN G. (1865–1923), Republican senator from Ohio and twenty-ninth president of the United States (1921–1923), remembered especially for his scandal-ridden administration. After graduating from Ohio Central College at age sixteen, Harding moved to Marion, Ohio, where in 1884 he began a successful venture as a newspaper publisher with the acquisition of the Marion *Star.* Hand-

some and congenial, Harding became widely known in the community as a fervent supporter of the Republican party.

Local prominence combined with oratorical skills to make Harding an attractive political candidate. Elected to the state senate in 1899 and 1901, he became Ohio's lieutenant governor in 1904. A conservative Democrat defeated Harding for governor in 1910 by capitalizing on revelations of Republican corruption. Harding achieved national recognition in 1912 with his ringing nomination of President William Howard Taft at the national convention, and he was elected to the U.S. Senate in 1914.

Harding loved being in the Senate but demonstrated little interest in the legislative process. He served with no distinction on various committees: Commerce, Claims, Coastal Defenses, Investigations of Trespasses on Indian Lands, and Sale of Meat Products. He supported wartime measures and woman suffrage. Though hardly a dry, Harding voted for the Eighteenth Amendment to satisfy powerful prohibitionist forces at home. He introduced 134 bills, 122 of them relating to local matters; his twelve national bills had little significance. Harding disliked controversy and was absent from 46 percent of roll-call votes. When voting, he supported his party 95 percent of the time. In May 1919, Harding became a member of the Foreign Relations Committee, where he opposed the League of Nations and voted against the Treaty of Versailles.

Harding announced his candidacy for the presidency in December 1919 primarily in order to strengthen his Ohio political base. But he quickly realized that the national candidates might negate each other at the convention and began to seek the nomination seriously, shrewdly asking delegates to name him their second choice if the convention deadlocked. When this occurred, the delegates turned to Harding, selecting Calvin Coolidge as his running mate.

Harding ran a conservative "front porch" campaign; his slogan, "Back to normalcy," set the tone. Wartime dislocations, postwar economic difficulties, and the fight over the Treaty of Versailles had weakened the Democrats, and Harding won in a landslide, receiving an unprecedented popular majority of 60.2 percent.

Harding made three excellent cabinet appointments—Charles Evans Hughes, Herbert Hoover, and Henry C. Wallace, as secretaries of State, Commerce, and Agriculture, respectively. But Secretary of the Treasury Andrew W. Mellon's economic policies during the 1920s contributed to the coming of the Great Depression, while Attorney General Harry M. Daugherty, Harding's political manager, and Secretary of the Interior Albert B. Fall, a Senate friend, turned out to be disastrous appointments. Rarely establishing policy himself, Harding allowed cabinet officers to run their departments, mediating any disagreements that occurred within the cabinet.

The Washington Conference (1921–1922), called to end a naval arms race and solve problems in the Far East, became the most important foreign policy achievement of Harding's administration. The conference produced history's first significant arms limitation agreement, though agreements concerning the Far East proved less successful.

Harding's relationship with the Republican-dominated Congress (303 Republican seats in the House and 55 in the Senate) reflected his conception of the presidency. He did not believe in dictating legislation to Congress; party leaders, in his view, worked out legislative matters in consultation with cabinet officers. His domestic policy was to reduce taxes, create sound fiscal policies, raise tariffs, limit immigration, examine agricultural problems, end interference with business, and assist veterans. Agricultural policy became a major area of contention because the congressional farm bloc wanted federal relief for farmers suffering from a depression that had begun in 1920. Mellon argued against providing aid. Eventually, the administration accepted modest relief measures after the farm bloc threatened to obstruct Congress. In 1921, Congress reduced taxes, limited immigration, and created the Veterans' Bureau, the General Accounting Office, and the Bureau of the Budget. The Fordney-McCumber Tariff Act (1922) restored high tariffs. In this way, the Harding administration established the Republican economic agenda for the decade.

Harding died on 2 August 1923 from complications caused by a heart attack. Harding's enormous personal popularity did not long survive him because serious scandals involving his administration soon became public. Although Harding did not know about the Teapot Dome scandal, he attempted to cover up other illegal activities, such as the influence-peddling of the "Ohio Gang" and malfeasance in the Veterans' Bureau. Revelations that Harding had carried on extramarital affairs coupled with the other scandals to ruin his reputation; and he is remembered as among the worst American presidents. The Republican party quickly distanced itself from Harding the man while fully embracing his politics of normalcy.

BIBLIOGRAPHY

Murray, Robert K. *The Harding Era: Warren G. Harding and His Administration*. 1969.
Trani, Eugene P., and David L. Wilson. *The Presidency of Warren G. Harding*. 1977.

DAVID L. WILSON

WARREN G. HARDING.   LIBRARY OF CONGRESS

HARPER, ROBERT G. (1765–1825), representative from South Carolina, senator from Maryland, Federalist leader. Harper was born near Fredericksburg, Virginia, but grew up on a North Carolina frontier farm. At the age of fifteen, he joined a cavalry troop to oppose British general Charles Cornwallis during the Revolution. Harper's peripatetic nature was revealed in his brief law study in Charleston after graduating from Princeton in 1785, his back-country legal practice, a term in the state legislature, and his unsuccessful land speculation. After filling a congressional vacancy from a central Carolina district in the Third Congress (1793–1795), he was returned to the House from the western district of Ninety-six in the Fourth Congress (1795–1797).

Harper increased his popularity by advocating the regulation of western land sales and the admission of Tennessee to the Union. He abandoned his pro-French and Republican sympathies to defend Washington's administration in the Jay's Treaty controversy. Harper was skilled and outspoken in debate and maintained contact with constituents through printed letters; he won reelection in 1796 and 1798. In the Fifth Congress (1979–1799), he was chairman of the House Ways and Means Committee. Harper ardently supported war against France in 1798 and approved of the Alien and Sedition Acts on broad constitutional grounds. He stood by Aaron Burr during the House vote to resolve the presidential election tie in 1801, finally acceding to Thomas Jefferson's election.

Harper retired from Congress in 1801, resumed his legal career in Baltimore, and argued many cases before the Supreme Court. Prominent socially, he continued to play a significant political role in Maryland and was elected U.S. senator in 1816. He resigned soon after taking office to become the Federalists' vice presidential candidate. Harper was deeply concerned about slavery and was active in the Maryland colonization movement, which promoted the settlement of free blacks in West Africa. He died in 1825. Eleven years later, a new town in Liberia was named after him.

BIBLIOGRAPHY

Broussard, James H. *The Southern Federalists, 1800–1816.* 1978.

Cox, Joseph W. *Robert Goodloe Harper: The Evolution of a Southern Federalist Congressman.* 1967.

WINFRED E. A. BERNHARD

HARRISON, BENJAMIN (1833–1901), Republican senator from Indiana and twenty-third president of the United States (1889–1893), who developed close working ties between Congress and

REPUBLICAN CAMPAIGN POSTER. Benjamin Harrison and Levi P. Morton as the 1888 party nominees for president and vice president.
LIBRARY OF CONGRESS

the White House. Harrison established a law office in Indianapolis, Indiana, in 1854. He supported the new Republican party and would be the party's nominee for governor in 1876, an election he narrowly lost. Colonel of an Indiana regiment during the Civil War, Harrison was part of the growing group of veterans in politics. In 1880 he led Indiana's delegates to the Republican nominating convention, where he supported James A. Garfield.

Harrison declined President Garfield's invitation to join his cabinet in 1881, opting instead to accept election to the U.S. Senate. His committee assignments included Indian Affairs, Military Affairs, Territories, and Rules; he later chaired the Military Affairs and Territories committees. To deal with the unprecedented surplus in the U.S. Treasury, Harrison proposed higher pensions for Union veterans and 25 percent lower tariffs, but neither course was taken. In lengthy speeches in 1882, because of previous experience on the Mississippi River Commission, he supported construction of levees to maintain the Mississippi's navigability. Like many senators, Harrison had problems with federal political appointments; they did not live up to his high expectations. He therefore advocated civil service reform and voted for the Pendleton bill, which became law in 1883. He voted against the Chinese Exclusion Act, which he thought unconstitutional.

Ever ready to see Republican strength in the Senate grow, Harrison supported the creation of two states from the Dakota territory and statehood for Washington, Montana, Wyoming, and Idaho, a program not achieved until his presidential administration. Harrison introduced the bill to set aside land that later made possible Grand Canyon National Park, and he supported government reclamation of transcontinental-railroad land grants. Harrison endorsed broad powers for the federal government, including federal railroad regulation, but not the unsuccessful Blair bill, designed to provide federal aid to common schools.

In 1885 Grover Cleveland became president and the Democrats regained control of Indiana politics. A redistricted legislature forecast an end to Harrison's senatorial tenure in 1887. But Cleveland's tariff message to Congress on 6 December 1887 reinvigorated Harrison's political career. He won the Republican nomination for president in 1888 and the election, while Republicans regained control in both houses of Congress. Major bills passed by Congress during his administration included the Sherman Antitrust Act, the McKinley Tariff and Silver Purchase acts, the Omnibus Statehood Act, and the land act (which Harrison insisted must create

national forests). Later he was more active in foreign affairs.

Not reelected in 1892, Harrison retired to his law office in Indianapolis. During his last decade he became more sympathetic to organized labor than he had been in the Senate or in the presidency. He accepted speaking engagements and wrote for publication, and in 1899 he pleaded Venezuela's case in a boundary dispute with England before an international court in Paris.

BIBLIOGRAPHY

Sievers, Harry J. *Benjamin Harrison, Hoosier Statesman: From the Civil War to the White House, 1865–1888.* 1959.

Socolofsky, Homer E., and Allan B. Spetter. *The Presidency of Benjamin Harrison.* 1987.

HOMER E. SOCOLOFSKY

HARRISON, WILLIAM HENRY

HARRISON, WILLIAM HENRY (1733–1841), delegate from the Northwest Territory, representative and senator from Ohio, hero of Tippecanoe, "log cabin" presidential candidate, ninth president of the United States, first president to die in office. Harrison was born in Charles City County, Virginia, attended Hampden-Sidney College, and studied medicine in Richmond. He joined the army in 1791, serving in the Northwest Territory before resigning his commission in 1798 to become territorial secretary.

Harrison's checkered political career was based in large part on personal rather than party affiliations and on his military record. Although he probably owed his 1798 secretarial appointment to Federalist representative Robert Goodloe Harper of South Carolina, a long-standing family friend, he subsequently allied himself with the Jeffersonian faction, which in 1799 elected him the Northwest territorial delegate to the Sixth Congress. His labors generated the 1800 Harrison Land Act, which facilitated credit for public land purchases and secured the creation of the Indiana Territory from part of the Northwest Territory. President John Adams appointed him governor and Indian commissioner of the new territory in 1800, a post he held until 1813. A narrow victory over Shawnee forces at Tippecanoe Creek in 1811 was the basis for Harrison's later fame as a military hero, and it prompted Speaker of the House of Representatives Henry Clay to sponsor his appointment as a major general in the U.S. Army during the War of 1812.

Harrison resigned his commission in 1814 and settled in North Bend, Ohio. He ran for the House

WILLIAM HENRY HARRISON. Mezzotint by John Sartain, 1841, after James R. Lambdin.   LIBRARY OF CONGRESS

growth of executive power under the Jacksonians, the Whigs touted Harrison as a frontier hero aloof from the corrupting intrigues of party politics. The log cabin became a powerful symbol of Harrison's supposed humble origins, and the slogan "Tippecanoe and Tyler, too" reminded voters of his military exploits. The intense popular campaign, which drew a record number of voters to the polls, resulted in a sweeping victory for the Whigs, who won not only the White House but both houses of Congress.

Bitterly disappointed at not receiving the 1840 Whig nomination, Clay attempted to dictate Harrison's agenda even before the new president took office on 4 March 1841. He attempted to control cabinet appointments and urged Harrison to call a special session of Congress to raze the Jacksonian fiscal system. Harrison in large part resisted Clay's pressure but did call a special session of the 27th Congress for 31 May 1841. He died—before the new Congress convened—on 4 April 1841.

BIBLIOGRAPHY

Friedman, Bernard. "William Henry Harrison: The People against the Parties." In *Gentlemen from Indiana: National Party Candidates, 1836–1940*. Edited by Ralph D. Gray. 1977.

Goebel, Dorothy Burne. *William Henry Harrison: A Political Biography*. 1926. Repr. 1974.

JO ANNE MCCORMICK QUATANNENS

in 1816, primarily to clear himself of charges of financial malfeasance during the war. In both the House (14th and 15th Congresses, 1816–1819) and the Senate (19th and 20th Congresses, 1825–1829), Harrison was an advocate on behalf of military personnel—he chaired the Senate Committee on Military Affairs during his brief Senate term—but never achieved distinction as a legislator. Although aligned with the anti-Jackson opposition emerging under Clay's leadership, he was not a strong party advocate.

Harrison was one of three Whig candidates in the 1836 presidential election. His strong showing in the West—he received more electoral votes there than either of his fellow Whigs—paved the way for his 1840 presidential bid. The 1840 campaign pitted Harrison against Democratic incumbent Martin Van Buren in a campaign that stressed personalities rather than issues. Pointing critically to the

HATCH ACT (1939; 53 Stat. 1147–1149). The tension between politics and administration is longstanding in the American federal government. Until the late 1800s, federal employment was governed by a spoils system, which viewed federal employment as reward for partisan loyalty and service. In 1883, with the passage of the Pendleton Act, Congress began to move toward a competitive, merit-based system of federal employment. The insulation of federal employees from partisan politics was extended by President Theodore Roosevelt, whose amendment to Civil Service Rule 1, in 1907, declared that persons covered by the federal merit system could take no "active part" in political management or political campaigns.

Thirty years later, the growth of government during the New Deal years again raised the specter of potential abuse of the civil service by politicians—in this case, President Franklin D. Roosevelt. In 1935, Congress began to debate the merits of legislation that would ban partisan political activity by members of the civil service. In 1939, Sen. Carl A. Hatch (D-N.M.) successfully championed the first of several Hatch acts, officially titled "An Act to Prevent Pernicious Political Activities." The most significant portion of the act provided that

> no officer or employee in the executive branch of the Federal Government, or any agency or department thereof, shall take part in political management or political campaigns. All such persons shall retain the right to vote as they may choose and to express their opinions on all political subjects.

In 1940, the provisions of the act were extended to state and local employees whose programs or activities were funded even in part by federal funds. In 1974, that provision was altered to forbid only actual candidacy for partisan office and specific efforts to influence the votes of others. In popular parlance, employees covered by Hatch Act provisions are said to be "hatched."

In the years since its initial passage, the Hatch Act has been subject to a variety of criticisms and challenges. The Supreme Court ruled in both *United Public Workers v. Mitchell* (1947) and *Civil Service Commission v. National Association of Letter Carriers* (1973) that the act is constitutional. Congress itself has been ambiguous about continuing to constrain political activity of federal employees and there have been numerous attempts to repeal key provisions. In 1976, Congress did pass legislation to "unhatch" federal employees, but the bill was vetoed by President Gerald R. Ford. In 1990, Congress passed similar legislation, which was vetoed by President George Bush. In both cases, the president noted that removing Hatch Act provisions was likely to lead to politicization of the federal civil service. Proponents of the repeal have generally argued that removing fundamental political "rights" from federal employees renders them essentially powerless to defend their own interests.

The controversy over the Hatch Act and the constraints it places on civil servants is likely to continue. Although the fear of returning to a spoils system if the act is repealed is very real to many members of Congress and to many civil servants, many other public employees in local, state, and federal government—and particularly public employee unions—continue to argue that their First Amendment rights are abrogated by Hatch Act constraints on their political activity.

[*See also* Civil Service Reform Act of 1978; Pendleton Act.]

BIBLIOGRAPHY

Benda, Peter M., and David H. Rosenbloom. "The Hatch Act and the Contemporary Public Service." In *Agenda for Excellence: Public Service in America*. Edited by Patricia W. Ingraham and Donald F. Kettl. 1992.

Eccles, James R. *The Hatch Act and the American Bureaucracy*. New York. 1981.

PATRICIA W. INGRAHAM

A GOOD HATCH. Sen. Carl A. Hatch (D-N.Mex.) portrayed as a hen nesting with a brood of chicks that depict provisions of the Hatch Act. Attorney General Frank Murphy, a progressive reformer and New Deal politician, looks on the "hatch" with approval. Clifford K. Berryman, 20 October 1939. LIBRARY OF CONGRESS

HAWAII. The territory of Hawaii was annexed by the United States in 1898, four years after the overthrow of the Hawaiian monarchy by American business leaders residing in Honolulu. During the territorial period, from 1898 to 1959, whites (*haole* in Hawaiian) controlled the large estates and the production of Hawaii's most important product, sugar. Through most of that period, they usually were able to influence congressional policies on the major issues affecting the territory: the importation of labor to work on the plantations, the allocation of quotas for marketing sugar, and the control of land. But in 1934 Hawaii was classified as a nondomestic producer of sugar, the practical effect of which was to cut the Hawaiian quota while increasing the amount of sugar that could be marketed by U.S. states. The leaders of the Hawaiian sugar in-

SIGNING OF THE HAWAIIAN STATEHOOD PROCLAMATION. *Seated, left to right,* Vice President Richard M. Nixon; President Dwight D. Eisenhower; House Speaker Sam Rayburn (D-Tex.); *standing, left to right,* Lorrin Thurston, chairman of the Hawaiian Statehood Commission; Edward Johnston, former secretary of the treasury of Hawaii (representing governor-elect William F. Quinn); Frederick A. Seaton, U.S. secretary of the Interior; senator-elect Oren E. Long (D-Hawaii); and representative-elect Daniel K. Inouye (D-Hawaii), August 1959.   SAM RAYBURN LIBRARY

dustry were thereby converted to the cause of statehood.

Congress held twenty hearings on Hawaiian statehood between 1935 and 1958, listening to more than one thousand witnesses. But opposition to statehood, based in part on the fear of admitting a new state with a majority nonwhite population, was strong. In the 1950s two other factors reinforced opposition: the fear of southern senators that the admission of Hawaii would bring two more pro–civil rights votes to that body and the concern by some members of both houses that Hawaii's largest labor organization, the International Longshoremen's and Warehousemen's Union, was dominated by communists.

Joining the business leaders (nearly all Republicans) in lobbying for statehood were the territory's Asian-American political leaders, most of whom

were Democrats. Prostatehood sentiment was enhanced in Congress by the record in World War II of the 442d Regimental Combat Team, made up of *nisei* (second-generation Japanese Americans born in the United States) who fought valiantly in Europe, proving their loyalty to the United States beyond question. With the election in 1956 of John A. (Jack) Burns, the first Democratic Hawaiian territorial delegate to Congress in modern times, a strategy was worked out with the Democratic Senate majority leader, Lyndon B. Johnson, and Democratic Speaker of the House Sam Rayburn, both of Texas, to push separate bills for Alaskan and Hawaiian statehood, allowing the Alaskan bill to be passed first. By acquiescing in the admission of Alaska, whose leaders were predominantly Republican, some Republican congressional opposition to Hawaiian statehood was removed; southerners Johnson and Rayburn lobbied strongly for statehood, eroding some southern Democratic opposition. After an overwhelming vote in both houses of the 85th Congress to admit Hawaii as a state, all that remained was for the voters of the territory to endorse the statehood bill in the June 1959 primary election, which they did by a margin of 17 to 1. All ethnic groups except native Hawaiians, many of them still anguishing over the destruction of the Hawaiian monarchy, welcomed statehood.

In 1960 Hawaiian voters surprisingly chose Republican businessman Hiram Fong, the first Chinese American to be elected to the U.S. Senate. They also elected Democrat Daniel K. Inouye, the first Japanese American to be seated in the House of Representatives. Inouye, a former war hero and veteran of the highly decorated 442d, became Hawaii's best-known political leader when as senator he served as cochairman of the select committee handling the Iran-contra investigation of 1987. By 1993 he had become one of the most senior U.S. senators. As of 1994, the state of Hawaii was generally regarded highly for its standards of government and its excellent health care system.

BIBLIOGRAPHY

Fuchs, Lawrence H. *Hawaii Pono.* 1961. Repr. 1983.
Ogawa, Dennis M. *Kodomo No Tama Ni: The Japanese Experience in Hawaii.* 1978.
Phillips, Paul C. *Hawaii's Democrats: Chasing the American Dream.* 1982.

LAWRENCE H. FUCHS

HAWLEY-SMOOT TARIFF ACT (1930; 46 Stat. 590–763). After ten months of debate, Congress enacted and President Hoover signed the Hawley-Smoot Tariff Act of 1930. The vote in Congress was along party lines: Republicans in the House voted 248 to 11 for passage and Democrats opposed by 140 to 22; in the Senate Republicans voted 50 to 5 for the measure and Democrats voted 30 to 8 against. Passage was 270 to 151 in the House, 58 to 35 in the Senate.

The act raised U.S. tariffs to their highest levels in history, helping to trigger a trade war and adding to the worldwide depression that destroyed the pattern of world trade. This led to competitive devaluations and controls on trade and financing throughout the world, while doing nothing to stop the decline in domestic prices and production.

During the 1920s U.S agriculture had been in a deep depression. Prices of agricultural products dropped by as much as 30 percent, while simultaneously prices of manufactured goods rose, and farmers were caught in the squeeze. The situation prompted President Hoover and the Republican leadership to propose further raising of tariffs on agricultural imports, even though the high rates of the Fordney-McCumber tariff of 1922 had failed to strengthen farm prices. This initiative spurred manufacturing interests to demand even greater protection. When Hoover realized what he had set in motion, he cautioned restraint, but to little avail.

Rep. Willis C. Hawley of Oregon introduced a bill in the House that ignored Hoover's advice, and Sen. Reed Smoot of Utah followed in the Senate. The result was an orgy of special-interest protectionism at the expense of rational economics and the national interest. Hearings lasted for months and produced seven thousand pages of testimony from over eleven hundred advocates of particular interests.

Senator Smoot took care of Utah's sugar beet interests; Sen. David A. Reed of Pennsylvania spoke for eastern manufacturers; and Sen. Hiram Bing-

"EVEN DISTRICTS SEEM UNGRATEFUL." Cartoon depicting a disheveled Rep. Willis C. Hawley (R-Oreg.) beset by the outpouring of criticism that followed the passage of the Hawley-Smoot Tariff Act. In particular, the drawing illustrates voter dissatisfaction over the inability of the high tariffs to stimulate the domestic economy. Hawley's long congressional career ended when he was voted out of office in the 1932 elections. Clifford K. Berryman, *Washington Evening Star*, 25 October 1930.

U.S. SENATE COLLECTION, CENTER FOR LEGISLATIVE ARCHIVES

ham of Connecticut added to the glossary of protectionism when he spoke of the need to take care of "aged industries."

Informed opinion was appalled at the result. The American Bankers' Association, leading newspapers, and a petition signed by more than one thousand economists warned of the consequences of Hawley-Smoot. Hoover had deep reservations as well, but he rationalized that the act's "flexible tariff provision" would permit reduction of the more exorbitant rates. The president was given authority in the 1922 act to "equalize the cost of production" of U.S. and foreign producers by means of flexible tariff adjustments; Hawley-Smoot liberalized this procedure to permit downward adjustments. The procedure proved so cumbersome, however, that it produced no significant reduction.

The high Hawley-Smoot tariff rates, averaging 60 percent of the value of dutiable imports, contributed substantially to the trade wars of the 1930s and, many claim, to the worldwide depression. While Hawley-Smoot's contribution to the depression has been exaggerated, the association between protectionism and economic decline has persisted in trade debates to this day.

[*See also* McKinley Tariff Act.]

BIBLIOGRAPHY

Barrie, Robert W. *Congress and the Executive: The Making of U.S. Foreign Trade Policy 1789–1986.* 1987.

Bauer, Raymond A., Ithiel de sola Pool, and Lewis Anthony Dexter. *American Business and Public Policy.* 1972.

Schattschneider, E. E. *Politics, Pressures, and the Tariff: A Study of Free Enterprise in Pressure Politics, as Shown in the 1929–1930 Revision of the Tariff.* 1935.

ROBERT W. BARRIE

HAYDEN, CARL (1877–1972), representative and senator from Arizona, president pro tempore of the Senate, chairman of the Committee on Appropriations, and champion of federal reclamation in the western United States. Native Arizonan Carl T. Hayden was one of the principal architects of federal reclamation in the twentieth century. Known as the "Silent Senator" for his avoidance of speeches on the floor of Congress, the Arizona Democrat had a longer combined service in the House and Senate (1912–1969) than any other person in U.S. history.

While Hayden developed a renowned expertise in the field of federal reclamation, he gained notori-

ety also in several other policy areas important to the growth and development of the western states. He championed, for example, federal highway legislation and was coauthor of the landmark Hayden-Cartwright Act of 1934. This New Deal measure established the formula for the distribution of federal aid for highways to the states on the basis of area rather than population. He introduced numerous measures that advanced mining operations throughout the country. His efforts provided fair prices, protection against unfairly competitive imports, and subsidization for strategic metals. He worked assiduously for social security legislation and in 1950 fostered an initiative to include American Indians within its framework.

Water and its use and distribution, more than any other issue, lay at the heart of Hayden's public career. During his first term in the House he obtained authorization for an engineering investigation that eventually led to the construction of Coolidge Dam on the Gila River and the San Carlos irrigation project. He also helped shape federal reclamation policy in its early years by authoring and securing passage of the provision that allows local water-use associations to take over the care, maintenance, and operation of federal reclamation projects. Finally, Hayden played a dominant role in shepherding passage of the Colorado River Basin Project Act of 1968, which, among other things, called for the construction of the Central Arizona Project. The legislation was the capstone of Hayden's political career.

BIBLIOGRAPHY

August, Jack L., Jr. "Carl Hayden, Arizona, and the Politics of Water Development in the Southwest, 1923–1928." *Pacific Historical Review* 58 (1989): 195–216.

August, Jack L., Jr. "Carl Hayden: Born a Politician." *Journal of Arizona History* 26 (1985): 117–124.

August, Jack L., Jr. "A Sterling Young Democrat: Carl Hayden's Road to Congress, 1900–1912." *Journal of Arizona History* 27 (1987): 117–142.

JACK L. AUGUST, JR.

HAYES, RUTHERFORD B. (1822–1893), Republican representative from Ohio, elected nineteenth president of the United States after a protracted congressional crisis over how the electoral votes in the election of 1876 should be counted, vigorous opponent of senatorial courtesy and of riders on appropriation bills. A war hero, Hayes was elect-

RUTHERFORD B. HAYES.
OFFICE OF THE ARCHITECT OF THE CAPITOL

ed by his Cincinnati constituents in 1864 to the 39th Congress, was reelected in 1866, and served from 1865 to 1867, when he resigned to run for governor of Ohio. Although regular in attendance and conscientious in his committee work (particularly on the Library Committee), Hayes rarely spoke in Congress and had no perceptible influence on his colleagues. He voted consistently for Radical Republican Reconstruction measures.

In 1876, while Hayes was serving his third term as governor, the Republican party nominated him for president. The Democrats named Gov. Samuel J. Tilden of New York. On the basis of actual votes cast Tilden appeared to have won the election, but the vote was close in South Carolina and Florida. In those states and in Louisiana, black Republicans were intimidated and prevented from voting. In approving the bipartisan Electoral Commission Act (1877), Congress created a body to decide which votes should be counted. The disputed ones were awarded to the Republicans by a partisan 8 to 7 vote. Filibustering by House Democrats prolonged the crisis until two days before Hayes took office.

As president, Hayes clashed with Republican senators—particularly Roscoe Conkling of New York—over control of federal field offices such as the New York Customhouse. When Hayes attempted to replace Conkling's head of the Customhouse, Chester A. Arthur, with Theodore Roosevelt the Senate rallied behind Conkling, upheld senatorial courtesy (that presidents should defer to the wishes of senators when making appointments in the field service), and would not confirm Roosevelt. Biding his time, Hayes dismissed Arthur after Congress adjourned in 1879. Later, after considerable lobbying by the administration, the Senate confirmed Hayes's nominee. By the close of the Hayes administration representatives and senators suggested but no longer dictated federal appointees in their districts and states.

Hayes also clashed with the Democratic Congress in the second half of his administration over riders on appropriations bills. To secure legislation that was obnoxious to Hayes—specifically, the repeal of laws designed to enforce the Fourteenth and Fifteenth Amendments to the Constitution—the Democrats added them to military and civil appropriations bills that had to be passed for the government to function. Hayes thought riders were wrong in principle because they were an attempt to deprive the president of the right to veto legislation. He also objected to their substance: they were designed to rid the polls of federal authorities, who were there to prevent fraud, intimidation, and violence against white and black Republicans by northern and southern Democrats. Hayes steadfastly vetoed appropriations bills that contained riders, and he rallied his party and the public to his side. Retreating, the Democrats passed the appropriations bills without the riders except for a few minor, face-saving gestures, which Hayes was willing to concede. With this victory and the one over Conkling, Hayes greatly enhanced the stature of the presidency in its dealings with Congress.

BIBLIOGRAPHY

Davison, Kenneth E. *The Presidency of Rutherford B. Hayes.* 1972.

Hoogenboom, Ari. *The Presidency of Rutherford B. Hayes.* 1988.

ARI HOOGENBOOM

HAYNE, ROBERT Y. (1791–1839), senator from South Carolina, a proponent of the doctrine of nullification. Hayne studied law in the office of Langdon Cheves, a prominent figure in state politics. After serving as a legislator and attorney general in South Carolina, Hayne in 1822 was elected

to the U.S. Senate as a "tariff for revenue" Democrat, and was reelected in 1828. Among his senatorial concerns were improving the navy and upholding the prerogatives of the Senate in matters relating to foreign relations. Hayne believed that the tariff was improper, unconstitutional, and promotive of intersectional conflict.

When a resolution was introduced in the Senate to limit the survey and sale of public land, he denounced the proposal as an attempt to deprive American citizens of the opportunity to improve their livelihood. He condemned what he saw as a growing trend toward the consolidation of federal power at the expense of the states. Sen. Daniel Webster of Massachusetts took the floor to refute Hayne's charges. During a nine-day period in January 1830, the two men clashed memorably over the interpretation of the Constitution and the nature of the Union. It was Hayne's contention that the Constitution represented a compact between the states and the federal government. Therefore, if Congress gave the sanction of law to an unauthorized or illegal action, then the individual states had the right to ignore or nullify such a law. Webster countered Hayne's arguments, most notably in his reply on 26 and 27 January, and Webster was believed by many observers to have won the debate. The doctrine of nullification, however, did not die.

When Vice President John C. Calhoun broke with the administration of President Andrew Jackson and resigned his office in 1832, Hayne also resigned, to make room for Calhoun in the Senate.

BIBLIOGRAPHY

Jervey, Theodore D. *Robert Y. Hayne and His Times*. 1909, 1966.
Langley, Harold D. "Robert Y. Hayne and the Navy." *South Carolina Historical Magazine* 82 (1981): 311–330.

HAROLD D. LANGLEY

HAYS, BROOKS (1898–1981), Democratic representative from Arkansas and a hero in the battle for racial desegregation in the South. Elected to Congress in 1942, Hays served until the end of 1958. He was one of only a handful of politically consequential white southerners at that time who attempted to improve the lot of blacks in all the states of the old Confederacy. Even before his election to Congress, Hays had gained local and national recognition by championing social legislation and executive action to help the disadvantaged. His political fortunes were strongly aided by his great oratorical ability and his humor in the tradition of Will Rogers. He served as president of the Southern Baptist Convention in 1957 and 1958.

As a member of the House Foreign Affairs Committee, he championed foreign aid, assistance to the Allies both before and after World War II, and better Canadian-American relations. He also offered the Arkansas Plan for Civil Rights in 1949, becoming the first white southern member of Congress to offer a civil rights plan. Although not enacted, it gained sympathetic attention from many, including President Harry S. Truman.

Hays arranged a meeting between Arkansas governor Orval Faubus and President Dwight D. Eisenhower in the autumn of 1957 in a desperate but unsuccessful effort to head off the constitutional confrontation that led Eisenhower to send troops to Little Rock, Arkansas, to enforce school integration. In a backlash to his efforts, Hays, whose congressional district included Little Rock, was defeated for reelection to a ninth term in a last minute write-in campaign. His opponent, who fanned the flames of racist hysteria, was widely believed to have benefited from corrupt electoral practices.

President Eisenhower honored Hays after his defeat by appointing this Democrat, who had supported Adlai E. Stevenson for the presidency, to the board of directors of the Tennessee Valley Authority. President John F. Kennedy later appointed Hays

ROBERT Y. HAYNE.   *PERLEY'S REMINISCENCES, VOL. 1*

first as assistant secretary of State and then as special assistant to the president, a post he also held under Lyndon B. Johnson, through 1966. President Kennedy is known to have said that if he were to write a sequel to his *Profiles in Courage,* Brooks Hays would be chapter one.

BIBLIOGRAPHY

Hays, Brooks. *Politics Is My Parish.* 1980.
Hays, Brooks. *A Southern Moderate Speaks.* 1959.

WARREN I. CIKINS

HAYS, WAYNE L. (1911–1989), Democratic representative from Ohio, chairman of the Committee on House Administration, and self-proclaimed "Mayor of the House." First elected in 1948, Hays reveled in controversy for much of his twenty-eight years in Congress. He resigned his House seat on 1 September 1976 under fire from the press and his colleagues for abusing his powers as a committee chairman.

By 1976 the House Administration Committee, an obscure housekeeping body when Hays took charge of it in 1971, had acquired sweeping authority over personnel, travel, office and equipment expenditures, and other perquisites available to House members. Hays's domain also included an array of House service operations, including restaurants and cafeterias, barber and beauty shops, and a stationery store.

The onetime schoolteacher arbitrarily dispensed favors such as liberal office and travel allowances to his supporters and threatened to withhold such considerations from those who opposed him. While complaining privately of Hays's power, a House majority allowed him to decree frequent and generous increases in their perquisites and then willingly absorb the blame whenever the public reacted angrily.

Hays also was notorious for lavish, expense-paid trips abroad as chairman of the International Operations Subcommittee of the Committee on International Relations. He occasionally took along House employees whose duties were unrelated to subcommittee work. In 1963, headwaiter Ernest Petinaud of the House dining room accompanied him to Paris.

Hays's fiefdom collapsed on 23 May 1976, when a House Administration subcommittee employee, Elizabeth Ray, told the *Washington Post* that Hays, in return for sexual favors, had put her on the payroll at $14,000 a year and provided her with an office despite her inability to type, file, or answer a telephone. Subsequent press reports focused on other abuses by Hays. He resigned his chairmanship on 18 June. In the aftermath, the House tightened its office and staff policies and opened more of its records to public scrutiny.

BIBLIOGRAPHY

Congressional Quarterly Inc. "Sexual Scandal." In *Congressional Quarterly's Guide to Congress.* 2d ed. 1976. Pp. 464–467.
U.S. House of Representatives. Commission on Administrative Review. *Communication from the Chairman.* 95th Cong., 1st sess., 1977.

DONALD C. BACON

HEALTH AND MEDICINE. Because the Constitution makes no mention of health or medicine, congressional activity in this field derives indirectly from Congress's power to regulate interstate commerce and from the injunction in the Preamble to "promote the general welfare." Despite the wealth of legislation since World War II, federal jurisdiction over health and medicine has been contested by advocates of states' rights, by private interest groups (notably physicians), and at times by the hospital, pharmaceutical, and insurance industries. Influential advocacy groups for federal involvement have included disease-oriented philanthropies, such as the American Cancer Society; organized labor; and professional groups strongly oriented toward education, public health, or research, such as the American Association of Medical Colleges, the American Public Health Association, and professional organizations of biomedical scientists. Federal programs providing funding and support for research, training, and services have fostered the development of active constituencies, including those for research, mental health, and prepaid group practice.

The posture of the executive has varied greatly, from strong advocacy of federal health legislation in the administrations of Harry S. Truman, John F. Kennedy, and Lyndon B. Johnson, to mild antagonism by the Nixon administration, to determined opposition in the administrations of Ronald Reagan and George Bush. Health spending has nevertheless increased during all administrations since 1933.

Congressional committees and subcommittees play the major role in mediating ongoing conflicts and shaping legislation in health and medicine. Historically, there are six of these: in the House, the Health and Environment Subcommittee of the Energy and Commerce Committee (formerly the Interstate and Foreign Commerce Committee); the Labor, Health and Human Services, and Education (formerly Labor and Health) Subcommittee of the Appropriations Committee; and, for the health care financing programs Medicare and Medicaid, the powerful Ways and Means Committee. In the Senate, they are the Labor and Human Resources Committee; the Labor, Health and Human Services, and Education (formerly Labor and Health) Subcommittee of the Appropriations Committee; and for financing, the Health for Families and the Uninsured Subcommittee of the Finance Committee. The Senate has a separate Environment and Public Works Committee. For both houses, the changes in the budget process following the Congressional Budget and Impoundment Control Act of 1974 diminished the powers of the appropriations and financing committees.

Committee and subcommittee chairs and ranking members of both parties have championed federal health legislation. Important leaders have included, in the House, J. Percy Priest (1941–1956; D-Tenn.), John E. Fogarty (1941–1967; D-R.I.), Paul G. Rogers (1955–1979; D-Fla.), Wilbur D. Mills (1939–1977; D-Ark.), and Henry A. Waxman (1975–; D-Calif.), and in the Senate, Claude Pepper (1936–1951; D-Fla.), Lister Hill (1938–1969; D-Ala.), Edward M. Kennedy (1962–; D-Mass.), Orrin G. Hatch (1977–; R-Utah), and Jacob K. Javits (1957–1981; R-N.Y.).

Federal health and medicine legislation covers six broad areas of activity: direct provision of services; funding and reimbursement for services; regulation of products and services; sponsorship of research; sponsorship of education and training; and planning and regulation of health care delivery. These activities have their roots in the Public Health Service (PHS).

The Public Health Service before 1930. Federal health care began with "An Act for the Relief of Sick and Disabled Seamen," signed 16 July 1798. Congress was forced to act in this matter of "commerce," after ten years of considering the matter, because no state or local authority claimed jurisdiction for sailors who arrived ill or injured in American port cities. The Marine Hospital Service (MHS), funded by deductions from seamen's pay, was made part of the Treasury Department.

By the time of the Civil War, the Marine Hospital Service was facing severe criticism for poor management and inadequate care. In 1870, the "Act to Reorganize the Marine Hospital Service" created the post of supervising surgeon general. The "Act to Regulate Appointments in the Marine Hospital Service," signed on 4 January 1889, established the Commissioned Corps, an elite group of qualified career officers dedicated to Service activities.

Those activities had greatly expanded. Inadequacies of state quarantine laws against infectious disease, dramatized by a deadly yellow fever epidemic in the Mississippi Valley in 1877, had forced Congress to legitimate federal quarantine enforcement in 1878. In addition to internal quarantine control, between 1891 and 1893 the MHS was authorized by quarantine acts to inspect incoming vessels and carry out medical screening of new immigrants.

The newly professional Service met its added challenges with enthusiasm, employing the new science of bacteriology as well as established public health methods. In 1887, Surgeon General John Hamilton opened a small "hygienic laboratory" at the Marine Hospital on Staten Island that required neither congressional notice nor special funding; it was moved to Washington in 1891. In 1894, Congress asked the lab director to investigate ventilation in the House of Representatives. He reported that the air was quite foul and the carpets saturated with tobacco.

In 1901, in a routine civil appropriations bill, Congress officially recognized the Hygienic Laboratory's research in "infectious and contagious diseases, and matters pertaining to the public health." In the following year, at the request of Sen. John C. Spooner (R-Wis.), Surgeon General Walter Wyman submitted a draft bill that became the Public Health and Marine Service Act of 1902. This major legislation renamed the Service (now the PHS), established a new Division of Scientific Research with an advisory board, and mandated the surgeon general to hold an annual meeting of state and territorial health officers and to collect birth, morbidity, and mortality statistics from the states. In 1912, the Public Health Service Act extended the Service's authority to "all the diseases of man" and the pollution of U.S. waters. Products of the Progressive era specifically written "to improve efficiency," these acts epitomized the prevailing faith in the methods of science and business organization, without overriding the traditional federal-state relationship.

A third law, the Biologics Control Act of 1902, assigned a new role to the PHS: the inspection and licensing of manufacturing establishments for product safety. The introduction of an antitoxin for diphtheria (1894) had saved many lives, but commercial production without supervision increased the possibility of contamination or inadequate potency. Incidents in St. Louis, Missouri, in 1901, where thirteen children died from contaminated diphtheria antitoxin, and in New Jersey, where nine deaths were caused by smallpox vaccine, created public alarm. The Medical Society of the District of Columbia drafted the bill with PHS input.

Using its new authority to study "matters pertaining to the public health," the PHS carried out many such projects in the 1910s and 1920s, without special congressional authorization or appropriation, to control and investigate a plague, Rocky Mountain spotted fever, and hookworm disease. Congress provided specific appropriations for work on trachoma and pellagra (1913), venereal disease (1917 and 1918), influenza (1918), and narcotics control (1929).

Surgeon General Hugh Cumming (1920–1936) was mainly concerned with administrative reform. He had successfully forestalled moves in 1922 and 1925, led by Sen. Reed Smoot (R-Utah), to combine the PHS with the Veterans' Bureau and curtail its authority. Cumming wanted to establish statutory language approving the detailing of PHS officers to assist other bureaus, state health departments, and university laboratories; to transform the advisory board into a national advisory council; to remedy inequities in pay and perquisites within the service; and to grant the secretary of the Treasury the authority to create new divisions.

Cumming formed an alliance with the National Health Council, a group of citizens and public health workers, and arranged to have a bill introduced in 1926 by Rep. James S. Parker (R-N.Y.), chair of the House Commerce Committee. In the same year, Sen. Joseph E. Ransdell (D-La.), chair of the Public Health Committee, introduced a bill to create a national institute of health to conduct basic medical research and to establish a fellowship program. This proposal was backed by a coalition of researchers and philanthropists.

Both bills languished in Congress for four years, facing determined opposition from Calvin Coolidge's Bureau of the Budget and apathy from everyone except Ransdell. Cumming and the Hygienic Laboratory director, George McCoy, were very interested in the Parker bill, but wary about the enormous expansion in funding and responsibility embodied in the Ransdell bill. Some other federal bureaus, milk producers, and drug manufactures were concerned about the language that appeared to empower the PHS to tighten and enforce regulations. The bill was therefore reworked to limit the role of the service vis-à-vis other agencies to "cooperation" and to fit the National Institute of Health (NIH) within the established mission of the Hygienic Laboratory.

In 1928, the Parker bill passed both houses, only to be vetoed by Coolidge over the question of executive authority. The president was apparently willing to support the Ransdell bill, but Smoot's objections prevented its passage that session. Herbert Hoover, an engineer with an interest in administration, was more supportive in 1929; outbreaks of influenza and psittacosis, and considerable congressional interest in cancer research, added impetus for passage. The Parker and Ransdell acts became law in 1930 and established the direction and organization of the PHS for the next forty years.

The PHS was now running four types of programs: (1) direct care to disabled mariners, lepers, narcotics addicts, and, after 1930, when Congress created the Federal Bureau of Prisons, prisoners (the PHS consulted with the Bureau of Indian Affairs on care for Native Americans, finally assuming full responsibility in 1955); (2) assistance to states through consultation, disease surveillance, and direct help with public health programs; (3) regulation of biologics and control of infectious diseases; and (4) research. Many of these functions were carried out without direct congressional authorization. After 1930, however, the PHS found it necessary to build alliances.

Health Legislation during the New Deal. New Deal legislation did not include much provision for health. Progressive interest in all areas of social reform had included agitation for better organization of health care services and for compulsory health insurance, which was initially proposed by the American Association for Labor Legislation in 1914. From 1927 to 1932, the Committee on the Costs of Medical Care, a prestigious group funded by foundations, published multiple volumes of data on the nation's health. The final report advocated a coordinated system of group practices based on regional medical schools and teaching hospitals and approved more attention to education and research. Because of the determined opposition of members representing the American Medical Association (AMA), it did not endorse compulsory health insurance, however. Despite considerable support within his administration for health insurance, Franklin D. Roosevelt refused to endanger the rest of his programs for so controversial an idea. National health insurance bills, repeatedly introduced from 1939 to 1943 by Senators Robert F. Wagner (D-N.Y.) and James E. Murray (D-Mont.) and Rep. John D. Dingell (D-Mich.), did not have strong administration support and were blocked by the coalition of Republicans and southern Democrats that had stalled the New Deal.

Some other proposals, harbingers of the future, had better luck. The progressive Sheppard-Towner Act of 1921—which offered grants from the Children's Bureau to the states to improve the "welfare and hygiene" of mothers and infants—had expired in 1929, in response to the opposition of the AMA and the PHS. However, a similar program for maternal and child health and crippled children became Title V of the Social Security Amendments of 1935. Title VI provided for PHS matching grants to state health departments, based on population and per capita income, to "build" state health departments and assist in training and in developing new services, including industrial hygiene. New venereal-disease legislation, in 1935 and 1938, funded research and control activities. The acts bore the stamp of Thomas Parran, who became head of the Venereal Disease Division in 1935 and surgeon general in 1936, and of Lewis R. Thompson, the assistant surgeon general. The acts were written to extend PHS authority without offending medical interest groups.

In 1937, the AMA was more wary of the bills, introduced by Rep. Maury Maverick (D-Tex.), Sen. Homer T. Bone (D-Wash.), and Rep. Warren G. Magnuson (D-Wash.), to establish and fund another institute dedicated categorically to cancer research. Reflecting the new interest of the scientific community in the problem of chronic disease, and the influence of the American Society for the Control of Cancer, the bill provided for additional PHS research and for a new program of extramural grants. The National Cancer Institute Act passed both houses unanimously.

The Pure Food and Drugs Act of 1906 had been the result of concern over adulterated food products, dramatized by several books and articles during the Progressive era. Authority to enforce the purity and correct labeling of products fell to Harvey Wiley, the energetic chief of the Bureau of Chemistry in the Board of Agriculture. However, the Supreme Court determined in 1911 that the bureau had no authority to judge the efficacy of a drug preparation, as that was purely a matter of opinion. The Sherley Amendment (1912) did prohibit "false and fraudulent claims" by manufacturers.

During the New Deal, the renamed Food and Drug Administration (FDA) drafted a bill with the support of Rexford Tugwell, assistant secretary of agriculture, to strengthen its enforcement powers.

The bill stalled in Congress for five years, until the deaths of more than one hundred people from a toxic sulfa preparation prompted a public outcry. The Food, Drug, and Cosmetic Act of 1938 banned interstate commerce in hazardous substances, required that new drugs be submitted to the FDA for approval, with proof of safety, and that they be appropriately labeled with directions for use and warnings of hazards. A drug would be exempt from some labeling requirements if sold by prescription only, which in time made physicians the controllers of the pharmaceutical market. In 1951, the Durham-Humphrey amendment was an attempt to make the FDA the arbiter of "prescription only" status, but pharmaceutical manufacturers lobbied successfully against the change.

World War II and Medical Care for Veterans. World War II stimulated new health programs, including a giant medical research program directed by the Committee on Medical Research (CMR) of the Office of Scientific Research and Development and the Children's Bureau's medical assistance program (EMIC) for the needy dependents of servicemen (which was supported by Congress but hotly opposed by the AMA). The Public Health Service was transferred to the Federal Security Agency in 1939 and reorganized by the Public Health Service Act of 1944. The latter bill included a provision (301[d]) for research grants to individuals and institutions in any area of PHS interest. When the Committee on Medical Research began closing its operations in 1945, its remaining contracts were transferred to the PHS and converted into the first grants under section 301(d). The NIH, with some difficulty, overcame the concerns of the Bureau of the Budget, enlisting support from its allies in Congress.

In 1946, Dr. Lawrence Kolb of the PHS Division of Mental Hygiene submitted, through Parran, a draft bill for a new National Neuropsychiatric Institute. It was supported by the American Psychiatric Association, the new "health lobby" organized by Albert and Mary Lasker, and buoyed by accomplishments in crisis-intervention therapy during the war. The National Mental Health Act of 1946, managed through Congress by Representative Priest and Senators Hill and Pepper, created a new research institute, the National Institute of Mental Health. It also included a provision for direct federal aid to state mental health agencies for demonstration projects, training grants, and community education.

Congress had attempted to provide for the needs

of aged and disabled naval and army veterans, first by using the Marine Hospitals (1799–1811) and later by authorizing the Naval Home (1833) and the U.S. Soldiers' Home (1851). The needs and voting power of 1.9 million Union veterans following the Civil War prompted new legislation (1866) establishing national homes for residential care; when necessary, the homes contracted for medical care with civilians. World War I sharply demonstrated the inadequacy of the medical services for servicemen and veterans. The War Risk Insurance Bureau (1917) provided for hospitalization and medical care for any veteran with a service-connected injury or disability, to be provided by the PHS. The service quickly found this additional responsibility overwhelming, and a new Veterans' Bureau was created in 1921, taking over sixty-two old and new PHS hospitals. Veterans' legislation in 1922 and 1924 authorized the bureau (renamed the Veterans Administration [VA] in 1930) to provide care not only for service-connected disabilities, but for tuberculosis and psychiatric disorders as well. This mandate was extended by the Veterans Administration Act of 1933, which approved VA care for any medical problem if the veteran was "unable to defray the necessary expenses."

After World War II, in 1946, amendments to the veterans' acts authorized larger funding levels, established a new Department of Medicine and Surgery, and officially recognized medical specialties. This department arranged contracts with medical schools to provide training and research opportunities in return for medical care.

The 1950s: Consensus and Incrementalism. In 1946, Congress's primary attention lay elsewhere. The Wagner-Murray-Dingell bills had included provisions for grants for hospital construction, an idea strongly backed by the American Hospital Association (AHA). George Bugbee of the AHA now began a strong lobbying effort in alliance with the PHS. Other support came from the health lobby, organized labor, the farm bureau federation, and the AMA. A bill based on a Parran draft was introduced by Senators Lister Hill and Harold H. Burton (D-Ohio). The powerful Robert A. Taft (R-Ohio) was wary of too much federal control. He insisted that states' rights and local control be retained in the bill, that funds be allocated according to state assessments of need, and that local hospital boards supply matching funds. Hill understood that the bill appealed to representatives from rural states, including many of the most conservative, and hoped for bipartisan support if he could win Taft's

backing. A funding formula devised by I. S. Falk of the Social Security Administration, to award the largest sums to the poorest states (determined by per capita income), convinced Taft. The Hill-Burton Act, officially Title VI of the Public Health Service Act, was signed in August 1946.

The Hill-Burton Act made plain the possibility of consensus among Congress, the "health lobby," and the medical profession. President Truman, Oscar Ewing of the Federal Security Agency, and their liberal allies hoped to extend this consensus by enacting a national health program and providing federal money to support construction, research, medical education, and national health insurance. However, the AMA allied with resurgent conservatives to defeat national health insurance and aid to medical education in 1949 and 1950; medical school deans also opposed the latter measure as inviting too much government control. The Hill-Burton funding plan remained acceptable to all parties. By its use of state plans, it subtly reoriented health services around base hospitals in each region, enhancing secondary and tertiary care at the expense of prevention and primary care.

The other goal on which the various interests reached consensus was funding for medical research. Parran and NIH director Rolla E. Dyer had been anxious for NIH (officially renamed the National Institutes of Health in 1948) to maintain research leadership and to avoid absorption into the proposed National Science Foundation, but they had also been hesitant to overextend their resources. Leonard Scheele, who became surgeon general in 1948, had no such qualms. He allied with Mary Lasker and her cohorts and with Pepper, Murray, and H. Styles Bridges (R-N.H.) in the Senate to pass the National Heart Institute bill in 1948; they used PHS contributions to research the preventative qualities of fluoride to argue for the National Institute for Dental Research. The coalition and the PHS record were convincing enough two years later to win passage of the Omnibus Medical Research Act of 1950, which not only set up two new institutes (the Institute of Neurological Diseases and Blindness, and the Institute of Arthritis and Metabolic Diseases), but left the creation of still others to the option of the surgeon general.

Throughout the 1950s, and particularly after 1955, Congress maintained strong bipartisan support for medical research. The respective chairs of the Senate and House subcommittees for health appropriations, Lister Hill and John Fogarty, invited the NIH witnesses to explain what use they might make of additional funds and encouraged them to describe how they might investigate the committees' latest medical interests. NIH directors William Sebrell and James Shannon and their staffs always had suggestions, and each year the administration's proposed budget was increased: in fiscal 1957 from $126 to $183 million, in fiscal 1958 from $190 to $211 million. NIH's grants to universities and teaching hospitals provided federal funding for training and equipment, thus indirectly subsidizing medical education and health services, as well as research.

Support for national health insurance appeared moribund, however. In 1950, Oscar Ewing encouraged I. S. Falk and Wilbur Cohen of the Social Security Administration to develop a proposal to serve as the first step toward an insurance plan: minimal hospitalization for elderly social security recipients, financed through a payroll tax. Although supported by organized labor, the bill, introduced yearly, was invariably routed to a quiet death in the House Ways and Means Committee. In 1958, however, a committee member, Aime J. Forand (D-R.I.), reintroduced the bill personally, and a new contest developed.

The 1960s: New Legislative Directions. The AMA's opposition to the Forand bill was shared by most conservative members of Congress and major interest groups, including the Chamber of Commerce and the American Legion. Critics pointed out that the bill was regressive and limited, not offering meaningful assistance to the "truly needy"; on the other hand, its broad coverage would extend to others who did not need it. The proposal was criticized as an abuse of federal power and an encroachment on states' rights. In 1960, a compromise bill, sponsored by Sen. Robert S. Kerr (D-Okla.) and Rep. Wilbur D. Mills, the powerful chairman of the Ways and Means Committee, offered matching funds to the states, drawn from general revenues, to be used to aid the elderly under state-determined guidelines. Only thirty-two states accepted these funds and only four provided full benefits. President John F. Kennedy backed a Forand-style bill in 1961, introduced by Sen. Clinton P. Anderson (D-N.Mex.) and Rep. Cecil R. King (D-Calif.); however, Mills controlled Ways and Means and was determined to report out only a bill that had bipartisan support.

The new administration was not the only factor for change in the early 1960s. Opinion polls indicated strong public support for health insurance for the elderly. PHS and NIH grants had nurtured a strong constituency of scientists and academic physicians supportive of federal health leadership. Mary Lasker and her health lobby were active. Medical school deans, represented by the American Association of Medical Colleges, were feeling financially pressured and talking about a physician shortage if funds for construction and tuition assistance were not available. The AMA, preoccupied with the specter of national health insurance, was cautiously favorable to support for medical education.

There were by now precedents for aid to education, including the 1958 Public Health Service Act Amendments, which offered formula grants to schools of public health, and the National Defense Education Act (1958), which provided undergraduate loans and construction and training grants to encourage study of the sciences. Determined efforts by the Department of Health, Education and Welfare (HEW), the successor to the Federal Security Agency, ensured the passage of the Health Professions Education Assistance Act of 1963; the act provided construction grants to medical schools and student loans.

President Kennedy was also interested in funding for new community mental health centers and research and treatment centers for mental retardation. A bill embodying both programs passed through Hill's committee in the Senate and that of Oren Harris (D-Ark.) in the House, but it was recommitted to the latter when the AMA announced its opposition to the community mental health center concept. That part of the bill provided construction funding and start-up funds for staffing, to be decreased as private and local sources took over. Hill and Harris agreed to reduce the authorizations and eliminate the staffing grants in the final measure, the Mental Retardation and Community Mental Health Centers Construction Act. Health centers for migrant workers aroused less furor and were authorized for grant funding in 1962.

A series of congressional hearings on prices and monopoly control of drug products had begun in 1959, with the Senate Judiciary Committee's Subcommittee on Antitrust and Monopoly of the Judiciary, chaired by Estes Kefauver (D-Tenn.). Kefauver was interested in controlling prices through mandatory patent licensing. However, the bill he submitted was substantially rewritten in the wake of the thalidomide disasters of 1962, when a toxic drug was kept off the U.S. market only by extraordinary FDA diligence. The Food and Drug

Amendments of 1962 made no mention of patent licensing; they did, however, authorize active FDA monitoring of new-drug applications, to determine efficacy as well as safety, and retroactive review of old drugs.

Kennedy's assassination, followed by the 1964 Democratic landslide and Lyndon B. Johnson's commitment to the War on Poverty, brought to Congress and the administration liberal Democrats interested in health, eager to innovate, and closely connected to the national biomedical community. Their new programs and laws supported the basic concepts of state or regional organization, centered on a research-oriented medical center.

This philosophy was best represented by two acts passed in 1965 and 1966. The Heart Disease, Cancer, and Stroke Amendments of 1965 (to the Public Health Service Act) were designed to fund and support regional cooperative programs for research and training, centered around leading medical schools and hospitals. The Regional Medical Program embodied the concept that hierarchical regional organization was crucial to the efficient control of chronic disease. The following year, the Comprehensive Health Planning Act (Partnership for Health) mandated a hierarchical design for state and local health planning agencies. Although in one sense it was an extension of the long PHS tradition of assistance to state and local authorities, this legislation created many new federal requirements for agency composition and functions.

The most dramatic event of the era was the enactment of the Social Security Amendments of 1965, which created Medicare and Medicaid. Recognizing that passage of the King-Anderson bill was now inevitable, Mills sought bipartisan consensus. He proposed to combine the hospital insurance plan with a voluntary plan (funded by general revenues and small premiums) for medical services and an expanded Kerr-Mills program for all medically indigent persons, to be administered through the states. The voluntary plan was based on a bill drafted by John W. Byrnes (R-Wisc.), the ranking Republican on Ways and Means. The revised bill, despite its added costs and complexity, passed both houses by solid majorities and was signed into law in July 1965.

Community medical health centers also resurfaced. The National Institute of Mental Health now had data indicating that many centers were stalled for lack of funds, especially in poorer areas. The AMA, assured by the American Psychiatric Association that the program was directed only toward the indigent, and distracted by Medicare, allowed the new Community Mental Health Centers Act to pass.

The Community Action Program, created by the Economic Opportunity Act of 1964, funded some demonstration community health centers in 1966. The centers provided medical services, trained local residents, and acted as a focus for community action. The PHS was interested enough to use section 314 (e) of the Comprehensive Health Planning Act, which authorized grants for new types of service projects, to create its own community center. With the migrant workers' health centers, the mental-health centers, and maternal and child health projects (extended in 1963 and 1965), Congress had now enacted multiple federal programs for provision of services to the general population.

Manpower legislation extended construction grants and student-loan funds to schools for nurses (1964) and allied health professionals (1966), and the Health Professions Educational Assistance Amendments of 1965 provided basic and special-improvement grants and scholarship funds for professional schools in addition to new scholarships. In 1970, a special effort by Senator Warren Magnuson, with some support from rural representatives, created the National Health Service Corps (the Emergency Health Personnel Act); a student enrolled in the corps received an educational "loan" to be forgiven in return for a period of work in an underserved area.

The 1970s and 1980s: Reversals and Power Struggles. The Public Health Service Act Amendments of 1970 not only created the Health Service Corps but also added new grant programs for communicable disease control, alcohol and drug abuse, and family planning. The Comprehensive Health Manpower Act of 1971 extended project grants for medical schools and created financial distress grants and a new system of capitation funding based on enrollment. Health policy continued to have a strong appeal in Congress, with Senators Edward Kennedy and Jacob Javits and Representative Paul Rogers taking over the leadership of the crucial subcommittees. Many expected that the planning, insurance, and funding programs of the 1970s had paved the way for national health insurance; more than two hundred proposals for increased federal coverage were introduced into the House.

However, neither the PHS nor the federal health program was as robust as it had been in the 1960s. The PHS was criticized by the Nixon administra-

Landmark Legislation in Health and Medicine

TITLE	YEAR ENACTED	REFERENCE NUMBER	DESCRIPTION
Public Health and Marine Service Act	1902	P.L. 57-23	Renamed the service, established the Division of Scientific Research, and formalized federal-state cooperation in public health.
Biologics Control Act	1902	P.L. 57-244	Provided for the inspection and licensing of vaccine, antisera, and antitoxin manufactories, to insure product safety and potency.
Pure Food and Drugs Act	1906	P.L. 59-384	Gave the Department of Agriculture authority to inspect and regulate food and drug producers in order to protect against adulteration, contamination, and fraudulent sales.
Public Health Service Amendments of 1930 (Parker Act)	1930	P.L. 71-106	Made important statutory changes enhancing the authority and facilitating the operations of the Service.
National Institute of Health Act (Ransdell Act)	1930	P.L. 71-251	Changed the name of the Hygienic Laboratory and authorized it to conduct basic medical research and to grant fellowships.
National Cancer Institute Act	1937	P.L. 75-244	Created a new categorical institute for PHS cancer research and extramural grants.
Public Health Service Act	1944	P.L. 78-410	Administrative act that established a broad, open-ended authorization for research funding to individuals and institutions.
National Mental Health Act	1946	P.L. 79-487	Created the National Institute of Mental Health; authorized direct federal aid to state agencies for training, education, and services.
Hospital Survey and Construction Act (Hill-Burton Act)	1946	P.L. 79-725	Provided matching funds to states for hospital construction based on state assessments of local needs.
Food and Drug Amendments of 1962 (Kefauver-Harris Amendments)	1962	P.L. 87-78	Gave the FDA stronger authority over new drugs, including review for efficacy, and the power to recall drugs.
Health Professions Education Assistance Act	1963	P.L. 88-129	Provided student loans and medical school construction grants.
Social Security Amendments of 1965 (Medicare and Medicaid)	1965	P.L. 89-97	Included a hospital insurance program for elderly Social Security recipients, funded from payroll taxes, and voluntary medical service insurance for the same group, funded by small premiums and general revenues; and expanded the Kerr-Mills program for all medically indigent individuals.
Comprehensive Health Planning Act (Partnership for Health)	1966	P.L. 89-749	Created a nationwide health planning design, based on local and state health planning agencies.
Public Health Service Amendments of 1972	1972	P.L. 92-603	Established a mechanism for Professional Standards Review Organizations (PSROs); mandated that hospitals receiving federal funds conduct Certificate of Need Reviews.
Omnibus Budget Reconciliation Act of 1981	1981	P.L. 97-35	Collapsed funding for many categorical grant programs into block grants to states; reduced funding for all health services programs; and increased local and state governance over remaining programs.
Tax Equity and Fiscal Responsibility Act	1982	P.L. 97-248	Tightened regulations on Medicare and Medicaid; introduced Medicare reimbursement based not on costs or charges, but on set rates for diagnostic related groups (DRGs).

tion as too independent and too powerful. Congress often expressed concern about the PHS's longtime responsibilities for industrial hygiene, where it was less forceful than the Department of Labor, and for environmental protection, to which it gave low priority. The Water Pollution Control Act of 1965, like the Clean Air Act of 1963, had established new federal regulatory authority; but the Water Pollution Control Administration was quickly moved to the Interior Department. New laws establishing the Occupational Health and Safety Administration in the Labor Department and an independent Environmental Protection Agency reduced PHS authority in these areas. Rising federal health-care costs, driven by Medicare and Medicaid reimbursement of "usual and customary" charges, were straining the budget. Even the NIH was under attack by the Lasker lobby for not having made greater progress against cancer and heart disease after more than thirty years of support.

After listening to the lobbyists' complaints, Senators Kennedy and Javits introduced a bill in 1971 to sever the National Cancer Institute (NCI) from NIH, make it responsible to the president, and increase its budget. Richard M. Nixon supported more cancer funding but was wary of creating another health empire. He submitted a counterproposal through Sen. Peter H. Dominick (R-Colo.) for a new NCI within NIH but reporting directly to the president. Representative Rogers, irritated by the tactics of the Lasker group and strongly lobbied by the biomedical community to preserve the structure of NIH, managed a revised version of the Dominick bill through to passage. The National Cancer Act of 1971 separated the NCI budget from the rest of HEW, and made the heads of NCI and NIH presidential appointees, but NCI was left within NIH. The net effect was to give the president more control over health-research policy.

Nixon's primary concern was with the overburdened health budget, which he attempted to address through increased regulation on the one hand, and program termination on the other. Congress was also troubled by high health costs, but it was supportive of research and services programs and resentful of Nixon's challenges to its prerogatives and authority in impounding funds already appropriated and restricting HEW access to congressional staff.

Congress attempted to use the regional model already developed to regulate abuses of Medicare, Medicaid, and Hill-Burton funds. Cases of Medicaid fraud and poor quality of care were reported very early, including a widely read 1969 Chicago Sun Times series on abuses at Cook County Hospital. In spring 1970, the AMA proposed a federally funded peer-review system operated through local medical societies. Sen. Wallace F. Bennett (R-Utah) introduced an amendment outlining a similar plan but establishing a direct relationship between HEW and local independent Professional Standards Review Organizations (PSROs) in designated areas. The PSRO amendment to the Social Security Act was signed in 1972.

In the same set of amendments, section 1122 mandated that hospitals receiving federal funds conduct reviews before purchasing equipment or expanding facilities and file a certificate of need demonstrating the necessity of the capital expenditure. Two years later, the complex Partnership for Health was replaced by the even more intricate Comprehensive Health Planning and Development Act of 1974. This act created a network of 205 local health systems agencies, overseen in each state by two state agencies, with a charge to develop a five-year health-systems implementation plan. All states were required to have Certificate of Need (CON) laws, mandating agency review of new facilities and equipment, in place by 1980. For most local agencies, this charge proved financially and logistically overwhelming.

In 1971, Nixon suggested an ambitious plan to cut health care costs, fostering the development of health maintenance organizations (HMOs), or prepaid group practice plans, to provide care for Medicare and Medicaid beneficiaries. This idea, which had been promoted by HEW and the Office of Management and Budget, later lost favor with the White House when the AMA pointed out its essential similarity to the "socialized, government-controlled" medical system it had been fighting for years. But Kennedy, Javits, Rogers, and Rep. William R. Roy (R-Kan.) adopted the plan with enthusiasm. An HMO option was added to Medicare and Medicaid, but viable HMO practices were scarce. After three years of congressional effort, the Health Maintenance Organization Act of 1973 created a small, experimental program to fund HMO development and enable insured employees to select an HMO plan where available.

The major battle between Congress and the executive branch began in 1972, when President Nixon announced his intention to terminate federal support for Hill-Burton, community health centers, mental health centers, and other programs; to reduce funds for remaining categorical grant programs; and to impound the currently appropriated funds. Congress reacted with fury, passing and repassing appropriations. In the Special Health Revenue Sharing Act of 1975, which was passed over Gerald R. Ford's veto, Congress ensured the survival of the grant programs for the interim, although under detailed legislative injunctions regarding planning, funding, and reimbursement. The health leaders were backed in this endeavor by the many representatives with ongoing programs in their own states, as well as by general congressional resentment of the president's tactics.

The administration of Jimmy Carter provided a brief respite from the debate, although concerns about cost containment were now dominant in most hearings on continuing programs. In 1981, however, Ronald Reagan announced plans to collapse all the twenty-six categorical health services programs (including migrant health, maternal and child health, community health centers, alcohol and drug abuse, and vaccination programs) into two block grants—for health services and preventive health—and to reduce funding by 25 percent. Senator Kennedy and Representative Henry Waxman (the new chair of the House Health Subcommittee), fought to save the programs. They were vigorously opposed in committee by conservatives in both parties, including Senators Orrin Hatch (R-Utah) and Phil Gramm (R-Tex.) and Representatives Edward R. Madigan (R-Ill.), James T. Broyhill (R-N.C.), and William E. Dannemeyer (R-Calif.). Waxman managed to negotiate three block grants: for preventive care, alcohol and drug abuse, and maternal and child health. Family planning, migrant workers' health centers, vaccination programs, and some others were retained as categorical grants. Community health centers were funded through a peculiar block grant of their own, which states could accept only to fund at existing levels. If they did not, the federal government would continue to fund the centers. This compromise was achieved only after the last-minute lobbying of representatives by Republican governors.

The bill containing these provisions, the Omnibus Budget Reconciliation Act of 1981, also reduced funding for the National Health Service Corps, local health systems agencies, capitation grants, and Medicaid; in several cases, it increased local and state governance over such programs as remained. Although the Reagan administration's goals were both to cut costs and to reduce federal regulation, the latter sometimes had to bow to the former, particularly in the Medicare and Medicaid

programs. The Tax Equity and Fiscal Responsibility Act of 1982 and Social Security Amendments of 1983 tightened regulations on both, including new peer-review requirements, and introduced Medicare reimbursement based not on cost or charges, but on set rates for diagnostic related groups (DRGs).

Presidents Reagan and Bush had the backing of the many conservative senators and representatives who shared their views. New health legislation had little chance of passage in their administrations. Kennedy and Waxman attempted to continue to support PHS grant programs and, to some extent, returned to the research emphasis of the 1950s. Waxman continually challenged and increased administration budget requests for AIDS research; in 1989, both Congress and the president agreed to fund the elaborate and expensive Human Genome Project. The abortion issue continued to be the basis for many unresolved issues, including consultation procedures in federally funded family planning clinics and the use of fetal tissue for research. Legislation in 1987 and 1988 to provide catastrophic health insurance coverage for Medicare recipients was derailed by the need for continuing payment reductions and by beneficiary protests over increased contributions.

In a successful initiative, congresswomen led by Senator Barbara Mikulski (D-Md.) and Representatives Patricia Schroeder (D-Colo.) and Olympia Snowe (R-Maine) joined other women's health activists in supporting the creation of a new Office for Research on Women's Health at NIH (the Women's Health Equity Act of 1991).

By the end of the Bush administration, the high costs of health care and large numbers of Americans without insurance coverage alarmed many observers, prompting demands for major health care reform by the federal government. President Bill Clinton made health care a priority of his new administration in 1993, announcing universal coverage as his goal and appointing Hillary Rodham Clinton to head a special task force to develop recommendations. The strong Republican minority in Congress, headed by Senator Robert Dole (R-Kans.), and with the frequent support of conservative Democrats, made it clear that they would challenge the president on any new funding proposals. A new congressional struggle over the thorny issue of government involvement in health care delivery, unresolved since the early years of the twentieth century, appeared likely to dominate the last decade as well, while the Public Health

Service prepared proudly to commemorate its bicentennial.

[*For discussion of related areas of public policy, see* Alcohol Policy; Family Policies; Medicare; Narcotics and Other Dangerous Drugs; Social Welfare and Poverty. *For discussion of the several congressional committees associated with the development of health and medical policy, see* Appropriations Committee, House; Appropriations Committee, Senate; Energy and Commerce Committee, House; Environment and Public Works Committee, Senate; Finance Committee, Senate; Labor and Human Resources Committee, Senate; Ways and Means Committee, House. *See also* Budget Process; Congressional Budget and Impoundment Control Act of 1974; Hospital Survey and Construction Act; Occupational Safety and Health Act of 1970; Pure Food and Drugs Act.]

BIBLIOGRAPHY

Bauman, Patricia. "The Formulation and Evolution of the Health Maintenance Organization Policy, 1970–73." *Social Science and Medicine* 10 (March–April 1976): 129–142.

Foley, Henry A., and Steven S. Sharfstein. *Madness and Government: Who Cares for the Mentally Ill?* 1983.

Fox, Daniel M. *Health Policies, Health Politics: The British and American Experiences 1911–1965.* 1986.

Harden, Victoria A. *Inventing the NIH: Federal Biomedical Research Policy, 1887–1937.* 1986.

Marmor, Theodore R. *The Politics of Medicare.* 1973.

Mullan, Fitzhugh. *Plagues and Politics: The Story of the United States Public Health Service.* 1989.

Price, David E. "Health and Environment." In *The Commerce Committees.* Edited by the Ralph Nader Congress Project. 1975. Pp. 252–278.

Redman, Eric. *The Dance of Legislation.* 1973.

Rettig, Richard A. *Cancer Crusade.* 1977.

Sardell, Alice. *The U.S. Experiment in Social Medicine: The Community Health Center Program, 1965–86.* 1988.

Strickland, Stephen P. *Politics, Science, and Dread Disease: A Short History of United States Medical Research Policy.* 1972.

Temin, Peter. *Taking Your Medicine: Drug Regulation in the United States.* 1980.

DANIEL M. FOX and MARCIA L. MELDRUM

HEARINGS. *See* Committees, *article on* Committee Hearings.

HEPBURN ACT (1906; 34 Stat. 584–595). An 1897 Supreme Court decision rendered the Interstate Commerce Commission (ICC) powerless, but within a decade Progressives, led by President Theodore Roosevelt, agitated for the end of railroad rate discrimination by giving the ICC the power to set maximum freight rates. In 1905, the ICC drew up a model bill for Roosevelt, Congress, and the public; by 1906 pressure for its adoption was so irresistible that even railroad officials were prepared to accept ICC maximum-rate regulation, with as much judicial review as they could get. Leaving the issue of judicial review to the courts, the Hepburn bill, named for Rep. William P. Hepburn (R-Iowa), was passed by the House on a vote of 346 to 7.

But several senators, led by Nelson W. Aldrich (R-R.I.), tried to secure a broad judicial review of rates set by the ICC. If they succeeded, the rate-setting power would be lodged in the courts. A narrow ju-

HEALTH CARE REFORM. President Bill Clinton speaks to Congress on health care, 22 September 1993. In the background are Vice President Al Gore, *left*, and House Speaker Thomas S. Foley (D-Wash.).

R. MICHAEL JENKINS, CONGRESSIONAL QUARTERLY INC.

HEPBURN BILL. Passed by the Senate after much amendment, the Hepburn bill limps past an approving teddy bear, who represents President Theodore Roosevelt, on its way to the House for a vote. Clifford K. Berryman, *Washington Post*, 15 May 1906.

U.S. SENATE COLLECTION, CENTER FOR LEGISLATIVE ARCHIVES

dicial review limited to questions of jurisdiction and method would make the ICC an independent regulatory commission having quasi-legislative, -executive, and -judicial powers. In the end the Senate left the extent of judicial review undetermined, and the bill passed with only three negative votes.

The Hepburn Act, which Roosevelt orchestrated into being, strengthened the ICC. Upon complaint the ICC could set a just-and-reasonable maximum rate that was binding on promulgation; its jurisdiction was widened to include express and sleeping-car companies, oil pipelines, and railroad switches, spurs, yards, depots, and terminals; its control over railroad accounting methods was increased. Despite the hopes of conservatives and the fears of Progressives, the Supreme Court adopted a narrow review policy, and the Hepburn Act transformed the ICC into an effective regulatory agency.

BIBLIOGRAPHY

Blum, John Morton. *The Republican Roosevelt*. 1954.
Hoogenboom, Ari, and Olive Hoogenboom. *A History of the ICC: From Panacea to Palliative*. 1976.

ARI HOOGENBOOM and OLIVE HOOGENBOOM

HIGHER EDUCATION ACT OF 1965 (79 Stat. 1219–1270).

Congress supported higher education in the nineteenth century through the establishment of the military academies and, in a much more substantial way, with the Morrill Act for land grant colleges. In the twentieth century, Congress provided further aid to higher education, especially after World War II, when the amount of research funding grew rapidly and the government embarked on large-scale student aid with the G.I. Bill. Still, the Higher Education Act (HEA) of 1965 (P.L. 89-329) was a landmark piece of legislation. It provided the first general program of undergraduate scholarships and loans, greatly increasing the federal investment in higher education. The G.I. Bill had covered only veterans, and the National Defense Education Act had assisted only students of high academic ability in areas considered relevant to national defense. HEA, however, partook of the mid-1960s concern for equal opportunity, reflected in the Elementary and Secondary Education Act passed the same year. Both education bills were considered central instruments in the war on poverty, and both reflected the theme of equal opportunity in President Lyndon B. Johnson's Great Society legislative program. Not only was eligibility for financial aid limited solely by family income under HEA, but there was a substantial program of outright scholarships, previously controversial in Congress.

HEA provided aid to assist libraries and train librarians, aid to "developing institutions" (aimed primarily at historically black colleges), aid to teacher training programs, and aid for the improvement of undergraduate instruction. But it was Title IV, for student aid, that got the most attention and, eventually, the most funding. A House committee noted "the appalling frequency with which a student is presently forced to forego the opportunity of postsecondary education because of inability to meet the costs."

In the late 1960s influential reports such as those of the Carnegie Commission on Higher Education and of Assistant Secretary of Health, Education and Welfare Alice Rivlin underscored the central priority of equal opportunity through scholarships and grants to individual students on the basis of need. The next major revision of federal higher education assistance occurred with the Education Amendments of 1972 (P.L. 92-318). In contrast to HEA, which a strongly Democratic Congress saw as crucial to the legislative program of a Democratic president, the higher education title of the 1972 Education Amendments was initiated by a Democratic

Congress faced by a Republican administration unenthusiastic about federal aid to poor students. Nonetheless, led by Claiborne Pell of Rhode Island, new chairman of the Senate Subcommittee on Education, Congress created a program of Basic Education Opportunity Grants and expanded other forms of student aid. Thus, federal policy toward higher education migrated from mostly institutional assistance to mostly individual student aid, which was 32 percent of all federal assistance in 1966 and 90 percent in 1986. This development set the terms of congressional debates about higher education assistance from the mid 1980s through the early 1990s, which focused on how much student assistance the federal government could afford and where the lines for eligibility should be drawn.

[See also Elementary and Secondary Education Act of 1965.]

BIBLIOGRAPHY

Gladieux, Lawrence E., and Thomas R. Wolanin. *Congress and the Colleges: The National Politics of Higher Education.* 1976.

Keppel, Francis. "The Higher Education Acts Contrasted, 1965–1986: Has Federal Policy Come of Age?" *Harvard Educational Review* 57 (1987): 49–67.

CARL F. KAESTLE

HIGHWAY SYSTEM. See Interstate Highway System.

HILL, LISTER (1894–1984), Democratic representative and senator from Alabama for forty-five years and sponsor of major legislation for federal programs in health and education. Son of a widely known Alabama physician, Joseph Lister Hill was reared in privileged circumstances. He earned his bachelor's degree from the University of Alabama and law degrees from that institution and from Columbia University Law School. Elected to the House of Representatives in 1923, largely owing to his father's connections, Hill, at twenty-eight, was the youngest member of that body. He became an ardent follower of a fellow representative of the American gentry, President Franklin D. Roosevelt, and in 1933 cosponsored, with Nebraska senator George W. Norris, the bill creating the Tennessee Valley Authority.

In 1938, Hill won the Senate seat formerly held by Hugo L. Black, Roosevelt's first appointee to the Supreme Court. In his campaign against former senator J. Thomas Heflin, Hill vigorously supported the pending federal law to create a minimum wage and a maximum work week. His victory, closely followed by that of Sen. Claude Pepper in Florida, broke the congressional logjam and led to passage of the Fair Labor Standards Act of 1938.

Democratic whip under Majority Leader Alben W. Barkley, Hill resigned this post in 1946 to avoid having to rally support for President Harry S. Truman's civil rights proposals. By this pragmatic decision, Hill retained his Senate base but relinquished his chance to become majority leader. His opposition to civil rights—a necessity to win political office in Alabama during that era—also forced Hill to give up ambitions for national office.

As a senior senator, Hill concentrated on areas far removed from civil rights. He and Alabama representative Carl A. Elliott won passage in 1958 of the National Defense Education Act, which still channels billions of federal dollars to provide college loans and improve U.S. education. Hill and Elliott also sponsored the 1956 Library Services Act, which provided federal funds to upgrade the nation's libraries.

Hill's chief focus, however, was health. He and a titular Republican cosponsor, Ohio senator Harold H. Burton, won passage in 1946 of the Hill-Burton Act, which forestalled Truman's proposal for national health insurance by providing federal funds for a vast hospital construction program, with many new hospitals targeted for rural areas. As chairman of the Senate Committee on Labor and Public Welfare, Hill, working with Rhode Island representative John E. Fogarty in the House, convinced Congress to commit billions to expand the National Institutes of Health, once an obscure governmental enterprise, into a medical research empire funding thousands of projects on the causes and control of major diseases and other health problems.

Rather than face a reelection campaign centered on racial issues, Hill retired in 1968. Although forced by practical politics to oppose all civil rights measures, Hill, through pathbreaking achievements in education and health, indirectly benefited average Americans of every race.

BIBLIOGRAPHY

Hamilton, Virginia Van der Veer. *Lister Hill: Statesman from the South.* 1987.

VIRGINIA VAN DER VEER HAMILTON

HILL-BURTON ACT. See Hospital Survey and Construction Act.

HINDS, ASHER C. (1863–1919), House parliamentary expert, Republican representative from Maine. Asher Crosby Hinds was first appointed by Speaker Thomas B. Reed as Clerk at the Speaker's Table in 1899. He was appointed again in 1895, at which time Hinds, "at the advice of the Speaker, who desired to make the position one of dignity and importance, began the study of parliamentary procedure." Hinds pursued this endeavor so diligently that he soon became the acknowledged expert on parliamentary procedure in the House and was reappointed by Speakers Reed, David B. Henderson, and Joseph G. Cannon. In several scholarly articles, Hinds traced the evolution of the Speaker's office, supported the power of the Speaker to appoint committees, and stressed that while the Speaker conducted the business of the House through his use and knowledge of the rules, a persistent and persuasive majority ultimately prevailed over the will of the Speaker.

Hinds's major contribution to the efficient operation of the House was the compilation in 1907 of five volumes of *Precedents of the House of Representatives*. This was perhaps the first instant authority available to the Speaker for helping the House avoid lengthy procedural arguments that delayed legislation. In his insightful introduction to that work, Hinds wrote that "the protection of the minority in its proper functions of examining, amending, and sometimes persuading the House to reject the propositions of the majority is an essential requirement of any sound system of procedure," but that "Mr. Jefferson wrote no one had seriously conceived that a minority might go further than this lofty and useful duty."

Hinds served as parliamentarian of the Republican National Conventions of 1900, 1904, and 1908. He became a representative from the 1st Congressional District of Maine in 1911 and served in the 62d through the 64th Congresses until his voluntary retirement.

BIBLIOGRAPHY

U.S. House of Representatives. *Hinds' Precedents of the House of Representatives of the United States*, by Asher C. Hinds. 5 vols. 59th Cong., 2d sess., 1907.

Charles W. Johnson

HISPANIC MEMBERS. Hispanics have been represented in Congress since the 1820s, and almost continuously since the 1850s. In 1993 seventeen Hispanics (3.9 percent of the House membership) were regular members of the House of Representatives, although in that year persons of Hispanic descent comprised 9 percent of the U.S. population.

Joseph M. Hernandez was the first Hispanic to serve in Congress. Born in St. Augustine, Florida, in 1793, when Florida was still a Spanish colony, he was elected as a delegate to the 17th Congress and served from September 1822 to March 1823.

In 1853 the newly created New Mexico territory sent its first delegate to Congress: Jose Manuel Gallegos, a popular priest. Miguel A. Otero, who succeeded Gallegos, was a more urbane and polished leader. He was reelected three times, serving in Congress from 1855 until 1861. The Hispanics who represented New Mexico as delegates to Congress between 1860 and 1900 were businessmen ranchers and landowners who were also active in politics.

Romualdo Pacheco, a Republican who was elected in 1877, was California's first Hispanic member of Congress, as well as the first Hispanic to be a regular voting member of Congress. He served three terms, leaving office in 1883.

The twentieth century saw the appearance of a succession of Hispanic delegates to Congress (known as resident commissioners) from Puerto Rico. Congressional delegates from Guam and the Virgin Islands have also been Hispanics and belonged to the Congressional Hispanic Caucus.

New Mexico became a state in 1912 and in 1914 Benigno "B.C." Hernandez was elected to its single seat in the U.S. House of Representatives. He was unsuccessful in his reelection effort in 1916 but won another term in 1918. Hernandez declined to seek reelection in 1920; he was succeeded by Republican Nestor Montoya, who served from 1921 until his death in 1923.

The 1920s also produced the first Hispanic U.S. senator. Octaviano A. Larrazolo, a former New Mexico governor (1919–1920), was elected in 1928 to fill the unexpired term of the late senator Andrieus A. Jones. Larrazolo declined to seek reelection in 1930 due to failing health.

The modern era of Hispanic representation in Congress began in 1930 with the election of liberal Democrat Dennis Chavez from New Mexico. In 1931 Chavez entered the House, where he served two terms. In 1935 he was appointed to the Senate, and he remained there until his death in 1962. Chavez's career was most notable for his long tenure as chairman of the Senate Public Works Committee, which during his chairmanship oversaw construction of numerous dams and federal

Hispanic Members of Congress

SENATORS	CONGRESS
Octaviano A. Larrazolo	71st
Dennis Chavez	74th–88th
Joseph M. Montoya	89th–94th

REPRESENTATIVES	CONGRESS
Romualdo Pacheco (R-Calif.)	45th–48th
Ladislas Lazaro (D-La.)	63d–70th
Benigno "B.C." Hernandez (R-N.Mex.)	64th–66th
Nestor Montoya (R-N.Mex.)	67th
Dennis Chavez (D-N.Mex.)	72d–73d
Joachim O. Fernandez (D-La.)	72d–76th
Antonio M. Fernandez (D-N.Mex.)	78th–84th
Joseph M. Montoya (D-N.Mex.)	85th–88th
Henry B. Gonzalez (D-Tex.)	87th–
Edward R. Roybal (D-Calif.)	88th–102d
E. "Kika" de la Garza (D-Tex.)	89th–
Manuel Lujan, Jr. (R-N.Mex.)	91st–101st
Herman Badillo (D-N.Y.)	92d–95th
Robert Garcia (D-N.Y.)	96th–102d
Matthew C. "Marty" Martinez (D-Calif.)	97th–
Esteban E. Torres (D-Calif.)	98th–
Solomon P. Ortiz (D-Tex.)	98th–
Bill Richardson (D-N.Mex.)	98th–
Albert Bustamante (D-Tex.)	99th–102d
Ileana Ros-Lehtinen (R-Fla.)	101st–
José E. Serrano (D-N.Y.)	102d–
Ed Pastor (D-Ariz.)	102d–
Lucille Roybal-Allard (D-Colo.)	103d–
Xavier Becerra (D-Calif.)	103d–
Frank Tejeda (D-Tex.)	103d–
Henry Bonilla (R-Tex.)	103d–
Lincoln Diaz-Balart (R-Fla.)	103d–
Luis V. Gutierrez (D-Ill.)	103d–
Robert Menendez (D-N.J.)	103d–
Nydia Velázquez (D-N.Y.)	103d–

SOURCE: Compiled by Maurilio E. Vigil

buildings and the initiation of the Interstate Highway System.

Joseph M. Montoya, also representing New Mexico, had an impact on Congress comparable to that of Senator Chavez. Montoya was reelected to the House three times and served in the Senate from 1965 to 1972. Montoya's advocacy of Hispanic concerns led him to sponsor the Bilingual Education Act of 1968 and the bill creating the Cabinet Committee on Opportunities for the Spanish-speaking. His Senate career was abruptly ended when he was defeated by astronaut Harrison H. Schmitt in 1976.

The decade of the 1960s was an important turning point for Hispanics in Congress. Before then, Hispanic representation had been limited to New Mexico and some isolated instances from Florida, Louisiana, and California. Now a larger and more varied group of Hispanic members appeared on the scene.

One of the more prominent new Hispanics was Henry B. Gonzales. He was elected to Congress from Texas's 20th District, encompassing San Antonio, in 1961, and through 1992 had been reelected continuously, sometimes without opposition and usually with resounding majorities. The colorful Gonzalez, known by the media for his occasional late-night oratory before an empty House chamber, is also the powerful chairman of the House Banking, Finance, and Urban Affairs Committee. Gonzalez triggered the congressional probe that uncovered the savings and loan scandal.

E. "Kika" de la Garza served six terms in the Texas House of Representatives before being elected to the 89th Congress from the 15th Congressional District that comprises the south Texas cities of Mission, McAllen, and Edinburg. De la Garza, a Democrat and chairman of the House Agriculture Committee, has been directly involved in most of the agricultural legislation passed since the 1980s.

Edward R. Roybal has been representing a Los Angeles district since 1962, and as chairman of the House Select Committee on Aging he has been influential in the development of policies for the elderly. Manuel Lujan, Jr., another original member of the "60's club," was something of an oddity as a Republican among the otherwise Hispanic Democrats in Congress. Elected to the House from New Mexico in 1968, the staunchly conservative Lujan often found himself in opposition to his Hispanic Democrat colleagues. He kept his seat until 1989, when he retired. He then became the secretary of the Interior.

New York's Puerto Rican community was represented in Congress for the first time in 1970 with the election of Herman Badillo. Badillo, who entered politics as borough president of the Bronx, ran unsuccessfully for mayor of New York before being elected to the House in 1970. A Democrat, he served four terms until his resignation in 1977 to become deputy mayor of New York City.

The Congressional Hispanic Caucus (CHC) was organized in 1976 in order "to monitor legislation and other government activity that affects Hispanics [and] to develop programs and other activities that would increase opportunities for Hispanics to participate in and contribute to the American political system." Although there are differing views concerning just how influential the CHC has been, its members have been quite vocal on immigration reform and civil rights legislation.

Developments in the 1980s and the early 1990s tripled the size of Hispanic congressional representation to the count of seventeen in 1993. Population growth and population shifts revealed in the 1980 and 1990 censuses increased the number of congressional seats of several "sun belt" states, leading to the creation of several new congressional districts with Hispanic concentrations. These trends led to the election of three additional Hispanic members from both Texas and California, the first two Hispanic members from Florida, one additional member from New York, and the first Hispanic members from Arizona, Illinois, and New Jersey. Hispanic members now comprise both men and women, representing both major political parties and every major region of the country.

Ileana Ros-Lehtinen, a Cuban American, was elected in 1989 to the Florida seat vacated by the late Rep. Claude Pepper; she was the first Hispanic woman elected to Congress. José E. Serrano was elected in 1990 to replace Robert Garcia as the representative of New York City's South Bronx, and in 1991 Arizona elected its first Hispanic member, Ed Pastor.

Most Hispanic members of Congress have been Democrats and have relied heavily on support from Hispanic constituencies. But their degree of attention to Hispanic issues has varied. While some (notably Chavez, Montoya, and Roybal) have been frequent and outspoken advocates for Hispanic concerns, others have been more subdued on ethnic minority issues. While uniting Hispanics in the House, the Congressional Hispanic Caucus has been a loose coalition with limited influence even in such key areas as immigration. Nonetheless individual members have exerted great power in their role as committee chairmen.

Hispanics now constitute a recognized group in Congress. Given such recent trends as population growth, immigration, increased political participation by Hispanics, and favorable congressional redistricting, the prospects for greater numbers and influence are high.

BIBLIOGRAPHY

Vigil, Maurilio E. "The Congressional Hispanic Caucus: Illusions and Realities of Power." *The Journal of Hispanic Policy* 4 (1989–1990): 19–30.

Vigil, Maurilio E. *Los Patrones: Profiles of Hispanic Political Leaders in New Mexico History.* 1980.

MAURILIO E. VIGIL

HISTORIANS OF THE HOUSE AND SENATE. For almost two hundred years Congress left to others the role of compiling and preserving its own rich history. Documents became lost or destroyed through indifference, and vital institutional memory diminished with each retirement or death. In 1975, the Senate sought to address those oversights by establishing the Senate Historical Office. The House, after hiring its first professional historian in 1983 primarily to direct House bicentennial observances, created in 1989 its own Office of the Historian of the House. Although given separate responsibilities, the nonpartisan offices, headed in 1994 by Senate historian Richard A. Baker and House historian Raymond W. Smock, have often worked together on historical preservation and information projects.

The Senate Historical Office, under the supervision of the secretary of the Senate and staffed by four historians and three research assistants, compiles information on key events, dates, statistics, and precedents. It provides reference services and produces publications for use by senators' offices, the press, scholars, and the public. A staff archivist advises senators and committees on cost-effective disposition of their noncurrent office files, assists researchers seeking access to Senate records, and publishes the *Guide to Research Collections of Former United States Senators* (1982).

Senate historians conduct oral history interviews with retired senior staff members and maintain biographical and bibliographical information on former senators. The office has published or contributed to several books, including Sen. Robert C. Byrd's four-volume history, *The Senate, 1789–1989,* and Sen. Bob Dole's *Historical Almanac of the United States Senate* (1991). It also compiles entries for the *Biographical Directory of the United States Congress,* last published in 1989, and makes available for research and publication its collection of some thirty thousand Senate photographs and other illustrations.

The Office of the Historian of the House, which operates under the direction of the House Speaker, took over the historical research and information functions of the House Office for the Bicentennial when that operation completed its principal mission and was abolished in 1989. Staffed by three historians and a research assistant, it provides general historical information to members of Congress, their staffs, the public, and the press. The House historical office and its predecessor have compiled, published, and contributed to a wide range of publications, including *Guide to Research Collections of Former Members of the United States House of Representatives, 1789–1987; Black Americans in Congress, 1870–1989; Women in Congress, 1917–1989;* and *Origins of the House of Representatives: A Documentary Record* (1990). The bicentennial office also prepared and edited sketches for the *Biographical Directory of the United States Congress, 1774–1989,* correcting errors from previous editions and adding new information, including committee chairmanships held by former and current House members and bibliographic citations. The 1989 edition marked the first time the biographical directory, published periodically since 1859, had been edited by professional historians.

BIBLIOGRAPHY

Baker, Richard A. "Documenting the History of the United States Senate." *Government Publications Review* (Fall 1983): 415–426.
U.S. House of Representatives. Office of the Historian. *Final Report of the Commission on the Bicentenary of the U.S. House of Representatives.* 101st Cong., 2d sess., 1990. H. Rep. 101–815.

DONALD C. BACON

HISTORY OF CONGRESS.

[*This entry surveys the foundation and history of the U.S. Congress during eight historical periods, beginning with the origins of its legislative practice in the seventeenth century:*

The Origins of Congress
The Road to Nationhood (1774–1801)
National Growth and Institutional Development (1801–1840)
Sectionalism and Nationalism (1840–1872)
The Age of the Machine (1872–1900)
Progressivism and Normalcy (1900–1933)
The Rise of the Modern State (1933–1964)
Congress Today and Tomorrow

For analytical discussion of congressional operations, practices, and traditions, see nine articles under the heading Congress. *For detailed discussion of the two houses of Congress, see* House of Representatives; Senate. *For general discussion of the relations of Congress with the other branches of the U.S. government, see* Constitution; Executive Branch; Judiciary and Congress; Legislative Branch; President and Congress. *See also various entries on special areas of public policy, particular legislative acts, particular congressional committees, and numerous leaders of Congress mentioned herein.*]

The Origins of Congress

Early in September 1774, delegations from twelve of Britain's thirteen mainland colonies met in Philadelphia to form the First Continental Congress. The term *congress,* in the usage of the time, meant a coming together of sovereign states. (In Europe it would continue to have this meaning in the nineteenth century, as in the Congress of Vienna [1814–1815].) And, indeed, each of these colonies had its own government, consisting of a governor, a council, and an elected assembly, whose structure and authority derived from a royal charter. (Georgia, a creation of Parliament, chose not to attend at this stage). The delegates represented colonies, not localities, and owed their appointments to the vote of their assemblies. Many of them were known to each other by repute, since the controversies of the previous few years had given rise to much intercolonial correspondence and a great deal of newspaper and pamphlet literature. Although few of them had actually met before, they quickly settled, with very little formality or disagreement about procedure, into a business routine that enabled them to confront the great questions that lay before them.

Coming together from distant regions with differing economic systems and social structures, these delegates nonetheless had two advantages: a common language and a shared political language of history and principles. Much of this political heritage had been acquired through the large measure of self-government exercised by the colonial assemblies, which in Virginia and most of New England had been in continuous or almost continuous existence for as much as a century and a half.

Thus the knowledge of parliamentary procedure, which made a silent but important contribution to the functioning of the Congress, was derived from long experience. It is not going too far to say that the confidence bred by generations of assembly rule filled these men with a passion for exercising power over their own domains. But in recent years this power had been challenged by the claims of the same British Parliament on which the assemblies had studiously modeled their own procedures and privileges. The conflict that brought the members of the Continental Congress together thus confronted them with a deep and complex conflict of loyalties and principles. Whatever their views on imperial government, none doubted the right of the assemblies to rule, almost exclusively, within their jurisdictions.

John Dickinson, in his *Letters from a Farmer in Pennsylvania* (1767), which was widely reprinted, had asserted the legislative and legal autonomy of the colonies in forceful terms. His was not an uncommon view. Yet at the same time, very few wished to deny the supremacy of Parliament over the whole empire or could have suggested an alternative system of government. These few were edging their way to the idea of the legal supremacy of the crown alone, but until 1774 they left their thoughts mainly unpublished. With several radical exceptions, most delegates had the common objective of persuading or coercing Britain into respecting their rights and privileges. This meant, to their thinking, a fundamental respect for the forms and procedures of government derived from their experience of the colonial assembly. If they achieved that aim, the First Continental Congress would also be the last. Hardly anyone expected it to be the origin of a totally new continental government.

Principles of Representation Affecting the American Colonies. England's earliest colonies, founded in the first three or four decades of the seventeenth century, were products of a period of unusual turbulence in parliamentary politics. Tudor and Stuart monarchs found it almost impossible to rule for long periods without the assistance of Parliament. The body was usually convened to vote taxes, an English right since 1340. Each session constituted a separate parliament; men spoke of "calling a parliament," not of Parliament as a continuous body. It could have no existence without the wish of the crown, and the monarch could always dissolve a sitting parliament. Precisely on this principle, royal governors dissolved colonial assemblies.

The theory of representation—insofar as anyone thought of reducing practice to theory—developed historically through the need to summon representatives to speak for and vote subsidies for their home communities. Every man in England was supposed to be represented in a parliament. But men, with their families, were not considered autonomous political individuals; they were members of communal groups that achieved formal status either in their counties, or shires, each of which sent to Parliament two members or "knights of the shire," or through their communes, or boroughs, which were represented according to the provisions of their charters—hence, etymologically, "the Commons." There was no entitlement to representation as an individual or in proportion to numbers, and this view was transported to the colonies and persisted in election laws governing the assemblies throughout the colonial era. New England's incorporated towns, regardless of their population, wealth, or tax contributions, were represented in the general assembly by two members elected at annual town meetings. In other provinces, people were represented, as in England, through their counties.

The major political excitements of Parliament during the period of the early North American settlements stemmed from local issues. Even important members of Parliament often used their influence more for local than for national purposes. But they were also becoming increasingly concerned about more general issues, and they were particularly affected by a severe economic depression around 1619. Many were also worried about royal favoritism toward the irresponsible Duke of Buckingham, whose influence passed from James I to his son Charles; by issues of foreign policy; and by religious conflicts intensified by Puritan suspicions of Arminian (or even Roman Catholic) influences on Charles. Some or all of these matters were likely to have been on the minds of early emigrants to America.

In a variety of constituencies in England, sharp contests were fought in elections for the parliaments of the 1620s, and older members or those who stood on hereditary or traditional claims could no longer count on being returned. Distant parts of the country showed increasing interest in parliamentary proceedings. After a series of quarrels, Charles ruled quite effectively without parliaments from 1629 to 1640. The legality of this procedure was a matter of dispute: the king had historical grounds for considering himself under no obligation to call a parliament if he could do without one. His opponents, however, took a different view and called this period "the eleven years tyranny."

The Puritans and other opponents of royal policy at home and the men who settled New England took this very much to heart. They were imbued with the belief that lawful government required the consent of the people freely given through their representatives. It was not a result of some democratic quality inherent in the American situation, but a direct transfer from old to new England when, in 1634, the freemen of Massachusetts Bay insisted on inspecting their royal charter, which revealed to them that they had rights of representation in the assembly. From that early date they elected their own representatives. The voting franchise, however, was limited to male members of the local Congregational churches.

This was not the first representative assembly to convene on American soil. In 1619, the Virginia Company in London, whose colony had been struggling for survival, instructed the governor to call an assembly as the most practical way to gain cooperation from the planters. After the dissolution of the company in 1624, the royal government managed the colony's affairs for four years without an assembly. A colony was a different proposition from a commercial company, however, and by 1628 a new assembly was thought the most practical method of dealing with the problems of defense as well as those of trade and general government. Assemblies were thenceforth a permanent feature of the government of Virginia—working always with the royal governor and his council. From 1634, the newly drawn counties became the principal basis of representation.

The thirteen continental colonies, as well as those of the West Indies, were founded for varying reasons over a period of more than a century, and thus their assemblies originated in somewhat differing ways. However, representative institutions always came into existence early in a colony's life, if not at the beginning. Seventeenth-century New York was ruled without an assembly for its first twenty years, but the fact that the proprietor was forced eventually to authorize an assembly for purposes of taxation reflected the difficulty of governing English subjects without some form of representation. The differences among the colonies were much less significant than the fact that throughout the colonial period of American development, representation through the elective branch of the assembly was a permanent and fundamental principle of legitimate government. Other methods, such as direct rule by a military governor, were tried but were never long-lived. No less significant is the fact that several of these assemblies had been established during the prolonged struggles between the crown and Parliament in England and met regularly, even when Parliament's role in English government was uncertain and far from secure. Britain's American colonists thus had long experience in support of their conviction that their assemblies represented their own collective interests whenever those interests appeared to differ from Britain's.

English Parliamentary Politics. The colonies had a large stake in the prolonged conflict between Parliament and the Tudor and Stuart monarchies.

The parliamentary side in England's civil wars consisted of much the same elements that had settled New England only a few years earlier. Certainly not all colonists made this identity their own; in Virginia there seems to have been much loyalty to the crown. But everywhere the cause of Parliament appeared to incorporate important aspects of the liberties the colonies held dear.

In Charles II's later years Parliament was consciously undermined, as the king believed increasingly that he could get by without parliamentary assistance. It would have been easy to believe by the 1680s that English government was moving in much the same absolutist direction as that of France under Louis XIV. This trend became more direct and ominous under James II, who carried the threat into the colonies by instituting a new form of unified royal government in a Dominion of New England that also included New York. The Massachusetts charter was invalidated by legal process. The abolition of New England's cherished assemblies, linked as it was to a policy of threatening the validity of land titles, united most of the colonists in the belief that the assembly had represented their interests against the crown's.

Those colonies that had been reconstructed under royal rule—New England and New York—could only view the Glorious Revolution of 1688 as a liberation, and the news from England was quickly followed by uprisings in America. They viewed Parliament's cause as their own and rejoiced in what they believed to be an identity of interests, a view their English contemporaries did not share. Here lay the roots of a misunderstanding that would deepen with the years.

Following the Glorious Revolution, England's Parliament—Great Britain's after 1707—gradually entrenched itself in the government of a nation that was now described as a limited or mixed monarchy. The assembly that had summoned William and Mary in 1688 from the Netherlands called itself a parliament, and a later parliament determined the Hanoverian succession. No monarch could ever again rule without a parliament, and a law requiring triennial elections reinforced the popular character of the representative element.

The parliamentary element in British government thus gradually grew more powerful as it also grew more oligarchic. The Septennial Act of 1716 lengthened the life of each parliament from three to seven years, greatly decreasing the influence of popular constituency opinion on the conduct of the House of Commons. This stood in sharp contrast to New

England, where annual elections continued to be the rule. Most other colonies gave their assemblies a somewhat longer span of life between elections. In Virginia, in a long interim between royal governors, the council ruled the colony from 1706 to 1710 entirely without an assembly, and it would have taken courage to predict that the assembly would eventually come to dominate the government. Yet once the assembly reconvened, it began to consolidate its power. It thus joined the mainstream of political development of the colonies with the advance of the eighteenth century.

The Conduct of Colonial Assemblies. Colonial "general assemblies" usually consisted of two houses, but the lower, elected ones are generally regarded as predecessors to the United States Congress. In Massachusetts, whose government, like that of Virginia, originated in a company charter, the assembly was called the Great and General Court. Initially the Massachusetts Bay Company made no provision for two legislative chambers. The magisterial "assistants" who sat with the governor also sat as members of the general court. They separated themselves from the elected representatives and began to function as an upper chamber in the early 1640s, after an unseemly quarrel over a lawsuit concerning the alleged abduction and slaughter of a poor widow's sow, in which the assistants and representatives voted on opposite sides. Virginia also eventually initiated a bicameral system, but as time went on, colony charters normally provided at the outset for both a lower and an upper house, the latter of which was also the governor's council. The emergence of bicameralism was the most significant development of the earlier period of assembly history.

The council consisted of a small and elite group of great landowners and merchants who functioned as a board of advisers to the governor, a final court of appeal, and an upper legislative chamber. In most cases—some of the New England colonies were exceptions—members owed their appointment to the crown, upon nomination by the governor. The council, which in some respects bore more resemblance to the English privy council than to the House of Lords, to which it was often likened, also advised the governor on, and in some cases served as the authority for, the important power to issue warrants for land grants. Although its members were drawn from the higher gentry, the nearest element to a colonial aristocracy, they could in no sense be said to represent the gentry as a class. But, apart from being nominated rather than elect-

ed, the council was simply too small and select to speak for the elite at large. Representatives of this group—and far more of them—found seats in the lower house.

In the developing crisis of the Revolution, the councils were unable to resist the pressure of popular opinion; they had neither the will nor the power to act as a restraining force. By 1775 the Virginia council, which had shown earlier signs of independence, felt constrained to declare that it harbored no designs inimical to the interests of the people. When the colonies sent their delegates to Philadelphia, there was no conception of a council or upper chamber in the structure of the Congress. Such a plan could apply only to a nation-state in which different chambers represented different estates of a single realm. That idea, which still prevailed in Britain and France, had no meaning where sovereign states were meeting as equals.

Elections. Elections to the lower house of assembly were annual events in New England and also in Pennsylvania. "Where annual elections end, tyranny begins," ran a popular New England slogan, which might have been held to imply that the beginnings of tyranny might be seen in colonies such as Virginia, where elections for a new House of Burgesses were called at irregular intervals—on average once in three years. Throughout New England, the elections were held at the annual town meetings, at which freeholders or persons qualified by the possession of a certain amount of personal property cast their votes under the eye of the moderator. South Carolina, on the other hand, had a secret ballot. Outside New England, the county was the unit of representation, and elections took place in the courthouse under the authority of the sheriff. The prevailing property qualification was a moderate freehold or its approximate equivalent in personal property. Many cases have been found, however, in which tenants cast their votes; a convention seems to have existed by which election officers were willing to consider long-term tenants as freeholders.

The extent of the suffrage franchise varied considerably from place to place. In round terms it may have amounted to as much as 75 percent of the adult men, everywhere excluding slaves and in southern colonies generally excluding all blacks. In Boston, the concentration of poor reduced the level to approximately 59 percent around the mid-eighteenth century. From the time of the Stamp Act crisis, radical leaders succeeded in stirring up an atmosphere in which more and more legally unqualified men were encouraged to vote. In 1772, "anything with the appearance of a man is admitted without scrutiny," said a sarcastic report of Governor Thomas Hutchinson of Massachusetts.

This leveling did not apply to the candidates, who, throughout the colonies, were normally drawn from among the more distinguished members of the recognized gentry or merchant classes. In 1758, for example, the young George Washington, a surveyor by trade and a soldier by avocation, confirmed his claim to elevated social status when he secured election to the Virginia House of Burgesses after several failures. In spite of colonial society's rough edges and occasional disorders, there remained a general disposition to defer to accepted social leadership. In provinces like New York or Virginia, where the great landlords or planters had some pretensions to aristocracy, they were expected to produce lavish quantities of liquor—usually rum—not so much as an outright bribe to voters but more as an expression of their own social standing. The self-assurance bred by this prevailing deference helped give the leadership the confidence it needed to challenge British authority.

Rules of procedure. Colonial assemblies do not seem to have possessed handbooks on parliamentary procedure. George Wythe, who served from 1769 to 1775 as clerk of the Virginia House of Burgesses, made a careful study of the rules of the British House of Commons, on which he modeled the procedure of his assembly. His law student Thomas Jefferson became absorbed in the same issues, and when he was vice president of the United States Jefferson wrote the first handbook of procedural guidance for the Senate, which became the standard work. [*See* Jefferson's Manual.]

The lack of formal guides, however, did not prevent the assemblies from learning to conduct their own procedures. Their early method was to deal with particular problems by appointing ad hoc committees, which dissolved when the matter in question was resolved by the house. Before the end of the seventeenth century, however, the Virginia assembly had discovered the art of establishing permanent committees to deal with specific classes of business. While this procedure had obvious advantages of drawing on specialized experience, it also tended to confide the more important matters to an inner circle. Socially weighty burgesses frequently occupied the more influential committee slots, often for long periods; in Virginia, a handful of members, nearly all from the province's great families, dominated the important committees through

most of the eighteenth century. This was a departure from the procedure of the British House of Commons, where the appointment of standing committees was merely ceremonial and a "grand committee," or Committee of the Whole House, was formed to discuss important issues.

Offices such as speaker and clerk were also usually occupied by socially prominent men. In Massachusetts these offices seldom slipped out of the control of Boston or the principal seaport towns. In Virginia one man, John Robinson, who also became treasurer, sat as speaker from 1738 to his death in 1766.

None of this kept the assemblies from being genuinely representative of and consciously sensitive to the numerous interests that demanded attention in addressing the economic, demographic, and in some cases religious questions of their societies. Thus the establishment of a land bank in Massachusetts in 1740—later rescinded by Parliament—was an act of the assembly against the wishes of the governor and a merchant minority. Conflicts between "parties" or "factions" organized around prominent families, such as the De Lanceys and the Livingstons in New York, also found their expression in assembly elections and politics. Until about the middle of the eighteenth century, the old Quaker "party" of Pennsylvania virtually ran the province. The yearly Quaker meeting arranged the tickets for forthcoming elections; it has been called the first closed primary. The Quakers lost their grip on assembly power over the issue of war supplies (a tender subject for Quaker consciences) in the mid 1750s, reflecting the changing balance of interests in the province at large.

Extent of powers. Colonial charters conferred extensive internal powers on the assemblies, though they were forbidden to make laws repugnant to the laws of England, and their acts were subject to scrutiny by the crown, which disallowed those of which for any reason it disapproved. This particularly applied to acts that were held to infringe the royal prerogative. The rise of assembly power gradually squeezed the council and confronted the governor.

This process became more self-conscious as assemblies increasingly claimed that within their own domains they were little parliaments, with all—in some cases more than—the rights and privileges of the Parliament of Great Britain. Prominent colonial lawyers such as Richard Bland of Virginia, James Otis of Massachusetts, and Daniel Delany of Maryland drew the comparison in pamphlets in 1764 and 1765. British authority had willingly conceded the fundamental principle that, as British subjects, colonists had a right to vote taxes through their own representatives. (What Britain asserted in the dispute between Parliament and the colonies over taxation was that all British subjects, colonial included, were "virtually" represented in Parliament). But the British regarded the colonial assemblies as having essentially the status of local corporations. In a dispute with New York in the late 1760s, Parliament actually threatened to suspend the assembly. Assemblies, for their part, pursued their claims to parliamentary status by asserting their exclusive right to originate and control money bills, eventually fighting off claims by the councils. They began by monitoring accounts, and by mid-century they were establishing the important principle that only the assembly could authorize expenditures of funds raised by taxation. They determined their own membership when elections were disputed and controlled their internal procedures.

The story, or at least the chronology, differed from colony to colony. In South Carolina this argument extended into the late 1760s and ended so inconclusively that no tax bill could be passed from 1768 until after independence. As early as the 1720s, Massachusetts disputed the governor's claim to exercise a veto over the assembly's choice of speaker. When this, among other points, led the crown to amend the charter with a supplementary document, a number of members voted against receiving it. On one notable occasion in 1733 the Massachusetts assembly requested the House of Commons to intercede with the crown to secure the withdrawal of a royal instruction to Lieutenant-Governor Dummer—an impertinence that the Commons promptly denounced. The incident illustrates the mistaken colonial belief that their assemblies and the House of Commons had a common interest against the crown, a view by then some forty years out of date. Massachusetts assemblies were notorious for wrangling with governors over salaries, which they used as a counter in bargaining for executive cooperation.

This record of self-assertion and self-aggrandizement can too easily be taken as evidence that colonial assemblies were consciously charting a course toward independence. This, as Governor Francis Fauquier of Virginia observed in 1760, was far from the truth. "Whoever charges them with acting upon a premeditated concerned plan, don't know them," he explained, "for they mean honestly, but are Expedient Mongers to the highest Degree." Members

of the assemblies were intent on exercising the dominant power within their own territories, but they were not directed by a sense of ultimate aims. Their mode of operation was opportunistic rather than preconceived; they were loyal to the crown, and although they occasionally probed the boundaries of parliamentary supremacy, they accepted the imperial system as a whole. The Continental Congress still held to these views in 1774.

The assemblies were in fact alert to the privileges of their position in relation to the people as much as in relation to their governors. For an editor or pamphleteer to criticize an assembly could be interpreted as a breach of privilege and was sometimes punished by imprisonment. The right to print votes and acts was assigned to a specified printer under the speaker's authority. Press reporting of assembly debates was entirely unknown in colonial America, although by the 1760s Americans had every opportunity to know that debates in Parliament were unofficially and illegally printed and widely read in Britain. On only a few occasions were records of assembly votes printed, and then usually for the purpose of affecting political loyalties or forthcoming elections.

Yet assemblies could never disclaim their basis in public support. Their ultimate reliance on the electoral system was evident when, in both New York and Pennsylvania in the 1740s and 1750s, the assemblies appealed to public opinion in quarrels with their governors. After the Stamp Act riots, Boston radicals used publicity as a means of exerting political pressure: they were instrumental in adding a public gallery to the assembly in 1766, from which Samuel Adams's supporters in the Boston crowd could intimidate representatives from country towns. Virginia had taken the same step two years earlier.

Assembly privacy could not be long maintained under these conditions, and when during the Stamp Act crisis town and county meetings began to issue instructions (which were sometimes written by assembly members themselves), they took an initiative that was incompatible with the principle of privacy. This conflict was resolved only when revolutionary constitutions officially proclaimed the public's right to knowledge of assembly proceedings, calling for open doors and publication of the record.

Precedents for these demands had appeared occasionally in earlier colonial days, when pamphleteers claimed that the people had a right to know what their legislators were doing. A tract linking representation to public knowledge was published in Boston in 1739; John Adams, writing as "Novanglus," renewed this claim in 1775. In New York, beginning in 1754, the speaker annually issued an order permitting the printing of the record of the assembly's proceedings, but this was only a chronicle of the events of the session. Before the Revolution, the people could consider themselves entitled to a report only at the end of the session; they had no constitutional right to know what went on from day to day.

The First Continental Congress. It was wholly in keeping with colonial tradition then, that one of the first decisions of the First Continental Congress, convened in September 1774, was to keep its proceedings secret. This freed the delegates from the pressures of local opinion in Philadelphia. It also served to conceal, at least temporarily, the divisions and dissensions within the Congress, difficulties that could have seriously impaired its public reputation and given encouragement to royal authorities. The policy of secrecy does not seem to have attracted criticism or even comment at the time.

After rejecting an invitation from Joseph Galloway, speaker of the Pennsylvania assembly, to meet in the State House, delegates accepted a rival invitation from Carpenters' Hall. This snub to Galloway, engineered by enemies in his own state, was followed by the appointment of a political enemy, Charles Thomson, as clerk. Thomson's method of keeping the record was to report only positive decisions; failed motions were omitted. The *Journal of the Continental Congress* is therefore an incomplete record. It was not part of Thomson's duty to report debates, of which we have glimpses in John Adams's *Diary* and occasional letters by members of the Congress.

Before they could proceed further, delegates also had to decide how to vote. Privincial delegations varied in size from two (New Hampshire) to five (New Jersey and South Carolina) and six (Virginia) and were chosen without particular concern for population; it would have been arbitrary to count heads within the Congress. It also seemed arbitrary, from the point of view of the larger and wealthier colonies, to count the separate delegations as equals, also without regard for the populations they represented. The latter course was chosen, however, for the practical reason that no accurate statistics existed by which either population or wealth could be ascertained. Delegates, as John Adams implied, could not trust each other's word on so serious a matter. The decision was held at the time to be temporary, but it gave the smaller colonies an entrenched position from which they could not later be dislodged and became a permanent feature of the structure of the Continental Congress. It may be said to have reappeared in the Constitution with the equality of the states in the U.S. Senate.

It was agreed that divine aid should be invoked, and an Anglican clergyman, the Reverend Jacob Duché, who was invited to offer prayers, preached to such effect that John Adams, a Congregationalist who had never heard a Church of England service, was deeply moved. Duché later became a Loyalist.

The small group of delegates who were privately eager to forward the cause of independence, including John and Samuel Adams from Massachusetts, Richard Henry Lee and George Wythe from Virginia, and Christopher Gadsden of South Carolina, had little influence with the great majority, who desired nothing more than to patch up the quarrel and persuade the British government to return to its old, relaxed, and apparently benign way of running the empire. The preferred manner of producing these results had been applied before, at the times of both the Stamp Act and the Townshend duties, and was what are now called economic sanctions. Through a series of embargoes, first on the importation of British goods, then, if need be, on all exports to Great Britain, the members hoped to create pressures on British merchants that would affect government policies. That the delegates never formally debated any form of military action demonstrates their cautious mood. When on 6 October the Massachusetts dispatch rider Paul Revere brought alarming news that General Thomas Gage, the British commander, was fortifying his army's position in Boston, Congress's reply was to urge restraint on both sides rather than encourage Boston to arm itself, as the radicals had hoped. Congress declined to advise whether Boston should be evacuated.

This conservatism reflected the anxieties felt by many delegates over the domestic consequences of encouraging revolt. Many men of substance were uneasily aware of stirrings of discontent that might overturn their authority and threaten property in their colonies. Others, though more confident of their domestic position, sincerely believed that the whole dispute could be settled without disloyalty to the crown. George Washington of Virginia, for one, was disturbed by rumors of the revolutionary purposes of the men from Massachusetts. On 28 September he sought reassurance from Samuel Adams, who succeeded in convincing him that the group had no such intentions.

Agreement was reached fairly soon on halting imports from Britain, Ireland, and—a painful deprivation—the British West Indies. Greater difficulties arose over exports. Virginia and South Carolina wanted time to harvest and export the next season's crops of tobacco and rice. After much wrangling, the date of nonexportation was delayed until 10 August 1775. The hope was that nonimportation and the threat of worse would bring the British government around in time to avert deeper sacrifices. When the South Carolina delegates reported home, they faced furious opposition from backcountry farmers who felt that the great coastal rice planters had put their own interests before all else.

Congress sent addresses pleading with the king and British people for recognition of the constitutional rights claimed by the colonists. Its strongest rhetorical declaration was given in "the Suffolk Resolves," a statement of colonial rights recently passed in Suffolk County, Massachusetts. The resolves went beyond the usual appeals to British constitutional and common law to include a claim to natural rights. The issue was divisive. Domestic conservatives, whatever they might have felt toward Britain, were cautious about declarations that might threaten their own supremacy if self-defense turned, as many feared, into domestic upheaval. On 11 October Congress advertised its own caution by denying that the resolves represented a willingness to countenance an attack on the governor in Massachusetts.

The most far-reaching proposal for resolving the entire problem of colonial relations with Britain was introduced by the arch-conservative Joseph Galloway, who reached back to the abortive Albany Plan of Union of 1754, and in a sense looked forward to the Constitution of the United States, by proposing a "grand council" or parliament for the colonies. This body, presided over by a crown-appointed president-general, to hold office during the crown's pleasure, would deal with all matters affecting more than one colony or relations with Britain. All legislation affecting America, whether initiated in Britain or the colonies, would be subject to agreement by both sides.

Genuine radicals had reason to view Galloway's plan with alarm, for it would provide a machinery for mediating all future disputes within the institutional context of the empire. The more conservative majority viewed it with discomfort because it would unsettle habitual domestic arrangements and would create an authority superior to the colonial assemblies on the American continent. The Continental Congress, itself such a body, was intended to meet only to resolve the present crisis and then dissolve.

After an initially favorable reception, the Galloway Plan was defeated on a second hearing and all reference to it was expunged from the records— an early and remarkable example of news manipulation. Galloway blamed the timidity of his supporters on the outright intimidation from the streets—the sort of demonstration Samuel Adams had so often orchestrated in Boston.

The most important outcome of the First Continental Congress was the adoption of the Continental Association. Americans, according to this declaration of grievances and intents, had suffered from British aggressions since "about 1763"—a date that left an open field for claimants of land grants from the crown before that year. In addition to nonimportation and nonexportation, the association pledged its adherents to promote frugality, to renounce extravagant ceremonies, and to encourage the breeding of sheep and the production of American goods. Before it dissolved, the Congress looked to its own succession. If the redress sought had not been granted, a second Congress was to be called in May 1775.

Long before this, in one of its earliest measures, the Congress authorized the creation of local committees throughout the colonies. These committees, through whose agency it transmitted and enforced its policies, gave the Congress a basis of popular authority transcending that of any individual assembly. The states could never have achieved independence without the basis of legitimacy authorized by the Congress. But the Congress could also use its authority through the committees to determine the limits of local action. The implications were far-reaching, perhaps revolutionary. Since the committees survived after the Congress had dissolved itself, they constituted a revolutionary foundation for the Second Continental Congress, which in July 1776 declared the independence of the United States.

On 27 October 1774, John Dickinson, the famous "Pennsylvania Farmer," wrote to Arthur Lee in London that Congress had broken up the day before. The colonists had taken such ground that Great Britain must relax, or involve herself in civil war. Dickinson's mood was, for him, unusually militant. But the vast majority of delegates had gone home in the hope that Britain would indeed relax and relent, leaving them free to return to the old ways of their familiar and beloved colonial assemblies.

The end they hoped for was not to be. Britain refused to respond to either persuasion or pressure, and after a winter of deepening crisis the Second Continental Congress met, again in Philadelphia, in May 1775. It needed no new grant of authority: the meeting proceeded smoothly from decisions taken by the First Congress six months before. There was no need to lay the groundwork for colonial cooperation; the machinery was already in place. There were new developments: an unconvincing offer of conciliation from Lord North's administration in Britain and the news of the bloodshed at Lexington and Concord in Massachusetts. In the ensuing months, Congress exerted its latent powers by raising an army, sending further dispatches to Britain, issuing its own currency, and opening negotiations with foreign powers. These were the embryonic beginnings of a new government of the continental colonies. The name "Congress" would survive in the Constitution of the United States—a step not yet imagined when the War of Independence began, or when, a year later, Congress assumed the power to declare the independence of the United States.

BIBLIOGRAPHY

Bailyn, Bernard. *The Origins of American Politics.* 1968.

Dinkin, Robert J. *Voting in Provincial America: A Study of Elections in the Thirteen Colonies, 1689–1776.* 1977.

Greene, Jack P. *The Quest for Power: The Lower Houses of Assembly in the Southern Royal Colonies, 1689–1776.* 1963.

Greene, Jack P. "Political Mimesis: A Consideration of the Historical and Cultural Roots of Legislative Behavior in the British Colonies in the Eighteenth Century." *American Historical Review* 75 (1969): 337–360.

Greene, Jack P. *Peripheries and Center: Constitutional Development in the Extended Politics of the British Empire and the United States, 1607–1788.* 1986.

Hirst, Derek. *The Representative of the People? Voters and Voting in England under the Early Stuarts.* 1975.

Russell, Conrad. *The Crisis of Parliaments: English History, 1509–1660.* 1971.

Pole, J. R. *Political Representation in England and the Origins of the American Republic.* 1966. Rept. 1971.

Pole, J. R. *The Gift of Government: Political Responsibility from the English Restoration to American Independence.* 1983.

Tully, Alan. "The Political Development of the Colonies after the Glorious Revolution." In *The Blackwell Encyclopedia of the American Revolution.* Edited by Jack P. Greene and J. R. Pole. 1991.

J. R. POLE

The Road to Nationhood (1774–1801)

In retrospect, it seems surprising that the members of the Federal Convention of 1787 decided to retain the name *congress* for the new national legislature that their proposed constitution would create. In the ordinary usage of the era, *congress* denoted a diplomatic assembly rather than a legislative body. That was the sense in which the name was first used to describe the one essential institution of central government that had operated since the British Parliament, by adopting the Coercive Acts of 1774, precipitated the crisis that led to American independence. Even before the Continental Congress first met at Philadelphia in September 1774, this institution had been heralded as "the collected wisdom of America" by patriot writers who evoked the language of the Book of Daniel to predict that its decisions would be obeyed as implicitly as "the laws of the Medes and Persians, which altereth not."

By 1787, however, an entirely different image of Congress had taken hold. Now it was often derided for its "imbecility," and the Framers at Philadelphia were intent on reconstituting a national representative body that would bear little resemblance to its predecessor. The legislature they designed was to be a truly national institution. In choosing to call it a *congress* still, they may have hoped that the continuity of names would disguise how different they hoped the two bodies would be.

During the first quarter century of American independence, then, not one but two congresses served as the locus of national politics. The Continental Congress (1774–1789) was primarily a revolutionary body whose authority rested more on the course of the struggle against Great Britain than on the formal powers it claimed with the adoption of the Articles of Confederation in 1781. By contrast, the new congress that assembled in New York in April 1789 was the product of the remarkable debates that had replaced the Articles with the Constitution. But during the first decade of its existence, the politics of this congress were still shaped by revolutionary forces—only now these forces originated in France.

The Continental Congress, 1774–1781. No subsequent congress commanded as much prestige and authority as the First Continental Congress of 1774 and its successor, the Second Continental Congress, which reconvened in Philadelphia in May 1775—at least until the latter's approval of the

Declaration of Independence was quickly followed by a string of military defeats and the first signs of the monetary inflation that would trouble the American cause for the next five years. This early deference to Congress reflected the severity of the shock the British government had delivered with its harsh reaction to the Boston Tea Party of December 1773, a reaction that pushed Americans to the brink of civil war. Within the short space of seven weeks, the delegates to the First Congress (representing every colony but Georgia) agreed upon a coherent set of demands and tactics around which colonial resistance could mobilize. When most of these same delegates returned to Philadelphia in the spring of 1775, fighting had already broken out in Massachusetts, and the Second Congress quickly organized a continental army and began to mobilize for war.

Potentially significant differences of opinion about the costs of winning independence and the prospects for reconciliation existed within Congress during this period, separating more militant delegates such as Samuel Adams, John Adams, and Richard Henry Lee from moderates like John Dickinson, James Wilson, and John Jay. But the delegates understood that their collective authority rested on their ability to maintain the image of unanimity they had inherited from the First Congress and, more important, on their capacity to allow the public sentiment toward independence to be driven by fresh British provocations rather than by impulsive acts of Congress. A shared sense of responsibility to "the common cause" thus restrained delegates from conveying their individual concerns about the course of resistance to their constituents in provincial conventions or to the people at large.

After 1776, memories of this early patriotic fervor provided the benchmark against which delegates to Congress measured both their own frustrations with an indecisive war and a mounting sense that popular enthusiasm for the struggle was abating. From 1775 on, Congress acted in a dual character. As a deliberative assembly of thirteen states—the United States in Congress Assembled—it retained overall direction of the war effort. But through an extensive apparatus of committees—some permanent, many ad hoc—Congress also exercised substantial administrative responsibility, framing and adopting countless measures designed to mobilize resources for the war. Many of these decisions took the form of resolutions and requisitions that Congress transmitted to the state governments in the confident expectation that they

in turn would act as its administrative auxiliaries by converting general recommendations into legislative acts applicable to the particular circumstances of their constituents.

This expectation reflected the popular patriotism of the period from 1774 to 1776. But as the war dragged on, imposing seemingly limitless burdens on the economy and thus on private citizens, it became more difficult for the states to meet their federal obligations. By 1778, congressional and state reliance on paper currency to pay the costs of war, coupled with shortages of various goods and commodities, produced a runaway inflation that no one knew how to control and that left masses of Americans aggrieved with government at every level.

Declining confidence in Congress also resulted from a series of disputes over foreign policy that erupted in 1778 and 1779 and proved too bitter for Congress to contain. In the first years of the Revolution, issues of foreign policy served as a unifying force among both the delegates and the American public—especially when Congress learned that the "peace" commissions that Britain sent to America in 1776 and 1778 lacked any real authority to respond to American demands. But the conclusion of the treaty of alliance with France in 1778 helped turn issues of foreign policy from a source of unity into a basis for factional disputes rooted in the distinct interests of the different regions of the Union. When the French minister to the United States urged Congress to define its terms of peace in 1779, he precipitated a protracted debate centered on the conflicting interests of New England and the South that spilled over into the press. For the first time it became evident that deep divisions existed among the delegates. This further deflated the residual image of Congress as the repository of "the collected wisdom" of the country.

Congress nonetheless remained the embodiment of American union, and it never lost the support required to maintain the war. By comparison with the early years, however, its reputation and influence had fallen sharply, and this mattered all the more because until 1781 its authority rested on a political rather than a constitutional foundation.

Congress under the Articles of Confederation, 1781–1789. Congress had set out to secure a constitutional basis for its power as early as June 1776, when a committee chaired by John Dickinson drafted Articles of Confederation to clarify the extent of its authority. But disputes over three intractable issues—the rule of voting in Congress, the formula for apportioning common expenses among the states, and the control of western lands—quickly led to stalemate. After that, other business preoccupied Congress until the fall of 1777, when its members, anxious to capitalize on the victory at Saratoga to complete an alliance with France, finally mustered the will to complete the Confederation. In doing so, however, they only laid the basis for future difficulties.

The decision to retain the principle of giving each state a single vote in Congress—adopted as an expedient in 1774—continued to rankle leaders of the more populous states. The formula for apportioning expenses among the states on the basis of the value of improved lands proved unworkable, and it complicated later efforts to provide Congress with adequate and independent sources of revenue. By refusing to vest Congress with authority over the interior lands claimed by various states, the Framers of the Articles of Confederation provoked a small group of "landless" states to delay the ratification of the Confederation, on the grounds that they would have to tax their citizens heavily to pay their share of the costs of the war. By 1779 only Maryland still withheld its assent; but it continued to do so until it finally acceded in February 1781, enabling the Articles to take effect on March 1.

As a first application of a theory of federalism, the Articles were a reasonably pragmatic attempt to divide basic responsibilities of governance between Congress and the states. In many ways, Congress could be regarded as the successor to the British crown, in the sense that its principal duties centered on the conduct of war and foreign relations, which were royal prerogatives under the British constitution. In these crucial areas, Congress was to all intents and purposes sovereign. On the other hand, the crown had also held the power to veto colonial legislation and to regulate the development

CONGRESS MOVING TO PHILADELPHIA. In the cartoon, published c. 1790, the congressional majority rides on the "ladder of preferment" that rests on the back of the alleged instigator of the move to Philadelphia, Sen. Robert Morris of Pennsylvania (labeled in the print as Robert Coffer). The majority is portrayed as looking forward to the financial gains to be reaped from the move, while the minority is led along by strings through their noses, skeptical of the majority's motivation for the move and questioning the political and practical benefits of going.   LIBRARY OF CONGRESS

of the interior, neither of which Congress could do. Nor did Congress have any authority to raise revenue, except by asking the states to levy taxes to meet their share of national expenses. Under the Articles, the states retained complete authority over their "internal police"—the entire body of domestic legislation, including the power of taxation, that regulated the ordinary affairs of the citizenry. At the behest of Thomas Burke of North Carolina, an early advocate of a states' rights theory of federalism, Congress adopted an additional explanatory article affirming that each state retained "its sovereignty, freedom, and independence, and every power, jurisdiction, and right, which is not by this confederation expressly delegated" to the Union.

Formal ratification of the Confederation had little impact on either the procedures or the politics of Congress. But the intervening years exposed flaws in the assumptions under which the Articles were drafted. The most important involved issues of revenue and other resources needed to sustain the war. After abandoning its scheme of currency finance in late 1779, Congress transferred to the states much of the responsibility for raising specific supplies needed by the army. But it still needed independent sources of revenue, not only to meet ongoing expenses but also to secure foreign loans. Shortly before the Confederation was ratified, Congress transmitted to the states its first proposed amendment to the Articles, which would allow it to collect a 5 percent impost (or duty) on goods imported from overseas. In the long term, Congress also hoped that it would be able to use western lands as a source of revenue and credit. By 1781 the individual states were beginning to cede their interior claims to the Union, gradually making possible the establishment of a national domain above the Ohio River.

The willingness of the claiming states to convey this territory to Congress represented perhaps the apex of its ability to embody national interests transcending the immediate goal of securing independence. But other issues on the congressional agenda after 1781 produced less encouraging results. The effort to secure the impost amendment of 1781 foundered on the initial dissent of Rhode Island. In April 1783, after prolonged debate driven by rumors of unrest in the army and the maneuvers of Robert Morris, whom Congress had appointed its first superintendent of finance in 1781, Congress approved a second set of amendments proposing a revised impost as well as an alteration in the formula for apportioning expenses. But these propos-

COMMEMORATIVE BRASS BUTTON. Issued for President George Washington's inauguration. The original states are represented by the circle of thirteen links.

COLLECTION OF DAVID J. AND JANICE L. FRENT

als also failed to gain the unanimous state ratification required for adoption.

What role would Congress play in American public life after the revolution it had been organized to direct was brought to a successful conclusion? Just as the creation of the national domain gave Congress significant domestic business to conduct, so new issues of foreign relations emerged in 1783 and 1784 to demonstrate the continuing need for an effective national government. The most important of these was trade. American merchants were eager to regain access to markets in the British West Indies and to enjoy the profits of commerce with the former mother country. But although American agricultural exports were welcome in Britain's island possessions, and British imports were eagerly sought by American consumers, American shippers found themselves excluded from both avenues of trade, while urban artisans suffered from the dumping of British manufactures on the domestic market.

The logical response to these conditions was to curtail the access of British ships and goods to American markets until imperial harbors were opened to American merchants. Under the Confederation, however, Congress lacked the authority to regulate either interstate or foreign commerce, and the partial and inconsistent efforts of individual states to act in its stead seemed only to demonstrate the need for uniform, national action. In the spring of 1784—shortly before adjourning for the first time since 1775—Congress accordingly proposed two additional amendments that would have given it limited authority to regulate foreign commerce. Again, however, neither amendment secured the requisite unanimous consent of the states. In the meantime, Britain seized on the failure of individual states to comply with peace treaty provisions relating to the rights of loyalists and creditors as justification for its commercial policy and its retention of important forts along the northern frontier. From these posts the British exercised influence over various Indian nations and thus threatened U.S. settlement of the interior.

Another major foreign policy issue arose in the Southwest in 1784, when Spain denied the United States access to the Gulf of Mexico through the Mississippi River. This action alarmed southern delegates to Congress, and they became even more disturbed in 1786 when John Jay, the secretary of foreign affairs, proposed that the United States abjure its claims to navigate the Mississippi in order to secure a commercial treaty with Spain. Jay's request triggered another protracted debate over foreign policy. More important, it created a stark division between northern and southern delegates to the Confederation Congress.

Caught between northern desire for strong action to advance U.S. commerce and southern concern over issues of territorial expansion, Congress encountered difficulties in the realm of foreign affairs that seemed to call into question the very idea of a coherent, identifiable national interest that it could effectively define and protect. The contrast with 1776 could not have been more profound. Once the embodiment of the idea of American union, Congress had become the locus for the Union's most dangerous conflicts. Its inability to define or pursue the national interest now seemed to threaten the concept of nationhood itself. Although many Americans remained oblivious to the implications of the issues, a small but influential segment of their political leadership became concerned that the Union itself was endangered and that the strategy of piecemeal reform of the Confederation that had been pursued thus far was not adequate to the divisive forces that had revealed themselves.

Creating a National Legislature, 1787–1789. The crucial point of departure for the delegates to the Federal Convention of 1787 was the conviction that the central defect of the Confederation lay in the dependence of the Continental Congress on the state legislatures not only for the approval of amendments to the Articles but also for the prompt execution of its ordinary resolutions. A few delegates thought it would be more prudent to give additional powers over revenue and commerce to the existing Congress, as the New Jersey Plan proposed to do. But from the outset the dominant sentiment lay with the advocates of the Virginia Plan. This proposed a new bicameral legislature empowered to adopt laws that would act directly upon the American population, rather than issue resolutions requiring the intermediate approval of the state assemblies. The legislature would consist of a lower house elected by the people, with representation allocated on a proportional scale yet to be determined, and an upper house elected by the lower house from candidates nominated by the state legislatures.

The Virginia Plan was the product of a systematic effort by James Madison to diagnose what he called the "vices of the political system of the United States." Drawing upon his own service in Congress and the Virginia assembly, Madison concluded that the great defect of the Confederation was its assumption—so plausible in 1776, so questionable after the experience of the war and four years of peace—that the state assemblies could be counted on to perceive and pursue the national interest. The naïveté of this assumption seemed most apparent when efforts to amend the Confederation triggered the requirement for unanimous state compliance, but it was nearly as evident when lesser matters were referred to the states. As a delegate to Congress in the early 1780s, Madison had toyed with the idea that it might be possible to vest Congress with power to coerce delinquent states into doing their duty. But by 1787, this seemed to him to be a formula not for government but for civil war.

In proposing that the union should be allowed to act legislatively upon its citizens, the Virginia Plan immediately led to two further propositions. The first was that the successor to the Continental Congress would have to be reconstituted as a legislature in the usual sense of the term—that is, as the bicameral body demanded by conventional constitutional theory—because only a divided body could be safely trusted with the power to legislate.

Second, because the legislature would act directly on citizens and their property, through the legislative power of taxation, justice dictated that representation and voting within it would have to be proportioned according to some formula other than the Confederation rule of one state, one vote. In the lower house, that formula would have to decide whether the entities to be represented were simply the citizens themselves or the people together with their property, whether measured by their contributions to the national treasury or, in the peculiar case of the southern states, by their property in the enslaved African American population. For the upper house, Madison believed that the principle of proportionality would be sufficiently honored simply by allowing its members to be elected by the lower house. Though he thought that it was possible to create a lower house relatively insulated from the parochial pressures of its electors, he was more deeply committed still to the establishment of a truly cosmopolitan senate, an institution that would be capable of defining and pursuing a broad conception of the national interest.

Madison's ideas, as refined in the Virginia Plan, were vulnerable on two grounds. Though he believed that the populous states of Virginia, Pennsylvania, and Massachusetts would approve the necessary increase in the legislative power of the union only if the "vicious" principle of equal state representation was abandoned in both houses of the proposed legislature, the delegates from the less populous states were equally adamant that their constituents would never be safe in a union in which they did not retain the privilege of the equal state vote in at least one house. And most delegates could not shake a residual conviction that the states deserved some voice in national government, whether they were regarded as cohesive communities, as corporate units, or simply as distinct governments whose cooperation would still be needed in the operations of any federal system.

Madison and his allies (James Wilson of Pennsylvania, Rufus King of Massachusetts, Alexander Hamilton of New York) answered these claims with powerful arguments that the small state delegates rarely met on their merits. They argued, for example, that differences of interest among the large states would preclude their establishing a federal condominium; that justice demanded proportional representation in both houses; and that a senate representing the state governments could never fulfill the cosmopolitan role they intended for it, including control over foreign relations. But the small state delegates, led by William Paterson of New Jersey and Oliver Ellsworth and Roger Sherman of Connecticut, remained unmoved. After securing an early decision (7 June) endorsing election of the Senate by the state legislatures, they held on another five weeks until, in the misnamed "great compromise" of 16 July, they gained the equal rule of voting they had demanded.

The Convention's other great decision on the formation of the new legislature concerned the apportionment of representation in the lower house. Here two considerations came into play. First, delegates from the southern states insisted, in terms that echoed the language of the small states, that their security required adoption of a formula that would count their half million slaves in the apportionment of representation; otherwise, the free white electorate of the South would be a permanent minority (relative to the electorate of the North) in the reconstituted union. Second, because the southern states could not rely on the goodwill of a legislature dominated by northern interests to reapportion seats equitably, this formula had to be fixed constitutionally rather than left to the political discretion of later Congresses.

In a tacit compromise worked out just prior to the crucial vote on the Senate, the Convention adopted a formula to count slaves as three-fifths of the free population for purposes of apportioning representation. To disguise the moral embarrassment that northern delegates felt over this decision, the Convention substituted the euphemism "other persons" for "slaves"; it further implied that its formula for representation derived from its decision to use the same ratio to calculate how "direct taxes" would be levied on the states. (By "direct taxes" the Convention appears to have meant quotas of contributions to the national treasury that would be assigned to the states in the same manner as the requisitions of the Continental Congress; in fact, few, if any, of the delegates thought that such taxes would ever be employed.)

So long as issues of apportionment were under debate, nearly all the delegates described the prospective powers of the new legislature in expansive terms. Once the apportionment of votes in the two houses was fixed, however, their language grew more moderate. From imagining the legislature as a nearly omnipotent body empowered (in the words of the Virginia Plan) to "legislate in all cases to which the separate States are incompetent, or in which the harmony of the United States may be interrupted by the exercise of individual [state] legislation," the delegates now spoke of a body whose authority would be supreme but whose responsibilities would be limited and enumerable. Its most important duties, most delegates agreed, would include regulating interstate and foreign commerce; raising armed forces; deciding when the nation would go to war; and regulating the development of the West. To carry out these functions, the legislature would need unrestricted powers of taxation. Late in the proceedings, the Convention added a handful of other powers designed to enable the national government to promote the general welfare by such useful means as granting copyrights and patents, developing post roads, and other lesser matters that found their way into Article I, section 8 of the Constitution. By the time the Convention adjourned on 17 September, however, the delegates understood that much of the burden of governance in the United States remained with the state legislatures that so many of them despised.

The concluding weeks of debate brought one other notable shift in the design of the new Congress. Growing reservations about the character of the Senate led to a significant transfer of authority from that chamber to the office of the president, whose election and powers were not conclusively determined until the final fortnight of debate. Partly in reaction to earlier decisions regarding its election and mode of voting, partly because some delegates perceived the Senate as the nursery of an "aristocracy," the broad power it was initially expected to exercise over foreign relations (through treaty making) and appointments was now shifted to the executive, who would act with the "advice and consent" of the Senate. This did not mean that the Framers had come to regard the presidency as the one branch of government best qualified to embody and represent the national interest. But it did establish a constitutional basis for the executive to make that claim. And as the events of the first decade of national politics under the Constitution demonstrated, when issues of foreign policy came to the fore, the executive commanded resources and advantages that Congress could rarely match.

Congress under the Constitution: The Early Years (1789–1801). The First Federal Congress of 1789 to 1790 is often described as a second session of the Constitutional Convention. It adopted legislation that organized executive departments of government and gave the national government its first reliable sources of revenue. At the strong urging of James Madison, now a representative from Virginia, it also proposed the constitutional amendments that came to be known as the Bill of Rights. At the same time, President Washington's appointment of Alexander Hamilton as the first secretary of the Treasury set the stage for crucial innovations

in relations between the executive and legislative branches of government and, with striking rapidity, the emergence of opposing factions in Congress that soon evolved into political parties actively competing for the allegiance of a popular electorate.

This first system of political parties was as innovative an achievement as any of the developments in constitutional theory that accompanied the War of Independence. The role of Congress in the process of party formation was complex. The first party system began as a division within Congress itself, as rival groups of congressmen coalesced first to support or oppose the Hamiltonian program and then divided again as issues of foreign policy came to the fore after 1793. Because congressmen themselves interpreted these disputes in ideological terms—that is, as disagreements over principles and not mere differences of opinion over discrete decisions—leaders on both sides sought to formulate and exploit issues with an eye to influencing the electorate in order to enhance their strength within Congress. Finally, the frustration that the opposition Jeffersonian Republicans met in their efforts to convert Congress into an effective check on the Federalist administrations of George Washington and John Adams led them to recognize that control of the presidency was essential to control of the government in general.

Taken by themselves, the central elements of the Hamiltonian financial program—the funding of the public debt left over from the Revolution, the assumption of the state debts, and the chartering of a national bank—probably would not have sustained deep partisanship either within Congress or among the electorate. In 1790, Hamilton's two leading rivals—Madison and Secretary of State Thomas Jefferson—were prepared to moderate their opposition to the assumption of state debts in exchange for assurances that the national capital authorized by the Constitution would be located along the Potomac. In 1793, however, the outbreak of war between Britain and revolutionary France created a fresh set of issues that compounded the original divisions over the Hamiltonian program and drove both factions to mobilize popular constituencies in efforts to influence the balance within Congress. For the Jeffersonian Republicans led by Madison and Jefferson, the turning point came with the furor over the treaty that Chief Justice John Jay negotiated with Britain in 1794. The Jay treaty resolved the outstanding issues dividing the two nations, and it preserved the ties of Anglo-American commerce that were so essential to Hamilton's financial system. But its conciliatory character made it offensive to large segments of the public. In the same way, the Federalists later exploited the quasi war with France of 1798 to buttress their position, until their excesses in using the Sedition Act to harry their critics laid the basis for the coalition that carried Jefferson and Aaron Burr to victory in the hotly contested presidential election of 1800.

In 1787 both Hamilton and Madison believed that the new government would work best if its deliberations were effectively insulated from the forces of public opinion. But by the mid 1790s they were leading well-organized efforts to rally voters to the banners of the rival Federalist and Jeffersonian Republican parties. Although both men saw themselves working within a constitutional framework, it is apparent that their interpretations of what the Constitution permitted or required diverged significantly. As a professed admirer of the eighteenth-century British constitution, in which ministers of state wielded patronage and influence to build governing coalitions, Secretary of the Treasury Hamilton sought to follow their example and use his office and policies, as well as the prestige of President Washington, to form a pro-administration party in Congress. By contrast, the more Jefferson and Madison struggled to counteract Hamilton's influence with Congress and the president, the more they subscribed to traditional republican principles emphasizing the importance of an uncorrupted, independent legislature.

After 1793, foreign policy gave these issues their particular focus. The strong claims that Hamilton made in defense of executive initiative and prerogative in foreign affairs, coupled with the institutional advantages the executive commanded in shaping foreign policy and conducting diplomacy, alarmed Republican leaders not only because their sympathies lay with France but also because of the fundamental questions of constitutional authority raised. In the mid 1790s, Madison repeatedly struggled to demonstrate that responsibility for foreign policy was as much the right of Congress as of the executive. But with turnover in the House so high as to make the relative strength of the contending parties always difficult to ascertain, with the Federalists in firm control of the Senate, and with Congress often left to react to developments that took place in its recess, the Republicans eventually learned that they had to extend the competition between the parties to the executive as well as the legislative branch of the national government. The election of 1800 thus marked a revolution in American politics not only

THOMAS JEFFERSON. As president, holding a copy of the Declaration of Independence.   LIBRARY OF CONGRESS

because it produced a peaceful transition in government despite the polemical passions of the 1790s, but also because it revealed the central place that the presidency would henceforth occupy in political competition.

[*See also* Anti-Federalists; Articles of Confederation; Bill of Rights; Constitutional Convention of 1787; Eleventh Amendment; Federalists; First Congress; Jeffersonian Republicans.]

BIBLIOGRAPHY

Bell, Rudolf M. *Party and Faction in American Politics: The House of Representatives, 1789–1801.* 1973.

Cunningham, Noble E., Jr. *The Jeffersonian Republicans: The Formation of Party Organization, 1789–1801.* 1957.

Henderson, H. James. *Party Politics in the Continental Congress.* 1974.

McDonald, Forrest. *The Presidency of George Washington.* 1974.

Marston, Jerrilyn Greene. *King and Congress: The Transfer of Political Legitimacy, 1774–1776.* 1987.

Rakove, Jack N. *The Beginnings of National Politics: An Interpretive History of the Continental Congress.* 1979.

Rakove, Jack N. "The Great Compromise: Ideas, Interests, and the Politics of Constitution Making." *William and Mary Quarterly* 44 (1987): 424–457.

JACK N. RAKOVE

National Growth and Institutional Development (1801–1840)

A new era in the history of Congress opened with the election of Thomas Jefferson as president of the United States. The "revolution of 1800," as Jefferson called it, brought the first transfer of power in the national government from one political party to another, both in the presidency and in Congress. When the Seventh Congress met in December 1801, it ushered in a period of party governance in which the Jeffersonian Republican majority looked to the president for leadership and the Republican legislative leaders worked with him to implement the administration's policies.

The Presidency, Congress, and Party Politics. In 1801 the Republican majority in the House of Representatives elected Nathaniel Macon of North Carolina, a longtime Jeffersonian Republican, Speaker of the House, and Macon named John Randolph of Roanoke chairman of the Committee of Ways and Means, the most influential standing committee of the House. President Jefferson had no role in Randolph's selection, but when Randolph became, in effect, the majority leader of the House, Jefferson sought to make him the administration's spokesman. Randolph was never comfortable in that role, and in 1806 he broke with the president and opposed his policies on the floor of the House. What followed illustrated the role that party had come to play in the operation of the House. At the next Congress in 1807, Macon, who had been Speaker since 1801, was not reelected to the post, and the newly elected Speaker, Joseph B. Varnum of Massachusetts, did not appoint Randolph chairman of the Ways and Means Committee.

Randolph's disaffection led Jefferson to seek another floor leader in Congress, and in 1806 he sought to persuade Barnabas Bidwell of Massachusetts to take up the task. "If the members are to know nothing but what is important enough to be put into a public message, and indifferent enough to be made known to all the world," Jefferson wrote to Bidwell, "if the Executive is to keep all other information to himself, and the house to plunge on in the dark, it becomes a government of chance and not of design." Jefferson explained: "I do not mean that any gentleman relinquishing his own judgment, should implicitly support all the measures of the administration; but that, where he does not disapprove of them he should not suffer them to go off in sleep, but bring them to the attention of the house and give them a fair chance." Jefferson's desire to have Bidwell assume a leadership role was forestalled, however, when Bidwell resigned from Congress in 1807.

Party influence in Congress during Jefferson's presidency (1801–1809) was aided by House rules under which the Speaker of the House appointed all standing and select committees, unless otherwise directed by the House. That Jefferson did not personally dictate the Speaker's choices for the standing committees was illustrated by Macon's appointment of his friend John Randolph to head Ways and Means. The Speaker also paid close attention to the party composition of committees. Macon appointed a Republican majority on every standing committee in 1801, a pattern that persisted as long as the Federalists posed any threat as an opposition party.

Jefferson's system of party management did not long survive his retirement from office in 1809. Although his successor, James Madison, had been the Republican leader in the early Congresses, he lacked the presidential skills of Jefferson and faced more difficult relations with Congress, as Republican divisions in Congress intensified and the War of 1812 divided the country. The emergence of Henry Clay, elected Speaker of the House in 1811, as a powerful congressional force contributed to a weakening of presidential influence in Congress.

After the end of the War of 1812, the influence of party in Congress greatly diminished, and the Federalist party faded away as an effective national force. One representative in 1816 observed: "Among the most auspicious appearances of the times, is the obliteration of party spirit. No question at the present session of Congress has been discussed or determined on the ground of party." Two years later, at the close of James Monroe's first year as president, Rep. John Tyler of Virginia believed that "party distractions have been entirely forgotten."

The demise of a system of two nationally competitive parties, however, did not eliminate factional

VIEW OF WASHINGTON, D.C. In the early 1800s.

groupings. Future presidential candidates competing to succeed Monroe sought to build support in Congress. Without the aid of a strong, nationally based party, presidential influence in Congress weakened. During the presidencies of Monroe and John Quincy Adams, the executive and legislative branches each held its ground.

There were very few periods of legislative tranquillity during the four decades of rapid national growth, territorial expansion, and economic change from 1801 to 1840. Until the end of the war with Great Britain in 1815, the most controversial measures before Congress were related to matters of foreign affairs: the Louisiana Purchase, the Jeffersonian embargo, and the declaration of war in 1812. Following the War of 1812 and the resumption of peace in Europe, Congress increasingly turned its attention to domestic concerns: the Bank of the United States, tariffs, roads and canals, western lands, and the continental expansion of the territory of the United States. With the eruption of

conflict over slavery in the controversy over the admission of Missouri into the Union, slavery emerged as the most divisive issue facing the nation and Congress.

During John Quincy Adams's presidency (1825–1829), two national political parties again took form. When Andrew Jackson assumed office after the hotly contested campaign of 1828, he attempted to reassert presidential dominance, and conflict between the two branches intensified. Jackson's Democratic party supporters had a strong majority in the House of Representatives in each of the four Congresses during his two terms as president (1829–1837), but in the Senate parties were closely balanced between the Democrats and the National Republicans, or Whigs. Thus, confirmation of presidential appointments often provoked confrontations with the president. Although most of Jackson's nominees were confirmed, Sen. Daniel Webster wrote privately at the end of Jackson's first year as president that but for fears of Jackson's popularity the Senate would have rejected more than half of his nominees. Before Jackson left the White House, a number of striking confrontations took place, including the rejection of Martin Van Buren as minister to Great Britain in 1832 and of Roger Taney to be associate justice of the Supreme Court in 1835.

Just as the controversy over slavery in Missouri and in the territories threatened to divide the Union in 1820, so did the conflict over the issue of protective tariffs in 1832, after a convention in South Carolina passed an ordinance of nullification. As with the Missouri crisis of 1820, the nullification crisis of 1832–1833 required the cooperation of the president and Congress.

Issues of banking policy, land policy, and tariff legislation continued to be major divisive issues throughout the administrations of Jackson and Martin Van Buren (1837–1841). There were few sharper encounters between Congress and the presidency in the early decades of the Republic than those between Jackson and Congress over the Bank of the United States. In the midst of the presidential campaign of 1832 Congress passed and Jackson vetoed the bill to recharter the bank, reigniting a controversy over banks that continued throughout Van Buren's presidency and beyond.

After Jackson followed his veto of the bill to recharter the Bank of the United States with the removal of government deposits from the bank, the Senate passed a resolution of censure introduced by Henry Clay. Three years later, Sen. Thomas Hart Benton led a successful move to expunge the censure resolution from the Senate Journal. The banking issue remained a major point of conflict, and Van Buren, during his first year as president, proposed an independent treasury. A split in Democratic party ranks kept it from passing until his last year in office, but the victory was short lived because Congress repealed the measure after Van Buren's defeat for reelection in 1840.

Committees in the House of Representatives. Much of the work of the early Congresses was done in and by committees. In 1801 the five standing committees in the House of Representatives were Elections, Claims, Commerce and Manufactures, Ways and Means, and Revisal and Unfinished Business. There was also a joint Senate-House Committee on Enrolled Bills. The Ways and Means Committee, with wide authority over revenues and appropriations, was the most important standing committee of the House, and a large portion of major legislation passed through it. In 1802 the du-

ties of the Ways and Means Committee were expanded to include serving as a watchdog committee with oversight of the expenditures and accountability of the executive departments. Next in influence was the Committee of Commerce and Manufactures. Its broad area of legislative concern meant that more petitions to Congress were referred to that committee than to any other except the Committee of Claims, to which all private claims were referred. Until a House committee on foreign affairs was created in 1822, international and diplomatic matters were referred to select committees, the Committee of Ways and Means, or the Committee of Commerce and Manufactures, thus adding to the influence of those bodies.

Before the end of Jefferson's two terms, four new standing committees were created by the House: Accounts, Public Lands, District of Columbia, and Post Office and Post Roads. A joint standing Committee on the Library of Congress also was established in 1806. Except for the Committee of Accounts, all of the new House standing committees evolved from select committees to which similar matters repeatedly had been referred. The Committee on Accounts, created in 1803, reflected the Jeffersonian emphasis on frugality; it sought to apply the same accountability to House expenditures as was required of executive departments. In 1805 the House gave the committee the additional responsibility of auditing the accounts of members for their travel to and from the capital and for their attendance in Congress.

In 1814 the responsibilities of the Ways and Means Committee in oversight of department expenditures were transferred to a newly created Committee of Public Expenditures. Two years later a major reorganization in the House of Representatives produced separate standing committees on expenditures for the State, Treasury, War, and Navy departments, the General Post Office, and public buildings. Speaker Clay led this move in order to establish closer legislative control over the executive. The growth of the standing committee system was more than a response to an expansion of House membership and an increase in work load; it demonstrated Congress's determination to maintain a major role in policy formation.

In the early 1820s a major expansion of the House committee structure led to the separation of Commerce and Manufactures into two committees and the establishment of standing committees on Agriculture, Military Affairs, Naval Affairs, Foreign Affairs, and Indian Affairs. By the time James Monroe left the presidential office in 1825 there were twenty-six standing committees in the House of Representatives. By 1840 there were thirty-three. Among the new additions were standing committees on Territories, Roads and Canals, and Patents—all reflections of the expanding nation and its economic growth.

The development of a standing committee system resulted in important changes in the way Congress performed its legislative role. In the early House the first referral of matters to the Committee of the Whole, in which the entire House sat as a committee, was common and implied an equality of members in legislating and the expression of majority will. Policy would be set by general deliberation, not by a few committee members. These decisions could then be sent to a committee to draft appropriate legislation. Early Congresses tightly controlled the power to report by bill, and did not automatically give committees that authority. The increase in the number of standing committees changed these procedures and underlying attitudes. Gradually the practice of making important decisions in the Committee of the Whole and assigning to committees the implementation, bill drafting, and working out of details gave way to referring substantive matters to standing committees. This change was so well advanced by 1816 that one member of congress protested on the floor of the House against "an unconquerable indisposition to alter, change, or modify anything reported by any one of the Standing Committees of the House." By the end of the 1820s first referral to the Committee of the Whole had largely disappeared, as members increasingly believed that the specialized knowledge of a standing committee promoted better legislation and that referring legislation first to the Committee of the Whole was a waste of time.

As the number of standing committees increased, the use of select committees declined. By the end of the 1820s the House was sending virtually all matters of public policy to standing committees, which were given the authority to report by bill at their own discretion. As members increasingly relied on standing committees, the Committee of the Whole became largely a reviewer and ratifier of committee decisions. This pattern tended to promote the influence of special interests, and to diminish the sense of legislating together for the common interest.

The expansion of standing committees also added to legislative oversight of the executive branch. In the years following the War of 1812, congressional committees—both standing and se-lect—became increasingly active in investigating administrative affairs. There were examinations of army expenditures on the northern frontier and the fiscal affairs of the post office in 1816. Two years later Congress inquired into Gen. Andrew Jackson's conduct in the Seminole War and the conduct of clerks in the executive departments. The General Post Office was a frequent target of review (as in 1821 and 1822), and a full-scale inquiry into the post office by both the House and the Senate in 1834 and 1835 led Jackson to replace the postmaster general.

The establishment of standing committees brought the first, although hesitant, movement toward the creation of committee staffs. Neither members of Congress nor early committees had staffs, leaving legislators highly dependent on executive departments for information and staff services. In 1803 the House of Representatives refused to appoint two clerks to serve its committees, and in 1815 it rejected a proposal to provide a clerk for each standing committee. Occasionally committee chairmen asked department heads to provide clerk services, and they also began to hire clerks on a per diem basis. The practice increased, and in 1838 the House adopted a rule that no committee was permitted to employ a clerk at public expense without first obtaining the approval of the House.

House Membership. Congressional membership during the period from 1801 to 1840 continued the pattern of high turnover displayed in earlier Congresses. The lowest percentage (33.2 percent) of first-term members in the House of Representatives during the period was in the 20th Congress (1827–1829). New House members made up 40 percent or more of thirteen and over 50 percent of three Congresses. The highest turnover occurred in 1817, when 59.2 percent of the representatives in Congress were new members. This unprecedented unseating of incumbents followed the passage of the act in 1816 to raise the pay of representatives and senators from six dollars per day—where it had been fixed since the First Congress—to $1,500 per year. The new salary was no more than that earned by many clerks in government offices, but the "salary grab" raised an outcry throughout the country and decimated incumbents at the polls. At the next session the act was speedily repealed, and replaced by eight dollars per diem.

Although the pay of members of Congress increased only meagerly, the demands on them grew substantially. Before the end of Madison's administration (1809–1817), members were increasingly complaining about the calls made upon them to attend to constituent business. Rep. Elijah Mills of Massachusetts wrote in 1815, "I have been constantly engaged in attending to some private business for my *constituents* and friends, who think they have a right to call on me for that purpose." In 1816 Rep. John McLean of Ohio complained that during the session "I never was more industriously engaged than in attending to the private business of others, when the house was not in session. There were three western mails a week, by which my principal letters were received—these often amounted to between thirty and forty, generally on business, which required my attention at the different offices." By the time Andrew Jackson took office in 1829, such matters had become for many members an oppressive burden.

Because they received low compensation for their own services, members of Congress not surprisingly were parsimonious with executive departments, continually demanding accounts of expenditures, while at the same time Congress was reluctant to provide additional clerks for government offices to gather the information and provide the reports they requested. Reflecting on his service in the Senate, one member remembered "when the proposition to have a clerk, or half a dozen clerks, added to one of the departments, would occasion debate for a week, under the administrations of Jackson and Van Buren. Such propositions never failed to be denounced as seeking to plunder the treasury."

The Senate. During Jefferson's presidency, the Senate existed mainly as an ancillary chamber, dominated by the executive and overshadowed by the House of Representatives. The upper house, whose members were directly responsible to the state legislatures that elected them, received less public notice than the House of Representatives, whose members were directly responsible to the voters. House debates were more extended and received fuller press coverage than those of the Senate. When Samuel L. Mitchill resigned his seat in the House in 1804 to enter the Senate, he wrote to his wife: "Henceforward you will read little of me in the Gazettes. Senators are less exposed to public view than Representatives. Nor have they near so much hard work and drudgery to perform."

While newspaper reporters recorded House debates, if a senator wanted his speech printed in the papers he had to write it out himself. Senator William Plumer of New Hampshire explained in 1806: "In the other House it is different—galleries are usually attended, frequently crouded, with spectators—Always one, often two, stenographers attend, and their speeches are reported in the gazettes." Yet greater prestige came with service in the Senate, and during Jefferson's administration, nine House members moved to the Senate, while no senator resigned to take a seat in the House.

The Senate committee system during the early years of the nineteenth century differed from that of the House of Representatives. Other than the joint committees on enrolled bills and the Library of Congress, there were only two standing committees in the Senate before 1816, and both were housekeeping committees—one on engrossed (final text of) bills, and the other to audit the contingent expenses of the Senate. Select committees elected by the full membership of the Senate performed most of its committee work.

Senate rules specified that "all committees shall be appointed by ballot, and a plurality of votes shall make a choice." Most committees were composed of three members, but for important matters, five-member committees were common. Each senator voted for as many persons as there were places on the committee, and the senator with the most votes served as chairman. "As our committees are all chosen by ballot, the influence and weight of a member can be very well measured by the number and importance of those upon which he is placed," Sen. John Quincy Adams recorded in his diary in 1805. Commonly the senator who introduced a matter was elected to the committee, and he was usually named chairman.

Vote tallies for committee elections show that most of the committee work was done by a group of leading senators (usually numbering about eight in the Jeffersonian Congresses). In the first session of the Ninth Congress (1805–1807) eight senators filled 325 (74 percent) of the 447 seats on 133 committees elected, and they constituted a majority of 102 (77 percent) of these committees. The same group of Senate leaders chaired 87 (72 percent) of the committees. The busiest senator, Abraham Baldwin of Georgia, served on 70 committees. In the first session of the Tenth Congress (1807–1809) John Quincy Adams served on 54 committees, more than any other senator, though in chairing 11 committees, he ranked fourth; Joseph Anderson of Tennessee ranked first, chairing 17 committees. Throughout Jefferson's presidency the Republican party dominated the Senate leadership, and the leadership group was highly stable.

The years between the close of Jefferson's presidency in 1809 and the beginning of Jackson's presi-

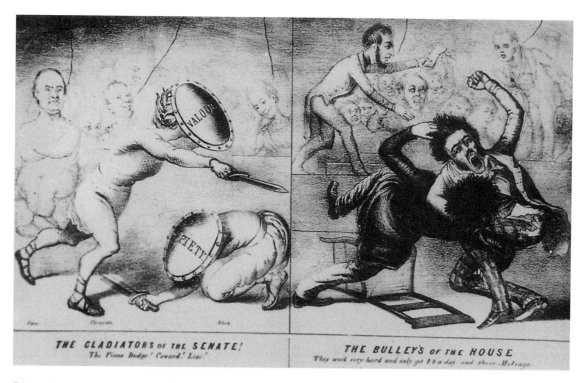

THE GLADIATORS OF THE SENATE!
The Pious Dodge! Coward! Liar!

THE BULLEYS OF THE HOUSE
They work very hard and only get $8 a day and their Mileage

"THE GLADIATORS OF THE SENATE! THE BULLEYS OF THE HOUSE." Political cartoon depicting the early-nineteenth-century belief that the Senate was the more dignified of the two houses of Congress, while the House of Representatives was rowdy and undisciplined.   LIBRARY OF CONGRESS

dency in 1829 have been described as marking a reconstitutive period in the Senate's history. It was a period during which the Senate was transformed from a reactive upper chamber to a proactive legislature. The Senate became less likely to approve routinely presidential nominations and domestic and foreign policy initiatives. President Madison was forced to reconsider cabinet appointments, and neither James Monroe nor John Quincy Adams found the Senate passive in matters of foreign affairs. The changes in the Senate that had begun during Madison's presidency (1809–1817) were maintained and extended during the Jackson (1829–1837) and Van Buren (1833–1837) presidencies, as the Senate challenged presidential nominees and policy initiatives. Following confirmation as Jackson's secretary of State in 1832, Edward Livingston complained about "an investigation in which my whole life was scrutinized and all the newspaper abuse examined . . . with all the force that party could give to them."

Among the major alterations in the way the Senate conducted its business was the transformation of its committee system. In 1816 the Senate created for the first time a system of standing committees.

Twelve were established: Foreign Relations, Finance, Commerce and Manufactures, Military Affairs, Militia, Naval Affairs, Public Lands, Claims, Judiciary, Post Office and Post Roads, Pensions, and the District of Columbia. In the 1820s Commerce and Manufactures was divided into separate committees, as in the House. New committees added later included Accounts, Indian Affairs, Agriculture, and Roads and Canals. By 1840 the Senate had twenty-two standing committees.

In 1823 the Senate began to experiment with permitting the presiding officer to appoint committees, unless otherwise ordered. The initial change was introduced while Daniel Tompkins, who rarely appeared in the Senate, was vice president. But when John C. Calhoun became vice president in 1825, he took the chair on the opening day of the 19th Congress and exercised the authority to appoint the standing committees. A few months later the Senate restored the old rule of choice by ballot, unless otherwise ordered. The Senate also experimented with giving the president pro tempore power to appoint committees, and tried other schemes, but repeatedly returned to election by ballot. By 1840, however, it was customary to suspend the rules requiring a ballot and to authorize the appointment of committees by the presiding officer or other designated officer of the Senate.

Congressional Growth and National Expansion. The expansion of organization and the widening legislative activity that characterized the Congress of the United States during the years between 1800 and 1840 must be viewed against the background of national population growth and territorial expansion. In the Seventh Congress (1801–1803), 106 members served in the House of Representatives. That number doubled to 213 after reapportionment following the census of 1820, and by 1840 the membership of the House was 242. In the Senate membership increased from 32 in 1801 to 52 in 1840. With the increase in population and in the number of states in the Union came an expansion of the role and activities of the national government. In taking office Thomas Jefferson had promised a government rigorously simple and frugal, but despite the reductions he made in the early years of his presidency, the government continued to expand along with the country. With the Louisiana Purchase, the territory of the nation doubled. Under President James Monroe, Florida was obtained and Secretary of State John Quincy Adams negotiated a transcontinental treaty line with Spain that extended the claims of the western border of the United States to the Pacific Ocean. By the time Monroe left office in 1825 there were twenty-four states, in contrast to sixteen when Jefferson was inaugurated in 1801. In 1840 there were twenty-six states. The population had increased from little more than five million in 1800 to nearly ten million in 1820 and to seventeen million in 1840.

Not all members of Congress welcomed the expanded role of Congress and the expansion of the activities of the national government; the fear of consolidating national power had deep roots in the Jeffersonian tradition. In 1827, Sen. Nathaniel Macon, who had represented North Carolina in one or the other of the houses of Congress since 1791, complained, "Formerly two men were sufficient for doorkeeper, etc., for the two houses, but now there is a regiment." Referring to the days when the Jeffersonian Republicans had opposed John Adams's administration, Macon asked: "If there was reason to be alarmed at the growing power of the General Government [then], how much more has taken place since?" On another occasion, Macon warned his Senate colleagues against "constantly gaining power by little bits. A wagon road was made under a treaty with an Indian tribe, twenty odd years ago;

and now it has become a great national object, to be kept up by large appropriations," he protested. "We thus go on by degrees, step by step, until we get almost unlimited power."

The Nominating Caucus and Presidential Elections. The period from 1800 to 1824 brought the rise and fall of the congressional nominating caucus, which named candidates for president and vice president. Both Republican and Federalist members of Congress nominated candidates in 1800, but only the dominant Republican caucus survived the Jeffersonian triumph in 1800. Although the assumption of the nominating authority by members of Congress was repeatedly challenged, the Republican congressional caucus nominated Jefferson in 1804, Madison in 1808 and 1812, and Monroe in 1816, by which time caucus nomination had become tantamount to election. The lack of organized opposition to Monroe's reelection in 1820 made the caucus superfluous, and before the election of 1824 presidential contenders were openly challenging its role. Although the caucus nominated William H. Crawford for president in 1824, the authority of the congressional nomination had vanished, and after 1832 it was superseded by the nominating convention.

Members of Congress in 1801 and 1825 played a more direct role in the election of the president of the United States than at any other time in American history. When no candidate received a majority of the electoral votes in the elections of 1800 and 1824, the election went to the House of Representatives for decision, the only such instances in American history. The 1800 electoral vote had resulted in a tie vote between Thomas Jefferson and Aaron Burr under the constitutional provision that did not permit separate balloting for president and vice president. It required thirty-six ballots in the House before Jefferson was elected president.

Ratification of the Twelfth Amendment before the next presidential election eliminated the possibility of a tie vote by providing for separate balloting for president and vice president. The possibility of multiple candidates dividing the electoral vote remained, however, and in 1824, none of the four candidates—Andrew Jackson, John Quincy Adams, William H. Crawford, and Henry Clay—received a majority of the electoral vote. The House of Representatives, with each state delegation having one vote, elected John Quincy Adams sixth president of the United States.

Presidential Veto. During the administrations of the seven presidents from Jefferson through Van

Buren, five of them vetoed a total of twenty-one bills passed by Congress, and none of these vetoes was overridden. Until the presidency of Andrew Jackson, presidents adhered to the view that the executive veto should be exercised only on the grounds of unconstitutionality or in cases of legislative encroachment on the executive branch. Neither Jefferson nor John Quincy Adams used the veto during their administrations, and Monroe and Van Buren each vetoed only one measure. In the years from 1801 through 1840, most of the vetoes came from two presidents: Madison and Jackson. Jackson's twelve vetoes exceeded the number of any previous president, a number that was not surpassed until the presidency of Andrew Johnson (1865–1869).

Madison's most important vetoes were his rejections of the bill to recharter the Bank of the United States in 1815 and of a bill for internal improvements, vetoed on his last day in office, 3 March 1817. Monroe's lone veto was of an internal improvement bill for the repair of the Cumberland Road. The most controversial and far reaching of Jackson's vetoes was of the bill to recharter the second Bank of the United States in July 1832. Jackson's other important vetoes included the rejection of several internal improvements measures. Van Buren's veto was of a minor measure relating to President Madison's papers.

Of even more importance than the measures that Jackson rejected was his view of the presidential veto power. In his second annual message to Congress on 6 December 1830, after having vetoed four measures passed during the previous session of Congress, he declared:

It is due to candor, as well as to my own feelings, that I should express the reluctance and anxiety which I must at all times experience in exercising the undoubted right of the Executive to withhold his assent from bills on other grounds than their constitutionality. That this right should not be exercised on slight occasions all will admit. It is only in matters of deep interest, when the principle involved may be justly regarded as next in importance to infractions of the Constitution itself, that such a step can be expected to meet with the approbation of the people.

The first president to assume this broader authority to exercise the veto power, Jackson began a new era in the relationship between the president and the Congress.

Petitioning Congress. Petitioning played a much more important role in the legislative process in the early Congresses than it has in the twentieth century. On matters about which Americans today would write their representatives and senators, citizens—and even aliens—in the early Republic petitioned Congress directly. Indeed, many of the standing committees in Congress evolved from the practice of referring similar petitions to the same committee; and a large portion of the work of the standing committees stemmed from petitions addressed to Congress.

Petitioners commonly addressed their memorials to both houses of Congress and directed them to members with requests that they be presented in each chamber. Petitions were handwritten or printed; all were signed, and frequently had pages of signatures attached. Petitioning efforts often were well organized, with printed copies widely circulated for the collection of signatures. Private claimants presented the largest number of petitions in the early Congresses, but those relating to commerce, manufactures, public lands, and post offices and post roads soon combined to outnumber private claims. Petitions for protection of various manufactured products kept the tariff issue before numerous sessions of Congress, and floods of new petitions poured in whenever Congress considered tariff revisions. Many of these were the product of well-organized efforts by special interest groups.

The volume and content of petitions sent to Congress contradicts the view that legislators were remote from their constituents and that the citizenry was indifferent to the national government. Proposed legislation frequently produced petitions on both sides of an issue, and new laws provoked petitions in response. Passage of the embargo of 1807 generated a large number of petitions seeking its repeal and a lesser number of memorials supporting it. The propositions introduced in Congress in 1819 and 1820 to prohibit slavery in Missouri and in the territories inspired one of the most extensive petitioning efforts up to that time. These petitions came from public meetings and from state legislatures, and although the Missouri Compromise settled, temporarily, the issue of slavery in Missouri and in the territories, antislavery groups continued to use the tactic of petitioning Congress.

By the mid 1830s Congress was overwhelmed with antislavery petitions. With the revival of political parties during Jackson's presidency, Whig members, who presented most of the antislavery petitions, sought to discredit and obstruct the Democrats, who controlled Congress. After the 24th Congress assembled in December 1835, a sharp increase in

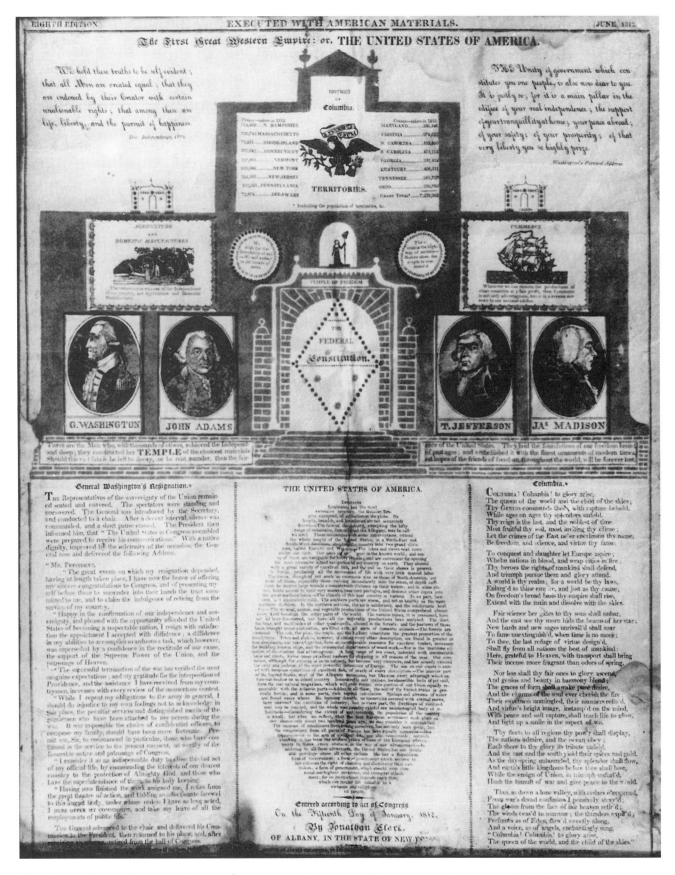

"THE FIRST GREAT WESTERN EMPIRE." An engraved print glorifying the United States, published in June 1812.

COLLECTION OF DAVID J. AND JANICE L. FRENT

petitions seeking the abolition of slavery and the slave trade in the District of Columbia consumed an increasing amount of Congress's time and produced growing acrimony. In May 1836 the House sought to restore tranquillity by adopting a rule that all petitions or resolutions, or any other papers relating to slavery or the abolition of slavery, be laid on the table, without being either printed or referred, and that no further action be taken on them. This gag rule ended neither the agitation nor the sending of antislavery petitions to Congress. Indeed, when those presented to Congress between December 1837 and April 1838 were stacked compactly in a room in the Capitol, they filled a space 20 by 30 by 14 feet. After the Democratic party lost control of Congress in the election of 1840 the Whigs enacted a new gag rule, but the measure did not for long silence the slavery issue in the halls of Congress.

The Congressional Community. Congressional sessions between 1800 and 1840 varied in length from three to seven months, but usually lasted four or five months. The first session of each Congress generally was the longest; Congress commonly convened early in December and adjourned at the end of April or in May. In some years the sessions dragged on until July, but not until the 1830s did this become common. The final session of each Congress had to adjourn before 4 March, when the congressional term ended. Because in most years members of Congress were in Washington, D.C., for only a few months, they commonly found temporary living quarters, usually in boardinghouses, many on Capitol Hill, others in Georgetown and elsewhere as the city grew. Members tended to group with friends from their own state or region and to board with those who shared similar political views. During Jefferson's presidency, when party divisions were sharp, Federalists and Republicans rarely boarded in the same house or hotel.

In the early decades of the nineteenth century, members of both houses spent much of their time in the legislative chambers. They had no private offices and were expected to remain until the House or Senate adjourned for the day. President Jefferson's invitations to dinner invited members of Congress to dine "at half after three, or whatever later hour the house may rise." Members of one house sometimes sat in on the debates in the other house. During Jefferson's presidency, Sen. John Quincy Adams frequently attended House debates after the Senate adjourned. During Madison's presidency the galleries were usually full when it was anticipated that Henry Clay or other powerful orators would be

speaking. In 1812 Henry Clay left the chair as Speaker of the House to argue for the declaration of war against Great Britain in an address that was widely published. Clay's powerful voice was also heard in later debates on the Missouri Compromise and other critical issues.

By Jackson's presidency some of the greatest orators of the day were in the Senate, among them Henry Clay, John C. Calhoun, and Daniel Webster. The attention of the capital centered on such debates as that between Daniel Webster of Massachusetts and Robert Y. Hayne of South Carolina in 1830. This debate, which started over the issue of public lands, broadened into one on states' rights and the origin and nature of the Constitution and the Union. Later, debates on the tariff, nullification, the bank, and public lands would make the Jacksonian era a golden age of Senate oratory.

Many members of the House of Representatives—especially those from southern and western states—reported regularly to their constituents in printed letters. Generally written near the close of a session—and in election years timed to arrive opportunely in their districts—the letters reported on the principal proceedings of Congress and offered the writer's views on the issues. Occasionally members commented on Congress itself. Few did so more frankly than Ephraim Bateman of New Jersey in a letter of 4 March 1819:

> There was much sound sense and some brilliancy of talent resident in the late congress. If I might be permitted, however, lightly to criticise, I should say that there was too large a proportion of professional gentlemen, and others not sufficiently conversant with the manner in which the main body of the yeomanry of the country gain their subsistence.
>
> Legal gentlemen, who have been accustomed to public speaking, can generally deliver their sentiments more fluently than others; but I have observed that the best of them seldom drop the lawyer. Upon assuming the legislative character, they seem to forget that they are not in court. . . . Although a certain portion of this class is necessary, yet, ever since I have been honoured with a seat in congress, we have had a redundancy of them, and stood in greater need of intelligent jurymen, than of additional solicitors.
>
> Wishing to be entirely frank . . . there were a few members of the congress of the United States, (to the honour of the American electors but few,) whose libidinous characters and dissipated habits were disgraceful.

Bateman's reference to a redundancy of lawyers in Congress was well founded, and the number of lawyers in the House continued to increase. During the decade in which he was writing the proportion of lawyers entering the House rose to 55 percent, and by 1840 it exceeded 63 percent. The educational background of members changed little during the same decades; the percentage of college-educated members remained near 40 percent. There was, however, a decline in the proportion of members who attended elite colleges, as the number of colleges and state universities increased.

To Virginia representative William C. Rives, taking his seat in the House for the first time in December 1823, Congress presented a more favorable impression than it had to Representative Bateman. Rives was struck with the beauty of the rebuilt Capitol. "The Hall of the House of Representatives is a most magnificent room of a semicircular form, surrounded with a row of beautiful pillars of variegated marble, the floor elegantly carpeted, and studded with mahogany desks and hair-bottomed mahogany chairs for the accommodation of the members," he wrote. "In general, the members seem to be entirely worthy of the handsome equipment with which they are surrounded. They are good-looking, well-dressed men, and those to whom I have been introduced are elegant and polished gentlemen."

Most members and visitors were impressed with the beauty of the Capitol, rebuilt after its destruction during the War of 1812. But the House chamber with its stone walls, tall marble columns, and dome was not well designed for legislative proceedings. In 1824, after two months in the House, Ohio representative Duncan McArthur observed:

With all this expence and grandure, the Hall is unfit for the purpose for which it was intended, as the debates cannot be heard by half the members, and it is seldom that a question put by the Speaker or Chairman, can be heard, or the bills or amendments read by the Clerk heard or understood by one half of the members. Consequently little attention is paid to business, and some times one half of the members are engaged in private conversation. And many motions are made and questions decided on, which many of the members, never hear, understand, or know any thing about.

Institutional Record. As the years passed, Congress displayed a growing awareness of the need to create and maintain an institutional record. As directed by the Constitution, both houses kept journals of their proceedings, but these were sketchy and contained no reports of debates. For years the debates were recorded only by stenogra-phers employed by the editors of the newspapers in which they were printed. On one occasion the House refused to appropriate $1,600 to have its debates recorded. The laws of each session were published, and each new member received a set when he took his seat in Congress. Otherwise the institutional record of Congress was found largely in the papers of the clerk of the House and the secretary of the Senate. The loss of many papers and documents when the British burned Washington, D.C., in 1814 awakened congressional interest in government records, and in 1817 Congress began systematic publication of documents. In 1819 it also published the journal of the Constitutional Convention of 1787, and in 1824 William W. Seaton and Joseph Gales, Jr., began publishing the proceedings of Congress in annual volumes. During the next decade these active publishers also collected the reports on debates in earlier Congresses and began the *Annals of Congress* in 1834. Congress in 1832 authorized the publication of the *American State Papers*, which ultimately totaled thirty-eight volumes. By 1840 the institutional record of Congress before 1824 had been reassembled, and the habit of preserving a full record of its activities was firmly established.

From 1801 to 1840, the internal history of Congress was marked by the development and growth of standing committees in both the House of Representatives and the Senate, and in each chamber committees played an increasingly dominant role in performing the business of Congress. The period was notable for the expansion of the oversight role of Congress and the elaboration of its investigative powers regarding executive departments. Constituent business also consumed larger and larger segments of the time of most individual members. Throughout the period, floor debates remained a major part of the legislative process, especially in regard to the most critical and controversial issues. By the time of Jackson's presidency, the Senate, with its smaller chamber and veteran political figures, had become a citadel of oratorical vigor and eloquence.

The most visible change in Congress during the four decades from 1801 to 1840 was the increase in the membership of both houses. The 20 seats added in the Senate by 1840 made the upper house with 52 senators closer in size to the House of Representatives in the First Congress (65 members) than to the Senate of 1801. With 242 members the House of Representatives constituted the largest house before 1870.

The institution of Congress evolved between 1801 and 1840 against a background of national growth and a changing political environment. The Federalist and Republican parties, nationally competitive in 1800, had given way on the national level by 1815 to a dominant Republican party. By 1820 many Americans were envisioning a society and government without political parties. But by 1830 a two-party system had emerged to impose on Congress the most nationally competitive two-party system the young Republic had experienced. With varying degrees of success Congress dealt with such controversial issues as the embargo, neutral rights, the War of 1812, the Bank of the United States, internal improvements, the tariff, public lands policy, the admission of Missouri into the Union, and the nullification crisis, but the unresolved issue of slavery hung heavily over the Congress of the United States as the decade of the 1830s came to a close. By 1840 the competition between the Congress and the executive for dominance in the national government had not ended, but the basic organization and procedures of the legislature had become firmly rooted.

[*See also* Anti-Federalists; Bank of the United States; Boardinghouses; Embargo; Federalists; Jeffersonian Republicans; Louisiana Purchase; Marbury v. Madison; Missouri Compromise; Nullification; Twelfth Amendment; War of 1812; Webster-Hayne Debate; West Florida.]

BIBLIOGRAPHY

Bogue Allan G., Jerome M. Clubb, Carroll R. McKibbin, and Santa A. Traugott. "Members of the House of Representatives and the Process of Modernization, 1789–1960." *Journal of American History* 63 (1976): 275–302.

Cooper, Joseph. *The Origins of the Standing Committees and the Development of the Modern House.* Rice University Studies, vol. 56, no. 3. 1970.

Cunningham, Noble E., Jr. *The Process of Government under Jefferson.* 1978.

Cunningham, Noble E., Jr., ed. *Circular Letters of Congressmen to Their Constituents, 1789–1829.* 3 vols. 1978.

Galloway, George B., and Sidney Wise. *History of the House of Representatives.* 2d ed. 1976.

Goodman, Perry M., and James S. Young. *The United States Congressional Directories, 1789–1840.* 1973.

Harlow, Ralph Volney. *The History of Legislative Methods in the Period before 1825.* 1917.

Polsby, Nelson W. "The Institutionalization of the U.S. House of Representatives." *American Political Science Review* 62 (1968): 144–168.

Swift, Elaine K. "Reconstitutive Change in the U.S. Congress: The Early Senate, 1789–1841." *Legislative Studies Quarterly* 14 (1989): 175–203.

Sydnor, Charles S. *The Development of Southern Sectionalism, 1819–1848.* 1948.

White, Leonard D. *The Jacksonians: A Study in Administrative History, 1829–1861.* 1954.

White, Leonard D. *The Jeffersonians: A Study in Administrative History, 1801–1829.* 1951.

Young, James Sterling. *The Washington Community, 1800–1828.* 1966.

NOBLE E. CUNNINGHAM, JR.

Sectionalism and Nationalism (1840–1872)

By 1840 the Jacksonian Democratic–Whig party system—the nation's second—was firmly in place. From 1840 to the early 1850s the parties vied for support throughout the Union over a cluster of social and economic issues. From the late 1840s, this party system began to deteriorate; it finally collapsed as the old issues on which it was based were eclipsed by the issue of slavery. The conflict over slavery led not only to secession, the Civil War, and Reconstruction, but also to the emergence of a new Democratic party–Republican party system in the mid to late 1850s—the nation's third party system. By the 1870s, Civil War issues were diminishing in importance, slowly being replaced by concerns related to the development of the modern commercial and industrial economy. Both the slavery issue and post–Civil War economic issues testified to the growing nationalization of American political and economic life.

Congress played a central role in these transformations: in the articulation of issues, the development of public policy, and even the administration of public affairs. Its structure changed to reflect its growing importance as the forum that instituted national social and economic policy. Its interaction with the presidency became the focal point of U.S. politics and decision making. The intensity of the conflict over slavery in particular strained congressional institutions and created tensions between Congress and the presidency. Congress not only coped with the crisis but by the 1870s remained very much what the Framers had wanted it to be: the first branch of government.

Intensifying Sectional Conflict, 1840–1861. By 1840 the institutional structure of both branches of Congress was well articulated, but the legislature's relationship with the executive was still developing. Both houses had a number of standing committees, among them Naval, Military, Foreign, and Indian Affairs; District of Columbia; Commerce and Manufactures; Post Office; Territories and Public Lands; and Judiciary. Minor committees took care of claims against the government, pensions, public buildings, and similar administrative functions. And there were expenditure committees to audit the spending of the executive departments and to influence their administration. The most important committees, Ways and Means in the House and Finance in the Senate, determined the system of taxation and made the appropriations that paid for governmental activities. Because of their control over appropriations, they influenced all policy areas, sometimes subverting decisions made by the other committees. Other committees became more or less important as public issues changed. Those dealing with the territories, for example, became crucial as the issue of slavery in the territories became prominent. Moreover, members from different states and regions might find different committees attractive depending on whether their constituents were more interested, for example, in internal improvements or in relations with the Indians.

Portions of the president's annual message to Congress on the state of the Union were referred to appropriate committees for consideration, as were his special messages and resolutions from state legislatures and petitions from ordinary citizens. Both houses routinely referred members' proposed bills to committees with the proper jurisdiction. Occasionally a jurisdictional dispute erupted over a particular subject or bill. Such disputes might be resolved by the appointment of special committees or simply be fought out on the floor.

On rare occasions a disputed matter might be resolved in the caucus of the majority party. Members of Congress generally agreed that caucus decisions were binding, possibly on all party members and certainly on those who had attended the caucus. For that very reason, such decisions were usually restricted to matters where it was essential to maintain party unity, as in determining candidates for congressional offices and, in the Senate, committee assignments. Rarely, when party unity was required on divisive issues of supreme importance, the caucus made fundamental decisions about procedure and policy.

In both houses, committees dominated the business on the floor. They considered and reported on presidential appointments to positions under their jurisdiction, which made some committees particularly attractive in an era when political patronage

was extremely important. Committees reported out bills and in each case appointed one member to manage the bill on the floor. Floor managers had to make sure that they retained control of their bills, marshaling support to turn back unwanted amendments and procedural motions and, in the House, to call the previous question, which limited debate.

Committees had to persuade legislators to suspend the rules to take up their measures or to designate a certain time for their consideration. The relative prestige of committees and the relative influence of their chairmen were important factors in the success of such maneuvering, as was skill in conciliating rival claimants for time. Senate leaders such as Henry Clay, John C. Calhoun, Stephen A. Douglas, and Robert M. T. Hunter gained their great reputations in part through their ability to gain and control the floor in order to guide their committees' proposals through the legislative thicket. House leaders were less well-known, but men such as James I. McKay, Samuel F. Vinton, Linn Boyd, and Thomas H. Bayly won the respect of their colleagues for the same talents.

Senate Rule XXXIV required the whole Senate to elect chairmen and members of its committees. But when the vice president, who presides over the Senate according to the Constitution, belonged to the same political party as the majority of senators, they delegated this job to him. After 1845, however, the parties agreed to elect slates selected by their caucuses, suspending Rule XXXIV by unanimous consent.

The Speaker named the chairmen and members of the House committees. Although the Speaker of the House had the crucial job of determining the makeup of committees, by the 1840s he was no longer the dominant figure Henry Clay had been in the early decades of the century. In fact, between 1841 and 1863 only one Speaker served a second term. In general, the Speaker had to satisfy his own party and the entire House as to his impartiality— that is, he had to reflect the distribution of power rather than to alter it.

Long-term incumbencies were still unusual, especially in the House. Even House Speakers usually had relatively brief congressional experience. John White of Kentucky, elected Speaker in 1841, had served only six years prior to his election. Only one Speaker elected between 1841 and 1859, Linn Boyd of Kentucky, had sat in Congress more than eight years. William Pennington of New Jersey, elected Speaker in 1859, had never served in Congress at all. The addition of new states led to a constant influx of first-term legislators, who made up more than half the members of almost every Congress even after the Civil War. The few experienced members accrued influence because of their knowledge of the institution and its rules.

In the Senate, a custom seems to have developed allowing a senator to retain his place on a committee unless he wanted a change. In general he rose according to seniority, often reaching the chairmanship. The rule was not a fixed one, but to remove a member (and especially a chairman) against his will was a serious matter; it was done only under extreme circumstances and usually proved traumatic.

The president exercised little direct influence on Congress, even when his party held the majority of the seats. Institutionally, the chief executive had direct input into the legislative process primarily through his messages and his power to veto legislation. But Andrew Jackson had expanded the power of the presidency between 1828 and 1836. Besides vetoing more legislation than any of his predecessors, he exercised a powerful informal influence. Through his vetoes and proclamations, he articulated political principles and positions, whose supporters organized the Democratic party to sustain him. He incorporated the principles and programs of his party into his messages to Congress, providing the legislative program of his party. To maintain his party organization, Jackson nominated party activists to federal offices.

The triumphant Whig party of 1840 opposed both Jackson's policies and his use of presidential power and influence to secure support for them. They blasted the "spoils system" as corrupt; they denounced executive "despotism." The Whigs did not expect their new president, William Henry Harrison, to lead their party. Harrison promised to avoid vetoes and to act on the advice of his cabinet, composed of Whig luminaries. The great Whig senator Henry Clay was expected to dominate Whig policy-making from his position as chairman of the Senate Finance Committee. He was to manage legislation to repeal the independent Treasury system created by the Democrats, to reestablish the national bank that Jackson had destroyed, and to distribute money from the sale of public lands to the states to foster "internal improvements" such as roads and canals. Clay was made chairman of a powerful select committee to shepherd his program through the Senate.

Harrison died soon after taking office, however, and was succeeded by Vice President John Tyler. It soon became clear that Tyler rejected the advice of his cabinet. He vetoed Clay's national bank legislation. Senate Whigs tried to conciliate the president by passing a modified national bank bill, reported by a new select committee independent of Clay's influence. But Tyler vetoed this bill too, against the advice of his cabinet, and nearly all the members of the cabinet resigned. Tyler then turned to a small coterie of fellow Virginians for support, nominated supporters to federal positions, and in general undermined the Whigs' ability to establish a legislative program. As a result, the Democrats soon returned to power in Congress, and many Whigs learned the importance of having an active president exerting party leadership.

This lesson was reinforced during the administration of James K. Polk. Polk defeated Clay for the presidency in 1844 largely by stressing the issue of territorial expansion. Maneuvering the United States into a war with Mexico, he acquired the northern territories of Mexico, including California and what became Arizona, New Mexico, Nevada, and parts of Utah and Colorado. Polk's administration also reestablished an independent Treasury to administer federal funds, eliminated most of the protective features of the tariff, and successfully vetoed various internal improvement bills.

These successes led to the establishment of presidential-congressional relations on a Democratic pattern in the 1840s and 1850s. It became customary to consult the party's senators about major appointments in their states and representatives about minor ones in their districts. Although many Whigs remained distrustful of executive power and political partisanship, most accepted the now-established system.

Despite the Democratic party's policy successes, Americans elected a Whig, Mexican War hero Zachary Taylor, to the presidency in 1848. Like Harrison, Taylor died soon after his election, and he was replaced by Millard Fillmore. Fillmore faced a Democratic Senate, but the patronage-based party system was so well entrenched that the senators generally recognized the president's right to appoint members of his own party to office, and they generally acquiesced as long as the nomination was not obnoxious.

Congress became the principal forum for developing the political issues on which the parties campaigned. Key legislative proposals were designed not only to make public policy but to articulate political principles. Members would make long speeches on particular bills, explaining how they

PEWTER-RIM MEDALLIONS. For the presidential campaigns of 1844. Lithograph portraits of presidential candidates Henry Clay (W-Ky.), *left*, and James K. Polk (D-Tenn.).

COLLECTION of DAVID J. and JANICE L. FRENT

related to the most fundamental principles of government. These were published in the *Congressional Globe*, with which Congress contracted to provide a verbatim record of debates after 1848. Newspapers carried detailed accounts of congressional activity, both in correspondence from Washington, which provided behind-the-scenes information about political maneuvering, and in long excerpts from the *Globe*. Newspapers were partisan and regularly carried the complete congressional speeches of their favorites.

The parties received different levels of support in different sections of the country, although these sectional differences became far more pronounced during the 1850s. The positions on economic and social questions taken by Whigs enabled them to elect proportionately more congressmen from New England and, usually, the mid-Atlantic states than from the South and West. But within the sections differing positions on local economic, social, and cultural issues led to widely divergent degrees of support from people of different localities, different economic interests, and different social backgrounds. The Whig and Democratic parties thus remained generally competitive in all parts of the country.

But the great successes of the Democratic Polk administration set in motion the events that led to the collapse of the second party system. The Mexican War brought the slavery issue to the center of U.S. politics. Up to this time both Democratic and Whig leaders worked assiduously to avoid this, insisting that slavery was a state issue rather than a national one. For several years the House had refused even to hear antislavery petitions, in apparent violation of the First Amendment's guarantee of the right of petition.

Now northern Whigs, their traditional political program in shambles, began to echo antislavery charges that the war was part of a conspiracy to expand slavery westward. Antislavery emotion ran so strong in the North that in 1846 northern Democrats joined Whigs in supporting a proposal offered directly from the floor of the House by Pennsylvania Democrat David Wilmot. The so-called Wilmot Proviso, offered as an amendment to a bill appropriating money to aid peace negotiations, guaranteed that any territory gained from Mexico would remain "free soil"—that is, free of slavery.

The Wilmot Proviso passed the House of Representatives on a sectional vote, with party lines breaking down completely. The Senate, evenly divided between representatives of slave and free states, blocked the measure. Like the House, it divided almost entirely along sectional lines. From

UNITED STATES SENATE CHAMBER. Engraving by Thomas Doney, 1846, after J. Whitehorne.   LIBRARY OF CONGRESS

1846 to 1850 the slavery issue disrupted discussions of what to do with territory acquired in the war.

The controversy strained congressional institutions. The two new antislavery senators elected in 1848, Salmon P. Chase of Ohio and John P. Hale of New Hampshire, objected to the traditional agreement between the parties over committee lists, forcing the tedious election of the chairmen and members of every committee. It took sixty-three ballots to elect a Speaker in the House, and this was possible only after the rules were changed to permit election by a plurality rather than a majority vote. In both houses, antislavery legislators were denied appointments to committees with jurisdiction over matters relating to slavery. In turn, they raised controversial slavery issues on the floor.

The conflict came to a head in 1850, as California petitioned for admission to the Union as a free state, which would for the first time have created a free-state majority in the Senate. Southern members blocked California's admission. Over the objection of Sen. Stephen A. Douglas (D-Ill.), the chairman of the Committee on Territories, the Senate created a select committee, chaired by Henry Clay (W-Ky.), to find a solution. The great leaders Clay and Daniel Webster (W-Mass.) urged compromise in magnificent orations, while the equally renowned John C. Calhoun (R-S.C.) demanded northern concessions. After Clay's compromise proposal failed, Democratic leaders led by Douglas cobbled it back together. They called their key element "popular sovereignty," allowing settlers in western territories to decide for themselves whether to permit slavery. They further conciliated the South by strengthening the federal law governing the recovery of fugitive slaves and courted the North by barring the slave trade in the territories.

Dissidents in both sections denounced this so-called Compromise of 1850 but its supporters in both parties carried the congressional elections of that year. By 1852 Democrats emerged as the party of compromise and Union, even in the South, where many Democrats had toyed with secession. But the Whig party's national unity had disintegrated. While southern Whigs tried to establish themselves as the party of Union, challenging the Democrats' newfound moderation, northern Whig voters began to drift. In 1852 the Whig vote collapsed and the Democrats recaptured the presidency. The result was the disintegration of the second party system and the development of the third.

The congressional elections of 1854 indicated a major realignment in voting patterns, with disparate groups of antislavery, nativist, and Whig members—most of whom coalesced into the new Republican party—outnumbering Democrats. By 1856 the Republicans were able to carry most of the northern states for their presidential candidate, as northern nativists abandoned their once-formidable political organizations.

The voting realignment that introduced the third party system polarized the parties along sectional lines. New England went from voting relatively Whiggish to voting overwhelmingly Republican. The shift was less dramatic but still significant in the rest of the North and in the West, which went from generally Democratic to largely Republican. At first the result was a sectionally polarized but evenly balanced Congress, with Democrats adding a minority of members from the North to their southern Democratic base.

The political tumult precipitated by the slavery issue continued to strain congressional institutions. As in 1849, in 1855 and again in 1859 no party was able to secure a clear majority in the House. Representatives balloted more than a hundred times without electing a Speaker before again changing the rules to permit election by a mere plurality.

Many southern Democrats and their allies could not abide the more radical of their Republican opponents. Democratic senators refused to assign Radical Republican senator Charles Sumner of Massachusetts to a committee, for example. Worse, in 1855 Sumner was brutally assaulted on the floor of the Senate by Rep. Preston S. Brooks of South Carolina. No senator intervened and the House refused to expel the assailant, who nonetheless resigned and was triumphantly reelected by his belli-

cose constituents. Southern members challenged Republicans to duels, and many members went to the chambers armed.

Congressional institutions helped to integrate the new anti-Democratic opposition. The importance of the speakership required Republicans to reach out to nativists, antislavery Democrats, and others to consolidate their forces in 1855. Their successful candidate, Nathaniel P. Banks of Massachusetts, carefully balanced his committee appointments to further the process. In the same Congress Republicans brought forward attractive legislative resolutions that united anti-Democratic forces behind the antislavery position as much as possible. Congressional institutions withstood the strain. The Speakers and Senate caucuses named committees representative of the whole Congress and allowed the minority to name its own members. Committees continued to report out legislation and Congress continued to follow established rules in considering it.

Pressed by the rising antislavery tide, from 1857 to 1860 President James Buchanan worked to maintain unified Democratic support for the increasingly proslavery Democratic political program. When the powerful Stephen Douglas broke with the administration over its proslavery policies, Buchanan removed the senator's allies from the federal civil service and appointed his enemies. In 1859 he helped persuade the Senate Democratic caucus to strip Douglas of the chairmanship of the Committee on Territories, an extreme step that even many of Douglas's critics denounced.

Instead of imposing unity, Buchanan's actions disrupted the party. Throughout the North, local Democratic politicians rallied to Douglas as the only Democratic leader untainted by subservience to the South. In 1860 the Democrats were unable to unite on a presidential candidate or a policy on slavery. Buchanan and his allies supported a prosouthern, proslavery ticket and platform, while Douglas represented most northern Democrats on his "popular sovereignty" platform. The division enabled the Republican candidate, Abraham Lincoln, to capture the presidency. Democrats, however, won control of Congress. A governmental stalemate would surely have followed, had not southern members left Congress as their states seceded from the Union.

Congress had failed to prevent secession and avoid Civil War. As the states of the Deep South seceded, each house created a select committee to forge a compromise. State delegations held caucus-

ARGUMENT OVER THE SECESSION OF MISSISSIPPI. Between Mississippi Democratic representative Albert G. Brown and Unionist representative John A. Wilcox in March 1851. As journalist Ben Perley Poore recalled the incident: "Mr. Brown, of Mississippi, delivered a long speech in the House upon the politics of that State, in which he defended the State Rights party and ridiculed the Union movement as unnecessary, no one then being in favor either of disunion or secession. This, one of his colleagues, Mr. Wilcox, denied. 'Do you mean,' said Mr. Brown, 'to assert that what I have said is false?' 'If you say,' bravely responded Mr. Wilcox, 'that there was no party in Mississippi at the recent election in favor of secession or disunion, you say what is false!' The last word was echoed by a ringing slap from Brown's open hand on the right cheek of Wilcox, who promptly returned the blow, and then the two men clinched each other in a fierce struggle" (vol. 1, pp. 394–395).

PERLEY'S REMINISCENCES, VOL. 1

es irrespective of party; separate moderate and southern extremist caucuses organized among Democrats. When the select committees failed to report acceptable compromises, desperate unionists turned to an extragovernmental conference of delegates sent from northern, border-state, and Upper South states. Only at the last minute did Congress finally pass a single compromise measure—a proposed constitutional amendment to forbid the federal government from abolishing slavery even through a constitutional amendment. But

events progressed too rapidly. In April 1861 South Carolina's militia fired on Fort Sumter; Lincoln called up troops to suppress the rebellion; and most of the rest of the slave states seceded and joined the Confederate States of America.

Civil War and Reconstruction, 1861–1872. The withdrawal of southern senators and representatives gave the Republicans control of the 37th Congress, which was not scheduled to meet until November 1861, eight months after Lincoln became president in March. Despite the crisis, Lincoln did not immediately call Congress into special session. Lincoln regarded secession and the war essentially as a breakdown in the execution of the laws of the United States, which, he believed, he as commander in chief had the primary responsibility for upholding. He did not convene Congress until 4 July 1861, nearly three months after the Confederates fired on Fort Sumter. In the meantime he called up armed forces and set the war in motion.

Lincoln recognized Congress's final authority to enact legislation to control war policy. But he regularly used his influence to dissuade the legislature from passing laws inconsistent with his actions. This led to conflict over the suspension of habeas corpus, the imposition of martial law, and especially policies regarding slavery and the reconstruction of the Union.

In the matters of habeas corpus and martial law, Congress tended to favor a more restrained and systematic approach. Lincoln wanted more flexibility; he managed to delay for two years passage of an act regulating the suspension of habeas corpus, and he retained control over areas under martial law. But when it came to emancipation and reconstruction, Republican members of Congress wanted more vigorous action. For a year and a half Lincoln resisted powerful pressures to support emancipation, denying that Congress had the power to abolish slavery. Finally, on 1 January 1863, he issued the Emancipation Proclamation as a presidential war measure freeing slaves behind rebel lines. He was even more adamant about keeping control of reconstruction through the exercise of his powers as commander in chief. He tenaciously fought congressional efforts to pass laws on the subject, killing the only one that did pass, the Wade-Davis bill, with a pocket veto.

As Lincoln conceded Congress's final authority on most matters, congressional leaders refrained from directly challenging the president's choice of military strategy and officers. Nevertheless, for most of the war Republican leaders in Congress were desperately unhappy with his choices. They distrusted professional officers and called for the appointment of former civilians to important military commands. They clamored for bolder strategies; they urged Lincoln to instruct local commanders to take more forceful actions against slavery and disloyalty. The chief institutional vehicle for this pressure was the Joint Committee on the Conduct of the War, created in 1861. Dominated by Radical Republicans, it put pressure on Lincoln and his generals and issued reports of southern atrocities that fired northern passions. The Republican congressional caucuses also played a role, pressing Lincoln to appoint a more radical cabinet and more aggressive generals.

The war worked significant changes in Congress. New Republican leaders emerged—always linked to their committee positions. Rep. Thaddeus Stevens (R-Pa.) became chairman of Ways and Means and thus the majority leader of the House. William Pitt Fessenden (R-Maine) took over the chairmanship of the Senate Finance Committee and became majority leader in that chamber. Lyman Trumbull (R-Ill.) chaired the Senate Judiciary Committee, wielding great influence over civil-military relations and, ultimately, Reconstruction policy. With firm control of Congress, the Republicans strengthened the speakership, reelecting Schuyler Colfax of Indiana to three terms in that position and then selecting James G. Blaine of Maine, who would play an active role in determining policy through his committee selections and parliamentary decisions.

Laying claim to a strong role in prosecuting the war, the various congressional committees that governed military and naval affairs worked closely with the Lincoln administration in appropriating money and deciding how to spend it and in confirming military promotions. They complemented the Joint Committee on the Conduct of the War, which tried to influence war policy more generally. Some of the future leaders of Congress and the nation, such as Blaine, future president James A. Garfield, and future vice president Henry Wilson and vice presidential candidate John A. Logan, began their careers as members and chairmen of these committees. The war also enhanced the prestige of the House and Senate Judiciary committees, which were responsible for framing legislation governing habeas corpus, defining citizens' rights, and proposing constitutional amendments.

The Republicans' antislavery principles were complemented by a conviction that the national government should take an active role in promoting economic development. During and after the war Congress passed laws subsidizing the construction of roads, railroads, and canals; the operation of ocean steamship lines; and the development of land-grant colleges. Congress appropriated money to dredge rivers and harbors; it reinstituted a protective tariff to foster industrial development; and, most important, it reorganized the national banking and currency system, regulating the amount of currency in circulation and its distribution around the country. By the end of the war, economic policymaking had shifted almost entirely to Washington. As never before, economic interests attended to Congress—hiring lobbyists, courting members, and subsidizing political activity. In turn, federal policies encouraged the development of a national market and economic system.

These activities increased the prestige of the House Committee on Rivers and Harbors and the Senate Commerce Committee. Each house created new committees with jurisdiction over railroads. The Senate created a new Committee on Manufactures. But of greatest general importance to the economy were the government's taxing, spending, and financial policies. The burden of developing and monitoring these policies proved too great for the House Ways and Means and the Senate Finance committees. In 1865 the House split the responsibility among three committees: Ways and Means, Appropriations, and Banking and Currency, which immediately became the three most prestigious committees in the House. The Senate created a new Appropriations Committee to take over the spending function from the Finance Committee; the Senate Appropriations Committee soon became second in influence only to the Finance Committee. Its chairman, John Sherman (R-Ohio), would be a leading figure in shaping U.S. public policy for more than thirty years.

The Civil War also raised the thorny issues regarding how to restore the Union and concerning the place of the freed slaves in postwar society. The House established a Select Committee on the Rebellious States, which proposed the Wade-Davis Reconstruction bill. The two houses created select committees to deal with issues surrounding the abolition of slavery, the Senate committee chaired by the great Radical Republican humanitarian Charles Sumner. They successfully proposed legislation establishing a Freedmen's Bureau to superintend the transition from slave to free labor in the South. By the war's end it was clear that for the first time the national government was going to play a significant role in defining and protecting the rights of Americans within the states.

The novelty of wartime issues and the creation of new committees led to conflict in Congress. In the House, the chairmen of Ways and Means and the new Appropriations Committee jockeyed for authority, especially after Thaddeus Stevens died in 1869. In both houses, committees complained that the new Appropriations committees were invading their jurisdiction by making substantive decisions through the appropriations process. Different committees claimed authority over reconstructing the Union. The jurisdiction of the Joint Committee on the Conduct of the War overlapped that of the various committees on military and naval affairs. The domain of the select committees on Slavery and Emancipation overlapped with that of the Judiciary committees. In general, Republicans of a radical bent—that is, who favored an aggressive war policy, thorough restructuring of southern institutions, and equal civil and political rights for African Americans—dominated the select committees created during the Civil War. Republicans of a more conservative persuasion predominated on the traditional standing committees. Thus the rivalries among committees reflected differing policy orientations. As the select committees dissolved at the war's end, conservative Republicans gained the upper hand in Congress.

Dealing with the place of the freed slaves in American society was made more difficult by the assassination of Lincoln and the succession to the presidency of Vice President Andrew Johnson. Johnson, a Democrat before the war, had been elected as a unionist and had never formally committed himself to the Republican party. The quarrel between Johnson and the Republicans over reconstruction ultimately led to the greatest conflict between presidential and congressional authority in the history of the United States. Like Lincoln, Johnson claimed authority to inaugurate a program of reconstruction; unlike his predecessor, however, he claimed sole and final authority. And the gulf between Johnson's views and those of congressional Republicans was much wider than that that had separated Congress from Lincoln.

Johnson was committed above all to reawakening the loyalty of former Confederates and restoring a Union in which the states retained their traditional areas of authority, free of federal interference. He was unsympathetic to the plight of black Americans, and unwilling to expand the power of the federal government to protect them against state legislation.

In the seven-month hiatus between Lincoln's assassination and the first meeting of the 39th Congress, Johnson superintended the reorganization of civil governments in the southern states, limiting voting rights to white southerners. When Congress met in December 1865, he pressed for the admission of southern congressmen and restoration of the Union. Congress responded by delaying restoration. To coordinate policy, Republicans created a Joint Committee on Reconstruction, made up of the most influential members of both houses, to investigate southern conditions. Working separately, the House and Senate Judiciary committees devised and won passage of civil rights legislation extending the life of the Freedmen's Bureau, defining citizenship to include African Americans, and securing equal civil rights for all persons in the United States. Meanwhile, the Joint Committee on Reconstruction framed and secured passage of the Fourteenth Amendment, which incorporated the definition and rights of U.S. citizenship into the Constitution.

In response Johnson declared war on the congressional majority. Unwilling to ally formally with the Democratic party, Johnson attempted to create a new, conservative unionist political organization of his own, utilizing his control over federal appointments in the effort. He began to purge federal officeholders who remained loyal Republicans, infuriating Republican leaders in Congress. They regarded patronage as a legitimate tool when used by an elected president to promote party unity and to further the policies endorsed by the constituency that had elected him. But Johnson was using patronage to create a personal following—in direct opposition to the wishes of those who had elected him. The voters confirmed that perception in 1866, when they overwhelmingly rejected Johnson's call to oust Republicans from Congress.

Emboldened by this mandate, Republicans in 1867 passed a series of Reconstruction acts placing the southern states under military control and reorganizing them on the basis of racially nondiscriminatory suffrage. They also limited Johnson's control over patronage by passing the Tenure of Office Act, which kept officeholders in place until the Senate confirmed their successors—except during recesses of Congress, when the president could replace officers temporarily.

But Johnson refused to concede the legitimacy of the Republican program, even though Republicans passed it over his veto. The laws were unconstitutional invasions of states' rights and the powers of the president, he insisted. Moreover, he challenged the legitimacy of Congress itself as long as it continued to exclude representatives of the southern state governments reconstituted under his authority.

To the Republicans' dismay, Johnson began a campaign to obstruct the Reconstruction acts and to gain control of the army. In the fall of 1867, while Congress was adjourned, he temporarily removed Secretary of War Edwin M. Stanton, who sympathized with Congress, naming Gen. Ulysses S. Grant to replace him. Then he began to replace the military commanders in the South with officers sympathetic to him. When the Senate refused to make Stanton's removal permanent, Johnson tried but failed to persuade Grant to retain the office. After Radical Republicans failed to muster the necessary votes to impeach him in December 1867, Johnson removed more military officers in the South and urged his allies there to take the offensive. Finally, in February 1868, he dismissed Stanton in apparent violation of the Tenure of Office Act, throwing down the gauntlet to Congress. This time, conservative and Radical Republicans in the House united to impeach him.

Although Republicans were confident of success when the impeachment proceedings moved to the Senate, their confidence soon dissipated. The threat of removal led Johnson to moderate his activities and enabled Republicans to complete the reconstruction process, reducing the crisis atmosphere. Over the objections of Radical Republicans who insisted that impeachment proceedings were essentially political, the trial served to establish their quasi-judicial character. The Senate turned itself into a "high court of impeachment" to hear evidence and legal arguments, with Chief Justice Salmon P. Chase presiding and setting the judicial tone. In the end, Johnson escaped conviction by a single vote, primarily because it was not clear that the Tenure of Office Act covered Stanton.

The election of Republican presidential candidate Ulysses S. Grant in 1868 ultimately meant a return to traditional party government. But for several years Grant tried to run a relatively apolitical administration, leaving Republicans in Congress adrift. Not until 1871, when the Republican malaise began to threaten Grant's prospects for reelection, did he take on the president's traditional role as party leader. He demonstrated his power by persuading the Senate to remove his bitter critic, Charles Sumner, from the chairmanship of the Senate Foreign Relations Committee and by providing firm leadership on domestic policy. With this the party regrouped, passing legislation that once more stressed the sectional issues on which its political appeal primarily rested.

But the struggle between Congress and Andrew Johnson led to a significant change in the Senate's role in Republican party politics. Under the Tenure of Office Act federal officeholders could retain their positions unless the Senate confirmed a replacement. As a result, every appointee considered his senator as his patron, no matter who had secured the initial appointment for him. The House tried to repeal the Tenure of Office Act in 1869, when Grant became president, but the Senate, unsurprisingly, blocked the effort. Such senators as Roscoe Conkling of New York, Simon Cameron of Pennsylvania, and Oliver H. P. T. Morton of Indiana soon commanded the corps of federal appointees in their states, evolving into bosses of their party machines and the principal links between local party organizations and the presidential administration. The system was strengthened by the principle of "senatorial courtesy," whereby senators agreed not to vote to confirm an appointee obnoxious to any senator of the president's party in whose state the appointee's jurisdiction lay.

At first this system promised more orderly, rational party mobilization. But by the mid 1870s senators commanded political baronies whose particular interests seriously threatened party unity. At the same time, new economic issues emerged to compete with the old wartime and postwar issues. (For example, many westerners and southerners challenged the banking and financial system that Republicans had established during the war.) Such issues, too, undermined Republican unity. Meanwhile, in the South, Democrats used fraud and violence to overthrow the Republican state governments and suppress the black vote. In the congressional elections of 1874 Democrats swept the South and reestablished their competitiveness in the North. For the first time since 1860 Democrats took control of the House of Representatives. For the next twenty years, the parties would be evenly balanced in Congress and in presidential elections.

[See also Civil War; Compromise of 1850; Congress of the Confederacy; Fifteenth Amendment; Fourteenth Amendment; Mexican War; Morrill Land-Grant College Act; Reconstruction; Secession; Sectionalism; Slavery; Thirteenth Amendment; Wilmot Proviso.]

BIBLIOGRAPHY

Alexander, Thomas B. *Sectional Stress and Party Strength: A Study of Roll Call Voting Patterns in the United States House of Representatives, 1836–1860.* 1967.

Benedict, Michael Les. *A Compromise of Principle: Congressional Republicans and Reconstruction, 1863–1869.* 1974.

Benedict, Michael Les. *The Impeachment and Trial of Andrew Johnson.* 1973.

Benedict, Michael Les. "The Party, Going Strong: Congress and Elections in the Mid-19th Century." *Congress and the Presidency* 9 (1981–1982): 37–60.

Bogue, Allan G. *The Earnest Men: Republicans of the Civil War Senate.* 1981.

Galloway, George B. *History of the House of Representatives.* 1961.

Holt, Michael F. *The Political Crisis of the 1850s.* 1978.

McCormick, Richard P. *The Second American Party System.* 1966.

Nichols, Roy Franklin. *The Disruption of American Democracy.* 1948.

Silbey, Joel H. "After 'The First Northern Victory': The Republican Party Comes to Congress, 1855–1856." *Journal of Interdisciplinary History* 20 (1989): 1–24.

Silbey, Joel H. *The Partisan Imperative: The Dynamics of American Politics before the Civil War.* 1985.

Silbey, Joel H. *The Shrine of Party: Congressional Voting Behavior, 1841–1852.* 1967.

MICHAEL LES BENEDICT

The Age of the Machine (1872–1900)

In the closing third of the nineteenth century, America's problems seemed particularly daunting. Just about any adult male could vote, but with political machines in the cities and professional politicians who defined the issues to suit themselves, democracy seemed less meaningful than ever. Almost nowhere could women vote, and, for all the guarantees of the Fourteenth and Fifteenth Amendments, blacks generally found themselves barred from the polls and denied the equal protection of the laws. Hoping to make a new life in the New World, immigrants by the millions brought over many of their old habits—too many for the taste of millions of immigrants' descendants already well settled in their small-town Protestant ways. Thanks to the industrial revolution, consumer goods had never been cheaper—and neither had employees' lives. Canting about manifest destiny and America's mission to civilize the savage, settlers drove the Indians off their lands and the government reservations "uplifted" them virtually into extinction. By the century's end, the greatest republic in the world seemed poised to become an empire, with the Philippines under its flag—but not, apparently, under its Bill of Rights.

Surely if an age needed statesmen, the Gilded Age

did: the several hundred elected representatives in the House, the seven dozen or so men chosen by state legislatures to fill the Senate. Yet what was the result?

The Case against Congress. "If every man in Congress should fall dead in his seat, it would be a God's blessing to the country," wrote "Pickaway" in the *Cincinnati Enquirer* of 20 June 1884, "and in less than two months there would be a set of men there just as wise and good as their predecessors."

A harsh judgment! But it was not all that uncommon in the late nineteenth century. Never very popular, Congress at that time acquired an indelible notoriety as a conclave of hirelings, windbags, mediocrities, and dawdlers. When members of the House sprawled in their chairs; put feet on their desks; abused doorkeepers; munched peanuts, apples, and toothpicks; sucked unlit cigars; spat tobacco on the carpet; and cleaned their fingernails with pocketknives, observers in the gallery found it hard to believe the country well represented. No matter who spoke, the chamber struck visitors as a broil of disorder. Desk lids slammed, pens scratched, outsiders paid calls on individual members, and gossip flowed continuously, no matter how persistently the Speaker pounded his gavel or the representative holding the floor held forth. With barrooms in the Senate cloakroom and below stairs, whiskey flowed as freely as oratory. When, as was often the case, half a dozen or more senators were drunk and kept resupplying themselves by trips downstairs, sessions ranged from confusion to pandemonium.

And yet, for all of these distractions, how the solons talked! It was child's play to fill up seventy pages of the *Congressional Globe* or, after 1873, the *Congressional Record* with a day's verbiage. Saturdays were special in the House. Then, representatives could hold forth with bunkum speeches that no one heeded, on any topic they pleased, often delivering addresses written up by Washington correspondents, whose scanty salary could use that extra fifty dollars. But even on other days of the week, debate ran unfettered by relevance, with a piece of Reconstruction legislation sidetracked into discussions of Ireland, Tom Moore's poetry, sausages, and scullions. In place of debate, more and more lawmakers by the 1870s were reading written texts, more ornate than everyday discussion but no more intelligent—which was the best justification for senators answering their mail during the session or taking a nap until a vote was called. Though one wit suggested taking away legislators' desks, nobody ever tried it. Forcing them to pay attention to each other would have constituted cruel and unusual punishment. Rarely did speeches change a single vote; by the late 1870s, reporters in the press gallery were providing bare summaries, and by the turn of the century, they were leaving them out of their reports altogether.

What they did write down were the set-tos. One Senate debate resulted in the ruling that the term "God-damned son of a bitch" ought not be applied by one member to another. Occasionally, House members described one another as thieves, hangmen, or hyenas. "Oh, Blaine, dry up!" Samuel S. "Sunset" Cox of New York screamed, as the distinguished sometime Speaker and presidential candidate James G. Blaine made a telling point in debate—and Cox was renowned as one of the shining lights of legislative repartee. (Not that his words appeared in the *Congressional Record*. But then, the *Record* never lived up to its name. It got bigger year by year; the 37th Congress produced 6,560 pages of discussion, the 41st Congress 12,824. Lawmakers were not speaking more, just inserting more. They withheld their own remarks "for revision"; sometimes they induced the stenographers to withhold their colleagues' as well, to make the repartee work more favorably in their own direction. Attempts to forbid the publication of bogus speeches got nowhere.)

Observers (like the young scholar Woodrow Wilson in his best-selling treatise, *Congressional Government*) freely admitted that there were no more Henry Clays left in either chamber, and among the postwar senators, scarcely a man outside of Massachusetts who rose beyond stump orator or wirepuller. Representatives survived by doling out local favors, chaperoning private claims and grievances through the appropriate agencies, and disbursing pumpkin seeds, grape slips, and government documents to constituents. Both ends of the Capitol became clearinghouses for office seekers; members touted their merits, blocked their selection, or protected them from dismissal. Patronage brokering and errand running scarcely encouraged the broad outlook among Congress members that Americans expected. If Democratic presidential candidate Winfield Scott Hancock looked like a fool in 1880 when he declared the tariff a local issue, what did that make Congress look like, when the tariff issue turned the floor into a free-for-all among defenders of parochial interests? It was all very well for William D. Kelley of Philadelphia, father of the House, to take such pride in protection for his dis-

trict's industry that he gloried in the nickname "Pig Iron," but while the member for collars and cuffs discussed rates with the member for sugar beets, who spoke for the United States?

Advancing the selfish private interests of their constituents, the lawmakers coddled their own as well. From the so-called salary grab of 1873, in which lame-duck members gave themselves a pay raise that was two years retroactive, to the purchase of sufficient independent Republican votes to carry Sen. Matthew S. Quay's reelection through the Pennsylvania legislature in 1901, the two houses were infamous for their corruption. Joseph Keppler's caricature of "The Bosses of the Senate" in

VYING FOR THE REPUBLICAN PRESIDENTIAL NOMINATION. For the 1888 election. Benjamin Harrison (R-Ind.), winner at the convention and in the November election, came from the Senate, as did most of his competitors for the nomination. The caption for the cartoon, published 4 June 1888, reads: "The Republican Cinderella— Who'll take the slippers?" The massive pair of slippers are labeled "Blaine's slippers," referring to Secretary of State James G. Blaine, who had narrowly lost in the 1884 presidential election and declined the nomination in 1888.

OFFICE OF THE HISTORIAN OF THE U.S. SENATE

1889 caught the public impression exactly: standing in the gallery behind a body of Lilliputian legislators, Brobdingnagian money-bag industrial trusts keep a jealous eye on proceedings. But how unnecessary, reformers cried at the century's end; why should the special interests manipulate the upper chamber when they could hold the seats directly? The Senate had become a House of Lords, a millionaires' club for Standard Oil directors, railroad presidents, and timber barons.

Stalemate. What Americans might reasonably have expected from such a body they generally seemed to get: ignorance, inattention, or worse. For example, after the House had done two readings and gone through a day of debate on a bill, its sponsor proposed adjournment so that members might actually read the measure before proceeding any further—for it had not been reduced to print. But not proceeding any further was a specialty of both branches. More and more things went undone: over 11,000 bills died with the end of the 1884–1885 session. The House calendar ran for nearly one hundred pages with measures that could not be handled for lack of time. House bills moved into the Senate, never to be heard from again. Of course, just getting a measure to the Senate was a challenge. In one session of the 45th Congress (1877–1879), the House Claims Committee had to handle 913 different cases. The unsworn testimony of claimants lay before members, and nothing more. With virtually no clerical staff and no money for summoning witnesses or gathering affidavits, the committee could consider a few cases, none of them thoroughly, and leave the rest for another Congress, which left them to the next, and so on. Only 163 claims were reported that session, and of these, Congress passed a dozen. More often than not, then, a committee report on a bill was no more than the glass case putting the corpse on display for friends of the deceased to pay respects. With so many forces for delay, controversy could stop a measure, and so most public legislation needed a pretty thorough gutting or a pretty strong demand to pass. Even then, bills moved at a snail's pace or, as one congressman snorted, in "mucilaginous majesty."

Corruption and imbecility were not, in fact, really to blame for the legislative logjam. Contrary to Wilson's lamentation, the Senate had quite a number of effective lawmakers, conscientious and sound of judgment. Many apprenticed at the other end of the Capitol; long before 1890, the Senate was living up to the description offered by Speaker Thomas B. Reed of Maine as the place where good representatives went when they died. Among Republicans, the compassion of Henry L. Dawes of Massachusetts, the financial expertise of John Sherman of Ohio and Nelson W. Aldrich of Rhode Island, and the talent for compromise of William B. Allison of Iowa compared favorably with senators of any era. Alongside the grotesques and one-termers in the House sat those whose mastery of day-to-day business thrust them into the unofficial leadership: Dawes; James A. Garfield of Ohio; and William S. Holman of Indiana, to name a few. As head of the House Claims Committee in the early 1870s, William B. Washburn of Massachusetts spoke rarely, but when he did, his words carried such weight that whatever his committee reported was as good as written into law. Still, there was indeed corruption; senators did buy their seats now and then. Some representatives sold themselves for a payoff, and others, like Aldrich, for a generous financial settlement from the Sugar Trust. But experience, local interest, and partisan allegiance held far more sway in the making of legislation.

What, then, were the real reasons for congressional ineffectiveness? Three stand out: political, procedural, and principled.

The political problem was twofold. First, too much of legislators' time went to gratifying individual constituents. Veterans wanted help getting pensions, distillers and merchants needed tax relief or special Treasury consideration, and always there were crowds of people whose right to payment the U.S. Court of Claims had not seen fit to grant. In 1880, lawmakers made some 40,000 written or verbal inquiries of the Pension Bureau; in 1891, the number had risen to 154,817—500 or more for every working day. Naturally, bustling around the departments on private matters took precious time. So did the welter of private legislation offered often to correct the callous treatment that the Pension Bureau and Claims Court meted out to worthy applicants. The 48th Congress (1883–1885) saw 598 special pension bills, and the 50th (1887–1889) 1015. As the burden of proposals grew heavier, more general legislation got crushed beneath a mountain of petty favors.

However, even if all the services for constituents had been lifted from members' backs, the rough balance between Democrats and Republicans stood in action's way. From 1861 to 1875, heavy Republican majorities allowed Congress to do just about anything that a presidential veto could not prevent—and Republican presidents were stepping in

JAMES A. GARFIELD (R-OHIO). Representative (1863–1881), president (1881). *PERLEY'S REMINISCENCES*, VOL. 2

gingerly, picking fights with the legislative branch. Then the "tidal wave" of 1874 swept in a Democratic House and a long period of divided authority. Tariff bills, silver-coinage proposals, even army appropriations and a bill to exclude Chinese immigrants stalled in one house, passed to die in the other, or perished beneath a presidential veto. Not until 1881 would the same party control the White House and both ends of the Capitol, and even then the president's party controlled the Senate by a wafer-thin margin. Not until 1889 would there be a Congress under strong enough partisan control to put through a legislative program. From 1875 to 1895, Democrats held every House but two (1881–1883 and 1889–1891) and the Republicans every Senate but one (1879–1881). A united opposition and a divided majority meant sure stalemate, and aside from objecting to whatever the other side tried to do, getting consensus inside the party took remarkable skills or strong majorities.

Activism would also require a change in the rules for conducting business. Without a quorum, nothing could be done, and the longer a session lasted, the less willing members were to show up for busi-ness. By August 1876, House Democrats were scrambling to bring in as many as one hundred absentees a day. A sergeant at arms could scour every bar and lobby for missing members, and if need be arraign them before the bar of the House, but their colleagues usually let the offenders off on the paltriest excuse, which made enforcement a farce. And there was nothing the sergeant at arms could do about congressmen sitting in the chamber and refusing to answer to their names, the so-called disappearing quorum, a choice ploy by the minority to halt action. Even so forceful a Republican Speaker as James G. Blaine (1869–1875) avoided a head-on attack on that tactic; after all, Republicans might avail themselves of it someday (as soon they did). Long experienced in the arts of obstruction, Democratic Speakers behaved even more timidly. By 1888, they found it virtually impossible to push through any public measure without unanimous consent and believed it unthinkable to propose any reform.

But was it even the responsibility of lawmakers to make laws without pressing need? Democrats insisted that overzealous government activism lay at the heart of so many national problems: subsidies handed out to railroads, tariff protection to industrial interests, bounties to steamship companies, pensions to worthy veterans and unworthy widows, and utopian schemes to promote equality for Negroes and Indians. Republicans, admittedly, saw government in more active terms and had plenty of ideas for using the public revenue, but even they allowed that legislating should have strict limits. Among Democrats, Holman was known as the great objector of the House, though Samuel J. Randall earned the nickname "the Brakeman" for his obstruction to jobbery. Among Senate Republicans, much the same could be said of George F. Edmunds of Vermont. A superb debater, he remained all negative, a carper and critic, to anything proposed by colleagues. Under his control, the Judiciary Committee was a slaughterhouse for legislation. There was nothing constructive in his statesmanship. When he declared his unwillingness to be president to George F. Hoar, the Massachusetts senator had a ready comeback. "But, Edmunds," he protested, "just think of the fun you would have vetoing bills."

A New Congress of Older Members. An effective Congress would need to overcome all three limitations on its power to act. So Congress did, although the change went unnoticed by outsiders, including Wilson.

Congress itself changed the most by changing less, that is, by lengthening the tenure of its members. Up to the Civil War, most representatives, especially outside the South, served a single term. In thirty Congresses before 1877, including twenty of the preceding twenty-two, newcomers constituted a majority. Even House veterans generally lasted no more than three terms. Having so many members fresh from the people may have been democratic, but it added to the confusion. When committees were chock-full of novitiates, unversed in the arcana of their assigned specialty, when the chairmen usually came straight from some other committee rather than doing time on the panel that they now led, business as usual was business handled clumsily and with painful slowness. The only people who knew legislation's ins and outs were the lobbyists; many of them, at least, were veterans of long standing. (Some, such as William E. Chandler of New Hampshire, would become lawmakers themselves.)

As a one-party South emerged in the late 1870s, the pattern began to change. Republican voters were bulldozed away from the polls by night riders and shotguns, and voting requirements were managed creatively enough to disqualify most blacks and the more unreliable white constituents; the white supremacist, post-Reconstruction Redeemer Democrats were not likely to be unseated. At the same time, northern incumbents with Civil War service found that a blue coat covered a multitude of sins, even present service in Congress. The years of parliamentary experience of the so-called Southern brigadiers, not their numbers in Congress, explained their growing influence in a legislature that was overwhelmingly nonsouthern. If other states wanted to match the influence on the Commerce Committee of a John H. Reagan of Texas, they would need to match his endurance record of sixteen years in the House. Starting in 1877, then, the House had a regular majority of repeat performers, and the proportions steadily grew. By 1900, two members in three had prior service. Not yet the fixed, rigid custom that it became after 1911, a seniority system nonetheless was beginning to develop in which committee chairs went to those with past committee service and time in rank earned its reward.

The reward was all the sweeter for the enhanced power that the committees wielded over legislation. Of course, certain committees had always enjoyed a special relationship with the executive departments doing the same business and had privileged access to the spoils. For years, a member's committee assignments had showed how much of a force to be reckoned with he was. The choicest House positions had long been on the two leading money committees, Ways and Means (getting) and Appropriations (spending); after that came Judiciary, Foreign Affairs, and Commerce. Now, the assignments became even more coveted, the perquisites more lavish. By the late 1870s, a chairman could expect preference in obtaining the floor. A decade later, as one observer grumbled, "nearly every Chairman of Committee gets the delirium tremens if he can not have a committee parlor."

Any committee could direct the flow of legislation simply by refusing to report bills that its members disliked. In the House, a member complained, lay two great burial grounds for revenue reform: the calendar of bills and the Ways and Means Committee. So they were, as long as Samuel J. Randall, a Pennsylvania protectionist, wielded the Speaker's gavel and kept his high-tariff friend, Fernando Wood of New York, handling money matters. Appropriations accumulated powers even more prodigious. Under the Holman Rule of 1876, the only riders allowed onto a money bill were those to cut spending. In effect, this left the Appropriations Committee with almost total discretion over the bills it reported.

Greater power did not mean broader jurisdiction, however. As legislative needs grew, the House and Senate divided their tasks among more committees, each with a narrower specialty. The Senate had forty-four standing committees in 1892, the House fifty. Between 1877 and 1885, the Appropriations Committee lost discretion over particular money bills to both Commerce and Agriculture. Then, in 1885, the committee lost oversight of just about every other revenue measure that could be allocated elsewhere. The Commerce Committee's management of internal improvement funding lasted all of six years, until 1883, when the House passed it to a newly formed body, the Rivers and Harbors Committee. Twelve years later, a heavy caseload of contested elections even split the duties of the House Elections Committee among three committees.

The second real change in committee power came with the creation of the House Rules Committee in 1880, a sign of the other great transformation in procedure that was necessary. Unless House business could be concluded, it scarcely mattered whether lawmakers knew better what they were doing, and for the House to be productive, the procedure of doing business would have to become less deliberative and more managed.

Reed's Rules—and Others'. In the House, managed procedure would require a Speaker with power enough to direct the chamber's business efficiently. That power had, in fact, been accumulating for some time. Until the 1860s, most Speakers held office briefly and with little effect. They were essentially parliamentarians. Many of them won after grueling contests or as compromise choices after deadlock had forced stronger candidates to withdraw. Having to pledge themselves before their selection to win over rivals in the party caucus, they found their discretion over committee appointments, printing contracts, even the choice of door-keepers, mortgaged out in advance.

The bitter partisanship of the Civil War period changed all that. Late in the 1880s, English visitor James Bryce marveled at the vast resources a Speaker had at his disposal:

> In calling upon members to speak he prefers those of his own side. He decides in their favour such points of order as are not distinctly covered by the rules. His authority over the arrangement of business is so large that he can frequently advance or postpone particular bills or motions in a way which determines their fate. Although he does not figure in party debates in the House, he may and does advise the other leaders of his party privately; and when they "go into caucus" . . . he is present and gives counsel. He is usually the most eminent member of the party who has a seat in the House, and is really, so far as the confidential direction of its policy goes, almost its leader.

Even cautious Speakers like John G. Carlisle of Kentucky (1883–1889) chose committee chairs inclined their way, though as time went on, the seniority system began to limit their range of choices. Pledged to reduce government revenue by tariff cuts rather than repealing the tobacco tax, Carlisle closed his eyes to any representative with different ideas to offer. "No man with that damned bill in his hand can ever secure recognition," he said—and no man did.

A strong-willed Speaker could go still farther in that direction, and three of them did. First came James G. Blaine of Maine (1869–1875), handsome and courteous and a master of parliamentary procedure. As presiding officer, he proved wonderfully self-possessed and, to outward appearances, scrupulously fair to the Democratic minority. Behind the scenes, however, Blaine steered matters where he wanted them to go. Members might get a mes-

sage from the Speaker, directing them on what bill to propose. If they preferred to follow their own agenda, they might find another member springing a point of procedure upon them to block consideration.

Using a list of speakers to guide him in according recognition, Blaine made discussion as orderly as he could. Yet, those whose goals did not suit the Speaker's might as well have been invisible for all the attention they got from the chair. Members with bills to propose would do well to clear their details with the Speaker if they wanted to be recognized. After 1880, the Rules Committee would play the same role in floor scheduling that Blaine's speaker's list did. Already by 1875, House members grumbled that the rules had been so tightened that the majority could hobble free debate.

This process, however, had only begun. Coming to power in late 1875, Democrats soon discovered that the high principles of Michael C. Kerr (1875–1876), the tuberculosis-wracked congressman from Indiana, made a poor substitute for forceful leadership in the chair. When Kerr died after a tumultuous, fruitless session, the party turned to Samuel J. Randall of Pennsylvania (1876–1881), the closest equivalent to Blaine on their side of the aisle. The new Speaker was quick to apply his discretion in recognizing members to break his own party's filibuster against counting the electoral votes in the disputed presidential election of 1876. House rules would need to be recodified and streamlined, and it was Randall who chose the committee that did the job and then made it a standing body with priority in bringing resolutions to the floor and complete power over any measure that touched on House procedures.

Greatest of all the innovative Speakers, however, was Thomas B. Reed of Maine (1889–1891 and 1895–1899). As bulky as President Grover Cleveland and much brighter, Reed was an uncommon politician, firmly holding principles though scorning to admit it. "One with God is always a majority," he once remarked, "but many a martyr has been burned at the stake while the votes were being counted." Behind the languid, drawling style that he affected, Reed had a zest for partisan warfare and a skill in parliamentary fencing that made him the most dangerous man on the Republican side of the hall throughout the 1880s.

His election as Speaker late in 1889 in a House only marginally Republican showed just how dangerous he could be. Party caucuses could keep the ranks united but, barring exceptional health and attendance among its members, could not carry on the business of legislating as long as the "disappearing quorum" permitted Democrats to stop action. On 29 January 1890, Reed ordered the clerk to count as present all members in the hall, regardless of their responses to the calling of the roll. Democrats were furious. They leaped to their feet, yelled, and waved their fists. "The Chair is making a statement of fact that the gentleman from Kentucky is present," said the "Czar" to one protestor. "Does he deny it?" Throughout the 51st Congress (1889–1891), Reed cracked down on dilatory motions and abuses of parliamentary procedure to stall business. Republicans followed his guidance; they rose when he motioned to them and sank into their chairs when he scowled them into silence.

Reed's real achievement, however, was institutional, not personal. Gradually, his Rules Committee converted the Speaker's actions into official regulations. The Speaker obtained the power to count quorums and reject obstructionism more or less as he saw fit. "Mack," the Speaker would inform Benton McMillin, one of the Democratic leaders, "here is an outrage [William] McKinley [of Ohio], [Joseph G.] Cannon [of Illinois] and myself are about to perpetrate. You will have time to prepare your screams and usual denunciations." The Rules Committee effectively made policy, set the agenda, and arranged the calendar. Its reports could not be filibustered. Reed's Rules raised a ruckus, but they survived. Overwhelmingly Democratic though the next House was, it accepted the new Rules Committee, and the one that followed ended up adopting the essential principle that wiped out the disappearing quorum as a way of getting around Reed's own roadblocks. The "Czar" could not have been made happier, unless it was by his own return to the chair in 1895.

In contrast to the House, where rules had been so well developed by 1907 that the House parliamentarian could publish a book of *Precedents* with 7,346 procedural points filling eight volumes, the Senate left things pretty much alone. Efforts to limit debate or set a general calendar beyond members' caprices came to nothing. What had changed by the mid 1880s was not rules but rulers. The parliamentary savvy and adept management of a few strong-willed men like Nelson W. Aldrich and William B. Allison on the Republican side and Arthur Pue Gorman of Maryland among the Democrats, combined with the tools of party discipline—caucuses, steering committees, and committees on committees—would make things go and, quite a lot of the time, make things stop. So influ-

ential was Aldrich that, when he was shepherding through a tariff bill in 1890, he made his party colleagues beg his permission before adding any other matter to the order of business.

Do-Something Congresses. Procedural change cleared the way for action within each house. But enacting party programs took something more: an end to the political stalemate and some limitation on the errand-running side of congressional service. In the late 1880s, Congress extended the U.S. Court of Claims's jurisdiction far enough to reduce lawmakers' responsibility for constituents' claims on Congress. The extension of pensions to virtually all Union veterans and their heirs in 1890 cut down on the constant, heavy flow of private pension bills. Similarly, the growing restrictions on the spoils system eased at least some of the pressure on legislators to act as the sponsor (or nemesis) of officeholders.

Even when the two major parties stood in rough balance, Congress had never been completely inactive. Bipartisan majorities passed the Pendleton Act in 1883, creating the rudiments of a professional civil service; adopted three laws restricting Chinese immigration (all over presidential vetoes); enacted a ban on contract labor from abroad in 1887; and set up the Interstate Commerce Commission, the first national regulatory agency, also in 1887. In addition, enemies of Treasury deflation made common cause in 1878 to inject some silver coin into the monetary system with the Bland-Allison Act, and a baffling coalition of interests adjusted the high protective tariff in 1883 in ways that pleased just about nobody. Both parties talked economy, and both poured out the pork for internal improvements.

And yet, much more might have been accomplished had one party dominated official Washington. Tariff reform came up over and over, only to be smothered. The best that could be said of the Mills bill in 1888, for example, was that it made an attractive campaign document. So long as the Senate stood by the high tariff duties already in force, the House measure would never go further than a Senate committee. Proposals to fund southern public education faced implacable Democratic opposition. So, after 1875, did any Republican effort to give black voters federal protection.

So it was no coincidence that the 51st Congress (1889–1891)—the first in fourteen years in which the same party held solid partisan majorities in both houses as well as control of the White House—should be the first in a generation to accomplish much. Reed's Republican House pushed through 611 public bills, many of them far-reaching pieces of legislation. Guided by Ways and Means chairman William McKinley, Congress raised tariff rates. The Sherman Antitrust Act put Congress on record against "combinations in restraint of trade," whatever that meant. (Many supporters probably assumed it meant nothing at all and lived to see their mistake.) To soothe the demands of the West, the Sherman Silver Purchase Act obligated the Treasury to buy 4.5 million ounces of silver each month, a modest and, as it turned out, sham step to expand the money supply. Six new states were admitted to the Union, all of them, by no coincidence, Republican. There was even one last attempt to extend federal protection to black southern voters by allowing federal circuit courts to supervise elections and investigate allegations of fraud and intimidation. But here Republican unity collapsed, and the Senate failed to pass the so-called force bill. Not until the Republicans regained the White House in 1897 would there again be such a chance to act—provided that those in power wanted action. But did they?

To the century's end, both parties were inclined to treat federal intervention in domestic, commercial, and local affairs as a last resort, suitable for problems that neither the marketplace nor state and local government could handle. Republicans, of course, were more disposed to federal activism to promote prosperity; they had little trouble raising duties higher than ever with the Dingley Tariff Act in 1897. Labor legislation, however, like a federal income tax or civil rights, was another matter.

There were a few stirrings of change. Southern Democrats obtained an income tax provision in 1894 as their price for supporting the wan Wilson-Gorman tariff reduction bill. (Neither measure outlived its infancy.) Already by 1900, there were murmurings within Republican ranks about the social and economic injustices spawned by a new industrial order. In time, they would swell to a mighty chorus in favor of government activism, but that time was nearly a decade away. With Reed's retirement in 1899, the House and Senate leadership fell into the hands of men suspicious of reform. Even after the rank and file had begun to shift, those in control had all the advantage that their new procedural powers afforded them to smother inconvenient measures before they could come to a vote. It would take presidential muscle to get things moving again.

The Slow Recovery of Executive Power. That muscle, as it happened, was growing even as Congress enhanced its own effectiveness, and the change, too, was easily overlooked by contemporaries, even Woodrow Wilson. Building on the wartime advance in executive powers, Andrew Johnson had tried to consolidate and even extend his prerogatives in peacetime. Instead, he crippled the presidency and came within one vote of being removed. Legislative supremacy remained the reality in domestic policy to the century's end. Presidents might exercise their authority in quieter ways—Grant became rather adept at what later historians would describe as the "hidden-hand presidency"—or would protect small territories of prerogative, but they could not go much beyond that. Even Grover Cleveland could do little more than propose a program and leave it to his legislative supporters to carry it out—which, in the case of tariff reform, they did on a stretcher.

A tight control over patronage and the executive branch's pocketbook kept Congress supreme. Theoretically, a president could choose whomever he liked for any of the tens of thousands of federal offices, subject to Senate confirmation in some cases and the empty requirements of an unenforced, loophole-ridden Tenure of Office Act, which allowed the Senate to challenge dismissals of civil officials. Practically, however, presidents needed to consult lawmakers on any local appointments and oblige them as far as possible. No executive, no roster of cabinet officers, could sift through the credentials of every applicant. A state's representatives felt that they knew better. As far as they were concerned, any job in their territory was their political property. Woe to the president who nominated a man for the Supreme Court without clearing the choice with the appropriate senators first! The nominee was sure to go down, as Cleveland's choices did out of courtesy to Sen. David B. Hill of New York (or, as Cleveland referred to him, "David B. D—d!").

Congress clung just as tightly to its power to manage the smallest details in departmental spending. Cabinet officers found themselves fettered with elaborate restrictions on how much money to allocate and where to spend it. Lawmakers set the salaries for petty officials, raised barriers against the transfer of funds within different offices in the same department, sequestered surpluses, and pored over the books looking for fraud. When one party controlled the White House and the other ran the legislative committees, Congress degenerated into what one wit described as "government by detective."

Civil service reform began to change the balance of power. Presidents welcomed the chance to reclaim their authority over appointments. Chafing at the way senators treated Treasury offices as their own private preserve, Rutherford B. Hayes challenged one of the strongest barons in the party, Roscoe Conkling of New York, by dismissing the officials of the New York customhouse. In a humiliating rebuke to one of its own members, the Senate then confirmed the president's replacement nominees. Two years later, when a new president put an open foe of Conkling's into the collector's office, the senator saw that the jig was up. Rather than watch his own power wane, he resigned, carrying his colleague Thomas C. Platt with him. Confronted by a belligerent President Cleveland in 1886, the Senate surrendered even its token authority to block dismissals and repealed the last vestiges of the Tenure of Office Act. Most important to the swinging power balance, the Pendleton Act of 1883 began the process of creating a bureaucracy independent of the lawmakers' control. Under the law, presidents could extend the act's provisions to cover additional government employees. And so the presidents did, never with more relish than in their last days in power, when a new president stood poised to cast out their nominees.

Step by step, presidents restored their prerogatives or added to them. Where Ulysses S. Grant vetoed 43 bills in eight years, Cleveland vetoed 301 of them in four, or three times as many as had every president up to 1885 combined. What was more striking was the idea, once anathema, that a president could reject a bill not just on constitutional grounds but because he disapproved of its policy. Add to his constitutional powers a willingness to cultivate friends in the press and on Capitol Hill, and a chief executive could become formidable. Grant lacked these skills, while Chester A. Arthur and Benjamin Harrison scorned them. As for Cleveland, he could barely hide his disdain for prominent legislators, nor they for him. One story told how the First Lady woke her husband to tell him that there were robbers in the house. "I think you are mistaken," the sleepy president is said to have responded. "There are no robbers in the House, but there are lots in the Senate." Only when William McKinley took office in 1897 did the courtship of Congress begin in earnest.

Still, to the century's end government policy remained where it had begun, with the barons of Capitol Hill. It was a telling moment in 1898 when McKinley, reluctant to take his country into war with Spain, found himself forced to follow Congress's lead. By the time McKinley won reelection in 1900, the United States had become that most peculiar of anomalies: an empire without an emperor.

Nor, for that matter, did it have a "czar." Disgusted with his party's foreign adventures, himself unable to control a majority clamoring for empire, Reed had quit public life. His death in 1902 was timely and, for a man so closely associated with an effective legislative branch, perhaps a merciful fate. He had seen Congress at the noonday of its power; watching the shadows lengthen might well have brought melancholy even to his cynical heart.

[See also Chinese Exclusion Policy; Dawes Severalty Act; Electoral Commission of 1877; Electoral Count Act; Interstate Commerce Act; McKinley Tariff Act; Pendleton Act; Populism; Reed's Rules; Sherman Antitrust Act; Sherman Silver Purchase Act; Silver Issue.]

BIBLIOGRAPHY

Alexander, DeAlva Stanwood. *History and Procedure of the House of Representatives.* 1916.

Bryce, James. *The American Commonwealth.* 2 vols. 1891.

Fiorina, Morris P., David W. Rhode, and Peter Wissel. "Historical Change in House Turnover." In *Congress in Change: Evolution and Reform.* Edited by Norman Ornstein. 1975.

Keller, Morton. *Affairs of State: Public Life in Late-Nineteenth-Century America.* 1977.

Morgan, H. Wayne. *From Hayes to McKinley: National Party Politics, 1877–1896.* 1969.

Polsby, Nelson W. "The Institutionalization of the U.S. House of Representatives." *American Political Science Review* 62 (1968): 144–168.

Polsby, Nelson W., Miriam Gallaher, and Barry Spencer Rundquist. "The Growth of the Seniority System in the U.S. House of Representatives." *American Political Science Review* 63 (1969): 787–807.

Robinson, William A. *Thomas B. Reed: Parliamentarian.* 1930.

Rothman, David J. *Politics and Power: The United States Senate, 1869–1901.* 1969.

Thompson, Margaret Susan. *The "Spider Web": Congress and Lobbying in the Age of Grant.* 1985.

Wander, W. Thomas. "Patterns of Change in the Congressional Budget Process, 1865–1974." *Congress and the Presidency* 9 (Autumn 1982): 501–527.

White, Leonard D. *The Republican Era, 1869–1901.* 1958.

MARK WAHLGREN SUMMERS

Progressivism and Normalcy (1900–1933)

By 1900 the Congress of the United States was an old and powerful American institution: as old as the Republic, and the dominant branch of the federal government. The decades after the Civil War had seen not the rise of a powerful national bureaucracy, as in other modern industrializing nations such as Germany and Great Britain, but rather the undisputed supremacy of the legislature. Woodrow Wilson thought in 1879 that there "could be no more despotic authority wielded under the forms of free government than our national Congress now exercises." And in his influential book *Congressional Government* (1885) he called Congress the "predominant and controlling force, the centre and source of all motive and of all regulative power." James Bryce's *The American Commonwealth* (1888) also dwelt on the primacy of Congress.

The Institution

There were a number of reasons for this preeminence. One was the substantial number of state and local party leaders who became senators and representatives, thereby making Congress the great gathering (and bargaining) place of the major party organizations that so dominated late-nineteenth-century U.S. politics. Closely related to this was Congress's nearly total control over budgetary and fiscal policy in an age of weak presidents, no strong and independent bureaucracy, and government expenditures (for such things as Civil War veterans' pensions and a patronage-infested postal service) that were keyed primarily to the demands of expensive party politics.

Party and Committee Government. The congressional ascendancy in government was fostered by the increasingly assertive leadership of the heads of the major committees and the Speaker of the House. This was in great part a response to the sheer growth of the membership—from 293 in 1870 to 391 in 1900—and of the congressional workload. More than eighty-one thousand public and private bills were introduced between 1891 and 1901, well over double the average of the 1870s. By the end of the century, permanent expenditures were allocated through 185 separate acts, including 13 major annual appropriations bills.

By 1900 the practical work of Congress had long been firmly entrenched in its committees. In the House, Wilson observed, "committee work is everything and discussion nothing but 'telling it to the country.'" Indeed, said Bryce, the House was "not so much a legislative body as a huge panel from which committees are selected." The most powerful and ambitious members chaired the key standing committees: Appropriations, Rules, and Ways and Means in the House; Appropriations and Finance in the Senate. Sen. Orville H. Platt of Connecticut observed in 1895: "I should care nothing for being President pro tempore [of the Senate], but I should care very much for a place on the Finance Committee."

It is not surprising that strong partisans ran Congress by the turn of the century. Republican Speaker Thomas B. Reed governed the House from 1889 to 1891 and from 1895 to 1899, in collaboration with the chairs of Appropriations and Ways and Means. Together they dominated the all-powerful Rules Committee, acting as "a masterful steering committee" that decided procedural questions and controlled committee assignments and the course of legislation. Reed as Speaker pushed through modifications in the rules of the House that gave him new and extensive power to limit the ability of the Democratic minority to block the passage of legislation.

The strong Republican ascendancy in national politics that emerged from the 1896 electoral contest between William McKinley and William Jennings Bryan strengthened this party-oriented style of congressional leadership. The first Republican party whip in the House was designated by Reed in 1897.

The Senate underwent a similar evolution. Woodrow Wilson in the 1880s called the body "a small, select, and leisurely House of Representatives." But only a few years later James Bryce was struck by its "modern, severe, and practical" character. Like the House, the late-nineteenth-century Senate came under more forceful leadership. From the mid 1880s on, the Republican Steering Committee (later called the Committee on Committees) controlled the all-important committee assignments, and took over the scheduling of legislative business. The Republican party caucus played an increasingly important role in shaping the legislative agenda. And strong figures such as William B. Allison of Iowa, chair of Appropriations from 1881 to 1908, Nelson W. Aldrich of Rhode Island, chair of Finance, Orville H. Platt of Connecticut, John C. Spooner of Wisconsin, and the Democrat Arthur Pue Gorman of Maryland, brought a previously unknown degree of party and procedural discipline to the upper chamber.

Increasing Institutionalization. Modern urban-industrial America emerged at the turn of the century: a time of great economic, social, and cultural change. A substantial political science literature

INFORMAL MEETING OF THE SENATE FOUR. *Left to right,* Orville H. Platt (R-Conn.), John C. Spooner (R-Wis.), William B. Allison (R-Iowa), and Nelson W. Aldrich (R-R.I.) at Aldrich's Newport, R.I., estate, 1903. Together, they largely controlled the direction of policy in the Republican-dominated Congress during William McKinley's presidency.

LIBRARY OF CONGRESS

agrees that this is also the time when the modern Congress appears, if we define the modern Congress as an institution dominated by the seniority system, strong committee chairs, and weakened party leadership.

But there is considerable disagreement over the pace and sources of this change. The common denominator that characterizes the modern Congress, it is generally agreed, is "institutionalization," which political scientist Nelson Polsby defines as the replacement of a particularist, discretionary legislative process by a universalist, automated one: that is to say, the rise of more general, systematic, and controlled ways of defining and doing the business of Congress.

Just when and why this happened is subject to debate. The apparent increase in recent years of autonomous and fractious legislators disinclined to party discipline suggests that rather than "the modern Congress," it would be better to speak of "the early and mid-twentieth century Congress," as distinct from the quite different sort of institution Congress is likely to be by the end of the century.

How, then, should the evolution of Congress as an institution in the years from 1900 to 1933 be described? In many respects, it was the continuation—indeed, the acceleration of trends already evident. More than ever before, the early twentieth-century Congress was a gathering of lawyers: two-thirds of the House and the Senate in the 57th Congress (1901–1903). And the rules of the House kept accumulating. In 1907, longtime House parliamentarian Asher C. Hinds published a five-volume work, *Precedents of the House of Representatives,* that codified 7,346 procedural technicalities, almost all of them restrictions on the members: a monument of sorts to the view that the House now was an institution firmly controlled by its leadership (although one congressman observed in 1908 that the rules had become so complicated that three quarters of the House's business was done outside them, through devices such as suspension, unanimous consent, riders on appropriations bills, and the like).

Most of all, the closely interconnected growth of longevity of service and seniority for committee chairmanships gave a distinctive character to the early-twentieth-century Congress. The gradual increase in the average length of members' terms during the late nineteenth century all but exploded: the modern pattern of low turnover came into effect.

The average number of first-term members in the 42d to 56th Congresses (1871–1899) was 42.6 percent; in the 57th to 72d Congresses (1901–1931), 22.9 percent; in the 73d to 89th Congresses (1933–1965), 20.9 percent. Successive new records for the totals of prior service in the House were established in 1900, 1904, 1906, and 1908; successive new lows for the proportion of new members were set in 1898, 1900, 1904, and 1908. The 57th Congress, elected in 1900, was the first in which more than two-thirds of the House consisted of returning representatives and in which the average term of congressional service was over three years.

Why this increase in longevity should have occurred around the turn of the century is a question that has been open to much speculation. According to one view, it was the product of a long-term institutionalization of Congress. Another emphasizes new term-lengthening developments such as the greater life expectancy of members, an earlier average age of entry into Congress, a greater willingness by members of Congress to spend their careers there, and a tendency for members to have greater knowledge of and provide greater service to their constituencies. Yet another explanation points to the sharp decline of competitive seats in the Republican North and the solidly Democratic South after the formative McKinley-Bryan election of 1896 and argues that in the twentieth century most congressional districts became more homogeneous ethnically, economically, and culturally, thus fostering longer terms in office.

Certainly sectional party loyalties were greatly reinforced after 1896—Democrats in the South, Republicans in the East and West—and these persisted until the Great Depression and the New Deal effected large-scale changes in party identity and ideological alignments. Party control of the House changed often in the late nineteenth century (in 1875, 1881, 1883, 1889, 1891, and 1895) but less frequently in the early twentieth (in 1911, 1919, and 1931).

The greater longevity of members of Congress in office had a number of consequences for Congress as an institution. House careers in particular were now likely to be lifelong; experience and clubbiness counted more than ever before. Prior to 1899 a Speaker of the House served in the chamber an average of six years before attaining that office; his post-1899 counterparts, twenty-six years.

But what was most important, with longevity came the strict seniority system for committee chairmanships. This was under way even before 1900: in the 47th Congress (1881–1883), seniority was followed in two House committee chairmanships and ignored in thirty-seven; by the 57th Congress (1901–1903), it was adhered to in forty-nine of fifty-seven committees. Between 1895 and 1910, the record for longevity was set or tied in the chairs of thirteen of fourteen of the top committees. Another indicator of change is that in 1904 the *Congressional Digest* shifted from an alphabetical listing of members of Congress to a listing in order of continuous service. By World War I, seniority had become the all-but-inviolable norm in the House.

Perhaps the most consequential product of strict seniority was the hammerlock that southern Democratic members secured on key House committees. Southerners held 28 of 59 committee chairs in 1917, 27 of 47 (and the speakership) in 1931, by which time major committee chairs had served an average of more than nine terms. By 1913 the Texas delegation alone included the already powerful future Speaker John Nance Garner, Agriculture chair Marvin Jones, Interstate and Foreign Commerce chair (and future Speaker) Sam Rayburn, Judiciary chair Hatton Summers, and Rivers and Harbors chair Joseph J. Mansfield.

There were other measures, too, of a more settled, matured, stable institution. Contested elections were frequent in the nineteenth century and were settled in an intensely partisan manner: up to 1907, only 3 of 382 were resolved in favor of the

The Republican Party is in Power

THE BOTTOM IS OUT OF THE "FULL DINNER PAIL"

COPYRIGHT 1908
J. M. ERMERINS.
DETROIT

Isn't a change desirable?

DEMOCRATIC PARTY CAMPAIGN POSTCARD, 1908. In the campaigns of 1896 and 1900, Republican candidates used the "full dinner pail" slogan to emphasize their party's perennial advocacy of full employment and prosperous factories. Following the panic of 1907, during which the stock market dropped drastically and many businesses failed, the Democrats capitalized on the Republicans' apparent failure to assure continued economic prosperity by using their old slogan against them.

COLLECTION OF DAVID J. AND JANICE L. FRENT

minority party candidate. Contested elections sharply declined in the early twentieth century, in part because of tougher election laws and the Australian ballot. And they were judged by Congress more frequently on the merits of the case.

New congressional districts—always a potential source of instability—also came to an end: in the 63d Congress (1913–1915) the present total of 435 House members was set. And blatant manipulation of legislative rules for party purposes became less common. Lewis Deschler served as House parliamentarian from 1928 to 1974, embodying the principle that the rules of the House be applied in a nonpartisan way.

Looked at in this way, the early-twentieth-century Congress reflected the pre–New Deal American polity at large: some structural and substantive response to a rapidly changing society, but change that was gradual and in sum did little to alter the character of Congress as an institution.

The Historical Experience

If we shift our focus from Congress as an institution to its more immediate, year-to-year experience as a legislative body, the picture changes. What we find is an ebb and flow in the strength of party leadership, and in the capacity of Congress to enact legislation, that is very similar to the experience of more recent decades. The tension between the pressures of social and economic change and the weight of institutional precedent was as much a part of congressional life during the first three decades of the twentieth century as it is at the century's close.

The reality of rapid social change came starkly into view around 1900. The Spanish-American War of 1898 and the imperialism controversy that followed it, the great consolidation movement in big business at the turn of the century, and the assassination of McKinley and Theodore Roosevelt's assumption to the presidency gave a new tone to national politics in general and to executive-legislative relations in particular.

McKinley's political career had centered on Congress before he became president; he was the pluperfect party man and worked easily with the Republican leadership. Roosevelt (to this day the nation's youngest president) came of age politically as a civil service reformer and (briefly) governor of New York. He had very much an executive-administrative rather than a legislative perspective on the practice of government.

Far more than his predecessors, Roosevelt tried to shift political power from the Republican party, the courts, and Congress to the presidency. He thought that the power of his office enabled him "to do anything that the needs of the nation demanded. . . . Under this interpretation of executive power, I did and caused to be done many things not previously done. . . . I did not usurp power, but I did greatly broaden the use of executive power." Inevitably this view raised constitutional issues, and led to occasional turf wars with Congress.

Nevertheless it would be a mistake to equate Roosevelt's presidential leadership with that of his distant cousin Franklin D. Roosevelt in the 1930s. The most important legislation of Theodore Roosevelt's presidency—the Newlands Reclamation Act, the Elkins Act (aimed at ending discriminatory pricing by railroads), the Pure Food and Drug Act—was as much the product of Congress's responding to particular interests and to a new national, media-fostered public opinion demanding reform, as to presidential leadership. The Hepburn Act, which substantially strengthened the authority of the Interstate Commerce Commission (ICC) to regulate railroad rates, was the product of complex negotiations between Theodore Roosevelt and congressional leaders Joseph G. Cannon and Nelson W. Aldrich, in which Roosevelt abandoned any effort for tariff reform in return for an expansion of the ICC's regulatory power.

The Progressive movement of the early twentieth century—that vast and varied effort, on the local, state, and national levels for a bewildering variety of social, economic, and political reforms—created a new and more tense relationship between the branches of government. This was evident in William Howard Taft's administration. On the face of it, Taft should have gotten on far better with Congress than did Roosevelt. A contemporary said that when a course of action was proposed to Roosevelt, he asked if the law forbade it; if not, then he was ready to proceed. Taft tended to ask if the law allowed it; if so, then he was ready to ask Congress if it should be done.

But Taft's conservative Republican ideology clashed with a growing Progressivism among both Democratic and Republican members of Congress. When Taft had the temerity in 1910 to propose the Commerce Court railroad regulation bill drafted by his attorney general, instead of leaving its construction to Congress, House Democrats attacked him for unduly expanding the power of the presidency. And when Gifford Pinchot, who headed the Forest Service, accused Taft's Interior secretary, Richard Ballinger, of unduly favoring corporate interests in his management of coal and water-power sites, insurgent Republicans such as Sen. Jonathan P. Dolliver of Iowa played a key role in making this a national political issue. On issues of rising importance such as immigration restriction and prohibition, Congress marched to its own (discordant) drummers.

This is not to say that the ties of party loyalty unraveled to the degree that they have in more recent decades. Despite the number and intensity of issues arising in the Progressive period, studies of roll-call votes reveal high levels of party coherence through the period. Indeed, one study of roll-call votes from 1881 to 1923 found that strong party voting (de-

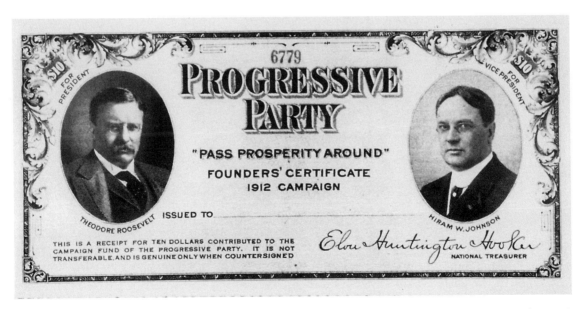

PROGRESSIVE PARTY FUND-RAISING. Paper certificate given for a ten dollar contribution to the 1912 Bull Moose campaign.   COLLECTION OF DAVID J. AND JANICE L. FRENT

fined as more than 90 percent of the members of one party voting alike) actually increased. The major trends of the time—the full emergence of the white, one-party South, the growing disaggregation of districts according to economic distinctions, such as between agricultural and industrial sectors, and along sectional and ethnocultural lines—appear to have fostered, and benefited from, the strong party leadership that characterized both houses of Congress through most of the late nineteenth and the early twentieth centuries. Long-term predominance of party leadership survived even the most important Progressive reforms of Congress as an institution: the Seventeenth Amendment providing for the direct election of senators and the revolt in the House against Speaker Cannon.

Direct Election of Senators. The movement for the popular election of senators was part of a larger impulse for direct democracy that expressed itself in the primary, initiative, referendum, and recall movements in the states and the ultimately successful state and national campaigns for woman suffrage. The Senate, chosen by state legislatures and conspicuous for a number of millionaire members sufficient to feed charges that it was a "rich man's club," was a tempting target. In Europe, too, members of upper houses came to be seen as obstacles to representative government and social change: in the British House of Lords, Lloyd George led the fight in 1911 to make that body more responsive to the popular will; in France, the Senate came under fire for being the repository of older politicians with a rural bias.

The House of Representatives, increasingly responsive to Democrats and reform-minded Republicans, voted for a direct election amendment six times between 1893 and 1911. The issue became an expression of the growing division between conservatives and liberals that would define so much of twentieth-century American political (and congressional) experience. Historian John W. Burgess commented in 1902 on the fact that the Republicans, "the once great nationalist party," generally opposed the direct election of senators while most Democrats, "members of the old States' Rights party," supported it.

In fact, popular selection of senators steadily grew: by 1912 twenty-nine states had party primaries to select senatorial candidates. Of the thirty senators whose terms expired in 1907, about a third were replaced by the primary system. State legislatures tended to adhere to these choices, to the extent that in 1908 the Republican legislature

in Oregon selected the winner of the Democratic primary.

A number of party machines resisted direct election, and some states'-rights southerners opposed federal regulation of elections (which might extend as well to black voting). But the strong public pressure for direct elections could not be ignored. Thirty state legislatures asked Congress to convene a constitutional convention for this purpose—an idea that wonderfully concentrated the minds of conservatives on the desirability of not opening such a Pandora's box. In 1911 the Senate finally went along with the House in endorsing the Seventeenth Amendment, and by 1913 enough states had ratified it to make direct election of senators the law.

One result was a temporary increase in turnover: in 1905, only thirteen of ninety members of the Senate were without previous experience; by 1914, about half were first-termers. But in the long run neither the increase of longevity in service nor the ties of party fealty were noticeably impeded by the change.

The Anti-Cannon "Revolt." The controversy over the power of House Speaker Cannon was even more intense. Cannon became Speaker in 1903, and by controlling the five-member Rules Committee he was able to determine the all-important committee assignments of the House, which he populated with like-thinking conservatives. Like Reed before him, Cannon was called a "czar," because he could count on the support of an ideologically cohesive and numerically dominant Republican House majority. Among his associates were James S. Sherman and Sereno E. Payne of New York, John Dalzell of Pennsylvania, Charles H. Grosvenor of Ohio, and Walter I. Smith of Iowa—all representatives of the core, "standpat" Republican party stretching across the upper North.

Cannon arbitrarily used his power to recognize (or not to recognize) members seeking the floor. With masterful employment of other parliamentary devices he was able to control the flow and content of the business of the House. One reflection of his authority was that the number of acts and resolutions passed by Congress declined from 6,249 in 1905–1907 to 235 in 1907–1909.

While not conspicuously issue oriented (he offered no significant piece of legislation in his forty-six-year House career), Cannon nevertheless served those conservative business interests, ensconced in his beloved Republican party, which felt most threatened by the Progressive impulse. Under his leadership the House assumed legislative supremacy over the Senate. (It was fitting that the first House office building, designed to accommodate an expanding legislative body, opened in 1909, and that congressional expenditures in these years increased more than threefold. It is appropriate, too, that the three main House office buildings bear the names of notable Speakers of the early and mid-twentieth century: Cannon, Nicholas Longworth, and Sam Rayburn.)

While in many respects he was only following in the footsteps of his powerful predecessor Reed, Cannon did so in a very different political environment. His conflict was not with an obdurate minority party seeking to block legislation, but with a majority Progressive coalition of Democrats and insurgent Republicans who wanted to end the Speaker's capacity to impede the legislative process. In 1910 that coalition, led by insurgent Republican George W. Norris of Nebraska, deprived Cannon of his power to appoint and control the Rules Committee and to keep bills from coming before the House. After the Democrats won the House in the 1910 election, they removed the Speaker from Rules and stripped him of his right to choose standing committees and recognize members on the floor.

But for all the high drama of institutional reform, the underlying problem of organizing and running a fractious legislative body of 435 members did not disappear. Indeed, as the demands of Progressive reform and then of mobilization for World War I placed increasingly substantive demands on Congress, the need for strong leadership grew.

Wilson's "Party Government." Congressional legislative activism flowered after Woodrow Wilson won the presidency in 1912. With a Democratic Congress during his first six years in office, he was able to extend the role of presidential leadership well beyond that of his predecessors. He broke new ground by personally delivering his first annual message to Congress, and even more so by proposing (and to a considerable degree having Congress enact) his extensive New Freedom legislative program.

In theory, the House Democratic caucus was supposed to pass on the party's agenda. But a different form of leadership quickly emerged. It is a telling comment on the new importance placed on the enactment of legislation that Ways and Means supplanted Rules as the most important House committee. The Democratic members of Ways and Means also served as the Committee on Committees, which had the critically important function—

previously the prerogative of the Speaker—of making committee assignments. This gave great power to Oscar W. Underwood of Alabama, the chairman of Ways and Means (and hence of the Committee on Committees) and majority floor leader.

Wilson bypassed Speaker James Beauchamp (Champ) Clark to deal primarily with Underwood and with relevant committee chairs. After Underwood went to the Senate in 1914, and was succeeded by Claude Kitchin of North Carolina, Wilson relied more on John Garner of Texas.

Republican representative Nicholas Longworth told his colleagues that they had become "a mere legislative amanuensis" of Wilson, copying down laws dictated by him. And certainly the Wilson administration, which secured such landmark measures as the Federal Bank Reserve Act, the Federal Trade Commission Act, the Clayton Antitrust Act, the Underwood tariff, the Smith-Lever agricultural aid law, the Federal Farm Loan Bank Act, the first child labor law, and the LaFollette Seamen's Act, can be said to have secured the first modern president-led legislative program.

After his 1916 reelection and U.S. entry into World War I in April 1917, Wilson's leadership and congressional responsiveness reached even greater heights. Acts were passed that gave the government unprecedented powers over agricultural, industrial, fiscal, and military mobilization, and over free speech and public opinion, often with only perfunctory congressional scrutiny.

From a broader historical perspective, however, the first third of the twentieth century was by no means a time of unalloyed growth in the power of the executive relative to Congress. None of the four constitutional amendments of the period—the Sixteenth (income tax), Seventeenth (direct election of senators), Eighteenth (prohibition), and Nineteenth (woman suffrage)—can be attributed primarily to presidential leadership. Wilson lost control of both houses of Congress after the 1918 election, and proceeded on a collision course with the Senate over the Versailles treaty and the League of Nations. The consequence was not only one of the great clashes between the executive and the legislature in U.S. history but also a substantial reassertion of congressional power after two decades of growing executive leadership.

Congress in the 1920s. Echoes of an older congressional culture became quite distinct in the wake of the Progressive period, raising some doubts as to just how thoroughgoing was the institution's "modernization." Despite its new legislative agenda during the Progressive years, Congress remained an institution strongly wedded to its traditional ways of thinking and behaving. An observer commented in 1914: "Congress is one of the few legislative bodies that attempts to do its work almost entirely without expert assistance—without the aid of parliamentary counsel, without bill drafting and revising machinery and without legislative and reference agencies." Wisconsin's state legislators had a bill-drafting bureau by 1905, but Congress's Legislative Reference Service was not established until 1914. And when a Republican congressional majority and a Republican president swept back into power from 1918 to 1920, the capacity of Congress to march to its own drummer was fully tested.

The Senate came to dominate the national political scene in the 1920s, and to make clear its independence from executive leadership in such issues as the World Court and the League of Nations, the Teapot Dome oil scandal, and the propaganda activities of large electric utilities companies. Its rejection of Charles Warren, Calvin Coolidge's nominee for attorney general, was the first refusal to confirm a cabinet choice since 1868.

After the Republicans regained control of Congress in 1919, they did little to alter its form and structure. Frederick H. Gillett of Massachusetts, the Speaker from 1919 to 1925, resembled Champ Clark in his deference to the institutional traditions of the House and the floor leadership of his party. The Republicans in 1919 created a five-man steering committee, chaired by their floor leader and excluding members of Rules and other committee chairmen. And the Committee on Committees, as had been the case under the Democrats, continued to be the chief arbiter of committee assignments.

The style of Congress during the 1920s was, arguably, closer to that of the nineteenth century than to that of the Progressive era just past. The presidents of the period—Warren G. Harding, Calvin Coolidge, Herbert Hoover—were almost as powerless to shape the course of Congress as their pre-1900 predecessors. Indeed, Harding's nomination in 1920 was very much the achievement of a handful of key Republican senators.

But there was at least one important difference. The autonomy of Congress rested not on its domination by state and local party bosses but on the dictates of seniority, now "transformed from an important consideration to a sovereign principle." This meant that while the authority of the president was weakened, so too (at least during the early

and mid 1920s) was that of the party leadership, since they could do little to award loyalty or punish disloyalty in the face of the all-powerful seniority system. Factionalism in the form of congressional voting blocs, whose leaders brokered and bargained outside of and across party lines, became a more visible element in Congress than ever before.

The first of these was the prohibition bloc, welded together before and during World War I in good part by the Anti-Saloon League and its talented chief lobbyist, Wayne Wheeler. For perhaps the first time since the Civil War, a major policy issue took form and was enacted into law outside the party system.

After World War I, a flurry of other special-interest groups left their mark on Congress. Organized veterans, reinvigorated in numbers and bolstered by a veterans' bloc in Congress, secured a pension law over Coolidge's veto. The Ku Klux Klan for a few years enlisted the sympathy and support of a number of members of Congress on issues such as immigration restriction.

The farm bloc was the most substantial example of special-interest factionalism in the Congress of the 1920s. World War I greatly stimulated an already well-developed network of farm organizations, which included the Farmers' National Council, the National Grange, the National Board of Farm Organizations, and most notably the American Farm Bureau Federation, whose Washington representative, Gary Silver, played a role as a congressional lobbyist strikingly similar to that of the Anti-Saloon League's Wheeler.

As farm prices slid, the Farm Bureau Federation pushed for a subsidy plan, which in effect would underwrite the dumping of crop surpluses in overseas markets. Its key supporters were a group of about thirty midwestern and Plains senators and almost as many representatives. What brought them together to act as an organized voting bloc was their shared sense that farm organizations, in particular the Farm Bureau Federation, were a better source of electoral support and access to their constituents than were the traditional party organizations.

Although the issues and techniques of the farm bloc later bore fruit in the agricultural support programs of the 1930s and after, the bloc failed to get its way in the 1920s, and faded in the latter part of the decade. President Coolidge twice vetoed the McNary-Haugen bills that embodied the Farm Bureau's support scheme, on the ground that this was price fixing on behalf of a special interest. And in fact the bloc was a partisan (Republican) and regional (midwestern) group. Southern farmers remained loyal to their Democratic party organizations.

By the mid 1920s the Republican party in Congress had regained a numerical and ideological predominance not seen since the turn of the century. The Republican House leadership became increasingly assertive during the mid and late 1920s, due primarily to the strength of the party's majority and the declining power of dissenting Republicans. The relative ideological conformity—at least compared to those of the Progressive era before and the New Deal era to come—among both Republicans and Democrats strengthened the authority of congressional party leaders. Nicholas Longworth, Gillett's successor as Speaker in 1925, was more forceful than any of his predecessors since Cannon. With his steering committee colleagues, floor leader John Q. Tilson of Connecticut, Rules chairman Bertrand H. Snell of New York, and James T. Begg of Ohio, Longworth sought, as Cannon had before him, to make the House a more efficient body.

But Longworth's style was collegial, not autocratic. He and his close friend Texas Democrat John Nance Garner had begun to meet for drinks—

WOMEN MEMBERS OF CONGRESS. *Left to right,* Representatives Alice M. Robertson (R-Okla.), Mae E. Nolan (R-Calif.), and Winnifred S. M. Huck (R-Ill.), on the steps of the Capitol, 1920s. They were preceded in the House by Jeannette Rankin (R-Mont.), the first woman elected to Congress. LIBRARY OF CONGRESS

"striking a blow for liberty," Garner called it—during the war. When Longworth became Speaker, they continued the practice in another Capitol hideaway, where they and a few other key members—who came to be known as the "Board of Education"—shared liquor, conviviality, and the informal working out of procedural and other House matters.

Congressional policy, like the institutional structure, also reflected the predominantly conservative political tone of the mid and late 1920s. That conservatism was expressed in the passage of a quota-based system of immigration restriction, reduced taxation, and, in particular, tariff policy.

The Fordney-McCumber (1922) and Hawley-Smoot (1931) tariffs bore witness to the power and persistence of traditional Republican protectionism. Despite the recent tendency of historians to describe politics and government in the 1920s in terms of an "associative" state, in which big business and government work hand in glove, the tariff laws of the decade were very much the product of traditional interest-group politics and a weak government. Hoover's close associate William Starr Meyers called the Fordney-McCumber Act "one of the most ill-drawn legislative acts of recent political history." And Hawley-Smoot was the product of a veritable orgy of special-interest protectionism worthy of any of its late-nineteenth-century predecessors.

On the eve of the Great Depression and the New Deal of the 1930s, it could reasonably be said that most senators and representatives had more in common with one another as members of Congress than they had differences as Republicans or Democrats. Congress, for all its institutional autonomy and potential legislative power, remained more responsive to local and particular than to national and general issues and interests. As a branch of the U.S. government, it might with equal accuracy be described either as a dog that did not bark or a dog whose bark was worse than its bite. Surely Cannon (who died in 1926) would have nodded approval of floor leader John Tilson's appraisal of the 69th Congress (1925–1927): "It will probably be said with truth that the most important work I have done during the session has been in the direction of preventing the passage of bad or unnecessary laws."

The New Deal Comes to Capitol Hill. The Great Depression led soon enough to a change of party domination over Congress. The House turned Democratic in 1930, the Senate in 1932, and with occasional exceptions they have remained so since. But for all the cataclysmic changes wrought in American politics and government by the Depression and the New Deal, the structure and culture of Congress changed little and slowly. After their 1930 victory the Democrats established a steering committee of their own. But as in the case of his friend Longworth before him, Garner, the new Speaker, relied on a small group of associates. Nor did Garner offer much congressional initiative in response to the Depression. A national sales tax (initially opposed by Garner, and ultimately rejected by the Senate) was the most conspicuous effort of the House. The major concerns of Senator Norris of Nebraska, perhaps the leading congressional liberal, were pre-Depression issues, such as an anti-injunction bill and the disposition of the government's World War I dam and nitrate plant at Muscle Shoals.

Franklin D. Roosevelt brought both an invigorated executive leadership and an abundant legislative program from 1933 on. But much of his program had to take account of congressional autonomy, strengthened now by the seniority system. Successful New Deal legislative endeavors, such as the Tennessee Valley Authority, agricultural policy, welfare and public works, and social security, of necessity showed a tender regard for congressional sensibilities. Proposals less responsive to those sensibilities, such as the Supreme Court–packing plan of 1937 and the Administrative Reorganization Act of 1937–1938, fell by the wayside. And when Roosevelt sought, in the wake of his sweeping 1936 election victory, to take on conservative Democratic congressional leaders in his 1938 primary "purge," the initiative proved one of his most notable failures.

Indeed, the rise of the New Deal was shadowed by the appearance of a comparably portentous development in U.S. politics and government: the "conservative coalition" of southern Democratic and midwestern Republican members of Congress that lasted from the late 1930s to (at least) the 1960s. Even the cataclysmic changes in American life from the 1930s to the 1960s did not in and of themselves work major changes in Congress.

At century's end, when Congress has become so staff-ridden, so culturally diverse, so free of party bonds, has that profound change occurred? Perhaps. But it would be wise not to underestimate the staying power, the persistence of forms and practices, of an institution so old and powerfully set in its ways.

[*See also* Anti-Saloon League; Eighteenth Amendment; Farm Bloc; League of Nations; New Freedom; Nineteenth Amendment; Progressive Movement; Seventeenth Amendment; Sixteenth Amendment; World War I.]

BIBLIOGRAPHY

Bensel, Richard F. *Sectionalism and American Political Development, 1880–1980.* 1984.

Brady, David W., and Phillip Althoff. "Party Voting in the United States House of Representatives: Elements of a Responsible Party System." *Journal of Politics* 36 (1974): 753–775.

Cooper, Joseph, and David W. Brady. "Institutional Context and Leadership Style: The House from Cannon to Rayburn." *American Political Science Review* 75 (1981): 411–425.

Hansen, John M. *Gaining Access: Congress and the Farm Lobby, 1918–1981.* 1991.

Peters, Ronald M., Jr. *The American Speakership.* 1990.

Polsby, Nelson. "The Institutionalization of the U.S. House of Representatives." *American Political Science Review* 62 (1968): 144–168.

MORTON KELLER

The Rise of the Modern State (1933–1964)

The Great Depression of 1929 confronted the Congress with one of the most severe challenges in its history. When the Depression hit, a Republican party committed to laissez-faire economics at home and neutrality abroad controlled the House, the Senate, and the presidency. Confronting the Republican party were congressional Democrats led largely by southerners who believed in states' rights and agrarian democracy. Nowhere in the national government in 1929 was there a strong voice and ready presence prepared to provide the nation with the assertive government it ultimately demanded as the global depression deepened.

For three years a conservative Congress and a Republican president sought to master the Depression by holding fast to free market principles. In the general and special elections of 1930 and 1931 the public swung its support toward the Democratic party, giving it a slight majority in the House of Representatives. House Democrats goaded Herbert Hoover and the Republicans for the nation's economic failures, held wide-ranging hearings, and proposed a variety of legislative proposals. But in truth neither the Democrats nor the Republicans had a coherent vision of the activist measures that might address the economic malaise. What the Democratic House did demonstrate during the 72d Congress (1931–1933), and what Democratic presidential nominee Franklin D. Roosevelt articulated in his New Deal rhetoric of 1932, was a greater willingness to question economic orthodoxy and to experiment with new approaches until a satisfactory solution was found. It was this willingness to experiment and to risk government activism that came to characterize the New Deal Democrats. The creation and consolidation of the activist state preoccupied Congress and the nation for thirty-two years, with the initial commitment to activism followed by a period of policy deadlock prolonged and complicated by World War II and the coming of the Cold War.

The New Deal Congress (1933–1936). The move to an activist American state began on Election Day, 1932. One-quarter of the American workforce was unemployed and the nation's banking system was in a downward spiral. The public responded by electing Roosevelt, with 57 percent of the popular vote, and by electing a solid Democratic Congress, with a 313 to 117 majority in the House and a 60 to 35 majority in the Senate. Unlike previous years, when most Democrats had hailed from the South, two-thirds of House Democrats and a majority of Senate Democrats were from the North. Despite the predominance of northerners in the 73d Congress, southern Democrats dominated congressional leadership and the key committees, owing to seniority. While southern Democrats were social conservatives, committed to southern segregation, both they and northern Democrats supported an activist response to the immediate economic crisis.

On Sunday, 5 March 1933, the day following his inauguration, Roosevelt called a special session of Congress to enact a plan reviving the nation's banking system. When Congress adjourned on 15 June 1933, ending Roosevelt's fabled Hundred Days, it had enacted fifteen major laws. In the popular mind, the Hundred Days was a period of unparalleled presidential initiative and congressional acquiescence in liberal policy-making. In reality, while the executive was quite active in drafting and lobbying for legislation, in virtually all of the legislative activity of the Hundred Days, according to Lawrence H. Chamberlain in *The President, Congress, and Legislation* (1946), the germ of the new laws had been supplied by the preceding Congress or in hearings and bills initiated by members during the Hundred Days. Congress continued to initiate and pass activist legislation during the regular session of 1934, much of which also reflected a congressional origin or considerable congressional influence, so that the 73d Congress (1933–1935) was one of the most active and creative in the nation's history. Out of it came the statutory foundations of the liberal activist state, including the National Industrial Recovery Act of 1933, the Agricultural Adjustment Act of 1933, the Tennessee Valley Authority Act of 1933, and the Securities Exchange Act of 1934.

In response to the legislative record of the 73d Congress and a subsequent slow but steady decline in unemployment, the nation in the 1934 elections voted to increase the congressional majority of a first-term president for only the second time in American history. Whereas the 73d Congress was noted for its response to economic emergency, a response that accepted the existing concentration of economic power, the 74th Congress (1935–1937) sought to create a more equitable distribution of social and economic power in the country. In this spirit the 74th Congress passed the Social Security Act, the National Labor Relations Act, and the Public Utility Holding Company Act. Combined with additional liberal legislation, these landmark bills demonstrated that the New Deal Congress was committed not simply to management of the Depression but to a long-term move toward activist involvement of government in the general economic life of the nation.

As the Congress and Roosevelt pushed forward on an expanded activist agenda, the nation polarized. On the right, business leaders led a conservative attack on the economic soundness, social desirability, and constitutional legitimacy of the New Deal. In Congress, the House Rules Committee, composed of business-oriented conservatives led by Chairman John J. O'Connor of New York, began in 1935 to oppose the New Deal on key rules requests, particular on the Utility Holding Act. On the left, Sen. Huey P. Long (D-La.) and others complained that the New Deal did not go far enough and thus kept the Democrats continually fearful of a radical revolt should the economy worsen. Most critically, during 1935 and 1936 the Supreme Court issued a series of decisions declaring key portions of the New Deal unconstitutional. The survival of the New Deal thus seemed dependent on changes in the Court.

Despite the gathering storm clouds, as the 1936 general elections approached the New Deal Congress could look back on a historic legacy. Congress and the presidency had laid the foundations of the modern activist state, in the process fundamentally altering the politics of Congress. First, the Democrats in Congress had created a new and more sys-

tematic conception of congressional party government. House Speaker Henry T. Rainey (D-Ill.) experimented in the 73d Congress with a party Steering Committee to direct party policy, and created a permanent whip organization composed of fifteen assistant whips. In the Senate, under the leadership of Joseph T. Robinson (D-Ark.), the Democrats created a more active and policy-oriented party caucus. And in both houses the expanded Democratic majority demonstrated a capacity to act in an innovative and rapid manner to pass party policies through committees and floor consideration. Second, the Congress embraced a close and intertwined relationship with the executive branch in the policy-making process, with the executive for the first time helping to initiate and draft a broad-scale legislative program, requesting that key legislation considered by Congress be cleared by a central agency within the executive branch, and utilizing a systematic liaison process whereby executive officials would lobby members of Congress for the passage of administration bills. Third, during Hoover's last year and then during the New Deal, Congress had responded to the management problems of a growing bureaucracy and to the complexities of the New Deal by using the legislative veto for the first time in American history.

Most critically, the New Deal Congress demonstrated the importance of the legislative body's long-term deliberative and lawmaking roles. Rather than being a rubber stamp for the executive branch, Congress played an essential part both in generating and in shaping the legislative agenda of the New Deal. The most important legacy of the New Deal Congress, then, was its demonstration of the vital role that a representative assembly can play in solving a domestic policy crisis so long as it is not obstructed by executive opposition and particularly when it is joined by a cooperative and energetic president. It was this legacy that the New Deal Democrats took to the American people in the 1936 general elections.

The Rise of the Conservative Coalition (1937–1940). Seldom has a general election produced such an extraordinary electoral mandate and contradictory policy tensions as was the case in 1936. The public reelected Roosevelt by the largest popular vote plurality in history and again increased the Democratic majority in Congress. In addition, the election produced a shift in the support base of the two parties. Whereas the New Deal victory of 1932 reflected a fairly even swing toward Democrats across all groups, the 1936 election produced a polarization of party support. The urban North and the lower classes swung behind the New Deal Democrats; the rural North and the upper classes swung for the free-market Republicans; the South continued to be committed largely to states' rights Democrats.

The end result of the election was a congressional Democratic party at considerable odds with itself. Its congressional majority consisted of northern and urban legislators committed to an expanded New Deal activism in behalf of urban social services, minorities, and labor. But its committee leadership generally consisted of rural and southern Democrats who had supported the early New Deal but now were suspicious of northern economic radicalism and concerned that a national government committed to social activism would intervene in southern segregation. Finally, the success of the New Deal in reducing the economic emergency led many commentators to believe that the time for a breathing spell in New Deal experimentation had arrived.

In response to the policy pressures of the expanding northern and urban base of the Democratic party, Roosevelt embraced an aggressive policy strategy during the second term. Most critically, he proposed a plan to Congress to pack the Supreme Court with up to five new justices. Southern Democrats in the Senate rapidly broke with the president out of fear that a New Deal Court would lead to an attack on segregation; progressives and western Democrats broke with him out of fear that Court packing would centralize too much power in the president's hands; and Republicans supported the existing Court as the best bulwark against New Deal measures. In July of 1937, this coalition of Senate forces defeated both Roosevelt's original plan and proposed compromises.

Following the Court battle, Roosevelt's effort later in 1937 to gain statutory authority to restructure the executive branch seemed additional proof of his imperious intentions, and a second battle with Congress ensued. This proposal was particularly objectionable to legislators, committees, and interest groups that had developed close political ties with existing agencies and were loath to let the president restructure government in ways that might upset "sweetheart relationships." The critical battleground became the House of Representatives, particularly the House Rules Committee. Led by Chairman O'Connor, the committee came to oppose Roosevelt's reorganization plan as an intolerable move toward dictatorship; it thus refused to grant any limit on debate over the plan, where-

upon O'Connor led the floor fight that defeated the bill.

The defeat of the Court and executive reorganization plans solidified the emergence of a conservative coalition in Congress. The dramatic conservative success in these battles was not matched during the 75th Congress (1937–1939) on votes that dealt directly with the spending programs of the New Deal. Liberal success on such votes resulted from the growth during Roosevelt's first term, and the electoral success in 1936, of a large number of organized interests served by and committed to the federal spending of the New Deal. Having tasted the fruits of expanded federal spending during the first Roosevelt term, such groups as farmers, relief workers, union members, and blacks were quick to realize the potential benefits of increased federal spending and to exert pressure upon their representatives. Thus in votes dealing not with executive power but with programmatic spending issues, the conservative coalition crumbled. In such votes, however, the New Deal coalition was increasingly dependent not on the president but on liberal pressure groups. The voting alignments within Congress thus shifted dramatically across policy areas to reflect not just the position of the legislators' parties but the economic and social interests of their constituents in particular legislation, a pattern that came to dominate congressional voting with the rise of the activist state.

Nowhere was this development clearer than in the election of 1938 and in Roosevelt's effort to purge the party of those unreliable Democrats who had opposed his Court-packing and executive reorganization plans. In response to Roosevelt's efforts, many if not most of these Democrats emphasized their loyalty to the New Deal while pointing to their independence, their dispassionate approach to issues, their freedom from "rubber stampism." The result was a resounding presidential defeat. Roosevelt was successful in purging only one objectionable Democrat, O'Connor, the chairman of the House Rules Committee.

The failure of Roosevelt's purge of conservative Democrats, combined with the large-scale Republican defeat of northern Democrats in 1938, encouraged conservatives during the 76th Congress (1939–1941) to oppose the president and challenge the New Deal itself. They succeeded in limiting Roosevelt's relief and housing programs, restraining new spending, upending tax reform, and pursuing unfriendly House investigations. On the other hand, most routine appropriations were untouched, presidential appointments were largely approved, and Congress passed a mild executive re-organization plan; under pressure from interest groups, Congress also continued its support of the Wagner and Fair Labor Standards acts. The New Deal thus survived the rise of the conservative coalition but enjoyed little new success. The pressing question was to be whether it would survive the coming of world war.

The Congressional Response to Global War (1941–1945). During the 1930s Congress had focused its energies largely on domestic problems and had sought to limit foreign entanglements that might lead it into war. The personal and financial costs associated with World War I had created a widespread desire for isolation and restraint in international relations, resulting in moves within Congress to ensure American neutrality in any future foreign war that might arise. This isolationist sentiment became law when Congress passed the Neutrality Act of 1935, which declared that whenever war broke out, the nation would embargo arms shipments to all belligerents.

Following Germany's invasion of Poland and the outbreak of a European war, Congress honored Roosevelt's request to repeal the arms embargo so that the nation might assist Great Britain and France. Despite the repeal, isolationist sentiment remained strong in Congress as the 1940 elections approached. While Roosevelt won his third term, and the Democrats maintained reduced majorities in the 77th Congress (1941–1943), isolationists continued to dominate Congress. Roosevelt convinced Congress to accept the lend-lease agreement—providing Britain with free weapons and matériel—in March of 1941. But as late as November isolationist sentiment in Congress was so strong that the House decision to repeal additional neutrality restrictions passed by only eighteen votes, 212 to 194, despite German attacks on U.S. ships and war clouds in the Pacific. All of this changed when Japan attacked Pearl Harbor on 7 December 1941.

Congress declared war on Japan on Monday, 8 December, and the nation then moved swiftly to enact the laws necessary to the prosecution of the war. These laws included the First and Second War Powers Acts, which together authorized the president to reorganize the government as he saw fit and to enforce regulations on controls over priority goals; an extension of the draft to include eighteen-year-olds; and revenue legislation to finance the war. Most controversially, Congress enacted price control legislation that led to great public dissatisfaction over the management of the war.

The public expressed dissatisfaction with the domestic impact of the early war policies in the 1942 general elections, which cut the Democrats' Senate margin by nine seats and, combined with subsequent special elections, reduced them to a two-vote margin in the House. The 1942 general election brought into office a number of conservative members of congress who then led a frontal assault on the New Deal. During the 78th Congress (1943–1945) conservatives succeeded in liquidating the Civilian Conservation Corps and the National Youth Administration, both of which had been created in the Depression to provide jobs and otherwise assist in recovery projects that the war seemed to make irrelevant. Social Security and other major foundations of the New Deal all survived, supported in particular by strong advocacy among labor groups and by effective leadership on the part of Speaker Sam Rayburn (D-Ark.), who had begun his long tenure in September of 1940, and by Senate majority leader Alban Barkley (D-Ky.).

The 78th Congress became deeply involved in the conduct of the war and in the plans for reconversion to peace after it. Perhaps the most central and delicate role of the wartime Congress was its control of purse strings and federal revenue. While stringent with domestic programs, Congress proved generous in providing money to conduct the war and showed itself willing to forgo detailed specification of appropriations, relying instead on close oversight of the use of funds.

While ultimately deferring to the executive branch on broad issues of wartime strategy and alliances, Congress provided both a forum for public discussion of these issues and oversight of administration actions. Thus perhaps the major strategic decision of the war was the relative emphasis to be placed on the Atlantic or Pacific phase of the war—whether to defeat Germany or Japan first. While Congress never voted directly on this issue, it debated it extensively in the spring of 1943. The open discussion on these issues, as well as on such subjects as the proposed invasion of Europe, was conducted for the most part in a dignified and supportive manner that served to lend an air of democratic legitimacy—if not formal congressional approval—to military strategy. The committees of Congress, particularly the Armed Services Committee, also maintained a close relationship with military leaders.

Most momentously for the structure of foreign policy in the postwar world, Congress involved itself in creating a new foreign policy for the nation. Because the coming of the war had discredited the preexisting isolationist policy, in 1943 Congress be-gan to concern itself with a new foreign policy that would outlast the war itself. In March of 1943 four senators introduced a bipartisan resolution in the Senate recommending that the United States take the initiative in creating a United Nations organiza-tion to keep the peace after the end of the war. This resolution caught the public imagination and sparked such widespread and growing support that the chairman of the Senate Foreign Relations Com-mittee, Tom T. Connally of Texas, introduced a sim-ilar resolution with the support of the Foreign Re-lations Committee; the Senate moved by a vote of 85 to 5 to adopt it. The House passed a similar res-olution, named for J. William Fulbright of Arkan-sas, by a vote of 360 to 29.

Finally, the 78th Congress was deeply involved in efforts to plan for the reconversion to peace. In 1943 each House created special reconversion com-mittees to develop appropriate plans. In 1944 Con-gress formally created the Office of War Mobili-zation and Reconversion (initially established by executive order) to act as supreme coordinator for war and peace; it also enacted laws to terminate unnecessary government contracts and to dispose of surplus war property. In addition, the 78th Con-gress gave close attention to the well-being of veter-ans by creating the GI Bill of Rights. By the end of 1944 Congress had enacted virtually all of the legis-lation that the nation would need for postwar re-conversion to occur.

The Postwar Adjustment (1945–1952). In the fall of 1944, as Allied victory in the war appeared certain, Roosevelt won his fourth term as President and the Democrats solidified their control of Con-gress. By April of 1945 Roosevelt was dead and Harry S. Truman was president; by September both Germany and Japan had surrendered and the na-tion was confronting the transition to postwar poli-tics. It had survived the bloodiest war in world his-tory with its representative institutions intact.

The ending of the war confronted Congress and the nation with staggering problems. With much of the world in shambles, the nation needed a foreign policy that would ensure its security over the com-ing decades. With the flood of military personnel back into the labor force, the nation needed domes-tic policies to help avoid a return of economic de-pression. And, following the great expansion of the power of the executive branch during the Depres-sion and world war, Congress itself needed to find ways to reassert its authority. Such reassertion was complicated by an outmoded organizational struc-

ture and by the continued effort of conservatives to use Senate filibusters and their dominance of the House Rules Committee to obstruct activist legisla-tion even when they were a minority of the Con-gress. Reassertion was further complicated by the 1946 elections, which gave control of both the House and Senate to the Republicans, so that for two critical years the nation was governed by a Democratic president confronting a Republican Congress. While the Democrats regained control of Congress in 1948, and Harry S. Truman retained the presidency, the ideological division between lib-erals and conservatives remained close until the end of Truman's presidency in 1953 and thus mag-nified the conservatives' obstructionist power.

Congress responded to the postwar challenges in three distinct ways. In the area of foreign policy, it embraced the internationalist approaches that had emerged during the war years with the Connally and Fulbright resolutions. The postwar solidifica-tion of a bipartisan internationalism began in Janu-ary of 1945, when Sen. Arthur H. Vandenberg, long a leading isolationist, announced his support of the Dumbarton Oaks treaty proposing the United Na-tions, taking with him in support of the U.N. the majority of Senate Republicans. His participation as a delegate to the San Francisco conference, to-gether with that of Senator Connally, solidified bi-partisan congressional cooperation with the exec-utive branch in the making of foreign policy. Thereafter the postwar Congress, whether Demo-cratic or Republican, joined with the president in creating a bipartisan foreign policy devoted to the re-construction of Europe through the Marshall Plan, the containment of communism through the main-tenance of a strong defense establishment at home, and a military presence throughout Europe and Asia. As Robert A. Dahl concluded in *Congress and Foreign Policy* (1950), the development of a collabo-rative spirit between Congress and the executive branch in foreign policy provided Congress with some surety that its preferences would be taken into account in policy decisions. Far from weaken-ing Congress, collaboration allowed Congress to ex-ercise influence at the level of high policy rather than of departmental details.

In the area of domestic policy, Congress took a quite different and more recalcitrant tack. Unlike the area of foreign policy, where the conservatives chose to acknowledge the lessons of the 1930s and early 1940s and embrace the internationalism sup-ported by a national majority, in domestic policy the conservatives chose obstruction, opposing both

THE "BIG FOUR." At the White House, 81st Congress, 1949. *Left to right*, Vice President Alben W. Barkley (D-Ky.), formerly Senate Democratic leader; House Speaker Sam Rayburn (D-Tex.); House majority leader John W. McCormack (D-Mass.); and Senate majority leader Scott W. Lucas (D-Ill.).   SAM RAYBURN LIBRARY

the expansionary policies of President Truman and even the more moderate compromises of congressional colleagues. Thus the passage of the Full Employment Act of 1946, designed to help ensure employment for all able-bodied Americans during the postwar years, occurred only through the crippling of many of its most vital elements. The Rules Committee in 1946 killed the Wagner-Ellender-Taft housing bill to provide for favorable Federal Housing Authority mortgage terms, research and development grants, public housing units, and urban redevelopment grants. During the Republican years of the 80th "Do-Nothing" Congress (1947–1949), the conservatives engaged in a battle of veto overrides with President Truman; he sustained sixty-nine vetoes in two years and protected the core of the New Deal while conservatives defeated him on six bills, including the Taft-Hartley Act to restrict

organized labor. And during Truman's second term, stalemate characterized the policy process, with Truman and the activist Democrats managing to win modest victories in the area of urban redevelopment, expansion of Social Security benefits, and increases in the minimum wage. These victories owed a special debt to the skillful House leadership of Sam Rayburn, who, despite the existence of a factionalized House, was increasingly seen as the most powerful and effective Speaker since Henry Clay.

Finally, throughout these years Congress sought to reorganize itself in ways designed to increase its policy-making capacities and assert its constitutional powers. A widespread belief existed within Congress that the growth in executive power during the Depression and World War II resulted in part from organizational arrangements and rules in

Congress that were inadequate to the demands of activist government planning. To address such problems, the 79th Congress (1945–1947) passed the Legislative Reorganization Act (LRA) of 1946, designed, among other things, to modernize the committee system of Congress by reducing the number of committees, clarifying their jurisdictions, and giving them, as well as individual members, more adequate staff allotments. In 1949, the House sought to address the problems with the Rules Committee by passing the Twenty-one Day Rule, which allowed committee legislation to bypass Rules under specified conditions. This rule was used during the 81st Congress (1949–1951) to gain the passage of such laws as statehood for Alaska and Hawaii but was revoked after the 1950 elections, when conservatives gained additional seats in the House. Likewise during 1949, Senate reforms sought to reduce the obstructive power of filibuster, in order to pass Truman's civil rights program over southern objections, by extending the cloture rule (Rule XXII) to cover all business with the exception of debate on Senate rules. The Senate adopted this change, but in exchange conservatives forced the Senate to accept a new rule that required the vote of two-thirds of the entire Senate membership, instead of two-thirds of those present and voting, in order to invoke cloture.

In the end, these reforms failed to resolve the organizational problems of Congress, but did set the reform agenda that Congress would confront over the next several decades. In addition, during the 80th Congress the members had passed and sent to the states for ultimate ratification the Twenty-second Amendment to the Constitution, which limited future presidents to two terms. This amendment was a Republican response to the four-term presidency of Franklin D. Roosevelt, a precedent that they feared future Democratic presidents would use to expand liberal dominance of national government. Ironically, the Republicans in 1952 would elect a president, Dwight D. Eisenhower, who proved as popular as Roosevelt and could have been a candidate for third-term consideration without the amendment.

The Survival of the New Deal Agenda (1953–1960). In the general election of 1952, the nation turned to Republican government after two decades of Democratic dominance, electing Eisenhower president in a landslide and giving him a Republican Congress. Since the late 1930s Republicans had vowed to cut back or destroy the New Deal, whose policies they increasingly compared to the socialist programs of the nation's Cold War ad-

versary, the Soviet Union. For eight years they would control the presidency and exercise considerable influence in Congress, first as the majority party and, following the 1954 election, which the Democrats won, in coalition with southern Democrats. These eight years, perhaps the most critical years for the survival of the New Deal programs following Roosevelt's death, were as disappointing to conservatives who dreamed of dismantling Roosevelt's legacy as were the Truman years to those liberals who dreamed of expanding state activism.

The 83d Congress (1953–1955) continued the bipartisan foreign policy of the Truman years and provided grudging but continuous funding for New Deal programs. In foreign policy the Congress supported Eisenhower's effort to end the Korean War and defeated—by one vote—the Bricker amendment to restrict the treaty-making power of the presidency. In domestic policy, rather than mounting a strong conservative program replacing Social Security, the minimum wage, and other liberal policies, the Republicans concentrated on modest departmental appropriations, on committee investigations by Sen. Joseph R. McCarthy (D-Wis.) and others exploring communist influence in government, and on approving a tax reduction bill favoring the wealthy. Once in power, the Republicans found the broad public sentiment for such New Deal programs as Social Security and agricultural price supports, and lobby pressure in their behalf, too strong to ignore, particularly in light of Eisenhower's passive approach to domestic policy-making. By accepting such programs, the Republicans implicitly validated the activist state and shifted the long-term domestic debate toward the character and funding of the programs, and to the expansion of state activism into new areas that might not so easily benefit from established interest group support.

In 1954 the public returned control of the House and Senate to the Democrats and thereby, with Eisenhower's reelection in 1956, set in motion a six-year period of divided party government. Again the conservative southern Democrats dominated the committee leadership positions within Congress, with moderate and liberal Democrats constituting the party's congressional majority. In the middle between these groups, serving as the House and Senate party leaders, were two Texas Democrats, Speaker Rayburn and Majority Leader Lyndon B. Johnson, who saw the survival and enhancement of the New Deal agenda as their party's chief goal. Rayburn and Johnson saw themselves not as programmatic innovators nor as organizational reformers but as brokerage politicians who, through accommodation and compromise, would ensure the passage of the party's domestic legislation as produced by the committees of Congress, which, following the 1946 LRA, had developed very distinctive legislative cultures that heavily shaped the decision-making process in different policy areas. Their great talents as a congressional team derived from their personal friendship, their understanding of the norms and folkways of Congress, their working relationship with key lobby groups, and their persuasive powers with fellow members. Their legislative record proved to be a modest but significant one, including the creation of the national interstate highway system, the National Defense Education Act, the continued protection and increased funding of such New Deal programs as Social Security and the minimum wage, and the passage of the Civil Rights Act of 1957, the first such act in eighty years. In foreign affairs they and the Democratic Congress continued bipartisan congressional support for the president.

Throughout the Rayburn-Johnson years, majority action on domestic legislation was hampered both by the threat and occasional use of the presidential veto and by the power of the conservative coalition in Congress. Rayburn and Johnson sought to deflect presidential opposition through consultation and compromise with Eisenhower, a strategy they followed successfully until the 1958 elections gave the Democrats a larger liberal majority; thereafter Rayburn and Johnson became more assertive and independent of the president and focused on shaping a Democratic record for the 1960 elections. Their overall success in working with the president was not matched, however, by their mastery of the congressional conservatives. Consistently throughout these years, conservatives used their control of the Rules Committee to dominate the House while in the Senate they resorted to the filibuster to obstruct legislation. Rayburn hesitated to reinstitute the Twenty-one Day Rule or to expand the Rules Committee, fearing a southern backlash that might splinter the party, and so the Rules Committee continued to block housing, civil rights, labor, medical care for the aged, and other social welfare legislation even during the 86th Congress (1959–1961), when Democrats had their largest liberal majority since 1936. Johnson, less tied to tradition than Rayburn and also committed to creating a more liberal image for his own presidential race in 1960, pushed through a modest revision of Rule XXII in 1959 allowing two-thirds of those present and voting to invoke cloture.

Despite the inability to limit the power of the obstructionists or to ensure majority control of congressional policy-making, the maintenance of a Democratic majority in the mid and late 1950s proved critical to the survival and eventual expansion of New Deal programs. First, in maintaining control of the congressional committees during the mid and late 1950s, the Democrats solidified their relationship with key liberal lobby groups and maintained leverage on executive agencies to respond to these groups; the Democrats thus were able to solidify a "subgovernment" politics in which executive agencies, interest groups, and congressional committees sustained the activist state by close and mutually beneficial cooperation not only in the passing of legislation but in the implementation and oversight of programs. Second, Democratic control of the committees allowed activist legislators to debate and draft a broad range of legislation that, while impossible to enact over conservative obstruction and Eisenhower's veto, would form the legislative agenda for the Democrats in the 1960s. Third, the struggle of the Democratic leadership with organizational obstruction, particularly in the late 1950s, when the moderates and liberals had an increased party majority, served to fuel demands for institutional reform; these calls gave rise to a growing popular awareness of organizational problems in Congress and to the creation of the Democratic Study Group in 1958, a subcaucus of liberal Democrats committed to reform. Finally, though their legislative success may have seemed limited in the late 1950s, the Democrats created an image of activism and policy inclusiveness; this image was to appeal to the nation in the 1960 general election and lead to a return to united Democratic control of government with the election of President John F. Kennedy.

The Activist Resurgence (1961–1964). Running on the promise to "get the country moving again," Senator Kennedy (D-Mass.) won the White House in November of 1960 by a narrow margin while Democrats retained control of the House and Senate with reduced majorities. After eight years of a Republican president, and after two decades of effort by conservatives to weaken the New Deal, Democratic activists were anxious to address the policy problems—in such areas as poverty and unemployment, urban decay, civil rights, medical care, and education—that they believed had festered and grown during the fourteen years of policy deadlock. They faced a difficult task. The numerical division in

Congress between the activists and the conservative coalition was virtually even. Conservatives continued to compare an activist liberal state to the socialized planning of the Soviet Union, thereby creating an explosive campaign issue against moderates who supported liberal legislation. The Rayburn-Johnson leadership team was no longer as potent due to Johnson's selection as vice president and Rayburn's failing health. And in seeking legislative victory the activists still faced conservative control of important committee positions within the Congress, particularly the House Rules Committee.

Following the election Kennedy and the Democratic leaders decided that success in an activist agenda required reform of the House Rules Committee. Based on Rayburn's recommendation, they decided that the most practical reform was to expand the Rules Committee from twelve to fifteen members, a strategy that would provide the leadership a shaky 8 to 7 margin on most bills. The fight over the Rules Committee expansion occurred in January of 1961, with the House voting for expansion by a margin of 217 to 212. The majority of southern Democrats united with Republicans to oppose the expansion, so that victory required the solid support of northern Democrats as well as loyal southerners. The passage of the expansion required not only Rayburn's complete effort, one of the last battles of his extraordinary career before his death a year later, but also the deep involvement of the new president and his key lieutenants, elaborate vote-gathering efforts by the House Democratic whip system, and the supplemental support of the Democratic Study Group.

The expansion of the Rules Committee, of course, did nothing to lessen the close margin between conservatives and liberals in the 87th Congress (1961–1962), a margin that remained close after the 1962 elections again produced a slightly reduced Democratic majority in Congress. As a result, party leaders and the president worked closely with the legislative committees to pass party legislation. In the House, Speaker John W. McCormack (D-Mass.), who succeeded Rayburn upon his death, stressed the development of unanimity among the Democrats in a standing committee before bringing a major bill to a floor vote. In the Senate, Mike Mansfield (D.-Mont.), the majority leader who succeeded Johnson, attempted to gain committee unanimity across Democrat and Republican lines. The stress on some form of committee unanimity was an attempt to use the politics of committee reciprocity as a way of overcoming the narrow ideological divisions that existed in both houses. The leaders argued that the members of all congressional committees should support one another's legislation so long as each committee reported its legislation by a near-unanimous vote and thus certified the legislation as gaining the broad approval of committee members who had most closely studied the legislation. This strategy allowed the Congress to pass legislation despite conservatives' attacks on the "socialist" character of activist legislation and the consequent electoral fears of many members. The House leaders also worked extensively with the party whip system and lobby groups to persuade members to support party legislation. In addition, party leaders in both houses enjoyed a close relationship with the White House liaison operation that helped bring the president's influence to bear in close congressional votes.

By November of 1963 Kennedy and his activist allies in Congress, building on the Democratic agenda that had emerged from the 86th Congress and adding to it some additional innovations, had amassed a creditable legislative record. In the area of foreign policy the Congress enacted the Peace Corps, passed the Trade Expansion Act, created the Arms Control and Disarmament Agency, and embraced the Alliance for Progress. In the area of domestic policy, Congress had passed the Area Redevelopment Act, a job retraining program, a rural and industrial development plan, an expansion of Social Security, and an increase in the minimum wage. Pending before the 88th Congress (1963–1965) were the most innovative tax cut in the nation's history and the most ambitious civil rights bill of the twentieth century; innovative domestic programs for youth employment, higher education, elementary and secondary school aid, and Medicare; a foreign aid bill; and a limited test ban treaty. It is debatable whether Congress and President Kennedy together would have succeeded in passing the bulk of this legislative agenda prior to the 1964 elections, but they clearly were moving in a committed manner to reinvigorate the liberal agenda inherited from the New Deal and to strengthen the nation's commitment to an activist state.

President Kennedy's assassination on 22 November 1963, and the elevation of Vice President Johnson to the presidency, dramatically altered policy deliberations in Congress. Utilizing the sense of national crisis that followed Kennedy's assassination, and that was magnified by the social and civil rights ferment of the early 1960s, Johnson threw the full force of his considerable political talents into passage of the activist program to honor the president's memory. In this effort Johnson benefited from his long experience in both the House and Senate and from a skillful White House liaison team. Johnson made civil rights his most important legislative goal, seeking to reassure the nation that he as a southerner would not fail to address the problem that had become the nation's most explosive domestic issue. Congress responded by enacting a series of liberal programs—including the Civil Rights Act of 1964, the Tax Reduction Act of 1964, and the Economic Opportunity Act of 1964 (which created the Job Corps and Vista)—that renewed the activist vision of the early New Deal. Johnson proved less successful in gaining the enactment of other activist liberal legislation, notably including Medicare, consumer protection, and education legislation; these items became central planks in the Democratic party platform as Johnson sought election to the presidency in his own right in 1964.

The Democratic victory of 1964 completed the resurgence of liberal activists to power and validated not only the activist state begun by Franklin Roosevelt and the New Deal Congress but legitimized the move toward racial equality. For almost thirty years congressional liberals had sought to break the power of conservatives who united in opposition to the New Deal during Roosevelt's second term and who thereafter used committee power and the Senate filibuster to obstruct majority consideration of activist legislation. Activists had succeeded during this time in protecting much of the New Deal from dismantlement by drawing on the legislative skills of congressional party leaders and on support from powerful lobby groups that pressured conservatives into funding key programs such as Social Security and the minimum wage. But only with the reform of the Rules Committee in 1961, the assassination of President Kennedy, and the subsequent landslide victory of Johnson were activist Democrats to regain the firm control of Congress that Roosevelt and New Deal Democrats enjoyed during his first term in office. The thirty-two years from the initial New Deal Congress to the activist resurgence of the 1960s thus demonstrated the great creative capacity of Congress to respond to deep domestic crises and war, its susceptibility to obstruction and policy deadlock during periods of ideological and partisan division in the government, its ability to sustain the existing programs of an activist state when supported by strong group interests even in the face of institutional gridlock, and its long-term responsiveness to popular demand for policy activism in the midst of renewed domestic crisis and united government.

[*See also* Cold War; Great Society; Korean War; New Deal; Peace Corps; Twenty-second Amendment; Twenty-third Amendment; World War II.]

BIBLIOGRAPHY

Bailey, Stephen K. *Congress Makes a Law: The Story behind the Employment Act of 1946.* 1950.

Dodd, Lawrence C., and Richard L. Schott. *Congress and the Administrative State.* 1979.

Fenno, Richard F., Jr. *The Power of the Purse.* 1966.

Hardeman, D. B., and Donald C. Bacon. *Rayburn: A Biography.* 1987.

Huitt, Ralph K., and Robert L. Peabody. *Congress: Two Decades of Analysis.* 1969.

Matthews, Donald R. *U.S. Senators and Their World.* 1960.

Mayhew, David R. *Party Loyalty among Congressmen.* 1966.

Patterson, James F. *Congressional Conservatism and the New Deal.* 1967.

Ripley, Randall. *Majority Leadership in Congress.* 1969.

Schlesinger, Arthur M., Jr. *The Age of Roosevelt.* 3 vols. 1957–1960.

Sundquist, James L. *Politics and Policy.* 1968.

Young, Roland. *Congressional Politics in the Second World War.* 1956.

LAWRENCE C. DODD

Congress Today and Tomorrow

When President John F. Kennedy was struck down by an assassin's bullet on that bright Friday afternoon of 22 November 1963, Congress and the nation were already on the threshold of a new era of politics and policy. The turbulent events that followed, however, could not have been predicted. Kennedy's successor, Lyndon B. Johnson, once the Senate's most powerful and feared floor leader, displayed in the White House a mastery of legislative politics unequaled by any president before or since. Congress not only approved Kennedy's unfinished New Frontier agenda but then entered new realms encompassed by Johnson's Great Society. Long-festering social and racial tensions broke into open violence. The escalating Vietnam War (1964–1975) polarized the nation. On Capitol Hill, structural and procedural changes were so rapid and numerous that scholars refer to the years 1965 to 1974 as the reform era.

The Kennedy assassination thus provides a useful landmark in the history of Congress. To understand

Congress in the years following that event, it is important to recall the character of the older Congress that it replaced.

The Era of the Barons

Since Franklin D. Roosevelt's second term, Congress had been dominated by a conservative coalition of southern Democrats and old guard Republicans. Congressional leaders overrepresented safe one-party regions (the Democratic rural South and Republican rural areas elsewhere). Their ranks swollen by malapportioned House districts and their power magnified by the seniority system, these conservatives constricted the domestic policy-making agenda, especially with regard to civil rights, health care, and social welfare legislation. Even into the Kennedy years, the conservative-dominated Congress stood in the way of activist presidents and their electoral constituencies. In his 1963 book *The Deadlock of Democracy,* political scientist James MacGregor Burns described American politics as a four-party system, with Democrats and Republicans each divided into a progressive, urban-centered, presidential wing and an obstructionist, rural, congressional oligarchy.

The two chambers were ruled by a coterie of senior committee chairmen, known as the barons or the old bulls. When Democrats held the majority (as they did in all but two congresses), these leaders spoke with a thick southern accent. In the House, there was crotchety Clarence Cannon (D-Mo.) of Appropriations, avuncular "Uncle" Carl Vinson (D-Ga.) of Armed Services, courtly but wily "Judge" Howard W. Smith (D-Va.) of Rules, and Wilbur D. Mills (D-Ark.) of Ways and Means, perhaps the most successful of the breed. Although southerners composed no more than 40 percent of the House during this period, they chaired 60 to 70 percent of the committees.

The Senate, which journalist William S. White described in 1956 as "the South's unending revenge upon the North for Gettysburg," was little different. The ruling elite of that chamber (sometimes called the "inner club") counted among its charter members Virginia's Harry Flood Byrd, Sr. (Finance), Arizona's Carl Hayden (Appropriations), Mississippi's James O. Eastland (Judiciary), and the chief southern strategist, Georgia's Richard B. Russell (Armed Services). In his study of the Senate, Donald R. Matthews (1960) found that "the seniority system's bias against urban liberals of both parties tends to be self-perpetuating." If they failed to smother a progressive bill in committee, conservatives could

talk it to death on the floor. The right to filibuster allowed the southern diehards to kill anti–poll tax, anti-lynching, and other civil rights bills.

The legislative workload throughout the post–World War II years reflected stable yet growing demands for legislative action (see figure 1). A large proportion of the bills and resolutions were routine: immigration, land claims, and private legislation. Eventually these matters were delegated in whole or in part to the executive branch. Internally, the key committees (the taxing and spending panels, plus Rules in the House) were cohesive groups—"corporate," Richard F. Fenno, Jr. (1973) called them—boasting firm leadership and rigorous internal norms of behavior. They kept a tight lid on new legislation, especially in fiscal affairs. The appropriations committees stood guard over the U.S. Treasury, holding in check the more rapacious inclinations of the program-oriented authorizing panels.

But social change eventually overran this tight system. The unprecedented post–World War II prosperity, coupled with dramatic demographic shifts—migration from farms to cities and suburbs, and the rise of the baby boomers, the children of the high-birthrate years between 1946 and 1964—fueled demands for new and expanded government services. Building slowly but steadily in the 1950s, these demands were voiced in the 1960s and 1970s by a series of mass movements: civil rights, feminism, consumerism, environmentalism, and opposition to the Vietnam War. Their demands were amplified by the era's rapid structural changes: reapportionment, widened citizen participation, social unrest, economic dislocations, and technological innovations in transportation and communications.

Urban and suburban progressives of both parties pressed for new laws dealing with race relations, schools, joblessness, welfare, transportation, and other issues. Activist senators and representatives championed their cause. At the core of the Senate's activist bloc were Minnesota's Hubert H. Humphrey, Illinois's Paul H. Douglas, Montana's James E. Murray, Pennsylvania's Joseph S. Clark, and Michigan's Patrick V. McNamara. All were Democrats; only one of them, Humphrey, could be considered a member of the Senate's inner circle, or "club." House activists, who in 1959 formed the Democratic Study Group (DSG), included Eugene J. McCarthy (Minn.) John A. Blatnik (Minn.), Chet Holifield (Calif.), Lee Metcalf (Mont.), and Frank Thompson, Jr. (N.J.). Waging guerrilla warfare on the barons, these mem-

Figure 1
U.S. Congress, Total Measures Introduced (80th Congress to 102d Congress)

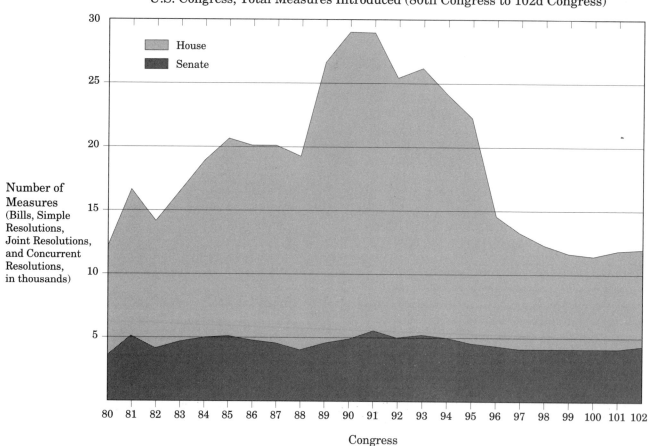

SOURCE: Carol Hardy-Vincent and Robert Moon, *Indicators of House of Representatives Workload and Activity* (Congressional Research Service, 13 April 1993), p. 9.

bers introduced bills, held hearings, pressed for floor action, and forged alliances with elements of the Democratic party's presidential wing (organized labor, for example). This process was described as "block-by-block building under the leadership of those making up the activist triangle in the Senate, the House, and the Democratic Advisory Council [a national party group]" (Sundquist, 1968, p. 415). Although Democrats oversaw most of the policy incubation, progressive Republicans such as Senators Jacob K. Javits (N.Y.) and Hugh Scott (Pa.) also played a role.

Thus the legislative groundwork for change had been laid by the time Kennedy entered the White House in 1961. But votes still were lacking to pass the bulk of the progressive agenda. Urban and suburban voters finally won parity in 1964, when the Supreme Court enunciated the "one person, one vote" principle to govern the drawing of district lines for state legislatures (*Reynolds v. Sims*, 1964) and for the House of Representatives (*Wesberry v. Sanders*, 1964). Even as President Kennedy traveled to Dallas, the old rural- and southern-dominated order was under siege.

Opening the Legislative Floodgates (1965–1978)

Political upheavals and structural reforms were thus conjoined with an ambitious and expansionary workload almost unique in the history of Congress. Presidential leadership added a crucial ingredient. It was the era of programmatic presidential themes: Kennedy's New Frontier, Johnson's Great Society, and Richard M. Nixon's New American Revolution. Although presidential leadership added a crucial ingredient, the legislative foundations had already been laid in the 1950s and early 1960s by activist senators and representatives and their allies outside of government.

The decade following 1964 brought an outpouring of congressional activity that had not been seen since the early New Deal days of the 1930s. There were landmark enactments in civil rights, education, medical insurance, employment and training, science and space, consumer protection, and the environment. Five new cabinet departments were created: Education; Energy; Health and Human Services; Housing and Urban Development; and Transportation. Four constitutional amendments were sent to the states to be ratified: the Twenty-fourth, Twenty-fifth, and Twenty-sixth Amendments, and the so-called Equal (Women's) Rights Amendment, which fell short of ratification. Legislative activity soared in those years by whatever measure one chooses to apply—bills introduced, hearings,

reports, hours in session, floor amendments, recorded floor votes, and measures passed. The processing of freestanding bills and resolutions became the centerpiece of individual, committee, and subcommittee work.

The reformist era did not end with President Johnson's retirement in 1969. To be sure, Johnson's success rate on Capitol Hill has not since been matched (see figure 2). Yet although his successors (Nixon, Gerald R. Ford, Jr., and Jimmy Carter in his first two years) pushed through fewer of their own priority bills, they could not stem the tide of new legislation flowing from Capitol Hill. One need only recount the legislative achievements of the Nixon years to show that the mutual hostility between the Republican president and the Democratic Congress did not stand in the way of significant enactments. The laws included a comprehensive tax code revision, the National Environmental Poli-

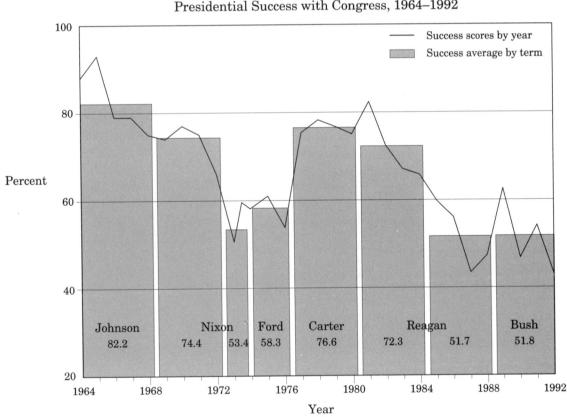

Figure 2
Presidential Success with Congress, 1964–1992

Note: "Presidential success" is a measure of how often the president won his way on roll-call votes on which he took a clear position.

SOURCE: *Congressional Quarterly Weekly Report*, 19 December 1992, pp. 3841–3843, 3896.

LET'S PUT ROBERT KENNEDY TO WORK FOR NEW YORK

CAMPAIGN POSTER. For Attorney General Robert F. Kennedy's (D-N.Y.) 1964 race for the Senate. Kennedy's brief Senate career (1965–1968) was propelled by his concern for civil rights issues, his opposition to President Lyndon B. Johnson's foreign policy, and the growing anti-war movement.

COLLECTION OF DAVID J. AND JANICE L. FRENT

cy Act of 1969, major air and water pollution control measures, endangered species protection, a comprehensive organized crime bill, postal reorganization, urban mass transit and rail reorganization plans, the Occupational Safety and Health Act of 1970 (OSHA), the Consumer Product Safety Act, the Comprehensive Employment and Training Act (CETA), the Federal Election Campaign Act of 1971, coastal zone management, the trans-Alaska pipeline, the War Powers Resolution of 1973 (passed over Nixon's veto), and the Congressional Budget and Impoundment Control Act of 1974—not to mention two constitutional amendments, the Twenty-sixth (eighteen-year-old vote) and the unratified Equal Rights Amendment.

The legislative juggernaut continued for at least two reasons. First, President Nixon saw his primary mission in foreign affairs and diplomacy, leaving his aides in the various domestic departments free to reach accommodations as best they could with Capitol Hill majorities. Second, the Nixon and Ford Congresses attempted extremely high numbers of veto overrides. Nixon may be remembered as a conservative president, but the legislative record of Congress during his administration was expansive and liberal.

Two defining events of this era were the Vietnam War (1964–1975) and the so-called Watergate affair (1972–1974). At the time both appeared to verify the hegemony of the "imperial presidency" in military and security affairs. Yet both ultimately enfeebled the presidency and had profound effects upon subsequent executive-legislative relations.

The Vietnam War. U.S. embroilment in an undeclared war in Southeast Asia began in 1959, when a handful of advisers were sent to help the South Vietnamese government resist attacks from pro-Communist North Vietnam. Lawmakers indulged the limited but mounting involvement, and in 1964 President Johnson persuaded Congress to approve the Gulf of Tonkin Resolution, affirming support for "all necessary measures to repel any armed attack against the forces of the U.S. . . . to prevent further aggression . . . and assist [any Southeast Asian country bound to us by a mutual security treaty]." This vague grant of authority passed the House 414 to 0 and the Senate 88 to 2. Over the following year Johnson escalated the Vietnam effort without consulting further with Congress; fortified by military stockpiles, the president could delay until spring 1966 before requesting funds specifically for the war. By that time Congress was in no position to halt the effort. Vietnam was a major war by any standard, no matter how hard Johnson and later Nixon tried to distance it from the American people. At the height of the war some 600,000 U.S. troops were engaged; 58,000 of them gave their lives.

Congress initially saw Vietnam as a vital outpost in the global war against communism. Sen. Frank J. Lausche (D-Ohio) called southeast Asia "our first line of defense; when an enemy attacks us there, he is, in principle, attacking us on our native land." But as troops and equipment poured into Vietnam, it became apparent that much more would be needed to resolve what was more a civil strife than a global confrontation. In 1966 Sen. J. William Fulbright's Foreign Relations Committee launched hearings that raised doubts about the war; by 1968 a significant portion of the electorate had lost its appetite for the endeavor. In March of that year, Johnson did so poorly in the New Hampshire presidential primary that he withdrew from the presidential race, becoming in effect a civilian casualty of the war. Riots and protests erupted as the war tore apart the nation's political fabric.

Backlash over Vietnam spawned the War Powers Resolution, enacted in 1973 over President Nixon's veto. (Once enacted, a joint resolution has the same legal standing as a statute derived from a bill.) The resolution provides that presidents must inform Congress promptly when they commit U.S. troops to hostile situations abroad. If Congress does not approve of the action within sixty to ninety days, the troops must be withdrawn. The resolution was an awkward compromise between executive and legislative authority; presidents and their advisers opposed any incursion of the commander in chief's prerogatives and resisted being tied down to a timetable of engagement. Nevertheless, through the end of 1992 presidents had reported to Congress on twenty-five occasions that troops had been deployed on foreign soil. (In other cases the military action was brief and no report was filed; in still others, the White House claimed that reports were not required because no hostilities were expected.) The War Powers Resolution remained controversial throughout the Cold War years, and in the 1990s its critics questioned its application to international peacekeeping efforts. But the resolution was explicitly invoked when Congress voted in January 1991 to authorize the Persian Gulf War.

The Watergate Affair. Presidential hubris surely lay behind the second great event of the period. In the summer of 1972 operatives connected with President Nixon's reelection campaign were caught breaking into the offices of the Democratic National Committee (then housed in a building in the Watergate complex). The resulting coverup, which eventually implicated the president himself, played itself out in the national press and on Capitol Hill over the next two years.

As new revelations surfaced, the Senate in February 1973 voted to investigate Watergate and other 1972 campaign abuses. The special committee's televised hearings, beginning in May 1973, rivaled the most colorful congressional inquiries of past eras. The panel's chair was Democrat Samuel J. Ervin, Jr., of North Carolina, a wily and pithy expert in constitutional law who proved more than a match for the collection of White House functionaries and petty criminals who paraded before the cameras. During one hearing it was revealed that the White House had installed a taping system to record Oval Office conversations. A bitter struggle ensued for control of the tapes: Nixon initially refused to release them, then published edited summaries, and finally was compelled by the Supreme Court (in *United States v. Nixon,* 1974) to deliver them all to the courts and Congress. By this time the House Judiciary Committee was debating impeachment, and on 27 July 1974 it approved three articles of impeachment. But before the articles could be presented to the full House, the tapes provided the smoking gun: proof that Nixon had approved the coverup from the outset. His congressional support evaporated; when he resigned as president on 9 August, he cited the absence of a "strong enough political base in Congress to justify continuing."

Watergate caused a major realignment in presidential-congressional relations. As Nixon's public standing eroded during 1973–1974, Congress's own popularity rose (see figure 3). Congressional Democrats grew bolder in challenging the administration's positions and in overriding vetoes (one such override was the War Powers Resolution). Subsequent presidents faced a reinvigorated, aggressive Congress insistent upon laying down restrictions on the executive branch. New ethics codes and campaign finance laws were enacted. Adversarial reporters pursued investigative journalism of the type that had exposed the Watergate story. The general public seemed to sustain a new level of cynicism toward politics and politicians.

Reform-Era Changes on Capitol Hill

The turbulent politics of the 1960s—the civil rights movement, political riots and assassinations, the Vietnam War, the resultant peace movement, and other citizen crusades—yielded not only new voting patterns and cleavages on Capitol Hill but also pressures for structural and procedural changes. "The political upheavals of the 1960s led to a new political agenda in the Congress," according to Barbara Sinclair, "and . . . the upheavals, combined with the new agenda, increased the saliency of politics to the mass electorate" (in Leroy N. Rieselbach, ed., *The Congressional System: Notes and Readings,* 2d ed., 1979, p. 334).

The reform politics of the 1960s and 1970s coincided with an era of Democratic party dominance on Capitol Hill. During those two decades, the Democrats maintained a 23-seat median advantage over

Figure 3
Public Assessments of Congress and Individual Representatives, 1963–1993

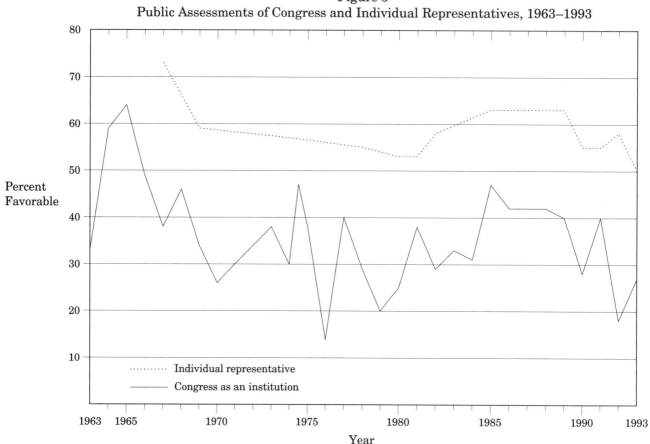

Note: The Gallup Organization's questions are "Do you approve of the way the U.S. Congress is handling its job? Do you approve or disapprove of the way the representative from your own congressional district is handling his/her job?" The Harris Survey's questions are: "How would you rate the job done this past year by [Congress][your member of Congress]—excellent, pretty good, only fair, or poor?" Responses are dichotomized as favorable ("excellent," "pretty good") or unfavorable ("only fair," "poor"). Graph lines indicate respondents approving or favorable of congressional performance.

SOURCES: Author's interpolations of surveys of the Gallup Organization and the Harris Survey for the years 1974–1992, as summarized in "Public Opinion and Demographic Report," *The American Enterprise* 3 (November/December 1992): 86–87. Data for 1993 are from Charles E. Cook, "Congress Rebounds in Polls after Years of Public Disregard," *Roll Call*, 4 February 1993, p. 8.

Republicans in the Senate and nearly a 100-seat advantage in the House. In the Great Society 89th Congress (1965–1967), the Democrats' margins in the two chambers were 36 and 155 seats, respectively. Later, the post-Watergate Democratic landslide of 1974 enabled liberal majorities on Capitol Hill to initiate many important structural changes. The cohesiveness of the Democrats was strengthened as old-time southern segregationists were replaced by New South moderates.

As barriers to new legislation were lowered, the cozy domains of the barons were pulled apart by what journalist Hedrick Smith (1988) called a "power earthquake." As with all historical periods, the boundaries of the reform era are imprecise. The

process of change began as early as the 1958 elections, which enlarged the Democrats' ranks by 16 senators and 51 representatives, many of them programmatic liberals. Both chambers felt an immediate impact. Senate majority leader Johnson's heavyhanded rule lightened perceptibly; in the House, liberal activists formally launched the Democratic Study Group (DSG), which spearheaded efforts for procedural reforms in the 1960s and 1970s. Two years later Johnson relinquished the Senate majority leadership to a liberal, Mike Mansfield (D-Mont.), whose mild-mannered, permissive style encouraged more and more senators, including newcomers, to take an active part in key decisions. Also in 1961, House Speaker Sam Rayburn won a closely fought contest to enlarge the Rules Committee in order to break the conservatives' hold on that powerful panel.

Assault on the Barons. Reform politics in the 1960s and early 1970s centered on efforts to give wider circles of legislators a "piece of the action." Little by little, reformers chipped away at the senior leaders' power. The attack on seniority came on several fronts. In several committees, revolts against arbitrary chairmen resulted in new committee rules limiting the chairman's authority. Meanwhile, the Democratic caucus reasserted its right to approve all committee assignments, including chairmanships. In 1974 three chairmen were actually denied renomination in the caucus. Although relatively few chairmen lost their posts after that, all of them were put on notice that erratic or arbitrary behavior could cost them support within the caucus. Meanwhile, subcommittees grew in number and autonomy, thus enlarging the number of leadership posts and further checking the committee chairmen's powers. Democratic caucus actions in 1971 and 1973 (the latter called the "subcommittee bill of rights") strengthened subcommittees by guaranteeing them staffs, fixed jurisdictions, and procedural safeguards.

The Senate's factional disputes were milder because committee leaders never monopolized business as much as they did in the House. Junior senators were more likely to chair subcommittees; all senators could employ floor tactics to influence matters outside their committee assignments. Yet junior senators agitated for bigger staffs and procedural benefits, which were granted in a series of chamber actions.

Capitol Hill staffs grew dramatically in the 1970s—seemingly a permanent legacy of the reform era, although staffing levels have remained virtually unchanged since 1980. Staffs were increased not only to help members cope with legislative and constituency demands but also to equalize members' leverage on legislation and influence within the chamber. Professional assistance was made available to all members, not just a few senior committee leaders. "House committee staffs were two and three-quarters times as large in 1979 as they were in 1970, and Senate committee staffs doubled over the same period" (Norman J. Ornstein et al., *Vital Statistics on Congress 1993–1994*, 1994, p. 122). By the 1990s some 2,300 people were employed by House committees and 1,150 by Senate committees.

Increases also occurred in other staff categories. Members' personal office staffs were enlarged to handle citizen mail and casework. Personal staff levels just about doubled in the 1970s and have remained virtually level since then. In the 1990s, about 11,500 persons served on representatives' and senators' personal staffs. Roughly two-fifths of the representatives' staffs and one-third of senators' staffs worked in state or district offices—a dramatic rise since the early 1970s. Congressional support agencies also grew during this period. Two new research agencies, the Congressional Budget Office (CBO) and the Office of Technology Assessment (OTA), were created in the mid 1970s to provide Congress with expert advice on increasingly complex economic and technological issues. In the 1970s two older agencies, the Congressional Research Service (CRS) and the General Accounting Office (GAO), were given expanded mandates and personnel.

The skirmishes over seniority yielded clear winners and losers. The winners were "backbenchers" of all types: mid-career members who now chaired subcommittees; junior members who had new staff and procedural aids at their disposal; and even the minority party, guaranteed a portion of committee staffs. In policy terms, Democratic liberals gained the most from the reforms, at least in the 1960s and 1970s. The losers were the old-style committee chairmen and the political philosophy many of them espoused: conservatism in foreign affairs, domestic programs, and civil rights.

Although the modern Congress's membership is remarkably stable by historical standards, there have occurred brief periods of high turnover—what might be called generational changings of the guard. The World War II generation that flocked to Capitol Hill in the 1940s came to leadership only in the 1960s. Another wave of new members arrived in the reform-era 1970s. "Career legislators retired in droves," writes Burdett Loomis of the 1970s, "which provided an infusion of new blood to a Congress that was primed to offer real opportunities to its incoming members" (*The New American Politician*, 1988, p. 26). The "Watergate Babies" elected in 1974, for example, dug into their jobs, solidified their constituency ties, and labored to decentralize power and perquisites on Capitol Hill. Many of them remained to emerge as leaders in the 1990s.

The Monroney-Madden Committee (1965–1966). By the 1960s, congressional reformism had moved from the scientific management focus of the 1940s to a factional power struggle pitting liberal activists against senior conservatives. Creating a second Joint Committee on the Organization of Congress was one of the demands presented to

Speaker John W. McCormack (D-Mass.) by the Democratic Study Group after the 1964 elections. Yet the panel's prime mover, Oklahoma's senator A. S. Mike Monroney, who had cochaired the earlier 1945–1946 effort, stressed management issues: the appropriations process, scheduling, and committee structures and work loads. After ten months, the committee reached unanimous agreement on sixty-six proposals that were incorporated into an omnibus bill. The heart of the bill was a "committee bill of rights," designed to regularize committee procedures, prevent the arbitrary exercise of chairmen's powers, and protect minority-party rights. Fiscal controls and congressional budget review were also parts of the bill. The Legislative Reference Service (renamed the Congressional Research Service) was to be enlarged in both size and mandate.

Even these centrist proposals faced unyielding resistance from entrenched committee leaders. Although the Senate accepted the reform package (after tempering some of its features), in the House the senior leaders put up stiffer resistance. The modest committee bill of rights was too radical for Speaker McCormack and his tight circle of senior committee leaders. So he referred the measure to the Rules Committee, which sat on it for more than three years. Not until mid 1970 did the measure reach the House floor, propelled by a bipartisan reform coalition centered in the liberal DSG and "Rumsfeld's Raiders," a group of reform-minded Republicans identified with Illinois representative Donald Rumsfeld. The final product was significantly strengthened on the floor when a series of amendments proposed by the reformers was adopted.

House and Senate Committee Realignments (1973–1977). By the 1970s, House and Senate committee systems were in serious disarray. Jurisdictional boundaries lagged behind emerging public issues and hampered attempts to coordinate policy responses to broad emerging issues. Internally, there were jurisdictional rivalries, scheduling conflicts, and intracommittee power struggles. Legislators themselves expressed acute frustration with committee structures. A 1973 survey of 101 House and Senate members found 81 percent dissatisfied with "committee jurisdictions and the way they are defined in Congress." In the mid 1970s, therefore, the two houses separately undertook to reorganize their committee structures.

The House effort, launched in 1973, was led by long-time reformer Richard W. Bolling (D-Mo.) and ranking Rules Committee member David T. Martin

(R-Nebr.). The panel's detailed, wide-ranging report, presented in March 1974, enunciated four goals for reorganized committees: coherent subject matter, balanced political interests, equal work loads, and political salability. The last point proved a stumbling block. The reform plan aroused noisy opposition from committee leaders who resisted any incursion on their domains, not to mention the staff members and lobby groups allied with the various committees. Opposition solidified within the Democratic caucus. In a close vote, the caucus referred the Bolling plan to its Committee on Organization, Study, and Review. Only a drumbeat of outside criticism kept the caucus panel from scuttling the plan altogether. Its hastily assembled substitute, containing many elements of the Bolling plan, was adopted in October 1974 and took effect the following January.

The Senate's committee realignment effort proved more successful. It was proposed and chaired by Senators Adlai E. Stevenson III (D-Ill.) and William E. Brock III (R-Tenn.). The group's plan, announced in October 1976, trimmed the number of committees, limited senators' assignments, and shifted scores of jurisdictional topics. The plan gained momentum from the 1976 elections, which delivered eighteen new senators in January 1977, the largest freshman class in a generation. After numerous adjustments to placate key senators and powerful interests, the final product was passed 89 to 1. In traditional style, the Senate had composed its differences and produced a consensus product.

Scandals and Reforms. Despite their brief duration, crises and scandals attract the intense public scrutiny that stirs up pressure for changes in Congress's ways of doing things. Election scandals in the early 1970s brought about the Federal Election Campaign Act of 1971 and its 1974 amendments. Revelations about misconduct by Secretary of the Senate Robert G. (Bobby) Baker led in 1964 to creation of a bipartisan panel that became the Senate's Ethics Committee. In 1967, responding to the case of Adam Clayton Powell, Jr. (D-N.Y.), the House established its bipartisan Committee on Standards of Official Conduct to recommend a code of conduct and later to enforce it. In 1976 another series of scandals targeted members' personal conduct. The most publicized was a sex-and-public payroll affair in which Wayne L. Hays (D-Ohio), chairman of the House Administration Committee, was accused of giving a woman, Elizabeth Ray, a staff job in exchange for sexual favors. The next year the House and Senate adopted separate but similar codes of ethics for members and employees. In 1978 Congress passed the Ethics in Government Act to enforce the codes and to apply their financial disclosure requirements to the other two branches of government.

The Postreform Era (1978–1990)

After the mid 1970s, economic stagnation and lagging productivity constricted the legislative agenda. Government tax receipts suffered, along with citizens' confidence in their economic future. Fiscal and revenue issues crowded out other matters, inhibiting program innovation and curtailing spending increases. On Capitol Hill, the budget process loomed ever more dominant, with increasingly detailed restrictions on spending and revenue-raising measures. Other outside forces impinging upon the legislative agenda included the end of the Cold War; tensions in developing nations, including terrorism; racial divisions; class polarization, including the growth of a disadvantaged underclass;

and demographic shifts, including migration, immigration, and an aging population.

Budgetary Preoccupations. The 1980s reversed the previous era's liberal activism. Government revenues were curtailed by lagging economic productivity, a pattern exaggerated after 1981 by tax cuts, program reallocations, and soaring deficits. As political scientists Benjamin Ginsberg and Martin Shefter have argued,

> The enormous deficit created by Republican fiscal policies exert constant downward pressure on the funding levels of domestic programs. To protect their favorite programs . . . lobbyists who represented such groups as farmers, organized labor, senior citizens, advocates of welfare spending, and local governments [were] compelled to engage in zero-sum conflict. . . . In other words, one group's gain has become another group's loss. (in Michael Nelson, ed., *The Presidency and the Political System,* 3d ed., 1990, p. 337)

As a result, few new programs could be launched, and few holdover domestic programs could win ad-

PERESTROIKA BUTTONS. Made in the Soviet Union and issued in a limited edition, these photographic buttons commemorated the 1987 summit between President Ronald Reagan and Soviet president Mikhail Gorbachev and the signing of the Intermediate Nuclear Forces Treaty. The treaty was easily passed by the Senate in 1987.   COLLECTION OF DAVID J. AND JANICE L. FRENT

ditional funding. Emphasis was also placed on reviewing, adjusting, refining, or cutting back existing programs. "There's not a whole lot of money for any kind of new programs," explained Sen. Thad Cochran (R-Miss.), "so we're holding oversight hearings on old programs . . . which may not be all that bad an idea."

Preoccupied by budget worries, lawmakers invested less of their energies in analyzing pressing public needs and fashioning legislative remedies. Fewer bills were sponsored by individual members: senators and representatives in the 1980s introduced only about as many measures as they had two generations earlier, when the barons were in charge (figure 1). Members' measures were less likely to survive the legislative gauntlet leading to final passage. "Congress doesn't do what it used to do, look at problems and try to fashion solutions," said Robert Reischauer, director of the Congressional Budget Office.

Low-Cost Stratagems. Key policy decisions were packaged into huge "megabills," thus permitting lawmakers politically to endorse tough provisions that would be unlikely to pass as freestanding measures. Devices for blame avoidance were embedded into legislation to distance lawmakers from the adverse effects of cutback politics. Examples included the 1983 rescue of the Social Security system, the 1986 tax reform act, and the 1990 budget package. All embodied potentially explosive issues, delicate political compromises, and high-level bargaining between congressional and executive-branch leaders. A 1988 law covering military base closures illustrated the techniques of cutback policy-making. To insulate the process from congressional pressures, a bipartisan commission was created to draw up lists of installations targeted for closure. To make the commission's recommendations difficult to overturn, the list would have to be accepted or rejected as a whole.

Because new programs faced long odds, many lawmakers capitalized on low-cost, high-return symbolic issues—patriotism, abortion, and family values, for example. Symbolic benefits were extracted also from noncontroversial commemorative resolutions designating certain days, weeks, or months in honor of causes or groups. Such measures comprised from a third to a half of all laws passed by Congress in the 1980s.

Reinvigorated Parties. Ironically, in view of the apparent decline of party loyalty among the electorate, party-line voting on Capitol Hill soared to modern-day highs. In a typical year, about half of all floor votes could be called party unity votes, in

which a majority of voting Republicans opposed a majority of voting Democrats. The average legislator voted with his or her party from three-fourths to four-fifths of the time. Levels of party voting still fell short of those in parliamentary systems or those in Congress during the "militant parties" era around the turn of the twentieth century. Yet heightened partisanship marked congressional politics after the 1960s, to the point where partisan gridlock became a buzzword of the 1992 campaigns.

The roots of the new partisanship were tangled. The major explanation is that shifts in the two parties' demographic bases yielded greater ideological unity among their officeholders. That is, Democratic members were more "liberal" and Republicans more "conservative" than in earlier years, when the strong conservative coalition of southern Democrats and Republicans blurred party lines. Without the corrosive issue of race to divide them, the Democrats coalesced around a left-of-center platform. The Republicans, by the same token, moved rightward as they captured conservative districts in the South and lost moderate-to-liberal areas in the Northeast and Midwest. The once-influential Republican moderate became an endangered species, especially in the House. The Republicans' revived

SEN. BEN NIGHTHORSE CAMPBELL (D-COLO.). *Left*, chatting with Rep. Jerry Lewis (R-Calif.) before a Senate Energy and Natural Resources Committee markup of a California desert bill, 29 September 1993.

R. MICHAEL JENKINS, CONGRESSIONAL QUARTERLY INC.

fortunes in the 1980s, especially their twelve-year lease on the White House (1981–1993) and their six years in the Senate majority (1981–1987), brought about not only a dramatic shift in legislative agenda priorities but also certain procedural innovations, especially those centered in a more exacting and cumbersome budgetary process.

Procedural innovations also heightened the partisanship of floor votes, particularly in the House. Omnibus budget packages tended to display partisan features that encouraged voting along party lines. House procedures especially sharpened partisanship. By controlling committees, scheduling issues, and using restrictive special rules to structure floor debate and voting, Democratic leaders could arrange for votes they were likely to win and avoid those they were apt to lose. Such tactics often foreordained party-line outcomes and raised the ire of the minority Republicans.

Party leaders in the process became markedly stronger than at any time since the revolt against Speaker Joseph G. Cannon in 1910. Leaders of the 1980s and 1990s benefited not only from the powers given them during the reform era, but from the widespread belief that they were the only people who could untangle jurisdictional overlaps, orchestrate the legislative schedule, negotiate with the White House, and produce legislative programs on which the parties could campaign.

The revival of party leadership did not occur overnight. Speaker Carl B. Albert (D-Okla.) embraced his new powers but was fearful lest he be faulted for exploiting them too aggressively. Thomas P. (Tip) O'Neill, Jr. (D-Mass.), who became Speaker in 1977, used his powers adroitly in trying to enact President Carter's programs. He then endured an uncomfortable period in 1981 and 1982, when Ronald Reagan's popularity and the Democrats' diminished ranks effectively denied him majority control. By 1983, however, O'Neill had taken a more aggressive stance in challenging the Reagan administration.

James C. Wright, Jr. (D-Tex.), O'Neill's successor, wielded his powers with parliamentary skill and combative partisanship to fulfill a domestic and foreign policy agenda. At one point he seized de facto control of the nation's Central American policy, coercing the Reagan administration into accepting multilateral negotiations to end Nicaraguan civil strife. "I entered into a joint declaration with the president, most of which I dictated," the Speaker boasted later. The Speaker pursued his goals so aggressively that his enemies determined to destroy him. "If Wright consolidates his power, he will be a very, very formidable man," declared Rep. Newt Gingrich (R-Ga.). "We have to take him on early to prevent that." Republican foes raised ethical charges against Wright, and eventually the Committee on Standards of Official Conduct charged him with several violations of House rules. Wright resigned in mid 1989.

Like Joseph Cannon in 1910, Wright had pushed his prerogatives beyond the limits of his colleagues' tolerance. Yet, whereas the Cannon revolt eclipsed the office for decades, Wright's fall left the speakership virtually intact. Although Wright's successor, Thomas S. Foley (D-Wash.), followed a more conciliatory path, most members continued to regard vigorous leadership as essential for realizing their own objectives, whether they were leaders or followers, majority or minority.

Yet Capitol Hill partisanship should not be overstated. Although party-line floor voting was on the rise, senators and representatives increasingly regarded their party obligations with the same ambivalence long exhibited by their constituents. Presidents and congressional party leaders had to bargain for votes in order to overcome the pervasive pressures that emanated from constituencies and organized groups of all stripes.

Divided Government. Democratic dominance on Capitol Hill coexisted during most of this period with Republican success in capturing the White House. By 1992, Democrats had won twenty straight House elections, capturing from 53 to 68 percent of the seats; their hold on the Senate was interrupted only by six years of Republican control (1981–1987). Meanwhile Republicans won six of the ten presidential contests, several by landslides. But whether because of voters' preferences or incumbent members' stratagems, Republican presidential successes had surprisingly little impact on party control of Congress.

Divided government—split partisan control of Congress and the presidency—occurred throughout four Republican presidencies: Nixon, Ford, Reagan, and Bush. (The Republicans controlled the Senate for six of Reagan's eight years.) Many commentators became convinced that divided government was a prescription for confusion, delay, and deadlock. To be sure, legislative productivity was affected by party control: presidents were invariably more successful in achieving their legislative goals if their partisans comfortably controlled both chambers (figure 2).

Yet party control remained an incomplete indicator of legislative achievement. Jimmy Carter's presidency showed that party control of both branches was no guarantee of interbranch harmony. By the same token, the Nixon-Ford period and the first year of Reagan's presidency witnessed legislative productivity far beyond what would be expected from divided government. Davidson (1991) found that legislative productivity levels corresponded very imperfectly with unified or divided party control. Likewise Mayhew (1991) concluded that unified or divided control made little difference in enactment of important legislation or launching of high-profile congressional investigations into executive-branch misdeeds.

The Crisis of the 1990s

Economic, social, and political unrest erupted in the early 1990s in what can only be called a crisis of governance. The symptoms included joblessness, riots, social unrest, and citizen alienation. One member of Congress called it a massive "civic temper tantrum." Public officials reacted with uncertainty and panic.

Although other institutions did not escape blame, Congress bore the largest share of public criticism. By the spring of 1992 only 17 percent of those questioned in a national survey approved of the way Congress was doing its job; 54 percent approved of their own representative's performance. Both figures were all-time lows. The unrest far exceeded the usual level of Congress bashing, and even the public criticisms of the 1960s and 1970s. It seemingly reflected not only outrage at scandals and distrust of politicians, but also a feeling that government was not working well and that the nation itself had strayed off course.

The crisis stemmed from both external forces and internal disruptions. Among the external factors were the long-term lag in the economy, social violence, political party disintegration, growth in the number and effectiveness of interest groups, more than a decade of divided party control of the legislative and executive branches, and the resultant stalemate in many domestic policy areas. Internally, members complained of abrasive partisanship (an ironic complaint in such an antiparty era), frustration, weariness, and interpersonal stress. In record numbers (for modern times), lawmakers opted out and retired.

Externally, Congress found few defenders in the press or among other political elites. Sympathetic or even serious coverage of the institution had declined in major national media outlets. Mainstream newspapers, magazines, and television networks were cutting back on their coverage of the national government, especially Congress. Following the canons of investigative journalism, reporters were increasingly on the alert for hints of scandal, wrongdoing, or corruption. Reports of possible ethics violations—more accessible to investigation than ever before through such mechanisms of public accountability as campaign finance reports—became easy targets for stories that, whether true or not, could bring unflattering coverage to elected officials. Members of Congress, not to mention the institution as a whole, were unable to mount a convincing defense. As one veteran reporter commented, "Congress, which gets trivial television attention, has no sense of news management and cannot speak with a clear voice."

To most critics, and even to many lawmakers themselves, the unhappy 102d Congress (1991–1993) symbolized the institution's faults. Unlike the preceding Congress, which had enacted half a dozen landmark laws despite its clashes with President Bush, this Congress was blamed for gridlock in Washington. Aside from a memorable January 1991 debate over entering the Persian Gulf War, its legislative output was thin. A combination of partisan posturing, presidential vetoes, and Senate filibusters waylaid dozens of agenda items: school reform, urban aid, gun control and other anticrime initiatives, abortion rights, fetal tissue research, easing of voter registration rules, additional funds for the savings and loan cleanup, and reforms in health care, campaign finance, and congressional procedures.

The two chambers also suffered from a series of scandals that, even more than legislative gridlock, fed the public's scorn. In late 1991, what turned into a seven-month furor erupted over House members' penalty-free overdrafts at their Capitol bank (actually, an old-fashioned payroll office). Although no public funds were lost in the transactions, average citizens reacted furiously at this seeming evidence of special privilege. A special prosecutor was named to investigate the affair, and the numbers and amounts of overdrafts were published. Half a dozen members with overdrafts were dumped in primary elections and another 19 in the general elections; many more found refuge in retirement. Of the 269 members with overdrafts, more than one in four (77) retired or were defeated for reelection or for another office. Among the 17 members whom the House ethics committee cited as having "abused their banking privileges," only 6 remained. Other reports highlighted members' unpaid bills at House restaurants and employee thefts and drug deals at its post office.

House leaders were at first slow to assess and

counteract the damage done by the scandals. Nervous Democrats faulted Speaker Thomas S. Foley's cerebral leadership; one of them took to the House floor to urge Foley to resign. Republicans gleefully pounced on the revelations as proof of the Democrats' misrule, even though a number of Republicans were implicated in the scandals. Soon the House sergeant at arms, the House official in charge of the bank, resigned, as did the House postmaster. Several postal employees pleaded guilty to various crimes, while a federal grand jury subpoenaed expense account records of three Democratic members as part of a long-running inquiry. Eventually a House administrator or Director of Nonlegislative and Financial Services was hired. With the 1992 elections the House scandals seemed to have run their course. After mounting a vigorous campaign to muster support among committee chairmen and to co-opt the newly elected members, Speaker Foley and his leadership team were reelected to their posts with scant opposition. Yet scandalous reports lingered: for example, the deposed sergeant at arms accused House Ways and Means chairman Dan Rostenkowski (D-Ill.) of diverting his office postage-stamp allowance into cash for personal use, and a lengthy inquiry ensued.

The Senate also attracted public scorn over several highly publicized events. First was the Keating Five ethics case, in which five senators intervened with federal regulators on behalf of failed savings and loan executive Charles H. Keating, Jr. The Senate ethics panel issued various levels of rebuke to the five. In October 1992 occurred the televised confirmation hearings concerning Supreme Court nominee Clarence Thomas, when the Judiciary Committee came under public fire for its handling of law professor Anita F. Hill's sexual harassment charges against the nominee. There was also a late-night vote in the Senate on a pay raise, guaranteed to raise public anger. Later, sexual harassment charges against Oregon's Bob Packwood produced further negative publicity and painful Senate debates.

In such an atmosphere, Congress was powerless to resist demands for reform. A new Joint Committee on the Organization of Congress, initially resisted by House Democratic leaders, was approved and during 1993 undertook to draw up a wide-ranging set of reform recommendations. (The panel's Senate and House contingents eventually went their own separate ways, and the most far-reaching reform topics fell victim to partisan and bicameral hostilities.) Revision of the outdated 1970s campaign finance law, advocated by most critics of the Hill, gained new momentum. The two parties, which enjoyed differing patterns of funding, strove to protect their advantages and curtail their opponents' resources. The outcome was a stalemate, as long as congressional Democrats could pass bills that were sure to be vetoed by Republican presidents. The balance of power shifted with the election of Democrat Bill Clinton, who promised to "change the way Washington works" and in May 1993 proposed his own reform plan. Yet partisan disputes, not to mention skepticism on the part of scholarly commentators, continued to plague efforts to reform the complex, high-stakes business of financing campaigns.

The 1992 crisis was distinctive because it lacked a clear or compelling political, partisan, factional, or even institutional agenda. Complaints about structures and procedures were legion. House Republicans, frustrated after nearly four decades of minority status, had an exhaustive list of complaints about how Democrats were managing the chamber. Sponsors of the Joint Committee on the Organization of Congress cited overstaffing, committee overlaps, budget strife, breakdowns in communication between the chambers and among the branches, lack of policy integration, and too much partisanship. Representative Lee H. Hamilton (D-Ind.), co-chairman of the joint committee, declared that "Congress increasingly seems bogged down and unable to tackle the main issues that Americans are concerned about—from jobs and crime to health care reform."

Yet little consensus existed upon the desired direction of the changes. Equally unclear was the extent to which institutional defects had contributed to the public's and the political, journalistic, and scholarly elite's discontent with Congress's performance. The perennial love-hate embrace between the American people and their elected lawmakers became, in the 1990s, unusually turbulent and unpredictable.

[See also Abscam; Great Society; House Bank; New Frontier; Organization of Congress Committee, Joint (1993); Peace Corps; Persian Gulf War; Twenty-fourth Amendment; Twenty-fifth Amendment; Twenty-sixth Amendment; Twenty-seventh Amendment; Vietnam War; Watergate.]

BIBLIOGRAPHY

Davidson, Roger H. "The Presidency and the Three Eras of the Modern Congress." In *Divided Democracy*. Edited by James A. Thurber. 1991.

Davidson, Roger H., and Walter J. Oleszek. *Congress against Itself.* 1977.

Davidson, Roger H., ed. *The Postreform Congress.* 1992.

Ginsberg, Benjamin, and Martin Shefter. *Politics by Other Means.* 1990.

Mayhew, David R. *Divided We Govern: Party Control, Lawmaking, and Investigations, 1946–1990.* 1991.

Peterson, Mark A. *Legislating Together: The White House and Capitol Hill from Eisenhower to Reagan.* 1990.

Rieselbach, Leroy N. *Congressional Reform.* 1986.

Rohde, David W. *Parties and Leaders in the Postreform House.* 1991.

Sinclair, Barbara. *Majority Leadership in the U.S. House.* 1983.

Sinclair, Barbara. *The Transformation of the U.S. Senate.* 1989.

Smith, Steven S. *Call to Order: Floor Politics in the House and Senate.* 1989.

Sundquist, James L. *The Decline and Resurgence of Congress.* 1981.

Sundquist, James L. *Politics and Policy: The Eisenhower, Kennedy, and Johnson Years.* 1968.

ROGER H. DAVIDSON

HOAR, GEORGE F.

HOAR, GEORGE F. (1826–1904), representative and senator from Massachusetts and a leader in the Republican party's Half-Breed faction, the wing of the party that, in the late nineteenth century, favored government activism to foster economic growth. Educated at Harvard College and Harvard Law School, George Frisbie Hoar served one term each in the lower and upper house of the Massachusetts legislature before entering the U.S. House of Representatives in 1869. After four terms he was elected in 1877 to the Senate, where he served until his death.

In response to industrialization and other economic and social changes, Hoar favored an expanded role for the federal government. Hailing from the industrial city of Worcester, he defended the interests of the manufacturers and laborers of his district and state by fervently supporting protective tariffs. He also championed other Republican principles, including a stable currency, federal aid to education, and the expansion of U.S. markets overseas.

In the House his committee service included membership on the Judiciary, Education and Labor, and Railways and Canals committees. During the presidential election dispute of 1876–1877, he was one of five House members on the Electoral Commission and joined the Republican majority in deciding the contest in favor of Rutherford B. Hayes over Samuel J. Tilden.

SENATORS GEORGE F. HOAR (R-MASS.), *RIGHT,* AND ARTHUR PUE GORMAN (D-MD.). Drawing from 1898 or 1899, predicting the forthcoming debate over the Treaty of Paris, which ended the Spanish-American War.

LIBRARY OF CONGRESS

In the Senate Hoar chaired the Judiciary Committee and the Committee on Privileges and Elections. Classed as a radical during Reconstruction and as an ardent supporter of black suffrage, Hoar was appalled by the continuing suppression of the black vote in the South in the post-Reconstruction years. In 1890 he was a principal architect of a bill calling for the policing of congressional elections by the federal courts. Defeated, the proposal was the last significant civil rights bill before the mid-twentieth century.

The climax of Hoar's Senate career came at the end of the nineteenth century, when he condemned imperialism and was one of only two Republican senators to oppose the Treaty of Paris, ending the Spanish-American War, and U.S. acquisition of the Philippines.

BIBLIOGRAPHY

Hoar, George F. *Autobiography of Seventy Years.* 1903.
Welch, Richard E., Jr. *George Frisbie Hoar and the Half-Breed Republicans.* 1971.

CHARLES W. CALHOUN

HOLIDAYS. *See* Federal Holidays.

HOMESTEAD ACT (1862; 12 Stat. 392–394). By 1861, when the 37th Congress (1861–1863) convened, many lawmakers had been urging passage of a homestead act—legislation granting free title to settlers on the public domain—for a decade and a half. In the 1850s the House had passed homestead legislation repeatedly, but just as frequently the measures had died in the Senate. In the summer of 1860 even that barrier was breached, but President James Buchanan vetoed the bill. The 1860 Republican platform pledged the party's support to the passage of homestead legislation, which was generally considered to have made a major contribution to Republican victories in the Midwest.

Early in the 37th Congress, Rep. Cyrus Aldrich (R-Minn.) introduced a homestead measure and had it referred to the Committee on Agriculture, of which he was a member. Since the House considered only military and related financial measures in its short summer session, it was not until December 1861 that the bill was brought to the floor. At that point a squabble developed between the Committee on Agriculture and the Committee on Public Lands, and the proposal was referred to the latter body, which reported a bill on 10 December 1861. The measure was then postponed to the first Monday in February 1862 by a highly sectional vote of 88 to 50, with almost all the representatives (regardless of party) from New England, the Middle States, the Border States, and the Far West voting to postpone. This vote probably represented the actual preferences of the members, many of whom (especially Republicans) could not afford to vote against the measure directly.

The proposal came back to the House floor in February 1862. In a dramatic move, Speaker Galusha A. Grow of Pennsylvania, a longtime proponent of homestead legislation, came down from the chair to speak in support of the measure. A week later, after several amendments, the bill passed with only sixteen negative votes, nine of them Republican.

The measure then went to the Senate, where it languished in the Committee on Public Lands until 25 March and then suffered further delays because of a crowded Senate calendar. Finally, after some amendment, it passed the Senate on 6 May 1862 by a vote of 33 to 7.

The measure then went back to the House, which called for a committee of conference (in this case apparently merely a parliamentary device to permit the attachment of a few other minor amendments). The conference committee's report was taken up in both houses on 15 May and passed without division or debate.

The act provided for the transfer of public lands to citizens of the United States, or to persons who had declared their intention to become citizens, on the payment of a $10 entry fee and the occupancy of the land for five years. Settlers could claim 160 acres of land valued for preemption at $1.25 per acre or 80 acres valued at $2.50 per acre. The claimants had to be at least twenty-one years old or the head of a household. The homestead claims could not be attached for prior debt.

Some difference of opinion exists among historians about the impact of the Homestead Act on the course of western expansion. There can be no doubt that enormous amounts of federal land were taken up under the terms of this act and later supplements. It can be argued, however, that the utility of the act was much diminished by the removal of large blocks of land from the public domain by the Morrill Land-Grant College Act (most of the land given to the states was sold to speculators) and the Pacific Railroad Acts. Consequently, the best-located and best-watered land could often be obtained only by purchase.

[*See also* Morrill Land-Grant College Act; Pacific Railroad Acts.]

BIBLIOGRAPHY

Curry, Leonard P. *Blueprint for Modern America: Nonmilitary Legislation of the First Civil War Congress.* 1968.
Robbins, Roy M. *Our Landed Heritage: The Public Domain, 1776–1936.* 1942.

LEONARD P. CURRY

HONORARIA. Payments in recognition of professional services for which there are no set fees are called honoraria. As applied to members of Congress and other officers and employees of the government, an honorarium has been defined as payment of money or anything of value for a speech, appearance, or article. The definition does not include reimbursements for travel and subsistence expenses, awards, gifts, book royalties, or stipends (payment for a series of speeches, appearances, and articles) when the payment is unrelated to an individual's official duties or status with the government (5 U.S.C.A., app. 7, sec. 505[3]).

In the United States the practice of providing honoraria does not appear to have begun until the early 1800s, when evidence appears of men being paid to deliver lectures. According to Robert Oliver (*History of Public Speaking*, 1965), the first lecture bureau was established in about 1873 by James B. Pond, who "converted the lecture business wholly and frankly to the aim of making money." The following year, the famous Chautauqua movement was launched, which earned lecturers large amounts of money through the early 1900s. This movement ended after the Great Depression, as Chautauquas began to be replaced by lecture bureaus.

By the 1950s payment to members of Congress for speeches was a widespread practice and cause for concern, as evidenced in the 1951 report (82d Cong., 1st sess.) of Sen. Paul H. Douglas's Senate Subcommittee on Ethical Standards in Government. The subcommittee explored the ramifications of a majority of members of Congress attempting to supplement their congressional salaries and posed several questions about the propriety of retainers, fees, and stipends.

By the late 1960s and early 1970s, when Senate and House rules required limited public disclosure about honoraria receipts, it was apparent that members were receiving substantial payments for speeches, writings, and appearances. Controversy and criticism intensified as members continued to supplement their salaries with progressively higher levels of income received from activities that diverted their attention from congressional responsibilities.

During the Watergate reform era, Congress enacted the Federal Election Campaign Act Amendments of 1974 (P.L. 93-443), which contained a provision limiting for the first time the honoraria of members of Congress as well as all officers and employees of the government. The law established an annual ceiling of $15,000 and an individual limit of $1,000 per speech, appearance, or article. The honoraria limitation was also seen as a way to prevent evasion of limits on campaign contributions.

For the next fifteen years, honoraria became increasingly controversial, even though not all members accepted these earnings. Congress periodically changed the annual honoraria ceiling for members. Representatives continuously had an honoraria limit, but senators had no annual honoraria restrictions between late 1981 and mid 1983. At other times, senators could receive yearly sums higher than the limits set for representatives. Congressional staff, after 1981, did not have any annual honoraria limits, only a $2,000 restriction per speech, appearance, or article.

The press and public continued to focus on these earnings. The widespread practice of groups with important stakes in the business of Congress paying honoraria to considerable numbers of members (sometimes merely for meeting or dining with them) cast a cloud over the entire system; the custom gave the appearance that honoraria had become another way for special interests to gain influence or access to members, and that members were using their official positions for personal gain. Even the practice of members' donating honoraria to charity was criticized. It was argued, further, that public disclosure of these fees was not a deterrent to the appearance of conflicts of interest.

It was also widely claimed that congressional salaries were inadequate. Periodically from 1976 to 1988, federal salary commissions and reform groups called for elimination of honoraria coupled with salary increases for members to alleviate the necessity to supplement congressional salaries. Critics advocated that Congress stop this "backdoor" payment.

Finally, after years of public controversy, Congress enacted the Ethics Reform Act of 1989 (P.L. 101-194). Effective January 1991, this law banned honoraria for all officers and employees of the three branches of government, except senators and Senate staff, and provided a 25 percent salary increase for top government officials, except senators.

The Senate opted for a salary lower than that of members of the House in return for the continuation of honoraria. The law, however, provided for senators' honoraria earnings to be decreased by the same amount as any future salary increases until their honoraria limit was less than or equal to 1 percent of their salary. At that point honoraria would be prohibited.

The Senate ultimately bowed to public pressure to eliminate honoraria. The 1992 Legislative Branch Appropriations Act (P.L. 102-90) prohibited honoraria earnings by members, officers, and employees of the Senate and adjusted senators' salaries to the same level as that of representatives. As a result, honoraria are now prohibited for all officers and employees of the three branches of government except enlisted military personnel.

Several efforts, however, are underway to relax the honoraria ban for rank-and-file career government employees (excluding members of Congress, cabinet officers, or federal judges) under certain conditions. One such condition is that the subject of the speech or article must not relate primarily to the policies or programs of the employee's office and must not involve the use of government resources or nonpublic government information.

BIBLIOGRAPHY

Association of the Bar of the City of New York. Special Committee on Congressional Ethics. *Congress and the Public Trust.* 1970. Pp. 197–201.

Congressional Quarterly Inc. *Congressional Quarterly's Guide to Congress.* 4th ed. Edited by Mary Cohn. 1991. Pp. 495, 635–649, 786–787, 791–793, 809–810.

Hook, Janet. "Senate's Ban on Honoraria Marks End of an Era." *Congressional Quarterly Weekly Report,* 20 July 1991, 1955–1961.

Solomon, Burt. "Bite Sized Favors." *National Journal* 11 October, 1986, pp. 2418–2422.

MILDRED LEHMANN AMER

HOOVER, HERBERT (1874–1964), secretary of Commerce, thirty-first president of the United States (1929–1933). While Herbert Hoover's admonition that Congress favored narrow, special interests and that the president stood for the whole people is largely correct, his obsessive practice of the admonition precluded a successful relationship between the executive and legislative branches during his presidency. Another irony attending his weak presidential liaison with Congress is that his decade of experience with Congress prior to 1929 should have given him an advantage.

As Woodrow Wilson's food administrator during World War I, Hoover, a Republican, secured much necessary legislation to forge a national food program. Despite this he scorned Congress, believing that in such an august institution there was "the same minority of maliciousness and trouble that

HERBERT HOOVER. *Front,* as president, leaving the Capitol on 31 May 1932 after making an unexpected appearance before the Senate. Hoover delivered an address to the Senate, appealing to its members to pass a sales tax measure and other legislation designed to balance the budget, reduce government expenditures, and help give relief to the unemployed. His relationship with Congress worsening in 1932, the legislation Hoover requested was not passed. He had to abandon his attempts at using a 2.5 percent manufacturing sales tax to help balance the budget, and he reluctantly supported $300 million in federal expenditures to provide relief to the states.

LIBRARY OF CONGRESS

there was in the rest of the world, and their opportunity was greater."

Perhaps because of his "bureaucratic" supremacy over Congress (as food administrator and later as secretary of Commerce), he believed he would achieve similar success as an electoral leader, especially as president. But as the nation's electoral leader, he faced the ever-present executive-legislative "deadlock of democracy," a deadlock exacerbated by the buildup of his antagonisms with congressional leaders over the previous decade. The explanations of such antagonisms are several-fold. He abhorred broker state politics, thus ignoring the need for compromise between divergent interests. He espoused corporatist ideas of balances, as between branches of government (and government, capital, and labor segments of society). His personality particularly precluded successful executive-congressional liaison. In the words of political scientist James David Barber, Hoover was an "active-negative" president—an active president without "political love," thus lacking an empathy for legislators so essential to the organization and implementation of a presidential program in Congress.

Prior to the stock market crash in October 1929, Hoover achieved some congressional support for his programs, not the least of which was the Agricultural Marketing Act, a $500 million program to advance the interests of agriculture. The passage of that legislation, however, had ominous implications. He gave so little direction to the passage of the legislation that it was almost rendered ineffective by various export tariff provisions. Hoover honestly believed that his electoral mandate would compel Congress to give him the agricultural program that he had called for in the presidential campaign.

When the Depression set in, especially after the midterm elections of 1930, Hoover's problems with Congress multiplied. Bad feelings surfaced almost immediately when a few liberal Democrats, and more insurgent Republicans, demanded a special session to address the worsening economic conditions. Hoover, always more comfortable when Congress was not in session, would not consider the notion of convening it. He felt his executive actions were quite sufficient to effect national recovery. And, when he realized he would need Congress to get approval for certain domestic and foreign actions, such as creation of the Reconstruction Finance Corporation (RFC) and a moratorium on foreign debts, he garnered enough prior congressional

commitments to ensure support when Congress next convened. Some members of Congress, including George W. Norris of Nebraska, were enraged by his ploy.

Hoover did achieve some executive and congressional action in the first months of 1932, if one considers the foreign debt moratorium, the Glass-Steagall Act, and the RFC Act. But from springtime on, a near deadlock ensued, particularly as related to such measures and revenue and relief legislation. As for the former, the president had to give up trying for a balanced budget based on a 2.5 percent manufacturing sales tax. On relief legislation the president very begrudgingly supported $300 million of relief to states.

If President Hoover's relationship with the 72d Congress was strained, it became intolerable in the lame-duck session after his defeat in the 1932 presidential race. His pleas for credit and banking legislation were ignored, especially by Democrats awaiting the new president, Franklin D. Roosevelt. When the president-elect requested Hoover's support for certain agricultural aid legislation, Hoover opposed it as adamantly as Democrats had opposed his outgoing legislative proposals. In short, Herbert Hoover's relationship to Congress was a model of an unsuccessful executive-congressional liaison.

BIBLIOGRAPHY

Burner, David. *Herbert Hoover: A Public Life.* 1979.
Fausold, Martin L. *The Presidency of Herbert C. Hoover.* 1985.
Wilson, Joan Hoff. *Herbert Hoover, Forgotten Progressive.* 1975.

MARTIN L. FAUSOLD

HOSPITAL SURVEY AND CONSTRUCTION ACT (1946; 60 Stat. 1040–1049).

As World War II ended, health reformers, who wanted to restructure the health care delivery system and institute national health insurance, and health services providers, who opposed both goals, agreed on the need for federal subsidy of hospital construction. George Bugbee, secretary of the American Hospital Association, allied his organization with the Public Health Service to lobby for a hospital bill, which was introduced by Senators Lister Hill (D-Ala.) and Harold H. Burton (D-Ohio). Other support came from health philanthropists, organized labor, the Farm Bureau Federation, and the American Medical Association. The powerful senator Robert A. Taft (R-Ohio), wary of federal control, insisted that states' rights and local control be retained, that funds be allocated according to states' assessments of need, and that local hospital boards supply matching funds. Hill understood that the bill appealed to representatives from rural states, including many strong conservatives, and hoped for bipartisan support if he could win Taft's backing. A funding formula, devised by I. S. Falk of the Social Security Administration to award the largest sums to the poorest states (determined by per-capita income), convinced Taft.

The Hospital Survey and Construction Act (Hill-Burton Act), Title VI of the Public Health Service Act, was signed in August 1946, after President Harry S. Truman decided not to risk a veto and thus try to pressure Congress into passing a more comprehensive package including national health insurance. Extended many times and amended to provide funding for outpatient departments, nursing homes, emergency rooms, and modernization of facilities, Hill-Burton provided $4 billion in grants and $1.9 billion in loans and loan guarantees to more than four thousand hospitals before it was finally allowed to expire in the late 1970s. The funding program subtly reoriented health services around regional hospitals throughout the country, particularly urban teaching institutions, enhancing secondary and tertiary care at the expense of prevention and primary care.

BIBLIOGRAPHY

Fox, Daniel M. *Health Policies, Health Politics: The British and American Experience, 1911–1965.* 1986.
Weeks, Lewis E., and Howard J. Berman. *Shapers of American Health Policy: An Oral History.* 1985.

DANIEL M. FOX and MARCIA L. MELDRUM

HOUSE ADMINISTRATION COMMITTEE.

The Committee on House Administration is one of only two committees (the other is Appropriations) with administrative as well as legislative responsibilities. Its administrative character is reflected in the scope of the committee's jurisdiction, which affects most internal operations of the House of Representatives. In this capacity, the committee is, along with the House administrator, the primary housekeeping agent of the House in overseeing internal fiscal and administrative operations of the House.

The committee's jurisdiction, responsibilities, and authorities emanate from the Legislative Reorganization acts of 1946 (P.L. 79-601) and 1970

(P.L. 91-510), the Rules of the House, *U.S. Statutes at Large* (other than the two reorganization acts), and House resolutions, customs, and precedents. The committee's broad spectrum covers issues ranging from campaign finance reform legislation to telephone service contracts and franked mail, orientation programs for new representatives and funding levels for all House committees to promulgation of rules and regulations relating to House accounts, office equipment, travel, pay, retirement, and member and committee and staff perquisites, just to cite a few examples.

The House Administration Committee was established 2 January 1947, pursuant to the Legislative Reorganization Act of 1946. In an effort to coordinate and streamline House operations, the act consolidated the administration of housekeeping functions within one committee. Before 1947, House administrative and management responsibilities were dispersed among ten select and standing committees. The act abolished these committees and transferred their functions to the new standing Committee on House Administration. The former committees and their dates of establishment were Accounts (1803); Disposition of Executive Papers (1889); Library (1809); Enrolled Bills (1789); Memorials (1929); Printing (1846); Election of the President, Vice President, and Representatives in Congress (1893); and Elections (1789, divided into three committees—Elections No. 1, No. 2, and No. 3—in 1895). The consolidation was one of the major steps toward modernization of the administrative and management operations of the House in the twentieth century.

From 1946 to the early 1970s, the committee's influence over day-to-day activities of the House grew considerably; under the chairmanship of Wayne L. Hays (D-Ohio, 1971–1976), the committee became one of the most powerful on Capitol Hill. This was due primarily to authority invested in the committee to fix the level of most allowances available to members, to determine and implement many services available to House offices, and, along with the Appropriations Committee, to set management policies of most internal operations of the House.

In 1976, however, Hays was forced to resign as chairman in the aftermath of problems related to payroll and allotment of member allowance. In reaction, Congress, along with the committee, in the following year approved several reforms that consolidated members' allowances and required that any adjustments in their allowances as recommended by the committee be approved by the

House. The House Administration Committee was directed to continue its oversight of allowances and House services, to continue to set and monitor policies for their use, and to adjust allowances and services to reflect fluctuations in cost of living and prices of goods. Other changes instituted by the committee required disclosure by members of expense allowance use and costs of foreign travel. Among the committee's more recent initiatives were modernizing the House computer system, updating the House telephone system, and ensuring live House television coverage.

Jurisdiction. The basic statement of the committee's jurisdiction is set forth in Rule X of the House, which defines the committee's jurisdiction over appropriations and expenditures from the House contingent fund; auditing and settling of accounts charged against the fund; hiring of staff by the House, including clerks for members and committees; management of the Library of Congress, and matters relating to the House Library, statuary and pictures, acceptance and purchase of art for the Capitol, the Botanic Garden, purchase of books and manuscripts, and erection of monuments to memorialize individuals; matters relating to the Smithsonian Institution and the incorporation of similar institutions; matters relating to printing and correction of the *Congressional Record;* measures relating to House accounts generally; measures relating to office space assignment; and measures relating to disposition of useless executive papers.

House Rules further specify authority over measures relating to election of the president, the vice president, and members of Congress, corrupt practices, contested elections, credentials and qualifications, and federal elections generally; measures relating to House services, including the House restaurant, parking facilities, and administration of House office buildings and of the House wing of the Capitol; measures relating to House members' travel; measures relating to the raising, reporting, and use of campaign contributions for House candidates; measures relating to pay, retirement, and other benefits of members, officers, and employees of Congress; examining all bills, amendments, and joint resolutions after passage by the House to see that they are correctly enrolled and when originated by the House delivered to the president; reporting members' travel to the sergeant at arms; and operating responsibility for House information systems.

The committee reports the annual expense resolution for committee studies and investigations, including foreign travel by House committee members and staff. At any time, the committee may require reports from individual House committees to account for expenditures authorized in the resolution. Further, the committee is required by law to maintain itemized reports of foreign travel expenditures.

Numerous matters within the purview of the committee's administrative responsibilities are explicitly named in law and resolution as requiring its approval. Items that fall within this category include preparation of job descriptions for employees of House officers, disposition of documents and furniture, appointment of Capitol police employed by the House, assignment to committee staffs of personnel on loan from executive agencies, procurement of consultants and training for staff, and acquisition of furniture. Rules and regulations promulgated by the committee for its responsibilities in these areas are published in a manual.

Structure. To assist the committee in carrying out its responsibilities, portions of its authority and functions are delegated to six subcommittees and House Information Systems. Subcommittees include Accounts; Administrative Oversight; Libraries and Memorials; Personnel and Police; Elections; and Office Systems. From time to time, committee leadership authorizes ad hoc subcommittees and task forces to deal with emerging issues. For example, in the 102d Congress (1991–1993), the committee leadership established the Task Force on Campaign Finance Reform and the Task Force for the Investigation of the House Post Office. The chairman and ranking minority member serve ex officio on all subcommittees. Additionally, committee members serve on the Joint Committee on Printing and the Joint Committee on the Library of Congress. The committee comprises twenty-one representatives.

The role of the committee in bringing technological innovation to the House was highlighted with introduction in 1971 of House Information Systems (HIS). Since then, HIS has been the main computer support for the House by providing services to members and committees, including assistance with mailing, private and public information data bases, district office communications, case work, financial disclosure preparation, and committee publications and accounting. Additionally, HIS serves House officers and related support entities, including the offices of postmaster, doorkeeper, clerk, sergeant at arms, and the House restaurant, and supports legislative and administrative functions of the House, including publication of calendars, legislative information, and audit support.

[*See also* Rules and Administration Committee, Senate.]

BIBLIOGRAPHY

U.S. House of Representatives. Committee on House Administration. *Calendar of Business of the Committee.* 103d Cong., 1st sess., 1994.

U.S. House of Representatives. Committee on House Administration. *Report on the Activities of the Committee on House Administration of the House of Representatives during the 102d Congress.* 102d Cong., 2d sess., 1992. H. Rep. 102–1083.

PAUL E. DWYER

HOUSE BANK. For a century and a half, the House bank was a facility in the Capitol where the pay of representatives was deposited into accounts and could be redeemed by them for cash. During the mid-twentieth century, a practice developed at the bank of allowing representatives to write checks on their bank accounts with little regard for whether their account balances were sufficient to cover their drafts. In 1991, the news media took note that members had been writing thousands of overdrafts on the bank, triggering a sensational scandal that led to abolition of the facility on 31 December 1991.

The affair, which began in September 1991 and raged intermittently throughout 1992, shook the House more severely than any previous scandal, with the possible exception of the 1972 Abscam affair. It is widely believed to have forced at least twenty-five representatives from office, through either retirement or defeat at the polls.

The banking facility's history and traditions of operation, in the view of many, made the final catastrophe inevitable. The bank originated as an informal operation of the House sergeant at arms in the early 1800s, when the Speaker charged that office with disbursing salaries. Sometime between 1830 and 1889, the sergeant at arms began allowing representatives to keep their pay on deposit rather than receive it all at once (though no interest was ever paid). Thus, the office of the sergeant at arms almost inadvertently became a sort of bank, although its informal evolution prevented the establishment of traditional banking practices at the facility, including regular audits.

The lack of common banking controls led to a series of thefts at the House bank over the next century and a half, the first of which occurred in 1889, when a cashier absconded with some $50,000. In 1947, a new scandal erupted over the bank when Kenneth Romney, the previous sergeant at arms, was convicted of lying to General Accounting Office investigators to hide two decades of embezzlement.

Regular GAO audits were first mandated in the aftermath of the Romney scandal, but controls remained weak overall. Around the same time, a practice developed at the bank routinely allowing House members to write overdrafts—in effect, taking short-term, no-interest loans—funded with the deposits of other representatives.

Beginning in 1954 and possibly even earlier, the General Accounting Office periodically voiced concerns about the overdrafts in reports to the House, but House leaders paid little heed. On 18 September 1991, however, the GAO published an unusually detailed report about the overdraft practice, stating that in a one-year period (from mid 1989 to mid 1990), a total of 8,331 overdrafts had been written, and that a group of 134 members had written 581 overdraft checks with face amounts of $1,000 or more. Questions about possible administrative and

HOUSE SCANDALS. Following the discovery of two decades of embezzlement from the House bank by former sergeant at arms Kenneth Romney, a new congressional scandal emerged concerning theft from the House stationery room. The political cartoon depicts the recurring Berryman figure John Q. Public offering brooms to Speaker Joseph W. Martin, Jr. (R-Mass.), so he can clean up the House. Clifford K. Berryman, *Washington Evening Star,* 23 January 1947.

U.S. SENATE COLLECTION, CENTER FOR LEGISLATIVE ARCHIVES

financial abuses by Sergeant at Arms Jack Russ were also raised. Press coverage of the report, which occurred in a climate of escalating controversy over other congressional perquisites and alleged ethical lapses, quickly touched off a tempest. On 3 October the House passed a resolution ordering the bank abolished and an investigation launched.

The investigation by the House Committee on Standards of Official Conduct ultimately led to a vote by the House on 13 March 1992 in favor of public disclosure of the number of overdrafts written by each House member in the two years prior to October 1991. Release of this information forced dozens of members to explain their seemingly irresponsible banking practices to hostile constituents who did not enjoy similar penalty-free banking privileges. Many members saw their perceived transgressions as too great a political liability and chose not to seek reelection. At least a dozen other members with records of significant numbers of overdrafts were defeated in primaries or in the November general election.

Amid the furor following release of the committee report in the spring of 1992, U.S. Attorney General William P. Barr appointed a prosecutor to probe possible criminal wrongdoing in the affair. The prosecutor promptly sought legally to compel the House to provide him its bank records, touching off a new controversy. Some representatives, including Speaker Thomas S. Foley, opposed providing the records on the ground that such an act would jeopardize the independence of the legislative branch. On 30 April, however, the House voted overwhelmingly to comply with the demand, and subsequent court challenges to that decision, on separation-of-powers grounds, were rejected. The prosecutor was ultimately unable to establish wrongdoing in the vast majority of cases. On 6 October 1993 former sergeant at arms Russ pleaded guilty to wire fraud and false statement charges related to misuse of House bank funds. He was later sentenced to two and a half years in prison. One congressman defeated in 1992, Carroll Hubbard, Jr., was convicted on 6 April 1994 of financial crimes uncovered during the bank probe and was later sentenced to prison.

The most significant effects of the House bank scandal were the heavy turnover in House membership that it fueled and the boost it gave to the movement for congressional reform and higher standards of ethical conduct. Some reforms, such as reduced patronage in the House bureaucracy

and appointment of a professional administrator to oversee House affairs, were enacted almost immediately, while others were taken up in the 103d Congress (1993–1995).

[*See also* Standards of Official Conduct Committee, House.]

BIBLIOGRAPHY

Kuntz, Phil. "The History of the House Bank: Scandal Waiting to Happen." *Congressional Quarterly Weekly Report*, 8 February 1992, pp. 282–289.

Simpson, Glenn R. "In the End, Over Half Members with More Than 100 Overdrafts Won't Be Back in 1993." *Roll Call*, 5 November 1992, p. 5.

U.S. House of Representatives. Committee on Standards of Official Conduct. *Inquiry into the Operation of the Bank of the Sergeant at Arms of the House of Representatives.* 102d Congress, 2d sess., 1992. H. Rept. 102-452.

GLENN R. SIMPSON

HOUSE OF REPRESENTATIVES. [*This entry includes three separate articles providing a general analysis of the House of Representatives as a legislative body:*

    An Overview
    Daily Sessions of the House
    House Rules and Procedures

For comparable treatment of the Senate, see Senate. *For broad discussion of congressional powers and practices, see nine articles under* Congress. *See* History of Congress *for eight articles that survey the history and development of Congress from its origins to the present.*]

An Overview

In his notes on the Constitutional Convention of 1787, James Madison called the proposed House of Representatives "the grand repository of the democratic principle of government." The House was designed to be the institution of national government most responsive to popular sentiment. Its members were given two-year terms, shorter than the six-year terms of senators and the four-year terms of presidents, and seats in the House were allocated to states based on population. Unlike the Senate, the presidency, and the Supreme Court, the House was to be directly elected by the people.

For more than a century, the House grew as the nation grew, maintaining a low ratio of representatives to constituents but creating a rapidly expanding legislative body. The House, which had sixty-five members in the First Congress, added seats every ten years, following the national census, to reflect population growth and the addition of new states. In 1911, when the House had 435 seats, Congress decided to halt the body's expansion and instead to reapportion seats among the states every ten years based on changes in relative population, while ensuring that each state had at least one seat. Nonvoting delegates have been added from American Samoa, the District of Columbia, Guam, and the Virgin Islands; a nonvoting resident commissioner represents Puerto Rico.

The House is assigned one special constitutional prerogative—the power to originate all legislation on taxation—in order to protect the people from a confiscatory, self-aggrandizing central government.

The House soon assumed the power to originate all appropriations (spending) legislation as well.

The "grand repository" was not fully trusted by the framers of the Constitution. It was feared that the House, with its short terms and direct mode of election, would react impulsively to shifting public opinion and parochial pressures and would not be a reliable judge of the general welfare. As Madison put it, the House "was liable to err . . . from fickleness and passion." Bicameralism and separation of powers were devised, in part, to make it difficult for the transient public passions registered in the House to be translated into public law. And the House was excluded from certain functions—ratification of treaties and confirmation of presidential nominees for the courts, diplomatic posts, and high government positions—that were given to the Senate.

HOUSE CHAMBER. Under repair, 1948.

These fundamental institutional features—term of office, constituency, size, and constitutional prerogatives and constraints—continue to shape the modern House. For example, the size of the House makes it difficult for the typical member to contribute much on most legislation. Indeed, there is a limit to how much collegial exchange and deliberation is feasible in the House. Policy-making responsibilities must be shouldered by smaller groups, whether committees, party leaders, or ad hoc task forces. When the House relies on committees, policy-making takes on a decentralized cast; when the majority party and its leaders dominate policy-making, it takes on a centralized look. The history of the House has often been characterized as oscillating between centralized and decentralized control.

Reliance on committees and subcommittees has, however, been the general tendency. Only occasionally, on important, highly partisan issues and when powerful people have held positions, have majority party leaders directed the process with a strong hand. The inclination toward a decentralized, committee-oriented process is partly a result of the need for a division of labor to manage a large work load. This system also meets the needs of individual members, who enjoy a process that enables them to contribute meaningfully to public policy, at least within certain policy areas, and to exercise special influence in areas of particular interest to themselves or their constituencies.

The Modern House. The basic institutional features of the House, as well as its tendency toward a decentralized process, are reflected in its modern rules, internal distribution of power, media attention, policy-making role, and capacity to change.

Rules and procedures. The House and its rules are recreated every two years. In early January, following each election, the House elects a new Speaker and adopts a set of rules. The last Speaker of the House, if he or she is reelected and his or her party remains in the majority, is routinely reelected to the position. The rules of the last Congress, usually with a few changes, are adopted again. Both the vote on the Speaker and the vote on the rules are party-line votes, as the two major parties nominate their own leaders for Speaker and usually differ over the content of the rules.

The rules of the modern House are more elaborate than those of the Senate. Because of its size, the House cannot afford unlimited debate and unrestricted amending activity, so its rules carefully limit and structure debate, and bar nongermane amendments. Floor debate and amending action on most important legislation occurs in the Committee of the Whole, where debate is severely limited but where business may be conducted with a quorum of only one hundred members. Generally, important legislation is brought to the floor and considered in the Committee of the Whole by special rules, written by the Rules Committee and supported by majority votes. Special rules allow the majority to impose its agenda and further structure or limit debate and amendments. And, unlike the Senate, the House has a previous question rule that allows a majority to bring debate to an end and force a vote.

The potential unwieldiness of the large House has led to the emergence of a powerful presiding officer. The Speaker, who gains the post by virtue of leading the majority party, refers legislation to committees, controls the recognition of members to speak or offer motions from the floor, makes parliamentary rulings, and appoints conference committee delegations in addition to exercising numerous powers within his or her party caucus. No other member of Congress, House or Senate, enjoys formal powers as great as those of the Speaker.

The strong speakership, along with rules allowing simple majorities to overcome procedural obstacles that minorities may place in their way, gives the House a strongly majoritarian character. The majority party and its leaders usually exercise control over the agenda. The minority party, small factions, and individual representatives have no effective options when facing a cohesive majority party. This stands in sharp contrast to the Senate, where minorities and individual senators have the means to obstruct rapid action by offering amendments and conducting extended debate.

Yet the full potential of majoritarian rule is seldom realized in the House. Divisions within the majority party often limit its ability to devise policy and push it through the House. Majority party leaders usually rely on committees to initiate legislative action and draft the details of legislation. Much of the central leaders' effort is devoted to facilitating the work of committees and managing the flow of legislation from committees and through the House floor. The House seems to operate most smoothly when committees and the majority party leadership operate in collaboration or partnership.

House rules and precedents reinforce the power of standing committees. The rules make it difficult to circumvent a committee by bringing a measure directly to the floor or by attaching the measure as an amendment to some other legislation. House

Organization of the House of Representatives

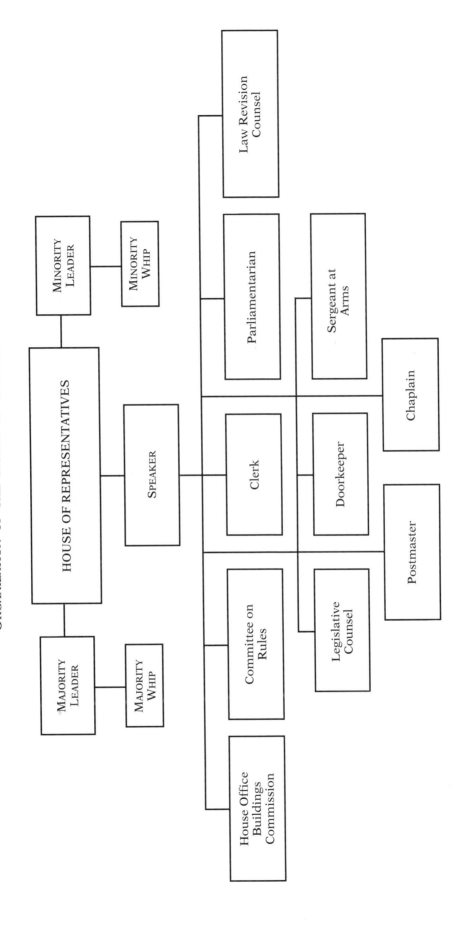

committees are granted a great deal of deference. Committee bill managers are granted advantages on the floor, and committee members dominate conference committee delegations. Committees also are advantaged by the expertise their members acquire through years of service, their relationships with interest groups and executive agencies, and their large professional staffs.

Media coverage. The typical representative lacks the influence and media visibility of the typical senator. The sheer size of the House reduces the formal power of the average representative. Majoritarian rules minimize the opportunities for individuals or factions to attract attention by employing obstructionist tactics. And the committee-centered process removes much of the action from the House floor to committee rooms, where legislative markups seldom draw the attention of visitors, print journalists, or the electronic media.

A study of television news coverage in the mid-1980s demonstrated that senators averaged six times as much attention as representatives. One reason for the differential is that few presidential candidates emerge from the House. The Senate is the home of a larger number of potential, current, and former presidential candidates, whose national visibility makes them attractive subjects for TV news and feature programs. Representatives are less frequently seen as the leading spokespersons for a point of view or cause. And the fact that senators typically make a greater effort to attract media attention plays a role as well. Senators, who generally face more sharply contested elections, must appeal to larger constituencies. Because they are frequently seeking to build a national base for a presidential bid, they work harder to appear on television news and interview programs.

In the middle decades of the twentieth century, the low-visibility, decentralized character of House decision making gave the House a technocratic flavor. The House, as Nelson Polsby noted in a 1970 essay, was a "highly specialized instrument for processing legislation." Policy-making was quietly dominated by senior members, particularly committee chairmen, who were disproportionately southern and conservative. Individual members were specialists in the subject matter of their committees and tended to be more expert than their counterparts in the Senate. They gained power by accruing seniority and waiting their turn to chair subcommittees and full committees. During this period, partisanship was muted in the House, particularly in the field of foreign policy, where the Cold War consensus after World War II kept the House in line with the president on most matters.

Changes since the 1960s. But the House is not immutable. To the contrary, important and dramatic change has occurred since the late 1960s. Perhaps most conspicuously, more representatives now seek to use television as a tool for generating attention for themselves and their causes. Though still a small proportion of the House, a number of representatives now have national visibility as leaders of certain factions or crusades. Recent House party leaders have hired media specialists, more aggressively sought to influence public opinion through the mass media, and sometimes incorporated explicit media strategies into their legislative plans. And spicy debates in televised floor sessions occasionally generate network news coverage. The House still lacks the coverage given the Senate, but it is not the nearly invisible institution it was at midcentury.

Below the surface of media coverage, the neatly decentralized, committee-oriented policy-making of the past has given way to a more fluid process. In the early 1970s, the grip of full committee chairs on committee action was loosened. Most committees were required for the first time to create subcommittees with guaranteed jurisdictions, bill referral, and staff. Committee chairs faced biennial election by the Democratic Caucus; between 1974 and 1990, six chairmen lost bids to be reelected to their posts. Since 1974, committee chairs have been less obstructionist and more sensitive to the preferences of the majority party caucus. Furthermore, new sunshine rules required committees to open most meetings to the public and required committees to maintain a public record of committee actions and voting.

At the same time, the Speaker gained new formal powers. He acquired new discretion to refer legislation to multiple committees, the ability to set deadlines for committee consideration in some circumstances, more influence over committee assignments, and firm control over the membership of the Rules Committee. Moreover, rank-and-file members gained more opportunities to participate thanks to the revitalization of the Democratic Caucus and rules changes that made it possible to record votes on floor amendments and that encouraged the Speaker to appoint larger conference delegations.

At first, the reforms of the 1970s appeared to have a strongly decentralizing effect. Committee government was replaced by subcommittee government, observers argued, and the House's ability to enact coherent legislation in a timely manner declined. Norms restraining participation among junior members and committee outsiders were weakened, and floor amendments to committee bills multiplied. The Speakers of the 1970s, Carl B. Albert (D-Okla.) and Thomas P. (Tip) O'Neill, Jr. (D-Mass.), did not exploit their new powers. The predictability and efficiency of midcentury gave way to a more fragmented, seemingly disorderly process.

Conditions changed in the 1980s and early 1990s. Tolerance of the chaos on the House floor wore thin. The legislative work load moderated as the policy agenda shifted to resolving serious fiscal problems. Democrats, who had suffered deep regional divisions in the 1960s and early 1970s, became more cohesive. The majority party Democrats of the House were thrown on the defensive as Republicans gained control of the White House (1981–1993) and Senate (1981–1987). Divided party control of the major institutions intensified conflict between the legislative and executive branches. Policy stalemate on fiscal, civil rights, environmental, and other issues was common. And attributing and avoiding blame for policy stalemate became a dominant strategy of both parties.

In response, the House became more partisan, more centralized, and more dependent on flexible special rules. Speaker O'Neill became more assertive in the 1980s, and his successor, James C. Wright, Jr. (D-Tex.), aggressively shaped the agenda of the House. These Speakers, along with Wright's successor, Thomas S. Foley (D-Wash.), more frequently sought special rules to limit and structure floor amendments. Budget rules and negotiations among top leaders on budget matters reduced the autonomy of committees and their subcommittees. Partisanship and the cohesiveness of the House Democrats further diminished the policy contributions of minority party Republicans, who, out of the majority since the years 1953 to 1955, became increasingly frustrated. The House of the 1980s and early 1990s looked so different from the decentralized one predicted in the 1970s that some observers began to refer to the "postreform" House.

In the postreform House, the decision-making process looks more flexible than it did in the tidy, committee-oriented process of midcentury. The Speaker uses multiple referral power more frequently to shape committee action on major legislation. The Speaker often appoints task forces of Democrats to design policy and generate support for the party. The task forces are extracommittee entities, composed of members and nonmembers of the committees with formal jurisdiction. Furthermore, the content of legislation is more frequently negotiated among contending factions and committees after a committee has reported the measure but before it is taken to the floor. Such negotiations, usually conducted under the direction of the Speaker, often lead the Rules Committee to structure floor action so as to advantage the negotiated product.

Many of these changes were reflected in the policy-making role of the House. The House, once less liberal and assertive than the Senate, became more liberal and assertive in the 1970s and 1980s. In the 1970s, liberated subcommittee chairs and rank-and-file members, bolstered by enlarged staffs, assumed more initiative in generating policy ideas. More House members ran for president, cultivated national constituencies, and became recognized policy leaders. The House became a more important source of policy ideas in both the domestic and foreign policy fields. Indeed, the House often led the Senate in challenging the foreign policies of Republican presidents. No longer is the House merely a "specialized instrument for processing legislation."

Essential Elements of House Politics. The record of recent decades illustrates several properties of House politics. First, House decision-making processes are quite malleable. They respond to external forces, particularly the nature of policy problems, electoral forces, and relations with the president and the Senate, and to internal factors, such as the expectations of a changing membership, the distribution of policy views within and between the parties, the personal style of individual Speakers, and inherited procedures and structures.

Second, the House is majoritarian. House policy majorities, particularly when a policy majority can be created from within the majority party, are usually able to gain House approval of their legislation. Generally, a cohesive majority party can establish rules and pass legislation that suit its needs. Cross-party majority coalitions face greater difficulty when they are opposed by the majority party leadership or committee leaders, who enjoy substantial parliamentary advantages. But even a determined cross-party majority coalition can eventually force action on its legislation or even impose new procedures. Many of the new budget procedures created in the 1980s and 1990s were the work of cross-party coalitions.

Third, floor decision making in the House is structured by formal rules. The House relies on its standing rules—and increasingly on special rules that supplant or supplement the standing rules—to guide virtually all floor action on legislation. In contrast, the Senate lacks detailed rules to order floor debate or limit floor amendments and must instead rely on unanimous consent agreements, which are negotiated on a case-by-case basis, to order floor activity.

The House's malleability, majoritarianism, and formality are related. In contrast to the Senate, where large minorities can block changes in the rules, the House may change its rules by simple majority vote. This allows House majorities to adjust the rules frequently to meet changing conditions, and it allows House majorities to grant procedural advantage to their own proposals by imposing special rules of their choosing.

Fourth, party considerations structure House decision-making processes. In both houses, the two major parties make committee assignments, sit on opposite sides of the center aisle on the floor, and usually serve as the basis for organizing floor debate. The House goes further by granting to the leader of the majority party the wide powers of the speakership. Consequently, the majority party leadership has the ability to set the agenda of the House without meaningful consultation with the minority.

Finally, the House is constrained by the demands of the rank-and-file membership. Party structure and majoritarianism might appear to be a formula for rule by central majority party leaders. Yet party leaders are severely constrained by the tolerance of the rank and file. House members know that the next election is never far away, and they realize that their reelection prospects turn on what they do for their constituencies. These considerations uncouple many members from their own party leaders. To be sure, the House is not as individualistic as the Senate, but it is far more individualistic than most other national legislatures. Its leaders and committees must, and usually do, operate within bounds acceptable to the majority of members.

House politics, then, usually represents some balance among competing pressures for centralization, decentralization, and a more collegial process. The size and work load of the House require the delegation of power to subgroups of members. The interests of individual members limit the extent to which power devolves to small groups of central leaders or committee members. House members have created a maze of formal rules and insisted on majority rule in order to limit the exercise of arbitrary power by advantaged groups.

BIBLIOGRAPHY

Bach, Stanley, and Steven S. Smith. *Managing Uncertainty in the House of Representatives.* 1988.

Davidson, Roger H., and Walter J. Oleszek. *Congress against Itself.* 1977.

Fenno, Richard F., Jr. "The Internal Distribution of Influence: The House." In *The Congress and America's Future*, edited by David B. Truman. 1965.

Jacobson, Gary. *The Politics of Congressional Elections.* 1987.

Madison, James. *Notes of Debates in the Federal Convention of 1787.* 1969.

Ornstein, Norman. "The House and Senate in a New Congress." In *The New Congress*, edited by Thomas Mann and Norman Ornstein. 1981.

Polsby, Nelson. "Strengthening Congress in National Policy Making." *Yale Review* (Summer 1970): 481–497.

Price, David E. *The Congressional Experience.* 1992.

Sinclair, Barbara. *Majority Leadership in the U.S. House.* 1983.

STEVEN S. SMITH

Daily Sessions of the House

A typical day in the House of Representatives begins with the opening of the cloakroom doors. The sergeant at arms enters the House chamber carrying the mace, an ebony and silver rod symbolizing his authority and that of the institution. He is followed by the Speaker of the House, who ascends the rostrum. The various clerks take their places at the lower two tiers. With the bang of the Speaker's gavel, the House convenes.

Normally the House convenes at noon, although the press of business may dictate an earlier, or occasionally a later, hour. The chaplain of the House, or a guest chaplain, delivers a prayer. The Speaker then announces his approval of the House Journal (the official record of the proceedings of the House) from the last day of session. At times, members may ask for a vote on the Speaker's approval of the Journal, a vote that is used more to discover who is present for that day's deliberations than actually to approve the Journal. Next, the Speaker chooses a member to lead the House in the Pledge of Allegiance.

One-minute speeches follow, alternating between majority and minority members. These speeches are popular for their value in publicizing a wide variety of subjects, both to constituents and to colleagues. How many one-minute speeches are permitted on any particular day depends on the Speaker's judgment of how pressing the day's agenda appears.

The House then turns to routine—that is, uncontroversial or minimally controversial—business. On the first and third Mondays of each month, the clerk will call the Consent Calendar. Uncontroversial bills expected to clear the House by unanimous consent with little or no debate are scheduled under this procedure. In addition to the 2 percent of all measures considered under the Consent Calendar procedure, the House calls up another 33 percent of its measures for consideration with a simple unanimous consent request, again with virtually no debate.

On the second and fourth Tuesdays of the month, the clerk calls the Private Calendar. About 4 percent of bills that reach the floor affect the welfare of private individuals only, and not the nation as a whole. They are considered with very little debate, and usually passed by voice vote.

Every Monday and every Tuesday of every week are considered "suspension days." Under the suspension procedure, it is in order to move to suspend the Rules of the House and pass legislation whether the measure is still in committee, pending on the calendar, or being held at the House desk. A motion to suspend limits debate on a measure to forty minutes and prohibits floor amendments. Adoption of a motion to suspend the rules and pass a bill requires two-thirds of those present to vote in the affirmative. The suspension procedure is used for approximately 35 percent of all measures that receive floor consideration. From the majority perspective, this method is popular because the committee version of the bill is protected from any further modification on the floor. From the minority perspective, the prohibition against amendments is a drawback, although the minority does gain the advantage of being able to defeat a measure with only one-third of the House in opposition, rather than the one-half normally required.

The House considers another 19 percent of legislation on the floor as "privileged matter." Under this procedure, debate is normally restricted to one hour and amendments are permitted only if the House defeats a motion calling for the previous question, a rare event.

In the early afternoon the House considers that day's planned agenda. The main piece of legislation chosen undoubtedly has some controversy attached to it, and amendments are expected. Or it may contain language that either raises or spends public money. For any of these reasons, the House considers the measure in a special legislative forum—the Committee of the Whole House on the State of the Union, better known simply as the Committee of the Whole. The House transforms itself into the committee through two simple steps. First, the Speaker leaves the rostrum and appoints a majority-party member to serve as the presiding officer in his stead. Second, the sergeant at arms lowers the mace. Both actions signal that the House is no longer meeting but has resolved into the Committee of the Whole. Although the chamber and membership stay the same, the more expeditious rules of debate and amendment utilized by committees can now govern.

Most significant and controversial measures considered in the Committee of the Whole are considered under the auspices of a "special rule," a resolution reported out of the House Committee on Rules, which must then be adopted by the House. It acts as a blueprint, setting the terms for debate and amendment of a specific bill. Some 7 percent of all measures are considered according to the provisions of a special rule.

The presiding officer, now addressed as "Mister [or Madam] Chairman," directs the clerk to designate the bill before the Committee. A period of general debate on the legislation then follows. Time for debate is evenly divided between the majority and minority sides. A majority and minority floor manager control and allocate the time for debate on their respective sides of the aisle.

After all time for general debate has been either utilized or yielded back to the chair, the clerk designates the first section of the bill as open for amendment. An amendment—a proposal to change the text of the bill—must be formally offered as either a motion to insert language, a motion to delete language, or a motion to strike out language and insert new text in that same place.

When all amendments have been disposed of, the Committee of the Whole disbands via a motion to rise and then resolves itself back into the House. The chairman leaves the rostrum and the Speaker returns. The mace is returned to its original position. The measure debated and amended in the Committee is now before the House for a vote on final passage. If desired, a minority member may at this point move to recommit the bill to the committee that originally had reported it to the House. The motion may be an indirect attempt to defeat the measure or, if it contains instructions, may be a final attempt to amend the bill. Once the recommittal motion has been disposed of, the House takes the vote on final passage of the measure.

It is now late afternoon or early evening. The majority leader and minority leader often engage in a short dialogue to inform the members about the remaining agenda for the week. Members may begin to leave the chamber and head for official dinners, receptions, or home knowing that no more votes will occur that day.

The House completes the day with a series of special order speeches. These speeches can be on any subject a member wishes. They vary in length from five minutes to the maximum time allowed, one hour. Members must get the unanimous consent of the House prior to delivering a special order speech. Because these speeches are considered nonlegislative debate and no votes are involved, the member giving the special order usually speaks to an empty chamber—but live television cameras in the chamber continue to ensure that there will be an audience. The last motion of the day—the motion to adjourn—is usually made by the member giving the last special order of the day. The Speaker pro tempore (substitute Speaker) and the clerks then leave the rostrum, and the day is over.

[*See also* Amending; Calendars; Committee of the Whole.]

BIBLIOGRAPHY

Congressional Quarterly. *Congress A to Z.* 1988. P. 189.
Green, Alan. *Gavel to Gavel: A Guide to the Televised Proceedings of Congress.* 1991.

ILONA B. NICKELS

House Rules and Procedures

The procedures followed by the House of Representatives are derived from several sources. First, the U.S. Constitution, while giving each house the authority to determine the rules of its proceedings, establishes certain basic requirements to which those rules must conform. Article I, section 5 provides that a quorum (a majority of each house) is necessary to do business. The yeas and nays may be demanded by one-fifth of those present, and votes so taken must be "entered on the Journal," that is, made a matter of public record.

The second source of House procedure is the Rules of the House, adopted by the body for each Congress. Many of these rules are readopted when each new Congress convenes in the January following its election. In the 103d Congress the House had fifty-one adopted rules. Some individual rules contain disparate and independent concepts so that in reality almost two hundred different precepts are expressed in the Rules. Of these, about thirty have their origins in the First Congress.

Some of the rules deal with the organization of the House. The duties of the five elected officers of the House (the Speaker, clerk, doorkeeper, sergeant at arms, and chaplain) are set forth. The number, jurisdiction, and oversight responsibilities of the House's twenty-two standing committees are specified.

Another category of rules is perhaps best termed administrative, or regulatory: prescribing how the House chamber and the galleries of the House may be used, providing for services of the House (how, for instance, its proceedings are to be recorded and broadcast), establishing a code of conduct for members and employees, and delineating how expenses of members and committees are to be accounted for.

Finally, there are rules that deal with the passage of legislation: detailing the motions to be utilized in the conduct of business on the floor and in committees, establishing the scope and time for debate and the amendment process, dealing with amendments made by the Senate, and reconciling differences between the content of House and Senate legislation.

One House rule specifically makes the provisions of Jefferson's Manual applicable to and binding on the House where its concepts are not inconsistent with the adopted rules. The Manual, compiled by Jefferson when he was vice president of the United States and thus president of the Senate and its presiding officer, is a restatement of the procedure of the British House of Commons during the period. Many of the principles set forth in the Manual, particularly those dealing with the conduct of debate in the House and the relationship between House and Senate, are followed today.

Finally, many statutes contain explicit rules for the conduct of certain types of legislative activity. The Legislative Reorganization acts of 1946 and 1970 and the Congressional Budget Act of 1974 are examples of laws that contain rules governing House and Senate consideration of certain legislation.

Undergirding these four sources of rules are the decisions of the Speakers and other presiding officers of the House (precedents of the House) interpreting the specific written rules. The House follows precedent when points of order or parliamentary inquiries are raised on the floor. The decisions rendered by the House itself (by its vote on an appeal) or by various presiding officers in ruling on points of order or answering parliamentary inquiries have been recorded, annotated, and published. *Hinds' Precedents, Cannon's Precedents, Deschler's Precedents,* and Deschler and Brown's

Procedure in the United States House of Representatives are such works. The compilation process is a continuous one, and the number of precedents created by rulings of the chair grows annually. Finding the applicable precedents to guide the chair in a contemporary ruling is one of the main tasks of the parliamentarian's office.

Steps in the Legislative Process. Rules and procedures affect all the stages in the legislative process: (1) introduction and referral of legislation; (2) committee consideration and reporting to the House; (3) consideration, debate, and passage; (4) action on Senate amendments, including conference consideration; and (5) transmittal of bills to the president, and action if the president vetoes a bill.

Introduction and referral. Legislative measures may be introduced by placing them in the "hopper," a receptacle placed at the rostrum of the House when it is in session (Rule XXII, clause 4). They may be introduced by one member, but public bills may be cosponsored.

Bills are referred by the Speaker (Rule XXII, clause 4) to the appropriate committees of jurisdiction. (The jurisdiction of the twenty-two standing committees is spelled out in Rule X, clause 1). The Speaker is required to refer a bill to all committees having jurisdiction (Rule X, clause 5). Measures may be referred to a single committee, to several concurrently, or to several in sequence (clause 5). The Speaker's authority (under clause 5) permits the division of a bill for reference (for example, by giving Title 1 to committee A, Title 2 to committee B, and so on) or, with the permission of the House, a bill's referral to a select committee that the Speaker would then appoint.

Certain committees are authorized to originate legislation without having it referred to them. Rule XI, clause 4, gives this privilege to the committees on Appropriations, Budget, House Administration, Rules, and Standards of Official Conduct. Bills that originate in this manner and are then reported to the House can be considered on the floor as "privileged" and do not have to be given a floor slot by the Committee on Rules (see Rule XI, clause 4[b]) or by some other scheduling mechanism such as suspension of the rules. Intervention of the Committee on Rules may be sought if the appropriation bill, for instance, requires protection from points of order, or if there is a desire to structure the process by which the bill may be amended.

Committee consideration and reporting to the House. Committee hearings, consideration, and amendment of bills are conducted in accordance with procedures broadly outlined in Rule XI, clause 2. In the interrogation of witnesses before committees and in the markup (amendment process) of bills, the five-minute rule is applied: each member recognized is entitled to five minutes to ask questions or to offer or debate an amendment. A committee can establish the quorum required for taking testimony as being as few as two members. For preliminary legislative steps (voting on amendments and other motions in markup), the quorum may be as low as one-third of the committee membership. For reporting a bill to the House, however, a majority of the members must be present. Proxies may be used for certain actions in committees, pursuant to committee-adopted rules, which must be consistent with the overall House rule on the subject (see Rule XI, clause 2[f]).

When all committees to which a measure has been referred have reported, the bill is assigned by the Speaker to one of the calendars of the House—the Union Calendar (or, more precisely and accurately, the calendar of the Committee of the Whole House on the State of the Union), the House Calendar, or the Private Calendar (see Rule XIII, clause 1). Measures that raise revenue, directly or indirectly spend money, or dispose of property go to the Union Calendar and must be considered in a Committee of the Whole (Rule XXIII, clause 3). The House Calendar is the repository of all other public measures.

Private bills, for the relief of an individual or a corporation, go to the Private Calendar. Bills on the House Calendar or Union Calendar that are thought to have no opposition can, at the request of a member, be placed on the Consent Calendar. Both the Private and Consent calendars are "called," that is, the bills on these calendars are considered without objection in the order on the calendars. The Consent Calendar is called on the first and third Mondays of each month (Rule XIII, clause 4), and the Private Calendar on the first and third Tuesdays (Rule XXIV, clause 6). If there is an objection to consideration of a bill on the Consent or Private calendar, other procedures must be employed to obtain floor consideration.

Consideration, debate, and passage. Rules exist that provide for calling bills on the House and Union calendars, but they are seldom utilized in modern practice. Calendar Wednesday (Rule XXIV, clause 7) does provide a mechanism for considering bills on the Union Calendar: the standing committees are called alphabetically and, when a bill is reached in the call, the chairman may call it up. House Calendar bills are eligible for consideration under Rule XXIV, clause 4 (the "morning hour" rule), but since there are more efficient ways to secure their consideration, this rule is not used.

The rules also set aside special days for the consideration of measures under suspension of the rules. On each Monday and Tuesday the Speaker has authority to recognize motions to suspend the rules (Rule XXVII, clause 1). Such motions require a two-thirds vote for adoption (two-thirds of those present and voting, a quorum being present) and can be used for a variety of legislative purposes: a bill may be brought directly to the floor, avoiding committee consideration, or any rule of the House that impedes passage can be circumvented. The motion may be to suspend the rules and pass a bill; to agree to Senate amendments to a House bill; or to suspend a measure and agree to a conference report on it. Debate is limited to forty minutes (twenty in favor, twenty opposed). When pending, the motion is not subject to amendment; although the proponent may include an amendment in the motion, as, for instance, "I move to suspend the rules and pass the reported bill with a further amendment that is at the desk." As a session of the House proceeds and committees have reported measures to the House, this mechanism is used to gain consideration and passage of a large proportion of House business. However, because of the supermajority required to adopt the motion, it is obviously not suited for the consideration of controversial legislation.

Finally, Rule XXIV, clause 8, permits the Committee on the District of Columbia to seek recognition on the second and fourth Mondays of the month to call up measures dealing with the District and reported by that committee.

Legislative measures in the House take several forms: most are introduced as House bills (noted in the *Congressional Record* and other documents as H.R., followed by an identifying number). Where the use of a preamble is necessary, the proper legislative vehicle is the House joint resolution (H.J. Res.). Both of these, when enacted, are sent to the president for his approval and become laws of the United States when so approved. Matters internal to the House, such as authorizing printing of a document for use by the House, can be in the form of House resolutions (H. Res.). If the concurrence of the Senate is necessary (e.g., to provide for an adjournment of the Congress or of either house for more than three days), the proper vehicle is the House concurrent resolution (H. Con. Res.). The Senate has similar nomenclature (S., S.J. Res.) for measures originating in that body.

Voting in the House can be by voice ("Those in favor will say 'Aye'; those opposed, 'No.'"); by division ("Those in favor will stand and remain standing until counted; those opposed will rise . . ."); by the yeas and nays (if supported by one-fifth of those present); or by recorded vote (if ordered by one-fifth of a quorum). (See Rule I, clause 5[a]; U.S. Constitution, Article I, section 5). The House uses electronic voting for taking the yeas and nays and record votes. On certain types of questions the Speaker has the authority to postpone the votes to a later time on the same or the next legislative day (see Rule I, clause 5[b]). This authority is customarily used on rules-suspension days, when roll-call votes (if ordered) on motions entertained and debated on Monday or Tuesday are postponed to and taken at an announced time within the next two legislative days. Votes then come in sequence without intervening debate, and can be reduced to five minutes each.

While there is a rule for the order of business on any legislative day (Rule XXIV, clause 1), the House, after prayer by the chaplain and approval of the Journal (see Rule XXIV, clause 1), normally interrupts that order to consider business that is privileged under other House rules. While appropriation bills and concurrent resolutions of the budget are often considered under the rule giving them privilege (Rule XI, clause 4), most major bills are brought to the floor pursuant to resolutions reported from the Committee on Rules, providing special orders for their consideration (see Rule XI, clause 4[b]). A typical special order will provide for consideration of the measure in the House or in Committee of the Whole, whichever is appropriate; specify a length of time for general debate on the bill; waive any points of order that would otherwise inhibit consideration of the measure; address the amendment process by making specific amendments in order or by prohibiting certain (or all) amendments; and provide that, at the conclusion of the amendment process, the bill shall be reported back to the House, where the previous question is considered as ordered to final passage (thereby prohibiting further debate or amendment in the House) except for one motion to recommit.

There are numerous patterns for these special orders. The design of a rule will depend on the legislative complexity of the subject, the political battleground anticipated, and the amount of floor time available in the House schedule. "Open" rules permit all germane amendments to be offered, whereas "closed" rules may prohibit all amendments except those offered by direction of the committee reporting the measure; variations on these forms are referred to as "modified open" or "modified closed" rules. Some rules, especially those that inhibit amendments or curtail the right of the minority in the House to offer a motion to recommit, may be opposed by factions of the House. An effort may be made to defeat the previous question on the rule in order to offer an amendment to it and change the procedures recommended by the Committee on Rules or to defeat the rule.

A special order of this character may be reported, as privileged, from the Committee on Rules (Rule XI, clause 4[b]). When called up for consideration, the resolution is debated for up to one hour, with time customarily divided equally between the member of the Committee on Rules calling up the resolution and a minority member of the Rules Committee. If the resolution is adopted, the House has thereby established a procedural framework for the consideration of the bill in question.

Without the discipline imposed by a special rule, consideration of a bill would be under the general rules of the House. Debate could conceivably proceed for up to 435 hours (if each member exercised his or her right to speak for one hour, the maximum time permitted). Following debate, the bill would be "read for amendment," that is, considered by section or paragraph for amendment, and any germane amendment could be offered.

The germaneness rule (Rule XVI, clause 7) is an important discipline that the House has imposed on itself since 1789. While parliamentary law at that time did not require that an amendment relate to the text under consideration (see *Hinds' Precedents*, V, section 5825), the House determined that such a rule was essential for orderly legislative procedure. The rule applies to whatever text is pending: a first-degree amendment must be germane to the bill under consideration, and a second-degree amendment must be germane to the primary or first-degree amendment. Hundreds of germaneness rulings have been made since 1789, and the chair, in ruling on a point of order, attempts to follow the applicable precedent. Several general principles emerge from the germaneness precedents: one individual proposition is not germane to another; a specific subject may not be amended by an amendment that is general in scope; an individual or specific addition or subtraction may be in order to a general proposition. The germaneness of an amendment must be determined from its text and not from some abstract "purpose." The rule is applied in House committees during markup and on the House floor when the bill is read for amend-

ment; it is sometimes also applied to have a separate vote on a Senate amendment not germane to a House bill, as well as on nongermane Senate amendments agreed to by conferees.

The Committee of the Whole House is a useful parliamentary fiction that permits business to be expedited. To an observer in the gallery, there is little discernible change when the House resolves into the Committee of the Whole. The Speaker appoints a member to preside over the deliberations of the Committee, the mace is lowered from its pedestal, and debate is directed to "Mr. (or Madam) Chairman," not to the Speaker. But the "invisible" changes in procedure are substantial: the quorum required in the full House is a majority of those members elected, sworn, and still living whose membership has not been terminated by resignation or action of the House. (See U.S. Constitution, Article I, section 5.) In a "full" House, a quorum is 218. But in Committee, under Rule XXIII, clause 2(a), the quorum is reduced to 100.

Debate in the Committee is of two types: general debate, during which each member can theoretically speak for one hour, and debate on amendments under the five-minute rule. The general debate is invariably limited to a reasonable period, either by a unanimous consent agreement entered into before the House resolves into Committee or by the terms of a special order reported from the Committee on Rules and adopted by the House. The five-minute rule (Rule XXIII, clause 5) permits any person offering an amendment to speak for five minutes in favor of it. A member opposed can have the same time to speak in opposition. Debate in this mode can be continued beyond the ten minutes by use of a pro forma amendment to "strike out the last word," which permits an additional ten minutes of debate. Pro forma amendments are normally considered as withdrawn after the debate thereon, so another can be offered, allowing more debate (in blocks of ten minutes) on a pending primary amendment.

In the Committee, the constitutional right for one-fifth of those present to demand the yeas and nays (U.S. Constitution, Article I, section 5) is not applicable, but a "record" vote (also taken by roll call or electronic device) can be demanded by twenty-five members (Rule XXIII, clause 2[b]). When the Committee of the Whole finishes the amendment process, it reports its work back to the full House, where separate votes may be demanded on those amendments adopted in the Committee, and where the vote on final passage occurs.

Pending the vote on final passage, one motion to

recommit the bill is in order. This motion, recognition for which is the right of someone who is opposed to the bill (Rule XVI, clause 4), is an important tool for the minority in the House, since it provides a last opportunity to shape the bill to its liking. If the motion is to recommit (to any committee) with instructions (that is, to amend or direct the committee to take certain further legislative action), it may be debated for ten minutes (five on each side), if demanded. A "straight" motion, without instructions, is not debatable.

The rules of the House specify the motions that can be entertained, as a matter of right, at appropriate times during sessions of the House and of the Committee of the Whole. When a question is under debate, the permissible motions, in their order of precedence, are the following: to adjourn (with its variations of equal privilege—the motion that when the House adjourns, it stand adjourned to a day and time certain, and the motion to authorize the Speaker to declare a recess); to lay on the table; to move for the previous question; to postpone to a day certain; to amend; to refer; and to postpone indefinitely. The first three of these motions—to adjourn, to table, and to move for the previous question—are not debatable. Understanding the precedence of the motions in Rule XVI, clause 4, is essential. If the House adopts a motion to adjourn, obviously no further actions on the matter under debate can be taken until the next legislative day. If the motion to table is adopted, the matter is thereby adversely disposed of, without debate. If the previous question is ordered, amendments and the other motions of lesser precedence are no longer in order. Knowing when to apply these various motions and using them to accomplish a legislative purpose is the essence of legislative strategy.

The *motion to lay on the table* is used in the House to dispose of a matter adversely, without debate. It is in order whenever a motion is pending that is either debatable or subject to amendment, but it is not used in the Committee of the Whole. It is useful in reaching a quick decision on a matter; an appeal from the decision of the chair, which is subject to debate in the House, is often laid on the table to get an immediate decision on the question of order. Privileged business, if presented unexpectedly, is often tabled (or referred) so that the House can continue its announced schedule.

The *motion for the previous question* is used to cut off debate and amendments and bring the House to an immediate vote on the underlying motion or question. For example, when a resolution providing for printing a document for the House is under debate, the member in charge will customarily move the previous question when he feels there has been sufficient explanation. If carried, no further debate is in order and the House then immediately has before it the question on the adoption of the resolution. If defeated, the manager loses the floor; a member opposing the previous question is entitled to recognition and can offer an amendment and have an hour to debate it. At the conclusion of that hour, the previous question can again be moved, and in this manner the House determines when a majority is ready to vote on the underlying resolution, without further amendment.

The two *motions to postpone*—to a day or time certain, and indefinitely—have quite different uses. The first obviously allows the House to influence its agenda. An example of its use can be found in the manner of dealing with a presidential veto. When the president vetoes a bill and returns it to the house of origin, the Constitution requires the house to "proceed to reconsider it" (Article I, section 7). This does not mean that the house has to vote immediately on the reconsideration ("the question is, shall the bill pass, the objections of the President to the contrary notwithstanding"); it can refer the matter to committee or postpone consideration indefinitely or to a day certain. Such motions are debatable under the hour rule.

The *motion to amend* is one of the most important legislative tools offered in Rule XVI. House rules permit one amendment at a time to be offered to pending text. But that amendment (the primary, or first-degree, amendment) can be amended, either by a second-degree amendment or by a substitute amendment. The substitute itself (which is not considered to be in the second degree) may also have one amendment offered to it. The "amendment tree," as it is called, can then have four components. When all these amendments are pending, the "tree" is fully developed; no further amendment is in order since it would be in the "third degree," which is specifically prohibited. Jefferson's Manual governs the order of voting on these amendments. When one of the second-degree amendments is adopted or rejected, another amendment can be offered to fill its place on the tree. In the House the motion to amend is debatable under the hour rule. In the Committee of the Whole the five-minute rule applies.

The parliamentary *motion to refer* is recognized in several House rules. When a matter is "under debate," the motion to refer has the precedence indicated above and is debatable within narrow limits: the debate must be focused on the question of referral and not on the merits of the underlying proposition. The motion can direct referral to any committee or committees. This motion is used by the House when a matter is before the body that has not had prior committee consideration. For instance, if a resolution is offered from the floor that raises a question of privilege of the House, the motion to refer is one of the preferred options. Likewise, when the president returns a vetoed bill, the House often refers the measure back to the committee from which it came rather than voting immediately on whether to override the president's veto.

The same rule (Rule XVI, clause 4) provides for a variation on the motion to refer after the previous question is ordered on a bill or joint resolution to final passage. One *motion to recommit* is guaranteed at this point, and the Speaker is instructed to recognize a member opposed to the measure to offer the motion. Debate on a simple or straight motion to recommit at this stage is precluded by the operation of the previous question on the bill "to final passage," but if the motion is to recommit with instructions, ten minutes of debate are specifically guaranteed, which can be extended to one hour if the manager of the bill so demands.

Rule XVII provides for a *motion to commit* or recommit pending the motion for the previous question or after it has been ordered, and the broader language of this form of the motion to refer covers resolutions as well as bills. The motion under this rule can be applied to Senate amendments and various other motions pending in the House.

The minority party in the House views the motion to recommit (after the previous question is ordered on a bill or joint resolution) as one of its basic protections. It is often used to state a party position, and when the motion includes "instructions" to the committee to report back to the House "forthwith" with a specified amendment, the manager of the bill does so immediately and the House then has the opportunity to vote on the amendment. The proposed amendment must be germane to the bill in its perfected form, as shaped by the action of amendments previously adopted in the Committee of the Whole or in the House. The rules otherwise restrict the use of the motion: a motion to recommit with instructions cannot change an amendment already adopted by the House. Hence, if a bill under consideration has been amended by a complete amendment in the nature of a substitute, the motion to recommit cannot further amend; for this reason, a special order addressing the consideration of a measure reported from a standing committee with an amendment in the nature of a substitute may specify that the motion may be "with or without instructions." The inclusion of this language, commonly utilized where the adoption of an amendment in the nature of a substitute is anticipated, is a further guarantee of the minority's use of the motion.

The *motion to reconsider* (Rule XVIII) may be made by a member who has been recorded on the prevailing side on a matter on the same or succeeding day. (If the vote is not of record, any member can make the motion). The motion is rarely utilized, however, and is customarily laid on the table following the vote on passage of a matter, thus assuring the finality of the vote. The chair normally states that "the bill is passed and without objection, a motion to reconsider is laid on the table." The measure or matter can then proceed to the next legislative step.

Action on Senate amendments. When a House measure is passed by the House, it is then sent to the Senate, which, using its own procedures, can consider and amend the House proposal. When the Senate sends the bill back to the House in amended form, the House must then act on the Senate amendments: it may accept or concur in the actions of the Senate (thus enabling the bill to be enrolled and sent to the president), or it may amend the Senate language and return it to the Senate. If the House does not approve or amend, it can either send its latest proposal back to the Senate or request a conference on the disagreeing votes.

The precedence of the various motions used in the House with respect to Senate amendments—the motions to amend, concur, disagree and request a conference, or disagree (motions in order before the stage of disagreement), and the motions to recede (from disagreement) and concur, to amend, to insist and request a conference, or to insist (motions in order after the stage of disagreement)—are set forth in Jefferson's Manual (section XLV; House Rules and Manual, section 528).

If the Senate agrees to the request for a conference, the Speaker (under Rule X, clause 6[f]) has the authority to appoint managers to represent the House at the conference. The conferees or managers from the two houses must stay within the differences submitted to them. Simply put, if the House has authorized a million dollars for a project, and the Senate two million, the conferees can accept the high or low figure or anything in between; but they cannot go outside these parameters. If they do, their report is subject to a point of order when called up in the House. Most conferences involve far more complex compromises than this illustration, but the same principle of the "scope of conference" applies (Rule XXVIII, clause 3).

When the conference report is filed in the House, it may be called up for consideration after it is printed and has been available for three days (Rule XXVIII, clause 2[a]). A conference report is debatable for an hour and must be adopted by a majority vote. If the House is acting first on the report, a motion to recommit the report to the committee of conference is in order prior to the vote on adoption. Since a conference report is in the nature of a contract between House and Senate, it cannot be amended, but the House managers can be "instructed" to attempt to preserve or compromise the House position.

On occasion, particularly when dealing with appropriations, the Senate may have added numerous amendments to the House bill, and the conferees may agree to some Senate amendments, compromise others, but remain in true (or technical) disagreement with respect to the remainder. When this occurs, it is often necessary to report a partial conference agreement. In this event, the conference report embodies those items on which agreement has been reached; items still in disagreement are brought up in the House for disposition after the conference report has been adopted. The House may recede from its disagreement and concur in the Senate amendment or recede and concur with a further amendment; or it can insist on its original position and see if the Senate will recede. If the Senate insists, a further conference may be required.

Transmittal of bills to the president. When all items in disagreement have been resolved, the bill is enrolled, signed by the Speaker and the president of the Senate, and sent to the president for consideration. If the president vetoes the bill (returns it to the house of origin without his signature), that house can address the question of reconsideration by using the permissible motions discussed above.

Points of Order. The Speaker decides all questions of order, subject to appeal to the House (Rule I, clause 4); in the Committee of the Whole, the chair fulfills this responsibility. A point of order can be raised against any motion or procedure that violates a House rule, but it must be raised in a timely manner, at the appropriate stage in the proceedings. Questions of order that the chair is frequently called on to decide include the following: (1) that an offered amendment is not germane (Rule XVI, clause 7); (2) that a provision in an appropriation bill or an amendment thereto changes existing law (often referred to as "legislating on an appropriation bill," prohibited by Rule XXI, clause 2), or that the appropriation is unauthorized (that is, that there is no law to support the appropriation, as required by Rule XXI, clause 2); (3) that a bill or amendment violates a requirement of the Congressional Budget Act; (4) that debate is proceeding in an unparliamentary manner; (5) that a bill reported from a committee other than Ways and Means carries a tax or tariff provision (prohibited by Rule XXI, clause 5[b]); and (6) that conferees have exceeded their authority by reporting matters not in disagreement between the House and Senate (Rule XXVIII, clause 3). Debate on a point of order is within the discretion of the chair. Appeals in the House are debatable but are subject to the motion to lay on the table. In the Committee of the Whole they are decided without debate, but the motion to table cannot be used in the Committee.

[*The preceding article is designed to provide an overview of rules of procedure. The encyclopedia includes numerous other entries on particular rules and procedures, which can be found by consulting the Synoptic Outline of Contents, the Glossary, and the Index at the back of volume 4. See also* Manuals of Procedure, *article on* House Manuals; Precedents, *article on* House Precedents; Rules Committee, House. *For comparable discussion of the Senate, see* Senate, *article on* Senate Rules and Procedures.]

BIBLIOGRAPHY

Luce, Robert. *Legislative Procedure.* 1922.
U.S. House of Representatives. *Cannon's Precedents of the House of Representatives of the United States,* by Clarence Cannon. 8 vols. 74th Cong., 1st sess., 1935.
U.S. House of Representatives. *Constitution, Jefferson's Manual, and Rules of the House of Representatives, 103d Congress.* Compiled by William Holmes Brown. 102d Cong., 2d sess., 1992. H. Doc. 102–405.
U.S. House of Representatives. *Hinds' Precedents of the House of Representatives of the United States,* by Asher C. Hinds. 5 vols. 59th Cong., 2d sess., 1907.
U.S. House of Representatives. *Procedure in the United States House of Representatives,* by Lewis Deschler and William Holmes Brown. 4th ed. 97th Cong., 2d sess., 1982.

WILLIAM HOLMES BROWN

HOUSE POST OFFICE. *See* Franking; Perquisites; Ethics and Corruption in Congress.

HOUSING ACTS. *See* Federal Housing Acts.

HOUSING POLICY. The people of the United States are among the best housed in the world, a condition that reflects rising income levels, strong consumer preference, and supportive national policies. These factors had by the late twentieth century enabled almost two out of three households to own their homes and to have far more space and amenities than their forebears.

At the same time, some Americans, particularly young families, cannot find affordable homes or rental units. Chronically poor and disadvantaged persons have serious housing problems: housing expenses that absorb too large a part of their income; dwellings lacking full kitchens or having other defects; and unsafe and trash-littered streets. Residential segregation of African Americans and other minorities persists in most cities. Homelessness was another problem in the early 1990s: half a million or more persons had access only to temporary shelter or were living on the street.

National policies impact on housing directly and indirectly. Indirect influences include macroeconomic policies that affect consumer income that can be spent on housing as well as mortgage interest rates. Transportation programs, such as the Federal-Aid Highway Act of 1956, facilitated the movement of jobs and housing to suburbs and lowered the demand for housing and business locations in central cities. The federal tax system has tended to encourage investment in housing, favored ownership over renting, and has given the largest tax benefits to owners in the highest income brackets.

Direct housing policies mainly address two problems: first, the risks to financial institutions in making long-term loans to home buyers and investors; and second, the inability of low-income and disadvantaged people to find decent, affordable shelter. The barriers that African Americans and other minority groups encounter in trying to buy, rent, or finance housing have also evoked executive orders and legislation.

A housing goal for the nation was proclaimed in the landmark Housing Act of 1949. The legislation called for "the realization as soon as feasible of the goal of a decent home and a suitable living environment for every American family. . . ." The Housing and Urban Development Act of 1968 reaffirmed this goal and set as a quantitative target the construction or rehabilitation of twenty-six million housing units over the following decade, including six million for low- and moderate-income families. While the goal and target were not binding, the concern was, for a time, reflected in federal budget decisions and program levels. But little was heard about housing goals in the 1980s, a time of deep cuts in housing assistance programs.

Legislative Milestones. The Federal Home Loan Bank Act (1932) laid the foundation for a federally regulated savings industry that would be the mainstay of residential mortgage finance over the next four decades. Local institutions that collected the savings of individuals and made home loans to their neighbors gained access to federally preferred credit through the Home Loan Banks in exchange for regulation of their borrowing and lending practices.

The system was rounded out in 1934 with the establishment by the National Housing Act of the Federal Savings and Loan Insurance Corporation (FSLIC). The FSLIC insured depositors, initially up to $5,000 and eventually up to $100,000, against loss on savings deposited in a member savings institution. This insurance, combined with a slightly more favorable rate of interest than available elsewhere, induced a growing number of individuals to place their savings in institutions specializing in mortgage lending.

A small premium paid by the savings associations was intended to cover expenses and risk of the FSLIC. In fact, most of the risk was borne by the federal government, but it was not until the 1980s that huge losses wiped out accumulated reserves and had to be met from general tax revenues. In *The Future of Housing* (1946), Charles Abrams was prescient in observing that risks in deposit insurance and mortgage insurance were socialized, while profits or surplus were retained by private entities.

The National Housing Act also gave birth to the Federal Housing Administration (FHA). The FHA pioneered the long-term mortgage loan that could be fully paid off by level payments without the need to refinance. This replaced the risky five-year rollover loans of the 1920s. Lenders were insured against loss on mortgage loans in the event of default by a borrower. The insurance premium was paid by the borrower. The FHA-insured and standardized loan became the basis for a nationwide home mortgage market. A savings bank with surplus funds, say in New England, could safely invest in FHA-insured mortgages on properties located in growth areas like California. From 1934 through 1992, FHA insured almost 21 million home mortgages, with 6.9 million in force at the end of 1992.

What should be done for families living in slum conditions and too poor to buy or rent decent dwellings? The answer, in 1937, was public housing. Labor groups and social reformers were the main supporters; realtors, home builders, and other industry groups were bitterly opposed. With Sen. Robert F. Wagner of New York leading the way, Congress passed the United States Housing Act of 1937 (sometimes referred to as the Wagner-Steagall Act after its sponsors, Senator Wagner and Rep. Henry B. Steagall of Alabama). The purposes of the act were to clear slums, to provide decent dwellings for low-income families, and to stimulate business activity.

Responsibility for construction or acquisition and management of the housing was vested in public housing agencies (PHAs) established under state laws. The PHAs issued tax-exempt bonds to cover development costs; the federal government made annual contributions to pay off the bonds. Tenants' rents were expected to meet operating expenses such as maintenance, repairs, and utilities. This was a workable formula in the early years of public housing, when tenants were mainly working class. From the beginning, however, PHAs had difficulty finding suitable locations for the low-rent developments because of neighborhood opposition. As a result, many projects were crammed onto undesirable sites, often in racially segregated neighborhoods.

Despite innovations in public policy and institutions, serious housing deficiencies were revealed by the 1940 Census of Housing: 38 percent of nonfarm housing needed major repairs or lacked basic plumbing; farm housing was worse, with more than eight out of ten units lacking running water, a private flush toilet, or central heating in the dwelling. The 1940 home ownership rate in nonfarm areas was lower than in 1930 (41 percent compared to 46 percent). The new financing and subsidy approaches had had only a few years to make inroads on the housing backlog, but the basic reasons for housing deprivation were low family incomes and high unemployment levels.

A huge housing shortage developed after the end of World War II as veterans returned home, found jobs, and began to marry and have children. Housing measures were designed to relieve these general shortages; savings accumulated during the war and rising incomes in the postwar years made the programs workable. A home loan guarantee program for veterans enacted in 1944 was widely used, and the FHA mortgage insurance programs moved into high gear. These loan guarantee programs gave impetus to suburban development and the departure of middle-income families from the central cities. At the same time, many entry-level workers were moving to the inner cities from the South and Puerto Rico.

To arrest and reverse the middle-class exodus and rebuild the central city tax base, a slum clearance and urban redevelopment program was launched by the Housing Act of 1949. The Housing Act of 1954 broadened the program to include neighborhood rehabilitation. Federal loans and grants were made available to cities and towns to clear blighted areas and to rehabilitate older housing and neighborhoods. These efforts met with limited success in some areas but failed in places where market demand was weak.

Opposition to urban renewal mounted among African Americans and other groups as thousands of families were uprooted from their neighborhoods. At the same time, vacant land was piling up in the clearance areas. Legislative changes in the mid 1960s shifted the emphasis of the program from large-scale clearance to neighborhood rehabilitation and provided more adequate relocation payments.

The surge in domestic legislation during the administrations of John F. Kennedy and Lyndon B. Johnson included mandates for the construction of housing for low- and moderate-income families; support for community and metropolitan planning that linked construction of housing, community facilities, and open spaces; and fair housing laws. The Department of Housing and Urban Development (HUD) was established in 1965 to orchestrate these programs; Robert C. Weaver, who had served since 1961 as housing administrator, was appointed by President Johnson to be the first secretary of HUD, and was the first African American to hold a cabinet post. The Housing and Urban Development Act of 1968 contained a huge quantitative target for housing production, and authorized large subsidy programs to meet low-income housing goals.

It fell to Richard M. Nixon and his Housing secretary, George Romney, to implement Johnson's 1968 law. Romney, a former auto industry executive, seized the new tools and launched a massive production effort. From 1969 through 1972, the government approved support for 1.6 million additional units of assisted housing for moderate- and low-income families, more than in all the years back to the New Deal.

These activities were brought to an abrupt halt by presidential order at the start of Nixon's second term in January 1973. Romney and his top aides were replaced, and a policy review group concluded that the suspended housing subsidy programs were too costly and basically inefficient. Congressional supporters were unable to get the urban housing programs restarted, but some rural housing activities were restored by court order.

Major shifts in subsidized housing and community development programs were introduced by the Housing and Community Development Act of 1974. A new rental assistance program (Section 8, an amendment to the United States Housing Act of 1937) became the main vehicle for helping low-income families obtain affordable housing. Payments could be made to private owners of newly built or existing housing on behalf of eligible families. Under provisions applicable in 1993, the tenant paid 30 percent of adjusted income (or more under some circumstances) toward the contract rent, and the government paid the balance. The rent could not exceed a fair market rent established and periodically revised by HUD.

The 1974 legislation was a compromise; the administration favored using existing housing, which was less expensive on a per-family basis; most tenant advocates urged new construction to add to the low-income housing supply. Initially, more funds and units were authorized for new or substantially rehabilitated housing under Section 8. After 1983, however, new construction under this program was reduced to a trickle, and eligible families were directed to existing housing.

The 1974 legislation also initiated a program of community development block grants that consolidated a number of categorical aids and allowed localities considerable flexibility in dealing with local problems. Among the HUD programs dropped were urban renewal, sewer and water grants (grants for construction of waste treatment works continued to be made by the Environmental Protection Agency), and open space land grants. Model cities, a program enacted in 1966 that was intended to demonstrate methods of integrating physical improvements and social assistance programs in the poorest city neighborhoods, was also terminated.

A major transformation in mortgage finance has occurred since the 1970s. Savings and loan associations have been replaced by mortgage pools and trusts as the main source of new capital for housing. Savings and loans, with their large portfolios of fixed-rate mortgages, were particularly vulnerable to a sustained rise in market interest rates, which began in the late 1970s as the Federal Reserve Board tightened monetary policy in order to curb inflation. Many depositors shifted their funds into Treasury bills and other higher-yielding market securities, a process called disintermediation.

Legislative and administrative responses to the changed economic environment included phasing out ceilings on interest rates that could be paid to depositors and allowing institutions to increase their investments in risky corporate debt securities, commercial real estate, and land loans. The changes came too late or in some cases worsened the problem, and many savings and loans failed. Estimated cleanup costs, borne largely by taxpayers, range between $165 billion and $195 billion.

New sources of funds for housing include pension funds, mutual funds, and trust departments of banks, attracted by the highly marketable mortgage-backed securities. The securities are typically guaranteed as to timely payment of interest and principal by the Government National Mortgage Association (Ginnie Mae) or government-sponsored enterprises, the Federal National Mortgage Association (Fannie Mae) or the Federal Home Loan Mortgage Corporation (Freddie Mac). The latter two organizations are publicly chartered but stockholder-owned companies authorized by legislation passed in 1968 and 1970.

Housing Policy and Programs in the 1990s. Designing and implementing a coherent housing policy has always proven elusive, and never more so than in the 1990s. Widely differing schools of thought were reflected in the 1990 Cranston-Gonzalez National Affordable Housing Act, which was fashioned by the Subcommittee on Housing and Urban Affairs of the Senate Committee on Banking, Housing and Urban Affairs and the Subcommittee on Housing and Community Development of the House Committee on Banking, Finance and Urban Affairs. One school, to which Senate lawmakers were responsive, backed housing block grants to state and local governments under a program called HOME Investment Partnerships. Participating jurisdictions must provide some matching money but have flexibility in the use of funds to carry out locally determined housing strategies. HUD's role is to monitor activities for consistency

Landmark Housing Legislation

TITLE	YEAR ENACTED	REFERENCE NUMBER	DESCRIPTION
Federal Home Loan Bank Act	1932	P.L. 72-304	Instituted the Federal Home Loan Bank system and laid foundation for a federally regulated savings industry specializing in financing home mortgages.
National Housing Act	1934	P.L. 73-479	Established the Federal Housing Administration, which insured institutional lenders against risk of default on residential mortgages. Created the Federal Savings and Loan Insurance Corporation, which insured deposits of member savings institutions.
United States Housing Act	1937	P.L. 75-412	Established the low-rent public housing program.
Servicemen's Readjustment Act (GI Bill)	1944	P.L. 78-346	Authorized benefits for veterans of the armed forces, including guarantes of home mortgage loans.
Housing Act of 1949	1949	P.L. 81-171	Established a national housing goal, enlarged the public housing program, initiated urban redevelopment grants.
Housing Act of 1954	1954	P.L. 83-560	Authorized urban renewal with emphasis on slum prevention, rehabilitation, and neighborhood conservation and related FHA financing programs. Provided grants for metropolitan and small community planning.
Housing Act of 1961	1961	P.L. 87-70	Introduced moderate-income rental housing program, grants for open-space land, demonstration program for low-income housing.
Housing and Urban Development Act of 1965	1965	P.L. 89-117	Established rent supplement program for low-income households. Permitted public housing authorities to lease private apartments for low-income families. Authorized grants for basic water and sewer facilities, neighborhood facilities, advance land acquisition for future public facilities. Provided mortgage insurance for land development.
Department of Housing and Urban Development Act	1965	P.L. 89-174	Created a new department to coordinate urban and housing activities of the federal government, giving urban interests a voice in the president's cabinet.
Demonstration Cities and Metropolitan Development Act	1966	P.L. 89-754	Referred to as Model Cities; intended to demonstrate methods of integrating physical and social programs in low-income sections of cities.
Civil Rights Act of 1968	1968	P.L. 90-284	Prohibited discrimination on the basis of race, color, religion, sex, or national origin in the sale, rental, or financing of housing.
Housing and Urban Development Act of 1968	1968	P.L. 90-448	Reaffirmed the national housing goal, set ten-year housing production targets. Established low-interest subsidy programs for home ownership and rental housing. Partitioned the Federal National Mortgage Association into a federally chartered, stockholder-owned secondary market enterprise (Fannie Mae) and a government agency (Ginnie Mae) to backstop residential mortgage programs. Authorized loan guarantees for new community development.

with the local strategies and for compliance with such federal laws as environmental protection and fair housing, not to make determinations on local applications project by project.

A second school—traditional supporters of low-income housing with ties to key House members—clung to the notion that a strong federal presence remains important to proper implementation of national housing policy. It was committed to continuing and strengthening established subsidy programs, such as public housing and rent certificates, and preserving the supply of assisted housing for

Landmark Housing Legislation (Continued)

TITLE	YEAR ENACTED	REFERENCE NUMBER	DESCRIPTION
Housing and Community Development Act of 1974	1974	P.L. 93-383	Created the community development block grant program in place of urban renewal, Model Cities, basic sewer and water grants, neighborhood facilities, open space land, and other categorical aids. Authorized Section 8 rental-assistance program for low-income families.
Depository Institutions Deregulation and Monetary Control Act	1980	P.L. 96-221	Phased out interest rate limitations on all accounts (Regulation Q). Raised federal insurance on accounts to $100,000. Permitted savings and loan associations to make consumer loans and offer other services.
Omnibus Budget Reconciliation Act	1981	P.L. 97-35	Limited additional budget authority for low-income housing. Targeted housing assistance to very low–income families. Increased tenant rent contributions to 30 percent of adjusted income.
Garn–St Germain Depository Institutions Act	1982	P.L. 97-320	Permitted savings and loan associations to diversify investments further away from home mortgage loans. Authorized federally insured money market deposit accounts.
Stewart B. McKinney Homeless Assistance Act	1987	P.L. 100-77	Authorized funds for shelter, health care, and food for homeless persons.
Fair Housing Amendments Act	1988	P.L. 100-430	Extended prohibition against discrimination in housing to families with children and to the handicapped. Required new multifamily housing to be designed to meet needs of handicapped. Strengthened fair housing enforcement machinery.
Financial Institutions Reform, Recovery, and Enforcement Act	1989	P.L. 101-73	Created new agencies to oversee savings and loan industry. Authorized funds to close insolvent savings institutions and reimburse insured depositors. Raised capital requirements of savings institutions and increased percentage of investments that must be in residential loans.
Cranston-Gonzalez National Affordable Housing Act	1990	P.L. 101-625	Established housing block grant program called HOME Investment Partnerships, National Homeownership Trust to help first-time home buyers, HOPE programs to enable low-income residents to manage and own their apartments, and supportive housing programs for the elderly, persons with disabilities, and the homeless.
Housing and Community Development Act of 1992	1992	P.L. 102-550	Reauthorized and amended programs enacted by the Cranston-Gonzalez Act. Raised FHA mortgage insurance limits on 1-to-4-family housing. Consolidated several programs for the homeless into a single Supportive Housing Program. Established new standards and enforcement machinery to assure safety and soundness of the Federal National Mortgage Association (Fannie Mae) and the Federal Home Loan Mortgage Corporation (Freddie Mac).

low- and moderate-income occupancy. Another of this school's objectives was to assist first-time home buyers, for whom a down payment subsidy and interest-reduction program, the National Homeownership Trust, was designed.

A third set of players called for a war on poverty through resident ownership of public and other government-assisted housing. President George Bush's HUD secretary, Jack Kemp, urged this approach, and succeeded in getting his HOPE program (Homeownership and Opportunity for People Everywhere) included in the 1990 legislation.

Members of all schools tended to agree that vulnerable groups, such as persons with disabilities and the frail elderly, need supportive services along with housing. There was consensus that able-bodied adults receiving housing subsidies should be encouraged to work their way out of public assistance. A "family self-sufficiency" provision enacted in 1990 required that public housing agencies enroll one assisted person in a training program for each additional family or unit receiving housing assistance.

In 1993, the Section 8 rent certificate and voucher programs assisted about 2.2 million households, and the older public housing program supported 1.4 million housing units. Another half million low- and moderate-income households were in rental housing erected under interest subsidy programs enacted in the 1960s. In rural areas, about 400,000 low-income families lived in rental housing assisted by the Farmers Home Administration. All together, 4.5 to 5 million lower-income households (about 12 million people) were receiving help under HUD and Farmers Home housing programs.

An even greater number were receiving housing help through welfare programs. At the end of 1992, 4.9 million families (14 million people) were enrolled in Aid to Families with Dependent Children (AFDC), and 5.4 million people—aged, blind, or disabled—were receiving payments under Supplemental Security Income (SSI). While some of these households also received housing assistance (about 1.6 million in 1989), those that did not get such aid typically spent 40 percent or more of their welfare checks on shelter. Dwellings occupied by most welfare recipients did not have to meet quality standards (required under HUD's programs), and so many were living in squalid quarters.

For mayors and other local officials who saw direct federal assistance to their communities cut back in the 1980s, retaining the community development block grant program was a high priority. This program was funded at $4 billion in 1993.

Advocates of fair housing won important legislative battles but remained disappointed with their limited impact. The Civil Rights Act of 1968 and other laws prohibited discrimination in housing because of race, color, religion, sex, or national origin. The Fair Housing Amendments Act of 1988 extended coverage to families with children and to the handicapped. Enforcement machinery was also strengthened in 1988.

Increasingly, housing markets were opening to middle-class families in the minority population, but most African American and Latino households continued to live in highly segregated city neighborhoods. Market testing showed that black families more frequently encountered discriminatory treatment than whites when seeking to buy or rent a house or apartment. A study by the Federal Reserve found that blacks were much less likely to get a home loan than whites with similar incomes. Practices in financing, selling, and renting residential real estate continued to fall far short of the spirit of the fair housing laws.

It is one thing to get an authorizing bill passed, another to get it funded and implemented. Appropriations committees have much say about which measures will be supported. A program of metropolitan development incentive grants was authorized by the Demonstration Cities and Metropolitan Development Act of 1966. It was designed to reward communities for carrying out areawide development activities in accordance with areawide comprehensive planning. Whether they were dubious about federal efforts to promote areawide planning or simply deemed the additional grants superfluous, the Appropriations committees declined to include funds for this purpose in HUD's budget. At a later date, a program to assist first-time buyers, the National Homeownership Trust, failed to receive an appropriation.

Advocacy groups and lawmakers have learned not to assume that laws are self-executing or can be handed over to a value-free bureaucracy. In the 1960s, old guard elements within the Federal Housing Administration resisted having to implement mortgage loan programs targeted to inner city neighborhoods and marginal borrowers. During the Bush administration, there were complaints that favored programs, such as HOPE, were getting so much attention that others were being neglected.

Rethinking Housing Policy. Even as new laws are barely implemented, debate goes on in Congress and elsewhere about the efficacy and fairness of current housing policy and programs. Some questions that may inform the emerging policy debate include the following.

How large a share of the nation's resources should be invested in housing? Housing represented 40 percent of the nation's private, fixed, reproducible, tangible wealth—$7 trillion—in 1991. Have we overinvested, thereby slighting investment in public infrastructure and private plant and equipment needed for economic growth?

About twenty-seven million taxpayers itemized their home mortgage interest payments in 1991;

the revenue cost of these deductions and other tax benefits to homeowners came to $66.9 billion for the year. At the other end of the income scale, approximately five million low- and moderate-income households occupied assisted rental housing requiring federal outlays of about $18 billion a year. Does this distribution of housing benefits constitute a balanced and equitable support system for housing?

Government analysts estimate the number of low-income households seriously needing but not receiving housing assistance at five million; another three to five million are eligible on an income basis. How many low-income Americans should be helped? Can a case be made for offering help to all eligible people, that is, for having an entitlement program? At what cost?

With limited funds available for housing, some say that the government should target help to the very poorest people. Others argue for assisting a wider range of lower-income households, citing the benefits of diversity and having role models for the most deeply disadvantaged, the lower subsidy costs per family, and the greater ease of managing the properties. Which view should prevail?

Legislation in the early 1990s sought to make welfare recipients more self-sufficient. Able-bodied adults were being pressured to enter remedial education and job training programs. What might be done to those who fail? How much should be expected of poor and disadvantaged persons who receive assistance of one type or another?

Production subsidy programs for low-income housing were severely reduced in the 1980s. It was argued that the housing problem is due to inadequate income, not lack of adequate dwellings, and that it is cheaper to provide rental assistance for use in existing housing than to build new housing. Others believe that some new construction may be needed for large families, the homeless, persons with disabilities, the frail elderly, and perhaps in some tight local housing markets. Can these positions be reconciled?

At one time, public-housing tenants paid 20 percent of their income for rent. That was raised to 25 percent, and later to 30 percent. Under a variation of Section 8 rental assistance, some families paid 40 percent or more. How much should low-income families be required to spend on housing?

What is decent housing? Should standards be the same for assisted housing as for nonassisted housing? Can we be satisfied with the lower quality of housing and higher rent burdens of people receiving help only through AFDC and SSI as compared with similar households who also get rental assistance from HUD?

Fair housing laws are on the books, yet discriminatory practices persist. Can more be done—should more be done—to foster fair housing and open occupancy practices?

Responsibility for delivering housing services has been shifting in recent years to residents of public housing and to nonprofit community housing development organizations. How much can be expected from these new players? Can they develop the expertise and avoid the mismanagement and corruption that stained earlier providers?

Observers expect the 1990s to be difficult years for assisted housing for three reasons. First, a chronic federal budget deficit will frustrate efforts of housing advocates to enlarge housing subsidy programs. Second, with slow economic growth projected for the decade, there will not be much of a social dividend to distribute. Third, disenchantment with the federal government generally and with the Department of Housing and Urban Development in particular runs deep. Advocates of housing for low- and moderate-income people will have to work with a more dispersed and perhaps less sensitive resource allocation system at state and local levels of government. But new and unforeseeable events could change the outlook. In other times, housing has been an instrument for dealing with a depressed economy, for facilitating movements of defense workers, for rewarding homesteaders and veterans, and for waging a war against poverty. Such a call could come again.

[See also Banking, Finance, and Urban Affairs Committee, House; Banking, Housing, and Urban Affairs Committee, Senate; Federal Housing Acts.]

BIBLIOGRAPHY

DiPasquale, Denise, and Langley C. Keyes, eds. *Building Foundations: Housing and Federal Policy.* 1990.

Downs, Anthony. *The Revolution in Real Estate Finance.* 1985.

Fish, Gertrude Sipperly, ed. *The Story of Housing.* 1979.

Hays, R. Allen. *The Federal Government and Urban Housing.* 1985.

McFarland, M. Carter. *The Federal Government and Urban Problems.* 1978.

National Housing Task Force. *A Decent Place to Live.* 1988.

Schussheim, Morton J. *The Modest Commitment to Cities.* 1974.

U.S. House of Representatives. Committee on Banking, Finance, and Urban Affairs. *Housing: A Reader.* Report prepared by Congressional Research Service. 98th Cong., 1st sess., 1983. Committee Print 98-5.

U.S. Department of Housing and Urban Development. *Housing in the Seventies.* 1974.

Wolman, Harold. *Politics of Federal Housing.* 1971.

MORTON J. SCHUSSHEIM

HOUSTON, SAM (1793–1863), representative from and governor of Tennessee, hero of the Texas revolution, president of the Republic of Texas, and U.S. senator from Texas. Sam Houston is one of the legendary figures in American history. His life was so remarkable that it seems like fiction rather than reality. As a teenager, Houston lived for three years with the Cherokee Indians in the Tennessee mountains. He later served with Andrew Jackson in the war against the Creek Indians and became Jackson's devoted supporter. Returning to civilian life,

he became an attorney and, with Jackson's backing, was elected to the U.S. House of Representatives in 1823.

In 1827, he was elected governor of Tennessee, only to resign two years later to return to live among the Cherokees after his wife of three months left him. Houston moved to Texas in 1832 and, with the creation of a provisional government there in 1835, was made a major general in the army. His army defeated the Mexican army at the battle of San Jacinto. With the creation of the independent Republic of Texas, Houston served two terms as its president. Houston was elected U.S. senator in 1846, shortly after Texas became a state. In the Senate, he was known for his Western dress and rough-hewn manner. His most notable position as a senator was his strong support of the Union. He opposed both northerners and southerners whom he feared were inciting people to civil war. His strong pro-Union position led him in 1859 to run successfully for governor of Texas against the incumbent, a secessionist. When Texas did secede and join the Confederacy, Houston refused to take an oath of allegiance and was removed from office. He retired to Huntsville, Texas, and died in 1863.

BIBLIOGRAPHY

Friend, Llerena B. *Sam Houston: The Great Designer.* 1954.

James, Marquis. *The Raven: A Biography of Sam Houston.* 1929.

ANTHONY CHAMPAGNE

SAM HOUSTON. Hero of the 1836 revolution in which the people of Texas fought for independence from Mexico, Houston was elected president of the short-lived independent Republic of Texas and was given the mandate to seek annexation to the Union. He represented Texas in the U.S. Senate from 1846 to 1859.   NATIONAL ARCHIVES

HULL, CORDELL (1871–1955), representative and senator from Tennessee, secretary of State, champion of multilateral trade agreements. Hull stands out among the southern political leaders who were influential in Congress and the nation during the first half of the twentieth century and who embraced a conservative domestic agenda and a liberal approach to world affairs. From 1907, when he first entered Congress, to 1944, when he resigned as secretary of State, Hull espoused equal and exact justice, the rule of law, and unfettered access to the world's markets, which was characteristic of Wilsonian liberal internationalists.

Born in Overton County, Tennessee, Hull attended college in Ohio. He earned a law degree from Cumberland University Law School in 1891, practiced law, saw military service during the Spanish-American War, and served on the Fifth Tennessee Judicial Circuit from 1903 to 1907. Hull served seven terms in the U.S. House of Representatives from Tennessee's 4th Congressional District, was defeated in the Warren G. Harding landslide, headed the Democratic National Committee from 1921 to 1923, then returned to Congress for four more terms. He won election to the U.S. Senate in 1930. A strong supporter of Franklin D. Roosevelt's presidential bid in 1932, he was recruited to be secretary of State by Roosevelt, who needed Hull's influence with Congress and the southern wing of the Democratic party.

Hull brought to public service a blend of Jeffersonian agrarianism and the low-tariff and antimonopoly radicalism popular in the 1890s. In his first speech before Congress, he called for "the suppression of lawless combinations and the proper curbing of corporate wealth." Five years later, urging the removal of trade barriers, he informed his colleagues that "economic wars are but the germs of real wars." Quickly making a name in Congress as author of the first income-tax statute in 1913 and of inheritance- and estate-tax legislation in 1916, he acquired influence (though some termed him the "Cassandra of Congress" for prophesying gloom and doom) and a reputation as an expert on fiscal matters and trade policy. Hull's advocacy of tariff reform and an open economic world was grounded in "vindictive evangelism," a call for the destruction of special privilege however constituted, rather than in an understanding of the complexities of international economics. He was, however, instrumental in steering through Congress the Reciprocal Trade Agreements Act of 1934, and he zealously supported a form of legalistic multilateralism throughout his tenure in the State Department.

During Roosevelt's first two administrations, Hull's links to the congressional leadership proved valuable in launching initiatives for improved relations with Latin America and East Asia and in curbing isolationists. By 1941, a combination of ill health, opposition to Roosevelt's decision to run for a third term, and the emergence of rivals within the White House circle shunted Hull to the sidelines.

BIBLIOGRAPHY

Drummond, Donald F. "Cordell Hull." In *An Uncertain Tradition: American Secretaries of State in the Twentieth Century.* Edited by Norman A. Graebner. 1961.
Hull, Cordell. *Memoirs.* 2 vols. 1948.

THEODORE A. WILSON

HUMOR AND SATIRE. [*This entry includes two articles. The first analyzes the history, purpose, and effect of levity in legislative debate. The second examines the long tradition of making Congress the object of ridicule.*]

In Congress

Congress has always been of two minds about the use of humor in political debate. Some members have followed the advice that Sen. Thomas Corwin once offered to Gen. James A. Garfield. "To succeed in life," the Ohio Republican asserted, "you must be solemn, solemn as an ass—all the great monuments are built over solemn asses." But not everyone has adhered to Corwin's dictum—certainly not Corwin himself. Although he complained that his irrepressible funniness kept him from becoming president, he nevertheless found fame as "the clown prince of Congress," and is generally regarded as the most affable member ever to serve in that body.

Corwin, a representative before becoming a senator in 1845, was just one in a long line of quick-witted men and women who have gained special recognition for their ability to see the lighter side of lawmaking. Such individuals—curiously rare in recent years—have helped to ease the tensions that inevitably arise in the legislative forum and, for this service, have traditionally been cherished and protected by other members.

With timely quip, clever ridicule, sarcastic retort, biting witticism, incisive epigram, outrageous hyperbole, and acerbic irony, such members have added, in the words of Rep. Samuel S. Cox, "momentary sparkle to the sluggish waters of debate." Cox himself was known for his wit and amusing doggerel, which he used mainly to poke fun at pompous colleagues. His treatise on the utility of humor in legislative debate remains the most thorough study to date of a seldom-examined aspect of Congress.

What Makes Congress Laugh. What provokes laughter among lawmakers is not the humor of a stand-up comedian or the antics of a buffoon. Instead, in a body that thrives on words and respects their power, it is wordplay—from subtle double entendre to scalding sarcasm—that most often wins a smile or a roar of appreciation. Brevity and originality are its heart and soul; quick, sharp thrusts are preferred over long, complex jokes, stories, and anecdotes. The witty retort that silences an opponent is almost certain to provoke a chuckle or at least an acknowledging groan from other members. Subtlety is highly admired, but outrageous exaggeration, sarcasm, and comical invective have always had their place. Ridicule, within certain limits, is considered, as John Randolph once observed, "as fair a weapon as any in the whole parliamentary armory." Cox uses the following exchange to illustrate classic congressional humor:

> First member: You cannot assail my record.
> Second member: I do not go into small matters.
> First member: I do for I shall answer.
> Second member: Then discuss yourself and magnify little things.

Congressional humor is highly perishable and, in many respects, an acquired taste. It turns largely on an unexpected phrase or an individual's spontaneous reaction to a particular circumstance. What struck Congress as funny in an earlier age might be totally inappropriate today. For instance, making fun of a fellow member's physical or intellectual impairments was standard fare in Congress a century ago. Today, the wittiest example of that genre can seem tasteless and unfunny, especially in print.

Humor's Long Precedence. Humor has been used in debate as long as Congress has existed. In the very first Congress, members lapsed into collective playfulness while considering appropriate titles for the new president and vice president. They literally laughed away monarchist proposals to anoint high officials of the new government with the trappings of royalty. The idea was quietly shelved after one lawmaker suggested "His Rotundity" as a fitting title for corpulent John Adams, the vice president.

Through much of its history, Congress thrived on humor that was rough and personal. Verbal jabs, intended to prick but not destroy an opponent, were freely exchanged, often to the delight of other members. Members thus assailed were expected to, and usually did, respond in kind. Much leeway was allowed, although mean-spirited remarks couched in humor—humor "with a poison dart," as one senator described it—were generally frowned upon. Indeed, in Congress's early years, it was risky for a member to go too far in humiliating another member. During the age of the *code duello*, which lasted into the 1850s, several lawmakers lost their lives in duels resulting from offensive remarks spoken in debate.

The Legacy of Randolph. Oblivious to such dangers was Virginia's John Randolph, whose singular wit and unpredictable nature enlivened the House and Senate from 1799 to 1829. An aristocrat whose high-pitched voice, scarecrow frame, and pasty countenance made him an oddity, Randolph entertained endlessly with his comically sarcastic, often bitter witticisms. Many tested him, but none were his equal. His verbal joustings with Rep. Tristam Burges of Rhode Island, a master of wit and sarcasm in his own right, were legion. Many lesser colleagues pestered Randolph and attacked his views in efforts to enhance their own reputations for debate. Such challenges he met with disdain. During debate on the Missouri question, for instance, an Ohio member repeatedly interrupted him with bellowing calls for a vote on the previous question, a motion not then in order. On the third such interruption, Randolph paused:

> Mr. Speaker, in the Netherlands a man of small capacity, with bits of wood and leather, will in a few moments construct a toy that, with the pressure of a finger and thumb, will cry, "Cuckoo! Cuckoo!" With less ingenuity, and with inferior materials, the people of Ohio have made a toy that, without much pressure, will cry "Previous question, Mr. Speaker! Previous question, Mr. Speaker!"

The House roared with laughter as the Virginian, after pointing a bony finger toward his antagonist, resumed his speech. Later, in the Senate, he ignored the pesky sniping of a recently arrived replacement for a senator who had died in office. Refusing to acknowledge the freshman's presence, Randolph casually referred in debate to the late senator "whose seat remains vacant." Informed on another occasion that a certain senator had been denouncing him, Randolph responded: "Denouncing me? That is strange. I have never done him a favor."

Congress in its first century never lacked for members who could inject humor into the heaviest situation. Daniel Webster used humor effectively to relieve the solemnity of his orations. His famous speech in reply to Sen. Robert Y. Hayne included an amusing burlesque of an imaginary attack on a federal customhouse by the South Carolina militia.

Henry Clay was at times "playful as a colt" and "liked to engage in stingless fun," according to Cox. "His mirth constantly restored and preserved the good temper of the Senate." As author Leon A. Harris has observed, he could also be cruel. Once, as a representative, Clay sat through a long, tiresome speech by Alexander Smyth. Pointing to Clay, Smyth intoned, "You, sir, speak for the present generation; I speak for posterity." Retorted Clay: "Yes, and you seem determined to speak until the arrival of your audience." Both Webster and Clay enjoyed teasing their dour colleague John C. Calhoun, who had little use for humor himself.

Clay's Kentucky has given Congress some of its best-loved humorists. For many years, members of Congress referred to a Kentucky style of humor, which derived from a tradition of personal warmth, an ability to play on the American weakness for burlesque, and an endless repertoire, passed from one generation to the next, of good stories. Corwin himself was Kentucky born. So was Abraham Lincoln, who earned his reputation as a humorist after leaving Congress. Corwin was preceded in Congress by Rep. Ben "Meat-Ax" Hardin, whose nickname alluded to his debating style, and was followed there by Rep. Proctor Knott, whose famous "Duluth" speech, which spoofed pork-barrel practices, still ranks as the funniest of its kind. Speaking in opposition to a road bill, Knott convulsed the House with a ludicrous description of his efforts to find Duluth, Minnesota, one of the bill's potential beneficiaries, on a map.

> . . . Duluth! The word fell upon my ear with peculiar and indescribable charm, like the gentle murmur of a low fountain stealing forth in the midst of roses, or the soft, sweet accents of an angel's whisper in the bright joyous dream of sleeping innocence. Duluth! 'Twas the name for which my soul had panted for years, as the hart panteth for the water-brooks. But where was Duluth? Never in all my limited reading had my vision been gladdened by seeing the celestial word in print . . . .

Another beloved Kentuckian was Sen. Alben W. Barkley, whose infectious jollity helped him win the vice presidency in 1948.

When Humor Reigned. Humor in Congress is said to have peaked in the 1840s. Entering its second half century, Congress reflected the nation's satisfaction with its progress and confidence in its future. Cox notes that the House, in high spirits despite mounting sectional friction, "laughed at everything." As a representative from Ohio (1857–1865) and later from New York (1869–1889), Cox did much to preserve that legacy in his time. Often needled about his smallness, he countered with rhyming epitaphs mocking his tormentors for their obesity ("Beneath this stone Owen Lovejoy lies, little in everything except in size. . . ."). Usually in this sparring he had the last word. But not always, as when Roswell G. Horr went Cox one better with a rhyme of his own:

> Beneath this slab lies the great Sam Cox.
> He was wise as an owl and grave as an ox.
> Think it not strange his turning to dust,
> For he swelled and he swelled 'til he finally "bust."
> Just where he's gone and how he fares
> Nobody knows and nobody cares.
> But wherever he is, be he angel or elf,
> Be sure, dear reader, he's puffing himself.

Edward Boykin, in *The Wit and Wisdom of Congress* (1961), records this incident: Angered in debate, a burly representative shouted at diminutive Alexander Stephens, "You little shrimp, I could swallow you whole." Retorted Stephens: "If you did you'd have more brains in your belly than you ever had in your head."

Night sessions, common in the nineteenth century, often degenerated into raucousness, depending, it was alleged, on how much liquor the members had consumed at dinner. House members especially enjoyed the routine of rounding up absentees. Some had to be dragooned from parties, restaurants, and taverns and brought before their peers to explain their truancy. The more outrageous the excuse, the better the miscreant's chances to be absolved of his crime. Even the debate on motions to bring in the absentees could provoke humor, as when a member proposed to insert the words *dead or alive*, which was followed by a motion to amend the amendment by striking the word *alive*.

Congress has had its share of punsters. John Randolph once observed, referring to Robert Wright and John Rea (pronounced "ray"), that the House had two anomalies: a Wright always wrong and a Rea without light. In the 1860s, Rep. Stevenson Archer, after responding to Oakes Ames's name as well as his own on a roll-call vote, apologized for the error, noting, "A better Archer would have had better aims." His colleagues, amused by his double vote, nicknamed him "Insatiable Archer."

Ridicule and Invective. Members perceived by their peers to be overly serious or self-righteous have been targets for much of Congress's humor and ridicule. Sen. Charles Sumner's preoccupation with his moral crusades, for instance, inspired Sen. Matthew Carpenter to comment: "He identifies himself so completely with the universe that he is not at all certain whether he is part of the universe or the universe is part of him." To a member who exclaimed, "I'm right; I know I'm right. So I say with Henry Clay, sir, I'd rather be right than president," Speaker Thomas B. Reed reportedly remarked: "The gentleman need not worry for he will never be either."

By far the most withering verbal assault by one member upon another in debate was Rep. James G. Blaine's rejoinder to a sarcastic remark by Roscoe Conkling, whose pomposity and fastidious grooming seemed to invite ridicule:

> As to the gentleman's cruel sarcasm, I hope he will not be too severe. The contempt of that large-minded gentleman is so wilting, his haughty dis-

dain, his grandiloquent swell, his majestic over-powering turkey-gobbler strut has been so crushing to myself and to all the members of the House, that I know it was an act of the grandest temerity for me to venture upon a controversy with him. But, sir, I know who is responsible for all this. I know that within the last five weeks, as members of the House will recollect, an extra strut has characterized the gentleman's bearing.

Blaine attributed the "extra strut" to a recent newspaper article satirically suggesting Conkling as a successor to House leader Henry Winter Davis. He continued:

The gentleman took it seriously, and it has given his strut added pomposity. The resemblance is great. It is striking. Hyperion to a Satyr, Thersites to a Bengal tiger, a whining puppy to a roaring lion. Shade of the mighty Davis, forgive the almost profanation of that jocose satire.

"The members of the House laughed with delight at Conkling's humiliation," wrote Neil MacNeil in *Forge of Democracy*. Conkling waited for eighteen years to get his revenge. His refusal to support Blaine, his party's presidential nominee, helped tip New York and the election to the Democrats in 1884.

Humor in the Modern Congress. While humor has not vanished entirely from congressional debate, it has grown sparse in recent decades. Various explanations have been offered, including that newer members are better educated, more professional, and therefore more serious-minded than their predecessors; that the current issues before Congress require solemnity; that members fear a hypercritical press; and that modern politics requires members to spend more time with constituents, at the expense of interacting with fellow lawmakers. In *The Fine Art of Political Wit*, author Leon A. Harris blames television for the general decline in the use of humor by politicians. The television industry's fear of offending people was taken to heart by office seekers when the medium became their principal means of reaching voters, he contends.

Still, Congress occasionally shows flashes of its former self. Freshman representative James Nussle was both funny and effective in his guise as the "Unknown Congressman" in 1991. Nussle placed a paper bag—with holes for eyes and mouth—over his head and informed colleagues he was returning home incognito because voters were outraged over the privileges enjoyed by members of Congress. Similarly, Rep. Silvio Conte wore a plastic pig snout to underscore his vocal objections to pork-barrel legislation.

William L. Hungate kept the House in stitches with his parodies, the most memorable of which he entitled "Down by the Old Watergate." When he retired in 1976, he left colleagues laughing with this departing sentiment: "May the future bring all the best to you, your family and friends, and may your mother never find out where you work." Several of Rep. Patricia Schroeder's clever labels and catch phrases became part of the American language in the 1980s. In labeling Ronald Reagan "the Teflon president," she expressed her Democratic party's frustration over Reagan's ability to deflect criticism.

Other lawmakers who have used humor effectively in recent times include Sen. Hubert H. Humphrey, who extolled "the politics of joy" in his 1968 presidential campaign; Sen. Everett M. Dirksen, who rhapsodized humorously on the virtues of the marigold; and Sen. Bob Dole, who in the 1980s and 1990s combined a dry, caustic wit with a professional comedian's sense of timing. House members still honor the memory of Rep. Brooks Hays, a soft-spoken Arkansan who illuminated his philosophy with humorous, apt anecdotes as he fought, sometimes alone among southern lawmakers, against extremist efforts to thwart desegregation in the 1950s.

For some thirty years, Rep. Morris K. Udall made masterly use of a gentle wit and a storehouse of timely anecdotes to soften and outmaneuver opponents of his legislative ideas. Udall understood humor's power as much as any lawmaker ever has. "A savvy pol can use humor to disarm his enemies, to rally his allies, to inform, rebut, educate, console, and convince," he wrote in 1988. "In my own career, I have used humor to help me get reelected fourteen times, and to attain passage of the 1977 strip-mining bill and the 1980 Alaska lands bill." When he retired in 1992, Congress lost its most convincing response to the argument that humor and serious lawmaking do not mix.

BIBLIOGRAPHY

Cox, Samuel S. *Why We Laugh.* 1876.
Harris, Leon A. *The Fine Art of Political Humor.* 1964.
MacNeil, Neil. *Forge of Democracy.* 1963.
Schutz, Charles E. *Political Humor from Aristophanes to Sam Ervin.* 1977.
Stout, Richard. "Foe of the Bon Mot: Politics." *New York Times Magazine,* 22 April 1956, p. 13.
Udall, Morris K. *Too Funny to Be President.* 1988.

DONALD C. BACON

About Congress

The American people like to grouse about the president, but they are even more censorious when it comes to Congress. Sometimes the criticism is deadly serious, but often it is lighthearted in nature. Judging from the hundreds of amusing stories about the national lawmakers that have accumulated in the years since Congress held its first meeting in New York City in April 1789, Americans have shared Mark Twain's belief that humor is the most effective form of criticism. "From the beginning of the Republic," sighed House Speaker Nicholas Longworth (R-Ohio), in an interview about Congress with the *Literary Digest* on 23 January 1926, "it has been the duty of every free-born voter to look down on us, and the duty of every free-born humorist to make jokes of us. Always there is something—and, in fact, almost always there is almost everything—wrong with us. We simply can not be right."

Satirists in every period of American history have enjoyed putting down the nation's legislators. "Suppose you were an idiot," wrote Mark Twain during the Gilded Age. "And suppose you were a member of Congress. But I repeat myself." Elsewhere he wrote: "It could probably be shown by facts and figures that there is no distinctly native American criminal class except Congress." Still elsewhere: "A jay hasn't got any more principle than a Congressman. A jay will lie, a jay will steal, a jay will deceive, a jay will betray, and four times out of five, a jay will go back on his solemnest promise." It is not surprising that Twain made congressional corruption a major target in the satirical novel *The Gilded Age* (1873), which he wrote with his friend Charles Dudley Warner. Twain overlooked the fact that there was more corruption in the administration of his hero Ulysses S. Grant than in Congress itself. But, as Speaker Longworth noted ruefully, Americans have always been harder on Congress than on the president.

In the 1920s and 1930s H. L. Mencken, the satirical Sage of Baltimore, was as caustic in his comments on Congress as Twain had been in the 1870s. The average representative, Mencken asserted,

> is an ignoramus. Having to choose between sense and nonsense, he chooses nonsense almost instinctively. Until he got to Washington, and began to meet lobbyists, bootleggers and the correspondents of newspapers, he had perhaps never met a single intelligent human being. As a Congressman, he remains below the salt. . . . When he is invited to a party, it is a sign that police sergeants are also invited. . . . His dream is to be chosen to go on a congressional junket, i.e., on a drunken holiday at government expense. . . . In brief, a knavish and preposterous nonentity, half way between a kleagle of the Ku Klux and a grand worthy bow-wow of the Knights of Zoroaster.

Mencken thought better of the Senate, at least for a time, and then decided that the adoption of the direct election of senators (as provided in the Seventeenth Amendment) in 1913 had resulted in filling the upper chamber with frauds, fanatics, poltroons, and scoundrels. He insisted that

> the average Senator, like the average Congressman, is simply a party hack, without ideas and without anything rationally describable as self-respect. His backbone has a sweet resiliency; he knows how to clap on false whiskers; it is quite impossible to forecast his actions even on a matter of the highest principle, without knowing what rewards are offered by the rival sides.

Mencken thought that if voters applied the right pressure, members of both Houses "would cheerfully be in favor of polygamy, astrology, or cannibalism." Balancing his comments, though, in the way Twain never did, he also insisted that if Franklin D. Roosevelt, one of his pet presidential hates, thought cannibalism would bring votes, "he would fatten up a missionary on the White House lawn."

Humorist Will Rogers was a kindlier and gentler observer of the movers and shakers on Capitol Hill than either Twain or Mencken. For Rogers, writing in the 1920s and 1930s, the legislative branch of government was "a never-ending source of amusement, amazement and discouragement." The American people, he wrote, have "come to feel the same way when Congress is in session as we do when the baby gets hold of a hammer. It's just a question of how much damage he can do before we take it away from him." Congress "is strange," he once mused. "A man gets up to speak and says nothing. Nobody listens . . . and then everybody disagrees." On another occasion he exclaimed: "But with Congress—every time they make a joke it's a law. And every time they make a law it's a joke." Still, the cowboy humorist took a genially tolerant attitude toward congressional shenanigans. "You know," he said, "Congressmen are the nicest fellows in the world to meet. I sometimes really wonder if they realize all the harm they do." But they did good, too, when it came to comedy. "I never lack material for my humor column," Rogers acknowledged gratefully, "when Congress is in session." Rogers believed in kidding, not kicking, the toilers on Capitol Hill. "Kid Congress and the Senate, don't scold 'em," he advised Franklin Roosevelt shortly after the 1932 election. "They are just children that's never grown up. They don't like to be corrected in company. Don't send messages to 'em, send candy."

In the late twentieth century, professional humorists were still teasing and taunting the nation's lawmakers. "Public regard for Congress, never high," reported *Newsweek* in December 1989, "has degenerated into late-night talk-show jokes." TV comedian Jay Leno, for one, mindful of the "ethics scandals" involving representatives who did favors for those who contributed to their campaign funds, announced that a toy company was "making action figures modeled after the U.S. Senate, and they are pretty realistic—each senator is sold separately." His was only one of numerous snide jokes about congressional venality making the rounds in the 1980s and 1990s.

There have, of course, always been some members of Congress on the take, especially during ages of greed like the 1870s, 1920s, and 1980s. And there have been plenty of windbags in the House and Senate through the years, as well as deadbeats, hypocrites, bigots, womanizers, boozers, liars, and slobs. But the majority of senators and representatives, it is safe to say, have taken their responsibilities seriously and worked hard for what they regarded as the nation's welfare. Still, Congress-baiting—like grumbling about government in general—is an old American sport, and most members of Congress have accepted it as a facet of their public position and have been gratified that so much of it was good-natured. Some of the best quips about Congress, in fact, originated on Capitol Hill.

The notion that there was something disreputable about being a member of Congress has long been a favorite theme in congressional humor. A nineteenth-century joke book told of two newly elected members of the House talking about their recent campaigns. "How did you ever come to run for Congress anyhow?" asked one. "Well, sir," said the other, "I did it to bring disgrace on an uncle of mine up in New York. You see, he treated me very bad when I was a boy, and I took a fearful vow that I would humiliate him, and I have done it." "What business is your uncle engaged in?" asked the first representative curiously. "He's making shoes in Auburn penitentiary," replied his companion. Less heavy-handed was the joke, circulating in the

1890s, about the senator who dozed off during roll call and, when the clerk called his name, woke up with a start and shouted: "Not guilty!" Better still, perhaps because it was based on an actual event, was the story, popular in the 1940s, about the precinct captain who explained to voters how to work the new-fangled voting machines during an off-year election. "Now, it's very simple," she said. "When it comes time to vote, you just take the lever beside the name of your candidate and pull and pull and pull. Electing a congressman," she concluded triumphantly, "is just like flushing the toilet!"

Sometimes the jokes—in books, magazines, newspapers, movies, and on radio and television—centered on congressional doubletalk. "Why did they provide the Capitol with a Rotunda?" went an old joke. "So that the statesmen will find it easier to run around in circles." The humorist's congressman—it is never a congresswoman, even after women began appearing on Capitol Hill—is almost invariably a waffler, straddler, equivocator, obfuscator. According to one tall tale, when an angry constituent sent a peremptory telegram to his representative demanding to know whether he was for or against universal military training, the latter wired back: "I certainly am." In another story, a reporter asked a senator, up for reelection, what he thought about the military-industrial complex and received the following reply: "I think I'm undecided—but I'm not sure." "Senator," the reporter is said to have exclaimed, "I congratulate you on the straightforward manner in which you dodged my question!"

Another solon, according to congressional folklore, who was an artful dodger, left a reporter speechless after an exchange about the economy. When the reporter asked for his views on inflation the representative declared: "I'm totally against inflation." "Well," said the reporter, "I guess you are for deflation." "No," said the representative, "I'm against that too." "Well," said the reporter, "what are you for?" The congressman thought for a moment and then announced: "I guess I'm foursquare for *flation!*" This little joke ended up in a comic movie, *The Senator Was Indiscreet* (1947), starring William Powell, about a blowhard senator who waffled, pandered, pontificated, and pussyfooted. (The movie was dedicated to "every politician who has ever jeopardized a baby's health with unsanitary kisses, who has ever delivered a three-hour Fourth of July oration about himself and George Washington, who has ever promised peace, pros-

CAPITOL STEPS. A satirical musical comedy troupe founded in 1981, made up of current and former congressional staffers, which lampoons and parodies national political figures.

KEN COBB, CAPITOL STEPS

perity, and triple movie features in exchange for a vote.")

The humorist's member of Congress was long winded as well as tricky tongued. One of Kentucky's senators, according to an old tale, was such a garrulous bore that his cry, "Mr. President," was the signal for a general exodus from both the Senate chamber and the visitors' gallery. But one day, when he rose to speak, a Kentucky colonel, who was an old friend of the senator, stationed himself in front of the gallery exit, a revolver in each hand, and forced visitors to remain seated until the senator had finished his remarks. Hours later, when the senator finally ended his speech and took his seat, the colonel put his pistols away and motioned for the visitors to leave. "Mister," sighed one man, as

he passed the colonel on his way out, "that was all right, no fault to find, but, *if it was to do over again, you might have to shoot!*" It was a Kentuckian, too, who starred in another old story, set in the 1870s, about congressional speechifying. This man was running for Congress for the first time, so the story goes, and while making the rounds stumbled onto a public hanging in one of the counties in his district. The sheriff invited him to occupy a seat on the gallows, along with the prisoner and his spiritual adviser, and, just before the fatal hour arrived, told the prisoner he had five minutes still to live and that it was his privilege, if he so desired, to address the crowd gathered below. The prisoner meekly declined, whereupon the congressional candidate jumped up and announced: "As the gentleman does not wish to speak, if he will kindly yield me his time, I will take this occasion to remark that I am a candidate for Congress, regularly nominated by the Democratic convention." At this point the prisoner cried out frantically: "Please hang me first, *and let him speak afterward!*"

The congressional persona beloved of the nation's funmakers is corrupt and dishonest ("so crooked you're going to have to screw him into the ground when he dies") as well as effusive and evasive. "A Congressional committee costs money," says one of Twain's characters in *The Gilded Age*, who was seeking congressional support for his navigation company. "Just reflect, for instance. A majority of the House committee, say $10,000 apiece—$40,000; a majority of the Senate committee, the same each—say, $40,000; a little extra to one or two chairmen of one or two such committees, say $10,000 each—$20,000; and there's $100,000 of the money gone, to begin with." Years later, it seems, the wheeling and dealing was subtler, according to humorists, but the story was the same. A lobbyist drove an elegant Rolls-Royce to the home of a senator, according to a tale popular in the 1970s, and announced: "Senator, my organization wants you to have this." The senator exploded; he said he was shocked to think that any organization had the impression he would accept anything that could be interpreted as a bribe in order to influence his vote on some upcoming legislation. The lobbyist backed off at once, apologized, and exclaimed: "You are absolutely right, Senator. It would be deplorable if such an interpretation could be made. And it could. But now, sir, what would you think if I were to tell you that we would like to *sell* you this car for fifty dollars?" "Oh," said the senator at once, "that's a different story. In that case, you can put me down for two!"

Congressional mendacity has also been a source of amusing stories about lawmakers. Back in the 1840s, according to congressional folklore, a North Carolina senator named Robert Strange, in his last illness, called for his son and told him: "I've decided what I want on my tombstone: 'Here lies an Honest Congressman.'" "And then your name?" asked the son. "No," said Strange, a twinkle in his eye, "that won't be necessary. People who read, 'Here lies an Honest Congressman' will say: 'That's Strange!'" Years later, Paul J. Fannin, the Republican senator from Arizona (1965–1977), enjoyed telling the story about the attorney who challenged a witness in a Texas courtroom on the ground that he didn't understand the obligation of an oath. "Do you know what will happen," the judge asked the

witness, "if you don't tell the truth?" "If I tell one lie," replied the witness, matter-of-factly, "I'll go to the state legislature. If I tell two, I'll go to Congress." The judge, according to Fannin's story, at once held the man qualified.

Senator Fannin wasn't the only lawmaker who liked to tease about his profession. Most members of Congress who wrote their memoirs upon retiring from office included a tale or two in their books ribbing their colleagues as well as themselves. In his autobiography, *In the Senate* (1978), New Hampshire's Norris Cotton recalled an incident that he thought revealed the odd impression the upper house made on many Americans. Once, he said, a senator was entertaining an elderly woman who was a constituent of his, and when he was called away on some urgent business, he asked his page to take her to the Senate gallery, identify the senators for her, and explain what was going on below. But the lad had been a page for only a short time and didn't really know much more about the Senate than the woman did. The Senate was busy that day; bells were continually ringing for quorum calls as well as for roll calls. Puzzled, the woman finally asked: "Why do these bells ring so constantly and so stridently?" "I'm not quite sure," said the boy uncertainly, and then, thinking it over, he suggested: "I think maybe one of them has escaped."

Most members of Congress have taken all the jesting and joshing in good humor. They have realized that poking fun at Congress was much of the time simply an expression of the old American custom of taking cracks at politics and government, while at the same time insisting theirs was the best system in the world. "I'm convinced," said Arizona representative Morris K. Udall in a book on congressional humor published in 1988,

that humor is as necessary to the health of our political discourse as it is in our private lives. Political humor leavens the public dialogue; it invigorates the body politic; it uplifts the national spirit. In a sprawling society where politicians often seem distant from those they represent, political humor is a bridge between the citizens and their government. . . . Humor is also the best antidote for the politicians' occupational disease: an inflated, overweening, suffocating sense of self-importance. . . . Nothing deflates a pompous ass quicker than a well-placed barb.

In the 1990s the nation's lawmakers seemed to be taking Udall's observations seriously. Talk show theater, as it was called, came to be an important forum for political discussion, and members of the

House and Senate turned up with increasing frequency on television shows like the "Late Show with David Letterman" with the definite purpose of demonstrating to the American people that they could be good-humored as well as deadly serious. "The humor part of the political appearance is no longer incidental," noted TV political satirist Mark Russell. "It's become part of the main endeavor." With C-SPAN covering congressional debates, moreover, some members of Congress began introducing sight gags as well as funny remarks into their speeches for the benefit of the cameras on the House and Senate floors. "Politicians are doing this to ingratiate themselves with the voters," explained Rep. Barney Frank, a Massachusetts Democrat known on Capitol Hill for his sense of humor. "There's a volatile mood out there. We're seen as pompous and self-important. Humor is a way to humanize ourselves."

BIBLIOGRAPHY

Boller, Paul F., Jr. *Congressional Anecdotes.* 1991.
Mencken, H. L. *Notes on Democracy.* 1926.
Sterling, Bryan. *The Best of Will Rogers.* 1979.
Twain, Mark. *The Gilded Age.* 1973.
Udall, Morris K. *Too Funny to Be President.* 1988.
Wiley, Alexander. *Laughing with Congress.* 1947.

PAUL F. BOLLER, JR.

HUMPHREY, HUBERT H. (1911–1978), senator from Minnesota (1949–1965, 1971–1978) and vice president of the United States (1965–1969). Hubert Humphrey was a dominant figure in the U.S. Senate from the late 1950s through the mid-1960s, first as a leading Democratic liberal and then as majority whip. He was the original sponsor of many major pieces of legislation, including those creating Medicare, the Peace Corps, the Food-for-Peace program, the Food Stamp program, and the Arms Control and Disarmament Agency.

He was an outspoken leader in the long struggle for civil rights legislation. He first drew national attention at the Democratic national convention of 1948 with a dramatic (and successful) plea for a strong civil rights plank in the party platform, and his greatest legislative achievement was to lead the long and difficult fight for enactment of the landmark Civil Rights Act of 1964.

Humphrey's Senate career was interrupted when he was elected vice president in 1964. He was the Democratic nominee for president in 1968, narrowly losing to Richard M. Nixon. Humphrey returned to the Senate in 1971 and served until his death in January 1978.

Hubert Horatio Humphrey, Jr., was born in the small town of Wallace, South Dakota, and he remained first and always a man of his region and his time—a child of the Great Plains and the Great Depression. He became a big-city mayor, a nationally known senator, and then a world figure, but he never forgot his small-town beginnings. His political heroes were William Jennings Bryan, Woodrow Wilson, and Franklin D. Roosevelt; he was a prairie populist, a progressive Democrat, an internationalist, and a fervent New Dealer.

The harsh depression years shaped his political beliefs. "I must say that the Depression left a lasting impression on me. Much of my politics has

HUBERT H. HUMPHREY. During a Senate Foreign Relations Committee hearing on the Limited Test Ban Treaty, August 1963.   LIBRARY OF CONGRESS

been conditioned by it," he said. "I learned more about economics from one South Dakota dust storm than I learned in seven years at the University. . . . I saw what happens when there's no money and no crops and then the drought hits. You see what happens to people."

Humphrey enrolled in the University of Minnesota in 1929 but dropped out after a year to help run the family drugstore. He was able to resume his education seven years later. After earning bachelor's and master's degrees in political science he went to work in 1940 in the Minnesota office of the Works Progress Administration (WPA).

He first sought elective office in 1943, when he ran for mayor of Minneapolis. He lost, but ran again in 1945 and won. He was reelected in 1947, then won a U.S. Senate seat in 1948 as the nominee of the recently merged Democratic and Farmer-Labor parties.

Humphrey's early months in the Senate were not happy. He chafed at the slow pace, the conservative atmosphere, the seniority system, and the political dominance of the South. He reacted by speaking too often and too long on too many subjects, and he later called it "the most miserable period of my life."

Gradually he adjusted to the Senate—and the Senate adjusted to him. He grew from a shrill, doctrinaire nonstop talker into one of the most accomplished and best-liked legislative leaders of his time. One of his new friends was particularly helpful to Humphrey's career: when Lyndon B. Johnson was elected Democratic leader in January 1953, he tapped Humphrey to be the link between the party's predominantly southern leadership and its small but growing northern liberal bloc.

The list of programs first proposed by Humphrey and later adopted by others amounts to a catalog of post–World War II liberalism. The first bill he introduced in the Senate, in 1949, was to establish a program of federal health insurance; it became law—as Medicare—sixteen years later. Humphrey was similarly ahead of the times in other areas of domestic concern, aid to developing nations, and arms control.

Both a liberal and anticommunist, he led a successful effort to end communist influence in the Minnesota Democratic party in the late 1940s, and in 1954 was the author of a controversial law making it a crime to belong to the Communist party. (Humphrey introduced this bill when he was running for reelection at the height of the McCarthy period. It was enacted despite its doubtful constitutionality.)

He had a deserved reputation as a man who could make a speech on virtually any subject. But the same prodigious energy, wide-ranging mind, and facile tongue that propelled his oratory also made him a tireless and effective advocate for his legislative interests. Humphrey saw himself as a tribune for those who had no voice in American society—people "of modest origin and limited financial means, who lack the power or the influence to fully control their own destiny."

Many of his proposals finally became law between 1961 and 1965, when Humphrey served as Democratic whip of the Senate. This period was the most productive of his political career. In his leadership position, he was one of the two or three most powerful senators; he had an influential voice in the legislative councils of the Kennedy and Johnson administrations.

Humphrey's single most impressive legislative achievement was to engineer the passage of the Civil Rights Act of 1964. He put together a bipartisan Senate majority large enough to obtain cloture and thus break a southern filibuster—the first time this had ever been achieved with a civil rights bill.

Humphrey was also deeply interested in foreign affairs. Many Americans became aware of him for the first time in December 1958, when he had an extraordinary eight-hour conversation with Soviet premier Nikita Khrushchev in the Kremlin. However, Humphrey's interest in this area was of long standing; as a youth he idolized Woodrow Wilson, and he sought and won a seat on the Foreign Relations Committee while still in his first term in the Senate.

Humphrey became the leading congressional proponent of U.S.-Soviet arms control negotiations. He sponsored and served as chairman of the Senate Disarmament Committee; he authored the law that established the Arms Control and Disarmament Agency in 1961; and he played the leading role in engineering bipartisan Senate approval of the first U.S.-Soviet nuclear agreement, the Limited Nuclear Test Ban Treaty of 1963.

Despite his success in the Senate, Humphrey repeatedly sought the presidency. He first ran in 1960, losing the Democratic nomination to John F. Kennedy. In 1964 he was chosen as vice president by Lyndon Johnson and became the Democratic presidential nominee in 1968 after Johnson withdrew as a candidate for reelection. Humphrey lost to Nixon in a campaign dominated by the bitter national debate over the Vietnam War. Throughout the race, Johnson loomed in the background; as his vice president, Humphrey was linked to the administration's support for the war.

Humphrey was again a presidential candidate in 1972, this time losing the nomination to George McGovern. He considered running in 1976, but—partly because of failing health—decided not to enter the race.

Although Humphrey had returned to the Senate in 1971, he never regained the dominant position he had occupied prior to 1965. His one major legislative achievement in this period was the Humphrey-Hawkins bill, finally enacted after his death, which established a framework for setting national economic goals.

In his final years, Humphrey came to be regarded as an elder statesman and wise counselor. He regularly took part in legislative meetings at the White House, and he became a trusted adviser to President Jimmy Carter. Humphrey was struggling with cancer, however; despite two major operations, he died on 13 January 1978. President Carter, in his eulogy, said Humphrey "always spoke up for the weak and the hungry, and for the victims of discrimination and poverty. . . . He was the most beloved of all Americans."

BIBLIOGRAPHY

Eisele, Albert. *Almost to the Presidency.* 1972.
Griffith, Winthrop. *Humphrey: A Candid Biography.* 1965.
Humphrey, Hubert H. *The Education of a Public Man.* 1976.
Solberg, Carl. *Hubert Humphrey.* 1984.

CHARLES W. BAILEY

HUNDRED DAYS CONGRESS. *See* New Deal.

HUNGER COMMITTEE, HOUSE SELECT. The Select Committee on Hunger was organized by the U.S. House of Representatives to study the special problem of hunger and malnutrition in America and around the world. The committee had no legislative jurisdiction; it was temporary and existed from 1984 to 1993.

The House of Representatives established the Select Committee on Hunger on 22 February 1984, in part to demonstrate representatives' concern about domestic and world hunger issues. Proponents also supported its creation because at the time eight separate House committees had jurisdiction over hunger, and the select committee provided a way to address hunger issues from a broader and more comprehensive perspective.

The Select Committee on Hunger was supported by both Democrats and Republicans. In 1984, the resolution that originally created the panel was co-sponsored by a bipartisan group of 258 representatives. The proposal passed the House by an overwhelmingly favorable vote of 309 to 78.

The Select Committee on Hunger had the authority to study a broad range of domestic and global food-related issues; its functions remained the same throughout the committee's history. The committee had authority to conduct a continuing comprehensive study and review of the problems of hunger and malnutrition, including but not limited to those issues addressed in the reports of the Presidential Commission on World Hunger and the Independent Commission on International Development Issues, issues that include: (1) the United States development and economic assistance program and the executive branch structure responsible for administering the program; (2) world food security; (3) trade relations between the United States and less developed countries; (4) food production and distribution; (5) corporate and agribusiness efforts to further international development; (6) policies of multilateral development banks and international development institutions; and (7) food assistance programs in the United States. The select committee also had authority to review any recommendations made by the president, or by any department or agency of the executive branch of the federal government, relating to programs or policies that affect hunger or malnutrition, and to recommend to the appropriate committees of the House legislation or other action the select committee considered necessary with respect to programs or policies that affected hunger or malnutrition.

During remarks in 1991, the committee's chair, Tony P. Hall (D-Ohio), described the committee as "the voice for the voiceless." That same year the *Washington Post* wrote that the committee "is the patron saint of forgotten causes." Topics of the committee's hearings during the 102d Congress reflected these characterizations, and included state and local perspectives on welfare reform, poverty alleviation through the World Bank, breast-feeding in the United States, urbanization in the developing world, homeless children, building assets to alleviate poverty, and microeconomic development strategies for rural areas.

Until 1993, representatives readily reconstituted the select committee at the beginning of each of four new Congresses, and the number of House members who could serve on the select committee was increased by each Congress. The House increased the size of the panel from seventeen members in 1984 to thirty-three members in 1991. However, the climate changed in the 103d Congress (1993–1995) and many members sought the end of all four existing House Select committees as a cost-saving measure. With a majority of the Congress in favor of disbanding the select committees, Speaker Thomas S. Foley (D-Wash.) saw no reason to bring the issue to a vote. He let the select committees, including the House Select Hunger Committee, quietly die when their authorization expired on 31 March 1993.

BIBLIOGRAPHY

Gugliotta, Guy. "Helping the Helpless by Power of Persuasion." *Washington Post*, 25 June 1991.

Wehr, Elizabeth. "House Creates Special Panel to Study Hunger." *Congressional Quarterly Weekly Report*, 25 February 1984, p. 466.

Alston, Chuck, and Richard Sammon. "Foley Foresees Quiet Death for Select Committees." *Congressional Quarterly Weekly Report*, 20 March 1993, p. 647.

MARY ETTA BOESL

HYDE AMENDMENTS. In response to the Supreme Court's abortion decision, *Roe v. Wade* (1973), Congress had by 1993 enacted more than twenty-five laws restricting the use of federal funds for abortions. The Appropriations Act of 1976 for the departments of Labor and of Health, Education, and Welfare contained restrictions that prohibited the use of federal funds for abortions, except when the life of the mother would be endangered by carrying the fetus to term. Some critics of the Hyde amendments (named for their original sponsor, Republican representative Henry J. Hyde of Illinois) argued that they denied equal protection of the law because they disproportionately affected poor and minority women. However, in *Harris v. McRae* (1980) and several other decisions the Supreme Court decided that Congress and the states are not constitutionally obligated to fund either elective or medically necessary abortions.

After *Harris* Congress adopted about ten other laws restricting the expenditure of federal funds for abortions. Because Congress is free to favor childbirth over abortion, it can appropriate funds for the former while denying assistance in obtaining the latter. President George Bush's Health and Human Services secretary, Louis Sullivan, added to the controversy by prohibiting the expenditure of federal money for family planning services that provided information about abortion. While Sullivan's opponents claimed that the rule stifled constitutionally permissible speech, his advocates argued that the regulation was a legitimate expression of the government's interest in promoting childbirth. Bill Clinton overturned this Bush administration policy as one of his first acts as president. As the struggle over abortion funding reveals, Congress and the nation remain deeply divided on the issue.

[*See also* Abortion.]

BIBLIOGRAPHY

Keynes, Edward, with Randall K. Miller. *The Court vs. Congress: Prayer, Busing, and Abortion.* 1989. Pp. 244–312.

EDWARD KEYNES

I

IDAHO. When the Territory of Washington was divided in 1863, Idaho became a territory in its own right. During the next few years, portions of the original Idaho Territory became the Montana and Wyoming territories. The current boundary became final in 1868. Idaho encompasses a huge geographical area, three hundred miles long on its southern border but sharply narrowing to only forty-five miles along the Canadian border. Idaho came into the Union on 3 July 1890 as the forty-third state.

Idaho's original constitution reflected the populism that swept the West during the 1890s. The main controversy was the inclusion of a clause that disfranchised religious practitioners of polygamy. The intent was to deprive the Mormons of southeastern Idaho of political influence, which became less of an issue after the Mormons publicly abandoned polygamy in 1890. During the territorial years, Idaho's politicians consisted of immigrants from other states and federal appointees.

For all of its history Idaho has had two congressional districts. Idaho's representatives have not distinguished themselves in the House because few have stayed there very long, typically quickly seeking to move on to the Senate. Gracie B. Pfost, a Democrat from northern Idaho, served throughout the 1950s but lost a Senate bid just as she gained power in the House. Another House member, Republican George Hansen, who served numerous non-successive terms from the late 1960s until the mid 1980s, embarrassed the state with his financial illegalities, which ultimately sent him to federal prison.

Idaho has, however, produced a number of distinguished members of the Senate. The first genuinely significant elected official was William E. Borah, the progressive Republican senator who served from 1907 until 1940. Borah rose to national prominence in the area of foreign policy. Always liberal on domestic issues, Borah became a leading isolationist during and after World War I. As chairman of the Senate Foreign Relations Committee throughout the 1920s he helped shape America's policy of nonentanglement. In 1936 Borah sought the Republican nomination for president but lost to Kansas governor Alfred M. Landon. Borah did support much of Franklin D. Roosevelt's New Deal. He died in office in 1940.

Borah was an idol of a young Boise lawyer, Frank Church. Church, at the age of thirty-two, was elected to the Senate in 1956 and served four distinguished terms as a Democratic senator. Although he is best known as a critic of the Vietnam War, Church chaired both the Senate Foreign Relations Committee and the Select Committee on Intelligence. However, from Idaho's point of view Church will be long remembered for his work on the Scenic and Wild Rivers Act, wilderness area legislation, and as a protector of the environment. Church lost his seat in the Republican landslide that accompanied Ronald Reagan's election to the presidency and died four years later.

After a number of years in the House, James A. McClure of Payette was elected to the first of three terms in the Senate in 1972. McClure gained notice as a moderate voice in the ongoing contest between environmentalists and developers. He also contributed significantly to the nation's attempt to create an energy policy.

Idaho has a small population but has contributed significantly to Congress in the twentieth century. Its delegation has a powerful legacy to uphold.

BIBLIOGRAPHY

Peterson, F. Ross. *Idaho: A Bicentennial History.* 1977.

Schwantes, Carlos. *In Mountain Shadows: A History of Idaho.* 1991.

Stapilus, Randy. *Paradox Politics: People and Power in Idaho.* 1988.

F. ROSS PETERSON

ILLINOIS. Illinois is the microcosm state. Since the 1820s its social and economic structures have reflected closely the national average. Combining national importance, because of its size, and remarkably high levels of interparty competition, the Illinois arena has sent more party leaders to Congress than any other state.

Admission to the Union in 1818 was uneventful, as Congress ignored the padding of census totals that brought the underpopulated frontier territory up to par. The state's first major political figure was Stephen A. Douglas, who wasted little time after his 1847 arrival in the Senate in becoming the dominant figure of the Democratic party. Demonstrating an unmatched mastery of coalition building, Douglas forged the Compromise of 1850 and ushered through the Kansas-Nebraska Act in 1854. He was victorious over Abraham Lincoln in his 1858 reelection bid and over President James Buchanan in his effort to seize control of the Democratic party in 1859–1860; as the presidential nominee, he carried only two states.

Downstate Illinois produced Henry T. Rainey, the majority leader of House Democrats who sabotaged the Hoover program in 1931 and 1932 and the Speaker who pushed through the first New Deal legislation in 1933 and 1934. Much less successful was Scott W. Lucas, a Democrat who found frustration in the job of Senate majority leader (1949–1950) until he was relieved of his seat by Everett M. Dirksen. The honey-tongued Dirksen was the Senate's minority leader from 1959 until his death in 1969.

Republican Joseph G. Cannon, in his half-century career in the House (1872–1890, 1892–1912, and 1914–1923) always seemed two decades behind the times. He was a powerful Speaker (1903–1910) until a coalition of Democrats and insurgent Republicans stripped the office of its control of the Rules Committee in retaliation for Cannon's disre-

REP. ELIHU B. WASHBURNE (R-ILL.). Served in the House from 1853 to 1869, resigned to become President Ulysses S. Grant's secretary of State, and shortly thereafter became a diplomatic minister to France.

PERLEY'S REMINISCENCES, VOL. 2

gard of the fledgling seniority system. House Republicans Leslie C. Arends (party whip 1943–1974) and Robert H. Michel (minority leader 1981–) have set records for years of tenure, radiance of amiability, and probability of being outvoted. No wonder several ambitious Illinois Republicans have moved from Congress into the cabinet (Donald Rumsfeld to Defense, Edward J. Derwinski to Veterans Affairs, Lynn Martin to Labor, Edward R. Madigan to Agriculture). The centralist skills Illinois politicians develop rarely allow for the requisite color or charisma to compete effectively for the White House, as John B. Anderson in 1980 and Paul Simon in 1988 quickly learned. An obvious exception was Abraham Lincoln, who showed little evidence of future greatness during his one term as a member of the House of Representatives from 1847 to 1849.

Mastery of legal and substantive technicality was the avenue to influence employed by numerous Illinois figures. Lyman Trumbull wrote much of the

Civil War legislation (including the Thirteenth and Fourteenth Amendments), while Shelby M. Cullom was a master of interstate commerce during his long Senate career (1883–1912). In recent decades Dan Rostenkowski moved from a minor figure in the Democratic machine controlled by Chicago mayor Richard Daley to party spokesman on taxation, both on camera and as chairman of the Ways and Means Committee.

Not all Illinois members so successfully navigated their careers. William Lorimer was expelled from the Senate in 1912 because of bribery in the legislature that elected him. After deep involvement in the savings and loan scandal, Frank Annunzio was ousted from a committee chairmanship. In 1985, at the age of eighty, Charles Melvin Price lost his chair of the House Armed Services Committee. On the whole, however, the Illinois delegation has learned to stick together and foster a knack for leadership.

BIBLIOGRAPHY

Jensen, Richard. *Illinois: A Bicentennial History.* 1978.

RICHARD JENSEN

IMMIGRATION ACT OF 1990 (104 Stat. 4978).

The Immigration Act of 1990 effected the first overhaul and expansion of the legal immigration system since 1965. The product of an unlikely alliance of ethnic groups, growers, business, labor, and human-rights advocates, the act set up a three-track visa system. Most visas further the traditionally favored goal of "family reunification"; 520,000 visas were allotted to several categories of relatives of citizens and permanent residents in 1992. (Inevitably that figure will expand since the number of visas for children, spouses, and parents of U.S. citizens is unlimited.) An additional 140,000 visas are based on job skills, and a final 40,000 (increasing to 55,000 in 1995) are "diversity" visas granted to nationals of countries that sent few immigrants to the United States under the 1965 law. Refugees and those seeking political asylum are admitted without respect to these ceilings. The new law for the first time caps the number of visas available to nonimmigrants who will work here temporarily and provides "temporary protected status," or safe haven from deportation, to Salvadorans already in the United States and to other groups designated by the attorney general. The law also facilitates the swift deportation of aliens convicted of certain crimes, especially drug-related felonies.

The 1990 act originated in the 1981 Report of the Select Commission on Immigration and Refugee Policy (SCIRP), established by Congress in 1979 and chaired by Theodore Hesburgh, then president of the University of Notre Dame. Some of SCIRP's congressional members, including Senators Edward M. Kennedy and Alan K. Simpson, helped shape the decade's immigration policies along many of the lines recommended in the SCIRP report.

Congress divided the SCIRP agenda in two, dealing with illegal immigration before legal admissions. In 1986 Congress enacted the Immigration Reform and Control Act (IRCA), which combined amnesty programs for undocumented aliens, agricultural workers, and Cuban-Haitian "entrants" who had lived in the United States for some time with employer sanctions designed to end the hiring of unauthorized workers, thereby reducing the principal incentive for illegal migration. In addition, the act created a temporary category of visas for nationals of countries "adversely affected" by the 1965 immigration law; this benefited primarily Irish emigrants. Despite its employer sanctions provisions, IRCA on balance expanded the number of immigrants with legal status. Having thus stemmed illegal migration—or so Congress liked to think— legislators turned to the legal immigration system. In 1988, Congress added another category of visas for nationals of countries "underrepresented" in the immigrant stream, a provision that ultimately favored aliens from the Indian subcontinent. This category, together with the "adversely affected" category created in 1986, became the "diversity" program in the 1990 act.

During the long gestation of the 1990 act, the House favored both expanding the number of immigrant visas and, in deference to organized labor, capping the number of visas granted to temporary workers. The House also included human-rights and safe-haven protections, while the Senate demanded a more skills-oriented admissions policy and stricter enforcement. The act was a delicate compromise. The immigration-expanding provisions of IRCA and the 1990 act have reversed the relatively restrictive policies that had prevailed since World War I.

BIBLIOGRAPHY

Schuck, Peter H. "The Politics of Rapid Legal Change: Immigration Policy in the 1980s." *Studies in American Political Development* 6 (Spring 1992): 37–92.

PETER SCHUCK

IMMIGRATION AND NATIONALITY ACT. *See* McCarran-Walter Immigration and Nationality Act.

IMMIGRATION AND NATURALIZATION SERVICE V. CHADHA (462 U.S. 919 [1983]).

On its face *Immigration and Naturalization Service v. Chadha* is about an immigrant's efforts to remain in the United States. Jagdish Chadha, an East Indian from Kenya, had come to the United States as a student in 1966. When his visa expired he was ordered to show cause why he should not be deported by the Immigration and Naturalization Service (INS). After hearing his case the INS in June 1974 granted him a "suspension of deportation" that allowed him to remain. The law under which the INS granted the suspension required that a report be submitted to Congress. If at any time during the next two sessions of Congress either house vetoed the suspension, Chadha would have to be deported. On 12 December 1975, the House of Representatives voted to veto Chadha's suspension. Facing deportation, Chadha appealed the case and found himself in the midst of a constitutional struggle between Congress and the executive branch.

The constitutional issue involved was the legitimacy of the legislative veto. Congress had added legislative veto provisions to nearly two hundred statutes, enabling it to exercise veto power by majority vote of both houses (a two-house veto), by majority vote of one house (a one-house veto), or by action of a single committee (a committee veto). The executive branch, especially the Department of Justice, believed that Congress could not take action that had the force of law unless it followed the presentment process set out in the Constitution. When the Justice Department, representing the INS, joined Chadha's attorney in arguing that the legislative veto was unconstitutional, both the Senate and House intervened in the case to defend its constitutionality.

On 23 June 1983, the Supreme Court by a vote of 7 to 2, ruled the legislative veto in the Immigration and Naturalization Act unconstitutional. As Chief Justice Warren Burger explained in his majority opinion, the Constitution provides "a single, finely wrought and exhaustively considered procedure" for exercise of the legislative power of the federal government. "Explicit and unambiguous provisions of the Constitution," he went on, "prescribe and define the respective functions of the Congress and of the executive in the legislative process." Any actions taken by either house, if "they contain matter which is properly to be regarded as legislative in character and effect," must conform with this constitutionally designed legislative process—passage by a majority of both Houses and presentment to the president. And lest there be any confusion as to what the Court considered to be "legislative in nature," Burger carefully spelled that out; legislative action, he stated, is any action that has the "purpose and effect of altering the legal rights, duties, and relations of persons outside the legislative branch." This broad definition effectively called into question the constitutionality of virtually every existing legislative veto. While recognizing the convenient nature of the shortcut offered by the veto in the *Chadha* case, which enabled Congress to share authority over aliens with the executive branch, Burger forcefully defended the "step-by-step, deliberate and deliberative process" for legislative action set out in the Constitution.

In a vehement dissent, Justice Byron White defended the legislative veto as "an important if not indispensable political invention that allows the president and Congress to resolve major constitutional policy differences, assures the accountability of independent regulatory agencies, and preserves Congress's control over lawmaking." Courts have employed a flexible interpretation of the Constitution to justify the broad delegation of what is effectively law-making power to executive branch and independent agencies, he stated. Therefore, White argued, it is wholly inappropriate for the Court to use a rigid interpretation of the Constitution to prevent Congress from possessing a necessary check on the unavoidably expanding power of the agencies. In White's view, neither the presentment clause nor the doctrine of separation of powers is violated by this "mechanism by which our elected representatives preserve their voice in the governance of the nation."

Congressional response to the Court's ruling was mixed. There were efforts to attempt to fashion a constitutional alternative to the one- and two-house versions of the veto that would include the president. For arms sales to foreign nations, Congress did amend the law changing its two-house veto provision to allow veto of an arms sale by joint resolution, a process that requires bicameral passage and presentment to the president. Congress also moved to restrain the president's ability to impound funds without congressional assent. In a few other cases Congress also moved to alter existing veto provisions into joint resolutions of approval or disapproval to conform to the Court's ruling. A joint resolution, though, whether of approval or disapproval of an executive action, is really just another name for a law. It does not give Congress the power to act without presidential involvement. In some cases, Congress added what clearly were committee-level vetoes to laws granting power to executive branch actors to reprogram funds from accounts set out in the law. Executive branch acquiesence to these provisions as the price for added flexibility has so far gone unchallenged in the courts. Though this committee form of the veto is the most pernicious constitutionally, perhaps the executive is willing to accept it secure in the knowledge that *Chadha* stands as a bar to such expansion of the veto as occurred in the past. Little else was done to replace the now unconstitutional provisions for legislative vetoes in most other laws. Constitutional amendment proposals to allow a legislative veto were introduced but went nowhere.

Congressional acquiescence to the *Chadha* decision is perhaps best explained by its timing. By 1983, the administration of Ronald Reagan had moved significantly to stem the growth of federal regulations. For those who believed the legislative veto was essential to curtail bureaucratic regulatory excess, the problem no longer seemed paramount. For those in Congress who were unhappy with administrative foot-dragging in implementation of the law—especially laws aimed at protecting the environment, consumer safety, and civil rights—the legislative veto was not the remedy. The legislative veto was a mechanism for stopping executive action, and what they needed was a prod, not a rein.

[*See also* Veto, *article on* Legislative Veto.]

BIBLIOGRAPHY

Craig, Barbara Hinkson. *Chadha: The Story of an Epic Constitutional Struggle*. 1988.
Gilmour, Robert S., and Barbara Hinkson Craig. "After the Congressional Veto: Assessing the Alternatives." *Journal of Policy Analysis and Management* 3 (1984): 373–392.

BARBARA HINKSON CRAIG

IMMIGRATION POLICY. Throughout the first half of the nineteenth century Congress paid little attention to immigration policy. But in 1819 it began requiring manifests of all passengers aboard ships coming to the United States, and so began generating immigration data. (Lawful land-border arrivals were not counted until the mid 1850s and

not with much completeness until after 1900.) A major reason for congressional inattention to immigration policy was the widely held belief that large numbers of immigrants were desirable, because, as President John Tyler said in an address to Congress in 1843, immigrants would "by their labor . . . swell the current of our wealth and power."

Chinese Exclusion Laws. Although there was considerable criticism of and opposition to immigrants, especially to the Irish at the time Tyler spoke, immigration restriction did not become a major issue in Congress until almost 200,000 Chinese arrived between 1861 and 1880 to work in mines and on farms and railroads. When it appeared that some Chinese women had been imported for prostitution, Congress in 1875 required masters of vessels to determine whether any immigrant had entered into a contract for "lewd or immoral purposes" and also prohibited the admission of Asian persons "without their free and voluntary consent" (18 Stat. 477). A rash of immigration bills was passed in 1882. One of them expanded the excludable classes from two to four, adding to convicts and those deemed immoral (specified in 1875) mental defectives (described as "lunatics" and "idiots.") and those unable to take care of themselves without becoming public charges (22 Stat. 214).

Responding to public pressure against Chinese immigration, Congress the same year overwhelmingly passed a bill to suspend the immigration of Chinese laborers, including skilled laborers, for ten years and to provide for the deportation of any Chinese person found unlawfully within the United States (22 Stat. 59). It also forbade state and federal courts from admitting resident Chinese to citizenship, clearing up an ambiguity in the 1790 statute that had denied naturalization to any nonwhite person.

With passage of the Immigration Act of 1882, Congress assumed clear responsibility for regulating and restricting immigration. In 1884 Congress responded to mounting public pressure against contract labor by making it unlawful for any person, company, partnership, or corporation to prepay the transportation or assist in the importation of aliens under contract or agreement to perform labor in the United States (23 Stat. 58). Exempt were skilled laborers entering to perform work that could not be obtained from American workers, professional actors and artists, and those assisting in the immigration of family members or personal friends.

Having enacted immigration restrictions, Congress set out to enforce them. Legislation passed in 1887 (24 Stat. 414) gave the secretary of the Treasury power to enforce the law restricting contract labor. In 1888 Congress suspended all Chinese immigration (not just laborers) for twenty years with the exception of officials, teachers, students, merchants, and tourists (25 Stat. 476). Another law made it illegal for any resident Chinese laborer who left the United States to return (25 Stat. 504).

Broadening of Restrictions. Restrictionist sentiment spread to European immigrants in the 1880s and 1890s, especially after an 1894 report by the House Judiciary Committee pointed out that although foreign-born individuals constituted less than 15 percent of the population, more than half of the white penitentiary convicts and residents of America's poorhouses were foreigners. Restrictionists argued that a literacy test would screen out people likely to become criminals or paupers and would impede the immigration of Italians, Jews, Hungarians, Greeks, and others they deemed less desirable than immigrants from Germany, France, and Scandinavia. President Grover Cleveland reported in 1896 that the proportion of illiteracy among immigrants older than fourteen had risen by more than one-third in one year, to 28.6 percent. Nevertheless, Cleveland, opposing literacy as a basis for selection, successfully vetoed a bill that would have excluded all those older than sixteen who could not read or write English or some other language. The president believed that the literacy barrier would exclude many desirable and needed immigrants.

The restrictionist movement was fueled in part by concern over the sheer volume of immigration. Nearly nine million immigrants entered the United States during the last twenty years of the nineteenth century. Cleveland's successor, Republican William McKinley, supported the literacy test, a measure endorsed by the American Federation of Labor.

But Congress, preoccupied with the war with Spain in Cuba, decided to establish a body, the Industrial Commission, to study immigration matters and make recommendations. (The Industrial Commission also was charged with examining various problems of U.S. industrialization, including trusts and labor.) The commission conducted extensive hearings and research and submitted its report in 1901. Congress enacted most of its recommendations in 1903, including a system for inspecting U.S. land borders, the exclusion and deportation of anarchists, the strengthening of the Chinese exclusion and contract labor laws, and the exclusion of anarchists or people who advocated the overthrow of government and of those attempting to bring prostitutes into the country (32 Stat. 176). Only two members of the commission had recommended a literacy test, and nothing was done on that issue.

In his message to Congress on 7 December 1903 President Theodore Roosevelt failed to make specific legislative proposals but warned Congress that it must eliminate immigration of the "wrong kind." A year later he became more specific, saying that the United States should not admit those whose standards of living, customs, and personal habits would lower the level of the American wage earner. In 1905, at the beginning of the 59th Congress, when immigration was rising to new heights, he suggested that it would be desirable if only natives of Canada and Mexico crossed U.S. borders. It was not enough, he said, to keep out anarchists; the country also needed to exclude those with anarchistic tendencies and all people of bad character, including the lazy and incompetent.

Congress responded by passing the Immigration Act of 20 February 1907 (34 Stat. 898). Additional categories of exclusion were added, including those with tuberculosis.

Dillingham Commission. Perhaps the most important part of the 1907 bill was the creation of a new commission to study immigration. It consisted of three House members, three senators, and three presidential appointees and became known as the Dillingham Commission after its chairman, Sen. William P. Dillingham (R-Vt.); like the Industrial Commission before it, the Dillingham Commission would prove to have a profound effect on legislation.

When the first session of the 61st Congress opened in 1909, concern about the size and composition of immigration was high. The foreign-born constituted more than 14 percent of the U.S. population, and one in every three people residing in the country was either someone who had been born in a foreign country or the child of foreign-born parents. The recommendations of the Dillingham Commission, presented in two summary volumes on 5 December 1910, were restrictionist. (Some detailed reports appeared earlier and others came later, for a total of forty-two volumes.)

After extended debate Congress in 1913 passed the so-called Dillingham bill, which included a provision proposed by the commission that any immigrant could be deported within five years after entering the country for crimes involving moral turpitude and for three years after entry for becoming a public charge. This modified the older requirement that immigrants who became public charges could be deported only for reasons that existed prior to entry. Also enacted was the exclusion of Asian persons from a barred zone known as the Asia-Pacific triangle.

The centerpiece of the bill was a literacy test to be given to all aliens older than sixteen. It required them to read a portion of the Constitution in either English or some other language or dialect. President William Howard Taft vetoed the bill, primarily because he opposed the literacy test, and by a slight margin the House of Representatives failed to overturn his veto. Taft was responding to employer groups and, to a lesser extent, newly organized immigrant ethnic groups that opposed restriction.

An alternative way of curtailing immigration recommended by the Dillingham Commission was the admission of immigrants based on a fixed percentage from each country, sharply reducing those from eastern and southern Europe (disproportionately Jewish, Catholic, or Eastern Orthodox in religion). But the literacy test had the advantage of simplicity over a national-origins formula, and many members of Congress believed that it would accomplish the same goal. Another comprehensive bill, including a literacy test, was passed in January 1915, but it was successfully vetoed by President Woodrow Wilson. Finally, in 1917 Congress passed the literacy test over Wilson's veto (39 Stat. 874). The act also barred Asian immigrants from a geographically defined zone (not yet including Japan).

Despite the literacy test, immigrants came from eastern and southern Europe in large numbers, bringing the total for the first two decades of the twentieth century to 14.5 million and accounting for more than 45 percent of the nation's total population growth. Wartime patriotism, postwar unemployment, and fear of radicalism strengthened popular (and hence congressional) anti-immigration sentiment.

In 1921 Congress adopted the Dillingham Commission's alternative to the literacy test, known as national-origins quotas. This legislation set annual quotas for each nationality group at 3 percent of the number of foreign-born people of that national origin enumerated in the 1910 census, except for Asians coming from a zone that now included Japan, who were barred. Exceptions to the quotas were made for aliens younger than eighteen who were the children of citizens and for aliens who had lived continuously for at least a year in countries of the Western Hemisphere (42 Stat. 5). With the sentiment for restriction growing even stronger, Congress passed the comprehensive Immigration Act of 1924 (43 Stat. 153), the main feature of which set national quotas at 2 percent of the 1890 foreign-born population for each nationality from the Eastern Hemisphere resident in the United States (the Western Hemisphere had no quotas). Immigration, which had been greater than 700,000 in 1924, dropped to fewer than 300,000 in 1925, and Italian, Polish, Greek, and Russian (mostly Jewish) immigration fell by 85 percent. The complicated formula was changed in 1927 and again in 1928, but the overall effect was the same. Although remembered now for its invidious racist assumptions about superior and inferior peoples, the 1924 act also allowed consular officials abroad to issue immigrant visas and defined the status of *immigrant* (permanent resident alien) and *nonimmigrant*.

World War II and After. Economic depression further curtailed already lowered numbers of immigrants in the 1930s. Indeed, in the early 1930s more people left than entered the United States. Although the basic policy of restriction remained intact, Congress began to chip away at it as a result of American involvement in World War II. Because China was an ally, Chinese exclusion was ended in 1943 (57 Stat. 600), and Chinese people or people of Chinese descent were assigned a quota of 105 per year. In the same spirit of friendship, legislation in 1946 gave nonquota status to the Chinese wives of American citizens (60 Stat. 975). Another act authorized the admission of people of races indigenous to India and of Filipinos or people of Filipino descent, making them eligible for naturalization (60 Stat. 416).

During the war, the United States also signed agreements with Mexico to establish a *bracero* program for Mexican workers to fill labor shortages, particularly in the West and Southwest—a tremendous spur to immigrants (who received permanent resident status) in the 1950s, 1960s, and 1970s. Illegal immigration, too, greatly expanded. The *bracero* program was suspended between 1947 and 1951, but it was begun again to meet labor shortages during the Korean War and lasted until President John F. Kennedy ended it in 1964.

Because the United States had no specific refugee policy, potential immigrants fleeing Nazism had to qualify under restrictive immigration quotas. Relatively few persecuted Jews and others were able to enter the United States during the war. The Displaced Persons Act of 1948 (62 Stat. 1009) was an attempt to respond to the large numbers of Europeans who had been turned into refugees by the war. Priority went to aliens qualified as farm laborers (a minimum of 30 percent of the visas issued pursuant to the act) and those who had other skills. Racial and religious factors also affected implementation of the bill: from 30 June 1948 to 1 July 1950, half of the German and Austrian quotas were made available exclusively to "persons of German ethnic origin who were born in Poland, Czechoslovakia, Hungary, Rumania, or Yugoslavia and who, on the effective date of the Act, resided in Germany or Austria."

Immigration Quotas. The national-origins quota system was maintained in the comprehensive McCarran-Walter Immigration and Nationality Act of 1952 (66 Stat. 163), passed over the veto of President Harry S. Truman. The president approved some aspects of the bill: codification of immigration and naturalization laws, establishment of limited quotas for Asian countries, removal of racial barriers to naturalization (meaning Asian immigrants became eligible for naturalization), and establishment of nonquota status for alien husbands of citizens and residents comparable to that given alien wives. But Truman objected to continuing the national-origins quota system because of its racial and religious distinctions and disliked many provisions making it easier to exclude and deport aliens.

Successive presidents—Dwight D. Eisenhower, John F. Kennedy, and Lyndon B. Johnson—asked Congress to end the national-origins quota system. Finally, it did so in the Immigration Act of 1965 (79 Stat. 911). In the new system a numerical ceiling of 170,000 immigrants per year was set for the Eastern Hemisphere, with no more than 20,000 visas annually for any one independent country. A preference system was created with emphasis on the admission of relatives of U.S. citizens and permanent resident aliens. It established four family relationship categories for a total of 170,000 immigrants from the Eastern Hemisphere. A ceiling (of 120,000 slots) was for the first time imposed on the Western Hemisphere, and in 1976 the preference system and the per-country limits were extended to these countries of origin as well. In 1967 the hemispheric ceilings were combined into a total worldwide ceiling of 290,000, not counting the minor children, spouses, and parents of U.S. citizens, who were admitted without numerical restriction. Included in the 290,000 were 17,000 visas set aside for refugees

fleeing communist or Middle Eastern countries (that number was eliminated in 1980 with the passage of the Refugee Act).

Refugee Influx. In the three decades following the end of World War II there was an explosion of refugee migrations, and Congress responded by enacting laws to allow "displaced persons," "parolees," "conditional entrants," and "refugee-escapees" —sometimes employing unused country quotas or mortgaging a country's future quotas—to be admitted to the United States on a selective basis. As a result of these individual acts—particularly those affecting Cubans and Vietnamese—hundreds of thousands of refugees came to the United States in the 1950s, 1960s, and 1970s. Responding to the ad hoc nature of these statutes, Congress for the first time passed comprehensive refugee legislation in 1980 (94 Stat. 102).

The Refugee Act of 1980 established procedures for consultation between the president and Congress on the numbers and allocations of refugees to be admitted in each fiscal year, as well as procedures for responding to emergency refugee situations; in conformity with the 1967 United Nations protocol on refugees, it defined a *refugee* as someone with "a well founded fear of being persecuted for reasons or race, religion, nationality, membership in a particular social group, or political opinion" should that person be returned to his or her home country. It also established a comprehensive program for domestic resettlement of refugees, and it created permanent resident status for them. The law anticipated that there would be a normal flow of fifty-seven thousand refugees and five thousand asylum seekers annually. These numbers proved to be unrealistically low, as an unprecedented number of refugees arrived in the United States during the 1980s. By the end of the decade it was customary for more than 100,000 to be admitted annually. The 1980 law also theoretically eliminated the ideological and geographic bases established in 1965 for admitting refugees. In practice, refugee numbers were allocated overwhelmingly to those fleeing communist oppression.

Congress also became preoccupied with growing numbers of illegal aliens coming to the United States from all over the world, especially those arriving from Mexico. Partly because of that concern, Congress established the Select Commission on Immigration and Refugee Policy, consisting of four members of the House, four from the Senate, four cabinet officers, and four appointed by the president, including its chair, who for most of the life of the commission was the Rev. Theodore M. Hesburgh.

Migrant Workers and Other Illegals. Under the Immigration and Nationality Act of 1952 it had become a crime to import, transport, or harbor an illegal alien. But one provision of the law (called the Texas Proviso) made it clear that to *employ* was not to *harbor.* Growers, ranchers, and other employers could continue to hire illegal aliens with impunity. The flow of illegal aliens accelerated rapidly in the late 1970s, and several bills designed to curb it were introduced. But passage was stymied in 1971 and 1973 in the Senate, where agribusiness interests were strongly represented. The key reform proposed by Presidents Gerald R. Ford and Jimmy

Carter was to impose civil sanctions on employers who knowingly and willfully hired illegal aliens. It was not until the U.S. Select Commission emphasized that tolerating large-scale undocumented immigration had pernicious social effects that a bipartisan coalition in Congress was able to enact legislation penalizing employers. Five and a half years after the Select Commission made its report, President Ronald Reagan signed the Immigration Reform and Control Act (IRCA) of 6 November 1986 (100 Stat. 3359).

The history of this legislation provides a classic example of multiple pressure groups at work. Growers were able to persuade Congress to enact a special agricultural program. But this time they

PRESIDENT LYNDON B. JOHNSON. Signing the Immigration and Nationality Act Amendments at a ceremony on Liberty Island, New York, 3 October 1965. The act was Congress's response to more than a decade of requests by presidential administrations for legislation ending national-origins immigration quotas.

YOICHI R. OKAMOTO, LYNDON BAINES JOHNSON LIBRARY

Landmark Immigration Policy Legislation

Title	Date Enacted	Reference Number	Description
Act of 3 March 1875	1875	18 Stat. 477	Established the policy of direct federal regulation of immigration by prohibiting entry to criminals and prostitutes and any Asian person without his or her free and voluntary consent.
Chinese Exclusion Act of 6 May 1882	1882	22 Stat. 58	Suspended immigration of Chinese laborers (not students, teachers, merchants, tourists) to the U.S. for ten years; provided for deportation of Chinese illegally in the U.S.; barred Chinese from naturalization. Chinese exclusion laws were repealed 17 December 1943.
Immigration Act of 3 March 1891	1891	26 Stat. 1084	The first comprehensive law for national control of immigration, establishing the Bureau of Immigration under the Treasury Department to administer all immigration laws (except the Chinese Exclusion Act). Also added to the inadmissible classes were persons likely to become public charges, those suffering from contagious diseases, and persons convicted of certain crimes.
Immigration Act of 3 March 1903	1903	32 Stat. 1213	Extensive codification of existing immigration law added to the list of inadmissible immigrants and provided for the exclusion of aliens on the grounds of proscribed opinions (e.g., anarchists or persons who believed in the overthrow of the U.S. government).
Immigration Act of 5 February 1917	1917	39 Stat. 874	Codified all previous exclusion provisions and added the exclusion of illiterate aliens from entry; created a "barred zone" (known as the Asia-Pacific triangle), natives of which were inadmissible.
Quota Law of 19 May 1921	1921	42 Stat. 5	The first quantitative immigration law; limited the number of aliens entering the U.S. to 3 percent of the number of foreign-born persons of that nationality who had lived in the U.S. in 1910; exempted those who had resided continuously for at least one year preceding their application in one of the independent countries of the Western Hemisphere.
Immigration Act of 26 May 1924	1924	42 Stat. 153	The first permanent limitation on immigration, establishing the national-origins quota system; set the annual quota of nationalities under the law at 2 percent of the number of foreign-born persons of such nationality resident in the U.S. in 1890 (total quota: 164,667). System established from 1 July 1929 to 31 December 1952 fixed quota for the Eastern Hemisphere at 150,000 and established family preferences within it. Wives and unmarried children under 18 of U.S. citizens and natives of Western Hemisphere countries were permitted to come without reference to quota. Established system for issuing immigration visas by American consular officials abroad.
Act of 14 June 1940	1940	54 Stat. 230	Permanently transferred the Immigration and Naturalization Service from the Department of Labor to the Department of Justice.
Act of 29 April 1943	1943	57 Stat. 70	Provided for the importation of temporary agricultural laborers to the U.S. from North, South, and Central America. The program served as the legal basis for the Mexican *bracero* program, which lasted through 1964.

Landmark Immigration Policy Legislation (Continued)

TITLE	DATE ENACTED	REFERENCE NUMBER	DESCRIPTION
Displaced Persons Act of 25 June 1948	1948	62 Stat. 1009	First major expression of U.S. policy for admitting persons fleeing persecution; permitted the admission of up to 205,000 displaced persons during the two-year period beginning 1 July 1948 (chargeable against future years' quotas).
Immigration and Nationality Act of 27 June 1952 (McCarran-Walter Act)	1952	66 Stat. 163	All immigration laws brought into one comprehensive statute. All races made eligible for naturalization; sex discrimination eliminated with respect to immigration; established quota preference for skilled aliens. Broadened the grounds for exclusion and deportation of aliens. Repealed the ban on contract labor (see Act of 30 March 1868) but added other qualitative exclusions.
Immigration and Nationality Act Amendments of 3 October 1965	1965	79 Stat. 911	Abolished the national-origins quota system, eliminating national origin, race, or ancestry as a basis for immigration. Established Eastern Hemisphere ceiling of 170,000 and Western Hemisphere ceiling of 120,000, except for immediate relatives of U.S. citizens and certain special immigrants. Established 20,000-per-country limit within numerical restrictions for Eastern Hemisphere, applied in 1976 to Western Hemisphere. Established seven-category preference system for relatives of U.S. citizens and permanent resident aliens in U.S. and for persons with special occupational skill.
Refugee Act of 17 March 1980	1980	94 Stat. 102	First omnibus refugee act enacted by Congress; established procedures for consultation with Congress by the president on numbers and allocation of refugees for each fiscal year. Defined refugees according to United Nations' 1967 protocol on refugees; established category of asylees; provided comprehensive program for domestic resettlement of refugees and for the adjustment of the status of refugees and asylees to immigrants.
Immigration Reform and Control Act of 6 November 1986	1986	100 Stat. 3359	Authorized legalization of illegal aliens who had resided in an unlawful status since 1 January 1982. Established sanctions prohibiting employers from knowingly hiring illegal aliens. Increased immigration by authorizing adjustments for Cubans and Haitians who had entered the U.S. without inspection prior to 1 January 1982, increasing number of immigrants admitted from dependent areas, and creating a small additional number for aliens from countries adversely affected by 1965 law.
Immigration Act of 29 November 1990	1990	104 Stat. 4978	A major overhaul of immigration law increasing total immigration under an overall flexible cap. Ratio of employment-based immigrants to family-sponsored immigration increased. All grounds for exclusion and deportation revised. Bar against admission of Communists as nonimmigrants and exclusion of aliens on foreign-policy grounds repealed. Attorney general authorized to grant temporary protective status to aliens of countries subject to armed conflict or natural disasters. Created new temporary-worker admissions categories. Recodified 32 grounds for exclusion into 9 categories.

were obliged to accept one that was fundamentally different from the *bracero* programs that had preceded it. The new program provided for legalization of special agricultural workers, who were free to work anywhere, even outside agriculture, and who were eligible to become resident aliens and citizens. Congress explicitly rejected the idea that a large body of foreign workers should—through either illegal migration or some variation of a guest-worker or *bracero* program—be confined by law to an essentially inferior status because they are aliens.

Congress also adopted the Select Commission's recommendation to legalize aliens who had earlier entered the United States illegally, choosing a cutoff date of 1 January 1982. And to deal with the possibility that employer sanctions would result in discrimination against foreign-sounding or -looking resident aliens and citizens, Congress established new civil rights protections by broadening the antidiscrimination provisions of the Civil Rights Act of 1964 to prohibit employment discrimination based on citizenship status or national origin.

But instituting sanctions against employers who willfully hired illegal aliens depended on there being a reliable method of identifying people eligible to work. Congress decided to require a combination of existing pieces of identification in response to the fear that a reliable system of identifying those eligible to work might lead to an abuse of civil liberties. This decision left open wide opportunities for fraud. After an initial period of diminished flows, the number of illegal aliens apprehended rose to levels close to what they had been before passage of IRCA.

Although its main aim was to curtail illegal immigration, the 1986 bill paved the way for many illegals to secure legal status. Between 1984 and 1989 the number of aliens granted permanent residence in the United States doubled. Most of the increase in 1989 was due to IRCA, which created several new categories of permanent residents, including Cubans and Haitians who had been paroled into the United States during the early 1980s. The 1986 act also changed from 1948 to 1972 the requisite date of eligibility for illegal aliens to show continuous residence in order to receive permanent residence immediately: nearly 59,000 aliens legalized their status under this provision.

The Door Is Reopened. Congress continued its pro-immigration policy, adopting other recommendations of the Select Commission in the 1990 immigration Reform Act (104 Stat. 4978). Greater numbers of slots were allocated to reunify families, thus reducing the waiting time for spouses and minor children of resident aliens. The number of immigrants admitted independent of family already in the United States almost tripled, from 54,000 to 140,000 a year. The 1990 law contained a provision establishing a safe haven for those already in the country who had fled civil war and natural disasters and was applied immediately to Salvadorans. And the restrictions in the Immigration and Nationality Act in 1952 that had so bothered Truman because they kept out immigrants and nonimmigrants because of their beliefs, membership in political parties, or sexual orientation were overturned. Other pro-immigration measures in the 1990 act included the granting of 55,000 visas annually for three years for the spouses and minor children of recently legalized aliens under IRCA; the expansion of visas for people from Hong Kong; the awarding of 40,000 visas a year for thirty-three countries that had had low rates of immigration in recent years; and allowing more time for newly legalized aliens to apply for permanent residence.

Under immigration policy as established by the Immigration Act of 1990, at least 700,000 visas would be issued annually through 1994. An overall flexible cap of 675,000 immigrants was established to take effect in 1995. Just over 71 percent of these visas would be for family-sponsored immigrants, about 21 percent for employment-based immigrants (including their families), and about 8 percent for immigrants from countries that had received few visas in previous years. Congress opened the front door to legal immigration more widely than it had been since the early 1900s. Although it increased civil and criminal penalties for those engaged in bringing illegal aliens to the United States and/or employing them, it failed to act on the issue of establishing a reliable system for identifying employees eligible to work, an issue it will probably revisit. The act created a nine-person commission on immigration reform whose final report is due at the end of 1997, virtually assuring another major reexamination of immigration policy by Congress by the year 2000.

[*See also* Chinese Exclusion Policy; Citizenship; Immigration Act of 1990; McCarran-Walter Immigration and Naturalization Act.]

BIBLIOGRAPHY

Aleinikoff, Thomas Alexander, and David A. Martin. *Immigration: Process and Policy*. 1985.

Higham, John. *Strangers in the Land: Patterns of American Nativism, 1860–1925.* 1963.

Hutchinson, E. P. *Legislative History of American Immigration Policy, 1789–1965.* 1981.

Portes, Alejandro, and Rubén G. Rumbaut. *Immigrant America: A Portrait.* 1990.

Reimers, David M. *Still the Golden Door: The Third World Comes to America.* 1991.

LAWRENCE H. FUCHS

IMPEACHMENT. The power to impeach high-ranking federal officers may be the most awesome, although one of the least used, power of the U.S. Congress. Designed to address wrongdoing of an official nature, the impeachment clauses of the U.S. Constitution endow the legislative branch with authority to impeach (formally indict or charge) and, after trial, to convict and remove from office the most powerful public servants, including the president and vice president, the chief justice, associate justices of the U.S. Supreme Court, other federal judges, and cabinet members. The remedies of removal from office and potential disqualification from holding any future federal office reflect the seriousness of betraying the public trust.

At the turn of the twentieth century, a British observer, Lord James Bryce, aptly described impeachment as being "like a hundred-ton gun which needs complex machinery to bring it into position, an enormous charge to fire it, and a large mark to aim at." The impeachment mechanism is powerful but awkward. Members of Congress who have participated in impeachments appear to derive little political mileage from the process and generally view their participation as a public duty rather than an opportunity for political advancement.

Constitutional Provisions. By its very nature the Constitution is a political document. Nowhere is this more evident than in the six impeachment clauses.

The delegates to the Constitutional Convention struggled for months over impeachment, and only after careful deliberation did they assign the power to the national legislature—and then with carefully crafted conditions for its exercise. Consensus was achieved on the basic text; other issues were left to be resolved by future generations. As Chief Justice William H. Rehnquist observed, "The framers were sufficiently practical to know that no charter of government could anticipate every future contingency, and they therefore left considerable room for 'play in the joints.'"

Delegation of the indictment power to the House of Representatives and the trial power to the Senate derived in part from the Framers' belief that independence and autonomy in the executive and judicial branches would be necessary to preserve liberty. The Framers were concerned almost exclusively with the applicability of impeachment to the president. Having established a single executive, the Framers' prevailing feeling was that impeachment would be a central element of executive responsibility. James Madison argued that some provision was indispensable to defend the community against "the perfidy of the chief magistrate."

Article III of the Constitution—the federal courts' beacon—provides in section 1 that "the Judges, both of the supreme and inferior Courts, shall hold their Offices during good Behaviour, and shall, at stated Times, receive for their Services, a Compensation, which shall not be diminished during their Continuance in Office." Consequently, federal judges hold their offices for life, without a fixed term. Their salaries cannot be reduced while they are in office, but they can be removed from office through impeachment.

In statements made after the Constitutional Convention, Alexander Hamilton noted in *Federalist* 73 that federal judges would be tried by the Senate, which he described as "consistent with the independence of the judicial character." Hamilton further observed in *Federalist* 78 that the judiciary will always be the branch least dangerous to the "political rights of the Constitution," and "all possible care is requisite to defend [the judiciary] against [the other branches'] attacks."

Unlike some constitutional provisions that charted entirely new directions in practices and procedures for the new nation, impeachment was a subject familiar to the Framers. Roughly six centuries of English experience with impeachment, as well as decades of state and colonial experiences, antedated the Constitutional Convention. The English model, firmly embedded in common law, was well known to the Framers. Like forks in a road, however, the old English and the new American systems deviated from each other. One of the most significant differences is American intolerance for the penal sanctions (fine, imprisonment, and perhaps even death) that, in England, attached to conviction. Further, American impeachment is limited to officeholders; the English system permitted the House of Commons to impeach any person (except members of the royal family) for any crime or misdemeanor whether the accused was a peer or a commoner. In short, the American remedy, aimed more at the office than the officeholder, tilts toward protecting the public interest as opposed to punishing the individual.

The scope of the impeachment power is succinctly set forth in Article II, section 4: "The President, Vice President and all civil Officers of the United States, shall be removed from Office on Impeachment for, and Conviction of, Treason, Bribery, or other high Crimes and Misdemeanors." This clause is the only provision in the U.S. Constitution that specifically authorizes the disciplining of executive and judicial branch officials.

There is debate over whether members of Congress can be subjected to impeachment. In 1797 the Senate dismissed charges against William Blount on jurisdictional grounds, finding that a senator is not an impeachable civil officer of the United States. Individual members can be removed from office through other means. Both houses of Congress are authorized to punish "Members for disorderly Behaviour and, with the Concurrence of two thirds, expel a Member" (Art. I, sec. 5).

Three provisions in Article I assign responsibility to the two houses of the Congress and provide minimal procedural requirements. Section 2 confers on the U.S. House of Representatives the "sole Power of Impeachment." The threshold power to determine whether impeachment is an appropriate remedy therefore lies in the collective wisdom of the body most representative of the people. Section 3 states that the U.S. Senate has the "sole Power to try all Impeachments" and also specifies that a two-thirds vote is required for conviction and removal. The Senate alone determines whether to convict on any article of impeachment voted by the House. If an article of impeachment is brought against the president, the chief justice of the United States presides at the Senate trial.

Section 3 also clarifies the consequence of a Senate conviction, providing that a judgment of conviction shall extend no further than removal from office and disqualification from enjoying any "Office of honor, Trust or Profit under the United States." Finally, section 3 provides that a convicted party may also be liable for criminal prosecution, trial, judgment, and punishment in a court of law.

The Constitution is otherwise silent on the procedures that the House and Senate may employ in impeachments, except to provide that "each House may determine the Rules of its Proceedings" (Art. I, sec. 5).

Of lesser significance are two phrases that mention impeachment in connection with other subjects. One provides that "The President . . . shall have Power to grant Reprieves and Pardons for Offenses against the United States, except in Cases of Impeachment" (Art. II, sec. 2). Another states that the trial of all crimes, except in cases of impeachment, shall be by a jury (Art. III, sec. 2).

Historical Experiences. In the United States, impeachment activity commenced almost immediately after independence and has continued at irregular intervals ever since. More than fifty impeachment proceedings have been initiated in the House, but only fourteen Senate impeachment trials have taken place. The following individuals have had articles of impeachment voted against them by the House for commission of a high crime or misdemeanor and have been tried by the Senate:

Sen. William Blount of Tennessee (impeachment proceeding held during 1798 and 1799)

U.S. District Judge John Pickering, District of New Hampshire (1803–1804)

Associate Justice Samuel Chase, U.S. Supreme Court (1804–1805)

U.S. District Judge James H. Peck, District of Missouri (1826–1831)

U.S. District Judge West H. Humphreys, District of Tennessee (1862)

President Andrew Johnson (1867–1868)

Secretary of War William W. Belknap (1876)

U.S. District Judge Charles Swayne, Northern District of Florida (1903–1905)

U.S. Circuit Judge Robert W. Archbald, U.S. Court of Appeals for the Third Circuit, then serving as associate judge of the U.S. Commerce Court (1912–1913)

U.S. District Judge Harold Louderback, Northern District of California (1932–1933)

U.S. District Judge Halsted Ritter, Southern District of Florida (1936)

U.S. District Judge Harry E. Claiborne, District of Nevada (1986)

U.S. District Judge Alcee L. Hastings, Southern District of Florida (1988–1989)

U.S. District Judge Walter L. Nixon, Jr., Southern District of Mississippi (1988–1989)

Of these fourteen people, seven (all federal district judges) were convicted by the Senate and removed from office: Pickering (drunkenness and senility), Humphreys (incitement to revolt and rebellion against the nation), Archbald (bribery), Ritter (kickbacks and tax evasion), Claiborne (tax evasion), Hastings (conspiracy to solicit a bribe), and Nixon (false statements to a grand jury).

After sensational trials, two famous impeachment proceedings resulted in Senate acquittals. President Andrew Johnson was charged with eleven articles, all but two relating to violations of the Tenure of Office Act, which required congressional consent for the removal of any public servant whose appointment was congressionally approved. The Senate failed by a single vote to reach the two-thirds necessary for conviction on three of the articles and adjourned without voting on the remaining eight. Justice Samuel Chase, accused of partisan conduct on the bench, was likewise acquitted after extremely contentious proceedings in the Senate. These two acquittals may be as important as all the convictions because, through these trials, the Senate created a body of precedents and knowledge about what factual circumstances are necessary for conviction and what circumstances fall short.

All members of Congress take essentially the same oath of office as federal judges: to defend and uphold the U.S. Constitution. The significance of the oath—constitutionally mandated by Article VI—is underscored by the fact that a term of office does not begin until an investiture ceremony is held. Furthermore, when sitting for the purpose of impeachment, senators are required to take an oath to do impartial justice according to the Constitution and laws. On a case-by-case basis, respect for these oaths has shown the Senate capable of distinguishing between a case warranting conviction and one warranting acquittal, ultimately contributing to maintenance of the vibrant and viable separation of powers envisioned by the Framers.

In a number of instances, the impeachment process has been commenced in the House, but resignation of the officer foreclosed further action. The foremost of these cases involved President Richard M. Nixon, who resigned from office in 1974 after the House Judiciary Committee approved three articles of impeachment relating to the Watergate affair (obstruction of justice, abuse of presidential power, and unconstitutional defi-

IMPEACHMENT TRIAL OF PRESIDENT ANDREW JOHNSON. Depiction of the opening session in the Senate chamber, 13 March 1868. After a drawing by James E. Taylor, *Frank Leslie's Illustrated Newspaper,* 28 March 1868.

LIBRARY OF CONGRESS

ance of House subpoenas). In 1873, impeachment was voted against a federal judge, Mark W. Delahay, but he resigned before actual articles of impeachment were approved. Another federal judge, George W. English, resigned in 1926 after articles of impeachment were voted but before a Senate trial. In 1876, Secretary of War William W. Belknap resigned from office two hours before the House voted to impeach him. The Senate voted to acquit Belknap because many senators questioned the authority of the Senate to try an individual no longer in office.

Legislative activity relating to the disciplining of federal officials has been sporadic but continuous throughout American history. The First Congress enacted a law providing that a federal judge convicted of a bribe will forever be disqualified from holding any office of honor, trust, or profit under the United States. The act of 1790 has never been enforced, and its constitutional validity has been questioned. Since the constitutional constructions of the First Congress are entitled to great weight, the 1790 act may support the view that statutory alternatives for removal and disqualification are constitutionally permissible.

The first constitutional amendment proposing a removal mechanism as an alternative to impeachment was introduced in 1791. Between 1807 and 1812 nine other constitutional amendments were proposed in the wake of the attempted removal of Justice Chase.

Debate continues unabated today. Some members of Congress argue, using Jefferson's words, that impeachment of federal judges is a "bungling business." Others respond that the process works well (albeit slowly), exactly as the Framers contemplated. Records from virtually all Congresses reveal that members have introduced proposals either to amend the Constitution or to establish statutory means for removal, with increased legislative activity most apparent immediately after each impeachment proceeding. Reform proposals, however, have always failed to garner the requisite support for final enactment.

Virtually every state provides for the removal of executive and judicial officers through impeachment. As is true nationally, the remedy is rarely used but nonetheless powerful. (In 1988, the Arizona state senate removed an incumbent governor, Evan Mecham, from office.) Exact procedures vary from state to state, and most states have adopted separate disciplinary procedures for judges. With these alternative mechanisms, impeachments of state judges are uncommon.

IMPEACHMENT TRIAL TICKET. For admission to President Andrew Johnson's trial. Intense public interest in the impeachment drew many spectators.

COLLECTION OF DAVID J. AND JANICE L. FRENT

Current Considerations. The Constitution is a living document, holding sway in a constantly changing society. Although U.S. government institutions and the statute books have been molded by constitutional dictates, many modern entities and laws would scarcely be recognizable by the Founders. The number of civil officers of the United States has grown dramatically. Since the resignation of President Nixon in August 1974, Congress has imposed an increasing number of ethical constraints on government officials, including outside income limitations and requirements relating to financial disclosure and conflicts of interest. Congress also established a mechanism and procedures within the judicial branch to consider and respond to complaints about the misconduct and disability of federal judges. Misbehaving judges may be disciplined short of removal from office, and if an impeachable offense may have been committed, a policy arm of the judiciary—the Judicial Conference—is authorized to transmit to Congress a certification stating this.

Since 1980 the U.S. Department of Justice has prosecuted five sitting federal judges. Three were impeached and removed. One of these, Alcee L. Hastings, was acquitted in his criminal trial but pursuant to a Judicial Conference certification was later impeached and removed from office. In 1992 he subsequently was elected by voters of the 23d Congressional District of Florida to serve in the U.S. House of Representatives, the body that previously impeached him, where he then sat among his former accusers. During his electoral campaign, Representative Hastings argued, among other things, that he—as an African American—had been targeted by prosecutors and deprived of constitutional rights. In 1993 Robert L. Collins, a judge convicted of bribery, resigned from judicial office in lieu of facing imminent impeachment proceedings in the House of Representatives.

Congress has adopted various efficiency measures, along with procedural safeguards for the rights of the accused. The House developed the practice of referring all impeachment resolutions to its Judiciary Committee, which decides whether to commence an investigation and ultimately whether to report articles of impeachment in the form of a resolution. Impeachment resolutions are considered matters of high constitutional privilege when offered on the House floor. All matters relating to impeachment—procedural and substantive, in the committee and the full House—are resolved by majority vote. Following the adoption of a resolution and articles, the House appoints managers to conduct the trial and notifies the Senate of its actions.

Throughout its first 150 years, the Senate exercised its trial authority by conducting proceedings before the full body. In the three impeachments from 1986 to 1989, the Senate acted pursuant to a rule adopted in 1935 and formed a trial committee of twelve senators to hear evidence. The committee prepared both a certified copy of the entire proceeding before it and an impartial statement of facts, along with a summary of evidence about contested issues of fact. Both documents, without recommendations, were distributed to the full Senate, which voted on the articles of impeachment after hearing closing arguments. This procedure was challenged by removed judge Walter L. Nixon, Jr., as being unconstitutional. The Supreme Court in *United States v. Nixon* (113 S. Ct. 732 [1993]) upheld the Senate's authority to determine the procedures it uses to conduct impeachment trials. The Court concluded that a challenge to the Senate's use of a trial committee to receive evidence was not judicially reviewable. Writing for the Court, Chief Justice Rehnquist observed that "judicial review would be inconsistent with the Framers' insistence that our system be one of checks and balances."

In one impeachment, that of Judge Harry E. Claiborne, the Senate rejected a notion incorporated in one of the articles—that a prior conviction for a criminal offense could serve both as a shortcut in the Senate trial and prevent the accused from contesting the facts underlying the conviction. After assessing the facts, the Senate nonetheless found Claiborne guilty of substantive offenses and removed him from office.

In spite of procedural refinements, impeachment remains cumbersome and time consuming. Impeachment cases present factual questions of a precise nature, calling on the House to inquire into the nature of conduct that might stimulate the charge of an impeachable offense; the Senate must sit in judgment, receiving evidence and assessing whether the case has been proved by the House managers. In the modern era Congress has a strictly limited amount of time to devote to legislative business, and impeachment proceedings may divert attention from pressing policy matters.

The arduous nature of impeachment minimizes the possibility that so serious a course will be pursued without fair and due deliberation by the elected officials themselves. By making impeachment difficult, the Constitution chills legislative intrusions into the business of the judicial and executive branches.

Remaining constant is the bedrock principle that the "awful discretion" (Hamilton's words) of impeachment rests solely with Congress. The president is constitutionally precluded from extending executive clemency to an individual in order to avoid congressional proceedings. And, as shown in the *Nixon* case, the federal courts have taken a hands-off view when asked to review impeachment decisions.

Unanswered Questions. In the 1980s, prosecutions of federal judges, convictions followed by imprisonment, and Senate removals increased public scrutiny of the process and placed pressure on Congress not only to devote time to specific impeachment cases but to examine the general subject as well. On 1 December 1990, Congress created the National Commission on Judicial Discipline and Removal, directing it to study issues related to judicial independence and accountability and to make recommendations for change, if necessary. Composed of members appointed by the three branches and the Conference of (state) Chief Justices, the commission duly filed its report in August 1993.

The commission concluded that impeachment of federal judges is a cumbersome process but intentionally made so by the Constitution. Despite its weight, the "hundred-ton gun" works. The commission recommended retention of the time-tested political mechanism of impeachment by the House and trial by the Senate as the sole appropriate means for the removal of life-tenured federal judges. Statutory alternatives, if enacted by Congress, would not pass constitutional muster. With implementation of procedural and administrative reforms in the House and Senate and development of a close working relationship among the branches of the federal government, however, the costs of impeachment can be reduced and the benefits augmented.

The commission's report and recommendations will no doubt be helpful to the Congress and the courts. However, the recommendations will not resolve all new problems of constitutional interpretation and application that will arise among the branches in cases of impeachment. By design, the Framers did not incorporate a fixed standard for impeachment into the Constitution. Rather, they drafted a general standard, one flexible enough to meet future circumstances and events that they could not foresee and one flexible enough to provoke persisting debate.

What then is an impeachable offense? Was Gerald R. Ford right when he answered, "The only honest answer is that an impeachable offense is whatever a majority of the House of Representatives considers it to be at a given moment in history; conviction results from whatever offense or offenses two-thirds of the other body considers to be sufficiently serious to require removal of the accused from office"? Is an indictable offense a requirement? The Constitution mandates that judges serve "during good Behaviour" and yet can be impeached for "high Crimes and Misdemeanors." Are these two conditions essentially the same standard? Could the Senate develop a summary procedure (a proverbial "flip of a coin") for disposition of impeachments? Did the Supreme Court's decision in *Nixon* address the issue of due process rights of the accused before the full Senate? How extensive is the House's investigative power in a duly authorized impeachment proceeding to obtain information from the executive and judicial branches? Would exercise of the House's sole power to impeach be judicially reviewable? The Constitution is silent on whether the House and Senate have the power to impeach and try an accused person who has resigned. Could the House still have impeached and the Senate tried President Richard M. Nixon after his resignation in 1974? Questions such as these will continue to be the subject of the ongoing debate over impeachment.

BIBLIOGRAPHY

Berger, Raoul. *Impeachment: The Constitutional Problems.* 1973.

Black, Charles. *Impeachment: A Handbook.* 1974.

Bushnell, Eleonore. *Crimes, Follies, and Misfortunes: The Federal Impeachment Trials.* 1992.

Gerhardt, Michael. "The Constitutional Limits to Impeachment and Its Alternatives." *Texas Law Review* 68 (1989): 1–104.

Grimes, Warren. "Hundred-Ton-Gun Control: Preserving Impeachment as the Exclusive Removal Mechanism for Federal Judges." *UCLA Law Review* 38 (1991): 1209–1255.

Hamilton, Alexander, James Madison, and John Jay. *The Federalist.* Edited by Clinton L. Rossiter. 1961.

Hoffer, Peter Charles, and N. E. H. Hull. *Impeachment in America, 1635–1805.* 1984.

National Commission on Judicial Discipline and Removal. *Report of the National Commission on Judicial Discipline and Removal.* 2 August 1993.

Rehnquist, William H. *Grand Inquests: The Historic Impeachments of Justice Samuel Chase and President Andrew Johnson.* 1992.

Symposium on Judicial Discipline and Impeachment. *University of Kentucky Law Journal* 76 (1987–1988): 633–859.

U.S. House of Representatives. Judiciary Committee. Staff of the Impeachment Inquiry. *Constitutional Grounds for Presidential Impeachment.* 93d Cong., 2d sess., February 1974.

MICHAEL J. REMINGTON

IMPLIED POWERS. Congress may make any law it deems necessary and proper to implement its enumerated powers (Article I, section 8 of the U.S. Constitution). The Framers' notion of implied powers provided the broad-scale authority required by the new legislative branch of government.

Implied powers gained credibility with the 1819 Supreme Court decision of *McCulloch v. Maryland* (17 U.S. [4 Wheat.] 316 [1819]). Maryland had placed a tax on the Baltimore branch of the Bank of the United States, objecting that the bank's charter was not expressly stated in the Constitution and arguing simultaneously for a limited interpretation of congressional power. The bank refused to comply on several grounds: Congress had the implied power to create the bank, and a state had no authority to tax an institution of the federal government. The Supreme Court upheld the bank's claims in an eloquent defense of national power written by Chief Justice John Marshall. Creating a bank, Marshall argued, was reasonable to accommodate such enumerated powers as regulating currency or encouraging interstate commerce. As Marshall wrote, "Let the end be legitimate, let it be within the scope of the Constitution, and all means which are appropriate . . . , which are not prohibited, . . . are constitutional."

The political controversy surrounding implied powers has been evident ever since. States' rights advocates have warned that Congress may expand its powers too far, so as to intrude upon the powers that are reserved for the states. Another facet of the controversy occurs over the precise means to achieve legislative ends or goals. For example, when Congress has the express constitutional power to raise and support armies and navies, does this imply that a draft policy is the most appropriate means to provide for national defense? The heart of the dilemma is thus the debate over the proper scope and means of implied legislative powers.

[See also Enumerated Powers; McCulloch v. Maryland.]

BIBLIOGRAPHY

Ducat, Craig, and Harold Chase. *Constitutional Interpretation: Powers of Government.* 1974.
Peltason, Jack W. *Understanding the Constitution.* 1994.

JANIS JUDSON

IMPOUNDMENT. In a news conference on 31 January 1973, President Richard M. Nixon raised a number of congressional and academic eyebrows by asserting that the "constitutional right for the President of the United States to impound funds . . . not to spend money, when the spending of money would mean either increasing prices or increasing taxes for all the people . . . is absolutely clear." Far from laying the issue to rest, Nixon's claim led to about eighty cases in the federal courts, almost all of which the administration lost. Congress also passed the Congressional Budget and Impoundment Control Act of 1974 to restrict presidential power.

Any discussion of impoundment requires a distinction among a variety of decisions by administrative officials. Some actions are legitimate exercises of executive power, while others trespass directly on the legislative domain. One type of impoundment consists of routine decisions for the purpose of efficient management—that is, saving money, accommodating changing events that make expenditures unnecessary, and satisfying basic managerial responsibilities. These impoundments provoke few controversies. If an agency can accomplish a legislative purpose by not spending all the funds appropriated, Congress does not object. Similarly, if Congress provides funds for some purpose but subsequent events make the expenditure unnecessary, it is reasonable for a president to withhold the funds. For example, in 1803 President

Thomas Jefferson withheld $50,000 that had been appropriated for gunboats. Because the Louisiana Purchase changed national security requirements, he saw no need to spend the money at that time. Neither did Congress. A year later, having taken the time to study the most recent models of gunboats, Jefferson released the funds.

In some cases, the president is required or directed by law to withhold funds under conditions and circumstances prescribed by Congress. The Omnibus Appropriations Act of 1950 directed President Harry S. Truman to cut the budget by not less than $550 million without impairing national defense. From 1967 to 1970, Congress enacted a number of spending ceilings on federal outlays, requiring Presidents Lyndon B. Johnson and Richard M. Nixon to withhold funds in accordance with the statutory budget-cutting formula. Similar cuts were required by the sequestration process of the Gramm-Rudman-Hollings acts of 1985 and 1987.

These types of impoundments are reported to Congress without triggering legislative objections. Congress has been quick to object, however, when an administration withholds funds simply because it disagrees with a statutory purpose. As the House Appropriations Committee noted in 1950, "There is no warrant or justification for the thwarting of a major policy of Congress by the impounding of funds." House Appropriations chairman George H. Mahon (D-Tex.) made a similar point the previous year: "Economy is one thing, and the abandonment of a policy and program of Congress another thing."

Presidents have provoked a number of clashes with Congress by withholding funds. Major collisions occurred from the administration of Franklin D. Roosevelt to that of Lyndon B. Johnson, but these confrontations were resolved through the regular political process: presidents announced the withholding of funds; Congress and its committees reacted with sharp criticism; and presidents backed down by finding a compromise.

A major change in this pattern of executive-legislative conflict occurred during the Nixon administration, which claimed the right to use impoundment to terminate programs in their entirety. In December 1972 and January 1973, major cancellations and cutbacks were announced. The programs affected by the Nixon impoundments included the Rural Environmental Assistance Program, the Water Bank Program, the emergency loan program of the Farmers Home Administration, the Rural Electrification Administration, rural water and sewer grants, and housing projects. The largest dollar amount came from the clean water program. The administration impounded exactly half of the $18 billion provided by Congress for a three-year period.

In court, the administration tested a number of theories to justify this exertion of presidential power. In almost every case, these theories were rejected by federal judges. The only case that reached the Supreme Court was *Train v. City of New York* (1975), involving the clean water program. The Court held that the administration was required to spend the full amount provided by Congress.

In response to the Nixon impoundments, Congress passed legislation in 1974 restricting the president's ability to withhold funds. The Impoundment Control Act of 1974 provides procedures for two types of impoundment: proposals to terminate funds (rescissions) and proposals to delay the expenditure of funds (deferrals). For rescissions, the president needs the support of both houses of Congress through a regular bill or joint resolution. He must obtain congressional approval within forty-five days of continuous session, which excludes legislative adjournments of more than three days.

The 1974 legislation places the burden on the president to secure congressional support for rescissions within a fixed number of days, but proposals have been introduced to give the president enhanced rescission powers. Under these plans, the president would propose rescissions, which would take effect after a specific number of days unless Congress disapproved by passing a bill or joint resolution. Enhanced rescission would reverse the burden, requiring Congress to act.

Regarding deferrals, the 1974 statute allowed either house of Congress to disapprove. This one-house legislative veto was, however, declared unconstitutional in 1983 by the Supreme Court in *Immigration and Naturalization Service v. Chadha*. For a few years, the Reagan administration limited itself to routine deferrals, but the spending cuts required by the Gramm-Rudman-Hollings Act of 1985 led to heavy use of policy deferrals. A federal appellate court in *City of New Haven v. United States* (809 F.2d 900 [D.C. Cir. 1987]) held that the legislative veto in the Impoundment Control Act could not be severed from the deferral authority. The statutory language and the legislative history of the act convinced the court that Congress would not have delegated deferral authority to the president without the check of a one-house veto. Thus, if the legislative veto was invalid, the deferral au-

thority fell with it. Congress promptly enacted that policy into law (101 Stat. 785) by restricting deferrals to routine, administrative actions. Presidents may not defer funds simply because they disagree with statutory policies.

[*See also* Congressional Budget and Impoundment Control Act of 1974; Immigration and Naturalization Service v. Chadha.]

BIBLIOGRAPHY

Fisher, Louis. *Presidential Spending Power.* 1975.
Pfiffner, James P. *The President, the Budget, and Congress: Impoundment and the 1974 Budget Act.* 1979.
Schick, Allen. *Congress and Money: Budgeting, Spending, and Taxing.* 1980.

LOUIS FISHER

IMPOUNDMENT CONTROL ACT OF 1974. *See* Congressional Budget and Impoundment Control Act of 1974.

INCUMBENCY. The dominant fact about elections to the House of Representatives is that incumbents who seek reelection almost always win. The high reelection rate (94 percent in the period from 1982 to 1992) has important consequences for congressional careers. Not only do incumbents generally win, but likely victory is an incentive to keep trying. Incumbents generally keep seeking reelection until presented with a compelling reason not to. In a typical election year, less than 10 percent of sitting House members actually retire. Those who voluntarily leave often do so to run for another office or to become lobbyists. Some quit because of illness or old age. Rarely do members leave because they prefer to abandon politics. Almost all representatives are, to use a pejorative term, "career politicians."

While several factors account for House incumbents' electoral success, attention tends to focus on one simple reason; incumbents exploit their advantage of incumbency over potential opponents. Incumbents can accrue an electoral advantage over potential challengers by utilizing their many perquisites of office, such as free mailing privileges (franking), generous travel allowances, and large staffs primarily devoted to servicing constituent needs. Also, incumbents have greater access than their opponents to publicity and campaign funds. As a result, incumbents have the wherewithal to generate favorable images for themselves among their constituents, while their opponents must fight an uphill battle for even minimal visibility.

Technically, "incumbency advantage" is the added increment to the vote margin that a candidate gains by virtue of being the incumbent. Or, put another way, incumbency advantage is the causal effect of incumbency on the vote. The best way to measure the advantage is to calculate the size of the "sophomore surge," that is, the percentage of the vote that candidates gain from their first victory (as nonincumbents) to their first reelection attempt (as incumbents). Adjusted for the national partisan trend, the average sophomore surge is a simple but accurate measure of the typical vote share gained from incumbency. In the 1970s and 1980s, the surge averaged about seven percentage points. That is, their incumbency status gave new incumbents about seven percentage points more than they otherwise would have won.

The seven-point sophomore surge represented an increase from a value of only about two percentage points in the 1950s. This growth occurred in part because of the decline of partisanship in the United States. As voters became more inclined to vote on the basis of the candidates themselves rather than on simple party affiliation, incumbency mattered more. Simultaneously, by increasing their own perquisites of office, House members kept themselves more in the public spotlight.

The incumbency advantage does not, however, accrue automatically. To earn it, incumbents must invest in the sort of activities that please their constituencies. Representatives who were elected by a slim margin have the most incentive to please their districts, and they are the ones who attend most carefully to district interests. As a result, they are the ones who earn the largest reward, in terms of added vote share, from being incumbents.

The incumbency advantage is not the only reason incumbents generally win. Even if incumbency offered no special electoral edge, most incumbent candidates would win reelection. First, and most obviously, many incumbents are almost guaranteed to win because they represent the majority party in their district. Every constituency has a particular partisan makeup, tilting to some degree to either the Democratic or Republican party. In districts where the majority always supports one party, the incumbent need do nothing special to stay elected other than to stay nominated. (Of course, this is not true of all districts; some are competitive.)

One overlooked reason incumbents win is that incumbency status is, in effect, earned at the ballot box. Beyond district partisanship or any national partisan trend, elections are won on the basis of which party can field the stronger candidate. Strong candidates tend to win, and by winning become incumbents. After winning, they survive until they falter or lose to even stronger candidates. But strong candidates tend to draw weak challengers. Politicians who are electorally strong tend to run for election to a new office when their prospects of victory are strongest—when there is an open seat, a weak incumbent, or the anticipation of a favorable electoral tide. When incumbents are strong candidates in their own right, they scare off strong challenges even without exploiting the added leverage of incumbency. When they do exploit the perquisites of incumbency, the chance that a strong challenge will arise is reduced even further.

Although the incumbency advantage is usually discussed in the context of House elections, it also plays some role in Senate elections. Incumbent senators are slightly more vulnerable to defeat (with an 87-percent reelection rate for 1982–1992) than House incumbents. Senators enjoy only a modest incumbency advantage, with an average sophomore surge of only about two percentage points. One possible reason for the relative weakness of the Senate incumbency advantage is that senatorial challengers achieve electoral visibility more easily than do House challengers. A senator can rarely win simply because he or she represents a state that is safe for his or her party. Unlike congressional districts, all states are to some extent competitive. Like House members, however, senators earn their incumbency at the ballot box. Most senators achieve reelection for no other reason than that they retain the electoral strengths that allowed them to win their first election as nonincumbents.

The 1992 election campaign was marked by an unusual surge of anti-incumbent and anti-Congress sentiment among the electorate. Still, when the primary and general elections were over, 88 percent of House incumbent candidates (and 82 percent from the Senate) had survived to serve another term. As always, it seemed that voters hate Congress but love their local representatives. But not to be ignored is 1992's high number of congressional retirements (15 percent in the House, 20 percent in the Senate). The retirement rate was highest (approaching one third) among incumbents connected to the "rubbergate" scandal involving bounced checks from the House bank. Incumbents of the 1990s appear to be less certain about making Congress their career. They must worry that if the voters do not get them directly, then maybe the movement for term limitations will.

[*See also* Members, *article on* Tenure and Turnover; Term Limitation.]

BIBLIOGRAPHY

Alford, John R., and David W. Brady. "Personal and Partisan Advantage in U.S. Congressional Elections." In *Congress Reconsidered.* 5th ed. Edited by Lawrence C. Dodd and Bruce I. Oppenheimer. 1993.

Erikson, Robert S., and Gerald C. Wright. "Voters, Candidates, and Issues, in U.S. Congressional Elections." In *Congress Reconsidered.* 5th ed. Edited by Lawrence C. Dodd and Bruce I. Oppenheimer. 1993.

Mayhew, David W. "Congressional Elections: The Case of the Vanishing Marginals. *Polity* 6 (1974): 295–317.

ROBERT S. ERIKSON

INDEPENDENTS. During much of its history, Congress has been a two-party institution, consisting of Federalists and Anti-Federalists in the earliest years and, since 1856, Democrats and Republicans. On occasion, however, third-party candidates, generically called independents have been elected. (Some care must be taken with this identification, since "Independent" has also been the name of a political party, and the word "Independent" has also been used as a prefix in party affiliations such as Independent Populist and the like.) Independents have rarely been large in number; in the twentieth century, they have never exceeded more than four per Congress in the Senate, and in the House they have reached double-digit levels only three times.

From the First Congress in 1789 until 1831, no third-party candidates were elected to either the House or the Senate. Then came a period, from 1831 to 1865, of relative party instability, during which there were few Congresses to which no independents were elected. From 1865 until 1871, no third-party candidates served in either chamber. Thereafter, until 1903, populist candidates of various stripes were elected, particularly to the House. During the next fifty years or so, some independent progressives and a few socialists were elected to various Congresses.

Since 1947, two-party hegemony has prevailed in Congress, with the occasional election of a third-party candidate, most frequently a sitting member moving away from a major party toward independence or affiliation with the other major party—for example, Wayne L. Morse (Oreg.), Harry F. Byrd, Jr. (Va.), and Strom Thurmond (S.C.).

Once elected, independents have usually affiliated with one of the major parties, usually the majority party, in order to receive committee assignments. Most have received equal consideration with party loyalists in receiving choice committee assignments, although they generally have received fairly junior slots, usually after majority member assignments were determined.

BIBLIOGRAPHY

Galloway, George B. *History of the House of Representatives.* 1961.

JUDY SCHNEIDER

INDIANA. The Indiana Territory was established on 7 May 1800, as part of the first division of the Northwest Territory. Indiana received its present boundaries at the urging of Jonathan Jennings, the territory's congressional delegate, who shifted the boundary ten miles northward to ensure full access to Lake Michigan. The passage to statehood was relatively untroubled, and Indiana became the nineteenth state on 11 December 1816.

Indiana's early senators and representatives were typical frontier congressmen, concerned with public lands and canals. After a brief dominance the Jacksonian Democrats were sharply challenged by the Whigs, and Indiana acquired a lasting reputation as a swing state. The first Hoosier to distinguish himself in Congress was George W. Julian, a forthright abolitionist and admired orator. Schuyler Colfax was a firm Republican whose good nature and generous campaign speeches for his colleagues led to his election as Speaker of the House for three terms, beginning in 1863. On the Democratic side Sen. Jesse D. Bright was a strong partisan whose pro-Confederate views led to his expulsion from the Senate in 1862.

Although Republicans dominated Indiana's congressional delegation from the Civil War until the New Deal, Democrats campaigned fiercely and were never humbled. Oliver H. P. T. Morton, the Civil War governor, served in the Senate as a strong Radical Republican from 1867 until 1877. Sen. Thomas A. Hendricks played a leading role among the outnumbered Democrats between 1863 and 1869. Daniel W. Voorhees, during his long service in both chambers, was a talented advocate for the northern wing of the Democratic party.

Because Indiana was a swing state both parties frequently nominated Hoosiers for vice president. Colfax, nominated by the Republicans in 1868, was

CAMPAIGN SIGN FROM INDIANA. Dan Quayle won a U.S. Senate seat in the 1980 election.

COLLECTION OF DAVID J. AND JANICE L. FRENT

first, followed by Hendricks for the Democrats in 1876 and 1884, the undistinguished former representative William H. English for the Democrats in 1880, and Sen. Charles W. Fairbanks for the Republicans in 1904 and 1916. John Worth Kern, the losing Democratic candidate for vice president in 1908, was successful in his effort for the Senate in 1911; the next year Gov. Thomas R. Marshall became vice president. Benjamin Harrison served in the Senate from 1881 until 1887 and became the successful Republican candidate for president in 1888.

Hoosier politics have traditionally been competitive: no senator has ever served more than three terms, and few representatives have acquired sufficient seniority for a major committee chairmanship. Kern became the Senate's first formally chosen majority leader in 1913. Although successful in Washington, he lost his bid for reelection in 1916. Louis Ludlow is remembered for his resolute antiwar proposals, particularly the so-called Ludlow amendment of 1935–1938, which would have required a national referendum to confirm a declaration of war.

During the Cold War era Indiana's fervid conservatism was exemplified by staunch Republicans such as Homer E. Capehart and William E. Jenner in the Senate and Charles A. Halleck in the House. Halleck served twice as majority leader (1947–1949 and 1953–1955) and for six years as minority leader (1959–1965). Democrats came to the fore after 1960, notably Sen. Birch Bayh and Rep. John Brademas, who became majority whip.

Indiana's House delegation increased rapidly to thirteen by 1872 and remained at that number until 1932, but afterward declined to ten. Throughout the twentieth century Indiana was characteristically midwestern, combining rural and industrial interests in a generally conservative blend. After 1916 it appeared that Indiana's reputation as a nursery of vice presidential candidates had lapsed, but the nomination of Dan Quayle in 1988 attracted renewed attention to the old tradition.

BIBLIOGRAPHY

Barrows, Robert G., ed. *Their Infinite Variety: Essays on Indiana Politicians*. 1981.
Bartholomew, Paul C. *The Indiana Third Congressional District*. 1970.
Gray, Ralph D., ed. *Gentlemen from Indiana: National Party Candidates, 1836–1940*. 1977.

PATRICK J. FURLONG

INDIAN AFFAIRS COMMITTEE, SENATE SELECT.

The Select Committee on Indian Affairs was created in 1977 by Senate Resolution 4 (95th Congress) as a temporary committee to consider all Indian matters (including American Indians and Alaska Natives), especially recommendations of the American Indian Policy Review Commission (AIPRC). Sen. James Abourezk (D-S.Dak.), sponsor of the bill creating AIPRC, became the Select Committee's first chairman. The committee was thrice extended (to 1984) before being made permanent by Senate Resolution 127 (98th Congress; 6 June 1984). From 1947 to 1977, the Senate handled Indian affairs through the Indian affairs subcommittee of the Interior and Insular Affairs Committee (predecessor to the Energy and Natural Resources Committee), and between 1820 and 1947 through the Indian Affairs Committee and various special committees. (In 1993 the committee was redesignated the Committee on Indian Affairs, dropping the "Select.")

The committee has jurisdiction over Indian affairs legislation and oversees executive agencies administering Indian affairs. It shares jurisdiction over Indian education and the Administration for Native Americans with the Labor and Human Resources Committee. The Energy and Natural Resources Committee retains jurisdiction over matters concerning the Alaska Native Claims Settlement Act. Some Native Hawaiian programs have also become committee responsibilities.

Starting with five members, the committee grew to ten by the 101st Congress (1989–1991), to sixteen in the 102d Congress (1991–1993), and to eighteen in the 103d (1993–1995). Most members come from states with Indian reservations, chiefly in the West. However, Democrat Daniel K. Inouye, chairman since the 100th Congress, is from Hawaii, which has indigenous Hawaiians but no Indian reservations. Since the 100th Congress, the committee has also had a vice chairman from the minority party.

The Indian Affairs Committee has no subcommittees, although between 1987 and 1989 it created a Special Committee on Investigations to investigate allegations of fraud, waste, and other failures to carry out the government's trust responsibility to Indians.

Many committee staff members and directors have been Indian. The committee has handled between 50 and 100 bills and held 40 to 65 hearings per Congress. To be more accessible to reservations, the committee holds many field hearings. The workload was heaviest in the 95th and 96th Congresses (1977–1981) because of AIPRC, and during the 100th to 102d Congresses (1987–1993), when the committee became more active.

Besides AIPRC consideration and the Special Committee's investigations, the committee's most significant activities have included consideration of the Indian Child Welfare Act (1978), the American Indian Religious Freedom Act (1978), the Tribal Self-Governance Demonstration Project (1988), and the Indian Gaming Regulatory Act (1988), as well as settlement of major land and water claims, restoration of federally terminated tribes, reform of Navajo-Hopi relocation, and creation of a national Indian museum and of programs on Indian substance abuse, forest management, and repatriation of burial remains.

Abourezk began a tradition of general support for Indian goals and sovereignty under federal law, although not without compromise with non-Indian interests. Under Inouye, the committee encouraged communication with tribal governments and national Indian organizations, cosponsoring a series of tribal leaders forums. It has been generally critical of executive agencies administering Indian programs (e.g., Bureau of Indian Affairs, Indian Health Service) and has pushed for increased federal spending for Indians. The committee under Inouye promoted bipartisanship. Most of the important splits within the Committee on Indian Affairs have mirrored attitudes toward Indian sovereignty, not partisan positions.

[See also Natural Resources Committee, House.]

BIBLIOGRAPHY

Jones, Richard S. *American Indian Policy: Background, Nature, History, Current Issues, Future Trends.* Congressional Research Service, Library of Congress. CRS Rept. 87-227 GOV. 1987.

Shea, Michael P. "Indians Skeptical of Report Urging Program Overhaul." *Congressional Quarterly Weekly Report,* 13 January 1990, p. 98.

U.S. Senate. *History of the Committee on Energy and Natural Resources, U.S. Senate, as of the 100th Congress, 1816–1988.* 100th Cong., 2d sess., 1989. S. Doc. 100-46.

ROGER WALKE

INDIAN POLICY. Because the Constitution stipulates that Congress "shall have power . . . to regulate commerce with foreign Nations, . . . and with the Indian tribes," the legislative branch has played a leading role in federal Indian policy-making throughout its history. Congress has set the terms for the unique political and legal relationship between Native Americans and the United States and has been responsible for developing federal programs to carry out the government's obligations to the continent's aboriginal people.

Establishing the Treaty System. On 25 May 1789, President George Washington forwarded his first executive message to the Senate. It was a report from Secretary of War Henry Knox containing two treaties between the United States and "certain northern and northwestern tribes" negotiated at Fort Harmar on the Muskingum River the previous winter. Following the president's recommendation that treaties with Indians should be handled in the same way as other international agreements, the Senate approved the agreements by a wide margin. In doing so, the legislators established a unique relationship between Native Americans and the national government, giving substance to the president's assertion that treaty making would insure that "Indian affairs would become uniform, and be directed by fixed and stable principles."

The Removal Era. As the nineteenth century began, federal Indian policy appeared to be operating on two parallel tracks. On the one hand, American officials continued to endorse the formal recognition of tribal groups through treaties. (Between 1800 and 1825, 113 Indian treaties were ratified by the Senate.) On the other hand, the rapid growth of English-speaking settlements and the surge of popular democracy in the new nation meant that Indian-settler relations would be increasingly affected

NATIVE AMERICAN DELEGATION TO WASHINGTON, D.C. Southern Cheyenne and Arapaho delegates, 1899.

SMITHSONIAN INSTITUTION

by the growing political power of western settlers and their representatives in Congress.

The centerpiece of federal administration of Indian affairs during the early nineteenth century was the Trade and Intercourse Acts, first passed in 1790 and revised regularly over the next four decades until a comprehensive version was adopted in 1834. These laws established federal controls over the Indian trade and prohibited the transfer of tribal land to non-Indians without federal approval. They also attempted to block the sale of liquor to Indians and to undercut the influence of unscrupulous fur traders. In 1824 Congress established the Indian Office to oversee relations with the tribes. With treaties in place, trade being regulated, and settlers acquiring land from federal officials who had acquired it from the tribes, few proposals were made to change the nation's Indian policy prior to 1830.

But with the election of westerner Andrew Jackson to the presidency in 1828 and the rising militancy of tribes such as the Cherokees and Seminoles, the two tracks of federal Indian policy began to converge. If the tribes refused to retreat voluntarily, settler complaints could no longer be satisfactorily resolved within the framework of the federal treaty system. If tribes accepted debilitating land sales, their governments would be disowned and would face their own rebellious radicals. The new politicians from the West began to rally around what they believed was a solution.

The new approach was articulated most fully by Sen. Hugh Lawson White of Tennessee, President Jackson's replacement in the Senate and chairman of the Senate Committee on Indian Affairs. In February 1830 White's committee issued a long report urging Congress to authorize negotiations that would lead to the removal of all Indians from lands east of the Mississippi. Two months later the Senate adopted White's proposal, authorizing the president to negotiate removal treaties and to spend up to $500,000 to carry them out. With House concurrence, the Removal Act became law on 28 May 1830.

While the removal of tribes under the 1830 act required substantial amounts of federal persuasion, intimidation, and—ultimately—military force, the process did not appear to shake Congress's commitment to the treaty system as the principal instrument of federal policy. Even the most notorious removal—the Cherokee "Trail of Tears" to Oklahoma—was accomplished with a treaty, the hated agreement signed by a minority of the tribe at New Echota in 1835. Similarly, the U.S. Supreme Court, which became the focus for a final confrontation between Georgia and the Cherokees, ruled that an Indian tribe was not a "foreign state" but a "domestic dependent nation." Thus treaties could not be absolutely binding, but they deserved respect.

The Emergence of Reservations. With Indian communities now relocated on the western border of the United States, members of Congress believed they had solved the "Indian problem." The Indian Office became a favorite source of political patronage, and tribal affairs receded from center stage in national politics. Then suddenly, during the space of a few months in 1846, war with Mexico and the settlement of the Oregon boundary dispute with Britain resulted in the incorporation of one million square miles of land and 250,000 additional native people within the new national boundaries. Then, the Mormon migrations of 1847 and the California gold rush of 1849 destroyed the old notion that the West would be the Indians' safe haven.

Congress responded to these events with two administrative reforms. First, the patent, land, pension, and Indian offices were taken from the Departments of State, Treasury, and War to form the Department of the Interior. Second, in February 1851, Congress approved the creation of three superintendencies to manage the tribes east of the Rockies and authorized the appointment of agents in New Mexico and Utah. Additional legislation created superintendencies for California, Oregon, and Texas. The Indian Office was changing from a bureau to supervise trade and diplomacy with tribes to a nationwide system of superintendents and agents charged with managing small groups of Native Americans who were being engulfed by a surging population of white settlers.

Indian commissioners during the 1850s advocated federally protected homes—or reservations—for the nation's tribes. Commissioner George W. Manypenny wrote in 1856 that the "wonderful emigration" to the West "blotted" native people out of existence "unless our great nation shall generously determine that the necessary provision shall at once be made, and appropriate steps be taken to designate suitable tracts or reservations of land, in proper localities, for permanent homes for and provide the means to colonize, them thereon."

Legislators responded by supporting the growth of the Indian Office bureaucracy and by ratifying treaties that attempted to provide for the tribes' transition to a "civilized" life. Central to many of these agreements were appropriations for agricultural education and religious training.

The Doolittle Committee and the End of Treaty Making. During the Civil War, the trends of the 1850s continued. In August 1862, the Dakota Sioux in southern Minnesota—who were on the verge of starvation because of the government's failure to supply promised annuities—successfully attacked their local agency and then attacked surrounding white settlements, killing more than 350. During the next two years, fighting broke out with Apaches and Navajos in Arizona, with plains and plateau tribes resisting the intrusion of miners into Montana and Idaho, and with the Cheyenne in Colorado. The latter conflict culminated in a surprise attack on a friendly Cheyenne camp by an undisciplined band of territorial militiamen on 29 November 1864. The Sand Creek massacre, in which at least 150 Indian people were slain, raised the fear that the tribes would be "blotted out of existence" if the westward movement continued with no change in federal policy.

The barbarity of the Sand Creek attack prompted two congressional investigations. More significant was a special committee created in March 1865 to examine "the condition of the Indian tribes and their treatment by the civil and military authorities of the United States." Chaired by Republican senator James R. Doolittle of Wisconsin, the committee criticized warfare against the Indian tribes and suggested that better "supervision and inspection" could overcome the lawlessness of the West and reverse the decline in native population. In the optimistic spirit of the early Reconstruction era, Congress thereupon authorized a new commission to "establish peace" with the hostile tribes in the West, which it did in 1867.

The Doolittle Committee also recommended "that the intercourse laws with the Indian tribes be thoroughly revised," preferably by placing tribal affairs in the hands of "an independent bureau or department." Acting in the same spirit, President Ulysses S. Grant in 1869 put agency appointments in the hands of Christian churches and promised to "bring all the Indians upon reservations, where they will live in houses, and have schoolhouses and churches, and will be pursuing peaceful and self-sustaining avocations. . . ." Supporters of the idea were quick to label it the "Peace Policy."

As the effort to orchestrate peace on western reservations gained momentum, the House of Representatives, shut out of Indian policy by the treaty prerogative of the Senate, began to assert that there was no longer any need to deal with Native Americans on the basis of the legal form of treaties. And so in March 1871, the 41st Congress, faced with a House of Representatives determined to exercise equal jurisdiction with the Senate in Indian affairs, inserted a brief rider to the Indian Appropriation Act stating that "hereafter no Indian nation or tribe within the territory of the United States shall be acknowledged or recognized as an independent nation, tribe, or power with whom the United States may contract by treaty."

The Assimilation Era. In the last decades of the nineteenth century, despite the fact that old treaties remained in force and new, congressional "agreements" were negotiated with several tribes, federal authorities adopted a growing array of procedures designed to destroy the coherence of Indian communities by individualizing and assimilating their people and property. During the 1870s and 1880s, a small group of legislators, led by Massachusetts senator Henry L. Dawes and other eastern reformers, searched for a politically acceptable policy that would save Indians from violence and displacement while allowing white expansion to continue. Dawes introduced a general allotment bill that became law in February 1887. The nation's first piece of general Indian legislation since 1834, the Dawes Severalty Act provided for the division of reservation lands into individual homesteads, the extension of U.S. citizenship to all who took a separate allotment, and the sale of all "surplus" real estate; that is, lands remaining after the assignment of homesteads to tribal members.

After 1887 the purpose of federal policy was to destroy community self-government and incorporate individual Native Americans into the general American population. In 1887 Senator Dawes had hoped that this process would be gradual and buttressed by government assistance. But over the next three decades, the Massachusetts senator's genteel expectations were superseded by the practical voices of men elected to represent people intent on rapid development of the Far West's economic resources.

Efforts to Reduce the Federal Role. From 1887 to 1930, a series of conflicts between western Indian communities and their new, non-Indian neighbors revealed the nature of the "development" envisioned by western politicians. Repeatedly, pressure to allot reservations overrode efforts to delay the division of tribal lands and slow the forces of "progress." In 1898 Congress passed the Curtis Act, which unilaterally terminated the tribal status of the "civilized tribes" in Indian Territory and opened

the way for Oklahoma to become a state. The tribes there resisted, but by 1907 over 100,000 people had been assigned 15,794,400 acres of real estate as homesteads. When Congress admitted Oklahoma to the Union on 17 September 1907, it abolished Indian reservations in the new state.

Typical of legislative attitudes during the years before World War I was the report of a special Joint Commission of Congress to Investigate Indian Affairs, created by resolution on 30 June 1913. The commission did not make legislative recommendations, offering instead a series of superficial suggestions. In the area of health care, for example, the commission stated that the "prevailing insanitary conditions of Indian life" would best be improved by enlisting the help of "public-spirited citizens who avow their interest in the welfare of the Indian race, and whose efforts are at present unorganized and therefore somewhat misdirected and unavailing." In 1920 another review of "the condition of Indian affairs in the Southwest and Northwest," submitted by a nine-person subcommittee of the House Indian Affairs Committee, reached similarly vacuous conclusions. After interviewing dozens of witnesses and traveling thousands of miles, the committee urged that Indians twenty-one years of age or older who had completed the seventh grade "have turned over to them anything due them from the Government and then be required to work out their own salvation."

In 1927 and 1928, the Senate debated creating another investigations subcommittee. Non-Indian reformers, including one outspoken young defender of Indian interests named John Collier, claimed that the Indian Office denied Indians the full rights of citizenship, while legislators like Wisconsin senator James A. Frear emphasized the need to end federal supervision. On 1 February 1928, the Senate authorized the creation of a subcommittee charged with making "a general survey of the condition of the Indians" and exploring "the relation of the Bureau of Indian Affairs to the persons and property of Indians." As the hundreds of pages of testimony began to accumulate, however, the only consistent theme in the subcommittee's deliberations appeared to be criticism of the Indian Office (now called the Bureau of Indian Affairs). Senators heard of waste, mismanagement, health problems, and Indian poverty. But few witnesses added anything beyond the well-established cries for efficiency, fairness, and reform of the mismanaged bureau.

The Indian Reorganization Act and the Termination Era. The 1934 Indian Reorganization Act, passed during the first years of Franklin D. Roo-

Landmark Legislation

Title	Year Enacted	Reference Number	Description
Trade and Intercourse Act	1790	1 Stat. 137–138	Established federal supremacy in relations with Indian tribes. The law regulated all trade with Indians, required all traders to obtain a license and follow prescribed rules of conduct, and prohibited states from acquiring Indian land without congressional approval.
Indian Removal Act	1830	4 Stat. 411–412	Authorized the president to initiate negotiations leading to the removal of eastern tribes to lands west of the Mississippi River. The law was a victory for western politicians and initiated a decade during which tribes in both the Great Lakes and the South were forcibly moved west.
Organization of the Department of Indian Affairs	1834	4 Stat. 735–738	Created an elaborate system of regional and local agents responsible for dealing with the tribes in their area. Located within the War Department, these agencies were to distribute payments called for in treaties and to encourage the "civilization" of the tribes. In 1849 the Indian Office was transferred to the new Department of Interior.
End of Treaty Making	1871	15 Stat. 566	This rider to the annual appropriations bill abolished the practice of treating agreements with tribes as treaties but stipulated that all existing treaties would remain in force.
Dawes Severalty Act (General Allotment Act)	1887	24 Stat. 388–391	Established the procedure for dividing all tribal lands into individual homesteads. It declared all "allotted" Indians to be citizens of the United States, and established a twenty-five-year period during which they could not sell land and local authorities could not tax it.
Indian Reorganization Act	1934	48 Stat. 984–988	Prohibited the Indian Office from authorizing additional allotments and permitted Indians to organize reservation governments; called for federal support for vocational and other advanced training and established a revolving fund that tribal governments could draw upon for community development projects.
Indian Self-Determination and Educational Assistance Act	1975	88 Stat. 2213–2217	Created a mechanism for tribal governments to contract with the Indian Office for the provision of educational and other services on reservations; established the precedent of local communities administering their own social service agencies rather than relying upon federal authorities.

sevelt's New Deal, is usually regarded as marking a shift in federal policy away from assimilation and toward a re-recognition of Indian tribes. While Commissioner of Indian Affairs John Collier, who wrote the proposal that formed the basis for the new law, was a visionary reformer, he was not in tune with congressional sentiment. Congress drastically altered Collier's original bill. In the view of most members of Congress, the Indian Reorganization Act was a statute largely consistent with previous attempts to "prepare" Indians for incorporation into the United States as marginal semicitizens.

John Collier's proposal called for an end to all future allotments, effectively repealing the Dawes Act, and charted an ambitious course of Indian self-rule. His draft bill granted the tribes the power to organize under charters and to function as "federal municipal corporations." These corporations would acquire all allotments on the death of their current owners, take over responsibility for administering many federal services within the reservation, operate courts, and have the power to compel the removal of government officials from the reservation.

By the time Congress passed the bill on 18 June 1934, many of Collier's proposals had been eliminated. The Indian Reorganization Act declared an end to the policy of allotments, but it severely restricted the powers and autonomy of the new tribal governments. The constitutions establishing them would require the approval of the secretary of the Interior; the governments would not have the power to compel the return of allotments to tribal ownership, nor would they be able to force the transfer of government officials or operate courts apart from the existing ones authorized by the Bureau of Indian Affairs. In sum, the established federal bureaucracy remained intact.

John Collier's influence gradually declined over the course of his remaining eleven years as commissioner. As tribal governments were organized and began to function, the representatives and senators who had supported Collier's reforms sensed a rising tide of Indian militancy and began to oppose the commissioner's reforms. The investigative subcommittee of the Senate Indian Affairs Committee, which had been created under Lynn J. Frazier (R-N.Dak.) in 1928, continued to meet through the 1930s and became a forum for airing complaints against Collier.

Despite their inability to rescind the Indian Reorganization Act, Collier's opponents gained support for terminating all federal aid to Indian tribes during the immediate postwar years. A number of specific administrative reforms reinforced this trend. In 1946 Congress responded to the growing number of tribes that wished to file suit against the federal government in the Court of Claims for compensation for unconscionable and illegal land seizures by creating the Indian Claims Commission. This quasi-judicial body would hear complaints and recommend settlements. While the commission offered Indians a forum for their grievances, it also aimed at settling all outstanding disputes quickly and extinguishing all claims against the United States. A reorganization of the Bureau of Indian Affairs in 1947, which created a series of area offices and decentralized many activities, had similar consequences. While the stated purpose of the effort was to increase efficiency, it actually helped achieve the goal of scaling back or ending the bureau's functions.

Placed on the defensive by nearly half a century of attacks from impatient legislators and reflecting Congress's general reaction to the New Deal, the Bureau of Indian Affairs began to echo its critics' arguments by calling for greater self-sufficiency and cutting federal services. Many favored a complete termination of federal involvement in Indian affairs. In May 1950, Dillon S. Myer, one of Collier's political enemies, became commissioner of Indian Affairs. As the former director of the War Reloca-

tion Authority, which supervised the internment of Japanese Americans during World War II, Myer had no background in Indian affairs and little sympathy for tribal communities. His replacement in the Eisenhower administration, Glenn L. Emmons, a banker from Gallup, New Mexico, shared Myer's attitudes and continued his policies.

The high point of this movement toward termination (the ending of all federal services and protection for tribes) came in the summer of 1953, when Congress adopted House Concurrent Resolution 108 and Public Law 280. The preamble to the concurrent resolution declared that "the Indians within the territorial limits of the United States should assume their full responsibilities as American citizens," a sentiment that pervaded the document. It promised to "free from federal supervision" a number of small tribes in California, Florida, New York, and Texas and to pursue the complete termination of others in Montana, North Dakota, Wisconsin, and Kansas. Public Law 280 replaced tribal with state jurisdiction in criminal prosecutions arising on most Indian reservations in California, Minnesota, Nebraska, Oregon, and Wisconsin. These two laws, and the specific termination of twelve tribes between 1954 and 1962, suggested that the federal commitment to tribes would continue to decline for the remainder of the twentieth century. Nothing in these statutes signaled the resurgence of tribes that in fact would characterize legislative and administrative life in the 1960s.

The Ervin and Kennedy Hearings and Their Aftermath. Most twentieth-century members of Congress interested in Indian affairs assumed that Indians belonged to a "vanishing race" that would soon disappear. But by 1960, it had become obvious that the United States contained very few "vanishing Americans." In 1900, the Indian population began to rise for the first time since 1492; in 1960, the census reported 523,000 Native Americans, up 47 percent from 1950. And when legislators encountered Indian leaders in the 1950s, it was usually in the context of Native American opposition to termination. Led by the National Congress of American Indians, an intertribal group formed in 1944, Indian leaders such as Helen Peterson, Joseph Garry, and D'Arcy McNickle showed remarkable unanimity on the issue. The goals of assimilation and termination had rested on the assumption that Indians ultimately wanted the same things as other Americans and that their "uplift" would cause them to disappear into the American melting pot. This assumption was contradicted by the persistence of native traditions in the twentieth century and by the Indians' repeated insistence on being recognized as a tribal people.

It was in this context that two Senate committees set out to investigate aspects of tribal life during the 1960s. In 1961, the Senate Judiciary Committee authorized Sen. Samuel J. Ervin, Jr., of North Carolina to conduct a series of hearings on the constitutional rights of American Indians. In four years of intermittent meetings, Ervin produced ample evidence that the courts operating on Indian reservations did not conform to legal practice. Defendants were rarely advised of their rights or represented by lawyers, and tribal judges had little formal training. But Ervin also learned that local Bureau of Indian Affairs officials either manipulated or ignored the proceedings of tribal courts, and that states such as California and Minnesota, which had been given jurisdiction over Indian reservations under Public Law 280, either discriminated against or ignored native communities.

In 1965 Senator Ervin introduced nine bills to "provide our Indian citizens with the rights and protections conferred upon all other American citizens." The North Carolina legislator's proposals focused primarily on reforms serving to bring tribal governments in line with the U.S. Constitution. But equally significant, Ervin recognized the failures of the states and the Bureau of Indian Affairs. He proposed that no more states be granted criminal jurisdiction over Indian reservations without tribal consent and that federal officials take steps to improve the administration of justice on the reservations.

Ervin's bills were debated off and on from 1965 to 1968. As the discussion progressed, however, the subject shifted from the issue of how to "improve" tribal courts and governments to how the federal government might reform these institutions while demonstrating its sensitivity to the continuing viability of Indian cultures.

When Ervin's bills won congressional approval as the Indian Civil Rights Act of 1968, it contained language supporting continued tribal self-government, a goal it urged the Bureau of Indian Affairs to support. Instead of requiring that tribes conform to the Constitution, the Indian Civil Rights Act listed ten specific limitations on the power of tribal governments. It also amended Public Law 280, requiring tribal consent to any further extensions of state jurisdiction over them, ordering the bureau to create a model code for the administration of justice on reservations, and stipulating that tribal con-

tracts for legal counsel would be automatically approved unless canceled by the secretary of the Interior within ninety days of being signed. Recognizing that some Indian governments are theocratic, the law also exempted tribes from the constitutional prohibition against the establishment of religion. In addition, concern for the tribes' cultural traditions and awareness of their small budgets led to an exemption from the requirement of free legal counsel for indigent defendants and the requirement that civil cases be tried before a jury.

In August 1967, while legislators and lobbyists were debating Senator Ervin's proposals for the reform of Indian courts, another Senate investigation of Indian affairs was getting under way. Launched at the height of the civil rights era, Sen. Robert F. Kennedy's investigation of Indian education, conducted by the Subcommittee on Indian Education of the Committee on Labor and Public Welfare, reflected the public's growing acceptance of tribal governments and tribal communities as permanent features of American life. Just as the Ervin Committee endorsed tribal self-government, so the Kennedy Committee came to the defense of Indian-run schools.

A week after the Indian Civil Rights Act cleared the Senate, the Kennedy panel held its first hearing. When the committee issued its final report in 1969 (chaired in the end by Robert Kennedy's brother, Edward), it urged the creation of a Senate Select Committee on the Human Needs of the American Indian, the convening of a White House conference on American Indian affairs, increased funding for curricula sensitive to Indian cultures, and greater supervision of state and local officials receiving federal funds for the education of Native Americans in the public schools. "One theme running through all our recommendations," the committee observed, "is increased Indian participation and control of their own educational programs. For far too long, the Nation has paid only token heed to the notion that Indians should have a strong voice in their own destiny."

The Policy of Self-Determination. The Indian Education Act of 1972 was the first congressional endorsement of the Kennedy Committee's call for greater Indian self-determination. The law required public school districts to involve parents and community members in the administration of federal funds for Indian children. Three years later, Congress went further by approving the Indian Self-Determination and Education Assistance Act, which added new requirements for Indian involvement in public school programs receiving federal funds. Declaring a desire for "maximum Indian participation" in programs "responsive to the needs and desires" of native communities, the act authorized tribes to sign contracts with federal agencies to administer government programs. The tribes responded eagerly to this new opportunity; five years after its passage, 370 contracts were in effect, providing $200 million worth of services to the Indian people.

The years since 1975 have been marked by substantial controversy. Indian politicians, commentators, and community leaders such as legal scholar Rennard Strickland and Apache leader Wendell Chino, and politicians such as Arizona representative Morris K. Udall have charged that the self-determination legislation of the 1970s was proving to be an empty promise. Programs are self-administered but underfunded, and the regulations under which grants are made to tribes are frequently written by hostile federal administrators.

Mirroring these frustrations are the arguments of those who say that tribal groups have been receiving an unfair and unrealistic amount of federal assistance. Led by non-Indian backlash organizations that have frequently formed in response to litigation (such as the effort of Puget Sound tribes to gain recognition for their off-reservation fishing rights during the 1970s) or to the success of Indians who operate legal gambling operations, this camp rejects what it considers to have been the radical reforms of the 1970s and urges a return to the philosophy of termination.

Despite the existence of these sharply contrasting views, congressional committees and Congress itself have held consistently—and cautiously—to self-determination as a policy objective. While attacked by some for having moved too quickly and by others for not having moved at all, legislators have held to a remarkably steady course. In 1975, at the urging of South Dakota senator James Abourezk, Congress created the American Indian Policy Review Commission. Its 1977 final report drew criticism from both Indian rights advocates and terminationists, but its ten volumes of work symbolized congressional concern for the future of Indian communities and legislative support for tribal self-government. In 1976 the Indian Health Care Improvement Act extended the ideas of the 1975 Self-Determination Act to a new area of tribal services by encouraging native organizations to manage their own clinics and hospitals. In 1977 the Senate reestablished its Select Committee on Indian Af-

fairs to oversee legislation affecting native people. A year later, two additional statutes—the Tribally Controlled Community College Educational Assistance Act and the Indian Child Welfare Act—provided support for other tribal institutions.

In the 1990s, after directing federal Indian policy for nearly two centuries, congressional leaders have returned to the idea that tribal governments should be self-governing. In this sense, they have appeared to return to the "fixed and stable principles" first articulated by George Washington in 1789. Undermining this goal has been the poverty of many Native American communities and the hostility of many non-Indians. Ironically, in the modern era, tribal autonomy is possible only with federal support. Self-determination will thus continue to be defended by appeals to federal officials and invocations of Congress's unique responsibility to the tribes.

[See also Dawes Severalty Act; Indian Affairs Committee, Senate Select; Indian Treaties; Natural Resources Committee, House.]

BIBLIOGRAPHY

Ball, Milner S. "Constitution, Court, Indian Tribes." *American Bar Foundation Research Journal* (Winter 1987): 3–139.
Bee, Robert. *The Politics of American Indian Policy.* 1982.
Brown, Anthony, ed. *New Directions in Federal Indian Policy: A Review of the American Indian Policy Review Commission.* 1979.
Deloria, Vine, Jr., and Clifford Lytle. *The Nations Within: The Past and Future of American Indian Sovereignty.* 1984.
Hoxie, Frederick E. *A Final Promise: The Campaign to Assimilate the Indians, 1880–1920.* 1984.
Prucha, Francis Paul. *The Great Father: The United States Government and the American Indian.* 1984.
Viola, Herman J. *Diplomats in Buckskin: A History of Indian Delegations in Washington City.* 1981.
Washburn, Wilcomb E., ed. *Handbook of North American Indians.* Vol. 4: *History of Indian-White Relations.* 1988.

FREDERICK E. HOXIE

INDIAN TREATIES. Between 1789 and 1871, representatives of the United States negotiated, and the Senate ratified, more than 370 treaties with Indian tribes. After 1871, when Congress passed a resolution declaring treaty making with Native Americans at an end, federal officials continued to negotiate agreements with tribal leaders and to submit them to the legislative branch for approval.

Fifty-six of these agreements were approved after 1871, and they have subsequently been upheld by federal courts as having the same effect as treaties (*Choate v. Trapp* [1912]).

No country has used treaty making as the basis for relations with an indigenous population as extensively as the United States. The Canadian government has ratified a much smaller number of "treaties and surrenders," but these have not always been considered the equivalent of international agreements. New Zealand authorities negotiated one agreement, the Treaty of Waitangi, with Maori chiefs, but no treaties transferred tribal land or power to national authorities in Australia, Mexico, South America, or Africa. There are two reasons for the unique history of treaty making in the United States.

First, there was ample precedent, particularly in the English colonies, for dealing with Indians by treaty. From the beginning of European settlement, imperial powers had sought to buttress their claims to land with legal documents. The Papal Bull of 4 May 1493 began this process by granting lands "found and to be found" to the Spanish Crown, but it continued during the rivalry among the Dutch, French, and English for control of the Atlantic seaboard. Each group attempted to ally itself with a local Indian community and to seal this alliance with a treaty. The Covenant Chain that bound British colonial officials and the Iroquois League into an alliance serving the interests of both groups was perhaps the most famous of these arrangements. It was sanctified by both written documents and Indian rituals. After the Revolution, it was only logical to continue formal relationships of this kind.

Second, treaties were a practical solution to a difficult political and diplomatic problem. When the First Congress assembled in New York in the spring of 1789, a series of treaties with Ohio Valley tribes awaited action. At the same time, a powerful alliance of Creeks in Georgia, supported with Spanish arms, appeared to threaten the country's southern border. President George Washington appeared before the Senate during the summer of 1789, urging legislators to "conciliate" these Indians and "attach them firmly to the United States" by authorizing a formal treaty with the Creeks. While several members resisted the proposal, the Senate acceded to the president's request, and an agreement was signed by Creek leader Alexander McGillivray and Washington the following year.

Not only did the Creek treaty avoid an expensive and bloody conflict, it gave Washington and the War Department the authority to prevent state and local militia from invading tribal lands and provoking a general war. Treaties both mollified the tribes and emphasized the extent to which Indian affairs was a federal, not a local, responsibility. Thus, the agreements appealed to Federalists like Washington and his political allies as well as to leaders like McGillivray.

Most Indian treaties fell into three categories. First were agreements in which tribes pledged their loyalty to the United States and both sides expressed their wish for friendship and trade. The treaty signed by representatives of nine different tribes near Fort Laramie, Wyoming, in 1851 is an example of this type. It outlined the extent of each tribe's domain, stipulated that $50,000 worth of supplies would be delivered to the tribes each year for a decade, and pledged each group to stop making war on the others. A second category of treaty ceded land to the United States in exchange for money and a clear title to a reservation. The "removal treaties" of the 1830s, for example, conveyed fee simple titles to western reservations to the Indian tribes in exchange for their sale of land and property east of the Mississippi. Finally, many treaties contained provisions intended to carry the tribes to "civilization." These often included promises of individual homesteads, farming instruction, schools, and other federal services. The "peace policy" treaties negotiated at Medicine Lodge Creek in 1867 and at Fort Laramie in 1868 are examples of this third type of agreement.

Congress began abrogating Indian treaties in the late nineteenth century, first with the Curtis Act, which unilaterally abolished tribal governments in Oklahoma, and later in land purchase statutes that violated individual agreements. Although tribal leaders protested, these actions were upheld by the U.S. Supreme Court in *Lone Wolf v. Hitchcock* (1903). Despite these actions, however, federal courts have consistently held that treaty provisions not explicitly repealed by Congress remain in effect. This position, expressed most fully in *United States v. Wheeler* (1978), has formed the basis for much litigation involving treaty rights to water, natural resources, and local self-government.

BIBLIOGRAPHY

Barsh, Russell L., and James Y. Henderson. *The Road: Indian Tribes and Political Freedom.* 1980.

Wilkinson, Charles F. *American Indians, Time and the Law: Native Societies in a Modern Constitutional Democracy.* 1987.

FREDERICK E. HOXIE